# PRODUCTION AND OPERATIONS MANAGEMENT

## THIRD EDITION

**KANISHKA BEDI**

*Professor*
*School of Business & Quality Management*
*Hamdan Bin Mohammed Smart University*
*Dubai, UAE*

OXFORD

UNIVERSITY PRESS

# OXFORD
### UNIVERSITY PRESS

Oxford University Press is a department of the University of Oxford.
It furthers the University's objective of excellence in research, scholarship,
and education by publishing worldwide. Oxford is a registered trade mark of
Oxford University Press in the UK and in certain other countries.

Published in India by
Oxford University Press
22 Workspace, 2nd Floor, 1/22 Asaf Ali Road, New Delhi 110 002

First Edition published in 2004
Third Edition published in 2013
Eighth impression 2023

ISBN-13: 978-0-19-807209-6
ISBN-10: 0-19-807209-0

Typeset in Times New Roman
by Anvi Composers, New Delhi 110063
Printed in India by Gopsons Papers Private Ltd., Sivakasi

For product information and current price, please visit www.india.oup.com

*To*

*My mother, Mrs Kusum Vipin Bedi, for all her sacrifices and love for me*

# Features of the Book

## Learning Objectives
Each chapter begins with learning objectives that focus on the learning and knowledge you should acquire by the end of the chapter.

**Learning Objectives**

After reading this chapter, you will be able to answer the following questions:
- How are products and services similar to each other?
- What is production and operations management?
- What are the various steps that should be followed by an entrepreneur in se manufacturing/service facility?
- What are the new concepts in process design?
- What are the latest trends in operations management in India?
- How can organizations make their operations environment friendly?
- What is automation? What are its advantages and disadvantages?

Production and operations management (POM) is defined as the design, operation, and improvement of the transformation process, which converts the various inputs into the desired outputs of products and services.

Production and operations management (POM) is defined as the design, operation, and improvement of the transformation process, which converts the various inputs into the desired outputs of products and services.

The term 'production and operations management' is being increasingly replaced by simply operations management, as the production function relating to the manufacturing organizations has become a part of operations. 'Operations management' is a broad term which includes manufacturing as well as service organizations. Operations management also highlights the increasing importance of the service industry in the overall business environment. There is a growing need for the application of the principles of operations management in the service industry.

## Sidebars
Important concepts appear as sidebars throughout the text for quick recapitulation, which will come handy for revision before exams.

## Solved Examples
The chapters include solved examples that will help you understand the concepts well and give you adequate practice before you start solving the various exercises given at the end of the chapters.

**Example 5.1**

Triveni Steels (P) Ltd is planning to start a new factory for manufacturing steel utensils. It is considering three location options, namely, Bokaro, Jamshedpur, and Bhilai. The fixed costs at the three locations have been estimated at ₹8.15 million, ₹7.377 million, and ₹7.903 million, respectively. The variable costs at the three locations are estimated at ₹500 per unit, ₹580 per unit, and ₹490 per unit, respectively. The factory will have an annual production capacity of 10,000 steel utensils and in the initial years it will operate at 75% efficiency. Find the best location option, which has the lowest total cost of production.

**Solution**

At 75% efficiency, the factory will annually produce
75% of 10,000 units = 7,500 units

**Table 5.1** Factor ratings for a leather goods manufacturing facility

| Factor | Factor ratings |
| --- | --- |
| Close proximity to markets | 3 |
| Close proximity | |
| Transportation f | |
| Basic amenities | |
| Acceptance of a | |
| Availability of c | |
| Low constructio | |
| Easy availability | |

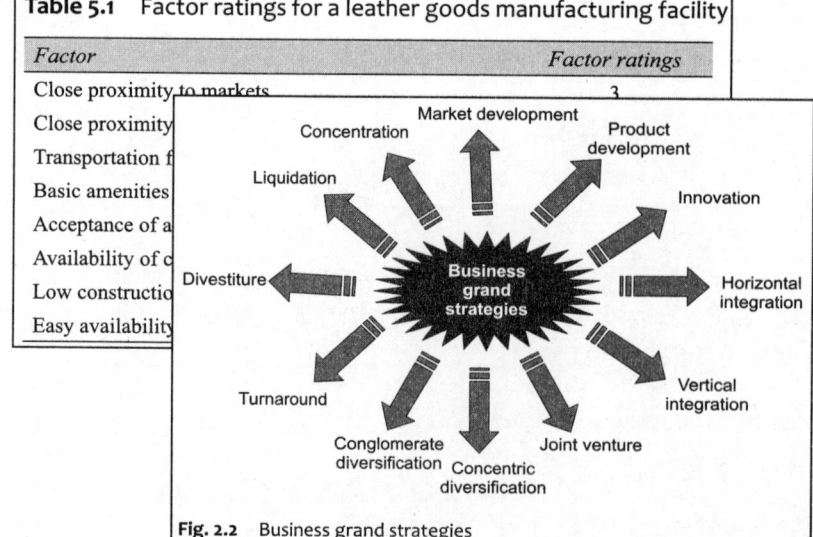

**Fig. 2.2** Business grand strategies

## Tables and Figures
All chapters contain tables and figures to illustrate the topics discussed in the chapter.

## Exhibits

The chapters contain exhibits that help in understanding the application of the theory discussed in the chapter.

**Exhibit 1.1    The Rise of Laxmi Niwas Mittal**

In 2006, Forbes magazine touted steel tycoon Laxmi Niwas Mittal as the fifth richest man in the world. Microsoft chief Bill Gates led the list for the twelfth year in a row with a net worth of US$50 billion followed by Warren Buffet, who had a net worth of US$42 billion. London-based Mittal, who still proudly flaunts an Indian passport, stood tall at the fifth position with a net worth of US$23.5 billion. In comparison, software giant Wipro's Chairman, Azim Premji, stood at number 25. Mukesh Ambani, the Chairman of Reliance Industries was at rank 56 and his brother Anil Ambani at rank 104.

problem, and decided to stay back to start the mill. Thus, Ispat Indo was born in Jakarta. There was no looking back after that for LN. During 1980s, LN started his acquisition spree worldwide by acquiring steel mills in Trinidad and Canada. The biggest coup came when he snapped up the loss-making Sibalsa Mill in Mexico for US$220 million in 1992. His acquisition of Chicago-based Inland Steel made Ispat International (now known as Mittal Steel) the third largest producer of steel in the world. He went ahead to acquire Stahlwerk Ruhrort GmbH (SRG), a steel maker in the Ruhr, and Walzdraht

## Summary

*Facility location planning* involves choosing the best place, from the available options, for setting up a plant/service facility. Various factors are responsible for making a production or service facility successful at a particular location. *Factor ratings* and *location ratings* help in selecting the better location options. *Break-even analysis* can be used for selecting locations that have lower break-even volumes. It can also be used for deciding upon the capacity of a plant, the number of plants, and the number of shifts for which the plants can be operated.

The final analysis boils down to the minimizatio of the transportation costs. The location optio with the minimum total transportation cost is t best option. The *simple median model and the cent of gravity method* are helpful for this purpose. T *transportation model* is even more accurate tha these models, but slightly difficult to use. For t final analysis of choosing the best service facili location, the *Ardalan heuristic* is most suitable. helps in finding a location that can cater to a lar population.

## Summary

The summary at the end of each chapter draws together the main concepts discussed within the chapter, which will help you to reflect and evaluate the important concepts discussed.

## Keywords

All technical terms have been explained at the end of each chapter, which will help you retain all the new terms that you have learnt in the chapter.

## Keywords

**Break-even point** is the point on the cost/revenue, namely, the volume of production, curve at which total revenue is equal to total cost. It corresponds to the break-even volume $V_{BE}$ on the x-axis. $V_{BE}$ represents the volume of output at which there is no profit and no loss. All the expenses incurred are completely covered by the revenues generated.

and equipment, etc. These costs remain constant despite the volume of production (number of units produced within a given duration).

**Revenue** is the money which comes into the firm by selling its products at their sales prices.

**Variable cost** is the cost of labour (directly involved in the production process) and raw material. As the

## Concept Review Questions

1. Define quality and quality control. How is quality control different from total quality control?
2. What are the various dimensions of quality? What are t
3. Nam saying qual
4. Wha diffe I and
5. Exp cont limi

7. Explain Taguchi's concept of
8. What is Six Sigma? How is it
9. How many types of sampling

## Objective Questions

**Choose the correct option**

1. The modern assembly line was invented by
   (a) Frederick W. Taylor
   (b) Taiichi Ohno
   (c) Henry Ford
   (d) W. Edwards Deming
2. Who propounded the just-in-time (JIT) production system?
   (a) Joseph M. Juran
   (b) Henry Ford
   (c) Frederick W. Taylor
   (d) Taiichi Ohno

   (b) computer numerically controlled
   (c) case numerically conducted
   (d) case not conducted

**State True or False**

5. Intermittent processes are assembly processes which are repetitive in nature.
6. Carbon emission is a measure of the amount of carbon dioxide gas emitted.
7. Job shop is a type of intermittent process.

**Fill in the blanks**

8. The transformation process consists of ___

## Exercises

A series of objective and concept review questions as well as project assignments highlight the major topics covered in the chapter, which can be used for review and classroom discussion.

## End-of-chapter Cases

Each chapter ends with one or more case studies designed to consolidate your understanding of the chapter subject and broaden your financial decision-making skills.

## CASE STUDY I

### Kishore Biyani and Big Bazaar

Kishore Biyani's saga starts with his family business in textiles, which he joined after graduating in commerce. In 1987, Biyani launched the first branded ready-made trousers brand known as Pantaloon through his company Pantaloon Fashions. The trousers were marketed through the Pantaloon Shoppe stores. By the time Pantaloon Fashions went public in 1992, it had 60 exclusive shops. Later, he started manufacturing garments under two more brands—John Miller and Bare. Despite good products and competitive pricing, the business seemed unviable due to high distribution

around ₹70 million in the first year, but beating all expectations, the store did a business of ₹100 million. This experience was an eye-opener for Biyani, who came to know that Indian market is 'under-retailed'.

The year 2001 saw Biyani's entry into the hypermarket concept adapted to Indian conditions in the form of Big Bazaar. During that time, Pantaloon's topline was around ₹1.8 billion. Big Bazaar required a lot of investment and the company had generated profits only worth ₹40 million. It was not feasible to raise money from the market as the share price was

# Preface to the Third Edition

Globalization has intensified competition in business, and organizations are continually trying to add more value to their products and services. Organizations are moving towards becoming more efficient, effective, and customer-focused than ever. World-class performance in operations is fundamental to a company's competitive success and long-term survival. Widely followed in organizations across the continents, the various tools and techniques offered by production and operations management helps streamline processes, minimize costs, maximize output and profitability, and facilitate managerial decision-making.

Governments and organizations have realized that they have to collaborate as the world is looking for answers from sustainable development initiatives. There has been increased focus on green energy, sustainable operations, and so on.

This subject area seeks to understand, examine, and optimize the processes practised at organizations. Product and process design, operations, and supply chain are some key aspects of production and operations management. The field includes the areas of facility location planning, product development, production, lean manufacturing, quality management, and operations strategies.

The book has been revised keeping in mind new developments in this area. The text continues to provide a well-defined approach to production and operations management. It strives to lucidly explain each topic, particularly those requiring statistical/mathematical treatment.

This edition features several new case studies that demonstrate the inter-linkages of operations with other functional areas of management. The professional journeys of many business luminaries have been included to allow the learners to have a glimpse of the management of operations along with other functional areas during the formative years of a business enterprise.

## About the Book

The book has been designed to serve as a comprehensive text on production and operations management that especially meets the requirements of MBA students. It introduces students to the basic concepts of production and operations management before moving on to topics such as operations strategies, new product development, facility location planning, and project management. The text provides in-depth coverage of topics such as aggregate planning, work design, demand forecasting, and operations scheduling. The book has been revised to provide learners with the contemporary approaches in the field. It is imperative for the learners to understand that operations cannot be managed in isolation and their close relationship with marketing, finance, human resources, etc. should be understood properly in order to manage them effectively.

## Key Features

- A unique blend of theory and practice, the text provides a step-by-step approach to each topic.
- Each chapter is exhaustive, with numerous organizational examples and exhibits.

- The chapters include numerous solved examples, classroom-tested cases, and end-chapter problems with critical-thinking elements, interesting activities like group discussions, and outdoor projects.

## New to This Edition

- Chapter on new product development
- New exhibits in all chapters
- Additional case studies
- New sections on facility location decisions and network design in the supply chain, calculating labour and machine requirements to achieve a capacity, earned value management (EVM), managing demand uncertainty, vendor relationship management, and more
- Sidebars for easy recall
- Objective-type questions in all chapters

## Online Resource Centre

The online resource centre continues to provide resources for students and lecturers and also links to additional resources.

The following resources are available to faculty members using this text:

- Instructor's Manual
- PowerPoint Slides

Students can now access the following as part of their study plan:

- Multiple Choice Questions
- Web Links
- Concept Flashcards
- MS Excel templates of various numerical examples covered in the book
- Digital site tours of Hero MotoCorp Ltd, NTPC, JCT Ltd, and the Bengaluru International Airport Project

## Extended Chapter Material

The third edition improves upon the coverage of the original edition, making the text much more comprehensive and lucid.

*Chapter 1 Introduction to Production and Operations Management*: History of production and operations management and The latest trends in operations management

*Chapter 2 Operations Strategies*: Centralization vs decentralization of authority and responsibility

**Chapter 3** is a new chapter on new product development.

***Chapter 4 Outsourcing and Offshoring***: The outsourcing process

***Chapter 5 Facility Location Planning***: Facility location decisions and network design in the supply chain

***Chapter 6 Facility Capacity and Layout Planning***: Determining the requirements of personnel and equipment

***Chapter 7 Project Management***: Earned value management (EVM)

***Chapter 8 Inventory Management***: The effect of demand uncertainty

***Chapter 9 Materials Requirement Planning, Just-in-time, and Supply Chain Management***: Understanding the supply chain

***Chapter 11 Aggregate Planning***: Vendor relationship management

***Chapter 12 Work Design***: Job task discretion

***Chapter 14 Quality Management***: Application of DMAIC

***Chapter 15 Demand Forecasting***: New product demand forecasting

***Chapter 16 Service Operations Management***: The dimensions of quality in services and Conformance to specifications

## Chapter Organization

The book contains 16 chapters, which provide comprehensive discussions on the various aspects of production and operations management.

*Chapter 1* presents an introduction to production and operations management, and includes topics such as steps in the production and operations process from the point of view of an entrepreneur and the evolution of this discipline in India. Other topics discussed in the chapter include the role and contribution of operations management in a business organization in the post-liberalization era and the emerging role of a production and operations manager in India.

*Chapter 2* on operations strategy emphasizes the importance of its alignment with the overall business strategy of the organization, while balancing it with other functional area strategies.

*Chapter 3* is a new chapter that is dedicated to new product development. The chapter discusses concepts such as robust design, quality function deployment, Kano's model, stage-gate new product development process, and mass customization.

*Chapter 4* discusses outsourcing and offshoring. It aims to make the readers abreast of the pitfalls of outsourcing and the ways to avoid the same.

*Chapter 5* discusses topics on facility location planning and covers, among other topics, locating foreign operations facilities, the transportation model using MS Excel, and the Ardalan heuristic for planning the location of service facilities.

*Chapter 6* on facility capacity and layout planning addresses the issues of facility capacity and layout planning and includes contemporary topics such as strategic capacity planning as a key to competitiveness.

*Chapter 7* on project management covers topics such as the role of project management in other functional areas of management, projects under resource constraints, limitations of CPM and PERT, and Microsoft Project.

*Chapter 8* on inventory management addresses topics such as the role of other functional departments in inventory management, multiple criteria ABC analysis, Monte Carlo simulation, in addition to the various inventory models.

*Chapter 9* on MRP, JIT, and SCM focuses on topics such as the hybrid MRP-JIT production system, Japanese supply chain management in practice—the *keiretsu,* comparison of the Japanese JIT supply chain management and the traditional US purchasing, e-procurement, and operating resource management.

*Chapter 10* on total productive maintenance emphasizes the utility of this philosophy, which has helped many Indian factories to enhance productivity and attain increased quality levels.

*Chapter 11* introduces aggregate planning and explains the methods of planning the quantity of products/ services to be produced, with discussions on rough-cut capacity planning, time fences, etc.

*Chapter 12* on work design explains job task discretion in addition to traditional topics such as methods analysis, stop watch time study, and work sampling.

*Chapter 13* on operations scheduling covers topics such as routing, prioritizing, dispatching, expediting, forward and backward scheduling, finite and infinite loading, and various methods of sequencing.

*Chapter 14* on quality management presents the key topics in the area of quality management and includes discussions on the concepts of statistical quality control, acceptance sampling, etc., as also natural tolerance limits, process capability ratio, process capability ratio for an off-centre process, Six Sigma, etc.

*Chapter 15* on demand forecasting introduces new product demand forecasting with trial-repeat models and competitive share models.

*Chapter 16* on service operations management covers the important aspects of service design, capacity, and quality. The service sector is growing at a much faster rate in the country as compared to the manufacturing sector. The chapter, therefore, discusses the various aspects of this significant sector. It also covers various aspects of service quality including its measurement using the SERVQUAL instrument.

**KANISHKA BEDI**

# Preface to the First Edition

Production and Operations Management (POM) involves managing the various activities, processes, and procedures related to the conversion of numerous production-related inputs into outputs. It is crucial for manufacturing as well as services organizations to implement POM practices effectively.

This subject is assuming greater importance with globalization, and with corporations expanding their operations worldwide. In this context, a postgraduate student of management is expected to be equipped with the latest theories and practices of POM. A production and operations manager, for instance, needs to decide where to locate new international facilities in order to address various markets simultaneously, while minimizing the overall cost of operations. The capacity and layout of the facility must be so planned that it can fight local competition effectively. Project management skills and techniques have to be applied to facilitate the establishment of operations facilities in time and within the given budget. In addition, many more methods of POM such as materials requirement planning (MRP), just-in-time (JIT), supply chain management (SCM), aggregate planning, work design, quality management, etc. need to be implemented in order to gain competitive advantage.

The Indian economy has experienced enormous development in POM practices since liberalization. Before liberalization, POM took a back seat, as the Licence Raj had created a seller's market, and whatever was produced had to be accepted by the Indian consumer. Quality and cost considerations were not important for companies in the earlier era, as greater emphasis was generally placed on lobbying to procure production licences. Liberalization has brought with it a lot of foreign MNCs into the country as well as world-class POM practices to be implemented by the domestic companies.

Of late, the term 'operations management' is gaining acceptability worldwide; it includes the production aspect. However, in India, the term 'production and operations management' is more popular and is taught as a core paper in all B-schools. This textbook includes all the latest developments in POM theories and concepts to guide the Indian manager effectively.

## Aim and Methodology

Designed to meet the requirements of MBA/PGDBA students by presenting concepts that are clearly explained through numerous examples of managerial applications, students of other degree courses such as BBA, B.Tech. (Industrial/Production/Mechanical Engineering), and ICWA will also find this book useful and relevant.

Popular software such as MS Excel, MS Project 2000, and SPSS 10.0 are extensively used to solve numerical problems and explain concepts of POM. This could provide the student an opportunity to use the latest software and acquire hands-on practice in solving problems in the shortest possible time, with great accuracy.

The book introduces various topics of the subject sequentially from the point of view of an entrepreneur. Each chapter starts with a brief introduction to the topic, deals with the established theories and concepts, and moves on to the latest developments in the field. This approach is necessary to ensure that students of diverse academic backgrounds, enrolled in any MBA programme, are able to grasp the concepts easily.

## Pedagogical Features

The book introduces this subject in the Indian context, taking examples and cases of world-class companies such as Maruti Udyog Ltd, Bajaj Tempo, Kirloskar, etc. At the same time, it discusses the contemporary theories and practices of POM in organizations such as GE, BMW, Boeing, Rolls-Royce, Airbus Industrie, Honda, Toyota, Volvo, Nestlé, ABB, Olivetti, GE, Harley-Davidson, Mitsubishi, etc. Every topic, particularly, those requiring statistical/mathematical treatment, is approached step by step to enable users to master the core concepts with ease.

Additional features of the book are chapter-end questions including numerous solved problems with critical-thinking elements, interesting practicals—such as group discussions and outdoor projects—and computer-based problems to facilitate hands-on practice. It is accompanied by an Instructor's Manual providing a teaching note for guidance on pedagogy, solutions to numerical problems, project assignments, and case questions.

**KANISHKA BEDI**

# Acknowledgements

I would like to express my profound gratitude to the following persons/organizations/publications without whose support and encouragement I would have not been able to complete this work.

Emerald group of journals (MCB University Press), UK; Taylor & Francis, UK; APICS, USA; The International Organization for Standardization (ISO), Geneva; The Bureau of Indian Standards (BIS), New Delhi; The Centre for Science and Environment (CSE), New Delhi; Airbus Industrie, France; The Boeing Company, USA; BMW; ABB; Hyundai; Rolls-Royce Plc; Harley Davidson; The Tata Group; Hero Honda Motors Ltd; NTPC; JCT Limited; BPCL; Bengaluru International Airport Limited (BIAL); Jet Airways; domain-b.com; rediff.com; *The Times of India*; Steelworld.com; *Business Week Online*; *The Hindu Business Line*; *Express Computer*; *Business World*; BBC News; *Fortune*; *Business Today*; *Business India*; *The Economic Times*; MoneyControl.com; and *Indian Management*.

Prof. Anders Segerstedt, Luleå University of Technology, Sweden, for contributing a couple of interesting numerical problems in Chapters 8 and 9. An international expert in materials requirement planning/aggregate production planning, Prof. Segerstedt has propounded the concept of cover time planning (CTP) and has been a constant source of inspiration for me.

Padma Bhushan Dr Ramdas Pai, Chairman, and Dr Ranjan Pai, CEO, Manipal Education and Medical Group for inspiring a great vision of providing Yeoman's service to the mankind. Mr T.V. Mohandas Pai, Chairman; Mr Vaitheeswaran S., CEO; and Mr Sivaramakrishan V., Executive President, Manipal Global Education for their kind encouragement. Dr Mukesh Aghi, CEO, L&T Infotech, and Former CEO, Universitas 21 Global (U21Global Graduate School), Singapore for his well-wishes and appreciation for my books. Mr Madan Padaki, Co-founder, MeritTrac and Former CEO, Erudient, for providing me opportunities to work on online education projects in the USA, which augmented my understanding of operations management in the developed world.

Prof. Carlos Alberto Torres, University of California, Los Angeles (UCLA) for providing excellent avenues of research. Prof. Michael A. Goldberg, Professor Emeritus, University of British Columbia and Former Chief Academic Officer, U21Global for whole-heartedly supporting me in all my research endeavours and for showering immense praise on the slightest of my achievements. Prof. Jeremy B. Williams, Director, Asia Pacific Management Centre, Griffith University, Australia—my friend, philosopher, and guide—who propounded the concept of digital storytelling in online learning. The genesis of digital plant/site tours included in this book can be traced to the joint research work undertaken by the two of us on this topic.

My mentors, Mr Nick Hutton, Former CEO, and Prof. Wing Lam, Vice Chancellor, GlobalNxt University for their unrelenting support and motivation in all my academic endeavours. My colleagues at GlobalNxt University, Prof. Habibullah Khan, Prof. Jason Fitzsimmons, Prof. Amy Wong, Prof. Evelyn Gullett, Prof. Alexandra Gray, Prof. Chinmoy Sahu, Prof. Kamna Malik, Prof. Mamta Bhandar, Prof. Mark Esposito, Mr Shrikant Sinha, Ms Kananjeet Kaur, and Ms Jessie Teo for their good wishes and extraordinary support. Ms Cecelia Lee, Librarian for maintaining excellent collection of journals, research databases, and books at the GlobalNxt University e-library. My former colleague at U21Global, Prof. Ken Wong, Ryerson University (Canada), for his generous motivational comments. Prof. Malay Bhattacharyya,

Indian Institute of Management Bangalore (IIMB), for his immense affection. While writing this book, I kept in mind his advice—'Always be simple in approach.' Prof. Sreeja Bhattacharyya, Christ University, Bangalore for always being kindness personified to me and extending every possible help as an elder sister from time to time. Prof. B. Mahadevan, IIMB, for his kind words of appreciation for my books.

My illustrious teacher, Prof. Asha Kaul, Indian Institute of Management Ahmedabad (IIMA) for her guidance and blessings. Dr N.K. Dhooper, Founder Director, Jaipuria Institute of Management (JIM), Lucknow for instilling the dream of writing this book and always showing me the right direction as a godfather. My Guru, Prof. R.S. Rastogi, previously professor in the Department of Business Administration, University of Lucknow, for introducing me to this wonderful world of production and operations management. His influence on me as a teacher is inexpressible. Prof. J.K. Sharma, OSD, Institute of Management Sciences, University of Lucknow—my teacher and guide—for his unstinted support. My mentors and teachers, Prof. S.R. Musanna, Director, JIM, Lucknow, and Prof. Pankaj Kumar, Indian Institute of Management, Lucknow (IIML), for all their immense affection and support.

Prof. Subrata Chakraborty, Former Director, JIM Lucknow (Formerly Director-in-Charge and Dean, IIM Lucknow) for his affection and encouragement. Prof. A.K. Sengupta, Director (MBA–Marketing Economics) and Mrs Kamna Sengupta, University of Lucknow, for their extraordinary backing. Prof. V.K. Chib, JIM Lucknow for his praise about my books. Prof. Sudarshan Seshanna, Alliance Business School, Bangalore for all his hand-holding in the process of writing this book. Mr P. Aravindakshan, Principal, Seth M.R. Jaipuria School, Lucknow for always inspiring me to become a teacher. Mr D.K. Tripathi, Librarian, and Mr R.M. Tiwari for the extraordinary collection of books and journals on production and operations management at the JIM library. Mr R.K. Nair and Mr Raju Verghese, JIM Lucknow for helping me in every possible way. Prof. J.N.S. Chandel, IILM Academy of Higher Learning, Lucknow for his blessings. My friend, Prof. Aurnob Roy, for sharing all my problems and joys. Prof. Freda Gnanaselvam, Principal, MMES Women's Art and Science College, Melvisharam, for her inquisitive emails regarding various topics in this book and for making me realize the untapped potential of a faculty learning community in this era of networked world. My friend Prof. Purnendu Mandal, Lamar University, Texas (USA) for his affection and unflinching support.

Dr Anadi Pande, Vice-President, Hero MotoCorp for his well-wishes and Mr Mahesh Kaikini for his permission to photograph their state-of-the-art plants at Dharuhera and Gurgaon and for meticulously explaining the intricate operations of their plant. Mr R.K. Jaiswal, AGM (TQM), NTPC, Lucknow, for organizing my tour of their Singrauli plant. Mr V.K. Malhotra, Maruti Udyog Limited, for providing insights into the contemporary operations management practices followed at their Gurgaon plant. My pal, Mr Prem Das Maheshwari, VP, IMT Ghaziabad CDL, for encouraging me all along.

This book would not have been possible without the immense affection and backing of my family. I profusely thank my mother Mrs Kusum Vipin Bedi and my father Mr Vipin Bedi for showering their eternal love and blessings upon me; my loving wife Dr Monika Bedi for patiently taking due care of me during the long spells of manuscript writing for my books and for making sacrifices to support my various academic endeavours; my daughter Siya and son Tanay for bringing joy and exhilaration to me; my brother-in-law Mr Vikas Kapoor, my sister Mrs Karishma Kapoor, and my nieces Vivika and Mehr for being a constant source of love and encouragement.

In the end, I express my heartfelt thanks to my friends at Oxford University Press for their great help in every possible way.

**KANISHKA BEDI**

# Brief Contents

# Detailed Contents

# List of Exhibits and Case Studies

# 1

# Introduction to Production and Operations Management

## Learning Objectives

After reading this chapter, you will be able to answer the following questions:
- How are products and services similar to each other?
- What is production and operations management?
- What are the various steps that should be followed by an entrepreneur in setting up a new manufacturing/service facility?
- What are the new concepts in process design?
- What are the latest trends in operations management in India?
- How can organizations make their operations environment friendly?
- What is automation? What are its advantages and disadvantages?
- What are the various duties and responsibilities of production and operations managers in India?

## History of Production and Operations Management

*Scientific management* started gaining momentum during the evolution of the industrial activity in Europe in the late nineteenth century. However, the concept had started taking roots much earlier—during the late eighteenth century. The fundamental objective of scientific management was to find better ways of improving the productivity in the factories, as Europe transitioned from small-scale handicraft industry to large-scale mass-production activities. Scientific management methods called for optimizing the way the tasks were performed and simplifying the tasks enough so that workers could be trained to perform their specialized sequence of motions in the one 'best' way. Thus, scientific management can be viewed as the basis for the operations management stream of the management thought.

The successful creation of the steam engine by James Watt (1736–1819), a Scottish inventor and mechanical engineer, served as a harbinger of the industrial revolution in Great Britain and the rest of the world. Having obtained the patent for the steam engine, Watt created a steam engine manufacturing company in

James Watt

partnership with Matthew Boulton in 1794. The company had a foundry called the Soho Foundry Works, which both the partners decided to put under the joint control of their sons, James Watt Jr and Matthew Robinson Boulton. Watt Jr and Robinson deployed systematic techniques, such as demand forecasting, facility layout and work flow, production planning, planned site selection, production standards, and standardization of product standards, to manage their foundry. They also created systems to determine costs and profits for each machine manufactured. They meticulously developed training programmes for their employees, systems for compensation based on work measurements, and also employee-welfare programmes like sickness benefit programme executed by a committee of elected employees (Pollard 1974).

Charles Babbage

Charles Babbage (1772–1871), a British mathematician, mechanical engineer, and inventor, was a firm believer of the merits of division of labour. He promoted the idea of profit sharing with workers based on their productivity and encouraged the use of employee suggestion schemes. He proposed the observational methods of studying manufacturing processes. His seminal work published in 1832—*On the Economy of Machinery and Manufactures*—is regarded as an important masterpiece of scientific management (Higgins 1991).

Robert Owen

Robert Owen (1771–1858), a British social reformer, is remembered for his reforms regarding child labour in factories, providing meals in the factories to on-the-job workers, and creating suitable housing facilities for the workers. He used visual displays like painted signboards with four different colours attached to machines, signifying various levels of productivity achieved by the individual workers working on those machines. These signboards served as *silent monitors* of worker productivity and everybody in the factory could easily see the accomplishment of a worker (Wren 1972).

Thomas Alva Edison

Thomas Alva Edison (1847–1931), an American inventor and businessman, made several significant inventions and set up the world's first industrial research laboratory. Some of his prominent inventions are the long-lasting electric bulb, motion picture camera, and the phonograph. He set up large-scale production and distribution of electric power to houses, offices, and factories, and, thus, revolutionized the way people lived their lives. Few people know that he was an ingenious entrepreneur, an exemplary marketer, and an excellent businessman.

Frederick Winslow Taylor

Frederick Winslow Taylor (1856–1915), an American mechanical engineer, is aptly hailed as the father of scientific management. His book *The Principles of Scientific Management* was published in 1911 and is regarded as a cornerstone of management thought. He is famous for his stop watch time studies, in which he measured the time taken by workers in performing various parts of a task. He argued that by such measurements, a standard time could be arrived at, which could be used to create benchmarks for others to follow. According to him, this careful scientific analysis of a task helps in finding 'one best way' of performing it. In one such interesting experiment, he developed the 'science of shovelling'. He observed that the same type and size of shovel was used by workers to lift material of different densities. He provided workers with shovels of various shapes and sizes, customized according to the densities of the material to be lifted. The productivity increased three to four times due to this innovation. Taylor believed

Henry Ford

Henry Laurence
Gantt

that the primary interest of the workers and an organization's management team was the same—the management team wants better productivity from the workers, while workers want higher wages. Workers can command higher wages because their work is measurable. Once the workers understand the benefits of scientific management, they would immediately develop a better mental attitude towards the management team, thus eliminating the need for constructive criticism and complaints (Taylor 1911).

Henry Ford (1863–1947), an American entrepreneur, engineer and innovator, is best known for his invention of the modern assembly line. During his early days, Ford worked for Edison Illuminating Company (founded by Thomas Alva Edison). His passion led to several experiments in creating an internal combustion engine, which eventually culminated in 1896 with the completion of his own self-propelled vehicle—the Quadricycle. He witnessed two failures to establish his own automobile manufacturing company before finally incorporating the Ford Motor Company in 1903. In 1908, he introduced his most successful Model T, which provided an affordable, reliable, and rugged means of transport to the masses. In his factory, Ford implemented several concepts of Frederick Taylor, including standardized and interchangeable parts, precision manufacturing, and division of labour. In 1913, he invented a continuous moving assembly line. His River Rouge factory was the first integrated automobile manufacturing facility in the world, with a steel mill, a glass factory, and an automated assembly line. All this resulted in drastic reduction in per unit cost of production of his cars, thus bringing them within the reach of the common man.

Henry Laurence Gantt (1861–1919), an American mechanical engineer, is famous for the Gantt charts invented by him for use in project management. These charts served as visual display to gauge the progress of various activities in a project and are still used extensively in project management and other applications. Gantt worked with Frederick W. Taylor from 1887 to 1893 at Midvale Steel and Bethlehem Steel. Earlier, Gantt was the roommate of Taylor at the Stevens Institute of Technology. Using his Gantt charts, Gantt was able to devise an incentive system to reward the workers who completed a task before the stipulated time. He also introduced incentive schemes for the supervisors who were able to train their workers well to enhance productivity.

Lillian Moller Gilbreth (1878–1972) and Frank Bunker Gilbreth (1868–1924), an American couple, were the pioneers in the field of industrial engineering. Lillian did a PhD in industrial psychology, while Frank had no formal education beyond high school. However, Frank had rare management insights and rose from being a bricklayer to a building contractor, an inventor, and eventually, to a management engineer/consultant along with his wife Lillian. Lillian served as an advisor to American presidents Hoover, Roosevelt, Eisenhower, Kennedy, and Johnson on matters of civil defence, war production, and rehabilitation of the physically handicapped. The husband–wife duo is credited with the evolution of time–motion studies, through which they developed the 'Laws of Motion Economy' having 22 principles dealing with the use of the human body, the workplace arrangement and tools and equipment design (Gilbreth and Gilbreth 1917).

In more recent times, W. Edwards Deming (1900–1993) and Joseph M. Juran (1904–2008) are hailed as quality gurus for their immense contributions to the field of production management. Both these gentlemen were instrumental in bringing Japan to the global world map for its quality products which were beyond competition during the 1980s compared to their Western counterparts. Deming and Juran (both of them Americans) lectured throughout Japan during the 1950s and 1960s, preaching the concepts of quality. Their preaching is hailed as the harbinger of total quality management (TQM) philosophy.

It is during this time that Taiichi Ohno (1912–1990), the then Vice-President of Toyota, invented the famed just-in-time (JIT) production method (known as the Toyota Production System during that time). JIT reduced the inventory in the factories drastically, thus reducing the overall cost of production even while improving the quality.

## Products and Services

All industries may be treated as service industries to an extent, some organizations more than others. Even purely manufacturing organizations do not just sell a product but provide some form of back-up, such as after-sales service, advice, warranty, repair, installation, or training. On the other hand, even in 'pure' service industries, such as banks, hospitals, education, and consultancies, there is often a product that changes hands. For example, banks talk about new product development, because they do have products—loan schemes, deposit schemes, various types of credit cards, other types of monetary instruments, etc. Hospitals provide products to the patients in the form of diagnoses and prescription reports. Similarly, consultancies provide reports of their findings, analyses, and recommendations to client organizations. In an educational set-up, a student may see the degree or diploma as the end product, while the institution's perception may be entirely different, as it may consider an enlightened student with appropriate knowledge and skills as the end product. Exhibits 1.1 and 1.2 chart the growth of two companies—Arcelor-Mittal, which produces steel, and Amazon.com, the online retailer that has redefined book selling.

---

### Exhibit 1.1    The Rise of Laxmi Niwas Mittal

In 2006, Forbes magazine touted steel tycoon Laxmi Niwas Mittal as the fifth richest man in the world. Microsoft chief Bill Gates led the list for the twelfth year in a row with a net worth of US$50 billion followed by Warren Buffet, who had a net worth of US$42 billion. London-based Mittal, who still proudly flaunts an Indian passport, stood tall at the fifth position with a net worth of US$23.5 billion. In comparison, software giant Wipro's Chairman, Azim Premji, stood at number 25. Mukesh Ambani, the Chairman of Reliance Industries was at rank 56 and his brother Anil Ambani at rank 104.

Laxmi Niwas Mittal (popularly known as LN) is today the richest Indian in the world. He has certainly come a long way from the days when he was asked by his father to visit Jakarta (Indonesia) during an excursion trip to cover Bangkok, Singapore, Hong Kong, and Tokyo. His father had bought land in Jakarta and was not able to go ahead with the creation of a steel mill due to electricity problems. LN visited the site, sorted out the electricity

problem, and decided to stay back to start the mill. Thus, Ispat Indo was born in Jakarta. There was no looking back after that for LN. During 1980s, LN started his acquisition spree worldwide by acquiring steel mills in Trinidad and Canada. The biggest coup came when he snapped up the loss-making Sibalsa Mill in Mexico for US$220 million in 1992. His acquisition of Chicago-based Inland Steel made Ispat International (now known as Mittal Steel) the third largest producer of steel in the world. He went ahead to acquire Stahlwerk Ruhrort GmbH (SRG), a steel maker in the Ruhr, and Walzdraht Hochfeld GmbH (WHG), a wire rod manufacturer in Duisburg. Both SRG and WHG belonged to the Thyssen group, a leading German industrial consortium. He continued to acquire steel mills in Algeria, South Africa, Romania, and the Czech Republic during the early 2000.

The most recent and also the most controversial has been the merger of Mittal Steel with its nearest rival

*(Contd)*

*Exhibit 1.1 Contd*

Arcelor. This deal has catapulted LN to the position of the world's biggest steel producer, currently producing about 10 per cent of the world's total steel production. The world's largest steel group Arcelor–Mittal has a capacity of 120 million tonnes (mt). In comparison, India currently produces about 33 mt of steel annually. India's largest producer SAIL produces about 9.5 mt. Tata Steel produces about 5 mt of steel currently. The huge steel capacity amassed by LN is working in his favour to satisfy the great demands in China, which of late has emerged as the manufacturing hub of the world. In all the steel mills acquired by him, he has had an alchemist's effect. He has turned all these around into giants churning out steel up to their highest capacities. His approach in this regard exemplifies the best operations management practices, which may be emulated by other organizations in the manufacturing sector for achieving the highest productivity and quality targets.

The story of Ispat Mexicana (Imexsa) is a trend-setter for Mittal Steel in its turnaround approach. LN is said to have mastered the art of converting mini mills into integrated producers through the use of scrap alternatives. In 1991, the Mexican government invited Ispat to bid for acquiring their Sicartsa steel plant due to Ispat's reputation of turning around Iscoot, a steel mill in Trinidad. LN sent a team of people from his Trindad and Indonesia plants representing all line and staff functions with a mandate to come up with a plan to turn around the plant. The team had clear instructions from LN to give 'solid' and 'do-able' recommendations so that the person making these could be easily called upon to implement the same.

The team's report disclosed technical problems plaguing the plant, running at about 20 per cent of its total capacity, producing low quality slabs, and having a demotivated workforce. The only saving grace for the plant was its relatively young workforce with an average age of 27 years and the supporting infrastructure. The final recommendation of the team was to bid for the plant, which LN did and won the Mexican government's approval for the same. It is interesting to note that Ispat also bid for 50 per cent equity stake in many of the businesses that supported the Sircartsa plant. For example, PMT, which produced welded pipes; Pena Colarada, which provided the plant with iron pellets; and Serciin, which distributed electricity and managed the deep water port facilities. This helped in integrating the various activities in the plant.

The main highlights of the Ispat bid were the company's promise to lay off a maximum of 10 per cent of the 1,000 strong workforce and a commitment to invest US$350 million with a penalty clause of US$50 million if the company failed to follow through its investment commitment.

Imexsa was taken over by Ispat on 1 January 1992, when the steel industry was laced with deep recession. The furnaces had to be shut down for a while due to the lack of orders from customers and lack of inventory storage space. Despite the shut down, only 70 workers were laid off, though eventually 270 workers were hired after the plant started producing at a much higher capacity than earlier. Mittal set the international benchmarks for operations before the new management of the acquired plant. If the management was unwilling to strive for these benchmarks, they were told to leave. In case of Imexsa, the management stayed. At Imexsa, the production planning manager presented two production plans to LN, of which one was quite conservative at 6,00,000 tonnes and was based upon the past experience of the manager, while the other was quite ambitious at 1.2 mt. LN advised him to go ahead with the 1.2 mt plan. When the manager expressed concerns about not finding markets for additional slabs produced under this plan, LN assured him that he would take care of that himself. LN used the Ispat Indo's sales network to scout for orders in the Asian markets and successfully ended up with an order of 4,00,000 tonnes per year from a Taiwanese steel manufacturer. Thus, Imexsa was able to increase its capacity utilization and focus on improving product quality.

The new management team instituted daily meetings to discuss the previous day's cost, volume, productivity, and quality performance. These meetings also discussed the current day's results and the following day's targets to be set for each department. The MD would usually pose technical questions to force the technical managers to think through problems and get to their root causes. For example, if too much steel was being consumed in the electric arc furnaces, the questions put up were—'Is leakage responsible for consuming this much amount of steel?', 'Is steel being lost in the slag?', 'How can we improve this by using the cheapest method in the world?', and 'Can we adapt any technology which may help us in doing so?'

The cost accounting systems existing at Imexsa before the takeover were designed to report aggregate production costs on a monthly basis and that too with a delay of about three weeks. The new management implemented Ispat's daily operations reporting systems

*(Contd)*

*Exhibit 1.1 Contd*

so that the day's figures became available by the next day morning. For example, to monitor raw material usage, the warehouse employees were asked to track the volume of raw material leaving the store every day and provide these figures to the accountants.

Another unique initiative adapted by Imexsa in 1996 was a systematic programme for making internal service agreements between its own departments and monitoring service delivery levels against these agreements. The head of the department taking services from internal services provider met them once a year to explain to them the service requirements and come up with specific measures of gauging the service to be rendered by them. The internal service providers were also given the opportunity to express any prerequisites required for the delivery of service. For example, the total preventive maintenance (TPM) department may require intimation from the production department at least one week in advance about scheduled downtime of the plant to carry out preventive maintenance activities. The head of the service department monitored the provision of service on a

daily basis and submitted a monthly report to the head of the department receiving the service to be signed off by him or her if the service delivery was satisfactory. Otherwise, on repeatedly failing to meet the service delivery requirements, the issue could be discussed in the daily meeting. At Imexsa, seldom did any issue reach that stage.

Imexsa increased its shipments from 5,28,000 tonnes to 9,29,000 tonnes and decreased the cash cost per tonne produced from US$253 to US$178. In 1992, it earned a small profit within the first year of its operation under Ispat. Shipments increased up to 3 mt from 1992 to 1998, while productivity increased from 2.62 to 0.97 man hours per tonne during this time.

No wonder that a JP Morgan study hailed Imexsa as the lowest cost producer of steel slabs in the world, while the media elevated it to the highest podium by publishing statements such as 'At Imexsa, Ispat makes Nucor's cost position look almost amateurish'. This is testified by the fact that Imexsa could sell a slab in America at US$135 a tonne, much below Nucor's cash cost of production at US$210 per tonne.

> Manufacturing provides a tangible and identifiable product, which is obtained as a result of a series of transformation processes subjected to it.

In manufacturing, we get a tangible and identifiable product, which is obtained as a result of a series of transformation processes subjected to it. In services, the end product is often intangible—amusement in a theme park, hospitality in a hotel, good education, etc.—but it is just as real. When we buy a television, we ignore its manufacturing processes, but focus only upon the features of the end product. The main difference is that in services it is the customer that has been processed. In the service industry, it is often the processes that are bought rather than the product. Some organizations may be considered as offering a hybrid of products and services to its customers. For example, in a restaurant, a customer expects good preparations of the food offered (a product) and good ambience of the place, good behaviour, and quick service on the part of the waiter (a service). Similarly, while flying in an aeroplane a customer gets a product for use (a seat in the plane) and services such as medical aid and refreshments from the attendant.

## Exhibit 1.2   Jeff Bezos and Amazon.com

Jeff Bezos graduated in electrical engineering and computer science from Princeton University. He turned down offers from Bell Labs and Intel to take up a job in an entrepreneurship endeavour of two Columbia University professors, who were building a cutting-edge telecommunications network for Wall Street firms. After some time, he left the company and started selling software to pension fund clients for Bankers Trust on Wall Street and eventually joined David Shaw's D.E. Shaw

Hedge Fund. Shaw, a trained computer scientist, was a pioneer in using computers to hunt for wrongly priced securities. Within five years, Bezos became the firm's youngest senior vice-president ever, at the age of 28.

While working at Shaw in 1994, Bezos read a study on the future popularity of the Internet and imagined that soon people could sell products on the Web and make money. He got obsessed with the idea, and after considering various items, decided to sell books on

*(Contd)*

*Exhibit 1.2 Contd*

the Internet. This was mainly because of the unique characteristic of books that almost every book was catalogued electronically, but no physical bookstore could carry them all.

In 1994, Bezos started Amazon.com and based his headquarters at Seattle for two reasons—it was a hub of software professionals and was very close to Roseburg, where the largest book distribution warehouse in the US was located. Bezos thought that in this way he would be able to give customers access to a giant selection without investing the time, expense, and hassle of opening warehouses and maintaining inventories of books. He was soon proved wrong and realized that in order to give a pleasant online buying experience to his customers, he had to control all the operations from start to finish on his own, and there was no way out except for opening his own warehouses.

Amazon's 8,40,000 sq ft warehouse at Nevada, USA, has technology as the key feature. Amazon now has six warehouses, each of which stores millions of books, CDs, toys, etc., and are completely computerized. The warehouses are very high-tech and take as many lines of code to run as Amazon's website does. Customers can log on to Amazon's website and choose books online. Then, an order form is filled online and submitted to Amazon's servers. The servers automatically send signals to workers' wireless receivers in the warehouse, telling them which items to pick off the shelves. The workers put these items into small packing boxes, affix shipping labels (bar codes) on the boxes, and put these on conveyor belts. Alongside the conveyors are scanners, which scan the shipping labels and automatically send the shipping report to the servers. The conveyor drops the boxes into the big containers of the courier company. The courier company delivers the boxes to the customers overnight. During the entire process, the computers generate reams of data such as which item gets plucked first, whether the weight is right for sending, wrongly boxed items, etc. The managers are expected to study this information in order to rectify any persisting problems.

The managers put warehouses to the maximum possible productive use. For example, a bottleneck has been overcome by redesigning the system so that workers now transfer orders arriving in green plastic bins to a conveyor belt that automatically drops them into appropriate containers for the courier company. This has enabled Amazon to increase the capacity of one of its facilities by 40 per cent. Its warehouses today can handle three times the volume they could in 1999,

and in the last three years the cost of operating them has fallen from nearly 20 per cent of its revenues to less than 10 per cent. The warehouses are so efficient that Amazon turns over its inventory 20 times a year compared to under 15 times for every other retailer. Jeff Bezos is very candid in saying, 'In the physical world it is the old saw: location, location, and location. The three most important things for us are technology, technology, and technology.'

In 2002, Amazon began offering software and website developers access to selected Amazon data such as pricing trends, gradually adding more and more until this year. At present the company is getting free help from more than 2,00,000 outside web developers, up 60 per cent from a year ago. These developers are building new services on top of Amazon technology, further feeding back into Amazon's core retail business. One service, Scanbuy, lets people check Amazon prices and compare them with those of other retailers on their cell phones.

In 2006, Bezos launched many more initiatives at Amazon. A new service known as Fulfillment lets small and midsize businesses send their inventory to Amazon warehouses. When a customer places an order, Amazon gets an automated signal to ship it without any mess, fuss, servers, software, or garages full of stuff. Amazon has started to rent out just about everything it uses to run its own business, from rack space in its 10 million square feet of warehouses worldwide to spare computing capacity on its thousands of servers, data storage on its disk drives, and even some of the millions of lines of software code it has written to coordinate all this.

On 24 August 2006, a new venture known as Elastic Compute Cloud was quietly launched in test mode by Bezos. Its service—cheap, raw computing power that could be tapped on demand over the Internet just like electricity. In less than five hours, hundreds of programmers, hoping to use the service to power their MySpace and Google wannabes, snapped up all the test slots. Bezos wants Amazon to run the messy technical and logistical parts of a business, using the same technologies and operations that power his US $10 billion online store. In the process, Bezos aims to transform Amazon into a twenty first century digital utility. Kindle, Amazon's electronic book reader, was launched in November 2007. Amazon has also introduced Kindle software for use on various devices and platforms. The company launched its Kindle store in China in September 2012.

*Sources*: Amazon.com (2012); Reuters (2012).

## The Product/Process Continuum

Various organizations can be placed on a continuum, whose extreme limits are product orientation (where the emphasis is on *what* the customer buys) and process orientation (where the emphasis is on *how* it is provided). The two extremes represent the 'pure' manufacturing and 'pure' service industries. In Fig. 1.1, the automobile manufacturers are shown at the product orientation extreme of the continuum. Next are the photocopier manufacturers and service providers. After-sales service is crucial for the customer in these cases as the parts of the photocopier are very expensive and available only with the manufacturing company. The secondary market does not exist for such parts, and service personnel are also not easily available as freelancers. Therefore, process orientation is present to some extent in this case as compared to automobile manufacturers.

Next on the continuum are the automobile retailers, who are mainly involved providing information to potential buyers through their sales staff in showrooms. They also provide after-sales services, warranty services, mobile service vans (providing on-site services), etc. Restaurants lie midway on the continuum as they provide food (product) as well as services to their customers. Consultancies and undertakers lie on the process orientation extreme of the continuum.

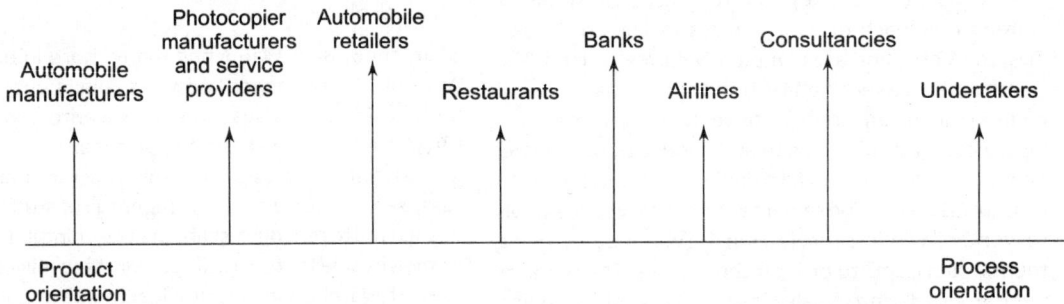

**Fig. 1.1** Organizations on a product/process continuum

## The Transformation Process

Every organization, be it a product or service organization, transforms certain inputs into outputs. For getting the desired output, the quality of the inputs has to be monitored. The quality of the actual output obtained also has to be continually compared with the desired output. As shown in Fig. 1.2, feedback mechanisms are required to monitor the performance of the transformation process. There may be some random disturbances hampering the transformation process of converting the inputs into desired outputs. These random disturbances are unexpected and sometimes not planned for. They are mostly due to external environment.

> Every organization, be it a product or service organization, transforms certain inputs into outputs.

Figure 1.3 shows the transformation process of an MBA institution, which is purely a service organization. Figure 1.4 shows the transformation process of a restaurant, which is a hybrid service and manufacturing organization. Figure 1.5 shows the transformation process of a refrigerator manufacturer, which is a purely manufacturing organization.

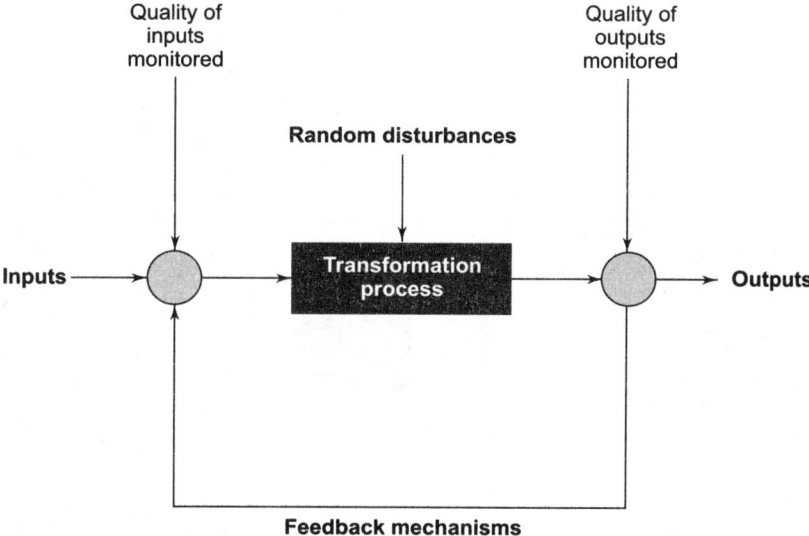

**Fig. 1.2**   Transformation process

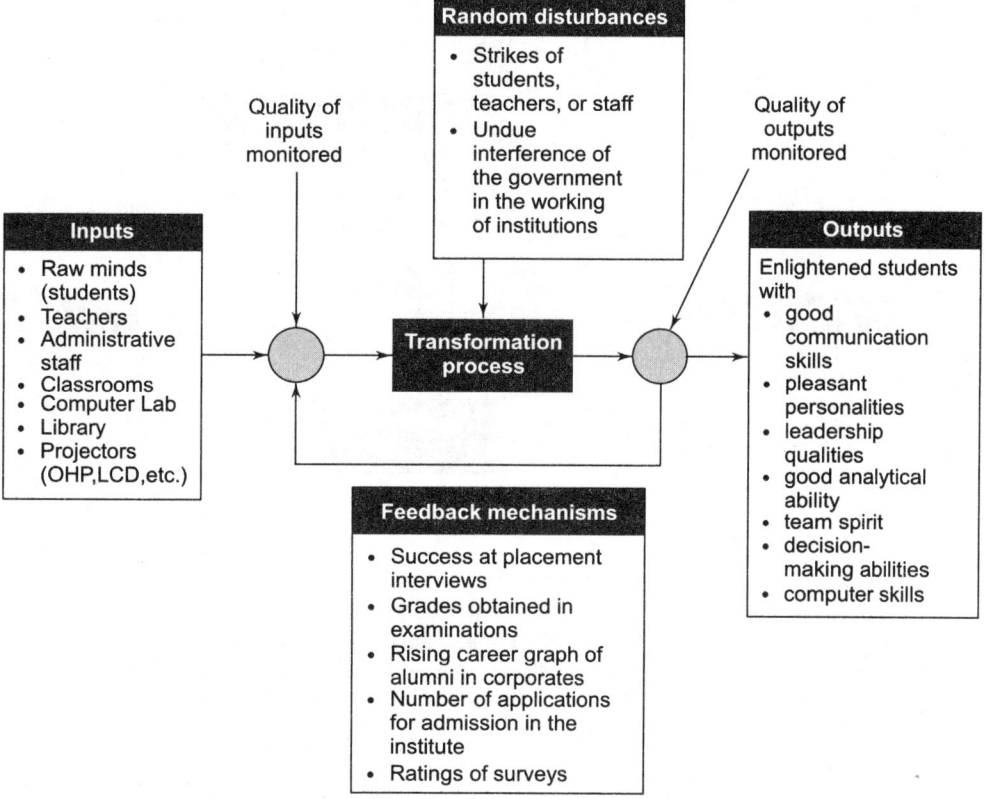

**Fig. 1.3**   Transformation process for a purely service organization (an MBA institution)

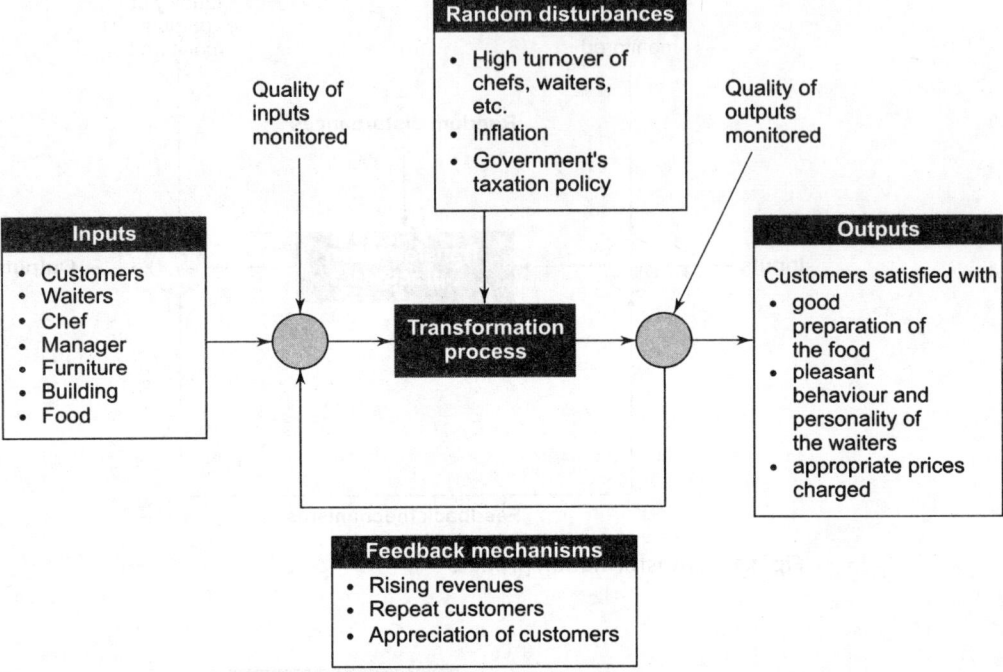

**Fig. 1.4**   Transformation process for a hybrid service and manufacturing organization (a restaurant)

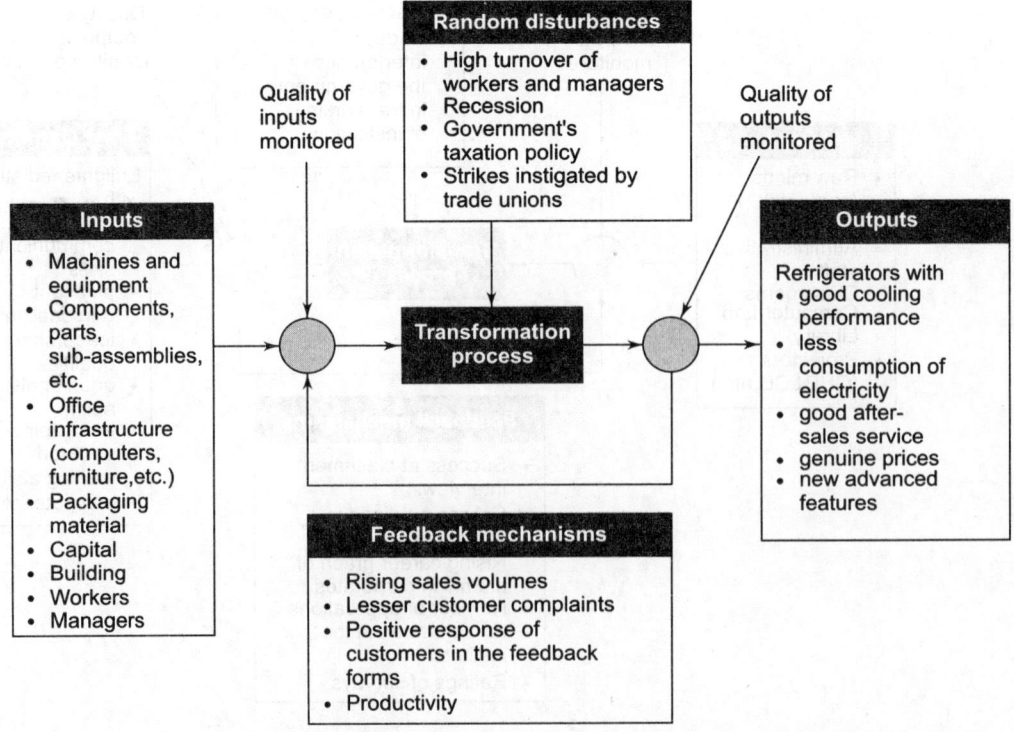

**Fig. 1.5**   Transformation process for a purely manufacturing organization (a refrigerator manufacturer)

# Production and Operations Management

Production and operations management (POM) is defined as the design, operation, and improvement of the transformation process, which converts the various inputs into the desired outputs of products and services.

The term 'production and operations management' is being increasingly replaced by simply operations management, as the production function relating to the manufacturing organizations has become a part of operations. 'Operations management' is a broad term which includes manufacturing as well as service organizations. Operations management also highlights the increasing importance of the service industry in the overall business environment. There is a growing need for the application of the principles of operations management in the service industry.

### The Operations Process from the Point of View of an Entrepreneur

This book addresses the various topics of POM in a logical sequence from the point of view of an entrepreneur who is planning to start a manufacturing/service unit (see Fig. 1.6). Entrepreneurship

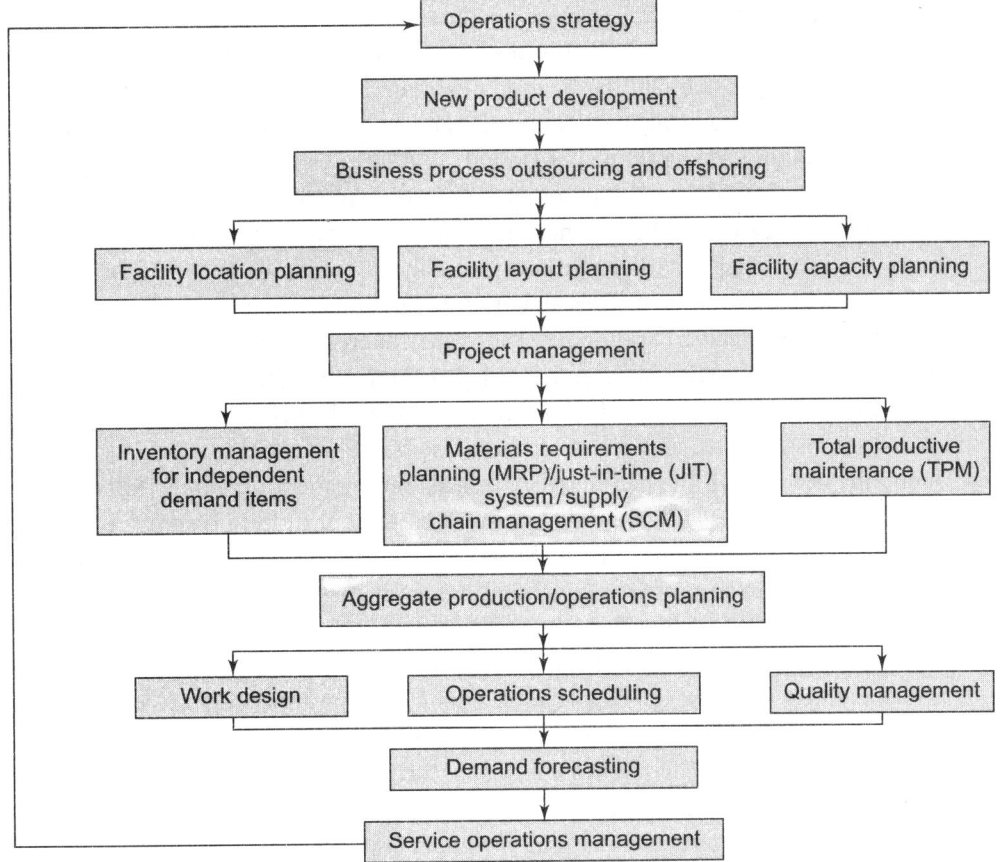

**Fig. 1.6**  Steps in the production/operations process from the point of veiw of an entrepreneur

Business process out-
sourcing and offshoring
are important features
of today's competitive
business environment.

represents the zenith of management principles and practice. An entrepreneur has to first decide about the operations strategy to be used in line with the overall business strategy of the firm. She or he has to decide if the focus in operations strategy would be on cost, quality, innovation, or to balance on all of them simultaneously. We shall study about operations strategies in Chapter 2. After deciding about the operations strategy best suited for him/her, the entrepreneur would develop a new product with unique attributes to distinguish with the similar products of the existing players in the market. This aspect of new product development would be covered in Chapter 3 of this book. In most instances, the entrepreneur does innovations in the product or process for an easy entry and a distinct product differentiation in the market place. Therefore, previous sales figures are not available for such products or services. Quantitative demand forecasting methods are not applicable under such situations. The initial estimates of demand are based upon qualitative methods and the instincts of the entrepreneur.

Business process outsourcing and offshoring are important features of today's competitive business environment. It is not an absolutely new concept in operations management, as managers always had to take decisions whether to 'make' or 'buy'. In the last one decade many organizations have adopted these practices. Chapter 4 covers this important aspect in detail.

Deciding the location of the facility is the next logical step and hence, Chapter 5 discusses facility location planning. The other consideration for the entrepreneur at the same time is the maximum capacity and, accordingly, the layout of the facility. These topics are covered in Chapter 6. In Fig. 1.6, note that facility location planning, facility capacity planning, and facility layout planning are all shown at the same level. This is so because all these decisions are dependent upon each other and should be performed simultaneously.

From the planning to the commissioning of a plant, it is a project to be handled by the entrepreneur. Later, as the business grows, the entrepreneur would come across projects of various kinds. Chapter 7 discusses project management in detail.

From where to source the raw material, in how much quantity and at what point of time are the issues to be decided upon next. These are covered in Chapter 8 on inventory management and Chapter 9 on MRP, JIT, and SCM. Inventory management focuses on the independent demand items, that is, items which are finished goods. Dependent demand items are components, parts, sub-assemblies, etc. These are called so because the demand of these items is dependent upon the demand of finished items. Materials requirement planning (MRP), just-in-time (JIT) and the hybrid MRP-JIT are the systems used to control the inventory of dependent demand items. Supply chain management (SCM) means having long-term relationship with suppliers and treating them as partners in overcoming competition. Chapter 10 discusses total productive maintenance (TPM), which is a key element of the JIT production system. It ensures that all the machines are well maintained. Hence, unexpected breakdowns resulting in production disruptions are prevented. All these concepts can be pursued by the entrepreneur simultaneously in order to save time. Hence, these are shown at the same level in Fig.1.6.

Once the raw material procurement issues have been addressed, production has to be planned. Chapter 11 deals with aggregate production operations planning. It may be noted here that MRP in not an input to aggregate planning. From an entrepreneur's point of view, while starting the business this sequence of deciding about MRP or JIT system may precede aggregate planning. Later, as the entrepreneur starts producing and selling the product or service, the sales data starts getting generated. This data helps in quantitative demand forecasting, which helps in aggregate production planning, that is, the quantity of goods to be produced. Then, the aggregate plan becomes an input for the MRP or JIT systems.

Once the production starts, it is to be checked whether the workers are performing with full efficiency or not. Chapter 12 on work design is based on this issue. In addition, the utilization of available resources in the best possible way is to be planned and controlled as discussed in Chapter 13 on operations scheduling.

The output generated by the production process has to be monitored during the process to ensure that it is according to the desired standards. The entrepreneur should know as to how to initiate and maintain a quality system in the organization. All these quality-related issues are discussed in Chapter 14 on quality management.

The entrepreneur is then concerned with demand forecasting discussed in Chapter 15. As the organization starts gaining experience in selling its products in the market, the marketing department becomes capable of providing the future demand forecasts.

As mentioned earlier in this chapter, services have certain aspects which make them different from products. An entrepreneur has to pay special attention to the service-related aspects of the operations in order to provide a valuable service experience to the customers. Therefore, there are certain approaches pertinent to service operations management. These approaches have been discussed in detail in Chapter 16.

## Process Design

The transformation process is used to convert inputs into desired outputs. The process can be of various types as shown in Fig. 1.7.

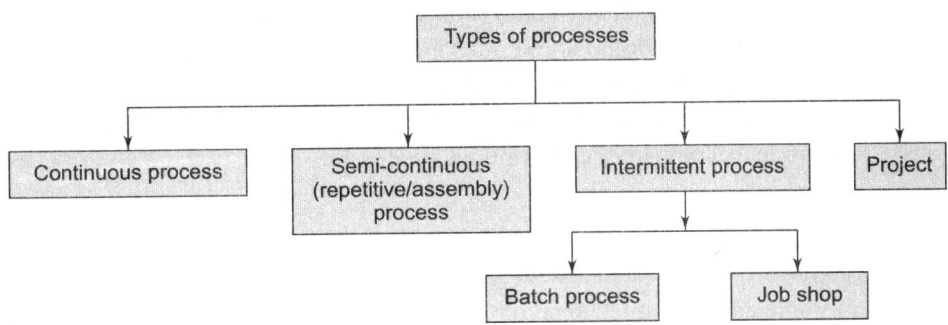

**Fig. 1.7**  Types of processes

### Continuous Process

> Intermittent processes stop at regular intervals of time because the product requires processing on a variety of machines.

The *continuous process,* as the name suggests, is continuous in nature. The set-up time for starting such processes is usually very long, and once started, they continue for a long duration. The products produced by such a process are highly standardized with almost no variety, and are measured on a continuous basis (tonnes per day, metre lengths per day, etc.) rather than in terms of discreet units. For example, urea, chemicals, steel, plastic, sugar, textiles, detergents, and other such industries are based on the continuous process and are, therefore, known as process industries.

### Semi-continuous Process

*Semi-continuous processes* are assembly processes, which are repetitive in nature. They produce high volume of output and the products produced have little variety. For example, automobiles, electronic items, white goods, etc. These processes require highly specialized machines, semi-skilled workers, and result in low cost per unit.

### Intermittent Process

As the name suggests, *intermittent processes* stop at regular intervals of time because the product requires processing on a variety of machines. The products made are of different varieties, thus making the production process slow in comparison to the continuous/semi-continuous process. Intermittent processes are of two types—batch process and job shop.

**Batch process**　This process is adopted when batches or lots of items are to be produced using the same set of machines in the same sequence. For example, in a bakery, a batch of salted biscuits may be made in the oven, followed by a batch of chocolate, followed by a batch of bread, and so on. The equipment used is the same in all the cases with the same processing steps, but cleaning and adjustments of the equipment may be required after each production run.

**Job shop**　This process can handle a larger variety of products than the batch process. The products may be so different from each other that their processing requirements may be varied processes, on different machines, in different sequences, and with different processing times. The batches of items produced in job shop may vary in size from large, comprising many units, to very small, comprising a single unit. For example, in a restaurant every customer gives a different order of dishes, which are prepared by different cooks using different utensils, ovens, etc., and different recipes. Job shop results in low volume of output at a given time, and thus costlier products compared to continuous processes.

### Projects

Projects are processes that handle very complex and unique sets of activities or tasks, which have to be completed in a limited span of time. For example, R&D projects, construction of plants, building complexes, implementation of specialized software in an organization, etc.

## Green Operations Management

The pace of industrialization in some parts of the world has been so rapid over the past few decades that it has produced an unprecedented impact upon the environment. China, in particular, seems to be choking on growth. Heavy smog in the atmosphere, polluted rivers, and deforestation are common in many parts of the country. People living in these affected regions are paying the price through medical problems, increased risk of incurable diseases like cancer, and breathlessness. The country is indeed heading towards a disaster in the making.

Another country that has far surpassed everyone's imagination in industrial growth over the past few decades is India. Multinational corporations (MNCs) have thronged the country to set up their facilities, as lack of stringent rules on environment makes it a lucrative facility location. The country is bestowed with natural resources, which again are being eyed by MNCs as attractive business propositions. The local populace in such regions is often given a raw deal, whereby neither their status of living changes due to industrialization in their region nor is their future secured. The story of Vedanta Aluminium Ltd in India echoes this gross neglect of environmental and social issues. Its aluminum factory in Odisha is extracting bauxite from the nearby hills, whose local populace is facing a serious threat of displacement and the greenery of the hills is quickly disappearing.

Sustainable development requires a responsible approach from organizations globally to make sure that the natural resources and the environment which we enjoy today remain available for our future generations. Unfortunately, most organizations today overlook this prime aspect in planning and managing their operations. Obviously, a lot of money can be saved by commercial organizations in the short term by exploiting natural resources and turning a blind eye towards the negative impacts produced by their operations on the natural environment. However, such organizations would be deemed by future generations as 'robbers', who deprived them of fresh air to breathe and clean water to drink. Gradually, organizations are realizing this important fact and, therefore, are focusing on corporate social responsibility (CSR).

A big question facing the environmental experts is how to reduce global warming. Is it through the use of alternative energy sources like solar, biofuel, or wind? In his new book *Hot, Flat and Crowded*, Thomas Friedman shares that creating an ecosystem to breed innovation in alternative sources is the only way forward. He argues that it is not because the human race had run out of stone that they stopped making stone tools. They did so because they had discovered bronze. Similarly, the world would not stop using fossil fuel when we would run out of it—it would still be there, but somebody would invent alternative sources of energy far better than fossil fuels.

## Carbon Credits and Carbon Trading

*Carbon emissions* and *carbon footprint* are terms associated with the air pollution generated by individuals/organizations/factories. The smoke emitted into the atmosphere by burning fossil fuels (such as coal, wood, petrol, diesel, kerosene, liquefied petroleum gas, etc.) contains carbon dioxide gas, which is one of the greenhouse gases (some other greenhouse gases are methane, nitrous oxide, etc.). Carbon emission is a measure of the amount of carbon dioxide gas emitted. In layman's terms, carbon footprint of an individual/organization is calculated on the basis of the average amount of fossil fuel used (directly or indirectly). For example, when we travel in a car or airplane using petrol, when we cook our food using liquefied natural gas (LNG), when we use electricity (generated through turbines run through fossil fuel), etc., we are leaving a carbon footprint on the planet earth. Naturally, it is not easy to accurately calculate absolute figures of carbon footprint for an individual or organization. However, the approximate carbon footprint figures do help in increasing awareness about the pollution created and to think of measures to minimize it.

Kyoto Protocol was a significant attempt by the international community to reduce the greenhouse gas emissions. It paved the way for *carbon credits*, whereby a company reducing air pollution below permissible limits can sell carbon credits to another company that is exceeding air pollution beyond the permissible limits. One tonne of carbon dioxide emission is treated as one unit of carbon credit.

The European Union was the torch-bearer in experimenting with the concept of *carbon trading*. The setting up of the European Climate Exchange was the first step in this direction. It provided an official platform for companies to trade carbon credits with each other. However, a major challenge was the low value (less than 50 cents) attributed to a carbon credit during the initial period, which did not inspire companies to take actual measures to control emissions. Hopefully, the market value of a carbon credit would rise substantially in the time to come, in order to overcome this issue. Taking a cue from the Europeans, the USA set up the Chicago Climate Exchange.

There are critics of the carbon credit and trading system, who argue that companies may use these mechanisms to exploit the developing countries. People involved in tree plantations in developing nations seeking carbon credits on behalf of MNCs, often crib about the fact that they got a raw deal in the process. Experts argue that such systems are in fact doing more damage to the environment than good. In their view, such systems encourage people to believe that they can continue to pollute the environment as long as they are 'offsetting' such acts by tree plantations, etc. However, the only way to reduce overall emissions realistically is to encourage people to actually avoid such acts that result in emissions in the first place.

### Reducing Emissions

Avoidance or reduction of the use of fossil fuels is the way forward to minimize carbon emissions. Various alternative energy options are available today—solar, wind, geothermal energy, and biofuels. Water as an energy source has been used since the time when large-scale generation of hydro-electric power became possible through conversion of hydro energy in order to run turbines, which convert it into electricity. However, in recent times, some of the hydro-electric projects have faced stiff resistance due to displacement of local populace at the location of the proposed dams. Sardar Sarovar Dam on river Narmada in India is a case in point—the dam witnessed severe opposition from the local population throughout its construction.

The construction industry should manage water resources better in order to avoid wastage during the construction process. The building designs should allow as much natural light as possible inside the building so as to reduce the power consumption during day time. Major hotel chains have redesigned the water-flushing systems in toilets so that they consume less water. They encourage their guests to reuse towels, bed sheets, and so on, to help reduce consumption of water and energy (in washing machines) used for washing. The famous catch line of Marriott Hotels 'Spirit to Serve' has undergone a transformation recently into—'Spirit to Preserve'. The hotel, which is renowned worldwide for its quality of service, is on the forefront of going green. Be it its laundry operations, use of fluorescent lamps, or creating sustainable hotel buildings, Marriott has demonstrated its whole-hearted willingness to contribute to this cause. Its latest 'Nobility of Nature' programme is helping to protect fresh water sources in Asia.

A large majority of vehicles today run on fossil fuels. Unfortunately, it is a major source of carbon emission. Transportation is an integral part of supply chains of major corporations. Thus, it is impossible to reduce the carbon footprint unless all supply partners resolve to do something about it jointly. One way is to make use of electric vehicles for transportation.

However, the electric-vehicle technology is still expensive and relatively cumbersome to maintain. Nevertheless, efforts are being made to overcome these challenges. Walmart, the famous American retail chain, has endeavoured over the past decade to imbibe the virtues of a green organization. In its latest efforts, it is asking its suppliers to go green in their operations. The company is aggressively positioning itself to drastically reduce greenhouse gas emissions all across its supply chain. The airline industry is usually an easy target of criticism for its carbon dioxide emissions. KLM is one of the world's few airlines that are on the forefront of reducing carbon dioxide emissions through their initiatives like Reduce–Control–Compensate. In November 2009, KLM became the world's first airline to test flying with biofuel. The airline has been a pioneer in CSR in the industry.

### Recycling

Recycling is increasingly becoming an important mechanism to reduce raw material consumption, energy, and pollution by processing the seemingly waste products into usable products. It is based on the premise that the resources required to produce a product from scratch would be much more compared to recycling the products. Not only does recycling help in removing waste products from homes and offices but also it converts them into reusable products. It is important to identify those products that are recyclable and those that are not. For example, paper bags are recyclable while most plastic bags are not. Therefore, people should be encouraged to use recyclable products rather than non-recyclable ones. Recycling of various types of products requires different types of processes and equipment. For example, recycling of computers involves separating various parts like the mother board, power supply, microprocessor, hard drive, etc. These different parts are subjected to varied processes of recycling.

McDonald's has faced severe criticisms for its so called 'junk' food. However, the company has taken unique CSR initiatives over the past couple of years. Be it opening of green building restaurant in Chicago, using disposable packaging or water management – the company is doing everything possible to project its image as a 'green' organization.

## Automation

Automation means replacing human labour with machines. The machines can be computers, robots, etc., which take care of the repetitive tasks. The extent of automation can range from partial to full (in which case no human labour is required at all). Figure 1.8 shows the advantages and disadvantges of automation. Exhibits 1.3 and 1.4 illustrate the benefits of automation at BMW and Force Motors.

*Computer-aided manufacturing* (CAM) is a form of automation in which computers are used in process control, ranging from controlling various machines to controlling even the process quality. *Computer numerically controlled* (CNC) machines are so called because they are controlled by a software program through a computer. A *flexible manufacturing system* (FMS) has a number of machines controlled simultaneously by a computer program in intermittent processes to process a variety of similar products. It is flexible to some extent, as the computer program can be modified to suit changes in processing requirements. *Computer-integrated manufacturing* (CIM) means integrating various other automation activities not only in the manufacturing

---

### Exhibit 1.3    BMW

Munich-based Baverische Motoren Werke (BMW) operates some of the most flexible and productive factories in the global auto industry. At BMW's Spartanburg plant (USA), to begin the painting process, each car body is prepared and cleaned through stages of fit hooks, brush wash, and degreasing. It then moves to the phosphate stage, where a crystalline structure of zinc, nickel, and manganese is formed that provides corrosion protection to the body. BMW is renowned worldwide for its built-to-order facilities. About 80 per cent of European BMW buyers custom-design their own cars, choosing everything from special engine configurations to headlights with sensors that track the bend in the road. The customers can change every detail on the car until five days before production. There are $10^{17}$ possible variations in a car for the customers to choose from. The computers at BMW can handle up to 1,20,000 customers per month, who keep changing their mind about what they want. Most of these last-minute changes are costly upgrades to bigger engines or more luxurious interiors.

*Source*: BMW.

---

### Exhibit 1.4    Force Motors

Pune-based Force Motors is one of the smallest automobile companies in India. The company was earlier known as Bajaj Tempo. It changed its name to Force Motors Ltd after the exit of its financial collaborator, Daimler Chrysler AG. It is also one of the most vertically integrated, possessing not only a state-of-the-art tool room and R&D capabilities, but also facilities to manufacture all critical parts such as engines, gearboxes, axles, and even hydraulic valves in-house. The company has mainly been a light commercial vehicle (LCV) manufacturer for over three decades. In 1999, it succeeded in indigenously designing and developing a range of latest generation tractors with many advanced features, from the concept stage to the production stage in a record time of 30 months—that too without any foreign collaboration. This is not new for Force Motors, where this is the way of life. The company had earlier developed three new LCV models and one new three-wheeler model.

The state-of-the-art tool room is backed by the latest CAD/CAM facilities. Force Motors has over a hundred CAD workstations for product design, analysis, simulation, etc. The initial product design is done using a number of CAD packages. For example, the engine of the tractor was designed by completely re-engineering the Mercedes OM 616 engine, which has been the powerhouse of Force Motors' LCVs for many years. Several radical changes were made in the engine design. For instance, it was converted into a direct injection engine from the indirect one. This resulted in more power, better combustion, and better fuel efficiency. A tractor needs a much higher torque compared to an automobile; therefore, the stroke of the engine was increased by redesigning the crankshaft. The bore and compression ratio was also altered. For the 35-hp tractor, the engine was truncated from four cylinders to three, while for the 45-hp tractor, all the cylinders were retained.

Once designs are frozen, the design data is used to design the dies for the parts using the CAD packages again. Then, the entire manufacturing process of the die is simulated on the computer to check for any fouling of the cutting tool. The computer also decides the optimum cutting speed for the maximum rate of material removal and desired finish. The entire data is then downloaded to a CNC die-sinking machine in the tool room. All the CNC machines are integrated, networked, and controlled by the CAD workstations in the R&D department. The machine operator clamps the raw material onto the machine bed and the cutting process is done automatically as the machine is controlled by computers, which have all the design data stored in them. Earlier when the manufacturing process was dependent on the skill of the operator, it used to take between three and six months to design and manufacture a die depending on the complexity. Now it takes hardly a month to do the same job.

*Source*: Force Motors (2012).

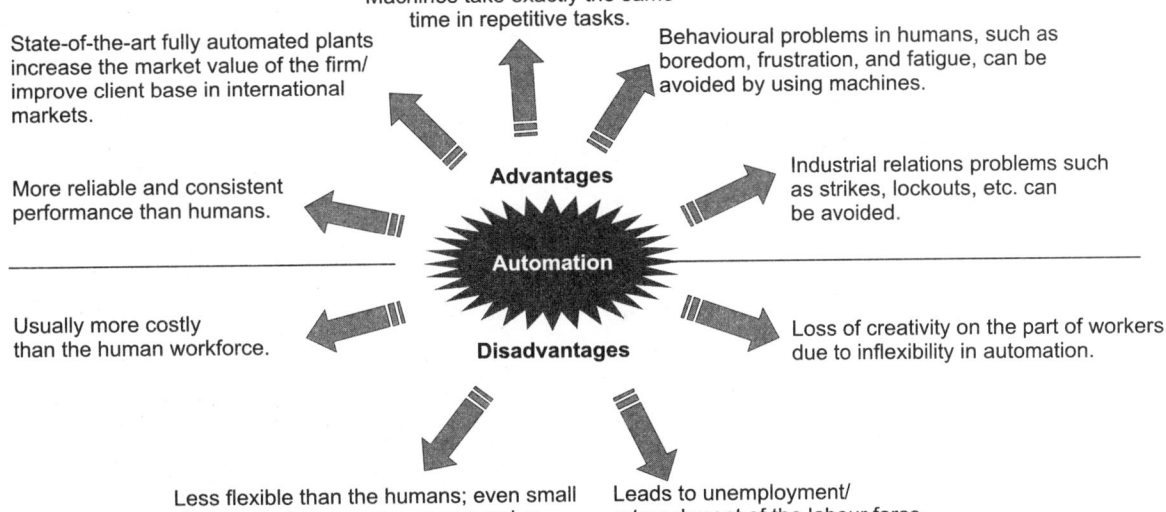

**Fig. 1.8** Advantages and disadvantages of automation

> Computer-aided manufacturing (CAM) is a form of automation in which computers are used in process control, ranging from controlling various machines to controlling the process quality.

department but also other departments such as engineering, purchase, materials, distribution, etc., so as to optimize the manufacturing capabilities of a firm up to the maximum extent possible.

*Enterprise resource planning* (ERP) softwares such as SAP R/3, Baan, Peoplesoft, etc. have provided the missing link between various functional departments providing higher efficiency in the operations processes. The main benefit of ERP implementation is that the repetition of data entry is eliminated completely. For example, if the purchase department has made some purchases from a supplier, the entries made by the purchase clerk in the purchase order form on the computer screen are automatically available at the relevant files in the accounts department (which can prepare for making payments), materials department (which can make preparations for receiving the goods), quality control department (which can make arrangements for quality inspection), and so on. Figure 1.9 shows the opening screen of SAP R/3. Note that the opening

> The main benefit of ERP implementation is that the repetition of data entry is eliminated completely.

screen shows the various modules in SAP R/3—office, logistics, accounting, human resources, and information systems.

## The Production Manager

### Duties and Responsibilities in Manufacturing Organizations

The following duties and responsibilities of production managers are prominently witnessed in manufacturing organizations:

1. Planning the geographical location of the factory
2. Purchasing production equipment
3. Layout of equipment within the factory
4. Designing production processes and equipment

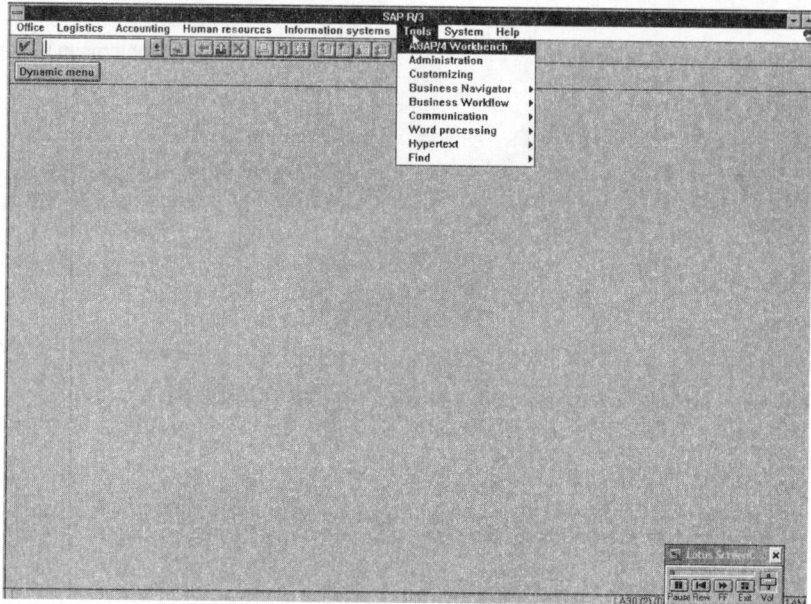

**Fig. 1.9**   Opening screen of SAP R/3

5. Product design
6. Desiging production work and establishing work standards
7. Capacity planning
8. Production planning and scheduling
9. Production control
10. Inventory management
11. Supply chain management
12. Quality control
13. Production equipment maintenance and repair
14. Measurement and monitoring of productivity
15. Industrial relations/personnel matters
16. Health and safety
17. Staff selection and training
18. Budgeting and capital planning

In 1986, Mohanty and Nair conducted a survey of 100 Indian companies having an annual turnover exceeding ₹6,00,000 from various sectors, both private and public, including chemicals, engineering, fertilizers, and textiles. The objective was to identify the critical decision areas in production management and to create a responsibility/activity matrix for Indian production managers so as to integrate the diversified decision areas. Some of the interesting findings of the survey are as follows.

1. The prime objectives of most production managers are to ensure customer satisfaction by meeting due dates and reducing the costs of production. For example, fertilizer industry production managers are generally found to be interested in minimizing wastage. Ensuring better working conditions for production employees was given low priority.

2. The major problems faced by production managers seem to be production scheduling and capacity planning. Despite the popular notion that availability of energy is a critical factor for industrial growth in India, production managers do not perceive it as a major problem. They have in fact developed working production schedules in restricted power supply situations.

3. Production managers in all industries have maximum responsibilities in the areas of production planning, scheduling, and production control, and spend their maximum time in these areas. Monitoring of productivity, for instance, is one of the important decision areas in the chemical industry. Quality control is also treated as an important decision area, and in certain industries, such as fertilizers, production managers spend most of their time on it.

4. Ironically, production managers are not involved in product design, with some exceptions in the textile industry. Historically, manufacturing systems have been separated from the product design function.

5. For a large majority of production managers, the most important part of their job is to ensure efficient utilization of resources, be it machines/equipment or human resources.

6. Computers are not yet perceived as important tools for decision support, and are also not likely to be in the near future. Subjective judgement and assessment are quite widely used in problem solving. However, with the exception of the textile sector, many managers do recognize the potential of quantitative techniques and modelling.

7. The extent of cooperation of other departments with the production department is shown in Table 1.1. There is little contact of the production managers with the board of directors; production is not considered to be a major contributor to corporate strategy in India. Production managers in process industries are more concerned about pollution control and, hence, the level of cooperation in this area is increasing day by day.

**Table 1.1**   Cooperation of other departments with the production department

| Decision area | Chemicals | Engineering | Fertilizers | Textiles |
|---|---|---|---|---|
| Marketing department | VI | III | III | Highest |
| Product design department | X | VII | IV | IV |
| R&D department | VIII | V | VII | V |
| Finance department | VII | IX | VII | VI |
| Personnel department | V | VI | IV | IV |
| Maintenance department | Highest | IV | Highest | III |
| Stores | IV | IV | VI | IV |
| Quality control department | III | Highest | II | IV |
| Production engineering department | X | VI | V | Lowest |
| Board of directors | Lowest | Lowest | Lowest | VIII |
| Other production departments | IX | II | VI | VII |
| Pollution control | II | VIII | Highest | II |

## Emerging Role of the Production and Operations Manager in India Today

After 1991, the liberalization in the country has brought about major changes in the business scenario. The entry of multinational corporations into almost every sphere of industry has created a sense of competition in the Indian industry. The role of the production and operations manager in India has increased manifold. Figure 1.10 shows the new dimensions which have been added to the responsibilities of the operations manager in India today. Go through Exhibit 1.5 to learn about IRCTC's online ticketing service.

**Fig. 1.10** Emerging role of the production and operations manager in India today

---

### Exhibit 1.5 Indian Railway Catering and Tourism Corporation Ltd

Indian Railways is the second largest rail network (under a single management) in the world after Russia, running over 14,500 trains daily throughout the country. Not long back, the Indian public had to stand in long queues for hours to get their journey tickets booked at the railway reservation counters. August 2002 witnessed a pleasant surprise from the marketing arm of Indian Railways, known as Indian Railway Catering and Tourism Corporation (IRCTC), which introduced its online ticketing services. No wonder that during the first month of this service, 3,343 tickets were sold online. By the end of the maiden year of its operations, the service sold 30,300 tickets valued at around ₹40 million.

The IRCTC reservation site allows passengers to buy tickets and pay for them using credit or debit cards; check train fares, routes, and availability in real-time; and receive alerts about rail schedules. Passengers can also track their tickets from the time of booking till third-party courier services make the delivery (under the i-ticketing option). Users register their credit card numbers and then book their tickets. The system dashes a query to the passenger reservation system to check for fares and availability. After the above process is done, it checks the validity of the credit card with the payment gateway. Once this verification is carried out,

it prints the physical ticket in Delhi. They are sorted out on a city-wise basis and sent by courier. From February 2006, IRCTC has given the passengers the option to take print-outs of their tickets (under the e-ticketing option), after booking is made. This has further eliminated the wait on part of the passengers to receive the tickets through the courier agency.

There were teething troubles during the initial launch of the online ticketing service, primarily due to the slow speed of dial-up Internet connections prevalent at that time. The IRCTC online booking portal works on the BroadVision e-commerce platform maintained by BroadVision Inc., which is a major provider of enterprise business portal applications and is based in California, USA. During the initial implementation stage, BroadVision had to overcome challenges relating to integration of the legacy system with the new reservation system and verifying credit card information real-time, as the booking had to be confirmed to the passenger on the portal immediately. The initial estimates of IRCTC of around 0.1 to 0.2 million hits on the portal for bookings and enquiries were based upon the numbers witnessed by online shopping sites. These estimates were instantly shattered when they were faced with over 1.3 million enquiries daily

*(Contd)*

*Exhibit 1.5 Contd*

converting into over 2,000 bookings daily. The result was jamming of networks and payment gateways. IRCTC had to instruct ICICI Bank and Citibank to upgrade their payment gateways to ensure smooth sailing for customers under this huge traffic.

IRCTC's success on the online ticketing front is enviable not only because it achieved this feat inspite of being a government organization, but also because of the complexities of the Indian railway system. On 13 July 2012, a record was created in the history of Indian Railways when a total of 4.96 lakh e-tickets were sold.

However, its reach is certainly going to be widened due to the easy availability of broadband Internet connections and increased used of credit cards by the Indian public.

As part of its customer-retention strategy, IRCTC has launched a loyalty program called 'Shubh Yatra' for frequent travellers. The online portal now offers flights and hotels booking facilities as part of its reservation services.

*Sources:* Jamal (2012); IRCTC (2013).

## POM in India: First 40 Years of the Republic

Would any entrepreneur or business house build a mini cement mill today with wet kiln technology, or a mini steel mill with an electric-arc or induction furnace, or a dimethyl terephthalate (DMT) plant, or a polyester plant of 10,000 tpa (tonnes per annum) capacity, or an auto plant with a production capacity of less than 2,000 cars per month, or a million-tonne oil refinery in the landlocked Gangetic basin? Forget building them, should you even dare to propose one at all, you would be laughed out of the stock market and bank boardrooms. In the last 12 years, that is, after liberalization, the change in the manufacturing sector in India is apparent as compared to the first 40 years of the Republic. There were times before liberalization when the government and the financial institutions not only encouraged such projects but also insisted on them.

The capacity of a facility is a strategic decision having long-lasting effects. The policy makers in the government before liberalization seemed to be bitten by the size bug and uniformly insisted on 'small is beautiful'. This led to fragmentation of capacity in all sectors of the economy. The worst examples are of mini cement plants and mini steel mills. While the service industry can survive and thrive to an extent when it is small, any kind of manufacturing must necessarily be large enough to achieve economies of scale. The licence holders masked higher in-built capacities when ordering plant and equipment, so that when the government allowed them to expand they could invoke the magical effects of 'in-house de-bottlenecking and technology absorption' and even claim some tax benefits under R&D efforts.

Facility location planning of various projects before liberalization was done by the government, and not by the entrepreneurs or bankers in the name of evenly spread industrial development of various regions. A classic example is the automotive industry. Even with restrictions on size in those days, Bajaj Auto, Force Motors, Kinetic Engineering, and Tata Motors seeded the growth of a large ancillary industry in the Pune-Pimpri-Chinchwad belt. But in capital intensive industries such as petrochemicals and telecommunication equipment, etc., where automation is the key to safety and quality, it makes no sense at all to dictate their location. Despite all the pressures from ministers and local MLAs, the managements of such plants have a limited scope for 'employment generation'.

There are many horror stories of governmental interference in the choice of manufacturing technology in the Licence Raj. Even the plan for plant modernization had to be approved by the government. Similarly, 'make or buy' was not a decision left to the management of an enterprise but to the government, especially if it involved import of some components or raw materials. The entire electronics

The capacity of a facility is a strategic decision having long-lasting effects.

Facility location planning of various projects before liberalization was done by the government.

industry in India missed the bus owing to interference from the Department of Electronics, even though India produced some of the best electrical, electronics, and communications specialists in the world.

Should we import liquid fuels for the energy-intensive industry or use local or imported coal? Should we use gas or imported naphtha for fertilizers? Can we import cheap South African or Australian coal and Brazilian iron ore for steel? All were redundant questions earlier, when the option of importing cheaper or better raw materials from anywhere in the world just did not exist. Today, if a plastic lubricant that can be made by one grade of high-density polyethyelene (HDPE) manufactured by, say, Reliance does not have satisfactory impact-resistance properties, the injection moulder will use an imported one from, say, Phillips, which might have the required properties. This situation not only provides better jerrycans to consumers but also drives Reliance to investigate polymer engineering and fine-tune its process parameters in order to satisfy its customers and retain its dominant position in every grade of plastics.

Could one collaborate with any foreign company, or buy a foreign technology for a mutually negotiated fee, or buy a foreign company itself, which might provide easier entry into the markets besides giving access to technology without becoming an NRI? No. All these were to be decided in Delhi. If Cipla, Essar Steel, or BPL has to buy a company in the US, Singapore, or France, they still have to cross a lot of hurdles.

Thus, if India is not a manufacturing powerhouse today despite its skilled labour and large domestic market and engineering capabilities, we have the first 40 years of the Republic and the Licence Raj to blame. If the Indian domestic industry has to come up strongly against the multinational threat, it has to start shunning old practices and adopting the latest ones. Amul has successfully used geographical information system to streamline its processes (Exhibit 1.6). Companies such as Cipla, Reliance, Tata Motors, Bajaj, Essar Steel, Hero MotoCorp, TVS, and a few others have been able to gain ground as world-class manufacturers by leaving all the  production and operations practices of the past 40 years behind them. The Online Resource Centre of the book includes digital plant tours of four organizations for your learning.

---

### Exhibit 1.6    Amul

Amul, started in 1946, is a pioneering concept in the dairy cooperative movement in India. The movement is synonymous with empowering farmers, especially rural women farmers. Due to this movement, today India has become the largest producer of milk in the world. This movement has been successfully replicated in about 70,000 villages in over 200 districts in India. Amul is also one of the largest food brands in India with an annual turnover of US$500 million, and with products ranging from milk, butter, ghee, cheese, chocolates, ice-creams, and pizzas. In 2005, Amul became the first Indian dairy products exporter to achieve a mark of ₹1 billion in revenues. The year 2005 ended with an export turnover of ₹1.15 billion—more than three times its export turnover as compared to the previous year. Quoting from the 2005 speech of the then Chairman

and the patriarch of the co-operative movement in India, Verghese Kurien, 'The diffusion of this visionary experiment has ensured the proliferation of numerous Amuls across India. Thus, Aavin, Him, Mahananda, Milma, Nandini, Omfed, Parag, Sanchi, Saras, Snowcap, Sudha, Verka, Vijaya, Vita—all are manifestations of Amul in its regional avatars.'

The cooperative has set new benchmarks in streamlining its operations by using automation and IT. Amul has installed about 3,000 automatic milk collection system units (AMCUS) at village societies to capture member information, milk fat content, volume of milk collected, and payment made to the member. This has ensured the highest level of transparency and real time data collection throughout the organization. Hundreds and thousands of farmers

*(Contd)*

*Exhibit 1.6 Contd*

throng its cooperative milk collection centres every day (morning and evening). They have been given plastic identification cards, which they insert in the AMCUS. The machine starts displaying the member's details on the computer monitor attached to it. The quantity of the milk brought by the farmer is measured. The machine also measures the fat content in the milk. Accordingly, the machine generates a printed slip to the farmer stating the value of the milk. This slip is carried to the adjacent payment counter and the full payment is received instantaneously.

Earlier, before automation, members were given paper passbooks and every time milk collection was done, the quantity of the milk supplied by the member was written on it. For measuring the fat content, a small sample of the milk was collected in a pouch to be taken to the lab for testing. This process normally used to take a week, only after which the farmer could receive the payment. Thus, it is obvious that this initiative has helped Amul to collect about 6 million litres of milk every day from around 2 million members with seamless accuracy and immediate payment. Milk being a perishable quantity, every minute saved in the collection process helps in its early preservation and subsequent value-adding processes. Even the end-products have a limited shelf life and hence, it is commendable for Amul to meticulously plan and execute all the operations with clock-work precision, especially in view of its mammoth scale of operations. The supply chain practices of Amul are akin to just-in-time (JIT) system and the rigorous time schedules followed by its 5000 odd trucks twice every day for bringing milk to about 200 milk processing plants qualify for Six Sigma level of precision.

Amul has implemented a customized ERP system designed by Tata Consultancy Services (TCS), which can be plugged into various points of the supply chain. Amul has connected all its offices and member dairies through VSATs and is in the process of web-enabling its entire supply chain (including transporters, member manufacturing units, suppliers, depots, and the entire field force) so as to capture key information at source and use it for decision-making.

A unique initiative of Amul is the use of geographical information system (GIS) by superimposing the product-wise sales data on the map of India demarcated into zones or depots in the GIS. This helps in sales and distribution planning. Amul's GIS also captures farmer-member census information including animal census data. This way Amul is able to extract information relating to milk production and productivity of animals region-wise in Gujarat. Not only has it helped in predicting milk production levels, but also in suggesting remedies for lower milk production rate in a region. This GIS is capable of being used for monitoring veterinary health and controlling the outbreak of diseases.

Amul has repeatedly redefined the way business is done. In its endeavour to eliminate middlemen and bring the producer–farmer closer to the end consumer, Amul has started a cyberstore gifting service capable of directly servicing customers in 125 cities across the country. Distributors can directly place orders through Amul's extranet known as Cyber Amul (www.amulb2b.com). As a result, Amul has been receiving queries from overseas agents for distributing its products in countries such as the US, UK, New Zealand, Singapore, and Thailand. Amul has recently become the world's biggest brand of vegetarian cheese, which is manufactured using rennet from either fungal or bacterial sources rather than animal sources.

The popularity of the brand is reflected in the cooperative's ₹11,660-crore turnover. In 2011, Amul was named the 'most trusted' brand in the food and beverages sector in *The Brand Trust Report*.

*Sources: Anon (2011); Anon (2012).*

## Latest Trends in Operations Management

Throughout this book, we shall be discussing contemporary ways of managing operations—be it the 'frugal engineering concepts' utilized by Tata in the creation of their 'Dream Car' Nano, or extensive leveraging of their supplier's designing skills by Mahindra for creating their Scorpio, XUV 500, and Xylo, or the direct-selling model innovated and exploited by Dell, or the supplier-exchange platform deployed by Ford in collaboration with General Motors and Chrysler in the USA. However, here we shall highlight how innovative approaches are helping to address some of the fundamental problems India (and the Indian sub-continent) have been grappling with for the past several decades.

First, let us keep in mind that the various functional areas of management are closely integrated with each other, namely operations, finance, marketing, and human resources. It is impossible to see an innovative approach purely from the perspective of a particular area of management. Even if an attempt is made to do so, it would mask important interplays that happen between the functional areas in order to create a viable and sustainable solution to address a problem.

Second, and more importantly, we shall focus our attention towards trends in operations management that are picking up in our country to deal with problems faced by the lowest strata of the society—the poor. We shall try to sensitize ourselves how innovative and entrepreneurial thinking on part of some social as well as commercial entrepreneurs has helped in alleviating the fundamental problems of impoverished people (Exhibit 1.7).

---

### Exhibit 1.7   Entrepreneurship and Social Change

**Muhammad Yunus and Grameen Bank**   In 2006, Muhammad Yunus received the Nobel Prize for Economics for his micro-finance schemes in Bangladesh. Till 1971, he was a professor of economics in the USA. However, when Bangladesh became a separate country in 1971, he returned to his homeland and joined a local university. The poverty-stricken people in the nearby villages provided this economics professor an opportunity to come face-to-face with harsh realities of life. The money lenders in these villages were exploiting the people such that their life was akin to 'slave workers'. Yunus turned from a teacher to a social entrepreneur and provided a shining example of how innovations at the grassroots can defy common logic and established systems. Traditional banks provide loans only to the rich and wealthy, who can mortgage properties/assets as guarantees against the loan applied for. In this system, the poverty-stricken people are completely deprived of availing the facility of availing loans from the conventional banks. Yunus changed this paradigm by applying the concept of 'micro-credit' for the poor and needy. His Grameen Bank or 'bank for the poor' neither has huge infrastructure nor swanky offices, but its outreach to the poor and needy is unprecedented. Interestingly, 97 per cent of Grameen Bank's customers are women. In the view of Yunus, a family benefits the most when women are given the opportunity of earning livelihood through the provision of loans. They are usually more responsible to take care of children in the household compared to male members in the family.

**Bindeshwar Pathak and Sulabh International**   In a developing country like India, till a few years back, people did not have the facilities of toilets at most of the public places even in the metropolitan cities. Wherever the government attempted to create such facilities, these were rendered highly unhygienic within no time due to lack of cleanliness and upkeep.

Dr Bindeshwar Pathak's organization Sulabh International developed 'pay and use' toilets at several places in many cities, towns, and villages across India. He used innovative toilet technology to use human excreta for creating biofuels, which is a source of energy. Not only did he create a sustainable system to address this basic public issue but also he liberated the community of scavengers from their pathetic conditions and social stigma.

**Ramesh Chauhan and Bisleri**   Ramesh Chauhan is a renowned entrepreneur, who created iconic brands such as ThumsUp, Limca, Maaza, and GoldSpot in the soft-drink segment during the 1980s. However, he later sold these brands and his factories to Coca-Cola Company, which entered the Indian market in 1993. Chauhan then shifted his attention to packaged water through his company Bisleri International.

Polyethylene terephthalate (popularly known as PET) bottles are used to package the mineral water by companies like Bisleri and its competitors. PET is non-biodegradable and is not traded even by 'raddiwalas'; thus, the rag pickers leave them as a waste. Therefore, PET was literally becoming an ecological hazard.

A couple of years back, Chauhan pilot-tested the idea of tying up with rag pickers of Dharavi, Mumbai, to collect PET bottles from waste and sell them directly to the collection centres of Bisleri. The PET bottles can be recycled for various uses like carpets, car parts, fabrics, road construction, and so on. Bisleri sells the PET bottles after processing to companies like Reliance Industries. Thus, not only Chauhan has created a model to collect and recycle the PET waste, but also provided a business opportunity to the rag pickers. The pilot testing was so successful that the model is now being expanded by Bisleri to cover the whole of national geography.

# Summary

Products and services organizations are similar to each other in many ways. Manufacturing organizations not only produce goods but also provide after-sales service, warranty service, etc. Similarly, service organizations produce products, for example, insurance companies talk of designing new insurance schemes. Both manufacturing and service organizations involve a transformation process in their production process, which converts various inputs into desired output, that is, goods and services. *Production and operations management* is the management of this transformation process. It is important to choose the right type of operations process depending upon the variety of products/services and the quantity produced. Organizations worldwide have started taking proactive steps to reduce environmental pollution through their operations. Exchange of carbon credits through carbon trading is just becoming a reality. *Automation* of facilities results in lot of advantages such as increase in productivity, no risk of worker strikes, etc., but there are disadvantages also, such as the loss of creativity on part of workers. After the liberalization of the country, the role of the operations manager has increased manifold. It has become more strategic in focus due to increased competition from the multinational corporations.

# References

Amazon.com 2012, http://www.amazon.com/, accessed on 30 January 2013.

Anon. 2005, 'Bajaj Tempo is Force Motors from now', *The Financial Express*, http://www.financialexpress.com/news/bajaj-tempo-is-force-motors-from-now/127870, accessed on 30 January 2013.

Anon. 2011, 'India's top 20 brands: Amul is No. 1', 7 July, http://www.rediff.com/business/slide-show/slide-show-1-indias-top-20-brands-amul-tops/20110707.htm, accessed on 30 January 2013.

Anon. 2012, *The Hindu*, 18 August, ttp://www.thehindubusinessline.com/industry-and-economy/marketing/article3791354.eceVipul Chaudhary elected GCMMF Chairman, accessed on 30 January 2013.

Force Motors, http://www.forcemotors.com/index.php/home/index, accessed on 30 January 2013.

Gilbreth, F.B. and Gilbreth L.M. 1917, *Applied Motion Study*, Sturgis and Walton, New York.

Higgins, J.M. 1991, *The Management Challenge: An Introduction to Management*, Macmillan, New York, pp. 33–61.

IRCTC 2013, http://www.irctc.co.in/loyalty.html, accessed on 30 January 2013.

Jamal, A. 2012, 'IRCTC registers highest-ever e-ticket sales', 24 July, http://articles.timesofindia.indiatimes.com/2012-07-24/internet/32826692_1_tatkal-tickets-advance-reservation-period-lakh-e-tickets, accessed on 30 January 2013.

Lee, M. 2012, 'Amazon launches Kindle store in China, could pave way for Kindle', Reuters, 13 December, http://www.reuters.com/article/2012/12/13/us-amazon-china-kindle-idUSBRE8BC0CF20121213, accessed on 30 January 2013.

Mohanty R.P. and J. Nair 1987, 'Responsibilities and activities in Indian production management', *International Journal of Operations and Production Management*, vol. 7, no. 3.

Pilkington A. 1999, 'Strategic alliance and dependency in design and manufacture—The Rover–Honda case', *International Journal of Operations and Production Management*, vol. 19, no. 5/6.

Pollard H.R. 1974, *Developments in Management Thought*, William Heinemann, London, 1974.

Schiessl M. 2008, 'Tulsi Tanti's Success Story: The Rise of Indian Wind Power', *Spiegel Online International*, 6 December, http://www.spiegel.de, accessed on 22 April 2009.

Taylor F.W. 1911, *Principles of Scientific Management*, Harper and Brothers, New York.

Wren D. 1972, *The Evolution of Management Thought*, New York: Ronald Press.

# Keywords

**Automation** means replacing human labour with machines.

**Batch process** is adopted when batches of items are to be produced using the same set of machines in the same sequence.

**Carbon credit** is the credit earned by a company that

is reducing air pollution below permissible limits. One tonne of carbon dioxide emission is treated as one unit of carbon credit.

**Computer numerically controlled (CNC)** machines are so called because they are controlled by a software program through a computer.

**Computer-aided design (CAD)** is a software which helps the designer to make the three-dimensional design of a product on the computer and visualize the design from various angles.

**Computer-aided manufacturing (CAM)** is a form of automation in which computers are used in process control, ranging from controlling various machines to controlling even the process quality.

**Computer-integrated manufacturing (CIM)** means integrating various other automation activities not only in the manufacturing department but also in other departments such as engineering, purchase, materials, distribution, etc., so as to optimize the manufacturing capabilities of the firm up to the maximum extent possible.

**Continuous process** The products produced by such a process are highly standardized with almost no variety and are measured on a continuous basis (tonnes per day, metre lengths per day, etc.) rather than in terms of discreet units.

**Flexible manufacturing system (FMS)** has a number of machines controlled simultaneously by a computer program in intermittent processes to process a variety of similar products. It is flexible to some extent, as the computer program can be modified to suit changes in processing requirements.

**Intermittent processes** stop at regular intervals of time because the product requires processing on a variety of machines. The products produced are of different varieties, thus making the production process slow in comparison to continuous/semi-continuous processes.

**Job shop** process can handle a larger variety of products than the batch process. The products may be so different from each other that their processing requirements may be varied processes, on different machines, in different sequences, and with different processing times.

**Production and operations management** is defined as the design, operation, and improvement of the transformation process.

**Projects** are processes that handle very complex and unique sets of activities or tasks, which have to be completed in a limited span of time.

**Semi-continuous processes** are assembly processes, which are repetitive in nature. They produce a high volume of output and the products produced have little variety.

**Transformation process** Every process in an organization, be it a product or a service organization, transforms certain inputs into outputs. This is called the transformation process.

## CASE STUDY I

# Kishore Biyani and Big Bazaar

Kishore Biyani's saga starts with his family business in textiles, which he joined after graduating in commerce. In 1987, Biyani launched the first branded ready-made trousers brand known as Pantaloon through his company Pantaloon Fashions. The trousers were marketed through the Pantaloon Shoppe stores. By the time Pantaloon Fashions went public in 1992, it had 60 exclusive shops. Later, he started manufacturing garments under two more brands—John Miller and Bare. Despite good products and competitive pricing, the business seemed unviable due to high distribution costs and margins. Therefore, in August 1997, Biyani decided to open his own store at Kolkata to market these brands. He was expecting to do business of around ₹70 million in the first year, but beating all expectations, the store did a business of ₹100 million.

This experience was an eye-opener for Biyani, who came to know that Indian market is 'under-retailed'.

The year 2001 saw Biyani's entry into the hypermarket concept adapted to Indian conditions in the form of Big Bazaar. During that time, Pantaloon's topline was around ₹1.8 billion. Big Bazaar required a lot of investment and the company had generated profits only worth ₹40 million. It was not feasible to raise money from the market as the share price was low at ₹18. This would have also meant the dilution of equity for the Biyani family, which held 40 per cent of the equity. Exposing himself to high-risk debt exposure, Biyani had to go for a loan of ₹1.2 billion. Failure of the Big Bazaar concept would have left the company in red. As it turned out, the first Big Bazaar at Mumbai clicked with the masses and pulled over 1,00,000 people within the first week of its operation. It thus paved the way for many more stores throughout the country.

Biyani wanted to give the Indian customer the feel of a local market place—narrow lanes, crowded marketplace, and customers bumping into each other and into commodities. Big Bazaar wears the look of intentional distinctive layout scheme designed by Biyani. He is quite clear that Indians like the hustle-bustle of the marketplace, which gives them a feeling that the goods being sold there are low-priced. The major challenge before the retailers in India was to dispel the myth in the minds of the Indian consumer that big shopping stores charge more prices for commodities, compared to the local *kirana* stores, due to high overhead costs. Big Bazaar and Biyani have been able to successfully overcome this challenge by way of clear communication to the public through their advertisement campaigns. The economies of scale enable big retailers to provide lower prices, discounts, and promotional gifts at their stores.

Biyani has exploited the economies of scale to the hilt, from raising finances to negotiating rentals for the store space. During his earlier days, he used to pay about ₹75 million for a 50,000 sq. ft store and would generate an annual turnover of ₹3.5 billion. Today, for a store of the same size, he spends about ₹40 million and generates a turnover of about ₹500–600 million. This may be partly attributed to the mall-making frenzy in the country, whereby builders prefer to rent their spaces to outlets, which have the ability to pull crowds. There was a time when Biyani had to do the interiors for the space after acquiring a leased space. Not anymore, as the builders are ready to provide fully-furnished stores to let him start the operations immediately.

Biyani has often tied up with manufacturers to bring down the selling price of the products sold in Big Bazaar. For example, there were days when the lowest price of a pair of denim jeans for their Bare brand used to be ₹695, while *Newport* used to be the cheapest brand in the market at ₹599. Big Bazaar contacted Arvind Mills to know whether they were willing to provide jeans at ₹299 per piece to them, if the company bought 1,00,000 units every month. Thus, Arvind created the Ruf-n-Tuf brand exclusively for Biyani's stores and got into a similar contract for T-shirts. Big Bazaar is able to engineer its own prices with its tie-ups with big manufacturers in the product categories of plastic, food, leather, etc.

In June 2002, Biyani started Food Bazaar within the Big Bazaars. Now Food Bazaar has several separate outlets. Biyani focuses on the 'farm to plate' concept in Food Bazaar. According to him Indians prize 'freshness' in their food. Therefore, while managers elsewhere in the country are focusing on creating a cold storage chain to preserve eatables, Biyani's vision is to have the farm next to his stores. The Food Bazaar at Ahmedabad has a full-fledged dairy having a capacity of 1000 litres a day and produces its own paneer and pasteurized milk. It also has a spice grinder and an *atta chakki* (flour mill). To quote Biyani on this aspect, 'Managers always complicate things. It is the MBA culture. B-Schools teach you how to manage complexity, but I don't think that is necessary. Life is quite simple.' Biyani has created in-house labels for certain products. For example, his stores sell the in-house ketchup brand for ₹38, while the nearest rival brand is priced at ₹58. By 2008, Biyani was ensuring to occupy 60 per cent of the shelf-space in his stores with in-house brands.

Another major decision taken by Big Bazaar was to use the traditional supply chain rather than developing its exclusive supply chain to replenish its stores, now located in every part of the country. The traditional supply chain is used by the small as well as big *kirana* stores and has various elements such as the manufacturer, clearing and forwarding (C&F) agents, distributors, wholesalers, and finally the *kirana* stores. Biyani chose this traditional supply chain not only because creating an exclusive distribution system is highly capital intensive, but also because the distributors play a major role in the traditional supply chain by operating at wafer-thin margins while utilizing their family-owned warehouses inherited from generations. Most of these distributors involve their family members into the business and are ready to provide goods even in small quantities by using inexpensive modes of transportation such as cycle rickshaws. By following this strategy, Big Bazaar runs the risk of facing shortages in scenarios where a particular product-related promotional scheme is launched in all its stores simultaneously. These distributors may then be swamped with orders from the stores, which may be beyond their capacities to handle. It is yet to be seen how this system works in the wake of competition from the new players such as Reliance, and Walmart (which is entering the Indian market in collaboration with Bharti). The R.P. Goenka (RPG) enterprises and the K. Raheja group have always been stiff rivals by way of retail outlets such as FoodWorld and Shoppers' Stop respectively.

Then there are relatively newer players in the arena such as Aditya Birla Group's More department stores. The mettle of the so called father of retailing in India, Kishore Biyani, would be tested in this final countdown.

## Discussion Questions

1. The layout of Big Bazaar stores is radically different from those in the West. Do you think this layout would be successful in the wake of the entry of big players such as Walmart in the Indian market?

2. Using the traditional supply chain has worked for Biyani so far. Do you think it would work in the future as Reliance has chosen to follow the exclusive supply chain route for its stores?

3. Do you think having a farm near Big Bazaar is a good idea? Do you think this concept would be operationally viable?

4. Biyani is ensuring to occupy 60 per cent of shelf space in his stores with in-house brands. Do you think it is a good idea?

## CASE STUDY II

# Tulsi Tanti—Green Energy, Clean Energy

The same kind of venturesome spirit that drives Tanti now was what set the Suzlon train in motion. Spurning their father's construction business in Gujarat, Tanti and his three siblings moved to textiles in the late 1980s. They started processing polyester yarn and then graduated to making furnishing fabrics.

The decision to shift again, into wind energy, was a brave one. The industry was in the dumps, as it had earned a bad reputation due to unscrupulous companies that lured customers with the bait of tax breaks. Projects were ill-conceived, and often left incomplete with no maintenance or service support to speak of. Banks wised up and stopped lending for wind power projects.

The brothers saw the opportunity for a producer not only to build the wind turbine but also to provide maintenance and service support—even operational—as well. The experience seems to have kept the brothers tight. 'We have a common store, but our kitchens are separate', is how Tulsi Tanti puts it, although even today they host each other daily at their respective flats.

Selling some family property, the Tantis put together $600,000 as seed capital to start Suzlon. They shopped around for technology in Europe, but no one was willing to give it without having an equity stake in the venture. Finally, Sudwind, a small German company, agreed, provided Suzlon bought ten turbines. Tanti convinced IPCL, a petrochemicals company that had been supplying raw materials for his yarn business, to sign up as Suzlon's first customer. Suzlon completed IPCL's 3.5-MW project using Sudwind's turbines within the three-month deadline. Tanti claims that ten years on, this first wind farm continues to run at 97 per cent efficiency.

But the four brothers, all engineers, wanted to prove their technical prowess by crafting their own turbine. Their research efforts got a boost when Sudwind went bust in 1997. They hired Sudwind's engineers and created an R&D centre in Germany. The subsequent acquisition of a manufacturer of rotor blades in the Netherlands gave them access to technology for a key component.

By 1999 Suzlon had introduced its partly home-grown turbine into the market. Today the company has three research sites in Germany, the Netherlands, and India, which are linked together. One important mission is to find ways of increasing output so that the cost per kilowatt of energy generated decreases.

At the same time, Tulsi Tanti is shrewdly consolidating his hold on component supplies, a critical success factor in this business. Recently, Suzlon acquired Hansen Transmissions Intl, a Belgian maker of wind turbine gearboxes, for US$565 million, thereby securing supplies of another key component. (Suzlon now makes two-thirds of its turbines in India; the remaining one-third is imported.)

Traditionally, wind power has depended on tax breaks to make it an attractive alternative to conventional energy. But Tanti insists that with the price of conventional power climbing, production costs today are almost the same. Suzlon's technology innovations and ability to substitute for expensive imports with cheaper domestic components has reduced costs in the last 10 years. 'We don't need government handouts to survive', he declares.

Wind power has its critics, one beef being the noise that neighbours of turbines have to endure.

But densely populated India in fact has large tracts of open land, mostly in remote rural areas. About 15 to 20 acres are needed for a 1-MW installation.

Suzlon has built Asia's largest wind farm, with an installed capacity of 500 MW, near Kanyakumari, on India's southernmost tip, where trade winds of 15 mph are common. The Ministry of Non-conventional Renewable Energy (MNRE) has created a 'wind atlas' for picking the best sites.

Suzlon Energy, the company Tanti founded in 1995, is already the world's fifth-largest wind turbine manufacturer, and Tanti himself, who is worth US$3 billion (€1.9 billion), is one of India's richest men. In 2005, Tanti converted his advantages over the competition into cash when he orchestrated a brilliant initial public offering. Suzlon raised US$340 million (€219 million) and, from one day to the next, catapulted its founder and his family in the realm of the subcontinent's ultra-rich. Tanti himself currently owns 16 per cent of Suzlon, while the family owns 66 per cent.

Acquisitions have made the company reach fifth place on the list, helped along by perhaps its greatest coup of all: In 2007, Tanti suddenly entered the bidding for Repower, a major German wind turbine producer, and ended up outbidding the French nuclear energy giant Areva. It was not cheap and it was a sensation. In May 2007, Suzlon paid €450 million (US$698 million) for 33.6 per cent of Repower. It was the largest acquisition an Indian company had ever made in Germany. On 8 December 2007, Tanti bought more shares of Repower held by Areva for US$543 million. In addition, Tantis have quietly bought Repower shares on the market in recent days, bringing their stake in the company to 66 per cent of its stock (Schiessl 2008).

On 18 April 2009, Tanti received the Canada India Foundation (CIF) Chanchlani Global India award 2009, instituted by Canada India Foundation, from Montek Singh Ahluwalia, Deputy Chairman of the Planning Commission of India, for his pioneering work globally to promote non-conventional sources of energy.

### Discussion Questions

1. Which aspects of operations management are critical for Suzlon?
2. According to you, how important is research and development to survive in the business of wind power energy?

## CASE STUDY III

# Rover–Honda

Rover, the British car maker belonging to the BLMC conglomerate (later renamed as BL) faced the problem of survival in the 1970s. No introduction of new models for a long time was a particularly acute problem for Rover. The existing range was tired and incompetent, and, because of financial weakness, investment had been severely curtailed for a number of years. Similarly, design resources had been cut and the specialist skills inherited from the separate companies had not been protected. BL had excess production capacity, but products with a poor reputation for quality and reliability. The only solution seemed to be collaboration with a foreign company which could provide its design expertise to Rover.

Honda soon emerged as the likeliest choice. Honda had design strengths in the areas in which BL had lost expertise and curtailed investment—engines and gearboxes. BL, for its part, possessed European design studios, something which particularly attracted the Japanese as a means of improving products by making them more attractive to customers both at home and abroad. In 1981, BL licensed an existing Honda model for assembly in the UK—the *Triumph Acclaim*.

The project involved the purchase of a replica Honda production facility and an agreement for the supply of major parts. *Acclaim* became a success in terms of sales in the UK, but most of the revenues generated went to Honda as a part of the agreement. The image of BL saw an upturn, though this venture did not have much impact on its capabilities.

*Acclaim* was followed by *Rover 200* in 1984. This product was more than a licensing deal, as BL was involved in the design of what was also to be a new Honda product. However, BL's design input was limited to making the 200 distinct from the *Ballade*, Honda's equivalent, with the key units—body and mechanics—designed by Honda. BL's job was only to adapt the design to take the existing O-series 1.6-litre engine and its matching gearbox. However, the biggest sellers, the 1.3-litre models, were powered by Honda units and thus, according to the contract agreement, Honda was again the main beneficiary. The agreement also contained the clause that *Rover 200* will be manufactured at BL's Longbridge plant, but after receiving a few units from this plant, Honda complained about the quality levels and terminated the agreement. In order to become self-reliant, BL's design engineers were initially concentrating upon developing the *Montego* and *Maestro* models as a replacement to the existing models. Due to the diversion of BL's resources to the *Rover* 200 project, these development projects became starved of resources.

After Rover 200, the series of models launched by the BL-Honda team were Rover 800, R8, and Rover 600/Honda Accord in 1987, 1990, and 1994, respectively. In all these projects, Honda had the upper hand in negotiations over design specifications and, more importantly, in contracts to supply engines and other parts. Rover continued to expend a great deal of its design resources in the continuous updating of its existing models, and this further weakened the firm's ability to replace its product range. BL and Honda maintained distance from each other, and developed separate product plans—Rover incorporating Honda models into its own plans when these were offered and Honda sharing some of the cost with Rover in return for lucrative manufacturing rights. There is little doubt that the injection of Honda—derived models and facilities supported BL, and allowed it to survive. However, Honda received a stunning blow when Rover was sold to BMW in 1995 (Pilkington 1999).

### Discussion Questions

1. What were the advantages derived by Honda from its relationship with BL?
2. Were there any commercial risks for Honda in sharing its design skills with BL?
3. What went wrong for Rover in regaining its design capabilities for replacing its existing fleet of models? Suggest a plan which Rover should have followed in this regard.

## Objective Questions

### Choose the correct option

1. The modern assembly line was invented by
   (a) Frederick W. Taylor
   (b) Taiichi Ohno
   (c) Henry Ford
   (d) W. Edwards Deming
2. Who propounded the just-in-time (JIT) production system?
   (a) Joseph M. Juran
   (b) Henry Ford
   (c) Frederick W. Taylor
   (d) Taiichi Ohno
3. The abbreviation CSR stands for
   (a) corporate social responsibility
   (b) computer social responsibility
   (c) corporate service relationship
   (d) company social relationship
4. The abbreviation CNC stands for
   (a) computer not controlled

(b) computer numerically controlled
(c) case numerically conducted
(d) case not conducted

### State True or False

5. Intermittent processes are assembly processes which are repetitive in nature.
6. Carbon emission is a measure of the amount of carbon dioxide gas emitted.
7. Job shop is a type of intermittent process.

### Fill in the blanks

8. The transformation process consists of _____ outputs, and feedback mechanism.
9. One _____ of carbon dioxide emission is treated as one unit of carbon credit.
10. _____ is increasingly becoming an important mechanism to reduce raw material consumption, energy, and pollution, by processing the seemingly waste products into usable products.

## Concept Review Questions

1. What are the similarities and differences between products and services?
2. What is the transformation process? Explain the transformation process in a bank.
3. Enumerate the various steps in production and operations management from the point of view of an entrepreneur.
4. Explain the role of the operations manager in India today.
5. How is a job shop different from the batch produc-

tion process?

6. What are the advantages and disadvantages of automation?

7. What are carbon credits and carbon trading?

8. Explain the ways in which organizations can reduce emissions that pollute the environment.

9. What is recycling? How does it help the environment?

## Project Assignment

Visit a nearby branch of a bank and observe the various inputs and outputs in the transformation process. Make a schematic diagram to represent the transformation process including the random disturbances and the feedback mechanisms. Also find out the quality monitors for monitoring the quality of inputs to the process. What type of process design is followed by the bank?

| Answers to Objective Questions | | | | |
|---|---|---|---|---|
| 1. (c) | 2. (d) | 3. (a) | 4. (b) | 5. False |
| 6. True | 7. True | 8. inputs | 9. tonne | 10. Recycling |

# 2

# Operations Strategies

**Learning Objectives**

After reading this chapter, you will be able to answer the following questions:
- How are operations strategies related to the business grand strategy?
- What are the various dimensions of operations for gaining competitive advantage?
- What is innovation? What type of research and development strategies may be adopted?
- How can we perform the strategic allocation of resources?

## Introduction

The year 1991 brought about a lot of changes in the Indian economy and the overall business environment in the country. During the liberalization process, many foreign multinational corporations (MNCs) started operations in India. Most of these operations were in the form of joint ventures (JVs) with Indian domestic companies.

It was not that all the JVs were started only after 1991. Some JVs, such as Maruti-Suzuki, TVS Suzuki, and Escorts Yamaha, had already started in the early and mid-1980s due to the decision of the Indian government to allow the entry of foreign MNCs in select sectors of the industry. These MNCs could set up JVs with Indian companies only if the Indian company held a majority stake.

This condition existed only in the 1980s. After 1991, the government continued more rigorously with its liberalization programme and most of the earlier restrictions, such as the majority stake of the Indian JV partner, were withdrawn by the government. Multinational corporations can now set up 100 per cent subsidiaries in India in most sectors of the economy. This has brought about a lot of competition, especially from the point of view of the domestic Indian industry. It has become a do or die situation for most of the Indian domestic companies, which had been operating for a long time in the seller's market of the Licence Raj.

Most of the JVs formed during the 1980s and 1990s have ended with the foreign MNC either taking full control of the venture or exiting the JV to set up its separate 100 per cent owned subsidiary in direct competition with the Indian partner. Joint ventures such as Hero Honda, Kinetic Honda, Shriram Honda, TVS Suzuki, and Escorts Yamaha, to name a few, are JVs which

> The operations department can play a significant role in achieving the long-term objectives of an organization's strategies.

have ended up in this manner. TVS and Kinetic deserve special mention because these two companies ensured that after the exit of their foreign JV partner, they were able to compete independently. These two companies have evolved an R&D set-up, which is capable of generating new models of their products continually. They have taken proper steps to learn the technical expertise of their foreign partners and have adopted their best practices.

In this context, it is high time the Indian domestic companies followed business strategies of survival and growth to face the competition effectively. The operations department can play a significant role in achieving the long-term objectives of these strategies. In this chapter, we will discuss various types of business strategies, operations strategies in line with the business strategies, and steps to be taken to ensure their successful implementation. Exhibit 2.1 discusses how Captain Gopinath started his low-cost airline, Air Deccan.

---

### Exhibit 2.1  Captain G.R. Gopinath

On 28 April 2007, Dominique Girard, the French Ambassador to India, conferred his Government's Order of Legion of Honour on Gorur R. Gopinath, Managing Director of Air Deccan, for revolutionizing the concept of flying and for enhancing trade relations between the two countries. The growth of the airline also contributed to increased trade relations between the two countries. ATR and Airbus became strategic components for Air Deccan's business. Long back, when Gopinath went to France to get an ATR aircraft, ATR did not take him seriously. However, the determination on his part made him realize his dream when Air Deccan started its first flight between Bangalore and Hubli with one ATR aircraft. Captain Gopinath says, 'My story—and Air Deccan's story—is the story of the new India, the India of possibilities. And it can be anybody's success story, in a country that is hungry for growth. All it needs is the ability to dream and the will to sustain that dream.'

As a child, Gopinath, today the founder of India's first low-cost airline, Air Deccan and Deccan 360, often used to go barefoot to class in his village school in Gorur, Karnataka, where his father was a school teacher. The young Gopinath joined the Indian Army and rose to the rank of Captain within eight years of service, before he decided to quit and return to his native place to become a farming entrepreneur.

During late 1970s, he landed at a place called Javagal, a couple of miles from Gorur, his ancestral village. All of 27, having just left the Indian Army, all he had with him was a tent, some utensils, bare necessities, and a boy called Raju. He had a stretch of barren land that his family had inherited as government compensation. At that time, he did not know that this would be his home for the next ten years. It was here that he started his married life with Bhargavi and had his first child, Pallavi.

When he returned home, his mind was afresh with memories of his village, where he was born and attended school, where his father was a teacher, where he played bare-foot in the paddy fields, and swam in the river Hemavati. However, he found the village in crisis. A dam had been built that flooded the ancestral lands. The government paid compensation in the form of a patch of land, which every villager decided to sell. Against the wishes of his family, Gopinath decided to take a look at this plot. When his family heard this, they took him for a lunatic. After all, he was an alumunus of the prestigious National Defence Academy and the Indian Military Academy. His father was initially against the idea, yet later he advised Gopi on crops and resources.

As an army man, Gopi had seen the life in tough places and wanted to start afresh. He knew it would be an arduous journey, but when he saw the land allotted to his family with shrubs and cacti all around, it justified his presence there. So he pitched his tent and pondered how to turn this patch into a profitable venture. Fortunately, the soil was fertile.

After an ineffective start at farming that landed him in debt, he refocused his efforts on sustainable eco-friendly crops that eventually succeeded. He was also awarded the prestigious Rolex International Award for Enterprise in 1996 for breaking new ground with organic farming. After his earlier farming disaster, Gopi set up a biogas plant in his farm and bought cows for milk and manure. Later on, he started silk worm farming. The low-cost formula formed its roots in the success of this venture.

*(Contd)*

*Exhibit 2.1 Contd*

At every step, life teaches you something. As Gopi was still learning to farm, he had 1,000 coconut trees. In the dry season, as there was no electricity, he carried water to the trees by hand, one pail on each side. Then one day he saw a *dhobi's* donkey carrying the entire load, and an idea struck him. He made a deal for four donkeys for ₹65 each per day and got his money's worth. Every morning, villagers gathered at his farm to see the 'mad farmer' tying pitches of water on his donkeys to water his plants!

Today, Gopi's farm is a secluded heaven. Tall palm and coconut trees grace the area. There are birds, bees, insects, cobras, and leopards too. Raju is still there and looks after the land. There is a mystical quality about being there. It gives Gopi time to think, read, and stand amidst the trees that he has planted.

At some point Gopi moved to Bangalore for his children's education. He bumped into an old friend from the army and together they realized that there was no company at that time offering customer-dedicated helicopter services. Gopi realized that he was staring at a goldmine. The idea took shape and he launched Deccan Aviation, his helicharter business. Gopi's dream got its wings and the helicopter service grew to become Air Deccan because Gopi could see what others failed to see—the needs of a billion people. He wanted to make every Indian fly at least once. He was no longer looking at a billion hungry people, he was looking at a billion hungry consumers. Thus, Air Deccan was formed as a unit of Deccan Aviation and began its operations in August 2003.

There can be no doubt that Air Deccan's business model flies some 15 million people travel by trains in India every day, with 3,00,000 of them travelling in first class; the airline hoped to get some of them to consider flying by offering rates that are the same and sometimes lower than the first class fares. That may sound simple, but the idea came to Gopinath, military hero, award-winning sericulturist, and collector of Kannada literature, on a 2002 holiday to the Grand Canyon. The epiphanic moment came at the Phoenix airport. 'I hadn't heard of C.K. Prahalad's theory of targeting people at the bottom of the (income) pyramid,' he says. 'All I knew was that the US, which had a population that was one fourth India's, boasted 40,000 flights and four million passengers a day.'

Lack of proper infrastructure was not the only problem in India. Although the quality of some airfields in the smaller towns leaves a lot to be desired, the fact is, they can be used for landing and taking off. For the record, India has around 400 airports that were not connected through any flights at all before Air Deccan began operations. For instance, Bellary in Northern Karnataka has a pre-World War II airport that can be used to land small airplanes, as does Dindigul to the south of Madurai in Tamil Nadu.

If the cost of leasing or purchasing planes is the same for everyone (it is), fuel costs are the same for everyone (they are), and airport landing fees the same (they too are), how was Air Deccan able to offer such low-cost tariffs? It was able to achieve this by cutting out all the frills. On Air Deccan flights, even water was not free. The exterior of the plane was sold to advertisers such as Sun Microsystems and NDTV, and the interiors to brands such as Chevrolet Tavera for in-flight promotion. Air Deccan did not offer frequent flyer programmes, nor did it put up people at hotels if a flight is cancelled (only the ticket value was refunded), it did not offer a cargo service (cargo delays turnaround time), and it used to fly point-to-point rather than follow the hub-and-spoke model, which has a cascading effect should one flight be delayed or cancelled. Then there is the choice of aircraft itself—ATR 42s make sense as they seat just 47 and the load factor can be improved. In addition, smaller airports lack the infrastructure to handle Boeings and Airbuses.

Air Deccan created history during August 2004 by flying passengers to Delhi from Bangalore for a fare of only ₹500, plus ₹200 as taxes. The Airbus A320 has a capacity of 180 passengers, and almost 100 of them boarded the inaugural Bangalore-Delhi Air Deccan flight by paying just ₹700. The budget airline offered 75 per cent of the seats at rates ranging between ₹500 and ₹5,000 and the remaining 25 per cent at around ₹7,500, which was 25 per cent less than the normal fare of ₹10,500 on any other airline. The new fare system devised by the airline was known as Dynafares. Passengers must book their tickets 90 days in advance of the date of flight to avail concessional fares.

In June 2005, Air Deccan introduced its ₹1 scheme. The logic behind offering two to three seats per flight at this symbolic fare was that it is better to provide seats at cheap rates, rather than flying with unoccupied seats. The catch behind the scheme was that only two to three seats per flight were made available. Also, the ticket cost to the customer amounted to ₹222 inclusive of taxes and not ₹1 as was the perception.

*(Contd)*

*Exhibit 2.1 Contd*

During June 2006, Air Deccan created another aviation history. It overtook the national carrier Indian to become the second-largest domestic airline in the country. Air Deccan's market share crept up to 21.2 per cent, from 19.4 per cent in May, while Indian's declined to 20.8 per cent, from 21.3 per cent in May 2006. The Mumbai-based Jet Airways, India's largest private airline, remained the market leader with a 32.3 per cent share in June 2006, down from 33.2 per cent in May.

Air Deccan was acquired by Vijay Mallya-promoted Kingfisher Airlines in 2007 and was eventually merged as the Kingfisher Red sub-brand. The low-cost tag was also gradually diluted in order to make the operations financially viable. However, newer airlines, such as SpiceJet and Indigo, still thrive on the Air Deccan model of low-cost airlines.

In November 2009, Gopinath started his new venture called Deccan 360, which provides transportation and logistics services to various industry verticals including pharmaceutical, machinery, manufacturing, retail, electronics, textile, and banking. The company prides itself in utilizing state-of-the-art technology to provide 24-hour express logistics support to organizations by connecting 47 cities nationwide. About 2 per cent of India's GDP is either lost or wasted in the absence of storage and cargo delivery infrastructure. With Deccan 360, Gopinath's mission is to overcome this chronic problem.

It seems Gopinath looks at his farm as a place not just to grow coconuts for profit, but to grow ideas, to plant experiments, fertilize them with imagination, and harvest the ideas that take root.

## Relationship between Business Grand Strategy and the Operations Strategy

Figure 2.1 shows a schematic diagram of the relationship between the business grand strategy and the operations strategy. The corporate mission statement of an organization sets out the basic purpose of its various activities. It identifies the scope of the firm in terms of the products/services it deals with, the markets in which it operates, and the technological areas it emphasizes. The corporate mission statement is a statement of the customers' needs to be satisfied by the company to project a positive image of the company and act as a guiding philosophy for the company's strategic decision makers.

The external environment of the company is constituted by various players such as the government, competitors, consumers, suppliers, and creditors. The external environment poses threats and offers opportunities to the company from time to time. For example, the government may start providing state-of-the-art infrastructure for some selective industry sectors at nominal rates, to promote it in some specific regions of the country (such as software development parks to promote the software industry). The creditors of the company such as banks and financial institutions may start giving loans at lower interest rates to the company, looking at its prospects in the future. The competitors of the company may have alliances with foreign multinationals to obtain the latest technology, which may render the existing production systems of the company obsolete.

A company should identify its competitive strengths and weaknesses to reap maximum benefit from the opportunities offered by the external environment, and to face the threats it poses comfortably. The competitive strengths of a company may be its technological patents obtained over the years due to its R&D efforts, its well-established physical distribution channels, the capital

> The corporate mission statement of an organization sets out the basic purpose of its various activities.

reserves it has accumulated over the years due to sustained profits, etc. The weaknesses of a firm may be its high debt burden, high inventory costs, obsolete technology, poor advertising campaigns, etc.

Strategic analysis and choice means matching competitive strength and weaknesses with the opportunities offered and threats posed by the external

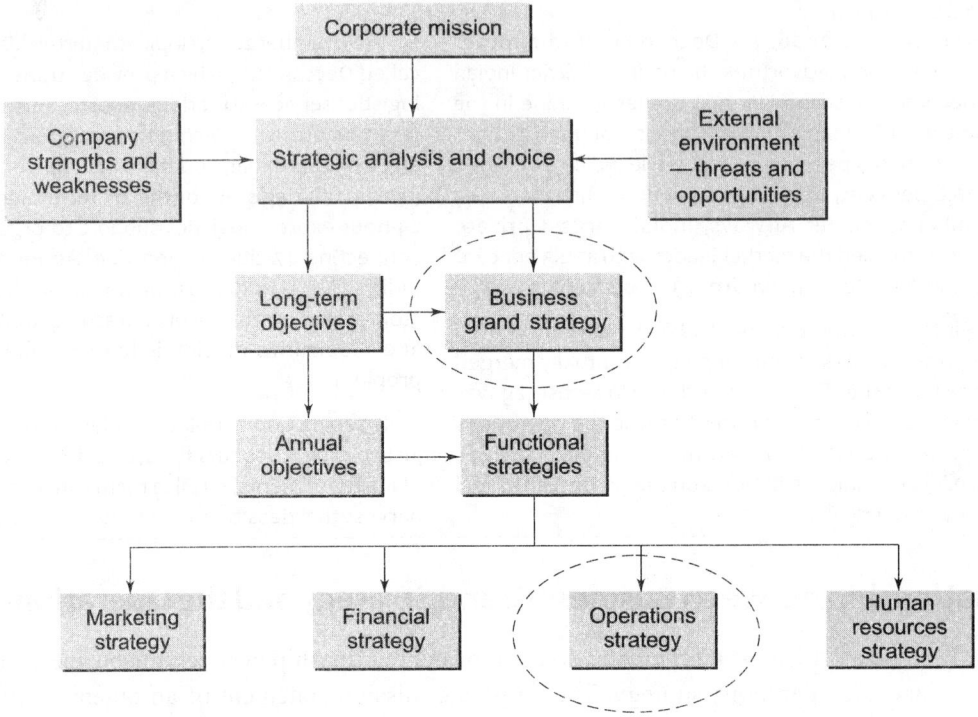

**Fig. 2.1** Relationship between the business grand strategy and the operations strategy

environment, keeping in view the corporate mission statement. Subsequently, it involves establishing the long-term objectives of the firm and choosing a business grand strategy from a set of various strategic options. The long-term objectives of the firm are the ones to be achieved normally in a duration of 5 to 10 years.

In some industries, the duration of long-term objectives may be smaller due to the industry being in the evolution or growth stage and, thus, experiencing unexpected changes in the market due to frequent technological innovations. For example, the computer and information technology industry may have long-term objectives covering a duration of three years. The long-term objectives of a firm may be to achieve market leadership from its current (number two) position in the market, to double the sales revenues in the coming five years with increases in each intervening year, to reduce the overall cost of operations by 30 per cent in the coming five years, etc.

Long-term objectives have to be broken down into annual objectives, which have a duration of one year. For example, the long-term objective of reduction in the overall cost of operations by 30 per cent in the coming five years can be broken down into an annual objective of reduction in the overall cost of operations every year by 6 per cent. A business grand strategy is a long-term plan of a company, which provides a road map for achieving its corporate objectives. Each functional department of the company, namely, operations, marketing, finance, and human resources, makes its functional strategies with respect to the business grand strategy and the annual objectives.

Long-term objectives have to be broken down into annual objectives, which have a duration of one year.

An operations strategy is a long-term plan for the production/operations function of a company, which acts as a guide for the operations functions to achieve annual business objectives.

An *operations strategy* is a long-term plan for the production/operations function of a company, which acts as a guide for the operations functions to achieve annual business objectives. Thus, the operations strategy of the company should always be in line with its business grand strategy. Operations strategies have various dimensions, which may have to be focused upon with respect to a particular grand strategy. In addition, different functional departments of the company may have conflicting objectives. In establishing the operations strategy of the company, the operations manager has to ensure that it should support the objectives and strategies of the other functional departments of the company.

## Operations Strategies for Particular Business Grand Strategies

There are twelve grand strategic options available as shown in Fig. 2.2. In the grand strategy of *concentration*, the firm concentrates on growing its current business with a single product only, based on a particular technology in a single market. This is the least risky strategy amongst the twelve grand strategies. Any new business has to use this strategy initially to establish itself firmly in a single market. The operations strategy with respect to the grand strategy of concentration will focus on keeping low inventory levels and lower costs of production to increase the usage rate of existing customers, and drawing competitors' customers towards the company's products. As the firm starts getting successful, it starts looking at the other strategies.

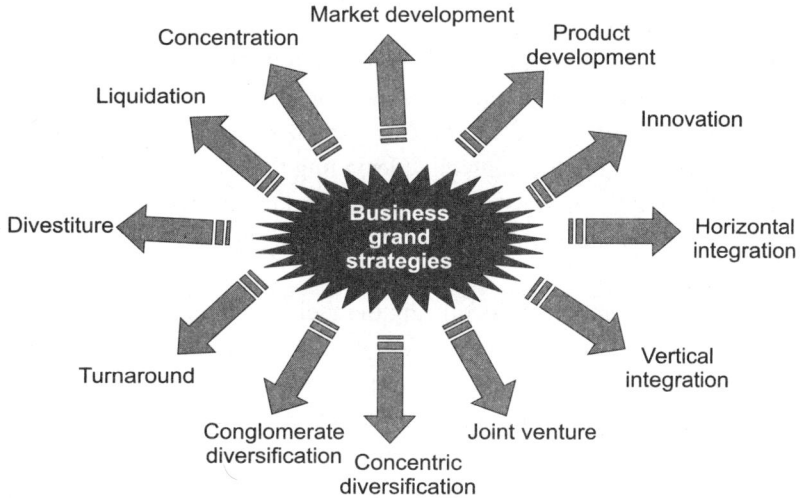

**Fig. 2.2** Business grand strategies

The second grand strategy is *market development*. As the name suggests, in this strategy the existing product of the company is launched in new markets (i.e., the geographical area is expanded). For example, a product successful in Maharashtra is launched in Gujarat and Karnataka. If it proves to be a success there too, the company launches it in the northern and eastern parts of the country, and so on. The operations strategy focuses on deciding whether to fulfil the demand of various markets from a single plant located at a central location, or to open new factories near major markets. This decision depends on the kind of product, for example, Pepsi and Coke prefer to have multiple bottling facilities near all markets in order to fulfil the demand promptly. On the other hand, automobile manufacturers prefer to have a single facility to fulfil the needs of a large geographical area, for example, a country.

The *product development* grand strategy involves developing new features of existing products for the present markets. This means extending the life cycle of existing products. Hyundai pursued this strategy in India with its *Santro* model. The *Santro Zip*, *Zipdrive*, *Xing*, *GL Plus*, etc. are sub-models having new features and substantial improvements in styling. The operations strategy in line with product development involves focusing on design changes and new features in the product through R&D, changes in the assembly line/production process according to the design changes in the product, etc.

*Innovation* is a grand strategy used by corporations such as Google, Sony, 3M, Honda, and Ranbaxy. In this strategy, the company innovates new products that render the existing products obsolete. These companies do not believe in fighting the competition in the maturity stage of the product by development, but in creating absolutely new products so as to rise above the competition as a leader. Sony invented the Walkman, compact handycam video camera, the digital camera, and many more products by following the grand strategy of innovation. Similarly, Honda invented fuel cell technology cars, the humanoid robot *Asimo,* and other innovative products. An operations strategy with respect to innovation will focus on establishing R&D facilities, that is, facility location, layout, project management of various R&D projects, etc.

*Horizontal integration* is a grand strategy in which the company expands through acquisitions of its competitors' facilities. This strategy helps in gaining market share by eliminating competitors, and acquiring access to new markets, technology, etc. The acquired firms deal in the same product as the acquiring company. In the Indian pharmaceutical industry, the Piramal group has expanded through many acquisitions. In 2008, Tata Motors acquired Jaguar and Land Rover in the UK from Ford Motor Company. An operations strategy in line with horizontal integration will involve focusing on redesigning the distribution system of products to different markets through the earlier as well as newly acquired plants. If the acquired facility has obsolete production systems, the operations strategy may involve redesigning the layout and modernization of the facility.

*Vertical integration* means acquiring the facilities of either the suppliers or the consumers in the supply chain. In place of acquisition, the company may start its operations from scratch for manufacturing its own raw material, or marketing its end products. For example, a cotton fabric manufacturer may start manufacturing its own raw material—the cotton filament yarn. This is called *backward vertical integration* (moving towards the raw material end). The cotton fabric manufacturer may also start manufacturing cotton shirts. This is called the *forward vertical integration* (moving towards the customer end).

Reliance Industries has done backward as well as forward vertical integration. It started producing its raw material PTA for manufacturing polyester filament yarn (backward integration). It started marketing its *Vimal* brand of clothing through its retail outlets throughout the country (forward integration). An operations strategy in vertical integration requires a lot of coordination between the various vertically integrated units. The production planning of various units should be synchronized with each other. Disruption of production at one unit may halt the production at other units, to which it is a supplier of raw material.

> Horizontal integration is a grand strategy in which the company expands through acquisitions of its competitors' facilities.

A *joint venture* (JV) is a grand strategy in which two or more firms team up to form a new firm to meet the competitive challenge effectively. Most JVs are formed to complement the strengths of one firm with the strengths of the other firm(s). In some situations, the government of a country makes it mandatory for foreign firms to operate in the country through a JV with a domestic company. In the mid-1980s, the Indian government had put such a condition before foreign MNCs. In 2007, Sunil Mittal-promoted Bharti Group entered into a 50:50 joint venture with Walmart Inc. to create wholesale cash-and-carry stores in India. It opened its wholesale store in Amritsar in 2009. The operations strategy for a JV involves focusing on the product/process choice, facility location and layout planning, project management, creating a supply chain for the venture, establishing MRP and aggregate production planning systems, etc.

> A joint venture (JV) is a grand strategy in which two or more firms team up to form a new firm to meet the competitive challenge effectively.

*Concentric diversification* means getting into new businesses related to the firm in terms of technology, markets, or products. For example, Archies Cards started with greeting cards at first and later ventured into gift items. The common distribution channels, advertising, and promotion for greeting cards as well as gift items were the main reason for this concentric diversification. In 2008, Microsoft acquired Skype in order to expand its presence in the web-based telecommunications space. This strategy focuses upon product/process choice, facility location and layout planning for the new products to be manufactured, project management, etc.

*Conglomerate diversification* means getting into new businesses completely unrelated to the existing business. For example, Reliance Industries was a textile company in the 1980s but later ventured into petrochemicals and telecom, completely unrelated to its existing business at that time. This grand strategy is a typical form of entrepreneurship, in which the operations strategy has to deal with all the aspects of production and operation management discussed in this book.

*Turnaround* means bringing back a firm from declining profits or increasing losses to prosperity. In a way, it means reversing the current negative trends, and thus the name 'turnaround'. Mohan Singh Oberoi (Oberoi Hotels) started his business by acquiring and turning around hotels (at Shimla and Kolkata) that were in the red. The turnaround grand strategy can be used in two ways: by cost reduction or by asset reduction.

Asset reduction can be done by selling off machinery, equipment, extra land, or buildings not directly essential to the basic activities of the company. Cost reduction can be achieved through reduction in the inventory cost, cuts in the advertising budgets, cuts in the benefits of senior employees, etc. The operations strategy here concerns the identification of assets to be disposed off, ways of reducing inventory cost, extending the life of machinery, leasing equipment in place of purchasing, etc. Many times, the cost reduction approach in the turnaround grand strategy is done by reducing R&D budgets. It is not necessary that such cost reduction will be useful for turnaround. On the other hand, the R&D effort may be directed towards the improvement of production processes to reduce costs. In 2009, General Motors (GM) could overcome its stage of near bankruptcy by getting a stimulus package from the US government. Since then, it has closed down several of its plants (asset reduction) and introduced several cost-cutting measures for turning around within the next few years.

> Divestiture is a grand strategy in which a business unit is sold off to another business house.

*Divestiture* is a grand strategy in which a business unit is sold off to another business house. The reason for sale may be the requirement of liquid cash for other crucial business units, or a wrong conglomerate diversification, which the company now feels is difficult to focus on and thus, better to sell off as a running concern to gain premium on the assets of the company being sold. In 1996, Lakme was divested by the Tata Group to Hindustan Unilever Ltd for the second reason, despite Lakme being a profitable business unit. In 2004, IBM divested its personal computer business to China's Lenovo Group.

*Liquidation* is the most disliked of all the twelve grand strategies discussed here. This strategy is the last resort, when all the efforts of turnaround have failed and the company is facing bankruptcy. In this strategy, the tangible assets of the company are sold off in parts or whole. For example, the major creditors of Daewoo in India—IDBI and ICICI—liquidated its plant at Surajpur (near Delhi) after it faced bankruptcy worldwide to a new company called Argentum.

The operations strategy with respect to the grand strategies of divestiture and liquidation focuses upon minimizing the losses of stakeholders by trying to sell off the company or its assets at the best possible prices.

## Coordination between Different Functional Strategies

An operations strategy cannot be successful without proper coordination with other functional departments of the organization. There are certain contradicting objectives between the various functional strategies. For example, the finance department may emphasize upon low levels of inventory to keep the capital tied up in inventory and, thus, the interest burden as low as possible. In this case, the operations strategy will also focus on keeping low levels of inventory. On the other hand, the marketing department will look forward to high levels of inventory, so that it is easier for them to make commitments to customers for prompt supply.

The marketing department will emphasize prompt delivery of products to customers, while the operations department will try to incur the lowest transportation cost by following the cheapest route and using full truckloads (which may take some more time in delivering to several customers using the same truck).

The marketing department will prefer short production runs, so that any variation in customer preferences may be promptly introduced in the product in the latest production run. In addition, it will reduce their burden of obsolete inventory in the warehouse as a result of fewer inventories (due to a short production run). On the other hand, the operations department will prefer long production runs to avoid frequent set-ups and, thus, high set-up cost.

The marketing department will emphasize on having separate warehouses near different markets to facilitate prompt supply to the customers in each market. In contrast, the operations strategy will focus on having a centralized warehouse at the plant so that it is easier to control the overall inventory, which would be relatively difficult if the inventory is scattered at different warehouses.

Therefore, while formulating the operations strategy with regard to a particular business grand strategy, the operations manager will have to coordinate with the other functional departments to ensure that there is no contradiction in functional strategies as explained above. This coordination between different functional strategies will ensure the success of the business grand strategy.

> An operations strategy cannot be successful without proper coordination with other functional departments of the organization.

## Operations Strategies in a Global Environment

We have so far discussed the business grand strategy and functional strategies. As an organization expands geographically within the country and diversifies

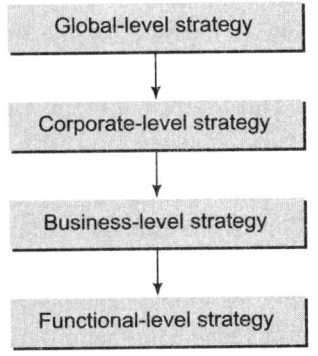

**Fig. 2.3** Relative position of the four levels of strategy

into various related and unrelated areas, it usually sets up a corporate headquarter that sets out 'corporate-level' strategies for all the group companies or divisions. When the company expands globally, it essentially becomes a multinational corporation (MNC). The global headquarter of the business group creates the 'global-level' strategy. Figure 2.3 captures the relative position of the four levels of strategies, namely global, corporate, business, and functional.

The global-level strategies can be of four types, depending upon the kind of control the global headquarter exercises on the local subsidiaries in different parts of the world. Higher the control of the global headquarters, the higher is 'centralization'. Higher the autonomy of the local subsidiaries, higher is 'decentralization'. Figure 2.4 captures the four types of global-level strategies on a scale with centralization and decentralization at the two extremes.

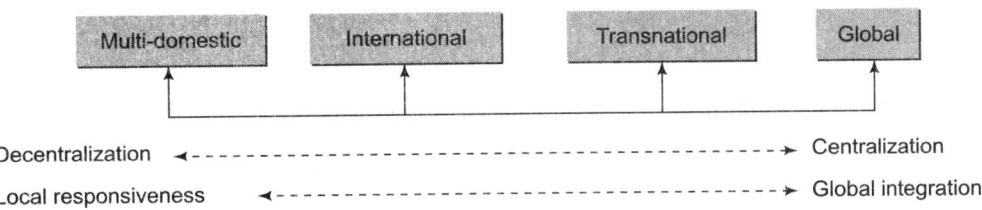

**Fig. 2.4** Four types of global-level strategies

**Multi-domestic strategy**  In this form of global-level strategy, the global headquarter creates wholly-owned subsidiaries in various countries and grants them almost full autonomy in designing new products as per the local requirements, and manufacturing and marketing them. However, the local subsidiary is provided with the core competencies of the global headquarter. Apart from that, the only link between the global headquarter and the local subsidiary is the transfer of profits and dividends. A global geographic organizational structure is used in this strategy with country heads responsible for all major decisions for their respective markets. A good example of multi-domestic strategy is Unilever, whose Indian subsidiary is called Hindustan Unilever Limited (HUL). HUL enjoys autonomy to great extent in terms of designing, manufacturing, and marketing products unique to the Indian market. HUL brands such as Annapurna, Taj Mahal, Brooke Bond Taaza, Hamam, Rexona, Pond's, and Lakme are specific to the Indian market. At the same time, it also manufactures and markets the global brands of Unilever, such as Sunsilk, Axe, Dove, Pepsodent, Lipton, and Knorr. Thus, the operations strategy in line with the multi-domestic strategy covers all aspects from product design and development, process design, facility location, layout and capacity, production planning, to quality management at the local subsidiary level.

**International strategy**  In this strategy, a local company forays into an international market without any modification in the product. The idea is to replicate the domestic success story in a foreign land. The manufacturing and distribution skills are transferred to the foreign subsidiary/ franchisee (in the 'host' country); however, the product development, R&D, and marketing are controlled by the headquarter (in the 'home' country). A global product group organizational structure is used in this strategy with global headquarters based upon product groups. For example, after its stupendous success in India, Airtel (promoted by Sunil Mittal) has ventured into the Sri Lankan market. Similarly, Coca Cola typically follows this strategy, whereby its soft drink products remain essentially the same in all the countries it operates. Thus, in this strategy, the operations strategy supporting the international strategy would focus on demand forecasting, production planning, facility location/layout/capacity, and supply chain efficiency.

**Global strategy**    In this strategy, a standardized product is produced in large volumes at a few low-cost global locations and is distributed throughout the world with minimal customization. Thus, this strategy exhibits very high degree of centralization, whereby the global headquarter controls every aspect of operations from product design and development to marketing and after-sales service. A global product group organizational structure is used in this strategy with global headquarters based upon product groups. The best example of this strategy is the personal computer industry. All major players, such as Hewlett-Packard (HP), Acer, and Lenovo, get their laptops assembled through contract manufacturers located in Taiwan and distribute them worldwide with little customization, such as  power chords and plugs, as per the country specifications.

**Transnational strategy**    This strategy tries to combine the benefits of the two extremes of global-level strategies, namely multi-domestic and global strategies, in order to strike a balance between local responsiveness and global integration. The global headquarter provides the core competencies (derived from various foreign divisions) to the low-cost foreign divisions, which use it to customize the products as per local requirements and create high-quality, low-cost products. A matrix organization structure is followed in the transnational strategy, whereby operations managers have dual reporting responsibility–one, to their local reporting head, and the other to their global headquarter's reporting manager. An example of transnational strategy is McDonald's in India, which has created several India-specific items in the menu, such as Mc Aloo Tikki, Mc Spicy Paneer, and Chicken Maharaja Mac. However, it still derives heavily from its global headquarter in terms of establishing, running, and maintaining its exclusive supply chain.

## Centralization vs Decentralization of Authority and Responsibility

Centralization and decentralization, just like delegation of authority, refer to the degree to which authority and responsibility is concentrated or dispersed. However, there is an important difference between the two concepts. Decentralization is a much broader concept and refers to the extent to which upper management delegates authority downward to divisions, branches, or lower-level organizational units, whereas delegation usually refers to the extent to which individual managers delegate authority and responsibility to the people reporting directly to them (Megginson et al. 1986). The delegation of authority should allocate commensurate *responsibility*, that is, when one is given 'rights', one also assumes a corresponding 'obligation' to perform (Robbins 1994). The decision of Alfred P. Sloan to decentralize General Motors (GM) in 1921 is considered as the first large-scale use of this approach (Dale 1955).

The concepts centralization and decentralization have been defined from three perspectives: hierarchical, concentration, and participation. In Steers' (Steers 1977) definition, centralization is viewed as the extent of power and authority held at the upper levels of an organization's hierarchy, while decentralization refers to the extent of power and authority extended down through the hierarchy. In contrast, the concentration approach is typified by the work of **Hage and Aiken** (1970), where centralization is defined as the concentration of power and decision-making in the hands of a small number of individuals, regardless of organization level. The participation perspective is characterized by Hage's (1980) assertion that the key to defining decentralization is the scope of actual participation or influence across hierarchical levels and substantive departments. In this approach, rather than the hierarchical position of the decision-maker or dispersion of decisions across levels, the extent to which members participate in the decision process was viewed as the discriminator between centralization and decentralization.

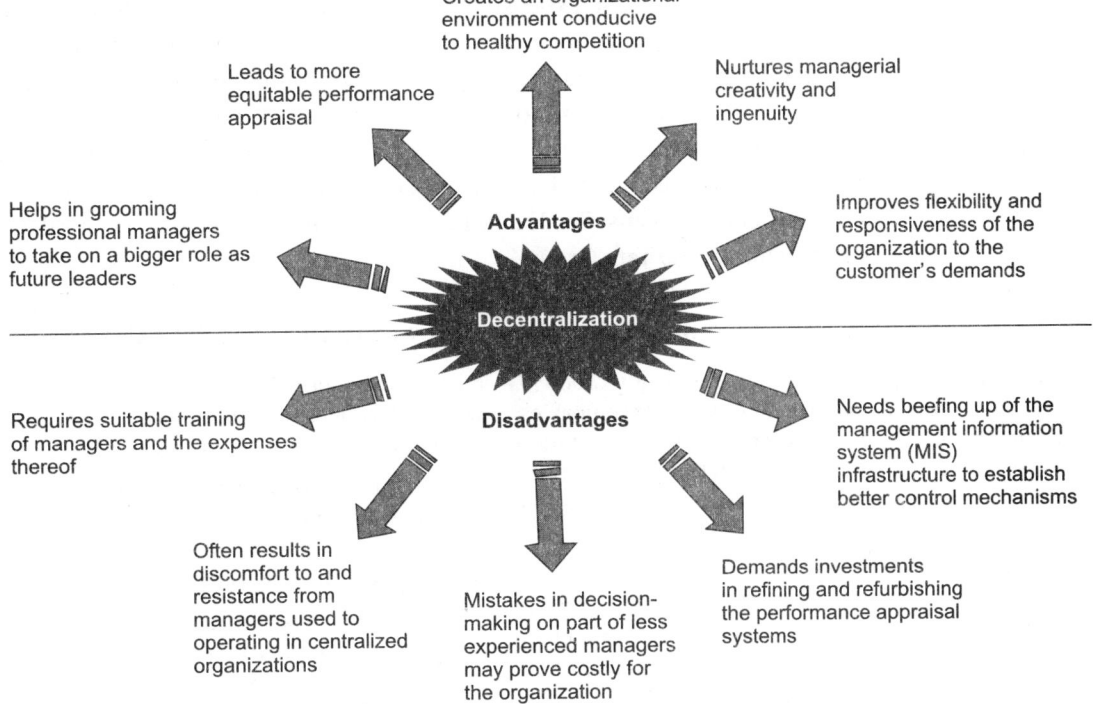

**Advantages**

Creates an organizational environment conducive to healthy competition

Leads to more equitable performance appraisal

Nurtures managerial creativity and ingenuity

Helps in grooming professional managers to take on a bigger role as future leaders

Improves flexibility and responsiveness of the organization to the customer's demands

**Decentralization**

**Disadvantages**

Requires suitable training of managers and the expenses thereof

Needs beefing up of the management information system (MIS) infrastructure to establish better control mechanisms

Often results in discomfort to and resistance from managers used to operating in centralized organizations

Mistakes in decision-making on part of less experienced managers may prove costly for the organization

Demands investments in refining and refurbishing the performance appraisal systems

**Fig. 2.5**   Advantages and disadvantages of decentralization

The various advantages and disadvantages of decentralization have been highlighted in Fig. 2.5. By virtue of its requirement for middle and lower managers to assume authority and responsibility (to take decisions), decentralization helps in grooming these managers to assume more important roles as future leaders of the organization. In a decentralized organization, the performance of the managers is gauged on the basis of results achieved and objectives met rather than just their personality. Hence, the performance appraisal systems become more equitable. The relatively liberal and open environment in a decentralized organization leads to healthy competition amongst managers, who vie with each other to achieve more for the organization by using the authority and responsibility vested in them. Such an environment also nurtures creativity and ingenuity by allowing the managers to think rationally and act responsibly for best possible outcomes. Last but not least, decentralization at times means quick decision-making by managers on the site locally rather than to wait for decisions from the headquarter (in a centralized organization). This results in improved flexibility and responsiveness to the customer's demands, which turns into a competitive advantage.

Decentralization has advantages as well as disadvantages. In order to make sure that the managers are well-equipped with proper skills of decision-making, suitable training programmes have to be provided to them before passing on the authority and responsibility to them. This also involves expenses in training and development. If a centralized organization is transformed into a decentralized one, the initial resistance and discomfort on part of managers used to operating in the centralized way a is natural. It is also expected that less experienced managers charged with the authority and responsibility in a decentralized organization may commit mistakes (especially in the beginning) which may prove expensive for the organization. The performance appraisal systems in a decentralized organization have to be refined and refurbished to capture the results achieved by managers with increased authority and responsibility. Proper control mechanisms are a must for a decentralized organization so that top managers may have ready access to the real-time data and information about the key initiatives taken by the managers in the lower rungs. Therefore, investments in MIS become imperative to aid the top management in having such efficient control mechanisms. See Exhibit 2.2 to know more about the decentralization and centralization structure at the Tata Group.

---

### Exhibit 2.2  Decentralization and Centralization at the Tata Group

J.R.D. Tata became the chairman of the Tata Group in 1938. Under his chairmanship, the number of companies in the Tata Group grew from 15 to over 100. Monetarily, the assets of Tata group grew from ₹62 crores to over ₹10,000 crores. He founded India's first commercial airline, Tata Airlines, in 1932, which in 1946 became Air India (now India's national airline).

In the 53 years that the late J.R.D. had been chairman of the group, Tata businesses were run in what even insiders call 'an unstructured manner'. J.R.D. picked his managers—the Russi Modys, the Darbari Seths, the Sumant Moolgaokars, the Ajit Kerkars—and gave them little short of complete control over their businesses. According to Fredie Mehta, an erstwhile director of Tata Sons, 'That was JRD's style. He had this genius of identifying and inspiring geniuses that he saw around him'.

Once he did that, J.R.D. would give them near-entrepreneurial freedom, rarely stepping in the way of their decisions. Such an approach had its pluses. His chief executives enjoyed tremendous opportunities to give vent to their entrepreneurial or managerial skills. And many of them emerged winners. For examples, Seth built the group's tea and chemicals businesses; Mody ran Tisco without even a whisper of industrial relations problems; the late Moolgaokar fashioned

Telco into an impressive engineering giant; Kerkar took a one-hotel operation and turned it into a 10,000-room international business.

But J.R.D.'s policy was like a double-edged sword. On the minus side, his managers got used to the freedom and ran their companies the way they wished, almost like they were their own little empires.

Ratan Tata, an architecture graduate from Cornell University, succeeded J.R.D. By the time Ratan Tata became Chairman in 1991, the group apex company Tata Sons hardly held sway over the bigger Tata companies because of its low shareholdings (Tatas held minority stakes in group companies ranging from 0.01 per cent to 15 per cent at that time). As over 80 percent of Tata Sons was held by charitable trusts, which could not subscribe to rights issues, the group had in the past tried to work on a proposal that could circumvent the problem. The idea was to get group companies to subscribe to fresh Tata Sons equity and thus enable the apex company to increase its holdings in the group companies. In the late eighties, that plan got stuck, chiefly because group satraps like Russi Mody resisted the move and Tata Sons shareholder Shapoorji Pallonji Mistry (a building magnate who holds 14 per cent) could not be persuaded to dilute his holding. However, after assuming charge, Ratan was successful in increasing the

*(Contd)*

*Exhibit 2.2 Contd*

shareholdings of Tata Sons in the group companies. Tata Sons determined that it would require raising a capital of ₹7 billion in 1995–96, to realize a 1 per cent increase in stake in each of the major Tata companies. To raise the necessary funds, Tata Sons invited subscriptions to a ₹3 million rights issue in September 1995. The shares were made available to Tata group affiliates (at a premium) through the renunciation of shares by various charitable trusts (having the rights). The additional money was raised by internal accruals, debt, and other strategies.

Ratan Tata's second parallel strategy to assume control of his empire was to oust J.R.D.'s entrepreneurial chieftains. A typical example is that of Ajit Kerkar's exit. Kerkar was instrumental in building IHL into a chain of classy hotels across the country, and is widely credited with having built Goa as the playground of the international tourist.

Ratan Tata also came up with the rule that the various outposts of the Tata group should pay the mother company a hefty sum (0.10% to 0.25% of each company's net income excluding taxes and non-operating, depending upon its association with the brand) for the use of the Tata brand name.

Rata Tata's success after the centralization of the Tata group is history. He revamped the operations of Tata steel and made it one of the lowest cost producers of the world. Under him, Tata Consultancy Service went public and Tata Motors was listed in the New York Stock Exchange. He shelled out US$435 million for Tetley Tea, making Tata the world's No. 2 tea company. He made the critics eat their words when he launched India's first indigenous car Indica. His ₹1 lakh 'dream car' Nano has caught international attention. His acquisitions of the Anglo-Dutch steelmaker Corus and iconic brands such as Jaguar and Land Rover in the UK have further accentuated his managerial might. Under Ratan Tata, the company touched almost all the new horizons—from telecom and teleservices to the Corus and South Africa ventures. At present, the group is headed by Cyrus P. Mistry, who was earlier Managing Director of the Shapoorji Pallonji group.

## Dimensions of Operations for Competitive Advantage

In order to gain competitive advantage against foreign MNCs, Indian corporates will have to attack them with operations improvements and innovations. It is worldwide experience that a company cannot be successful in world markets unless it is successful in its home turf. Therefore, Indian corporates will have to face competition from foreign MNCs head on. The following dimensions of operations management require attention from Indian corporates.

### Product/Service Quality

This is one dimension on the basis of which Japanese companies established their stranglehold in the international markets during the 1970s and 1980s. This one dimension is lacking to a great extent in Indian companies. During the Licence Raj (the period before the mid-1980s), the Indian consumer's perception of the quality of products and services was very different from what it is today. This was a time, for example, when there were only two main models of cars available in the Indian markets—*Ambassador* of Hindustan Motors and *Premier Padmini* of Premier Automobiles. Thus, the Indian customer had only two models of cars to choose from and be satisfied with their quality. In addition, for the quality available, the cost of cars was so high that an average Indian middle-class family could never afford to have a car.

In the two-wheeler market, Bajaj scooter was a symbol of quality during those times. The government did not allow Bajaj Auto to expand its production capacity to meet the huge demand of scooters by Indian consumers, who had to book a scooter for years before getting it. Otherwise, they had to pay a heavy premium in the black market to get it quickly.

The Licence Raj may be termed as a dark period for Indian consumers. Licences were given only to influential business houses in good terms with the particular government in power. Many times, business houses with licences did not start their ventures because they had given false projections to the government in order to win licences, and later found that their projects were not viable. The losers in the game were the consumers.

The entry of foreign MNCs after liberalization of the economy was a boon for consumers. First, they started getting world-class quality products and services; second, the Indian companies had to change their old style of operations in order to survive in the market. Indian business houses have definitely made sweeping changes, which are now evident from their world-class products.

The success of Tata *Indica* and Mahindra *Scorpio* deserve special mention. Tata *Indica* faced some teething troubles in terms of quality in the initial years after its launch. It was positioned in the most competitive segment of the Indian car market—the Hyundai *Santro*, Daewoo *Matiz*, Maruti *Zen* segment. Soon, the erstwhile Tata Engineering (now Tata Motors) made drastic improvements in its new model named *Indica V2*, which became quite a success. One important reason for *Indica*'s success was its diesel version, which was introduced at a time when no other company had a diesel version. Later, Maruti posed competition to it with its diesel version, but in vain. *Indica* still remains a popular choice for consumers opting for the cheaper diesel car compared to the expensive petrol. Tata Motors introduced its small car Nano that created waves internationally for its world-class styling and frugal engineering resulting in an unbelievable launch price of ₹1 lakh.

Mahindra *Scorpio* is another success story of an Indian company, Mahindra & Mahindra (M&M) facing direct competition in the multi-utility vehicle (MUV) category from the likes of Toyota (*Qualis*), Hyundai, Honda, GM (Chevrolet *Tavera*), and Tata (*Safari*). M&M has been in the MUV segment for a long time. Tata Motor's models like *Sumo* and *Safari* posed competition to its models, but the real threat came with the introduction of Toyota Kirloskar Motor's *Qualis*. It highlighted the quality perception of Indian consumers with regard to MUVs, which were so far considered to be rugged but not sophisticated vehicles. With the success of *Scorpio* and more recently Xylo and XUV 500, which have world-class quality parameters, M&M has proven that it is striving for excellence in quality.

Indian companies will have to not only reach the quality benchmarks established by their foreign MNC competitors, but also surpass them. Foreign MNCs have successful operations worldwide and have established themselves strongly in India also. They have inherent advantages compared to Indian companies, such as the benefits of currency imbalances, experience of establishing facilities worldwide, and making defect-free products using stringent quality measures such as Six Sigma, kaizen, etc. The big question to be answered is: Can Indian companies beat them on the quality front through innovations in quality? They have been successful to some extent, as is evident from the following statement made by Jack Welch, Former CEO, General Electric about Azim Premji's Wipro: 'From the first day in dealing with Wipro, there's been nothing but quality, character, highest integrity, and highest quality work. As a joint venture, you wouldn't find a better partner. As a supplier, you wouldn't find a higher quality partner.'

## Cost of Production

Cost of production is another dimension which can be critical for gaining competitive advantage over adversaries. In the 1980s, Gulshan Kumar's Super Cassettes Industries created ripples in the Indian music industry by introducing its T-series brand of audio cassettes. There was a major

> Cost of production is
> another dimension
> which can be critical
> for gaining competi-
> tive advantage over
> adversaries.

difference in the price of a T-series cassette and that of the market leader HMV at that time. These cassettes were of moderate quality but costed less. There is always a section of consumers who prefer products low on price and moderate in quality. T-series became a major success story, which in a way revolutionized the Indian music industry. Another example of low-cost operations strategy is that of Nirma. Karsenbhai Patel of Nirma taught a lesson to a giant like HUL (HLL earlier) in the 1980s by launching a low-price detergent with the brand name 'Nirma'.

It is a great misconception that India has the advantage of cheap and abundant labour. The fact is that Indian labour is very low in terms of productivity. This means there is great scope of improvement in the productivity of employees by proper training. There is a great need for measuring productivity, and then taking steps to increase it. A rise in productivity will lead to lower costs of production.

## Delivery Speed and Reliability

Courier companies are most affected by this dimension of competitive advantage. In India, the concept of couriers is also a result of the process of liberalization. The Indian postal service dominated the postal scene before liberalization. Still, there are not many Indian courier companies which can boast of innovating courier operations in India like FedEx did in the US. FedEx owns its own planes operating in many countries, moving cargo from one place to the other, and making overnight courier deliveries at most locations. Reliability is the characteristic of a supplier to deliver on promised time. How many Indian suppliers have the capability to become just-in-time (JIT) suppliers to other companies? JIT requires a lot of discipline and coordination at different levels in the organization. Indian companies have to definitely establish systems to ensure high delivery speed and reliability.

## Introduction of New Products/Features/Models

Consumers in the Indian market are becoming more and more demanding. Companies have to be on the move all the time to improvise their products, adding more features at lower prices to beat the rivals, especially foreign MNCs. However, there is no scope of complacency for Indian companies as foreign counterparts like LG are also focusing upon the operations dimension by introducing models like 3-D television.

South Korean MNC Samsung has been regularly introducing latest features in its Galaxy series of phones and tabs, which its arch rival Apple is currently finding hard to catch up with. As a result, Samsung is increasingly gaining market share worldwide. For example, the recently launched Samsung Galaxy camera combines the features of a mobile phone with a standard camera.

Indian companies will have to focus on this dimension of competitive advantage to ward off foreign MNC competition.

## After-sales Service

> JIT requires a lot of
> discipline and coordina-
> tion at different levels in
> the organization.

This is so far the most neglected dimension in India. After-sales service can take Indian companies where they want to be. How many Indian companies keep in touch with the consumer after a product or service has been sold? In the automotives sector, the dealers' service stations usually provide three free services to their customers. After these free services, the customers prefer to have their vehicles serviced by unorganized service centres rather than going to authorized ones. This is due to two reasons. First, dealers control authorized service stations as they wish to, the automotive company has little interest in their operations. Second, most of these service centres provide spurious spare parts, but charge the prices of the original company-packed spares. In other words, dealer-controlled service stations have failed to establish credibility in the minds of customers and gain their loyalty. However, in more recent times, Indian companies have started paying attention to this critical aspect of customer relationship management (CRM).

## Innovation Management

> 'I think there is a world market for may be five computers.'
>
> –Thomas Watson, Chairman of IBM (1943)

Innovation is the use of new knowledge to offer a new product or service that consumers want. It involves invention as well as commercialization. The new knowledge can be technological or market-related. Technological knowledge is knowledge of components, linkages between components, methods, processes, and techniques that go into a product or service. Market-related knowledge is knowledge of distribution channels, product applications and consumer expectations, preferences, needs, and wants.

### Research and Development

The research and development of a new product or process takes place in various stages, namely, basic research, applied research, developmental research, and finally commercialization. Basic or fundamental research is concerned with the discovery of new scientific ideas, concepts, facts, and theories that may or may not have an immediate practical application and relevance. For example, the basic research on computers and initial programming languages was done without knowing the practical uses of these new technologies. Companies involved in basic research face long-term risk with potentially no payout or long payback periods, and need to have enough capital to exploit discoveries through applied research, development, and commercialization. Most of these companies obtain patents and, if faced with lack of funds or know-how to exploit these discoveries, give licences to other companies to do so in return for licence royalties.

Applied research involves finding practical applications of new scientific knowledge as a result of basic research in different spheres of business and society. For example, a personal computer, microcomputers used in cars, photocopiers, computers used in space shuttles, satellites, etc. are all results of applied research, done after the basic research of a computer and initial programming languages.

Developmental research means the utilization of completed research toward new or improved products, machines, equipment, and processes. It consists of design drawings, manufacturing specifications, construction and testing of prototypes, upgrade, extension, and production engineering. Commercialization is the last stage, when the results of applied research and development are incorporated in new or improved products, processes, and services in large-scale commercial production and use.

> Innovation is the use of new knowledge to offer a new product or service that consumers want.

### Offensive or Defensive R&D Strategies

> Offensive R&D strategy is followed by companies which are leaders in technology and strive to retain their leadership position.

Offensive R&D strategy is followed by companies that are leaders in technology and strive to retain their leadership position. These are companies which perform breakthrough research of innovative products to render the existing products in the market redundant. The R&D approach here is to be 'first to market'. Companies such as Texas Instruments, Sony, Microsoft, Intel, 3M, and Honda come under this category (Exhibit 2.3). The R&D investments of these companies range between 10 per cent –20 per cent of the gross profit. These companies are involved in basic as well as applied research. For example, Honda has made huge investments in R&D for developing a humanoid robot called *Asimo,* despite robots not being direct products in its commercial product line. Similarly, Honda has invested billions of dollars in developing the latest fuel cell technology car with zero emissions.

Defensive R&D strategy is followed by companies which prefer to be followers rather than leaders by using the basic research done by others to perform product modifications. In this approach, companies buy the R&D effort of others (such as universities, government, or independent research labs). Such companies buy patents or seek licences by paying royalties to companies that have done the basic research. The approach here is to avoid the high risk involved in basic research and concentrate only upon the less risky applied and developmental research. For example, Matsushita Electric, Hitachi, Kodak, etc. are companies following the defensive R&D strategy. It is important to mention here that it is common for companies initially following the defensive R&D strategy to eventually get into the offensive R&D mode. A typical example here is that of Samsung, which followed a defensive R&D strategy for decades before following an offensive strategy in recent times.

---

#### Exhibit 2.3    3M

3M was founded in 1902 at the Lake Superior town of Two Harbors, Minnesota. Five businessmen agreed to mine a mineral deposit for grinding-wheel abrasives. However, the deposits proved to be of little value, and the new Minnesota Mining and Manufacturing Company quickly moved to nearby Duluth to focus on sandpaper products

Years of struggle ensued until the company could master quality production and a supply chain. New investors were attracted to 3M, such as Lucius Ordway, who moved the company to St Paul in 1910. Early technical and marketing innovations began to produce successes and, in 1916, the company paid its first dividend—6 cents a share. The world's first waterproof sandpaper, which eased the health problem of sanding dust, was developed in the early 1920s. A major milestone occurred in 1925 when Richard G. Drew, a young lab assistant, invented masking tape—an innovative step toward diversification and the first of many Scotch brand pressure-sensitive tapes.

In the following years, technical progress resulted in Scotch® cellophane tape for box sealing. Customers began to find many additional uses including consumer applications. Drawing on its expertise in bonding mineral grit to sandpaper, 3M brought out new adhesives to replace tacks in bonding upholstery, and sound-deadening materials for the auto industry's new metal-framed cars.

The roofing granule business (ceramic-coated bits of rock) was developed in response to a need to make asphalt shingles last longer. In the early 1940s, 3M was diverted into defence equipment for World War II, which was followed by new ventures, such as Scotchlite™ reflective sheeting for highway markings, magnetic sound recording tape, filament adhesive tape, and the start of 3M's involvement in graphic arts with offset printing plates.

In the 1950s, 3M introduced the Thermo-Fax™ copying process, Scotchgard™ fabric protector, videotape,

*(Contd)*

*Exhibit 2.3 Contd*

Scotch-Brite® cleaning pads, and several new electro-mechanical products. In the 1960s, dry-silver microfilm, photographic products, carbonless papers, overhead projection systems, and a rapidly growing health care business of medical and dental products were introduced. The markets further expanded in the 1970s and 1980s into pharmaceuticals, radiology, energy control, the office market, etc., and globally to almost every country in the world.

The 1990s set new sales records of over US $15 billion annually, and about 30 per cent of the sales coming from products created within the past four years. In 2012, the company clocked US$29.6 billion in revenues. 3M's growth has come through a desire to participate in a large number of markets where the company can make a significant contribution from core technologies, rather than be dominant in just a few markets.

*Source*: 3M (2012).

## Recognizing the Potential of an Innovation

In 1970, Intel's Co-founder and Chairman, Gordon Moore, rejected a proposal to build a personal computer using Intel's microprocessor. He later said, 'I personally didn't see anything useful in it [the personal computer], so we never gave it another thought.' In 1978, when Intel started designing the 80286, the fifth member of its now famous family of microprocessors, its list of major applications of the microprocessor did not even include personal computers. In 1994, Intel made US $2.28 billion in profits on a revenue of US$11.52 billion, and in 1995, it made US$3.6 billion in profits on a revenue of US$16.2 billion, most of it from selling its microprocessor to be used in personal computers.

Not many firms are as lucky as Intel to recognize the potential of an innovation and make profits from it. Xerox is one such firm. Long before Apple Computers was founded, and eight years before IBM introduced a personal computer, Xerox's Palo Alto Research Center (PARC) built the first personal computer in 1973. It also developed the first hand-held mouse and the first graphics-oriented monitor, both of which would later form the basis for Apple's Macintosh and, later, Microsoft's Windows.

Xerox also invented the first word-processing program many years before Microsoft was founded, and obviously much before it dreamt of its best-selling Microsoft Word. The first laser printer, local area network, and object-oriented programming language were also from Xerox. Of course, the first computer workstation was also built at Xerox. Since many opportunities are never recognized, we may never know whether Xerox blew most of its opportunities. The only reason we know of its blunders is that someone else eventually exploited them. If no one had, it would be difficult to tell whether these were, indeed, opportunities.

Xerox is certainly not alone. IBM invented the RISC (reduced instruction set computer) microprocessor in 1975 and sat on it for decades. Then in 1981 it chose to use Intel's microprocessor in its personal computer. In 1995, 20 years after inventing RISC, IBM tried to use it to dethrone Intel, which it had helped crown king in the PC world (leaving its RISC processor to rot on the shelf). It was also trying to use RISC in its other product lines (servers, mainframes, and supercomputers), having done so with workstations in 1990. In 1983, it had seen RISC only as a technology for workstations—not PCs, minicomputers, mainframes, or supercomputers. IBM also helped crown Microsoft the king of PC software by giving it the rights to DOS, when it could have either bought it outright or introduced its own operating system.

In some ways, what Intel, Xerox, and IBM faced were more opportunities for new businesses than threats to existing businesses. Exhibit 2.4 traces how Microsoft charted its path of innovation. In the Xerox case, billions of dollars were left on the table, but Xerox's main copier business

| Exhibit 2.4 | Microsoft |

The PC has made people and companies associated with it rich. These are the manufacturers, suppliers, and numerous others, who supply chips and other components.

In fact, those who have profited the most from the PC are not manufacturers, but others who are associated with it. In 2012, Intel, the top supplier of microprocessor chips for PCs, made US$11 billion in profits on revenue of US$53.34 billion; and Microsoft, the maker of PC software, earned US$16.97 billion on revenue of US$73.72 billion. On the other hand, Lenovo, one of the largest PC makers, made only US$472 million on sales of US$29.57 billion.

Microsoft's biggest break came when IBM decided to enter the PC market and sought Microsoft's help for developing programming languages for the latter's soon-to-be launched PC.

While discussing how they would meet their commitments to IBM, it was decided that Microsoft would buy an operating system called Q-DOS from Seattle Computer, and sell it to IBM. Microsoft paid US$50,000 for the operating system, and sold it to IBM for US$1,86,000. However, the terms of the contract were in Microsoft's favour—it retained the right to license DOS to other PC makers. This decision turned very profitable for Microsoft as many firms entered PC manufacturing and it sold its operating system to these new players. DOS on the PC came with two advanced versions of BASIC, ran all the applications software available on the machine, and was priced at US$40. CP/M-86, the rival operating system, was priced at US$240. Microsoft actively pursued PC manufacturing firms and provided them a 50 per cent discount over the list price.

DOS emerged as a standard for PC operating systems and became Microsoft's chief source of revenue. It started exploiting the standard since 1981, after Apple announced using IBM software for its Macintosh. Developing applications programs for the Macintosh gave Microsoft an opportunity to understand GUI technology. Microsoft used its strengths to develop the Microsoft Windows operating system, a GUI-based operating system that is compatible with DOS and therefore, the huge installed base of PCs and applications that run on them. The 1990 version was very successful and Microsoft quickly developed versions of its Microsoft Word and Excel for the PC, and later the popular Microsoft Windows 95.

*Sources:* Afuah (1998); Lenovo (2012); Intel (2012); and Microsoft (2012).

was not threatened by the firm's inability to exploit the laser printer, the workstation, and other information technology inventions.

## Allocating Resources to Strategic Alternatives

All the organizations have limited resources. The operations manager is expected to produce goods/services of acceptable quality within budgeted cost and on scheduled time using minimal resources. While taking decisions regarding facility location, layout and capacity, production planning, materials requirement planning, etc., the operations manager inevitably faces the problem of scarce resources. Linear programming is a technique which helps the operations manager to allocate resources to strategic alternatives in the best possible way.

### Linear Programming

> Linear programming is a technique which helps the operations manager to allocate resources to strategic alternatives in the best possible way.

Linear programming (LP) is a technique which may be applied in the following resource allocation decisions:

1. Product mix (deciding the combination of products/services leading to maximum profit)
2. Ingredient mix (deciding the quantity of ingredients to be used in the product leading to minimum cost)

3. Transportation problems (deciding the distribution plan of goods/services leading to minimum transportation cost)
4. Aggregate production planning (deciding the quantity of products/services to be produced so that the overall cost is minimum)
5. Assignment problems (to assign man or machine resources to various activities to minimize the total cost or maximize the profit)

An LP problem is characterized by the following typical characteristics:

1. There should be a well-defined objective function (usually to minimize the cost or maximize the profits).
2. There should be alternative courses of action.
3. There should be resource constraints in achieving the objective function.
4. The objective function as well as the constraints must be expressed as linear functions (of the form $y = a + bx$, which is the equation of a straight line).

## Linear Programming with MS Excel

The first step in LP problems is the formulation of the problem, that is, expressing the objective function and the constraints mathematically. The variables in any LP problem are always non-negative, that is, they cannot assume negative values. Thus, these are called the non-negative constraints. Once the LP problem has been formulated, we can solve it using the following methods:

1. The graphical method
2. The simplex method
3. Microsoft Excel Solver

We will use the MS Excel Solver to solve our LP problems. Let us take up an example to understand the solution of an LP problem.

### Example 2.1

Laxmi Flour Mills is based at Nagpur and specializes in making flour of three grades $X$, $Y$, and $Z$. It has two flour mills $A$ and $B$, for which the costs of running per day are ₹1,000 and ₹2,000, respectively. It has received a contract from Swastik Flour Suppliers, which markets flour in branded packets throughout the country. In the contract, Laxmi has to supply Swastik with 20, 18, and 25 quintals of flour grades $X$, $Y$, and $Z$, respectively. Everyday, mill $A$ produces 4, 3, and 2 quintals, while mill $B$ produces 2, 2, and 10 quintals of flour grades $X$, $Y$, and $Z$, respectively. Determine the number of days for which mills $A$ and $B$ should be operated in order to fulfil the contract most economically.

### Solution

Let us assume that mill $A$ is operated for $a$ number of days and mill $B$ is operated for $b$ number of days so that the overall cost is minimum. The cost of running mill $A$ per day is ₹1,000. Therefore, the cost of running mill $A$ for $a$ days will be ₹1,000$a$. Similarly, the cost of running mill $B$ per day is Rs 2,000. Therefore, the cost of running mill $B$ for $b$ days will be Rs 2,000$b$. The total cost (TC) is given by

> The first step in LP problems is the formulation of the problem.

$$TC = 1,000a + 2,000b$$

This cost is to be minimized. Thus, the objective function may be expressed as

$$\text{Minimize } 1{,}000a + 2{,}000b$$

The problem requires Laxmi to supply 20, 18, and 25 quintals of flour grades *X*, *Y*, and *Z*, respectively. Mill *A* produces 4 quintals of grade *X* flour per day. Therefore, in *a* days it will produce 4*a* quintals of grade *X* flour. Similarly, mill *B* produces 2 quintals of grade *X* flour per day. Therefore, in *b* days it will produce 2*b* quintals of grade *X* flour. The total grade *X* flour produced by mills *A* and *B* together is given by

$$4a + 2b$$

This amount of flour produced should be more than or equal to the 20 quintal requirement of grade *X* flour in the contract. Thus, this constraint can be expressed as

$$4a + 2b \geq 20$$

Similarly, for grade *Y* and grade *Z* flours, we can express the constraints as

$$3a + 2b \geq 18 \qquad 2a + 10b \geq 25$$

The number of days for which the two mills should be operated, that is, *a* and *b*, should always be non-negative. Therefore, we have two more constraints called the non-negative constraints, which may be expressed as

$$a \geq 0 \qquad b \geq 0$$

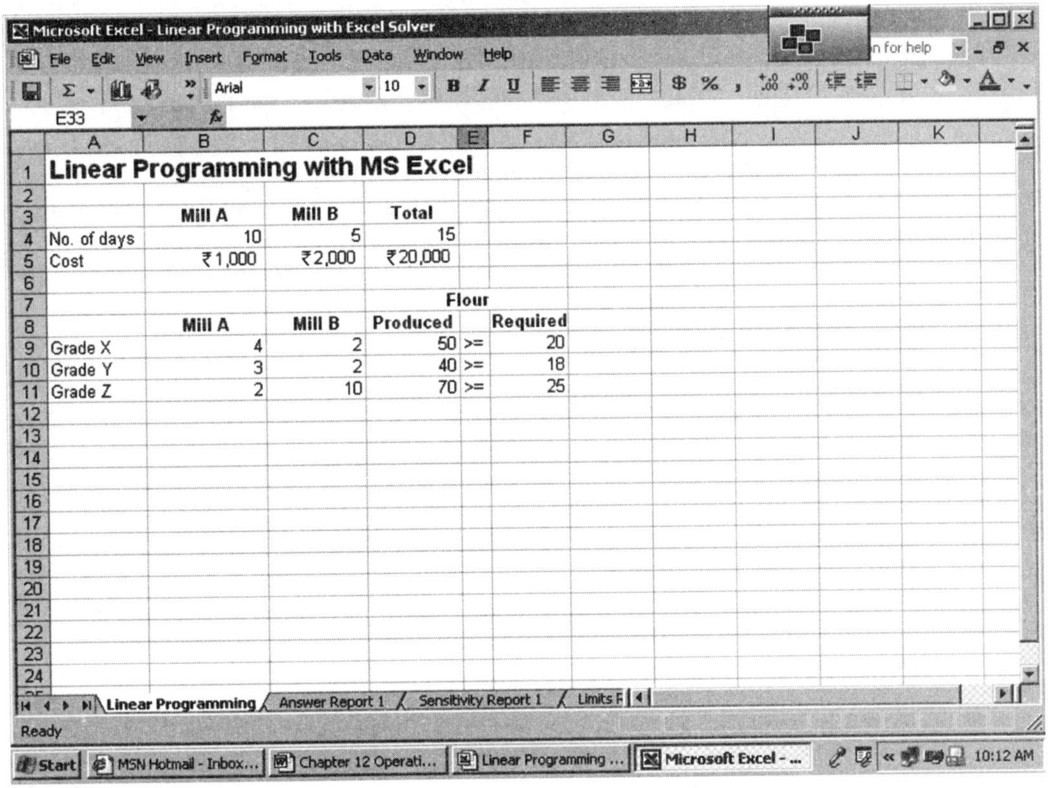


| | Mill A | Mill B | Total |
|---|---|---|---|
| No. of days | 10 | 5 | 15 |
| Cost | ₹1,000 | ₹2,000 | ₹20,000 |

| | Mill A | Mill B | Flour Produced | | Required |
|---|---|---|---|---|---|
| Grade X | 4 | 2 | 50 | >= | 20 |
| Grade Y | 3 | 2 | 40 | >= | 18 |
| Grade Z | 2 | 10 | 70 | >= | 25 |

**Fig. 2.6** Linear programming with MS Excel

The given problem may thus be expressed as
Objective function: Minimize $1{,}000a + 2{,}000b$

Subject to the constraints

$$4a + 2b \geq 20 \qquad 3a + 2b \geq 18 \qquad 2a + 10b \geq 25 \qquad a \geq 0 \qquad b \geq 0$$

We have to find the values of the number of days $a$ and $b$ for which mills $A$ and $B$, respectively, have to be operated so that the total cost is minimum.

Let us solve the given problem using MS Excel. As shown in Fig. 2.6, the costs of operating mills $A$ and $B$ are shown in cells B5 and C5 as ₹1,000 and ₹2,000, respectively. Cells B4 and C4 show the assumed values of the number of days $a$ and $b$ for which mills $A$ and $B$ have to be operated as 10 and 5 (these values are assumed randomly, as the optimal values will be generated by MS Excel). In cell D4, enter the formula **=SUM(B4:C4)** to get the sum of $a$ and $b$ as 15. In cell D5, enter the formula **=B4*B5+C4*C5** to arrive at the total cost (the objective function $1,000a + 2,000b$) of ₹20,000 (i.e., $1000 \times 10 + 2000 \times 5$). This value is to be minimized by choosing optimal values of $a$ and $b$. The software will change the values in cells B4 and C4 to arrive at the minimum total cost in cell D5.

Let us now express the constraints in rows 9–11. The first constraint is $4a + 2b \geq 20$. Write the coefficients 4 and 2 of $a$ and $b$ in cells B9 and C9, respectively. The right-hand side of this equation, 20 is entered in cell F9, which represents the quantity of flour $X$ required according to the contract. Enter the formula **=B9*$B$4+C9*$C$4** in cell E9 to get 50 quintals ($4 \times 10 + 2 \times 5$) as the total quantity of grade $X$ flour produced by mills $A$ and $B$ in 10 and 5 days, respectively. Note that while assuming the values of $a$ and $b$ in cells B4 and C4, one has to take care that the value appearing in cell D9 should be greater than or equal to the value in cell F9 (the $\geq$ symbol is shown in cell E9, in between cells D9 and F9).

Similarly, we enter the other two constraints shown in rows 10 and 11. The non-negative constraints will be entered in the solver of MS Excel. Having represented our problem in the MS Excel worksheet, we are ready to use the solver to find a solution to the problem. Click on the **Tools** in the toolbar and choose **Solver** from the pull-down menu. The **Solver Parameters** dialog box shown in Fig. 2.7 appears. If the solver option is not available in the pull-down menu, select **Add-Ins**. In the **Add-Ins** dialog box select **Solver Add-in** and click on **OK**. The solver add-in will be intalled for use.

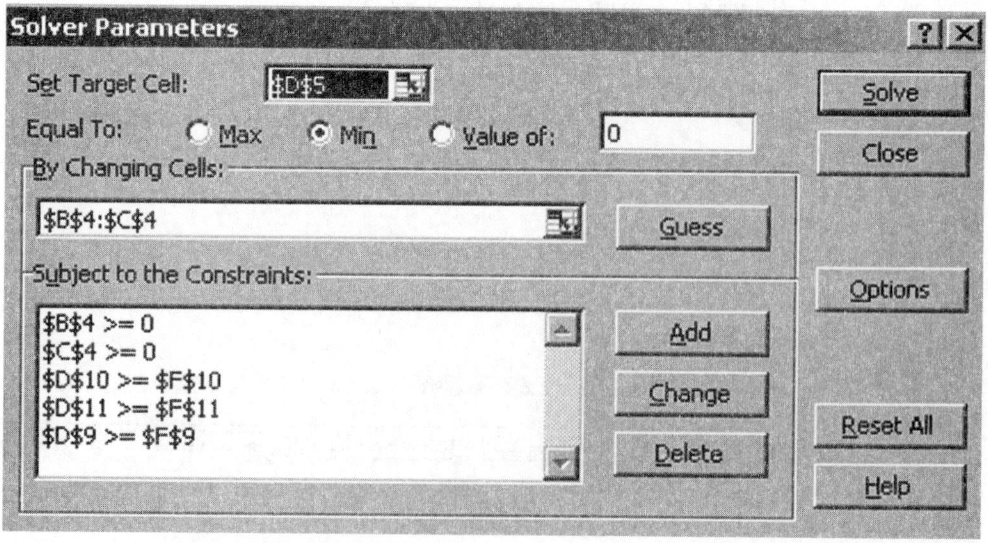

**Fig. 2.7** Solver parameters

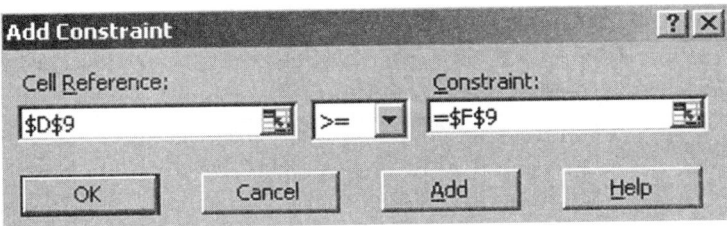

**Fig. 2.8**  Add Constraint option

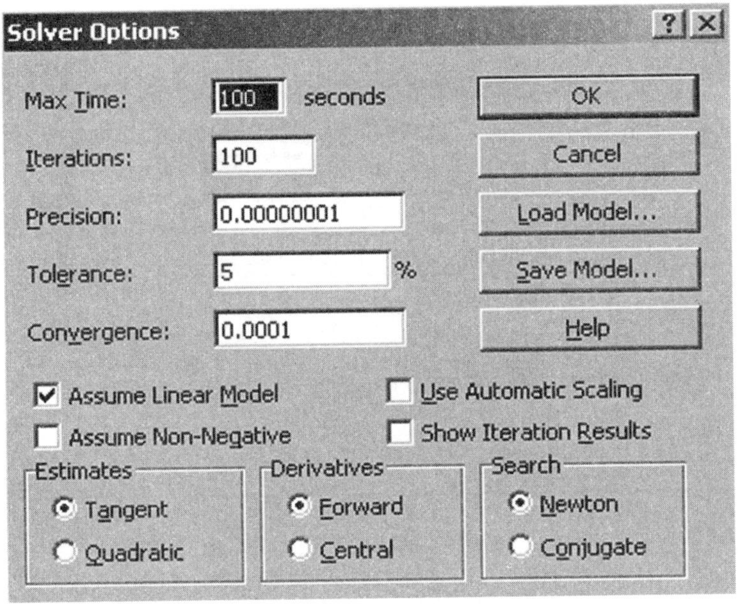

**Fig. 2.9**  Solver Options

In the **Solver Parameters** dialog box, **Set Target Cell** as cell D5. This is the total cost, which is to be minimized. Hence, select the radio button for **Equal To** to **Min**. Note that while solving a maximization problem (e.g., profit to be maximized), we will have to select the **Max** radio button. Click on the small arrow button in the text box **By Changing Cells**. The dialog box shrinks; in the worksheet, select cells B4 and C4, as these cell values have to be changed by the solver to obtain optimal values such that the total cost is minimum. Remember that the initial values in these cells have been randomly assumed as 10 and 5, respectively. Now click on **Add** so that a dialog box titled **Add Constraint** shown in Fig. 2.8 appears.

For this dialog box, select cell D9 in the worksheet so that **$D$9** appears in the **Cell Reference** text box. Choose the >= sign from the pull-down menu. Then select cell F9 in the worksheet so that it appears in the **Constraint** text box. Click on **Add**, and in the same way enter the other constraints in the problems, including the non-negative constraints. After entering all the constraints, click on **OK** so that the dialog box disappears. The constraints so entered are shown in the **Subject to the Constraints** text box as shown in Fig. 2.7. In the **Solver Parameters** dialog box, click on **Options** to get the **Solver Options** dialog box shown in Fig. 2.9.

In this dialog box, keep all the default entries intact. Select the check box for **Assume Linear Model,** as we solve the problem using LP. Click on **OK** so that the dialog box disappears. In the **Solver Parameters** dialog box, click on **Solve** so that the **Solver Results** dialog box shown in Fig. 2.10 appears.

Select the **Answer, Sensitivity**, and **Limits** options in the **Reports** text box. Click on **OK** to get the optimal values of *a* and *b* (the number of days for which mills *A* and *B* should be operated to minimize the total cost) in cells B4 and C4 as 5 and 1.5 days, respectively. The minimum total cost ₹8,000 is shown in cell D5. The answer, sensitivity, and limits reports can be seen by clicking on these buttons, which appear at the bottom of the workbook as shown in the figure. Note that the quantity of flour of grades *X, Y,* and *Z* produced is shown in cells D9, D10, and D11 as 23, 18, and 25, respectively. These values are either greater than or equal to the required amounts of these grades according to the contract, shown in cells F9, F10, and F11 as 20, 18, and 25, respectively.

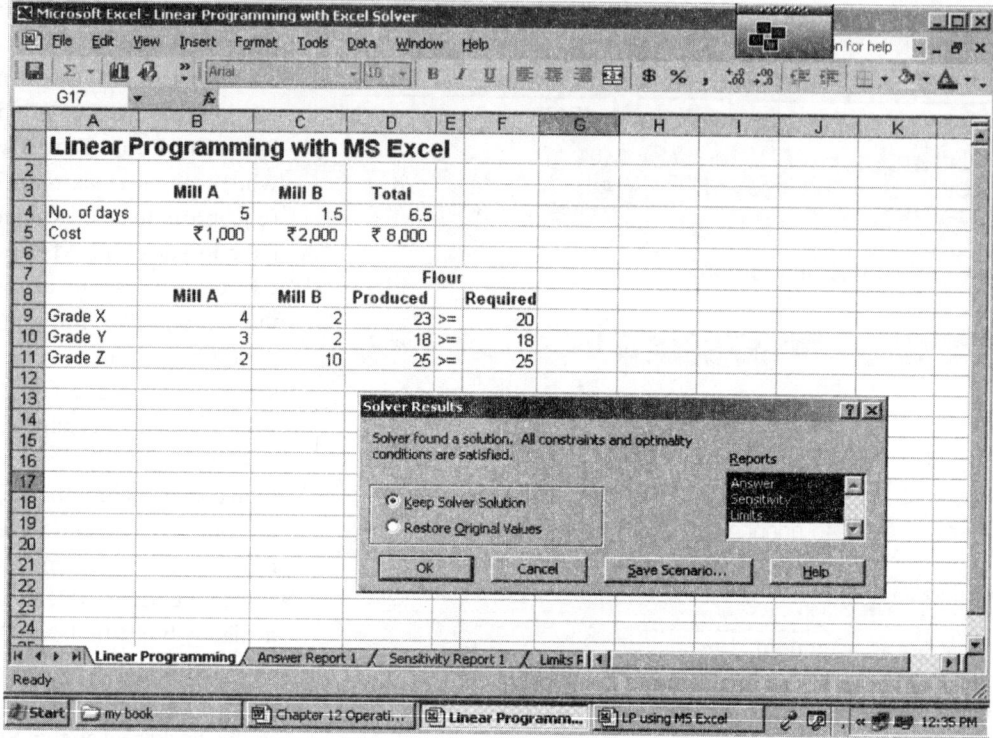

**Fig. 2.10** Solver Results

## Summary

The *corporate mission statement* of a business house sets out the basic purpose of its various activities. It identifies the scope of the firm in terms of the products/services it deals with, the markets in which it operates, and the technological areas it emphasizes. A *business grand strategy* is a long-term plan of a company, which provides a road map for achieving its corporate objectives. An *operations strategy* is a long-term plan for the production/operations function of a company, which acts as a guide for the operations required to achieve annual business objectives.

The business grand strategy is formed considering the corporate mission, the opportunities offered, and threats posed by the external environment, and the strengths and weaknesses of the company. There are twelve grand strategies: concentration, market development, product development, innovation, horizontal integration, vertical integration, joint venture, concentric diversification, conglomerate diversification, turnaround, divestiture, and liquidation. The operations strategy formulated should be in line with the business grand strategy and should be formed in coordination with other functional departments. This is important in order to avoid any conflicting objectives of functional strategies.

The global-level strategies can be of four types, depending upon the kind of control the global headquarter exercises on the local subsidiaries in different parts of the world. These are multi-domestic, international, global, and transnational. Decentralization refers to the extent to which upper management delegates authority downward to divisions, branches, or lower-level organizational units.

There are various *dimensions of operations* which may be used for competitive advantage: product/service quality, cost of production, delivery speed and reliability, fast introduction of new products/models/features, after-sales service, etc.

*Innovation* is the use of new knowledge to develop a new product or service that consumers want. It involves invention as well as commercialization. A company may pursue either *offensive* or *defensive*

*R&D strategies*. An offensive strategy is to be 'first to market' or a leader in innovations, while a defensive strategy makes a company a close second or follower in terms of technology. Resources are scarce and therefore, it is very important to strategically allocate resources, which is done by using *linear programming*.

## References

Afuah, Allan 1998, *Innovation Management—Strategies, Implementation, and Profits*, Oxford University Press, New York, pp. 150–153.

Dale, E. 1955, 'Centralization versus decentralization', *Advanced Management*, June, pp. 11–16.

Hage, J. 1980, *Theories of Organizations*, Wiley, New York.

Hage J. and M. Aiken 1970, *Social Change in Complex Organizations*, Random House, New York.

Megginson, L.C., D.C. Mosley, and P.H. Pietri Jr 1986, *Management: Concepts and Applications*, Second Edition, Harper & Row, New York.

Robbins, S.P. (1994), *Management*, Fourth Edition, Prentice Hall, Englewood Cliffs, NJ.

Smith, D.J. 2003, 'Strategic alliances and competitive strategies in the European aerospace industry: The case of BMW Rolls-Royce GmbH', *European Business Review*, vol. 15, no. 4, pp. 262–276.

Steers, R.M. 1977, *Organizational Effectiveness: A Behavioral View*, Goodyear, Santa Monica, CA.

'3M 2011 Annual Report, Form 10-K, Filing Date Feb 16', 2012, http://pdf.secdatabase.com/319/0001104659-12-010566.pdf, accessed on 30 January 2013.

http://www.intc.com/releasedetail.cfm?ReleaseID=734198&ReleasesType=Financial News, accessed on 4 March 2012.

'Lenovo Reports Fourth Quarter and Record Full Year 2011/12', Resultshttp://www.lenovo.com/ww/lenovo/pdf/Lenovo-earnings-press-release-4Q(Jan-March2012)and-FY-Eng(final).pdf, accessed on 4 March 2012.

http://view.officeapps.live.com/op/view.aspx?src=http://www.microsoft.com/investor/Downloads/Investor Services/Information for Investors/2012_Proxy_Statement.docx, accessed on 4 March 2012.

## Keywords

**Applied research** involves finding practical applications of new scientific knowledge as a result of basic research in different spheres of business and society.

**Basic or fundamental research** is concerned with the discovery of new scientific ideas, concepts, facts, and theories that may or may not have an immediate practical application and relevance.

**Business grand strategy** is a long-term plan of a company, which provides a road map for achieving its corporate objectives.

**Concentration** is a grand strategy in which a firm concentrates on growing its current business with a single product only, based on a particular technology in a single market.

**Concentric diversification** means getting into new businesses related to the firm in terms of technology, markets, or products.

**Conglomerate diversification** means getting into new businesses completely unrelated to the existing business.

**Corporate mission statement** of a business house sets out the basic purpose of its various activities.

It identifies the scope of the firm in terms of the products/services it deals with, the markets in which it operates, and the technological areas it emphasizes.

**Developmental research** means the utilization of completed research toward new or improved products, machines, equipment, and processes. It consists of design drawings, manufacturing specifications, construction and testing of prototypes, upgrade, extension, and production engineering.

**Divestiture** is a grand strategy in which a business unit is sold off to another business house. The reason for sale may be the requirement of liquid cash for other crucial business units, or a wrong conglomerate diversification, which the company now feels is difficult to focus on and, thus, better to sell off as a running concern to gain premium on the assets of the company being sold.

**Horizontal integration** is a grand strategy in which the company expands through acquisitions of its competitors' facilities. This strategy helps in gaining market share, by eliminating competitors, and access to new markets, technology, etc. The acquired firms deal in the same product as the acquiring company.

In **multi-domestic** form of global-level strategy, the global headquarter creates wholly-owned subsidiaries in various countries and grants them almost full autonomy in designing new products as per the local requirements, while also manufacturing and marketing them.

In an **international strategy**, a local company forays into an international market without any modification in the product.

In a **global strategy**, a standardized product is produced in large volumes at a few low-cost global locations and is distributed throughout the world with minimal customization.

**Transnational strategy** tries to combine the benefits of the two extremes of global-level strategies, namely multi-domestic and global strategies, in order to strike a balance between local responsiveness and global integration.

**Decentralization** refers to the extent to which upper management delegates authority downward to divisions, branches, or lower-level organizational units.

**Innovation** is a grand strategy in which the company innovates new products that render the existing products obsolete. These companies do not believe in fighting the competition in the maturity stage of the product by development, but in creating absolutely new products so as to rise above the competition as a leader.

**Joint venture (JV)** is a grand strategy in which two or more firms team up to form a new firm to meet the competitive challenge effectively. Most JVs are formed to complement the strengths of one firm with the strengths of the other firm(s).

**Liquidation** is the last resort, when all the efforts of turnaround have failed and the company is facing bankruptcy. In this strategy, the tangible assets of the company are sold off in parts or whole.

**Market development** is launching an existing product of the company in new markets (i.e., the geographical area is expanded).

**Operations strategy** is the long-term plan for the production/operations function of a company, which acts as a guide for the operations functions required to achieve annual business objectives.

**Product development** involves developing new features of existing products for the present markets. This means extending the life cycle of existing products.

**Turnaround** means bringing back a firm from declining profits or increasing losses to prosperity.

**Vertical integration** means acquiring the facilities of either the suppliers or the consumers in the supply chain. In place of acquisition, the company may start its operations from scratch for manufacturing its own raw material, or marketing is end products.

## CASE STUDY I

## Videocon—The True Indian Multinational

The late Nandlal Madhavlal Dhoot, a wealthy farmer in Maharashtra, initiated his sons, Venugopal, Padeepkumar, and Rajkumar in the family business, Videocon Electronics. His eldest son, Venugopal N. Dhoot, acquired one of India's first licences in 1984 to make colour televisions (CTVs). In 1985, through a technical tie-up with Toshiba Corporation of Japan, Venugopal formed Videocon International Limited and launched India's first colour television. Videocon, the US$2.5 billion group controlled by the Dhoots, now makes everything from washing machines to VCRs to MP3 players. Videocon bought a colour picture tube business from France's Thomson and a refrigerator unit from Sweden's Electrolux. The group has lucrative interests in oil exploration too.

Videocon's units in India have a capacity to churn out 4.5 million CTVs, 2.5 million refrigerators, 1 million washing machines, and 3,00,000 ACs. Its overseas plant in Oman manufactures 1,00,000 ACs per annum. In terms of components, in India, it manufactures 5 million compressors per annum, 24 million glass panels, and 6 million glass funnels. It is interesting to note that glass shells command margins as high as 30 per cent.

Till 2005, Videocon's individual businesses had clear identities. It started in 1984 as a branded manufacturer of consumer durables. In 1995, it ventured into contract manufacturing and oil exploration. The consumer electronics and oil businesses were separate entities with separate balance sheets. Things changed in 2005 when Videocon merged its oil subsidiary, Petrocon into the flagship Videocon Industries Limited (VIL). Now, it has a balance sheet that has the combined numbers of both consumer electronics as well as oil. It is clear that this was primarily done to use oil revenues to shore up the sagging consumer electronics business. Nevertheless, it is unusual. This move has raised questions about whether Videocon is trying out too many things. An indication of market sentiment can be obtained from the fact that the company's market capitalization of ₹96.55 million is less than even its estimated sales (put out by domestic brokerages) of ₹114.44 million in FY06 (it has an October-September financial calendar).

Videocon argues that while the oil business is highly profitable, it does not have the wherewithal to ramp up it significantly. According to Videocon, 'Consumer durables is definitely not as profitable as oil and gas, but if we were to expand our oil business, how would we do so?' Bidding for oil fields is becoming increasingly difficult because of the entrance of new players in the market and the government's permission to national oil companies to bid for the blocks. The bids are heading skywards due to expectations that the oil prices would soar higher in the near future. In other words, oil will probably never become the group's core business. Oil exploration is expensive and large players invest billions of dollars without the certainty of success. The supply is limited, pricing is controlled, and the industry is sensitive to political developments. Still, the dependence of the group's future on oil cannot be ignored. A fall in oil prices will impact the bottom line hugely, especially as the sector has fixed costs.

There is a stated intent to buy companies that have traditionally been engaged in research; that is why Videocon acquired Daewoo Electronics in 2006. However, the brands acquired by the company are at the manufacturing end of a business. For example, though Videocon bought Thomson's factories, the erstwhile French behemoth sold its brand to China's TCL. That means Videocon will not be able to use the Thomson label, even though it may be making TVs in Thomson's factories. This strategy is not entirely ill-conceived. After all there is a huge opportunity in contract manufacturing, reckoned at US$220 billion and it includes original design manufacturing too.

Videocon's entry into original equipment manufacturing (OEM) was different from that of global leaders such as Samsung and LG. The global companies first built strength in contract manufacturing and then graduated to being brand leaders. After the Videocon brand suffered a serious setback in India to LG and Samsung in the mid-1990s, the Dhoots focused on manufacturing. They started by manufacturing for licensed brands such as Toshiba, Hyundai Electronics, York, and Akai, and then for domestic brands such as Onida, Salora, and Crown. The group now has 26 OEM customers.

Industry observers feel that even India holds enough opportunity in OEM. According to iSuppli, contract manufacturers' supplies to consumer electronics companies in India touched US$236 million in 2004. Expectedly, Videocon has plans to expand OEM manufacturing in India. As branded players such as Philips move out of the manufacturing space in the sub-continent, Videocon could have a larger share of the Indian contract manufacturing pie.

Global contract manufacturing for CTVs is dominated by Turkish players such as the US$2.9 billion Vestel. The US$1.4 billion Beko Elektronik and the US$550 million Profilo Telra together have a 90 per cent market share of the European market. Chinese players such as Changhong and Skyworth are also in the fray.

While domestic players such as BPL and Onida saw their market share falling, the Dhoots followed a strategy of joining hands with the enemy. They entered into alliances with Akai, Sansui, Kenstar, Hyundai, Toshiba, York, and Kenwood to either manufacture or market their brands. In addition, the multiple branding strategy with the success of their Sansui brand paid off as Videocon managed to hold on to a combined market share of around 29 per cent, with LG at 26 per cent, and Samsung at around 24 per cent, according to company sources. However, industry sources put Videocon's combined market share around 24 to 25 per cent, with the two Korean companies sharing more than 50 per cent.

Credit must be given to the Dhoots. They not only set up a strong distribution and dealer network but, by entering into alliances, ensured that their manufacturing capacities were kept busy. In addition, Videocon followed the strategy of backward integration by getting into manufacturing of components such as electron guns and metal parts; deflection yokes for CTVs and compressors; and electric motors and plastic components for household appliances such as washing machines, refrigerators, and ACs. The group integrated further to get into the manufacture of glass panels and funnels, the key components for the manufacture of colour picture tubes. Videocon enjoys a unique synergy in the global CTV business from glass to cathode ray tubes (CRTs) to

CTVs. Together with other components for household appliances, this high degree of backward integration bestows upon the company a unique benefit over competition.

Venugopal Dhoot seems to have perfected the art of acquiring companies without paying much money. He bought 92 per cent of the Indian operations of Swedish major Electrolux for ₹500 crore. In a back-to-back deal, Electrolux picked up a 5 per cent stake in VIL for ₹4.15 billion. A year later, France-based Thomson sold its colour picture tubes facilities to Videocon for €240 million (around ₹12 billion at that time). In turn, it picked up a 14 per cent stake in VIL. As of September 2006, the promoter holding in VIL stood at 73 per cent.

What is it that these foreign majors have seen that they chose to sell their holdings in their businesses yet pick up a stake in the acquirer's flagship? The answers are not easy to come by.

Venugopal seems to hold the key to this puzzle. According to him, to have long-term success in this business, one has to be integrated end-to-end on a low-cost base. Videocon has acquired only low-cost assets in Mexico, China, and Poland. Thomson invested in Videocon because the business was seen as lucrative, based on a global scale integration of critical components on a low-cost base, with support of the steady cash flows from oil and gas businesses. Moreover, Thomson strategically wanted to remain in this business; hence, they acquired the stake in Videocon. The company believed in Videocon's strategy and felt that Dhoots were the right players to integrate and turnaround the business.

Industry sources do not buy the Dhoots' strategy of lapping up 'distressed' CRT capacities in the international arena at a time when there is no growth in demand for CRTs and the customers are demonstrating a qualitative shift in consumer preference towards flat, slim, LCD, and plasma televisions. Large multinationals generally exit a market segment once the prevalent technology matures and dies. Such companies do not mind exiting at any price. Thomson began to bleed as CRT prices came down to Chinese levels, but the costs remained European. In any case, Thomson wanted to exit the television and tube business and its deal with Videocon was a good strategy for the company.

There are some divergent views though. According to some industry observers, 'They (the Dhoots) have taken a cue from "think big, think global". They are aspiring to be the Ambanis of electronics.' With the acquisition of Thomson's facilities and Daewoo,

Videocon has brands that will help it to tap European and American markets. The company will not have to spend time and money to establish its own brand from scratch. Due to the huge price difference between LCD and plasma models and the conventional models, the CRT market will continue to hold its own. Since multinational companies in the LCD and plasma segment have invested huge sums of money in R&D, the prices are unlikely to come down drastically.

Analysts point out that the immediate worry for Videocon would be to find enough customers for the huge installed capacity of cathode ray picture tubes. While growth in the developed markets is driven by new technology products, the Indian market already has a sizeable installed capacity of picture tubes with well-entrenched players such as Samtel and Hotline. Thereby, supplying picture tubes to the Indian market from overseas units may not be an easy task. In addition, it would be some time before Videocon is able to produce newer products such as slim tubes. Dhoot, however, says that though the market for conventional picture tubes may be on the decline, it still accounts for over 85 per cent of picture tubes sales. He expects the growth to come in from developing regions such as the Commonwealth of Independent States (CIS), Eastern Europe, and Latin America.

There is a significant price difference between a conventional CTV and a premium product such as LCD or plasma TVs. The narrowing of this gap is still a few years away. Till that time there will be takers for the conventional television in developing countries in Asia, Europe, and Africa. Videocon should be able to set up lines for new products by that time and cater to the needs of diverse markets. The eventual success of the acquisition would depend on how quickly Videocon is able to adapt to technological changes.

Dhoot aims at deriving optimal value out of CRT assets. In case of televisions, he intends to be present in the global brand space through the Daewoo acquisition. He plans to build on Videocon's strong domestic position, especially in the emerging markets of this world, where the demand is being led by the increasing propensity of the erstwhile non-consumers to consumers. He also intends to build further on the OEM route. Videocon already has a presence in European markets through its operations based at Anagni in Italy. The company plans to sell 1.5 million TV sets with plasma, LCD, and CRT technologies. To complete its TV vertical, it will be present in the LCD space, by setting up a plasma panel line in Italy. This is already underway and soon, it will be one of the only six companies in the world producing plasma panels. A large project of LCD panel production facility is underway and the details with the Italian government are being worked out.

What were the strategies deployed to turn around the Thomson plants? One of the first areas Videocon looked into was the procurement side. Glass is the key component in the making CRTs and it has the largest facility in the world at a single location (at Bharuch, in India). Videocon is the lowest cost producer of glass globally due to a combination of low energy, manpower, and raw material costs. This was leveraged against the existing suppliers of glass to the erstwhile Thomson plants. The benefits were quite significant. In the first year, Videocon was able to save more than €25 million. Consolidation of CRT capacities in America and Europe has also helped its plants in Mexico and Poland. Inventory and working capital management also played a part in the process.

The newly-acquired Thomson units are supplying picture tubes to global consumer electronics majors with key customers being TCL and the Turkey-based Vestel. Globally, margins in the picture tube business have been under immense pressure with prices of picture tubes declining, while raw material prices have not come down proportionately. Videocon's strategy for integrating its glass shells unit may do well to lower cost of production. In addition, geographically, the company's acquired plants are at strategic locations with Mexico catering to the entire North American Free Trade Agreement (NAFTA) region, two units catering to Europe, and two in China where the bulk of CTV production has been shifted. However, one has to keep in mind that globally the cathode picture tube is seeing huge inventory pile-ups. In addition, the cost of maintaining a plant in Western markets is much higher than in India.

According to Dhoot, another very significant advantage of the acquisition is that it includes R&D centres and access to over 2,000 patents. This would enable the group to launch new products to counter the threat posed by the conventional television market being rapidly overtaken by high-tech products in overseas markets. In fact, it has already set up a line for plasma television at its unit in Italy, which it bought earlier from Thomson. This facility initially used to manufacture CRTs. The CRT lines are planned to be relocated to India. It will soon be rolling out high-tech products such as LCD, plasma, slim tube, and other flat panel display lines. The new technologies would help the company further consolidate its position in the Indian CTV market. The plant will churn out 1,00,000 pieces per annum. Meanwhile, it is currently into the assembly of ACs. It has come up with a technology breakthrough in LCD back-lighting. This should see the light of day soon. This new technology, besides giving better picture quality, consumes less power, is much slimmer and environment-friendly (as it is mercury-free), and comes at a much lower cost. The strategy here is to have a local supplier base for existing imports from Japan, Korea, and Taiwan.

Currently, the Mexico plant manufactures tubes catering to the Latin American markets. This plant too will manufacture ACs. Chinese facilities have already started making profits after the takeover by Videocon. While other plants are fully owned under the special purpose vehicle (SPV) floated at the time of takeover, there is a minority stake (about 8%) left with the local partner In China.

The Chinese plants produce about 11 million tubes from its two facilities in Foshan and Dongguan, in southern China. Sourcing and sales were earlier centralized from Paris (the Thomson headquarters). Once it moved to regional sourcing and given autonomy, it saw a drop in costs. Since the owners are big suppliers of glass, which constitutes about 20 per cent of the input costs, the company was in a much better position to bargain with locals.

With the roadmap of having Daewoo as its in-house brand for the global market and a major part of the cathode ray tube or colour picture tube (CPT) capacity to be used for contract manufacturing, Videocon will have to compete with the likes of Vestel PDP, Beko Electronik, and Profilo Telra, all of whom are in the contract manufacturing sphere.

### Discussion Questions

1. Which grand business strategies have been followed by Videocon in India? According to you, should it continue with the same business strategies or make changes in the future?
2. How has Videocon aligned its operations strategies with the business strategies adapted by it?
3. Which dimensions of operations would be most crucial to focus on for Videocon in the times to come for competitive advantage? Discuss.
4. As Videocon is expanding its operations worldwide, which of the four global-level strategies should it follow?

CASE STUDY II

# Indian 'Scorpio' Stings the World

J.C. Mahindra and K.C. Mahindra, the founders of the Mahindra Group, had the same ambition—to prove to themselves and the world that Indians were capable of being the best at whatever they chose to do. Accordingly, they gave up their professional careers at TISCO and Martin Burn respectively, and risked becoming entrepreneurs by setting up their own company—Mahindra & Mahindra (M&M). It was under their inspiring leadership that M&M made the first indigenous utility vehicle (UV) in the country in 1949.

Interestingly, J.C. Mahindra and K.C. Mahindra believed in globalization decades before it had become a buzzword. Even in the fifties, the company had British and German engineers on its rolls, and international tie-ups with Mitsubishi, Willys, Perrine, and Chrysler. Every venture they set up delivered satisfactory financial results and their company has grown into one of India's largest corporate groups. Even today the group is driven by the same vision that drove the entrepreneurs then.

Today, M&M is India's largest sport utility vehicle (SUV) maker and ranks about 25th in terms of the world's automakers. It started building Willys Jeeps for the Indian market in 1954 and eventually built its own SUV—the Scorpio—based on the Willys Jeep. About twelve years ago, M&M was the only SUV maker in India. Now the company holds about 50 per cent share of the segment.

The company has broken the unspoken rule that says automakers must design, engineer, and test their own vehicles, while spending hundreds of millions of dollars in the process. Along the way such companies provide contracts to suppliers who will build the components for them. M&M, instead, tried something suppliers had been suggesting for years. The company built a brand new vehicle with virtually 100 per cent supplier involvement from concept to reality for US$120 million. This included improvements to the plant. The new Mahindra Scorpio SUV had all of its major systems designed directly by suppliers with the only input from M&M being performance specifications and programme cost. Design and engineering of systems was done by suppliers, as was testing, validation, and materials selection. Sourcing and engineering locations were also chosen by suppliers.

When M&M decided fifteen years ago to talk about the next generation SUV, it had a big decision to make.

Global companies were coming to India in search of local partners. Many companies had talks with M&M, but in the end the automaker decided to move forward alone. After a lot of soul searching, M&M decided that it did not want to become an Indian subsidiary of a large multinational. It wanted to grow itself into a global player for SUVs in the low and medium segments.

Having decided to remain independent and become a global player, M&M decided about its products. The idea for a world class vehicle was born in 1996. Back then, it was but a small idea. It grew to become M&M's most ambitious and prestigious project. So much so that it embarked on what even a global car major would think twice about attempting—an all new engine in an all new vehicle. The company was clear that products based on ancient technology could not see the company through to the new millennium. It had two options. At that time Mahindra did not have the expertise to do a brand new product. However, developing that expertise was an option. The second was to outsource product development to one of the boutiques in Europe. This option was very expensive and, therefore, the company decided to develop a new product. The company had very little experience at product development at that time. It had never done a major facelift, let alone develop a new product.

After conducting market research, styling and features for the new Scorpio started taking shape. The company also realized that they did not have the expertise to develop the vehicle, and time to hire and train new people. It decided to leverage the strength of the suppliers who were available in India in the field of global product development.

In 1996–1997, tier one suppliers realized that supply contract volumes that brought them to India were not materializing. Their large, newly built facilities were not being used to capacity. They had capacity they wanted to utilize and M&M was able to tap into that need. The company decided to sign up with major suppliers for system development.

'It is easier to make what you can sell than to sell what you have made', this was the guiding force of integrated design and manufacturing (IDAM). It was conceived, working hand in hand with one of its suppliers CSC, UK (formerly Lucas Engineering) to streamline the delivery of a world class, zero defect, trouble-free product. Whether it is putting world class systems and manufacturing processes in place, delivering a unique buying experience to the customer, providing process expertise to its vendors, IDAM is at the core of every process at M&M. A result of its continued customer focus, IDAM gives customers the product they want.

## Market Research

The IDAM process begins where it should—with the customer. Before going to the drawing board, M&M met a large number of customers and understood their key buying factors using the quality function deployment (QFD) process. Then it converted these findings into product specifications and put them on the design block. 'For the customer, by the customer, of the customer', describes M&M's customer focus. Before the company even went to the design block, it went to the customer. It interviewed people, asked for their opinions, found out what they were looking for, and even went back to them to keep itself abreast of changing tastes and demands. It later evolved key buying factors and arrived at a list of product features as desired by customers.

## Design and Development

Once the design team had an idea of what the customer was looking for, it prepared styling themes. After this stage, the best vendors in the field were involved in product development and design. 'Luxury should not be an accessory. It should be standard equipment,' based upon this premise, the company decided to develop its product. The Scorpio has the absolute plush comfort of the Lear seats and the exquisite interiors from US; the fluently flowing exteriors from Visteon, US; the suspension system from Samlip, Korea that glides over speed breakers, ditches, potholes, and other such impediments; the all-absorbing shock absorbers from Armstrong; the sophisticated audio system from Kenwood; the assurance of Bridgestone for tyres; the latches and door-closing mechanisms that shut with a hush, from Meritor, UK; and the air conditioning from BEHR, Germany. The petrol version of Scorpio has the Renault engine that traces its lineage to a world class, racing heritage.

The company divided the IDAM team into 19 cross-functional design teams. Each team had a single head, accountable for the team's progress. The teams were fully empowered for decision-making, except when the decisions might impact the functioning of other teams. All this helped to create a seamlessly integrated product.

## Testing and Validation

Mahindra & Mahindra built 74 vehicles for the testing and validation phase. The company used extremely rigorous processes for testing and retesting. Every component was checked and re-checked to reach the best combination of form and function. Then under different climatic conditions, over one million kilometres of diverse terrain was covered, including, the army testing grounds and internationally reputed testing grounds in Belgium and Korea. This 'survival of the fittest' testing and validation was done using Sequential Testing and Examination Plan (STEP). After several trials the best combination of design and performance was evolved.

## Implementation

The main aim of this stage was to arrive at the best combination of design and customer features, and to iron out any rough edge. Any problem at this stage was sent back to the validation stage. This was done in the tool development, vendor development, and actual implementation stages. All these changes were checked in the pilot batch.

## Manufacturing Support

Mahindra & Mahindra has set up a world-class manufacturing facility in Nashik. With an investment of ₹6 billion, this facility spans 120 acres and has everything to deliver an impeccable product with a press shop by Fukui; dyes from Fuji, Japan; jig and fixtures in the body shop by Wooshin, Korea; a tester line (in the trim chassis final line) by Fori Automation, US; and a paint shop in collaboration with Durr, Germany.

The company did not stop at manufacturing a world-class product. From dealer development programmes to exclusively designed showrooms that go beyond mere product display, it focused entirely on the customer. The company strives to make each customer experience unique. Its showrooms across the country stand testimony to this focus.

Mahindra & Mahindra had 120 members in its Scorpio team. This team had an average age of 27 years so while M&M had immense drive, it also had the experience to reinforce it. Working under Dr Pawan Goenka, who was earlier with General Motors' engine research department at its R&D centre in Warren, Michigan, the team delivered the almost impossible. The company with its 120 people and external engineering consultants was responsible for the initial styling, body engineering, chassis and frame design, and vehicle integration.

Qualis, the name derived from quality and service, was introduced by Toyota in India on 11 January 2000. Despite its unexciting looks (it was jokingly called bread-box-on wheels) and old technology (the model was 15 year old when introduced in India), Qualis did exceedingly well in India. Produced from the Toyota Kirloskar Motors' (TKM) sprawling plant at Bidadi, near Bangalore, Qualis quickly redefined the multi utility vehicle (MUV) segment in India with 33 per cent market share in the category. Its sales, however, stagnated at around 3,100 vehicles per month in 2004–05. Toyota Kirloskar Motors sold 28,000 vehicle in the first nine months in the face of stiff competition from Mahindra Scorpio, which was launched during late 2002. This forced Toyota to replace it with a new vehicle—Innova. According to industry experts, Innova lacks the top-end punch of the Scorpio. It does not have the same spring in its step as the Scorpio and the performance figures prove this. It is a clear second behind in the dash to 100 kph, and in-gear acceleration figures are also a notch below the Scorpio. Interestingly, the experts feel, Innova closes the gap past 120 kph, possibly because of its sleeker shape.

As the Scorpio brand started improving on its equity, the M&M shop floor was still burning midnight oil. This time around the project was to improve on the product. Between July 2003 and January 2004, the brand was subjected to new product developments. Quieter engines were introduced after adopting the chain drive engine system. The seats were improved, and the new two-toned look was developed. Later, Scorpio installed a common rail diesel engine to meet the Bharat Stage (BS) III auto emission norms.

In April 2006, Mahindra launched an upgraded Scorpio by dubbing it the 'all-new' Scorpio. The car has 43 new features, most of which are aesthetic including new front bumpers, a new tail-light cluster, and an air-scoop on the bonnet. Yet, there are some crucial engineering changes as well, including a new rear suspension, which was jointly developed with Lotus, UK.

The Mahindra Scorpio is today sold across the world in countries such as Malaysia, South Africa, Russia, Italy, France, Spain, and Portugal. In Western Europe, so as not to confuse the vehicle with a previous Ford vehicle of the same name, it is marketed as the Mahindra Goa.

### Discussion Questions

1. What is so unique about the IDAM process adapted by M&M? Which process do other car manufacturers follow while designing new products?
2. What kind of risks does M&M face by outsourcing the designing of various parts of Scorpio to vendors?
3. Which business strategy was followed by M&M while developing the Scorpio? Was the company's operations strategy in line with this business strategy?
4. Mahindra Scorpio and Toyota Innova belong to two different categories of cars, namely SUVs and MUVs respectively. Are these cars still cutting into each other' market share?

---

## CASE STUDY III

# BMW Rolls-Royce

BMW Rolls-Royce GmbH was established on 1 July 1990 as a JV between the German car maker BMW AG (50.5 per cent) and UK's Rolls-Royce (49.5 per cent). Although BMW began life as a manufacturer of aero-engines and was Germany's leading producer of jet engines in the second World War, it severed its links with aerospace in the 1960s, and by 1990 its activities were confined to the automotive industry.

Although Rolls-Royce was one of the Big Three aircraft engine manufacturers in the world in terms of size as measured by turnover, which stood at US$4.1 billion in 1990, it was almost half the size of its two US rivals—General Electric with a turnover of US$7.6 billion and Pratt & Whitney with a turnover of US$7.3 billion. The purpose of the JV was to develop a new engine core for aircrafts—the BR700, which would provide the basis of a family of engines covering the (12,000–14,000)-lb thrust market segment and was designed to replace Rolls-Royce's successful Tay engine.

The BR700 core engine was formally launched on 31 March 1991. It drew heavily on Rolls–Royce's other engine programmes. The new core was run successfully for the first time in August 1993. The entry of the BR710 engine into service in late 1996 marked the transition of BMW Rolls-Royce GmbH from a company that developed aero-engines to one that manufactured them. Production built up rapidly and the output in 1997 was 100 engines, all BR710 for Gulfstream V corporate jets. Production of engines for the Global Express corporate jet commenced in 1998. In 1999, the larger BR715 engine went into production and entered service on the Boeing 717-200 regional jet.

These developments reflected a rapid build-up in production. By 1999, production had almost doubled to 200 engines a year. In the same year the JV moved up to a three-shift operation. Thus, by 1999 the objective of developing a new engine core that could be used as the basis of a family of new engines had been achieved, and two engines—the 14,000-lb thrust BR710 and the 18,000-lb thrust BR715—had been designed, developed, certificated, and put into service.

BMW Rolls-Royce GmbH performed well in terms of sales too. By late 1999, nearly 10 years after the JV was first announced, BMW Rolls-Royce GmbH had orders for 1,000 engines. This compares with the projected sales of 3,000 for the period 1996–2010. The first engine in the BR700 series, the 14,000-lb thrust BR710, was launched in 1992. Production commenced in 1996 and this was quickly reflected in the JV's turnover, which increased tenfold between 1995 and 1999. Hence, BMW Rolls-Royce GmbH had achieved one-third of its targeted sales within a comparatively short time and was well on target to achieve the sales total planned for 2010.

Not only was the level of total engine orders strong, the JV had by 1999 notched up these sales on four different aircraft applications. These included the Gulfstream V corporate jet, the Global Express corporate jet, the Boeing 717-200 (formerly designated the MD-95) 100-seat regional airliner, and the British Aerospace Nimrod 2000 maritime patrol aircraft. In addition, all four of these applications were single-sourced. That is, in each instance, the BMW Rolls-Royce GmbH engine was the only one used on that airframe. There was no rival engine that its customers could specify. Although single-sourcing is more likely to occur with corporate jet and regional airliner applications because customers do not have large aircraft fleets that justify multiple-sourcing, this was impressive. It was a measure of the airframe manufacturers' confidence in the new engine and also pointed to the prospect of greater profitability for the BR700 series engine because of the absence of competition.

While the JV proved successful in terms of its technical ability to develop new engines, and the overall level of sales was well on target by the late 1990s, penetration into specific market segments did not turn out as planned when the JV was established in 1990. The JV's business plan envisaged sales of 3,000 engines over the period 1996–2010. Having achieved orders for 1,000 engines by 1999, BMW Rolls-Royce GmbH was well on target. However, the mix of engines envisaged that the 3,000 engines would be split in favour of the regional jet market, with only 700 engines being sold in the corporate jet market.

In reality the engines were split the other way round, with the corporate jet sector taking two-thirds of the sales. This pattern led to greater than expected success in the corporate jet sector and disappointing results in the regional jet market. BMW Rolls-Royce GmbH's success in corporate jets came early. Having the BR710 engine selected by both the manufacturers of a new generation of ultra-long range, 'heavy iron' corporate jets meant that the JV dominated this market segment.

In November 1999, Rolls-Royce bought out BMW's stake, effectively ending ten years of JV operation, although the JV continues to function as Rolls-Royce Deutschland (Smith 2003).

### Discussion Questions

1. What were the reasons for Rolls-Royce entering into a JV with BMW?
2. Is it correct for a car manufacturer like BMW to start manufacturing aircraft engines?
3. Why did BMW pull out of the JV despite it bing successful?

## Objective Questions

### Choose the correct option

1. Strategic analysis and choice does not involve
   (a) corporate mission
   (b) company strengths and weaknesses
   (c) invention
   (d) external threats and opportunities
2. The use of new knowledge to develop a new product or service that consumers want is called

(a) innovation
(b) discovery
(c) invention
(d) research

3. A grand strategy in which two or more firms team up to form a new firm is called
   (a) concentration
   (b) joint venture
   (c) divestiture
   (d) liquidation

4. The external environment of a company is not constituted by
   (a) government
   (b) employees
   (c) competitors
   (d) suppliers

## State True or False

5. Applied research involves finding practical applications of new scientific knowledge as a result of basic research in different spheres of business and society.

6. In a global strategy, a local company forays into an international market without any modification in the product.

7. In the grand strategy of market development, an existing product of the company is launched in new markets.

## Fill in the blanks

8. _____ integration is a grand strategy in which a company expands through acquisition of its competitor's facilities.

9. In _____ strategy, the global headquarter creates wholly-owned subsidiaries in various countries and grants them almost full autonomy in designing new products as per the local requirements, and also in manufacturing and marketing them.

10. _____ R&D strategy is followed by companies which are leaders in technology and strive to retain their leadership position.

## Concept Review Questions

1. What is operations strategy? Explain the relationship between operations strategy and business grand strategy using a schematic diagram.

2. Why is it important to coordinate various functional strategies while formulating an operations strategy?

3. What are global-level, corporate-level, business-level, and functional-level strategies?

4. Explain the four types of global-level strategies with suitable examples.

5. What is innovation? What are the various stages of research and development?

6. Explain offensive and defensive R&D strategies.

7. Explain the various dimensions of operations for competitive advantage.

8. How can we strategically allocate resources? What is linear programming?

## Numerical Problems

1. Raj Furniture is a prominent furniture manufacturer at Bhubaneshwar and specializes in making dining tables and reading tables. It uses 20 sq. ft of wooden board and 15 labour-hours for making a dining table, while it uses 5 sq. ft of wooden board and 10 labour-hours for making a reading table. Each dining table sold contributes ₹1,000 to the profit margin, while each reading table sold contributes ₹500 to the profit margin. If the available resources are 500 sq. ft of wooden board and 600 labour-hours, determine how many dining tables and reading tables should be made in order to maximize the profit.

2. Super Plastics is based at Noida and manufactures three plastic parts $X$, $Y$, and $Z$ for automotive manufacturers. It has two machines $A$ and $B$, either of which may be used to manufacture the three parts and for which the costs of running per day are ₹4,000 and ₹5,000, respectively. Super Plastics has received a contract from Awadh Automotives, which manufactures three-wheelers to supply 25, 50, and 60 ('000 units) of parts $X$, $Y$, and $Z$, respectively. Everyday, machine $A$ produces 6, 6, and 4 ('000 units), while machine $B$ produces 3, 4, and 8 ('000 units) of parts $X$, $Y$, and $Z$, respectively. Determine the number of days for which machines $A$ and $B$ should be operated in order to fulfil the contract most economically.

# Project Assignments

1. Visit the websites of Infosys and Wipro. Develop their growth charts in chronological order. Compare and discuss their business operations and find important differences and similarities. In addition, decide which competitive operations dimension is focused upon by these companies.
2. Visit the office of a company near you and meet the seniormost manager in the company. Discuss with him the business grand strategy followed by the company and the corresponding operations strategies. Find out which competitive dimensions of operations they are focusing upon and why? Prepare a detailed report clearly highlighting the focus of operation.

## Answers to Objective Questions

| | | | | |
|---|---|---|---|---|
| 1. (c) | 2. (a) | 3. (b) | 4. (b) | 5. True |
| 6. False | 7. True | 8. Horizontal | 9. multi-domestic | 10. Offensive |

# 3

# New Product Development

**Learning Objectives**

After reading this chapter, you will be able to answer the following questions:
- What are the various aspects of product design to be considered while designing new products?
- How can new products be designed to be robust?
- How can quality be incorporated in the design stage of new products?
- How can we delight customers with innovative features in new products?
- Can we combine customization and mass production together to allow unprecedented choice for customers?
- What steps should be followed in new product development?

## INTRODUCTION

Developing new products (the term 'product' has been used to imply 'products and services' throughout the chapter) requires substantial strategic intent, capital, and scientific human resource on part of organizations. Not all organizations can afford to have these basic requirements of new product development; and that is why, we find that most organizations act just as 'followers' to the other few that are 'leaders in innovation'. Today, organizations such as Apple, Google, and Samsung are at the forefront of new product development. Not long back, companies such as Sony, Microsoft, and Toyota were synonymous with new product development.

Today, the challenges of new product development are enhanced due to short product life cycles, frequent changes in customer preferences, and the requirement of global outreach of products for swift market penetration. At that, the risk of product imitation by competitors despite the protection of copyrights and patents in various global geographies cannot be ruled out. Often corporations have to plunge into lengthy and costly legal battles over infringement of patents and copyrights. The legal tussle between Apple and Samsung over the technology used in Samsung Galaxy devices is a case in point.

The twentieth century was primarily led by the West in terms of innovation and new product development. Be it innovation in terms of fast food chains such as McDonald's, KFC, Burger King, Dunkin Donuts, and Starbucks, retail chain formats such as Walmart, Tesco, Carrefour, and IKEA, the concepts of

> New product development requires significant strategic intent, capital, and scientific human resource on part of organizations.

<table>
<tr><td colspan="2" align="center">**Exhibit 3.1  Facebook and Mark Zuckerberg**</td></tr>
</table>

Mark Zuckerberg is the co-founder, Chairman, and CEO of the social networking site Facebook. Mark was informally trained in computer programming at an early age. His first home-made product was a stripped-down version of the contemporary chat messenger, which allowed his family at home to communicate with his dentist father at the dental clinic.

When kids of his age used to play computer games, Mark used to create them. During his high school years, he created an innovative music player that used artificial intelligence to track the listening habits of the user. This player called Synapse caught the attention of Microsoft and AOL, who wanted to acquire it and recruit Mark as their employee. However, Mark chose to pursue his higher education at Harvard University instead.

During his sophomore year in the Computer Science and Psychology programme at Harvard, he created an application for campus students called CourseMatch, which provided visibility to the students about other students' choices of courses and form study groups. Sometime later, he created a program called FaceMash that allowed students at the Harvard campus to choose a better looking person out of the two photos chosen randomly from any of the nine houses. It is claimed that Mark hacked into the protected areas of the Harvard University computer network to gain access to the student photographs of the various houses. FaceMash became an immediate success at the campus, but Mark faced expulsion from the university on charges of computer

hacking. Later, these charges were dropped against him.

During early 2004, Mark created 'The Facebook', to which about half of the Harvard campus population subscribed quickly. Within the next few months, the membership was extended to other colleges and universities including the Ivy League institutions such as Stanford, Columbia, and Yale. Facebook was launched in 2004 and within a year, it extended its memberships to the high schools. On 26 September 2006, Facebook ('the' was dropped from the company name) allowed anybody to join provided they are 13 years or above and hold a valid email ID. As of September 2012, Facebook had more than one billion active users worldwide.

From the new product development perspective, there is a clear gradual testing, validation, and launch of the initial versions of the 'product' in small populations (within campuses) before the market geography was expanded. It also accentuates the fact that if an innovative product has acceptability in the market, getting funds is not difficult—Facebook received its first funding from PayPal co-founder Peter Theil as soon as it was incorporated in 2004. Later, in 2007, Microsoft purchased 1.6 per cent of its shares for US$240 million, thus projecting its implied value to US$15 billion. By November 2010, the company's value rose to about US$41 billion and by the time it introduced its initial public offering (IPO) in May 2012, its share prices had risen to US$38, thus making it a US$104 billion company.

amusement parks such as Disneyland, Universal Studios, and Sea World, or products such as iPhone, iPad, Google Android, and BlackBerry—the West has dominated the innovation space.

During the past few decades, the designs of new products developed in the West have been used by corporations for manufacturing in developing nations such as China and India to derive advantages of low manufacturing costs. This has exposed these developing nations to state-of-the-art technologies, designs, and manufacturing methods. Gradually, these countries are augmenting their design and development capabilities and it would not be surprising if during the coming few decades, seeds of innovation are sown and a culture of innovation is developed in Asian countries. Till that time, the Western domination of the innovation space shall continue. See Exhibit 3.1 to know more about Facebook's origin.

## Product Design

Figure 3.1 shows the concepts involved in product design.

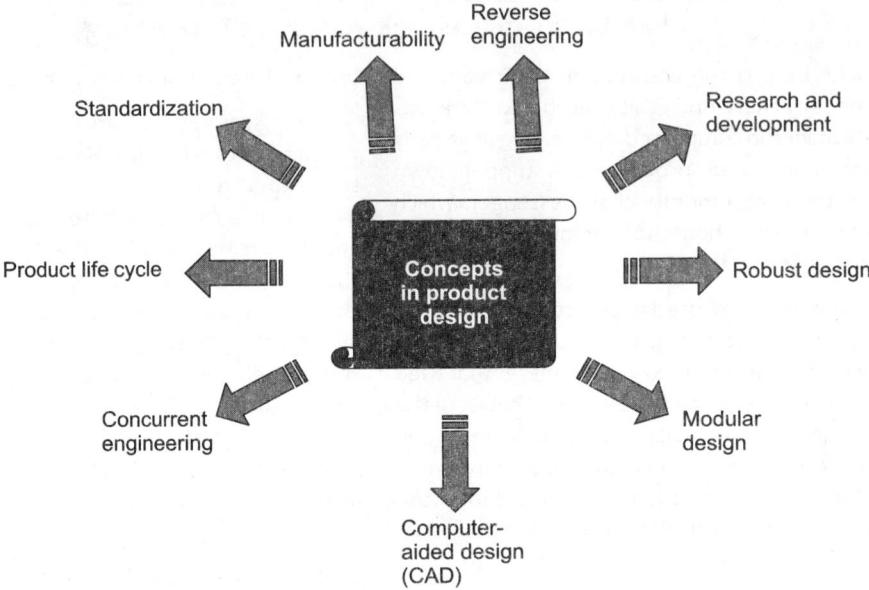

**Fig. 3.1** Concepts in product design

### Research and Development

The design of new products is done by the *Research and Development* (R&D) department of organizations with the help of many other departments. In R&D, *fundamental research* is the advancement of the state of knowledge in a subject, though it may not be practically converted into commercial applications. For example, when Newton found the law of gravity, it was a fundamental research, which did not have immediate applications. In the course of time, many commercial applications of the law such as space rocket propulsion and high-speed elevators came into existence.

*Applied research* has the objective of developing commercial applications. Most of the corporate houses have a R&D department devoted for this purpose. *Development* is the process of converting the results of applied research into useful commercial applications.

### Reverse Engineering

*Reverse engineering* is the process of carefully dismantling an existing product (of a competitor) step by step in order to understand the unique underlying concepts. It helps in designing new products, which are better than those of the competitors. In the field of consumer electronics, Sony Corp. is at the forefront in designing new innovative items such as the Walkman, Handycam, digital cameras, etc. Many other companies have to follow the reverse engineering approach in order to break Sony's monopoly of new products in the shortest possible time.

> Reverse engineering is the process of carefully dismantling an existing product (of a competitor) step by step in order to understand the unique underlying concepts.

### Manufacturability

*Manufacturability* implies designing a product in such a way that its manufacturing/assembling can be done easily. While designing a new product, the manufacturing capabilities (such as existing machines, equipment, skills of workers, etc.) of the organization have to be kept in mind. If the required capabilities do not exist, the management can consider enhancing the production capabilities by making more investments.

## Standardization

*Standardization* refers to less variety in the design of products, that is, new products are designed such that there is no major variation from the existing products. For example, all computers and typewriters have the same arrangement of keys in the keyboard because it has become a standard that consumers are used to. Although many other more efficient designs of keyboard keys are available, no company is willing to take the risk of deviating from this standard. Lack of standardization creates problems such as the NTSC and PAL standards in TVs and VCRs. In computers, different operating systems such as Windows and Linux have resulted in major compatibility issues. On the other hand, standardization has benefits such as lower design cost due to use of existing components/parts and easy availability of components for replacement if any defects arise.

Modular design is another type of standardization, which means designing a product in parts or modules. The modules are sub-assemblies of different components and parts. For example, in personal computers there are separate modules (small boxes inside which there are various integrated components) for the motherboard, the hard disk, power supply, CD drive, floppy drive, etc. Whenever a defect occurs, an entire module can be replaced by a new one, though it may be slightly more expensive than searching for the defective component in a non-modular design and replacing it. It is easier to find the defect because the investigation is limited only to a particular module. This approach reduces a lot of the effort and time required to design the product. The inventory management of modules is simple in comparison to that of a large number of different components in a non-modular design.

## Robust Design

*Robust design* means designing a product that is operational in varying environmental conditions. For example, if you compare a car with a jeep (a four-wheel drive), the jeep is more robust in design as it can even be used efficiently on hilly areas with poor road conditions. The Japanese engineer Genichi Taguchi emphasized that it is easier to create a product with robust design rather than making changes in the environment to suit the product.

## Concurrent Engineering

*Concurrent engineering* is the product design approach in which the design team includes personnel from the marketing department (to specify the customer requirements), engineering department (to look at the feasibility of the design), production department (to suggest if production capability exists for the design), materials department (to give inputs about material availability according to design specifications), and finance department (to suggest financial feasibility of the design) in addition to the design department. This approach is radically opposite to the classical sequential product design approach in which the design process takes place in stages, moving from one department to the other. Concurrent engineering saves a lot of time and effort,

> A robust design ensures a product that is operational in varying environmental conditions.

> The product life cycle has five stages spread throughout the life of a product.

unlike the sequential approach in which feedback between departments, at times leading to rejections of the suggested designs at later stages, results in the wastage of a lot of time and effort.

### Computer-aided Design

*Computer-aided design* (CAD) is a software which helps the designer to make the 3-D design of a product on the computer and visualize the design from various angles. In the earlier times, when CAD softwares were not available, design engineers had to make designs from various angles (say, front, back, side, top, bottom views of the product/components) on paper charts by using rulers and other equipment, which was tedious and time consuming. The designs made on CAD can be seen at different workstations through intranets simultaneously. Also, these can be transmitted to distant locations (for comments of experts, etc.) using the Internet.

### Life Cycle of a Product

The *product life cycle* has five stages spread throughout the life of a product. These are incubation, growth, maturity, saturation, and decline (Fig. 3.2). The duration of the life of a product depends upon the type of product. The *incubation* stage witnesses a low demand of the product owing to the customer's unawareness about the new product. As the awareness increases and new features are added to the product over a period of time, the demand starts growing and this phase is called the *growth* phase of the life cycle. Next follows the *maturity* stage, when the demand tends to become stable and even new features do not appeal much to the masses, leading to the *saturation* phase and eventually the *decline* phase.

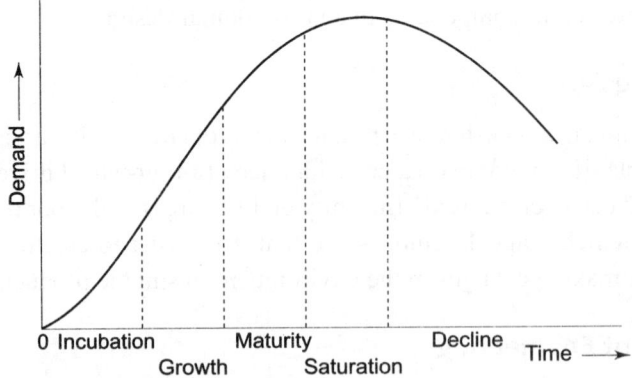

**Fig. 3.2** Product life cycle

## Robust Design and Taguchi's Quality Loss Function

> According to Taguchi, the cost of variability is zero only at the target or aimed-at value.

Genichi Taguchi is accredited with introducing the customer's point of view in the statistical quality control involving the specification limits for a product. According to the traditional view, if the product variables are within the specification limits, the product is of good quality. If the product variables cross these specification limits even slightly, the product becomes non-conforming or defective (as shown by the dotted lines in Fig. 3.3). The cost of variability is zero within the specification limits and it soars as soon as the specification limits are reached. Taguchi argued that the customer is not bothered about a product having a variable just within the specification limits or just outside the specification limits. Practically, it hardly makes a difference from the customer's point of view. Taguchi pointed out that the difference between the target or aimed-at value and lower specification limit (LSL) or upper specification limit (USL) (i.e., the variation) is large enough leading to a loss of quality. According to Taguchi, the incremental cost of variation (loss of quality) from the customer's point of view is not abrupt but gradual (as shown by the bold curve in Fig. 3.3). The cost of variability is zero only at the target or aimed-at value. The customers are becoming more and more demanding in terms of quality and any type of variation has to be reduced as much as possible, starting from the design stage of the product. Taguchi proposed that the design of the product should be robust enough so that any variation in the environment do not affect the performance of the product, that is, it should be insensitive to such variations.

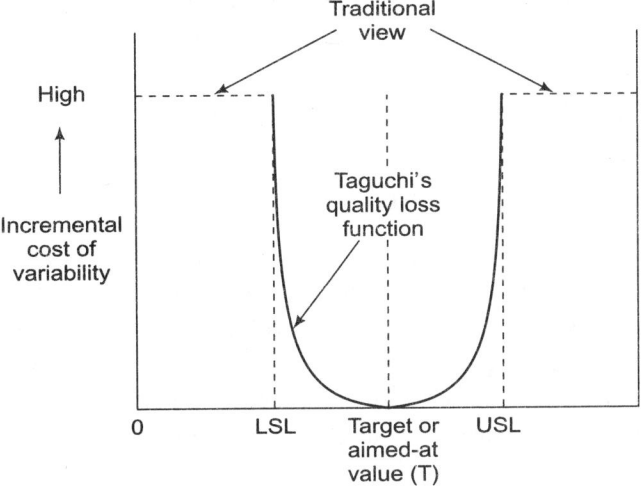

**Fig. 3.3** Traditional and Taguchi's views of cost of variability

The cost of variability is represented by Taguchi's loss function according to the following equation:

$$L(x) = k\,(x - T)^2 \tag{3.1}$$

Here,

L $(x)$ is the loss function

$x$ is the parameter under consideration

T is the target or aimed-at value of the parameter $x$

k is the proportionality constant

In this loss function equation, we notice that the loss would be zero only when the parameter value x exactly equals the target value T. Thus, the designers of the product have to strive for minimizing the loss function by bringing the parameter value x as close as possible to the target value T.

*Robust design* means designing a product such that it is operational in varying environmental conditions. For example, there are superior digital cameras that function properly in all weather conditions. Taguchi emphasized that it is easier to create a product with robust design rather than making changes in the environment to suit the product. In the creation of a robust design, Taguchi recommends three steps, namely system design, parameter design, and tolerance design. In the system design phase, the design engineer uses his practical and engineering knowledge to create design of the product according to the customer's requirements (specified by the marketing department of the company). The key considerations here are choice of the raw materials and components, availability of machines required for processing, capacity of the facility, determining the assembly sequence of the product, etc. In the next parameter design phase, identification of influential parameters of different components, parts, and sub-assemblies is done and their targeted or aimed-at or nominal values are determined. Also, the noise variables are identified and optimal settings of the controllable variables are established so as to minimize the effect of noise variables. The role of experimental design using Taguchi method is very prominent here. In the third and the last tolerance design phase, tolerances or specification limits are specified for those parameters, which show significant variability from the desired target value. This facilitates in taking measures so as to reduce the variation further, what could not be achieved in the parameter design phase. Also, in the tolerance design phase, the tolerances for those variables are eased-up, which do not have significant effect upon the response variable. Thus, the associated costs can be reduced further in this way.

## Quality Function Deployment

The American Society for Quality Control defines *quality function deployment* (QFD) as a 'structured method in which customer requirements are translated into appropriate technical requirements for each stage of product development and production. The QFD process is often referred to as 'listening to the voice of the customer' (Bemowski 1992). QFD is a method that determines customer requirements, deploys quality improvement resources to meet those requirements, and measures customer satisfaction to determine success. QFD is suitable not only for designing products but also for designing services. Thus, its applications span manufacturing as well as services organizations.

The word 'function' in QFD refers to a function analysis of the business process phases in order to improve the quality of the product development process itself. It does not refer to product function in this context. It is regrettable that this part of QFD, which is essential to gaining long-term buy-in, implementation, and compliance, has been completely overlooked by most QFD practitioners outside Japan. This type of function analysis and process mapping has recently found a renewed use in the so-called 'swim-lane' charts used in Six Sigma (Akao 2003).

QFD has its origins at Bridgestone Tire Kurume plant, where the Quality Chart was used for the first time in 1966. There are references to application of this technique during the 1970s at Mitsubishi Heavy Industries, Komatsu, Fuji, Isuzu, Konica, and Matsushita (Mizuno and Akao 1994). Yogi Akao (1972), a professor at Asahi University, Tokyo, has been credited with developing this technique to the present form. India has shown a strong interest in QFD both in its world-class software industry and in manufacturing industries such as trucks, automobiles, and farm tractors. India has hosted several QFD Green Belt and QFD Black Belt courses in both public and private forums (Akao and Mazur 2003).

> QFD is suitable not only for designing products but also for designing services.

## Applications of QFD

In 1987, the QFD Research Group of the Japanese Society of Quality Control (JSQC) led by Akao published a final survey report on the status of QFD application among 80 Japanese companies (Akao et al. 1987; Akao and Ohfuji 1989). The companies surveyed listed the following as the purpose of using QFD:

- Setting design quality and planned quality
- Benchmarking competitive products
- New product development that sets the company apart from its competitors
- Analysing and accumulating market quality information
- Communicating quality-related information to later processes
- Deploying design intent into manufacturing
- Identifying control points for the *gemba* (a Japanese term that refers to the place where source information can be learned)
- Reducing initial quality problems
- Reducing design changes
- Cutting development time
- Reducing development costs
- Expanding the market share

Yoshizawa (1997) listed the following two points as the significance of QFD in industry:

1. QFD has redefined quality control in manufacturing by moving it upstream to quality control for development and design. It has shifted the focus of total quality management (TQM) from process-oriented quality assurance (QA) to design-oriented QA and in the creation of a product development system.
2. QFD has provided a communication tool for designers. Engineers, positioned midway between marketing and production, need to take a leadership role in new product development. QFD is a powerful tool for engineers to build a system for product development.

Figure 3.4 shows the various steps in designing the QFD house of quality. See Exhibit 3.2 for more on the QFD practices at Toyota.

---

### Exhibit 3.2   QFD at Toyota

Toyota was trying to establish its foothold in the American markets during the 1970s. The Americans perceived Toyota cars as cheap, but of low quality due to its rusting problems. Toyota successfully employed QFD to devise painting techniques to overcome this rusting problem. QFD also helped Toyota with the door problems in their pickup trucks. The company conducted focus group interviews of some of its truck customers, who revealed that the truck doors posed problems in hilly terrain. When the trucks were parked downhill, on opening, the heavy doors would pull away from the passengers and were difficult to manage. Also, a lot of effort was required to close the door against the pull of gravity. Similarly, when the trucks were parked uphill, the same force of gravity would not let the heavy doors open easily. By using QFD, the company came up with the idea of introducing notches that hold the doors in the open position. Today, QFD has become an integral part of the design process of every new product/model of the company.

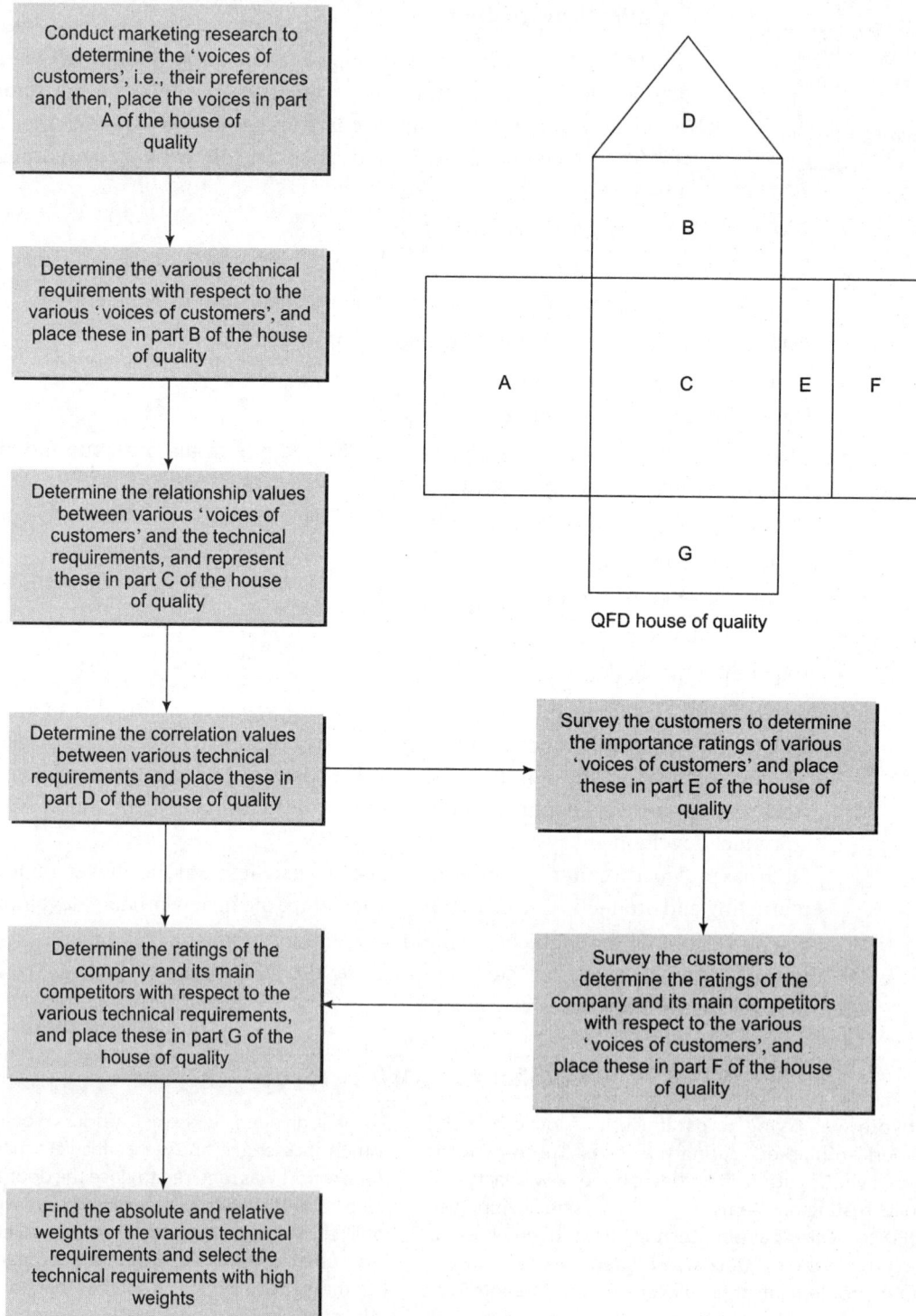

Fig. 3.4 Steps in designing the QFD house of quality

# Kano's Model

During the process of determining the 'voices of customers', it is possible that some of the root wants of customers may not get revealed. Kano et al. (1984) developed a very useful diagram for characterizing customer needs, which can help us gain a profound understanding of customer satisfaction (see Fig. 3.5). The *x*-axis represents the performance of the product and the *y*-axis represents the level of satisfaction attained by the customer. The model divides product features into the following three distinct categories, each of which affects customer satisfaction in a different way.

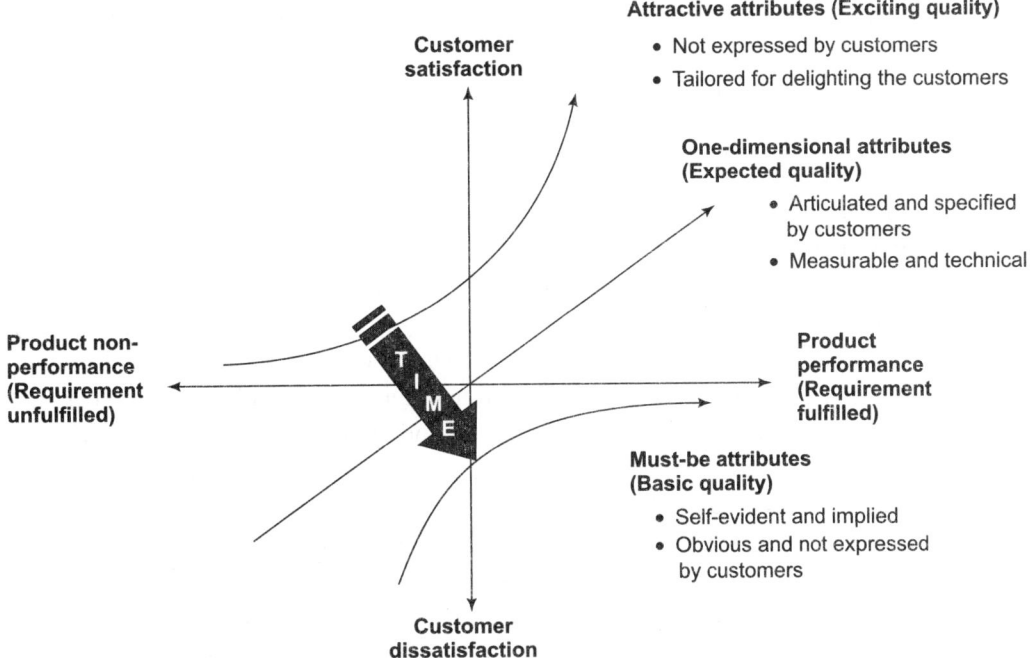

**Fig. 3.5**  Kano's model

**Must-be attributes (Basic quality)**  Customers take them for granted when fulfilled. However, if the product does not meet this basic need sufficiently, the customer may become very dissatisfied. For example, when a customer goes to buy a new television, 'S-band and hyper band' are such attributes. If a television does not have these attributes, it will not receive all channels having frequency in this range. Many years back, it was not a standard feature of colour televisions in India. But over the period of time, this feature has been incorporated in all televisions available in the market. Customers seldom mention these features in the interviews and the presence of these features does not enhance their satisfaction level much. Unless there is a recent personal bad experience with an attribute of such a product, these attributes seldom come to the mind of the customers during the interview process. This is shown by the lower curve in Fig. 3.5, which represents the must-be attributes. Note that with the increase in performance of the product (along +ve *x*-axis) with respect to these attributes (i.e., the company tries to improve upon these attributes), the increase in satisfaction (along +ve *y*-axis) is much lower compared to the two curves shown above this curve. On the contrary, when these attributes are absent (we move towards the tail of this curve), the satisfaction level falls drastically resulting in extreme dissatisfaction.

**One-dimensional attributes (Expected quality)**   These attributes result in customer satisfaction when fulfilled, and dissatisfaction when not fulfilled in equal proportions with respect to the performance of the product (see the straight line curve of one-dimensional attributes in Fig. 3.5). The better the attributes, the better the customer likes them, for example, a television with 300 channels will satisfy the customers more compared to a 100-channel television. Similarly, a TV with 1,200-watt sound system will be more satisfying to the customer compared to a 400-watt sound system television. These attributes are also known as spoken qualities as these attributes are mentioned by the customers in the interview process. The customers expect that the companies should keep on improvising these existing attributes of the product. These attributes are important in the QFD process as knowing the expectations of the customers on these fronts can help the company increase customer satisfaction.

**Attractive attributes (Exciting quality)**   The absence of attractive attributes does not cause dissatisfaction because they are not expected by customers who may be unaware of such product features. However, strong achievement in these attributes delights customers, for example, excellent processing power, sharper displays, or holographic keyboards of smartphones. In today's competitive environment, with so many brands available in the market with almost similar features, it has become more and more important for the companies to find new attractive attributes for the customers to compel them in buying their products. It is not enough to aim for satisfying the customer with only the must-be and spoken attributes. The attractive attributes, in fact, help the customers to choose the company's brand out of the gamut of brands available in the market, thus avoiding the confusion of choice on part of the customer.

It should be noted that the same attribute may change category over time. Specifically, attractive attributes can become one-dimensional attributes and then further become must-be attributes. For example, surfing the Internet using mobile phones is quite common today. Earlier, smartphones were used by only businessmen; however as many as 40 million smartphones may have been in use early this year in India (Nielsen 2013). People can now use phones to do things that were unimaginable a decade back—such as watch movies, play games, and download videos.

Thus, in the coming years, this feature may be considered as one-dimensional and eventually, a must-be attribute. Inherent in Kano's thinking is that customer needs and consequently product attributes are dynamic rather than static. This means that the companies have to strive for developing innovative features (attractive attributes) on a continual basis. Thus, by the time an attractive attribute becomes a one-dimensional attribute, the company should come up with a new attractive attribute in order to gain competitive advantage. Note that in Fig. 3.5 the curve for attractive attributes steeply rises signifying greater customer satisfaction for small increments in product performance with respect to these parameters.

The lesson for the designers from Kano's model is that they should ensure 'must-be' attributes in the new product being designed by them through a careful analysis (or reengineering) of existing products in the marketplace. They need to capture 'voices of the customers' to ensure that 'one-dimensional' attributes are incorporated in the new designs. In addition, they should strive towards innovating features which are not even imagined by the customers, so that the customers may get a pleasant surprise when new products are introduced. It must be noted that as time progresses, the 'attractive' attributes automatically become 'one-dimensional' and later, qualify as a 'must-be' attribute (as the competitors ape these features and they become common place). This is depicted by the bold arrow with time embossed over it in Fig. 3.5.

## Stage-gate New Product Development Process

Cooper (1990) proposed the stage-gate system for new product development, which has become quite popular in all types of industries today. Kodak, General Electric, Bombardier, Motorola, Lucas, and Rolls-Royce are some of the companies that have benefited extensively from this approach by tweaking it to their unique requirements (Phillips et al. 1999). There are five gates in the standard approach suggested by Cooper, as shown in Fig. 3.6. These gates are hypothetical, but serve an important mechanism to ensure that the deliverables (or milestones) expected by that stage of the new product development (NPD) process are achieved. Then only the NPD process can go to the next stage. It is recommended that each gate should be manned by senior management (who act as gatekeepers) and have significant authority to approve or disapprove the migration of the project to the next stage.

The five gates in this approach demarcate the following six stages of the NPD process:

*Stage 1—Idea generation* This is the first stage of the NPD process, wherein various ideas of new products are considered. A checklist of various criteria, such as alignment with strategic goals, budgets required, and potential of competitive advantage, is useful at this stage. Some of these criteria may be classified as 'definitely required' and others as 'desirable' to screen the ideas to the next stage. Points can be assigned to an idea on all such criteria and a weighted average taken to compare with other ideas. Ideas with higher overall weighted score stand a good chance of moving to the next stage.

*Stage 2—Initial assessment* Ideas that reach this stage after screening through Gate 1 are subjected to the next stage of initial assessment. It comprises a quick assessment of the market potential and technical feasibility of the proposed idea. Exploratory survey methods such as focus group interviews and secondary data sources are used for this purpose. Technical feasibility of the idea is ascertained by considering the in-house expertise, production facilities, availability of materials, etc. At Gate 2, the criteria for screening can be set as 'definitely required' and 'desirable'. Some basis financial parameters like payback period can also be considered for screening of ideas at Gate 2.

*Stage 3—Comprehensive business planning* After passing through Gate 2, an idea is subjected to comprehensive business planning that involves thorough financial analysis coupled with deciding the target market, customer preferences (through extensive market research), and converting them into relevant technical specifications. This stage is crucial for 'go ahead' or shelving the idea, as after passing Gate 3, the NPD project is destined to incur heavy capital expenses that are irreversible in most instances.

Idea generation is the first stage of the new product development process.

*Stage 4—Design and development* Having passed Gate 3, the product idea is set to take a tangible existence in the form of detailed designs and development. The specifications generated in the earlier stages are taken into consideration while creating the designs of the product. Detailed marketing

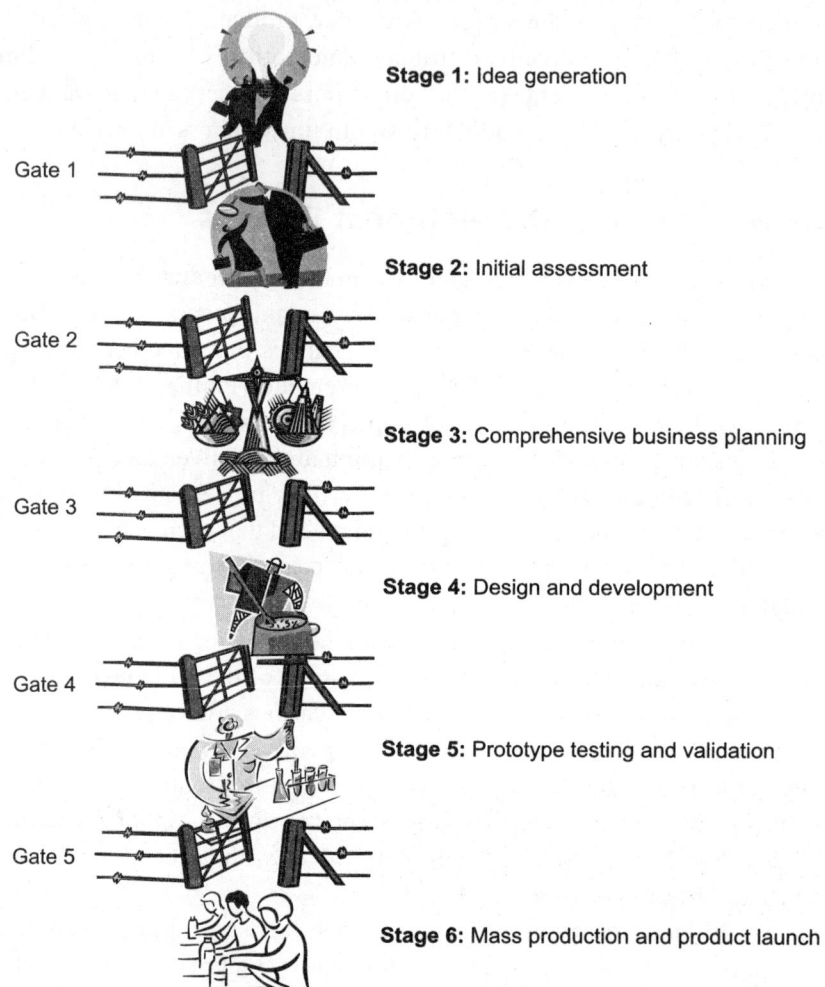

**Stage 1:** Idea generation

Gate 1

**Stage 2:** Initial assessment

Gate 2

**Stage 3:** Comprehensive business planning

Gate 3

**Stage 4:** Design and development

Gate 4

**Stage 5:** Prototype testing and validation

Gate 5

**Stage 6:** Mass production and product launch

**Fig. 3.6** Stage-gate process in new product development

plans, production plans, and financial plans are simultaneously prepared at this stage. Gate 4 acts as post-development review, wherein it is checked whether the development work has been conducted with due consideration to quality.

*Stage 5—Prototype testing and validation* A sample prototype of the product is created and tested to check how closely it matches the specifications and designs created in the earlier stages. The performance of the product in test conditions as well as field conditions is checked. A pilot market testing is done in a small geographical area to check the acceptability of the product in the market and to refine it further on the basis of the feedback received. A trial production run is conducted to preempt any teething troubles during subsequent stage of large scale production. Costing of the product is done and fresh revenue projections are done in order to ascertain the viability of the product. Gate 5 acts as the decision point whereby the top management may decide to shelve the product project even at this stage if found unviable.

> Exploratory survey methods such as focus group interviews and secondary data sources are used in the initial assessment phase.

A post-launch review is used in assessing the overall success/failure of the product.

**Stage 6—Mass production and product launch**    After passing through Gate 5, the product is produced on large scale and is simultaneously launched in the market. The initial sales trends are carefully monitored and production plans are adjusted accordingly. The product development project is terminated soon after. Post-launch review is done to assess the overall success/failure of the product and key learning for future NPD projects are recorded.

## Mass Customization

Pine (1993) proposed a radical way of production called mass customization, which literally means 'customization for the masses', or in other words, large-scale customization. Mass customization is basically an amalgamation of two traditional paradigms in production, namely craft production and mass production.

Craft production is heavily dependent upon the skills of the craftsman, who acquire such skills through apprenticeship and experience over a period of time. These craftsmen enjoy flexibility and creativity in the organizations they work for and that environment allows them to create unique objects as per the requirements of the customer. Paintings, sculptors, furniture, hand-made garments, hand-made shoes, etc., are usually a result of craft production. In India, we have several centres that are famous for their craft production. For example, Lucknow is famous for its *chikan* embroidered garments; Benaras (now Varanasi) and Mysore are renowned for their silk sarees; Saharanpur for its wood work; Moradabad for its brass utensils, etc. Craft production typically results in high variety of goods with high cost of production. Organizations engaged in craft production have less control over quality and cost, due to their heavy dependence on highly skilled workers. However, their clientele values the uniqueness and novelty of the products produced.

Mass production, on the other hand, has its genesis in Henry Ford's attempt to produce Model T on large scale during the early 1900s. He offered little variety to his customers, created a standardized product, and contained the cost of production such that a car came within the reach of the common man. A famous phrase used by him was, 'I can offer any colour of the car to my customers as long as it is black.' He invented the moving assembly line, exploited the concept of specialization of labour and integrated his factories from raw material up to the finished products stage, in order to produce high quality, low priced, and a standard product to the customers. In later decades, many companies across the world aped his concept of mass production and successfully replicated this operations strategy. In this strategy, per unit cost of production is typically low; the variety of products is minimal; and quality is high.

Pine (1993) argues that it is possible to derive the benefits of craft production and mass production by combining them seamlessly in the form of mass customization. However, it may be possible to use mass customization for manufacturing few select products.

### Concept of Modularity in Mass Customization

Pine (1993) recommends a modular approach to mass customization. In his view, each module within the product should be assigned a team of specialists in that area. These specialists should use their creative skills to come up with different variants of a module, which when fitted with

> The cost of assembling the modules should be kept to a minimum in order to keep the operations at economical levels.

other modules, provide distinct products akin to craft production. However, in order to achieve the merits of mass production at the same time, the variants of a module should fit in seamlessly with other modules so that the customer is not able to feel any anomaly therein. The cost of creating these variants of a module should also be contained in such a way that the benefits of mass production are retained in mass customization. Specifically, Pine advises the managers of modules to keep in mind the following key issues in mass customization.

**Swift integration**   Modules should quickly be fitted together with other modules without wasting any time so that the response to the customer's requests is almost instantaneous.

**Snug fitting**   Various modules constituting the customized product should be fitted snugly so that highest customer satisfaction is achieved.

**Economical operation**   Cost of assembling the modules should be kept to a minimal in order to keep the operations at economical levels.

**Camaraderie**   Mass customization is next to impossible in the absence of team work and camaraderie within a team constituted for a given module as well as between various teams for other modules. The level of coordination and communication should be such that no time is wasted at any stage after the customer order is received.

A typical example of mass customization is Dell. It utilizes the modular designs in computers, with each module assigned to either in-house or external vendor teams. Its online portal allows the customers with innumerable options of modules (such as hard drive, power supply, motherboard, CD drive, and RAM) to choose from and as soon as the order is placed online by the customer, all the teams automatically receive information about the specifications of the modules chosen by the customer.

## Mass Customization and Supply Chain Management

Mass customization requires highest level of coordination and camaraderie not only amongst internal teams but also across the supply chain. Dell has strategically partnered with its suppliers to achieve stringent levels of lead time, quality, cost, and customization. Its state-of-the-art information systems provide seamless and real-time flow of information all across the supply chain. Pine (1993) addresses the supply chain in the mass customization context as *dynamic networks* due to the agility that is required on part of various modular teams (internal as well as external). He also recommends postponement or delayed differentiation (concepts discussed later in Chapter 9 on MRP, JIT, and SCM) for mass customization, which again is used quite successfully by companies like Dell.

> Mass customization requires the highest level of coordination and teamwork not only amongst internal teams but across the supply chain.

In India, Tata Sky is offering its customers to choose channels as they wish. This level of choice in direct-to-home (DTH) systems is unprecedented. Naturally, it calls for various contractual agreements with channels to allow the Tata Sky customers to customize their portfolio of channels as per their unique preferences. In addition, it requires leading-edge technology to implement such a scheme promptly so that customers do not have to wait for such customization experience. Thus, mass customization is gradually catching up in the Indian market as well.

## Summary

Global competition in today's globalized world has made it increasingly difficult for organizations to develop new products that live up to the expectations of customers, who are demanding more and more value for their money. A long-term strategic vision coupled with necessary capital and human resources are imperative for new product development. *Product designing* involves various new concepts such as concurrent engineering, modular design, standardization, etc. The concept of robust design propounded by Genichi Taguchi has become much more relevant today, when customers are becoming less and less tolerant of products that are below their expectations. Quality needs to be built into the product right at the design stage and quality function deployment (QFD) becomes a great tool in this regard. There are organizations like Apple that look beyond customer satisfaction and aim at delighting them with innovative features in their products. This is typically what Kano's model envisages to do. The stage-gate process for new product development has gained acceptance in the industry of late, in which five successive gates are prescribed and a new product being developed must satisfactorily pass through a particular gate in order to move on to the next stage of product development. Mass customization is another new concept that leverages the good attributes of mass production and customization at the same time. Few organizations worldwide have been able to successfully use mass customization as a new product development strategy to their advantage.

## References

Akao, Yogi 1972, 'New product development and quality Assurance', *Standardisation and Quality Control*, vol. 25, April, pp. 7–14,.

Akao, Y., T. Ohfuji, and T. Naoi 1987, 'Survey and reviews on quality function deployment in Japan', *Proceedings of the International Conference for Quality Control*, JUSE and IAQ, Tokyo, pp. 171–176.

Akao, Y., T. Naoi, and T. Ohfuji 1989, 'Survey of the status of quality deployment—report from the quality deployment research committee', (in Japanese), *Quality Control*, vol. 19, no. 1, pp. 35–44.

Akao, Y. and G.H. Mazur 2003, 'The leading edge in QFD: past, present and future', *International Journal of Quality and Reliability Management*, vol. 20, no. 1, pp. 20–35.

Bemowski, K. 1992, 'The quality glossary', *Quality Progress*, February, American Society for Quality (ASQ), Millwaukee, WI. p. 26.

Burrows, P. 2004, 'The seed of Apple's innovation', *Business Week*, 12 December.

Cooper, R.G. 1990, 'Stage-gate systems: a new tool for managing new products', *Business Horizons*, May–June.

Halliday, D. 1983, 'Steve Paul Jobs', *Current Biography*, 5 February, H.W. Wilson Company, The Bronx, New York.

Kano N., N. Seraku, F. Takahashi, and S. Tsuji 1984, 'Attractive quality and must-be quality', Hinshitsu (*Quality, The Journal of Japanese Society for Quality Control*), vol. 14, no. 2, 39–48.

Mizuno S. and Y. Akao 1994, *QFD: The Customer Driven Approach to Quality Planning and Deployment*, Asian Productivity Organisation.

Neisen (2013), 'Smartphones keep users in India plugged in', http://www.nielsen.com/us/en/newswire/2013/smartphones-keep-users-in-india-plugged-in.html, accessed on 14 March 2013.

Phillips, R., K. Neailey, and T. Broughton 1999, 'A comparative study of six stage-gate approaches to product development', *Integrated Manufacturing Systems*, Bradford, vol. 10, issue 5, p. 289.

Pine, J. B., II. 1993 *Mass Customization*, Harvard University Business School Press.

Thomke, Stefan H. and Barbara Feinberg 2010, 'Design thinking and innovation at Apple', *Harvard Business School*.

Yoshizawa, T. 1997, 'Origins and development of internationalization of QFD', (in Japanese), *Proceedings of the 6th Symposium on QFD*, Tokyo.

## Keywords

**Applied research** is done with the objective of developing commercial applications.

**Concurrent engineering** is the product design approach in which the design team includes personnel from various departments such as marketing, engineering, production, finance, and materials in addition to the design department.

**Development** is the process of converting the results of applied research into useful commercial applications.

**Fundamental research** is the advancement of the state of knowledge in a subject, though it may not be practically converted into commercial applications.

**Manufacturability** implies designing a product in such a way that its manufacturing/assembling can be done easily.

**Mass customization** is basically an amalgamation of two traditional paradigms in production, namely craft production and mass production.

**Modular design** is another type of standardization, which means designing a product in parts or modules. The modules are sub-assemblies of different components and parts.

**Product life cycle** has five stages spread throughout the life of a product. These are incubation, growth, maturity, saturation, and decline.

**Quality function deployment** is defined as a structured method in which customer requirements are translated into appropriate technical requirements for each stage of product development and production.

**Reverse engineering** is the process of carefully dismantling an existing product (of a competitor) step by step in order to understand the unique underlying concepts.

**Robust design** means designing a product such that it is operational in varying environmental conditions.

**Standardization** refers to less variety in product design, that is, new products are designed such that there is no major variation from existing products.

## CASE STUDY I

# Steve Jobs and Apple

Late Steve Jobs completed education only till high school when he dropped out from Reed College, Oregon. Another dropout from the University of California at Berkeley was Stephen Wozniak, who started working for Hewlett-Packard (HP) and came in contact of a summer intern there—Jobs. Wozniak was an engineering wizard, who was influenced by Jobs to quit his job at HP and start a new venture. Thus, Apple Computer Corporation was founded by Jobs along with Wozniak in 1976 in his car garage. At that time, nobody had imagined that large computers hitherto confined to scientific installations could be configured for personal use by individuals. The Apple 1 computer designed and created by the duo received orders of 25 units from a local electronics retailer (Halliday 1983) and from thereon, the story of the first personal computer was started. Rest is now history.

Apple's approach to designing new products is rather unconventional, as if symbolizing the exotic leadership style of Jobs. In Steve's words, 'Simplicity is the ultimate sophistication.' A typical example is the iPod, which was designed to play music through a miniature device and do nothing else. The platform strategy is clearly evident in the use of OSX operating system in Macintosh, PCs, iPhone, and iPad. In fact, iPad is a natural extension of the iPhone in terms of the touch screen and other common user interfaces/applications. This promotes reusability of parts, components, software, etc., while ensuring less training time on part of existing customers using Apple products. Future applicability of current products through cross-pollination of internal ideas and technologies is an important aspect of Apple designs. Another facet of its approach is 'participatory design' whereby customers play an active role in the design process. In the development stages, the experiences and problems faced by a sample set of customers using a software/product are meticulously observed. The focus then shifts to finding simple yet effective solutions to such problems for improvising the designs. The customer involvement is 'iterative' in nature, that is, their experiences are continually monitored to identify the scope for further improvement. This explains the progressive release of latest versions of products, taking for example iPhone 4 that has innovative features such as video calling with FaceTime, retina display with 960-by-640 resolution, HD video recording, 5-megapixel camera with LED flash, dual-mic noise suppression, and much more. What sets Apple products apart from competition is their aesthetic appeal. The pristine white colour almost became synonymous with Apple products with 'snow white skin', when the company introduced vibrant colours in some of its products like iPods (Thomke and Feinberg 2010). This simply shows the flexibility and dynamism in Apple designs rather than getting trapped in the statics of currently successful designs. The future outlook and boldness is clearly a hallmark of Apple's designs, which always leaves the competition to do lots of catching up.

Experts argue that Apple products are not radical innovations but improvisations of existing products in the market. According to them, neither was iPod the first MP3 player nor was iPhone the first smartphone with a touchscreen (Palm Treo was). iPad was not the first tablet either. It is clearly a much refined descendent of another Apple product called Newton. The bottom line is that Apple not only learns from its own mistakes, but also from its competitor's mistakes. Apple's mission is clearly not to be the first, but to be the best.

Jobs' idea of innovation in design is aptly captured by his statement below:

'The system is that there is no system. That doesn't mean we don't have process. Apple is a very disciplined company, and we have great processes. But that's not what it's about. Process makes you more efficient. But innovation comes from people meeting up in the hallways or calling each other at 10:30 at night with a new idea, or because they realized something that shoots holes in how we've been thinking about a problem. It's adhoc meetings of six people called by someone who thinks he has figured out the coolest new thing ever and who wants to know what other people think of his idea. And it comes from saying no to 1,000 things to make sure we don't get on the wrong track or try to do too much. We're always thinking about new markets we could enter, but it's only by saying no that you can concentrate on the things that are really important' (Burrows 2004).

### Discussion Questions

1. Do you agree with Apple's strategy of creating their iPad only in two colours—black and white?
2. Apple's approach to product development has been to build upon existing technologies. Do you think it is high time that Apple started innovating new technologies on its own?
3. When asked what consumer and market research Apple had done to guide the development of the iPad, its former CEO Late Steve Jobs replied, 'None. It isn't the consumers' job to know what they want.' Do you agree with this statement from Jobs?

---

## CASE STUDY II

## Singapore Changi International Airport Terminal 4

Singapore is one of the smallest countries in the world in terms of geographical area and yet one of the most developed nations. Its economy is heavily based on the service industry and it has successfully projected itself as an epitome of service excellence.

Known as one of the four 'Asian Tigers,' Singapore has established itself as a hub of tourism in South-East Asia. Three organizations that deserve to be credited for such a stupendous feat are Singapore Tourism Board, Singapore Airlines, and Changi International Airport Singapore.

With about 370 accolades and awards under its belt, Changi Airport Singapore is today an international benchmark in terms of service quality. It has been consistently ranked as the World's Official 5-Star Airport by Skytrax that conducts annual online surveys of passengers to rate airlines and airports globally.

Currently, the Hong Kong International Airport and Incheon Airport, Seoul are the only other airports that enjoy the coveted 5-Star ranking by Skytrax. The Skytrax airport online survey takes traveller's feedback on various criteria such as website and ground transportation, security and immigration service, passenger arrivals, departures and transit, terminal comfort and terminal facilities, shopping, food and beverage.

Changi Airport had humble beginnings in 1981 and over the years has grown to handle a passenger volume of 42 million in 2010. The seventh busiest international airport today, with more than 100 airlines operating from it and a flight taking off or landing in roughly every 100 seconds, Changi Airport is a major air hub in Asia.

A passenger landing at Changi Airport for the very first time is usually amazed by the impeccable terminal arrival areas, soothing background music, courteous staff, and the best of facilities. The arrival as well as departure areas of its terminals provide an exemplary shopping experience to the travellers. It has always been a step ahead of competition, be it providing free Internet Wi-fi services, installing leg massage chairs near its boarding gates, or well-organized and guided taxi boarding points.

With over 70,000 square metres of commercial space across its three terminals, Changi Airport is also one of Singapore's best places for shopping and dining. The airport has also become a favourite destination for Singapore residents, especially families.

In order to keep pace with burgeoning passenger volumes, Terminal 3 (T3) was planned meticulously to surprise the passengers with even better quality of services and facilities. It exemplifies the vision of its top management to maintain Changi Airport's enviable position of the world's most admired airports.

The state-of-the-art technology used in T3 has well complemented its robust infrastructure, such as baggage handling and high speed transfer system, which uses underground tunnels to make the baggage reach the conveyor belts in the arrival hall in most instances even before the passengers reach the baggage pick-up area. T3 was one of the few terminals across the globe to have dedicated infrastructure to handle the mammoth-sized Airbus A380 aircraft.

Lee Seow Hiang, the Board Director and CEO of Changi Airports Group (CAG), is preparing the blueprint of Terminal 4 (T4) for Changi Airport Singapore. He desires that T4 should redefine operational and service excellence that Changi is today synonymous with.

### Discussion Questions

1. Identify the critical to quality (CTQs) characteristics of airports from the perspective of passengers.
2. Ascertain how Changi Airport Singapore has hitherto been able to fulfil the CTQs identified earlier.
3. Compare how Changi Airport Singapore has fared on these CTQs vis-à-vis other comparable airports.
4. Apply Kano's model of customer service delight to explore which innovative features in the proposed T4 should be incorporated in its blueprint.
5. Suggest any continuous improvement (CI) tool that may be helpful in keeping Changi Airport Singapore ahead of competition.

## Objective Questions

### Choose the correct option

1. Which one of the following is not a way of idea generation?
   (a) Gathering new ideas from employees and customers
   (b) Research-based methods of collecting ideas
   (c) Understanding competitor's service offerings
   (d) Requesting competitors to share their business ideas
2. The concept that the manufacturing process determined during the design phase of a product would help in bringing in more efficiency and quality, is called
   (a) design for logistics
   (b) design for quality
   (c) design for cost
   (d) design for manufacturing

### State True or False

3. A famous phrase used by Henry Ford was, 'I can offer any colour of the car to my customers as long as it is white.'
4. It is possible to use mass customization for manufacturing all types of products.
5. The supply chain in the mass customization context is like a *dynamic network* due to the agility that is required on part of various modular teams (internal as well as external).
6. Using CAD, the designers of products can easily create 3-D diagrams as per the specifications of the customers/ clients.

### Fill in the blank

7. Mass customization is basically an amalgamation of two traditional paradigms in production, namely _____ and mass production.

## Concept Review Questions

1. Briefly explain the following terms related to new product development:
   (a) Modular design
   (b) Reverse engineering
   (c) Concurrent engineering
   (d) Standardization

2. What is robust design? Explain Taguchi's quality loss function.
3. What is the concurrent engineering approach in product design? How is it different from the classical sequential design approach?
4. What is a product life cycle? Does every product or service have a life cycle of the same duration? Can the life cycle of a product be extended? How?
5. Explain what is meant by modular design and robust design of a product.

6. Explain the terms reverse engineering and standardization.
7. What is quality function deployment? How does it capture the 'voice of the customer'?
8. Using a schematic diagram, explain the Kano's model and related concept of customer's delight.
9. Explain the six stages of the stage-gate process of new product development.
10. What is mass customization? What are the key issues in mass customization?

## Project Assignments

1. Complete the first three stages of the stage-gate process in developing a new social networking site such as LinkedIn, Facebook, or Twitter, while keeping a particular target customer segment in mind.

2. Suggest how you can make the design of an air cooler robust in performance. How can we say that an air cooler has a great extent of standardization? Form groups and discuss the processes required to arrive at the most effective design.

| Answers to Objective Questions | | | | |
|---|---|---|---|---|
| 1. (d) | 2. (d) | 3. False | 4. False | 5. True |
| 6. True | 7. craft production | | | |

# 4

# Outsourcing and Offshoring

## Learning Objectives

After reading this chapter, you will be able to answer the following questions:
- What are outsourcing and offshoring?
- How has India suddenly become the international hub of outsourcing and offshoring?
- Why do organizations go for outsourcing?
- What are the business processes typically outsourced?
- What are the steps in the outsourcing process?
- How to avoid any pitfalls in outsourcing?

## India as an Outsourcing and Offshoring Destination

India has been the world's leading offshore destination. In 2006 it accounted for 65 per cent of the global industry in offshore IT and 46 per cent of the global business process offshoring industry. India, the global leader in outsourcing services—including software development and call centres—employs about 3,50,000 people in an industry that earned US$6.7 billion in the year ended March 2005. It is believed that India can sustain its global leadership position, grow its offshore IT and business process outsourcing (BPO) industries at an annual rate greater than 25 per cent, and generate export revenues of about US$60 billion (this does not include exports of software products) by 2010. At this rate, the IT and the BPO sector can contribute 1 per cent per year to GDP growth for the next five years. They would employ nearly 2.3 million people and provide indirect employment for another approximately 6.5 million workers.

India's offshoring companies could well become one of the world's great export industries, at par with France's luxury goods industry, Japan's automotive sector, and Taiwan's electronics manufacturing sector. Over the past years, India's offshore companies have proven to be significant economic growth engines. They have grown roughly three-fold between 2000 and 2004, from US$4.0 billion in 2000 to US$12.8 billion in 2004, accounting for 6 per cent of the increase in GDP between 2000 and 2004 (NASSCOM–McKinsey 2005).

Manufacturing offshoring to low-cost countries (LCCs), is a well-established trend, with US$1,300–US$1,400 billion worth of manufactured goods exported from LCCs in 2002. Low-cost countries such as India, China, Thailand, Poland, Mexico, Turkey, Brazil, Indonesia, Russia, Philippines, South Africa, Malaysia, and Taiwan have wage rates less than a third of the US. In 2002, China's manufacturing exports were US$300 billion, Taiwan's US$145 billion, Mexico's US$140 billion, Malaysia's US$78 billion, and Thailand's US$55 billion. India lagged far behind, with only US$40 billion in the export of manufactured goods.

Despite its modest start, India can and should aspire to become one of the three largest exporters of manufactured goods among LCCs by 2015. This will require growing the exports of manufactured goods from US$40 billion in 2002 to approximately US$300 billion by 2015, and consequently increasing India's share of world manufacturing trade from the current 0.8 per cent to 3.5 per cent by 2015. In-depth assessment shows that out of the targeted exports of US$300 billion, US$70–US$90 billion could be captured from just four sectors—apparel, auto components, specialty chemicals, and electrical and electronic products. India's exports in these sectors were US$10 billion in 2002 (CII–McKinsey 2003).

Indian companies topped the 2007 Global Services 100 list of the best IT and BPO companies in the world with 36 companies making the grade. *Global Services* magazine compiles the list on the basis of a survey across 18 countries. The US came second with 32 companies. However, over a dozen US companies service their clients largely through BPO offices based in India. It is noteworthy that

- Tata Consultancy Services (TCS) was rated number one among the top 10 best performing IT service providers;
- Polaris Software Labs led the list of top 10 specialty application development providers;
- Hinduja TMS was rated the best performing call centre provider; and
- US-based Genpact was rated the number one firm in human capital development and best performing BPO. Genpact employs thousands of people in India.

India remains an IT outsourcing powerhouse, with US$17.7 billion in software and IT services exports in 2005, compared with US$3.6 billion for China and US$1 billion for Russia. However, the competition is catching up fast. Philippines is one such country. As a former US colony, Philippines has strong cultural affinities with Americans, and Filipinos have a knack for mimicking North American accents—a big advantage for clients. One of the first questions service providers are asked (from callers) is, 'Are you in India?' The way things are growing in the Philippines, more and more callers are going to hear the answer 'no'.

China is catching up with India in providing call centre services. The number of employees at call centres in China is likely to rise 22 per cent in 2007 to 1,58,000, while in India the workforce is seen rising at the rate of 16 per cent to 3,12,500. China seems particularly competitive in the call centres, with hourly costs per employee of just US$3.62, against US$4.24 in India and US$18.46 in Singapore. Twenty nine per cent of call centres in China serviced international markets, against 33 per cent in India. As many as 93 per cent of call centres in China require their agents to speak in English.

Latin-American countries such as Mexico, Brazil, Argentina, Chile, and Nicaragua are beefing up their outsourcing infrastructure and have coined a new term 'near-shoring', to indicate their advantage of closer physical proximity to the US. Three years ago, the Mexican giant Softtek bought General Electric's (GE) Mexico-based IT operations. In the process, it absorbed nearly 1,000 engineers. As a result, Softtek became the company's main nearshore solution for IT work in Latin America, performing support and maintenance for GE's commercial finance and energy groups. Since then, Softtek's revenues have been growing 40 per cent annually and hit US$146 million in 2005, with more than half of the business from US clients. Now, the company has 3,500 employees, mostly engineers, making it the largest IT outsourcer in Latin America. Softtek, based in Monterrey, Mexico, has offices in the US, Argentina, Brazil, Colombia, Peru, Puerto Rico, Venezuela, and Spain. GE still outsources 90 per cent of its IT work to India, sending just 6 per cent to Mexico. However, as India's costs rise, Mexico will look cheaper and better. Due to US legislative restrictions, certain kinds of projects involving sensitive aviation and energy technology are more likely to be outsourced to Mexico than to India, a nuclear-power nation. However, the recent nuclear energy-related alliances between US and India have again tilted the fortunes in favour of India.

## Banking Industry and Outsourcing

The banking industry worldwide has embraced outsourcing in a major way. However, each one of them may adapt a different format. ABN AMRO (acquired by Barclays of UK), the largest bank of Netherlands having a worldwide presence, had experimented with outsourcing by granting an outsourcing contract worth US$1.2 billion (for 5 years duration) to the American company, EDS for software development and maintenance. The results were lukewarm as later the bank realized that outsourcing requires a broader strategic approach rather than a piecemeal approach. It gained from this experience that outsourcing should not only focus on saving costs but also on improving service quality. When it embarked upon its next major restructuring of banking operations and back-office revamping, it followed a cautious approach.

The bank invited proposals for outsourcing the monitoring of data centres worldwide, as well as the maintenance, support, and development of IT applications. It was aiming at the development of a seamless system where the retail, private, and investment-banking parts of the bank's businesses worldwide would be integrated on the same technology platform. The bank did not rush into a decision. Instead, the management took a year to evaluate the responses and evolved a strategy in the meantime. Finally, in September 2005, the bank announced that its US$2.1 billion, five-year deal, would be spread largely among three players. IBM Global Services would take on the data-centre work and some software development, while India's TCS and Infosys Technologies would handle the rest.

The bank knew that it had to retrench its IT workforce, but it decided to go about it in a phased manner. It tried to convince its IT staff that they had a brighter future in a technology company than in a bank. It provided retraining to many of them and even granted a generous severance package. The outsourcing is already showing its positive results with the bank's London-based Chief Information Officer, Lars Gustavsson commenting, 'Outsourcing isn't just strategic and tactical. Once you make a move, the invisible hand gets to work.' The bank's profit for the year 2006 was €4,780 million, up 7.6 per cent as compared to the 2005 results.

For Germany headquartered Deutsche Bank, outsourcing is a strategic issue, 'If you don't do it you won't survive.' It uses a staff of 150 at Luxoft, a Russian IT services company, for 27 different projects. Luxoft manages projects such as systems for managing client relationships. The bank outsources its back-office and analytical work to India. According to the bank, at present, labour arbitrage provides significant advantages. However, in 12 or 15 years, costs in India, may be on par with London or New York. The labour arbitrage story is temporary. The real story is about recruiting talent. China and India are the two largest labour markets in the world. If a company recruits only from London, Chicago, or San Francisco, they will lose out because these places are a tiny part of the population. For greater returns, companies need to recruit in Pune, Harbin, or Shanghai.

The bank is clear about the fact that outsourcing a process, which is not working, is a real recipe for disaster. Despite having its development centre in Moscow, the bank outsourced its software in Russia. The bank's rationale is—to do work in India, you must have scale. If you have a 25-person operation and put nine of those jobs in India, that is a bad idea. While the labour cost is attractive, the infrastructure cost will never break even. You need to have a group big enough to amortize the costs. In Russia, the team is relatively small. Since Moscow is only three hours from London, it was easy to get in and out. The bank could get a small group there without being burdened with huge costs. In terms of skill levels, both Russia and India have strengths. The maths and science tradition of the old Soviet Union is an advantage. Russia has a history of technical innovation and there is a constant demand to be innovative and creative. In India, the situation is different. Indians are incredibly process-focused. Indians can work with great care, but with the plan that is given to them.

For the Bank of America (BoA), in addition to huge cost savings, outsourcing provided with a $24 \times 7$ work regime, thanks to the time zone difference between India and the US. Programmers in California could hand work overnight to colleagues in India, who handed it back the next morning. The pitch books (containing data and analysis), to be prepared for creating presentations to American clients, are passed to Indian colleagues in the evening, who return the ready material for use the next morning. Another advantage derived by BoA is the easier upgradation of its legacy systems based upon old programming languages such as COBOL. It is hard to find professionals adept at these languages in the US these days, while there are organizations in India having their full departments devoted to these.

The bank has begun to shift more and more 'commodity' tasks around the globe. Some treasury functions such as reconciling small discrepancies in corporate accounts have been shifted from London to India. The bank has also relocated a letter of credit processing facility from Hong Kong to China. At present, BoA is looking at offshoring its call centre work to Mexico, where calls from Spanish-speaking customers in the US will be handled.

The London-based Hong Kong Shanghai Banking Corporation (HSBC) Bank follows a hybrid model of outsourcing. The bank has its software development centres in five Indian cities, China, and Brazil. In 2002, HSBC opened its Pune software centre, with just 30 people working on software maintenance. Since then, the centre's workforce has grown to 2,500, and now it develops software for the company's operations worldwide. Although HSBC's software centre is an in-house, captive centre, it operates like an independent contractor, getting paid market rates for whatever it does for the bank.

In 2003, HSBC acquired US financier Household Finance. Household Finance had a partnership with an offshore software services provider, Kanbay, also based in Pune, which developed consumer-lending software for the company. So HSBC now had its own captive development centre, as well as an independent contractor. HSBC did not consider Kanbay as a threat to its own captive centre. Instead, the bank worked with Kanbay, gave its management a room at HSBC's Pune premises, and included them in management meetings. Kanbay and HSBC devised a plan to partner on projects. Now the two groups work together on about 35

---

### Exhibit 4.1 Insourcing Strategy of Lenovo, while Rivals Outsource

The Chinese computer manufacturer Lenovo came to limelight in 2005, when it acquired the laptop business of IBM. Before that, Lenovo did not sell computers outside China. However, the acquisition of IBM's laptop division helped Lenovo expand globally in an unprecedented way. In 2011, it became the second largest personal computer (PC) manufacturer in the world while commanding a 12.9 per cent market share. It made a whopping US$29.6 billion of revenue in the financial year 2011. Lenovo has since emerged as the sole well-known Chinese consumer brand name in the international market.

All the rivals of Lenovo, including Apple Inc. and Hewlett Packard (HP), have increasingly outsourced their assembling operations to contract manufacturers in China . For example, Apple outsourced most of its manufacturing to the Taiwan-based company Foxconn Technology Group. However, Lenovo chose to keep all its manufacturing in-house. Its principal operations including research centres are in Beijing (China), Morrisville (North Carolina, USA), and Singapore. It

has eight company-owned factories including Beijing, Shanghai, Xiamen, Shenzhen, and Chengdu in China. According to its president and chief executive officer Yang Yuanqing, 'Selling PCs is like selling fresh fruit. The speed of innovation is very fast, so you must know how to keep up with the pace, control inventory, to match supply with demand and handle very fast turnover'. Thus, vertically integrated factories of Lenovo help in quickly adapting to changing customer preferences for its products and in providing greater end-to-end control that improves performance in all the key areas including pioneering new technology, cost management, delivery cycle times, and product quality.

During late 2011, the computer industry faced an acute shortage of certain types of hard drives due to floods in Thailand. Lenovo took advantage of the situation by quickly shifting the mix of products in its pipeline to focus on products for which the hard drives were available, and prioritize products that had higher profit margins. As a result, it gained market share at the expense of its arch rival HP in that quarter.

---

projects. It is a commercial relationship—if HSBC needs to borrow Kanbay's insurance-software expert, the bank pays for the work. There is a lot of commitment from both sides to stay on the path and stay honest.

There have been exceptions, like Lenovo, who have chosen to keep all their manufacturing in-house (Exhibit 4.1).

## Outsourcing, Offshoring, Near-shoring, and Farm-shoring

Outsourcing is not a new management concept, as traditionally, organizations have taken make or buy decisions in view of optimizing their processes for a better and cheaper product or service. Outsourcing has come into the limelight in recent times due to the unprecedented development and growth of the communication technologies such as the Internet, emails, video-conferencing, etc. The new technologies have brought the world closer. This has provided unlimited options to organizations to explore the best and cheapest sourcing options worldwide. This includes sourcing of human resources having better skill-sets and lower labour costs. The service industry has been the biggest beneficiary of this revolution as it does not require movement of tangible goods from one part of the world to the other. Rather most of its supplies can be easily moved real-time to and from any place in the world using state-of-the-art communication technologies. With a vast pool of an English-speaking population, developing countries such as India are natural destinations for outsourcing.

Over the past few decades, this interchange of ideas throughout the globe has helped the West in understanding the untapped technical potential of the developing nations in the East. This

> The term offshoring is referred to the outsourcing of business processes to a location distant from the service consumers.

has led many Western MNCs to set up their bases in Asia to derive maximum advantage of the labour arbitrage and, more importantly, the talent of the people in the East. The term *offshoring* is referred to the outsourcing of business processes to a location distant from the service consumers. *Near-shoring* is a term coined by Latin-American countries to refer to their close proximity to the US and other major service consumers. *Farm-shoring* refers to the placement of jobs in low-cost regions of the service recipient's home country.

There has been a lot of public outcry in developed countries against offshoring of many processes to developing nations such as India. Offshoring has led to huge layoffs in the service recipient's home country. Cohen and Young (2006) quote a contradictory statement given by a senior executive of a process manufacturing company that has been criticized for moving service jobs to India—'If you compare the numbers of employees my company has in India with the company's revenues derived from India, then you would have to conclude that India is underserved in terms of jobs. If anyone has a right to complain, it's the Indians. We've offshored jobs from India to the US if you really look at the numbers!'

Figure 4.1 shows the various ways of business process execution. It may be noted that an organization can use a combination of these ways to optimize its business process execution system.

## Reasons for Outsourcing

Figure 4.2 shows the various reasons behind an organization's outsourcing decisions. The first and foremost reason is usually cost reduction. A reduction in the cost of overall operations can be achieved by offshoring to developing countries. As mentioned earlier, availability of cheaper

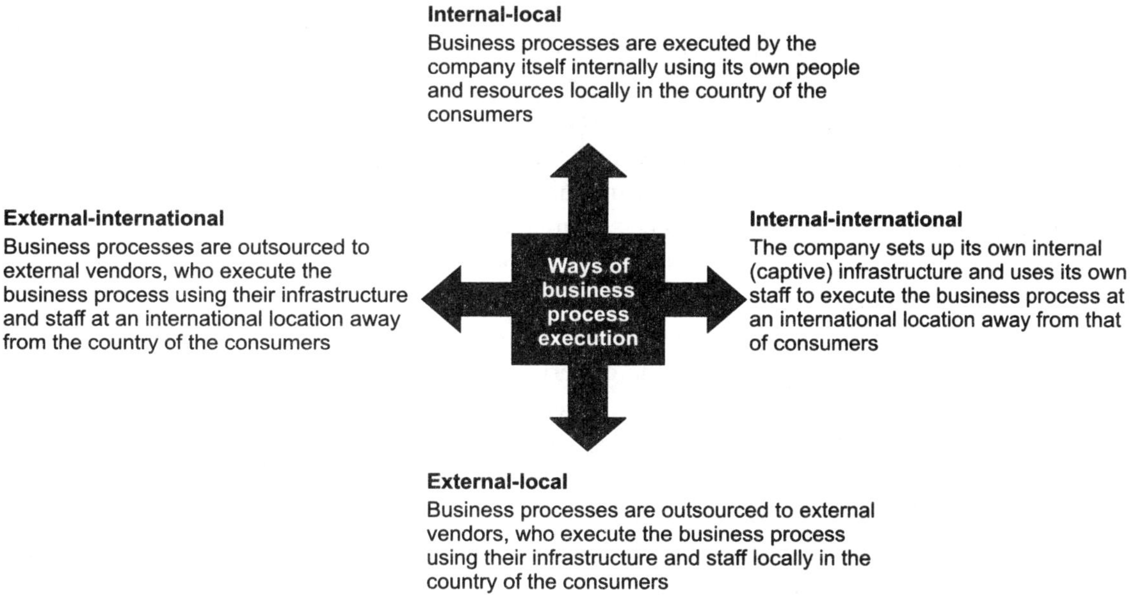

**Internal-local**
Business processes are executed by the company itself internally using its own people and resources locally in the country of the consumers

**External-international**
Business processes are outsourced to external vendors, who execute the business process using their infrastructure and staff at an international location away from the country of the consumers

**Ways of business process execution**

**Internal-international**
The company sets up its own internal (captive) infrastructure and uses its own staff to execute the business process at an international location away from that of consumers

**External-local**
Business processes are outsourced to external vendors, who execute the business process using their infrastructure and staff locally in the country of the consumers

*Source:* Adapted from Cohen and Young (2006).
**Fig. 4.1** Ways of business process execution

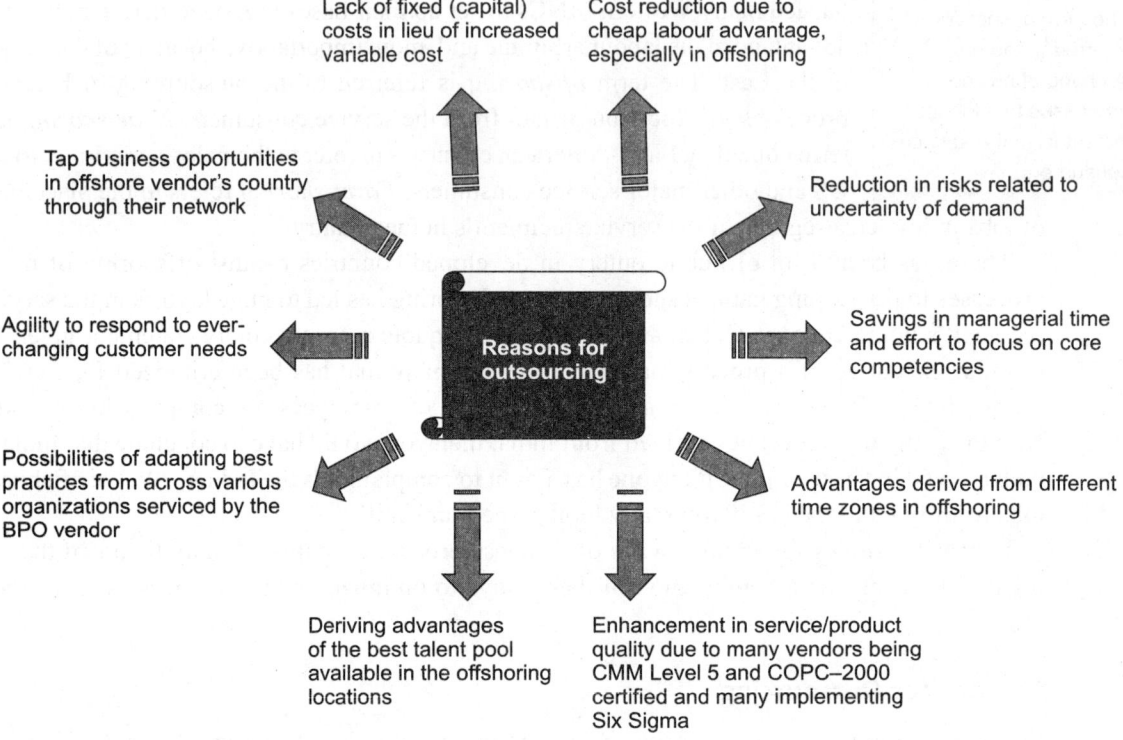

**Fig. 4.2**   Reasons for outsourcing

labour makes them attractive destinations. This advantage may not be that pronounced when outsourcing is done to local vendors within the same country or region. The low-cost labour advantage in developing nations such as India and China is also seen as transient in nature, which would eventually fade away, as the labour costs in these developing economies would come at par with those in the Western world. For the time being, this is a major reason for offshoring.

Another reason for outsourcing is the absence of capital expenditure (fixed costs) for the creation of a facility and related infrastructure compared to the case whereby the organization decides to perform the business processes in-house. Although, these savings in the fixed costs do result in increased variable costs as the vendor would charge some margins for delivery of outsourced products or services. The lack of fixed costs helps in the reduction of risks related to demand fluctuations, especially low levels of demand for the company's products and services. When the demand for these products or services is low in an outsourcing arrangement, the company can reduce its supply orders to the vendor for the ancillary products or services supplied. Thus, the demand fluctuation risk is shifted to the outsourcing vendor up to some extent.

When a company outsources its processes, it focuses upon its core competencies rather than wasting time and effort on peripheral support activities, which can be taken care of by outsourcing vendors. In most instances, the outsourcing vendors have their core competencies in these outsourced support activities. Thus, outsourcing helps in achieving better efficiencies and productivity in the overall outsourcer–vendor system.

The time zone difference between the location of the outsourcer and offshore vendor is a major advantage. It helps in reducing the lead times in execution of business processes. In many such arrangements, it becomes a $24 \times 7$ working and output generation for the organization, which is a great competitive advantage.

As mentioned earlier, many outsourcing vendors, especially in India, have developed their core competency in executing many ancillary support operations for outsourcing organizations. Many of these vendors in India have attained

> Outsourcing helps in achieving better efficiencies and productivity in the overall outsourcer–vendor system.

the highest level 5 CMM (Capability Maturity Model propounded by Carnegie Mellon University) certification and COPC–2000 (Customer Operations Performance Center Inc., USA) certification. COPC–2000 is particularly helpful for BPO organizations in attaining the highest service quality levels. Many vendors in India are implementing Six Sigma as an organization-wide quality system to enhance their service/product quality much beyond any certification. This aspect is going to be a major differentiating factor for the Indian BPO industry compared to its rivals in the times to come, when the labour cost advantage would fade away due to rising salaries of BPO employees in India.

The huge population of developing countries, such as India and China, has become an advantage due to a vast pool of talented and qualified professionals. India has an inherent advantage over China due to its English-speaking population. In developed countries, on the other hand, there is a scarcity of such professionals due to the declining interest in science and engineering education there. Thus, it is expensive and difficult to hire and retain such professionals. Professionals in these countries see call centre jobs as low profile, which is not the case in developing nations. In India, for example, many MBAs do not have any issues in taking up BPO jobs at least during the initial years of their career. In fact, many of them dream about creating their own entrepreneurial ventures and the initial years of stay in the BPO industry provides them ground-level experience. Thus, due to offshoring, the outsourcers get access to this vast pool of talented human resources.

BPO organizations normally service many clients simultaneously. Therefore, they are more likely to come across the best practices of many organizations. These practices can become benchmarks and can be replicated elsewhere. Hence, BPO companies are in a position to suggest process improvements and innovations in their domain of processes. Such improvements help BPO companies to develop their core competencies in handling such processes in an efficient and cost-effective manner. The clients, on the other hand, can focus on their core processes for improvements and innovation. This results in a win-win situation for both the stakeholders.

It is a well known fact that in today's competitive world the customer's needs and expectations do not remain static. Outsourcing helps organizations to become more agile in responding to the constantly changing needs of its customers. Vendors can satisfy customer expectations by revamping their infrastructure and retraining their employees accordingly.

Last but not the least, clients can possibly gain opportunities of new business in the country of their offshore partner (vendor) by exploiting their links and network. This is especially true for organizations having a limited presence in their offshore vendor's country. But some companies have found that the opposite works well for them. See Exhibit 4.2 to learn more about HUL's outsourcing activities.

## Outsourced Business Processes

The typical business processes that are outsourced are mostly routine repetitive tasks. Though, there have been instances in which high-end tasks such as engineering, design, and R&D are

## Exhibit 4.2    HUL: From Outsourcing to Insourcing

FMCG giant Hindustan Unilevers Limited (HUL), the Indian subsidiary of Unilever, is taking a U-turn of sorts on outsourcing. Outsourcing or sub-contracting the manufacture of products from third parties has been an integral part of the business model for FMCG companies in India for many years. Hindustan Unilevers Limited is better known for its marketing prowess than for its manufacturing capabilities. However, indications from HUL suggest that it is stepping up its own manufacturing capabilities, while reducing the proportion of goods outsourced from third parties. Evidence of this is available in the financial statements of the company. In the first half of 2002, HUL's outlay on 'purchase of goods' (which represents the outsourced component), nearly halved, compared to the corresponding previous period. It plunged from ₹14.04 billion in the first half of 2001 to ₹7.51 billion in the first half of 2002. The reason attributed to this steep fall in outsourcing is the establishment of new high-technology manufacturing facilities in 2001, which have helped to increase HUL's manufacturing capabilities. In the year 2001, HUL commissioned seven new units producing detergents, personal products, and beverages.

From the year 2004 onwards, the company started reducing sourcing of various processed foods from third parties in a phased way. It is planning to set up comprehensive food factories. The move is aimed at optimizing costs and synergizing operations. For example, the company's Nasik-based ice cream factory now makes jams and squashes too. Since ice-cream is a seasonal product, the company can utilize its production capacity by equipping the factory with capabilities to make other products such as jams and squashes. Similarly, the Mumbai factory, which earlier produced only Knorr soups, is also being utilized for other culinary products.

Not very long back, HUL had closed down three company-owned food factories to opt for the third party manufacturers. However, the company now feels that if it has to meet its growth plans, it would require flexibility in production cycles and centres of manufacturing excellence. The company's own manufacturing facilities would also give it the flexibility to innovate, produce, and alter plans. The company has set up a hub in Bangalore for planning, sourcing, and production scheduling to ensure efficient inventory management.

outsourced. For example, for the first time, with the 787, Boeing is outsourcing more than 70 per cent of the airframe and is giving all aircraft suppliers the responsibility for doing the detailed engineering designs. The Japanese and Italians are designing and building the composite fuselage sections and the wings. The Russians are contributing key engineering talent—particularly in the area of designing titanium aircraft parts. The aerospace giant has turned to Russian aircraft engineers and Indian software professional because of their high technical skills and lower salaries. Boeing is often required to swap manufacturing work in countries such as China and India in exchange for aircraft sales—a term known as an offset agreement.

Figure 4.3 shows the typical business processes that are outsourced. The functions such as customer service are most frequently outsourced. These functions require excellent English communication skills to respond to the email and telephonic queries of the client's customers. Countries such as India, Philippines, Singapore, and Malaysia have this advantage in their favour. The language skills are especially important while conducting marketing research and tele-marketing for the client.

The transaction processing tasks are related to data entry jobs such as entering data related to credit cards, loans, cheques, sales orders, and then, reconciliation of the same. At times, certain high-end jobs such as data mining and decision support are also outsourced to experienced and capable vendors in this category. The security concerns related to the leakage of sensitive customer information such as credit card details are key issues in this category of outsourced tasks. The Indian BPO industry is addressing this issue quite seriously by implementing stringent measures. For example, before entering the facilities of Wipro Spectramind, the BPO of Wipro Ltd

The typical business processes that are outsourced are mostly routine repetitive tasks.

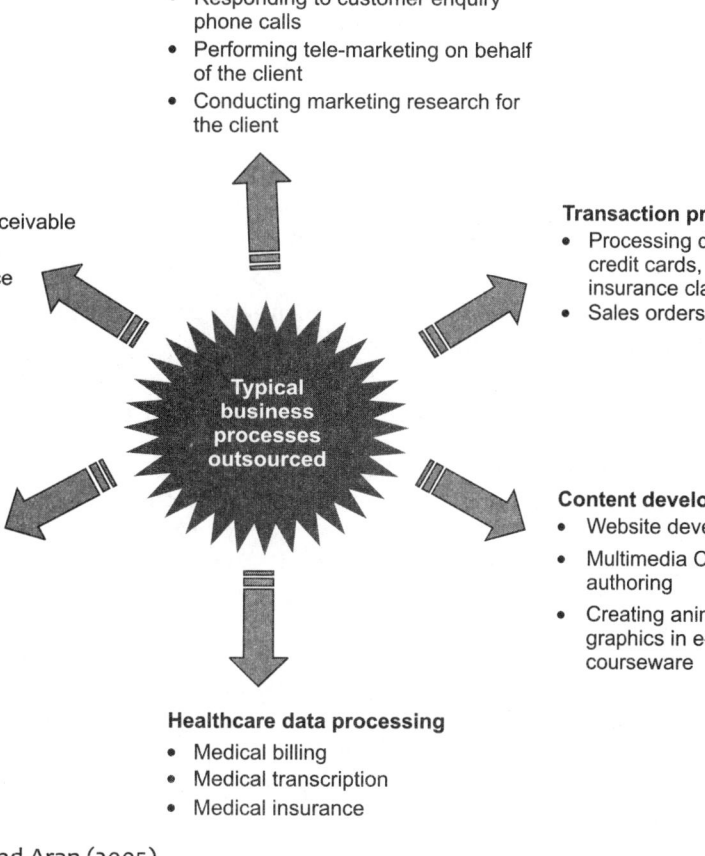

**Customer service**
- Providing responses to the email queries of the client's customers
- Responding to customer enquiry phone calls
- Performing tele-marketing on behalf of the client
- Conducting marketing research for the client

**Financial data processing**
- Managing accounts payable/receivable
- Bill processing
- Tax calculations and compliance with the local tax laws
- Financial reporting
- Cash management

**Transaction processing**
- Processing data related to credit cards, loans, checks, insurance claims, etc.
- Sales orders processing

**HR-related data processing**
- Processing payrolls
- Managing employee records
- Benefits administration
- Calculation of bonuses, commissions, taxes, etc. of employees
- Maintaining performance appraisal related record
- Recruitment and training
- Ensuring compliance of local labour laws

Typical business processes outsourced

**Content development**
- Website development
- Multimedia CD/ DVD authoring
- Creating animations and graphics in e-learning courseware

**Healthcare data processing**
- Medical billing
- Medical transcription
- Medical insurance

*Source:* Adapted from Patel and Aran (2005).

**Fig. 4.3** Typical business processes outsourced

in Bangalore, employees are frisked, mobile phone use is prohibited, and technology is used to monitor and record data records accessed through employee computers. All the facilities of Spectramind are fully monitored by electronic surveillance. In an effort to increase information security, Indian BPO companies now conduct thorough background employee checks, often even looking at school and college records. They also do a lot of hiring through referrals by their current employees, which helps them in getting people whose credentials are easily verified.

In the category of content development, tasks such as website development, graphics, animation, and multimedia CD/DVD authoring are outsourced. Contemporary sophisticated application software helps content developers to execute these tasks with ease without the need for actual programming skills.

Healthcare data processing tasks such as medical transcription were one of the first processes outsourced to India. In medical transcription, the voice-recorded reports of the patients by the physicians or other healthcare professionals are transcribed or converted into text by the BPOs for ready reference by the medical experts later. It requires good listening skills on part of the BPO employee performing such tasks, especially comprehending the foreign accents.

The human resources (HR) related processing tasks such as generation of pay rolls, benefits administration (for example, perks, medical allowances, etc.), calculation of taxes, bonus, commissions of employees, and entering performance appraisal records, are the most commonly outsourced tasks. Companies sometimes outsource higher-end functions such as recruitment and training, and compliance with the local labour laws. In offshoring, the vendor is more experienced and capable in undertaking these tasks economically for some part of the operations of the client existing in the vendor's country.

The financial data processing tasks such as managing accounts payables/receivables, bill processing, tax calculations, asset management, cash management, and financial reporting are non-core functions, which can be outsourced. Compliance with local taxation laws is offshored to the vendors, who are in a better position to protect the interests of the client, who has operations in the vendor's country. Even government-owned enterprises have discovered the benefits of outsourcing (refer to Exhibit 4.3).

---

### Exhibit 4.3  Southern Railways' Outsourcing Model

It was one of the firsts for Indian Railways, when in 2003 Southern Railways outsourced a portion of its critical call centre operation, the '133' Railway public service, which provides train arrival and departure information, to LatticeBridge Infotech Private Limited, a Chennai-based software firm. There is nothing new about organizations outsourcing their non-core processes to vendors, but what about the model in which the client is paid a share of revenue for outsourcing by the vendor? Amazing, but Southern Railway not only saved ₹5 million on investment in infrastructure and a further 15 per cent of investment every year that would have been spent on maintenance, but also gets this part of the revenue generated by the vendor.

In the outsourcing model adopted by the Southern Railways, the software company not only provides the '133' service for free to the Railways, but also shares revenue. The vendor earns revenue by playing advertisements while a caller waits for information. According to the deal, the vendor, and not the client, brings in advertisers.

Customers who call the service can get relevant information by asking for the train names. They need not remember the train numbers of almost 140 trains in the Chennai division. Launched in 2003, the 133-service uses automatic speech recognition (ASR) technology. It allows a computer to identify the words that a person speaks into a microphone or telephone. On dialing 133, the system greets the passenger and asks for the language. Once the language—English or Tamil—is chosen, simple queries are asked, and passengers give responses to queries by simply speaking to the system. The system gives relevant information to user. The system typically takes 10–15 seconds to retrieve the requested information. There are advertisements during the information retrieval period. The call centre handles about 20,000 queries a day with about 25 people working in shifts. This has meant an annual savings of ₹2 million for the Southern Railways.

Inspired by the success of Southern Railways on this front, the Indian Railway Catering and Tourism Corporation (IRCTC), in a bid to attract more tourists has set up four call centres across the four zones in India. The call centre is able to handle 20 million calls each day. It has however, outsourced the functioning of these call centres to a consortium comprising Spanco Telesystems, Stracon Backoffice Solutions Limited, and BSNL. IRCTC and the consortium will work on a revenue neutral model for ten years. The centre became operational in March 2007. The project was implemented at an approximate cost of ₹800 million. Spanco Telesystems is the system integrator, Stracon provides backend support, and BSNL is the telecom service provider. The technology is based on Nortel Networks platform.

The cordial voices that willingly impart information on train arrivals and departures will now facilitate ticket and hotel reservations, tour maps, guides, and even a complete travelogue. It aims to provide a packaged tour, complete with hotel and cab reservations.

## The Outsourcing Process

Outsourcing of an activity by an organization requires key decisions at various steps of the outsourcing process (McIvor 2000). As shown in Fig. 4.4, the first step is to decide if an activity is core to an organization or not. For example, banking operations are core to a bank, while running canteens at branch premises is a non-core activity. In most instances, it would be worthwhile to outsource such non-core activities, as shown in the first decision node of Fig. 4.4. However, if an activity being considered for outsourcing is a core activity for an organization, the next step recommends benchmarking it against potential external vendors.

In an example of a bank, answering credit card-related queries of customers may be deemed as core to the banking operations. However, there may be some external vendors, who may be more proficient in performing these activities on various performance parameters such as time to answer the calls, quality of responses to the customer queries, and less waiting time of calls. Thus, comparing this process on various parameters with the benchmarks of external vendors would be helpful for the bank in knowing if there are areas of improvement when the process is performed in-house.

The next step in Fig. 4.4 calls for performing a total cost analysis of such core activities that are being considered for outsourcing. Usually, organizations perform costing for functional areas such as marketing, finance, human resource, and operations. Therefore, in such instances, it is unclear as to which activity has consumed overall how much resource and in turn has incurred how much cost. Activity-based costing (ABC) is useful in this regard, whereby cost calculations are performed for each activity separately. ABC is based on the premise that each activity consumes resources, which add up to the cost for that activity. Thus, a comparison of costs involved in performing a core activity in-house and by using an external vendor gives a good idea of the merits of outsourcing that activity.

The key question to be answered by the decision-makers at the next step is, 'Is the company more competent than external vendors in performing the core activity?' If the answer is no, another key decision node is—'Would the company like to invest in developing this activity into a competitive advantage in future?' A 'yes' to this question calls for keeping the activity in-house, while a 'no' prompts strategically outsourcing this activity to the outside vendor. A 'yes' for whether the company is more competent than external vendors leads to another decision node—'Will the company be able to sustain this competitive advantage in future?' A 'yes' suggests that the company should keep the activity in-house, while a 'no' here means outsourcing to outside vendors.

The last two steps in the outsourcing process (Fig. 4.4) require meticulous identification, comparison, and eventual selection of the best vendor for performing the outsourced activity. Various performance criteria, past experience/record of the vendors in performing such activities, fee quoted by them, and so on are criteria that must be considered in selecting the optimal outsourcing alternative.

## Avoiding Outsourcing Pitfalls

In view of the intense competition that our Indian BPO industry is likely to face in the years to come, it is imperative for us to avoid outsourcing pitfalls in the contracts with foreign clients. Figure 4.5 shows the ways of avoiding commonly encountered pitfalls in outsourcing relationsips.

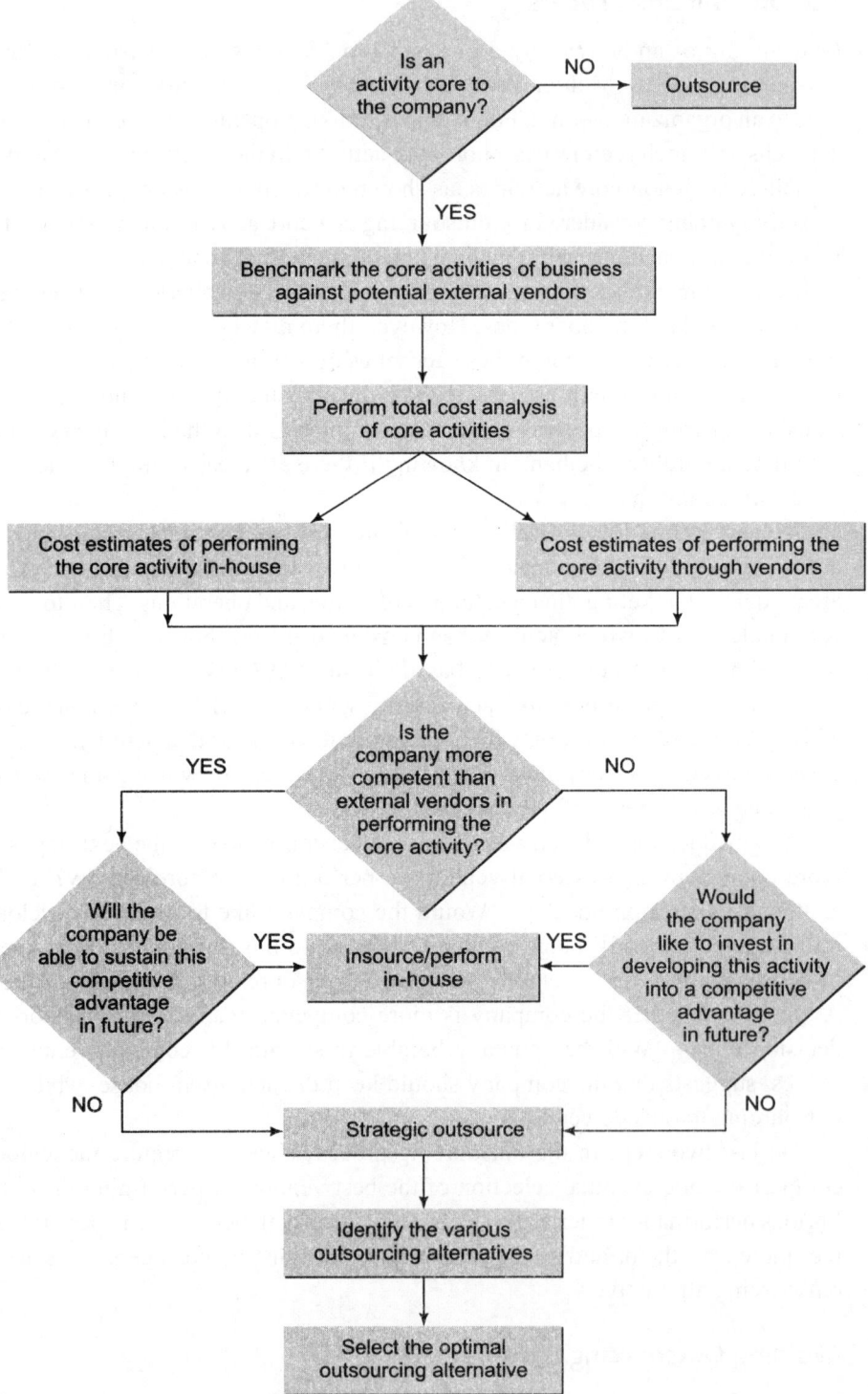

**Fig. 4.4**   The outsourcing process

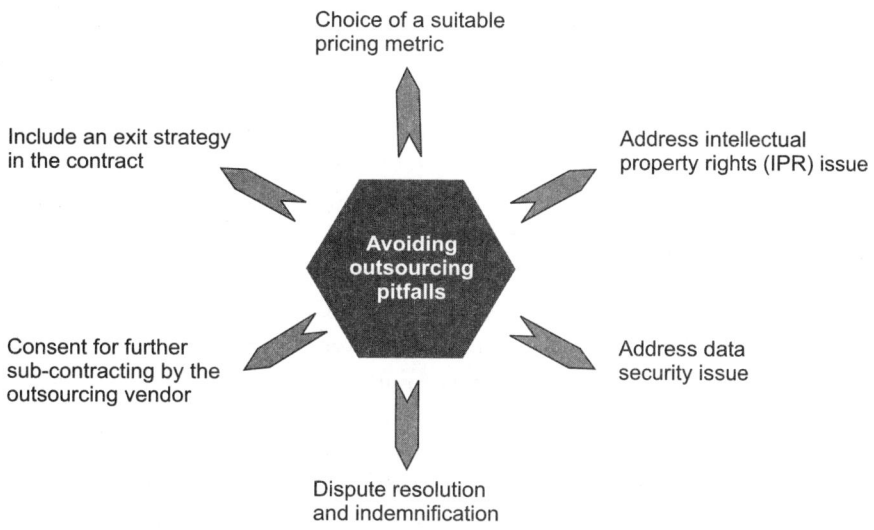

**Fig. 4.5**  Avoiding outsourcing pitfalls

Pricing is an issue, which often leads to strained outsourcing relationships between the client and the vendor. The foreign exchange fluctuations have a direct impact on the pricing in outsourcing contracts with foreign MNCs. Therefore, proper choice of a suitable pricing metric is important. Corbett (2001) opines that the pricing should not be dealt in outsourcing contracts with common metrics such as fixed price per unit (for example, per call attended by the call centre), prices based upon cost plus profit margin, or variable price per unit based on consumption ranges. This is because the client and the vendor have divergent interests; eventually ending the relationship sooner or later.

The outsourcer would always 'shop around' for other vendors willing to provide similar service for a lesser price and start decreasing the service volumes to the vendor currently under contract. Similarly, the vendors would always try to increase the volume of service sought by clients and decrease the cost of provision of the service to maximize their profits. These diverging interests are the recipe for failure of an outsourcing contract. Therefore, it is better to link pricing to 'gain sharing' by both the parties. Corbett (2001) suggests linking the pricing to the per cent savings or per cent revenue realized by the client or production targets (business volumes) of the client. As evident, these metrics require a high level of trust and transparency between the two partners.

Intellectual property rights (IPR) is a big issue in the Western world. This is especially true for organizations, which are outsourcing some of their high-end processes such as software development, R&D, industrial designs, and product designs. While entering into an outsourcing agreement, these organizations are concerned about having certain clauses in the contract relating to

- intellectual property that is already in existence at the time of entering the outsourcing contract;
- intellectual property that is likely to be developed during the outsourcing partnership; and
- restrictions upon the vendor from disclosing the client's intellectual property and other relevant information.

> It is better to link pricing to 'gain sharing' by both the vendor and the outsource.

Indian BPO companies must take utmost care in ensuring that these clauses are adhered to. This will help in avoiding a strained relationship with the outsourcer. Countries such as China, Russia, and Mexico are among the most popular countries for outsourcing; they also have the weakest intellectual property laws. On the other hand, protection of IPR in India continues to be strengthened. There is a well-established statutory, administrative, and judicial framework to safeguard rights, whether they relate to patents, trademarks, copyright, or industrial designs. Well-known international trademarks have been protected in India even though they are not registered in India.

The Indian trademarks law has been extended to services too. Computer software companies have successfully curtailed piracy through court orders. Computer databases have been protected. The courts, under the doctrine of breach of confidentiality, accorded an extensive protection of trade secrets. Right to privacy, which is not protected even in all developed countries, has been recognized in India. Various steps are being taken by the Government of India to strengthen and modernize intellectual property administration system, including patent information services, trademark registration, and patent offices in India.

Data security and privacy is another important concern for outsourcers. Data relating to identification of the outsourcer's customers, such as name, address, and social security number is highly confidential. If these details are leaked to outsiders by any employee of the vendor, it can be highly embarrassing for the outsourcer. Second, some details such as credit card information may lead to fraud and result in liabilities for the outsourcer.

It is in the interest of the outsourcer to understand data privacy laws of the vendor's country. In case the host country does not have sophisticated data privacy laws, vendors can be required to adhere to some international jurisdiction (for example, the European Union) through adequate clauses in the outsourcing contract. The safest option for the outsourcer to avoid any jurisdiction is to take the direct consent from its customers on a form to be signed by them to allow offshoring of data. Though, this is easier said than done.

The Indian BPO industry has beefed up its security to address the data security issue after some stray incidents were reported against it. Indian BPOs are already lining up to implement the best practices by using international certification as proof of security compliance. The country's top non-captive BPO companies such as ICICI OneSource, WNS, and Wipro Spectramind have got BS7799, which addresses physical security, information security, and business continuity management. In addition, companies are also looking at country specific certification. For example, Wipro has been certified for the UK Data Protection Act for UK processes. The Indian BPO industry has proposed the following changes in the Indian jurisdiction to the government for crimes related to data security:

- Implement a strong data protection regime. The IT Act 2000 was conceived to make e-commerce possible. It is, however, inadequate in tackling data security.
- Serious rise in the quantum of punishment. Currently a three-year imprisonment and ₹2,00,000 fine is imposed. This should be scaled up to at least seven years.
- India needs to expand and extend statutory powers to deal with compensation. The damage that can be claimed currently under Section 43 of the IT Act is ₹10 million. This needs to be increased to at least ₹500 million.
- The IT Act and the Indian Penal Code are not equipped to deal with data security issues. Data related crimes need a new set of laws. Currently Section 66 dealing with hacking is invoked in cases of data thefts. Data theft is not restricted to hacking.
- India needs to provide statutory protection for confidentiality.

> It is necessary to include an exit strategy in the outsourcing contract.

It is necessary to include clauses related to any dispute resolution. Some countries require that any dispute between the two parties in a contract have to be litigated in their land. Therefore, it may become hugely expensive for an Indian BPO to fight a case in a foreign country. It is always better to include clauses in the contract to specify how the litigation would be handled in case of a dispute between the two parties (after understanding the prevalent laws in the countries of the outsourcer and the vendor). It is a good idea to include clauses relating to arbitration for dispute resolution to avoid the courts. Outsourcers should include an indemnity clause in the contract to ensure that they are not held liable for the negligent or wilful conduct, or omissions of the supplier. This indemnity clause should be broad enough to insulate the outsourcer from an aggrieved third party, who would like to include the outsourcer in any civil or criminal offence.

Sometimes, the outsourcing vendor tries to subcontract the tasks outsourced by the outsourcer to a third party (sub-contractor). It is in the interest of the outsourcer to include clauses in the contract to ensure that the vendor has to take the written consent of the outsourcer before undertaking any such sub-contracting to third parties. Also, the outsourcers must retain the right of reviewing any such sub-contracting arrangement that the vendor would like to get into with a third party.

Though it may seem pessimistic to talk about breaking a relationship when it is being created, it is necessary to include an exit strategy in the outsourcing contract. It is prudent to specify the life (duration) of the contract. In view of the rapidly changing business environment today, it is better to keep the duration small (for example, two to three years). In case one of the two parties in the contract chooses to end the agreement before the termination date specified in the contract, there should be clauses for financial compensation to the other party to cover the costs of the affected party. Issues, such as who would own the equipment purchased during the agreement, who would own the IP created during the agreement, and the fate of employees who were transitioned from the outsourcer to the vendor, should be clearly spelled out in the exit strategy.

## Summary

India is currently the international hub of outsourcing and offshoring. Organizations worldwide are attracted to outsource their business processes to developing countries such as India and China due to low labour costs. This advantage is only transitory and would fade away in due course of time when the labour costs in these countries would come at par with those in the western world. The quality of outsourced services has become the critical factor. India has already started facing competition in this arena from countries such as China, Russia, Philippines, Mexico, Brazil, and so on. The Latin-American countries have coined the term 'near-shoring' to project their advantage of close physical proximity to the world's biggest outsourcing nation– the US. The reasons for outsourcing span from labour cost advantage to advantages derived from different time zones and so on. Major chunk of the business processes outsourced are in categories such as customer service, transaction processing, content development, healthcare data processing, HR-related data processing, and financial data processing. The steps recommended in the outsourcing process should be followed meticulously for outsourcing activities. For a long-lasting outsourcing relationship between the outsourcer and the vendor, there are certain pitfalls which should be avoided. Pricing is one such issue, which should be based upon metrics based upon 'gain sharing' to motivate both the parties to strive for improvement of the outsourced process. The outsourcing contract must have an exit strategy in place for amicable termination of the outsourcing contract, in case of unforeseen circumstances. India needs to further refine its laws relating to data security and intellectual property in view of the outsourcing boom and the related concerns of the outsourcing organizations based in the western world.

# References

CII–McKinsey Report 2003, 'Made in India: The next big manufacturing exports opportunity', http://www.mckinsey.com/locations/india/mckinseyonindia/pdf/Made_in_India.pdf, accessed in February 2007.

Cohen, L. and A. Young 2006, *Multisourcing: Moving Beyond Outsourcing to Achieve Growth and Agility*, Harvard Business School Press, Boston, Massachusetts.

Corbett, M.F., et al. 2001, 'Pricing models that share gains', as cited in Hillary, M.K. 2005, *Outsourcing to India: The Offshore Advantage*, 2nd edn, Springer (India), New Delhi.

McIvor, R. 2000, 'A practical framework for understanding the outsourcing process', *Supply Chain Management*, vol. 5, issue 1, p. 22.

NASSCOM–McKinsey Report 2005, 'Extending India's leadership of the Global IT and BPO Industries', http://www.mckinsey.com/locations/india/mckinseyonindia/pdf/NASSCOM_McKinsey_Report_2005.pdf, accessed on 4 February 2007.

Patel, A.B. and H. Aran 2005, *Outsourcing Success: The Management Imperative*, Palgrave Macmillan, New York.

# Keywords

**Farm-shoring** refers to the placement of jobs in low-cost regions of the service recipient's home country.

**Medical transcription** refers to the process of transcription or conversion of voice-recorded medical reports into text by the BPOs for ready reference by the medical experts later.

**Near-shoring** is a term coined by the Latin-American countries to refer to their close proximity to the US and other major service consumers.

**Offshoring** refers to the outsourcing of business processes to a location distant from the service consumers.

## CASE STUDY

## Sunil Bharti Mittal and Bharti Airtel

Sunil Bharti Mittal was awarded the Padma Bhushan by the President of India in 2006. Other eminent business personalities to receive this honour in 2006 include the Pepsi Chief, Indra Nooyi, and the Chairman of Suzuki Motor Corporation, Osamu Suzuki. Sunil is not only a successful first-generation entrepreneur, but also a generous philanthropist. He has funded about 50 schools in Madhya Pradesh and has donated ₹200 million to IIT Delhi for setting up the Bharti School of Technology and Management. Success seems to come easily to Sunil Mittal, but few people know his real story, which also has huge disappointments and frustration besides the Midas touch he is known for.

Sunil's father, Sat Paul Mittal, was in active politics in Punjab and had been elected a Member of Parliament (MP) from the Congress Party. Sat Paul, a *bania*, married a *khatri* lady and was, thus, denounced by his community for this inter-caste marriage. Their children including Sunil used the surname 'Bharti' for a long time and could regain their surname 'Mittal' much later. The early life of Sunil was spent in Ludhiana, which is a manufacturing hub, in Punjab. He graduated

from Panjab University and founded his enterprise known as 'Bharti' as a first-generation entrepreneur in 1976 at the age of 18. He borrowed ₹70,000 from his father and started manufacturing crankshafts for local bicycle manufacturing organizations in Ludhiana. During the next three years, he diversified into manufacturing yarn and stainless-steel sheets used for surgical utensils.

Sunil seems to enjoy the thrill of being a serial entrepreneur. What else could explain the fact that despite his successful ventures in Ludhiana, he sold off his factories there in 1980 to move to Mumbai and started afresh. His initial forays in Mumbai were into trading commodities such as brass, imported stainless-steel, plastics, and zip fasteners. Lady luck smiled again on Sunil in 1982 when he struck a deal with Suzuki Motor Corporation of Japan to become an exclusive agent in India for their electric power generators. Sunil was aware of the power shortage in most Indian cities and saw a great potential in providing this alternative to the companies and homes. As an adept businessman, he created a good distribution system with offices in the four metros of the country. Sales started climbing and it seemed as if there was no stopping him.

The big blow came in 1984, when the Government of India gave licences to the big industrial houses of Shriram and Birla to manufacture gensets in India with the collaboration of Honda and Yamaha respectively. These were the initial days of the liberalization process in India and without any warning, the government declared the import of gensets illegal. This was despite the fact known to everybody that it would take several years for the licensees to erect their facilities to manufacture gensets.

Under these unforeseen circumstances, the entrepreneurial acumen in Sunil pushed him to visit markets in Japan, Korea, and Taiwan. As luck would have it, these were going to be the defining moments for his entrepreneurial career as he was about to embark upon the telecom sector, which would become his identity for a long time to come.

Sunil came across a new telephone instrument in Taiwan, which did not have the circular dialing system but delicate push buttons instead. The sharp business mind of Sunil gave him a sense of success with this technology in India. Within the next few days, he found a supplier of these instruments and signed a contract. There were a few hurdles but it was not difficult for him to overcome them. It was not possible to import these fully assembled instruments due to the government restrictions. Sunil found the route of importing these legally by disassembling these gadgets in Taiwan, sending these components to major cities in India, and later assembling these back to their original form.

Within months, he started selling these instruments in India with a German-sounding brand name, Mittbrau, which meant Mittal Brothers. Bharti's business started flourishing again. Sometime later, the government granted licences to 52 other firms to manufacture touch-tone phones in India. This time around Sunil got a licence and simultaneously diversified into manufacturing fax machines, answering machines, and cordless phones. Most of the other licensee firms (big conglomerates), even after getting the licences, were not focusing much on this low profile business. This went in favour of Bharti as it continued to grow and years later became India's largest manufacturer of these instruments, while its rivals perished.

Sunil's bet of the lifetime came around in 1992 after the government embarked upon a major liberalization programme during 1991.

In 1992, the government invited licence bids for operating mobile phone networks in various parts of the country. Sunil was new to this technology. He delegated the management of his factories to his brothers and himself went to London to understand the intricacies of this potential business opportunity. With the help of world-class experts, he filed a tender with the Government of India for launching his mobile phone network.

Bharti won the licences for setting up its mobile phone networks in the four largest cities in India. Some of the disgruntled competitors, who could not get the licences, went to courts against Bharti. Eventually, Bharti could go ahead with its network only in Delhi. It was a blessing in disguise for Sunil, who had underestimated the capital required for setting up the network at ₹25 million per city. In reality, the cost was around four times higher. Sunil financed this new venture and put up the network in Delhi. Thus, Bharti Airtel was born, which launched its services, with the brand name Airtel.

In the subsequent years, when the government again invited bids for mobile networks in B-category cities, Sunil chose to sit back and relax. The competitors went berserk in tendering sky-high bids, only to realize their mistakes later. Within a couple of years of setting up their expensive networks, many of these rivals went into losses and divested their assets to Bharti Airtel, which was waiting for this right moment to enter these circles.

Many thought that the entry of conglomerates such as Reliance and Tatas into mobile telephony would wipe away Bharti. All these years Sunil has proved that he can maintain a slender lead above his arch-rivals. Bharti is currently the market leader after having captured 20 per cent of the market share. The revenues are over US$4 billion up from US$510 million in 2003. By the end of June 2006, Bharti Airtel had 24.58 million customers, including over 23 million mobile phone users, with fixed-line and broadband customers making up the remainder. Sunil could manage this unimaginable feat partly due to some innovative outsourcing practices adapted by Bharti during recent times.

With the kind of growth in customer base Bharti was experiencing in 2003, it was difficult to keep pace in terms of network expansion. Every time the company had to plan the network expansion, the onerous process of tendering and negotiating with the key vendors would start. This consumed valuable time and resources of the company. More importantly, the time consumed in identifying the need for capacity expansion, tendering, negotiating, choosing the suppliers, granting the tender, and implementation process would take from six months to a year. During this time, the services to the customers would be affected in terms of network jams, delays in call connection, or breaks/disturbances in calls. This could be detrimental to the survival and growth of a company aspiring to provide excellent customer service. Bharti's major vendors of telecom network equipment were Sweden's Ericsson, Germany's Siemens, and Finland's Nokia. It is a general tendency on part of the vendors to try to sell as much equipment as possible, while the network operators look forward to having minimum equipment with highest capacity utilization and coverage.

Bharti was struggling to keep pace with its burgeoning IT requirements too. The increasing need to upscale the existing hardware and software every now and then was a big headache for the internal IT department. It was painful to know that expensive software purchased just a year ago had become obsolete to handle the new requirements of the organization. Bharti required IT services to support the functioning of its telecom network, such as switching systems; to capture data related to customer service, such as, usage, network reliability, and quality; and to facilitate internal business functioning related to billing, financial reporting, salary/wages administration, etc. The company initially approached vendors such as IBM, HP, and Oracle according to the emerging requirements. The costs related to this approach were highly unpredictable. This posed a challenge before Bharti to offer its services at the most competitive prices to its customers.

Outsourcing was recommended as a solution to these issues by Akhil Gupta, the Joint Managing Director of Bharti Airtel. The idea was not very appealing to a majority of the members of the Board of Directors. Outsourcing as a concept was not new, but the company had not outsourced its core operations till then. As if that was not enough, Akhil was proposing to initiate negotiations with all the foreign vendors for this purpose. Major MNCs worldwide were outsourcing their business processes to Indian IT and BPO organizations and here was this Indian company thinking of outsourcing its 'core' processes to the foreign organizations. The idea of this 'reverse outsourcing' was supported by Sunil, who had the experience of dealing with many foreign organizations during his various entrepreneurial endeavours. According to him, in case of any problem in a switch in the network, there was hardly anything that Bharti's technicians could do to detect and correct the problem. They had to call a technician

from Ericsson to repair it. Since Ericsson manufactures these switches, its technicians are trained well. Hence, Bharti decided to outsource these processes to such companies.

In March 2004, Bharti entered into a US$400 million contract with Ericsson, Siemens, and Nokia. According to this contract, these vendors would be completely responsible for the design and installation requirements of Bharti's network. They would be making their own investments in creating this capacity in Bharti's network. The investments would be based on the projected customer demand in a region and would be paid by Bharti only after the capacity utilization by its customers.

The vendors were also made responsible for maintenance of the network at the highest level of service quality with prompt action in case of problems. To protect the interests of the vendors, the contract has clauses, which specify the increase in payment per unit of capacity if the usage density of the installed capacity turns out to be less than anticipated. The entire ancillary infrastructure such as air-conditioning, power back-up, and towers were created by Bharti in order to be equally involved in the capacity enhancement process.

In 2004, Bharti also partnered with IBM in a US$750 million deal for the design, installation, and maintenance of Bharti's IT requirements for a period of ten years (five years with an extension clause of five more years). This is a unique agreement based upon revenue sharing arrangement between the two partners. Bharti banked upon the 'on-demand' business concept propounded by IBM. It was understandable for Sunil to tie-up with foreign MNCs for design, installation, and maintenance of telecom network and equipment. It came as a surprise to many when he overlooked Indian IT bigwigs such as Infosys, Wipro, and TCS for its IT-related requirements. In Sunil's own words, 'It is hard for two Indians to partner well. They have not done this kind of a thing earlier. They are new. I am new'.

In this partnership with IBM, both partners understand that the spirit of this tie-up is more important than the contract per se. It is difficult to capture all the length and breadth of the actual operations involved in the contract. Therefore, both partners have set up a joint steering committee to oversee the smooth implementation of the agreement and to resolve any issues that come up at various levels.

Encouraged by the success of its outsourcing partnerships, Bharti Airtel entered into first ever landmark agreement in August 2005 to outsource its call centre operations to some of the best international BPOs. These strategic partnerships with four international BPOs—Hinduja TMT (HTMT), IBM Daksh, Mphasis, and TeleTech Services were aimed at significantly enhanced quality of customer service delivery to Airtel customers across the country. As part of this initiative, HTMT set up the contact centres in Chennai and Hyderabad; IBM Daksh in Chandigarh, Calcutta, and Pune; TeleTech in National Capital Region (NCR); and Mphasis in NCR and Bangalore.

Bharti also entered into a landmark technology outsourcing arrangement with Nortel, wherein Nortel will deliver technology and expert resources required to provide world-class customer services to Bharti's customers through voice, advanced speech recognition, multimedia contact centre, unified messaging, computer–telephony integration, IP-enabled video communications, and receiving and routing calls to the respective customer service partners. While all the four partners will operationally manage inbound call centre operations of Bharti, the technologies for call routing, prioritization and IVR, will be managed by Nortel. Upon completion of definitive documentation, Nortel expects to provide innovative natural speech recognition solutions, in local languages, to help Bharti enhance its customer satisfaction and increase its revenues, while reducing operating costs.

These agreements were based on a partnership approach, the value of which is based on customer growth, traffic, and service level agreements. The scope of the agreement extends to operationally managing Bharti's call centre covering inbound voice operations in 23 circles across India. This partnership was aimed to enable Airtel to channelise its resources and expertise to its core areas of product innovation, value added services, marketing, brand building, and customer delight innovations, while simultaneously providing world-class mobile services.

In 2006, Bharti Airtel signed a US$100 million deal with IBM under which the latter will create a unified content and application delivery platform to allow Airtel deliver a suite of innovative products, services, and applications to its customers. IBM's service delivery platform (SDP) will permit Bharti to bring its various value added services into one common platform and facilitate better customer service experience through service personalization, single access point, single sign-on, etc. The service delivery platform will enhance the spectrum of content, application, and services and integrate them across all of its service lines. It will present a consistent presentation of services to the customers, who will be able to access them through multiple channels such as SMS, MMS, WAP, web, and broad band.

Sunil's penchant for outsourcing does not end here. In November 2006, he announced an agreement with Google that enables Bharti's wireless customers to use its technology to search the web. Just when people started thinking that Airtel was the biggest climb Sunil could make, he announced an equal partnership with the American retail chain giant Walmart to launch retail stores in India. The joint venture of Bharti with Walmart operates 18 'cash-and-carry' stores in Punjab and Andhra Pradesh, which supply to wholesalers, retailers, restaurants, and *kirana* stores. With the government allowing up to 51 per cent stake of foreign partners in multi-brand retail in 2012, it is expected that Walmart would further extend its relationship with Bharti Airtel in expanding its India operations in the coming years.

Early 2007 saw Bharti's biggest rival in the Indian retailing space, Reliance, outsourcing its telecom requirements to Bharti Airtel. Reliance Retail has inked a deal with Bharti Airtel to source mobile and enterprise communication services. This includes mobile, broadband, and leased line services for its retail venture, expected to have a network of 8,000 stores. All these stores would be connected to each other and to the logistics chains in order to meet Reliance Retail's high-end communication needs. These telecom solutions will also be put to captive use for Bharti–Walmart.

Bharti Airtel continues to pursue its outsourcing strategy by awarding long-term contracts to its partners. In 2011, it awarded a more than US$1.5 billion contract to IBM to manage its information technology (IT) requirements for employees in 16 countries across Africa, which is its relatively new market. Similarly, in April 2012 it entered into a 5-year agreement with Avaya to manage the IT requirements of its business process outsourcing (BPO) partners across 80 locations. Under this agreement, Avaya will build a contact centre cloud facility that will link all BPOs that serve Bharti customers, and allow them to provide customer services through video calls and enable them to address complaints registered through social media. In this contract with Avaya, in place of revenue sharing, Bharti Airtel would use 'pay-as-you-go' model linked to usage of services and resulting in economies of scale.

In the years to come, Sunil Mittal is likely to reinvent himself and Bharti to create new frontiers of success with his entrepreneurial acumen.

## Discussion Questions

1. Which approach to outsourcing is better in your view—that of Bharti Airtel, which chose to partner with IBM, a foreign MNC, or that of Reliance Retail, which preferred to partner with Bharti Airtel than any foreign MNC?

2. What potential threats do you foresee with Bharti Airtel having outsourced even its core activities?

3. Is it possible to have a new model for organizations having all their functions outsourced and themselves performing the role of a moderator between all the vendors?

# Objective Questions

### Choose the correct option

1. The transfer, through foreign direct investment or subcontracting, of all or part of the production of services to another country with the intention to re-import them to the home country is called
   (a) near-shoring
   (b) offshoring
   (c) right-shoring
   (d) insourcing

2. Outsourcing service activities to a foreign, lower-wage country that is relatively close in distance or time zone (or both) is called
   (a) near-shoring
   (b) offshoring
   (c) right-shoring
   (d) insourcing

3. This process of conversion of recorded voice of the doctor into a nicely typed, written record is called
   (a) medical record
   (b) medical transcription
   (c) medical history
   (d) medical chemistry

4. Which one of the following is not a prominent global outsourcing destination?
   (a) Botswana
   (b) The Philippines
   (c) China
   (d) India

5. Which city has recently been adjudged as Asia's top outsourcing city?
   (a) Bangalore
   (b) Shanghai
   (c) Cebu City
   (d) Kuala Lumpur

6. The integrated factory concept was first used during the early 1900s by
   (a) General Motors
   (b) Ford Motor Company
   (c) BMW
   (d) Volkswagon

7. Outsourcing to a vendor located in another country is called
   (a) offshoring
   (b) near-shoring
   (c) farm-shoring
   (d) insourcing

### State True or False

8. LCL country means low-cost labour country.

### Fill in the blanks

9. A canteen or mess in a hospital would be considered as a _____ activity.

10. Taken together, _____ and the total cost analysis provide a holistic picture as to whether the company is more competent at performing the core activity than external vendors or not.

# Concept Review Questions

1. Why has India become the world's favourite off-shoring destination? What should be done to the competition from other countries eyeing to capture the outsourcing pie from India?

2. What is outsourcing? How is it different from off-shoring?

3. What are the various ways of business process execution in terms of internal-external processing and local-international locations?

4. Why do organizations outsource their business processes?

5. What kind of processes are easy targets of outsourcing by organizations?

6. Explain the steps in the outsourcing process.

7. Explain the precautions to be taken while entering into an outsourcing contract with foreign outsourcers.

# Project Assignment

While organizing various activities in Indian marriages, it is observed that the trend these days is to outsource many activities to outside vendors, for example, the marriage hall, catering, logistics, transportation, etc. Identify all such activities in a typical Indian marriage that can be outsourced (as many as possible). Contact such service providers in your city and find out the average price charged by them for providing such services. Arrive at an estimate of total expenses involved in organizing the marriage through this outsourcing arrangement. Consider the other extreme in which you decide to undertake as many activities as possible in the marriage yourself. Try to arrive at an estimate of savings expected to be made by you in this option. Compare the costs in the two options. Discuss the pros and cons of the two options amongst a group of students in your class.

| Answers to Objective Questions | | | | |
|---|---|---|---|---|
| 1. (b) | 2. (a) | 3. (b) | 4. (a) | 5. (c) |
| 6. (b) | 7. (a) | 8. True | 9. non-core | 10. benchmarking |

# 5

# Facility Location Planning

**Learning Objectives**

After reading this chapter, you will be able to answer the following questions:
- Why is it important to plan the location of a new facility?
- What are the operations strategies for having multiple facilities?
- What are the factors to be considered in facility location planning?
- What are the factors to be considered in the facility location planning of international facilities?
- Which models and techniques are useful in this context?
- How do facility location decisions influence network design in the supply chain?

## Introduction

A factory or a plant is the manufacturing facility of a company. A warehouse is the storage facility of a manufacturing or a distribution company. The offices of a service sector company such as a courier company, a bank, or an insurance company are its facilities. The facility location decision is very important for big business houses as well as new entrepreneurs. Wrong location of the facility may lead to a failure of the complete project. Figure 5.1 shows the repercussions of setting up a facility without proper facility location planning (Exhibit 5.1). Figure 5.2 shows the various steps to be followed in proper facility location planning. Various factors can be considered for making the facility location decision. In this chapter, we will study these factors and the relevant models and techniques. Before that, let us study the three operations strategies followed by organizations for having multiple facilities.

## Operations Strategies for Multiple Facilities

There are three strategies for the organizations to have more than one facility for pursuing their operations.

### Separate Facilities for Different Products/Services

Wrong location of the facility may lead to a failure of the complete project.

Companies which are into diversified product/service ranges prefer to have separate facilities for each of them. Each facility takes care of the entire population (markets) or total geographical area for a particular product/service.

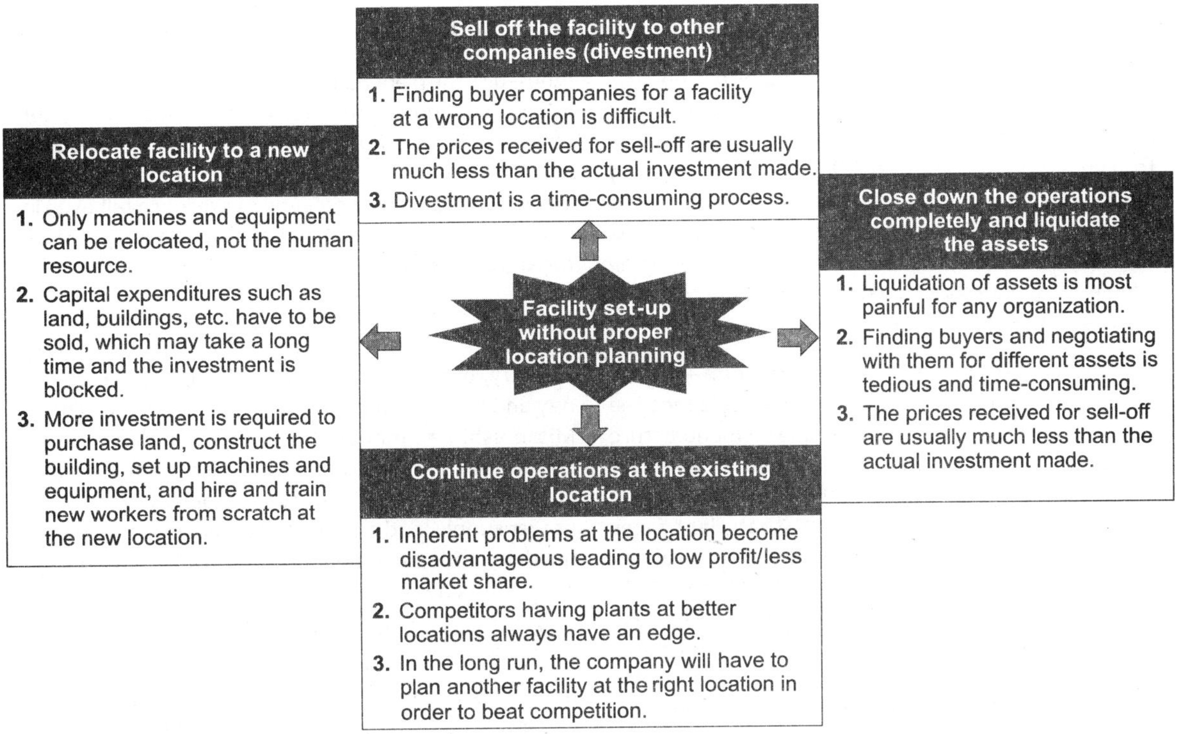

Sell off the facility to other companies (divestment)
1. Finding buyer companies for a facility at a wrong location is difficult.
2. The prices received for sell-off are usually much less than the actual investment made.
3. Divestment is a time-consuming process.
Relocate facility to a new location
1. Only machines and equipment can be relocated, not the human resource.
2. Capital expenditures such as land, buildings, etc. have to be sold, which may take a long time and the investment is blocked.
3. More investment is required to purchase land, construct the building, set up machines and equipment, and hire and train new workers from scratch at the new location.
Facility set-up without proper location planning
Close down the operations completely and liquidate the assets
1. Liquidation of assets is most painful for any organization.
2. Finding buyers and negotiating with them for different assets is tedious and time-consuming.
3. The prices received for sell-off are usually much less than the actual investment made.
Continue operations at the existing location
1. Inherent problems at the location become disadvantageous leading to low profit/less market share.
2. Competitors having plants at better locations always have an edge.
3. In the long run, the company will have to plan another facility at the right location in order to beat competition.

**Fig. 5.1** Problems due to improper facility location planning

Generate a list of alternative location options for the facility.
Find out factors relevant to the facility being planned.
Screen better location options using factor and location rating analysis.
Screen better location options using break-even (economic) analysis.
Apply simple median model for finding location with least overall transportation cost.
Apply centre of gravity model for finding location with least overall transportation cost.
Apply transportation model for finding location with least overall transportation cost.
Apply Ardalan heuristic to choose the best location for service operations.
Best location chosen.
Initial screening of locations
Final selection process

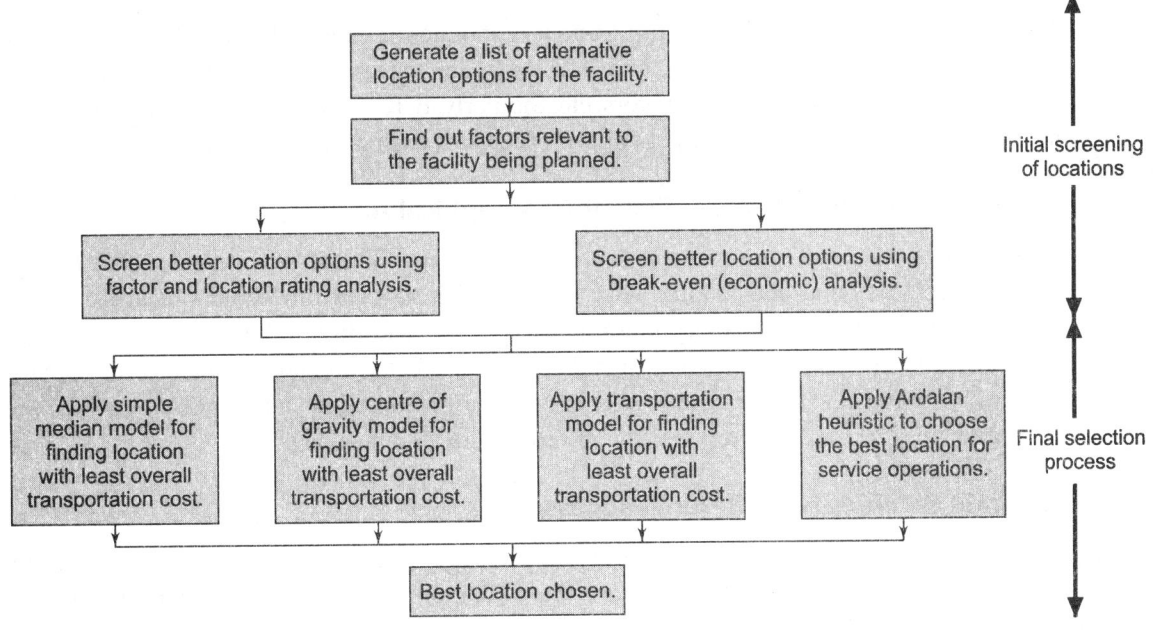

**Fig. 5.2** Steps in facility location planning

---

### Exhibit 5.1 Mitsubishi at Haldia

In 1997, when the US$14 billion Mitsubishi Chemical Corporation zeroed in on Haldia (West Bengal) to mark the beginning of their Indian adventure with a foreign direct investment (FDI) of ₹1,475 crore, they did so with the world in mind. At that time, Haldia was often in the headlines because of the massive Haldia Petrochemicals project, which was constantly facing problems. Mitsubishi entered quietly and put together a unique and remarkable project at Haldia.

The Japanese conglomerate has a custom—it builds all its pure terephthalic acid (PTA) plants facing the sea (PTA is a basic raw material used in the manufacture of polyester products). It made a small exception—in Haldia, the estuarine township of West Bengal, their 4,25,000 tonnes per annum (tpa) plant faces river Hooghly. The company's Managing Director, Takaharu Fukumoto, says with a touch of humour, 'To the Japanese the river here almost looks like the sea'. However, the Japanese are not given to emotional decision-making and are known for precision. The choice of Haldia in itself is a testimony to the potential of this fast-growing industrial river port, and the window of opportunities it presents to the investor.

During the first three years of its commissioning (2001–03), the plant had already crossed ₹15,000 million in turnover and commanded a market share of 35 per cent in the domestic PTA market. The quality standards of Mitsubishi are so high that the plant is making a mark in the international market and its presence felt even in China, arguably the market with the maximum potential for any polyester product.

Another feature of the plant is its environment-friendliness. PTA has often been considered a dirty industry, but with the use of truly high-end technology and highly specialized water treatment facilities, Mitsubishi has managed not only to eliminate all impurities from its product, but also from the effluents. The element of self-containment with its own power supply, and a dedicated pipeline ensuring connectivity with the Haldia port add to the company's competitiveness.

Mitsubishi enhanced its capacity to 4,70,000 tonnes in December 2003. With the growing demand for polyester products, it decided to go for another expansion project in 2006. The 8,00,000-tonne purified terephthalic acid plant at an investment amount of around ₹1,962 crore started its commercial production in March 2010.

---

This is done to avoid confusion and bring about economies of scale. White goods manufacturing companies such as LG, Videocon, and BPL have separate plants for colour TVs, washing machines, microwave ovens, refrigerators, etc. Similarly, ICICI, which is into banking, insurance, mutual funds, etc., has a separate network of offices for each of these segments.

### Separate Facilities to Serve Different Geographical Areas

Pepsi and Coca-Cola offer a perfect example of this strategy. Both these companies have bottling plants scattered all over the country, which cater to different regions/geographical areas. This strategy reduces the overall transportation cost and the lead time for supplying goods in the markets (Exhibit 5.2). Prompt action can be taken to deal with sudden changes in demand. Service sector organizations such as banks, insurance companies, hospitals, and courier services also have multiple offices to serve different regions/geographical areas.

### Separate Facilities for Different Processes

Companies which are into diversified product/ service ranges prefer to have separate facilities for each of them.

Many colour TV manufacturers have separate facilities for manufacturing picture tubes, which are major components used in the manufacture of a TV set. The Aditya Birla group has a separate factory at Jagdishpur (in UP) for manufacturing plastic sacks, which are supplied to the Indo-Gulf Fertilizers Factory, also at Jagdishpur. These sacks are used to package the

---

### Exhibit 5.2  Wipro in Himachal

In 2005, Wipro set up a manufacturing facility for its flagship brand Santoor toilet soap at Baddi in Himachal Pradesh. The Baddi plant supplies 25 per cent of the total volume of its Santoor brand and contributes 20 per cent of the company's toilet soap production.

According to Azim Premji, Chairman, Wipro, 'We selected Himachal Pradesh for setting up the toilet soap manufacturing unit after a long and careful analysis and we are happy to be here. The advantages we saw were good rail and road connectivity, good quality power, good water, and above all positive attitude of people including the government here.' Wipro experienced 33 per cent growth in the year prior to setting up this plant with Punjab, Haryana, and Himachal Pradesh consumers strongly endorsing their recently launched Wipro Safewash liquid detergent.

Wipro has also ensured that its third party suppliers of Santoor, Wipro Talcum powder, Wipro Safewash liquid detergent, and other toilet soap suppliers also shift to Himachal Pradesh.

The Himachal Pradesh plant is Wipro Consumer Care & Lighting's third toilet soap manufacturing unit in the country. Besides the new plant in Baddi, Wipro manufactures toilet soaps at its plants in Amalner, Maharashtra and Tumkur, Karnataka. Wipro's other factories are in Aurangabad where Wipro Consumer Care and Lighting manufactures lighting products, and in Pondicherry where Wipro Infotech manufactures computers.

The company is servicing the growing markets of the north and some part of west through this new plant, which produces almost 5,00,000 units or 50 tonnes per day. Almost 50 per cent of the total Glucovita production also comes from the Himachal Pradesh unit. It is a critical plant location for the company as the company hopes to consolidate its position in north. The market in north India is a 'weak' market for some of the company's brands. The company as a whole generated 3,000 jobs in the region, both directly through the plant and indirectly through third party employment generation.

---

urea manufactured by them. Similarly, companies such as Reliance Industries, which are into backward integration, that is, which manufacture their own raw materials, also tend to have separate facilities for the production of such items.

Another example is that of RPG, which has separate factories for manufacturing tyres (CEAT tyres) and carbon black (Philips Carbon Black Ltd). Carbon black is a major raw material used in the production of tyres. This strategy helps to avoid confusion at the main manufacturing set-up. At the same time, a lot of coordination is required between such plants, as these serve as feeder units to other plants.

In the service sector, banks and insurance companies have their central/head offices, where the main activity is designing various financial instruments/policies. These offices are analogous to feeder units in the manufacturing sector. These offices design new instruments, which are marketed by the various regional offices of the company.

## Factors Affecting Facility Location Planning

The following factors (Fig. 5.3) should be considered while evaluating a location for starting a new facility.

> When the customers/ markets are located near the plant, products can be easily supplied to them.

**Proximity to customers (markets)**   When the customers/markets are located near the plant, products can be easily supplied to them. This reduces the cost of the product as the transportation cost is not added to it. The product, thus, competes well with the competitors' product. Most of the small ancillary units are located near the big automotive factories. The big factories are the institutional customers of small parts, components, or sub-assemblies from these ancillary units. Pune has many such ancillary units because of the presence of big auto factories such as Bajaj Auto Limited and Kinetic Engineering Ltd.

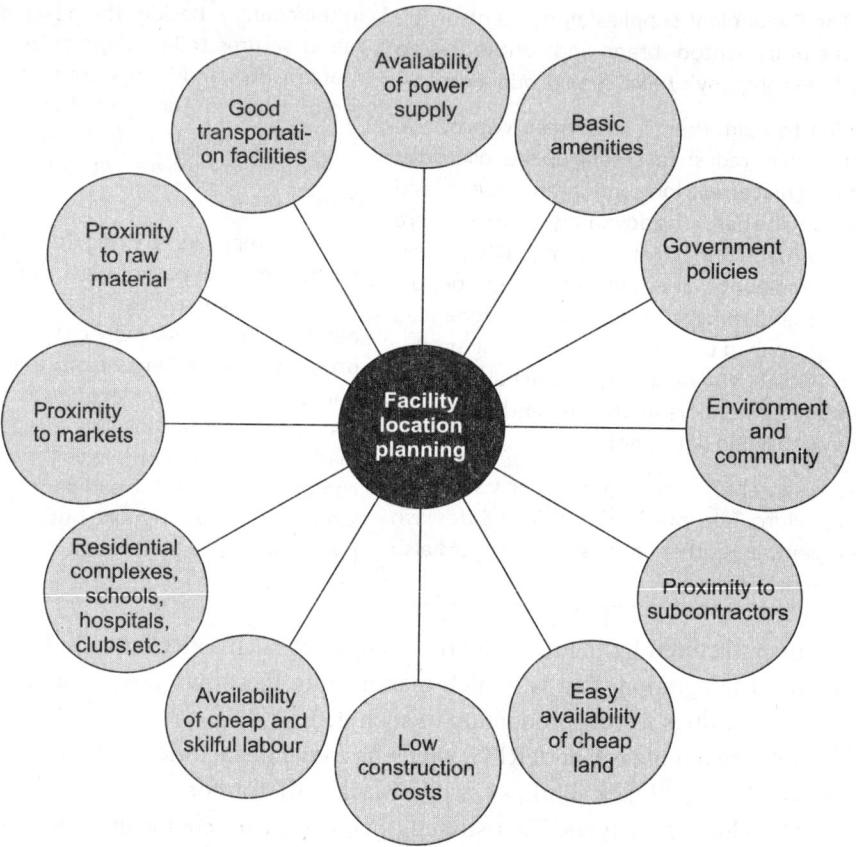

**Fig. 5.3** Factors affecting facility location planning

Proximity to markets allows companies to meet any sudden spurt in demand, thus providing an advantage over competitors located at far-off places. The response time to such demand is of prime importance for service sector organizations such as hospitals, clinics, nursing homes, post offices, banks, and insurance companies. These organizations locate their facilities/offices in high-population zones so that they are able to serve a large number of customers.

**Proximity to raw material** Most textile units are located in Gujarat and Maharashtra because these are the largest cotton-growing areas in the country. Iron and steel plants are located in Bihar and Orissa because of the large presence of iron ore mines in these regions. Easy access to coal, the raw material required for power generation in the process, is an added advantage. Raw material is thus cheaper because of negligible transportation cost. Also, it becomes easier to control its quality.

> Proximity to markets allows companies to meet any sudden spurt in demand.

**Good transportation facilities** Regions near metro cities have the advantage of good transportation facilities as they have good rail, air, water, and road transportation networks. Cities such as Mumbai and Chennai have been industrial and business hubs for a long time as they are located on the seashore.

**Availability of power supply**   Uninterrupted power supply is a basic requirement of most industries. Some factories have to set up their own captive power plants if located in areas with power problems. For example, the factories of HINDALCO (Aditya Birla Group) as well as Kanoria Chemical Industries Ltd at Renukoot (UP) have their own captive power plants.

**Basic amenities**   The area for location of the plant should have water supply lines managed by the local municipal corporation. Roads up to the factory premises are always desirable. These basic amenities are very useful even during the construction period of the plant. Other amenities desired are sanitation facilities such as sewer lines, and drainage system.

**Government policies**   The governments of states such as Maharashtra, Gujarat, and Karnataka have been very successful in inducing big business houses to set up their plants in these states. Local taxation policies and various promotional efforts help in increasing the industrial activity in the region. Pondicherry and Daman and Diu are examples of 'no sales tax regions' and, therefore, we find that most of the companies have their offices/warehouses located there.

Many state governments promote industrial activities in their regions by creating Industry Development Zones (Exhibit 5.3). Various facilities are provided by the government; for example, the governments of Karnataka, Andhra Pradesh, and UP have created software development parks, where facilities such as high-speed internet, servers, etc. are provided to software companies at subsidized rates.

Agriculture is one area that gets maximum subsidies from the central as well as state governments. Various processing plants of agricultural and horticultural products have these advantages. Before locating such plants in a region, the existing government policies of that place must be considered.

**Environmental and community considerations**   Many state governments have strict environmental policies in place, which have to be followed by the industries operating there. The people residing in the area should not be against the idea of having a plant in their region as the effluents from a factory spoil the natural environment of the region. Opposition from the community regarding the construction of a plant in their region can disrupt the whole project.

The Sardar Sarovar Dam project is an example where opposition from the local people had led to complete disruption in the construction of the dam over the Narmada river. After the Union Carbide factory disaster in Bhopal, every new factory there faces close scrutiny on the environmental front.

**Proximity to subcontractors**   The presence of small ancillary units manufacturing small components/sub-assemblies is important for any new factory. If a new auto plant is set up in Gurgaon, where the Maruti Suzuki plant is already located, it will get the advantage of the subcontractors existing there. These subcontractors can immediately start supplying the components required by the new plant for starting its production process.

The presence of small ancillary units manufacturing small components/sub-assemblies is important for any new factory.

**Easy availability of cheap land**   Land is the basic necessity for the construction of a new plant. Regions such as UP, Bihar, and Orissa may be lucrative for big companies because of this. Still, because of many other factors, companies prefer costly land near Mumbai, Pune, Ahmedabad, etc.

---

### Exhibit 5.3    Hero MotoCorp

The pro-industry policies of the Uttaranchal government are set to make it a haven for industrial activity. Major industrial houses such as Tata and Mahindra & Mahindra have already made huge investments in their new plants in the state. Cut-throat competition in the auto industry is prompting companies to look for ways to minimize costs. Tax waivers by governments such as in Uttaranchal are a real boon in this scenario. Plants in Uttaranchal are exempt from excise duty for the first 10 years. These plants also enjoy the benefit of zero income tax for the first five years and are 30 per cent exempt for the next five years.

Hero MotoCorp, earlier Hero Honda, the country's largest two-wheeler manufacturer, was awaiting the approval from the Rajasthan government to set up its new plant in Jaipur. In the meantime, its closest rival Bajaj auto announced its decision to set up its new plant in Pantnagar, Uttaranchal, a tax-free zone. This announcement from Bajaj seems to have prompted Hero MotoCorp to change its plans and it opted for Uttaranchal to set up its 1.5 million units a year plant in Haridwar. Hero commissioned this plant in April 2008.

The Hero plant and its main ancillaries are located on a 275 acre plot at the Integrated Industrial Estate in Haridwar, developed by the State Industrial Development Corporation of Uttaranchal Ltd. The company has already expanded capacity at its existing plants in Gurgaon and Dharuhera by an additional 9,00,000 units. Uttaranchal was chosen as a location for the plant taking into consideration a number of factors including the existing support infrastructure available and the tax sops offered by the government. These lead to improvement in operating margins.

Experts are of the view that these auto majors are unlikely to pass on the benefits of tax savings to the customers. Most of them will wait for these new plants to break-even during the coming three to four years before reducing the prices. However, Hero hopes the competition in the market would be driven by new product models than by discounts. With rising input costs and thinner margins, any price war triggered by lower tax would negate the gains of setting up capacity in tax-free havens such as Uttaranchal and Himachal Pradesh.

In June 2012, Hero MotoCorp announced that it would set up its fourth plant at Neemrana (Rajasthan), its fifth plant in Gujarat, and an R&D centre in Jaipur (Rajasthan) with an investment of ₹2,575 crore. These facilities would be commissioned sometime in 2014. It is interesting to note that the company has chosen to have all its plants in the north or west of the country despite the fact its products are sold all over the country.

---

**Less construction costs**   Construction costs of a plant may be low at a particular place due to cheap labour available there. The construction material may also be cheaper at another place. Such places are obviously preferred for locating a plant.

**Availability of cheap, skilful, and efficient labour**   India and other developing nations appear to have cheap labour. However, the reality is that labour turns out to be expensive here because it is not efficient when compared to the labour in developed countries. Multinational companies prefer China over India to set up their global sourcing bases because the labour in China has become more skilful and efficient as a result of increased industrial activity in the past few decades.

> The construction costs of a plant may be low at a particular place due to cheap labour available there.

### Residential complexes, schools, hospitals, clubs, etc.

Usually new factories are given land in remote villages by the state governments. Proper facilities such as residential complexes, schools, hospitals, clubs, etc. are not available for the managers of these plants and their families at such places. Under such situations, companies have to create these facilities on their own. The TISCO factory at Jamshedpur is the first example of this kind in India, where the company has created all such facilities for its employees. In UP, Indian Telephone Industries (Mankapur), HINDALCO (Renukoot), Indo-Gulf Fertilizers (Jagdishpur), and Kanoria Chemical Industries are similar

> If a new factory is set up at a place where all facilities already exist, fixed costs can be saved by the company.

examples. If a new factory is set up at a place where all such facilities already exist, fixed costs can be saved by the company.

## Locating Foreign Operations Facilities

Globalization has made consumers expect the best products at the lowest prices, irrespective of where they are produced. Companies are under competitive pressure to engage in global production and service operations due to the rapid growth of global markets. Recent changes in world politics and economy have made facility location decisions even more significant and challenging (Canel and Khumawala 1996).

**Fig. 5.4** Factors affecting international facility location planning

The following factors (Fig. 5.4) should be considered while evaluating international location options for a facility.

> Companies are under competitive pressure to engage in global production and service operations due to the rapid growth of global markets.

**Trade barriers** The government in some countries imposes trade barriers on the import of the products of foreign companies. The imported products thus become expensive due to import duties imposed and at times unavailable due to restrictions imposed in the form of quotas. In such situations, foreign companies can overcome these trade barriers by producing the goods locally in that country.

> If a foreign company has a large customer base in a country, it may be beneficial for the company to start operations locally in that country.

**International customers**   If a foreign company has a large customer base in a country, it may be beneficial for the company to start operations locally in that country. This way the company can serve the customers better and thus gain their loyalty.

**International competition**   If a company's competitors are starting or already have operations facilities in a country, it is natural for the company to start operations in that country.

**Regulations**   Harsh regulatory measures imposed by the government of a country can be avoided by starting operations facilities in another country.

**Additional resources**   International locations provide organizations with access to a host of additional resources such as natural resources, skilled human resources, and technologies.

**Lower costs**   The overall cost of operations may be lower at certain foreign locations due to low cost of labour, material, transportation, financing, etc.

**Incentives**   In order to promote FDI, the central and state governments in certain countries provide industrial infrastructure, insurance, tax exemptions/reductions, interest-free/subsidized loans, etc. to foreign companies willing to establish operations facilities in their region (Exhibit 5.4).

**Exploitation of firm-specific advantages**   Internationally famous brands and technologies of an organization can easily get established in a new country when it starts a new base of operations.

**Economies of scale**   More facilities in different countries imply more demand for the products, resulting in the economies of scale due to the large combined scale of production in all the facilities taken together.

**Synergy**   Past learning experiences and benefits from setting up facilities in some countries can be useful in setting up new facilities in other countries.

**Power and prestige**   The market value of the firm may soar as international operations are deemed prestigious by investors.

**Offensive in competitor's home country**   Initiating operations at the competitor's home country may at times force the competitor to concentrate more on the home turf and wind up or downsize its international operations.

## Factor and Location Ratings

The factors affecting the facility location decision discussed earlier are all important for any type of industry. At the same time, the importance of each of these factors may vary for different types of plants. According to the requirements of a new plant, a set of these factors is considered. These factors are rated from 1 to 5 to indicate the importance attached to them. A rating of 5 is given to the most important factor and a rating of 1 is given to the least important one. These are called *factor ratings*.

> Past learning experiences and benefits from setting up facilities in some countries can be useful in setting up new facilities in other countries.

Let us consider three location options for a new leather goods manufacturing facility being commissioned by a company. These location options are, say, Unnao (near Kanpur), Noida, and Gorakhpur. Table 5.1 gives the factors considered important for a leather goods manufacturing facility and their factor ratings.

## Exhibit 5.4 Biocon in Andhra Pradesh

Kiran Mazumdar-Shaw was born on 23 March 1953 in Bangalore. She had her schooling at Bishop Cotton Girls School and Mount Carmel College at Bangalore. After completing her B.Sc. in Zoology from Bangalore University in 1973, she went to Ballarat University in Melbourne, Australia and qualified as a master brewer.

Kiran Mazumdar-Shaw started her professional career as a trainee brewer in Carlton & United Beverages in 1974. In 1978, she joined as Trainee Manager with Biocon Biochemicals Limited in Ireland. In the same year, Mazumdar-Shaw founded Biocon India, in collaboration with Biocon Biochemicals Limited, with a capital of ₹10,000. She initially faced many problems regarding funds for her business. Banks were hesitant to give a loan to her as biotechnology was a totally new field at that time and she was a woman entrepreneur, which was a rare phenomenon.

Biocon's initial operation was to extract an enzyme from papaya. Under Mazumdar-Shaw's stewardship Biocon transformed from an industrial enzymes company to an integrated biopharmaceutical company with strategic research initiatives. In 1989, Unilever PLC acquired the Ireland-based Biocon Biochemicals Ltd and merged it with its subsidiary, Quest International. Later, in 1998, Unilever sold its specialty chemicals division (including Quest International) to ICI. However, Unilever agreed to sell its shareholding in Biocon India to the Indian promoters. Hence, Biocon India became an independent entity. Today, Biocon is recognized as India's pioneering biotech enterprise. In 2004, Biocon floated its initial public offering (IPO) and the issue was over-subscribed by over 30 times. Post-IPO, Mazumdar-Shaw held close to 40 per cent of the stock of the company. She is regarded as India's richest woman with an estimated worth of ₹21 billion. She is currently the CMD of Biocon and is ranked 16th in the Billionaire Club. She has also received an honorary Doctorate of Science, from her alma mater, Ballarat University, in recognition of her pre-eminent contributions to the field of biotechnology. Recently she also received an Honorary Doctorate from the Manipal Academy of Higher Education (MAHE), in recognition of her outstanding achievements in biotechnology and industrial enzymes. She is married to John Shaw, a Scotsman and Indophile, who headed Madura Coats, a leading textiles MNC, from 1991–1998 as Chairman and Managing Director. John Shaw has since joined Biocon as Director, International Business, and is the Vice Chairman of the Board.

In April 2006, Biocon invested ₹1 billion in collaboration with Cuba's Centre for Molecular Immunology to make monoclonal antibodies for cancer and autoimmune diseases. This joint venture is named Biocon Biopharmaceuticals Biologics. It is India's largest multi-product biologics facility and is located in Bangalore's Biocon Park. The 1,20,000 sq. ft building, spread over three floors, comprises process, laboratory, and technical support areas. It is regarded as a significant advancement in terms of technical sophistication over the company's existing facilities and comprises three distinct modules. The state-of-the-art facility is designed to manufacture a broad range of novel and bio-similar therapeutic products through large scale cell culture fermentation for the treatment of cancer, auto-immune, and metabolic diseases. The facility is also designed to cater to contract manufacturing needs of international bio-pharmaceutical companies.

In February 2007, Mazumdar-Shaw preferred to set up a ₹10 billion manufacturing facility at Jawahar Pharma City, a special economic zone (SEZ) in Andhra Pradesh near Vishakhapatnam (also known as Vizag) over Bangalore. According to her, 'Karnataka does not provide any infrastructural support for industries such as ours, while Andhra Pradesh is keen to do so. In Bangalore, IT and hardware sector get all the support. Karnataka does not seem to be aware of the needs of our industry. Effluent treatment is expensive, captive power generation is also very costly. The state has become too expensive. Hence, we have thought of an alternative location for our second facility in India. But we will continue to invest in the Bangalore facility as far as R&D is concerned. We have decided to carry out only research activities at our Bangalore facility. All manufacturing-related work will be done at Vizag.'

Biocon also set up a centre on a 10 acre plot in the Hyderabad biotech SEZ developed by the Andhra Pradesh State Industrial Infrastructure Corporation. The SEZ in Andhra Pradesh has a state-of-the-art effluent treatment plant with marine discharge facility. The state has promised Biocon uninterrupted power and water supply. It has been keen to get Mazumdar-Shaw invest in the state ever since it realized the biotech major is unhappy over Bangalore's infrastructure.

**Table 5.1** Factor ratings for a leather goods manufacturing facility

| Factor | Factor ratings |
|---|---|
| Close proximity to markets | 3 |
| Close proximity to raw material (leather) | 5 |
| Transportation facilities | 4 |
| Basic amenities | 2 |
| Acceptance of a leather factory by the local people | 4 |
| Availability of cheap land | 3 |
| Low construction costs | 1 |
| Easy availability of cheap and skill ful/efficient labour | 3 |

Now, with respect to each of the three locations, let us give each of these factors another rating, called the *location rating*, according to the benefits a particular location option offers. Location ratings vary from 1 to 10. A rating of 10 is given to the most beneficial factor at that particular location. Similarly, a rating of 1 is given to the least beneficial factor at that location. Table 5.2 gives the location ratings for the leather goods manufacturing facility.

Hence, we observe that the total score of Unnao is the highest, followed by Noida. This technique is used for screening locations with higher scores, which are then subjected to final analysis for finding the best location option (Table 5.2).

**Table 5.2** Location ratings for a leather goods manufacturing facility

| Factor | Factor ratings | Location ratings | | |
|---|---|---|---|---|
| | | Unnao | Noida | Gorakhpur |
| Proximity to markets | 3 | 4 | 6 | 3 |
| Proximity to raw material (leather) | 5 | 10 | 5 | 4 |
| Transportation facilities | 4 | 9 | 10 | 5 |
| Basic amenities | 2 | 6 | 7 | 6 |
| Acceptance of a leather factory by the local people | 4 | 8 | 3 | 7 |
| Availability of cheap land | 3 | 7 | 2 | 8 |
| Low construction costs | 1 | 5 | 1 | 6 |
| Easy availability of cheap and skillful/efficient labour | 3 | 3 | 8 | 4 |

For each location, let us find the product of factor and location ratings:

| Unnao | Noida | Gorakhpur |
|---|---|---|
| $3 \times 4 = 12$ | $3 \times 6 = 18$ | $3 \times 3 = 9$ |
| $5 \times 10 = 50$ | $5 \times 5 = 25$ | $5 \times 4 = 20$ |
| $4 \times 9 = 36$ | $4 \times 10 = 40$ | $4 \times 5 = 20$ |
| $2 \times 6 = 12$ | $2 \times 7 = 14$ | $2 \times 6 = 12$ |
| $4 \times 8 = 32$ | $4 \times 3 = 12$ | $4 \times 7 = 28$ |
| $3 \times 7 = 21$ | $3 \times 2 = 6$ | $3 \times 8 = 24$ |
| $1 \times 5 = 5$ | $1 \times 1 = 1$ | $1 \times 6 = 6$ |
| $3 \times 3 = 9$ | $3 \times 8 = 24$ | $3 \times 4 = 12$ |
| 177 | 140 | 131 |

# Break-even Analysis for Facility Location Planning

The conversion process from inputs to outputs involves two types of costs, namely, the fixed cost and the variable cost. Fixed costs are the capital expenditures (long-term investments in fixed assets), for example, cost of land, construction of building, and cost of machines and equipment. These costs remain constant, irrespective of the volume of production (number of units produced within a given duration) (Fig. 5.5).

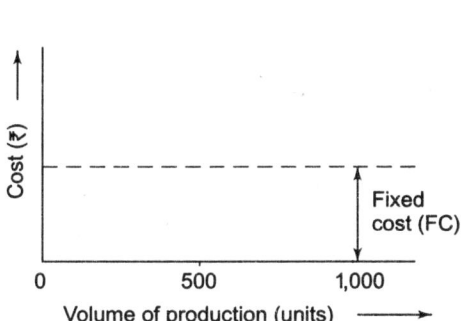

**Fig. 5.5** Volume of production vs cost

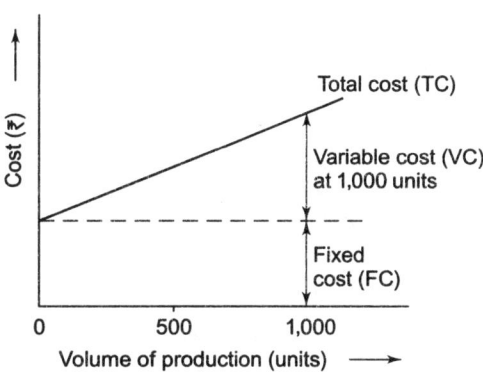

**Fig. 5.6** Total cost as a sum of fixed and variable costs

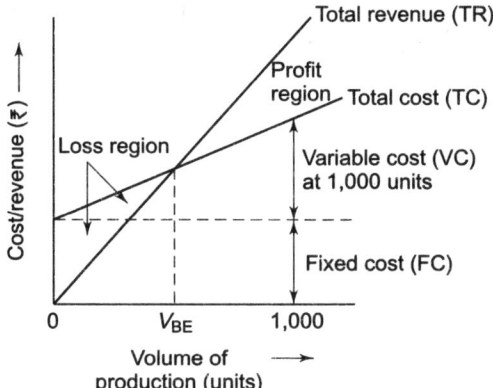

**Fig. 5.7** Graph showing TR, TC, and the break-even volume $V_{BE}$

In Fig. 5.5, we see that at the production of zero units, 500 units, and 1,000 units, the fixed cost remains the same. Variable cost is the cost of labour (directly involved in the production process) and raw material. As the volume of production increases, more labour and raw material are required for production and, thus, the variable cost increases.

When the variable cost (VC) is added to the fixed cost (FC), we get the total cost (TC) at a particular volume of production (Fig. 5.6).

We now draw the total revenue (TR) curve. Revenue is the money that comes into a firm when it sells its products at sales price. The TR curve is a straight line from the origin at a particular slope, which represents the sales price of an item (Fig. 5.7).

Figure 5.7 shows that the region where TR is more than TC is the region of profit, while the region where TR is less than TC is the region of loss. The point at which TR = TC is the *break-even point*, which corresponds to the *break-even volume* $V_{BE}$ at the x-axis. $V_{BE}$ represents the volume of output at which there is no profit and no loss. All the expenses incurred are completely covered by the revenue generated.

An organization always prefers to have a low break-even volume so that its investments can be completely recovered soon. In facility location planning, a location at which the break-even volume is lower is preferred. The fixed cost and the variable costs may be different at different location options and,

> The conversion process from inputs to outputs involves two types of costs, namely fixed cost and the variable cost.

> Revenue is the money that comes into a firm when it sells its products at sales price.

hence, these options may have different values of $V_{BE}$ (Fig. 5.8). Clearly,. in Fig. 5.8, the best location option is location 4, with visibly the lest value of $V_{BE}$ [Fig. 5.8(d)].

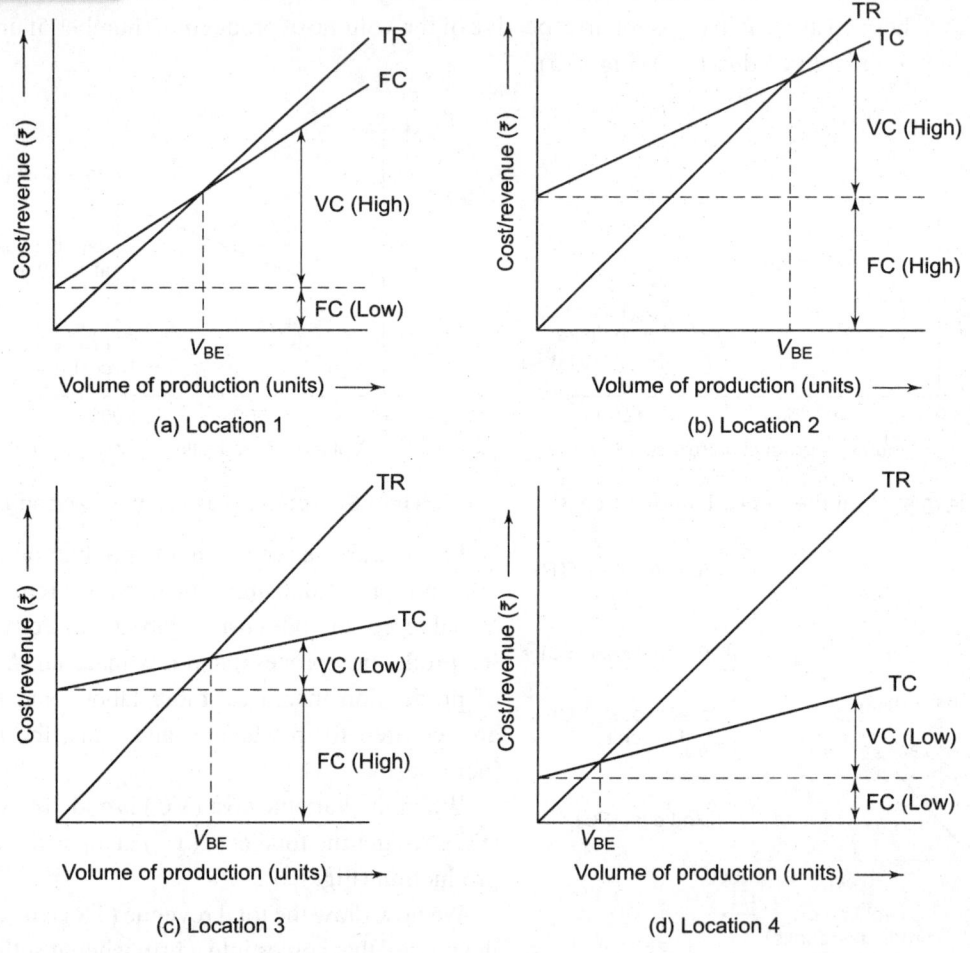

**Fig. 5.8** $V_{BE}$ at four different locations

As shown earlier in Fig. 5.2, break-even analysis is more suitable for screening the better location options rather than for selecting the best one.

### Facility Experiencing Very High Demand Increasing at a High Rate

> Break-even analysis is useful for deciding upon capacity expansion of the facility, creating more facilities, and operating them in more shifts.

When the demand of products manufactured/services offered by a facility is very high and is increasing at a high rate, break-even analysis is useful for deciding upon capacity expansion of the facility, creating more facilities, and operating them in more shifts.

Let us consider an example. A company has recently commissioned a plant called plant $X$ for manufacturing a popular product. The product has high demand in the market. The plant has a break-even point $V_{BE}(X)$ and its maximum capacity of production is $V_{max}(X)$ with a total cost of TC($X$) (Fig. 5.9).

The company's brand gains more popularity, and to meet further demand, the company decides to run plant X in two shifts. Now, the total cost curve has a steeper slope for the double shift because the labour unions have negotiated with the management for giving higher wages to the workers operating in the night shift. The variable cost also increases because of more wear and tear of the machines and equipment and, thus, higher maintenace cost is incurred (Fig. 5.10).

Plant $X$ now produces a maximum of $V_{max}(X)_{DS}$ units by incurring a total cost of TC($X$)$_{DS}$.

The demand for the product keeps on soaring, compelling the company to expand the capacity of the plant by incurring a fixed cost FC($X$)$_{exp}$ (Fig. 5.11).

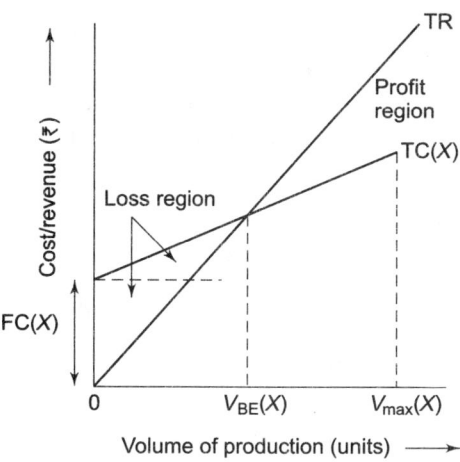

**Fig. 5.9** Graph showing initial values of $V_{BE}$ and $V_{max}$ for plant X

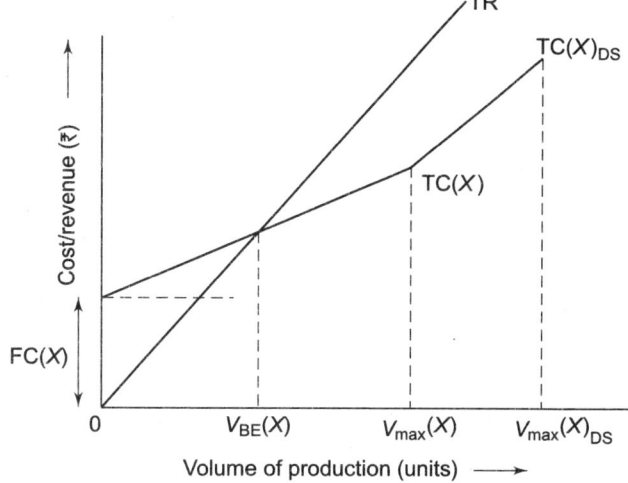

**Fig. 5.10** Graph depicting change in $V_{max}$ after plant X introduces a double shift

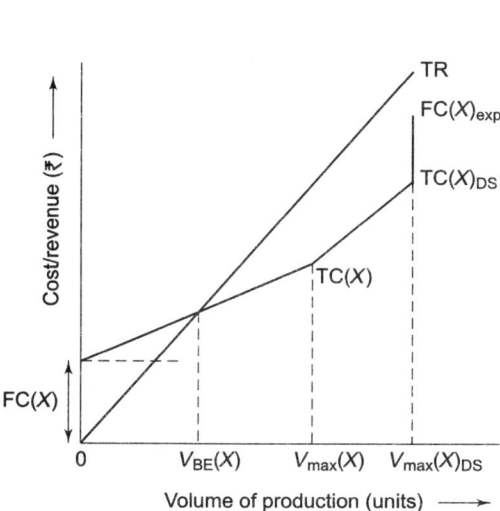

**Fig. 5.11** Graph showing expansion of plant X with fixed cost FC(X)$_{exp}$

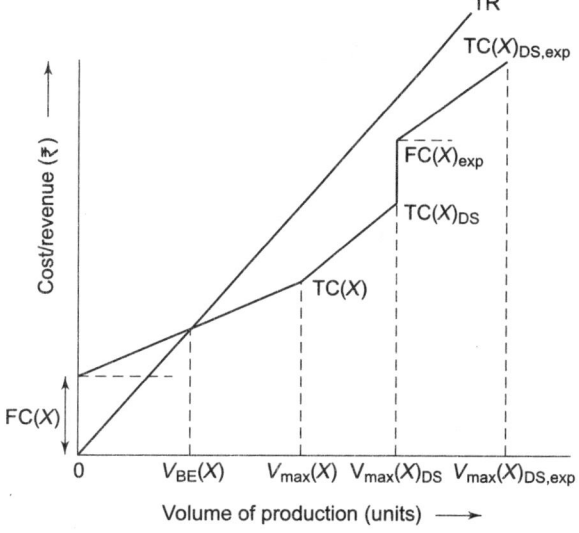

**Fig. 5.12** Graph depicting plant X operating in its full capacity

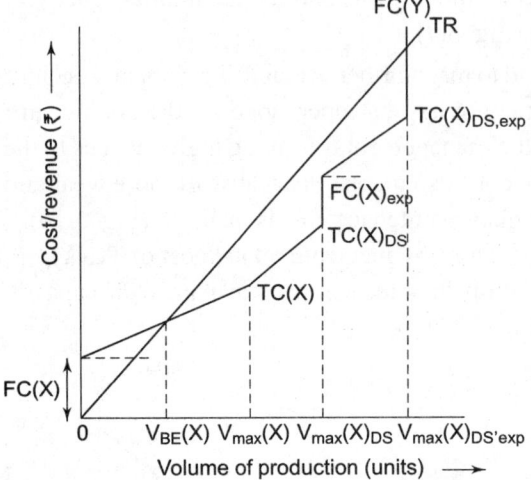

**Fig. 5.13** Graph depicting the commissioning of a second plant Y

Once the plant starts operating in its fully expanded capacity, it produces a maximum of $V_{\max}(X)_{DS,\exp}$ items with a total cost of $TC(X)_{DS,\exp}$ (Fig. 5.12).

The company has now been able to capture a large market share. To retain its market position, it decides to commission a second plant, $Y$, by incurring a fixed cost of $FC(Y)$ (Fig. 5.13). Plant $Y$, after commissioning, increases the production capacity of the company to $V_{\max}((X)_{DS,\exp} + (Y))$ with a total cost of $TC((X)_{DS,\exp} + (Y))$. The combined break-even point of the two plants is $V_{BE}((X)_{DS,\exp} + (Y))$ (Fig. 5.14).

The company knows that, if need be, it can operate plant $Y$ also in two shifts pushing the maximum production capacity to $V_{\max}((X)_{DS,\exp} + (Y)_{DS})$ units by incurring a total cost of $TC((X_{DS,\exp} + (Y)_{DS})$ (see Fig. 5.15).

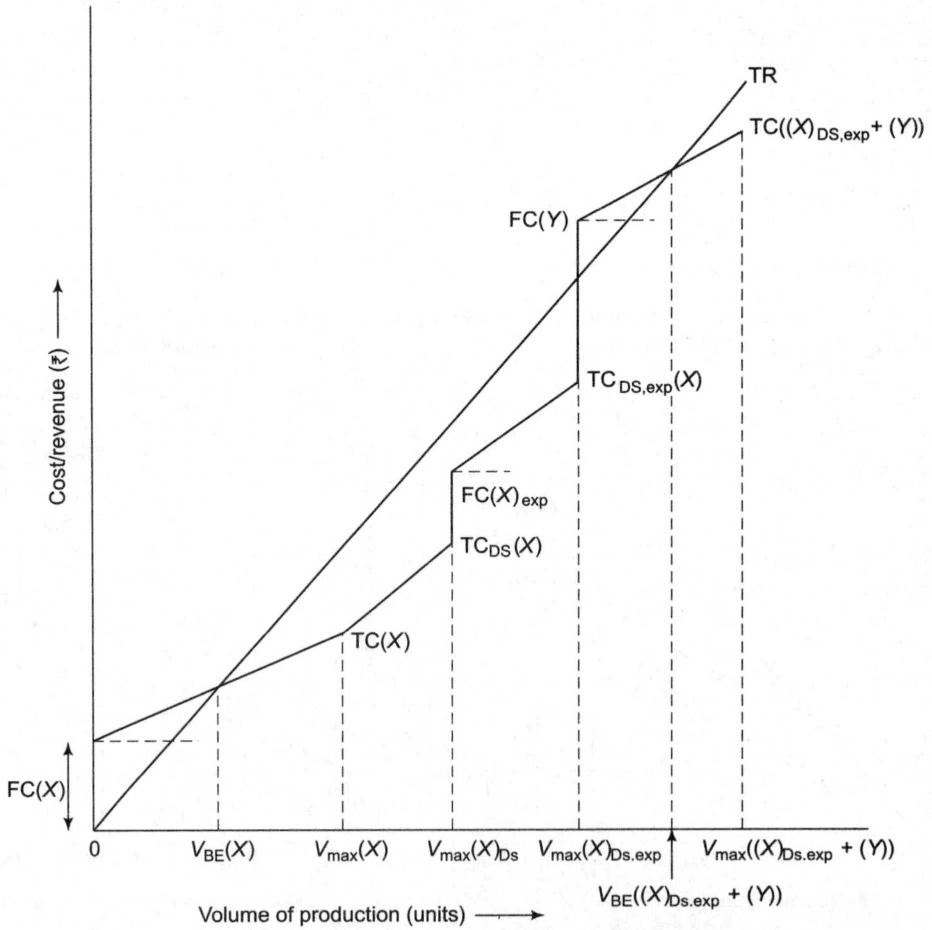

**Fig. 5.14** Increased production capacity after commissioning of plant Y

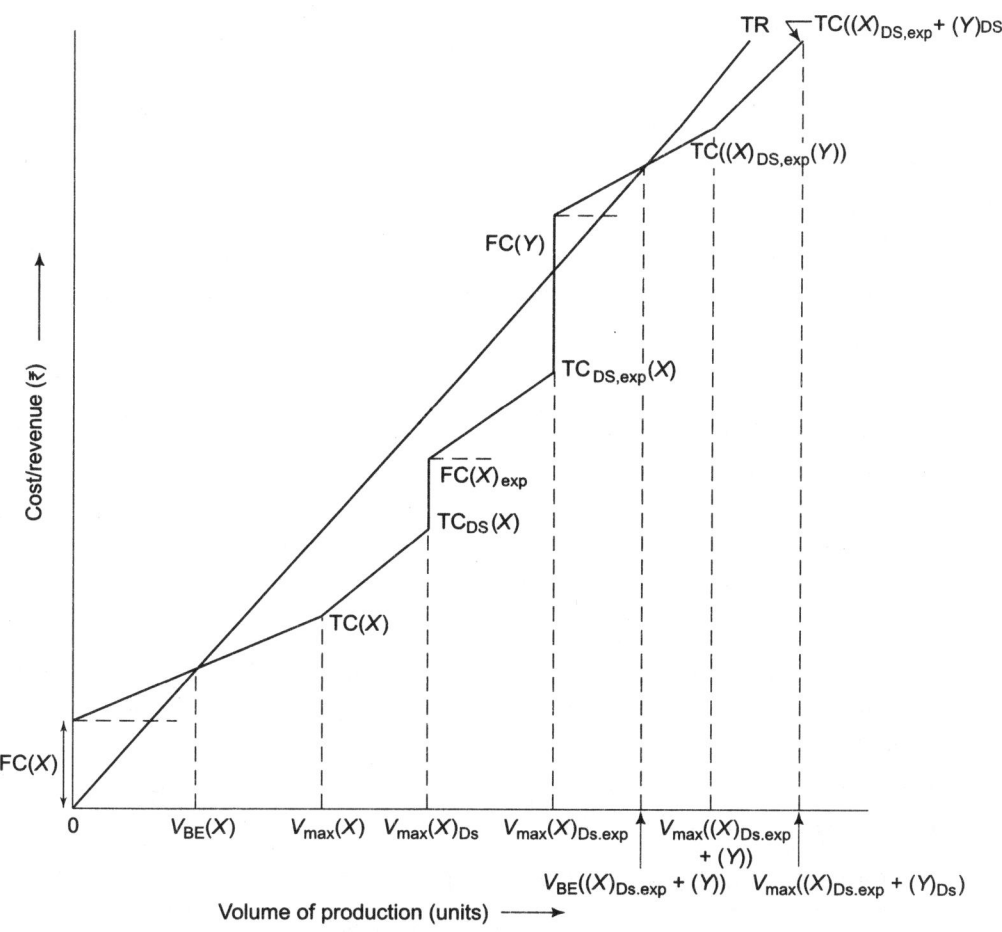

**Fig. 5.15** Change in V_max after plant Y introduces a double shift

### Example 5.1

Triveni Steels (P) Ltd is planning to start a new factory for manufacturing steel utensils. It is considering three location options, namely, Bokaro, Jamshedpur, and Bhilai. The fixed costs at the three locations have been estimated at ₹8.15 million, ₹7.377 million, and ₹7.903 million, respectively. The variable costs at the three locations are estimated at ₹500 per unit, ₹580 per unit, and ₹490 per unit, respectively. The factory will have an annual production capacity of 10,000 steel utensils and in the initial years it will operate at 75% efficiency. Find the best location option, which has the lowest total cost of production.

### Solution

At 75% efficiency, the factory will annually produce

$$75\% \text{ of } 10,000 \text{ units} = 7,500 \text{ units}$$

Total production cost

$$TC = FC + VC \times \text{no. of units}$$

For Bokaro,

$$TC = 81,50,000 + 500 \times 7,500 = 81,50,000 + 37,50,000 = ₹1,19,00,000$$

For Jamshedpur,
$$TC = 73,77,000 + 580 \times 7,500 = 73,77,000 + 43,50,000 = ₹1,17,27,000$$
For Bhilai,
$$TC = 79,03,000 + 490 \times 7,500 = 79,03,000 + 36,75,000 = ₹1,15,78,000$$
Hence, Bhilai is the best location from the economic point of view, as the total cost is minimum there.

### Example 5.2

Sigma Instruments (P) Ltd is considering three locations for its new factory—Faridabad, Kolkata, and New Delhi. The estimates of different costs for the three location options are shown in Table 5.3.

**Table 5.3**

|  | Faridabad | Kolkata | New Delhi |
|---|---|---|---|
| Transportation cost (₹per unit) | 10 | 20 | 9 |
| Cost of materials (₹per unit) | 120 | 110 | 100 |
| Taxes (₹per year) | 40,000 | 35,000 | 45,000 |
| Cost of construction of the factory (₹) | 5 million | 4 million | 4.7 million |
| Electricity (₹ per year) | 22,000 | 15,000 | 25,000 |
| Labour (₹ per unit) | 26 | 21 | 23 |

The company has financed the construction cost of the factory by a loan from the State Bank of India at 15% interest per annum. Find the economically best location option for the production of 5,000–10,000 units.

### Solution

Fixed cost (per annum):

**Table 5.4**  Comparison of fixed costs

|  | Faridabad | Kolkata | New Delhi |
|---|---|---|---|
| Cost of construction of the factory (₹) (15% of investment) | 7,50,000 | 6,00,000 | 7,05,000 |
| Electricity (₹ per year) | 22,000 | 15,000 | 25,000 |
| Taxes (₹ per year) | 40,000 | 35,000 | 45,000 |
|  | 8,12,000 | 6,50,000 | 7,75,000 |

Variable cost (per unit):

**Table 5.5**  Comparison of variable costs

|  | Faridabad | Kolkata | New Delhi |
|---|---|---|---|
| Transportation cost (₹ per unit) | 10 | 20 | 9 |
| Cost of materials (₹ per unit) | 120 | 110 | 100 |
| Labour (₹ per unit) | 26 | 21 | 23 |
|  | 156 | 151 | 132 |

Let us calculate the total cost of production for 5,000 units for each of the three location options using the costs given in Tables 5.4 and 5.5.

For Faridabad,
$$TC = FC + VC \times \text{no. of units} = 8,12,000 + 156 \times 5,000$$
$$= 8,12,000 + 7,80,000 = ₹15,92,000$$

For Kolkata,

$$TC = FC + VC \times \text{no. of units} = 6,50,000 + 151 \times 5,000$$
$$= 6,50,000 + 7,55,000 = ₹14,05,000$$

For New Delhi,

$$TC = FC + VC \times \text{no. of units} = 775,000 + 132 \times 5,000$$
$$= 7,75,000 + 6,60,000 = ₹14,35,000$$

Let us now calculate the total cost of production for 10,000 units for each of the three location options (Table 5.6).

For Faridabad,

$$TC = FC + VC \times \text{no. of units} = 8,12,000 + 156 \times 10,000$$
$$= 8,12,000 + 15,60,000 = ₹23,72,000$$

For Kolkata,

$$TC = FC + VC \times \text{no. of units} = 6,50,000 + 151 \times 10,000$$
$$= 6,50,000 + 15,10,000 = ₹21,60,000$$

For New Delhi,

$$TC = FC + VC \times \text{no. of units} = 7,75,000 + 132 \times 10,000$$
$$= 7,75,000 + 13,20,000 = ₹20,95,000$$

**Table 5.6**   Total cost of production (in ₹) at three locations

| Units | Faridabad | Kolkata | New Delhi |
|---|---|---|---|
| 0 | 8,12,000 | 6,50,000 | 7,75,000 |
| 5,000 | 15,92,000 | 14,05,000 | 14,35,000 |
| 10,000 | 23,72,000 | 21,60,000 | 20,95,000 |

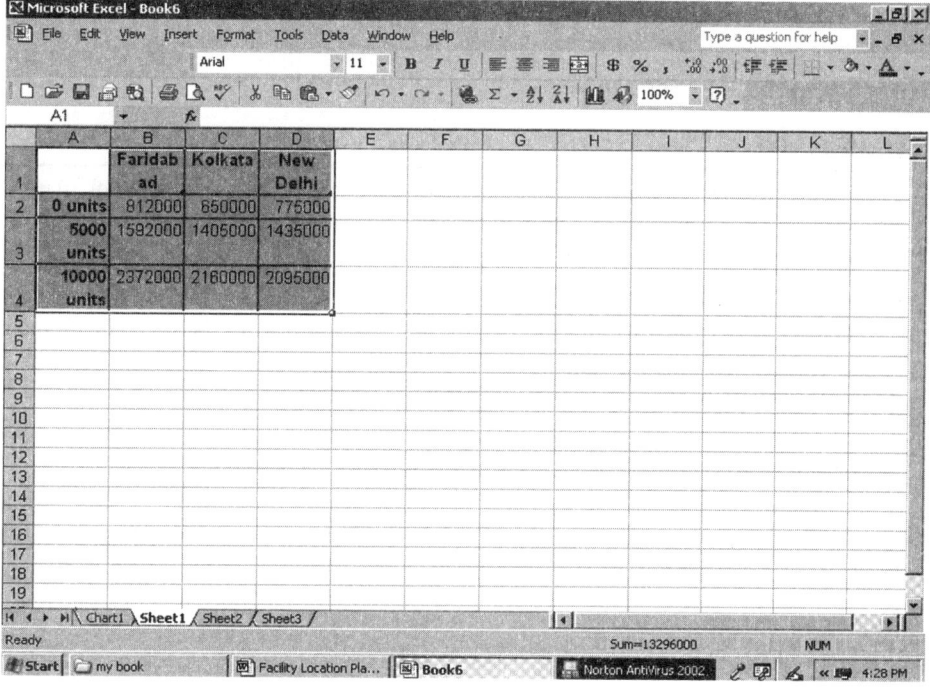

**Fig. 5.16**   MS Excel workheet showing data from Table 5.6

Copy Table 5.6 and paste it in a MS Excel worksheet as shown in Fig. 5.16. Select all the columns in the worksheet and then click on the **Insert** button in the toolbar. From the pull-down menu, select **Chart**. A chart wizard guides us through to get the chart shown in Fig. 5.17.

In the chart, we see that Kolkata is the most economical location for a production capacity of around 6,000 units or less (as its total cost curve is below the curves for New Delhi and Faridabad). For a production capacity of more than 6,000 units, New Delhi is the most economical location.

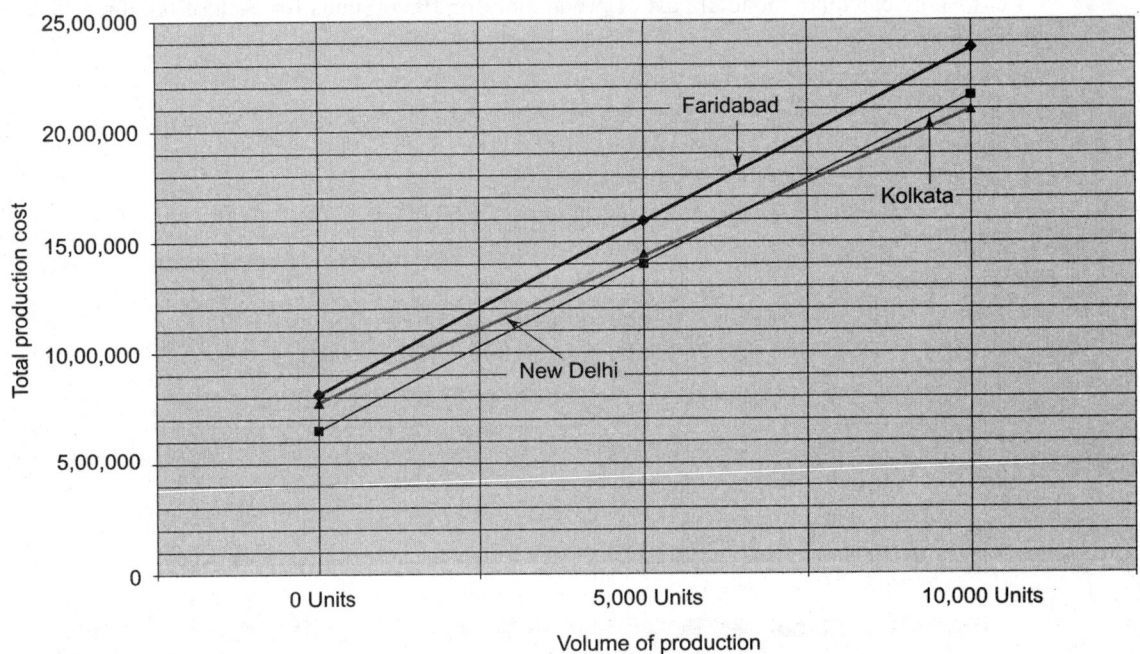

**Fig. 5.17**   Chart showing total production cost vs volume of production

### Example 5.3

Time Clocks Ltd is considering two location options for locating its new clock manufacturing facility, Pune and Noida. The company has its existing manufacturing facility at Chennai, which caters to the markets in the southern part of the country. The new plant will cater to the northern and central regions of the country.

The company estimates that the FC and VC at Pune for the facility are ₹2 million and ₹30 per clock, respectively. On the other hand, at Noida, the FC and VC are estimated at ₹1.8 million and ₹40 per clock, respectively.

The sales revenue estimates are also different for the two locations because of the consumers' perception of the quality of products manufactured at Pune being better. A clock can be sold for ₹100 if manufactured at Noida, and the same clock can fetch ₹120 if manufactured at Pune.

The management of the company will choose that location option for its new facility at which the break-even volume is lower. Which option should the company choose according to this criterion?

### Solution

Table 5.7 shows the estimates for Noida.

**Table 5.7**    TC and TR at Noida

| Volume of production (n) (1,000 units) | Total cost (₹) = FC + VC × n = 18,00,000 + 40 × n | Total revenue (₹) = selling price × n = 100 × n |
|---|---|---|
| 0 | 18,00,000 | 0 |
| 10 | 22,00,000 | 10,00,000 |
| 20 | 26,00,000 | 20,00,000 |
| 30 | 30,00,000 | 30,00,000 |
| 40 | 34,00,000 | 40,00,000 |
| 50 | 38,00,000 | 50,00,000 |

Table 5.8 shows the estimates for Pune.

**Table 5.8**    TC and TR at Pune

| Volume of production (n) (1,000 units) | Total cost (₹) = FC + VC × n = 20,00,000 + 30 × n | Total revenue (₹) = selling price × n = 120 × n |
|---|---|---|
| 0 | 20,00,000 | 0 |
| 10 | 23,00,000 | 12,00,000 |
| 20 | 26,00,000 | 24,00,000 |
| 30 | 29,00,000 | 36,00,000 |
| 40 | 32,00,000 | 48,00,000 |
| 50 | 35,00,000 | 60,00,000 |

From Figs 5.18(b) and 5.19(b), we see that the break-even volume for Pune is 22,000 units as compared to 30,000 units for Noida. Therefore, Pune is a better locaion according to this criterion.

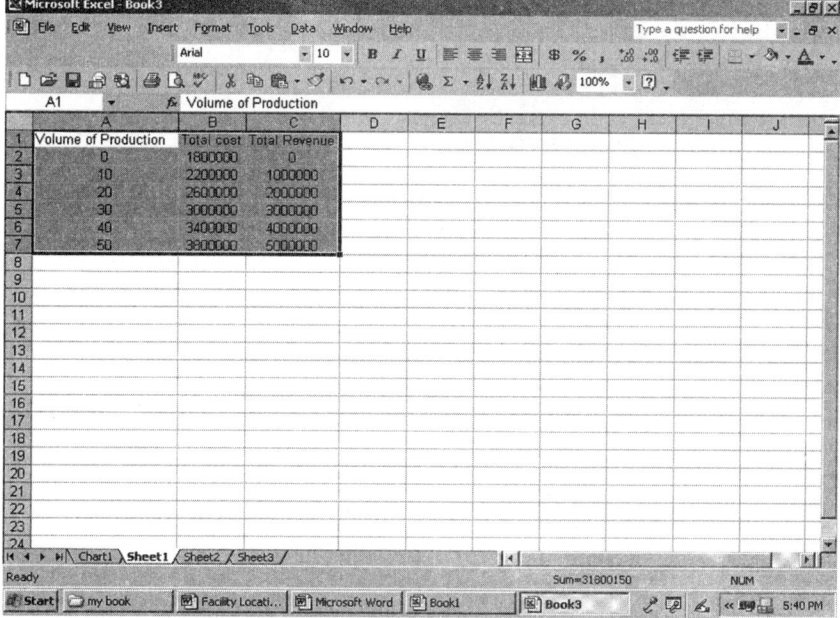

**Fig. 5.18(a)**    MS Excel workheet showing data from Table 5.7

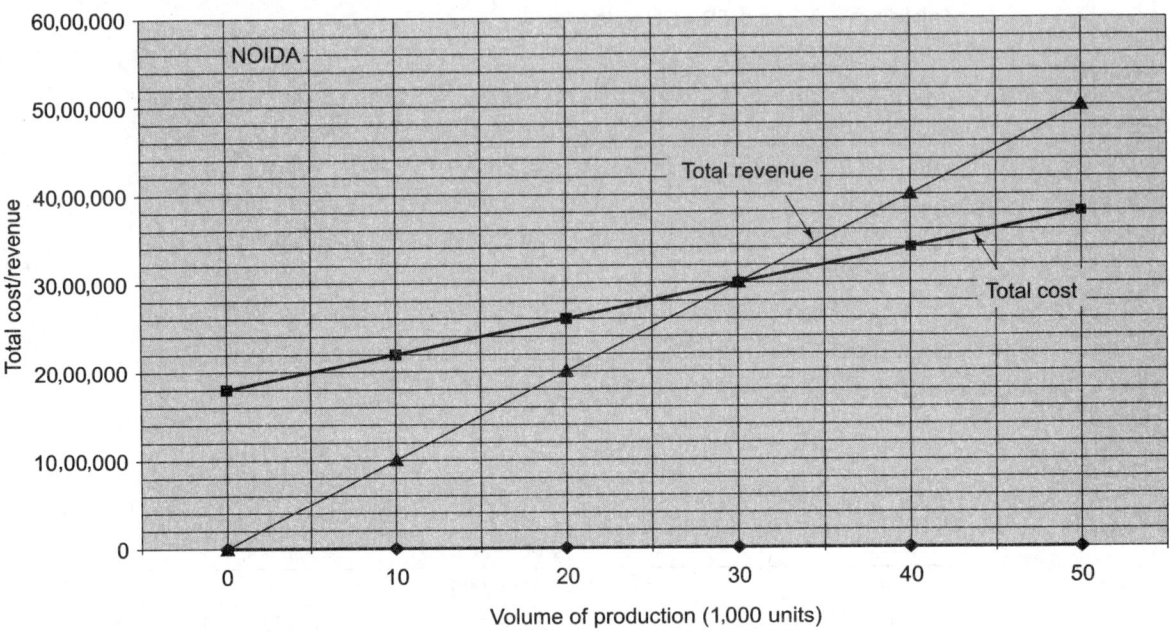

**Fig. 5.18(b)** Chart showing volume of production (n) vs total cost/revenue for Noida

**Fig. 5.19(a)** MS Excel workheet showing data from Table 5.8

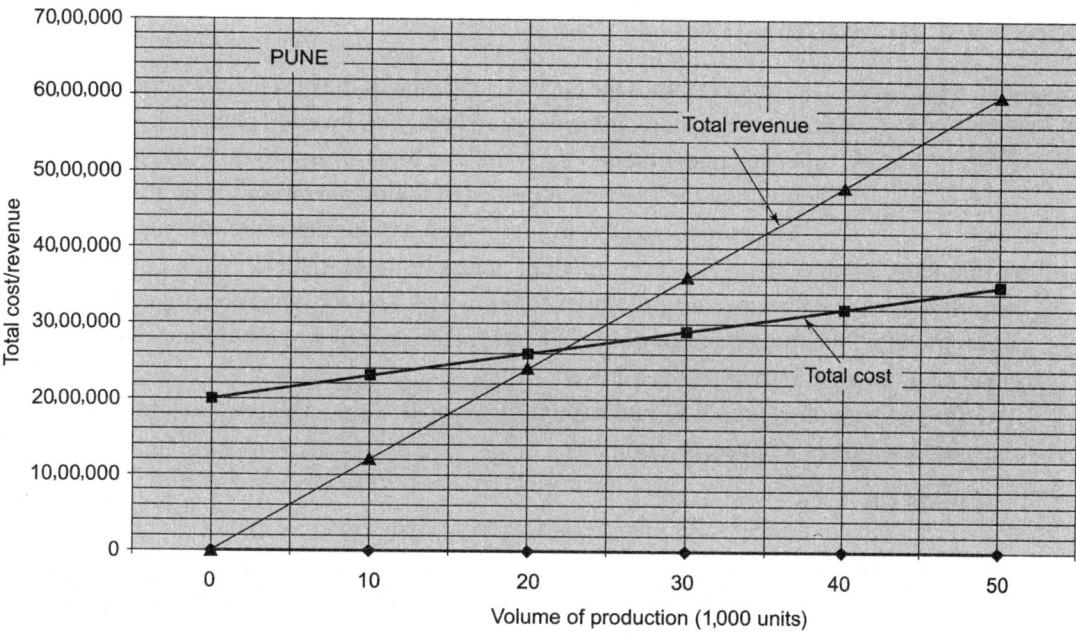

**Fig. 5.19(b)** Chart showing volume of production (n) vs total cost/revenue for Pune

Companies have sometimes taken decisions to look for other locations based on labour unrest (Exhibit 5.5).

---

### Exhibit 5.5  Maruti Suzuki in Gujarat

On 18 July 2012, in an unprecedented agitation by workers at the Manesar (Haryana) plant of Maruti Suzuki Ltd, an HR manager was burnt to death, while 100 persons were injured in clashes. The disparity between wages given to the permanent and temporary workers is said to be one of the reasons for these violent protests. The Manesar plant was locked out for a month by Maruti, which incurred per day loss of about ₹80 crores due to the lockout. The plant was reopened amidst heavy security on 21 August 2012 with a curtailed worker strength of 300, which could achieve only 10 per cent of the production capacity. Earlier, about 500 workers were sacked by the company on grounds of disciplinary action. Maruti would gradually increase the worker strength in the plant after suitably modifying its hiring policies. The plant manufactures the popular Swift and D'zire models and its lockout/reduced production before the festive season impacted Maruti's profitability.

During the past several years, other factories in Haryana and Delhi/NCR region have witnessed violent protests by workers. In 2005, about 150 people were seriously injured in clashes between police and agitating workers at the Gurgaon (Haryana) plant of Honda Motorcycle and Scooters India (HMSI). In September 2008, the chief executive officer of an Italian MNC Graziano was bludgeoned to death by agitating workers who were dismissed a month earlier.

Having seen unwarranted agitations by worker unions earlier at its Gurgaon plant, Maruti Suzuki was already considering setting up its new plant in Gujarat. The incident at Manesar seems to have provided a further push to this process. On 25 August 2012, Osamu Suzuki, the Chairman of Suzuki Motor Corp., visited the proposed 700-acre site at Hansalpur near Mehsana (Gujarat). Officials of the Gujarat state government accompanied him and promised full support in setting up the proposed plant, such as conversion of the metre gauge railway line between Kadi and Bharurachi to broad gauge and setting up of power sub-stations, to meet the requirements of the proposed plant. Maruti Suzuki was pleased with the welcoming gestures shown by the local people there and planned to set up the new plant with a capacity to roll out 2.5 lakh cars annually by 2015–2016 at an investment of ₹4,000 crore.

## Simple Median Model

Transportation cost is a major consideration in facility location planning.

This model is used for the final selection of the best location option. Transportation cost is a major consideration in facility location planning. This model helps to locate a new facility such that the total transportation cost between the new facility and the existing facilities of the organization is minimum.

The model is very simple in application; therefore, the name of the model has the term 'simple' in it. The term 'median' refers to the statistical median of the loads to be transported between the existing facilities and the new facility. The model has the simplifying assumption that the movement of goods can take place only in two directions, namely, the $x$ and $y$ axes. No diagonal movement is allowed.

Let us take up an example to understand this model. Table 5.9 gives information about the existing facilities of a beverage company.

**Table 5.9**

| Facility (F) | Coordinate location (x,y) | Cost (C) of moving one unit by unit distance (₹) | Annual load (L) (units) |
|---|---|---|---|
| Bareilly | (10,80) | 10 | 452 |
| Shahjahanpur | (30,60) | 10 | 678 |
| Gonda | (80,50) | 10 | 483 |
| Kanpur | (50,10) | 10 | 711 |
| Sultanpur | (80,10) | 10 | 539 |
| | | | 2,863 |

The existing facilities may be the factories, warehouses, or markets of the company. The company wants to know where it should locate its new plant. The annual load (in units) is the goods to be moved between a facility (*F*) and the new plant (NP). Plot the existing facilities of the company on the coordinate axes as shown in Fig. 5.20.

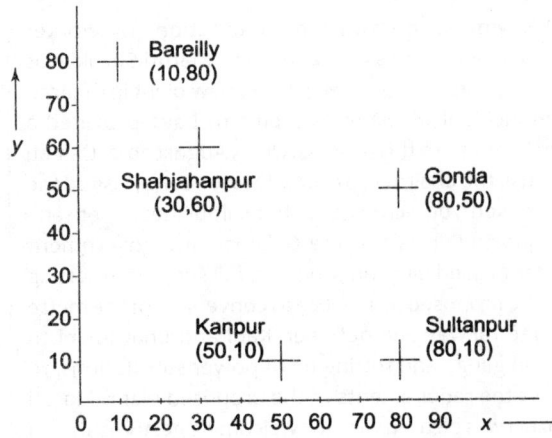

**Fig. 5.20**  Plot of existing facilities for the simple median model

The simple median model can be used in three steps.

**Step 1: Find the median load**   Add the annual loads given for all the existing facilities. The sum is 2,863 units. This is an odd number. Assume that the loads are marked with identification numbers starting from 1 to 2,863. Hence, we may say that the loads are arranged in the ascending order of numbering (a requirement for finding the median). For odd numbers, the median is the

$$\frac{(n+1)}{2} \text{ th item}$$

Therefore, (2,863 + 1)/2, that is, 1,432 units, is the median load.

For even number of loads, the average of two items in the centre of the series of items in ascending order is the median load.

**Step 2: Find the x-coordinate of the new plant**   Move from the extreme left towards the right along the positive $x$-axis. In doing so, we come across Bareilly first, being located at the extreme left of the $x$-axis. Assume that loads 1–452 have to be moved between Bareilly and the NP as Bareilly's annual load is 452. This range does not include the median load 1,432. Therefore, we move further towards the right and come across Shahjahanpur next. Assume that loads 453–1,130 (678 is the annual load for Shahjahanpur) are moved between Shahjahanpur and the NP. This range does not include the median load 1,432. We move again towards the right and come across Kanpur now. Assume that loads 1,131–1,842 (712 is the annual load for Kanpur) are moved between Kanpur and the NP. This range includes the median load 1,432. Therefore, the $x$-coordinate of the new plant is same as the $x$-coordinate of Kanpur, that is, 50.

$$x_0 = 50$$

**Step 3: Find the y-coordinate of the new plant**   Move from the bottom along the positive $y$-axis. In doing so, we come first across Kanpur and Sultanpur simultaneously. Assume that loads 1–1,250 have to be moved between Kanpur and the NP, and Sultanpur and the NP (as Kanpur and Sultanpur have annual loads of 711 and 539, respectively). This range does not include the median load 1,432. Therefore, we move further upwards and come across Gonda next. Assume that loads 1,251–1,733 (483 is the annual load for Gonda) are moved between Gonda and the NP. This range includes the median load 1,432. Therefore, the $y$-coordinate of the new plant is same as the $y$-coordinate of Gonda, that is, 50.

$$y_0 = 50$$

As shown in Fig. 5.21, the route to be followed between, say, the NP and Bareilly is represented by a dotted line. The total distance here is

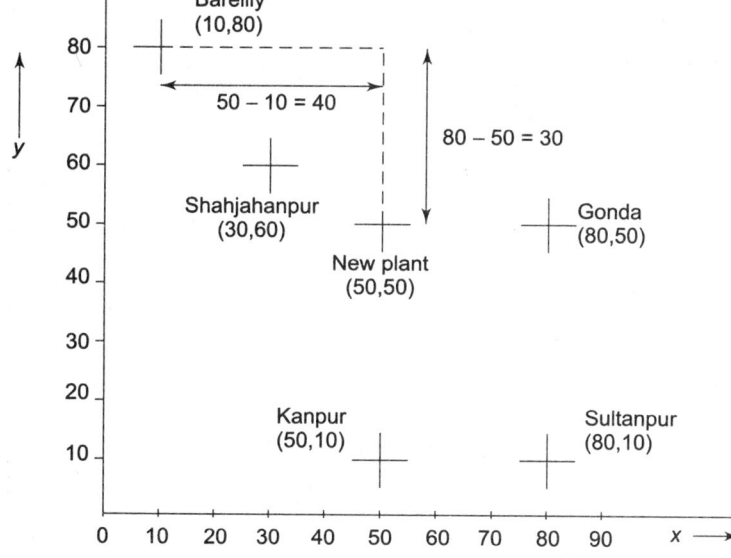

**Fig. 5.21**   Route to be followed between NP and Bareilly

$$|50 - x| + |y - 50|$$
$$= |50 - 10| + |80 - 50|$$
$$= 40 + 30 = 70$$

$(x, y)$ are the coordinates of the existing facility. The parallel lines in $|50 - x|$ mean that only the magnitude of the difference is to be considered, and if the difference is negative, the negative sign is dropped. Similarly, we find the distance between the NP and other existing facilities. Let us now find the total transportation cost involved. Table 5.10 gives the minimum transportation cost for the optimal ocation of the new plant (50,50).

**Table 5.10**

| Facility (F) | Coordinate location (x,y) | Distance (D) | Cost (C) of moving one unit by unit distance (₹) | Annual load (L) (units) | Transportation cost (₹) T = DCL |
|---|---|---|---|---|---|
| Bareilly | (10,80) | 70 | 10 | 452 | 3,16,400 |
| Shahjahanpur | (30,60) | 30 | 10 | 678 | 2,03,400 |
| Gonda | (80,50) | 30 | 10 | 483 | 1,44,900 |
| Kanpur | (50,10) | 40 | 10 | 711 | 2,84,400 |
| Sultanpur | (80,10) | 70 | 10 | 539 | 3,77,300 |
| | | | | | 13,26,400 |

## The Centre of Gravity Method

The centre of gravity method is also simple in approach. The coordinates of the new plant $(x_0, y_0)$ accordig to this method are given by

$$x_0 = \frac{\sum x_i L_i}{\sum L_i} \qquad\qquad y_0 = \frac{\sum y_i L_i}{\sum L_i}$$

where $(x_i, y_i)$ are the coordinates of existing facilities and $L_i$ represent the loads to be transported between the existing facilities and the new plant.

The $x$, $y$ coordinates of the new plant $(x_0, y_0)$ are found by taking the weighted average of the $x,y$ coordinates of all the existing facilities. The loads $L_i$ to be carried between existing facilities and the new plant are the weights used in these calculations, as shown by the above formulae.

Let us consider the same example that we had considered in the simple median model (see Table 5.9).

$$x_0 = \frac{(10 \times 452) + (30 \times 678) + (80 \times 483) + (50 \times 711) + (80 \times 539)}{452 + 678 + 483 + 711 + 539}$$

$$= \frac{4,520 + 20,340 + 38,640 + 35,550 + 43,120}{2,863}$$

$$= \frac{142,170}{2,863} = 49.66$$

$$y_0 = \frac{(80 \times 452) + (60 \times 678) + (50 + 483) + (10 \times 711) + (10 \times 539)}{452 + 678 + 483 + 711 + 539}$$

$$= \frac{36,160 + 40,680 + 24,150 + 7,110 + 5,390}{2,863}$$

$$= \frac{113,490}{2,863} = 39.64$$

# Transportation Model Using MS Excel

The transportation model using MS Excel is based upon linear programming and is much more complicated than the simple median model and the centre of gravity model.

This model is based upon linear programming and is much more complicated than the simple median model and the centre of gravity model. At the same time, it is much more accurate in finding the total transportation cost. Thus, this model is useful for finding the best location with the minimum transportation cost. The complexity of using this model manually can be overcome by using a computer spreadsheet software such as MS Excel, which is what we will use to solve these problems. Let us take up an example to understand the use of this model in facility location planning.

### Example 5.4

Mileage Tyres Ltd has four production facilities located at Chennai (C), Ahmedabad (A), Bhopal (BHO), and Lucknow (L). The company has three major sources of raw materials for its plants at New Delhi (ND), Kolkata (K), and Bhubaneshwar (BHU). It wants a fourth source of raw materials and has identified two options—Bangalore (BANG) and Mumbai (M). Both these suppliers can supply a maximum of 2,000 units of raw material per year.

The company has constructed two tables showing the annual requirement of plants and annual capacity of raw material suppliers. One table (Table 5.11) includes Bangalore as the raw material supplier and the other table (Table 5.12) includes Mumbai as the raw material supplier. The data in the table are the costs of transportation of a unit load of raw material from a raw material supplier to a plant.

Table 5.11 shows that ₹500 is the cost of moving a unit load of raw material from New Delhi to Chennai. Similarly, ₹700 is the cost of moving a unit load of raw material from Kolkata to Chennai. The Chennai plant requires 2,500 units of the raw material annually. Similarly, the Ahmedabad plant requires 1,500 units of the raw material annually. The New Delhi supplier can supply a maximum of 3,500 units annually, and so on.

**Table 5.11**  Transportation costs (in ₹ per unit load) (Bangalore as one of the suppliers)

| Destination → Source ↓ | Chennai | Ahmedabad | Bhopal | Lucknow | **Availability** |
|---|---|---|---|---|---|
| New Delhi | 500 | 300 | 400 | 150 | **3,500** |
| Kolkata | 700 | 600 | 300 | 450 | **1,000** |
| Bhubaneshwar | 100 | 600 | 250 | 550 | **4,500** |
| Bangalore | 200 | 700 | 400 | 750 | **2,000** |
| **Requirement** | **2,500** | **1,500** | **3,000** | **4,000** | **11,000** |

**Table 5.12**  Transportation costs (in ₹ per unit load) (Mumbai as one of the suppliers)

| Destination → Source ↓ | Chennai | Ahmedabad | Bhopal | Lucknow | **Availability** |
|---|---|---|---|---|---|
| New Delhi | 500 | 300 | 400 | 150 | **3,500** |
| Kolkata | 700 | 600 | 300 | 450 | **1,000** |
| Bhubaneshwar | 100 | 600 | 250 | 550 | **4,500** |
| Mumbai | 550 | 200 | 250 | 650 | **2,000** |
| **Requirement** | **2,500** | **1,500** | **3,000** | **4,000** | **11,000** |

Let us place the transportation cost table for the Bangalore option in a MS Excel worksheet as shown in Fig. 5.22. In this figure, the first table contains a formula in cell F6. It is for the sum of cells F2, F3, F4, and F5. Select all these cells including the empty cell F6 and then click on the summation sign in the toolbar. The sum, that is, 11,000, is shown in cell F6.

| | A | B | C | D | E | F | G |
|---|---|---|---|---|---|---|---|
| 1 | From / To | C | A | BHO | L | Availability | |
| 2 | ND | 500 | 300 | 400 | 150 | 3500 | |
| 3 | K | 700 | 600 | 300 | 450 | 1000 | |
| 4 | BHU | 100 | 600 | 250 | 550 | 4500 | |
| 5 | BANG | 200 | 700 | 400 | 750 | 2000 | |
| 6 | Requirement | 2500 | 1500 | 3000 | 4000 | 11000 | |
| 7 | | | | | | | |
| 8 | ND | 2500 | 1000 | 0 | 0 | 3500 | |
| 9 | K | 0 | 500 | 500 | 0 | 1000 | |
| 10 | BHU | 0 | 0 | 2500 | 2000 | 4500 | |
| 11 | BANG | 0 | 0 | 0 | 2000 | 2000 | |
| 12 | Requirement | 2500 | 1500 | 3000 | 4000 | 11000 | 11000 |
| 13 | | | | | | | |
| 14 | ND | 1250000 | 300000 | 0 | 0 | | |
| 15 | K | 0 | 300000 | 150000 | 0 | | |
| 16 | BHU | 0 | 0 | 625000 | 1100000 | | |
| 17 | BANG | 0 | 0 | 0 | 1500000 | | |
| 18 | | | | | | 5225000 | |
| 19 | | | | | | | |
| 20 | | | | | | | |
| 21 | | Transportation Model using MS Excel | | | | | |

**Fig. 5.22** MS Excel worksheet showing the Bangalore option

Let us first calculate the initial basic feasible solution using the north-west corner method in Fig. 5.23. In this method, we start assigning values in the table from the north-west (NW) corner. The NW corner in step 1 of Fig. 5.23 is cell B6. Note that we have shown the availability of raw materials in column F and the requirements in row 10. The total requirement is the same as the total availability, shown in cell F10 as 11,000. The availability of raw materials corresponding to cell B6 is 3,500 units (cell F6) and the requirement is 2,500 units (cell B10). Assign the smaller of these two values, that is, 2,500 to cell B6. This means the requirement of Chennai (2,500 units) has been satisfied completely, but New Delhi still has 1,000 units (3,500 – 2,500) available to be supplied to any other facility. Assign zero to cells B7, B8, and B9 so that the total of the first column in this table is 2,500 units (the total requirement of Chennai).

Now, move to cell C6 corresponding to which the requirement is 1,500 units. Assign the 1,000 units available at New Delhi to cell C6. Thus, New Delhi has no more units available and we assign zero to cells D6 and E6 so that the sum of units in row 1 of this table is 3,500 units (the total availability at New Delhi). Copy the table completed so far in step 1, before starting step 2, into the worksheet in Fig. 5.23 for the sake of clarity, and proceed further. This will not be required once the procedure is understood. All these steps can be performed easily in a single table.

In step 2 of Fig. 5.23, the availability corresponding to cell C17 is 1,000 units and the requirement is 1,500 units (from Ahmedabad). Out of these 1,500 units, we had assigned 1,000 units to cell C6 earlier (i.e., cell C16 in step 2). Thus, only 500 units are effectively required at Ahmedabad. Assign these 500 units to cell C17. There is no further requirement now at Ahmedabad, hence assign zero to cells C18 and C19. In cell D17, the availability is 500 units (1,000 – 500) and the requirement is 3,000 units. Therefore, assign the smaller of the two values, that is, 500 to cell C17. No more raw material is available at Kanpur. Hence assign zero to cell E17.

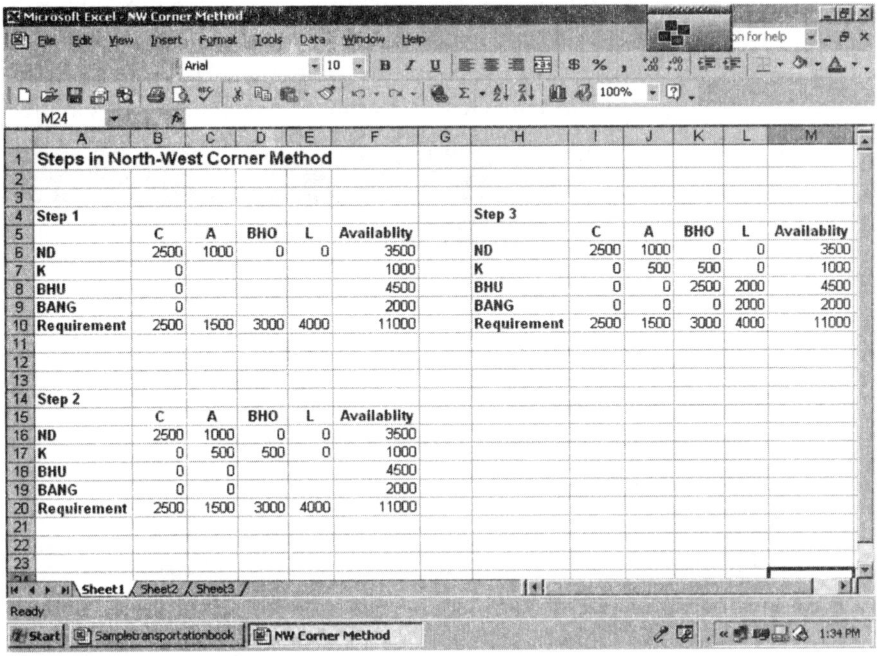

**Fig. 5.23**  Steps used in the north-west corner method

In step 3, at cell K8, the net requirement at Bhopal is 2,500 (3,000 – 500) and the availability at Bhubaneshwar is 4,500 units. Assign the smaller of these two values, that is, 2,500, to cell K8. The requirement at Bhopal is satisfied completely at 3,000 units and we assign zero to cell K9. At cell L8, the net availability is 2,000 units (4,500 – 2,500) and the requirement is 4,000 units. Assign the smaller of the two values, that is, 2,000, to cell L8. At cell L9, the net requirement is 2,000 units (4,000 – 2,000) and the availability is also 2,000 units. Assign 2,000 to cell L9. Thus, the requirements and availabilities at all the cells are satisfied and we have obtained the initial basic feasible solution.

In the second table of Fig. 5.22, we show the initial basic feasible solution using the NW corner method. Find the sum of all the columns and rows using the summation sign as explained before. Also, the sum of row 12 can be found in cell F12. For computing the sum of cells F8, F9, F10, and F11, select cell G12. Enter the sign = in it. Then write the formula **SUM(F8:F11)** and press **Enter**. The sum 11,000 is displayed in cell G12.

Every cell in the third table of Fig. 5.22 is the product of the corresponding cells in the upper two tables. For instance, in cell C14 you will have to write **=C2*C8** and press **Enter**. The product 12,50,000 will be displayed. This value means that for transporting 2,500 units from New Delhi to Chennai at the rate of ₹500 per unit load, the total cost is ₹12,50,000 annually. Similarly, the product value in each cell of this table is to be determined. In cell F18, find the sum of all the cells in this table by writing the formula **=SUM(C14:E17)** and pressing the **Enter** button. 52,25,000 is displayed in this cell.

Now, we need to install the **Solver** add-in for solving this transportation problem. Select the **Add-Ins** sub-menu from the **Tools** menu in the toolbar. In the dialog box which appears, select all the check boxes and click on **OK**. The **Solver** is installed and is ready for use. Now, select the **Solver** option from the **Tools** menu. The **Solver** dialog box as shown in Fig. 5.24 is displayed on screen. You can move the **Solver** dialog box at a suitable place on the screen by dragging the blue strip on top of the dialog box using the left mouse button. This is important so that the contents of the tables on the worksheet are clearly visible for filling the entries in the **Solver** dialog box.

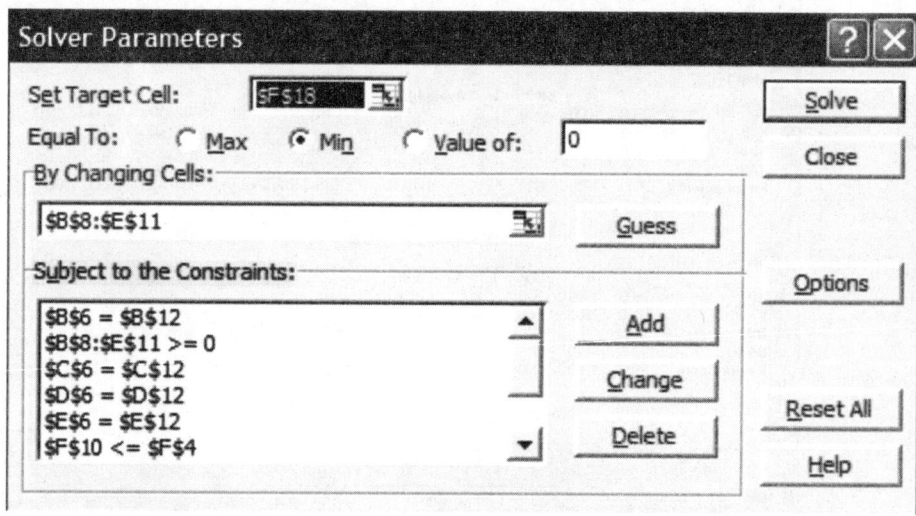

**Fig. 5.24** The Solver dialog box

The **Target cell** has been set as F18 as shown in Fig. 5.24. This is the total transportation cost, which is to be minimized. Hence, in the dialog box, select the **Min** radio button. Click on the text box **By Changing Cells** and then select cells B8 to E11 by clicking and dragging. Automatically **$B$8:$E$11** appears in the text box. Now, click on the **Add** button for adding the constraints to the problem. A dialo box as shown in Fig. 5.25 appears.

The following constraints have to be entered using this **Add Constraint** dialog box:

| | | | |
|---|---|---|---|
| B6 = B12 | C6 = C12 | D6 = D12 | E6 = E12 |
| B8:E11 >= 0 | F10 <= F4 | F8 <= F2 | F9 <= F3 |
| F11 <= F5 | | | |

This dialog box is helpful, as the constraints do not have to be entered using the $ sign repeatedly.

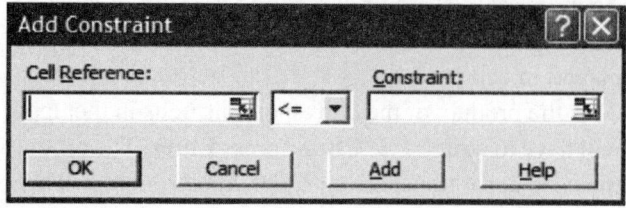

**Fig. 5.25** The Add Constraint dialog box

We have to simply select a cell on the worksheet and it is automatically displayed in the text box of the dialog box. Also, a suitable logical operator can be selected using the pull-down menu in the dialog box. Click on the **Add** button to add a constraint to the **Solver** dialog box, and after adding all the constraints, click on **OK** so that the **Solver**

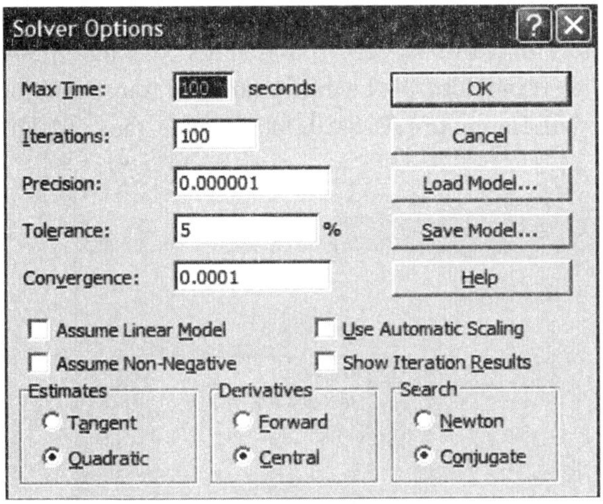


**Fig. 5.26** Solver Options dialog box

dialog box appears with all the constraints.

In the Solver dialog box, click on the **Options** button. A new dialog box **Solver Options** appears as shown in Fig. 5.26. Note that two options each are given for **Estimates, Derivatives,** and **Search**. We may have to use various combinations of these options to get a feasible solution to the transportation problem using the solver. By trial and error, we should only consider the combination that results in a solution with the least total cost. A solution may contain any value with E in any cell. For example, 5.68E-5 means $5.68 \times 10^{-5}$.

For our problem, the options selected as shown in Fig. 5.26 give a feasible solution. As managers, we need not get into the details of these options. Click on **OK** on the **Solver Options** dialog box to get the main **Solver** dialog box. Now, click on the **Solve** button to get the solution as shown in Fig. 5.27. Note that the minimum total transportation cost is ₹28,50,000 in the target cell F18. Three types of reports, namely, **Answer**, **Sensitivity**, and **Limits** reports, can also be generated, provided any of these options are selected in the final dialog box **Solver Results** shown in Fig. 5.28.

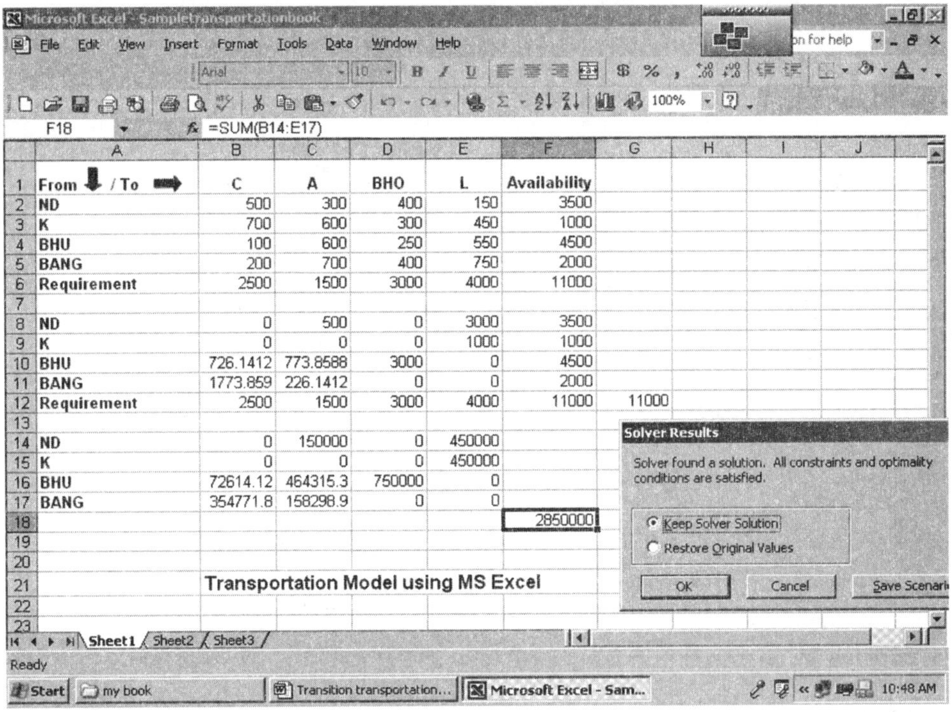


| | A | B | C | D | E | F | G |
|---|---|---|---|---|---|---|---|
| 1 | From / To | C | A | BHO | L | Availability | |
| 2 | ND | 500 | 300 | 400 | 150 | 3500 | |
| 3 | K | 700 | 600 | 300 | 450 | 1000 | |
| 4 | BHU | 100 | 600 | 250 | 550 | 4500 | |
| 5 | BANG | 200 | 700 | 400 | 750 | 2000 | |
| 6 | Requirement | 2500 | 1500 | 3000 | 4000 | 11000 | |
| 7 | | | | | | | |
| 8 | ND | 0 | 500 | 0 | 3000 | 3500 | |
| 9 | K | 0 | 0 | 0 | 1000 | 1000 | |
| 10 | BHU | 726.1412 | 773.8588 | 3000 | 0 | 4500 | |
| 11 | BANG | 1773.859 | 226.1412 | 0 | 0 | 2000 | |
| 12 | Requirement | 2500 | 1500 | 3000 | 4000 | 11000 | 11000 |
| 13 | | | | | | | |
| 14 | ND | 0 | 150000 | 0 | 450000 | | |
| 15 | K | 0 | 0 | 0 | 450000 | | |
| 16 | BHU | 72614.12 | 464315.3 | 750000 | 0 | | |
| 17 | BANG | 354771.8 | 158298.9 | 0 | 0 | | |
| 18 | | | | | | 2850000 | |

**Fig. 5.27** MS Excel worksheet showing the minimum total transportation cost with the Bangalore option

Repeat the above procedure for finding the minimum total transportation cost for the table with Mumbai as one of the sourcing options. This value is ₹20,75,000 (Figs 5.29 and 5.30). Clearly, Mumbai is a better sourcing option than Bangalore, as the minimum total transportation cost with Mumbai (₹20,75,000) is lesser than with Bangalore (₹28,50,000). Hence, the company should have the new facility at Mumbai.

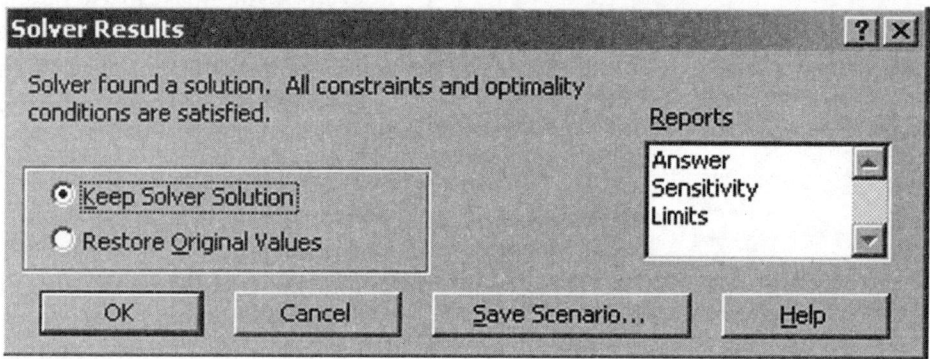

Fig. 5.28 Solver Results dialog box

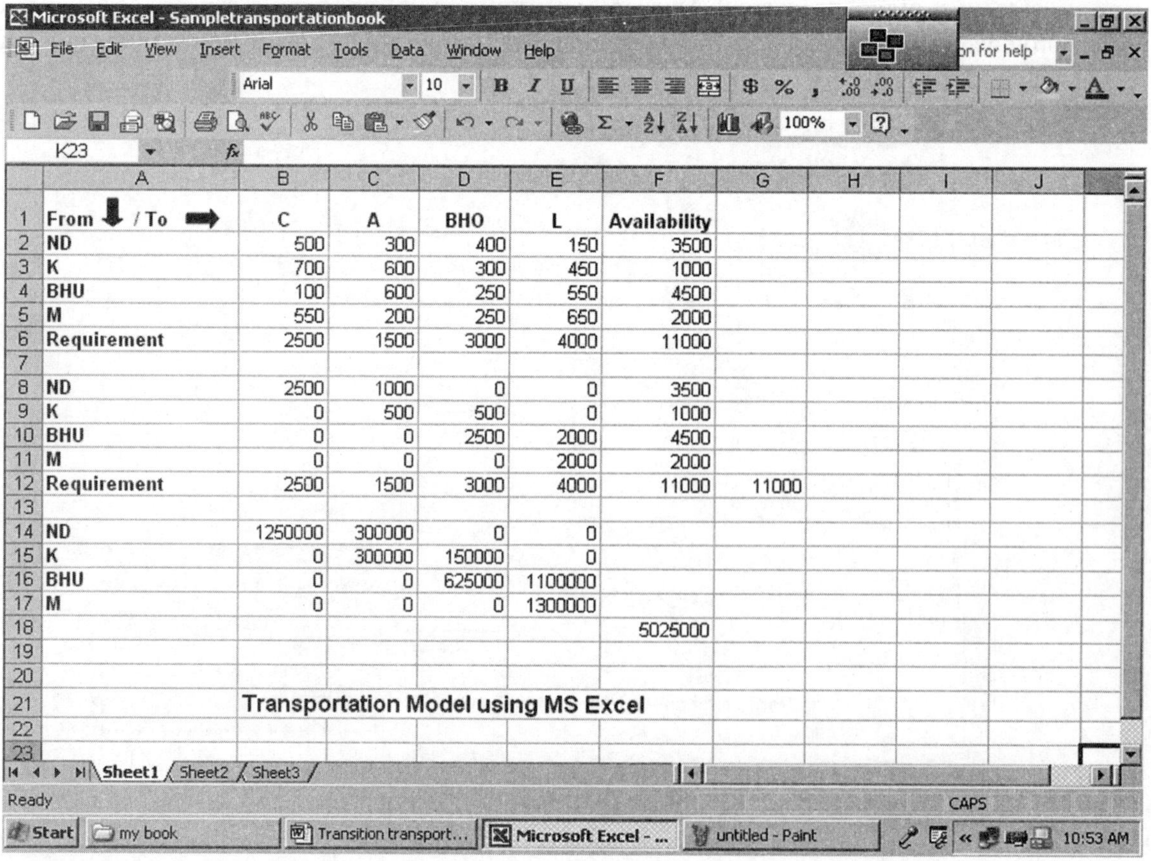

| | A | B | C | D | E | F | G |
|---|---|---|---|---|---|---|---|
| 1 | From / To | C | A | BHO | L | Availability | |
| 2 | ND | 500 | 300 | 400 | 150 | 3500 | |
| 3 | K | 700 | 600 | 300 | 450 | 1000 | |
| 4 | BHU | 100 | 600 | 250 | 550 | 4500 | |
| 5 | M | 550 | 200 | 250 | 650 | 2000 | |
| 6 | Requirement | 2500 | 1500 | 3000 | 4000 | 11000 | |
| 7 | | | | | | | |
| 8 | ND | 2500 | 1000 | 0 | 0 | 3500 | |
| 9 | K | 0 | 500 | 500 | 0 | 1000 | |
| 10 | BHU | 0 | 0 | 2500 | 2000 | 4500 | |
| 11 | M | 0 | 0 | 0 | 2000 | 2000 | |
| 12 | Requirement | 2500 | 1500 | 3000 | 4000 | 11000 | 11000 |
| 13 | | | | | | | |
| 14 | ND | 1250000 | 300000 | 0 | 0 | | |
| 15 | K | 0 | 300000 | 150000 | 0 | | |
| 16 | BHU | 0 | 0 | 625000 | 1100000 | | |
| 17 | M | 0 | 0 | 0 | 1300000 | | |
| 18 | | | | | | 5025000 | |
| 21 | | Transportation Model using MS Excel | | | | | |

Fig. 5.29 MS Excel worksheet showing the Mumbai option

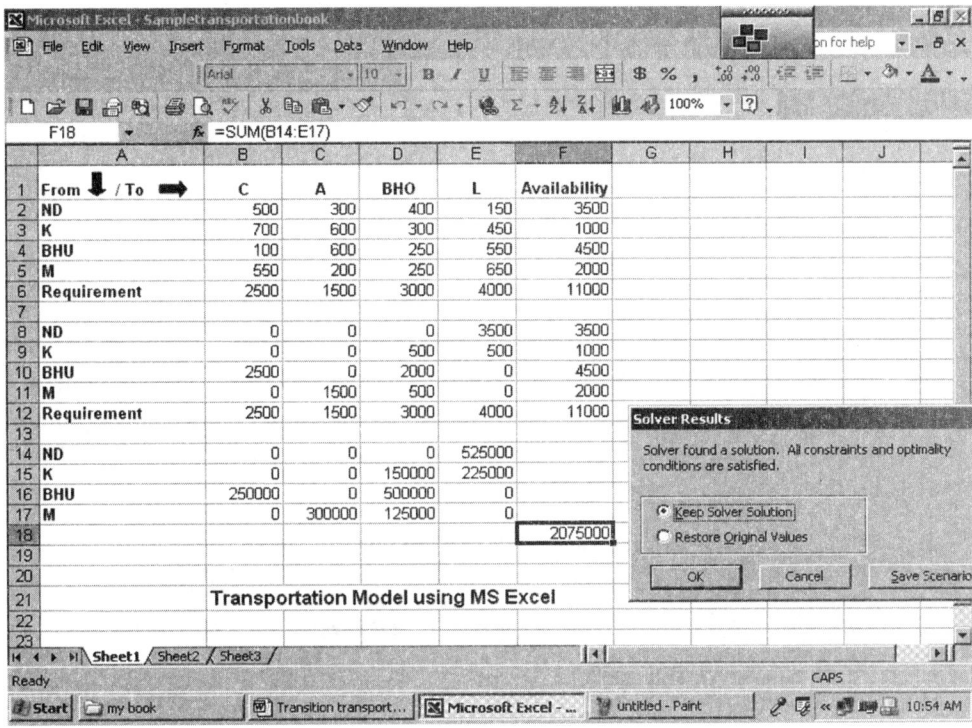

**Fig. 5.30**  MS Excel worksheet showing the minimum total transportation cost with the Mumbai option

# Ardalan Heuristic for Location Planning of Service Facilities

The Ardalan heuristic is used in making decisions regarding the location of service facilities, such as post offices, banks, medical clinics/hospitals, etc., so that a large population can benefit from these facilities (Ardalan 1984, 1988). From the business point of view, the heuristic helps in deciding the location of facilities, such as fuel service stations (petrol pumps), departmental stores, etc., so that these are accessible to people from a number of nearby locations, thus resulting in high profits.

Let us take up an example to understand this heuristic. State Bank of India is planning to open its rural branches in four villages/towns, which are located close to each other. (SBI already has its branches at these locations. This example is for illustration only.) It has the policy of having rural branches (which are not very profitable to the bank from the investment point of view) to serve its social objectives.

> The Ardalan heuristic is used in making decisions regarding the location of service facilities, so that a large population can benefit from these facilities.

SBI decides that it would first open only one branch in any one of these four places. Depending upon the performance of this branch, it may open a second, third, and fourth branch in the remaining places over a period of time. It wants to determine the sequence in which the branches should be opened in the four places, namely, Bachchrawan, Maharajganj, Pehremau, and Raebareli. The distance between each of these places, their populations, and weights attached (according to the bank's social criteria) are given in Table 5.13.

**Table 5.13**

| Location | Distance to | | | | Population (in thousands) | Weights |
|---|---|---|---|---|---|---|
| | *Bachchrawan* | *Maharajganj* | *Pehremau* | *Raebareli* | | |
| Bachchrawan | 0 | 8 | 12 | 10 | 10 | 0.7 |
| Maharajganj | 8 | 0 | 15 | 6 | 11 | 1.2 |
| Pehremau | 12 | 15 | 0 | 11 | 5 | 1.1 |
| Raebareli | 10 | 6 | 11 | 0 | 8 | 0.9 |

The Ardalan heuristic can be applied as follows.

***Step 1*** Take the products of the distances, population, and weights for the corresponding places in every cell of the table and place the product values in the respective cells of the table (see Table 5.14). The total cost here is equivalent to the sum of all the weighted population distances in a column (for a place). Maharajganj, with the lowest total cost, is the best location for the first branch of SBI.

**Table 5.14** Weighted population distances

| Location | Weighted population distances to | | | |
|---|---|---|---|---|
| | *Bachchrawan* | *Maharajganj* | *Pehremau* | *Raebareli* |
| Bachchrawan | 0 | 56 | 84 | 70 |
| Maharajganj | 105.6 | 0 | 198 | 79.2 |
| Pehremau | 66 | 82.5 | 0 | 60.5 |
| Raebareli | 72 | 43.2 | 79.2 | 0 |
| | 243.6 | 181.7 | 361.2 | 209.7 |

***Step 2*** Columnwise, compare the cell values of all other locations with that of Maharajganj. If the cell value is less than or equal to that of Maharajganj, keep it as it is. Otherwise, replace it with the cell value of Maharajganj (Table 5.15).

**Table 5.15** Modification of Table 5.14 following step 2

| Location | Weighted population distances to | | | |
|---|---|---|---|---|
| | *Bachchrawan* | *Maharajganj* | *Pehremau* | *Raebareli* |
| Bachchrawan | 0 | 56 | 56 | 56 |
| Maharajganj | 0 | 0 | 0 | 0 |
| Pehremau | 66 | 82. | 0 | 60.5 |
| Raebareli | 43.2 | 43.2 | 43.2 | 0 |
| | 109.2 | 181.7 | 99.2 | 116.5 |

This procedure has been followed because a person at Bachchrawan would not like to go to a branch at Pehremau or at Raebareli, because of the higher costs involved. Therefore, the cost value of the cell of Maharajganj replaces the values for Pehremau and Raebareli.

The total cost of Pehremau is now the lowest. Therefore, the second branch of SBI should be opened at Pehremau. The column for Maharajganj can be deleted now as Maharajganj was selected already for the location of the first branch, and its costs have been already adjusted.

***Step 3*** Repeat step 2 for the reduced table (Table 5.16).

**Table 5.16** Modification of Table 5.15 following step 2

| Location | Weighted population distances to | | |
| --- | --- | --- | --- |
| | *Bachchrawan* | *Pehremau* | *Raebareli* |
| Bachchrawan | 0 | 56 | 56 |
| Maharajganj | 0 | 0 | 0 |
| Pehremau | 0 | 0 | 0 |
| Raebareli | 43.2 | 43.2 | 0 |
| | 43.2 | 99.2 | 56 |

Now, Bachchrawan is selected for the third branch because of its lowest cost. The last remaining place Raebareli can have the last (fourth) branch of SBI.

## Facility Location Decisions and Network Design in the Supply Chain

With increasing fuel prices, transportation costs increase and add up to the overall prices of the products being transported across the supply chain. A supply chain is a network of facilities,such as factories, warehouses, distribution centres (DCs), and retail outlets, which may be owned and operated by different parties. Strategic locations of these facilities in a region help not only in optimizing the transportation cost but also in improving the response time to key markets. A better response time to replenish goods to markets can provide a distinct competitive advantage to firms. For example, retail chains such as Big Bazaar, Food World, and More create DCs at strategic locations to quickly transport goods to their several retail stores in a given region. The numbers and locations of these DCs determine the response time and the overall transportation costs involved.

If a single DC is created by a company to take care of all retail stores throughout India, possibly it can be located at a central location like Bhopal so that the response time from this DC to any corner of the country would be about five to six days.

If the company decides to have two DCs to address the needs of the retail stores more quickly, a hypothetical horizontal line can be drawn at the centre of the map of India indicating two large regions—north and south. Perhaps, one DC can be located at Lucknow and the other at Bangalore to cater to the retail stores in their respective north and south regions with a response time of three to four days.

Similarly, the number of DCs can be increased to four in order to cover four regions—north, east, south, and west/central with an even better response time of one to two day(s). Possibly, Delhi/NCR can be chosen for northern DC, Kolkata for eastern DC, Bangalore for southern DC, and Bhopal for western/central DC.

It must, however, be noted that more number of DCs require higher capital expenditure. Thus, a better response time comes at a cost and the decision about the number of facilities should be taken with due diligence.

# Summary

*Facility location planning* involves choosing the best place, from the available options, for setting up a plant/service facility. Various factors are responsible for making a production or service facility successful at a particular location. *Factor ratings* and *location ratings* help in selecting the better location options. *Break-even analysis* can be used for selecting locations that have lower break-even volumes. It can also be used for deciding upon the capacity of a plant, the number of plants, and the number of shifts for which the plants can be operated.

The final analysis boils down to the minimization of the transportation costs. The location option with the minimum total transportation cost is the best option. The *simple median model and the centre of gravity method* are helpful for this purpose. The *transportation model* is even more accurate than these models, but slightly difficult to use. For the final analysis of choosing the best service facility location, the *Ardalan heuristic* is most suitable. It helps in finding a location that can cater to a large population.

# References

Ardalan, Alireza 1984, 'An efficient heuristic for service facility location', *Proceedings of the Northeast Decision Sciences Institute Conference*, pp. 181,182.

Ardalan, Alireza 1988, 'A comparison of heuristic methods for service facility locations', *International Journal of Operations and Production Management*, vol. 8, no. 2, p. 52.

Canel, C. and B.M. Khumawala 1996, 'A mixed-integer programming approach for the international facilities location problem', *International Journal of Operations and Production Management*, vol. 16, no. 3, p. 62.

# Keywords

**Break-even point** is the point on the cost/revenue, namely, the volume of production, curve at which total revenue is equal to total cost. It corresponds to the break-even volume $V_{BE}$ on the x-axis. $V_{BE}$ represents the volume of output at which there is no profit and no loss. All the expenses incurred are completely covered by the revenues generated.

**Fixed costs** are capital expenditures (long-term investments in fixed assets), for example, purchase of land, construction of building, purchase of machines and equipment, etc. These costs remain constant despite the volume of production (number of units produced within a given duration).

**Revenue** is the money which comes into the firm by selling its products at their sales prices.

**Variable cost** is the cost of labour (directly involved in the production process) and raw material. As the volume of production increases, more labour and raw material is required for production and, thus, variable cost increases.

---

## CASE STUDY I

## Tata's Nano Plant Location

The 'dream car' project of the Tata group, one of India's largest and most respected business conglomerates, was to be located in West Bengal. In 2005–06 the group had revenues of US$21.9 billion—the equivalent of about 2.8 per cent of the country's GDP—and a market capitalization of US$46.9 billion. Former Chairman Ratan Tata wanted to create a car to be sold in the Indian markets with a price tag of ₹1,00,000. Tatas used their cost-saving engineering skills and surprised the world in 2009 with the launch of their 'dream car'—Nano.

Tatas always wanted to have a car manufacturing facility, but during the early 1940s, they lost the race to B.M. Birla and Walchund Hirachand, who secured the British Government's permission to establish their car factories in India. Hindustan Motors Limited (HML), India's pioneering automobile manufacturing company was established just before Indian independence, in 1942 by B.M. Birla. Commencing operations in a small assembly plant in Port Okha near Gujarat, the manufacturing facilities later moved to Uttarpara, West Bengal in 1948, where it began the production of the Ambassador cars. Premier Automobiles was founded by the visionary and entrepreneur par excellence, Walchand Hirachand Doshi, in 1944. In collaboration with the Chrysler Corporation, India's first car rolled out of the Premier factory in 1947. In collaboration with Fiat SpA, Italy, Premier first started assembling the Fiat 500 in India. Tatas had to wait for almost six decades before their maiden car Indica was launched in 1999. Indica's success gave confidence to Ratan Tata to go ahead with his ₹1,00,000 dream car.

During early 2006, Tatas started scouting for a good location for their dream car plant. The three states initially looking lucrative for the location were Karnataka, West Bengal, and Uttaranchal. Dharwad in Karnataka had the advantage of geographic location, being located between Bangalore and Pune (where Tatas have major facilities). The Karnataka government also offered water and power tariff sops and agreed to Tata's proposed move to build a township near the scheduled facility.

The West Bengal government, which was then in an industrialization drive in the state, enticed the Tatas with various subsidies and sops. It tried to convince Tatas to set up the factory in the backward district of West Midnapore near Kharagpur. In today's competitive environment, the car Tatas would be manufacturing would be the cheapest car available in the country, and the task they have undertaken is very challenging. Hence, they have taken into consideration all aspects, including logistics. Since the price factor is so important in this project, the choice of location is very critical. Apart from the availability of proper infrastructure and skilled labour, the company has to take into consideration social infrastructure such as proximity of educational institutions for the children of its employees. Out of the six different places offered by the West Bengal government, the company found Singur, about 50 kilometres north-west of Kolkata to be the most suitable.

If a particular company wants a big chunk of land for setting up a large plant, it is not possible for it to purchase land from each and every farmer. This is particularly true in West Bengal where fragmentation of land is very high. The state government came forward to acquire the land for the project. When the opposition raised issues against it, the government gave the justification that it is for a public purpose.

According to the government, industrialization means employment generation and development of society. The entire people of the state will be benefited from the new project. Therefore, the land acquisition was in public interest.

Setting a healthy precedent, the West Bengal government agreed to pay compensation to farmers for acquiring their land at a generous rate—almost 150 per cent more than the prevailing market price. This was much more than what most other state governments had ordained as the price to be paid for acquiring land from farmers for setting up industries or special economic zones. For instance, owners of single-crop land in Singur got ₹8,40,000 per acre and ₹1.2 million an acre if the land was used for double-cropping, while in Maharashtra, farmers got only ₹24,000 an acre. However, this comparison may not be appropriate.

The land in Singur has a greater market value as it is close to the National Highway No. 2, connecting Kolkata with Delhi, and the land in question in Maharashtra may not enjoy a similar advantage. Yet, it has to be conceded that the compensation package decided by the West Bengal government is generous and an important factor in convincing over 9,000 land-owners at Singur (over 94 per cent of the total land to be acquired). These farmers have agreed to the deal and have already received their compensation money from the state government. Land acquisition in Singur has been completed and the land has been handed over to the West Bengal Industrial Development Corporation (WBIDC). Till 2 December 2006, ₹766.4 million had been disbursed as compensation to the farmers who had lost their land. Around 9,020 farmers have received compensation for 635 acres of land. Eighty-eight recorded *bargadars* (sharecroppers) have already received a payment of ₹1.7 million and the number of persons yet to receive payment, till 2 December 2006, was around 3,000.

Another allegation by the opposition against the then state government is that land acquired for a private enterprise cannot be considered a public purpose. It is further alleged that the acquisition of land has not followed the established procedure of the company making advance payment. Instead the company was given the land at a very concessional rate payable within the next 20 years. All this was apparently being kept a secret by the government. The government, however, refuted these allegations and vouched for its transparency in following the procedures laid out for the industrialization of the state. According to government agencies, 'If you see the zig-zag way the map for the project site has been drawn, you will understand the pains we have taken to ensure the exclusion of the most fertile tracts of land in the region as well as homestead lands. This is not an ideal map for a factory site, and it took a lot of persuasion by us for the Tatas to accept this.'

Thirdly, there is a perception that the Tata small car project has acquired land far in excess of what it actually requires to set up a factory of that capacity. Maruti Udyog is situated in a total land area of 300 acres and has an installed capacity of 3,50,000 cars a year. The Singur land being handed over to the Tatas is three times more than what Maruti Udyog has and that too for producing only 1,00,000 cars. The question in everyone's mind is why the Tatas need 997 acres of land and whether there are other facilities that are being planned in that same area. Due to such issues, questions on the justification of allocating the Singur land to the Tatas will continue to be raised.

Agitations against the project started immediately after the fencing of the land was done. Singur's uneasy peace was shattered during early February 2007 as pro-farmland forces clashed with the police in phases throughout the day. It was a grim reminder of the fact that the Tatas' problems there are still far from over. For a group that has just tripped the mighty CSN of Brazil at the Corus sweepstakes in the United Kingdom, this small village in Hooghly continues to be a problem. It is alleged that the people of Singur offered Tata a plot of land on the other side of the village. This land is low-lying and needed to be filled up. According to the villagers, 'But the Tatas want everything on a platter. They don't want to spend money, so they want land which is fertile and the lifeline of the people. Why should the farmers of Singur subsidize Tata's one-lakh rupee car?'

The state government received an unequivocal support by Ratan Tata, who has said his group will not move out of West Bengal. The company cited the example of Uttaranchal where the company was the first to set up a huge plant. Land prices in the state had gone up 25 times in the last 10 months as other automobile companies followed suit. The farmers of Uttaranchal have gained from such opportunities. The company has also approached NGOs and *panchayats* in Singur to provide training to locals at Ramakrishna Mission for developing technical skills in areas such as, carpentry, plumbing, electrician, and simple fitting jobs. According to them, if the need arises, key

employees from Tata Motors plant can travel from Jamshedpur and impart training to students. This will bring to focus the skill sets required for jobs at an auto plant and how these tasks are carried out on a regular basis.

Tata Motors has also proposed a weekly forum meeting where farmers meet company executives and clear doubts. It also plans to replicate some of the programmes initiated in Pune and Jamshedpur for people in Singur. As part of other initiatives to connect with the people, the company is organizing special training programmes for women in areas such as tailoring, making, hand gloves garments, food products, and handicrafts. Tata Motors also plans to introduce technical subjects in local secondary schools by providing infrastructure support, sports facilities, career guidance, and a teachers' training programme.

Some of the opposition parties are still not satisfied and are not restricting their agitation only to Singur. They have gone ahead to urge the people of Nandigram to be united against the government's move to acquire multi-crop land for the proposed SEZ by the Indonesia-based Salim Group.

Despite all the efforts of Tata Motors to resolve the deadlock in Singur (West Bengal), frequent agitations instigated by the opposition parties marred the Singur plant project. During late 2008, the company took the tough decision to relocate this facility to Sanand in Gujarat. The plot in Singur is still under litigation and is more or less a sunk cost for Tata Motors. Built in a record time of 14 months, the 725-acre Sanand plant was commissioned in June 2010 and continues to be a highly productive plant for Tata Nano production.

## Discussion Questions

1. Why did Tatas prefer to locate their 'dream car' plant at Singur, West Bengal despite other equally good options such as Dharwad and Uttaranchal?
2. Tatas should have considered Pune and Jamshedpur, where they already had multiple facilities and several ancillary units, for locating this new plant. Do you agree with this statement?
3. Tatas have often chosen wrong locations for their plants, such as the one at Lucknow, which is also marred with controversies. Discuss.
4. How do you think the problems at Singur can be amicably resolved by Tatas for earliest constrution of their plant?

# Toyota in China

Toyota Motor Corp. entered the auto market in China in 1998, through a 50:50 joint venture with state-owned First Automotive Works Corp. (FAW), China's biggest automobile manufacturer. Toyota was a late entrant in the Chinese market where Volkswagen and General Motors Corp. were then holding the no. 1 and no. 2 slots, respectively.

The Toyota factory sits on a tiny plot of land, alongside grimy FAW workshops, near the north-eastern port city of Tianjin. With a capacity of just 1,00,000 cars annually, its small scale makes it something of a laboratory. The company feels as if the Chinese government has punished it for spurning a Chinese overture in the 1980s—when the Japanese company was busy expanding in the US.

Toyota preferred youngsters for the Tianjin plant in place of the FAW veterans, even though its operation stands in the shadow of the aging FAW factory. The average employee age is 21, which Toyota officials feel makes for a more malleable workforce, amenable to learning the 'Toyota way' teamwork, respect for authority, and techniques of kaizen, or continuous improvement. Toyota needed to school its new employees quickly in the basics of auto manufacturing and assembly. As the opening day of the Tianjin factory in October 2002 drew closer, it became clear that the workers lacked a skill even more fundamental than the precision welding, bolting, and fine-tuning required to build cars that meet Toyota's stiff quality standards. Most of the employees had never driven a car in their lives.

Ever resourceful, Toyota's managers placed a stripped-down demonstration of its Vios Subcompact on the factory floor to let workers get the feel of the machines they were building. The company dispatched a score of experienced technical hands from its most productive Japanese plants to serve as factory drill sergeants in Tianjin, as part of the effort to teach 'Toyota 101' to the 1,300 odd workers at the Vios plant. At Tianjin, assembly line staffers had to build their own workbenches, component bins, and trolleys from kits shipped from Japan, to learn teamwork and responsibility. Months before the first Vios rolled off the line, the teams practised assembling and taking apart prototypes over and over again. All the new employees had to go through a weeklong programme of seminars on the Toyota culture and wrist exercises to build up muscles for the assembly line.

The Tianjin plant does not have the same level of automation as the company's Japanese factories, despite it being Toyota's newest plant in China. Toyota did not import state-of-the-art robots and other expensive equipment from Japan. Instead the company relied heavily on manual assembly, in part because labour in China is much cheaper, but also because Toyota wants its Chinese workers to learn how to do things by hand first. The company feels if too much automation is introduced in a plant too soon, quality can suffer because workers do not get a chance to learn from their mistakes. Though the company's officials say that in some countries, Toyota has never been able to reach the quality levels of Japan, in Tianjin, Toyota's goal is nothing less than matching the quality of Japanese factories—or even exceeding it.

By 2003, Vios had become so popular that the company had a backlog of 16,000 orders in China. For the Tianjin plant, so far the going has been slow, as the company has built only 1,500 Vios sedans per month since production commenced in October 2002. This is largely because it has taken time for workers to master the kind of meticulous work-manship Toyota demands. In 2002, Toyota had to import 50,000 odd cars from Japan to be sold in China in contrast to Volkswagen, which sold 5,11,000, and GM, which sold 1,10,000. With the success of the Tianjin facility, Toyota has earned plenty of goodwill from Beijing and has been given the nod to build a second, larger factory across town.

In June 2004, Toyota established Tianjin FAW Toyota Motor Co. It is the second joint venture the company has set up with its partner, China FAW Group Corporation. A line-off ceremony was held at the subsidiary's second factory in the Tianjin Economic and Technological Development Area. In this factory, Toyota began manufacturing its new Reiz model. Reiz is the second model produced at the factory, after the Crown that has been assembled since March 2005. The first factory of Tianjin FAW Toyota Motor has been producing Corolla vehicles since February 2004, in addition to producing the Vios.

In September 2004, Guangzhou Toyota Motor Co., Ltd (GTMC) co-established by Guangzhou Automobile Group Co. Ltd (Guangzhou Automobile) of China and Toyota Motor Cooperation (TMC) started construction of a new plant in Guangzhou. Located at Guangzhou's

Nansha Economic and Technological Development Zone of Guangdong Province, GTMC involves 1.3 billion Yuan with a 50–50 equity participation by Guangzhou Automobile and TMC. The Camry will be produced in GTMC's newest plant in Nansha, a port city 65 km north of Hong Kong on the Pearl River. This southern region around Guangzhou has become an offshore Japanese car manufacturing hub that is challenging Shanghai's self-designated status as China's auto city, with Toyota, Nissan, and Honda all building up joint ventures, accompanied by dozens if not hundreds of parts suppliers.

In 2007, the venture, based in Guangzhou, planned to increase the number of its dealers to 167 throughout the country. Guangzhou Toyota is more eager to seek expansion in second-tier cities than Tianjin FAW Toyota Motor Co. Experts are of the view that Guangzhou Toyota is inferior to FAW Toyota in sales networking in bigger cities. In fact, FAW Toyota started expansion into second-tier cities in central and western areas since 2006. It spared no efforts in enhancing services in regions such as Xinjiang. For instance, it quickly set up repair stores in those regions. It had a relatively smooth expansion thanks to the strong sales network

of its Chinese parent FAW, one of the nation's top three auto manufacturers and sellers.

In 2012, the territorial dispute between China and Japan over a few islands impacted the car sales and production of all Japanese companies operating in China. The month of October 2012 witnessed Toyota cutting production in its Chinese factories by as much as 50 per cent. Its arch rivals in China have benefited immensely from this unexpected windfall.

### Discussion Questions

1. Discuss the major advantages and disadvantages of Tianjin as a location for Toyota's maiden venture in China.
2. 'The real reason of low automation of the Tianjin plant was that Toyota was awaiting a response from the Chinese government for a bigger facility.' Comment.
3. Could Toyota avoid delays in full-swing production at Tianjin due to unskilled workforce there, had the company hired most of the FAW veterans?
4. Toyota's JV with Guangzhou Automobile is an indication of its growing distances with the other JV partner FAW. What is your take on this statement?

## Objective Questions

### Choose the correct option

1. Which one of the following is not an operations strategy for multiple facilities?
   (a) Separate facilities for different clients
   (b) Separate facilities for different products/services
   (c) Separate facilities to serve different geographical areas
   (d) Separate facilities for different processes
2. Which one of the following is not a factor affecting facility location planning?
   (a) Good transportation facilities
   (b) Proximity to raw material
   (c) Proximity to markets
   (d) Proximity to government offices
3. Which one of the following is not a factor affecting international facility location planning?
   (a) International competition
   (b) Power and prestige
   (c) Racial superiority
   (d) Low costs
4. Which one of the following is not considered in the

break-even analysis for facility location planning?
   (a) Fixed costs
   (b) Features of the product
   (c) Variable costs
   (d) Volume of production

### State True or False

5. Factor and location ratings are used to screen for better location options.
6. Easy availability of cheap land is not a factor considered in facility location planning.
7. Offensive in competitor's home is a factor considered in international facility location planning.

### Fill in the blanks

8. The Simple Median Model helps in locating a new facility such that the total _____ cost between the new facility and the existing facilities of the organization is the minimum.
9. Ardalan Heuristic is used for location planning of _____.
10. The point at which total revenue and total cost curves meet each other is called the _____ point.

# Concept Review Questions

1. Explain the factors affecting facility location planning.
2. What are the repercussions if location of a facility is not planned at all?
3. Explain the various steps in facility location planning.
4. What are the factors affecting the location planning of international facilities?
5. What are factor ratings and location ratings? How are these useful in facility location planning?
6. What do you understand by break-even point? What are fixed and variable costs?
7. How can break-even analysis be useful in facility location planning? How can you decide upon the number of plants required, expansion of plants, and the number of shifts for operating plants using break-even analysis?
8. What is the simple median model? How is it used to find the best location of plants?
9. How is the location planning of service facilities different from the location planning of manufacturing facilities? Write a short note on the Ardalan heuristic.
10. How do the number of facilities and their location influence network design in the supply chain?

# Numerical Problems

1. Santro Electronics is considering two locations for its audio equipment factory. One location option is Ahmedabad and the other is Chennai. At Ahmedabad, the fixed cost of the factory is estimated at ₹1 million and the variable cost at ₹1,200 per audio equipment manufactured. At Chennai, the fixed cost of the factory is estimated at ₹1.2 million and the variable cost at ₹1,100 per audio equipment manufactured. The selling price of the equipment will be ₹3,000 per unit irrespective of the place of manufacture. Decide which location is best for the factory using break-even analysis.
2. MK Bond Paper manufactures photocopier paper. It is evaluating two location options for its new facility. The first location option is Dehradun, where the fixed cost of the facility will be ₹2 million and the variable cost will be ₹200 per ream of paper. The second location option is Hyderabad, where the fixed cost of the facility will be ₹2.5 million and the variable cost will be ₹170 per ream of paper. The factory will produce 10,000 reams of paper in the first year of production. The company will decide the location depending upon the lower cost of production in the first year. Which location should the company choose?
3. Gem Paper Ltd is a major paper manufacturer with its factory located at $X$ location (24, 15). It has its major warehouses located at $Y$ (5, 10) and $Z$ (10, 5). The company is planning a new major distribution centre at a location that is easily accessible to all its three existing facilities. The annual load to be transported between the proposed new facility and $X$, $Y$, and $Z$ has been estimated as 720, 340, and 250 million units of paper boxes (of standard size), respectively. You have been hired by the company as a consultant to help them decide about the location of the proposed new facility.
4. Udhampur Distilleries Ltd has four existing facilities—$W$, $X$, $Y$, and $Z$. The details of these facilities are given in Table 5.17. The company wants to locate a new facility such that the total transportation cost is the minimum. Advise the management of the company about the best possible location using the simple median model. Also, find the total transportation cost.

**Table 5.17**

| Existing facility F | Annual loads between F and new facility (units) | Cost of moving one unit by unit distance (₹) | Coordinate location (x,y) |
|---|---|---|---|
| $W$ | 279 | 10 | (20,30) |
| $X$ | 473 | 10 | (70,10) |
| $Y$ | 350 | 10 | (50,40) |
| $Z$ | 266 | 10 | (10,80) |

5. Solve Problem 3 using the centre of gravity model.
6. Godavari Automotives is an automotive manufacturer, having its factories in $W$, $X$, $Y$, and $Z$ locations. It sources components/parts/sub-assemblies from

its suppliers based in *K, L, M,* and *N.* Table 5.18 shows the cost of transporting a unit of standard boxes containing components/parts/sub-assemblies between any two locations. The annual requirement at each factory is given in the lower-most row of the table. Similarly, the maximum capacities of the suppliers are shown in the right-most column under 'Availability'.

**Table 5.18**

| To → From↓ | W | X | Y | Z | Availability |
|---|---|---|---|---|---|
| K | 520 | 460 | 250 | 170 | 1,500 |
| L | 240 | 390 | 410 | 210 | 3,000 |
| M | 310 | 270 | 530 | 480 | 4,500 |
| N | 450 | 180 | 330 | 360 | 3,000 |
| Requirement | 1,500 | 5,000 | 3,500 | 2,000 | 12,000 |

You have been hired as a consultant to advice Godavari Automotives as to how many boxes should be shipped from which suppliers so that the overall transportation cost is the minimum.

7. The Government of India has identified five tribal communities located near each other in the north-eastern region of the country. The population of all the five communities are almost equal to each other, and to the government, all the five communities are equally important from the social point of view. The government plans to provide medical dispensaries in any three of these communities. Therefore, the remaining communities will have to travel to these three locations for getting the services of a dispensary. The travel costs (in ₹ per person) between various communities are given in Table 5.19.

**Table 5.19**

| Destination → Source ↓ | A | B | C | D | E |
|---|---|---|---|---|---|
| A | 0 | 20 | 15 | 10 | 5 |
| B | 25 | 0 | 24 | 8 | 18 |
| C | 15 | 22 | 0 | 12 | 20 |
| D | 10 | 9 | 11 | 0 | 5 |
| E | 6 | 18 | 20 | 7 | 0 |

Using the Ardalan heuristic, advise the government about the three locations where dispensaries should be opened. Also, find the total travel cost involved.

## Project Assignments

1. Visit any three factories/service facilities in your city and meet the concerned operations managers. Ask them about the factors considered by the company in locating the facility. Did they perform the analysis techniques discussed in this chapter? Tell them about the techniques and models discussed here and take their opinion regarding their use.

2. Visit the websites of five major organizations in your region. Find out where their facilities are located. Form discussion groups to analyse the rationale behind the location of these facilities.

| Answers to Objective Questions | | | | |
|---|---|---|---|---|
| 1. (a) | 2. (d) | 3. (c) | 4. (b) | 5. True |
| 6. False | 7. True | 8. transportation | 9. service facilities | 10. break-even |

# 6

# Facility Capacity and Layout Planning

## Learning Objectives

After reading this chapter, you will be able to answer the following questions:
- What is the need for facility capacity planning?
- What models and techniques can be used to plan the capacity of a facility?
- What strategy can be adopted to meet the future capacity requirements?
- How many types of facility layouts are there?
- What models and techniques can be used to plan the layout of a facility?

## Capacity and Capacity Planning

The capacity of a facility is defined as the maximum load that can be handled by it during a given period. The load can be expressed in terms of the amount of input or output. For example, the capacity of a sugar mill can be expressed in terms of the tonnes of sugar cane (input) crushed per day or in terms of the tonnes of sugar (output) produced per day.

When a company produces many products or services, the measure of capacity in terms of output may not be suitable. For example, a plastic goods manufacturing unit may produce tables, chairs, jugs, toys, etc. It would be impractical to express the capacity of such a factory in terms of the output of each product produced, for example, 100 tables per day, 200 chairs per day, 1,000 jugs per day, and 1,000 toys per day. The suitable measure here is in terms of the input, that is, the amount of plastic processed per day. Hence, we may say that the measure of capacity is dependent upon the suitability of the situation.

> The capacity of a facility is defined as the maximum load that can be handled by it during a given period.

### Need for Facility Capacity Planning

Facility capacity planning is needed for various reasons as shown in Fig. 6.1. A low capacity of the facility may result in costs of under-capacity, especially during periods of high demand of the product. This cost is mainly due to the loss of potential profit. It has also been observed that the minimum average unit cost of a product is higher for small plants compared to large plants.

> A low capacity of the facility may result in costs of under-capacity, especially during periods of high demand of the product.

Similarly, over-capacity of the plant means less number of units of the product are produced due to a lower demand as compared to the capacity available. Again, the unit cost of the product will tend to rise, as the fixed costs of the

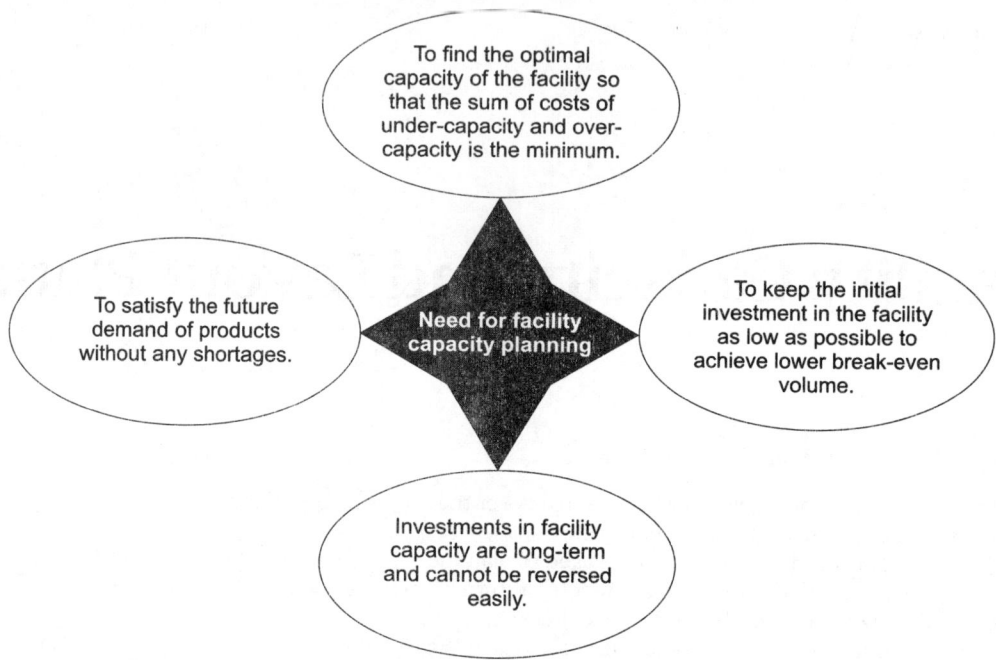

**Fig. 6.1**   Need for facility capacity planning

> The optimal capacity of the facility is thus the capacity at which the sum of the costs of under-capacity and over-capacity is the minimum.

> Effective capacity is the maximum rate of output which can be achieved under the constraints. It is always lower than the design capacity.

facility will be divided amongst less number of units of the product. The optimal capacity of the facility is thus the capacity at which the sum of the costs of under-capacity and over-capacity is the minimum.

We have already studied break-even analysis in Chapter 5. This theory is useful in facility capacity planning and also in determining the capacity at which the break-even volume is low. Low break-even volume is desirable for new facilities so as to recover the investments as early as possible through the revenue generated by selling the products.

## Types of Capacity

There are three types of capacity.

**Design capacity**   As the name suggests, this is the capacity designed for the facility. It depends upon the number and capacity of machines and equipment, coupled with labour. It represents the maximum rate of output that can be achieved under ideal conditions.

**Effective capacity**   In reality, if a facility is used to make different products, a set-up time will be required between batches of different products to be produced. These set-ups are required to replace the raw material and components for the new batch of a different product to be processed on the machines. Also, the machines may require adjustments, oiling, cleaning, etc. Some units of initial output may be lost in quality testing. Thus, it is not practically feasible to achieve design capacity. What can be achieved is the effective capacity. Thus, effective capacity is the maximum rate of output which can be achieved under the above constraints. It is always lower than the design capacity.

> Actual capacity cannot be increased beyond the effective capacity as it is the maximum limit of actual capacity.

**Actual capacity**    This is the maximum output rate which is actually achieved under the constraints of machine breakdowns, labour inefficiencies and absenteeism, defective products, late deliveries of materials by the supplier, and so on. Actual capacity can be equal to or less than the effective capacity.

There are two measures of system performance based upon these types of capacity.

$$\text{Efficiency} = \frac{\text{Actual output}}{\text{Effective capacity}}$$

$$\text{Capacity utilization} = \frac{\text{Actual output}}{\text{Design capacity}}$$

In the formula for utilization, design capacity is constant. Therefore, utilization can be increased only by increasing the actual output. Actual capacity cannot be increased beyond the effective capacity as it is the maximum limit of actual capacity. Thus, for increasing the utilization, effective capacity has also to be increased (Exhibit 6.1). Figure 6.2 shows various ways of increasing the effective capacity and, thus, increasing the capacity utilizaion.

## Role of Forecasting in Capacity Planning

The marketing department plays a major role in providing demand forecasts based on which both long-term as well as short-term capacity planning can be done. Figure 6.3 shows the different demand patterns or trends possible in a demand forecast provided by the marketing department.

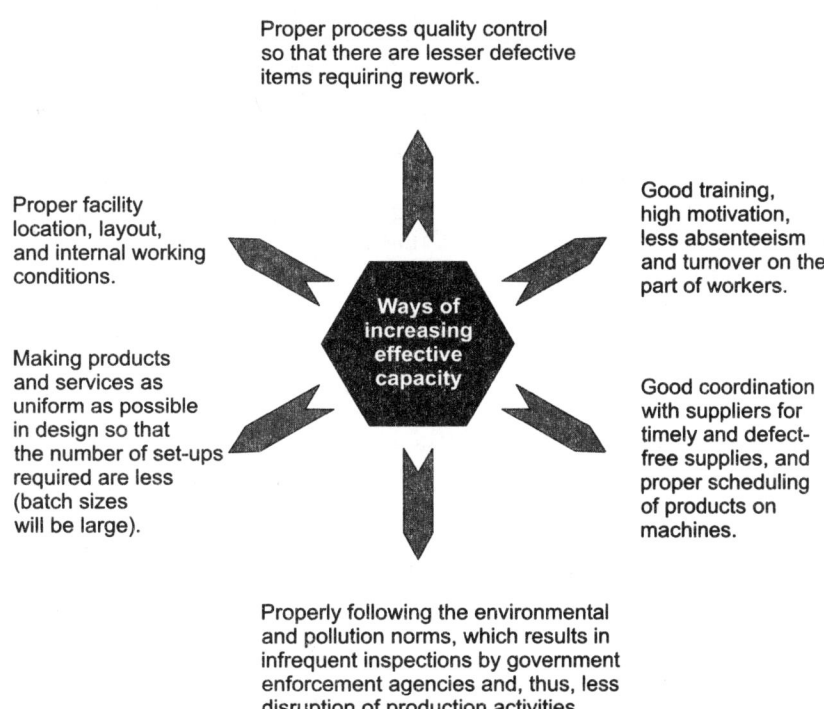

**Fig. 6.2**    Ways of increasing effective capacity

## Exhibit 6.1 Indian Textile Industry

The textile industry in India is the country's second largest industry, after agriculture. It provides direct employment to about 35 million people. It is also India's largest foreign export earner, accounting for 35 per cent of the gross export earnings in trade.

Trade restrictions had kept the textile industry from soaring to the heights it is capable of. However, all that changed from 1 January 2005, when quota-based restrictions for textile exports to the US and European nations were lifted. The Indian textile industry now has the opportunity to realize its full potential and the sector is already eyeing an export target of US$80 billion by 2020.

For more than three decades, the Multi-Fibre Arrangement (MFA) governed world trade in textiles and garments. Under the MFA, many industrial countries, through bilateral agreements or unilateral actions, established quotas on imports of textiles and clothing from more competitive developing countries. MFA was to initially operate for a limited period of four years and was primarily meant to provide breathing time to the textile industries of the developed countries to make structural readjustments. However, the MFA quota regime got extended time and again for varying periods. From 1987 onwards, vegetable fibres and silk-blend products were added to the scope of MFA.

The integration of the textile sector into the mainstream of World Trade Organization (General Agreement on Tariffs and Trade 1994) disciplines was embodied in an agreement on textiles and clothing which was negotiated during the Uruguay Round. The Agreement on Textiles and Clothing was a major boon for countries such as India and Bangladesh. Exports of textiles account for about 20 per cent of total exports from India and represent the largest net foreign exchange earner.

With the abolition of quotas and globalization in full swing, the market is now exposed to global competition. Indian manufacturers and exporters now have to compete with global players and also face emerging tariff and non-tariff barriers. Yet with its speed of operation, skill, quality of products, and low-cost labour, the industry is gearing up to reap rich rewards in the new era.

Ludhiana in Punjab is famous for its hosiery products. The city is aiming to carve a big slice of world textile trade for itself. A manufacturer such as Venus Garments, which supplies to GAP and Walmart, is still not clear about the shape of the emerging market. Companies have realized that the key to enhanced exports lies in capacity enhancement. In anticipation of growth, Venus has increased its garment production from 10,000 pieces to 15,000 pieces a day, besides increasing dyeing capacity from 8 tonnes to 12 tonnes a day. Similarly, Superfine Knitters has also doubled its production capacity from 2,000 garments per day. Abhishek Industries, which had revenues of 20 million in 1985, is now aiming to touch ₹2,000 billion in two years. Due to its locational disadvantage, Ludhiana's industry has lost out to other hosiery centres such as Tirupur in Tamil Nadu, which has an export market of over ₹50 billion. Ludhiana faces a disadvantage of its hosiery being costlier by about 5 per cent due to transport expenses to the ports (for export). However, the city continues to enjoy a strong advantage on the labour front. With migrant skilled and semi-skilled labour in good supply from states such as UP and Bihar, the textile sector is assured of adequate human resources at Ludhiana.

Nearly 60 per cent of the country's total knitwear exports come from Tirupur, which has an export market of more than ₹50 billion. Every month, buyers from more than 35 countries visit Tirupur because the town can deliver customized samples of knitted garments in less than 12 hours, and up to half a million pieces in a matter of days. Fifty six per cent of India's total knitwear exports are from Tirupur. The Export Import Policy of 2002–2007 made laudable tribute to Tirupur for its contribution to Indian exports and calls it a 'town of export excellence'.

New, modern apparel parks have been set up in Tirupur. Earlier, the town was dotted with tiny shops crammed with old sewing machines. Now the old sewing machines have been discarded. Earlier, machines used for the production of knitted garments were ordered from towns such as Ludhiana in Punjab. These days, most garment exporters import these machines from countries such as the US, UK, Germany, Japan, Italy, France, and Taiwan. As a testimony to the changing market scenario, nearly 250 garment manufacturers in Tirupur have imported close to 10,000 machines. An imported knitting machine costs anything between ₹1.5 million to ₹7.5 million. As compared to this, an Indian machine is available for ₹75,000. The

*(Contd)*

*Exhibit 6.1 Contd*

imported machines, with computerized jacquards, offer productivity levels that are six or seven times higher than those of Indian machines. Many exporters have realized that such machines are needed for better and modern knitted designs. Thus, they have stopped using Indian machines.

In Tirupur, Astro Apparel's owner Venkat is not among those buying new machinery. In fact, he has no plans to expand capacity. He believes that the real issue is labour productivity. Venkat believes that without adding a single new piece of machinery, it is possible to grow the company's turnover from the current ₹90 million to ₹150 million within a year. In October 2005, Venkat was part of a 32-member team that visited the Guangzhou province in China. Organized by the local office of the Textile Committee, the visit was meant to expose them to the best practices and the scale of Chinese garment factories. The experience was an eye-opener for Venkat. When he visited the factories, he found that Chinese workers did not even look up from their work when a visitor came in. He also found that the costs of labour and raw material were almost the same as back home. The crucial difference was productivity. According to Venkat, using the same machinery, the Chinese worker had a 200–250 per cent higher productivity.

Back in Tirupur, Venkat began to secretly monitor his workers' productivity levels. However, once the workers got to know this, they stopped working. They were not keen on productivity-linked wages. Venkat is facing a peculiar situation today. Typically, his order flow is such that his factory operates at full capacity for eight months in a year. During this period, workers often have to work overtime, mostly till 9 p.m.

In 2005, managers from Sara Lee, the leading global lingerie brand, visited his factory and were impressed by the facilities. Not only were they willing to make him an approved supplier, they were ready to place an immediate order that would keep his factory running for the entire year. The only requirement was that Venkat would have to shut his factory by 6 p.m. This was in keeping with Sara Lee's good production practices worldwide. Now, this was a win–win arrangement. His calculations showed that his workers would earn far more if they worked fewer hours, but for the entire year. The workers were not able to see the point and Venkat had to eventually decline the order from Sara

Lee. According to him, 'The labourers' attitude in Tirupur is just not conducive. By stepping up productivity, we can produce 150 per cent with the same machines and the labourers will also earn more. But it is just too difficult to convince them.'

Adopting international practices is already helping others such as the Bangalore-based Fibres and Fabric International. The company's Chairman and Managing Director, Anupam Kothari, hired an Italian technician a few months ago to look after the high-tech machines in his factory. The result—the downtime in his critical operations is now negligible. Says Kothari, 'The Italian technician did not come cheap, but we raised our efficiency a few notches almost overnight. We understood the difference between buying technology and using technology.'

Kothari is sparing no efforts for his next expansion. Soon, he will decide who will construct his factory—L&T or Gammon. The machines will be imported and the company plans to set up a state-of-the-art water recycling plant costing ₹60 million. That would increase the cost of water five times, but would ensure a high degree of social compliance—a selling proposition to the company's eco-friendly buyers from the Netherlands and Germany.

On the face of it, Kothari is going against the grain of cost-conscious manufacturing. However, in reality, he has cracked the pricing code. By focusing on the fashion denim market, Kothari has carved a niche for himself. He commanded an average price of €14.43 for each of the 2 million jeans he sold last year. This is more than double the industry average of €7. He commands a premium in the high-fashion jeans market too. Here, a dress would typically retail at €200 and above. Now, given the high inventory holding costs, most European retailers prefer to deal with suppliers who can replenish stocks in short lead times. Kothari's flexible manufacturing system allows him to cut lead times to just two weeks—unheard of in the Indian industry. Costs are understandably higher, but then it earns Kothari nearly €35 per pair. It is almost twice the price commanded by some Chinese manufacturers who are unable to offer the same level of service.

The World Trade Organization estimates that with the abolition of the quota system, China-made textile products would now account for half of all American clothing imports. During the quota regime, China's

*(Contd)*

*Exhibit 6.1 Contd*

share of the US textile market was 17 per cent. The Indian textile industry too is changing. A state-of-the-art apparel park, the Netaji Apparel Park, has been established on the outskirts of Tirupur. It is a huge expanse of 60 concrete factories that have cost more than ₹2.5 billion. The Netaji Apparel Park is India's first, largest, and most modern textile cluster that matches China's textile industry in production quality and quantity. There are no power breakdowns and water shortage in the park. The textile units in the park supply their wares to some of the world's leading retail chains, such as, Walmart, Marks & Spencer, and C&A. Welspun India Ltd, one of the world's largest producers of terry towel products, is building a US$220 million factory in Gujarat. Arvind Mills Ltd, Asia's largest producer of denim, has set up new plants in Bangalore and Ahmedabad. Gujarat-based Super Spinning Mills Ltd has acquired two sick textile mills in Madurai to cater to the US market. According to the Economist Intelligence Unit, while China, too, has a growing population of young, trainable people, the wages in India are lower than in China by about 30 per cent. However, China scores over India in its productivity levels, which are unquestionably better. Our wages may be marginally lower, but given our dated labour laws, so is our productivity. This means that product cost per employee is better in China.

China's other big advantage over India is scale. Chinese textile companies have built up huge capacities, thanks to the inflow of foreign direct investment over the last few years. China's spinning capacity is estimated at 53 million spindles compared to India's 39 million. In weaving, China's is estimated to have 1,60,000 shuttle-less looms compared to India's 20,000 (now being increased to 50,000–60,000). While fresh investments are being made in building new plants in India to make terry towels, T-shirts, and tuxedos, the investments are probably not enough to measure up against China.

*Sources:* Aron (2005); CCI (2012).

Four types of general trends are possible in demand forecasts: growth, decline, cyclical, and stable. The *growth* trend in demand forecast is an indicator of capacity expansion requirements in the future. Under this situation, provisions should be made for capacity expansions in the future. For example, the area of the factory premises should be kept large enough when the plant

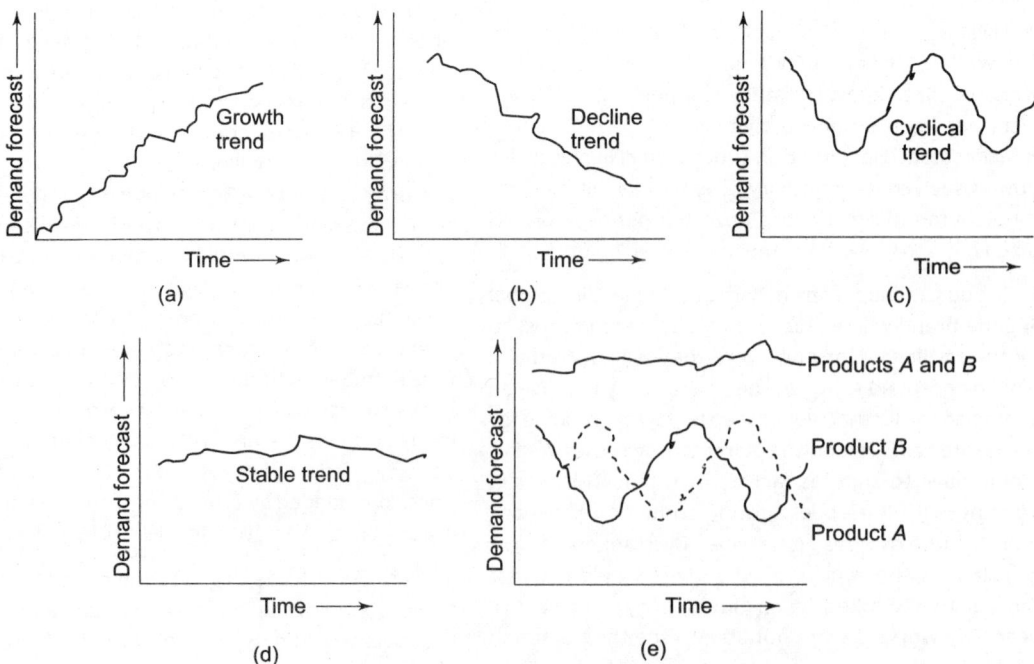

**Fig. 6.3**  Trends in demand forecasts

Four types of general trends are possible in demand forecasts: growth, decline, cyclical, and stable.

is built, keeping in view the future expansion possible. The *decline* trend of a product indicates that in the future, the company will have to think of utilizing the existing capacity in the processing of some new products. The *cyclical* demand trend of a product requires the company to produce some other product which has an opposite cyclical demand, so that the crests of the demand pattern of one product can be balanced by the troughs of the demand pattern of another product.

Figure 6.3(e) shows two products *A* and *B* which have opposite cyclical demand patterns, so that the combined demand pattern of the two products is fairly stable. For example, a company manufacturing water coolers as well as blower room heaters will experience this kind of a situation.

Capacity expansion is not the only solution for growing demand trend. Other possible measures are meeting the growing demand by overtime on part of workers and running the plant in more shifts, giving subcontracts to other small manufacturers, or accumulating inventory during periods of low demand for utilization during periods of high demand. Mature products and services have more predictable demand patterns compared to new products.

Exhibit 6.2 discusses the aspects of capacity expansion and design enhancement of Bengaluru International Airport.

### Exhibit 6.2 Capacity Expansion and Design Enhancement of Bengaluru International Airport

Bengaluru International Airport completed three successful years of operations in June 2011. Handling 33,000 passenger movements and 330 air traffic movements daily, the airport is growing at an annual rate of 18 per cent, which is higher than the national average of 16 per cent and is one of the busiest and most progressive airports in the country today.

Bengaluru International Airport Limited (BIAL) unveiled designs and details of the Terminal 1 (T1) expansion with enhanced capacity to cater to the rapidly growing passenger traffic in Bangalore.

The expansion of the existing T1 has been designed to enhance the operational performance in order to handle the increase of passenger traffic from now till 2015 (Table 6.1). The traffic is estimated to increase from the current 10.6 million passengers annually to approximately 17 million passengers. The expansion is scheduled to be completed in 18 months from the commencement of its construction in June 2011 at an estimated cost of ₹1,000 crores.

**Table 6.1** The refurbished T1 will be bigger and better

| Particulars | Current infrastructure | Post expansion |
| --- | --- | --- |
| Terminal area | 73,347 sq mtrs | 1,50,556 sq mtrs |
| Check in counters | 53 | 90 |
| CUSS | 18 | 30 |
| Emigration counters (Out-bound) | 18 | 24 |
| Immigration counters (In-bound) | 18 | 24 |
| Domestic security pedestals | 16 | 32 |
| International security pedestals | 10 | 16 |
| Aircraft aerobriges | 8 Code-C or 4 Code-E | 15 Code-C or 7 Code-E & 1 Code-F |
| Baggage reclaim belts | 9 | 15 |
| Domestic | 5 | 7 |
| International | 4 | 8 |

*(Contd)*

*Exhibit 6.2 Contd*

The construction partners for this project chosen are Larsen & Toubro, through an international competitive bidding process.

The enhanced T1 will be spread over an area of approximately 1,34,000 square metres. Designed by HOK, an architectural firm, along with several leading international architects, planners, urban designers, landscape architects, and engineering consultants, the expanded T1 would sport an enhanced and modern design elevation. The architectural concept is based on the idea of a dramatic swooping and curving roof, under which the building sits. The roof is the unifying element for new and existing facilities, bringing both together as one composition. It also forms a dramatic canopy to the main entrance, offering passengers and the public a giant covered area, protected from the weather outside. The undulating wave form provides the terminal with greater physical presence.

The expansion of the existing terminal marks a significant milestone for Bengaluru International Airport and is a step towards giving the city an airport that caters to its global aspirations. The radiant interiors and breathtaking exteriors will be designed to mirror the rich culture of Karnataka and the vibrant colors of the garden city.

*Sources:* Anon (2010); (2011).

## Optimal Capacity Determination

For a given capacity of a plant, the average unit cost of production of a product decreases as the output rate (say, in number of units produced per year) increases [Fig. 6.4(a)]. This happens because we know that the fixed cost incurred in the plant, machinery, equipment, etc. remains constant through changes in the volume of output. When a large number of units of the product are produced, these fixed costs get divided uniformly in the large number of units. Therefore, the average cost per unit of the product decreases.

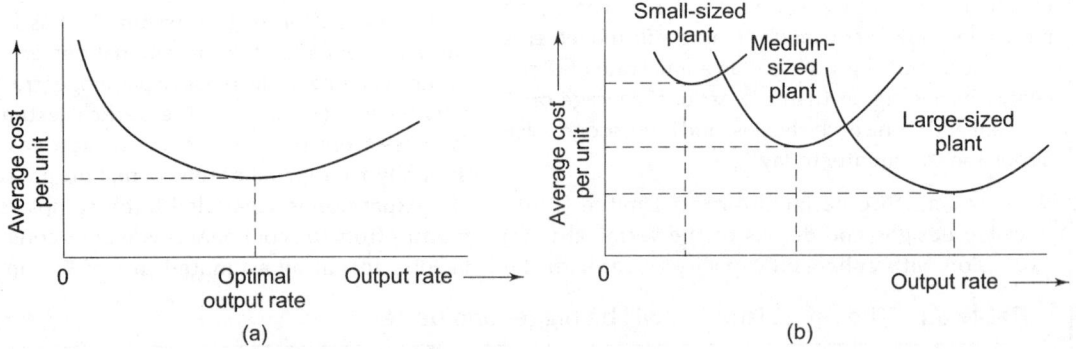

**Fig. 6.4** Optimal capacity determination

When the rate of output is increased beyond a particular limit, the average unit cost starts rising because of more frequent equipment breakdowns, fatigue in workers resulting in more defective items, scheduling problems, inventory problems, etc. This particular limit of the output rate is called the *optimum output rate*, for which the average unit cost of the product is the minimum.

There is a relationship between the optimum output rate, minimum average unit cost of a product, and the capacity of the plant. As shown in Fig. 6.4(b), for plants with small design capacity (small-sized plant), the optimum output rate is the lowest and the minimum average unit cost of the product is the highest compared to medium-sized and large-sized plants.

> There is a relationship between the optimum output rate, minimum average unit cost of a product, and the capacity of the plant.

Thus, while determining the optimal capacity of a new facility, three important factors have to be kept in mind. These are the demand forecast,

> The capacity should be kept at the minimum expected demand level and provisions should be made to introduce some flexibility in the facility in order to meet higher demands than the maximum capacity of the facility.

available capital and other resources, and the minimum average unit cost desired to keep the competitors at bay.

## Strategic Capacity Planning as a Key to Competitiveness

The large and significantly idle industrial base available in the US prior to World War II provided the foundation for America's worldwide economic dominance following this global conflict. The industrial capacity of the US, formerly dedicated to the war effort (approximately 60%), was used for the production of consumer goods and industrial equipment to meet pending demands not only at home, but also abroad. The capacity was still so high relative to the demand at prevailing prices that many industries accumulated excessive inventories during the 1950s. This scenario changed in the 1960s and 1970s, as the growing industrial output of countries recovering from the destruction of war slackened the demand for American imports and contributed to growing inventories in the US during this period.

An example of rising inventories and excess industrial capacity is the American steel industry. By the mid-1960s, foreign steel imports were having an alarming impact on American steel production, primarily because foreign steel could be purchased for less. It was assumed foreign steel was less costly to produce because of the newer, more efficient, and technologically advanced mills located in Japan and West Germany. No one had noted that these mills at that time were also more efficient because they were mostly operating at full capacity.

Thus, one reason why American steel became increasingly more expensive relative to foreign steel was that the cost of the ever-increasing excess capacity had to be spread over fewer and fewer units of production. The large capital investment in the modernization of the American steel industry did not reverse the balance of trade in this industry. The primary reason for this failure might be that the strategic planning for this modernization included an ever-present extra capacity for the newer facilities, resulting in increased production costs.

On the other hand, in the late 1940s, Japan had a worldwide reputation for cheap and shoddy goods. The economic planners in Japan knew that a healthy and thriving economy depended on manufacturing for export. The first step towards economic recovery, then, required the building of a new image for high-quality and dependable Japanese products at competitive prices. Therefore, a national economic strategy emerged to accomplish this objective. Their success in attaining these goals is evident worldwide. One key to their gains in the world marketplace might be traced to their ability to operate many production facilities at or near full capacity most of the time.

A lesson can be taken by organizations from this discussion in strategizing the capacity of a new facility so as to meet the future demand. The capacity should be kept at the minimum expected demand level and provisions should be made to introduce some flexibility in the facility in order to meet higher demands than the maximum capacity of the facility. The case of Nestle, which follows, demonstrates how it has followed this strategy to gain flexibility in its capacity to meet seasonal fluctuations in demand (Exhibit 6.3).

**Determining the requirements of personnel and equipment**   Personnel and equipment are necessary resources forming the long-term capacity of a facility. It is not easy to find suitably qualified and experienced personnel in the specialized areas of production. At the same time, it requires considerable planning and effort to create a healthy work environment in an organization

---

### Exhibit 6.3　Nestlé

The Nestlé Beverages plant in Suffolk, Virginia (USA) roasts, grinds, and packages a variety of coffees. The plant contains two separate facilities. One facility has a large capacity with continuous process lines for producing their primary brand. This line has one batch stage, roasting, but the batches are large enough (measured in 1,000 lb) to keep the rest of the line running in a continuous process fashion. The other facility is designed to run small batches of approximately 400 lb. This line is designed as a strict batch processing operation. The roasters are designed to process 400 lb, at a time, and instead of feeding into a continuous process operation, the roasted beans are stored in specially designed hoppers. These hoppers are on wheels so that they may be stored as work-in-process (WIP). These WIP batches are then scheduled through the grinding and packaging stages according to promised delivery dates.

Nestlé did not design the plant with two separate facilities strictly for capacity reasons. The primary reason was to allow them to run small batches of specialty coffees for smaller customers. The large continuous process facility could produce for the base demand, while the batch facility could be used to adjust to fluctuations in demand caused by seasonal or cyclical influences. Although it is more expensive to produce 1 lb of coffee on the batch line than on the continuous process line, producing 1 lb of coffee according to the actual schedule of demand is cheaper to the combined facilities compared to the continuous process facility (if a double-shift operation is considered), because of the flexibility of the small batch line.

*Source:* Hammesfahr et al. (1993).

---

to attract and retain talent. Similarly, the quantity of equipment and machines to be utilized in production calls for meticulous planning and analysis, keeping in view the long-term demand projections.

Let us take an example to understand how the requirements of personnel (labour) and equipment (or machines) are determined on the basis of demand forecasts in the long-term (Jacobs et al. 2009).

***Arriving at demand forecasts for products***　Zenith Electricals is a manufacturer of electrical appliances in Faridabad (Haryana). It has three major products—air coolers, ceiling fans, and table fans. It manufactures all these three products as an original equipment manufacturer (OEM) for a major retailer of electrical equipment, which sources these products from Zenith, brands them with its own name, and sells in markets in the Northern India. Zenith also manufactures and sells its unbranded products, with little modifications in the design. Upon insistence from its major institutional customer, it is contemplating about creating a new factory in Bangalore to address the needs of the markets in southern India. For this new facility, its marketing department has provided the yearly demand forecasts for the coming six years, as shown in Fig. 6.5 in the following screenshot of MS Excel. The forecasts have been categorized on the basis of branded products (to be supplied to the institutional customer) and the unbranded products (to be sold to other retail customers).

Figure 6.6 in the screenshot shows the composite demand forecasts for the three products—air coolers, ceiling fans, and table fans. This data is generated by entering the formula =B5+B10 in Cell B18 and then by dragging this cell along Row 18 so that the rest of the values appear automatically for this row. Similarly, the values are generated for Rows 19 and 20.

Let us now work out the machine capacity for these products.

### Example 6.1

Zenith sources the armatures of air coolers and ceiling and table fans from an external supplier. In its own facility, it primarily performs the production of sheet metal parts (such as the steel body of

| ▲ | A | B | C | D | E | F | G |
|---|---|---|---|---|---|---|---|
| 1 | | | | | | | |
| 2 | | | | | | | |
| 3 | | Year 1 | Year 2 | Year 3 | Year 4 | Year 5 | Year 6 |
| 4 | Branded | | | | | | |
| 5 | Air Coolers | 10000 | 12500 | 14000 | 16000 | 18000 | 21000 |
| 6 | Ceiling Fans | 15000 | 17000 | 19500 | 22000 | 25000 | 28000 |
| 7 | Table Fans | 5000 | 6500 | 8000 | 9000 | 11000 | 13000 |
| 8 | | | | | | | |
| 9 | Unbranded | | | | | | |
| 10 | Air Coolers | 3500 | 3800 | 4300 | 4700 | 5000 | 5600 |
| 11 | Ceiling Fans | 4000 | 4400 | 5200 | 6000 | 6400 | 6900 |
| 12 | Table Fans | 500 | 700 | 1000 | 1400 | 1700 | 2000 |
| 13 | | | | | | | |
| 14 | | | | | | | |
| 15 | | | | | | | |
| 16 | | | | | | | |
| 17 | | Year 1 | Year 2 | Year 3 | Year 4 | Year 5 | Year 6 |
| 18 | Air Coolers | 13500 | 16300 | 18300 | 20700 | 23000 | 26600 |
| 19 | Ceiling Fans | 19000 | 21400 | 24700 | 28000 | 31400 | 34900 |
| 20 | Table Fans | 5500 | 7200 | 9000 | 10400 | 12700 | 15000 |

**Fig. 6.5**   Demand forecast for product categories

**Fig. 6.6**   Composite demand forecast for products

air coolers and wings of fans) and assembling for all the three products. For this purpose, it uses different kinds of pressing machines. Figure 6.7 shown in the MS Excel screenshot shows the capacity of each of these pressing machines (in units per year of products produced). For the new proposed facility in Bangalore, it has tentatively earmarked the number of machines to be procured as shown in Column C of Fig. 6.7. Column D shows the total machine capacity (Capacity of each machine × No. of machines), while Column E shows the number of operators required on each machine.

***Calculating the labour and machine requirements***   In Fig. 6.8, we perform the calculations for capacity utilization, machine requirement, and labour requirement for each of the six years in future. Capacity utilization is defined as the ratio of the capacity used to the maximum capacity.

$$\text{Capacity utilization} = \frac{\text{Capacity used}}{\text{Maximum capacity}}$$

Let us perform the calculation for air coolers first. The maximum (machine) capacity for air coolers is shown in Cell D27 as 30,000, while 13,500 is the (expected) capacity to be used in Year 1 (as shown in Cell B18). Therefore, in Cell B36, we enter the formula =B18/D27 to arrive at the value 0.45. Thus, in Year 1, only 45 per cent of the maximum capacity would be utilized. We drag this cell across Row 36 to get the corresponding values automatically for the remaining five years. Note that capacity utilization for Year 6 is 88.67 per cent, thus leaving a capacity cushion of about 11.33 per cent. Capacity cushion is defined as follows:

$$\text{Capacity cushion} = 1 - \text{Capacity utilization}$$

Thus, some amount of capacity cushion should be maintained in order to safeguard against unexpected demand surges in a given time period.

Next, we find the machine requirement by multiplying the capacity utilization with the number of machines available. In Cell B37, we enter the formula =B36*3, where 3 is the number of machines proposed to be procured for manufacturing air coolers (as given in Cell C27). We get the value 1.35 signifying that we would actually require 1.35 machine to fulfil the demand in Year 1. We drag this cell across Row 37 to get the corresponding values automatically for the remaining five years. Thus, we observe that two machines would suffice for fulfilling the demand during the first three years of the planning horizon and the third machine should be procured just before the beginning of Year 4 for satisfying the demand during the remaining three years.

| | A | B | C | D | E | F | G |
|---|---|---|---|---|---|---|---|
| 25 | | | | | | | |
| 26 | | Machine Capacity (units per year) | No. of Machines | Total Machine Capacity | No. of operators on each machine | | |
| 27 | Air Coolers | 10000 | 3 | 30000 | 4 | | |
| 28 | Ceiling Fans | 15000 | 3 | 45000 | 2 | | |
| 29 | Table Fans | 10000 | 2 | 20000 | 2 | | |
| 30 | | | | | | | |
| 31 | | | | | | | |
| 32 | | | | | | | |
| 33 | | | | | | | |
| 34 | | Year 1 | Year 2 | Year 3 | Year 4 | Year 5 | Year 6 |
| 35 | Air Coolers | | | | | | |
| 36 | Capacity Utilization | 0.45 | 0.543333 | 0.61 | 0.69 | 0.766667 | 0.886667 |
| 37 | Machine Requirement | 1.35 | 1.63 | 1.83 | 2.07 | 2.3 | 2.66 |
| 38 | Labour Requirement | 5.4 | 6.52 | 7.32 | 8.28 | 9.2 | 10.64 |

**Fig. 6.7** Machine capacity and operator requirement on each machine

| | A | B | C | D | E | F | G |
|---|---|---|---|---|---|---|---|
| 40 | | | | | | | |
| 41 | | Year 1 | Year 2 | Year 3 | Year 4 | Year 5 | Year 6 |
| 42 | Ceiling Fans | | | | | | |
| 43 | Capacity Utilization | 0.422222 | 0.475556 | 0.548889 | 0.622222 | 0.697778 | 0.775556 |
| 44 | Machine Requirement | 1.266667 | 1.426667 | 1.646667 | 1.866667 | 2.093333 | 2.326667 |
| 45 | Labour Requirement | 2.533333 | 2.853333 | 3.293333 | 3.733333 | 4.186667 | 4.653333 |
| 46 | | | | | | | |
| 47 | | | | | | | |
| 48 | | Year 1 | Year 2 | Year 3 | Year 4 | Year 5 | Year 6 |
| 49 | Table Fans | | | | | | |
| 50 | Capacity Utilization | 0.275 | 0.36 | 0.45 | 0.52 | 0.635 | 0.75 |
| 51 | Machine Requirement | 0.55 | 0.72 | 0.9 | 1.04 | 1.27 | 1.5 |
| 52 | Labour Requirement | 1.1 | 1.44 | 1.8 | 2.08 | 2.54 | 3 |

**Fig. 6.8** Calculation of labour and machine requirement

Finally, we find the labour requirement by multiplying the machine requirement with the number of operators required on each machine. In Cell B38, we enter the formula =B37*4, where 4 is the number of operators required on a machine for manufacturing air coolers (as given in Cell E27). The value 5.4 suggests that we would require 6 operators in Year 1. We drag this cell towards row 38 for automatically arriving at the remaining values in this row. Thus, the recruitment of personnel can be planned accordingly—6 operators required in Year 1; 7 operators required in Year 2 (one operator to be recruited at the beginning of Year 2 as 6 operators from Year 1 would still continue); 8 operators in Year 3; 9 operators in Year 4, 10 operators in Year 5; and 11 operators in Year 6.

We perform calculations for capacity utilization and machine and labour requirement for manufacturing ceiling and table fans in a similar way as shown in Fig. 6.8 in the MS Excel screenshot.

# Decision Tree Analysis in Facility Capacity Planning

> Decision tree analysis is a technique used to analyse decision situations that are sequential in nature.

Decision tree analysis is a technique used to analyse decision situations that are sequential in nature. This means that decisions have to be taken one after the other in a sequence. In this technique, a diagram is made to represent the various decision options and their outcomes. The diagram resembles a tree with various branches coming out from the main stem and, therefore, it is called a decision tree.

In the decision tree diagram, small rectangles are used to represent the points of decision called *decision nodes*. Here a choice is to be made for the best decision option from a set of options branching out from this node. Small circles are used to represent the points of outcomes or events as a result of choosing a decision option. These circles are called *event* or *outcome nodes*. Various outcomes branch out from these nodes. These outcomes are not under the control of the decision maker and any one of these may occur according to the probabilities assigned to them. Probabilities are assigned to these outcomes on the basis of past experience or by expert judgements.

The decision tree is analysed for the best decision sequence by the *rollback technique*. In this technique, the decision nodes in the later part of the tree are analysed first and then those in the earlier part. Hence, the name rollback technique. Decision tree analysis is a useful technique for capacity planning of facilities.

## *Example 6.2*

Delight Café is a popular fast food centre at Park Street, Kolkata. It has a heavy rush of customers during the lunch and dinner hours on all days. The proprietor of Delight, Ashok Mukherjee, is considering expansion of the space in the restaurant so that more tables may be accommodated. This will require an investment of ₹0.6 million. Another option being considered by Mukherjee is opening a new fast food centre at Tollygunj, another locality in Kolkata, where he is getting a prime location and where it seems the demand for Delight's food is pretty high. This option requires an investment of ₹0.7 million.

Mukherjee does not have the capital to undertake both the investments simultaneously. He can undertake any one option at this time and if it results in strong demand from customers, he can go ahead with the other option too, or stop any further investment. Both the options lead to complete loss of investment if there is weak demand from the customers. There is a 60 per cent chance of strong demand after capacity expansion of the existing facility and it will result in a profit of ₹1 million (over investment). After creating the new facility at Tollygunj, there is an 80 per cent chance of strong demand and it will result in a profit of ₹0.9 million (over investment). Give your advice to Mukherjee about the best course of action using decision tree analysis.

## *Solution*

Initially there are three decision options for Mukherjee—expand the existing facility, create another facility at a new location, or do nothing. Make a small rectangle to represent decision node 1 and three lines emerging out from it to show the three decision options as shown in Fig. 6.9. Note that the 'do nothing' option results in ₹0 as it requires no investment and gives no profit.

The 'Expand the existing facility' decision option results in two outcomes or events. Either the demand will be strong with a probability of 0.6 and a profit of

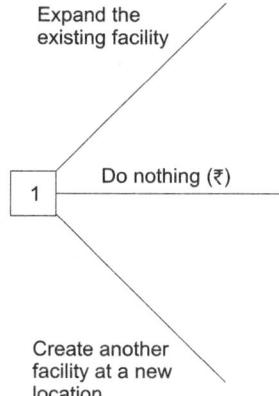

Expand the existing facility

Do nothing (₹)

Create another facility at a new location

**Fig. 6.9**

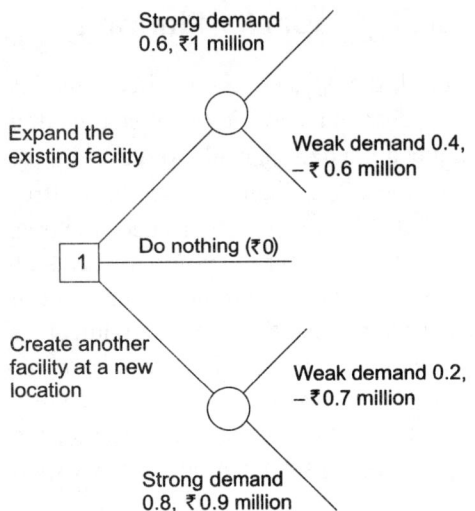

**Fig. 6.10**

₹1 million, or the demand will be weak with a probability of 0.4 and a loss of the ₹0.6 million investment. Similarly, the 'Create another facility at a new location' decision option results in two outcomes or events. Either the demand will be strong with a probability of 0.8 and a profit of ₹0.9 million, or the demand will be weak with a probability of 0.2 and a loss of the ₹0.7 million investment. We make small circles to represent event nodes at the end of these two decision options and branch out the outcomes from it as shown in Fig. 6.10.

The weak demand event will lead to no further action on Mukherjee's part. The strong demand event will lead to another decision node, where the decision options are either to stop, resulting in zero profit, or to undertake the other investment (Fig. 6.11).

At this stage, the 'Expand the existing facility' and 'Create another facility at a new location' decision options will again result in the same two outcomes each as before (Fig. 6.12). The decision tree diagram is made, and now we need to choose either decision node 2 or decision node 3 as both are at the same distance from the starting node 1. The rollback technique requires the decision nodes at later stages in the decision tree to be evaluated first and, therefore, we evalueate node 2.

At node 2, there are two alternatives—'Create another facility at a new location' and 'Stop'. These alternatives are shown in the first table of the Excel spreadsheet shown in Fig. 6.13. The outcomes of the alternative 'Create another facility at a new location', that is, strong demand and weak demand are also shown along with their probabilities of occurrence (0.8 and 0.2, respectively) and conditional values (₹0.9 million and ₹0.7 million, respectively).

To obtain the expected value for each outcome, multiply the conditional value with the corresponding probability (enter the formula =**C3*D3** in cell E3). Sum up the expected values of the two outcomes in cell E5 (by selecting the cells E3, E4 and E5 and then clicking on the summation sign Σ in the toolbar) to get the total value as ₹0.58 million.

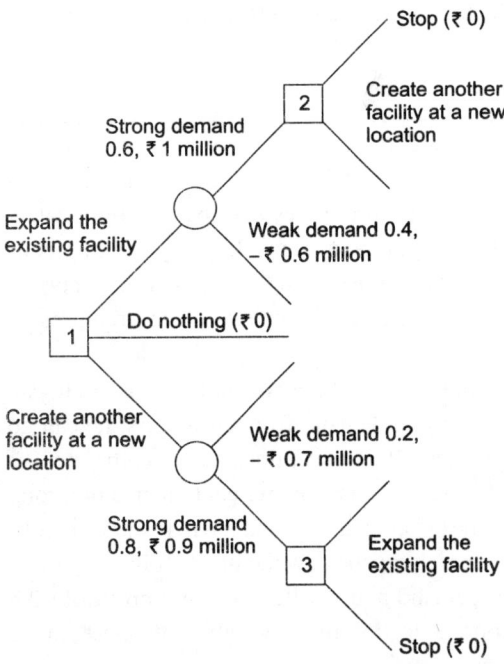

**Fig. 6.11**

For the 'Stop' alternative there is no outcome and its conditional value is ₹0. Thus, its expected value is also 0. On comparing the expected values of the two alternatives at node 2, we find that the value ₹0.58 million is a better option than ₹0. Hence, we cancel the 'Stop' option by striking off this path (Fig. 6.14) and choose 'Create another facility at another location'. ₹0.58 is now the expected value a node 2.

Repeat the above procedure for node 3 and choose the option 'Expand the existing facility' with the expected value of ₹0.36 million as shown in Fig. 6.14. Now, consider node 1, which has three decision options. Construct a table for node 1 on MS Excel as shown in Fig. 6.13. Note that for the

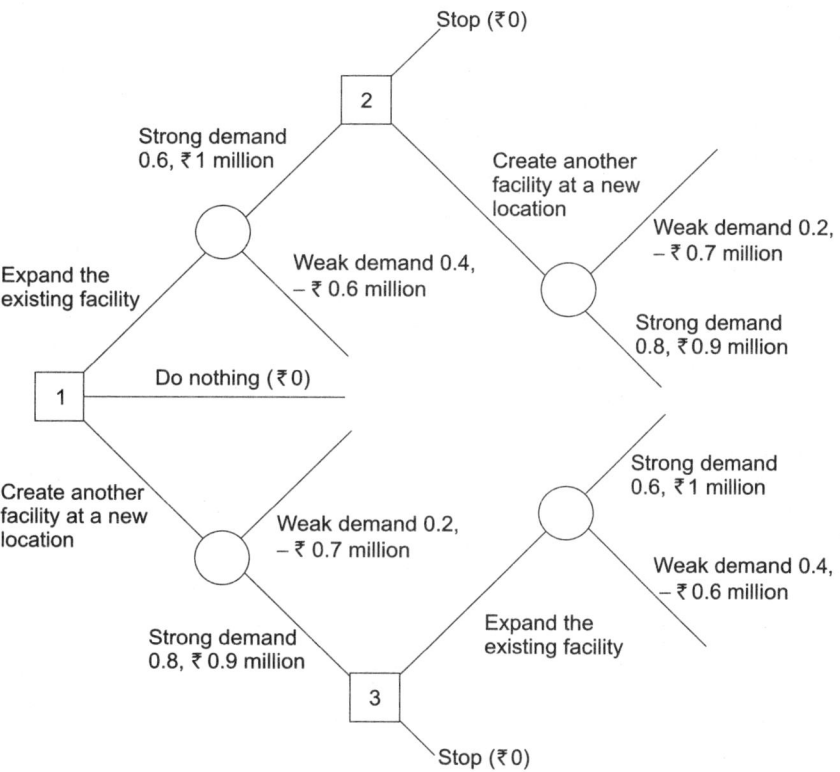

**Fig. 6.12**

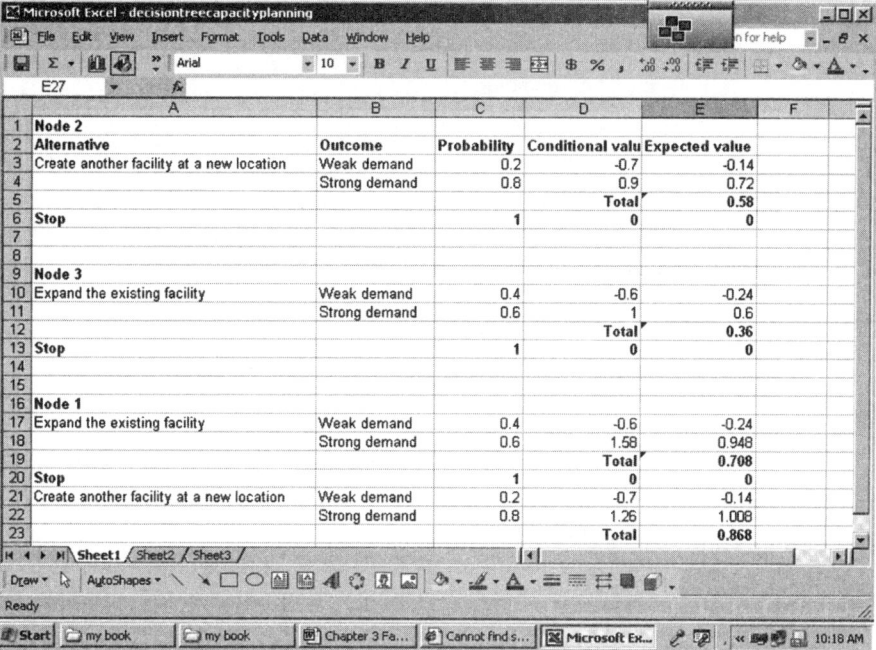

**Fig. 6.13** MS Excel worksheet for decision tree analysis

'Expand the existing facility' option and its strong demand event, we have added the ₹0.58 million expected value to the ₹1 million conditional value of the strong demand event to get a conditional value of ₹1.58 million for this event.

Similarly, for the 'create another facility at a new location' option and its strong demand event, we have added the ₹0.36 million expected value to the ₹0.9 million conditional value of the strong demand event to get a conditional value of ₹1.26 million for this event. Thus, for node 1 we get three expected values for the three decision options as ₹0.708 million, 0, and ₹0.868 million. The value ₹0.868 million is the highest for the option 'create another facility at a new location'. Therefore, this is the best option and we strike off the other two options as shown in Fig. 6.14.

Hence, our advice to Mukherjee is that he should create another facility at Tollygunj in Kolkata and if there is strong demand for his fast food there, he should expand his existing facility. Otherwise, he should stop any further investment.

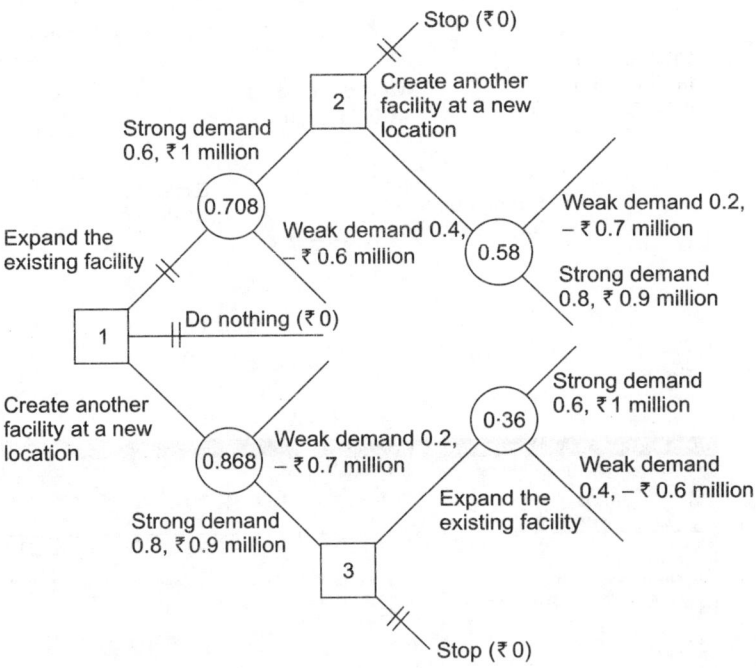

**Fig. 6.14**   Decision tree diagram displaying the paths that cannot be used and the expected values (encircled in millions)

# Facility Layout Planning

The layout of a facility is the physical location of the various departments/units of the facility within the premises of the facility. The departments may be located based on some considerations such as less walking distance, logical sequence of the processing requirements of the product, or any special requirements such as emergency services. The entries and exits to the premises also have a critical importance in the layout planning of facilities. There are four types of basic layouts: product, process, fixed-position, and cellular layouts.

> The layout of a facility is the physical location of the various departments/units of the facility within the premises of the facility.

## Product Layout

A product layout is suitable when a product having standard features is to be produced in large volumes. The production process thus involves repetitive tasks to be performed on items arranged in a sequence. The specialized machines and equipment are arranged one after the other in the order of sequence required in the production process, such that a production line is formed by them. This production line is often called the assembly line.

*Courtesy:* BMW. Used with permission.

At BMW's Spartanburg plant (USA), Power Train is a separate sub-assembly area, where the engine and transmission, front and rear axles, and drive shafts are assembled. This entire sub-assembly (also called the power train) is transferred for assembly with the underbody of the car. As shown in the picture above, the power train is just below the underbody of the car hanging above. The platform on which power train is put is raised to reach the underbody and the workers join the two together. After the marriage, the exhaust, under-hood connections, and battery hook-up are completed.

The assembly line has a mechanized moving platform or the conveyor, which moves at regular intervals of time. The basic structures of the products to be manufactured in the raw form (e.g., the chassis of cars in an automobile final assembly line) are placed on the conveyor at equal distances from each other (Exhibit 6.4). Across the conveyor, there are workstations

which have the required machines, equipment, components, sub-assemblies, tools, and workers to perform the assembling tasks on the basic structure of the product (Fig. 6.15).

As shown in Fig. 6.15, the chassis of (say) cars are arranged on the conveyor one after the other at equal distances. The conveyor has brought car 1 in front

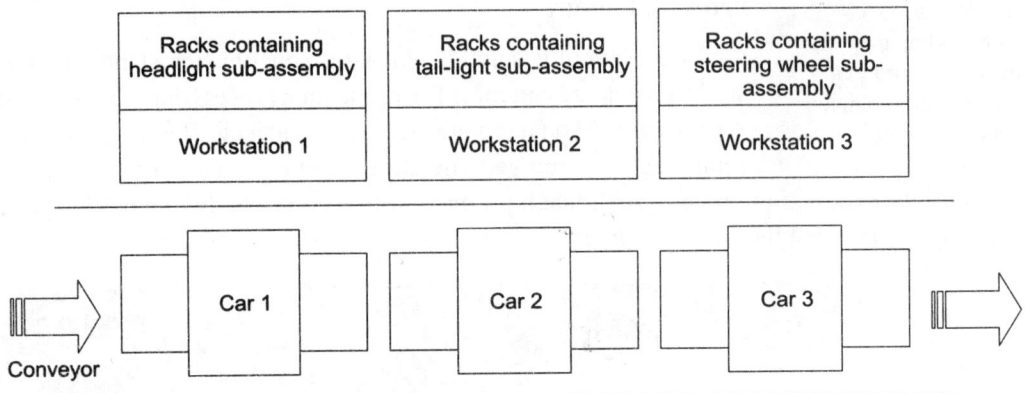

**Fig. 6.15**   An assembly line (product layout)

of workstation 1, car 2 in front of workstation 2, and car 3 in front of workstation 3. At workstation 1, the worker assembles the headlight sub-assembly (called so because it is itself made by assembling small components such as the reflector, bulb, holder, etc.) to the chassis of car 1. At workstation 2, the worker attaches the tail light to car 2. At workstation 3, the worker fits the steering wheel inside car 3.

After the workers finish their tasks, the conveyor is ready to move. It takes car 1 to workstation 2, car 2 to workstation 3, and car 3 off the assembly line (as workstation 3 is shown as the last workstation). If car 0 was placed before car 1 on the conveyor, it now comes to workstation 1. The respective tasks are performed once again at the workstations on the chassis of cars before them. This process continues so that finished cars (such as car 3 earlier) keep coming off the assembly line.

The total performance time of tasks assigned to each workstation should be almost equal. This is necessary because the conveyor moves after a definite period of time. In addition, the tasks should be assigned to successive workstations according to the required sequence, for example, the steering wheel sub-assembly can be fitted only after the steering rod (which controls the sidewise movement of the front wheels of a car) is in place. Figure 6.16 shows the advantages and disadvantages of a product layout.

**The U-shaped assembly line**   As shown in Fig. 6.17, a U-shaped assembly line is useful particularly when there is a single worker in the line taking care of all the workstations. The U shape of the line reduces the  walking distance of the worker almost by half. The U-shaped line is being successfully used by Matsushita Electric Co. of Japan by using a single worker in the line. More workers can also be used in such a line.

The closeness of the workstations allows workers to help a fellow worker catch up, especially one working on the station just opposite. This increases teamwork among workers. At the same time, many workstations close to each other may result in conversations, noise, etc., resulting in distraction from work. The U-shaped line reduces material handling as the entry and exit points of the material on the line are nearby. A trolley which brings the raw material for the line may take back the finished goods in a single round.

> The total performance time of tasks assigned to each workstation should be almost equal.

> A U-shaped assembly line is useful particularly when there is a single worker in the line taking care of all the worksta-tions.

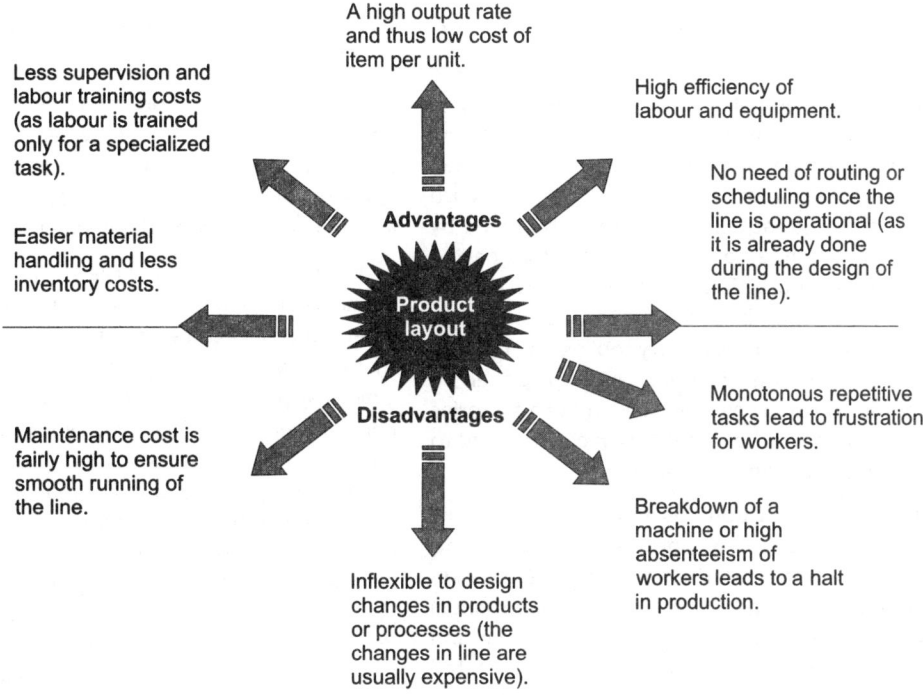

**Fig. 6.16** Advantages and disadvantages of product layout

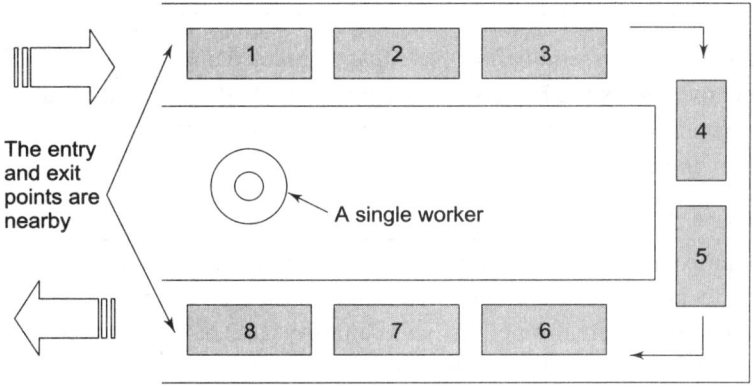

**Fig. 6.17** A U-shaped assembly line

**Assembly line balancing** The assembly line can be efficient only when tasks are assigned to different workstations in such a way that, as far as possible, the total processing times at these workstations are equal. This is so because the conveyor moves at regular intervals of time and, therefore, the time available for each workstation to complete its set of assigned tasks is the same. This is achieved by assembly line balancing.

> The time for which a basic structure of the product is available before a workstation is called the cycle time.

The time for which a basic structure of the product is available before a workstation is called the *cycle time*. In fact, it is the time after which the conveyor moves. Cycle time is defined as the time period after which completed

---

### Exhibit 6.4   Henry Ford—The Inventor of the Assembly Line

In 1913, Henry Ford employed up to 1,000 people simply to move material in his automobile factory, an occupation that was to be virtually eliminated in a new building with an improved layout and with mechanized and gravity-based material-handling systems. Ford discovered that great economies could be made by moving stocks to the assembly staff rather than having them leave their work places to get materials. He also noted that costs could be greatly reduced by providing the workers with all the necessary tooling and thereby eliminating tool rooms. The great emphasis placed on efficiency in transporting materials in Ford factories seems to have been the motivating factor that led to the development of an assembly line.

Before 1913, production was done in a process line, which embodied calculated, progressive movement, but no continuous flow. The assembly line appears to have been founded by making the earlier manual approaches more structured and rigorous first, and then, mechanized and continuous. It was first instituted on 1 April 1913 in a manually driven, worker-paced form, and soon developed to a mechanically driven form and spread throughout other suitable operations in the factory. The impact of the assembly line was to reduce direct labour input from 728 minutes to 93 minutes per car within a year. Ford later went even further and designed his factories to allow delivery directly to the production line. The greatest distance any material had to be trucked was 20 ft, this being the distance from the incoming freight car to the first conveyor.

Ford engineers conserved space by using very detailed floor plans and positioned equipment such that when a machine comes into the factory, it is placed so that the material coming from an operation will be as exactly as possible in position for the succeeding one. Ford himself said, 'They (machines) are scientifically arranged, not only in the sequence of operations, but to give every man and every machine every square inch of space that he/it requires and ... not ... more'. Ford was extremely conscious that space in his factory was valuable and sought to exploit it as completely as possible without giving any more to work in progress than was necessary. Ford emphasizes 'dividing and subdividing operations, keeping the work in motion—those are the keynotes of production', in a perspective that leaves no room for excessive or idle inventories.

*Source:* Wilson (1995).

---

units come off the assembly line. Note that completed units will be available after each movement of the conveyor, as the basic structure being worked upon at the last workstation will become a completed unit in that time. Let us try to understand the steps in assembly line balancing by the following example.

### Example 6.3

WorldStar Appliances Ltd is based at New Delhi and manufactures the BlueLine range of mixer/grinders for household use. It sources the outer plastic bodies of the mixers, electrical wires, electrical plugs, etc. from external suppliers. This company is ISO 9001 certified and has a large market share in the northern parts of the country. The assembly line of this factory has a number of tasks to be performed according to the precedence requirements given in Table 6.2.

*Step 1: Find the bottleneck operation and the minimum cycle time*   A *bottleneck operation* is the task requiring the longest operation time. It is called so because assuming that the tasks cannot be split into parts, this task has to be assigned to a workstation and the cycle time cannot be less than the duration of this task. Thus, the duration of the bottleneck operation is the minimum possible cycle time.

In our example, the bottleneck operation is task C, which requires a task time of 5 minutes (the longest time among the set of given tasks). Thus, the minimum cycle time for this assembly line design is 5 minutes. This cycle time is called the minimum cycle time because if the cycle time is kept less than 5 minutes (say, 4 minutes), then task C cannot be accommodated at any workstation (as the basic structure will be available before a workstation for only 4 minutes and task C requires 5 minutes).

> A bottleneck operation is the task requiring the longest operation time.

**Table 6.2**

| Task | Description | Precedence requirement(s) | Task time (min) |
|---|---|---|---|
| A | Fixing the electrical motor assembly over the plastic base | – | 4 |
| B | Inserting the rubber blocks in the slots below the plastic base | – | 2 |
| C | Connecting the electrical lead to the electric motor assembly | – | 5 |
| D | Attaching the outer plastic cover over the motor assembly and to the plastic base using screws | A, C | 3 |
| E | Fixing the electrical on/off switch over the plastic cover | D | 4 |
| F | Attaching the plastic circular rotator on top of the mixer, which moves another rotator inside the jar attachment (which is attached to the mixer) | D | 2 |
| G | Final inspection of the mixer | B, E, F | 3 |
| H | Packing the mixer unit with jar attachments | G | 2 |
| | | | 25 |

***Step 2: Find the theoretical minimum number of workstations required for the assignment of tasks***    Table 6.2 shows that the sum of task times of all the given tasks is 25 minutes. The cycle time is 5 minutes, that is, each workstation will have 5 minutes available for the performance of each task. Therefore, for a total of 25 minutes of performance time for all the tasks on the assembly line,

$$\text{Theoretical minimum number of workstations} = \frac{\text{Total performance time}}{\text{Cycle time}}$$

$$= \frac{25}{5} = 5 \text{ workstations}$$

***Step 3: Apply a heuristic to assign tasks to workstations***    The heuristic (a set of rules) we will use to assign tasks to the workstations is called the *longest operation time* (LOT) rule. This heuristic is called so because it gives the top priority of assignment to the task requiring the longest operation time. In our example, task *C* requires the longest operation time of 5 minutes (the bottleneck operation); therefore, this task has the highest priority of assignment at the first workstation. Table 6.2 shows that task *C* does not have the precedence requirement of any other task, that is, there is no need of any other task to be completed for the execution of task *C*. Therefore, task *C* can be assigned to the first workstation. We make Table 6.3 to start the assignment of tasks to the workstations.

*Heuristic step 1*    In the first heuristic step, *C* is the eligible task for the first workstation and is assigned to it (Table 6.3). The task time of *C* is 5 minutes. The time available on station 1 is 5 minutes as the cycle time is 5 minutes. Therefore, there is no time left on station 1 after the assignment of task *C* to it and, hence, no more tasks are assigned to this station.

**Table 6.3**

| Heuristic step | Workstation | Eligible task | Task assigned | Task time (min) | Remaining time available on the workstation (min) | Remaining eligible tasks |
|---|---|---|---|---|---|---|
| 1 | 1 | C | C | 5 | – | – |

*Heuristic step 2* Consider the next station, that is, workstation 2. Table 6.2 shows that tasks *A* and *E* now require the longest time of 4 minutes each. Task *A* has no precedence requirement, but task *E* requires task *D* to be completed before it can itself be assigned to any workstation. Task *D* has not been assigned earlier and, therefore, task *E* is not eligible for this workstation. Only task *A* is the eligible task for workstation 2 and is hence assigned to it (Table 6.4). Station 2 has 1 minute remaining, but there is no task in the given set requiring 1 minute for execution. Therefore, no other task is eligible for this workstation.

**Table 6.4**

| Heuristic step | Workstation | Eligible task | Task assigned | Task time (min) | Remaining time available on the workstation (min) | Remaining eligible tasks |
|---|---|---|---|---|---|---|
| 1 | 1 | C | C | 5 | – | – |
| 2 | 2 | A | A | 4 | 1 | – |

*Heuristic step 3* For workstation 3, we see that task *E* requires the longest task time of 4 minutes and has to be given top assignment priority. It has the precedence requirement of task *D* as discussed earlier. Therefore, task *D* becomes eligible at this workstation and is assigned to it (Table 6.5). Task *D* has a duration of 3 minutes and there are 2 minutes remaining on workstation 3. From Table 6.1, notice that tasks *B* and *F* each require 2 minutes. There is no precedence requirement for task *B* and that of task *F* is task *D*, which is already assigned on workstation 3. Therefore, both *B* and *F* become the remaining eligible tasks at workstation 3. This means that in the next heuristic step, we need to consider workstation 3 again.

**Table 6.5**

| Heuristic step | Workstation | Eligible task | Task assigned | Task time (min) | Remaining time available on the workstation (min) | Remaining eligible tasks |
|---|---|---|---|---|---|---|
| 1 | 1 | C | C | 5 | – | – |
| 2 | 2 | A | A | 4 | 1 | – |
| 3 | 3 | D | D | 3 | 2 | B, F |

*Heuristic step 4* At workstation 3, the eligible tasks are *B* and *F* (which were the remaining eligible tasks in heuristic step 3). We can assign any one of these tasks now as both have the same task time of 2 minutes. We choose task *F* and assign it to workstation 3 (Table 6.6). There is no remaining time on this workstation and, therefore, there is no remaining eligible task for it.

**Table 6.6**

| Heuristic step | Workstation | Eligible task | Task assigned | Task time (min) | Remaining time available on the workstation (min) | Remaining eligible tasks |
|---|---|---|---|---|---|---|
| 1 | 1 | C | C | 5 | – | – |
| 2 | 2 | A | A | 4 | 1 | – |
| 3 | 3 | D | D | 3 | 2 | B, F |
| 4 | 3 | B, F | F | 2 | – | – |

*Heuristic step 5* Consider workstation 4 now. Task *E* now requires the longest time of 4 minutes and is eligible for assignment at this station as its precedence requirement of task *D* is already satisfied. Therefore, we assign task *E* to station 4 (Table 6.7). One minute remains at station 4, but there is no task requiring 1 minute. Hence, there are no other entries in this heuristic step.

**Table 6.7**

| Heuristic step | Workstation | Eligible task | Task assigned | Task time (min) | Remaining time available on the workstation (min) | Remaining eligible tasks |
|---|---|---|---|---|---|---|
| 1 | 1 | C | C | 5 | – | – |
| 2 | 2 | A | A | 4 | 1 | – |
| 3 | 3 | D | D | 3 | 2 | B, F |
| 4 | 3 | B, F | F | 2 | – | – |
| 5 | 4 | E | E | 4 | 1 | – |

*Heuristic steps 6–8* Repeat the above-explained process to get Table 6.8. Note that we have used six workstations for the assignment of all the tasks (in contrast to five workstations theoretically determined earlier; this explains why this is called the *theoretical minimum*).

**Table 6.8**

| Heuristic step | Workstation | Eligible task | Task assigned | Task time (min) | Remaining time available on the workstation (min) | Remaining eligible tasks |
|---|---|---|---|---|---|---|
| 1 | 1 | C | C | 5 | – | – |
| 2 | 2 | A | A | 4 | 1 | – |
| 3 | 3 | D | D | 3 | 2 | B, F |
| 4 | 3 | B, F | F | 2 | – | – |
| 5 | 4 | E | E | 4 | 1 | – |
| 6 | 5 | B | B | 2 | 3 | G |
| 7 | 5 | G | G | 3 | – | – |
| 8 | 6 | H | H | 2 | 3 | – |

Figure 6.18 shows the tasks assigned to the six workstations. Let us now find the efficiency of this assembly line design using the data in Table 6.9.

**Table 6.9**

| | Workstation | | | | | | |
|---|---|---|---|---|---|---|---|
| | 1 | 2 | 3 | 4 | 5 | 6 | Total |
| Available time (min) | 5 | 5 | 5 | 5 | 5 | 5 | 30 |
| Performance time (min) | 5 | 4 | 5 | 4 | 5 | 2 | 25 |
| Idle time (min) | 0 | 1 | 0 | 1 | 0 | 3 | 5 |

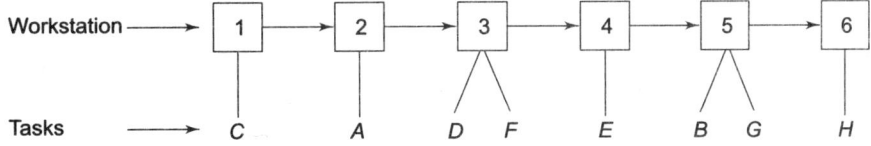

**Fig. 6.18** Assignment of tasks to workstations

$$\text{Efficiency of the line} = \frac{\text{Performance time}}{\text{Available time}} \times 100$$

$$= \frac{25}{30} \times 100 = 83.33\%$$

Thus, the line has a high efficiency of 83.33%. Ideally, the efficiency should be 100%, but practically this is not feasible in the given problem.

## Process Layout

In a process layout, general-purpose machines are arranged in no particular sequence, as the processing requirements and sequence are different for the various types of products to be manufactured.

In a process layout, general-purpose machines are arranged in no particular sequence, as the processing requirements and sequence are different for the various types of products to be manufactured. These machines include the lathe machine, drilling machine, milling machine, grinding machine, etc., which handle different types of processing requirements. In a production set-up, such a layout is also called a machine shop or job shop.

A good example of a process layout can be seen at any Maruti Service Station. Here, separate departments (areas) with general-purpose machines are assigned for dent corrections, painting, wheel alignment, oil replacement, engine correction, electrical check-up, interiors, washing, cleaning, etc. Different Maruti cars have different service requirements and are thus taken to different departments according to a schedule decided upon by the service supervisor (Fig. 6.19).

Process layout is particularly suitable when different products are produced in lots or batches. This is called *intermittent manufacturing*. The demand of items is not high enough to warrant continuous manufacturing. Process layout is very commonly found in service set-ups such as

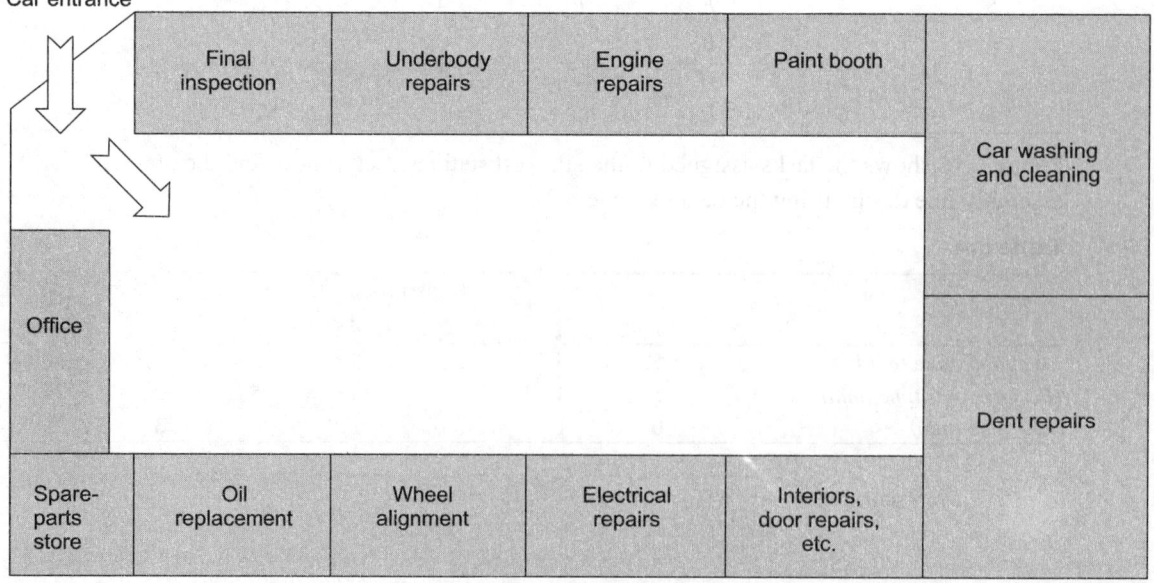

**Fig. 6.19** Process layout of an automobile service station

banks, hospitals, post offices, universities, libraries, etc. Figure 6.20 shows the various advantages and disadvantages of a process layout.

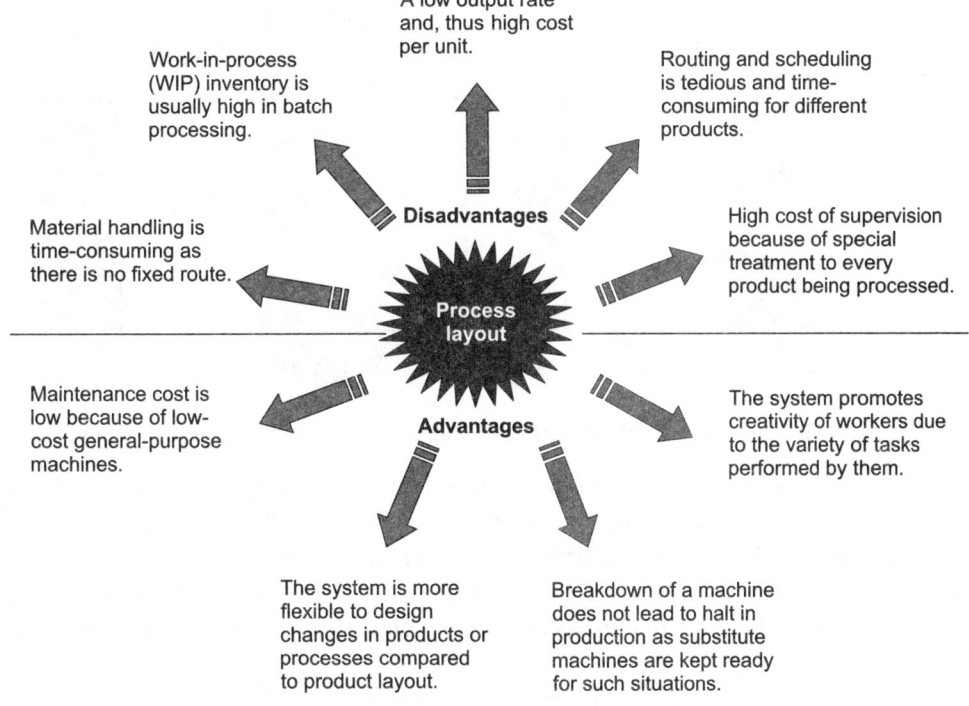

**Fig. 6.20** Advantages and disadvantages of process layout

## Fixed-position Layout

In this layout, the product is very bulky, heavy, large, or has a fixed position. For example, the construction of a building, dam, or a plant (these have fixed positions); drilling of crude oil (again a fixed-position site); or construction of an aeroplane, a ship, or a rocket (large, bulky). Thus, machines, equipment, raw materials, workers, etc. have to be taken to the site of the product. The important aspect is the placement of all these things inside or around the product so that no overcrowding takes place. Equipment, raw materials, and worker teams are brought to the site according to a time schedule for better utilization of the space available (Fig. 6.21).

## Cellular Layout and Group Technology

We have seen that both product and process layouts have their advantages and disadvantages. Product layout is desirable by most organizations, but the low volume and the variety of their products does not warrant it. Therefore, they have no choice but to go in for good old batch processing on process layout. Product layout and process layout represent the two extremes of layout techniques. An intermediate layout called cellular layout has evolved now to aid manufacturers with intermittent manufacturing of a high variety of products with the advantages of a product layout.

> Process layout is particularly suitable when different products are produced in lots or batches.

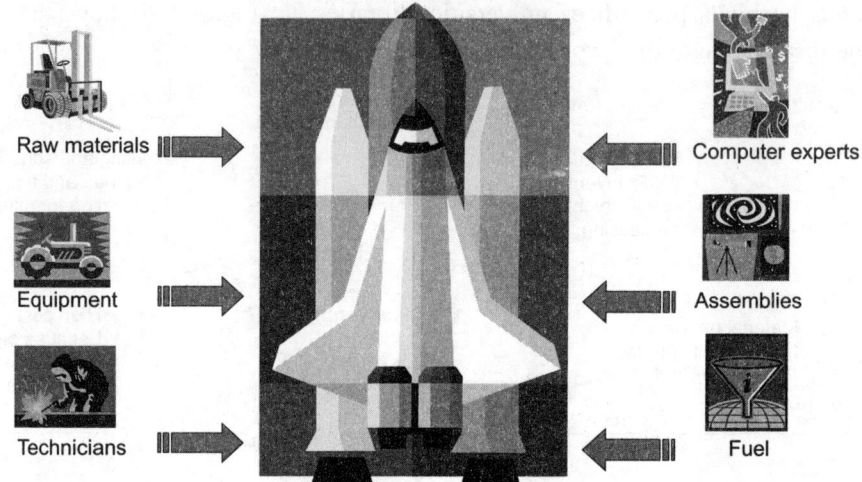

**Fig. 6.21**   Schematic diagram to show the fixed-position layout of a space shuttle

Let us take an example to understand cellular layout. Figure 6.22 shows the typical process layout of a factory which has six departments, namely, lathe, foundry, fitting, drilling, welding, and paint. Each of these departments has general-purpose machines required for processing products manufactured by the factory. Figure 6.22 shows how different products are routed through different departments according to their differing processig requirements.

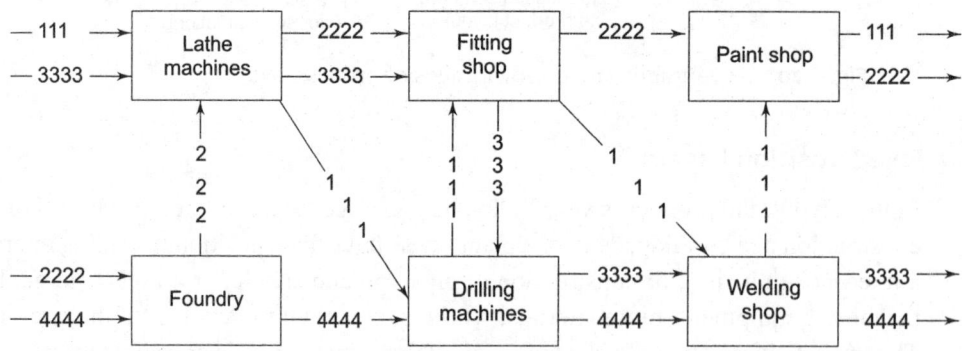

**Fig. 6.22**   Typical process layout of a factory

In a cellular layout of the same factory (Fig. 6.23), groups of items with similar processing requirements are identified, and separate manufacturing cells are formed for each group, which contain the required machines in the desired sequence. There is no conveyor or mechanized moving platform in the cells to carry items from one machine to the other, as in the product layout. The identification of similar groups of items is an important aspect of cellular layout and is called *group technology* (GT). Exhibit 6.5 discusses the production process of Airbus and Boeing.

> The identification of similar groups of items is an important aspect of cellular layout and is called group technology (GT).

In GT, groups of items can be formed either according to similarities in their design (external features such as size, shape, use, etc.) or according to similarities in their manufacturing process. This is a time-consuming and tedious task, which can be accomplished by the following methods:

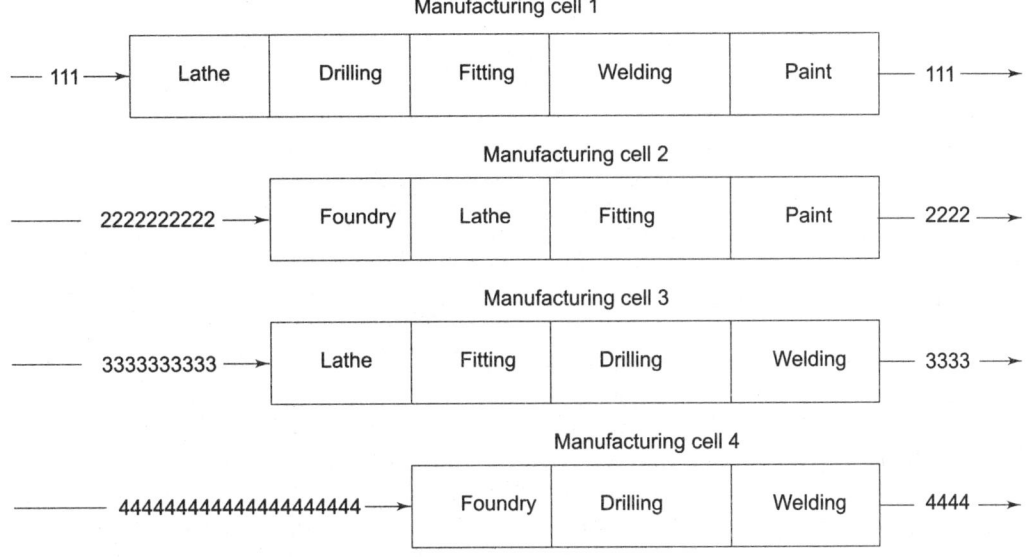

**Fig. 6.23** Cellular layout of the same factory

> Before switching over to a cellular layout from a process layout, the production manager must do proper cost and time comparisons to derive the maximum advantages of cellular manufacturing.

1. Visual inspection method (for grouping items according to design similarities), which is very simple in application but not very accurate.
2. Examination of design and production data (for grouping items according to design similarities), which is more complex to implement than visual inspection, but much more accurate.
3. Analysis of the production flow of items (for grouping items according to manufacturing process similarities).

Before switching over to a cellular layout from a process layout, the production manager must do proper cost and time comparisons to derive the maximum advantages of cellular manufacturing.

---

### Exhibit 6.5   Production Process Transformation of Airbus and Boeing

The lean manufacturing process of Airbus manufactures aircrafts in a moving production line. This is a break from the civil aviation industry practice of building aircrafts in 'docks'. Building aircrafts in docks had drawbacks, as teams would often get in each other's way if coordination was lax. This resulted in significant delays. For over a year, Airbus has been operating a moving production line inspired by production methods used by car makers such as Japan's Toyota Motor Corporation. These methods have been implemented to complete sections for its family of single-aisle short to medium-haul aircraft.

Airbus' arch-rival, Boeing Co, adopted a moving production line system in 2002 for final assembly of its 737 single-aisle model, and recently, it started the final assembly of the wide-body 777. Airbus' production line, by contrast, is involved at an earlier stage in the aircraft manufacturing process. Empty fuselage shells are installed with critical flight systems, such as flight-control, and passenger systems, such as electrical and electronics systems, hydraulics, air conditioning, and water. The finished sections are then moved to a final assembly line where the nose, wings, and tail sections are installed.

The new production technique has reduced the time necessary to manufacture a fuselage section by

*(Contd)*

*Exhibit 6.5 Contd*

40 per cent to around five days, thanks to a system where the sections move sideways through the plant on rails at a speed of one metre an hour. Overall, there has been a cost reduction of around 30 per cent as compared to previous manufacturing techniques. This has led to improvement in quality and reduction in waste. The company now has much greater flexibility to adjust production to its order book. This aspect is very important for the European company. With a bulging order book for the A320 and versions that are highly prized by low-cost airlines, Airbus has decided to increase the output of its A318m, A319m, A320, and A321 models gradually to 36 a month by the end of 2008 from 30 at the end of 2006. Over 2,000 orders have been booked in the last two years, and a further increase in production to around 40 a month is possible.

The single-aisle plant at Hamburg, which also makes sub-assemblies for the A380, is already working flat out. The paint shop is working with four daily shifts, and assembly operations with two or three shifts. With this new process in place, components remain on their jigs and move at a speed of one metre per hour from the first to the last of nine workstations in all. In contrast to assembly work in fixed docks, the fuselages will no longer have to be moved onto the next individual workstation by crane. This means that there is no need to interrupt the work process as was the case up to now.

The first moving line was set up at the Broughton A320 Family plant in North Wales in 2002. Wings built there move forward every 13 hours through each of the 11 assembly stations. The process has helped save up to 250 hours of 'waiting' per wing set, while helping improve quality and efficiency.

Boeing is introducing radical new transport equipment for moving big fuselage barrels within its Everett plant, a key part of its plan to make the production of 777 jets more efficient and flexible by shifting to a moving assembly line. Boeing began work to transform its 777 assembly line into a leaner and more efficient production system. This initial use of a moving line during final assembly represents substantial progress with this transformation effort. Assembled one-by-one, it takes 26 days to assemble the 777's three million constituent parts, but with a moving production

line, the aim is to cut that time to just eight days. For now, the moving assembly line is used only during final assembly positions for the airplane, moving it at a steady pace of 1.6 inches per minute during production.

Boeing is in the process of deploying the first of a set of new 55 tonne wheeled trolleys, slung low to the ground and known as 'crawlers'. They are highly maneuverable, capable of rotating aircraft sections full circle and can expand or contract to fit the different fuselage lengths of various 777 models.

Currently, the 777 fuselage sections are lifted by crane into heavy, fixed structures that hold them in place while hydraulic, electrical, and other systems are installed. These sections are then lifted out by crane to another structure where the sections are joined together. The crawlers do the work of both the cranes and the fixed structures.

The fuselage sections sit in two cradles atop the crawlers, and mechanics standing on attached work platforms install the systems as they move forward at a rate of 1.8 inches per minute, following a white line on the factory floor. The ultimate goal of the ambitious 777 production line remake, explicitly modelled on the Toyota production system, is to have a moving line from this point through final assembly. Starting 2007, the crawlers—this time moving at a rate of 10 feet per minute—transfer completed fuselage sections from systems installation over to the tooling where the aircraft sections are finally joined together.

The current process of using a crane for these major transfers limits the weight of the airplane sections that can be moved. With the crawlers, Boeing will be able to move heavier pieces without causing distortion to the airplane structure. This allows mechanics to install seats, stow bins, and other interior fittings earlier in the assembly process.

The net impact on the 777, according to internal company documents, will be to reduce the number of work-flow days—the total time spent on assembling one jet—from the current 20 days to 16 days by the middle of next year, to 15 days a year later, then further out to just 12 days. That dramatic shortening of build time will allow Boeing to adjust the production rate according to the level of orders.

> The assignment model is a heuristic which is used to assign machines to various locations in such a way that the total material-handling cost is the minimum.

## The Assignment Model in Layout Planning

The assignment model is a heuristic which is used to assign machines to various locations in such a way that the total material-handling cost is the minimum. The various steps in the assignment heuristic can be understood with the help of Example 6.4.

### *Example 6.4*

Brar Auto Components is a Ludhiana-based firm which is adding an annex to its existing facility for capacity expansion of the facility. It has to install five machines—$M_1$, a lathe machine; $M_2$, a drilling machine; $M_3$, a grinding machine; $M_4$, a punch press; and $M_5$, a welding machine. The annex has five locations at which these machines may be installed. The plant manager has calculated various material-handling costs in ₹per hour with respect to various combinations of machines and locations as shown in Table 6.10.

**Table 6.10**

| | *A* | *B* | *C* | *D* | *E* |
|---|---|---|---|---|---|
| $M_1$ | 74 | 34 | 15 | 66 | 38 |
| $M_2$ | 52 | 67 | 92 | 84 | 41 |
| $M_3$ | 59 | 73 | 87 | 70 | 18 |
| $M_4$ | 22 | 50 | 28 | 37 | 24 |
| $M_5$ | 29 | 93 | 82 | 55 | *M* |

The welding machine $M_5$ cannot be installed at location *E* due to its huge size; therefore, Table 5.9 contains the value *M* (a very large value of the cost) in the cell for machine $M_5$ and location *E*. Assign the machines to locations such that the total material-handling cost is the minimum. Find also the total minimum material-handling cost.

### *Solution*

The assignment heuristic can be applied in the following steps.

***Step 1*** Find the smallest value in every row and subtract it from each cell value in the corresponding row (Fig. 6.24). For example, in the first row the smallest value is 15; subtract 15 from each cell value of the first row. Similarly, the smallest value in the second row is 41, which is subtracted from each cell value of the second row. Thus, the revised table shown in Fig. 6.24 (step 1) is obtained.

| | A | B | C | D | E |
|---|---|---|---|---|---|
| M1 | 74 | 34 | 15 | 66 | 38 |
| M2 | 52 | 67 | 92 | 84 | 41 |
| M3 | 59 | 73 | 87 | 70 | 18 |
| M4 | 22 | 50 | 28 | 37 | 24 |
| M5 | 29 | 93 | 82 | 55 | M |

Step 1

| | A | B | C | D | E |
|---|---|---|---|---|---|
| M1 | 59 | 19 | 0 | 51 | 23 |
| M2 | 11 | 26 | 51 | 43 | 0 |
| M3 | 41 | 55 | 69 | 52 | 0 |
| M4 | 0 | 28 | 6 | 15 | 2 |
| M5 | 0 | 64 | 53 | 26 | M |

Step 2

| | A | B | C | D | E |
|---|---|---|---|---|---|
| M1 | 59 | 0 | 0 | 36 | 23 |
| M2 | 11 | 7 | 51 | 28 | 0 |
| M3 | 41 | 36 | 69 | 37 | 0 |
| M4 | 0 | 9 | 6 | 0 | 2 |
| M5 | 0 | 45 | 53 | 11 | M |

Step 3

| | A | B | C | D | E |
|---|---|---|---|---|---|
| M1 | 59 | 0 | 0 | 36 | 23 |
| M2 | 11 | 7 | 51 | 28 | 0 |
| M3 | 41 | 36 | 69 | 37 | 0 |
| M4 | 0 | 9 | 6 | 0 | 2 |
| M5 | 0 | 45 | 53 | 11 | M |

Step 4

| | A | B | C | D | E |
|---|---|---|---|---|---|
| M1 | 66 | 0 | 0 | 36 | 30 |
| M2 | 11 | 0 | 44 | 21 | 0 |
| M3 | 41 | 29 | 62 | 30 | 0 |
| M4 | 7 | 9 | 6 | 0 | 9 |
| M5 | 0 | 38 | 46 | 4 | M |

Step 5

| | A | B | C | D | E |
|---|---|---|---|---|---|
| M1 | 66 | 0 | 0 | 36 | 30 |
| M2 | 11 | 0 | 44 | 21 | 0 |
| M3 | 41 | 29 | 62 | 30 | 0 |
| M4 | 7 | 9 | 6 | 0 | 9 |
| M5 | 0 | 38 | 46 | 4 | M |

**Fig. 6.24** Application of the assignment heuristic

***Step 2*** Find the smallest value in every column and subtract it from each cell value in the corresponding column. For example, in the first column the smallest value is 0; subtract 0 from each cell value of the first column. Similarly, the smallest value in the second column is 19, which is subtracted from each cell value of the second column. Thus, the revised table shown in Fig. 6.24 (step 2) is obtained.

***Step 3*** Make horizontal and vertical lines to cover all the zeros in the table as shown by grey shaded rectangles in the figure (step 3). The lines drawn can be all horizontal, all vertical, or a combination of horizontal and vertical lines in whatever way possible. If the number of lines required to cover all the zeros in the table is equal to the number of machines (or the number of locations, as both are equal), the optimal solution has been obtained and we can skip step 4 and directly go to step 5. In our example, the number of lines required to cover all zeros is four, that is, less than the number of machines. Therefore, we follow step 4.

***Step 4*** Select the smallest value out of those not covered by any of the lines. In our example, it is 7. Subtract this value from all the values not covered by any of the lines (i.e., 7, 51, 28, 36, 69, 37, 45, 53, and 11) and add it to those at the intersection of any two lines (i.e., 59, 23, 0, and 2). Again, make horizontal and vertical lines to cover all the zeros in the table (Fig. 6.24, step 4). If the number of lines required to cover all the zeros in the table is equal to the number of machines (or the number of locations), the optimal solution has been obtained. In our example, five lines now cover all the zeros (equal to the number of machines). Hence, the optimal solution has been obtained.

***Step 5*** A single zero in any row or column is assigned first. For example, the fifth row contains a single zero, which is assigned (shaded grey in Fig. 6.24, step 5). This means that machine $M_5$ has been assigned to location $A$. Similarly, the third and fourth rows contain single zeros, which are assigned, implying that machines $M_3$ and $M_4$ have been assigned to locations $E$ and $D$, respectively. The first and second rows contain zeros in two cells; therefore, we try to find a column which contains any of these single zeros. The third column contains a single zero, which is assigned, implying that machine $M_1$ is assigned to location $C$. Shade the other zero in the first row dark grey. Now, excluding this dark grey shaded zero, there is a single zero in the second column and it is assigned. Thus, machine $M_2$ is assigned to location $B$. Shade the other zero in the second row dark grey. Hence, all the machines have been assigned to the given locations—$M_1$ to $C$, $M_2$ to $B$, $M_3$ to $E$, $M_4$ to $D$, and $M_5$ to $A$. The total minimum material-handling costs can be found by adding the costs from Table 6.10, with respect to the assigned cells in the table shown in Fig. 6.24 (step 5). Thus, the minimum total cost is $15 + 67 + 18 + 37 + 29 = ₹166$ per hour.

## Load–Distance Analysis in Process Layouts

In process layouts, two or more layouts can be compared to find out the layout which minimizes the total load–distance value of the various products manufactured. Here, *load* means the total number of units of different products any department processes. *Distance* means the distance between any two departments. Let us try to understand this technique called load–distance analysis in Example 6.5.

### Example 6.5

Figure 6.25 shows two layout options of a facility. The distance between any two adjacent departments is 10 m. No diagonal movement is possible, for example, if a load has to be moved from department 7 to department 5 in layout $A$, it can be either through departments 8, 9, and 6 or through departments

Layout *A*

| 1 | 2 | 5 |
|---|---|---|
| 3 | 4 | 6 |
| 7 | 8 | 9 |

Layout *B*

| 5 | 3 | 4 |
|---|---|---|
| 9 | 6 | 1 |
| 2 | 7 | 8 |

**Fig. 6.25** Layout options

**Table 6.11**

| Product | Department processing sequence | Quantity per month |
|---|---|---|
| *V* | 5-7-2-9 | 4,000 |
| *W* | 4-6-3-7-8-9 | 1,000 |
| *X* | 1-2-7-8 | 2,000 |
| *Y* | 5-2-1-7-9 | 3,000 |
| *Z* | 3-4-7-8-9 | 1,000 |

3, 1, and 2 by travelling a distance of 40 m. Table 6.11 shows the department processing sequence of various products and their quantity produced per month. Which layout is better in terms of lower total load–distance value?

### Solution

Find the total distance to be travelled by a product while getting processed in the various departments according to the given processing sequence (Table 6.12).

**Table 6.12** Distances travelled in layouts A and B

| Product | Department processing sequence | Quanity per month | Distance (m) Layout A | Distance (m) Layout B |
|---|---|---|---|---|
| *V* | 5-7-2-9 | 4,000 | 40 + 30 + 30 = 100 | 30 + 10 + 10 = 50 |
| *W* | 4-6-3-7-8-9 | 1,000 | 10 + 20 + 10 + 10 + 10 = 60 | 20 + 10 + 20 + 10 + 30 = 90 |
| *X* | 1-2-7-8 | 2,000 | 10 + 30 + 10 = 50 | 30 + 10 + 10 = 50 |
| *Y* | 5-2-1-7-9 | 3,000 | 10 + 10 + 20 + 20 = 60 | 20 + 30 + 20 + 20 = 90 |
| *Z* | 3-4-7-8-9 | 1,000 | 10 + 20 + 10 + 10 = 50 | 10 + 30 + 10 + 30 = 80 |

Now multiply the load, that is, the quantity of various products to be manufactured with the distances calculated in Table 6.12 for the two layouts. The total load–distance value for layout *B* is less than that of layout *A* (Table 6.13). Therefore, layout *B* is better than *A*.

**Table 6.13** Product of quantity and distance

| Product | Quantity | Quantity × distance Layout A | Quantity × distance Layout B |
|---|---|---|---|
| *V* | 4,000 | 4,00,000 | 2,00,000 |
| *W* | 1,000 | 60,000 | 90,000 |
| *X* | 2,000 | 1,00,000 | 1,00,000 |
| *Y* | 3,000 | 1,80,000 | 2,70,000 |
| *Z* | 1,000 | 50,000 | 80,000 |
| | | 7,90,000 | 7,40,000 |

> Closeness ratings are used to reflect the desirability of having one department near another.

## Closeness Ratings

Closeness ratings are used to reflect the desirability of having one department near another. These are very effective tools in service facility layout planning.

**Table 6.14** Closeness ratings

| Closeness rating | Importance |
|---|---|
| 1 | Absolutely necessary |
| 2 | Highly important |
| 3 | Important |
| 4 | Slightly important |
| 5 | Unimportant |
| 6 | Undesirable |

For example, in an MBA institution, it is desirable to have the library and computer centre as close as possible to the lecture theatres. The boys' and girls' hostel should be as far apart as possible. The girls' hostel is usually made near the teachers' residential premises. Thus, for any two departments, a closeness rating can be chosen from Table 6.14.

### Example 6.6

Municipal Hospital has made the matrix shown in Fig. 6.26(a) to show the closeness ratings of the various departments for its proposed new building. The matrix shows, for example, the closeness rating between departments $D1$ and $D2$ as 2, departments $D1$ and $D3$ as 4, $D1$ and $D8$ as 5, and so on. Make a layout for the hospital building keeping in view the various closeness ratings.

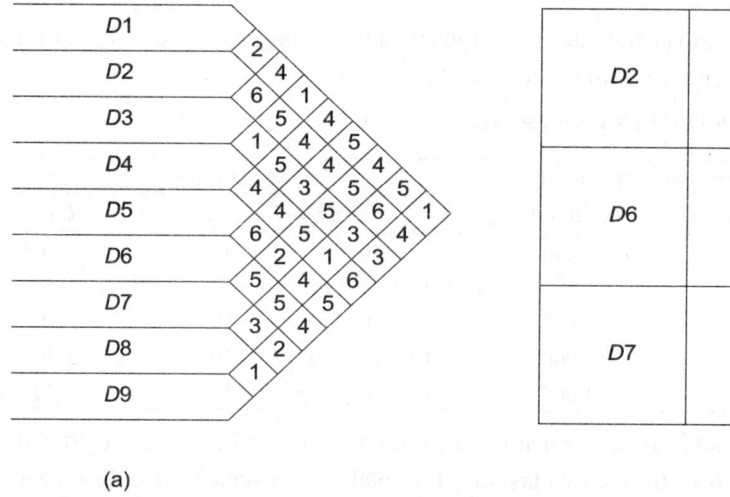

(a)

| | | |
|---|---|---|
| D2 | D4 | D3 |
| D6 | D1 | D8 |
| D7 | D9 | D5 |

(b)

**Fig. 6.26** (a) Matrix of closeness ratings and (b) layout plan of Municipal Hospital

### Solution

Make a list of department pairs with ratings 1 and 6.

| Rating 1 | Rating 6 |
|---|---|
| D1–D4 | D2–D3 |
| D3–D4 | D5–D6 |

| Rating 1 | Rating 6 |
|---|---|
| D1–D9 | D2–D8 |
| D4–D8 | D4–D9 |
| D8–D9 | |

**Fig. 6.27** Network of departments with rating 1

Now make a network of departments having the rating 1, with the department occurring most frequently ($D4$) at the centre (Fig. 6.27). Similarly, make a network of departments having the rating 6, with the department occurring most frequently ($D2$) at the centre (Fig. 6.28).

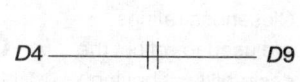

**Fig. 6.28** Network of departments with rating 6

Now, keeping in view the above networks, subjectively place the departments in the nine cells as shown in Fig. 6.26(b). Note that even the cells whose corners touch each other are considered to be close to each other. This placement satisfies all the conditions of not only departments with ratings 1 and 6, but also those with other ratings. While making the placements, we have to consider only ratings 1 and 6, the other ratings being automatically satisfied.

Closeness ratings require a trial and error method for placement of depart-ments. Therefore, some layout problems may require the use of computer software such as ALDEP (automated layout design programs) and CORELAP (computerized relationship layout planning). These are based upon the closeness ratings method. Another software, CRAFT (computerized relative allocation of facilities), is based upon the load–distance analysis and minimizes the material-handling cost in allocating departments in the layout.

## Summary

The capacity of a facility is the maximum load that can be handled by it during a given period. *Facility capacity planning* is important because it is a long-term decision which requires substantial investments and cannot be reversed easily. There are three types of capacities: design, effective, and actual. Managers should devote maximum attention to the enhancement of the effective capacity of the facility.

*Demand forecasting* trends help in capacity decisions for the future. The optimal capacity of the facility should be determined such that the total costs of under-capacity and over-capacity can be minimized as much as possible. *Strategic capacity planning* is the key to competitiveness, and emphasizes on flexibility in the capacity of the facility to accommodate future fluctuations in the demand of the product/service. *Decision tree analysis* and break-even analysis are helpful tools in capacity decision making.

There are three basic types of layouts: product, process, and fixed. *Product layout* is useful for producing large quantities of a product having standardized features. Product layout has a conveyor (a moving platform) on which the basic structures of the product are arranged at regular intervals and are subjected to different assembly operations by workers at the workstations arranged alongside the conveyor. This is called an assembly line. Assembly line balancing means assigning tasks to workstations in such a way that, as far as possible, their processing times are equal.

*Process layout* is suitable when a variety of products are to be processed using the standard machines. *Fixed-position* layout is required when the product is very bulky or heavy such as an aeroplane or a space shuttle. The basic structure of the product remains fixed at a location and all the required materials—tools, equipment, expert technicians, etc.—are brought to this location for performing the various processes on the basic structure. *Cellular layout and group technology* is the latest extension of the process layout. In service as well as manufacturing settings, *closeness ratings* of various departments are useful for planning the layout.

## References

Anon. 2005, 'Boom time for Indian textiles!',http://www.rediff.com/money/2005/feb/10bspec.htm, accessed on 1 February 2013.

Anon. 2010, 'Bengaluru airport's Terminal-1 expansion plan unveiled', Rediff.com, 19 August http://www.rediff.com/money/slide-show/slide-show-1-bengaluru-airport-terminal-1-expansion-plan-unveiled/20100819.htm, accessed on 19 March 2013.

Anon. 2011, 'BIAL to expand facilities at passenger terminal this year', *The Hindu*, 24 May, http://www.hindu.com/2011/05/24/stories/2011052459680700.htm, accessed on 19 March 2013.

CCI 2012, A brief report on textile industry, March 2012, http://www.cci.in/pdf/surveys_reports/Textile-Industry-in-India.pdf, accessed on 1 February 2013.

Hammesfahr, R.D. Jack, James A. Pope, and Alireza Ardalan 1993,'Strategic planning for production capacity', *International Journal of Operations and Production Management*, vol. 13, no. 5.

Jacobs, F. Robert, Richard B. Chase, and Nicholas J. Aquilano2009,*Operations and Supply Management*, Twelfth Edition, McGraw-Hill International, New York.

Mair, A. 1994, 'Honda's global flexifactory network',

*International Journal of Operations and Production Management*, vol. 14, no. 3.

Wilson, James M. 1995, 'Henry Ford's Just-in-Time system', *International Journal of Operations and Production Management*, vol. 15, no. 12.

## Keywords

**Actual capacity** is the maximum output rate that is actually achieved under the constraints of machine breakdowns, labour inefficiencies and absenteeism, defective products, late deliveries of materials by the supplier, and so on. Actual capacity can be equal to or less than the effective capacity.

**Assembly line balancing** means assigning tasks to workstations in such a way that the performance time of the tasks assigned at each workstation can be made as similar as possible.

**Assignment model** is a heuristic used to assign machines to various locations in such a way that the total material-handling cost is the minimum.

**Capacity** is defined as the maximum load that can be handled by a facility during a given period. The load can be expressed in terms of the inputs or outputs.

**Capacity utilization** is the ratio of actual output to design capacity.

**Closeness ratings** are used to reflect the desirability of having one department near another.

**Cycle time** is defined as the time period after which completed units come off the assembly line.

**Decision tree analysis** is a technique used to analyse decision situations that are sequential in nature.

**Design capacity** represents the maximum rate of output that can be achieved under ideal conditions.

**Effective capacity** is the maximum rate of output that can be practically achieved under the constraints of time consumed in set-ups, oiling and cleaning, defective items, etc. Effective capacity is always lesser than the design capacity.

**Efficiency** is the ratio of actual output to effective capacity.

**Group technology** is the identification of similar groups of items as an important aspect of cellular layout.

**Layout** of a facility is the physical location of various departments/units of the facility in the premises of the facility.

**Rollback technique** is a method in which the decision nodes in the later part of the decision tree are analysed before the decision nodes in the earlier part.

**Theoretical minimum number of workstations** is a ratio of the total performance time to the cycle time.

## CASE STUDY I

## Kingfisher Airlines and Its Over-capacity Woes

Kingfisher Airlines Limited was started with a lot of fanfare in 2005, when its promoter Vijay Mallya christened it after the famous 'Kingfisher' brand of beer owned by his flagship United Breweries (UB) Group. The flamboyant Mallya boasted of providing a unique flying experience to Indian flyers.

Within a few years, Kingfisher Airlines became synonymous with exemplary flying experience envisaged by Mallya. The in-flight gourmet cuisine, smiling on-ground and in-flight staff, and on-time performance made it the envy of other airlines. In addition to its King Club loyalty programme for frequent flyers, the airline also started 'Little wings', an initiative that allowed even young flyers between the ages of 3 and 12 years to earn mile points.

Kingfisher Airlines soon started growing at a phenomenal rate, opening flights in new sectors within India and abroad. The airline placed orders of new planes to Airbus including the gigantic A380. To satiate its hunger for growth, Kingfisher ordered 127 aircrafts from Airbus (including the A380 superjumbos) and 38 aircrafts from ATR. In their attempt to take the airline to India's number one status, the airline management did not realize that they had started overlooking the unprofitable routes that they were plying upon with dwindling load factor.

At a key juncture in its growth phase, Mallya acquired the low-cost carrier Air Deccan from its promoter Captain G.R. Gopinath. Air Deccan was bleeding with losses at that time, and Mallya was quick to take it over before merging it with Kingfisher Airlines. Air Deccan planes were repainted to don the 'Kingfisher Red' logos. It was a strategic move to slightly elevate the level of the low-cost carrier to bring it closer to the Kingfisher brand. Passengers flying in the new sub-brand had to pay a little more, but received complimentary snacks and drink, coupled with Kingfisher hospitality.

During the 2009 global recession as well, there were no signs of slowing down for Kingfisher Airlines. There was occasional news, however, that oil companies had stopped giving fuel to the airline on credit, and therefore, Kingfisher had to take fuel from them on 'cash and carry' mode. It was only in late 2011 that the airline's fortunes began dwindling. News of sudden cancellation of its several flights gripped the country. Passengers were stranded at the airports without any information. The initial response of the airline to the media was that several of the aircraft of the airlines were being sent for reconfiguration to include more business-class seats. However, this reasoning was unpalatable as such moves by airlines are normally done in a much planned manner.

When abrupt cancellations of Kingfisher flights continued for several consecutive days, the Directorate General of Civil Aviation (DGCA) summoned its chief executive officer (CEO) several times for explanation. Every time promises were made for restoration of the flight schedule, but never kept. In order to streamline the operations, several Kingfisher aircrafts were grounded in order to rationalize the routes upon which it operated.

In February 2012, the Income Tax Department froze the accounts of Kingfisher Airlines for not depositing the tax deducted at source for its employees. This forced the airline to cancel several of its flights and completely shut down operations at several airports. Mallya was seen on news channels offering reasons for the industry's bad times due to adverse government policies like hefty sales tax on fuel. Banks refused to lend any further money to the airline unless Mallya came up with a viable plan to bring the airline back on track.

Soon, the airline was crippled as employees and pilots began agitations due to non-payment of salaries. To further the tension, the International Air Transport Association (IATA) annulled its membership due to frequent cancellation of its international flights without prior notice to the passengers or travel agents and non-payment of its dues. This was a major blow to the airline, as most travel agents stopped accepting bookings for Kingfisher Airlines. The No. 1 airline of yesteryears started curtailing its routes over the next few months to become India's smallest airline.

In September 2012, the government provided some hope by bringing in a legislation to allow the airlines to attract foreign direct investment (FDI) up to 49 per cent. Kingfisher Airlines was likely to be the biggest gainer due to this legislation. However, the next challenge was to find a suitable buyer of equity in a severely bleeding airline.

The disgruntled employees of the airline grounded the operations of Kingfisher in October 2012, when they went on strike for non-payment of their salaries for the previous seven months. This served as a severe blow to the beleaguered airline, as the management had to declare a temporary lockout. The airline remains grounded since then, with its creditors starting to liquidate its assets.

### Discussion Questions

1. Do you think Kingfisher Airlines started flying on international routes too early since the time of its inception?
2. Did the acquisition of Air Deccan by Kingfisher Airlines resulted in excessive seat capacity?
3. Was Kingfisher Airlines too aggressive in placing orders for so many new aircrafts when it was already having a bloated capacity?
4. Discuss how the airline's King Club loyalty programme could be utilized for improving the overall yield and aircraft seat utilization.

---

## CASE STUDY II

# Honda's Mixed Model Assembly Lines

Honda has two major car manufacturing facilities in Japan—one at Sayama, north of Tokyo, and the other at Suzuka, west of Nagoya. The Sayama plant is the oldest one and its two assembly lines can make up to 6,00,000 vehicles a year. Suzuka's three assembly lines have a maximum capacity of around 8,00,000 vehicles a year. The production lines at both the plants are capable enough of making various models of cars simultaneously. For instance, at Sayama, seven types of cars can be assembled on the same assembly line—the basic *Accord*, *Prelude*, and *Legend*, the two-door *Legend*, the *Accord*-derived *Accord Inspire*, *Vigor*, and *Ascot*. The main advantage of the mixed model assembly line is that the declining demand for one model can be counter-balanced with increased demand for others.

Mixed models on single lines is no longer a novelty in the automobile industry. Toyota has a better-known variant of such an assembly line. Toyota arranges different models one after the other on the conveyors across the line to balance the workload for workers and to balance the delivery of parts. On the other hand, Honda has always produced in lots (typically in factors of 60 cars) of one model at a time and the cars are exactly the same in all respects (e.g., red *Civics*, left-hand drive, to be exported to Europe).

At Sayama, several batches of different derivative *Accords* may be manufactured before the line is switched to make *Preludes* for several batches. Models may be switched on the line three or four times in a day. This system allows easy planning of the supply of parts and at the same time offers flexibility in manufacturing according to fluctuating demand patterns.

Unlike the Toyota system of mixing the cars to accommodate the workers who stay at fixed work stations or in fixed groups, the Honda production system reorganizes the workforce, when necessary, with groups of workers moving about the assembly line to balance the workload. While designing a new model, it is kept in mind that it will be produced on the existing line with the same fixed equipment across the line. This is necessary to avoid staggering investments for making changes in the existing assembly line to suit the design requirements of a new model.

There are, however, a few limitations of such a sys-tem. For example, the dimensions of the Honda *Accord* station wagon, introduced at Honda's Marysville plant (USA), were designed to fit the existing production equipment. Hence, the third compartment was not very large and the rear window sloped forward.

Honda is also known for the complete metamorphosis of its Suzuka plant. This plant was opened in 1960 for manufacturing motorcycles. By the mid-1980s, Suzuka became the highest output motorcycle factory in the world. The same plant had started producing automobiles in 1967. Today this plant manufactures only automobiles after the motorcycle production was transferred completely to the exclusive motorcycle plant at Kumamoto in 1991 (Mair 1994).

## Discussion Questions

1. Critically compare the mixed model assembly lines of Honda and Toyota. Which approach is better according to you?
2. Suppose Honda wants to follow Toyota's mixed model assembly system of having different models of cars arranged one after the other on the assembly line instead of producing a batch of a single model for a few hours. Assume that Honda's *City* and *Accord* models have to be produced on the assembly line and the chassis of both require a different type of drilling to be done in the fabrication line. The drilling time for the *City* chassis (say, C) is 2 minutes and the *Accord chassis* (say, A) is 6 minutes. The final assembly requires the number of C's to be twice the number of A's. In what balanced sequence should the chassis of C and A be arranged on the fabrication line so that C = 2A? Assume eight working hours per day.
3. What are the disadvantages of mixed model assembly?

## Objective Questions

### Choose the correct option

1. Trucks used for transportation of goods have maximum capacity expressed in terms of
   (a) volume
   (b) mass
   (c) weight
   (d) output
2. A demand forecast trend that has crests and troughs is
   (a) cyclical trend
   (b) stable trend
   (c) growth trend
   (d) decline trend
3. The optimal output rate corresponds to the
   (a) maximum absolute cost per unit
   (b) minimum absolute cost per unit
   (c) maximum average cost per unit
   (d) minimum average cost per unit
4. Which one of the following is not a type of capacity?
   (a) design capacity
   (b) intended capacity
   (c) effective capacity
   (d) actual capacity

## State True or False

5. The phenomenon of economies of scale is explained by the fact that as the size of the plant increases from small to medium, the fixed costs get further distributed in large number of units produced (higher output rate).
6. Effective capacity is the maximum possible capacity under ideal conditions.
7. Imparting proper training to the workers on new machines and equipment so that the wastages in trial-runs are minimal is one of the measures to increase the effective capacity.

## Fill in the blanks

8. Capacity cushion = 1 – _____
9. Efficiency = Actual capacity ÷ _____
10. An assembly line is based on a _____ layout.

## Concept Review Questions

1. What is meant by the capacity of a facility? In what ways can the capacity of a facility be measured? Why is capacity requirements planning required for a facility?
2. Explain the different types of capacity of a facility. How can the effective capacity of a facility be increased?
3. Explain the various factors to be considered in the determination of the optimal capacity of a facility.
4. What is the role of forecasting in capacity requirements planning?
5. How is strategic capacity planning a key to competitiveness? Give your views.
6. How many types of basic layouts are there for a facility? Briefly explain each of them.
7. What is an assembly line? What are the advantages and disadvantages of product layout?
8. How is a U-shaped assembly line different from a regular assembly line? What are its advantages?
9. What is meant by assembly line balancing? Define cycle time and explain its various implications.
10. What is a cellular layout? How is it different from a process layout? How is group technology useful in cellular layout?

## Numerical Problems

1. A company manufactures two products A and B. It also markets the two products under two different brand names X and Y. The marketing department of the company has provided the demand forecasts for the coming five years as shown in Table 6.15.

**Table 6.15** Demand forecast for product categories

|            | Year 1 | Year 2 | Year 3 | Year 4 | Year 5 |
|------------|--------|--------|--------|--------|--------|
| *Brand X*  |        |        |        |        |        |
| Product A  | 5,400  | 6,300  | 7,200  | 8,000  | 8,700  |
| Product B  | 4,100  | 5,000  | 6,100  | 6,800  | 7,300  |
| *Brand Y*  |        |        |        |        |        |
| Product A  | 16,400 | 19,500 | 21,700 | 23,500 | 25,600 |
| Product B  | 1,450  | 1,710  | 2,170  | 2,360  | 2,540  |

The machine capacity per year and the operator requirements on each machine are given in Table 6.16.

**Table 6.16** Machine capacity and operator requirement on each machine

|           | Machine capacity (units per year) | No. of machines | Total machine capacity | No. of operators on each machine |
|-----------|-----------------------------------|-----------------|------------------------|----------------------------------|
| Product A | 10,000                            | 4               | 40,000                 | 3                                |
| Product B | 5,000                             | 2               | 10,000                 | 1                                |

Determine the capacity utilization and machine and operator requirements to make sure that the demand projections for the coming five years are met.

2. The R&D division of Medico Pharma, a pharmaceutical firm based at Ahmedabad, has invented an Ayurvedic medicine for curing HIV-positive

patients. Medico is faced with three decision options—to manufacture the drug, to sell the idea to some other firm, or to conduct a market study before taking any action. If it decides to manufacture the drug outright, the drug has a 60 per cent chance of success with a profit of ₹1.2 million, while its failure will result in a loss of ₹0.2 million. If the company conducts a market study, there is an 80 per cent chance that the study will give a positive report (favourable to the launch of the drug). After the positive report of the study, if the company manufactures the drug, there are 70 per cent chances that the drug will be a success, leading to a profit of ₹1 million, while a failure will result in a loss of ₹0.3 million. After the negative report of the study, if the company manufactures the drug, there are 30 per cent chances that the drug will be a success leading to a profit of ₹1 million, while a failure will result in a loss of ₹0.3 million. A competitor firm is willing to pay ₹0.5 million if Medico sells the idea to it before

the market study; ₹0.6 million if Medico conducts the study, revealing positive results; and ₹0.4 million if Medico conducts the study, revealing negative results. What course of action should Medico follow? Give your advice using the decision tree analysis.

3. VXL Motorcycles Ltd is a Chennai-based company manufacturing motorcycles for the Indian domestic market. The factory has separate assembly lines for engine assembly operations and the final assembly operation of motorcycles. In the final assembly operation of the motorcycles, the tasks given in Table 6.17 are performed according to the given precedence requirements. The production supervisor of the company has prepared a layout of the assembly line as shown in Fig. 6.29.
   (a) Determine whether this is a good assembly line design or not.
   (b) If not, make a new design of the assembly line.
   (c) Find the efficiency of the new design.
   (d) How many motorcycles can be produced per day?

**Table 6.17**

| Task | Description | Precedence requirement(s) | Task time (min) |
|---|---|---|---|
| A | Attaching the fuel tank to the chassis of the bike | – | 20 |
| B | Fixing the seat behind the fuel tank | A | 10 |
| C | Electric bulbs fitted in the headlight assembly | – | 5 |
| D | Headlight assembly attached to the front handle | C | 10 |
| E | Speedometer installation over the headlight | D | 15 |
| F | Electric bulbs fitted in the backlight assembly | – | 5 |
| G | Backlight assembly attached to the mudguard of the back wheel | F | 10 |
| H | Engine assembly fixed below the fuel tank | A | 30 |
| I | Tyres and tubes fitted on the wheels | – | 10 |
| J | Wheels attached to the axle on the chassis | I | 5 |
| K | Final inspection | B E, G, H,J | 30 |
| | | | 150 |

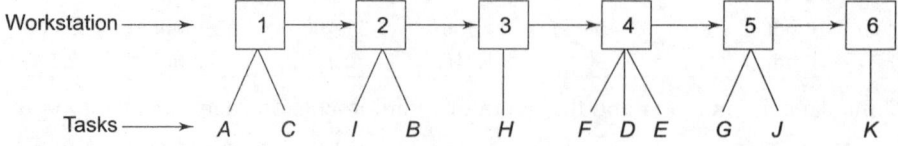

**Fig. 6.29**

4. Table 6.18 gives details about the various tasks in an assembling operation.
   (a) Find the theoretical minimum cycle time.
   (b) Find the theoretical minimum number of workstations.
   (c) Assign tasks to workstations using the LOT rule.
   (d) Calculate the efficiency of the assembly line.

**Table 6.18**

| Task | Precedence requirement(s) | Task time (min) |
|---|---|---|
| A | – | 10 |
| B | C | 20 |

*(Contd)*

Table 6.18 Contd

| Task | Precedence requirement(s) | Task time (min) |
|------|---------------------------|-----------------|
| C | A | 30 |
| D | A, C | 15 |
| E | A | 10 |
| F | B | 20 |
| G | D | 10 |
| H | G | 15 |
| I | G, H | 15 |

5. There are four location options for three new machines to be installed in a factory. The material-handling costs in ₹per hour are given in Table 6.19. Allocate the machines to locations such that the total material-handling cost is the lowest. Also, find this minimum cost. (**Hint:** Add a fourth row for a dummy machine IV with all the cell values as zero).

**Table 6.19**

| Locations | W | X | Y | Z |
|-----------|-----|-----|-----|-----|
| Machine I | 54 | 14 | 37 | 41 |
| Machine II | 32 | 49 | 26 | 13 |
| Machine III | 17 | 21 | 23 | 33 |

6. Figure 6.30 shows two layout options for a facility. The distance between any two adjacent departments is 10 m. No diagonal movement is possible. Table

Layout *A*

| 5 | 4 | 2 |
|---|---|---|
| 3 | 1 | 6 |

Layout *B*

| 4 | 3 | 6 |
|---|---|---|
| 5 | 2 | 1 |

**Fig. 6.30** Layout options

6.20 shows the department processing sequence of various products and their quantities produced per month. Which layout is better in terms of lower total load–distance value?

**Table 6.20**

| Product | Department processing processing | Quantity per month (units) |
|---------|----------------------------------|----------------------------|
| M | 6-4-3 | 1,000 |
| N | 1-5-2 | 2,000 |
| O | 4-2-6 | 3,000 |

7. Figure 6.31 gives the closeness ratings between various departments of a bank. Allocate the nine departments to the nine cells of a rectangular layout according to the given closeness ratings.

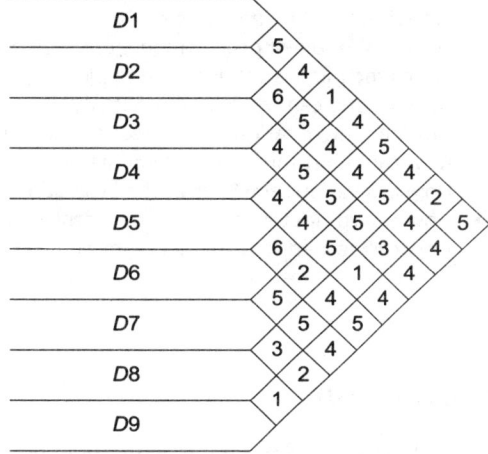

**Fig. 6.31** Matrix of closeness ratings between departments of a bank

# Project Assignments

1. Make a layout of the building of your institute. Identify and label various rooms and halls in the diagram of the layout. Suggest modifications in the assignment of various rooms and halls in order to improve efficiency in terms of walking distance. Brainstorm the various modifications suggested in the class and prepare an action plan for implementation.

2. Visit a hotel/lodge near you and find out the number of rooms it has for customers (capacity of the hotel). Ask them about the occupancy rate of the hotel, and about the seasonal factors which influence the rate. If the occupancy is low, suggest measures to improve it.

## Answers to Objective Questions

1. (c)      2. (a)      3. (d)      4. (b)

5. True      6. False      7. True      8. Capacity utilization

9. Effective capacity      10. product

# 7

# Project Management

## Learning Objectives

After reading this chapter, you will be able to answer the following questions:
- What is a project?
- What is project management?
- What is the role of project management in functional areas?
- Which techniques are available to plan projects?
- By how long can we delay any activity of the project such that it still gets completed in scheduled time?
- How can the duration of a project be reduced by adding more resources to it?
- How can the resource requirements be kept almost constant throughout the duration of the project?
- How can various activities of the project be scheduled under constrained availability of resources?
- How can computer software be helpful in planning projects?
- How can earned value management help in tracking the progress of projects?

## Introduction

Projects and project management have been defined in various ways. Munns and Bjeirmi (1996) define a *project* as the achievement of a specific objective which involves a series of activities and tasks that consume resources, and *project management* as the process of controlling the achievement of project objectives.

The British Standard for Project Management BS6079 (Atkinson 1999) defines project management as 'The planning, monitoring and control of all aspects of a project and the motivation of all those involved in it to achieve the project objectives on time and to the specified cost, quality and performance'.

The UK Association of Project Management (APM) defines project management as (Atkinson 1999) 'The planning, organization, monitoring and control of all aspects of a project and the motivation of all those involved to achieve the project objectives safely and within agreed time, cost, and performance criteria. The project manager is the single point of responsibility for achieving this'.

Munns and Bjeirmi (1996) define a project as the achievement of a specific objective which involves a series of activities and tasks that consume resources.

Managers have to handle various projects during their careers. A software consultant may need to implement a database management project, a construction manager may have to handle the construction project of a building, a scientist in the research and development department of an organization may

Planning a project requires identification of the various activities involved in the project, and the sequence in which these activities have to be performed.

be given a research project, and similarly, for an entrepreneur, starting a new business or a manufacturing unit is a project.

Planning a project requires identification of the various activities involved in the project and the sequence in which these activities have to be performed. A well-planned project leads to completion in the scheduled time, thus avoiding unnecessary delays and extra costs. See Exhibit 7.1 to know how the International Space Station project was planned.

## Exhibit 7.1    The International Space Station

The International Space Station (ISS) has been built with an estimated cost of €100 billion. This project is an epitome of international cooperation with many countries making contributions to it, with the US and Russia being the primary contributors. Led by the US, the ISS draws upon the scientific and technological resources of 16 nations—Canada, Japan, Russia, 11 nations of the European Space Agency (ESA), and Brazil.

More than four times as large as the Russian Mir space station, the completed ISS will have a mass of about 10,40,000 pounds. It will measure 356 feet across and 290 feet long, with almost an acre of solar panels to provide electrical power to six state-of-the-art laboratories. The scheduled completion date of ISS is 2016.

The Russian Mir Space Station was extensively used by the American space agency, NASA to gain experience about various aspects of creating and managing a new space station. This was made possible by the cooperation of Russia, which later became a major partner in the creation of the ISS. That included valuable experience in international crew training activities, the

International Space Station photographed following separation from the Space Shuttle Discovery on 19 December 2006

*(Contd)*

*Exhibit 7.1 Contd*

operation of an international space programme, and the challenges of long duration spaceflight for astronauts and ground controllers. Dealing with the real-time challenges experienced during Shuttle-Mir missions has resulted in an unprecedented cooperation and trust between the US and Russian space programmes, and that cooperation and trust has enhanced the development of ISS.

The construction of ISS is now far behind the original planned schedule for completion in 2004 or 2005. This is mainly due to the halting of all NASA Shuttle flights following the Columbia disaster (the shuttle carrying the astronaut of Indian origin, Kalpana Chawla) in early 2003. However, there had been prior delays partly due to Shuttle problems, and partly due to delays stemming from the Russian space agency's budget constraints.

By the beginning of 2006 many changes were made to the originally planned ISS. Modules and other structures had been cancelled or replaced, and the number of Shuttle flights to the ISS had been reduced from previously planned numbers. Nevertheless, the

ISS would have more than 80 per cent of its design as planned earlier. Throughout the 1990s, construction delays hit the project, budget projections were heavily revised, and the ISS structure was modified frequently. The ISS has been, as of today, far more expensive than originally anticipated. The ESA estimates the overall cost from the start of the project in the late 1980s to the prospective end in 2016 to be in the region of US$130 billion (€100 billion).

By 2006, four space tourists had been to the ISS, each spending US$20 million. All these tourists went aboard Russian supply missions. There has also been a space wedding when cosmonaut Yuri Malenchenko on the station married Ekaterina Dmitrieva, who was in Texas.

The six laboratories of ISS will lead to discoveries in medicine, materials, and fundamental science that will benefit people all over the world. Through its research and technology, the station will also serve as an indispensable step in preparation for future human space exploration.

# Role of Project Management in Other Functional Areas of Management

All the functional areas of management involve projects of different types as shown in Fig. 7.1. Project management skills are thus required by all managers—be it a financial manager, a marketing manager, an HRD manager, or an information systems manager. A manager should be a good project team member as well as a good project leader.

## Types of Projects

The various types of projects are described in this section.

**Projects by size**    Payne and Turner (1999) have categorized projects into four types according to their sizes:

1. Major projects    2. Large projects    3. Medium projects    4. Small projects

A major project is one whose value is roughly equal to the capital of the parent organization. A large project has a value roughly equal to one-tenth the capital of the parent organization, and so on. A major project is ten times larger than a large project, a medium project is ten times smaller, and a small project is further ten times smaller (Table 7.1).

**Projects by resource type**    Turner and Cochrane (1993) developed the matrix shown in Fig. 7.2 to classify projects into four categories according to the different approaches to their planning and control (Table 7.2).

A major project is one whose value is roughly equal to the capital of the parent organization.

Turner (1993) describes a project to build a warehouse in a Regional Health Authority in the UK. The authority was switching over from a system where each hospital bought and stored its supplies to a system with regional buying

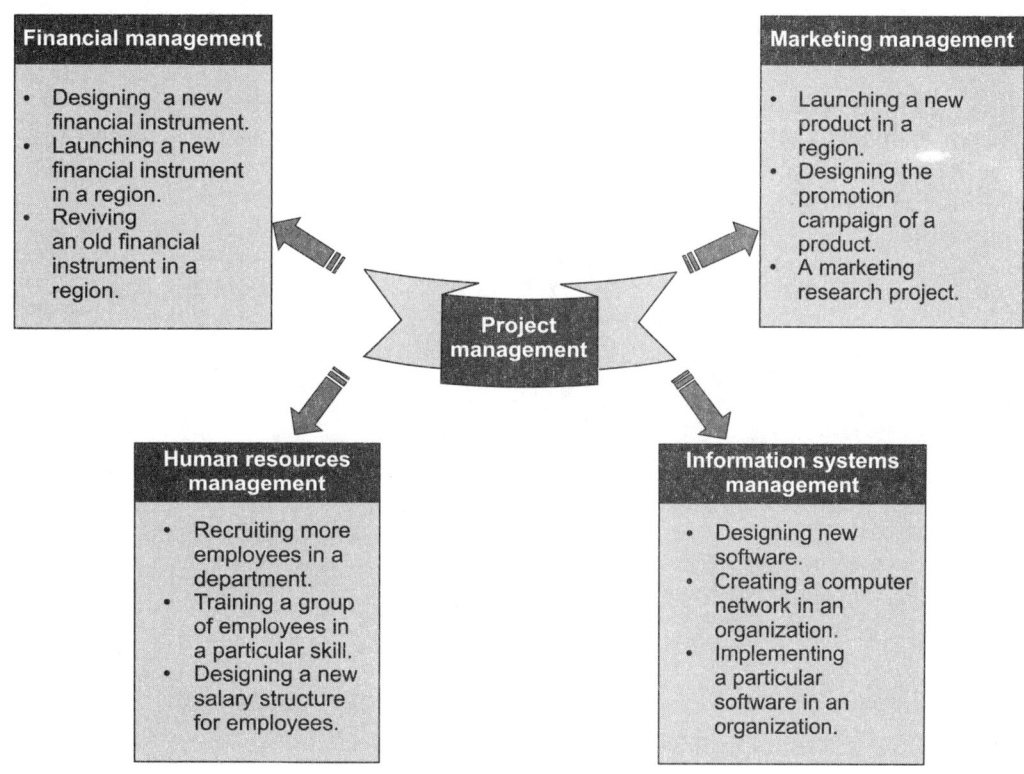

**Fig. 7.1**  The role of project management in various functional areas of management

**Table 7.1**  Characteristics of various types of projects

| *Small to medium projects* | *Large projects* | *Major projects* |
| --- | --- | --- |
| • Main emphasis is on the prioritization of resources across several projects. | • Major emphasis is on the coordination of the complex sequence of activities and balancing resources across these activities. | • Main emphasis is on coordinating the activities of people across several sub-projects. |
| • Small projects cannot stand the bureaucracy of procedures designed for larger projects. | • Large projects have much greater data management requirements than small to medium projects. | • Emphasis is also on managing the considerable risk (as failure of the project will sink the parent organization). |

and storing of materials. The benefit was a reduction in overall stock holdings, rather than each hospital being stocked up to peak demand, enabling the region to smooth out individual peaks and troughs. The project was divided into 22 sub-projects:

- Construction of the warehouse (Type 1 building project)
- Creation of the establishment to run the warehouse (Type 2 logistics project)
- Creating computer systems to operate the warehouse (Type 3 information systems project)
- Redeployment and training of people (Type 4 personnel project)

- Changing the buying function from each hospital to each region (Type 4 organizational change)
- Changing the budget from hospital-based to region-based (Type 3 systems)
- Implementing the changes in 15 hospitals (Type 4 organizational change)
- Commissioning the warehouse (Type 2 logistics)

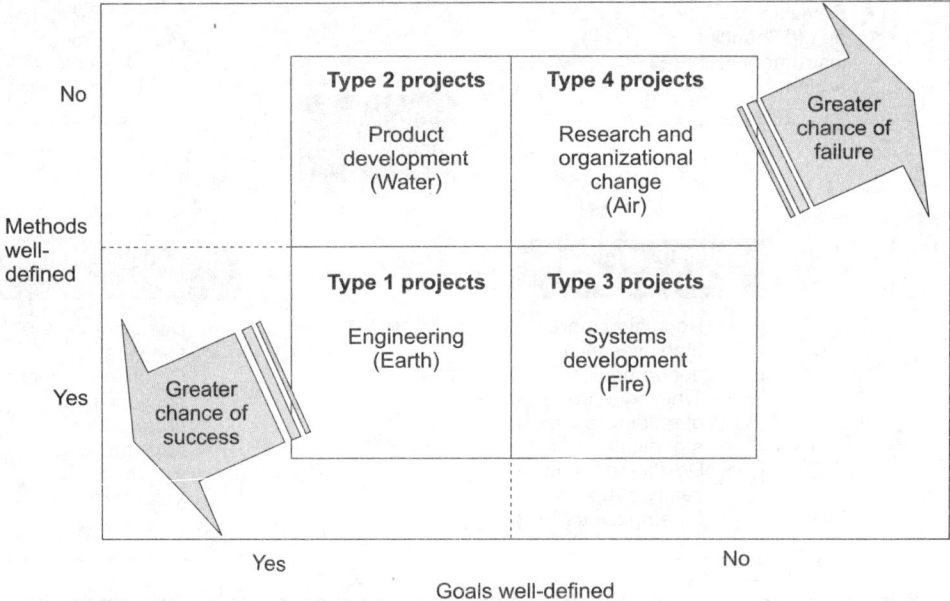

**Fig. 7.2**  Turner and Cochrane's goals and methods matrix

**Table 7.2**  Classification of projects according to planning and control

| *Type 1 (engineering projects)* | *Type 2 (product development projects)* | *Type 3 (information systems projects)* | *Type 4 (research and organizational change projects)* |
|---|---|---|---|
| • Most common type of projects, e.g., in engineering, construction and building industries. | • Goals are well-understood, but identifying the method of achieving the goals is the main point of the project, e.g., projects in electronics and manufacturing industries. | • Goals are poorly defined; the planning approaches tend to depend on the project life cycle. | • These projects tend to be managed as *Type* 2 or *Type* 3 projects depending on their nature. |
| • Have well-defined goals and methods of achieving those goals. | • Plans for projects are best based on a *bills of material* (*product-breakdown structure*), based on *breakdown structure*), based on known goals (the eventually desired product). | • Milestone-based approach to planning is adopted; milestones represent completion of life-cycle stages. | • Research projects tend to be managed as *Type* 3 projects. |
| • Lend themselves to activity-based approaches to planning. | • Milestone-based approach to planning, where milestones represent components of the desired product. | | • Organizational change projects tend to be man-aged as *Type* 2 projects. |

See Exhibit 7.2 to learn about the Bengaluru International Airport project.

## Exhibit 7.2 Bengaluru International Airport Project

The new Bengaluru International Airport Ltd (BIAL) is envisioned to meet the growing aviation needs of the city through the development of a passenger-friendly, well-operated, and financially sound airport. Located east of the Bangalore-Hyderabad national highway (NH7), the new airport is 37 kilometres away from Bangalore and 4 kilometres south of Devanahalli. The site spans an area of 3,900 acres and comprises all the modern amenities a traveller is looking for in terms of convenience, comfort, and connectivty.

The Bengaluru International Airport as of November 2006
*Source*: Wikipedia (2008).

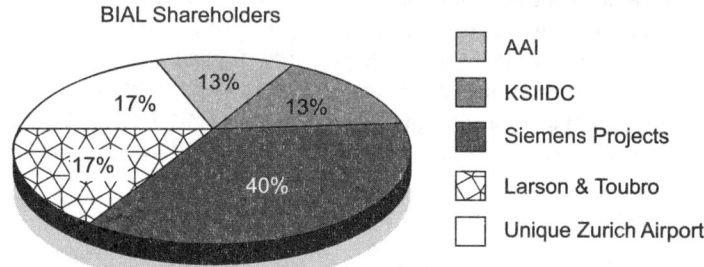

**Fig. 7.3** Shareholding pattern of BIAL

The BIAL shareholding pattern consists of private promoters holding 74 per cent equity stake and the state holding the remaining 26 per cent. The private promoters include Siemens Projects Ventures, Larsen & Toubro (L&T), and Unique Zurich Airport. The two state promoters are the Karnataka State Investment and Industrial Development Corporation (KSIIDC) and the Airports Authority of India. The shareholding pattern of BIAL is depicted in Fig. 7.3.

The design and business plans of BIAL are based on two passenger traffic forecasts:

- SH&E UK, appointed by KSIIDC in the year 2000.
- Lufthansa Consulting (LHC), appointed by BIAL

*(Contd)*

*Exhibit 7.2 Contd*

in the year 2002 to revalidate the SH&E traffic forecast.

With the passenger traffic at the existing HAL airport increasing from 2.3 million in 2001 to approximately 5 million in 2005, BIAL appointed LHC once more in 2005 to update the traffic forecast and develop planning parameters. In an extensive report conducted by LHC, the potential traffic flow from 2005 to 2025 was analysed. The new forecast showed a significant increase in passenger figures and aircraft movements in the coming years. These revised forecasts for passenger and cargo traffic are shown in Table 7.3.

**Table 7.3** Revised forecasts for passenger and cargo traffic

**Total passengers**

| Scenario | 2005 | 2010 | 2015 | 2020 | 2025 |
|---|---|---|---|---|---|
| Optimistic | 46,13,742 | 1,01,90,762 | 1,39,22,812 | 1,81,93,819 | 2,34,44,066 |
| Most likely | 44,70,904 | 85,40,579 | 1,13,69,184 | 1,45,36,743 | 1,84,41,082 |
| Conservative | 43,28,258 | 71,44,506 | 97,77,469 | 1,22,84,213 | 1,53,77,190 |

**Total cargo (tonnes)**

| Scenario | 2005 | 2010 | 2015 | 2020 | 2025 |
|---|---|---|---|---|---|
| Optimistic | 1,24,904 | 2,57,263 | 3,34,795 | 4,26,367 | 5,38,844 |
| Most likely | 1,22,157 | 2,34,017 | 2,99,303 | 3,75,118 | 4,69,179 |
| Conservative | 1,18,378 | 1,98,565 | 2,55,033 | 3,16,118 | 3,91,855 |

It was evident from LHC's revised projections that during the last few years, Bangalore has experienced a strong growth in traffic at its existing HAL airport with prominent international airlines, such as, Air France, British Airways, Gulf Air, Jetstar Asia Airways, KLM, Lufthansa, Malaysian Airlines, Royal Nepal Airlines, Singapore Airlines, and Sri Lankan Airlines already operating from Bangalore. The study estimated the international airport's opening year (2008) traffic flow to be around 6.7 million passengers. Given the new traffic figures, the facilities proposed initially were deemed to be grossly inadequate to cater to the new peak hour demand. Since the task of giving a final shape to agreements had taken three years and aviation requirements had changed during the interregnum, the design of the project was changed and scope extended.

Figure 7.4(a) shows the initial design, while Fig. 7.4(b) shows the revised design of the airpot.

The redesign saw an increase in the size of the terminal, number of aircraft stands, new taxiway layouts, and landside infrastructure. The redesign was incorporated into the original project schedule.

Construction of the airport began on 2 July 2005 and continued, including the testing phase, for 33 months. The project progressed well according to the time schedule of the project, which is shown in Fig. 7.5. The total project cost of BIAL stood at ₹19.3 billion. The redesigning entailed an additional capital investment of about ₹5 billion over and above the original project cost of ₹14.11 billion. The selected partners of BIAL will invest an additional ₹7 billion on infrastructure. Phase

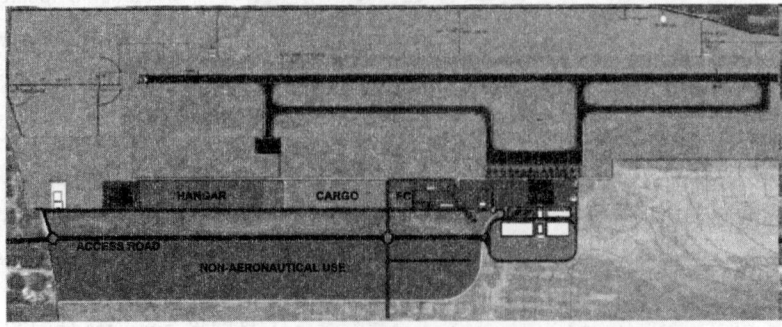

**Fig. 7.4(a)** Initial design of the Bengaluru International Airport

*(Contd)*

*Exhibit 7.2 Contd*

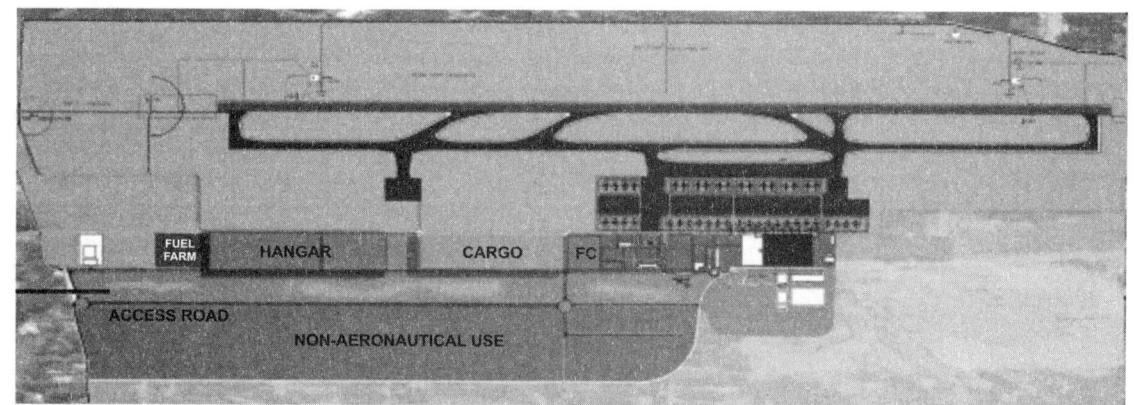

**Fig. 7.4(b)**   Revised design keeping in view the increased traffic projections

I of the proposed airport is expected to be ready by 2008, and Phase II by 2015.

The airport development plan is staggered across several phases. The initial phase of development was completed by 2008. It includes a passenger terminal, a 4,000 metre runway, entrance/exit taxiways, isolation bay, airside road system, two-way access road, air traffic complex, aeronautical equipment, rescue and fire-fighting facilities, airline support facilities, fuel farm, terminal parking, administration and maintenance buildings, ground equipment maintenance area, cargo complex, and boundary/security wall.

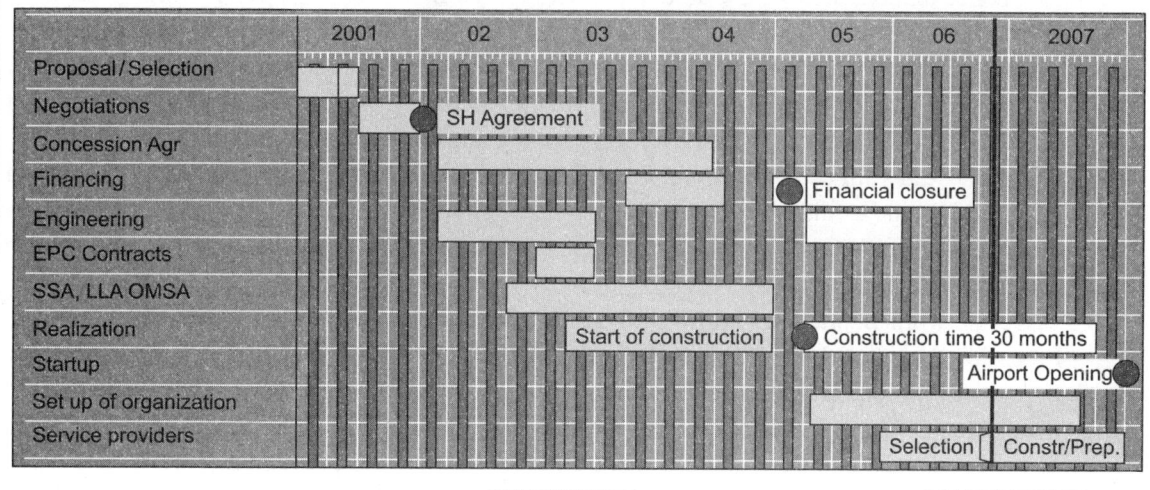

**Fig. 7.5**   The time schedule of the Bengaluru International Airport project

## Network Diagrams

> An event or node marks the beginning or end of an activity and is represented by a small circle in the network diagram.

A network diagram represents the various activities of a project. An *event* or *node* marks the beginning or end of an activity, and is represented by a small circle in the network diagram. An activity is represented by an arrow, preferably a straight line arrow. There can be only one activity between any two nodes.

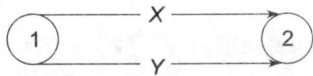

**Fig. 7.6** An invalid network diagram

Therefore, the representation shown in Fig. 7.6 is not permitted for two activities $X$ and $Y$ between the same two events 1 and 2.

The same situation can be represented by using a special activity called a *dummy activity*. A dummy activity is a hypothetical activity (i.e., does not exist practically), which does not require any type of resource (man, machine, materials, capital, etc.). Also, the duration of a dummy activity is always zero. Similarly, a dummy event is an imaginary event. The situation shown in Fig. 7.6 can thus be shown by using a dummy activity and a dummy event as in Fig.7.7.(a)

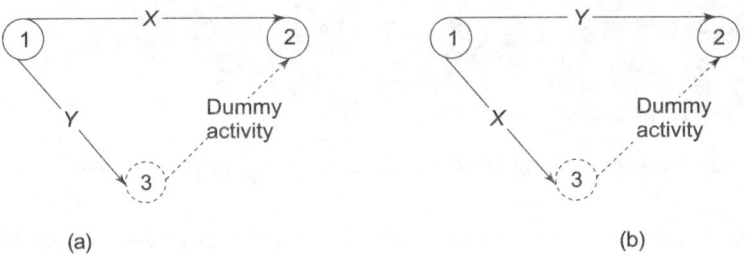

**Fig. 7.7** Dummy activity and event

In Fig. 7.7(a), activity $X$ is shown between nodes 1 and 2 as in Fig. 7.6. Make a dummy event 3 (shown by a dotted circle). Then join nodes 1 and 3 by an arrow, which represents activity $Y$. Join nodes 3 and 2 also with a dotted arrow to represent a dummy activity. Event 1 marks the beginning of activities $X$ and $Y$ simultaneously. Event 2 marks the end of activity $X$. The dummy event 3 marks the end of activity $Y$ and also the beginning of the dummy activity. The dummy activity gets over at node 2. Thus, node 2 marks the end of activity $X$ as well as the dummy activity. Just after activity $Y$ gets over, the dummy activity gets started. As the dummy activity does not use any time and resource, nodes 2 and 3 practically coincide with each other, and the situation is same as that in Fig. 7.6. The representation in Fig. 7.7(a) is permissible according to the rules of networking, but the representation in Fig. 7.6 is not. This situation can also be represented as in Fig. 7.7(b).

The network diagram in Fig. 7.8 shows the various activities in the construction of a building. Preparing a map of the building and purchasing the land for it are the two initial activities of the project, which can be started simultaneously at node 1. A dummy activity is used between nodes 2 and 3. The subsequent simultaneously occurring activities, that is, ordering for the bricks, cement, etc. and digging the foundations, are started at node 2. The remaining part of this network diagram is self-explanatory. As is evident, in the construction of a network diagram, the logical sequence of activities is very essential. Hence, in every project, the precedence requirement for every activity (which activity or activities should be over before starting a particular activity) has to be determined for making the network diagram.

## Critical Path Method

In construction projects, project managers can accurately predict how much time a particular activity will take based on past experience with similar projects. Such projects, in which the

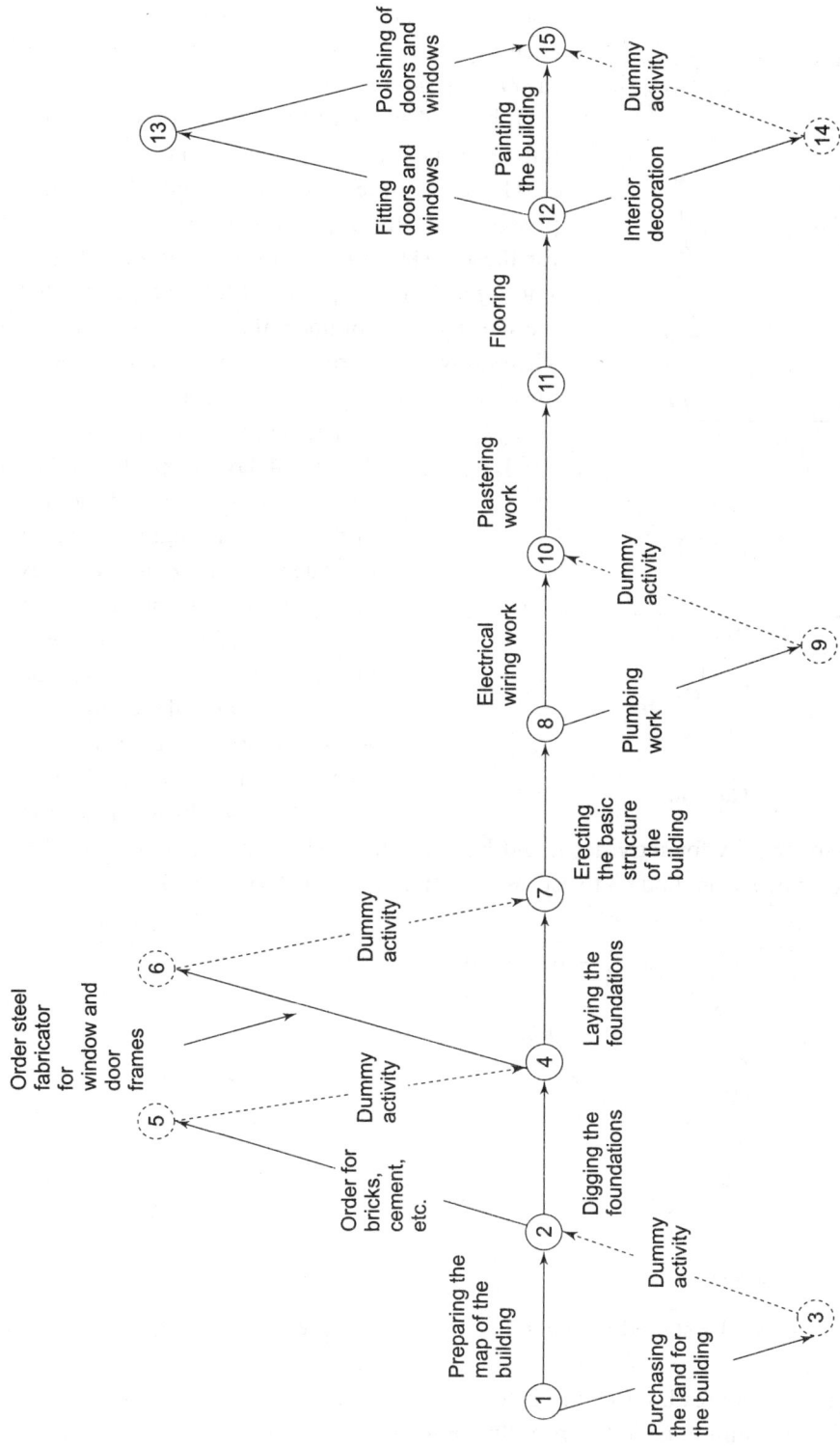

**Fig. 7.8**   Network diagram of a construction project

**Table 7.4**

| Task | Time (days) | Required predecessor(s) |
|------|-------------|-------------------------|
| A | 2 | – |
| B | 3 | – |
| C | 4 | – |
| D | 1 | A |
| E | 2 | B |
| F | 5 | B |
| G | 7 | C |
| H | 2 | D,E |
| I | 3 | F,G |
| J | 1 | H,I |

duration of various activities can be determined with great accuracy, can be planned with the help of a technique called the *critical path method* (CPM).

Table 7.4 shows the various tasks in a project, their duration, and required predecessors.

The first three tasks *A*, *B*, and *C* do not require any predecessor, that is, no other task needs to be completed for these tasks to get started. Therefore, these become the starting tasks of the project. Make a small circle to represent the starting event or node of the project. Mark this node as 1. Then draw three arrows starting from this node to represent the activities *A*, *B*, and *C* (Fig.7.9).

The duration of activities *A*, *B*, and *C* are 2, 3, and 4 days, respectively. We show these along with the names of the three activities in the network diagram. Activity *D* has the precedence requirement of activity *A*. This means that *D* can be started only when A gets over. Make a small circle at the end of the arrow for activity *A* to represent event 2. Event 2 marks the completion of activity *A*. Therefore, draw an arrow from node 2 to represent activity D (Fig. 7.10).

Table 7.4 shows that the required predecessor activity for activities *E* and *F* is *B*. Activity *B* gets completed in event 3. Therefore, draw two arrows from node 3 to represent activities *E* and *F* (Fig. 7.11).

**Fig. 7.9**  **Fig. 7.10**

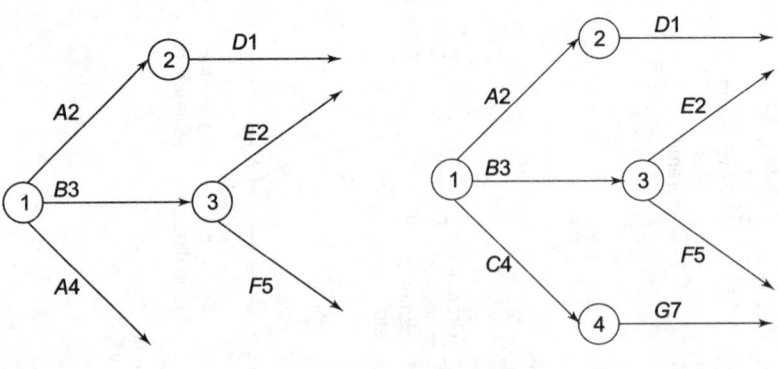

**Fig. 7.11**  **Fig. 7.12**

Activity *G* can be started at event 4 as its required predecessor is *C*, which ends at node 4 (Fig. 7.12).

Activity *H* requires both *D* and *E* to be over before it starts. Therefore join arrows *D* and *E* to end at a common node 5. From this new event 5, draw an arrow to represent activity *H* (Fig. 7.13).

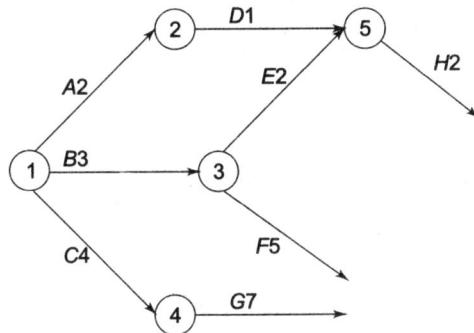

**Fig. 7.13**

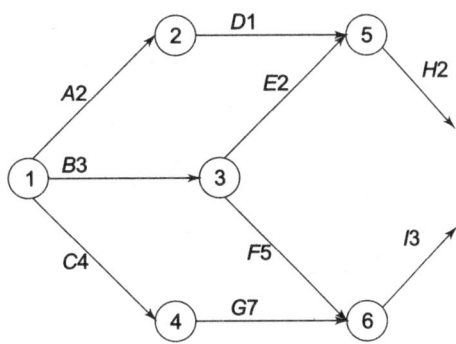

**Fig. 7.14**

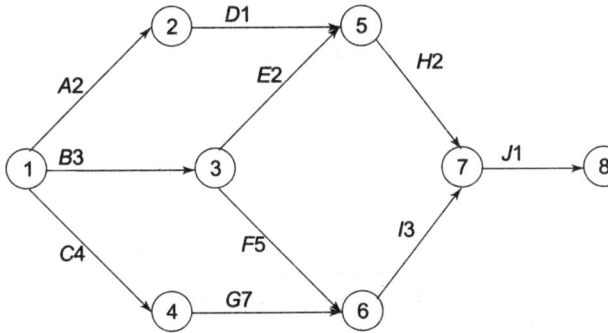

**Fig. 7.15**

Similarly, activity *I* requires both *F* and *G* to be over before it starts. Therefore join arrows *F* and *G* to end at a common node 6. From event 6, draw an arrow to represent activity *I* (Fig. 7.14).

Activity *J* similarly requires both *H* and *I* to be over before it starts. Therefore join arrows *H* and *I* to end at a common node 7. Event 7 marks the end of both activities *H* and *I*. From event 7, draw an arrow to represent activity *J*. Activity *J* ends at node 8, which becomes the last node of the project (Fig. 7.15).

### Critical Path

> The critical path is defined as the longest duration path between the first and the last nodes of a project.

The critical path is defined as the longest duration path between the first and the last nodes of a project. In the project described in Table 7.4, these nodes are 1 and 8. Different paths are possible between these nodes.

While tracing a path from the first node to the last node, one should always move along the direction of the arrows. The duration of a path is simply the sum of the duration of all the activities on the path.

From Table 7.5, we find that among all the possible paths, the longest duration is 15 days for the path 1-4-6-7-8 (*CGIJ*). Therefore, this is the critical path. Mark this critical path in the network diagram with double arrows (Fig. 7.16). *The duration of a project is always the same as the duration of its critical path.*

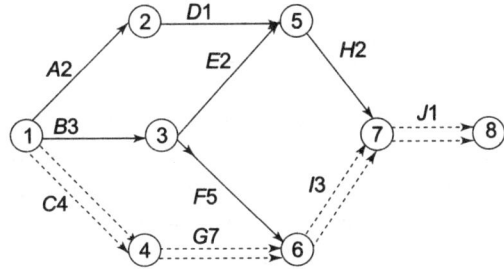

**Fig. 7.16** The critical path marked by double arrows

**Table 7.5**

| *Path* | *Duration (days)* |
|---|---|
| 1-2-5-7-8 (*ADHJ*) | $2 + 1 + 2 + 1 = 6$ |
| 1-3-5-7-8 (*BEHJ*) | $3 + 2 + 2 + 1 = 8$ |
| 1-3-6-7-8 (*BFIJ*) | $3 + 5 + 3 + 1 = 12$ |
| 1-4-6-7-8 (*CGIJ*) | $4 + 7 + 3 + 1 = 15$ |

## Example 7.1

A project has activities with duration and precedence requirements as given in Table 7.6. Draw the network diagram for this project.

**Table 7.6**

| Activity | Predecessor(s) | Duration (weeks) |
|----------|----------------|------------------|
| A | – | 7 |
| B | A | 8 |
| C | A | 10 |
| D | A | 6 |
| E | A | 2 |
| F | B,C | 5 |
| G | F,D,E | 8 |
| H | E | 7 |
| I | F | 5 |
| J | I,G,H | 2 |

**Solution**

The network diagram is shown in Fig. 7.17.

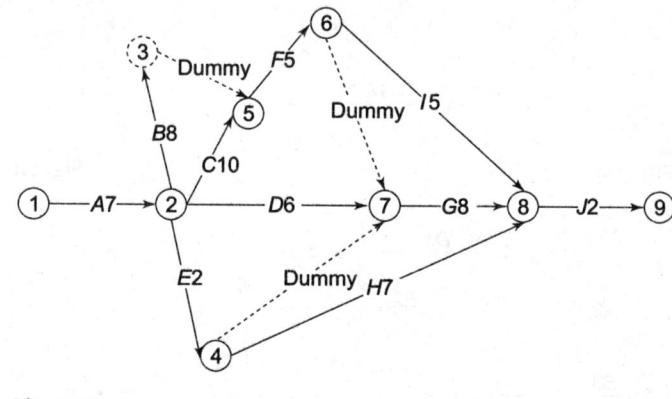

**Fig. 7.17**

## Example 7.2

A project has the characteristics shown in Table 7.7. Draw the network diagram of the project and find the duration of the project.

**Table 7.7**

| Activity | Predecessor(s) | Time (weeks) |
|----------|----------------|--------------|
| A | – | 7 |
| B | A | 10 |
| C | A | 12 |
| D | B | 3 |
| E | B | 8 |
| F | B | 7 |
| G | F | 2 |
| H | D,E | 5 |
| I | C | 13 |
| J | C | 6 |
| K | H | 14 |
| L | E,F | 5 |

**Solution**

The network diagram is shown in Fig. 7.18.

**Table 7.8**

| Path | Time (weeks) |
|------|--------------|
| 1-2-3-4-9-11 (ABDHK) | 39 |
| 1-2-3-5-8-11 (ABEL) | 30 |
| 1-2-3-6-8-11 (ABFL) | 29 |
| 1-2-3-6-11 (ABFG) | 26 |
| 1-2-7-11 (ACI) | 32 |
| 1-2-7-10-11 (ACJ) | 25 |
| **1-2-3-5-4-9-11 (ABEHK)** | **44** |

Table 7.8 shows the various paths. The critical path is *ABEHK* with a duration of 44 weeks. Therefore, the duration of the project is 44 weeks. In the construction of the network diagram, if we use dummies as shown in Fig. 7.19, the precedence requirement of activity *G* is not correctly met. Activity *G* has been given a precedence of only activity F, but Fig. 7.19 shows the precedence of both activities *E* (through the dummy) and *F* for activity *G*, which is wrong.

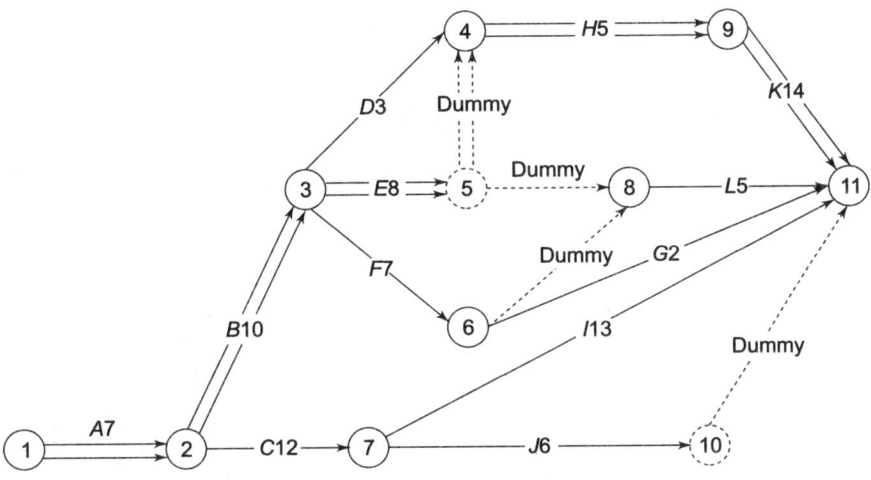

**Fig. 7.18**

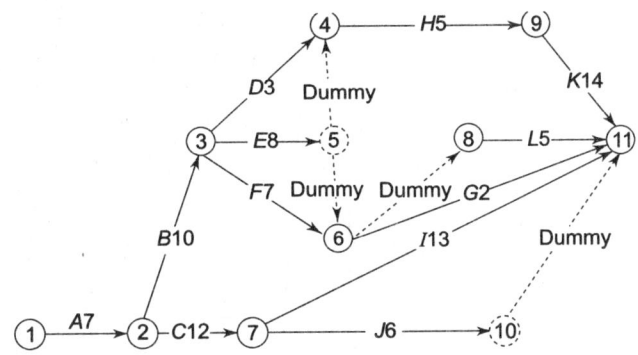

**Fig. 7.19**  Invalid network diagram for the project in Example 7.2

### Example 7.3*

Universal Transmissions (P) Ltd is based in Mumbai and employs around 45 people. It manufactures and assembles transmission systems (clutch systems and gear boxes) for two-wheelers. It gets 60% of its orders from Indian auto companies and the rest from some European companies. Universal is in the process of implementing just-in-time (JIT) in its factory. The consultants hired by them have given their recommendations and identified various activities with precedence requirements in this project (Table 7.9). They have also prepared a network diagram to aid themselves in the implementation of JIT (Fig. 7.20).

**Table 7.9**

| Task ID | Recommendations | Activities | Codes | Predecessor(s) |
|---------|-----------------|------------|-------|----------------|
| 1 | Reduction of the back-order risk from the key suppliers | Intimation of production plans to key suppliers | 1.1 | 2.1, 2.2 |
| 2 | Increase in buyer responsibilities | Training sessions for the buyer | 2.1 | 23.2 |
|  |  | Implications of the buyer in strategic decisions regarding the supply process | 2.2 | 23.2 |

*(Contd)*

* Adapted from Gelinas (1999).

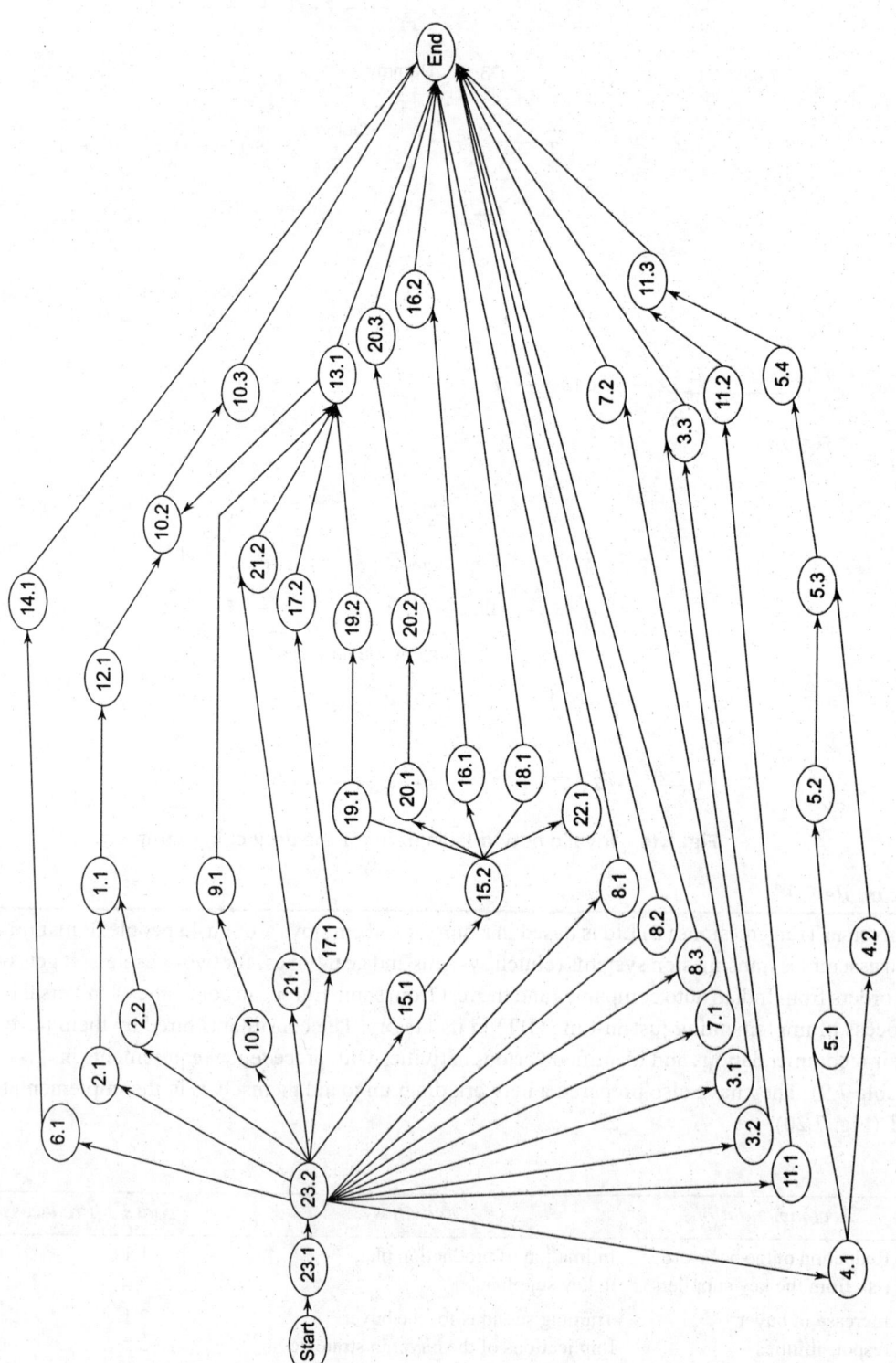

**Fig. 7.20**

*Table 7.9 Contd*

| Task ID | Recommendations | Activities | Codes | Predecessor(s) |
|---------|-----------------|------------|-------|----------------|
| 3 | Improvement of monitoring and control of distribution activities | Elimination of undue delays in Europe | 3.1 | 23.2 |
| | | Elaboration of an evaluation grid for the European distributors | 3.2 | 23.2 |
| | | Activity reports for the European distributors | 3.3 | 3.1, 3.2 |
| 4 | Reduction of set-up times | Analysis of the set-up times | 4.1 | 23.2 |
| | | Objectives definition | 4.2 | 4.1 |
| 5 | Reduction in the variance of the operation time | Analysis of the causes for the variance | 5.1 | 4.1 |
| | | Identification of the assignable causes | 5.2 | 5.1 |
| | | Study of the actual operation methods | 5.3 | 4.2, 5.2 |
| | | Determination of standard times | 5.4 | 5.3 |
| 6 | Maintenance improvement | Implementation of a preventive maintenance programme | 6.1 | 23.2 |
| 7 | Improvements in safety conditions | Definition of objectives and elaboration of incentive strategies | 7.1 | 23.2 |
| | | Financing an information programme | 7.2 | 7.1 |
| 8 | Improvement in operators' safety conditions | Enforcement of safety measures | 8.1 | 23.2 |
| | | First-aid resource availability | 8.2 | 23.2 |
| | | Fire extinguisher localization analysis | 8.3 | 23.2 |
| 9 | ISO 9001 implementation | Engagement in the certification process | 9.1 | 10.1 |
| 10 | Conception reorganization | Establishment of internal norms | 10.1 | 23.2 |
| | | Incorporation of production constraints into the conception process | 10.2 | 13.1, 12.1 |
| | | Revision of the die-casting conception | 10.3 | 10.2 |
| 11 | Improvement of the planning hardware and software | Real-time treatment of the information by the actual software | 11.1 | 23.2 |
| | | Buying a new production-oriented software | 11.2 | 11.1 |
| | | Software implementation | 11.3 | 11.2, 5.4 |
| 12 | Evaluation of the suppliers and subcontractors | Elaboration of an evaluation grid | 12.1 | 1.1 |
| 13 | Improvement of the problem resolution process | Involvement of the employees in the process | 13.1 | 9.1, 21.2, 17.2, |
| 14 | Improvement of working procedures | Documentation of working procedures | 14.1 | 6.1 |
| 15 | Improvement of human resources management | Training in human resources management | 15.1 | 23.2 |
| | | Creation of a position in human resources management | 15.2 | 15.1 |
| 16 | Implementation of monitoring tools for internal needs as well as for benchmarking | Identification of appropriate indicators | 16.1 | 15.2 |
| | | Data collection | 16.2 | 16.1 |
| 17 | Implementation of a monitoring tool for claims | Identification of appropriate indicators | 17.1 | 23.2 |
| | | Data collection | 17.2 | 17.1 |

*(Contd)*

*Table 7.9 Contd*

| Task ID | Recommendations | Activities | Codes | Predecessor(s) |
|---|---|---|---|---|
| 18 | Documentation of the human resources management function | Tasks and activities description | 18.1 | 15.2 |
| 19 | Expertise transfer pro- gramme among employees | Identification of critical expertise Coaching sessions | 19.1 19.2 | 15.2 19.1 |
| 20 | Training planning for the next two years | Identification of priorities | 20.1 | 15.2 |
| | | Identification of available resources | 20.2 | 20.1 |
| | | Elaboration of the training plan | 20.3 | 20.2 |
| 21 | Constitution of a coordination committee | Planning reunion Information diffusion in the internal journal | 21.1 21.2 | 23.2 21.1 |
| 22 | Modification of the vocation of the internal journal | Diffusion of strategic, economic, operational, and social information | 22.1 | 15.2 |
| 23 | Priority identification in strategic planning | Identification of possible strategies Identification of accepted strategies | 23.1 23.2 | – 23.1 |

## Earliest Start and Finish Times

> The earliest start and finish times of an activity are based on the condition that every activity will be started and finished as early as possible.

The earliest start and finish times of an activity are based on the condition that every activity will be started and finished as early as possible. Assume that the first event of the project takes place immediately, that is, right now or at time instant 0. The earliest start and finish times of an activity are shown in square brackets adjacent to the name of the activity. The first number in the square bracket represents the earliest start time and the second number after the comma represents the earliest finish time. Therefore, in our example, we show the earliest start time of the three activities *A*, *B*, and *C* as 0 (Fig. 7.21). Activity *A* takes 2 days for its execution; therefore, it can be finished on the day 2 at the earliest. Similarly, activity *B* can be completed only on day 3, as three days are required for it. The earliest finish time of activity *C* is 4 days.

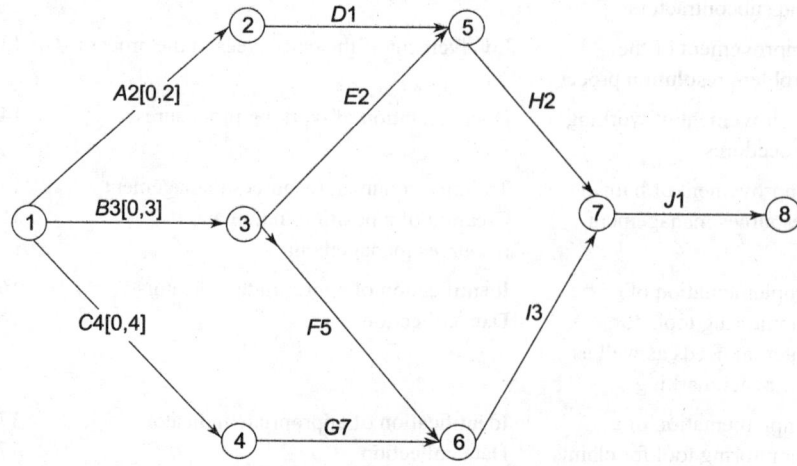

**Fig. 7.21**   Earliest start and finish times

Activity *D* can be started as early as possible on day 2, just after activity *A* gets over. It requires one day. Therefore, at the earliest, activity *D* will finish on day 3. Similarly, activity *G* can be started as early as possible on day 4, just after activity *C* gets over. It requires seven days, therefore activity *G* finishes on day 11 at the earliest. Similarly, activities *E* and *F* can be started as early as possible on the day 3, just after activity *B* gets over. At the earliest, activities *E* and *F* will finish on day 5 and day 8, respectively (Fig 7.22).

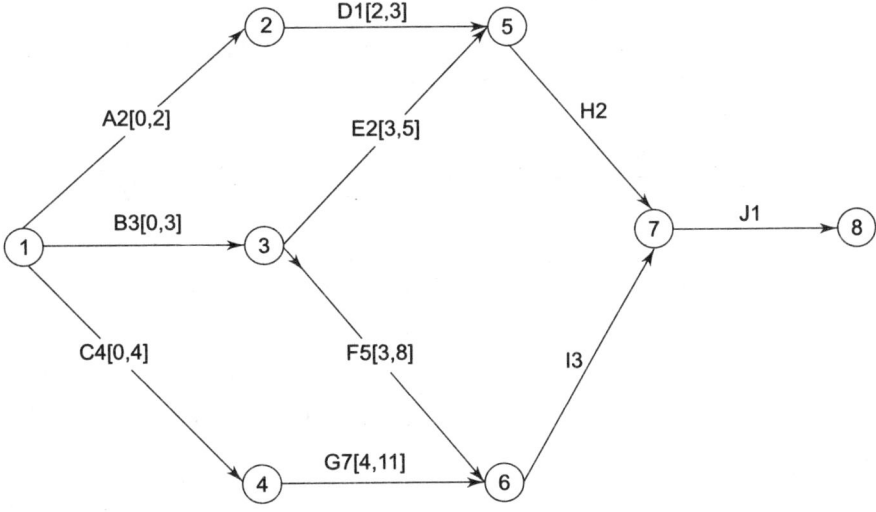

**Fig. 7.22**

Event 5 can take place only when both activities *D* and *E* get over. *D* gets over as early as possible on day 3 and *E* gets over as early as possible on day 5. Therefore, both the activities are over by day 5. Event 5 takes place on day 5 and immediately activity *H* can start. The earliest start (ES) time for activity *H* is 5 and the earliest finish (EF) time is 7 (Fig. 7.23).

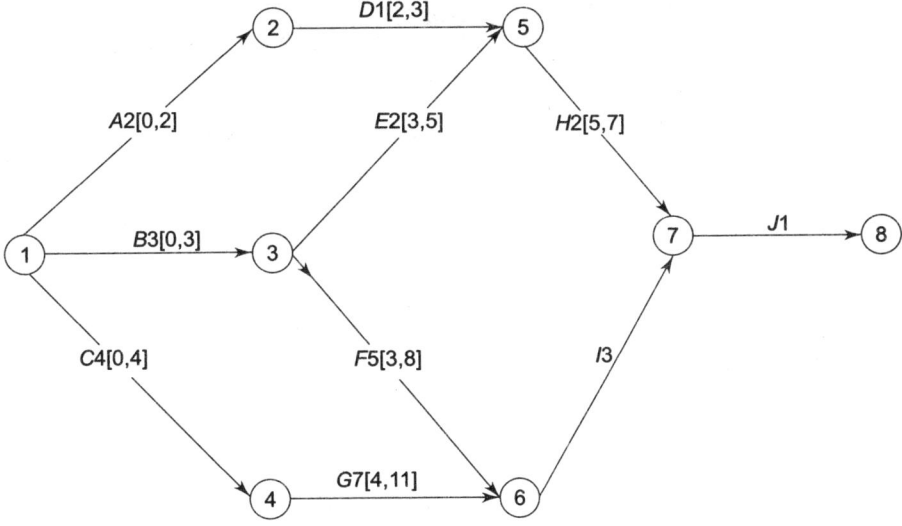

**Fig. 7.23**

Similarly, event 6 will take place only when both activities *F* and *G* get over. *F* gets over as early as possible on day 8 and *G* gets over as early as possible on day 11. Therefore, both the activities are over by day 11. Event 6 takes place on day 11 and immediately activity *I* can start. The ES and EF times for activity *I* are, therefore, 11 and 14, respectively (Fig. 7.24).

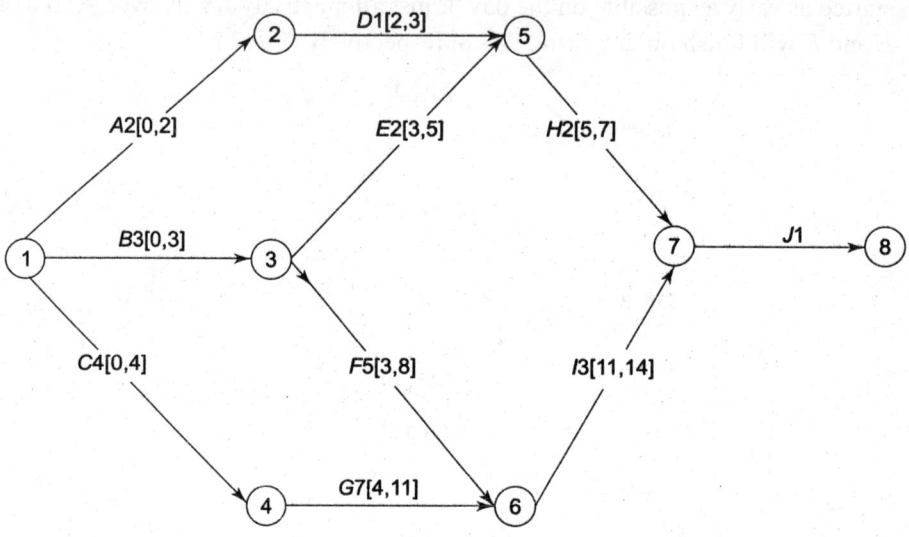

**Fig. 7.24**

Event 7 will take place only when both activities *H* and *I* get over. *H* gets over as early as possible on day 7, and I gets over as early as possible on day 14. Therefore, both the activities are over by day 14. Event 7 takes place on day 14 and immediately activity *J* can start. Therefore, the ES and EF times for activity *J* are 14 and 15, respectively (Fig. 7.25).

Thus, the end node of the project, that is, node 8, takes place on day 15. Therefore, the duration of the project is 15 days.

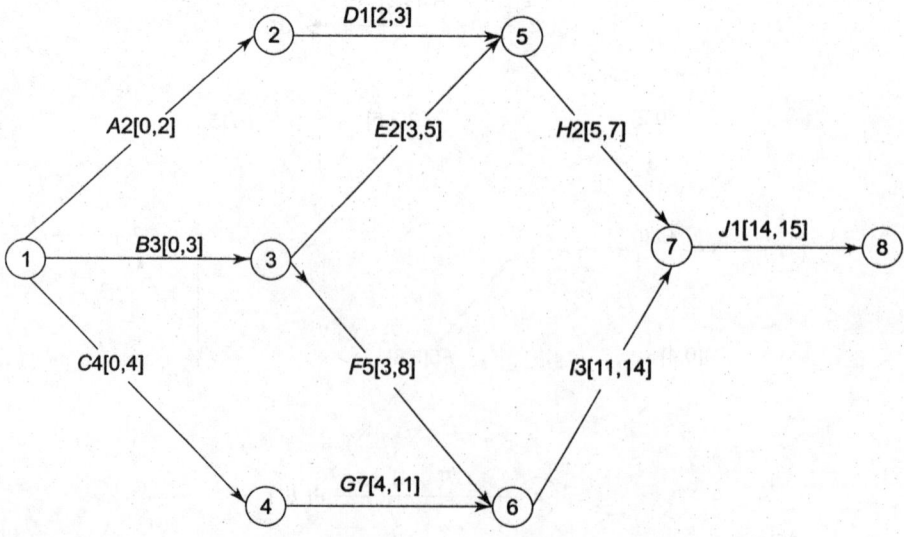

**Fig. 7.25**

## Latest Start and Finish Times

The latest start (LS) and latest finish (LF) times of an activity are based upon the condition that every activity will be started and finished as late as possible, but the project will still get completed in the scheduled time.

In our example, the project has to be over on day 15. Therefore, for the last activity *J* of the project, we put the latest finish time as 15. Activity *J* requires one day and hence its latest start time will be 15 − 1=14 (Fig. 7.26).

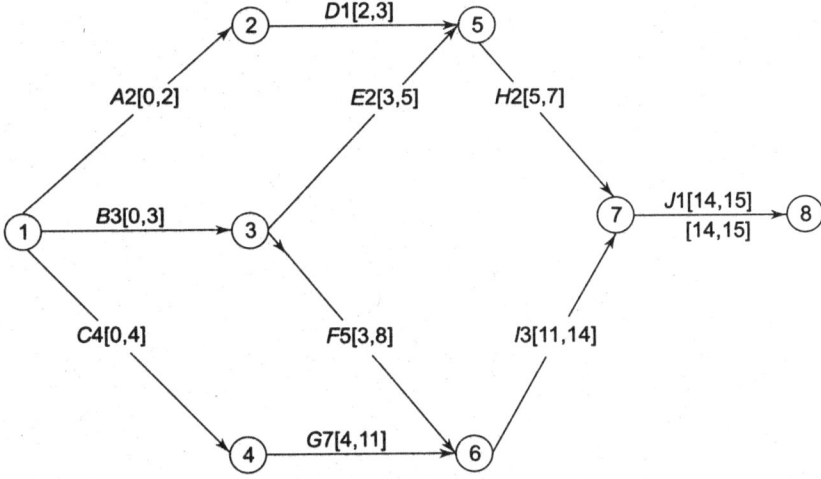

**Fig. 7.26**

For activity *J* to be started as late as possible on day 14, its preceding activities *H* and *I* should be over as late as possible on day 14. Therefore, the LF times of both *H* and *I* are 14. According to the time required for these activities, the LS times for *H* and *I* are 12 and 11, respectively (Fig. 7.27).

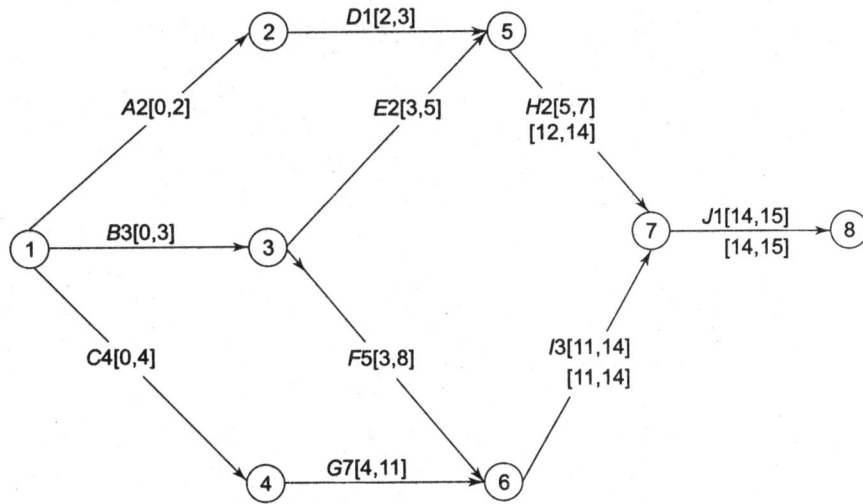

**Fig. 7.27**

For activity *H* to be started as late as possible on day 12, its preceding activities *D* and *E* should be over as late as possible on day 12. Therefore, the LF times of both *D* and *E* are 12. According to the duration of these activities, the LS times for *D* and *E*, are 11 and 10, respectively (Fig. 7.28).

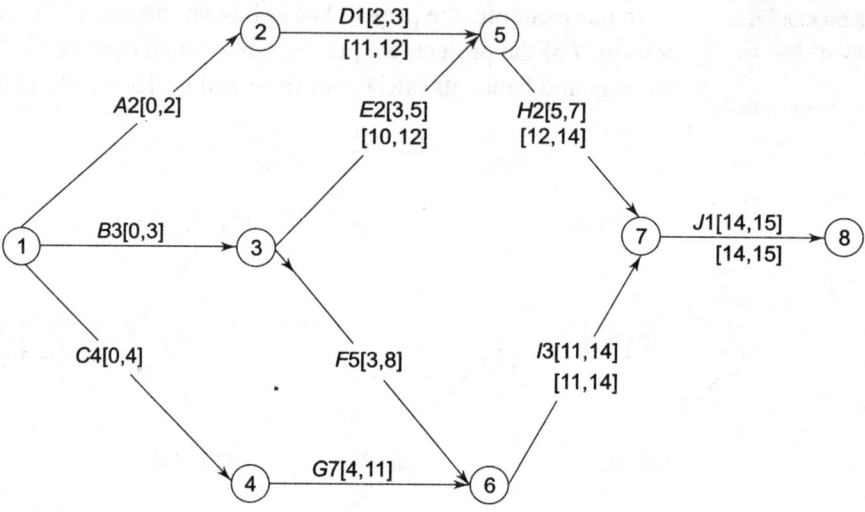

**Fig. 7.28**

For activity *I* to be started as late as possible on day 11, its preceding activities *F* and *G* should be over as late as possible on day 11. Therefore, the LF times of both *F* and *G* are 11. According to the duration of these activities, the LS times for *F* and *G* are 6 and 4, respectively (Fig. 7.29).

Activities *E* and *F* have LS times of 10 and 6, respectively. Hence their preceding activity *B* should get over as late as possible on day 6. Therefore, the LF time of activity *B* is 6; its LS time is 3 (Fig. 7.30).

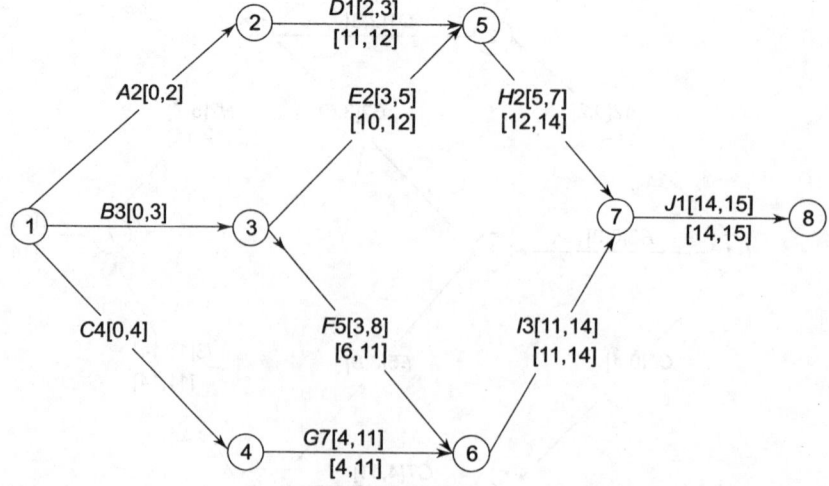

**Fig. 7.29**

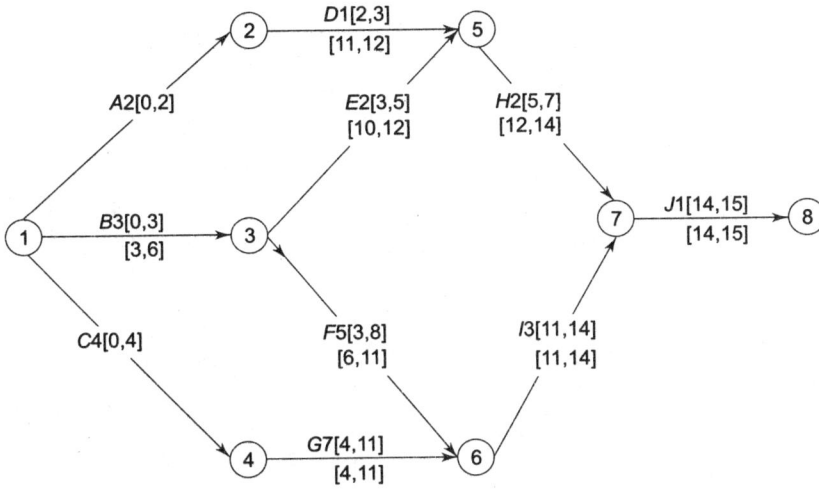

**Fig. 7.30**

The timely completion of critical activities is important for the timely completion of the project.

*A* is the preceding activity for activity *D*. For *D* to start as late as possible on day 11, activity *A* should be over as late as possible on day 11. Therefore, the LF time of *A* is 11 and its LS time is 9 as it requires two days. Similarly, for *G* to be started as late as possible on day 4, activity *C* should be over as late as possible on day 4. Therefore, the LF time of *C* is 4, its LS time is 0 as it requires four days (Fig. 7.31).

There are a few activities in the network diagram for which the earliest and latest times are exactly the same. These activities are *C*, *G*, *I*, and *J*. These are the critical activities in the project and constitute the critical path (Fig. 7.32). The earliest and latest times are same for these activities because they cannot be delayed by even a single day without delaying the project completion. Hence, these are called critical activities, as their timely completion is critical for the timely completion of the project.

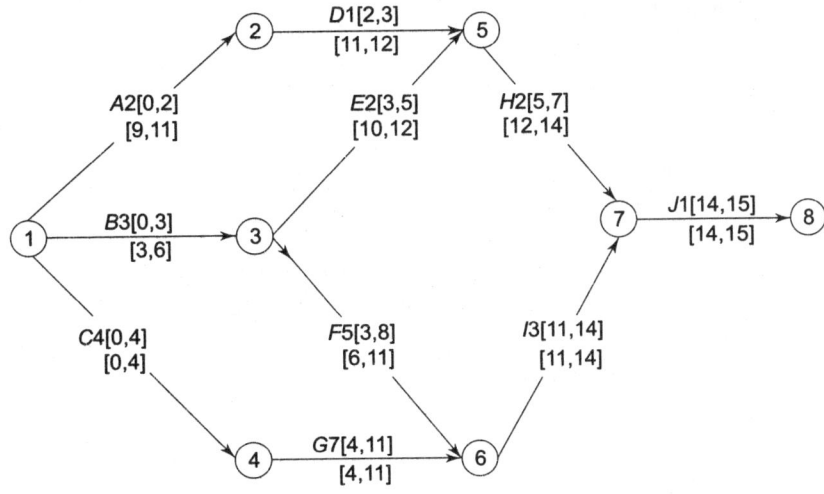

**Fig. 7.31**

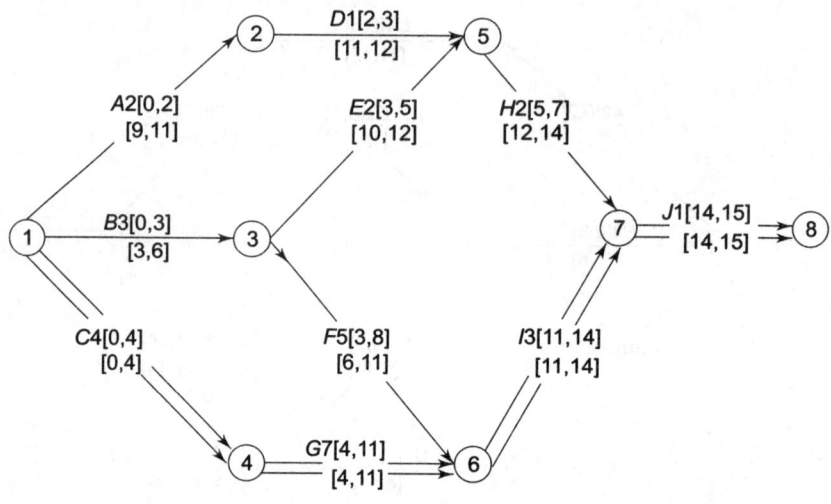

**Fig. 7.32** Critical activities C, G, I, J forming the critical path

> The total float of an activity is the maximum amount of delay that can be permitted in its execution without introducing any delay in the completion of the project.

**Float of an activity** The total float of an activity is the maximum amount of delay that can be permitted in its execution without introducing any delay in the completion of the project. It is helpful to find the float of various activities in the project because the project manager then has some flexibility in implementing the project. By calculating the floats, he knows how much an activity can be delayed without disturbing the project completion schedule.

The simplest formula for calculating the total float (TF) of an activity is

$$TF = LS_{i-j} - ES_{i-j} \tag{7.1}$$

where $i$ and $j$ are the start and end nodes for the activity. For the project represented by the network diagram in Fig. 7.33, let us find the total float using Eqn (7.1). Recall that the LS time for an activity $i$-$j$ (activity $A$ can also be called activity 1-2 because it exists between nodes 1 and 2) is the first number in the lower square bracket. We know that for critical activities, the total float is always zero. This can be verified from Eqn (7.1). In the network of Fig. 7.33, the TF of $A$, $J$, and $M$ is zero.

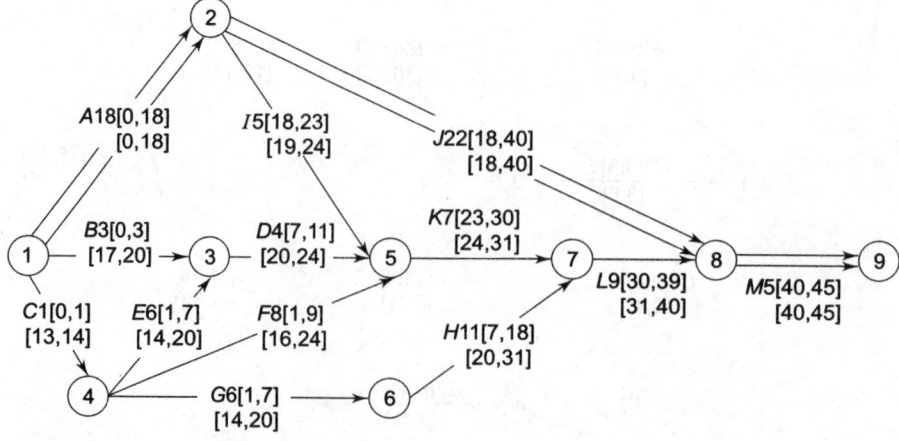

**Fig. 7.33**

| Activity | | | TF | | Activity | | | TF | |
|---|---|---|---|---|---|---|---|---|---|
| A | | | | 0 | H | 20 | − | 7 = | 13 |
| B | 17 | − | 0 = | 17 | I | 19 | − | 18 = | 1 |
| C | 13 | − | 0 = | 13 | J | | | | 0 |
| D | 20 | − | 7 = | 13 | K | 24 | − | 23 = | 1 |
| E | 14 | − | 1 = | 13 | L | 31 | − | 30 = | 1 |
| F | 16 | − | 1 = | 15 | M | | | | 0 |
| G | 14 | − | 1 = | 13 | | | | | |

The total float can also be calculated as

$$TF = LF_{i\text{-}j} - EF_{i\text{-}j} \qquad (7.2)$$

For activity $F$, TF $= 16 - 1 = 15$ days. The following formula can also be used:

TF = (total time available for an activity) − (total time required for its execution)

$$= (LF_{i\text{-}j} - ES_{i\text{-}j}) - t_{i\text{-}j} \qquad (7.3)$$

For activity $F$, TF $= (24 - 1) - 8 = 15$ days. Equations (7.2) and (7.3) gave the same result as Eqn (7.1). Therefore, to find the TF of an activity, one should always use the simplest formula [En (7.1)].

Figure 7.34 shows that, as an option, the total float (delay) of activity $F$ can be utilized before it starts (case 1), so that $F$ starts at its LS time and finishes at its LF time. Another option (case 2) is the start of activity $F$ at its ES time and end at its EF time. The TF of 15 days is utilized before its succeeding activity $K$ starts. The third option shown (case 3) is the partial utilization (5 days) of the TF, then the execution (8 days) of $F$, and finally the utilization of the remaining (10 days) TF. For partial utilization of TF, many more combinations like this one are possible.

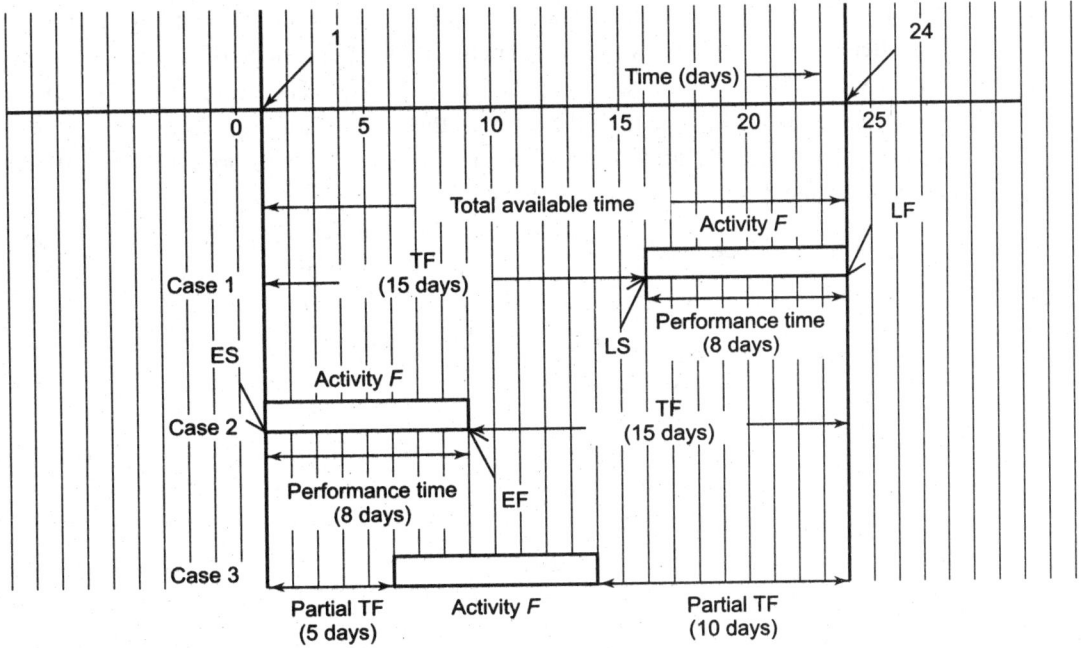

**Fig. 7.34**   Different options for the utilization of TF

> The slack of an event is equivalent to the float of an activity.

**Slack of an event** The slack of an event is equivalent to the *float* of an activity. It is defined as the maximum possible delay in the occurrence of an event.

Slack of an event = (latest occurrence time of the event)

– (earliest occurrence time of the event)

| Event | Slack |
|---|---|
| 1 | 0 |
| 2 | 0 |
| 3 | 20 – 7 = 13 |
| 4 | 14 – 1 = 13 |
| 5 | 1 |
| 6 | 20 – 7 = 13 |
| 7 | 31 – 30 = 1 |
| 8 | 0 |
| 9 | 0 |

The latest occurrence (LO) and earliest occurrence (EO) times of an event are always dependent upon the activities ending at this event. For example, three activities, namely, $I$, $D$, and $F$, end at node 5 in Fig. 7.33. Their EF times are 23, 11, and 9, respectively. Therefore, all the three activities get over on day 23, and event 5 also occurs on day 23 (EO time of event 5).

Similarly, the LF times of the three activities are all 24. Therefore, the LO time of event 5 is day 24. Hence, the slack of event 5 = 24 – 23 = 1 day.

The slack values of all events lying on the critical path is always zero. Therefore, in Fig. 7.33 the slack of events 1, 2, 8, and 9 is zero. The values of slack of the remaining events are shown above.

**Interfering and free floats of an activity** The TF of an activity is composed of two parts: *interfering float* (IF) and *free float* (FF).

$$TF = IF + FF$$

The IF of an activity is defined as that part of the TF which, when used, affects the floats of the following activities. Similarly, FF of an activity is defined as that part of the TF which when used does not affect the floats of the following activities.

*Head slack* or IF means the slack of a head event (event touching the head of the arrow representing the activity). For example, for activity $F$, event 5 is the head event (Fig. 7.33) and we have determined its slack as one day. Therefore, the head slack of activity $F$ is one day.

For activity $F$, IF = head slack = 1 day and TF = 15 days. Therefore, FF = TF – IF = 15 – 1 = 14 days. Table 7.10 shows the IF and FF for all the activities in Fig. 7.33.

For critical activities, IF and FF are zero since TF is zero. Therefore, in Table 7.10, for critical activities $A$, $J$, and $M$, write zero for IF and FF.

**Table 7.10** Interfering and free floats

| Activity | TF | Head event | IF (head slack) | FF |
|---|---|---|---|---|
| A | 0 | – | 0 | 0 |
| B | 17 | 3 | 13 | 4 |
| C | 13 | 4 | 13 | 0 |
| D | 13 | 5 | 1 | 12 |
| E | 13 | 3 | 13 | 0 |
| F | 15 | 5 | 1 | 14 |
| G | 13 | 6 | 13 | 0 |
| H | 13 | 7 | 1 | 12 |
| I | 1 | 5 | 1 | 0 |
| J | 0 | – | 0 | 0 |
| K | 1 | 7 | 1 | 0 |
| L | 1 | 8 | 0 | 1 |
| M | 0 | – | 0 | 0 |

Let us now try to understand the meaning of the IF and FF of an activity using the time diagram for activity $F$ in Fig. 7.35. Case 1 shows that the FF of 14 days is utilized before starting activity $F$. Activity $F$ starts on day 15 and gets over on day 23. Activity $F$ is followed by activity $K$, whose ES time is 23. Therefore, activity $K$ can be started on the same day and it (and its float) is not affected at all by the delay in the start of activity $F$.

Case 2 shows that both the FF (14 days) and IF (1 day) are utilized before activity $F$, which starts on day 16 and gets over on day 24. Now the succeeding activity $K$ (with ES time 23) cannot start at its ES time; it can start only on day 24.

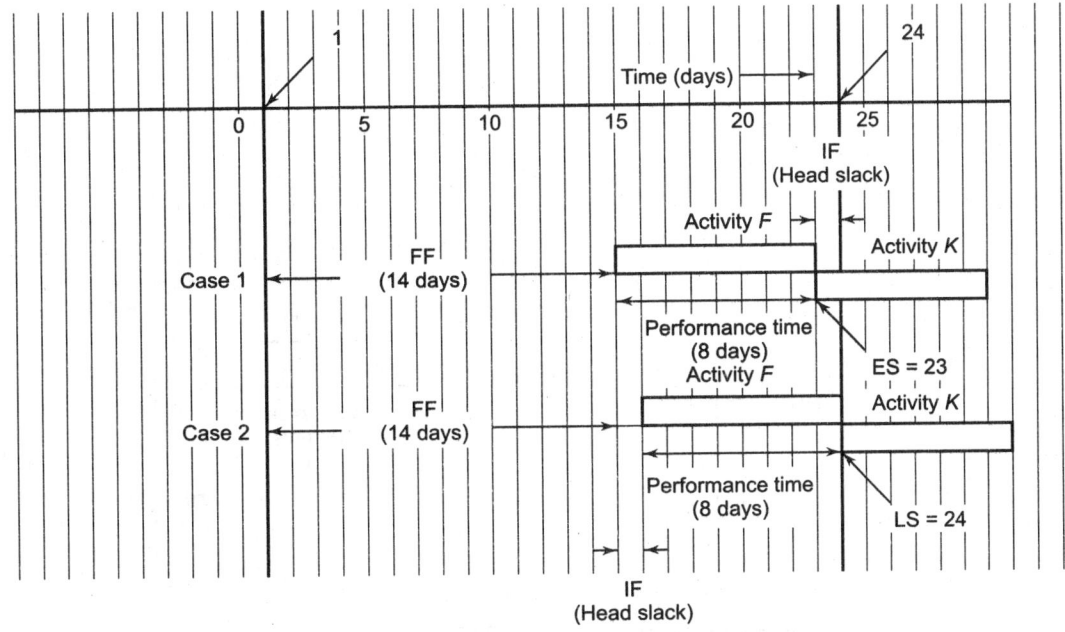

**Fig. 7.35** Time diagram showing free float (FF) and interfering float (IF)

> The independent float of an activity is the delay possible in it without affecting the preceding and following activities.

Note that activity $K$ is affected by activity $F$, and its TF of one day has been reduced to zero. This has happened because of the use of the IF of activity $F$. The IF of an activity interferes with its succeeding activities and hence its name.

**Independent float of an activity** The independent float of an activity is the delay possible in it without affecting the preceding and following activities. The tail event occurs as late as possible and the head event occurs as early as possible. Under this condition, the excess time over the performance time of the activity is called the independent float (IDF).

**Table 7.11**

| Activity | FF | Tail slack | IDF | Remarks |
|----------|-----|--------------|-----|------------------|
| A | 0 | Not required | 0 | |
| B | 4 | 0 | 4 | |
| C | 0 | Not required | 0 | |
| D | 12 | 13 | 0 | −1, taken as 0 |
| E | 0 | Not required | 0 | |
| F | 14 | 13 | 1 | |
| G | 0 | Not required | 0 | |
| H | 12 | 13 | 0 | −1, taken as 0 |
| I | 0 | Not required | 0 | |
| J | 0 | Not required | 0 | |
| K | 0 | Not required | 0 | |
| L | 1 | 1 | 0 | |
| M | 0 | Not required | 0 | |

Let us try to understand this float by using the time diagram (Fig. 7.36) for activity $F$, its predecessor activity $C$, and successor activity $K$. Activity C takes place as late as possible (at its LS and LF times) and activity K takes place as early as possible (at its ES and EF times).

Independent float of an activity can easily be calculated by using the following formula:

$$\text{IDF} = \text{FF} - \text{tail slack} \qquad (7.4)$$

The *tail slack* of an activity is the slack of the tail event of that activity. If the IDF comes out to be a negative value, we take it as zero. All the activities for which FF is zero will have zero IDF according to Eqn (7.4). IDF can also be calculated using Eqn (7.5) given below.

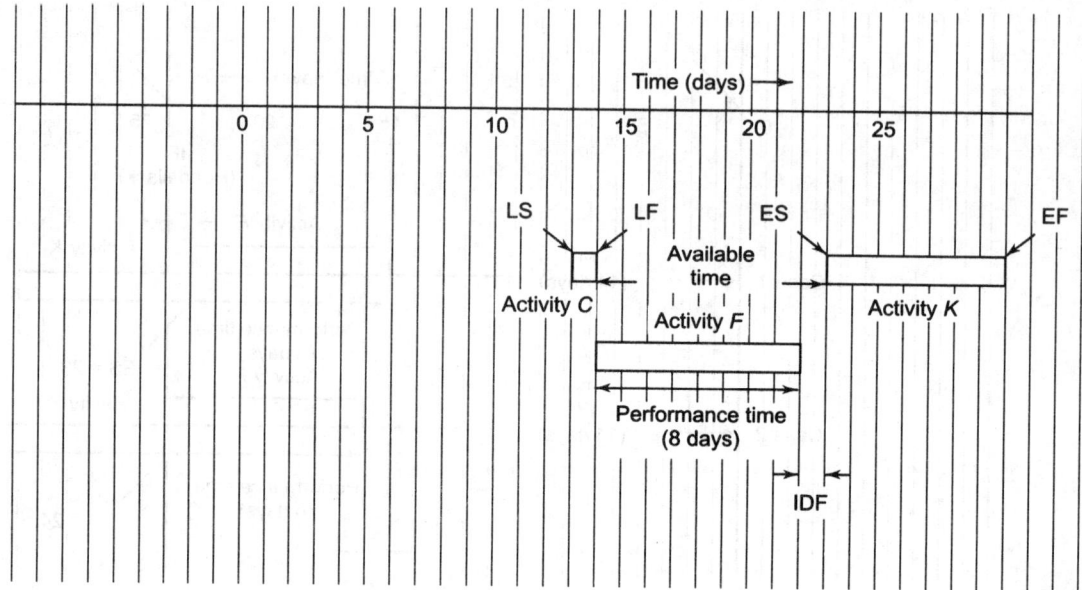

**Fig. 7.36** Time diagram showing independent float (IDF)

$$IDF = \text{(available time for activity } i\text{-}j) - \text{(performance time for activity } i\text{-}j)$$
$$= (ES_{j\text{-}k} - LF_{h\text{-}i}) - t_{i\text{-}j} \qquad (7.5)$$

where $i\text{-}j$ is the activity for which the IDF is to be found, for example, activity $F$; $h\text{-}i$ is the predecessor of activity $i\text{-}j$, for example, activity $C$; and $j\text{-}k$ is the successor of activity $i\text{-}j$, for example, activity $K$.

For activity $F$, IDF = (23 –14) – 8 = 9 – 8 = 1 day. The IDFs of all the activities in Fig. 7.33 are shown in Table 7.11.

See Exhibit 7.3 to understand the cost implications of project management.

---

### Exhibit 7.3 Delhi Commonwealth Games

The 2010 version of the Commonwealth Games Federation (Delhi 2010) was held in New Delhi, India, from 3 October 2010 to 14 October 2010. The event, traditionally marked with sporting fervour and celebrations all across the Commonwealth Nations, comprised various sports competitions across 12 days.

In 2003, India won the bid to host the games in New Delhi after beating its closest rival Canada. India had previously successfully hosted the 1982 Asian Games in New Delhi. Winning the bid to host the prestigious games was marked with jubilation. However, there were apprehensions as well, regarding whether Delhi would be able to pull off the games successfully.

On 10 February 2005, the Organising Committee (OC) of the Commonwealth Games 2010 (CWG 2010)

was constituted with the President of the Indian Olympic Association (IOA) Suresh Kalmadi as the Chairman of its Executive Board. The OC set itself the goal of conducting the best CWG to date, including the provision of impeccable service standards to athletes, officials, and the public, in close collaboration with its partners.

By December 2009, it became evident that many of the projects associated with CWG 2010 were delayed. The Chief Minister of Delhi, Sheila Dikshit, had earlier said that work was going on and money might even be saved. However, realising the glaring irregularities, she warned of stern action against contractors of the CWG projects and reiterated that the games should be a grand success. She also expressed nervousness about

*(Contd)*

*Exhibit 7.3 Contd*

the slow pace of the related projects. Interestingly, officials had been optimistic of the overall progress of preparations though they were troubled by the frequently extended deadlines. The Group of Ministers (GoM) and other committee members had expressed satisfaction about the developments. Nevertheless, their optimism was short lived, when in August 2010, merely two months before the scheduled inauguration of the games, the roofs of several newly constructed games venues started leaking due to heavy rainfall. While the concerned officials continued giving fake assurances, media coverage exposed the lack of preparedness of several venues.

A 40 per cent budget escalation for CWG 2010 was reported, from ₹22,000 crores in 2006 to ₹30,000 crores in 2010.

As if the time delays, cost overruns, and quality issues were not enough, the OC was hit by a corruption scandal during early August 2010. It was alleged that several equipment and utilities for the games were 'hired' at prices far above the 'buying price' of such items. In a news update, Delhi's health directorate issued a circular, blacklisting two companies, and ordered the government hospitals and departments to avoid buying medical equipment from them. It was discovered that free services from prominent clinics and practitioners were rejected, allowing monopoly by such companies.

As the furore over hosting games of such mammoth scale increased, the Indian government rejected the proposal of the IOA to bid for hosting the 2019 Asian Games.

## Programme Evaluation and Review Technique

> Programme evaluation and review technique (PERT) is applied in projects where the duration of various activities cannot be predicted with certainty.

*Programme evaluation and review technique* (PERT) is applied in projects where the duration of various activities cannot be predicted with certainty. CPM and PERT are very similar in application after the time estimates have been arrived at. PERT is especially suitable for research and development (R & D) projects. Researchers are usually not sure as to how much time a particular research activity will take; they have to arrive at three time estimates for each activity based on their past experience.

**Optimistic time estimate (a)**  This is the shortest possible time estimate of an activity. It is based upon the premise that everything will go right for the earliest completion of the activity.

**Pessimistic time estimate (b)**  This is the longest possible time estimate of an activity. It is based upon the premise that there may be hindrances in the completion of the activity.

**Most likely time estimate (m)**  This is the time estimate that has the highest probability of occurrence. This is based upon the gut feeling or hunch of the project manager.

These three time estimates are clubbed together into a single time estimate by taking a weighted average. This combined estimate is called the expected time estimate ($t_e$) of the activity. A weight of 4 (weight is the importance attached to a value) is attached to $m$ and weights of 1 each are attached to $a$ and $b$. $t_e$ can thus be found by using the following formula:

$$t_e = \frac{a + 4m + b}{6} \tag{7.6}$$

In order to view the weights attached, Eqn (7.6) can b written as

$$t_e = \frac{1 \times a + 4 \times m + 1 \times b}{6}$$

The denominator has the sum of all these weights, that is, $1 + 4 + 1 = 6$. These values have been found suitable according to researches conducted with various types of projects.

The probability distribution curve of the duration of an activity is represented by a curve known as the *beta curve* (Fig. 7.37).

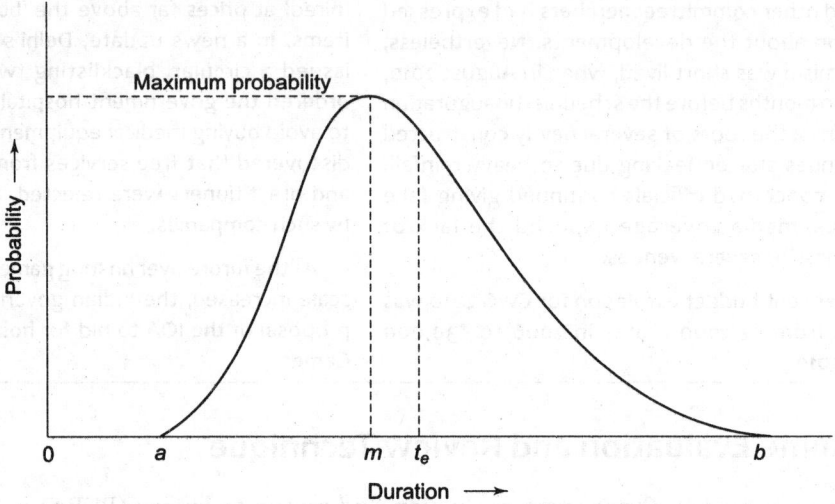

**Fig. 7.37**  Beta curve

The beta curve shown in Fig. 7.37 is dispersed around the average value $t_e$. This means that when this activity is actually implemented, it may take any time between $a$ and $b$. The dispersion of the curve as measured by its standard deviation is given by

$$\sigma = \frac{b - a}{6}$$

so that its variance is

$$\sigma^2 = \left(\frac{b - a}{6}\right)^2$$

For a project, the expected duration ($T$) is the sum of the expected duration ($t_e$) of all the *critical activities*.

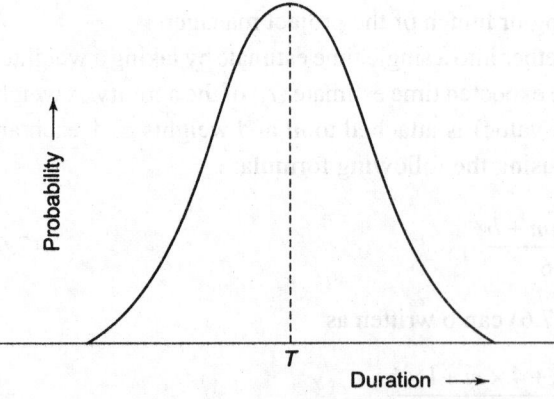

**Fig. 7.38**  Expected time duration of a project given by a normal distribution curve

Let us assume that a project has critical activities 1, 2, 3, ..., $k$. Then

$$T = t_{e1} + t_{e2} + t_{e3} + \cdots + t_{ek}$$

Similarly, the variance ($\sigma_T$) of the expected duration ($T$) of the project is the sum of the variances of all the critical activities.

$$\sigma_T^2 = \sigma_1^2 + \sigma_2^2 + \sigma_3^2 + \cdots + \sigma_k^2$$

The *central limit theorem* of statistics states that for a large number of critical activities (30 or more) in a project, the expected duration ($T$) of the project may be assumed to follow a normal distribution curve for all practical purposes (see Fig. 7.38).

The discussion so far will be clear with the help of the following example.

### *Example 7.4*

Table 7.12 gives details about the various activities of a project.

**Table 7.12**

| Activity | Node | a | m | b |
|----------|------|----|----|----|
| A | 1-2 | 10 | 11 | 12 |
| B | 2-3 | 6 | 10 | 14 |
| C | 2-4 | 5 | 8 | 11 |
| D | 2-5 | 1 | 5 | 9 |
| E | 3-6 | 3 | 5 | 13 |
| F | 4-6 | 4 | 9 | 14 |
| G | 5-7 | 1 | 2 | 3 |
| H | 6-7 | 3 | 7 | 11 |
| I | 7-8 | 9 | 12 | 15 |
| J | 7-9 | 3 | 5 | 7 |

Find (a) the critical path of the project and its expected duration, and (b) the probability that the project will be completed within 50 days.

### *Solution*

First, let us find the expected duration of all the activities. For activity $A$,

$$t_e = \frac{a + 4m + b}{6} = \frac{10 + (14 \times 11) + 12}{6} = 11$$

Table 7.13 shows the expected duration of all the activities:

**Table 7.13**

| Activity | Node | a | m | b | $t_e$ |
|----------|------|----|----|----|----|
| A | 1-2 | 10 | 11 | 12 | 11 |
| B | 2-3 | 6 | 10 | 14 | 10 |
| C | 2-4 | 5 | 8 | 11 | 8 |
| D | 2-5 | 1 | 5 | 9 | 5 |
| E | 3-6 | 3 | 5 | 13 | 6 |
| F | 4-6 | 4 | 9 | 14 | 9 |
| G | 5-7 | 1 | 2 | 3 | 2 |
| H | 6-7 | 3 | 7 | 11 | 7 |
| I | 7-8 | 9 | 12 | 15 | 12 |
| J | 7-9 | 3 | 5 | 7 | 5 |

Using the values of $t_e$ from Table 7.13, draw a network diagram as shown in Fig. 7.39.

Let us now find the critical path:

| Path | Duration (days) |
|------|-----------------|
| 1-2-3-6-7-8-9 | 11 + 10 + 6 + 7 + 12 = 46 |
| 1-2-3-6-7-9 | 11 + 10 + 6 + 7 + 5 = 39 |
| **1-2-4-6-7-8-9** | **11 + 8 + 9 + 7 + 12 = 47** |
| 1-2-4-6-7-9 | 11 + 8 + 9 + 7 + 5 = 40 |
| 1-2-5-7-9 | 11 + 5 + 2 + 5 = 23 |
| 1-2-5-7-8-9 | 11 + 5 + 2 + 12 = 30 |

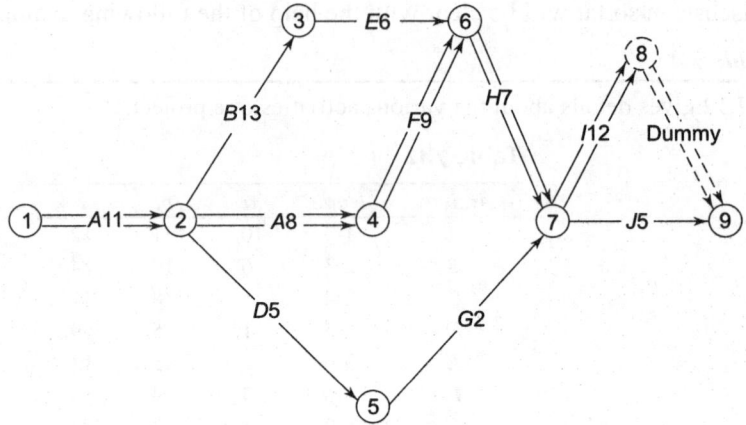

**Fig. 7.39**

The expected duration (*T*) of the project is 47 days as the critical path is 1-2-4-6-7-8-9. Now find the variances of only the critical activities, that is, 1-2, 2-4, 4-6, 6-7, 7-8, and 8-9. For activity 1-2,

$$\sigma = \frac{b-a}{6} = \frac{12-10}{6} = \frac{2}{6} = \frac{1}{3}$$

$$\sigma^2 = \left(\frac{1}{3}\right)^2 = \frac{1}{9}$$

Table 7.14 shows the variances of all the critical activities:

**Table 7.14**

| Activity | Node | a | m | b | $t_e$ | $\sigma^2$ |
|---|---|---|---|---|---|---|
| A | 1-2 | 10 | 11 | 12 | 11 | 1/9 |
| B | 2-3 | 6 | 10 | 14 | 10 | |
| C | 2-4 | 5 | 8 | 11 | 8 | 1 |
| D | 2-5 | 1 | 5 | 9 | 5 | |
| E | 3-6 | 3 | 5 | 13 | 6 | |
| F | 4-6 | 4 | 9 | 14 | 9 | 25/9 |
| G | 5-7 | 1 | 2 | 3 | 2 | |
| H | 6-7 | 3 | 7 | 11 | 7 | 16/9 |
| I | 7-8 | 9 | 12 | 15 | 12 | 1 |
| J | 7-9 | 3 | 5 | 7 | 5 | |

The variance of the duration of the project is the sum of the variances of the critical activities. Therefore,

$$\sigma^2 = \frac{1}{9} + 1 + \frac{25}{9} + \frac{16}{9} + 1 = \frac{1+9+25+16+9}{9} + \frac{60}{9}$$

$$\sigma = \sqrt{6.67} = 2.582$$

Let us now find the probability that the project will be completed within 50 days (Fig. 7.40). Let us calculate the *z*-value for *t* = 50 days.

$$z = \frac{t-T}{\sigma} = \frac{50-47}{2.582} = \frac{3}{2.582} = 1.16$$

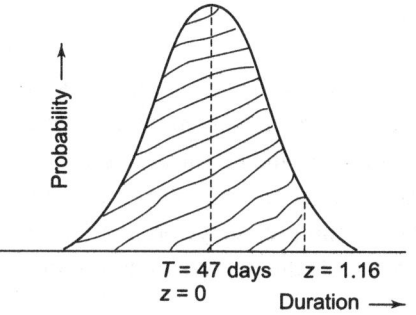

**Fig. 7.40**

From the z-table (table for areas under the normal curve given in Table A of the Appendix), the area between $z = 0$ and $z = 1.16$ is 0.3770. (Look at the first column of the table, which shows the values of $z$. Our value of $z$ is 1.16, with 1.1 as the first two digits. Therefore, choose the value of $z$ in the first column as 1.1. The values in the top row of the table represent the digit in the second decimal place in the $z$-value. In our $z$-value 1.16, the digit in the second decimal place is 6. Therefore find the value of the area that belongs to the column for the digit 6 and the row for the value 1.1. This value is 0.3770.). We know that the total shaded area in Fig. 7.40 represents the probability that the project will get completed within 50 days.

Shaded area = (area on the left of central line for $z = 0$)
+ (area between $z = 0$ and $z = 1.16$)

Therefore, the total shaded area under the curve = 0.5 + 0.3770 = 0.877. Hence the probability that the project will be completed within 50 days is 87.7 per cent.

## Limitations of CPM and PERT

CPM and PERT have been criticized in the past for the following reasons:

1. It is difficult to identify the various activities in complex projects, that is, to clearly define the start and end points of activities is not easy. In complex projects, a network diagram made during the planning stage may require new/modified activities due to changes in the project over a period of time.

2. In certain types of projects, it is not possible to sequence all the activities according to precedence requirements. For example, in the construction of a road, the various activities are performed in a predetermined sequence. Each portion of the road requires some or all of these activities. It is difficult to represent the various activities by standard networking procedures because most activities can start on parts of the road before their corresponding predecessors have been completed on all 'preceding parts' of the road.

3. The critical path is focused on only to control the duration of the project. There may also be certain non-critical paths, which can become critical when some of the activities get delayed.

4. The duration of activities in PERT have been assumed to follow a beta curve, and the variance of the project duration is equal to the sum of the variances of all the critical activities.

However, according to Avraham Stub (1997), the popularity of network-based project management techniques and the large number of software packages based on these techniques indicate that network models are useful for many types of projects. Furthermore, the volume of research in this area indicates that the assumptions in CPM and PERT are acceptable to many researchers as well. Stub has presented a *project segmentation model*, which is useful in projects like the road construction project mentioned above.

## Crashing of a Project

All projects have two types of costs: direct cost and indirect cost. Project direct cost is the direct cost involved in all the activities of the project. Activity direct cost is the cost of materials,

Crashing of a project means intentionally reducing the duration of a project by allocating more resources to it.

The limit beyond which the duration of the activity does not decrease by adding any amount of resources is called the crash time.

labour (salaries, wages, overtime cost, hiring and firing cost, etc.), and machines and equipment.

Project indirect cost is mainly the cost of supervision during the implementation of the project. The salaries paid to the project manager/supervisor, etc., miscellaneous costs due to delays in the project, and rewards to the project team members for its early completion are indirect costs. Project indirect cost is dependent upon the length of duration of the project. A project having a longer duration will have a higher indirect cost (due to supervision required for longer duration).

*Crashing of a project* means intentionally reducing the duration of a project by allocating more resources to it. A project can be crashed by crashing its critical activities (because the duration of a project is dependent upon the duration of its critical activities). We know that by adding more resources, the duration of an activity can be reduced. If an activity gets completed in 10 days with 5 men working on it, the same activity can be finished in (say) 6 days with 10 men. The initial direct cost was 50 man-days (5 men × 10 days) and now it is 60 man-days (10 men × 6 days). Therefore, the direct cost has increased by 10 man-days. At the same time, because of the decrease in duration of the activity by 4 days, the indirect cost (cost of supervision) decreases. Hence, observe that the direct and indirect costs are inversely proportional to each other, that is, when one increases, the other decreases.

An activity can be crashed by adding more resources only up to a definite limit. Beyond this limit, the duration of the activity does not decrease by adding more resources. This is due to decreasing efficiency of labour and also increasing confusion due to a large number of resources. In our example, if we increase the number of workers to 15, the same activity can be done in five days; but by adding five more men (so that 20 men work on this activity), the activity time may not decrease. The limit beyond which the duration of the activity does not decrease by adding any amount of resources is called the *crash time* and the corresponding direct cost is called the *crash cost*. Figure 7.41 depicts the direct cost with respect to duration (in our example) on a graph.

The *normal time* shown in the graph (10 days) can be defined as the duration of an activity when the minimum possible resources required for its performance are deployed. The corresponding minimum direct cost is called the normal cost.

In the actual time-cost curve, note that for crashing the activity from 10 days to 9 days, the incremental direct cost involved is approximately ₹2. On the other hand, for crashing the activity from 6 days to 5 days, the incremental cost is ₹20. This means that the cost of crashing keeps on increasing as the crash time is approached. For the sake of simplicity, in problems of crashing, assume

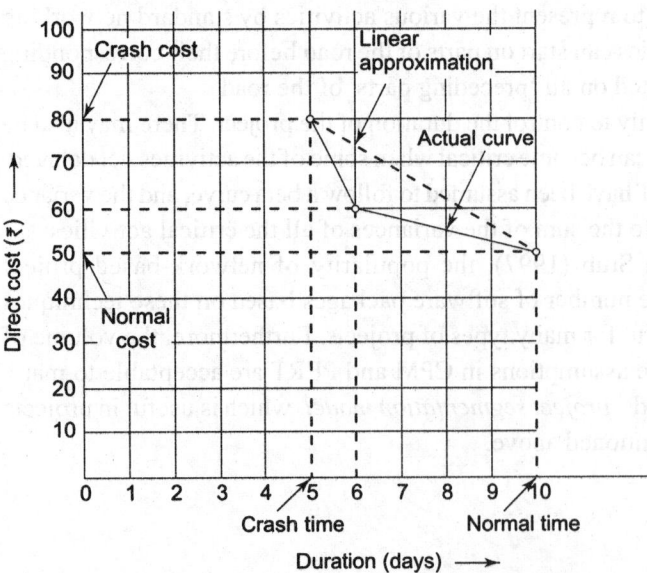

**Fig. 7.41**   Direct cost with respect to duration of an activity

that the linear approximation of the actual curve (shown by a dotted straight line in the graph) is followed. This linear approximation curve has a constant slope representing a constant incremental cost of crashing.

$$\text{Incremental cost of crashing} = \frac{\text{crash cost} - \text{normal cost}}{\text{noraml time} - \text{crash time}}$$

$$= \frac{₹(80-50)}{(10-5)\text{ days}} = \frac{₹30}{5\text{ days}} = ₹6\text{ per day}$$

During the process of crashing of a project, the critical path may get changed. At some stage of crashing, there may even be two or more critical paths (having the same duration) simultaneously. In such situations, one activity is chosen from each of the critical paths and these activities are crashed by unit time to reduce the duration of the project by unit time. Let us take up an example to understand the process of crashing.

### Example 7.5

Table 7.15 gives the normal time, crash time, and incremental cost of crashing for various activities in a project.

**Table 7.15**

| Activity | Nodes | Normal time (days) | Crash time (days) | Incremental cost of crashing (₹/day) |
|----------|-------|--------------------|-------------------|--------------------------------------|
| A | 1-2 | 6 | 5 | 50 |
| B | 1-3 | 8 | 7 | 100 |
| C | 2-5 | 9 | 8 | 80 |
| D | 2-4 | 11 | 7 | 60 |
| E | 3-4 | 5 | 1 | 90 |
| F | 3-6 | 7 | 7 | – |
| G | 4-7 | 8 | 2 | 40 |
| H | 6-7 | 3 | 3 | – |
| I | 5-7 | 7 | 6 | 100 |
| J | 7-8 | 2 | 1 | 50 |

The total normal cost for performing the 10 given activities = ₹2,000, cost of supervision = ₹100 per day, penalty = ₹300 per day over 25 days, reward = ₹200 per day for less than or equal to 21 days.

Find the minimum possible duration of the project and the related total cost, and the minimum total cost and the related duration of the project. Draw a graph using MS Excel for the duration of the project versus total cost.

### Solution

The network diagram for the project is shown in Fig. 7.42. For an activity, its normal time is shown outside the parentheses adjacent to the activity and its crash time is shown inside the parentheses. Let us find the duration of the different paths possible between nodes 1 and 8.

| Path | Normal time | Crash time |
|------|-------------|------------|
| 1-2-5-7-8 | 24 | 20 |
| **1-2-4-7-8** | **27** | **15** |
| 1-3-4-7-8 | 23 | 11 |
| 1-3-6-7-8 | 20 | 18 |

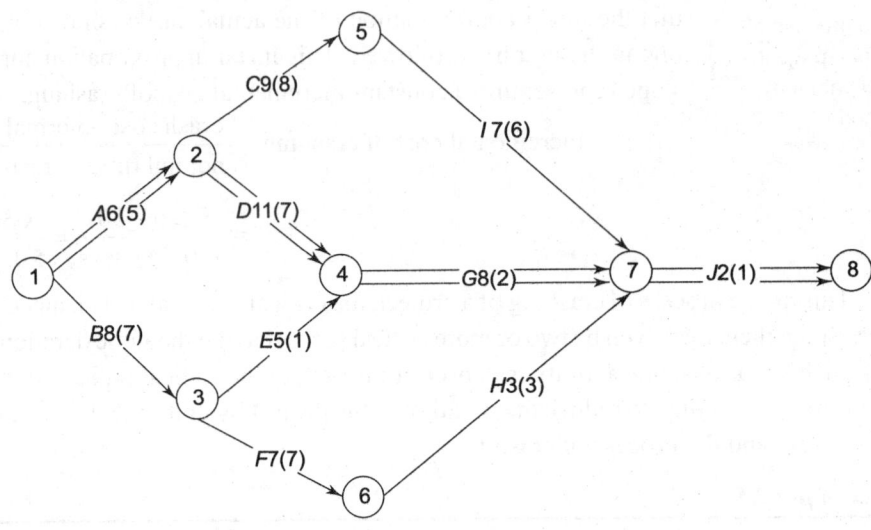

**Fig. 7.42**

Thus, the critical path is 1-2-4-7-8, as its normal time is the highest at 27 days. In Table 7.16, for the project duration of 27 days, the normal cost is ₹2,000, which is also the total direct cost. The cost of supervision at the rate of ₹100 will be ₹2,700 for 27 days. The penalty is ₹300 per day over 25 days. With a duration of 27 days, we are exceeding the 25 days duration by 2 days. Thus the penalty will be ₹600 for these 2 days. The total indirect cost is ₹2,700 + ₹600 = ₹3,300.

The total cost is the sum of the total direct cost and the total indirect cost. Hence for 27 days, the total cost is ₹2,000 + ₹3,300 = ₹5,300. At the end of each crashing, Table 7.16 is updated according to the duration of the project. Remember that the cost of crashing in Table 7.16 is the cumulative cost of crashing, that is, as we proceed with the process of crashing, we add the cost of crashing to the value in the previous duration of the project.

**Table 7.16**   The effect of crashing on direct and indirect costs

| Duration (days) | Crashing | Normal cost | Crashing cost | Total direct cost | Supervision | Penalty | Reward | Total indirect cost | Total cost (₹) |
|---|---|---|---|---|---|---|---|---|---|
| | | | Direct cost (₹) | | | Indirect cost (₹) | | | |
| 27 | – | 2,000 | – | 2,000 | 2,700 | 600 | – | 3,300 | 5,300 |
| 26 | I | 2,000 | 40 | 2,040 | 2,600 | 300 | – | 2,900 | 4,940 |
| 25 | II | 2,000 | 80 | 2,080 | 2,500 | – | – | 2,500 | 4,580 |
| 24 | III | 2,000 | 120 | 2,120 | 2,400 | – | – | 2,400 | 4,520 |
| 23 | IV | 2,000 | 170 | 2,170 | 2,300 | – | – | 2,300 | 4,470 |
| 22 | V | 2,000 | 220 | 2,220 | 2,200 | – | – | 2,200 | 4,420 |
| 21 | VI | 2,000 | 340 | 2,340 | 2,100 | – | 200 | 2,300 | 4,640 |
| 20 | VII | 2,000 | 480 | 2,480 | 2,000 | – | 400 | 2,400 | 4,880 |

*First crashing*   1-2-4-7-8 is the critical path with a duration of 27 days (Fig. 7.42). The various activities on this path are as follows.

| Activity | Nodes | Crashing cost (₹/day) |
|---|---|---|
| A | 1-2 | 50 |
| D | 2-4 | 60 |
| **G** | **4-7** | **40** |
| J | 7-8 | 50 |

Crash *G* (4-7) by one day, as its cost of crashing is the lowest (Fig. 7.43). In Table 7.16, the cost of crashing shows ₹40. The total cost now becomes ₹4,940.

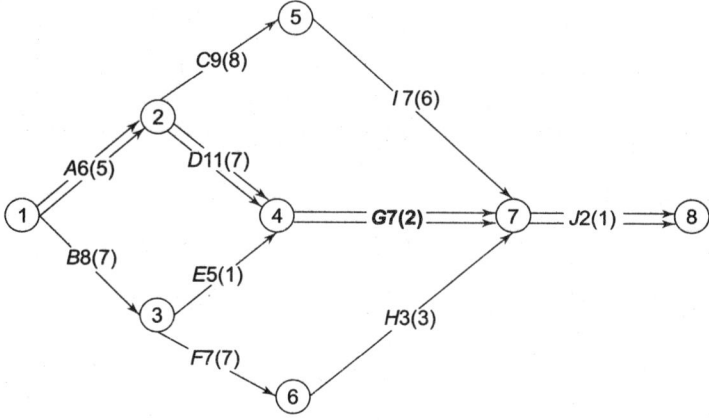

**Fig. 7.43**

***Second crashing*** 1-2-4-7-8 is still the critical path with a duration of 26 days. The duration of various paths are revised as shown below. Again crash *G* (4-7) by one day (Fig. 7.44). The total cost in Table 7.16 is now ₹4,580.

| Path | Normal time | Crash time |
|---|---|---|
| 1-2-5-7-8 | 24 | 20 |
| **1-2-4-7-8** | **26** | **15** |
| 1-3-4-7-8 | 22 | 11 |
| 1-3-6-7-8 | 20 | 18 |

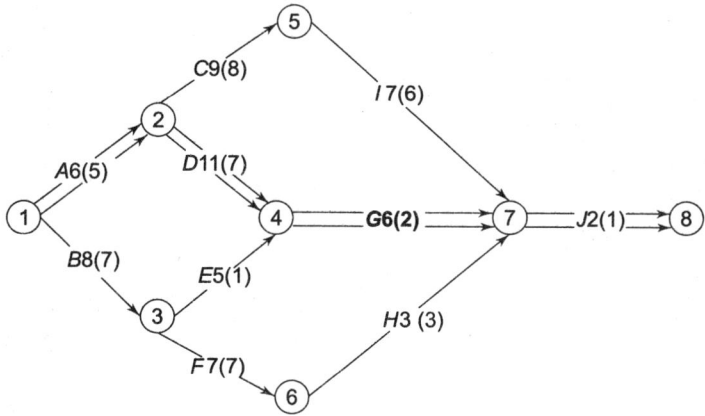

**Fig. 7.44**

***Third crashing*** 1-2-4-7-8 is still the critical path with a duration of 25 days. Again crash *G* (4-7) by a day (Fig. 7.45). The total cost in Table 7.16 is now ₹4,520.

| Path | Normal time | Crash time |
|------|-------------|------------|
| 1-2-5-7-8 | 24 | 20 |
| **1-2-4-7-8** | **25** | **15** |
| 1-3-4-7-8 | 21 | 11 |
| 1-3-6-7-8 | 20 | 18 |

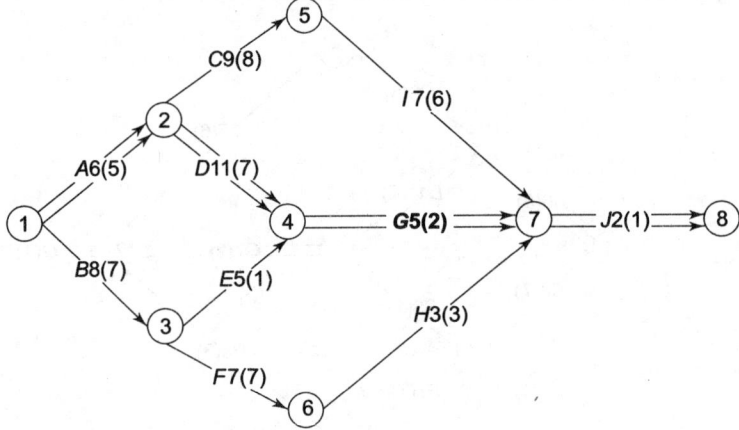

**Fig. 7.45**

***Fourth crashing*** Now there are two critical paths, namely, 1-2-5-7-8 and 1-2-4-7-8 with a duration of 24 days (Fig. 7.46).

| Path | Normal time | Crash time |
|------|-------------|------------|
| **1-2-5-7-8** | **24** | **20** |
| **1-2-4-7-8** | **24** | **15** |
| 1-3-4-7-8 | 20 | 11 |
| 1-3-6-7-8 | 20 | 18 |

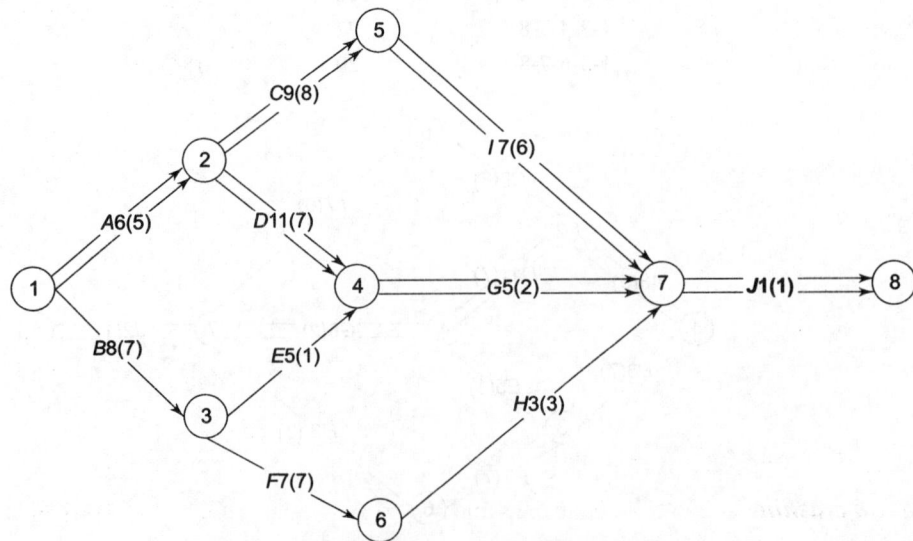

**Fig. 7.46**

Let us crash $J$ (7-8) for ₹50. The total cost in Table 7.16 now becomes ₹4,470. The costs of crashing various combinations are given below:

| Combination | Crashing cost (₹) |
|---|---|
| 1-2 | 50 |
| **7-8** | **50** |
| 2-5,2-4 | 80 + 60 = 140 |
| 2-5,4-7 | 80 + 40 = 120 |
| 5-7,2-4 | 100 + 60 = 160 |
| 5-7,4-7 | 100 + 40 = 140 |

***Fifth crashing***    We still have the same two critical paths, namely, 1-2-5-7-8 and 1-2-4-7-8, with a duration of 23 days. Activity $J$ (7-8) cannot be crashed further, as it has attained its crash time of one day.

| Path | Normal time | Crash time |
|---|---|---|
| **1-2-5-7-8** | **23** | **20** |
| **1-2-4-7-8** | **23** | **15** |
| 1-3-4-7-8 | 19 | 11 |
| 1-3-6-7-8 | 19 | 18 |

Therefore, crash $A$ (1-2) for ₹50 (Fig. 7.47). The total cost in Table 7.16 is now ₹4,420.

| Combination | Crashing cost (₹) |
|---|---|
| **1-2** | **50** |
| 2-5,2-4 | 80 + 60 = 140 |
| 2-5,4-7 | 80 + 40 = 120 |
| 5-7,2-4 | 100 + 60 = 160 |
| 5-7,4-7 | 100 + 40 = 140 |

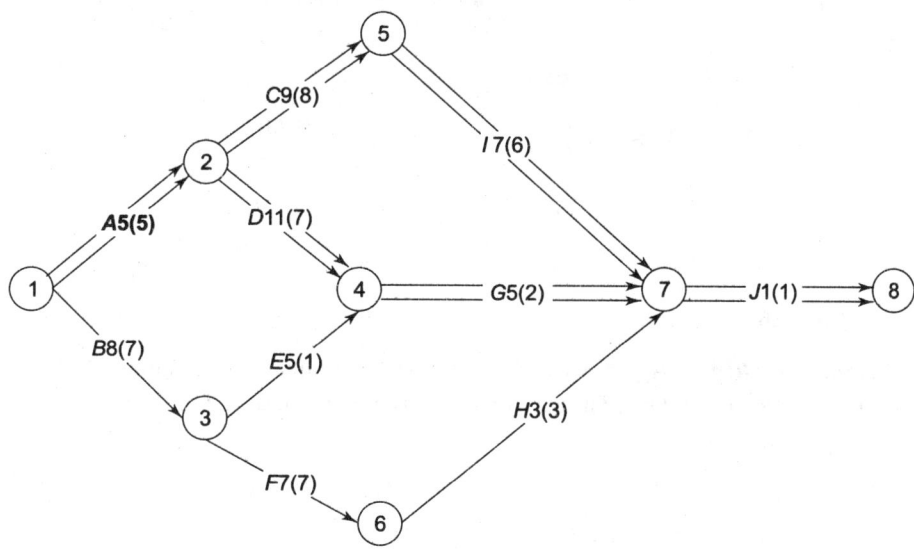

**Fig. 7.47**

***Sixth crashing***    Again we have the same two critical paths, namely, 1-2-5-7-8 and 1-2-4-7-8, with a duration of 22 days.

| Path | Normal time | Crash time |
|---|---|---|
| **1-2-5-7-8** | **22** | **20** |
| **1-2-4-7-8** | **22** | **15** |
| 1-3-4-7-8 | 19 | 11 |
| 1-3-6-7-8 | 19 | 18 |

Activity $A$ (1-2) cannot be crashed further as it has attained its crash time of five days (Fig. 7.48). Hence choose the combination 2-5,4-7 for crashing at ₹120. The total cost in Table 7.16 now becomes ₹4,640.

| Combination | Crashing cost (₹) |
|---|---|
| 2-5,2-4 | 80 + 60 = 140 |
| **2-5,4-7** | **80 + 40 = 120** |
| 5-7,2-4 | 100 + 60 = 160 |
| 5-7,4-7 | 100 + 40 = 140 |

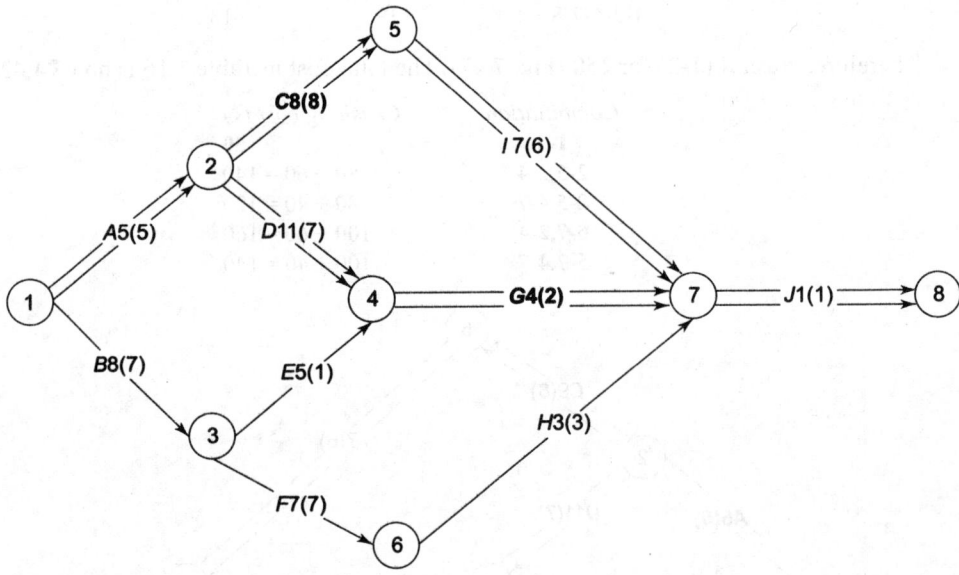

**Fig. 7.48**

***Seventh crashing*** Again, we have the same two critical paths, namely, 1-2-5-7-8 and 1-2-4-7-8, with a duration of 21 days. The activity $C$ (2-5) cannot be crashed further, as it has attained its normal time of eight days.

| Path | Normal time | Crash time |
|---|---|---|
| **1-2-5-7-8** | **21** | **20** |
| **1-2-4-7-8** | **21** | **15** |
| 1-3-4-7-8 | 18 | 11 |
| 1-3-6-7-8 | 19 | 18 |

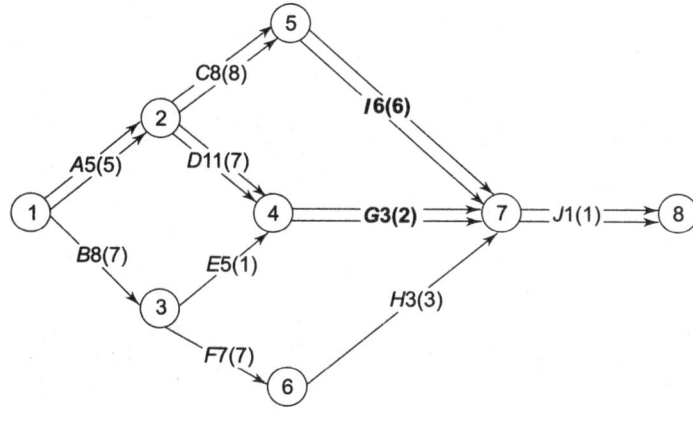

**Fig. 7.49**

Choose the combination 5-7, 4-7 for crashing at ₹140. The total cost in Table 7.16 is finally ₹4,880.

| Combination | Crashing cost (₹) |
|---|---|
| 5-7,2-4 | 100 + 60 = 160 |
| **5-7,4-7** | **100 + 40 = 140** |

Again, we have two critical paths, namely, 1-2-5-7-8 and 1-2-4-7-8, with a duration of 20 days (Fig. 7.49):

| Path | Normal time | Crash time |
|---|---|---|
| **1-2-5-7-8** | **20** | **20** |
| **1-2-4-7-8** | **20** | **15** |
| 1-3-4-7-8 | 17 | 11 |
| 1-3-6-7-8 | 19 | 18 |

Note that the minimum total cost is ₹4,420 for 22 days duration. The minimum possible duration of the project is 20 days with a cost of ₹4,880. Now paste the columns for duration, total direct cost, total indirect cost, and the overall total cost in an MS Excel worksheet as shown in Fig. 7.50. Select all the columns in the worksheet and then click on the **Insert** button in the toolbar. From the pull-down menu, select **chart**. A chart wizard guides us through to get the chart shown in Fig. 7.51.

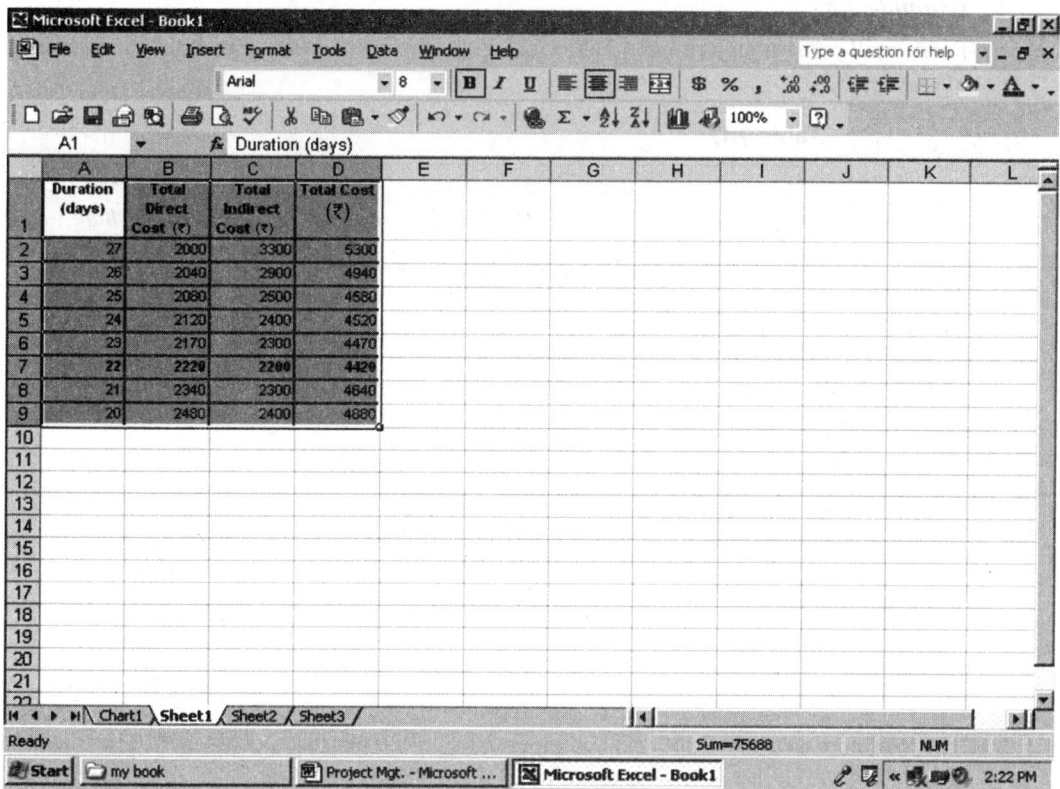

**Fig. 7.50**

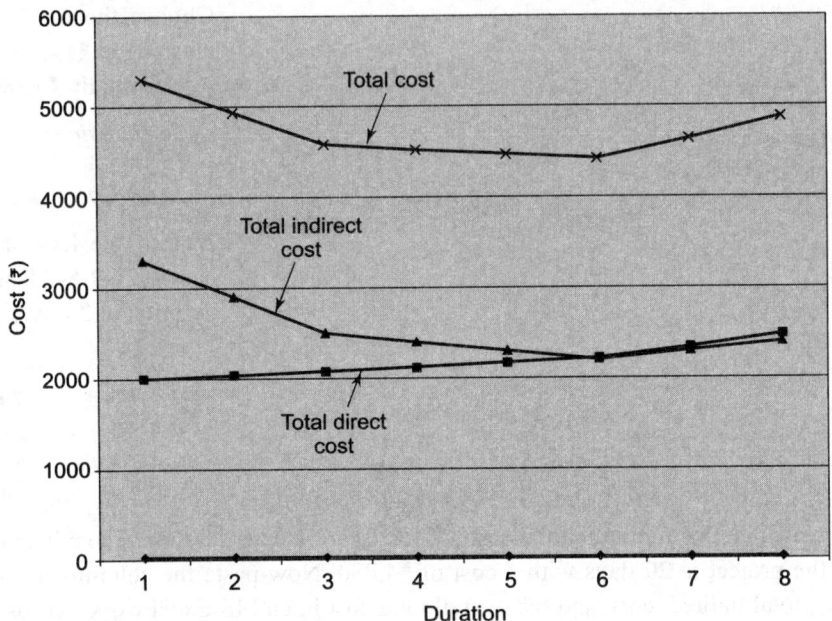

**Fig. 7.51**

## Example 7.6

For a small construction project, Table 7.17 gives the normal time, crash time, and incremental cost of crashing.

**Table 7.17**

| Activity | Nodes | Normal duration (days) | Crash duration (days) | Incremental cost of crashing (₹/day) |
|----------|-------|------------------------|-----------------------|--------------------------------------|
| A | 1-2 | 5 | 3 | 40 |
| B | 1-3 | 4 | 2 | 10 |
| C | 1-4 | 7 | 5 | 20 |
| D | 2-3 | 4 | 2 | 30 |
| E | 4-3 | 3 | 2 | 50 |
| F | 2-5 | 2 | 2 | – |
| G | 3-5 | 7 | 5 | 20 |
| H | 3-6 | 3 | 1 | 10 |
| I | 4-6 | 4 | 3 | 30 |
| J | 5-6 | 6 | 5 | 40 |

The total normal cost = ₹500, cost of supervision = ₹20 per day, penalty = ₹10 per day over 20 days, reward = ₹10 per day below or equal to 18 days. Crash the duration of the project and find (a) the duration of the project with minimum total cost and (b) the minimum possible duration of the project.

**Solution**

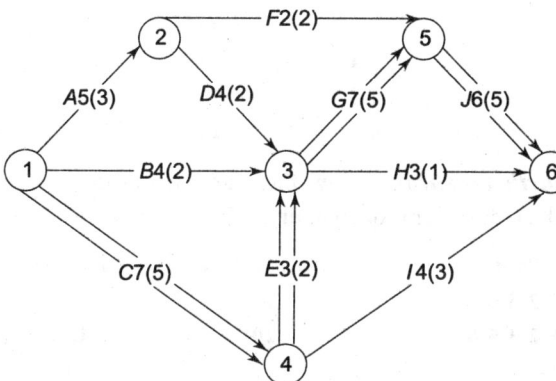

**Fig. 7.52**

**First crashing** 1-4-3-5-6 is the critical path with 23 days (Fig. 7.52):

| Path | Normal time | Crash time |
|------|-------------|------------|
| 1-2-5-6 | 13 | 10 |
| 1-2-3-5-6 | 22 | 15 |
| 1-3-6 | 7 | 3 |
| 1-4-3-6 | 13 | 8 |
| 1-4-6 | 11 | 8 |
| 1-3-5-6 | 17 | 12 |
| **1-4-3-5-6** | **23** | **17** |

Crash 3-5 by one day (Fig. 7.53):

| Activity | Crashing cost (₹) |
|----------|-------------------|
| 1-4 | 20 |
| 4-3 | 50 |
| **3-5** | **20** |
| 5-6 | 40 |

**Second crashing** 1-4-3-5-6 is still the critical path with 22 days:

| Path | Normal time | Crash time |
|------|-------------|------------|
| 1-2-5-6 | 13 | 10 |
| 1-2-3-5-6 | 21 | 15 |
| 1-3-6 | 7 | 3 |
| 1-4-3-6 | 13 | 8 |
| 1-4-6 | 11 | 8 |
| 1-3-5-6 | 16 | 12 |
| **1-4-3-5-6** | **22** | **17** |

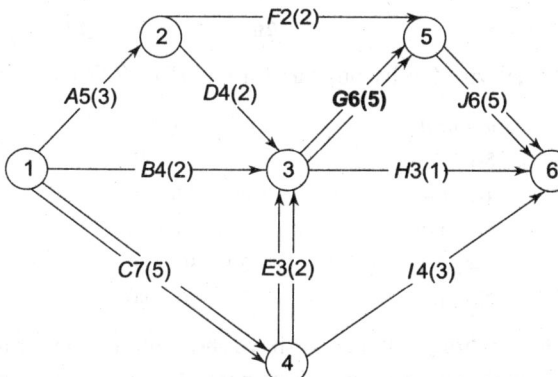

**Fig. 7.53**

Crash 3-5 again by one day (Fig. 7.54).

**Third crashing** 1-4-3-5-6 still remains the critical path with 21 days:

| Path | Normal time | Crash time |
|------|-------------|------------|
| 1-2-5-6 | 13 | 10 |
| 1-2-3-5-6 | 20 | 15 |
| 1-3-6 | 7 | 3 |
| 1-4-3-6 | 13 | 8 |
| 1-4-6 | 11 | 8 |
| 1-3-5-6 | 15 | 12 |
| **1-4-3-5-6** | **21** | **17** |

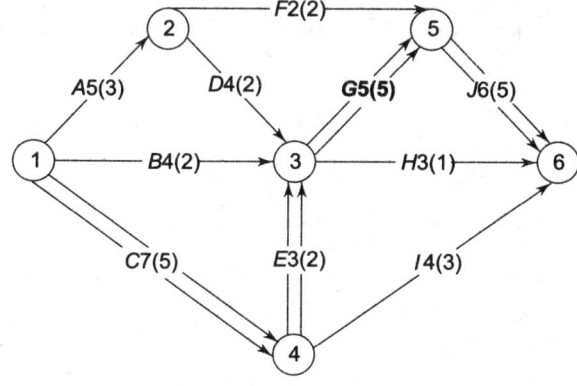

**Fig. 7.54**

Activity 3-5 cannot be crashed further, as it has attained its normal time of five days. Hence, crash 1-4 by one day for ₹20 (Fig. 7.55).

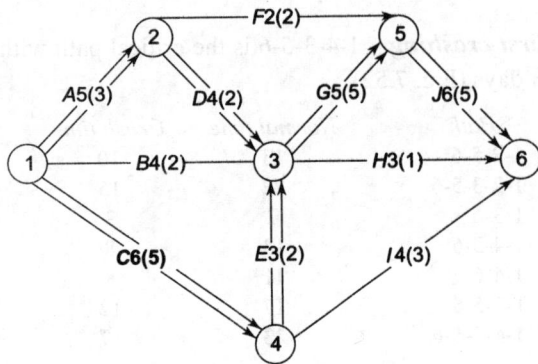

**Fig. 7.55**

| Activity | Crashing cost (₹) |
|----------|-------------------|
| **1-4**  | **20** |
| 4-3      | 50 |
| 5-6      | 40 |

***Fourth crashing*** Now there are two critical paths with 20 days duration, namely, 1-2-3-5-6 and 1-4-3-5-6.

| Path | Normal time | Crash time |
|------|-------------|------------|
| 1-2-5-6 | 13 | 10 |
| **1-2-3-5-6** | **20** | **15** |
| 1-3-6 | 7 | 3 |
| 1-4-3-6 | 12 | 8 |
| 1-4-6 | 10 | 8 |
| 1-3-5-6 | 15 | 12 |
| **1-4-3-5-6** | **20** | **17** |

Crash activity 5-6 by one day for ₹40 (Fig. 7.56).

| Combination | Crashing cost (₹) |
|-------------|-------------------|
| **5-6**     | **40** |
| 1-2, 1-4    | 40 + 20 = 60 |
| 1-2, 4-3    | 40 + 50 = 90 |
| 1-4, 2-3    | 20 + 30 = 50 |
| 2-3, 4-3    | 30 + 50 = 80 |

***Fifth crashing*** We again have the same two critical paths with 19 days duration, namely, 1-2-3-5-6 and 1-4-3-5-6:

| Path | Normal time | Crash time |
|------|-------------|------------|
| 1-2-5-6 | 12 | 10 |
| **1-2-3-5-6** | **19** | **15** |
| 1-3-6 | 7 | 3 |
| 1-4-3-6 | 12 | 8 |
| 1-4-6 | 10 | 8 |
| 1-3-5-6 | 14 | 12 |
| **1-4-3-5-6** | **19** | **17** |

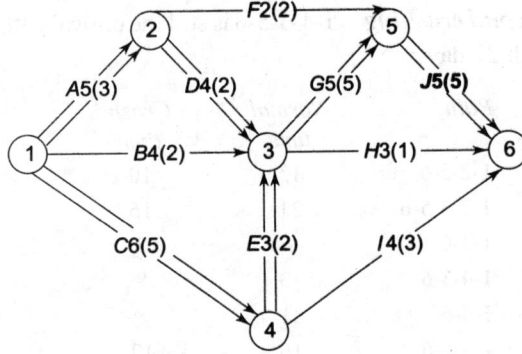

**Fig. 7.56**

Activity 5-6 cannot be crashed further. Hence, crash activities 1-4 and 2-3 simultaneously for ₹50 (Fig. 7.57).

| Combination | Crashing cost (₹) |
|-------------|-------------------|
| 1-2, 1-4    | 40 + 20 = 60 |
| 1-2, 4-3    | 40 + 50 = 90 |
| **1-4, 2-3** | **20 + 30 = 50** |
| 2-3, 4-3    | 30 + 50 = 80 |

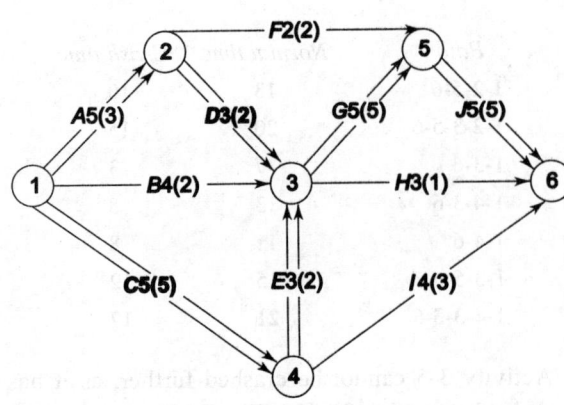

**Fig. 7.57**

***Sixth crashing*** Again, we have the same two critical paths with 18 days duration, namely, 1-2-3-5-6 and 1-4-3-5-6.

| Path | Normal time | Crash time |
|------|-------------|------------|
| 1-2-5-6 | 12 | 10 |
| **1-2-3-5-6** | **18** | **15** |
| 1-3-6 | 7 | 3 |
| 1-4-3-6 | 11 | 8 |
| 1-4-6 | 9 | 8 |
| 1-3-5-6 | 14 | 12 |
| **1-4-3-5-6** | **18** | **17** |

Activity 1-4 cannot be crashed further. We can choose any of the following two combinations for crashing.

| Combination | Crashing cost (₹) |
|-------------|-------------------|
| 1-2, 4-3 | 40 + 50 = 90 |
| **2-3, 4-3** | **30 + 50 = 80** |

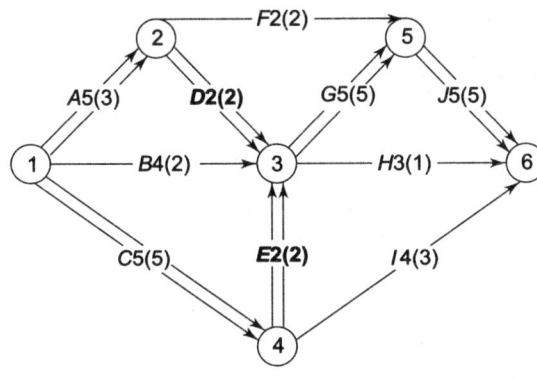

**Fig. 7.58**

Crash activities 2-3 and 4-3 simultaneously for ₹80 (Fig. 7.58). No further crashing of the project can take place, as the critical path 1-4-3-5-6 has now attained its crash time of 17 days.

| Path | Normal time | Crash time |
|------|-------------|------------|
| 1-2-5-6 | 12 | 10 |
| 1-2-3-5-6 | 17 | 15 |
| 1-3-6 | 7 | 3 |
| 1-4-3-6 | 10 | 8 |
| 1-4-6 | 9 | 8 |
| 1-3-5-6 | 14 | 12 |
| **1-4-3-5-6** | **17** | **17** |

Table 7.18 shows the effect of crashing on the direct and indirect costs. Note that the minimum total cost is ₹960 for the project duration of 20 days. The minimum possible duration of the project is 17 days with a cost of ₹1,090.

**Table 7.18**

| Duration (days) | Crashing | Direct cost (₹) | | | Indirect cost (₹) | | | | Total cost (₹) |
|---|---|---|---|---|---|---|---|---|---|
| | | Normal cost | Cost of crashing | Total direct cost | Supervision | Penalty | Reward | Total indirect cost | |
| 23 | – | 500 | – | 500 | 460 | 30 | – | 490 | 990 |
| 22 | I | 500 | 20 | 520 | 440 | 20 | – | 460 | 980 |
| 21 | II | 500 | 40 | 540 | 420 | 10 | – | 430 | 970 |
| 20 | III | 500 | 60 | 560 | 400 | – | – | 400 | 960 |
| 19 | IV | 500 | 100 | 600 | 380 | – | – | 380 | 980 |
| 18 | V | 500 | 150 | 650 | 360 | – | 10 | 370 | 1,020 |
| 17 | VI | 500 | 230 | 730 | 340 | – | 20 | 360 | 1,090 |

> The process of re-scheduling activities in order to level the resources throughout the project is called resource levelling.

## Resource Levelling

Uniform usage of resources throughout the duration of a project is most desirable by every organization. This is because frequent fluctuations in resource requirements lead to increase in costs. For example, fluctuations in the human resource requirement of a project result in hiring, training, and laying-off cost. Therefore, it is desirable that during the complete duration of a project, the resources requirement is uniformly distributed. This requires that the activities in the project be rescheduled such that the project completion time is unchanged. The process of rescheduling activities in order to level the resources throughout the project is called *resource levelling*. Let us understand the technique of resource levelling in a project by taking up the following example.

### Example 7.7

The network diagram in Fig. 7.59 shows the various activities in a project. The duration of an activity (in days) is shown outside parentheses, while the labour requirements is shown inside parentheses. Reschedule these activities so that the labour requirements are levelled as far as possoble throughout the duration of the project (keeping the project duration constant).

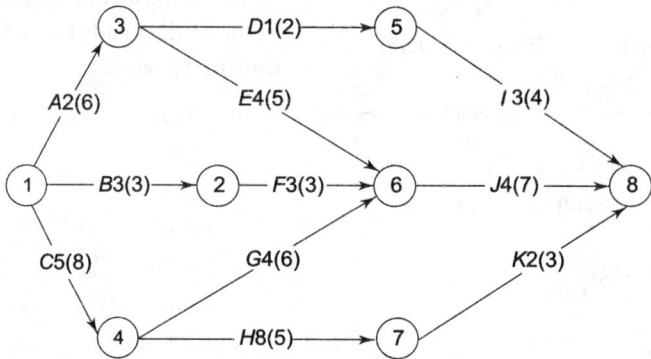

**Fig. 7.59**

### Solution

| Path | Duration |
|------|----------|
| 1-3-5-8 | 6 |
| 1-3-6-8 | 10 |
| 1-2-6-8 | 10 |
| 1-4-6-8 | 13 |
| **1-4-7-8** | **15** |

The critical path is 1-4-7-8 with a duration of 15 days. Plot these critical activities, namely, 1-4, 4-7, and 7-8, on the duration axis according to their respective duration as shown in Fig. 7.60(a) (here the length of an arrow represents the duration of an activity). In Fig. 7.59, activities $G$ and $J$ come between critical nodes 4 and 8. Therefore, these are shown slightly above the time axis to avoid overlapping with the critical activities. The excess times over the performance times of activities $G$ and $J$ are shown by dotted lines between nodes 4 and 8. Node 6 is shown at the completion of activity $G$. Between nodes 1 and 6, we have activities $A$ and $E$ as shown in the figure. We also have activities $B$ and $F$ between nodes 1 and 6. Finally, we have activities $D$ and I between nodes 3 and 8. Only the labour requirements of the various activities are shown in Fig. 7.60(a). Figure 7.60(b) shows a graph for the labour requirements on each day. As shown in the figure, this graph has a hill-like structure, which is to be levelled as much as possible.

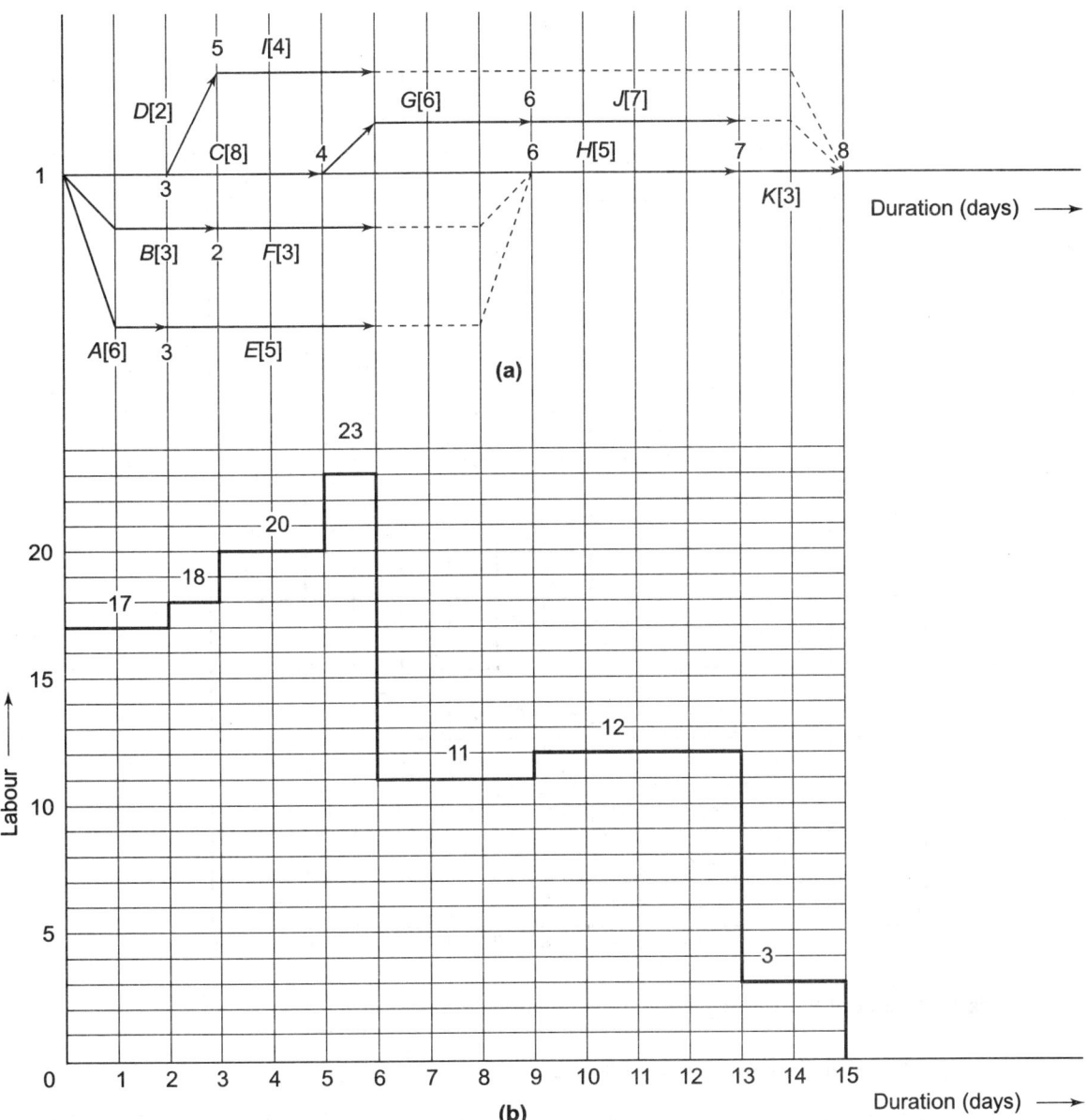

**Fig. 7.60**  (a) Activity-time diagram (b) Labour requirements graph

For resource levelling, move activities *G* and *J* along the dotted line towards the extreme right so that the level of labour requirement during this interval can be raised (Fig. 7.61). Note that event 6 will now take place on day 11 in place of day 9. Similarly, move activities *D* and *I* along the dotted line towards the extreme right; notice that between days 5 to 9, the labour level will go down. To avoid this, move activity *E* into this time interval and shift activities *B* and *F* towards the right by one day each. Now make the labour graph again and observe that the labour requirement has smoothened up to a great extent. It is practically not possible to level the labour requirement exactly at a particular level. Therefore, we have arrived at the optimal solution.

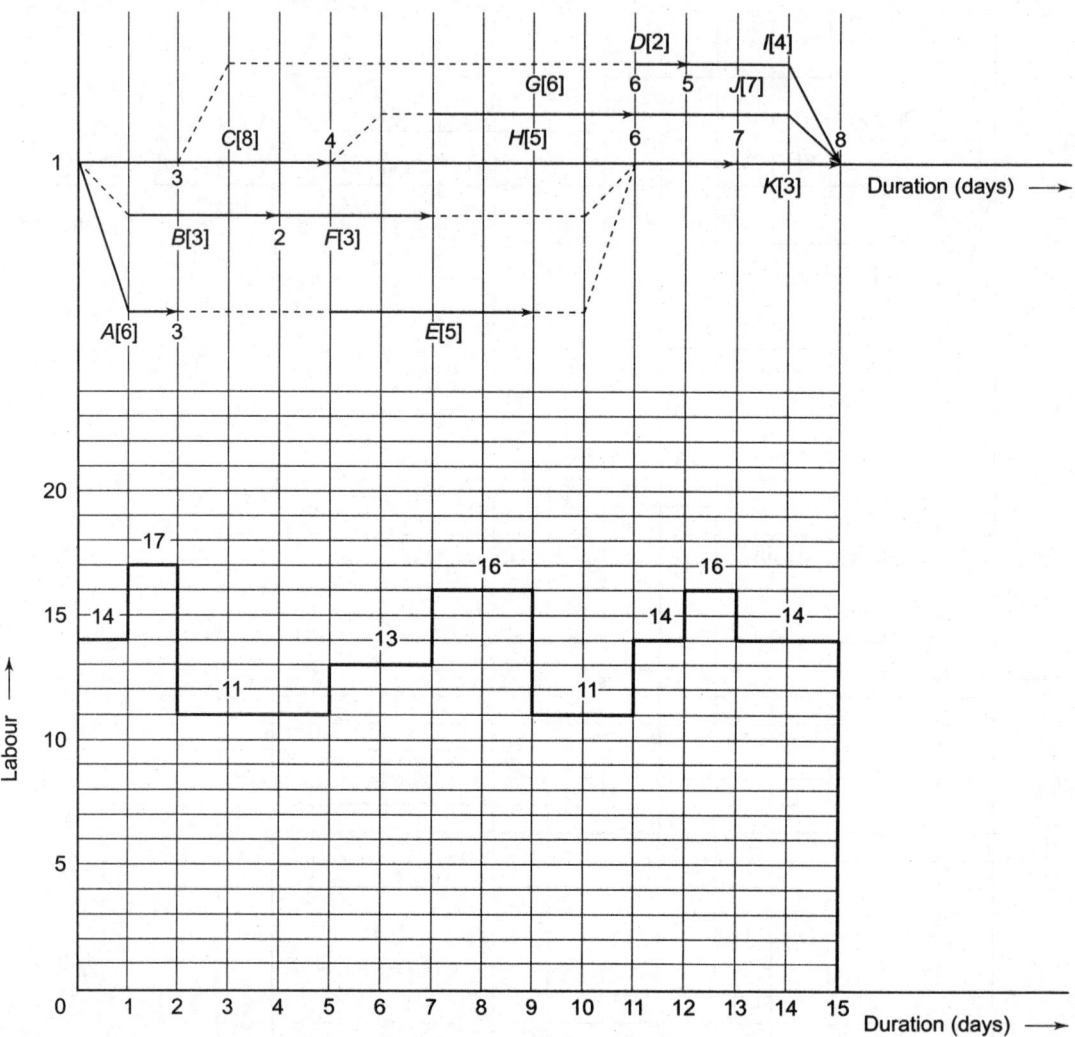

**Fig. 7.61** Smoothing of the labour graph due to resource levelling

## Projects under Resource Constraints

Organizations usually do not have unlimited resources. They have to manage projects under the given resource constraints. An allowance may be made for the project completion date to be extended while planning, keeping in view the limited resources. Activities can be rescheduled such that available resources are utilized up to the maximum extent possible. The following criteria are followed for rescheduling the activities:

1. The activity for which the LS time is the minimum is scheduled first.

2. In case two or more activities have the same LS time, the activity with the smallest duration is scheduled first so as to reduce the waiting time of subsequent activities.

3. Finally, if there is a tie between both the LS time and the duration of two or more activities, the activity requiring maximum resources is scheduled first so that maximum utilization of resources takes place.

> Activities can be rescheduled such that available resources are utilized up to the maximum extent possible.

Let us take up an example to understand the process of rescheduling activities under given resource constraints. The network diagram in Fig. 7.62 shows a project for which various details are given in Table 7.19.

**Table 7.19**

| Nodes | Activity | Duration (days) | LS time (days) | Men | Machines |
|---|---|---|---|---|---|
| 1-2 | A | 3 | 1 | 5 | X, Y |
| 1-3 | B | 6 | 0 | 10 | Z |
| 1-4 | C | 8 | 3 | 10 | Y |
| 1-5 | D | 1 | 5 | 5 | X |
| 2-6 | E | 7 | 4 | 20 | Y, Z |
| 3-7 | F | 10 | 6 | 15 | Y |
| 4-7 | G | 5 | 11 | 5 | X |
| 5-8 | H | 9 | 6 | 10 | X, Y, Z |
| 6-7 | I | 5 | 11 | 10 | X, Z |
| 6-9 | J | 4 | 14 | 20 | X |
| 7-9 | K | 2 | 16 | 10 | Y |
| 8-9 | L | 3 | 15 | 10 | |

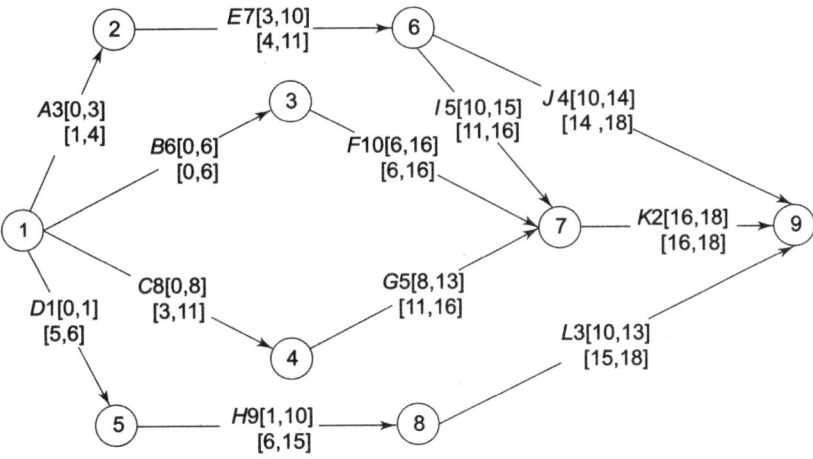

**Fig. 7.62**

The maximum resources available are as follows:

| Resource | Quantity available |
|---|---|
| Labour | 20 |
| Equipment X | 1 |
| Equipment Y | 1 |
| Equipment Z | 1 |

An activity resource allocation schedule has to be prepared under the given resource constraints.

We define an *eligible activity set* (EAS) as that group of activities, which have become eligible for scheduling because their predecessors have already

We define an eligible activity set (EAS) as that group of activities, which have become eligible for scheduling because their predecessors have already been scheduled earlier.

been scheduled earlier. At halt 1, that is, time $t = 0$, activities 1-2, 1-3, 1-4, and 1-5 are in the EAS, as these activities do not have any predecessors. The *ordered activity set* (OAS) is a group of activities for which the required resources are available at a given instant of time for the given halt. Only the activities from the EAS become a part of the OAS in a sequence according to the criteria laid earlier.

At halt 1, all the resources are available as no activity has been scheduled. The smallest LS time is 0 for activity 1-3 and, therefore, it enters the OAS first, followed by 1-2, 1-4 and 1-5 for which the LS times are 1, 3, and 5, respectively. As mentioned in the schedule below, activity 1-3 is scheduled for 6 days, as it has the lowest value of LS time at 0, and its resources required are plotted on a graph shown in Fig. 7.63. At the same halt 1, schedule activity 1-2 as its required resources are available at halt 1, time $t = 0$. Plot these resources on the graph (Fig. 7.63).

Note that after activity 1-3 is scheduled, activity 3-7 becomes eligible and enters the EAS. It has been marked with an asterisk to show that it has entered the EAS after its predecessor (1-3) activity is scheduled at this halt. Similarly, after activity 1-2 is scheduled, activity 2-6 becomes eligible and enters the EAS. No equipment is available now at $t = 0$ despite labour (5) still being available. Thus, the new activities in the EAS cannot enter the OAS. Therefore, no other activity can be scheduled at $t = 0$

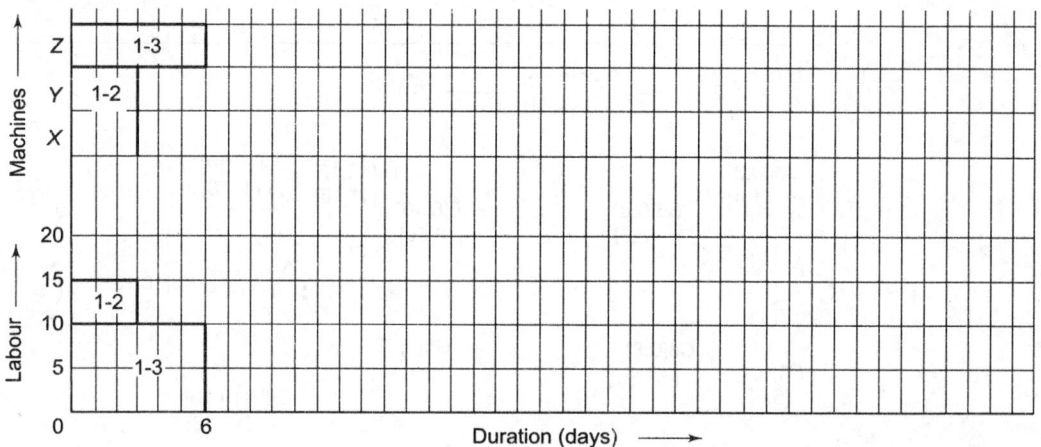

**Fig. 7.63** Halt 1

**Halt 1, $t = 0$:**

| EAS | Duration | LS time | OAS |
|-----|----------|---------|-----|
| 1-2 | 3 | 1 | 1-3 |
| 1-3 | 6 | 0 | 1-2 |
| 1-4 | 8 | 3 | 1-4 |
| 1-5 | 1 | 5 | 1-5 |
| 3-7* | 10 | 6 | – |
| 2-6* | 7 | 4 | – |

**Schedule: 1-3 for 6 days with 10 men and machine $Z$; 1-2 for 3 days with 5 men, machines $X$ and $Y$.**

**Halt 2, $t = 3$:**

| EAS | Duration | LS time | OAS |
|-----|----------|---------|-----|
| 1-4 | 8 | 3 | 1-4 |
| 1-5 | 1 | 5 | 1-5 |
| 3-7 | 10 | 6 | – |
| 2-6 | 7 | 4 | – |
| 4-7* | 5 | 11 | – |

**Schedule: 1-4 for 8 days with 10 men and machine $Y$.**

In Fig. 7.63 we see that some resources become available at $t = 3$ after activity 1-2 is over. Hence, our next halt for scheduling the activities will take place at $t = 3$.

Activities 1-4, 1-5, 3-7, and 2-6 are part of the EAS from the earlier halt. These are included now in the EAS at halt 2. The resources required by activities 1-4 and 1-5 are available at this halt. Activities 3-7 and 2-6 require 15 and 20 men, respectively, which are not available at $t = 3$ and will be available only at $t = 6$ (see Fig. 7.63). Hence, these activities do not enter the OAS at halt 2.

Activities 1-4 and 1-5 enter the OAS in the same sequence, as their LS times are 3 and 5, respectively (note that the LS times of all the activities always remain the same as calculated in the network diagram earlier). Activities 1-4 is scheduled for 8 days and its resources are plotted on the graph (Fig. 7.64). Note that activity 4-7 enters the EAS at halt 2 after activity 1-4 has been scheduled. No other activity in the OAS can be scheduled at this halt, as the resources required by these are not available. At halt 3, activities 1-5 and 4-7 enter the OAS; activity 1-5 is scheduled, as it has a lower value of LS time (Fig. 7.65). Activity 5-8 enters the EAS after activity 1-5 is scheduled at this halt. No other activity can be scheduled at this halt, as the resources required by these are not available. The scheduling process discussed earlier is followed further.

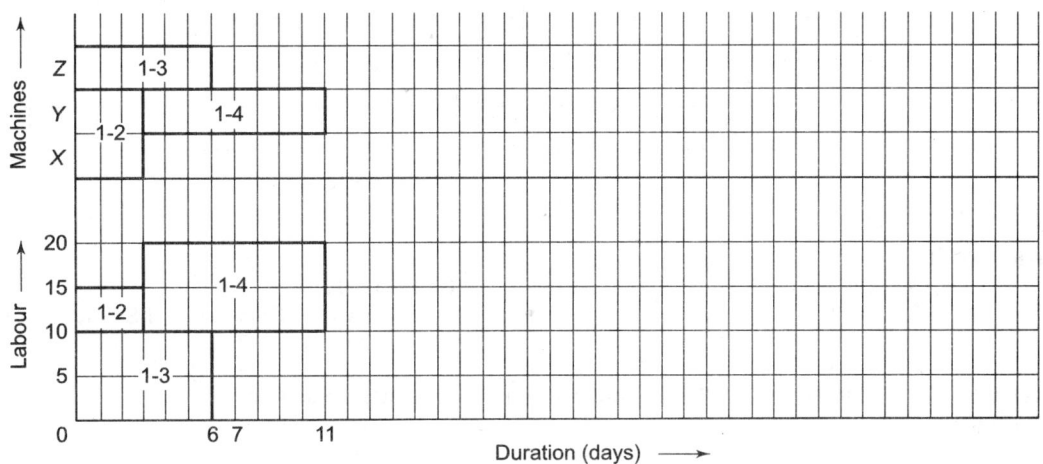

**Fig. 7.64**   Activity 1-4 scheduled at halt 2

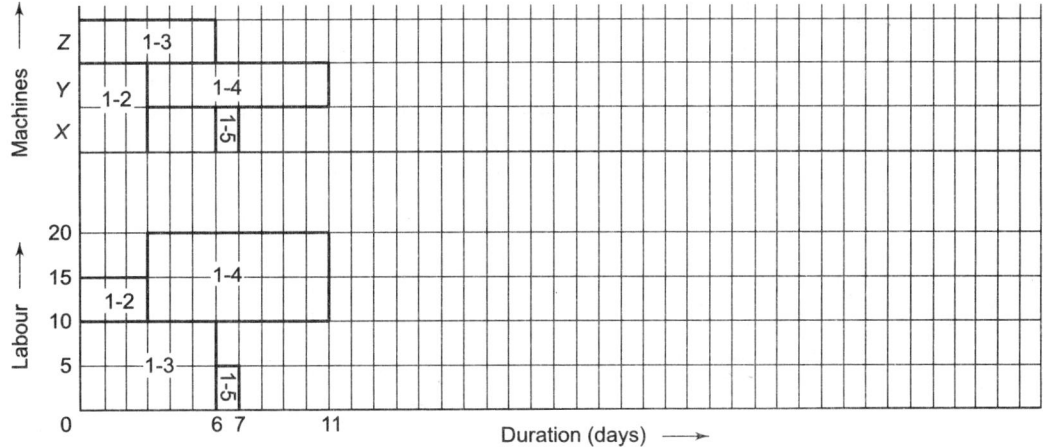

**Fig. 7.65**   Activity 1-5 scheduled at halt 2

**Halt 3, $t = 6$:**

| EAS | Duration | LS time | OAS |
|-----|----------|---------|-----|
| 1-5 | 1 | 5 | 1-5 |
| 3-7 | 10 | 6 | 4-7 |
| 2-6 | 7 | 4 | – |
| 4-7 | 5 | 11 | – |
| 5-8* | 9 | 6 | – |

Schedule: 1-5 for 1 day with 5 men and machine $X$ (Fig. 7.65).

**Halt 4, $t = 7$:**

| EAS | Duration | LS time | OAS |
|-----|----------|---------|-----|
| 3-7 | 10 | 6 | 4-7 |
| 2-6 | 7 | 4 | – |
| 4-7 | 5 | 11 | – |
| 5-8 | 9 | 6 | – |

Schedule: 4-7 for 5 days with 5 men and machine $X$ (Fig. 7.66)

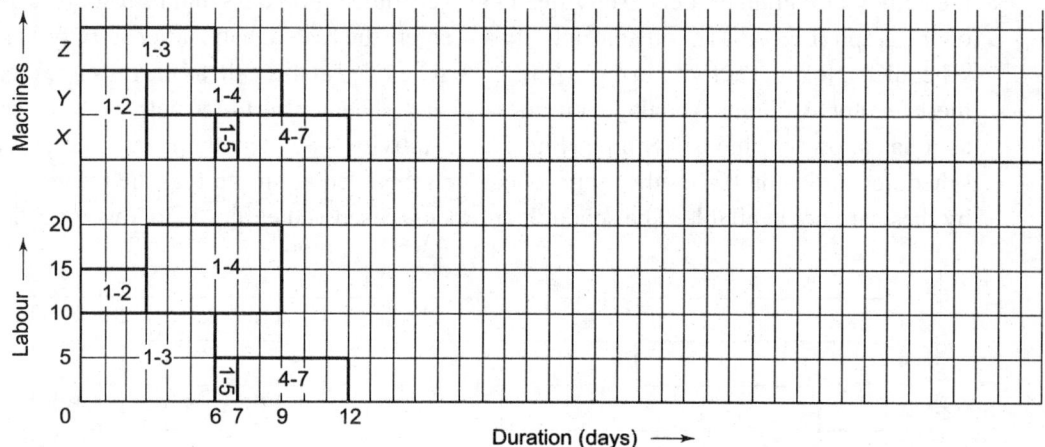

**Fig. 7.66**  Halt 4

**Halt 5, $t = 11$:**

| EAS | Duration | LS time | OAS |
|-----|----------|---------|-----|
| 3-7 | 10 | 6 | 3-7 |
| 2-6 | 7 | 4 | – |
| 5-8 | 9 | 6 | – |

Schedule: 3-7 for 10 days with 15 men and machine $Y$ (Fig. 7.67).

**Half 6, t = 12:**

| EAS | Duration | LS time | OAS |
|-----|----------|---------|-----|
| 2-6 | 7 | 4 | – |
| 5-8 | 9 | 6 | – |

Schedule: no activity.

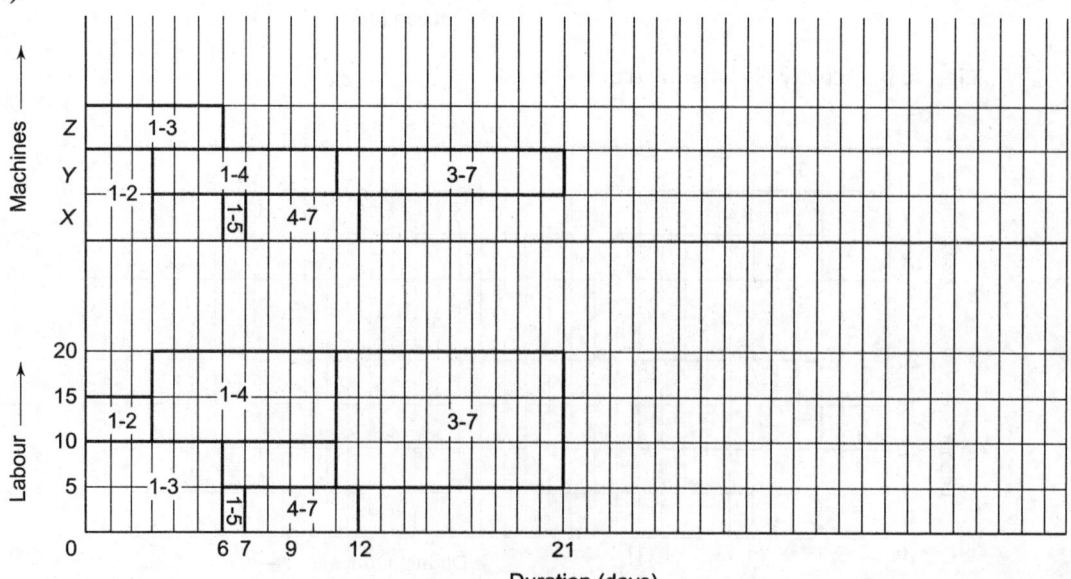

**Fig. 7.67**  Halt 5

**Halt 7, t = 21:**

| EAS | Duration | LS time | OAS |
|-----|----------|---------|-----|
| 2-6 | 7 | 4 | 2-6 |
| 5-8 | 9 | 6 | 5-8 |
| 6-7* | 5 | 11 | – |
| 6-9* | 4 | 14 | – |

Schedule: 2-6 for 7 days with 20 men and machines *Y* and *Z* (Fig. 7.68).

**Halt 8, t = 28:**

| EAS | Duration | LS time | OAS |
|-----|----------|---------|-----|
| 5-8 | 9 | 6 | 5-8 |
| 6-7 | 5 | 11 | 6-7 |
| 6-9 | 4 | 14 | 6-9 |
| 8-9* | 3 | 15 | – |

Schedule: 5-8 for 9 days with 10 men and machines *X*, *Y*, and *Z* (Fig. 7.69)

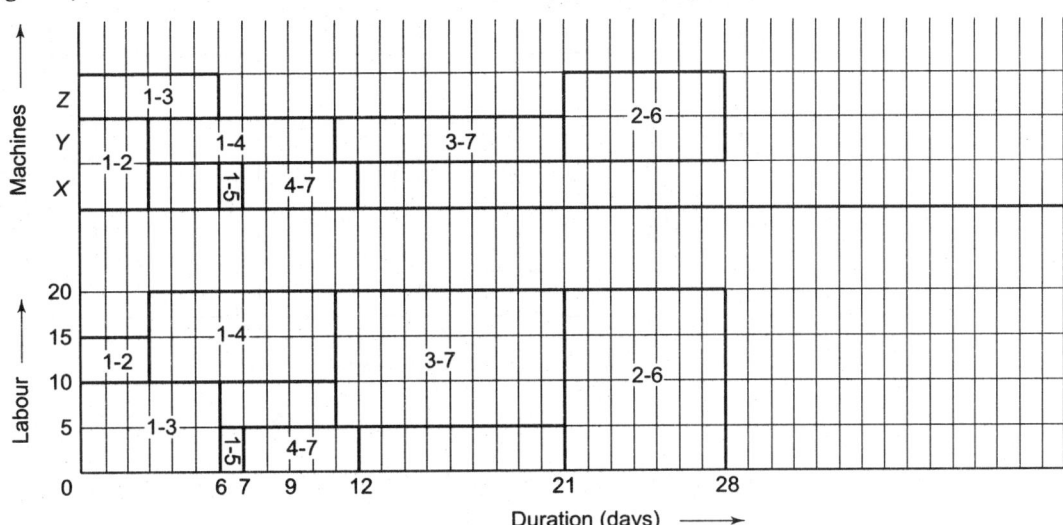

**Fig. 7.68**    Halt 7

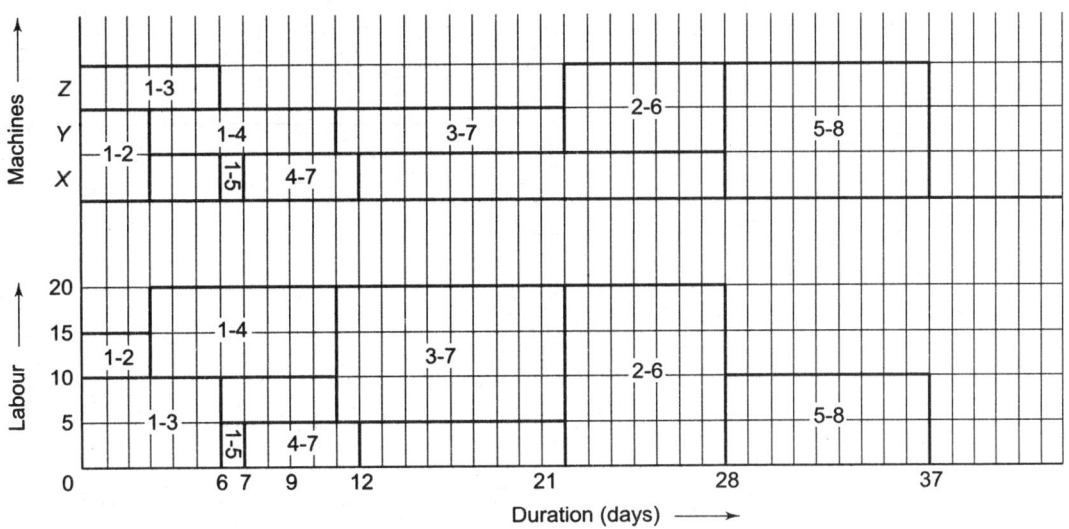

**Fig. 7.69**    Halt 8

**Halt 9, t = 37:**

| EAS | Duration | LS time | OAS |
|-----|----------|---------|-----|
| 6-7 | 5 | 11 | 6-7 |
| 6-9 | 4 | 14 | 6-9 |

**Halt 10, t = 40:**

| EAS | Duration | LS time | OAS |
|-----|----------|---------|-----|
| 6-9 | 4 | 14 | 7-9 |
| 7-9 | 2 | 16 | – |

| 8-9 | 3 | 15 | 8-9 |
| 7-9* | 2 | 16 | – |

**Schedule: 6-7 for 5 days with 10 men and machines *X* and *Z*; 8-9 for 3 days with 10 men and machine *Y* (Fig. 7.70).**

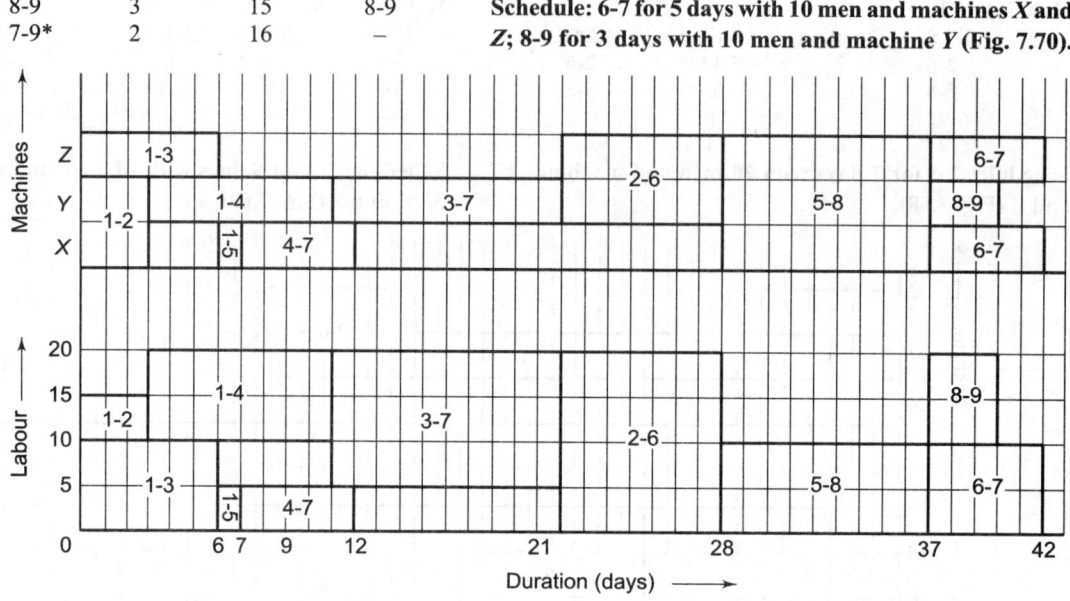

**Fig. 7.70**   Halt 9

**Schedule: 7-9 for 2 days with 10 men and machine *Y* (Fig. 7.71)**

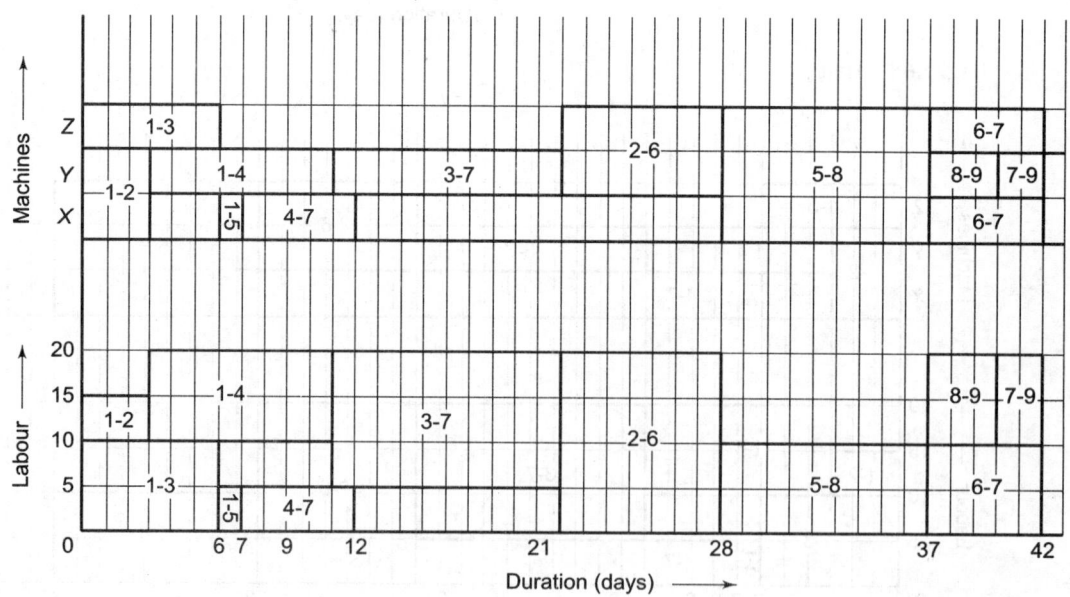

**Fig. 7.71**   Halt 10

**Halt 11, *t* = 42:**

| EAS | Duration | LS time | OAS |
|-----|----------|---------|-----|
| 6-9 | 4 | 14 | 6-9 |

**Schedule: 6-9 for 4 days with 20 men and machine *X* (Fig. 7.72).**

Thus, under the given resource constraints, the project can be completed in 46 days.

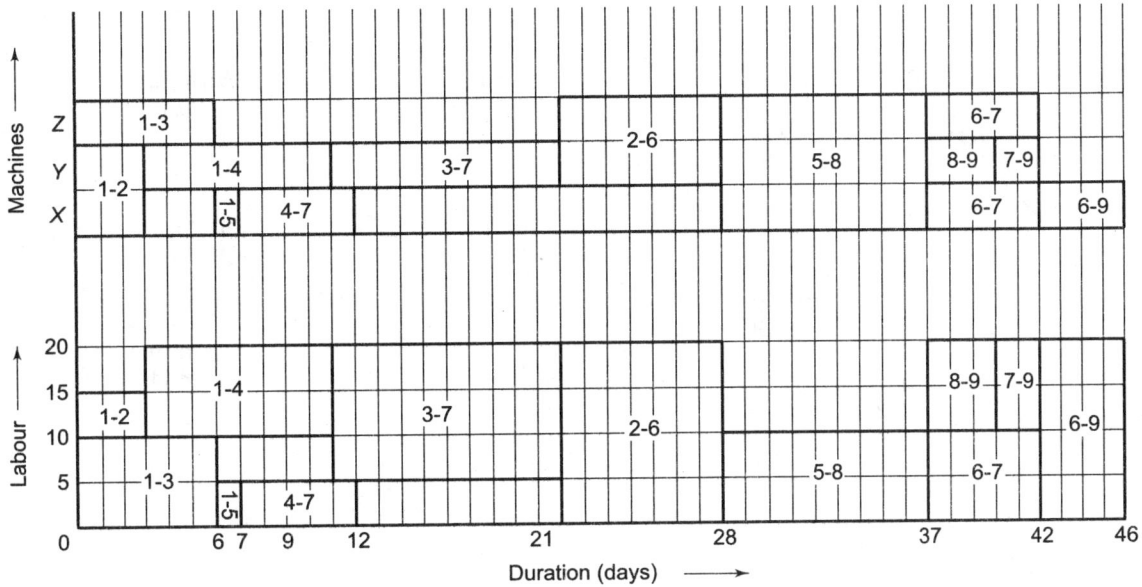

**Fig. 7.72**  Halt 11

## Example 7.8

Table 7.20 shows the details of a project. The maximum resources available are 50 men, one crane, one drilling machine, and one mortar mixing machine. Prepare an activity resource allocation schedule under the given resource constraints. Find the duration of the project.

**Table 7.20**

| Activity | Nodes | Duration (days) | LS time (days) | Resources |
|----------|-------|-----------------|----------------|-----------|
| A | 1-2 | 2 | 0 | 20 men, crane |
| B | 1-3 | 3 | 1 | 10 men, drilling machine |
| C | 2-4 | 3 | 2 | 40 men, mortar mixing machine |
| D | 3-4 | 1 | 4 | 20 men, crane |
| E | 4-5 | 5 | 5 | 30 men, mortar mixing machine |
| F | 4-6 | 2 | 9 | 10 men, crane |
| G | 4-7 | 1 | 7 | 50 men, drilling machine |
| H | 5-8 | 4 | 10 | 20 men, mortar mixing machine |
| I | 6-8 | 3 | 11 | 40 men, crane |
| J | 7-8 | 6 | 8 | 30 men, drilling machine |

## Solution

Figure 7.73 shows the network diagram of the project based on the details given in Table 7.20.

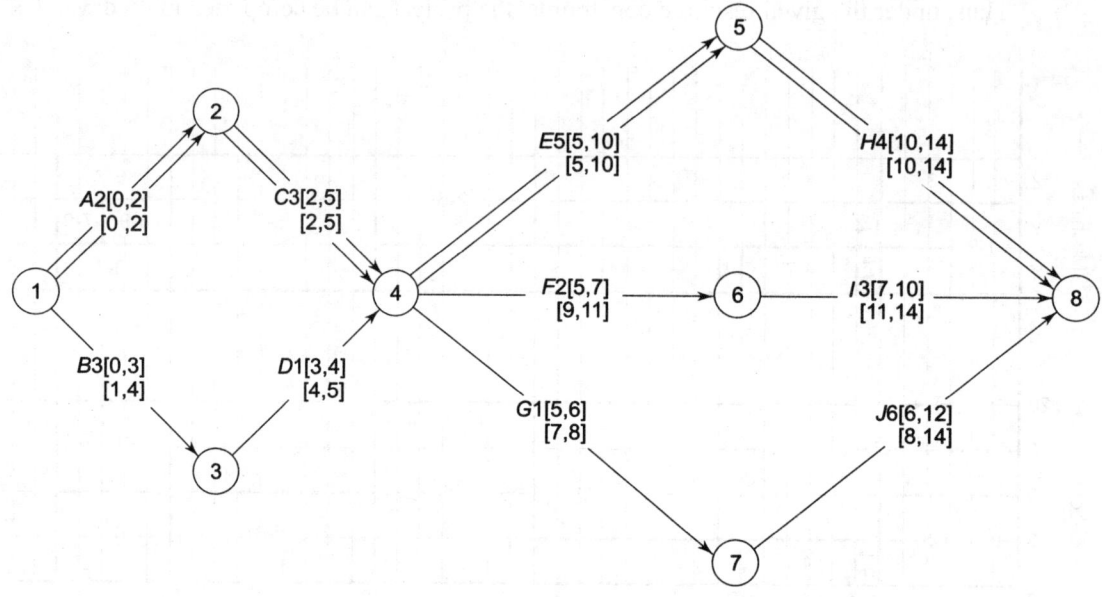

**Fig. 7.73**

**Halt 1, *t* = 0:**

| EAS | Duration | LS time | OAS |
|-----|----------|---------|-----|
| 1-2 | 2 | 0 | 1-2 |
| 1-3 | 3 | 1 | 1-3 |
| 2-4* | 3 | 2 | – |
| 3-4* | 1 | 4 | – |

Schedule: 1-2 for 2 days with 20 men and one crane; 1-3 for 3 days with 10 men and one drilling machine.

**Halt 2, *t* = 2:**

| EAS | Duration | LS time | OAS |
|-----|----------|---------|-----|
| 2-4 | 3 | 2 | 2-4 |
| 3-4 | 1 | 4 | 3-4 |

Schedule: 2-4 for 3 days with 40 men and one mortar mixing machine.

**Halt 3, *t* = 3:**

| EAS | Duration | LS time | OAS |
|-----|----------|---------|-----|
| 3-4 | 1 | 4 | – |

Schedule: no activity.

**Halt 4, *t* = 5:**

| EAS | Duration | LS time | OAS |
|-----|----------|---------|-----|
| 3-4 | 1 | 4 | 3-4 |
| 4-5* | 5 | 5 | 4-5* |
| 4-6* | 2 | 9 | – |
| 4-7* | 1 | 7 | – |
| 5-8* | 4 | 10 | – |

Schedule: 3-4 for 1 day with 20 men and one crane; 4-5 for 5 days with 30 men and one mortar mixing machine.

**Halt 5, *t* = 6:**

| EAS | Duration | LS time | OAS |
|-----|----------|---------|-----|
| 4-6 | 2 | 9 | 4-6 |
| 4-7 | 1 | 7 | – |
| 5-8 | 4 | 10 | – |
| 6-8* | 3 | 11 | – |

Schedule: 4-6 for 2 days with 10 men and one crane.

**Halt 6, *t* = 8:**

| EAS | Duration | LS time | OAS |
|-----|----------|---------|-----|
| 4-7 | 1 | 7 | – |
| 5-8 | 4 | 10 | – |
| 6-8 | 3 | 11 | – |

Schedule: no activity.

**Halt 7, *t* = 10:**

| EAS | Duration | LS time | OAS |
|-----|----------|---------|-----|
| 4-7 | 1 | 7 | 4-7 |
| 5-8 | 4 | 10 | 5-8 |
| 6-8 | 3 | 11 | 6-8 |
| 7-8* | 6 | 8 | |

Schedule: 4-7 for 1 day with 50 men and one drilling machine.

**Halt 8, *t* = 11:**

| EAS | Duration | LS time | OAS |
|-----|----------|---------|-----|
| 5-8 | 4 | 10 | 7-8 |
| 6-8 | 3 | 11 | 5-8 |
| 7-8 | 6 | 8 | 6-8 |

Schedule: 7-8 for 6 days with 30 men and one drilling machine; 5-8 for 4 days with 20 men and one mortar mixing machine.

**Halt 9, *t* = 15:**

| EAS | Duration | LS time | OAS |
|-----|----------|---------|-----|
| 6-8 | 3 | 11 | – |

Schedule: no activity.

**Halt 10, *t* = 17:**

| EAS | Duration | LS time | OAS |
|-----|----------|---------|-----|
| 6-8 | 3 | 11 | 68 |

Schedule: 6-8 for 3 days with 40 men and one crane.

Therefore, the duration of the project is 20 days. Figure 7.74 shows the resource graph of the schedule made

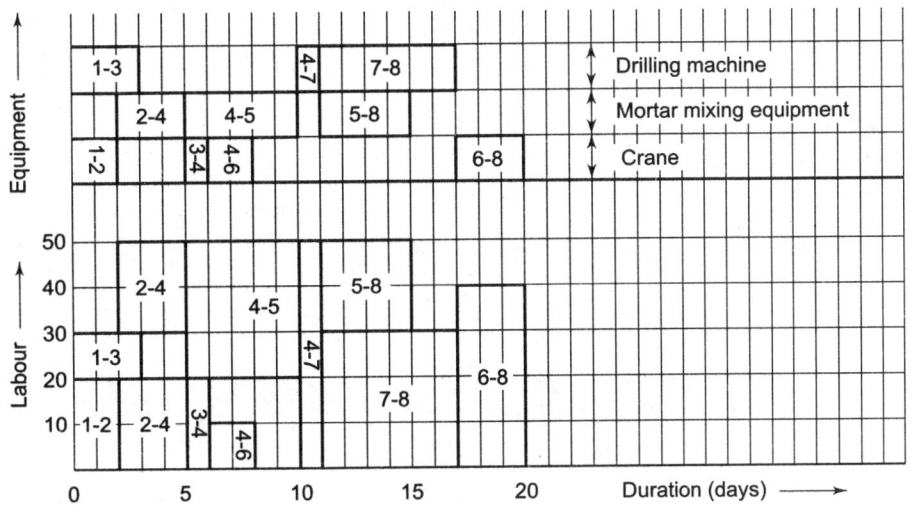

**Fig. 7.74**

# Microsoft Project

MS Project is a premiere software package used for planning and controlling projects. The opening screen of MS Project is shown in Fig. 7.75. The view shown is known as the Gantt view. This is because a Gantt chart (a bar diagram) is automatically prepared in this view according to the information filled-in about activities.

Let us plan a new project using MS Project. To do so, click on **File** in the toolbar and then select **New**. A dialog box appears on the screen asking you whether to start a blank project or not. Click on **OK**.

A new dialog box appears as shown in Fig. 7.76, asking you to fill in the project information. Let us assume we want to plan for a building construction project. The project manager has identified the tasks, with the duration, precedence requirements, and required resources given in Table 7.21.

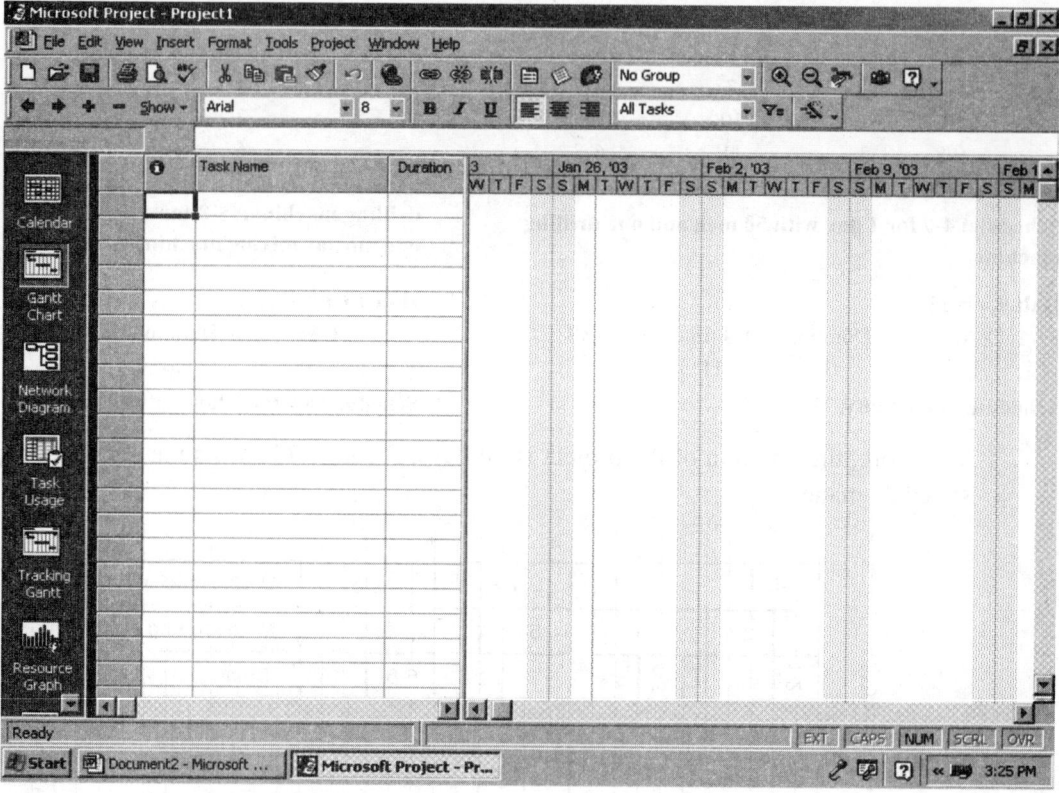

**Fig. 7.75** Opening screen of MS Project

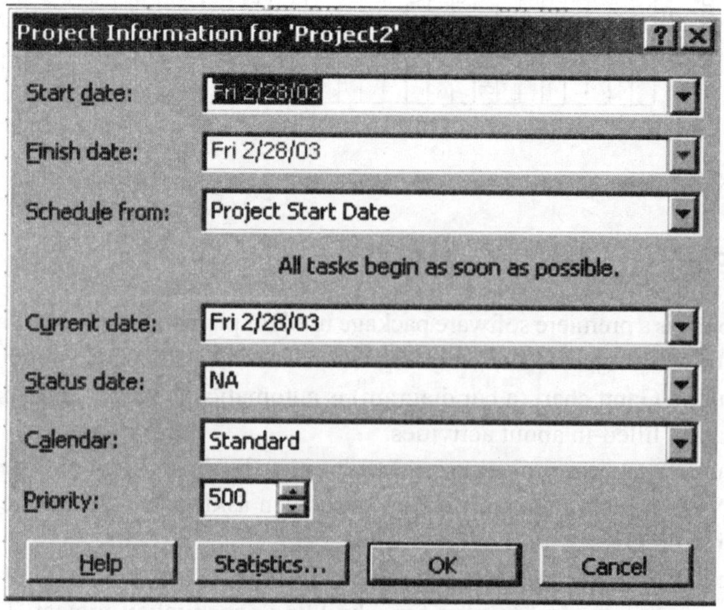

**Fig. 7.76** The Project Information dialog box

**Table 7.21**

| Task ID | Task name | Duration (days) | Precedence requirement | Resources required |
|---|---|---|---|---|
| 1 | Preparing the map of the building | 5 | – | architect, project manager |
| 2 | Purchasing the land for the building | 26 | – | assistant, project manager |
| 3 | Placing the order and receiving bricks, cement, mortar, etc. | 2 | 1, 2 | assistant |
| 4 | Digging the foundations | 10 | 1, 2 | 30 labourers, assistant |
| 5 | Placing the order and receiving goods from windows and door-frame fabricators | 10 | 3, 4 | assistant |
| 6 | Laying the foundation | 15 | 3, 4 | 35 labourers, assistant, 5 mortar mixing machines |
| 7 | Erecting the basic structure of the building | 60 | 5, 6 | 50 labourers, assistant, crane, 5 mortar mixing machines |
| 8 | Plumbing work | 6 | 7 | 6 plumbers, assistant |
| 9 | Electrical wiring work | 5 | 7 | 8 electricians, assistant |
| 10 | Plastering the basic structure | 20 | 8, 9 | 50 labourers, assistant, crane, 5 mortar mixing machines |
| 11 | Flooring | 15 | 10 | 40 labourers, assistant, crane, 5 mortar mixing machines |
| 12 | Placing the order and receiving the doors and windows | 10 | 11 | Assistant |
| 13 | Painting the building | 18 | 11 | 20 labourers, assistant |
| 14 | Interior decoration | 12 | 11 | 30 labourers, assistant, project manager |
| 15 | Polishing doors and windows | 6 | 12 | 20 labourers, assistant |

Fill only the **Start date** as 13 February 2004 (in the format 2/13/04) in the dialog box, and leave the rest of the text boxes as they are, that is, with default values. The finish date will be automatically calculated by MS Project after all the information regarding the tasks has been filled in.

Upon clicking the **OK** button in the **Project Information** dialog box, it disappears. We have the Gantt chart on the screen (Fig. 7.75). Double-click on the first row of the field **Task Name**. A dialog box as shown in Figs 7.77(a) and 7.77(b) appears asking for **Task Information**.

Fill the information about the first task in the project, namely, 'Preparing the map of the building', in the dialog box. Information about predecessors, resources, etc. has to be keyed in. While filling the resources, pay attention to the spellings and capitalization (upper case/lower case) of the names of resources, MS Project may mistake these as two different resources. Also, the number of units of any resource is given as a percentage, for example, one labourer means 100 per cent. Similarly, 30 labourers mean 3,000 per cent.

The identification numbers of tasks are automatically generated by MS Project (MSP). While filling the predecessors of a task, we simply need to use these IDs and the rest is done by MSP. Leave the **Advanced and Notes** tabs unchanged. For the first two tasks, if you see the **Advanced** tab, you will find that the constraint type in these tasks is 'Start no earlier than'. This constraint

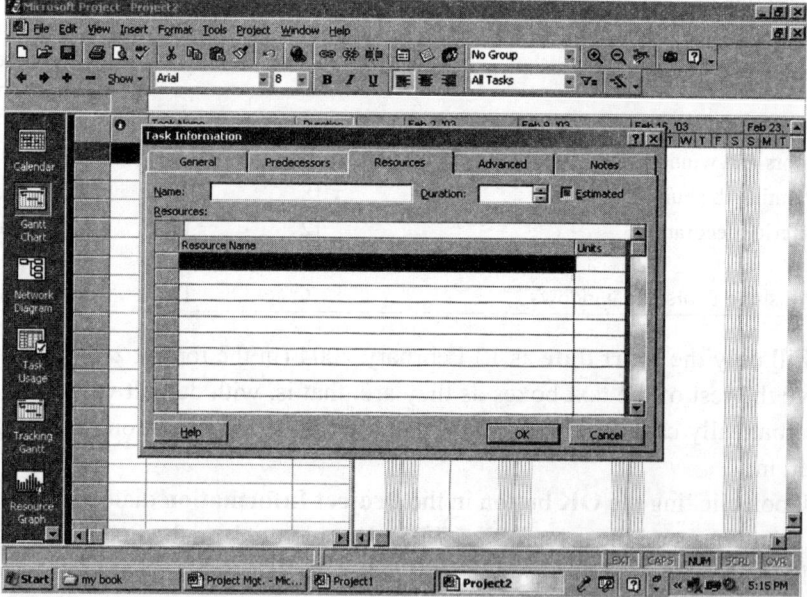

**Fig. 7.77(a)** Task Information dialog box

**Fig. 7.77(b)** Task Information dialog box

is there by default because we had specified the project start date as 2/13/04. Therefore, the first two tasks have to start no earlier than 2/13/04. For the rest of the tasks, the default constraint type is 'As soon as possible'.

As you keep on filling the information about the tasks, the Gantt chart is automatically created by MSP (Fig. 7.78). You can see that, by default, Saturday and Sunday are taken as holidays (shown shaded here). In India, we normally have working Saturdays, therefore the calendar being used by default needs to be changed.

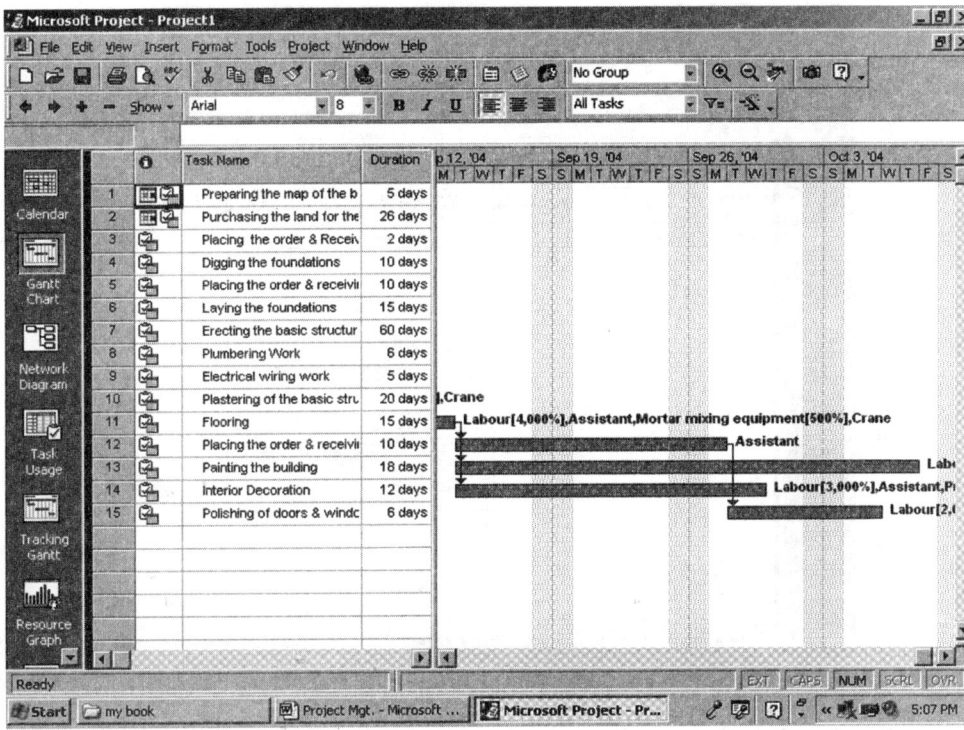

**Fig. 7.78**  Automatic Gantt chart creation

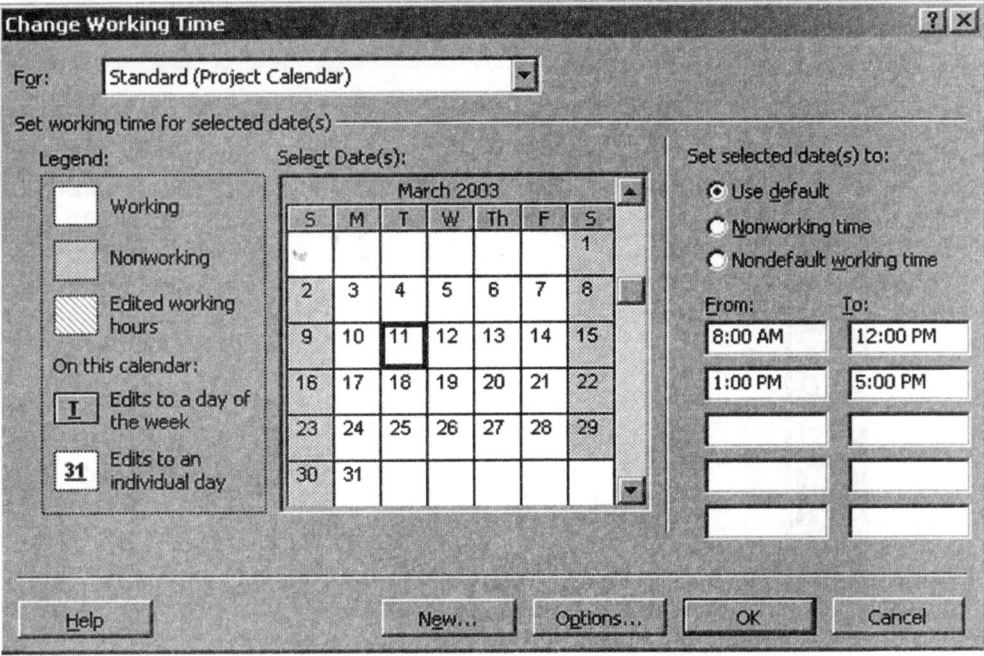

**Fig. 7.79**  Change Working Time dialog box

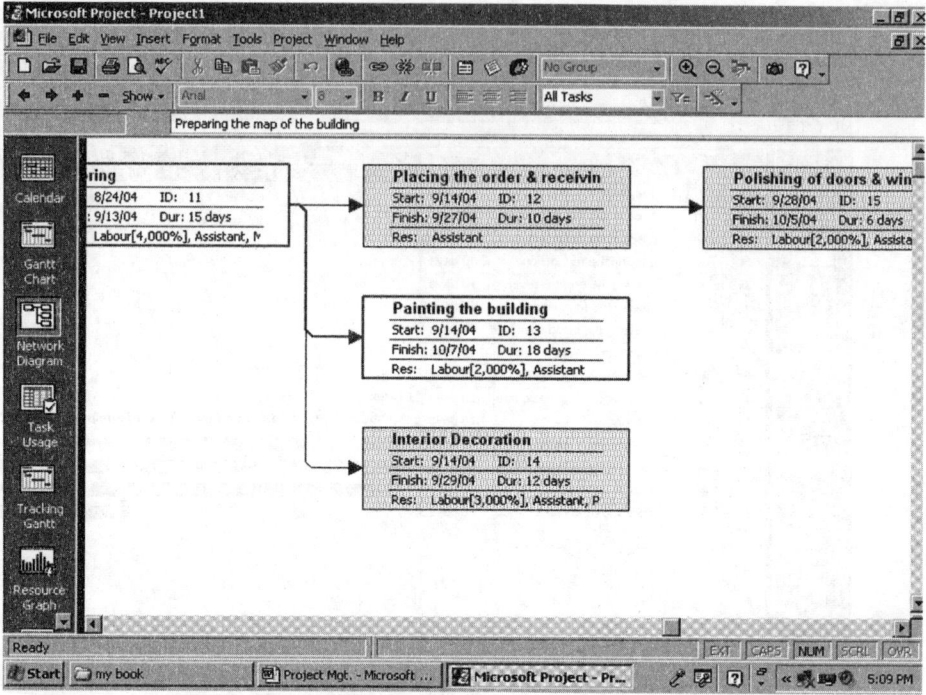

Fig. 7.80 Network diagram created by MSP

| | Resource Name | Type | Material Label | Initials | Group | Max. Units | Std. Rate | Ovt. Rate |
|---|---|---|---|---|---|---|---|---|
| 1 | Architect | Work | | A | | 100% | $0.00/hr | $0.00/hr |
| 2 | Project Manager | Work | | P | | 100% | $0.00/hr | $0.00/hr |
| 3 | Assistant | Work | | A | | 100% | $0.00/hr | $0.00/hr |
| 4 | Labour | Work | | L | | 100% | $0.00/hr | $0.00/hr |
| 5 | Crane | Work | | C | | 100% | $0.00/hr | $0.00/hr |
| 6 | Mortar mixing equi | Work | | M | | 100% | $0.00/hr | $0.00/hr |
| 7 | Plumber | Work | | P | | 100% | $0.00/hr | $0.00/hr |
| 8 | Electrician | Work | | E | | 100% | $0.00/hr | $0.00/hr |

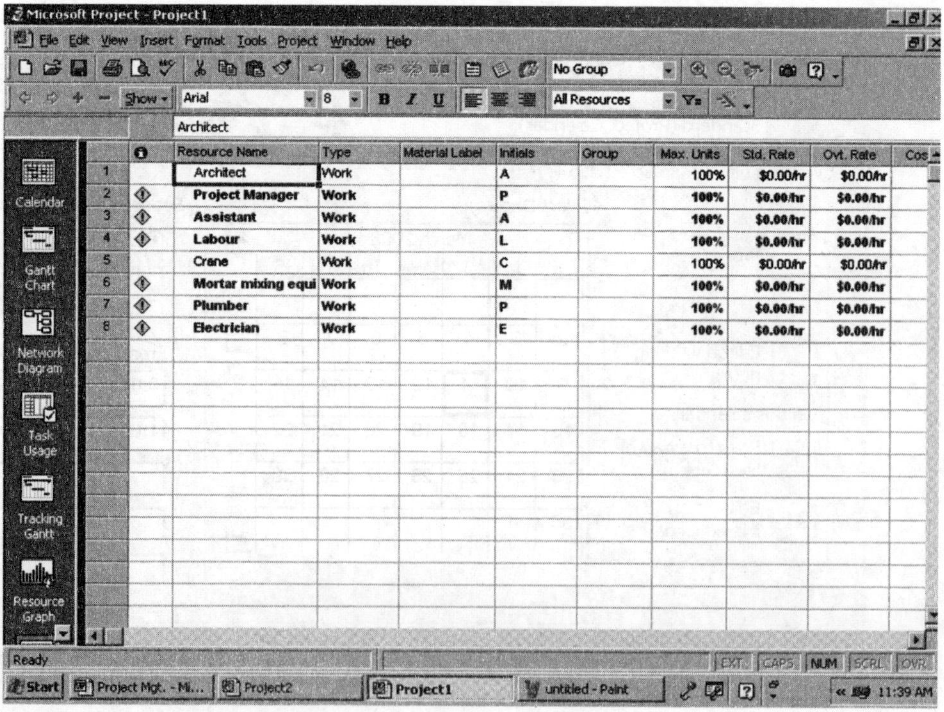

Fig. 7.81 Resource sheet generated by MSP

Click on Tools and then select **Change Working Time**. The dialog box shown in Fig. 7.79 appears. Click on **S** for Saturday, the whole column of Saturdays in the calendar gets selected. Then select the radio button for **Nondefault working time** and click on **OK**. You can now see in the Gantt chart that Saturdays have become working days. Similarly, we can mark holidays on certain dates according to the Indian calendar as **Non-working time**. Note that in the Gantt chart, the project finish date is Saturday, 28 August 2004.

Click on the **Network Diagram** button given in the left column of the screen shown in Fig. 7.78. The network diagram of our project is shown in Fig. 7.80. Now click on the **Resource Sheet** button given in the left column of the screen. The resource sheet (Fig. 7.81) takes the maximum number of units of a resource, by default, as unity (100%). Therefore, the rows of almost all the resources appear in red (on your screen), indicating a scarcity of these resources. We therefore increase the **Max. Units** of these resources (indicating the maximum units of a resource available) as follows:

| Resource name | Max. units (%) |
|---|---|
| Architect | 100 |
| Project Manager | 100 |
| Assistant | 300 |
| Labour | 4,000 |
| Crane | 100 |
| Mortar mixing equipment | 500 |
| Plumber | 1,000 |
| Electrician | 1,000 |

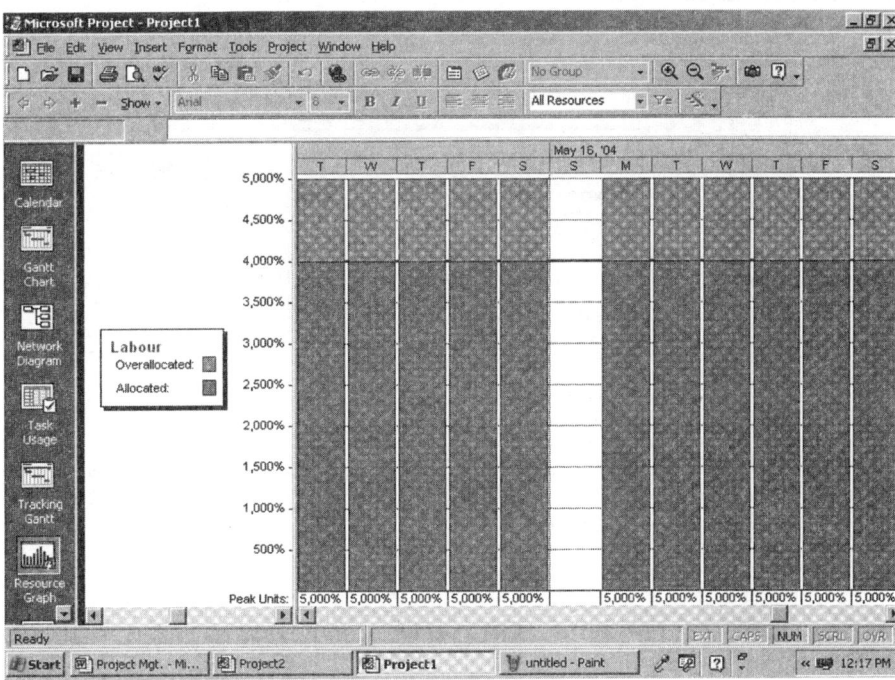

**Fig. 7.82**   Resource graph generated by MSP

We see that in the resource sheet, the rows for Project Manager and Labour are still red. An exclamation mark is also shown by MSP in the **i** field. When you hold the cursor over this mark, an information box appears displaying ,'This resource has to be leveled on a day-to-day basis'.

Now, click on the **Resource Graph** button given in the left column of the screen. The graph generated for the various resources used is shown in Fig. 7.82 (scroll for various resources and dates by using the scroll buttons at the bottom). Here also, note that some resources are over-allocated (shown in red).

Next, click on the **Resource Usage** button given in the left column of the screen. The details about the various activities in which the various resources are used are shown in Fig. 7.83.

The network diagram already shows the critical path represented by red-lined boxes. To see the critical path in the Gantt chart, click on **Format**. Then select **Gantt Chart Wizard**. The dialog box of the wizard appears, which prompts you to click on **Next**. In the next dialog box, select the radio button of **Critical Path**. Keep clicking on the **Next** buttons until the dialog box asks you to **Format it**. Upon clicking the **Format it** button, the critical path becomes red in colour on the Gantt chart.

The resource sheet still shows all the rows in red, implying that many resources are over-allocated. To remove this over-allocation, MSP has a feature called **Resource Leveling**. In the Gantt chart view, click on the **Tools** pull-down menu. Choose the **Resource Leveling** option. The dialog box shown in Fig. 7.84 appears. Choose the **Automatic** radio button. Notice that three levelling options are given. Click on the **Level Now** button after choosing one or more levelling options and notice the changes in the Gantt chart as well as the resource sheet. MSP handles resource levelling and resources under constraint problems in a different way, compared to our earlier discussion.

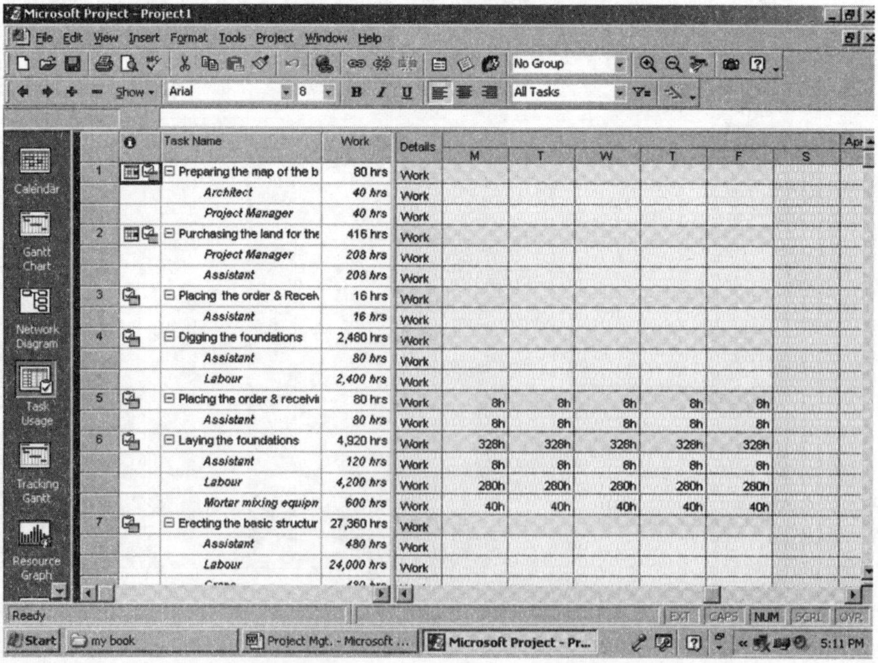

**Fig. 7.83** Resource usage details

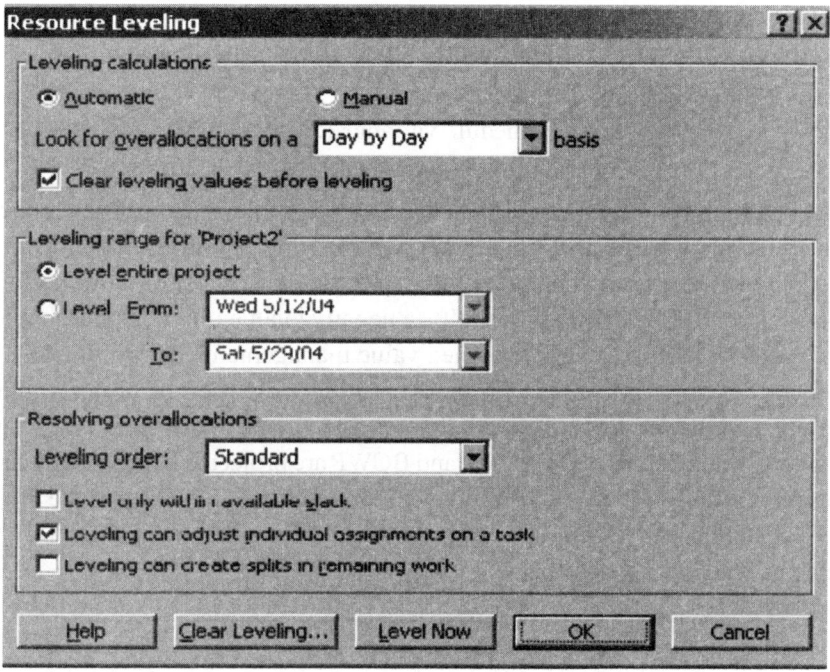

**Fig. 7.84** Resource Leveling dialog box

Exhibit 7.4 discusses the project management techniques that are practised in India.

## Earned Value Management (EVM) for Tracking of Projects

The earned value management (EVM) is an effective technique of tracking the progress of projects. Earned value comprises three dimensions:

**Budgeted cost of work scheduled (BCWS)**   It is the sum of the cost budget for all the activities in the baseline (original) plan of the project at any specific future point in time. Thus, this is the budgeted (planned) cost as per the project plan for a part of the project to be completed in a given time frame. For example, the BCWS for all activities in a product development project till Day 5 from commencement is say ₹2.0 lakh.

**Budgeted cost of work performed (BCWP)**   When a project is under implementation, a certain part of the project is completed at a given point in time. The budgeted (planned) cost of all the activities performed till that point in time is called BCWP. In our earlier example of product development project, let us say that BCWP till Day 5 is ₹1.2 lakh.

**Actual cost of work performed (ACWP)**   It is the actual cost incurred in implementing a part of the project till a given point in time. Let us assume that in the example of product development project, the ACWP is ₹1.7 lakh till Day 5.

The above three dimensions help us in controlling the time as well as cost of implementation of a project. Cost variance (CV) and schedule variance (SV) are two parameters particularly helpful here:

$$\text{Cost variance (CV)} = \text{BCWP} - \text{ACWP}$$

In our example, $\text{CV} = 1.2 - 1.7 = -0.5$

This suggests that more cost has been actually incurred by about ₹0.5 lakh compared to the budget of activities (work) performed till Day 5. Negative value of CV indicates being over budget and is obviously undesirable.

$$\text{Schedule variance (SV)} = \text{BCWP} - \text{BCWS}$$
$$\text{In our example, SV} = 1.2 - 2.0 = -0.8$$

A negative value of SV indicates that less work has been performed compared to what was scheduled to be performed till a given point in time. In our example, work worth ₹2.0 lakh of cost should have been completed till Day 5, while the cost of work performed till this day is less—worth ₹1.2 lakh only. Naturally, a negative value of SV is undesirable.

Figure 7.85 shows a simple earned value management chart to illustrate our example of the product development project. In practical implementation of projects, the curves of BCWS, ACWP, and BCWP are rarely straight lines as depicted in this simplistic example. In the current example, when the curves of ACWP and BCWP are projected along straight lines till the scheduled completion date of Day 15, the projected SV swells to ₹2.5 lakh and the projected CV increases to ₹1.5 lakh. Clearly, steps should be taken by the project manager on Day 5 to catch up on the delay as well as cost overrun.

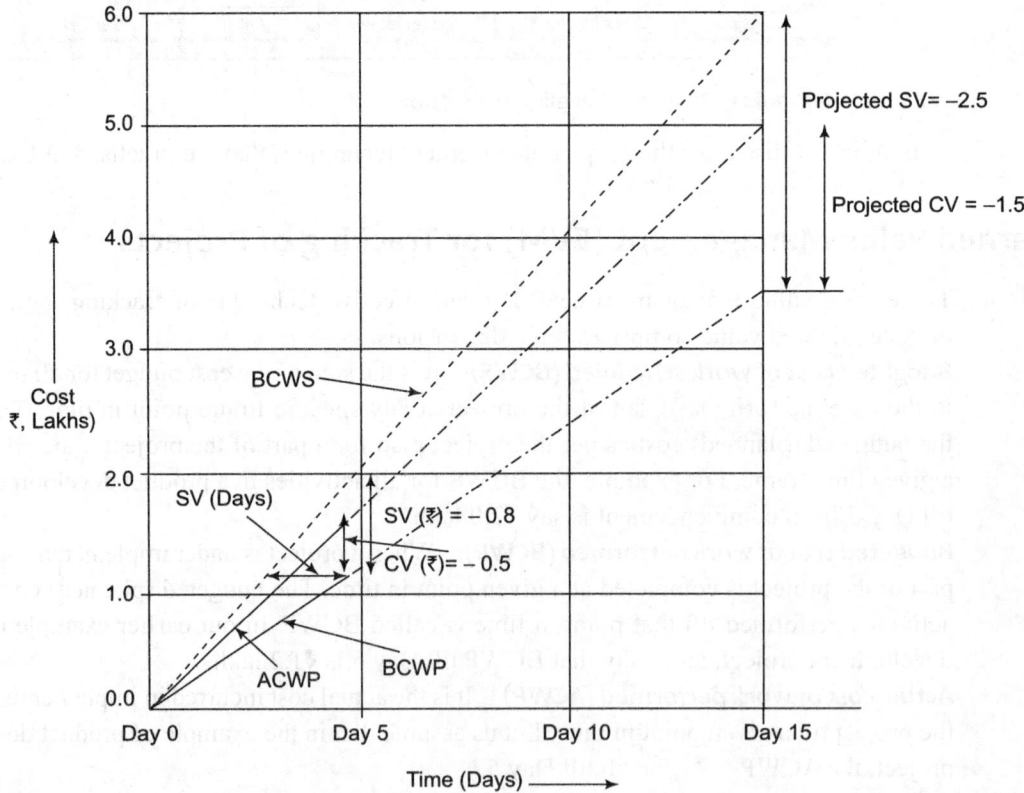

**Fig. 7.85** A simple earned value management chart

## Exhibit 7.4  Indian Industry

Reliance Industries is famous for the timely completion of all their projects. Be it the commissioning of new plants or the launching of Reliance India Mobile. A study by McKinsey has revealed that the timely completion of a project or a new product launch in the market is more important than budget overruns. According to them, a project that is on time but over-budget by 50 per cent will earn 4 per cent less than an on-budget project. On the other hand, an on-budget project which is six months late will earn 33 per cent less than an on-time project.

The Indian industry, in general, and the public sector, in particular, is plagued with the problem of delays in project completion. It has also been found that while estimating activity duration, project managers tend to inflate activity time estimates in order to be sure that the activity gets completed in time. Project managers tend to add more safety time for activities having greater uncertainty, which may cause a shift in the critical path of the project. During implementation, they will then concentrate more on an incorrect critical path.

Goldratt (1997) has suggested that instead of inflating individual activities in a project, it is better to add a project buffer before the finish time, as shown in the Fig. 7.86.

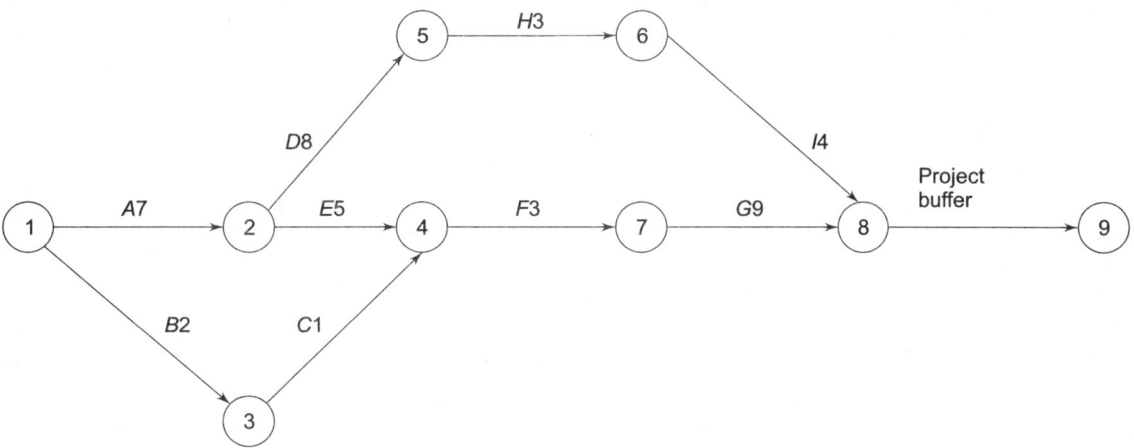

**Fig. 7.86**  Network diagram showing project buffer

Hoel and Taylor (1999) have suggested methods of finding the optimal duration of a project buffer by using simulation techniques. If a non-critical path becomes critical due to uncertainty in certain activity times, the problem does not get affected because of the project buffer. The project buffer applies for all the critical paths.

In our domestic industry, project planners should be advised to provide accurate estimates of activity duration. Goldratt's idea of the project buffer should be used and the effective reduction in the project completion time will lead to strategic benefits.

Gupta and Sravat (1998) have presented the factors which are impeding the development of private power projects in developing countries like India:

- high country/political risk
- unstable economic/fiscal environment
- highly bureaucratic system
- poor credibility of power purchaser
- fuel suppliers and transporters, which are state-owned monopolies
- immature capital markets, especially the long-term debt market

Further, they have suggested that multilateral financial institutions should participate in private power projects by way of equity. This will greatly enhance investor confidence, and the chances of the project financing of these projects being successful. The Government of India should ensure that incidents similar to Dabhol Power Project do not repeat, otherwise an investor would consider India a high

*(Contd)*

*Exhibit 7.4 Contd*

risk country, and the cost of international capital will escalate.

In his research, De (2001) has emphasized the importance of *project termination* in the life cycle of a project. According to his study, the key problems faced by Indian project managers in terminating projects are:

- negotiating claims with clients
- compliance with statutory requirements
- receipt of final installment of payment
- performance guarantee tests
- handling claims of suppliers

The termination phase is the formal closeout of a project after the conceptualization, planning, and execution stages. Some of the problems that are faced during termination are the results of laying insufficient emphasis on critical success factors, such as

- project audit
- contingency plans
- lack of proper communication mechanisms across the various phases in the project life cycle

De's study also suggests that during the termination of a project, the problems faced by private-sector corporations are as severe as those faced by public-sector companies, though this result is contrary to the popular perception about the laxity of public-sector companies.

Project management in India assumed importance in the early 1980s, when the Government of India started its liberalization programme by allowing multinational corporations to have a minority stake in joint ventures (JVs) with Indian companies in certain identified sectors. This was the time when companies such as Hero Honda, TVS Suzuki, etc. came into existence. These companies emphasized

the importance of project management in the Indian industry by commissioning their plants in record time, launching their world-class products in the Indian market, and further by continuous improvements in the subsequent models launched by them.

Prior to the early 1980s, the Licence Raj in India mainly created monopolies in almost every sector, with public-sector companies leading the show in most areas. These monopolies were so protected by the government that late completion of projects, budget overruns and improper implementation seldom posed any problem. The products or services provided by such monopolies had to be accepted by the consumer whether these were delivered late, lacked in quality, or had high prices. Project management took a back seat during the Licence Raj in India.

After 1991, the real liberalization was initiated by the Government of India, when MNCs were allowed to have a majority stake in JVs in many sectors of the industry. Many more MNCs such as Daewoo, Hyundai, LG implemented their Indian projects. The Indian software industry started growing by handling various international software implementation/development projects.

In the current context, Indian software companies such as Wipro, Infosys, and many more have shown to the world that the indian industry has come of age in the application of various models and techniques of project management in order to gain superiority in the international market place. Still there are many sectors, especially the infrastructure projects in which the Government of India has majority stakes, where project management principles have to be used effectively to ensure the success of projects.

# Summary

*Project management* can be defined as the process of controlling the achievement of the project objectives. A project can be divided into various activities or phases. If the duration of various activities in a project can be estimated with some certainty from past experience, the *critical path method* (CPM) can be used to plan the project. Otherwise, when these cannot be estimated from past experience (e.g., in research and development projects), three time estimates, namely, the *optimistic time* ($a$), the *most likely time* ($m$), and the *pessimistic time* ($b$), are used. The technique used

in such situations is called *programme evaluation and review technique* (PERT). Both these techniques (CPM as well as PERT) are based on the use of network diagrams in order to plan and monitor projects.

Projects involve two types of costs, namely, *direct and indirect costs*. The direct cost is the cost of raw materials, tools and equipment, and labour (wages, overtime, hiring, and laying-off costs). The indirect cost is the cost of project supervision, penalties for late completion, and rewards for early completion. Direct and indirect costs are inversely proportional to each other, that is, when one increases, the other decreases.

The process of intentionally decreasing the duration of the project by adding more resources to the activities of the project is called *crashing*. The requirement of resources in the implementation of a project may vary from time to time during the project. These fluctuations in resource requirements are undesirable to organizations. Thus, the activities may be rescheduled, keeping the duration of the project constant. This process is known as *resource levelling*. In situations where resources are limited, activities have to be rescheduled with optimal utilization of resources, but in this case the duration of the project may get extended further.

*MS Project* is a popular software used in project management. It is a user-friendly software for making network diagrams, assigning resources, levelling the resources, etc. while planning projects. It is also useful for monitoring the progress of projects during their implementation.

Earned value management is an effective way of tracking the progress of projects in terms of cost variance (CV) and schedule variance (SV).

## References

Atkinson, Roger 1999, 'Project management: Cost, time and quality, two best guesses and a phenomenon, its time to accept other success criteria', *International Journal of Project Management*, vol. 17, no. 6, pp. 337–342.

De, P.K. 2001, 'Project termination practices in Indian industry: A statistical review', *International Journal of Project Management*, vol. 19, no. 2, pp. 119–126.

Gelinas, Rene 1999, 'The Just-in-Time implementation project', *International Journal of Project Management*, vol. 17, no. 3, pp. 171–179.

Goldratt, E.M. 1997, *Critical Chain*, North River Press, Great Barrington, MA.

Gupta, Jyoti P. and Anil K. Sravat 1998, 'Development and project financing of private power projects in developing countries: A case study of India', *International Journal of Project Management*, vol. 16, no. 2, pp. 99–105.

Hoel, Kjersti and Sam G. Taylor 1999, 'Quantifying buffers for project schedules', *Production and Inventory Management Journal*, vol. 40, no. 2, second quarter.

Munns, A.K. and B.F. Bjeirmi 1996, 'The role of project management in achieving project success', *International Journal of Project Management*, vol. 14, no. 2, pp. 81–87.

Payne, John H. and J. Rodney Turner 1999, 'Company-wide project management: The planning and control of programmes of projects of different type', *International Journal of Project Management*, vol. 17, no. 1, pp. 55–59.

Stub, Avraham 1997, 'Project segmentation—A tool for project management', *International Journal of Project Management*, vol. 15, no. 1, pp. 15–19.

Turner, J.R. 1993, The *Handbook of Project-based Management*, McGraw-Hill, Maidenhead, UK.

Turner, J.R. and R.A. Cochrane 1993, 'The goals and methods matrix: Coping with projects with ill-defined goals and/or methods of achieving them', *International Journal of Project Management*, vol. 11, no. 2.

## Keywords

**Actual cost of work performed (ACWP)** is the actual cost incurred in implementing a part of the project till a given point in time.

**Beta curve** is the probability distribution curve of the duration of an activity.

**Budgeted cost of work scheduled (BCWS)** is the sum of cost budget for all the activities in the baseline (original) plan of the project at any specific future point in time.

**Budgeted cost of work performed (BCWP)** When a project is under implementation, a certain part of the project is completed at a given point in time. The budgeted (planned) cost of all the activities performed till that point of time is called BCWP.

**Crash time** is the limit beyond which the duration of an activity does not decrease by adding any amount of resources. The corresponding direct cost is called the **crash cost**.

**Crashing** of a project means intentionally reducing the duration of a project by allocating more resources to it.

**Critical path** is the longest duration path between the start and the end nodes of a project.

**Critical path method (CPM)** is a technique used to plan projects in which the duration of various activities can be determined up to great accuracy.

**Cost variance (CV)** is the difference between BCWP and ACWP.

**Dummy activity** is a hypothetical activity (i.e., does not exist practically), which does not require any resource (men, machine, materials, capital, etc.) for its performance. The duration of a dummy activity is also always zero. Similarly, a dummy event is an imaginary event.

**Earliest start (ES) and earliest finish (EF) times** of an activity are based on the condition that every activity would be started and finished as early as possible.

**Eligible activity set (EAS)** is that group of activities which become eligible for scheduling because their predecessors have already been scheduled earlier.

**Free float (FF)** of an activity is defined as that part of the total float which when used does not affect the floats of the successor activities.

**Independent float (IDF)** of an activity is the delay possible in an activity without affecting the preceding and succeeding activities. The tail event occurs as late as possible and the head event occurs as early as possible. Under this condition, the excess time over the performance time of the activity is called the independent float.

**Interfering float (IF)** of an activity is defined as that part of the total float which when used affects the floats of the successor activities.

**Latest start (LS) and latest finish (LF) times** of an activity are based upon the condition that every activity would be started and finished as late as possible, provided the project still gets completed in the scheduled time.

**Most likely time estimate** ($m$) is the time estimate which has the highest probability of occurrence. This is based upon the gut feeling or hunch of the project manager.

**Normal time** of an activity is the duration of an activity when the minimum possible resources required for its performance are deployed for it. The corresponding minimum direct cost is called the **normal cost**.

**Optimistic time estimate** ($a$) is the shortest possible time estimate of an activity. It is based upon the premise that everything will go right for the earliest completion of the activity.

**Ordered activity set (OAS)** is a group of activities for which the required resources are available at a given instant of time for the given halt.

**Pessimistic time estimate** ($b$) is the longest possible time estimate of an activity. It is based upon the premise that there may be hindrances in the completion of the activity.

**Programme evaluation and review technique (PERT)** is applied in projects where the duration of various activities is not known.

**Project direct cost** is the direct cost involved in all the activities of the project. Activity direct cost is the cost of materials, cost of labour (salaries, wages, overtime cost, hiring and firing cost, etc.), and the cost of machines and equipment.

**Project indirect cost** is mainly the cost of supervision during the implementation of the project. The salaries paid to the project manager/supervisor, etc., miscellaneous costs due to delays in the project, and rewards to the project team members for its early completion are indirect costs.

**Project management** is the process of controlling the achievement of project objectives.

**Projects** are the achievement of a specific objective which involve a series of activities and tasks that consume resources.

**Resource levelling** is the process of rescheduling the activities of a project in order to level the resources throughout the project.

**Schedule variance (SV)** is the difference between BCWP and BCWS.

**Slack** of an event is same as the float of an activity. It is defined as the maximum delay possible in the occurrence of an event.

**Total float (TF)** of an activity is the maximum amount of delay which can be introduced in the execution of the activity, provided the project gets completed in time (as scheduled).

---

CASE STUDY I

# Sreedharan and the Delhi Metro Rail Project

'I was instrumental here in proposing your name for this decoration to my authorities. But it is the President of the French Republic himself, who, having naturally accepted my proposal, went out of his way to make sure that your good name was put on his personal quota,' the French Ambassador to India, Dominique Girard, said while presenting E. Sreedharan with France's Knight of the Legion Honour in 2005. French President Jacques Chirac had gone out of his way to ensure Delhi Metro MD, E Sreedharan, was enlisted on his personal quota for France's most prestigious civilian awards. The Legion of Honour, instituted in 1802 by Napoleon Bonaparte, was originally awarded in France to soldiers for exceptional bravery.

Elattuvalapil Sreedharan was born in Chattanur, a small village near Palakkad in Kerala. In school, he was the classmate of the former Chief Election Commissioner of India, T.N. Seshan. He later studied at the Victoria College in Palakkad and then graduated as an engineer from the Government Engineering College, Kakinada (now Jawahar Lal Nehru Technological University). After a short tenure as a lecturer in civil engineering at the Kerala Polytechnic in Kozhikode and a year at the Bombay Port Trust as an apprentice, he joined the Indian Railways in its Service of Engineers. His first assignment was in the Southern Railway as a Probationary Assistant Engineer in December 1954.

In 1963, disaster struck Rameshwaram when tidal waves washed away the Pamban bridge connecting it with mainland Tamil Nadu. A passenger train was swept away, killing hundreds of persons. The Southern Railway decided to restore the bridge and set a target of six months. General Manager B.C. Ganguly advanced the deadline by three months and the Railway Board assigned the task to Sreedharan, then a 31-year-old Executive Engineer. It was a tough task as it was an old bridge, built by the British in late nineteenth century, with 146 spans and a Scherzer-A steel girder, which opens up for large vessels to pass under the bridge. Sreedharan took up the challenge and advanced the deadline by a month, making the task tougher. The bridge was functional in 46 days.

In 1970, as the Deputy Chief Engineer, he was put in charge for implementation, planning, and design of the Calcutta metro, the first ever metro in India. Sreedharan, who has been in the Indian Railways for 50 years, had successfully completed another mega-project, the Konkan railway between Maharashtra and Mangalore, prior to taking up the Delhi Metro Rail Project. The idea of Konkan rail-line was first mooted in 1990 by then Railway Minister, George Fernandes, in a meeting with Railway Board members. After stating it, Fernandes himself dismissed it as impossible. A month later, Sreedharan went to Fernandes with a well-charted out plan. 'I told him that we will have to work in a different fashion,' he

recalls. Probably his enthusiasm infected Fernandes, who got cabinet approval for the project within three days. Maharashtra and Kerala immediately agreed to the project, but Karnataka Chief Minister, Virendra Patil, objected. Sreedharan, then a member of the Railway Board, went to Maharashtra, Karnataka, Goa, and Kerala and got all the necessary approvals before his 'retirement'. However, Fernandes wanted him to head the West Coast Railway. Thus, the Konkan Rail Corporation was born. It created an engineering marvel by laying a rail network across the mountainous Western Ghats. Under his stewardship, the company executed its mandate in seven years. The project was unique in many respects. It was the first major project in India to be undertaken on a Build-Operate-Transfer (BOT) basis; the organization structure was different from that of a typical Indian Railway set-up; the project had 93 tunnels along a length of 82 km and involved tunneling through soft soil. The total project covered 760 km and had over 150 bridges. That a public sector project could be completed without significant cost and time overruns was considered an achievement by many.

Sreedharan did not stop there. A lot of people were sceptical about Delhi's metro project. The chaos created by a small, one-line metro in Kolkata for a decade and a half was well-known. However, Sreedharan took up the Delhi Metro Rail project. Sreedharan took up this task as the Managing Director (MD) of the Delhi Metro Rail Corporation (DMRC) in November 1997 on the condition that he should be allowed to choose his own team. He was allowed a fair degree of autonomy. Financial powers were vested with the MD. Also, the MD was the last authority on tenders. Another precondition was minimum interference of the government. The work culture was designed to reduce dependence on government subsidies and hence, there was minimal scope for interference from the government in decision-making. Soon the message was clear that there were no free lunches or freebies. The organization, therefore, was able to resist pressures from many quarters. Upon completion of the project, even the Prime Minister bought a ticket for enjoying a ride on the Metro.

Sreedharan seems to have mastered the art of dealing with political pressures. While sharing his experiences on this front during his DMRC tenure, he says, 'We had to recruit many people at DMRC. Then a lot of pressure used to come for promotions in the organization. The main areas were contract awarding, staff recruitment, land acquisition—when you decide on a particular route and try to acquire the land, politicians immediately want you to shift the alignment, "why don't you save this shop? Why don't you save that house?" This sort of thing used to come. But we never changed any decision simply because somebody wants it. If it was required technically or from a professional angle, yes, we do it. Not because anybody wants it. They (politicians) want some people to be appointed and I don't. Similarly contracts; I do exactly what is required. Of late, politicians know I cannot be maneuvered or managed that way. But now I have seen that they respect these qualities. They know this is good for the country, good for the organization. Ultimately if the organization succeeds, the credit goes to the politician. So they are very happy about it. In the initial years, we had a lot of interference now it is gradually tapering off.'

Any other project of this magnitude (see Figure 7.87) might have got bogged down in litigations, but not so with the DMRC. Although there are about 400 cases pending in various courts, no stay order has been given till date. That meant the DMRC could go about executing its work without worrying too much about cost escalation or project delay.

In ensuring minimum inconvenience to motorists and pedestrians alike, the DMRC successfully converted a challenge into an opportunity. That paid dividends too. All utilities were diverted in advance to ensure that there was no disruption of water, electricity, sewerage, and telephone connections during the construction of the area. Barricades were put up. An alternate traffic plan was drawn up with the help of the Indian Institute of Technology, Delhi, and in collaboration with Delhi Police. New roads were built or the existing roads widened to accommodate traffic.

The DMRC organized community interaction programmes for redressing problems that arose

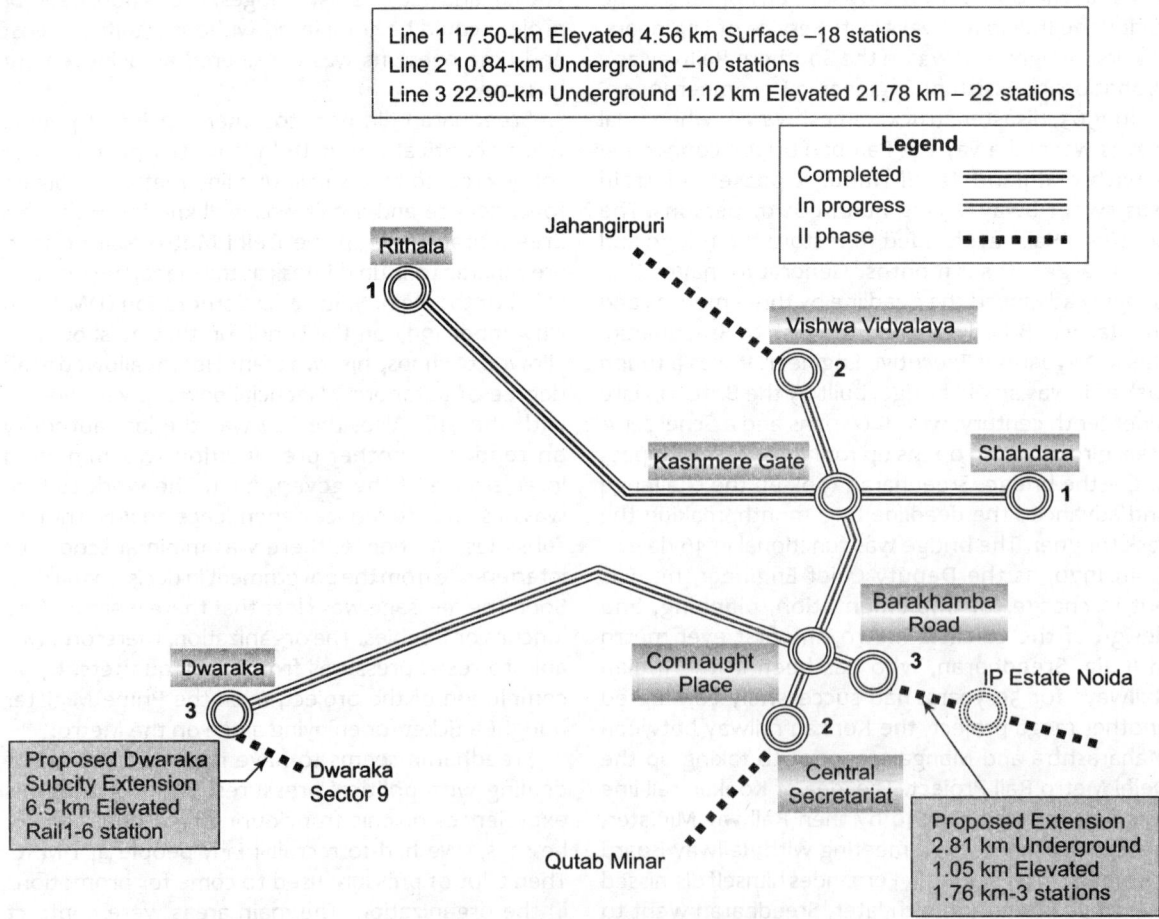

Line 1 17.50-km Elevated 4.56 km Surface –18 stations
Line 2 10.84-km Underground –10 stations
Line 3 22.90-km Underground 1.12 km Elevated 21.78 km – 22 stations

**Fig. 7.87** Sketch Map of Phase I and II of Delhi Metro Rail (not to scale and alignment)

among the local people. Every Monday, heads of department would meet and set new or review targets. DMRC has also devised a reverse clock to overtly display the exact number of days remaining to complete any particular task in the project.

The DMRC has also secured ISO 14001 certification for adhering to environment protection norms and the OSHSAS 18001 certification for meeting world standards in protecting the health of workers and passengers. Another hallmark of its operations has been labour standards. It employs 45 persons per kilometre of work. This ratio is one-third of that of the organizations elsewhere in the country

A detailed environmental impact assessment has been done in 2004 to minimize the negative environmental impact of the project during its construction stage. For every tree cut during construction, the DMRC is planting 10 trees in advance. Around 26,000 trees have been planted in Najafgarh, Isapur, and Rebla Khanpur. Through proper care, 30 per cent of trees in the alignment have been saved.

Installation of storm water drains for disposal of wastewater, monitoring air and noise pollution, disposal of excavated materials are some of the measures taken during construction to minimize the damage to the environment and inconvenience to the public.

The Delhi Metro project, which surprisingly is consuming over 70 per cent of all the cement and steel being used in the capital these days, managed to tide over a recent quantum jump in the price of steel by anticipating the rise and guaranteeing the orders placed by the contractors with the Steel Authority of India Ltd (SAIL).

It was only through some foresight and close monitoring of the prices that DMRC managed to anticipate the rise. The DMRC took the unique initiative of stepping in and assuring SAIL that all the steel being sought by the contractors would be paid for.

Due to this initiative, the various contractors working on the project received the supply of steel at almost the prevailing rates before the prices went up. The steel price had shot up from around ₹18,000 per tonne to around ₹30,000 per tonne within May to July 2004. While the rise has affected many other projects, the Delhi Metro project has smoothly 'sailed' over it. Normally in such an event the contractors get panicky. They either demand an increase in the contract amount or delay the construction in the hope that at a later stage they may be able to purchase the raw material at a lower price. In both the cases, the projects inadvertently suffer. However, with the

Delhi Metro project, neither of this happened as the contractors—wise with their experience of working on the project—understood the need to place orders immediately rather than play a waiting game.

As for the guarantee furnished by DMRC with SAIL, which actually clinched the deal for the contractors, DMRC had offered to make immediate payments to avoid any cost over-runs. It was given that the amount would be subsequently adjusted with the contractor's final payment.

It is this aspect of financial management of the project, which has prevented cost overruns and delays in completion of various sections till now. Every detail of the payment to be made and the contract amount is given in the tender document. All the contractors had been given the freedom to decide on how they would construct the project and give the estimate of the costs, labour, and quantity of material required.

While the penalty clauses were included in the contract to ensure timely completion, the DMRC also provided a counter-guarantee. It stipulated that if the payment was delayed, DMRC would pay interest on the amount. This has prevented delays in payments to the contractors. To facilitate the continuation of the construction work, DMRC also releases 80 per cent of the bill amount within 72 hours of its submission.

As for the rest of the 20 per cent, it is disbursed within the next 25 days after detailed scrutiny. To prevent any misuse of this clause, it has also been decided beforehand that till the entire 100 per cent of the first bill is not disbursed, no payment will be made on subsequent bills. Contractors found inflating bills run the risk of being heavily penalized and being deprived of the 80 per cent quick payment arrangement.

The carrot-and-stick policy appears to have worked very well. However, what really makes the difference is how DMRC handles its contractors and how other government departments handle them. While in the Metro project, the bills are prepared by the contractors and senior Metro officials subsequently scrutinize them, in many government departments these bills are usually prepared by the junior engineers or other engineers of the concerned departments. This leads to many of the problems plaguing various infrastructure projects.

Although, it might seem like a smooth sailing for DMRC all along, actually it was not so easy to implement the project. The Delhi Metro project ran through hard times in August 2004 and the progress of the work on the underground Metro Corridor connecting Delhi Main station to Chawri Bazar station appeared in deep trouble as the Rock Tunnel Boring Machine (TBM) deployed on the section struggled to move even 2 metres per day as against the anticipated advancement of 6 metres per day.

'The rocks we encountered under the surface were really tough to deal with. While mostly the rocks were so hard that it was difficult to scrape them, there was also a lot of variation in their composition and at some places the boulders underneath threatened to fall on the Rock TBM and damage it,' said the Chief Project Manager, Mangu Singh, while explaining the problem.

Although the contractors initially tried to overcome the challenge by making some adjustments to the Rock TBM, it still struggled to move on at the desired pace. Fearing that the slow progress could affect the timely completion of the corridor, the DMRC asked the contractors to go in for modification of the TBM. However, as two months passed in the process, they were forced to think about other alternatives as well.

Fortunately, while everything appeared gloomy, the progress of the other two Earth Press Balance Machines gave a ray of hope. Realizing that these machines were progressing almost 50 per cent faster than the anticipated speed of 8 metres per day, and therefore just one of them would be able to complete the tunnelling work between Patel Chowk and New Delhi station, DMRC directed one of them be taken off and modified into a Rock TBM. It was then put to work on the parallel tunnel from the Delhi Main station.

Simultaneously, Mr Singh said, 'The new Austrian tunnelling method—with which the Chawri Bazar station was to be constructed as per the plan—was also employed from both sides on the two tunnels connecting New Delhi station to the Chawri Bazar station. The smart moves paid rich dividend and the multi-pronged strategy has now almost covered up for the initial delay.'

According to Mr Singh, all this was made possible by the fact that the terms of the 'fixed term contract' as given in the tender had spelt out to the last detail the manner any crisis would be tackled. As in the entire Delhi Metro project, here too the contractor—a consortium of five companies headed by Dyckerhoff and Widmann AG of Germany—had made the design of this section after undertaking the geo-technical investigation and then quoted the price.

As such, according to the terms, it was also the responsibility of the contractor to ensure timely completion of the project in whichever way possible. Since there was no vagueness in the contract, each party knew its role and responsibility and so there was no misunderstanding despite several technical and cost adjustments being needed to ride through Delhi's tough interiors.

More recently, DMRC faced another challenge and an unavoidable delay resulting into a dark spot on its impeccable reputation. The short 2.81 km upcoming section of the Delhi Metro railway network from Barakhamba near Connaught Place to Indraprastha beyond ITO—with stations in between at Mandi House and Pragati Maidan—has become a major cause of embarrassment for DMRC. Although it has completed all other sections of the network so far on time and won many accolades for maintaining an impeccable track record in this respect, the delay on this particular stretch is now expected to extend up to six months.

While a number of reasons, including 'red tape', have been cited for the delay, the primary one is the issue of how the Metro tracks should go over the Indian Railways' overhead lines near ITO. These lines were curving and the Metro emerging from underground on Sikandra Road had to climb on to elevated viaducts to go over them. Since the area involved was huge and the railway tracks were also curving, as many as 400 drawings were prepared before the plan was finalized.

Inauguration of this section, originally scheduled for March 2006, had to be scheduled for September 2006. The primary reason for the delay has been problems relating to crossing the railway line at ITO. There has been a delay in work at the crossing. Though DMRC could have started operations up to Pragati Maidan in June by changing the signaling system, the costs involved would have been huge and it would have made operations on the section unviable. So it was decided that the section up to Indraprastha, which would serve as the gateway to East Delhi and Noida, be opened at one go in September.

However, this is not the first time this section has been plagued by problems. Last year the Delhi Government sat over a file, pertaining to grant of 200 square yards of land belonging to Indraprastha Thermal Power Station to DMRC for construction of a circulation area for the Indraprastha railway station, for five months.

Although it was known then that any delay would jeopardize timely completion of this vital line, the approval file was stuck at the Department of Power for nearly six months. While DMRC was able to get the necessary nod from the Delhi Government, even that did not help as problems with the railways on taking the Metro tracks over the railway line cropped up and led to further delay for the project.

There were a few lessons for DMRC, which tried to

blindly ape certain international practices adopted by the designers of Metro Rails worldwide. For lines 1 and 2, there are no public toilets at many stations. For line 3 it has toilets for the public at every metro station. DMRC did not do it for line 1 and 2 because it followed the normal international practice where public toilets are not provided at every station. Public toilets are provided just outside the important train junctions. However, it later realized that this was not good for the city. Hereafter, all the stations on the new lines will have public toilets. The general experience in India is that toilets are not properly cleaned and maintained. DMRC did not want this to happen in its stations, but now, DMRC officials find that once people have started respecting a system, they do not dirty it.

DMRC has adapted some unique practices with its suppliers and contractors. DMRC inserts a clause into the contract with its suppliers that they must have an Indian partner. Consequently, the DMRC procured the trains from Bharat Earth Movers Limited, Bangalore,

and elevators, which were produced indigenously. Another feature is the punctuality with which the DMRC pays its contractors, who are addressed by DMRC as associates. However, the real marvel of the Delhi Metro project stems from two counts. First is the way in which a foreign dependent project has been localized and re-engineered. This was done by roping in Indian companies as consortium members at each stage of the project. Table 7.22 shows the major international contractors of DMRC and their Indian partners.

Over the course of the seven year venture, several capabilities have been acquired by the Indian partners. In 2002, the Indian engineering firm, Bharat Earth Movers Ltd (BEML) signed a contract with South Korean firm Rotem for manufacturing rust-proof fibre-reinforced interiors steel coaches within India under a transfer of technology agreement. DMRC procured 240 coaches of which 60 (4 trains) are manufactured in Rotem, Korea. A year later, BEML released the first

**Table 7.22**   Major international contractors of DMRC and their Indian partners

| Operation | Contractors | Indian partners |
| --- | --- | --- |
| Civil works; Ventilation and air conditioning | Kumagai Gumi Co., Shimizu Corporation Itochu Corporation, (Japan); Samsung Corporation (Korea); Skanska International (Sweden); Dyckerhoff & Windmann (Germany) | IRCON International Hindustan Construction Co. Larsen & Toubro Ltd |
| Supply of coaches and engine | Mitsubishi Corporation, Japan; KOROS, Korea; | Bharat Earth Movers |
| Signalling and communication | Alstom Transport, France; Alcatel, Portugal; Sumitomo Corporation, Japan | Alstom Transport |
| Traction and power distribution technology | Corba, ELIOP, Spain | IRCON International |
| Supply, installation, testing, and commission of power supply | | ABB Ltd, Best and Crompton Engineering Ltd |
| Supply, installation, testing, and commissioning of ballast less tract | MVM, Australia | IRCON International |

rake comprising two engines and four trailer coaches. The company will manufacture the other 180 coaches (45 trains). Starting with the local assembly and testing of a few trains, BEML will manufacture the coach shell, traction motor, converter–inverter unit, battery, passenger announcement and information system, air-conditioning units, and seats. This will help in acquiring capability and avoiding import of trains for the forthcoming metro projects in Bangalore, Ahmedabad, Mumbai, and Hyderabad.

Alongside the manufacturing practices, project management processes have also been transferred seamlessly. When the metro project started, a five-member consortium managed it. Four of them were global firms—Pacific Consultants International, Railway Technical Services, Tonichi Engineering Consultants from Japan; and Parson Brinkerhoff International from the US. Rail India Technical and Economic Services (RITES) was the only Indian consultant. Now, for the final stretch of the metro project, DMRC and RITES are confident enough to navigate the venture alone, even though the third stretch will pass through some of the most congested areas of Delhi. Better still, DMRC's domain expertise acquired over the last seven years is now being used to develop feasibility studies for other metro projects. The studies include route alignment, utility mapping, and projected demand for transport in the next five decades, soil testing, environmental impact, and system designing.

For example, the West Bengal government asked DMRC to prepare a detailed project report to connect Kolkata's existing metro rail with Howrah, an industrial hub on the other side of the river Hooghly, which runs through the city. DMRC will use construction and technology similar to that used in the English Channel for linking UK with France through Metro Rail.

At another level, RITES, on behalf of Delhi Metro Rail Corporation, is in the process of completing a detailed project report for the southern cities of Bangalore and Hyderabad. Other metro projects in the pipeline include the western cities of Mumbai and Ahmedabad, the northern city of Lucknow, and the southern cities of Thiruvananthapuram and Kochi.

An important reason why DMRC's skills are being taken to other cities is the cost factor. At a presentation made to the Andhra Pradesh government in 2003, Sreedharan pointed out that the cost of a 39.45 km metro project in Hyderabad was estimated at US$712 million at April 2003 prices, which translated into a per km cost of US$18 million. 'The cost of the Delhi metro project at US$2.3 billion for 66 kms of tracks is higher since most of the technology has been sourced from abroad,' Sreedharan said during the presentation.

With over 80 per cent of the DMRC project completed, the swanky air conditioned trains and modern stations are changing the transportation system in the nation's capital city. Costing around ₹10,570 crore (₹105.70 billion), the project is expected to save ₹600 crore to ₹700 crore (₹6 billion to ₹7 billion) on the total cost, and more importantly, is slated to be completed on time. DMRC not only brings in experience and lower costs, it also shows the rest of India and the world how to complete a world-class project within time. Notably, Sreedharan was invited by the Pakistan Government in March 2007 to enlighten them with his vast experience in developing a metro rail for the city of Karachi.

On its fourth birthday in 2006, DMRC was given the mandate for undertaking the extremely challenging task of completing a hundred kilometres of Metro Rail corridors in the National Capital Region within the next 42 months. This is to meet the target of the completion ahead of the Commonwealth Games in 2010. Such a mammoth Metro Rail construction project had never been undertaken in such a short span of time anywhere else in the world. What made it all the more challenging was that the work would also involve tackling urban odds such as diversion of huge electricity lines, intricate telephone cables, water and sewage drains, and ensuring the very minimum cutting of trees. On 31 December 2011, Sreedharan retired as DMRC Chief and assumed the role of its Principal Advisor.

## Discussion Questions

1. How according to you the crisis of Metro tracks going over the Indian Railways' overhead lines near ITO should have been avoided by DMRC?

2. In your view, is it a right decision on the part of DMRC to now provide public toilets at all its stations by violating the international norm of not providing toilets at all stations?

3. It is always beneficial for a public sector enterprise to deal with public sector suppliers and contractors. Otherwise, it would have been impossible for a private enterprise to tackle the escalating steel prices problem, the way DMRC handled it by convincing its PSU supplier SAIL. Discuss.

# Dabhol Power Project

In 1991, India embarked upon a major liberalization programme. In continuation of its efforts to boost foreign direct investment in the infrastructure sector, the Government of India (GoI) took the initiative in May 1992. It invited an internationally recognized independent developer of power to consider setting up a power plant in India with imported liquefied natural gas (LNG).

| Source | Amount (in million US $) |
|---|---|
| **Debt/Loan** | **643** |
| US Exim Bank | 298 |
| OPIC | 100 |
| Bank of America and ABN-AMRO Bank | 150 |
| Syndicate of Indian Banks led by IDBI | 95 |
| **Equity** | **277** |
| Enron Corporation (80%) | 221.6 |
| General Electric (10%) | 27.7 |
| Bechtel USA (10%) | 27.7 |
| | **920.0** |

The project consisted of the design, engineering, construction, commissioning, and commercial operation of a 2,015 MW natural-gas-fired combine-cycle power station in two phases. The first phase was planned to have a generating capacity of 695 MW. It included the development of harbour and fuel oil facilities. The second phase would have a generating capacity of 1,320 and consisted of building the necessary infrastructure for off-loading, storage, and re-gasification facilities.

Thus, the Dabhol Power Project was given to an Indian company, Dabhol Power Company (DPC). The equity was provided by a consortium of foreign companies (in which Enron Corporation was the lead member, with Bechtel Enterprises Inc., and General Electric Company as members) and other Indian equity participants (see table). The debt was provided by export credit agencies and multilateral agencies.

The project was to be connected to the Maharashtra State Electricity Board (MSEB) grid through a 400 KV transmission system.

The power purchase agreement (PPA) was signed between DPC and MSEB in (the end of) 1993 for a period of 20 years. There were severe penalties for non-performance in the PPA. The DPC had to commission the project within 33 months (1,005 days) from the date of financial closure, failing which they would pay the penalty. The Government of Maharashtra (GoM) gave the guarantee for the payment obligation of MSEB, supported by a counter-guarantee from the GoI. The financial closing of the project took place in March 1995, about a year after the issuance of the basic information memorandum (BIM).

In August 1995, during the construction of the project, the opposition party came to power in Maharashtra and decided to repudiate the first phase and cancel the second phase. The matter went to court, but the Supreme Court upheld the validity of the contract. DPC initiated arbitration proceedings in London against the GoM. The GoM had to set up a group to negotiate the revival of the project (both phases I and II) with DPC in November 1995. Eventually, GoM cleared both the phases of the project in January 1996 with slight changes in the contract. The capacity of the project was increased to 2,450. It was decided that the fuel to be used would be naphtha, and the gasification plant was removed.

In November 2000, MSEB was purchasing electricity from DPC (Phase I was operational and Phase II was 80 per cent complete by then) at the rate of ₹7.80 per kWh (or unit), although according to DPC the average tariff worked out to be ₹4.94 per unit. At that time, the mean cost of supply in Maharashtra was ₹2.90 per unit, the comparative cost of Tata Electricity companies was ₹1.25 per unit, and of Bombay Suburban Electricity Supply (BSES), ₹2 per unit. MSEB was in the red with losses of ₹16,810 million in 1999–2000 and around ₹15,000 million in 2000–01. The GoM was not in a financial position to give subsidies to MSEB. According to the PPA, MSEB had to pay a fixed capacity charge of ₹945.9 million per month to DPC for phase I, whether it purchased power from DPC or not. Both the then Energy Secretary and Secretary (Finance) had cautioned the state government about the financial health of MSEB and the contractual payments it had to make to MSEB according to the PPA, before it was cleared. According to the new state government, while the project had been envisaged to tackle Maharashtra's enormous power shortfall of 2,400 MW, its purpose seemed to have been defeated because of its prohibitive cost, which the consumer might have to bear.

Barely 24 months after the project went live, DPC downed shutters after Enron filed for bankruptcy in 2001. But with US$2.1 billion (₹96.44 billion) sunk in the ground, the other promoters —GE and Bechtel — came up with a revival plan. The plan was to increase their holdings (10 per cent each) and rope in NTPC to replace Enron. Another dimension to the problem was that MSEB wanted the effective price per unit to be lowered from ₹5.20 to ₹4, and to pick up 70 per cent and not 90 per cent as in the original agreement – of the power generated by DPC.

After long deliberations between the stakeholders and the GoI, Ratnagiri Gas and Power Limited (RGPPL), a special purpose joint venture between NTPC, Gail India (GAIL), and the Maharashtra government was set up on 8 July 2005 (Fig. 7.88)

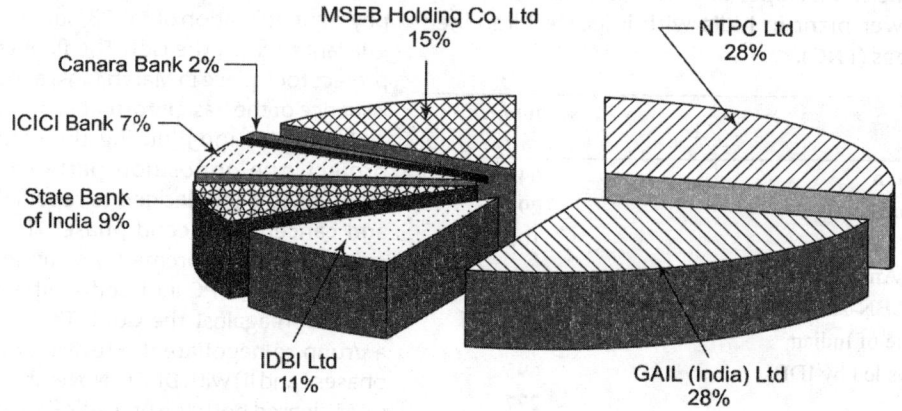

**Fig. 7.88** Shareholding pattern of RGPPL

Nevertheless, the Dabhol project—perhaps one of the most expensive power stations ever built if the cost of construction, time lags, wasted effort, and bitter litigation is added—is finding it hard to break the jinx and start generating power.

More cost overruns, uncertain fuel supply, and bickering among owners are now threatening to delay the restart of the 2,184 MW project ahead of October 2006, a humid month in which power consumption shoots up in Maharashtra.

It was estimated at the beginning of the year 2006 that the cost of completing the project and setting up a liquefied natural gas (LNG) terminal on the Ratnagiri coast would be between ₹8.7 billion and ₹13.85 billion. RGPPL told lenders that the cost could rise up to ₹25 billion. Lenders are of the view that they can put up a brand new 500 MW power plant with this money. There is no question of funding more than previously agreed.

The biggest hurdle is LNG supply. GAIL, which is in charge of the gas terminal near the power station, has not been able to get suppliers from Oman or Qatar to deliver the fuel at Dabhol. These suppliers have agreed to provide gas at Dahej on the Gujarat coast, where Petronet LNG, which is partly owned by GAIL,

has facilities to receive and pipe out the fuel. Petronet has promised 1.2 mBtu (million British thermal units) gas from December 2006 onwards for two years. However, it needs to be carried to Dabhol.

GAIL, which has connectivity between Dahej and Panvel, is laying a 187 km pipeline to transport gas to Dabhol. The contract worth ₹1.64 billion has already been awarded to Punj Lloyd. The company wants to recover that cost by charging RGPPL, US$1 per mBtu of gas. Its partner NTPC is unwilling to pay anything extra. Moreover, GAIL has still not indicated when it will be able to supply the fuel.

According to RGPPL, GAIL would have had to anyway lay the tube for piping LNG from Dabhol when the facility is complete two years from now. It is expected to cost a little more than ₹8 billion. The power project has import, storage, and re-gasification facility for 5 mBtu of LNG. The complete project would require 2.1 mBtu of gas and GAIL can sell the rest outside.

GAIL is of the view that the company's mandate was only to supply gas from 2008 onwards. On the issue of LNG transportation cost, it will be decided by the tariff commission.

RGPPL had committed to start the second unit of the three unit power stations in June, the third unit in September, and the first unit, which needed extensive repairs, in December, 2006. While the June restart took place on schedule using naphtha stored on site as feedstock, the generators had to be shut down when the stock was used. Naphtha is expensive and would make the project unviable.

While RGPPL has not gone to the government explaining the cost escalation, it is looking at ways to keep them under check. This is due to the government directives that overruns were unacceptable.

In August 2012, overcoming all problems witnessed by it since its inception, Dabhol Power Station turned profitable and RGPPL presented a 5 per cent dividend cheque to the Maharashtra government.

### Discussion Questions

1. What were the types of risks faced by the Dabhol Power Company in their project?
2. Was the PPA drafted in favour of DPC? Comment.
3. What are the main problems plaguing the 'ill-fated' Dabhol Power Project (DPP)?
4. Suggest ways to make the DPP more profitable.

## Objective Questions

### Choose the correct option

1. Which one of the following is not a project type by size?
   (a) large project
   (b) medium project
   (c) small project
   (d) miniature project
2. Which one of the following is not a project type by resource?
   (a) product development
   (b) engineering
   (c) management
   (d) systems development
3. Critical path in a network diagram is the one with:
   (a) shortest duration
   (b) average duration
   (c) median duration
   (d) longest duration
4. PERT is:
   (a) programme evaluation and review technique
   (b) project evaluation and review technique
   (c) programme evaluation and rewind technique
   (d) people evaluation and rewind technique

### State True or False

5. Project indirect cost is mainly the cost of supervision during the implementation of the project.
6. The process of rescheduling the activities in order to level the time throughout the project is called resources levelling.
7. The slack of an event is equivalent to the float of an activity.

### Fill in the blanks

8. _____ of an activity is the maximum amount of delay that can be permitted in its execution without introducing any delay in the completion of the project.
9. Reduction in the overall time duration of a project by deploying more resources is called _____.
10. _____ value management is an effective technique to track the progress of projects.

## Concept Review Questions

1. Why are dummy activities and dummy events used in the network diagrams of projects?
2. Explain the different types of projects. Also explain the role of project management in other functional areas of management.
3. What is a critical path? How is it important in a network diagram?
4. 'Over a period of time, CPM and PERT have become almost similar in application.' Justify this statement.
5. What do you understand by 'crashing' of a project? What are the direct and indirect costs in a project?
6. Why is it important to 'level' the resources in a project? How is it done?
7. What is an eligible activity set? How is it different from an ordered activity set?
8. What is incremental cost of crashing? Explain the time-cost curve for the duration of an activity in the process of crashing.
9. Explain the different views of a project as shown in MS Project 2000.
10. Can you perform resource levelling using MS Project 2000? How is it different from the levelling

done manually by using the activity-time graph?
11. Explain the three dimensions of earned value management and highlight how it helps in project tracking.

# Numerical Problems

1. Irfan Bearings (P) Ltd is considering the replacement of the old machines in their factory by new advanced machines. The production manager has identified the activities given in Table 7.23 for this project. Draw the network diagram of the project and find the critical path with its duration.

**Table 7.23**

| Activity code | Activity description | Time (days) | Precedence requirements |
|---|---|---|---|
| A | Analysis of costing with respect to purchase of new machines and sale of old machines as scrap | 2 | – |
| B | Approval of budget for purchase of new machines | 3 | A |
| C | Invite quotation of prices for new machines and choose the supplier with best prices | 7 | B |
| D | Invite tenders for sale of old machines | 7 | B |
| E | Advertise for additional new workers required for operating the new machines | 6 | B |
| F | Place the order for new machines | 2 | C |
| G | Select and train the new workers hired | 3 | E |
| H | Sell old machines to the selected buyer | 1 | D |
| I | Install the new machines | 4 | H, F |
| J | Start production | 2 | G, I |

2. Table 7.24 gives the details of a project.

**Table 7.24**

| Activity | Duration (days) | Required predecessor |
|---|---|---|
| A | 2 | – |
| B | 5 | – |
| C | 3 | A |
| D | 1 | A |
| E | 4 | B |
| F | 3 | B |
| G | 7 | C |
| H | 5 | D |
| I | 1 | E |
| J | 2 | F |
| K | 2 | G, H, I, J |
| L | 5 | G, H, I, J |
| M | 4 | K |
| N | 2 | L |

(a) Draw the network diagram of the project.
(b) Determine the critical path and duration of the project.

(c) Find the total float, interfering float, free float, and independent float of all the activities in the network.

3. A project involves the activities given in Table 7.25, with the given duration and precedence requirements. Find the various types of floats of all the activities in the network.

**Table 7.25**

| Activity | Duration (weeks) | Precedence requirements |
|---|---|---|
| A | 1 | – |
| B | 7 | – |
| C | 4 | A |
| D | 3 | A |
| E | 6 | B |
| F | 2 | B |
| G | 9 | C, D, E |
| H | 3 | F |
| I | 11 | G, H |

4. Find the various types of floats for the various activities in Problem 1.

5. A computer software implementation project has the activities given in Table 7.26. Find the free and independent floats for all the activities in the project.

**Table 7.26**

| Activity | Duration (days) | Predecessor(s) |
|----------|-----------------|----------------|
| A | 5 | – |
| B | 6 | A |
| C | 1 | A |
| D | 4 | B |
| E | 1 | B |
| F | 2 | C |
| G | 3 | C |
| H | 1 | B |
| I | 5 | D, E |
| J | 1 | D, E |
| K | 4 | F, G, H, I |
| L | 2 | E |
| M | 2 | G |
| N | 2 | J, K, L, M |

6. Draw a network diagram for the project detailed by Table 7.27. Find the total float, head slack, interfering float, free float, tail slack, and the independent float of all the activities in the network.

**Table 7.27**

| Activity | Duration (weeks) | Predecessor(s) |
|----------|------------------|----------------|
| A | 2 | – |
| B | 20 | – |
| C | 6 | – |
| D | 7 | A |
| E | 16 | B |
| F | 11 | B |
| G | 5 | C |
| H | 12 | D, E |
| I | 2 | G, F |
| J | 22 | I, H |

7. Systems Software (P) Ltd is planning to develop a new software. It has identified the activities given in Table 7.28 for this project, and has estimated three time estimates (in days) for every activity. Find the expected duration of the project and the probability that the project will be completed within 30 days.

**Table 7.28**

| Activity | Description | Predecessor(s) | a | m | b |
|----------|-------------|----------------|---|---|---|
| A | Plan the objectives of the project | – | 1 | 2 | 3 |
| B | Choose the appropriate operating system | A | 3 | 5 | 7 |
| C | Generate algorithm | A | 6 | 10 | 14 |
| D | Choose a suitable programming language (C++/ Java/Basic) | A | 4 | 6 | 8 |
| E | Write the program | B, C, D | 8 | 9 | 10 |
| F | Test the software | E | 2 | 4 | 6 |
| G | Get the approval for commercialization | F | 1 | 3 | 5 |

8. A project has the details given in Table 7.29. The total normal cost = ₹500, cost of supervision = ₹30 per day, and penalty = ₹10 per day over 14 days. Crash the duration of the project and find (a) the duration of the project with minimum total cost and (b) the minimum possible duration of the project.

**Table 7.29**

| Activity | Nodes | Normal time (days) | Crash time (days) | Incremental cost of crashing (₹/day) |
|----------|-------|--------------------|--------------------|--------------------------------------|
| A | 1-3 | 3 | 1 | 60 |
| B | 1-2 | 4 | 3 | 20 |

*(Contd)*

Table 7.29 Contd

| Activity | Nodes | Normal time (days) | Crash time (days) | Incremental cost of crashing (₹/day) |
|----------|-------|-------------------|-------------------|--------------------------------------|
| C | 2-3 | 3 | 2 | 40 |
| D | 2-5 | 5 | 4 | 50 |
| E | 2-4 | 6 | 3 | 30 |
| F | 3-5 | 4 | 3 | 20 |
| G | 4-6 | 5 | 4 | 50 |
| H | 3-6 | 3 | 2 | 40 |
| I | 5-6 | 5 | 4 | 30 |

9. A project has the activities given in Table 7.30. The maximum resources available are 40 men, one of resource 1, and one of resource 2. Prepare an activity resource allocation schedule under the given resource constraints. Find also the duration of the project.

Table 7.30

| Activity | Nodes | Duration (days) | Precedence | Men | Resource 1 | Resource 2 |
|----------|-------|-----------------|------------|-----|------------|------------|
| A | 1-2 | 3 | – | 20 | Yes | No |
| B | 1-3 | 7 | – | 10 | No | Yes |
| C | 1-4 | 6 | – | 10 | Yes | No |
| D | 2-5 | 4 | A | 30 | Yes | No |
| E | 2-7 | 5 | A | 20 | Yes | Yes |
| F | 2-3 | 4 | A | 10 | No | Yes |
| G | 3-4 | 5 | B, F | 10 | Yes | No |
| H | 3-7 | 4 | B, F | 20 | No | Yes |
| I | 4-7 | 2 | C, G | 10 | Yes | Yes |
| J | 4-6 | 4 | C, G | 30 | No | Yes |

10. A building construction project is planned to be completed in three months with a total budget of ₹60 lakh. After Month 1 of implementation, BCWS is estimated at ₹20 lakh. However, ACWP is found to be ₹25 lakh and BCWP is ₹18 lakh at the end of Month1. Calculate the cost variance (CV) and schedule variance (SV). Is the project progressing well?

11. A software development project is planned to be completed in four weeks with a total budget of ₹3 crores. After Week 2 of implementation, BCWS is estimated at ₹1.5 crores. However, ACWP is found to be ₹1.4 crores and BCWP is ₹1.6 crores at the end of Week 2. Calculate the cost variance (CV) and schedule variance (SV). Is the project progressing well?

## Project Assignments

1. Read the following situation and then perform the activities given in the end.

Dileep Narula is the CEO and MD of a Noida-based software exports company—Infozone Ltd. It specializes in database management systems (DBMS). The company has an annual turnover of

₹1,000 million and most of its clients are located in the US and the middle-east. It is facing immediate crisis because some of its regular clients have stopped taking its services because of the economic slowdown in the US. Dileep knows very well that in order to create a new client base for the company, he will have to take some strong marketing measures.

It is 9 a.m. and Dileep is already in his office. He knows his Vice-President (Marketing), Ujjwal Deshpande, also comes to office a bit earlier than the scheduled 10 a.m. He picks up the phone, dials Deshpande's number, and as expected he is there.

*Dileep:* How are you Ujjwal? Can you please come to my office?

*Ujjwal:* Good morning, Sir. I'll be there in a moment.

Ujjwal arrives in Dileep's office in a while.

*Ujjwal:* Good morning, Sir.

*Dileep:* Good morning. Please have a seat.

Ujjwal takes a seat and, looking at Dileep's expression, understands the urgency of the matter.

*Dileep:* Ujjwal, as you are aware, we are losing our clients. What are your suggestions for creating a new client base especially in the US?

*Ujjwal:* I have been thinking a lot during the past couple of days about this matter. I know that we have to create a new awareness about the expertise and competence of our company in the US. The conventional ways of doing so, such as advertising about the services of the company, are not proving worthwhile in the present scenario. I have thought of an innovative way of getting more clients.

*Dileep:* And what is that?

*Ujjwal:* We can hold a national conference on 'Database Management Systems in 2005' in the US. We can invite speakers from leading US Universities and from the US and Indian corporate houses. The speakers can also be from the clients who have left us, and also from potential clients. They can share the benefits gained by their organizations after the implementation of DBMS.

*Dileep:* That is an excellent idea. We can get sponsorships from other organizations also to cover the costs. The company will get good publicity, as the organizers and also we will come across delegates of many concerns, who may become our clients. Ujjwal, you have to plan this project and make this conference a big success. Can you give me the detailed plan by tomorrow morning?

*Ujjwal:* Yes Dileep, I will try my best.

*Dileep:* I think we can schedule the conference on 25 and 26 November this year. I want mails to be dispatched to the speakers by 25 August, with their consent mail deadline mentioned as 20 September. The brochures to be sent to various organizations for delegates can be printed later. I would like to review the progress of the preparations of the conference on 25 September and 15 November.

*Ujjwal:* I will see you tomorrow morning with the project plan.

Ujjwal leaves Dileep's chamber and, on the way to his room, decides to assign the task of making the conference plan to a young MBA he had hired a few days back.

(a) Assume that you are the young MBA hired recently by Ujjwal Deshpande. Prepare the list of tasks, required precedences, required resources, and their duration.

(b) Using Microsoft Project, prepare the project network diagram keeping in view the constraints mentioned in the case.

(c) Perform resource levelling for the entire duration of the project.

2. Find a live construction project in your city. It may be a skyscraper, a flyover, a bridge, or a new factory/plant being constructed. Interact with the project manager and ask him about the techniques he or his superiors have adapted in planning the project. How did they estimate the duration of the project? Did they use CPM/PERT? If not, discuss with them the uses of CPM and PERT. Did they ever crash the project during implementation by adding more resources to it? Are the human resources/equipment requirements uniformly distributed throughout the duration of the project?

## Answers to Objective Questions

| | | | | |
|---|---|---|---|---|
| 1. (d) | 2. (c) | 3. (d) | 4. (a) | 5. True |
| 6. False | 7. True | 8. Total float | 9. crashing | 10. Earned |

# 8

# Inventory Management

## Learning Objectives

After reading this chapter, you will be able to answer the following questions:
- What is an inventory?
- What are the uses of inventory?
- What is the role of other functional departments in inventory management?
- What are the types of costs associated with an inventory?
- How are these costs related to each other?
- How can an inventory be managed by retailers and manufacturers?
- What measures can be taken to avoid stock outs?
- Why do some retailers intentionally create shortages of certain items?
- Do we need to pay strict attention to managing the inventories of all the items in the organization?
- Can we simulate an inventory system to get some useful results?
- How can demand uncertainty be managed for better inventory management?

## Introduction

An inventory is the stock of idle resources in a firm for future use. In organizations, inventories can be of various types. Manufacturing organizations, typically, have inventories of raw materials, components, sub-assemblies (e.g., the headlight assembly for cars at Maruti Udyog Ltd is supplied by Lucas-TVS Ltd), tools and equipment, semi-finished goods, finished goods, etc.

In service organizations, such as banks, financial institutions, hospitals, etc., the inventory consists of various items to be used in the various service operations. For example, hospitals have inventories of medical equipment such as syringes, glucose bottles (drip), etc. and other accessories such as bandages, cotton, spirit, etc. in addition to various types of medicines. In banks, there are inventories of various types of forms (for various banking operations), brochures and pamphlets (for details of various banking instruments), etc. Banks also have inventories of currency notes and coins.

The inventory is maintained by organizations to avoid the stock out of an item. A *stock out*

> A stock out is undesirable for manufacturers because it halts the production process.

is undesirable for manufacturers because it halts the production process. For retailers, a stock out of any item results, first, in the loss of potential profit (which they could gain by selling the product) and, second (more importantly), in the loss of goodwill on part of the customer. A customer who did not get an item in

A low level of inventory may result in shortages or stock outs.

one retail store may go to another, where he gets the item. The customer may start going only to this new store in the future. This results in a reduction in the market share of the first retail store. Hence, a stock out has to be avoided and, therefore, inventories should be maintained at proper levels.

How much should the proper level of the inventory of an item be? This question has to be answered for the inventory of every item. A low level of inventory may result in shortages or stock outs. On the other hand, a high level of inventory has its own disadvantages. A high level of inventory involves tying up of more capital, for which, probably, the interest has to be paid to the bank. Even if the capital employed here is out of the reserves of the company, the opportunity cost of the capital is equivalent to the interest payment (the same capital could be put in a bank to earn interest). Therefore, the inventory of an item should be neither too high nor too less. It should be just optimal, that is, at the best possible level for an item (Exhibit 8.1). There are two questions to be answered by the materials manager:

1. How much should the size of the order placed to the supplier be?
2. When should the order be placed?

There are various inventory management models for answering these questions. Before discussing these models, let us first know the uses of inventory.

---

### Exhibit 8.1    Apollo Tyres

Named after the Greek Sun God, Apollo Tyres has created a niche for itself in the Indian tyre market. After three decades of consistent growth, Apollo Tyres Ltd is India's premier tyre manufacturing company. The company's history dates back to the early nineteen seventies. The company's licence was obtained in 1972 by Mathew T. Marattukalam and Jacob Thomas. In 1974, the company was taken over by Dr Raunaq Singh. The tyre project was implemented in 1976 in Perambra, Kerala. The commercial production began in 1977 with an installed capacity of 4,20,000 tyres and tubes each. Today, the company has four factories and has acquired Dunlop South Africa on 30 January 2006.

The company has been showing impressive results quarter by quarter due to unprecedented growth in the automobile sector in the country. During the first quarter of 2006–07, the high prices of its major raw material, natural rubber, resulted in increasing the overall cost of production. It was not a typical case with Apollo Tyres. All the major players in the industry were affected in the same way. During the later part of this quarter, the rubber prices declined from its peak. Nevertheless, its prices were still higher compared to earlier quarters with an average price of ₹93 per kg. Therefore, the prices were up by about five to ten per cent.

Advance booking of the rubber requirement for a quarter with the suppliers is not possible because it is primarily a spot market. It is not a market where a company can book its entire requirement for a quarter in advance. The ratio between imports and the domestic raw material consumption at Apollo Tyres for a quarter is normally 40:60. Apollo Tyres was holding about 20 days inventory of natural rubber at the starting of the first quarter in 2006–07.

It is interesting to analyse the effect of changes in raw material prices on the company's operations. For example, if rubber prices started cooling off in the second quarter of 2006–07, after how many days or how many months, does it reflect in the company's operations? Apollo Tyres typically stores natural rubber inventory for about fifteen days to three weeks. In this time frame, the figure will be reflected in the profit and loss account of the company. On the other hand, for the raw materials, which are linked to crude materials, the lag could be on an average about a quarter. This is so because all those raw materials are not a direct product of crude. For example, tyre cord is manufactured from caprolactam, which comes from benzene, which in turn comes from crude. Hence, it takes about a quarter for the cost effect to be reflected in the company's financial statements.

In process industries, such as the tyre industry, it is difficult to practice just-in-time (JIT) production system (discussed in the next chapter). Raw material

*(Contd)*

*Exhibit 8.1 Contd*

inventories have to be maintained for 15–20 days in the tyre manufacturing facilities to ensure enough raw materials for a production run as seen above in the case of Apollo Tyres.

The original equipment manufacturers (OEMs) such as car manufacturers are major customers of the tyre industry. These automotive factories pursue JIT production systems and expect their suppliers to supply JIT. Tyre manufacturers often come at the end of the supply chain and are unable to force their suppliers to supply JIT as most of their raw material comes from natural resources such as natural rubber. These natural resources cannot be grown JIT. Hence, inventories are a part and parcel of such process industries.

## Uses of Inventory

Inventory has various uses as shown in Fig. 8.1. Let us discuss these one by one.

**Anticipation inventory**   This is the fundamental use of maintaining the inventory of an item. It is to satisfy the customer demand, that is, to ensure that no customer is disappointed by not getting the desired item at any point of time. Enough inventories of items should exist to meet the expected or anticipated demand of customers.

**Cycle stock**   The inventory manager has to determine the quantities of items to be stocked by using models like the economic order quantity (EOQ) model discussed later. This model minimizes the total cost of inventory. Thus the stock of items stored as inventory to meet an inventory cycle determined by an inventory model is called the *cycle stock*.

> Enough inventories of items should exist to meet the expected or anticipated demand of customers.

**Safety or buffer stock**   To protect against fluctuations of demand and abrupt increases in the time taken by the suppliers to supply the items, some stock

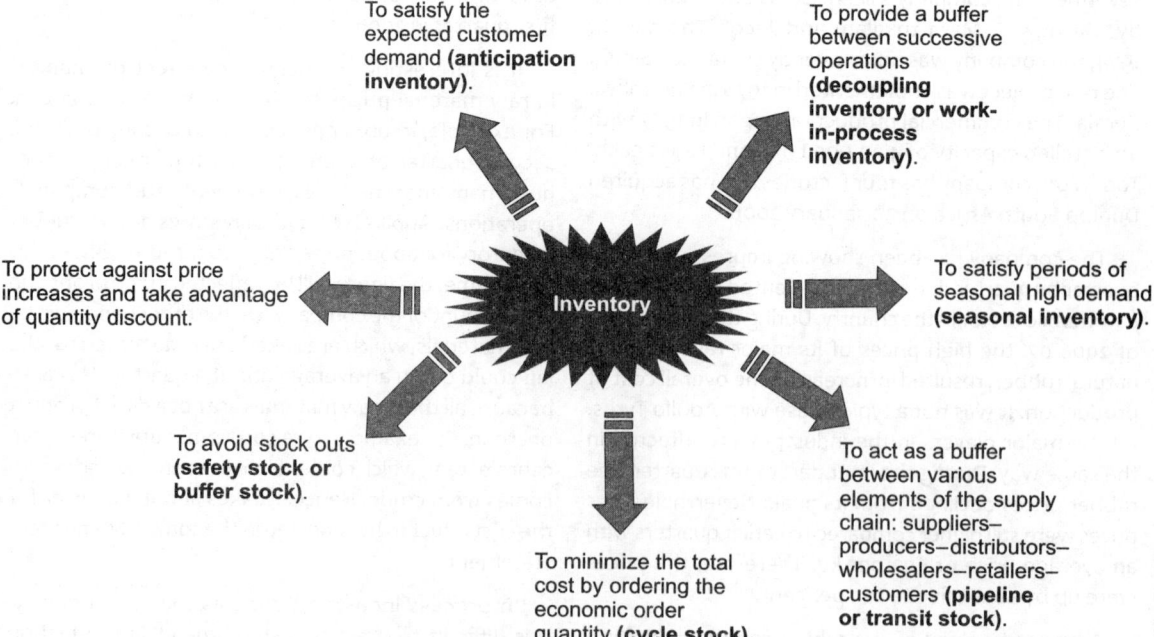

To satisfy the expected customer demand **(anticipation inventory)**.

To provide a buffer between successive operations **(decoupling inventory or work-in-process inventory)**.

To protect against price increases and take advantage of quantity discount.

To satisfy periods of seasonal high demand **(seasonal inventory)**.

To avoid stock outs **(safety stock or buffer stock)**.

To minimize the total cost by ordering the economic order quantity **(cycle stock)**.

To act as a buffer between various elements of the supply chain: suppliers–producers–distributors–wholesalers–retailers–customers **(pipeline or transit stock)**.

**Fig. 8.1**   Uses of inventory

known as the *safety or buffer stock* is maintained in excess of the anticipation inventory.

**Inventory for quantity discounts/future price increases**   Suppliers often offer discounts for bulk purchases. To take advantage of such discounts, organizations opt for large quantities of items, which have to be stored as inventory. In view of expected price increases, organizations go for bulk purchases, to reap the benefits of lower costs of their finished goods compared to those of the competitors in the future. At times it is beneficial to order according to full-truck load, when suppliers are located at distant places. The freight charges are discounted by truck operators if the quantity is enough to fill a truck completely.

**Decoupling or work-in-process inventory**   When operations take place in a sequence, for example, semi-finished goods being operated upon by machines one after the other in sequence, inventories of semi-finished goods pile up near each machine. These inventories are at times desirable, as in the case of a machine breakdown; the remaining machines can continue their operations for some time during which the faulty machine can be corrected. Such inventories are called *decoupling inventories*, as these decouple (de-link) the various processes of operations from each other. Decoupling inventories are becoming less popular, as organizations have realized that these inventories involve a lot of cost, which can be avoided by concentrating more on avoiding breakdowns or reducing the time required to service these breakdowns.

**Seasonal inventory**   Festivals are bonanza time for most organizations, before which preparations in the form of proper inventory of items have to be made to meet the anticipated heavy demand. For example, the Deepawali season witnesses inventories of crackers being piled up by cracker manufacturers, distributors, and so on. Certain types of items are seasonal in nature, for example, umbrellas, raincoats, etc. are required in the rainy season; air conditioners, air coolers, etc. during summers; and heaters, blowers, woollen garments, etc. during winters. Inventories of these items are stocked by firms before the start of the season. Hence, these inventories are called *seasonal inventories*.

**Pipeline or transit stock**   When stocks are moved between the various elements of the supply chain, that is, between suppliers, manufacturers, distributors, wholesalers, and the end customers, they are called *pipeline* or *transit stock*. During the transportation period between two places, these stocks do not serve any purpose. Therefore, organizations try to reduce the transit (movement) time of these stocks as much as possible.

## Role of Other Functional Departments

In an organization, no department can operate in complete isolation. The various departments have to support each other for successful functioning. As shown in Fig. 8.2, the materials department gets various types of support from other departments, namely, the finance department, the marketing department, the human resources department, and the information systems department. A big organization normally has a separate purchasing department, materials department, quality-control department, engineering department, manufacturing department, etc. For the sake of simplicity, in Fig. 8.2, we have not shown the role of these departments, which are closely intertwined with the materials department.

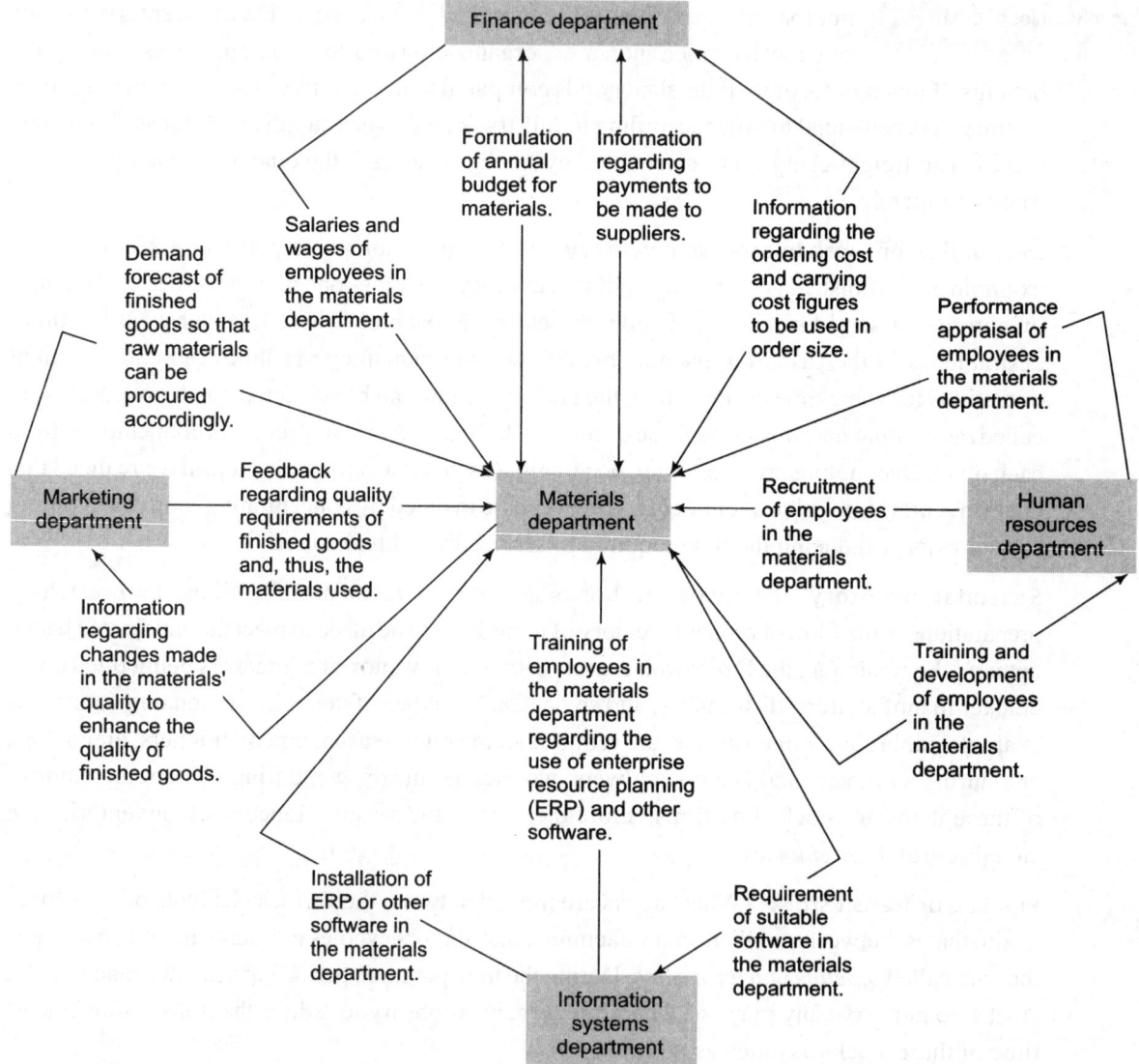

**Fig. 8.2**  Role of other functional departments in inventory management

## Types of Costs

There are basically two types of costs related to inventories. These are
1. ordering cost, and
2. carrying or holding cost.

## Ordering Cost

Ordering cost (OC) per order is the cost of placing a single order. The purchase department of the organization is responsible for placing orders to the suppliers. The purchase department incurs the following costs every year:

- salary to the employees
- cost of miscellaneous office items such as stationery, postage, etc. and expenses such as telephone bills, electricity bills, internet expenses, etc.
- rent of the office space where the department is located (or the opportunity cost if the office space is owned, that is, the space could be lent to any other company to earn rent)
- opportunity cost of furniture, computers, software, hardware, etc.

It is found that approximately 80 per cent of the purchase department costs are for placing orders, following up, and receiving of materials. Approximately 25 per cent of the stationery used in the purchase department is prorated (allocated) for the paper used for processing purchase orders (POs). Likewise, other expenses such as telephone, telex, Internet, and postage can also be prorated based on the share of these costs involved in order processing. All these costs can be summed up for the previous financial year. The sum is divided by the total number of orders placed in that year. The result is the OC per order, to be used for calculations related to inventory in the current year. The figure is only a rough estimate of the average OC, which is not appropriate for our calculation. Instead, we require the marginal or incremental cost of placing an order. In other words, we need the amount by which the OC would increase if we placed one more order per period, or the amount we would save if we placed one less order per period.

Most of the purchase department costs are fixed costs (office space, computers, furniture, staff on contracts, etc.) and, hence, are not affected by the placement of one more order. Therefore, we should not consider any fixed costs in the calculation of the OC per order, but only the variable costs (such as telephone, telex, Internet, postage, stationery, etc.). In the marginal method, simple linear regression would be the most straightforward technique to separate fixed OCs from variable OCs, where the estimated regression line would be

$$\text{Total estimated OC} = \text{Fixed OC} + (\text{Variable OC per order}) \times (\text{Number of orders}) \quad (8.1)$$

In regression analysis, we plot all the given values on a graph by plotting the number of orders on the *x*-axis and the relevant expenditure along the *y*-axis. Then, we find a best-fit line (a straight line) for the given data called the regression line. This line is based upon the least-squares method, which will be used by MS Excel automatically in our calculations. In symbolic form, the regression equation is written as

$$y = a + bx$$

This is the equation of a straight line. Here *y* is the total estimated OC, *a* is the fixed OC, *b* is the variable OC per order, and *x* is the number of orders.

> Ordering cost (OC) per order is the cost of placing a single order.

> Most of the purchase department costs are fixed costs and, hence, are not affected by the placement of one more order.

The marginal cost per order can be calculated using regression analysis as explained in the following example.

### Example 8.1

Table 8.1 shows data to be used for calculating OC using the marginal method. A similar approach can be used to demonstrate the effect on carying cost.

**Table 8.1**

| Year | No. of orders (x) | Relevant expenditure (y) (₹) |
|------|------|------|
| 1 | 2,563 | 38,05,715 |
| 2 | 2,986 | 41,94,269 |
| 3 | 3,297 | 43,31,260 |

Fill in the values of x (number of orders) and y (relevant expenditure) for the three years in columns A and B of an MS Excel worksheet, as shown in Fig. 8.3. Click on the **Tools** option on the toolbar. Select **Data Analysis** from the pull-down menu. If the **Data Analysis** option is not available, select **Add-Ins**. The dialog box shown in Fig. 8.4 appears on screen. Select the check box for **Analysis ToolPak** and click on **OK**. Now select the **Data Analysis** option from the pull-down menu of **Tools**. The dialog box shown in Fig. 8.5 appears.

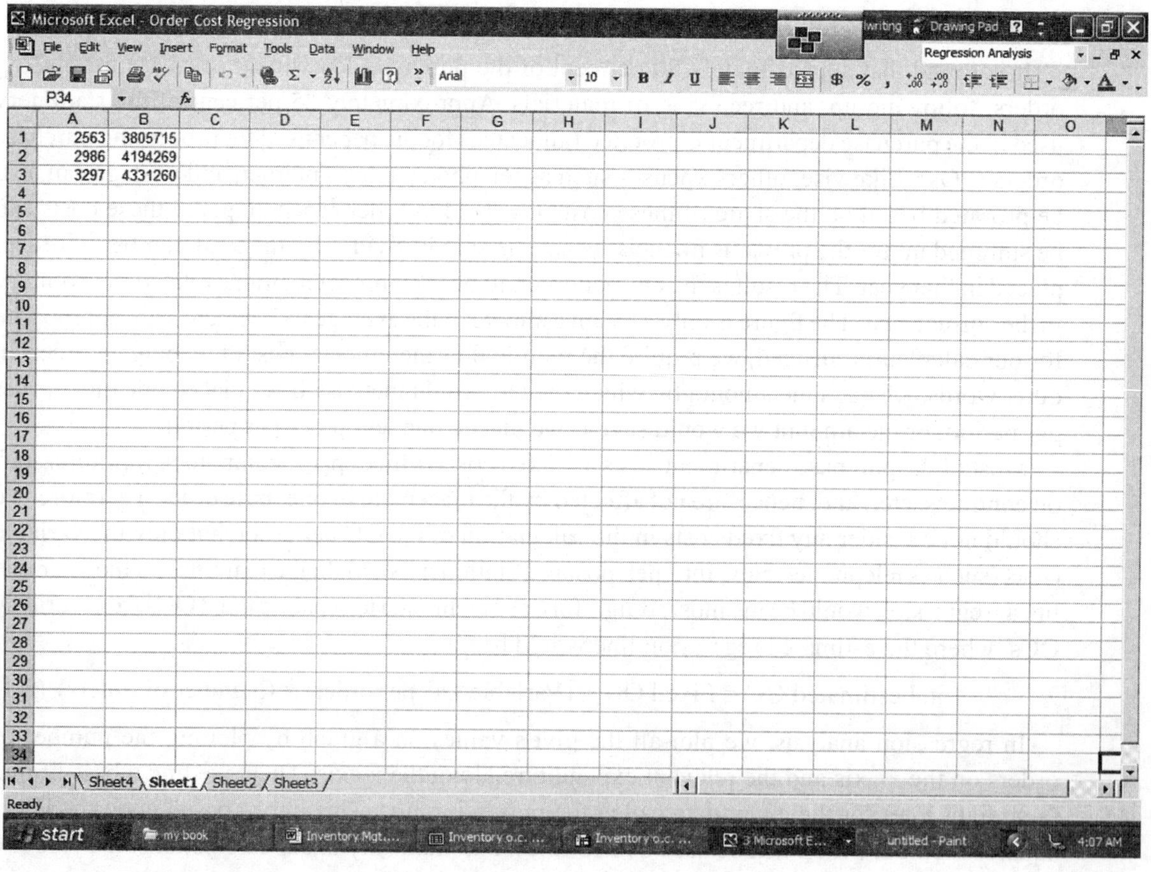

**Fig. 8.3**   Calculation of ordering costs

In Fig. 8.5 choose **Regression** from the list of **Analysis Tools** and click on **OK**. The dialog box shown in Fig. 8.6 appears. Select column B in Fig. 8.3 by clicking on cell B1 and then dragging the cursor down to cell B3. Click on the button with the arrow alongside the text box for **Input Y Range:** in the dialog box of Fig. 8.6. The values **$B$1:$B$3** automatically appear in this text box. Repeat this procedure by selecting column A, so that values **$A$1:$A$3** appear in the **Input X Range:** text box. In the **Output options**, the **New Worksheet Ply:** radio button is selected by default. Let it remain as it is. In the **Residuals** select the check box of **Line Fit Plots** and then click on **OK**. The screen shown in Fig. 8.7 appears.

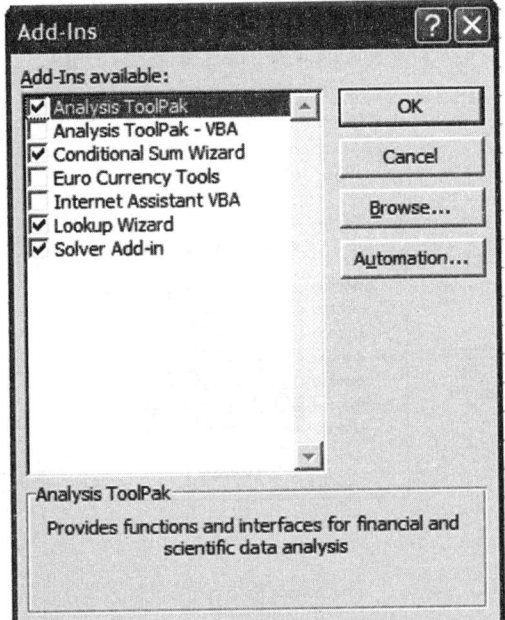

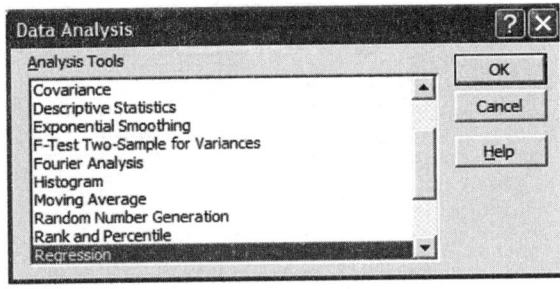

**Fig. 8.4** Add-Ins dialog box

**Fig. 8.5** Data Analysis dialog box

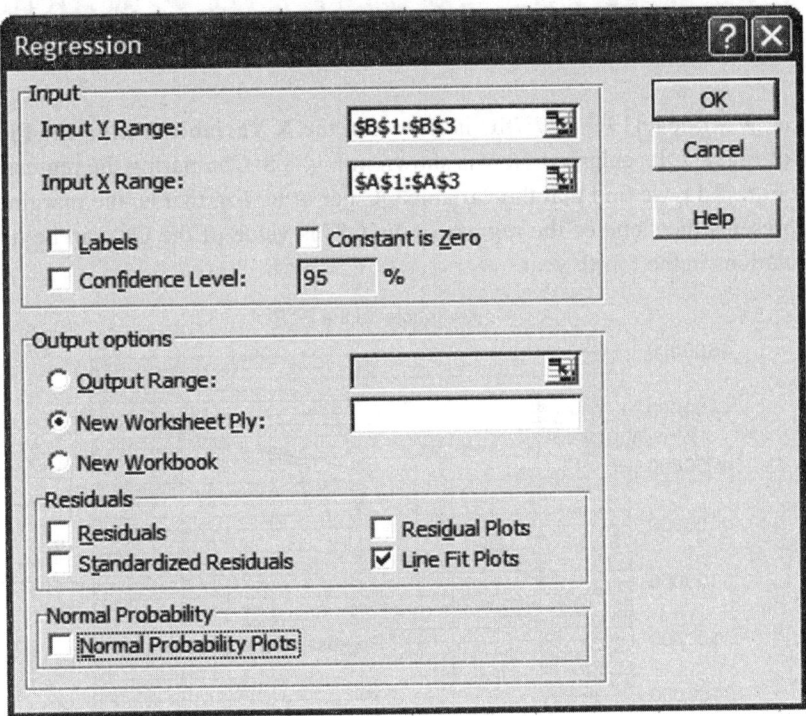

**Fig. 8.6** Regression dialog box

In Fig. 8.7, the values in cells B17 and B18 are useful to us. These are the values of constants $a$ and $b$ in the regression equation. Thus, $a = 19,64,419$ and $b = 727.7861$. The regression equation $y = a + bx$,

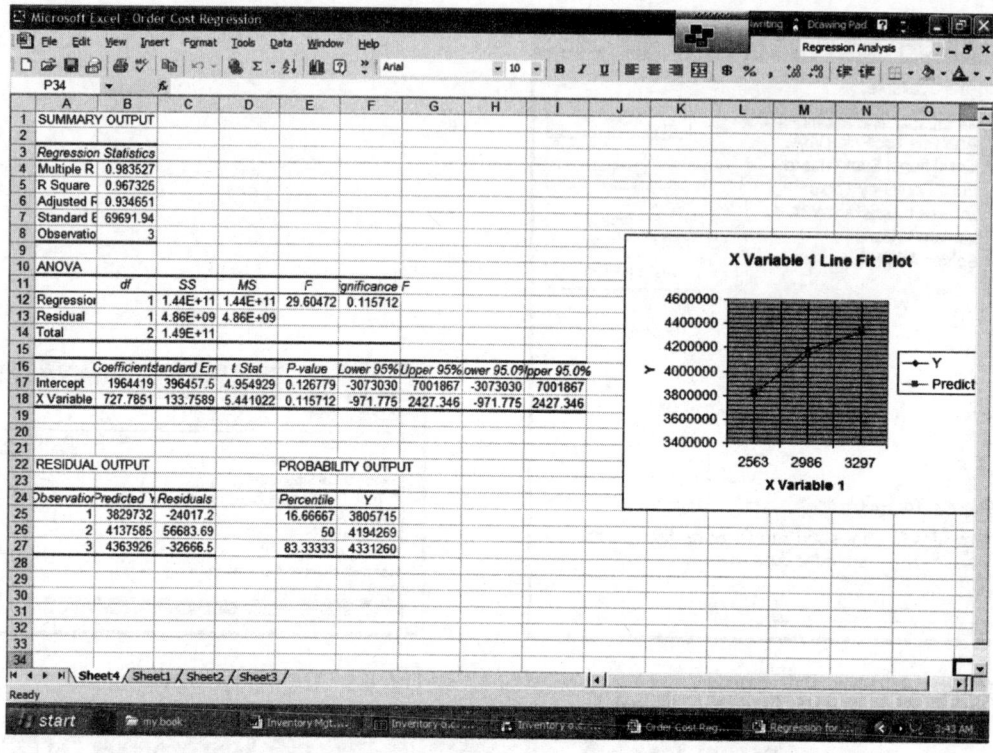

**Fig. 8.7** Regression analysis in MS Excel

that is, $y = 19,64,419 + 727.78x$, is shown in the **X Variable 1 Line Fit Plot** shown on the right side of Fig. 8.7. Its enlarged view is shown in Fig. 8.8. Comparing the regression equation obtained with Eqn (8.1), we find that the variable OC per order ($a$), that is, the marginal OC, is ₹727.78 and it represents the slope of the regression line. This value of the OC can be used for inventory cost calculations in the fourth year.

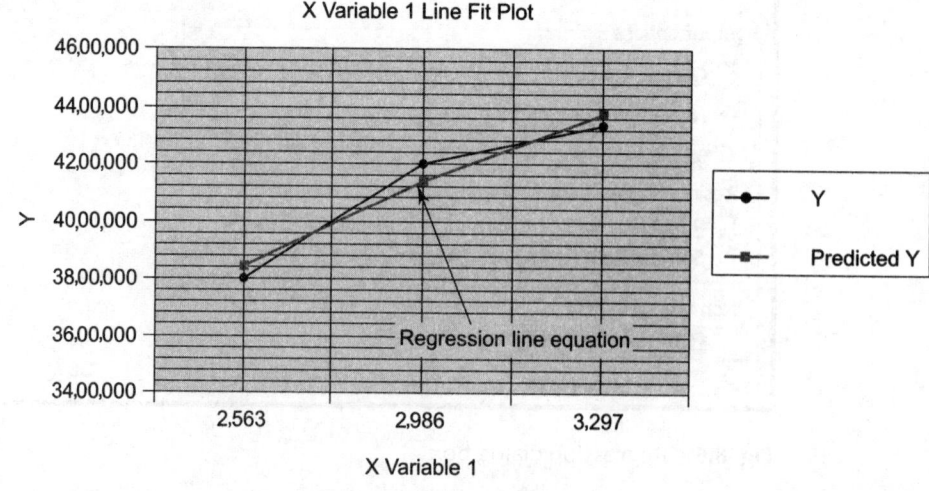

**Fig. 8.8** Enlarged view of the regression equation

### Carrying/Holding Cost

Carrying cost (CC) is the cost of storing the inventory in the warehouse. It consists of

- the rent of the warehouse (or the opportunity cost of the warehouse, if it is owned by the company; the company could have given the warehouse to any other company on rent)
- cost of capital tied up in inventory (interest charges or the opportunity cost)
- maintenance cost of the warehouse, such as electricity, air conditioning (if required for perishable items), security, etc.
- cost of damages (if items get damaged by mishandling)
- cost of obsolescence (if during the storage period of items, the demand for these items in the market gets exhausted due to some better or substitute products introduced by the competitors)

As explained in the marginal OC calculation, the marginal CC should be calculated using regression analysis. Regression analysis separates the fixed CC from the variable CC. In inventory CC calculations, only the variable marginal CC value should be used. CC can be expressed in two ways:

1. Money spent in carrying a unit item for unit duration (say, one year) in the warehouse.
2. Percentage of (monetary) value of the average inventory during a given period of time (say, one year). For example, if 100 items are stored on an average for one year and each item costs ₹2, the value of the average inventory will be ₹2 × 100 = ₹200. The CC can be expressed as 5% of the average inventory value, that is, 5% of ₹200 = ₹10.

## Inventory Management Systems

As shown in Fig. 8.9, there are basically two types of inventory management systems: *independent demand and dependent demand*. Let us take up an example to understand these systems. Consider a motorbike manufacturing company which has to perform the demand forecasting of motorbikes for future months. For the next month, the demand forecast is, say, 2,000 motorbikes. In a motorbike, two tyres, one speedometer, and four side-indicator lights are used. Therefore, the company orders 4,000 tyres (2,000 × 2), 2,000 speedometers (2,000 × 1), and 8,000 side-indicator lights (2,000 × 4) to its suppliers. Thus the demand of tyres, speedometers, and side-indicator lights is dependent upon the demand of motorbikes. Therefore, the inventory of these items is called *dependent demand inventory* and the inventory management system (IMS) is aptly called *dependent demand* IMS. On the other hand, the demand of motorbikes is determined directly by the demand forecast and is not dependent upon the demand of any other item. Hence, the inventory of motorbikes here is called *independent demand inventory* and its IMS is called *independent demand* IMS.

Dependent demand inventory is defined as the inventory of items that are the components, parts, or sub-assemblies of finished goods. Independent demand inventory is defined as the inventory of finished goods.

> Carrying cost (CC) is the cost of storing the inventory in the warehouse

As shown in Fig. 8.9, dependent demand IMS can be of three types, namely, material requirements planning (MRP), just-in-time (JIT), or a hybrid of the two. We will discuss these systems in detail in Chapter 9. Here we will focus on independent demand IMS only.

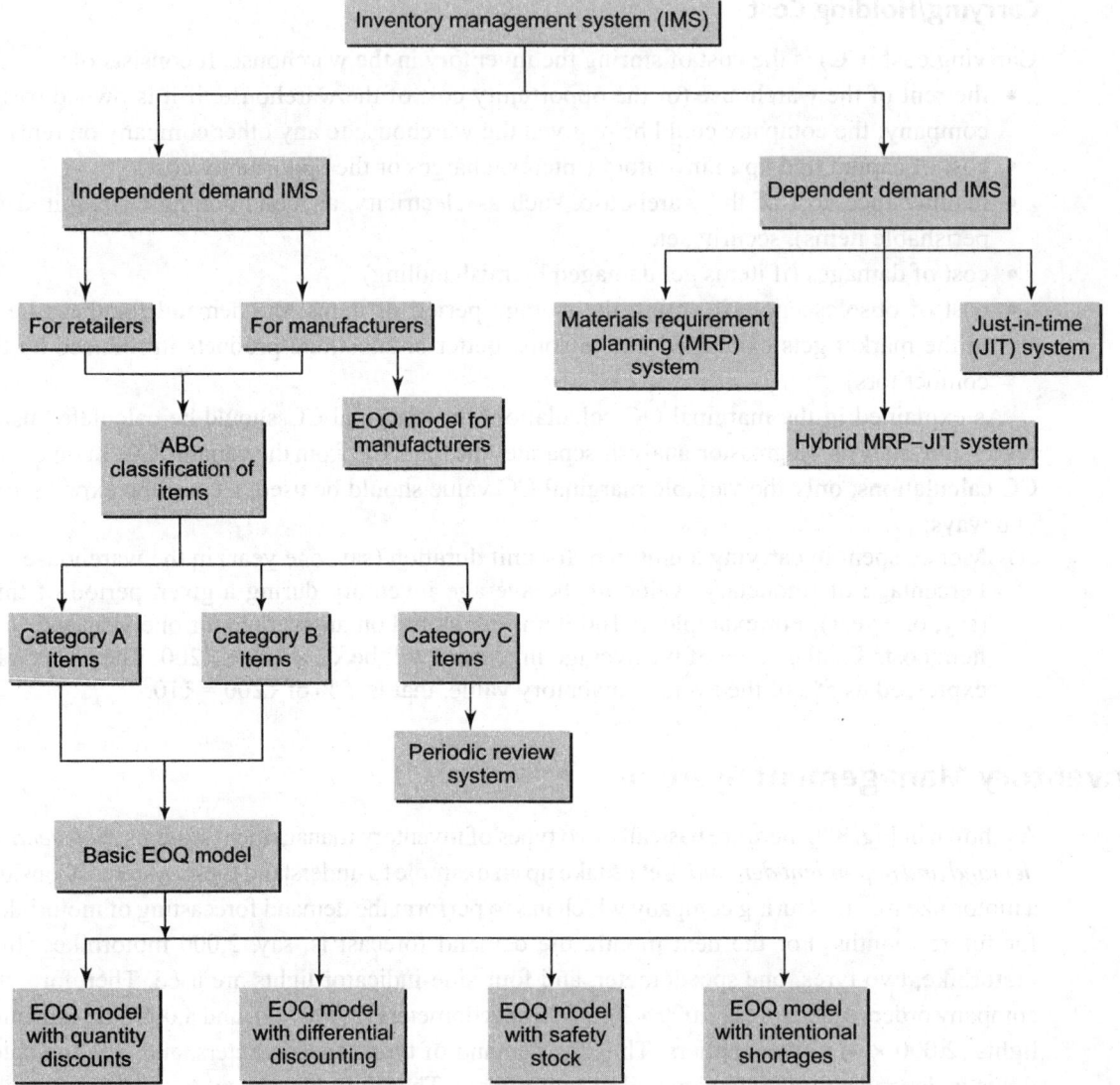

**Fig. 8.9** Types of inventory management systems

Independent demand systems can be further categorized into two categories: 'for retailers' and 'for manufacturers'. For manufacturers, we will study the production economic order quantity (EOQ) model, which is an extension of the basic EOQ model. For retailers as well as manufacturers, items have to be categorized into three classes, A, B, and C, according to the level of inventory control to be exercised with their inventories (*ABC classification*). Category A and B items require a stricter inventory control than category C items. Therefore, category C items are subjected to a *periodic review system*. Category A and B items are dealt with using the basic EOQ model, which can be classified further into the following types depending upon the requirements:

1. EOQ with quantity discounts
2. EOQ with differential discounting

3. EOQ with safety stock
4. EOQ with intentional shortages

We will first discuss the basic EOQ model and then its extensions, including the EOQ model for manufacturers, followed by the ABC analysis. Eventually, we will take up Monte Carlo simulation, which is a generic technique and can be applied to inventory management for getting useful results.

### Retailer's Model of Inventory Management (EOQ Model)

The EOQ model is based on the following assumptions:
1. The annual demand of the item is constant and known.
2. The annual demand of the item is uniformly distributed throughout the year. This means that the consumption takes place at a constant rate. For example, if the annual demand for an item is 3,650 units, then the rate of consumption is 10 units per day, considering there are 365 days in the year. Practically, it is not possible that every day exactly 10 units are demanded, neither more nor less. This is a simplifying assumption in the model.
3. The lead time is zero. *Lead time* is the time gap between placing the order and receiving the items from the supplier. In practical situations, the supplier always takes some time to supply the goods. This is an assumption to simplify the understanding of the model. Here it is assumed that the supplier supplies as soon as the order is placed.

Let $A$ be the annual demand, $Q$ the economic order quantity (the optimal size of the order, for which the total inventory cost is the minimum), $o$ the OC (in ₹) per order, and $c$ the CC (in ₹) per unit per year.

Figure 8.10 shows the relationship between time and the level of inventory for the EOQ model. The first order is placed for $Q$ items and the goods are supplied immediately by the supplier, as the lead time is zero. At time instant 0, the inventory level builds up to its maximum at $Q$ items.

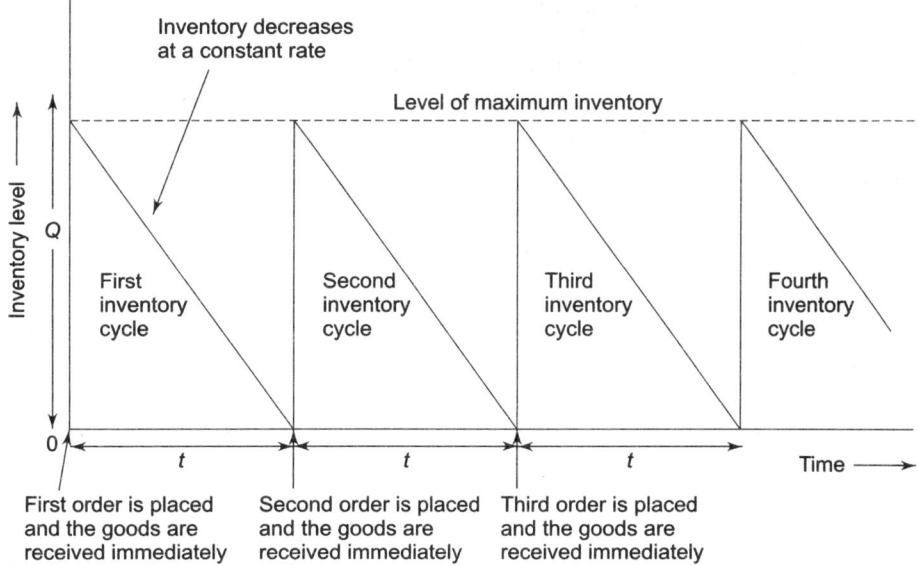

**Fig. 8.10** Relationship between time and the level of inventory in the EOQ model

As time progresses, the inventory level starts decreasing at a constant rate (see the constant downward slope in Fig. 8.10) due to the uniform consumption rate.

Eventually after time $t$, the inventory becomes zero. $t$ is called the *cycle time* of an inventory cycle. The second order is placed and, again, the supplier immediately supplies the goods. The inventory again builds to the maximum. These cycles continue further.

The level of inventory keeps on changing continuously with the passage of time. Therefore, we have to find the average inventory during one year. Let us take up an example. Assume that the level of inventory is constant throughout the year at 100 units and the CC per unit is ₹3 per year. This situation is depicted in Fig. 8.11.

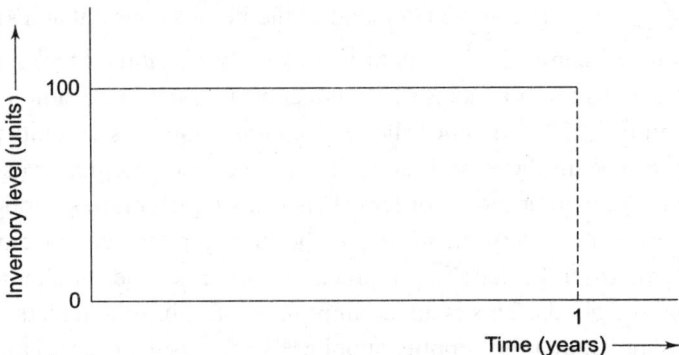

**Fig. 8.11**

In this situation, the total annual CC is ₹3 per unit × 100 units = ₹300. We see that it is very easy to find the annual CC in this situation. In our EOQ model, if we find the average level of inventory during the year, the annual CC can be calculated exactly as shown above. The average inventory can be calculated as follows:

$$\text{Average inventory} = \frac{\text{Maximum inventory} + \text{Minimum inventory}}{2}$$

In Fig. 8.10, the minimum inventory = 0. Therefore,

$$\text{Average inventory} = \frac{\text{Maximum inventory} + 0}{2} = \frac{\text{Maximum inventory}}{2}$$

Here the maximum inventory is $Q$ items. Therefore,

$$\text{Average inventory} = \frac{Q}{2}$$

$$\text{Annual CC} = \text{Average inventory} \times \text{CC per unit per year}$$

$$= \frac{Q}{2} \times c$$

$$\text{Annual OC} = \text{No. of orders per year} \times \text{OC per order}$$

$$= \frac{A\,(\text{units}/\text{year})}{Q\,(\text{units}/\text{order})} \times o\,(₹/\text{order})$$

$$= \frac{A}{Q}\,(\text{order}/\text{year}) \times o\,(₹/\text{order}) \quad = \frac{A}{Q} \times o\,(₹/\text{year})$$

Total annual inventory cost $(T)$ = Annual OC + Annual CC

$$= \frac{Ao}{Q} + \frac{Qc}{2}$$

Costs are minimized by the managers in an organization. Therefore, we have to minimize the total inventory cost $T$. The derivation below shows how $T$ can be minimized using differential calculus. However, as managers, we need not know this derivation; its end result is more useful.

$$T = \frac{Ao}{Q} + \frac{Qc}{2}$$

The first differential coefficient of $T$ with respect to $Q$ is

$$\frac{dT}{dQ} = -\frac{Ao}{Q^2} + \frac{c}{2}$$

The second differential coefficient of $T$ with respect to $Q$ is

$$\frac{d^2T}{dQ^2} = \frac{2Ao}{Q^3}$$

This is positive, implying that $T$ is minimum. To find the condition for minimization of $T$, equate the first differential coefficient to zero:

$$\frac{dT}{dQ} = 0 \qquad \Rightarrow \qquad -\frac{Ao}{Q^2} + \frac{c}{2} = 0$$

$$\Rightarrow \qquad -\frac{Ao}{Q^2} = -\frac{c}{2} \qquad \Rightarrow \qquad \frac{Ao}{Q} = \frac{Qc}{2}$$

$$\Rightarrow \qquad \text{Total OC } (P) = \text{Total CC } (R)$$

Therefore, the total inventory cost is minimum only when the total OC is equal to the total CC.

$$\frac{Ao}{Q} = \frac{Qc}{2} \qquad \Rightarrow \qquad Q^2 = \frac{2Ao}{c}$$

$$\Rightarrow \qquad Q = \sqrt{\frac{2Ao}{c}}$$

This is the expression for the economic order quantity $Q$. It is so called because when this quantity is ordered, it is most economical with respect to the total inventory cost.

Let us take up an example here. Assume that for an item, $A$ = 10,000 units, $o$ = ₹8 per order, $c$ = ₹4 unit per year. For EOQ, total OC $(P)$ = total CC$(R)$

$$\Rightarrow \qquad \frac{Ao}{Q} = \frac{Qc}{2} \qquad \Rightarrow \qquad \frac{10,000}{Q} \times 8 = \frac{Q}{2} \times 4$$

$$\Rightarrow \qquad Q^2 = 40,000 \qquad \therefore \qquad Q = 200 \text{ units}$$

The optimal number of orders per year = $A/Q$ = 10,000/200 = 50.

Tables 8.2(a) and 8.2(b) show the calculation of total CC and total inventory cost $(T)$ for the following values of number of orders in a year: 20, 40, 50, 80, and 100.

**Table 8.2(a)**  Calculation of total CC

| No. of orders (n) | Maximum inventory (Q = A/n) | Average inventory (Qc/2) | Total CC (Q/2) (₹) |
|---|---|---|---|
| 20 | 500 | 250 | 1,000 |
| 40 | 250 | 125 | 500 |
| 50 | 200 | 100 | 400 |
| 80 | 125 | 62.5 | 250 |
| 100 | 100 | 50 | 200 |

**Table 8.2(b)**  Calculation of total inventory cost

| No. of orders (n) | Total OC (₹) | Total CC (₹) | Total inventory cost (T) (₹) |
|---|---|---|---|
| 20 | 160 | 1,000 | 1,160 |
| 40 | 320 | 500 | 820 |
| **50** | **400** | **400** | **800** |
| 80 | 640 | 250 | 910 |
| 100 | 800 | 200 | 1,000 |

From Table 8.2(b) note that the total inventory cost is minimum at ₹800 for 50 orders in a year. Observe also that $T$ is minimum only when

$$P = R = ₹400$$

Using the above table, let us make a graph to understand the relationship between the three types of costs, namely, $P$, $R$, $T$, and the number of orders in a year. Copy Table 8.2(b) and paste it in an MS Excel worksheet as shown in Fig. 8.12. Select all the columns in the worksheet and then click on the **Insert** menu in the toolbar. From the pull-down menu, select **chart**. A chart wizard guides us through to get the chart shown in Fig. 8.13.

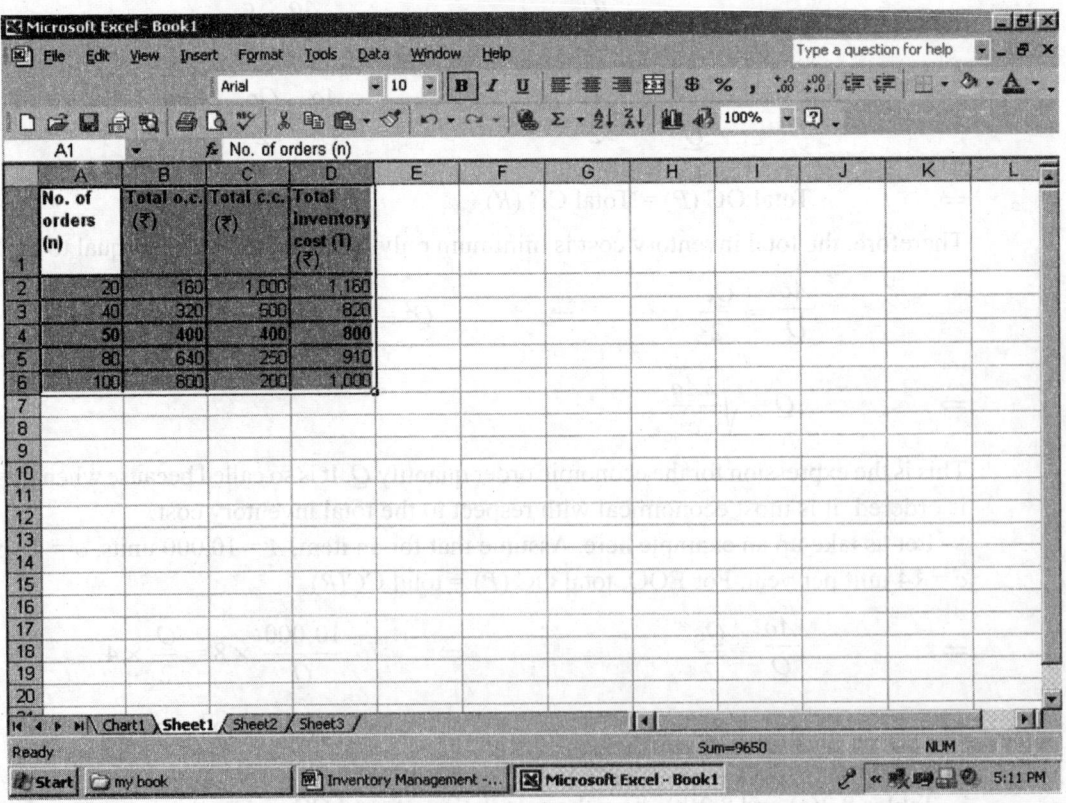

**Fig. 8.12**

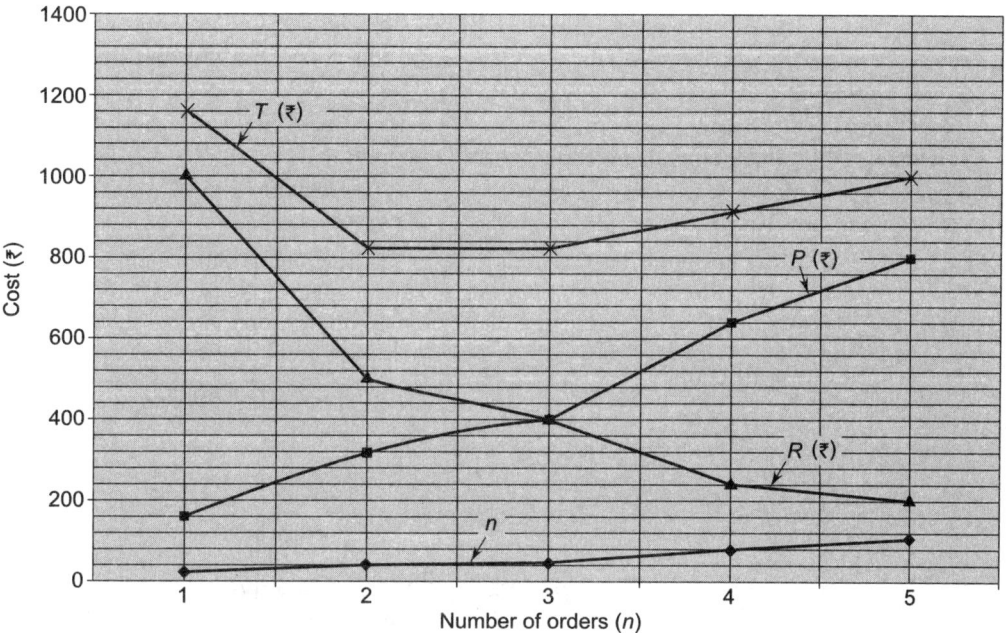

**Fig. 8.13**   Cost vs number of orders

From the graph in Fig. 8.13, we notice the following:

1. As $n$ increases, $P$ increases.
2. As $n$ increases, $R$ decreases.
3. As $n$ increases, $T$ first decreases, then reaches a minimum value (for 50 orders, where $P = R = ₹400$), and eventually starts increasing.

### *Example 8.2*

Yantra India Ltd is a supplier of speedometers to Speed Auto Ltd—manufacturers of 60 cc two-wheelers. It supplies 20,000 speedometers to Speed Auto annually. At Speed Auto, the OC per order is ₹5 and the CC is 2.5% of the average inventory value. The price of a single unit is ₹200. The company presently has a policy of placing 10 orders every year. Advise the management of Speed Auto as to whether it should continue with its present policy or switch over to the EOQ model.

### *Solution*

$A = 20,000$ units; $o = ₹5$; $c = 2.5\%$ of inventory value; price per unit $= ₹200$.

Whenever the CC is given as a percentage, convert it into ₹ per unit per year. Let us say there is a single speedometer to be stored in the inventory for one year. The inventory value (monetary) in this case will be ₹200, that is, the price of a single speedometer (one unit).

$$2.5\% \text{ of inventory value} = 2.5\% \text{ of } ₹200 = \frac{2.5}{100} \times 200 = ₹5$$

Therefore, the CC is ₹5 per unit per year.

Let us do the inventory cost calculations for the current inventory policy: 20,000 items are procured in 10 orders in a year. Therefore the company procures $20,000/10 = 2,000$ items per order, which becomes the maximum inventory to be stored. The average inventory to be stored $= 2,000/2 = 1,000$ units. Therefore,

$$\text{Total (annual) CC, } R = \text{Average inventory} \times CC$$
$$= 1,000 \times ₹5 = ₹5,000$$

Total (annual) OC, $P$, for placing 10 orders $= no$
$$= 10 \times ₹5 = ₹50$$

Hence,  Total (annual) inventory cost $(T) = P + R$
$$= ₹50 + ₹5,000$$

$\therefore$  $T_{existing} = ₹5,050$

Let us now do the inventory cost calculations for the EOQ model, in which

$$P = R \qquad \Rightarrow \qquad \frac{Ao}{Q} = \frac{Qc}{2}$$

$$\Rightarrow \qquad \frac{20,000 \times 5}{Q} = \frac{Q \times 5}{2} \qquad \Rightarrow \qquad Q^2 = 40,000$$

$\therefore$  $Q = 200$ units

Now,  $R = \dfrac{Qc}{2} = \dfrac{200 \times 5}{2} = ₹500$

$$P = \frac{Ao}{Q} = \frac{20,000 \times 5}{200} = ₹500$$

$$T = P + R = ₹500 + ₹500$$

$\therefore$  $T_{EOQ} = ₹1,000$

Clearly,

$$T_{EOQ} < T_{existing}$$

The management of the company should be advised to immediately switch over to the EOQ model.

### Example 8.3

Zen Bicycles Ltd sources 3,000 seat covers for its bicycles from an outside supplier. The OC is ₹10 per order and the CC is ₹6 per unit per year. The company has 300 working days per year. Find the (a) EOQ, (b) number of orders per year, (c) total inventory cost, (d) number of inventory cycles in a year, and (e) the duration of an inventory cycle.

### Solution

(a) Here, $A = 3,000$; $o = ₹10$ per order; $c = ₹6$ per unit per year. For EOQ

$$P = R \qquad \Rightarrow \qquad \frac{Ao}{Q} = \frac{Qc}{2}$$

$$\Rightarrow \qquad \frac{3,000 \times 10}{Q} = \frac{Q \times 6}{2} \qquad \Rightarrow \qquad Q^2 = 10,000$$

$\therefore$  $Q = 100$ units

(b) Number of orders per year $= \dfrac{A}{Q} = \dfrac{3,000}{100} = 30$

(c)  $R = \dfrac{Qc}{2} = \dfrac{100 \times 6}{2} = ₹300$

$\therefore$  $P = R = ₹300$

$$T = P + R = ₹300 + ₹300$$

$$T_{EOQ} = ₹600$$

(d) Number of inventory cycles in a year = Number of orders per year = 30

(e) Duration of one iventory cycle = $\dfrac{Q}{A}$ = $\dfrac{100 \text{ units}}{3,000 \text{ units/year}}$ = $\dfrac{1}{30}$ year

$$= \dfrac{300}{30} \text{ days} = 10 \text{ days}$$

The duration can also be calculated in another way. The maximum inventory of $Q = 100$ units is consumed at a constant rate of 10 units per day. This constant rate can be calculated as follows. The annual demand is 3,000 units and there are 300 working days in a year. Therefore, the demand per day = 3,000/300 = 10 units. Hence the maximum inventory of $Q = 100$ units will last for

$$\dfrac{100 \text{ units/cycle}}{10 \text{ units/day}} = 10 \text{ days/cycle}$$

Therefore the duration of one inventory cycle = 10 days.

**Quantity discounts**  It is a common observation while purchasing items that suppliers offer discounts on bulk purchases. They specify a particular percentage of discount if items equal to or more than a particular quantity are purchased. Hence, such discounts are called *quantity discounts*.

The purchaser has to compare the EOQ model with the discount option, that is, the total inventory costs are compared in both the options. The option having the lower total inventory cost is selected and adopted.

### Example 8.4

Trinity Hospital at Bangalore sources 20,000 disposable syringes every year from a supplier. The OC per order is ₹100 and the CC is ₹1 per unit per year. The price of a syringe is ₹5. The supplier offers a 5% discount if purchases are made in lots of 10,000 syringes or more. Determine whether the discount model is better than the EOQ model in this situation.

### Solution

$A = 20,000$ units; $o = $ ₹100 per order; $c = $ ₹1 per unit per year; price per unit = ₹5.

**EOQ model:**

$$P = R$$

$\Rightarrow \qquad \dfrac{Ao}{Q} = \dfrac{Qc}{2} \qquad \Rightarrow \qquad \dfrac{20,000 \times 100}{Q} = \dfrac{Q \times 1}{2}$

$\Rightarrow \qquad Q^2 = 4,000,000 \qquad \therefore \qquad\qquad\qquad Q = 2,000$ units

Now, $\qquad\qquad R = \dfrac{Qc}{2} = \dfrac{2,000 \times 1}{2} = \text{Rs } 1,000$

$$P = R = ₹1,000$$

$$\text{Cost of syringes} = 20,000 \times ₹5$$

$$= ₹1,00,000$$

$$\text{Total cost, } T_{\text{EOQ}} = \text{Cost of syringes} + P + R$$

$$= ₹1,00,000 + ₹1,000 + ₹1,000$$

$$= ₹1,02,000$$

**Discount model:**

$A = 20,000$ units. Therefore, two orders (of 10,000 units each) can be placed to get 20,000 units in a year.

$$P = \text{Number of orders} \times \text{OC per order}$$
$$= 2 \times ₹100 = ₹200$$

Maximum inventory = 10,000 units (because in one order 10,000 units will be supplied by the supplier)

$$\text{Average inventory} = \frac{\text{Maximum inventory}}{2} = \frac{10,000}{2} = 5,000 \text{ units}$$

$$R = \text{Average inventory} \times \text{CC per unit per year}$$
$$= 5,000 \times ₹1 = ₹5,000$$

Now, Cost of 20,000 syringes = ₹1,00,000

Discount @ 5% = 5% of ₹1,00,000

$$= \frac{5}{100} \times 1,00,000 = ₹5,000$$

Therefore,

Net cost of 20,000 syringes after discount = ₹1,00,000 – ₹5,000 = ₹95,000

Total cost after discount, $T_{\text{discount}}$ = Net cost of 20,000 syringes + $P + R$
$$T = ₹95,000 + ₹200 + ₹5,000$$
$$= ₹1,00,200$$

$$\therefore \qquad T_{\text{discount}} < T_{\text{EOQ}}$$

Hence, the hospital should implement the discount model.

---

**Differential discounting**    A supplier may offer different discounts for different quantities of an item. This is called *differential discounting*. In this situation, every discount option and the EOQ option are considered separately and the associated total cost is calculated. Then, a comparison of the total cost for the different options is made. The option with the least total cost is selected and adopted by the company.

### Example 8.5

Microcosm Softwares Ltd sources 9,000 blank CDs annually from a supplier. The OC per order is ₹10 and each CD costs ₹20. The CC is 10% of the CD price. The supplier offers the following discounts:

| Quantity | Discount |
|----------|----------|
| 100–449 | 2% |
| 450–899 | 4% |
| 900 and above | 5% |

Evaluate the various discount options and also the EOQ option, and advise the management of Microcosm about the best inventory policy for CDs.

### Solution

$A = 9,000$ units; $o = ₹10$ per order; price per CD = ₹20; $c = 10\%$ of item price = 10% of ₹20 = 10/100 $\times 20 = ₹2$ per unit per year.

**EOQ model:**

$$P = R$$

$$\Rightarrow \quad \frac{Ao}{Q} = \frac{Qc}{2} \qquad \Rightarrow \qquad \frac{9,000 \times 10}{Q} = \frac{Q \times 2}{2}$$

$$\Rightarrow \quad Q^2 = 90,000 \qquad \therefore \qquad Q = 300 \text{ units}$$

Now, $\quad R = \dfrac{Qc}{2} = \dfrac{300 \times 2}{2} = ₹300$

$P = R = ₹300$

Cost of CDs (@ ₹20 each) = $9{,}000 \times ₹20 = ₹1{,}80{,}000$

Since the EOQ of 300 units falls in the range 100–449 units, a 2% discount on ₹1,80,000— ₹3,600—will be availed. Therefore, the net cost of 9,000 CDs after discount is ₹1,80,000 – ₹3,600 = ₹1,76,400.

$\therefore \qquad T_{EOQ} = $ Net cost of CDs $+ P + R$

$\qquad\qquad = ₹1{,}76{,}400 + ₹300 + ₹300 = ₹1{,}77{,}000 \qquad\qquad (8.2)$

**2% discount option:**

For 100–449 units, a discount of 2% is available. We consider the lower limit, that is, 100 CDs in an order for availing the 2% discount. Therefore, 90 orders of 100 CDs each have to be placed in a year to get 9,000 CDs. The maximum inventory is 100 CDs (to be stored).

$$\text{Average inventory} = \frac{\text{Maximum inventory}}{2} = \frac{100}{2} = 50 \text{ units}$$

$R = $ Average inventory $\times\ c = 50 \times ₹2 = ₹100$

$P = 90 \times ₹10 = ₹900$

Cost of 9,000 CDs (@ ₹20 each) = $9{,}000 \times ₹20 = ₹1{,}80{,}000$

Discount @ 2% = 2% of ₹1,80,000

$$= \frac{2}{100} \times 1{,}80{,}000 = ₹3{,}600$$

Therefore,

Net cost of 9,000 CDs after discount = ₹1,80,000 – ₹3,600 = ₹1,76,400

Total cost after discount, $T_{2\%} = $ Net cost of 9,000 CDs $+ P + R$

$\qquad\qquad = ₹1{,}76{,}400 + ₹900 + ₹100$

$\qquad\qquad = ₹1{,}77{,}400 \qquad\qquad (8.3)$

This means whenever the EOQ falls within a discount range, there is no need of considering the lower limit of that range. This is because the EOQ with discount will invariably result in a lower overall cost.

**4% discount option:**

For 450–899 units, a discount of 4% is available. We consider the lower limit, that is, 450 CDs in an order for availing the 4% discount. Therefore, 20 orders of 450 CDs each have to be placed in a year to get 9,000 CDs. The maximum inventory is 450 CDs (to be stored).

$$\text{Average inventory} = \frac{\text{Maximum inventory}}{2} = \frac{450}{2} = 225 \text{ units}$$

$R = $ Average inventory $\times c = 225 \times ₹2$

$\qquad = ₹450$

$P = 20 \times ₹10 = ₹200$

Cost of 9,000 CDs (@ ₹20 each) = $9{,}000 \times ₹20 = ₹1{,}80{,}000$

Discount @ 4% = 4% of ₹1,80,000 = $\dfrac{4}{100} \times 1{,}80{,}000$

$\qquad = ₹7{,}200$

Therefore,

Net cost of 9,000 CDs after discount = ₹1,80,000 – ₹7,200 = ₹1,72,800

Total cost after discount, $T_{4\%}$ = Net cost of 9,000 CDs + $P$ + $R$
$$= ₹1,72,800 + ₹200 + ₹450$$
$$= ₹1,73,450 \qquad (8.4)$$

**5% discount option:**

For 900 and more units, a discount of 5% is available. We consider the lower limit, that is, 900 CDs in an order for availing the 5% discount. Therefore, 10 orders of 900 CDs each have to be placed in a year to get 9,000 CDs. The maximum inventory is 900 CDs (to be stored).

$$\text{Average inventory} = \frac{\text{Maximum inventory}}{2} = \frac{900}{2} = 450 \text{ units}$$

$$R = \text{Average inventory} \times c = 450 \times ₹2 = ₹900$$
$$P = 10 \times ₹10 = ₹100$$
Cost of 9,000 CDs (@ ₹20 each) = 9,000 × ₹20 = ₹180,000

$$\text{Discount @ 5\%} = 5\% \text{ of } ₹1,80,000 = \frac{5}{100} \times 1,80,000 = ₹9,000$$

Therefore,

Net cost of 9,000 CDs after discount = ₹1,80,000 − ₹9,000 = ₹1,71,000

Total cost after discount, $T_{5\%}$ = Net cost of 9,000 CDs + $P$ + $R$
$$= ₹1,71,000 + ₹100 + ₹900$$
$$= ₹1,72,000 \qquad (8.5)$$

Comparing Eqns (8.2)–(8.5), we find that 5% is the best discount option with an order size of 900 units.

---

| |
|---|
| Safety stock is defined as a hedge (protection) against the possibility of a stock out. |

### Safety stock

We have seen that the simplifying assumptions in the EOQ model are far from being real. In practical situations, the demand of items may fluctuate at any point of time. In addition, suppliers always need some *lead time* to supply the goods.

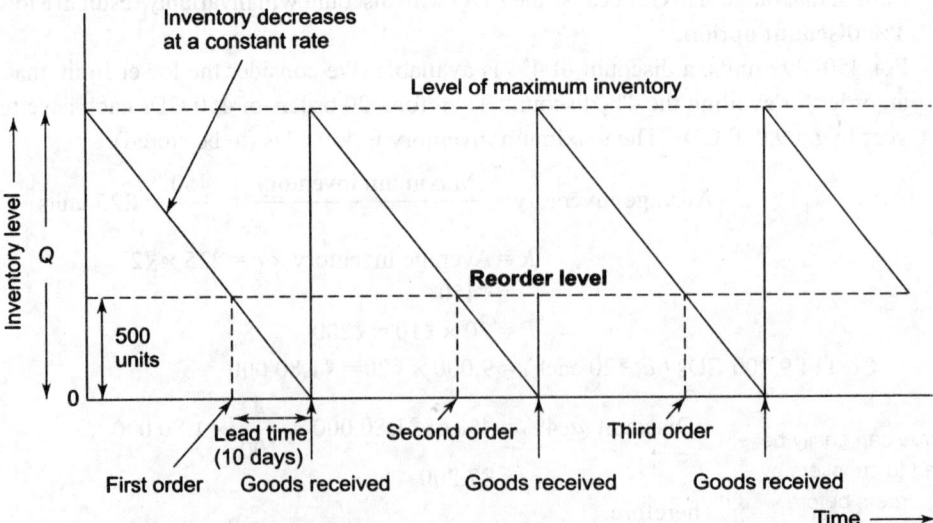

**Fig. 8.14** Lead time being provided by fixing a reorder level

Lead time can easily be provided to suppliers by placing orders before the inventory becomes zero. For example, if the lead time of an item is 10 days, the order can be placed 10 days before the inventory becomes zero. Let the uniform consumption rate of an inventory be 50 units per day. Therefore, during the 10 days of lead time, 500 units of the item will be consumed (10 days × 50 units per day). Hence, for this item, we can fix the *reorder level* as 500 units, that is, whenever the inventory level falls to 500 units, we know that the order has to be placed (Fig. 8.14).

A stock out may still occur sometimes because of any of the following reasons: (a) excessive consumption of inventory during lead time, (b) undue stretching of lead time by the supplier. In Fig. 8.15, we see that the slope of the line representing the consumption rate increases due to a rise in demand during the lead time. The inventory gets depleted completely in, say, 7 days, while it was expected to last for 10 days (normal lead time). Therefore, there is a stock out for 3 days.

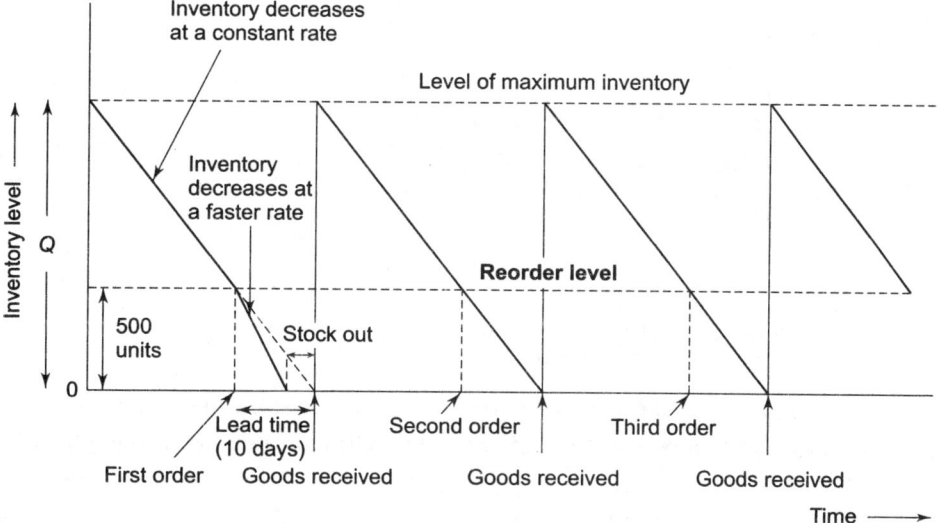

**Fig. 8.15** Excessive consumption of inventory during lead time, leading to a stock out

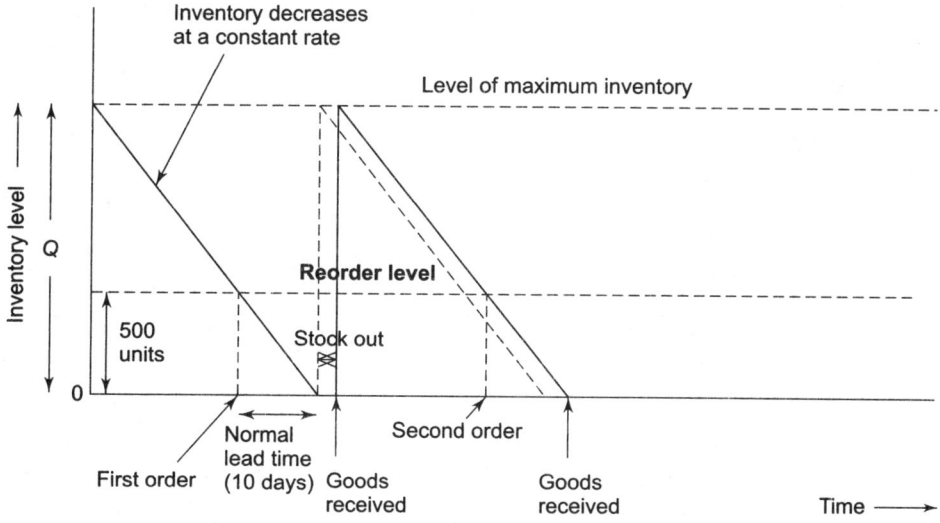

**Fig. 8.16** Undue stretching of lead time by the supplier, leading to a stock out

In Fig. 8.16, we observe that when the supplier unexpectedly takes more (say, 3 more days) than the normal lead time (10 days) to supply the goods, a stock out happens for 3 days.

We know that a stock out is undesirable for the various reasons discussed earlier. To avoid a stock out, extra stock of items is maintained throughout the year. This extra stock is called the *safety stock*. Safety stock is defined as a hedge (protection) against the possibility of a stock out.

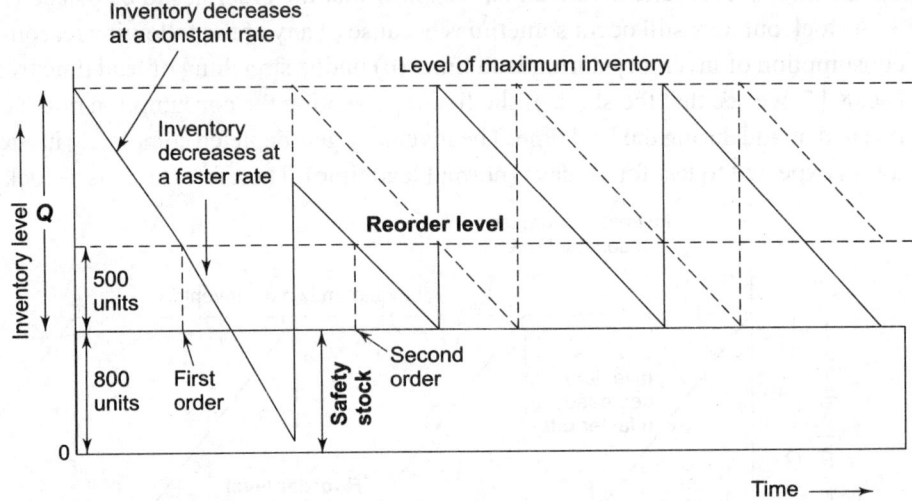

**Fig. 8.17**   Safety stock avoids a stock out caused by excessive consumption of inventory during the lead time

Figures 8.17 and 8.18 show that due to the safety stock, a stock-out situation is completely avoided. The reorder level now becomes 1,300 (500 + 800) units due to the safety stock of 800 units.

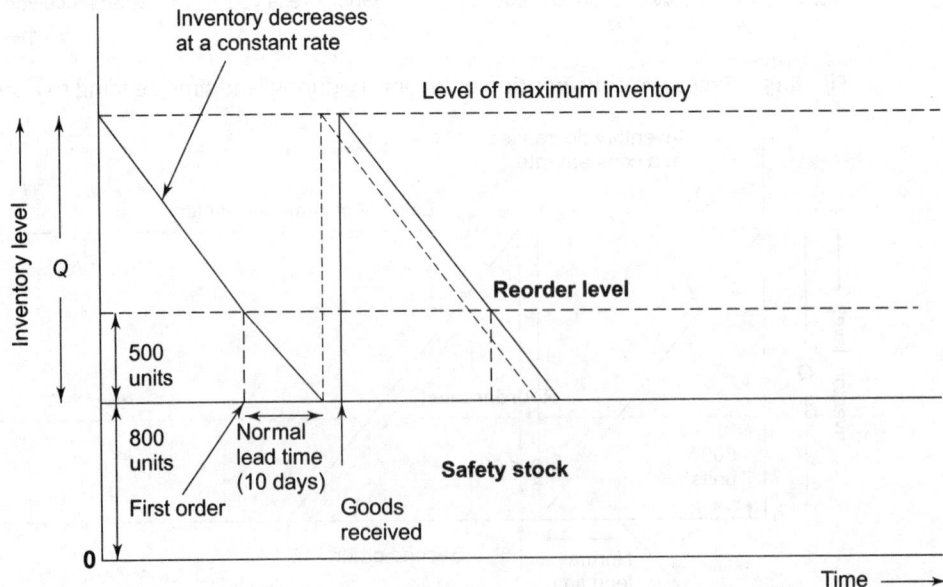

**Fig. 8.18**   Safety stock avoids a stock out caused by undue stretching of the lead time by the supplier

## Example 8.6

For a special component outsourced to a vendor and used in textile machinery manufactured by Luxmi Machine Tool Works at Coimbatore, we have the following situation:

| | |
|---|---|
| Yearly demand | 3,00,000 units |
| Purchase quantity | 1,00,000 units |
| Safety stock | 50,000 units |

The ordering cost, independent of purchase quantity, is ₹1,500 for each purchase. The (purchase) price of the component is ₹75/unit. Annual holding cost is 20% of the value of the component (inventory interest rate 20%). Assuming 230 working days per year, calculate:

(a) The number of purchases during a year
(b) Average inventory level (including the safety stock)
(c) Inventory turnover
(d) Average days of supply in inventory (known as cover time)
(e) Reorder point if the lead time is 15 working days
(f) Total inventory costs per year and total inventory costs per working day with purchase quantity 1,00,000 units
(g) Economic order quantity (EOQ)
(h) Total inventory costs per year and total inventory costs per working day with EOQ and with a safety stock decreased to 5,000 units.

## Solution

| | A | B | C | D | E | F | G | H | I | J | K | L | M | N |
|---|---|---|---|---|---|---|---|---|---|---|---|---|---|---|
| 1 | | A = | 300000 | units | | | | | | | | | | |
| 2 | | o = | 1500 | ₹ | | | | | | | | | | |
| 3 | | Price = | 75 | ₹ / unit | | | | | | | | | | |
| 4 | | c = | 20 | % of ₹75 = | | 15 | ₹/unit/year | | | | | | | |
| 5 | | Purchase quantity = | | 100000 | units/ order | | | | | | | | | |
| 6 | | Safety stock = | | 50000 | units | | | Lead time = | | 15 | days | | | |
| 7 | | No. of working days per year = | | 230 | | | | | | | | | | |
| 8 | | | | | | | | | | | | | | |
| 9 | a) The number of purchases during a year = A / Purchase quantity = | | | | | | 300000/100000= | | | 3 | | | | |
| 10 | | | | | | | | | | | | | | |
| 11 | b) Max. inventory = Purchase quantity per order + Safety stock | | | | | 150000 | | | Min. inventory = Safety stock = | | 50000 | | | |
| 12 | Average inventory level (including the safety stock) = (Max. inventory + Min. inventory) / 2 = | | | | | | | | 100000 | units | | | | |
| 13 | | | | | | | | | | | | | | |
| 14 | c) Inventory turnover = A / Average inventory = | | | | | | 3 | times per year | | | | | | |
| 15 | | | | | | | | | | | | | | |
| 16 | d) Average days of supply in inventory (known as cover-time) = (Average inventory / A) x No. of working days per year = | | | | | | | | | | | | 76.6667 | working days |
| 17 | | | | | | | | | | | | | | |
| 18 | e) Reorder point = Rate of consumption of inventory (units per day) x Lead time + Safety stock | | | | | | | | | | | | | |
| 19 | | = (A / No. of working days per annum) x Lead time + Safety stock = | | | | | | | 69565.2 | units | | | | |
| 20 | | | | | | | | | | | | | | |
| 21 | f) Total inventory cost = Total o.c. + Total c.c | | | | | | | | | | | | | |
| 22 | | | | | | | | | | | | | | |
| 23 | Total o.c. = No. of orders (purchases) during the year x o = ₹ | | | | | 4500 | | | | | | | | |
| 24 | Total c.c. = Average inventory x c = | | | | | ₹ | 1500000 | | | | | | | |
| 25 | | | | | | ₹ | 1504500 | Total inventory cost = Total o.c. + Total c.c | | | | | | |
| 26 | | | | | | ₹ | 6541.3 | Total inventory cost per working day = Total inventory cost/ No. of working days | | | | | | |
| 27 | | | | | | | | | | | | | | |
| 28 | g) EOQ = Q = √ (2Ao / c) | | | | | | | | | | | | | |
| 29 | Q² = | 6E+07 | | | | | | | | | | | | |
| 30 | Q = | 7745.97 | | | | | | | | | | | | |
| 31 | | | | | | | | | | | | | | |
| 32 | h) For EOQ, Total inventory cost = Total o.c. + Total c.c + c.c. of safety stock | | | | | | | | New level of safety stock = | | 5000 | | | |
| 33 | | | | | | | | | | | | | | |
| 34 | | | | o.c. = (A/Q) x o = | | 58094.8 | | | | | | | Full Scree ▼ x | |
| 35 | | | | c.c. = o.c. = | | 58094.8 | | | | | | | Close Full Screen | |
| 36 | c.c. of safety stock = New level of safety stock x c = | | | | | 75000 | | | | | | | | |
| 37 | | | | | ₹ | 191190 | Total inventory cost | | | | | | | |
| 38 | | | | | ₹ | 831.259 | Total inventory cost per working day = Total inventory cost/ No. of working days | | | | | | | |

> Stock-out cost is mainly the loss of potential profit and of goodwill on the customer's part.

*Optimum level of safety stock* A low level of safety stock can lead to a stock out. On the other hand, a high level of safety stock unnecessarily ties up capital. Therefore, we need to determine the optimum level of safety stock, which should be neither low nor high, but just right.

Safety stock involves two types of costs: (a) CC of the safety stock and (b) stock-out cost. Stock-out cost is mainly the loss of potential profit and of goodwill on the customer's part. It can be quantified in monetary terms using the previous financial year's stock-out experiences.

The above-mentioned costs are inversely related to each other:

$$\text{CC of safety stock} \propto \frac{1}{\text{Stock-out cost}}$$

When a high safety stock is maintained, it has a high CC. The possibility or the risk of a stock out will be less due to high safety stock. This corresponds to low stock-out cost. Research shows that the total cost of safety stock (= CC of safety stock + stock-out cost) is minimum only when

$$\text{CC of safety stock} = \text{Stock-out cost} \tag{8.6}$$

Equation (8.6) corresponds to the optimum level of safety stock.

In the following example, we will keep the normal lead time constant. The supplier supplies during the normal lead time. The demand during lead time may vary, leading to the possibility of a stock out.

### Example 8.7

**Table 8.3**

| Consumption during lead time (units) | Probability |
|---|---|
| 1,000 | 0.01 |
| 2,000 | 0.03 |
| 3,000 | 0.07 |
| 4,000 | 0.14 |
| 5,000 | 0.61 |
| 6,000 | 0.04 |
| 7,000 | 0.07 |
| 8,000 | 0.03 |
| | 1.00 |

A local chocolate distributor at Allahabad deals with a popular brand called Chocostik. The normal lead time taken by suppliers of Chocostik is 10 days. The normal consumption of inventory during lead time is 500 units per day. There are 10 inventory cycles per year. Table 8.3 shows the consumption pattern of Chocostik during lead time (from the past 100 observations). The CC is ₹1 per unit per year. The stock-out cost is ₹2 per unit short. Find the optimum level of safety stock for Chocostik.

### Solution

The normal consumption of Chocostik during lead time
= 10 days (lead time) × 500 units/day = 5,000 units
Observe from Table 8.3 that out of 100 observations, the consumption during lead time is 5,000 units or less 86 (= 61 + 14 + 7 + 3 + 1) times.

Therefore, even if no safety stock is maintained, there is an 86% chance that a stock out will not happen. At the same time there is a 14% (100% − 86%) chance that stock out will happen. Let us calculate the total cost of safety stock for the following cases:

Case 1: No safety stock
Case 2: 1,000 units of safety stock
Case 3: 2,000 units of safety stock
Case 4: 3,000 units of safety stock

First, we calculate the annual stock-out cost for the four cases. The calculations for cases 1–3 (Table 8.4) can be understood as follows. In case 1, when the consumption during lead time is

6,000 units, a stock out occurs for 1,000 units, as no safety stock is maintained, stock-out cost at the rate of ₹2 per unit short = 1,000 × 2. There are 10 inventory cycles per year. Therefore, the annual stock-out cost = 10 × 1,000 × 2. There is a 4% chance of this happening. Therefore, the expected annual stock-out cost = 0.04 × 10 × 1,000 × 2 = ₹800. In case 4, no stock out is possible. Therefore, there is no stock-out cost.

**Table 8.4**  Annual stock-out cost calculations for cases 1–3

| Lead-time consumption leading to a stock out (units) | Number of units short (compared to normal consumption of 5,000 units) | Probability | Expected annual stock-out cost (₹) |
|---|---|---|---|
| **Case 1** | | | |
| 6,000 | 1,000 | 0.04 | 10 × 1,000 × 0.04 × 2 = 800 |
| 7,000 | 2,000 | 0.07 | 10 × 2,000 × 0.07 × 2 = 2,800 |
| 8,000 | 3,000 | 0.03 | 10 × 3,000 × 0.03 × 2 = 1,800 |
| | | | 5,400 |
| **Case 2** | | | |
| 7,000 | 1,000 | 0.07 | 10 × 1,000 × 0.07 × 2 = 1,400 |
| 8,000 | 2,000 | 0.03 | 10 × 2,000 × 0.03 × 2 = 1,200 |
| | | | 2,600 |
| **Case 3** | | | |
| 8,000 | 1,000 | 0.03 | 10 × 1,000 × 0.03 × 2 = 600 |
| | | | 800 |

**Table 8.5**

| Safety stock level (units) | CC of safety stock (₹) | Stock-out cost (₹) | Total safety stock cost (₹) |
|---|---|---|---|
| 0 | 0 | 5,400 | 5,400 |
| 1,000 | 1,000 | 2,600 | 3,600 |
| **2,000** | **2,000** | **600** | **2,600** |
| 3,000 | 3,000 | 0 | 3,000 |

Hence, from Table 8.5 we conclude that the minimum total safety stock cost is ₹2,600 for 2,000 units. Hence, 2,000 units is the optimum level of safety stock.

### Example 8.8

**Table 8.6**

| Number of units | Price (₹/unit) |
|---|---|
| 50–99 | 2,000 |
| 100–149 | 1,900 |
| 150 and above | 1,800 |

Exide Batteries is offering discounted prices to its retailers for the following quantities of car batteries (Table 8.6). A retailer of the company at Jhansi has an annual demand of 2,500 units. The CC of batteries estimated by the retailer according to past experiences is 10% of the inventory value and the OC is estimated as ₹100 per order. Determine the size of the order the retailer should place with Exide so that the total inventory cost is minimum.

### Solution

Let us first determine the EOQ, starting with the lowest price of ₹1,800 per unit. For this price, CC = 10% of ₹1,800 = ₹180.

Now, $\dfrac{Ao}{Q} = \dfrac{Qc}{2}$ $\Rightarrow$ $\dfrac{2,500 \times 100}{Q} = \dfrac{Q \times 180}{2}$

$\Rightarrow$ $Q^2 = \dfrac{2,50,000}{90}$ $\Rightarrow$ $Q = 52.7 \approx 53$ units

This order size of 53 units does not fall in the range 150 units and above for the price of ₹1,800. Hence, this solution is not feasible.

For the price of ₹1,900, CC = 10% of ₹1,900 = ₹190.

$$\dfrac{Ao}{Q} = \dfrac{Qc}{2} \qquad \Rightarrow \qquad \dfrac{2,500 \times 100}{Q} = \dfrac{Q \times 190}{2}$$

$\Rightarrow$ $Q^2 = \dfrac{2,50,000}{95}$ $\Rightarrow$ $Q = 51.3 \approx 52$ units

This order size of 52 units does not fall in the range 100–149 units for ₹1,900. Hence, this solution is also not feasible.

For the price of ₹2,000, CC = 10% of ₹2,000 = ₹200.

$$\dfrac{Ao}{Q} = \dfrac{Qc}{2} \qquad \Rightarrow \qquad \dfrac{2,500}{Q} \times 100 = \dfrac{Q}{2} \times 200$$

$\Rightarrow$ $Q^2 = \dfrac{2,50,000}{100}$ $\Rightarrow$ $Q = 50$

This order size of 50 units falls in the range 50–99 units for ₹2,000. Thus, this solution is feasible and the EOQ is 50 units. Let us now calculate the total inventory cost for this order size.

$$T = \text{Price of a unit} \times A + \dfrac{Ao}{Q} + \dfrac{Qc}{2}$$

$$= 2,000 \times 2,500 + \dfrac{2,500}{50} \times 100 + \dfrac{50}{2} \times 200$$

$$= 50,00,000 + 5,000 + 5,000 = \text{Rs } 50,10,000$$

The total inventory cost for 100 units (lower limit of the range 100–149) at the price of ₹1,900 is

$$T = \text{Price of a unit} \times A + \dfrac{Ao}{Q} + \dfrac{Qc}{2}$$

$$= 1,900 \times 2,500 + \dfrac{2,500}{100} \times 100 + \dfrac{100}{2} \times 190$$

$$= 47,50,000 + 2,500 + 9,500 = ₹47,62,000$$

The total inventory cost for 150 units (lower limit of the range 150 and above) at the price of ₹1,800 is

$$T = \text{Price of a unit} \times A + \dfrac{Ao}{Q} + \dfrac{Qc}{2}$$

$$= 1,800 \times 2,500 + \dfrac{2,500}{150} \times 100 + \dfrac{150}{2} \times 180$$

$$= 45,00,000 + 1,666.7 + 13,500 = \text{Rs } 45,15,166.7$$

Hence, we note that the total inventory cost is minimum for the order size of 150 units. Therefore, the retailer should opt for an order size of 150 units.

## Example 8.9

Alliance Tyres is a distributor of MRF Tyres in Ludhiana. For the Zigma brand of radial tyres used in Maruti 800, Table 8.7 shows its observations of the distribution of demand during lead time (DDLT) in the past. The CC of a tyre unsold during the lead time is estimated to be ₹50 and the stock-out cost is estimated at ₹100. Find the optimum level of safety stock that will involve the minimum expected cost.

**Table 8.7**

| DDLT (units) | Frequency |
|--------------|-----------|
| 5 | 7 |
| 6 | 21 |
| 7 | 27 |
| 8 | 31 |
| 9 | 14 |
| | 100 |

### Solution

The given frequencies can be converted into probabilities as shown in Table 8.8.

**Table 8.8**

| DDLT (units) | Frequency | Probability |
|--------------|-----------|-------------|
| 5 | 7 | 0.07 |
| 6 | 21 | 0.21 |
| 7 | 27 | 0.27 |
| 8 | 31 | 0.31 |
| 9 | 14 | 0.14 |
| | 100 | 1.00 |

Let us now determine the optimum reorder level among the five options—5, 6, 7, 8, and 9 units—using Table 8.8.

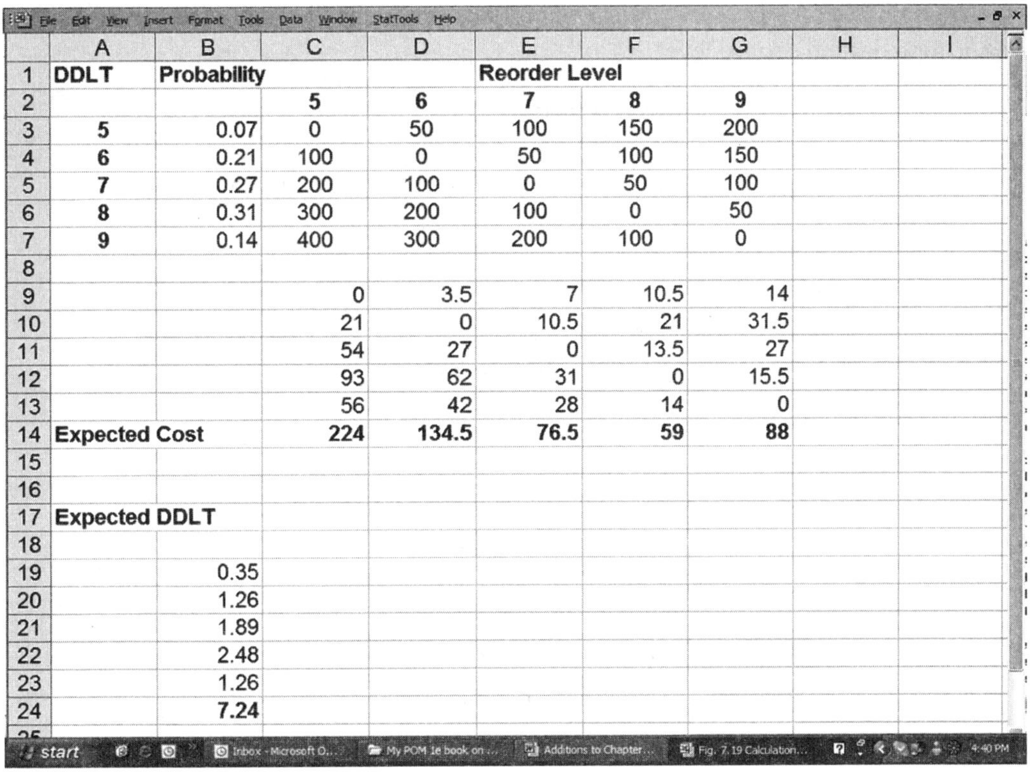

| | A | B | C | D | E | F | G | H | I |
|---|---|---|---|---|---|---|---|---|---|
| 1 | DDLT | Probability | | | Reorder Level | | | | |
| 2 | | | 5 | 6 | 7 | 8 | 9 | | |
| 3 | 5 | 0.07 | 0 | 50 | 100 | 150 | 200 | | |
| 4 | 6 | 0.21 | 100 | 0 | 50 | 100 | 150 | | |
| 5 | 7 | 0.27 | 200 | 100 | 0 | 50 | 100 | | |
| 6 | 8 | 0.31 | 300 | 200 | 100 | 0 | 50 | | |
| 7 | 9 | 0.14 | 400 | 300 | 200 | 100 | 0 | | |
| 8 | | | | | | | | | |
| 9 | | | 0 | 3.5 | 7 | 10.5 | 14 | | |
| 10 | | | 21 | 0 | 10.5 | 21 | 31.5 | | |
| 11 | | | 54 | 27 | 0 | 13.5 | 27 | | |
| 12 | | | 93 | 62 | 31 | 0 | 15.5 | | |
| 13 | | | 56 | 42 | 28 | 14 | 0 | | |
| 14 | Expected Cost | | 224 | 134.5 | 76.5 | 59 | 88 | | |
| 15 | | | | | | | | | |
| 16 | | | | | | | | | |
| 17 | Expected DDLT | | | | | | | | |
| 18 | | | | | | | | | |
| 19 | | 0.35 | | | | | | | |
| 20 | | 1.26 | | | | | | | |
| 21 | | 1.89 | | | | | | | |
| 22 | | 2.48 | | | | | | | |
| 23 | | 1.26 | | | | | | | |
| 24 | | 7.24 | | | | | | | |

**Fig. 8.19** Calculation of expected costs and DDLT

Figure 8.19 shows that when the reorder level is 7 units and the DDLT is 5 units, 2 tyres (7 − 5 = 2) remain unsold during lead time. Therefore, a CC of ₹100 is shown in cell E3 (at the rate of ₹50 per unit unsold). Similarly, when the reorder level is 5 units and the DDLT is 9 units, there is a shortage of 4 tyres (9 − 5 = 4). Hence, cell C7 shows a stock-out cost of ₹400 (at the rate of ₹100 per unit short). In the same way, the values in the remaining cells of the table can be calculated.

Cell C9 is the product of cells B3 and C3. The cells in rows 9–13 calculate the expected cost by multiplying the probabilities with the corresponding cell values. Click on cell C9, write =, click on cell B3, write * to represent the product operator, then click on cell C3, and press **enter**. The value 0 (0.07 × 0 = 0) is displayed in cell C9. Select cell C9 and drag up to cell C13 to get the values shown.

Row 14 shows the total expected cost for all the reorder values. This is the sum of columns C, D, E, F, and G between rows 9–13. Select any column between these rows and include an extra cell below, for example, select cells C9–C14 and click on the summation sign in the toolbar. The sum will be displayed in cell C14 as 224. Similarly, find the total expected cost for all the columns.

Observe that the expected cost is minimum for the reorder level of 8 units at ₹59. Therefore, this is the optimum reorder level. The safety stock is given as follows:

Optimum safety stock = Optimum reorder level − Expected DDLT

The expected DDLT can be found from Table 8.8 as follows:

$$0.07 \times 5 + 0.21 \times 6 + 0.27 \times 7 + 0.31 \times 8 + 0.14 \times 9 = 7.24$$

The screenshot in Fig. 8.19 also shows the calculation of expected DDLT in cell B24. Thus, the optimum safety stock = 8 units − 7.24 units = 0.76 units ≈ 1 unit.

***Safety stock determination when DDLT follows normal distribution curve*** When DDLT is assumed to follow *normal distribution*, the optimum level of safety stock can be determined for a desired service level.

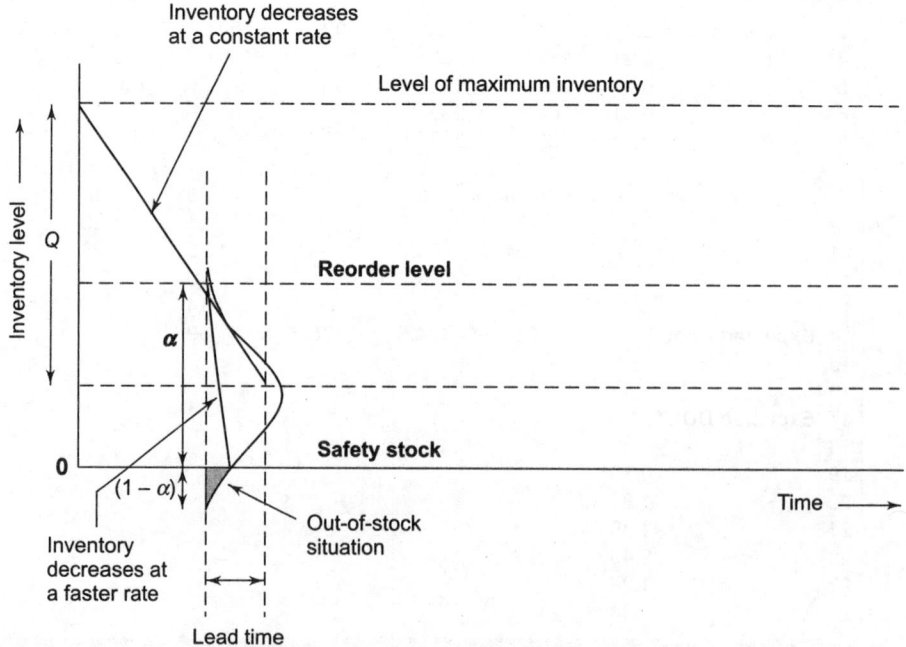

**Fig. 8.20**  Normal distribution curve representing DDLT

$$\text{Service level (\%)} = \frac{\text{Number of units given to customers without any delay}}{\text{Number of units demanded by customers}} \times 100$$

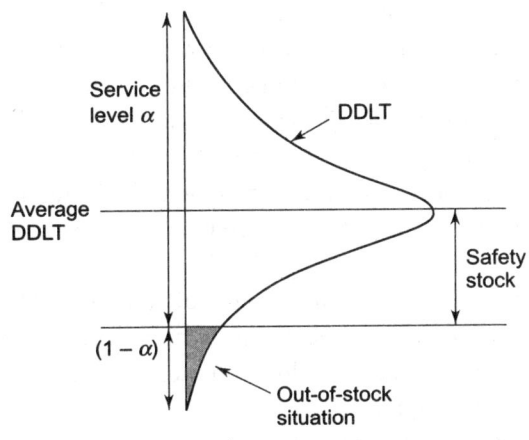

**Fig. 8.21** Dependence of DDLT on the service level

From the above formula, we see that the highest and most desirable service level is 100%. However, practically, the service level may vary between 0% and 100%. Figure 8.20 shows a normal distribution curve during lead time. This curve represents the DDLT. The highest point on a normal distribution curve corresponds to the average or mean value. Here, the highest point on the curve corresponds to the average DDLT.

Figure 8.21 shows that the level of safety stock depends on the service level $\alpha$. The non-shaded area under the normal distribution curve represents the service level. If the desired service level is $\alpha$, we have to find the value of $z$ for this service level. Then, the level of safety stock is given by $z\sigma$, where $\sigma$ is the standard deviation of the normal distribution curve for DDLT.

### Example 8.10

It is given that the DDLT for an item follows a normal distribution curve with an average value of 100 units and a standard deviation of 10 units. Find the optimum level of safety stock for a 90% service level.

### Solution

A 90% service level means we have to find the $z$-value corresponding to an area of 0.4 between the mean and desired service level (Fig. 8.22). This value of $z$ is 1.28. Therefore,

$$\text{Optimum level of safety stock} = z\sigma$$
$$= 1.28 \times 10 = 12.8 \text{ units} \approx 13 \text{ units}$$

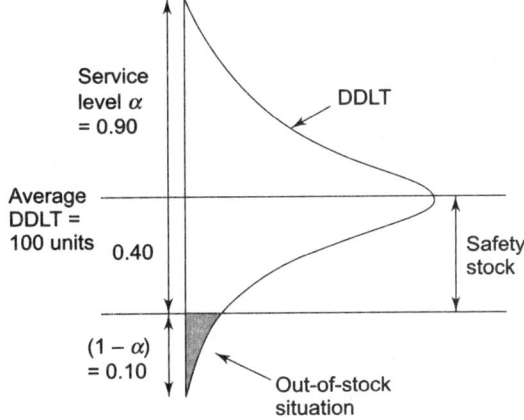

**Fig. 8.22**

The cost of shortages is mainly due to loss in goodwill on the customers' part, which depends on how long they have waited to receive the goods.

**EOQ model with intentional shortages**   Normally shortages are undesirable for retailers, but in some situations, they can be intentionally created by retailers dealing in very expensive items. This is because the CC of expensive items is very high. It may be so high that the cost of stock out or shortages may be comparatively very less. For example, the distributors of heavy industrial equipment keep on receiving back-orders from their customers, but the equipment is supplied only after a period of waiting time. The customers are also willing to wait in such cases, probably because there are no better options available to them.

After accumulating many back-orders, the distributors place the order to the manufacturers. On receiving the goods, the distributors first supply the back-orders. The remaining items form the inventory for the future.

There are three types of costs in this model: (a) OC, (b) CC, and (c) cost of shortages. The cost of shortages is mainly due to loss in goodwill on the customers' part, which depends on how long they have waited to receive the goods. It also includes the loss of potential profit due to the switching of the customers to competitors. In this model,

$$\text{Total inventory cost} = \text{Total OC} + \text{Total CC} + \text{Total cost of shortages} \qquad (8.7)$$

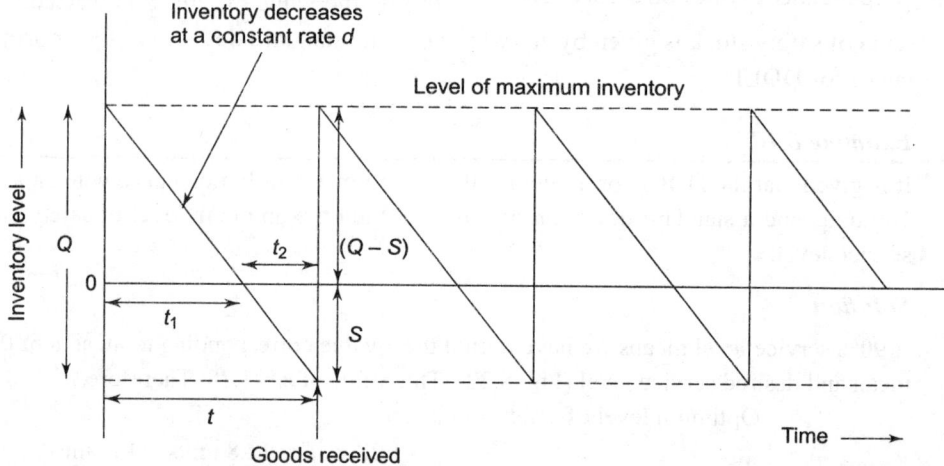

**Fig. 8.23**   EOQ model with intentional shortages

Figure 8.23 shows this model. Here, $S$ is the maximum shortage (maximum number of units short), $t$ the time period of one inventory cycle, $t_1$ the fraction of time during which customers are served immediately with items in the inventory, $t_2$ the fraction of time during which there is a stock out and back-orders are received, and $d$ is the rate of demand (say, in units per day).

*Total annual OC*

$$P = \frac{Ao}{Q}$$

***Total annual CC***   As seen in Fig. 8.23, $Q$ items are ordered in one inventory cycle. Out of these $Q$ items, $S$ items are immediately consumed to fulfil the back-order. The remaining $(Q-S)$ items form the maximum inventory, which lasts for time $t_1$. Therefore, the average inventory is $(Q-S)/2$. The quantity $(Q-S)$ lasts for time $t_1$. Therefore,

$$\text{CC during } t_1 = \frac{Q-S}{2} ct_1 \tag{8.8}$$

The inventory is consumed at a constant rate of $d$ units/day. Therefore, at this rate, $(Q-S)$ units are consumed in $t_1$ days. Therefore,

$$Q - S = dt1 \tag{8.9}$$

At the same rate, $Q$ units are also consumed in $t$ days. Therefore,

$$Q = dt \tag{8.10}$$

Dividing Eqn (8.9) by Eqn (8.10), we have

$$\frac{Q-S}{Q} = \frac{dt_1}{dt} \qquad \Rightarrow \qquad \frac{Q-S}{Q} = \frac{t_1}{t}$$

$$\Rightarrow \qquad t_1 = \frac{(Q-S)t}{Q}$$

Substituting this value in Eqn (8.8), we have

$$\text{CC during } t_1 = \frac{(Q-S)c}{2} \frac{(Q-S)t}{Q} = \frac{(Q-S)^2}{2Q} ct$$

Let there be $N$ inventory cycles in one year. Then,

$$R = \frac{(Q-S)^2 ctN}{2Q}$$

Now, $tN = 1$ year. Therefore,

$$R = \frac{(Q-S)^2 c}{2Q}$$

***Total annual cost of shortages*** Let $k$ be the cost of shortages per unit per year and $G$ the total annual cost of shortages. The maximum shortage $S$ is created at the rate of $d$ units/day in time $t_2$. Therefore,

$$S = dt_2 \tag{8.11}$$

We also know that

$$Q = dt \tag{8.12}$$

Dividing Eqn (8.12) by Eqn (8.11), we get

$$\frac{Q}{S} = \frac{t}{t_2} \qquad \Rightarrow \qquad t_2 = \frac{St}{Q}$$

Since $S$ is the maximum shortage, the average shortage is $S/2$. Therefore, the cost of shortages in $t_2$,

$$= \frac{Skt_2}{2}$$

Substituting the value of $t_2$, we have

$$\text{Cost of shortages in } t_2, = \frac{Sk}{2} \frac{St}{Q}$$

For $N$ inventory cycles in a year,

$$G = \frac{S^2 ktN}{2Q}$$

Now $tN = 1$ year. Therefore,

$$G = \frac{S^2 k}{2Q}$$

Equation (8.7) now becomes

$$T = P + R + G$$

$$= \frac{Ao}{Q} + \frac{(Q-S)^2 c}{2Q} + \frac{S^2 k}{2Q} \tag{8.13}$$

Now, the total inventory cost $T$ is to be minimized. It depends on two variables $Q$ and $S$; all the other values remain constant. Using differential calculus to minimize $T$, we get the following values of $Q$ and $S$:

$$Q = \sqrt{\frac{2Ao}{c} \frac{(c+k)}{k}} \tag{8.14}$$

$$S = \frac{cQ}{c+k} \tag{8.15}$$

Substituting these values of $Q$ and $S$ in Eqn (8.13), we get

$$T = \sqrt{\frac{2Aock}{c+k}} \tag{8.16}$$

The equation for $Q$ here is similar to that of the simple EOQ model (retailer's model), where $Q$ $\sqrt{2Ao/c}$. However, Eqn (8.14) has an additional term $\sqrt{(c+k)/k}$. When the cost of shortages $k$ is very high compared to $c$, the term $\sqrt{(c+k)/k}$ tends to unity. In that case, the EOQ ($Q$) here takes the same value as that in the simple EOQ model.

### Example 8.11

Vishal Computer Sales (P) Ltd is a leading dealer of computer servers and networking devices at Raipur. Servers are expensive machines and, therefore, Vishal follows a back-ordering policy. The CC is ₹50,000 per server per year and the OC is ₹1,200 per order. The cost of shortage per server is estimated at ₹20,000. The annual demand of servers is 300 units. Find (a) the optimal order quantity under the EOQ model with intentional shortages, (b) the maximum shortage level, and (c) the maximum inventory level. (d) If the lead time is 7 days and the DDLT is 3 units, what is the reorder level?

### Solution

(a)

$$Q = \sqrt{\frac{2Ao}{c} \frac{(c+k)}{k}}$$

$$= \sqrt{\frac{2 \times 300 \times 1,200}{50,000} \times \frac{50,000 + 20,000}{20,000}}$$

$$= \frac{12}{\sqrt{10}} \times \sqrt{\frac{7}{2}}$$

$$= 12 \times \sqrt{0.35}$$

$$= 7.1 \text{ units per order} \approx 7 \text{ units per order}$$

(b)
$$S = \frac{cQ}{c + k}$$

$$= \frac{50,000 \times 7}{50,000 + 20,000}$$

$$= 5 \text{ units}$$

(c)  Maximum inventory $= Q - S = 7 - 5 = 2$ units

(d)  Reorder level $=$ DDLT $-$ Maximum shortage

$$= 3 - 5 = -2$$

Therefore, when the back-order of two units is received, an order for 7 servers should be placed. See Exhibit 8.2 to know how the lack of inventory management at government granaries has resulted in wastage.

---

**Exhibit 8.2    India's Irony: Excessive Production, yet Hunger Deaths Continue Unabated**

The Food and Agriculture Organization (FAO) of the United Nations estimated that about 230 million Indians remain hungry daily. With 21 per cent of its population undernourished, nearly 44 per cent of children under five years of age are underweight and 7 per cent of them dying before they reach the age of five years, India stands among the world's most hunger-ridden countries.

This is despite the fact that Punjab and Haryana, collectively known as the 'granary of India', have had record production of wheat over the last five years. Ironically, India does not have proper storage capacity for this stockpile, resulting in millions of tonnes of grain rotting in open space. Nor does the government have policies in place to quickly disburse this stockpile to the poor and needy before it is wasted.

According to experts, for the last 25 years the storage capacity has not been upgraded at all. Part of the grain is officially stored outside storehouses, where the possibility of rotting or other forms of destruction is quite high. There are often not enough sacks and tarpaulins, and sometimes the grain is just dumped.

Part of the problem lies in the fact that the govern-ment buys rice and wheat from the farmers at a guaranteed price to provide economic security to them. This buying price for wheat has increased by about 70 per cent since 2007. This situation is lucrative enough for the farmers who choose to grow paddy and wheat in their fields compared to any other crop. Naturally, this has resulted in bumper harvest of these crops over the past half a decade in India.

Wheat procured in this manner becomes uncompetitive in pricing in the international markets after adding freight and storage costs. Thus, exporting it becomes unviable as its free on board (FOB) price of US$346 per tonne is way ahead of the international buying price of around US$260.

In 2010, the Supreme Court of India directed the government to distribute the wheat free of cost to the poor rather than let it go waste. However, the government failed to practically implement this directive due to the inefficient public distribution system based on ration cards and lack of will on the part of the state governments to buy the grain for distribution under the food welfare programme.

*Source:* Varma (2012).

---

## Production Model of Inventory Management (Manufacturer's Model)

In a manufacturing organization, when the production starts for a batch or lot of items, the inventory of that item starts building up. In one production run, one lot of items is produced. The production model of inventory management is based on the following assumptions:

1. The annual demand of the item is known and uniformly distributed throughout the year.
2. The production and sales of items take place simultaneously.

3. The demand of the item is not high enough to warrant continuous production. Therefore items are produced in lots or batches only.

Let $s$ be the set-up cost per production run, $Q$ the EOQ (optimum size of a production run, that is, the optimum number of units produced in a lot), $p$ the rate of production (number of items produced per day), and $d$ the rate of demand (number of items sold per day). Therefore, $(p - d)$ is the rate of accumulation of inventory (on any particular day, the items produced are more than the items demanded, hence the excess items over demand form the inventory) (see Fig. 8.24).

$$\text{Duration of a production run} = \frac{Q \,(\text{units})}{p \,(\text{units per day})}$$

$$= \frac{Q}{p} \,\text{days/production run}$$

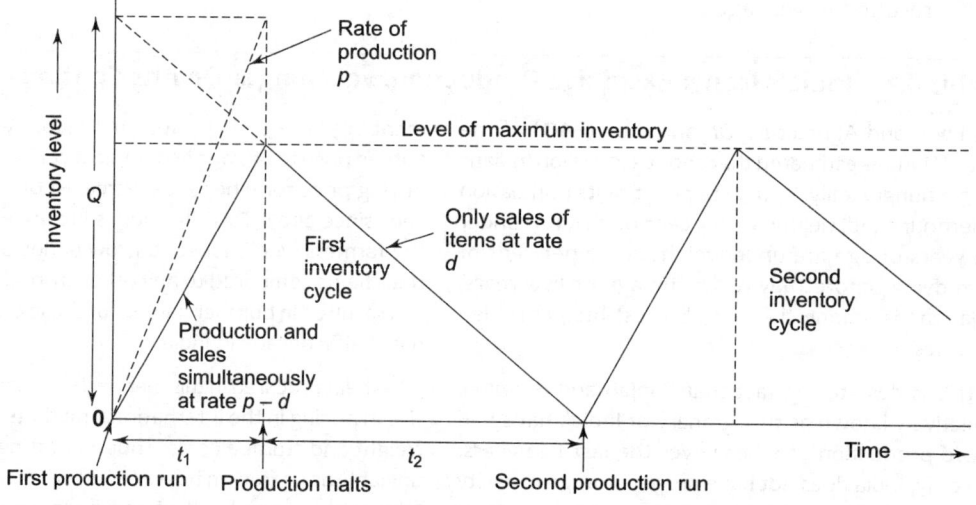

**Fig. 8.24** Production model of inventory management

Maximum units added to inventory per production run (maximum inventory)

$$= \frac{Q}{p}\,(p - d)$$

Therefore,

$$\text{Average inventory} = \frac{1}{2}\frac{Q}{p}(p - d)$$

Hence,

$$R = \frac{1}{2}\frac{Q}{p}(p - d)c$$

$$\text{Total set-up cost} = \text{Number of Set-ups} \times \text{Set-up cost per production run}$$

$$= \frac{As}{Q}$$

$$T = \text{Total set-up cost} + R = \frac{As}{Q} + \frac{1}{2}\frac{Q}{p}\,(p - d)c$$

The total cost is to be minimized

$$\frac{dT}{dQ} = -\frac{As}{Q^2} + \frac{1}{2}\frac{(p-d)c}{p}$$

$$\frac{d^2T}{dQ^2} = +\frac{2As}{Q^3}$$

The second derivative is positive, which means $T$ is minimum when

$$\frac{dT}{dQ} = 0 \qquad\qquad \Rightarrow \frac{dT}{dQ} = -\frac{As}{Q^2} + \frac{1}{2}\frac{(p-d)c}{p} = 0$$

$$\Rightarrow \qquad \frac{As}{Q} = \frac{1}{2}(p-d)\frac{Qc}{p}$$

Now, the total set-up cost is the same as the total CC. Therefore,

$$Q^2 = \frac{2Asp}{(p-d)c} \qquad\qquad \Rightarrow Q = \sqrt{\frac{2Asp}{(p-d)c}}$$

## Example 8.12

Singhvi Bottlers (P) Ltd is the sole bottler of Pepsi at Nagpur. The annual demand of Pepsi at Nagpur is 2,00,000 bottles. The CC of the inventory of bottled Pepsi is ₹10 per bottle per year. The set-up cost per bottling run is ₹1,000. The rate of production is 1,000 bottles per day and the rate of demand is 600 bottles per day. Find the optimum size of a bottling run, that is, the number of bottles that should be manufactured in one production run.

### Solution

Total set-up cost = Total CC

$$\Rightarrow \qquad \frac{A}{Q}s = \frac{1}{2}(p-d)\frac{Qc}{p}$$

$$\Rightarrow \qquad \frac{2,00,000}{Q} \times 1,000 = \frac{1}{2} \times (1,000 - 600) \times \frac{Q}{1,000} \times 10$$

$$\Rightarrow \qquad Q = \sqrt{\frac{2 \times 2,00,000 \times 1,000}{10} \times \frac{1,000}{400}} = \frac{2 \times 1,000 \times 100}{20}$$

$$= 10,000 \text{ bottles}$$

## Example 8.13

For a special ingredient YZ150 used in the manufacture of a detergent at Kolkata-based Bengal Chemicals, the following figures are prevailing:

| | |
|---|---|
| Yearly demand | 2,60,000 kg |
| Production quantity | 50,000 kg |
| Safety stock | 20,000 kg |

The set-up cost, independent of quantity, is ₹2000 for each production batch. The price of the ingredient is ₹150 per kg. Annual holding cost is 15 per cent of the value of the ingredient (inventory interest rate 15 per cent). Assuming 230 working days per year, calculate:

(a) The number of production batches during a year
(b) Average inventory level (including the safety stock)
(c) Inventory turnover
(d) Average days of supply in inventory (cover time)
(e) Reorder point if the lead time is 10 working days
(f) Total inventory costs per year and total inventory costs per working day with production quantity 50,000 kg
(g) EOQ (pure)
(h) The company can produce YZ150 at a production rate 7,500 kg per working day. Determine the economic production lot size. Assuming that the safety stock is decreased to 10,000 kg, calculate the new number of production batches per year, average days of supply in inventory, and the new total costs per working day and year.

**Solution**

| | A | B | C | D | E | F | G | H | I | J | K | L | M | N |
|---|---|---|---|---|---|---|---|---|---|---|---|---|---|---|
| 1 | | A = | 300000 | units | | | | | | | | | | |
| 2 | | o = | 1500 | ₹ | | | | | | | | | | |
| 3 | | Price = | 75 | ₹ / unit | | | | | | | | | | |
| 4 | | c = | 20 | % of ₹75 = | | 15 | ₹/unit/year | | | | | | | |
| 5 | | Purchase quantity = | 100000 | units/ order | | | | | | | | | | |
| 6 | | Safety stock = | 50000 | units | | | Lead time = | | | 15 | days | | | |
| 7 | | No. of working days per year = | | 230 | | | | | | | | | | |
| 8 | | | | | | | | | | | | | | |
| 9 | a) The number of purchases during a year = A / Purchase quantity = | | | | | | 300000/100000= | | | 3 | | | | |
| 10 | | | | | | | | | | | | | | |
| 11 | b) Max. inventory = Purchase quantity per order + Safety stock | | | | | 150000 | | Min. inventory = Safety stock = | | | | 50000 | | |
| 12 | Average inventory level (including the safety stock) = (Max. inventory + Min. inventory) / 2 = | | | | | | | | 100000 units | | | | | |
| 13 | | | | | | | | | | | | | | |
| 14 | c) Inventory turnover = A / Average inventory = | | | | | | 3 times per year | | | | | | | |
| 15 | | | | | | | | | | | | | | |
| 16 | d) Average days of supply in inventory (known as cover-time) = (Average inventory / A) x No. of working days per year = | | | | | | | | | | | | 76.6667 working days | |
| 17 | | | | | | | | | | | | | | |
| 18 | e) Reorder point = Rate of consumption of inventory (units per day) x Lead time + Safety stock | | | | | | | | | | | | | |
| 19 | | = (A / No. of working days per annum) x Lead time + Safety stock = | | | | | | | 69565.2 units | | | | | |
| 20 | | | | | | | | | | | | | | |
| 21 | f) Total inventory cost = Total o.c. + Total c.c | | | | | | | | | | | | | |
| 22 | | | | | | | | | | | | | | |
| 23 | Total o.c. = No. of orders (purchases) during the year x o = ₹ | | | | | | 4500 | | | | | | | |
| 24 | Total c.c. = Average inventory x c = | | | | | ₹ | 1500000 | | | | | | | |
| 25 | | | | | | ₹ | 1504500 | Total inventory cost = Total o.c. + Total c.c | | | | | | |
| 26 | | | | | | ₹ | 6541.3 | Total inventory cost per working day = Total inventory cost/ No. of working days | | | | | | |
| 27 | | | | | | | | | | | | | | |
| 28 | g) EOQ = Q = √ (2Ao / c) | | | | | | | | | | | | | |
| 29 | Q² = | 6E+07 | | | | | | | | | | | | |
| 30 | Q = | 7745.97 | | | | | | | | | | | | |
| 31 | | | | | | | | | | | | | | |
| 32 | h) For EOQ, Total inventory cost = Total o.c. + Total c.c + c.c. of safety stock | | | | | | | | | New level of safety stock = | | | 5000 | |
| 33 | | | | | | | | | | | | | | |
| 34 | | | | o.c. = (A/Q) x o = | | 58094.8 | | | | | | | Full Scre▼ x | |
| 35 | | | | c.c. = o.c. = | | 58094.8 | | | | | | | Close Full Screen | |
| 36 | c.c. of safety stock = New level of safety stock x c = | | | | | 75000 | | | | | | | | |
| 37 | | | | ₹ | | 191190 | Total inventory cost | | | | | | | |
| 38 | | | | ₹ | | 831.259 | Total inventory cost per working day = Total inventory cost/ No. of working days | | | | | | | |

*(Spreadsheet window menu bar: File Edit View Insert Format Tools Data Window StatTools Help)*

*(Taskbar: start — Inbo... Tran... Docu... Addit... Prod... Chap... In-en... 11:54PM)*

## ABC Analysis

A great variety of items is required in large organizations, for which inventories are maintained. It is not practical to have very stringent inventory control for each and every item. Therefore, all items are categorized into three categories, namely, A, B, and C on the basis of their consumption or usage values.

Consumption value (CV) = Unit price of an item × No. of units consumed per annum   (8.17)

Items are categorized according to the following criterion: category A has a high CV, category B has a moderate CV, and category C has a low CV. This classification is done using a curve known as the *ABC distribution curve* or the *Pareto curve*.

*Category A* items are subjected to strict inventory control. The EOQ model is used to determine the order size and the reorder level. A proper issuing system is maintained for such items, and workers requiring these items have to get them issued at the issue counter. *Category C* items have a low CV. Therefore the inventory control is not at all strict for such items. Such items are normally kept in an open area inside the factory, from where workers can take them according to their requirements. A periodic monitoring mechanism is established for such items, and quantities almost double the EOQ are ordered at one time. *Category B* items are subjected to an intermediate inventory control, neither as strict as that for category A, nor as casual as that for category C items.

### Example 8.14

Table 8.9 shows the details of ten items in a factory. Categorize them into categories A, B, and C according to their usage values.

**Table 8.9**

| Item ID | Unit price (₹) | No. of units per year |
|---------|---------------|----------------------|
| a | 5 | 1,000 |
| b | 10 | 10 |
| c | 7 | 5 |
| d | 750 | 100 |
| e | 5 | 2,000 |
| f | 1 | 150 |
| g | 8 | 1,500 |
| h | 6 | 10,000 |
| i | 30 | 20 |
| j | 4 | 9,000 |

### Solution

Calculate the CVs using Eqn (8.17). For example, for item *a*, the CV is ₹5,000 (₹5 × 1,000). Calculate also the percentage of the CV of each item (Table 8.10).

**Table 8.10**   Calculation of CV

| Item ID | Unit price (₹) | No. of units per year | CV (units) | CV (%) |
|---------|---------------|----------------------|-----------|--------|
| a | 5 | 1,000 | 5,000 | 2.514 |
| b | 10 | 10 | 100 | 0.050 |
| c | 7 | 5 | 35 | 0.018 |
| d | 750 | 100 | 75,000 | 37.710 |
| e | 5 | 2,000 | 10,000 | 5.028 |
| f | 1 | 150 | 150 | 0.075 |
| g | 8 | 1,500 | 12,000 | 6.034 |
| h | 6 | 10,000 | 60,000 | 30.168 |
| i | 30 | 20 | 600 | 0.302 |
| j | 4 | 9,000 | 36,000 | 18.101 |
|   |   |   | 1,98,885 | 100.000 |

Now rank the items starting with the item having the highest consumption percentage. Find also the cumulative consumption percentage, as it will be plotted along the *y*-axis of the Pareto curve. Plot the items at equal distances from each other along the *x*-axis. For placing these 10 items, we have divided the *x*-axis into 10 equal parts (Table 8.11).

**Table 8.11**

| Item ID | Consumption value (%) | Cumulative consumption (%) | Space for items on the x-axis (%) | Cumulative space for items on the x-axis (%) |
|---------|------------------------|-----------------------------|------------------------------------|----------------------------------------------|
| *d* | 37.710 | 37.710 | 10 | 10 |
| *h* | 30.168 | 67.878 | 10 | 20 |
| *j* | 18.101 | 85.979 | 10 | 30 |
| *g* | 6.034 | 92.013 | 10 | 40 |
| *e* | 5.028 | 97.041 | 10 | 50 |
| *a* | 2.514 | 99.555 | 10 | 60 |
| *i* | 0.302 | 99.857 | 10 | 70 |
| *f* | 0.075 | 99.932 | 10 | 80 |
| *b* | 0.050 | 99.982 | 10 | 90 |
| *c* | 0.018 | 100.000 | 10 | 100 |

We choose the software program SPSS 10.0 to make the ABC distribution curve as SPSS graphs are easy to manipulate. Copy the columns for *Cumulative space for items on the x-axis* and *Consumption value* from Table 8.11 and paste them in the SPSS 10.0 worksheet as shown in Fig. 8.25. From the SPSS Data Editor toolbar, select **Graphs**, then **Interactive**, and finally **Line** in the pull-down menu. A dialog box as shown in Fig. 8.25 appears. In the **Assign Variables** tab drag **var00001** to the *x*-axis and **var00002** to the *y*-axis, as shown in the dialog box. Click on **OK** to get a graph as shown in Figs 8.26(a) and 8.26(b).

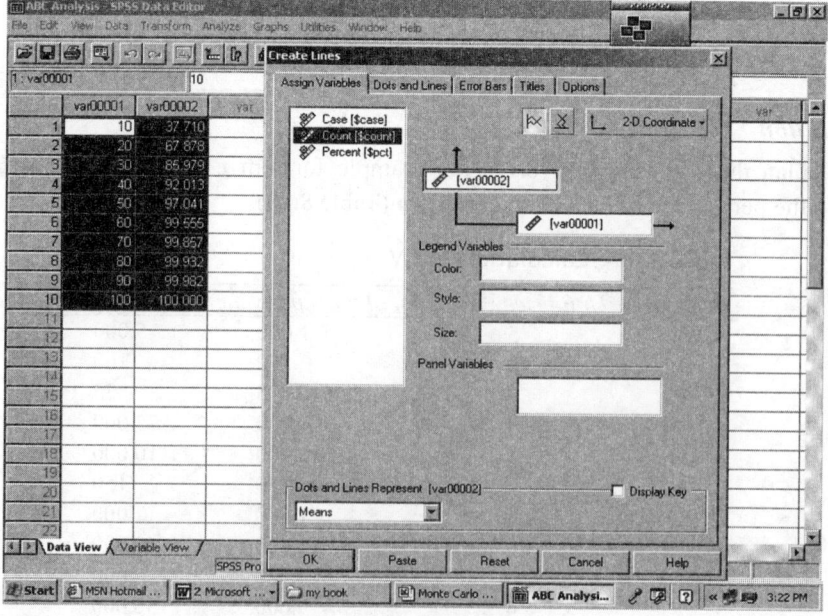

**Fig. 8.25** The Create Lines dailog box in SPSS 1.0

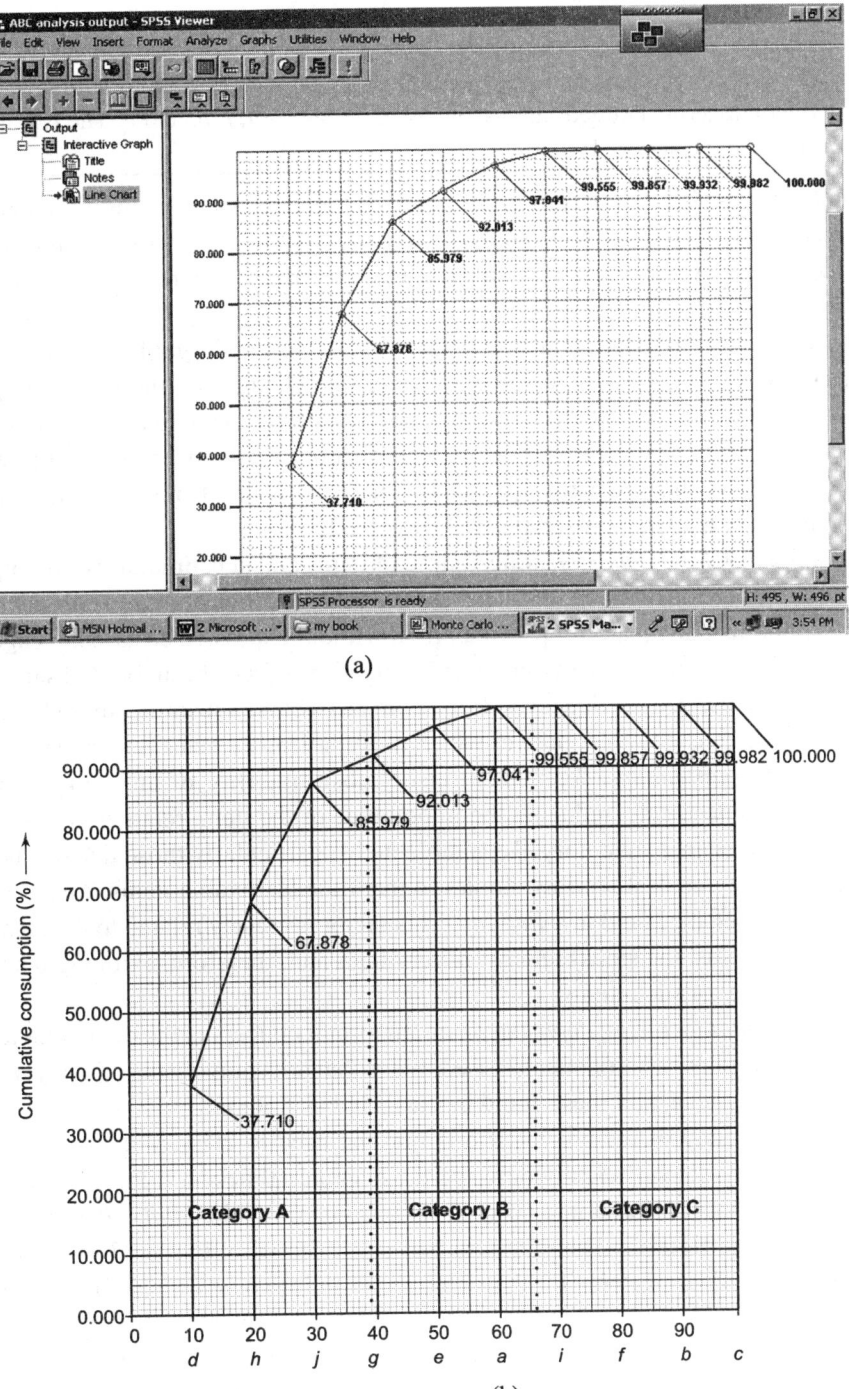

**Fig. 8.26** Cumulative consumption graph

After plotting the curve, we have to identify two points on the curve for dividing it into the three categories. For category A items, the slope of the curve is very steep and for category C items, the curve is almost flat (parallel to the x-axis). Category B items lie in-between category A and C items.

Move along the curve from the origin and find that the curve is very steep up to item *j*. Mark this point on the curve with a vertical dotted line—category A items are *d*, *h*, and *j*. Now move along the curve from the other end and find that the curve is flat enough up to item *i*. Mark this point on the curve with a vertical dotted line—category C items are *i*, *f*, *b*, and *c*. The remaining items, namely *g*, *e*, and *a*, are category B items.

---

**Multiple criteria ABC analysis** The criterion for categorizing items discussed so far is the usage (consumption) value in ABC analysis. In reality, many more criteria may be important. Let us now discuss various other criteria a materials manager may have to consider in practical ABC analysis (Flores and Whybark 1986).

Items in the inventory could be categorized on how susceptible they are to obsolescence and/or how likely they are to be subjected to design changes by the *engineering department*. For example, high-tech parts like microprocessors in personal computers are subject to obsolescence as technological developments occur. A number of items may be under study and may be subject to engineering changes in the near future. These items should be maintained under close scrutiny by inventory managers if scrap is to be avoided.

In the *purchase department*, lead time of items and substitutability are important criteria for the categorization of items. Both the length of the lead time and its variability could be important in maintaining adequate supply of an item without excessive costs. The length of the lead time decides the response time to a crisis and variability affects the amount of safety stock required to provide the desired service level. If the item has a close substitute, more flexibility and reduced response time is possible, both of which make inventory management easier.

In the *maintenance department* also, substitutability of an item provides flexibility in response to problems, reducing the importance of the item, relative to less substitutable items in the maintenance inventory. Repairable items, particularly those that can be repaired quickly, provide a degree of flexibility similar to that of substitutable items. Another possible criterion in the maintenance field is *criticality*. This factor is closely related to the idea of stock-out cost. For some items, the stock-out cost is very high and, therefore, extra vigilance is warranted for the inventory of such items.

In the *manufacturing department*, an important concept is the commonality of items. This is a measure of how a component is used. Items that are components of many products can impact the assembly area, and these could be classified as A items.

Although any of the above criteria may be used to classify items as A, B, or C, a single measure may not sufficiently describe the managerial needs. It may be desirable to take more than one of these criteria into account at the same time; the *joint criteria matrix* is useful here.

**Joint criteria matrix** The joint criteria matrix shown in Fig. 8.27 uses the *criticality classes and usage values* of items for their classification into nine cells. Table 8.12 shows 10 items in a factory classified as shown in the figure. However, we have to reclassify the items (as shown by the arrows), so that there are only three categories corresponding to cells AA, BB, and CC. In practice, managerial judgement is used to achieve the reclassification on an item-by-item basis. The arrows in Fig. 8.27 show how items 2; 10; and 6, 7, and 9 are moved to cells AA, BB, and CC, respectively, so that there are only three classes of items as in the usual ABC analysis. Practically, not all potential criteria are equally important in managing an

> The joint criteria matrix uses the criticality classes and usage values of items for their classification into nine cells.

inventory; just two criteria need to be included in the analysis usually, one of which should be the usage value of the items.

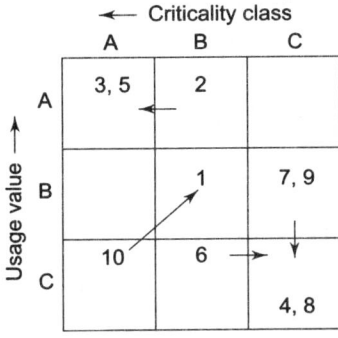

**Fig. 8.27**   Joint criteria matrix

**Table 8.12**

| Item | Criticality | Usage value |
|------|-------------|-------------|
| 1 | B | B |
| 2 | B | A |
| 3 | A | A |
| 4 | C | C |
| 5 | A | A |
| 6 | B | C |
| 7 | C | B |
| 8 | C | C |
| 9 | C | B |
| 10 | A | C |

**Periodic review system**   As discussed in ABC analysis, category C items are subjected to periodic reviews for replenishment. Periodic review means checking the inventory level after a regular interval of time. The desired/target inventory level and the present inventory level are compared. In such inspections, the order size for replenishment is determined using the following formula:

Order size = Desired/Target inventory level − Present inventory level

Desired/Target inventory level = Average demand during the review period
+ Average DDLT + Safety stock

It is important to determine the optimal time interval for these reviews. The EOQ model is helpful in doing so. In this model, let $t$ be the periodic review time interval. If $t$ is expressed as a fraction of a year, the demand during this time would be $At$, where $A$ is the annual demand. Hence this becomes the maximum inventory, and the average inventory is $At/2$.

$$\text{Annual OC, } P = no = (A/At) \times o = o/t$$

$$\text{Annual CC, } R = (At/2) \times c$$

$$\text{Total cost, } T = P + R = \frac{o}{t} + \frac{Atc}{2}$$

$$\frac{dT}{dt} = -\frac{o}{t^2} + \frac{Ac}{2} = 0$$

$$\Rightarrow \qquad \frac{Ac}{2} = \frac{o}{t^2}$$

$$\Rightarrow \qquad t^2 = \frac{2o}{Ac}$$

Therefore, the optimal time interval for periodic review,

$$t = \sqrt{\frac{2o}{Ac}}$$

### Example 8.15

The annual demand of an item is 20,000 units. Its OC is ₹200 per order and CC is ₹8 per unit per year. Assuming that there are 320 working days in a year, find the optimal time interval for the periodic review.

### Solution

$A$ = 20,000 units; $o$ = ₹200 per order; $c$ = ₹8 per unit per year. Then, the optimal interval for periodic review is

$$t = \sqrt{\frac{2o}{Ac}} = \sqrt{\frac{2 \times 200}{20,000 \times 8}} = \sqrt{\frac{1}{400}} = \frac{1}{20} \text{ year}$$

For 320 working days in a year,

$$t = \frac{320}{20} \text{ days} = 16 \text{ days}$$

Therefore, after every 16 working days, a review is required.

## Monte Carlo Simulation in Inventory Management

*Simulation* is the theoretical imitation of a real practical process. When a process has many variables, it becomes difficult to analyse. Simulation is a useful tool for processes such as rocket propulsions and space shuttle testing before launch, which involves a lot of time, effort, and money.

In inventory management, simulation is used to find the optimal order size and the optimum reorder level (so that the total inventory cost is minimum), when both the consumption during lead time as well as the lead time are variables. Monte Carlo simulation can be applied when the variables assume values (collectively exhaustive) only according to past experiences, so that the probabilities of occurrence of these values are also known. The term *collectively exhaustive* means that all the possible values (according to past experience) have to be considered. No value can be ignored. The sum of probabilities of occurrence of these values should be 1.

**Table 8.13**

| Lead time (days) | Observation |
|---|---|
| 1 | 4 |
| 2 | 17 |
| 3 | 36 |
| 4 | 25 |
| 5 | 10 |
| 6 | 8 |
| | 100 |

In order to understand the process of simulation, let us take up an example. Table 8.13 shows the lead times a distributor takes (according to 100 past observations) for supplying a consignment of the copies of a book to a bookseller.

From this table, we can find the probabilities of lead-time values. We also find the cumulative probabilities, and fix ranges for all the lead-time values as shown in Table 8.14. These ranges are fixed using the cumulative probability values as shown.

Observe that the decimals in these ranges have been dropped. These ranges are fixed for a definite purpose, which is to choose a random number from random-number tables or generated by software (such as MS Excel, SPSS, etc.). In a random-number table (see Table B of the Appendix), any number may appear randomly anywhere in the table. The table shown has two-digit random numbers: We require two-digit random numbers, as the probability values in our example have two digits after the decimal and, thus, the ranges also have two digits.

Simulation is the theoretical imitation of a real practical process.

**Table 8.14**

| Lead time (days) | Observations | Probability | Cumulative probability | Range |
|---|---|---|---|---|
| 1 | 4 | 0.04 | 0.04 | 00–03 |
| 2 | 17 | 0.17 | 0.21 | 04–20 |
| 3 | 36 | 0.36 | 0.57 | 21–56 |
| 4 | 25 | 0.25 | 0.82 | 57–81 |
| 5 | 10 | 0.10 | 0.92 | 82–91 |
| 6 | 8 | 0.08 | 1.00 | 92–99 |
| | 100 | 1.00 | | |

**Table 8.15**

| DDLT (units) | Observations |
|---|---|
| 10 | 2 |
| 15 | 3 |
| 20 | 19 |
| 25 | 41 |
| 30 | 23 |
| 35 | 5 |
| 40 | 4 |
| 45 | 2 |
| 50 | 1 |
| | 100 |

For choosing random numbers, we can start randomly from any point in the table, either vertically or horizontally. A random number chosen may fall in any one of the ranges fixed; the corresponding lead time will be chosen. The last range in our example (92–99) ends in 99, as the highest two-digit random number is 99. The ranges have been fixed in such a way that the last one ends in 99.

If the probabilities have more than two digits after the decimal (and thus the ranges have more than two digits), we choose random numbers with the same number of digits from the table. For example, if three-digit random numbers are chosen (starting from the top left corner of the table), the first number will be 221, the next will be 193, and so on.

Table 8.15 gives the DDLT experienced by the bookseller (according to past 100 observations).

We repeat the procedure discussed earlier with lead time for finding the probability, cumulative probability, and range for all the values that DDLT may assume (see Table 8.16).

**Table 8.16**

| DDLT (units) | Observations | Probability | Cumulative probability | Range |
|---|---|---|---|---|
| 10 | 2 | 0.02 | 0.02 | 00–01 |
| 15 | 3 | 0.03 | 0.05 | 02–04 |
| 20 | 19 | 0.19 | 0.24 | 05–23 |
| 25 | 41 | 0.41 | 0.65 | 24–64 |
| 30 | 23 | 0.23 | 0.88 | 65–87 |
| 35 | 5 | 0.05 | 0.93 | 88–92 |
| 40 | 4 | 0.04 | 0.97 | 93–96 |
| 45 | 2 | 0.02 | 0.99 | 97–98 |
| 50 | 1 | 0.01 | 1.00 | 99 |
| | 100 | 1.00 | | |

It is given that $c = ₹1$ per book per day, $o = ₹60$ per order, and $k = ₹20$ per book short. Let us assume that the bookseller wants to evaluate the three options given in Table 8.17 and then choose the best option. The simulations for these three options are shown in MS Excel worksheets.

**Table 8.17**

| | Option 1 | Option 2 | Option 3 |
|---|---|---|---|
| Opening inventory (units) | 150 | 150 | 150 |
| Reorder level (units) | 50 | 100 | 50 |
| Order size (units) | 100 | 50 | 50 |

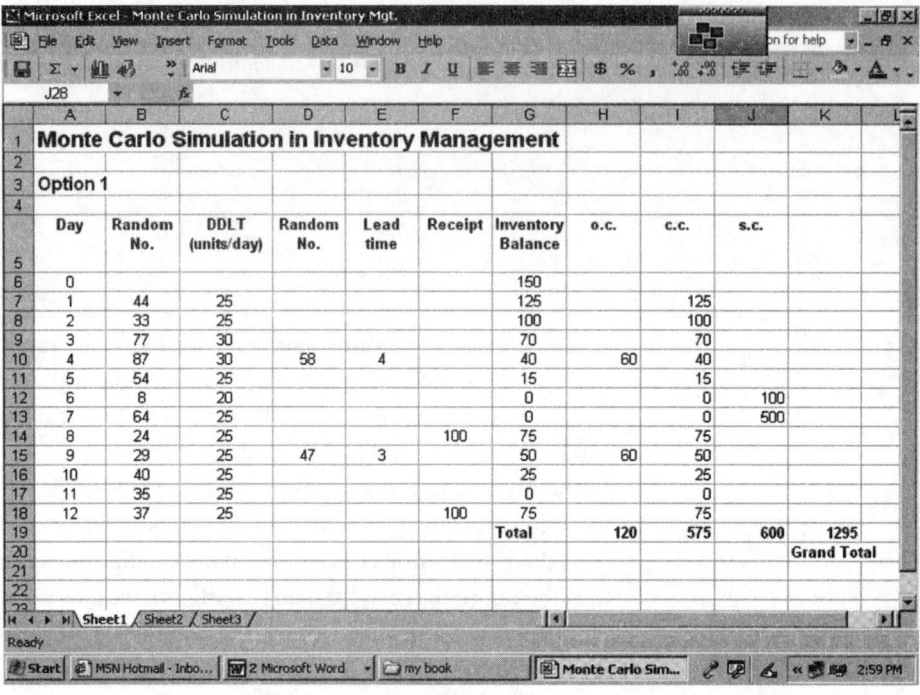

(a)

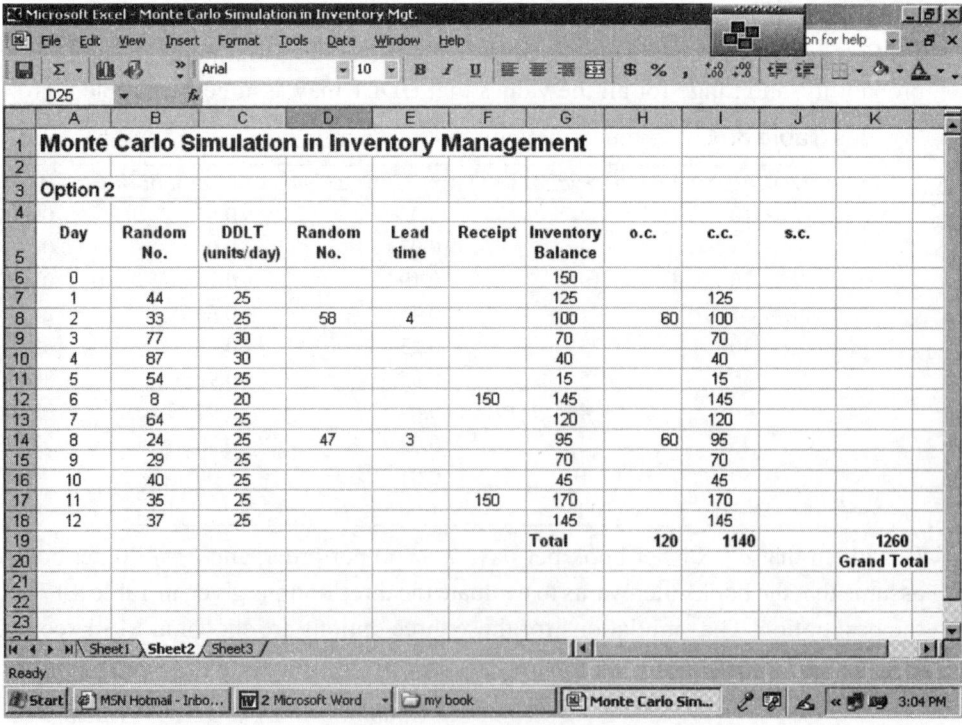

(b)

**Fig 8.28** (Contd)

The spreadsheet shows:

**Monte Carlo Simulation in Inventory Management**

**Option 3**

| Day | Random No. | DDLT (units/day) | Random No. | Lead time | Receipt | Inventory Balance | o.c. | c.c. | s.c. |
|-----|-----------|------------------|-----------|-----------|---------|-------------------|------|------|------|
| 0 | | | | | | 150 | | | |
| 1 | 44 | 25 | | | | 125 | | 125 | |
| 2 | 33 | 25 | | | | 100 | | 100 | |
| 3 | 77 | 30 | | | | 70 | | 70 | |
| 4 | 87 | 30 | 58 | 4 | | 40 | 60 | 40 | |
| 5 | 54 | 25 | | | | 15 | | 15 | |
| 6 | 8 | 20 | | | | 0 | | 0 | 100 |
| 7 | 64 | 25 | | | | 0 | | 0 | 500 |
| 8 | 24 | 25 | 47 | 3 | 50 | 25 | 60 | 25 | |
| 9 | 29 | 25 | | | | 0 | | 0 | |
| 10 | 40 | 25 | | | | 0 | | 0 | 500 |
| 11 | 35 | 25 | 23 | 3 | 50 | 25 | 60 | 25 | |
| 12 | 37 | 25 | | | | 0 | | 0 | |
| | | | | | | **Total** | **180** | **400** | **1100** |
| | | | | | | | | | **1680** Grand Total |

(c)

**Fig. 8.28**  Monte Carlo simulation (a) option 1, (b) option 2, (c) option 3

In Fig. 8.28(a) (for option 1), we start from day 0 to show an inventory balance of 150 units before day 1. For day 0, we have not shown the CC because these costs are considered day 1 onwards only. For day 1, choose a random number from the random-number table, say, 44 from column 11 and row 11 of the table. Let this be the starting point (the next number is 33). In Table 8.16, 44 falls in the range 24–64. The corresponding value of DDLT is 27. Hence, in the worksheet place 25 in the third column. The reorder level is 50 units for option 1 (Table 8.17). Hence, there is no need to choose a random number for lead time, and the fourth, fifth, and sixth columns for day 1 will remain empty. Out of a balance of 150 units on day 0, 25 units have been consumed on day 1. Therefore, we have a balance of 125 units on day 1. The CC at the rate of ₹1 per unit per day is ₹125 for this balance. For day 1, the OC and shortage cost (SC) are both zero.

For day 2, choose the next random number from the table. This number is 33 and again it falls in the range 24–64 in Table 8.16. Hence, 25 units are consumed on day 2. The balance is 100 units (125 – 25) for which the CC is ₹100.

For day 3, repeat the same process; the CC is ₹70. On day 4, the random number selected is 87, for which the demand in Table 8.16 is 30 units. The balance is 40 units (70 – 30). This balance is less than the reorder level (50 units). Therefore, on day 4, an order has to be placed. Pick up a random number for selecting the lead time. This time we start selecting random numbers from column 21 and row 1 of the table; the number selected is 58. From Table 8.14, we see that 58 falls in the range 57–81. The lead time corresponding to this range is 4 days. Put these values 58 and 4 in the appropriate place for day 4 in the worksheet. The OC for day 4 is ₹60 (because of the order placed on day 4), CC is ₹40, and SC is nil. The reorder size is 100 units for option

1. These 100 units will be received four days after day 4, that is, on day 8. Therefore, we place 100 units in the Receipt column of day 8.

For day 5, the random number is 54 and DDLT is 25 units. The balance inventory on this day is 15 units (40 − 25 = 15) and the CC is ₹15. On day 6, the random number is 08 and the corresponding DDLT is 20 units. Only 15 units are available in the inventory after day 5, while the demand on day 6 is 20 units. Therefore, there is a shortage of 5 units on day 6. The SC at the rate of ₹20 per unit short is ₹100 (5 × ₹20). The inventory level balance on day 6 is zero. Hence, the CC is also zero.

On day 7, the random number is 64 and DDLT is 25. The inventory balance is zero and there is a shortage of 25 units, for which the SC is ₹500 (25 × ₹20). The CC is zero as is the OC. On day 8, the random number is 24 and DDLT is 25 units. On the basis of order placed on day 4, 100 units are received. Therefore, the demand of 25 units on day 8 is satisfied and the inventory balance becomes 75 (100 − 25 = 75). The CC is ₹75.

This process is repeated up to day 12 and the sums of OC, CC, and SC are ₹120, ₹575, and ₹600, respectively. The total inventory cost is the sum of these three costs, which is ₹1,295 for option 1.

Similarly, we find the total inventory cost for options 2 and 3 (using the same random numbers as in option 1), shown in Figs 8.28(b) and 8.28(c). For option 2, the total inventory cost is ₹(120 + 1,140) = ₹1,260, and for option 3 it is ₹(180 + 400 + 1,100) = ₹1,680. Therefore option 2 provides the minimum total inventory cost and, hence, is the best option.

The above example is just for illustration and, hence, we have considered only 12 days for the simulation exercise. The results are accurate only when the simulation for every option is done for a very large number (thousands) of days. This can only be done by using computer simulation software.

# Managing Demand Uncertainty

### Effect of Demand Uncertainty

The fundamental lacuna of the economic order quantity (EOQ) model is that it assumes that demand is known and certain. In reality, this seldom happens. Most organizations deem that demand can be predicted with great certainty and that is why they create their production and inventory plans months ahead of the selling season by relying heavily on demand forecasts. This is despite the cognizance of the fact that forecasts may seldom prove to be sacrosanct.

In recent times, demand uncertainty has further increased due to short product life cycles. Take the example of the computer industry—almost every year, we find a plethora of new models of computers with innovative features thronging the market. The product variety in the market is huge with many players competing neck-to-neck. Which model or product will click in the market is highly unpredictable.

In order to reduce demand uncertainty, the following three points should be kept in mind by the production and inventory planners.

1. Always treat demand forecasts as unreliable.
2. Take cognizance of the fact that longer the planning horizon, more is the likelihood of the demand forecasts being inaccurate.

3. Try to arrive at aggregate forecasts by combining forecasts for various models of a product in order to increase the overall accuracy.

## Multiple Order Opportunities

In most instances, there are opportunities to place orders whenever the need be. Such instances come under multiple order opportunities. For example, if you are a distributor of refrigerators, you place the order to the manufacturer to deliver more units whenever you come to know that your stock has fallen below a certain level. However, this may not be possible in single ordering systems where there is a single opportunity to place the order. For example, a retailer of fire crackers normally has the opportunity of placing the order to the manufacturers only once—just before the Diwali season. Due to this seasonal demand, fire cracker manufacturers do not manufacture during the rest of the year and, hence, do not accept orders from the retailers during that time.

In situations of multiple order opportunities, the demand patterns are randomly distributed throughout the year. Also, the lead time taken by suppliers to supply the goods may vary depending upon the kind of demand rush being experienced by the manufacturer at that point in time. This clearly adds to the complexity of managing the inventory in the supply chain.

## Continuous and Periodic Review Policies

In a continuous review policy, the status of inventory is monitored continuously and a new order is placed to the suppliers as soon as the inventory falls below a certain level, known as the *reorder point*. This policy was hitherto justifiable for high-value–low-volume items. However, contemporary technologies like *radio frequency* identification (RFID) have made it feasible to continuously monitor the level of inventory on a real-time basis even for moderate-value–moderate-volume items.

In a periodic review policy, inventory is monitored at regular fixed intervals of time. Usually, this policy is executed for low-value–non-critical items required in large volumes. At the time of a periodic review, a top-up stock is ordered to the suppliers in order to bring the level of inventory to a specified pre-determined threshold level.

## Centralized vs Decentralized Systems

In a decentralized inventory system, the inventory is scattered at different locations (say, at multiple warehouses) to promptly respond to the customer needs (when each warehouse is strategically located close to the respective markets/customers). Customer responsiveness is quite high; however, due to diseconomies of scale the overall inventory is higher (at all the warehouses taken together). Also, it is relatively more difficult to manage the inventory due to reduced visibility across multiple locations. However, this issue can be taken care of by using contemporary IT systems that help in real-time tracking of inventory at multiple dispersed locations.

In a centralized inventory system, inventory is kept at a single location (say, a single warehouse), which is used to address several markets simultaneously. Naturally, there are economies of scale and relatively less overall inventory is required. Such systems are easier to manage as the available inventory is easily visible at the single location. However, customer responsiveness is reduced in this case, as distances to some markets/customers would obviously be higher.

### Risk Pooling

When an organization moves from a decentralized inventory system to a centralized inventory system, generally less overall safety stock is required to be maintained at the centralized location compared to the safety stocks required to be maintained at separate locations in a decentralization system. This is so because the overall 'risk' is reduced due to the 'pooling' of the inventory at a centralized location. This concept is, therefore, called *risk pooling*.

The following three kinds of situations may happen with risk pooling depending upon the correlation between demands at separate locations (say, markets).

**When demands are not correlated (independent demand)**   When demands at various markets are independent of each other, the possibility of these markets experiencing extreme demands at the same time is very less. Therefore, in a pooled (centralized) system, overall less safety stock can be maintained.

**When demands are positively correlated to each other**   In this scenario, the benefits of risk pooling would not be present. This is so because extreme demand situation may happen simultaneously at various locations. In this scenario, the safety stocks required at separate locations combined together would be the same as the overall safety stock required at a centralized location. For example, before a festival season, the demand at various locations may rise simultaneously.

**When demands are negatively correlated to each other**   The benefits of risk pooling are most pronounced in this scenario. This is so because the rise in demand at a particular location would happen with a simultaneous slump in demand at another location. This scenario prevails when the same set of customers choose between either of the two locations both of which are in their close vicinity.

## Summary

The main objective of inventory management is to ensure that the inventory level is neither too high nor too low, that is, it should be just optimal so that the total cost is minimum. The *economic order quantity* (EOQ) model helps in finding this optimal level of inventory. The optimal order size suggested by the EOQ model and any discount option being offered by the supplier are compared, and the best option is selected on the basis of least total cost. A proper level of *safety stock* should be maintained to avoid a stock out.

*Stock outs* may be created intentionally sometimes due to the high carrying cost (CC) of certain items. In the model for intentional shortages, one determines the optimal order size in order to minimize the total cost. The *production model of inventory* helps in determining the optimal size of a production lot when sales and production take place simultaneously.

The inventories of a great variety of items are to be maintained in an organization. The same level of strict inventory control cannot be exercised for every item. Therefore, items are classified into categories A, B, and C based on relevant criteria. A *periodic review system* is applied to category C items; the optimal time interval between periodic checks can be determined using the EOQ model.

*Monte Carlo simulation* is the ultimate solution for finding the optimal inventory system under a condition of many variables. It requires the use of simulation software to get accurate results.

Demand uncertainty can be managed by centralization and risk pooling in certain situations.

## References

Ashayeri, J., R. Heuts, A. Jansen, and B. Szczerba 1996, 'Inventory management of repairable service parts for personal computers', *International Journal of Operations and Production Management*, vol. 16, no. 12.

Flores, Benito E. and D. Clay Whybark 1986, 'Multiple criteria ABC analysis', *International Journal of Operations and Production Management*, vol. 6, no. 3, p. 38.

Varma, S. 2012, 'Superpower? 230 million Indians go hungry daily',http://articles.timesofindia. indiatimes.com/2012-01-15/india/30629637_1_ anganwadi-workers-ghi-number-of-hungry-people, accessed on 13 March 2013.

# Keywords

**Anticipation inventory** is maintained to satisfy customer demand, that is, to ensure that no customer is disappointed by not getting the desired item at any point of time.

**Carrying/holding cost** is the cost of storing the inventory in the warehouse.

**Cost of shortages** is the cost mainly due to loss in goodwill on the customers' part, which depends on how long they have waited to receive the goods. It also includes, the loss of potential profit due to the customers switching to competitors.

**Cycle stock** is the stock of items stored as inventory to meet an inventory cycle determined by an inventory model.

**Decoupling inventories** decouple (de-link) the various processes of operations from each other. When operations take place in a sequence, for example, semi-finished goods being operated upon by machines one after the other in sequence, (decoupling) inventories of semi-finished goods pile up near each machine.

**Dependent demand inventory** is the inventory of items that are components, parts, or sub-assemblies of finished goods.

**Differential discounting** refers to a supplier offering different discounts for different quantities of an item.

**Economic order quantity (EOQ)** is the optimal size of an order, for which the total inventory cost is minimum.

**Independent demand inventory** is the inventory of finished goods.

**Inventory** is the stock of idle resources in a firm for future use.

**Lead time** is the gap between the time of placing the order and the time of receiving the items from the supplier.

**Ordering cost per order** is the cost of placing a single order.

**Pipeline/transit stock** is stock that is moved between the various elements of the supply chain, that is, between suppliers, manufacturers, distributors, wholesalers, and the end users.

**Quantity discount** is a particular percentage of discount offered when a quantity of items equal to or more than a specified quantity is purchased.

**Safety stock** is defined as a hedge (protection) against the possibility of a stock out.

**Safety/buffer stock** is extra stock maintained in excess of the anticipation inventory, in order to protect against demand fluctuations and abrupt increases in the time taken by the suppliers to supply the items.

**Seasonal inventories** are inventories of items that are relevant in a particular season, stocked by firms before the start of that season.

**Simulation** is the theoretical imitation of a real practical process.

## CASE STUDY I

## Pantaloon—Revolutionizing Inventory Management in Indian Retailing

Kishore Biyani, the Indian retail living legend, has taught the industry a few lessons in inventory management. The retail industry thrives on managing the inventory of various items stocked and displayed in the retail stores. One of the biggest challenges is to keep track of ever-changing customer preferences, and accordingly, to achieve quick inventory turnaround. The promptness of replenishment of the inventories of hundreds of items in a retail store is a very crucial factor. The competition in the retailing industry is all set to intensify with the entry of many big Indian companies such as Reliance, Bharti (jointly with Walmart) and so on. Biyani is redefining the way inventory is managed in retailing and these revolutionary initiatives are all set to make his flagship Pantaloon a leader in Indian retail business.

Big and fast seems to be Kishore Biyani's mantra. Pantaloon has grown from mere ₹900 million in revenues in 1998 to a 55 store spread in nineteen cities with expected annual revenues of ₹11 billion, in the span of a mere seven years. During 2004, Pantaloon's stock price more than tripled and crossed ₹900 in April 2005. The company's sales are at an all time high, with revenues increasing by almost five times in the last five years. Biyani is now perfectly poised to push accelerated growth and cash in further on the retail boom that is spreading through urban India.

To leverage the growth in the retail industry, most other players were furiously setting up malls and expanding their chain of stores. According to Biyani, such companies were following a similar format to reach the same customers. In contrast, he decided to build a differentiated retail model. Therefore, he went back to the drawing board and developed three new highly successful retail formats. The new stores were designed to get maximum share of consumers' wallets.

In lifestyle retailing, the company's flagship brand Pantaloon was already synonymous with apparel merchandising. Biyani designed a new format known as Central. It is a seamless mall that offers apparel, fashion, and entertainment targeted at the rapidly expanding middle class market. Big Bazaar has already carved a niche for itself in value retailing and Food Bazaar is synonymous with food and grocery retail. He then spent the next few years rapidly setting up these stores across urban India. By June 2006, Biyani had set up fifty Food Bazaars, thirty five Big Bazaars, twenty Pantaloons, and six Centrals occupying close to 3.5 million sq. ft of retail space.

Meanwhile, Biyani is also focusing on inventory management. According to him retailing involves anticipating demand on a particular day (short-term demand) as well as while opening new stores (long-term demand). Hence, he has focused on reducing stock build up. Currently his inventory is around 75 days, down from 112 days in 2000–2001. To improve efficiency, he has assigned category managers for every product group. The category managers are responsible for managing the lifecycle of a product group and meeting sales targets.

Biyani is concentrating on economies of scale. He says, 'I think our biggest efficiency is in terms of our buying costs. We can get as much as we want, which is where we score over smaller retailers with lower cost structures. We buy huge quantities and have proven our ability to pay. We are also able to promote a brand/label in a store.'

Over the years, Pantaloons has been through a few makeovers. Biyani is junking the old positioning of 'India's family store' and is planning to target the youth instead. His consumer insight is, like always, a shade radical, 'Within a family, people were thinking and dressing and acting very differently. Which is why I believe studying Indian consumers by demographics and psychographics is a waste of time. We should look at communities—techies, metrosexuals, etc.'

Hence, Pantaloons will now be about affordable fashion. 'Fashion from Pantaloons' is the new punch line of the company. In the next few years, according to Biyani, Pantaloons will be the Indian equivalent of Spanish fashion retailer Zara. Internationally, in the business of fashion retailing, while the margins on individual garments are high, the final margins are low. That is because unsold stocks have to be liquidated through heavy discounting. For instance, it takes 90–120 days to design and ship a new line of fashion merchandise. This means two things. One, the company will be forced to order in lots of 90–120 days, lest it runs out of stock halfway. Two, if fashion changes, the company will be saddled with inventory, which then has to be liquidated. Says Biyani, 'If the margins on every garment are 50 per cent, but I am going to sell half of them after a 12 per cent markdown, my margins are already down to 44 per cent.' Therefore, the company is trying to crash the time to market from 90 days to about 21 days.

Zara has a neat model that lets it launch new lines in less than 21 days. What made it possible is that it had its own factories. Biyani is doing something similar. Faster manufacturing will let the company stock less inventory, which will make it more responsive to market changes, while reducing the quantity of stocks to be sold at a discount. At the same time, sales will rise due to faster arrival of fresh stocks. According to Biyani, 'We can up our margins by 5–6 per cent.' Right now, he has brought the time lag down from 90 days to 40.

Biyani's new strategy for Big Bazaar also centres on fashion, but with an orientation towards large volumes. It will retail what Biyani calls 'commoditised' fashion—blue jeans and white shirts. Biyani is planning to buy these garments in large quantities and sell them at low prices. Pantaloons has jeans from Bare at ₹695 and above. Newport, priced at ₹599, was the cheapest pair of jeans in the market. Biyani contacted Arvind Mills to manufacture 1,00,000 units of Pantaloons jeans at ₹299. Hence, Ruf-n-Tuf was born. The brand will now be only available at Big Bazaar. Biyani has a similar deal with Arvind Mills for T-shirts.

Biyani's retailing model will have lean operations. Pantaloon will carry no stocks. The inventory will lie with the manufacturer and replenished just-in-time. In businesses, such as, plastics, leather, food technologies, where there are not any large manufacturers, Pantaloon is trying to engineer its own low prices. For ketchup, it has an in-house label for ₹38 as opposed to an industry average of ₹58 for the same size.

Biyani's current passion is improving inventory management. Although the entire stock for grocery is replenished thirty times, and garment stocks are replenished six times annually, he is not satisfied. Explains Biyani, 'This will be the key differentiator between the winners and losers because it reduces working capital requirement and improves return on capital.' If Biyani gets it right, his retail juggernaut could well be unstoppable.

Kishore Biyani is on to another idea, and he is not letting go of it because it could change the face of the retail business. The goal is simple—to dramatically reduce the time it takes from when a product is conceived to the time it takes to get to the stores. His target is 45 days flat. In the world of fashion, it takes four to six months for an approved idea to make it to the stores. Biyani says that forecasting trends has too many variables and the chances of miscalculating customer needs are high. In such cases stores are stuck with large quantities of unsold inventories. 'The aim of "mind to market" is to respond to the demand of the market rather than try to forecast it months in advance,' he says. Pantaloon has already started pilot projects. In October 2004, the company detected a demand for trendier trousers. It launched Fashion 'F' Trousers based on this in December that year. To cater to the demand, all departments—design (he has hired fresh design graduates to work with him), production, category managers, marketing and fabrication—came together on the project plan. The team created a range of fashion styles and jointly agreed upon the fabrics that would be used, and the various price points at which the products would be launched. Says Biyani, 'We were able to put these trousers on the shelves of our stores all over India in 40 days.' At margins of 65 per cent, the pick-up offered great returns. No wonder Biyani's already on to the next project—where the lead time will be a meagre 22 days. Only Spanish retailer Zara's 15 day lead time is faster.

Much has been written about radio frequency identification (RFID) and what it can do for manufacturers—improve production operations, asset utilization, forecasting, inventory accuracy, and customer satisfaction by pinpointing the location and status of products as they move through the manufacturing and retail value chain. Taking a cue from this, in 2005, Pantaloon piloted an RFID project at one its warehouses in Tarapur using 1,000 RFID tags. The company started from where it matters the most—by implementing the technology at the warehouse.

Pantaloon went in for RFID for its simplicity of tagging, efficacy of use, product buffering, ability to keep track of over-produced items, and ability to monitor product-line lead time at the warehouse and fast-moving product-lines. The company selected a few lines of apparel, primarily shirts and trousers, for its RFID pilot. The RFID application developed by Wipro Infotech was tailored to the overall solution in line with Pantaloon's business processes and IT landscape (from the factory outward to the warehouse inward and from the warehouse outward) in order to capture real-time data. The application is integrated with Oracle database 10g and middleware along with an implementation of the RFID hardware. It integrates with the existing IT infrastructure, the in-house developed Retail Enterprise Manager.

At the factory outlet, RFID tags are attached to the merchandise and the data is written to them. When the RFID-tagged merchandise comes through the inward gate, all related information such as purchase and delivery orders are fed in the inward terminals in real-time. After collating the requirements of specific outlets with the merchandise in the warehouse, the items allocated for different outlets are transported. The tags are removed once the RFID-tagged goods pass through the outward terminal. The pilot was implemented at a cost of ₹3 million, which included the hardware cost (a writer, 2 tag readers, and 1,000 tags) and the cost of system integration.

Although with a few hiccups, Pantaloon has enjoyed certain benefits. Recording of data became smooth at the inward and outward terminals, which helped to save time and gain accuracy. Before the implementation, the possibility of scanning incorrect goods was much higher. Earlier, each item used to be scanned through the barcode recorder. After the RFID implementation, the time saved on the same is about 80 per cent in inward warehouse processing and 12 per cent in outward processing. Real-time visibility of items during all stages of the supply chain improved to 98 per cent.

Pantaloon now aims to extend the application to production routing and scheduling, product recall and returns, and real-time data for category managers for effective forecasting. Pantaloon expects that the RFID application will further help it to improve the shopping experience, store layout, and any inventory situation. Going forward, it sees the use of RFID technology to improve collaboration across its supply chain right up to the point of sale.

Recently, Pantaloon's management faced a unique problem—most of the time consumers complained of big queues that made them wait for long hours. It was, hence, essential to find out innovative and creative ways to make the shopping experience more convenient and delightful for customers. This resulted in the implementation of a full-transaction queue-busting solution with mobile checkouts.

With the deployment of the queue-busting system, Pantaloon expected the store's customer satisfaction levels to go up with the decrease in waiting time. This usually results in consumers buying more goods and, in turn, increasing the store's turnover. The other objective of the deployment was to increase customer satisfaction and loyalty by adding shopping delight.

Pantaloon proceeded with the transactions using handheld devices such as PT 40 scanners and a handy terminal. PT 40 is compact—almost the size of a cell phone with an integrated bar code laser. The device weighs approximately 119 grams and can store up to 2 MB of data memory. It can support task-switching of up to four applications (on an average). It also comes with a program generator to develop Windows-based applications. Servers running Windows were deployed at the backend. As the customers do shopping, the store attendants use this hand-held device to help them out with billing simultaneously. The scanners would read the bar codes on consumer goods and convert the information to text files. This data gets stored in the handheld device. Later when the customer is finished with the shopping, the data stored in the handheld scanner gets transferred to the cash tills after it is docked to the POS.

This contributed in saving time and energy for customers and customer care executives at the billing desk. The customer only had to pay his or her bills and move on to the exit. Investments that save time for customers are repaid many times over by generating repeat visits, increased sales, and strengthened customer loyalty.

By implementing mobile queue busting systems Pantaloon was able to streamline its store operations and improve customer satisfaction. It was also able to motivate the store floor workforce to become more productive and obtain rapid return on investment over a period of time. Pantaloon could maximize its revenue opportunities in various ways. First and foremost, transaction, authorization, and processing times were drastically reduced. The final and most important objective of a retail outlet is to enhance its brand image, which was also achieved with this implementation.

### Discussion Questions

1. The traditional retailer's model of inventory management (EOQ model) seems to be rendered obsolete by contemporary retail stores such as Pantaloon. Discuss.
2. Is there a scope of applying the ABC classification of inventory in the modern retail stores?
3. What should Kishore Biyani do further to match Spanish retailer Zara's 15 day lead time?
4. What should the 'local small retailers' do to safeguard themselves from the onslaught of big players such as Pantaloon?

## CASE STUDY II

## OLIVETTI

Olivetti is an Italian multinational company, which is renowned worldwide for its computers, monitors, printers, and other peripheral devices. In the Netherlands, its sales head office is located at Leiden, while the after-sales-service office is based at Nieuwegein. The service office controls the Olivetti service activities of the whole country and plays an important role in the management of the spare-parts inventory required for the service operations.

The Nieuwegein facility stores inventories of repairable service parts (called modules) and irreparable components separately. There are inventories of about 11,000 different components, out of which almost 50 per cent of the components have a positive inventory status at any given time. The components occupy about 25 per cent of the inventory space. Olivetti has developed an inventory management system for these components called SigerC. SigerC is based upon forecasting the requirement of components using *double- exponential smoothing* and generating orders using the classical EOQ model. Over a period of time, SigerC has proved to be reliable enough.

Apart from components, the Nieuwegein facility stocks inventories of around 2,500 different types of repairable modules, out of which around 1,500 are frequently demanded. SigerC is not used for the inventory of these repairable modules. The inventory of modules utilizes the remaining 75 per cent of the inventory space and is worth about 100 times the inventory of the components, thus warranting good inventory control of modules.

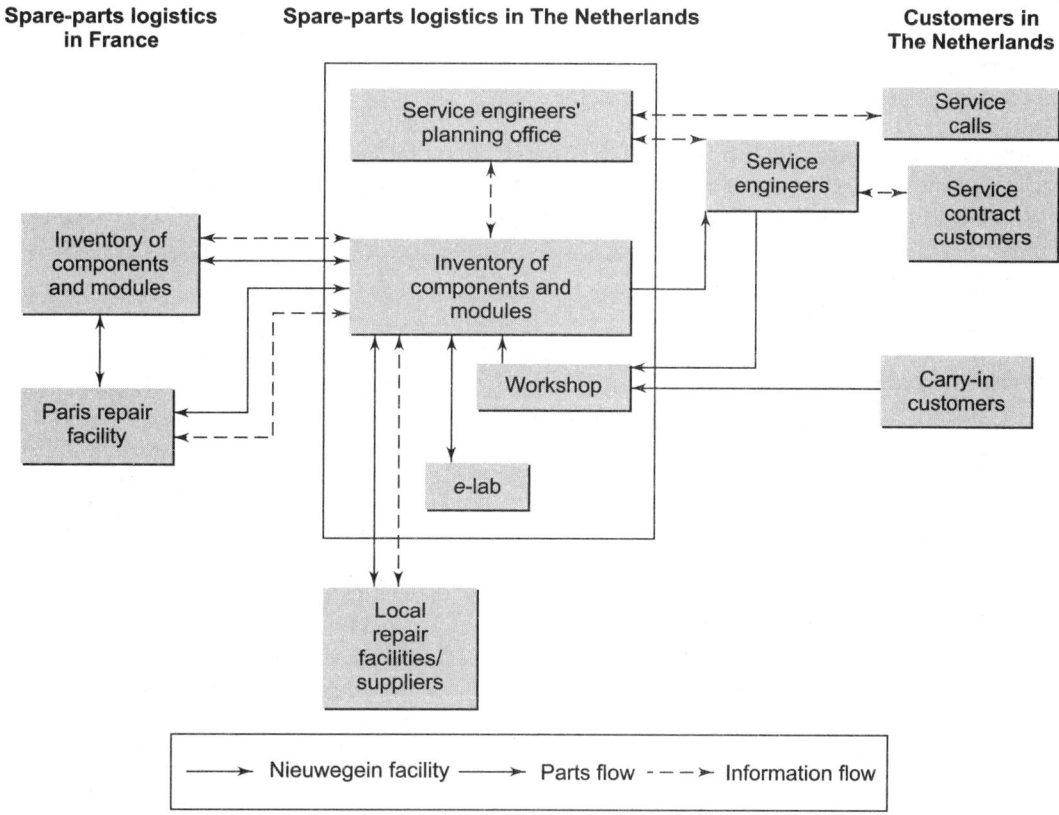

Olivetti has two repair facilities for modules—one is located in the Netherlands and the other at Paris, France. Usually, a repair is performed locally, but more complex repairs or large batches of repairable modules are sent to the Paris facility. The non-Olivetti parts are sent to external repair facilities. Around 90 per cent of the repairable modules are required by customers who have a service contract with Olivetti. The figure shows the logistics of the spare-parts inventory.

When a customer complaint is received in the form of a phone call at the Nieuwegein facility, a rough diagnosis of the problem is done and a service engineer is assigned. The service response time mentioned in the service contract has to be fulfilled under any circumstance. The service has to be provided within two, four, or eight hours after receipt of a phone call as mentioned in the service contract. Therefore, a small portion of the modules inventory lies for a maximum of one day with the service engineers to meet such short response-time service contracts.

Suppose a number of modules are given to a service engineer on Monday evening according to the nature of complaints received from customers. The engineer services the customer complaint on Tuesday by replacing the modules, if required, with new ones. The remaining modules will stay with him until Wednesday evening and, if not required for the day after, will be returned to Nieuwegein along with the defective modules on Thursday morning. Thus it takes around three days in all to re book the correct modules in inventory at Nieuwegein.

The defective modules are either repaired locally or sent to Paris. A safety stock of four days is kept at Nieuwegein, keeping in view the re-booking time of correct modules by service engineers, and the possible delays by the repair facility at Paris. When an inventory of repaired modules exists at the repair facility in Paris, it exchanges the defective modules with good ones on the same day (exchange option). Otherwise, the facility repairs these modules and returns them to Nieuwegein in about ten days (pure repair option).

Olivetti maintains a database of the flow of logistics using its software called Olivetti Board Repair Decentral (OLBORD). According to the nature of complaint made by a customer, a specialist uses his past experience and the back-order list to decide which defective module should be sent to which repair facility, as the real defect is not known. An estimate of the repair time can then be made. A fraction of

the defective modules is considered to be scrap and, hence, from time to time, new modules have to be procured (Ashayeri et al. 1996).

### Discussion Questions

1. Olivetti faces problems in deciding how many modules should be sent to the repair facilities and when. What measures should the management of Olivetti take in this regard?
2. Advise Olivetti about how many new modules should be purchased by its Nieuwegein service facility and when.
3. Suggest an inventory control system to Olivetti for managing the inventory of repairable moules.

## Objective Questions

### Choose the correct option

1. Multiple order opportunities throughout the year may not be available in case of
   (a) colour TVs
   (b) cars
   (c) fire crackers
   (d) cement
2. Inventory should be
   (a) high
   (b) low
   (c) optimal
   (d) conventional
3. The cost associated with storing the inventory in a warehouse is
   (a) holding cost
   (b) ordering cost
   (c) fixed cost
   (d) set-up cost
4. Oiling of machines after a production run would constitute
   (a) carrying cost

   (b) set-up cost
   (c) ordering cost
   (d) fixed cost

### State True or False

5. All costs incurred by the purchasing department are considered for calculating the ordering cost.
6. The EOQ model is also called the manufacturer's model.
7. Safety stock is defined as the stock that is maintained over and above the EOQ level in order to avoid stock out.

### Fill in the blanks

8. _____ is stock of idle resources.
9. Maintaining the safety stock involves _____ cost for the amount of units in the safety stock.
10. In a _____ system, a top-up stock is ordered to the suppliers in order to bring the level of inventory to a specified pre-determined threshold level.

## Concept Review Questions

1. What is inventory? Why is inventory management required in organizations? What are the uses of inventory?
2. What is the optimum level of inventory? Explain the kind of problems faced when very high or very low inventory is maintained for items.
3. What are ordering and carrying costs? What are their constituents?
4. Explain the relationship between ordering and

   carrying costs graphically.
5. What is economic order quantity (EOQ)? Explain the EOQ model of inventory with its simplifying assumptions.
6. How is the producer's model of inventory different from the retailer's model? Derive an expression for the EOQ in the producer's model.
7. 'Shortages are undesirable, but some organizations create shortages intentionally'—Do you agree with

this statement? Why? Derive an expression for total cost in the inventory model for intentional shortages.

8. What do you understand by safety stock? How is the optimal level of safety stock determined?

9. Why is the ABC classification of items done? How is the ABC distribution curve (Pareto curve) drawn?

10. What do you understand by simulation? How is simulation useful in inventory management?

11. Enumerate the three points to be kept in mind by production and inventory planners to reduce demand uncertainty.

12. Briefly explain (a) continuous and periodic review policies and (b) centralized versus decentralized systems.

## Numerical Problems

1. Plasma Cosmetics (P) Ltd has an annual requirement of 10,000 units of special glass bottles for its nail polish brand Glitter & Glow. A bottle has a CC of ₹10 per unit per year. The OC per order is ₹500. Calculate the total inventory cost for the following values of number of orders: 1, 5, 10, 20, and 25. Plot the various costs with respect to these orders on a graph using MS Excel. Also, find the EOQ from the graph.

2. A bookseller buys 2,500 copies of a book *Operations Management* every year. The OC is ₹1,000 per order. The CC is 5% of the inventory value. The price of a copy of the book is ₹400. The publisher of the book offers 1% discount if purchases are made in lots of 1,250 or more. Should the bookseller opt for the discount option or follow the EOQ model?

3. Navketan Griha Udyog is a manufacturer of the Swad brand of spices and is based at Indore. A 100-g pack of its chilli powder is priced at ₹20 for its suppliers. One of its suppliers purchases 16,000 packs per annum. The supplier incurs an OC of ₹180 per order and a CC of 5% of the inventory value. Navketan offers discounts for the following ranges of bulk purchases to its suppliers: 0.5% for 3,000–4,999 units and 1% for 5,000 and more units. Which discount option is the best one for its suppliers from the total cost point of view? Is it better than the EOQ option?

4. Oriflame Cosmetics is offering price discounts to its customers if they purchase their 100-ml packs of shampoo in the following quantity ranges: ₹50/unit for 10–19 units, ₹45/unit for 20–29 units, and ₹40/unit for 30 and more units. The CC of a pack of shampoo is estimated at 10% of the inventory value and the OC is ₹50. A customer has an annual demand of 100 packs of shampoo. Suggest the most economical order size for this customer.

5. For a component outsourced to a vendor and used in the colour television sets manufactured by Videocon at its Aurangabad factory, we have the following situation:

| | |
|---|---|
| Yearly demand | 9,00,000 units |
| Purchase quantity | 2,00,000 units |
| Safety stock | 30,000 units |

The ordering cost, independent of purchase quantity, is ₹1000 for each purchase. The (purchase) price of the component is ₹200/unit. Annual holding cost is 25% of the value of the component (inventory interest rate 25%). Assuming 225 working days per year, calculate:

(a) The number of purchases during a year
(b) Average inventory level (including the safety stock)
(c) Inventory turnover
(d) Average days of supply in inventory (known as cover time)
(e) Reorder point if the lead time is 10 working days
(f) Total inventory costs per year and total inventory costs per working day with purchase quantity 2,00,000 units
(g) Economic order quantity (EOQ)
(h) Total inventory costs per year and total inventory costs per working day with EOQ and with a safety stock decreased to 4000 units.

6. For a special component outsourced to a vendor and used in automobiles manufactured by Zenon Motors at Pune, we have the following situation.

| | |
|---|---|
| Yearly demand | 5,00,000 units |
| Purchase quantity | 1,50,000 units |
| Safety stock | 50,000 units |

The ordering cost, independent of purchase quantity, is ₹2,000 for each purchase. The (purchase) price of the component is ₹100/unit. Annual holding cost is 20% of the value of the component (inventory interest rate 20%). Assuming 235 working days per year, calculate the following.

(a) The number of purchases during a year
(b) Average inventory level (including the safety stock)
(c) Inventory turnover
(d) Average days of supply in inventory (known as cover time)

(e) Reorder point if the lead time is 15 working days

(f) Total inventory costs per year and total inventory costs per working day with purchase quantity 1,50,000 units

(g) Economic order quantity

(h) Total inventory costs per year and total inventory costs per working day with EOQ and with a safety stock decreased to 10,000 units.

7. SKF bicycles sources ball bearings for the bicycles it manufactures from a supplier based at Jalandhar. The normal usage of ball bearings during the lead time of 5 days is 70 units/day. It has been observed in the past that the DDLT varies according to Table 8.18. There are five inventory cycles per year. The CC is ₹2 per unit per year and the stock-out cost is ₹5 per unit short. Find the optimum level of safety stock for the ball bearings to be maintained by SKF.

**Table 8.18**

| DDLT (units) | Probability |
|---|---|
| 200 | 0.02 |
| 250 | 0.11 |
| 300 | 0.29 |
| 350 | 0.46 |
| 400 | 0.09 |
| 450 | 0.03 |
| | 1.00 |

8. Durable Furnitures is a firm at New Delhi known for the world-class furniture it markets. Its Safex brand of almirahs is particularly very popular in Delhi. Its DDLT follows the probability distribution given in Table 8.19. The stock-out cost of an almirah during lead time is estimated at ₹300 and the CC of an almirah unsold during lead time is ₹100. Calculate the optimum level of safety stock which minimizes the total cost.

**Table 8.19**

| DDLT (units) | Probability |
|---|---|
| 10 | 0.18 |
| 11 | 0.37 |
| 12 | 0.25 |
| 13 | 0.20 |
| | 1.00 |

9. Banarasi Silk Sari is a major production house of silk saris at Varanasi. The rate of production of saris is 120 units per day, while the rate of demand is 80 saris per day. Annually 50,000 saris are sold by Banarasi Silk. The CC is ₹150 per sari per year and the set-up cost of the factory is ₹600 per production run. How many saris should be manufactured in a production run such that the total inventory cost is minimum?

10. For a special ingredient Carbon Black used in the tyre manufacturing at JK Tyres, the following figures are prevailing:

| | |
|---|---|
| Yearly demand | 5,00,000 kg |
| Production quantity | 75,000 kg |
| Safety stock | 25,000 kg |

The set-up cost, independent of quantity, is ₹3500 for each production batch. The price of the ingredient is ₹300 per kg. Annual holding cost is 10% of the value of the ingredient (inventory interest rate 10%). Assuming 225 working days per year, calculate:

(a) The number of production batches during a year

(b) Average inventory level (including the safety stock)

(c) Inventory turnover

(d) Average days of supply in inventory (cover-time)

(e) Reorder point if the lead time is 10 working days

(f) Total inventory costs per year and total inventory costs per working day with production quantity 75,000 kg

(g) EOQ (pure)

(h) The company can produce Carbon Black at a production rate 4,000 kg per working day. Determine the economic production lot size. Assuming that the safety stock is decreased to 15,000 kg, calculate the new number of production batches per year, average days of supply in inventory, and the new total costs per working day and year.

11. For a special ingredient used in the manufacturing of tyres at Speed Tyres Ltd, Chennai, the following figures are prevailing.

| | |
|---|---|
| Yearly demand | 3,50,000 kg |
| Production quantity | 80,000 kg |
| Safety stock | 30,000 kg |

The set-up cost, independent of quantity, is ₹5,000 for each production batch. The price of the ingredient is ₹200 per kg. Annual holding cost is 15% of the value of the ingredient (inventory interest rate 15%). Assuming 235 working days per year, calculate the following.

(a) the number of production batches during a year

(b) average inventory level (including the safety stock)

(c) inventory turnover

(d) Average days of supply in inventory (cover-time)

(e) Reorder point if the lead time is 10 working days

(f) Total inventory costs per year and total inventory costs per working day with production quantity 80,000 kg

(g) Economic order quantity (pure)

(h) The company can produce the ingredient at a production rate 7,500 kg per working day. Determine the economic production lot size. Assuming that the safety stock is decreased to 15,000 kg, calculate the new number of production batches per year, average days of supply in inventory, and the new total costs per working day and year.

12. Audio Visual Devices Inc. is a multinational firm dealing with multimedia projectors of various brands. It markets projectors of Sony, 3M, and Panasonic to organizations having different types of presentation needs. These projectors are costly devices in the range of ₹0.2–0.5 million. The CC is ₹90,000 per projector per year, while the stock-out cost is ₹2,000 per unit short. The annual demand of projectors is 200 units with an OC of ₹100 per order. Calculate (a) The optimal order quantity under the EOQ model with intentional shortages, (b) the maximum shortage level, and (c) the maximum inventory level.

13. A wholesaler of Gillette Shaving Products observes that the demand of shaving razors during the lead time of 10 days is normally distributed with a mean value of 5,000 units and a standard deviation of 400 units. What is the service level expected by the wholesaler if he has a safety stock of 1,000 units.

Find also the safety stock required to be maintained if the wholesaler wants to maintain a 90% service level.

14. Escorts Tractors Ltd does the ABC classification of the various components and parts it uses for assembling its tractors. For category C items, it uses periodic checks and replenishes accordingly. For one such item, the CC is ₹2 per unit per year and the OC is ₹50 per order. The annual demand is 20,000 units for this item. Find the optimal interval of periodic review if there are 300 working days in a year.

15. Classify the ten items in Table 8.20 into A, B, and C categories according to their usage values. Draw the ABC distribution curve. Item 8 has a high criticality class, that is, a shortage of this item may lead to a complete halt in the production process. What special treatment can be given to this item?

**Table 8.20**

| Item ID | Unit price (₹) | Annual usage (units) |
|---------|----------------|----------------------|
| 1 | 5 | 100,000 |
| 2 | 35 | 2,600 |
| 3 | 79 | 420 |
| 4 | 68 | 13,600 |
| 5 | 800 | 210 |
| 6 | 2,300 | 670 |
| 7 | 450 | 76 |
| 8 | 6 | 400 |
| 9 | 92 | 6,100 |
| 10 | 3 | 250,000 |

## Project Assignments

1. Visit any hospital near your place and find out what type of inventories are maintained there. Do they perform ABC analysis? Do they follow the EOQ model? Do they carry a safety stock of items? Form discussion groups in the class and analyse the type of inventories maintained.

2. Visit any manufacturing factory near your place and study their methods of production lot sizing. Is the manufacturer's EOQ model useful to them?

# Materials Requirement Planning, Just-in-time, and Supply Chain Management

**Learning Objectives**

After reading this chapter, you will be able to answer the following questions:
- What is material requirements planning (MRP)?
- What models and techniques can be used to plan material requirements?
- What is the just-in-time (JIT) system? What are the benefits of JIT?
- Can MRP and JIT be used together in a plant?
- What is supply chain management? How is it different from purchasing and procurement?
- What role does technology play in the procurement of goods in the present context?
- What are the supply chain strategies that can be pursued by organizations?

## Materials Requirement Planning (MRP)

In assembly operations of products (finished goods), there are many items which are themselves sub-assemblies. These sub-assemblies are made by joining small components. The requirements of these components depend on the number of finished goods to be produced. Therefore, these components are called *dependent demand* items. Materials requirement planning (MRP) is a system used for planning the future requirements of dependent demand items. This planning is done based on three inputs:

1. Number of items already in the inventory (*inventory status*)
2. Number of finished goods to be produced in the near future using these items (*master production schedule*)
3. Number of units of the item required for manufacturing a single unit of the finished product (*bill of materials*)

To understand the new terms mentioned above—master production schedule (MPS) and bill of materials (BOM)—we must first understand a related term, *product structure*.

**Product structure**   The product structure shows a product's build-up. It shows diagrammatically the components required to assemble it, their numbers, and the sequence of assembly.

Let us take up an example. A sub-assembly *A* is made by joining one unit of component *B* and two units of component *C* (Fig. 9.1). Therefore, if 100 units of sub-assembly *A* are to be manufactured, 100 units of component *B* and 200 units of component *C* are required.

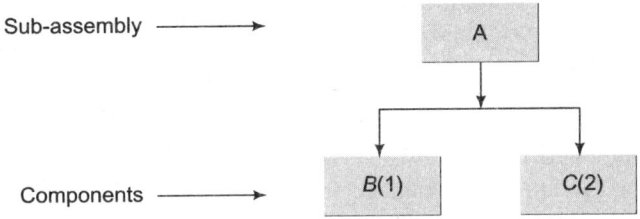

**Fig. 9.1** Product structure of sub-assembly A

Hence, we see that the requirement of components *B* and *C* depends on the requirement of sub-assembly *A*. The requirement of sub-assembly *A*, in turn, may depend on the requirement of the finished product *X* (Fig. 9.2). Exhibit 9.1 discusses the supply chain initiatives at Ashok Leyland.

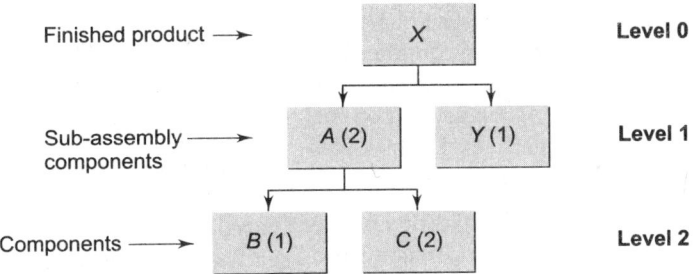

**Fig. 9.2** Product structure of product X

Now, if 100 units of product *X* are to be manufactured, the following would be required:

| Sub-assemblies/components | Number of units |
|---|---|
| *Y* | $1 \times$ no. of units of $X = 1 \times 100 = 100$ |
| *A* | $2 \times$ no. of units of $X = 2 \times 100 = 200$ |
| *B* | $1 \times$ no. of units of $A = 1 \times 200 = 200$ |
| *C* | $2 \times$ no. of units of $A = 2 \times 200 = 400$ |

## Exhibit 9.1   Ashok Leyland

The origin of Ashok Leyland can be traced to the urge for self-reliance felt by independent India. Pandit Jawaharlal Nehru, the then Prime Minister, persuaded Mr Raghunandan Saran, an industrialist, to enter automobile manufacture. In 1948, Ashok Motors was set up in what was then Madras (now Chennai), for the assembly of Austin Cars. The company's destiny and name changed soon with equity participation by British Leyland. Ashok Leyland commenced manufacture of commercial vehicles in 1950. In 1987, the overseas holding by Land Rover Leyland International Holdings Limited (LRLIH) was taken over by a joint venture between the Hinduja Group and IVECO Fiat SpA, part of the Fiat Group and Europe's leading truck manufacturer. In the journey towards global standards of quality, Ashok Leyland reached a major milestone in 1993 when it became the first company in India's automobile history to win the ISO 9002 certification. The more comprehensive ISO 9001 certification came in 1994. ISO 14001certification for all vehicle manufacturing units

*(Contd)*

*Exhibit 9.1 Contd*

was awarded to the company in 2002.

Ashok Leyland implemented JIT in its unique way in 1999. Barely eighteen months before the implementation of JIT, Ashok Leyland was fighting for survival. The truck-maker's supply chain was creaking under the recession—it had eaten away 17.62 per cent of its revenues in one year—forcing the company to helplessly allow inventories to tower. The results were showing on working capital—it had climbed from 33.34 per cent of sales in 1993–94 to 58.81 per cent in 1997–98. At the same time, net profits had crashed from ₹1.25 billion to a meagre ₹184.1 million. Thus began Project Oscars—named after optimizing supply chain and rationalizing sourcing—aimed at vendor-selection and development, better planning and scheduling, and inventory control processes. The system in operation until then was push-planning, resulting in up to 45 days of inventories of components compared to between 3 and 5 days globally. This happened because components were ordered by Ashok Leyland on the basis of an annual production-schedule, which was going haywire as demand plummeted.

Project Oscars began with a classification of the 5,000 odd components used by the company into category A (amounting to 75 per cent of the total cost of components), category B (amounting to 18 per cent), and category C (amounting to 7 per cent), with their suppliers also being classified accordingly. Then, Ashok Leyland devised different delivery systems for each category, aimed at cutting inventory-holdings.

The showpiece—a courier system for JIT supplies of category A items. The system proceeds as follows—the plant sends a JIT card, specifying the part number, quantity, and the unloading location, using courier, fax, or email to the supplier, who promptly dispatches the required consignment directly to the assembly-line. To evaluate Ashok Leyland's requirement, Project Oscars devised a funnel-planning system, covering six weeks of requirements. The broadest part stands for the tentative requirements of the last two weeks out of the six. The middle part stands for the semi-frozen requirement for the middle two weeks. The narrowest part stands for the frozen requirement for the first two weeks. Hence, the vendor already knows roughly when to expect the JIT card.

To reward vendors for conforming to the schedule, Project Oscars planned a reduction in their numbers from 607 to 200 over a three year time-frame. Ashok Leyland was looking at giving a minimum business of ₹10 million to each supplier involved in the process. The company also provides technological inputs for troubleshooting on the suppliers' shop floors, enabling them to cut their costs. Simultaneously, Project Oscars initiated a pull-based system on the Ashok Leyland's shop floor, where each stage produces only as much as the next stage needs. Thus, only when a new chassis is loaded does the request go out for the supply of an engine assembly, for the front and rear axle assembly-lines, and for the components that go into them. The results of this de-buffering—savings of ₹85 million a year and a lean supply chain.

## Inputs in MRP

There are three inputs required by the MRP processing logic (computer-based or manual) (see Fig. 9.3):

1. Bill of materials (BOM)
2. Master production schedule (MPS)
3. Inventory status

**Bill of materials**   Bill of materials is a document which tells us about an item's product structure, showing the sequence in which components/sub-assemblies are assembled and their required numbers. It also contains details about the workstations at which the item is assembled.

We have already discussed the product structure. Let us take up another example. Figure 9.4 shows the product structure of a product *M*. Note that the sub-assembly *N* appears at level 1 as well as level 2 of the product structure. When a computer program reads a BOM of a product, it starts from the top

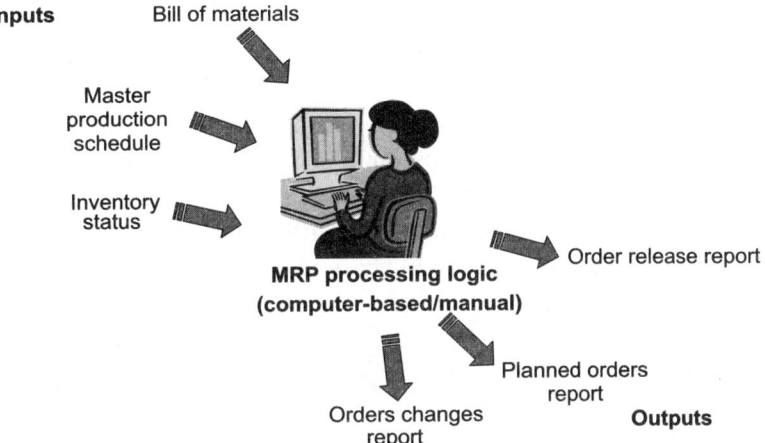

**Fig. 9.3** Inputs and outputs in MRP

level, that is, level 0. As it moves downward, it counts the different items it encounters down the product-structure tree. If an item appears in more than one level, its number of units cannot be determined unless the computer scan reaches the lowest level. This results in inefficiency of the program.

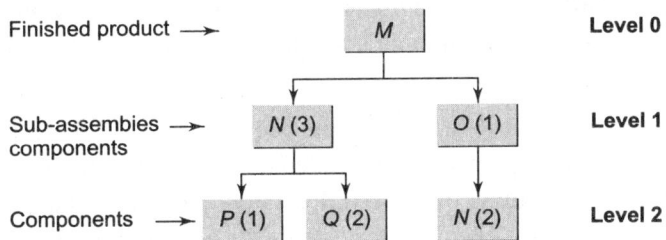

**Fig. 9.4** Product structure of product *M*

To avoid this, a procedure known as *low-level coding* is adapted. The product structure is redrawn and the item which appears at different levels is brought down to its lowest level. In Fig. 9.4, we bring the sub-assembly *N* at level 1 to level 2. Note also that the sub-assembly *N* which was already at level 2 can be expanded into its full form, that is, broken down into its components *P* and *Q* (Fig. 9.5).

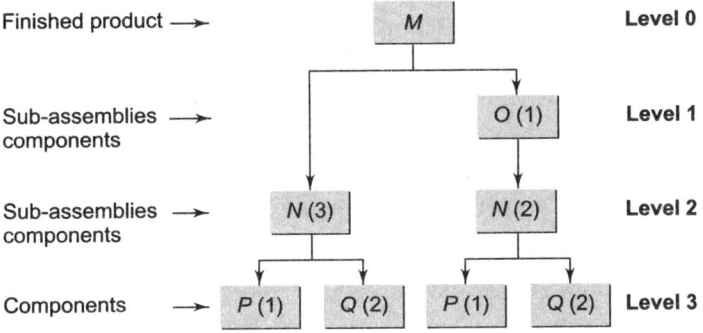

**Fig. 9.5** Modified product structure of product *M*

**Master production schedule**  An *aggregate production plan* tells us how many units of a product have to be manufactured in the coming 6–18 months on a weekly or monthly basis. For example, Table 9.1 shows the number of cars to be produced by Hyundai in the coming six months.

Therefore, this table shows the monthly aggregate production plan of Hyundai. The MPS is an extension of the aggregate production plan. It tells us the number of units of different models of a product to be manufactured on a weekly or monthly basis. If the aggregate plan is given in months, the MPS

**Table 9.1**

| Month | No. of cars |
|-------|-------------|
| Jan. | 10,000 |
| Feb. | 12,000 |
| March | 8,000 |
| April | 11,000 |
| May | 7,000 |
| June | 12,000 |

**Table 9.2**

| Weeks of January | I | II | III | IV | Total |
|------------------|-----|-----|-----|-----|-------|
| Santro | 1,200 | 2,000 | 2,500 | 700 | **6,400** |
| Accent | 700 | 950 | 1,300 | 250 | **3,200** |
| Sonata | 100 | 50 | 200 | 50 | **400** |
| | **2,000** | **3,000** | **4,000** | **1,000** | **10,000** |

may divide it further into weeks. Let us assume, in our example, that the MPS for the month of January is as shown in Table 9.2.

Further, the MPS can contain information on sub-models of a model, for example, in a given week, how many *Santros* will be made with power steering, how many with power windows, and so on.

**Inventory status**  This is the third input required in MRP. It tells us about the status of the inventory of an item at present, or in a given interval of time in the coming future. This includes scheduled receipts of units of item in that interval of time as a result of orders placed in the recent past to suppliers. The inventory status file also contains details about the supplier of the item, the lead time taken by him to supply the item, and the size of each order to be placed to him (determined earlier).

## Outputs in MRP

The following three types of outputs (reports) are generated by the MRP processing logic (Fig. 9.3):

1. Planned orders report    2. Order release report    3. Order changes report

**Planned orders report**  This report gives information about planned orders to be released on some future date or during a given interval of time. This report is helpful in preparing for the funds required for payments to the suppliers in the future according to the dates and order sizes. For example, suppose March is the current month and the finance manager wants to see what quantities of raw material purchases have to be made in June; this report helps him to do so and prepare for funds required in June for making payments to the suppliers.

**Order release report**  This report gives information about planned orders to be released on the present date. It helps the purchase managers to release purchase orders (POs) to the suppliers. This is the most common report generated by the MRP processing logic and it helps the purchase manager to keep track of the

The order change report provides the purchase manager with information about all such changes to be made in the open orders with the suppliers.

POs that have to be sent on a particular day. The MRP logic makes use of the lead time of items in determining the release date of orders, so that goods are supplied by the time the items are required for production.

**Order change report**   Open orders are those which have been placed in the past, and the supplier of the items is preparing for these supplies to be made to the company. During the lead time, the MPS of the company may fluctuate. For example, some customers cancel their orders, leading to a revision of the MPS. Because of this change in demand, open orders have to be revised, that is, suppliers are told to either cancel the orders placed earlier by the company, postpone them for some time, or reduce the order size to suit the current requirement. The order change report provides the purchase manager with information about all such changes to be made in the open orders with the suppliers.

### General format of an MRP report

Item identification: 786, Bearing

Lead time: 1 week

Available inventory: 100 units (at the begining of week 1)

Lot size: Lot-for-lot

Safety stock: 0

Allocated: 0

Low-level code: 1

Report date: 0

| | | | | Period (weeks) | | | | | |
|---|---|---|---|---|---|---|---|---|---|
| | | 1 | 2 | 3 | 4 | 5 | 6 | 7 | 8 |
| *Gross requirements* | | | | | 450 | | | 600 | |
| *Scheduled receipts* | | | | | | | | | |
| *Available inventory* | | 100 | 100 | 100 | 100 | | | | |
| *Net requirements* | | | | | 350 | | | 600 | |
| *Planned order receipts* | | | | | 350 | | | 600 | |
| *Planned order releases* | | | | 350 | | | 600 | | |

In the preceding sample MRP report, the lot size given is lot-for-lot. This means that whenever an order is placed with the supplier, its size will exactly match the production requirements. In the sample report, *gross requirements* are derived by the MRP logic from the MPS input. As the name suggests, these are the total or gross requirements in the given weeks. Here, the gross requirement of item 786 is 450 units in week 4 and 600 units in week 7. *Scheduled receipts* refer to orders that were placed earlier than the time span shown in the report; these may be received in any week shown in the report. In our sample, no such receipt is due in the weeks considered. Therefore there are no entries in this row of the table.

*Available inventory* shows the current status of the inventory of item 786 as 100 units in week

Scheduled receipts refer to orders that were placed earlier than the time span shown in the report.

1. This inventory level continues in weeks 2, 3, and 4, as there was no gross requirement in weeks 1, 2, and 3. In week 4, 450 units are required. Hence, in week 4, we subtract 100 units of available inventory from the gross requirement of 450 units to get a *net requirement* of 350 units, that is, 350 units of item 786 are required for the production process in week 4.

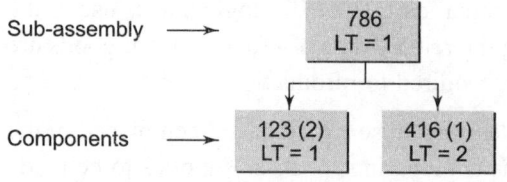

Sub-assembly ⟶ 786, LT = 1

Components ⟶ 123 (2), LT = 1 | 416 (1), LT = 2

**Fig. 9.6** Product structure of sub-assembly 786

Similarly, in week 7 the gross requirement is 600 units with no scheduled receipts and available inventory. Thus, the net requirement in week 7 is 600 units. Also, the *planned order receipts* for weeks 4 and 7 are 350 units and 600 units, respectively, as the lot-for-lot system is followed. This means that this many units should be received by the company from the supplier by the start of weeks 4 and 7. The lead time of item 786 is given as 1 week. Therefore, for receiving the items at the start of weeks 4 and 7, the orders to the suppliers will have to be released by weeks 3 and 6, respectively (one week in advance). These releases of orders are called *planned order releases*.

Let us now assume that item 786 has the product structure shown in Fig. 9.6, and it is currently the beginning of week 1 in the time horizon. The MPS of item 786 shows its requirements of 450 units in week 4 and 600 units in week 7 [Fig. 9.7(a)]. In the MRP report of this item, these become the gross requirements in weeks 4 and 7. Let us assume there are 100 units of this item as available inventory in week 1. Thus this inventory will continue as it is in weeks 1, 2, 3, and 4. In week 4, the requirement of this item is 450 units, therefore the 100 units in inventory will be consumed in this week, leaving a net requirement of 350 units (450 – 100) for this item. In the weeks beyond the fourth, no inventory will be available.

**Master production schedule for item 786**

| Period (weeks) | 1 | 2 | 3 | 4 | 5 | 6 | 7 | 8 |
|---|---|---|---|---|---|---|---|---|
| Gross requirements | | | | 450 | | | 600 | |

**MRP report for item 786, L T = 1 week**

| | | | | | | | | |
|---|---|---|---|---|---|---|---|---|
| Gross requirements | | | | 450 | | | 600 | |
| Scheduled receipts | | | | | | | | |
| Available inventory | 100 | 100 | 100 | 100 | | | | |
| Net requirements | | | | 350 | | | 600 | |
| Planned order receipts | | | | 350 | | | 600 | |
| Planned order releases | | | 350 | | | 600 | | |

**MRP report for item 123 (2), LT = 1 week**

| | | | | | | | | |
|---|---|---|---|---|---|---|---|---|
| Gross requirements | | | 700 | | | 1200 | | |
| Scheduled receipts | | | | | | | | |
| Available inventory | | | | | | | | |
| Net requirements | | | 700 | | | 1200 | | |
| Planned order receipts | | | 700 | | | 1200 | | |
| Planned order releases | | 700 | | | 1200 | | | |

**MRP report for item 416 (1), LT = 2 weeks**

| | | | | | | | | |
|---|---|---|---|---|---|---|---|---|
| Gross requirements | | | 350 | | | 600 | | |
| Scheduled receipts | | | | | | | | |
| Available inventory | | | | | | | | |
| Net requirements | | | 350 | | | 600 | | |
| Planned order receipts | | | 350 | | | 600 | | |
| Planned order releases | 350 | | | 600 | | | | |

**Fig. 9.7(a)**

Figure 9.7(a) shows no available inventory during weeks 5, 6, 7, and 8. The net requirement in week 7 is same as the gross requirement of 600 units. Therefore, we should have 350 and 600 units of this item at the beginning of weeks 4 and 7, respectively. The planned order receipts are, thus, 350 and 600 units in weeks 4 and 7, respectively. The lead time (LT) of this item is given as 1 week, therefore the orders have to be released one week before the planned order receipts. Thus, the planned order releases are in weeks 3 and 6 for 350 units and 600 units, respectively.

Each unit of item 786 is made by two units of item 123 and one unit of item 416 (Fig. 9.6). As shown by arrows in Fig. 9.7(a), the gross requirement of item 123 is 700 units (350 × 2) and 1,200 units (600 × 2) in weeks 3 and 6, respectively. It has an LT of 1 week and the planned order releases are in weeks 2 and 5, respectively. Note that the planned order releases and receipts are lot-for-lot, that is, exactly same as the gross requirements. Similarly, the MRP report for item 416 can be generated. Figure 9.7(b) shows that if the lot size is constant at multiples of 500 units for item 123 and multiples of 200 units for item 416, the excess of the order size over gross requirement becomes the available inventory in the coming weeks.

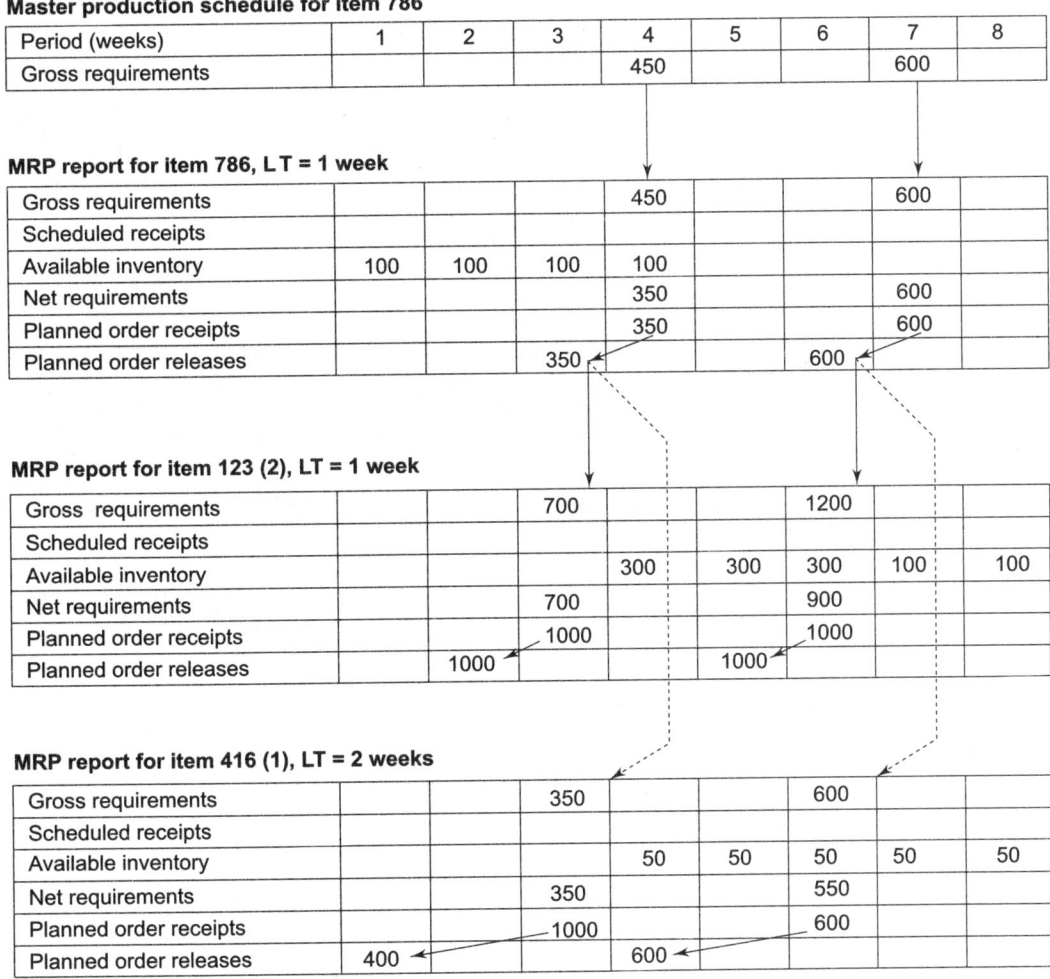

**Master production schedule for item 786**

| Period (weeks) | 1 | 2 | 3 | 4 | 5 | 6 | 7 | 8 |
|---|---|---|---|---|---|---|---|---|
| Gross requirements | | | | 450 | | | 600 | |

**MRP report for item 786, LT = 1 week**

| | | | | | | | | |
|---|---|---|---|---|---|---|---|---|
| Gross requirements | | | | 450 | | | 600 | |
| Scheduled receipts | | | | | | | | |
| Available inventory | 100 | 100 | 100 | 100 | | | | |
| Net requirements | | | | 350 | | | 600 | |
| Planned order receipts | | | | 350 | | | 600 | |
| Planned order releases | | | 350 | | | 600 | | |

**MRP report for item 123 (2), LT = 1 week**

| | | | | | | | | |
|---|---|---|---|---|---|---|---|---|
| Gross requirements | | | 700 | | | 1200 | | |
| Scheduled receipts | | | | | | | | |
| Available inventory | | | | 300 | 300 | 300 | 100 | 100 |
| Net requirements | | | 700 | | | 900 | | |
| Planned order receipts | | | 1000 | | | 1000 | | |
| Planned order releases | | 1000 | | | 1000 | | | |

**MRP report for item 416 (1), LT = 2 weeks**

| | | | | | | | | |
|---|---|---|---|---|---|---|---|---|
| Gross requirements | | | 350 | | | 600 | | |
| Scheduled receipts | | | | | | | | |
| Available inventory | | | | 50 | 50 | 50 | 50 | 50 |
| Net requirements | | | 350 | | | 550 | | |
| Planned order receipts | | | 1000 | | | 600 | | |
| Planned order releases | 400 | | 600 | | | | | |

**Fig. 9.7(b)**

### Example 9.1

Items *A*, *B*, *C*, and *D* have the following bill of materials (product stuctures):
*A* and *B* are end-items. Component *D* is used both in items *B* and *C*
(and hence, in item *A* too). To manufacture 1 unit of *A*, 1 unit of *C*
is required and to manufacture 1 unit of *C*, 1 unit of *D* is consumed.
The manufacturing of 1 unit of *B* requires 2 units of *D*. Fixed order
quantities are used in production.

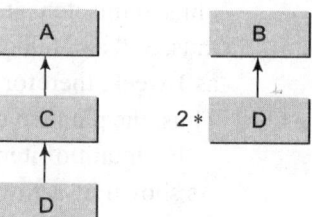

Other notable important specifics:

| Item | Lead-time in time periods | Order quantity |
|------|---------------------------|----------------|
| *A*  | 1  | 25 |
| *B*  | 2  | 15 |
| *C*  | 4  | 50 |
| *D*  | 3  | 75 |

Use the data given in the Master Production Schedules for end-items *A* and *B* (Fig. 9.8) to complete the
MRP calculations (in the tables given in Fig. 9.8) for the next 25 time periods for items *A*, *B*,*C*, and *D*.

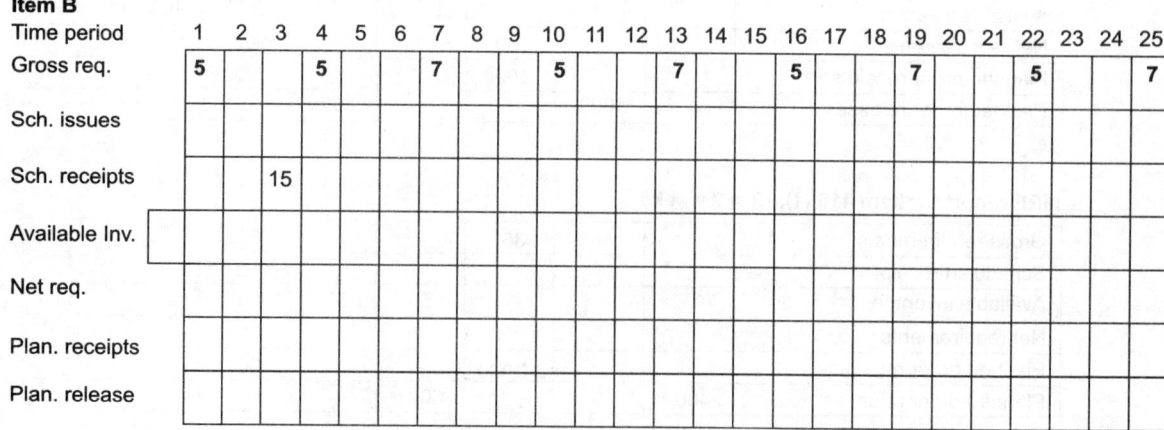

**Item A**

| Time period | 1 | 2 | 3 | 4 | 5 | 6 | 7 | 8 | 9 | 10 | 11 | 12 | 13 | 14 | 15 | 16 | 17 | 18 | 19 | 20 | 21 | 22 | 23 | 24 | 25 |
|-------------|---|---|---|---|---|---|---|---|---|----|----|----|----|----|----|----|----|----|----|----|----|----|----|----|----|
| Gross req. | 10 |  | 25 |  | 10 |  | 15 |  | 10 |  | 25 |  |  | 10 |  | 15 |  | 10 |  | 15 |  | 10 |  | 15 | 10 |
| Sch. issues | | | | | | | | | | | | | | | | | | | | | | | | | |
| Sch. receipts | 20 | | | | | | | | | | | | | | | | | | | | | | | | |
| Available Inv. | 10 | | | | | | | | | | | | | | | | | | | | | | | | |
| Net req. | | | | | | | | | | | | | | | | | | | | | | | | | |
| Plan. receipts | | | | | | | | | | | | | | | | | | | | | | | | | |
| Plan. release | | | | | | | | | | | | | | | | | | | | | | | | | |

**Item B**

| Time period | 1 | 2 | 3 | 4 | 5 | 6 | 7 | 8 | 9 | 10 | 11 | 12 | 13 | 14 | 15 | 16 | 17 | 18 | 19 | 20 | 21 | 22 | 23 | 24 | 25 |
|-------------|---|---|---|---|---|---|---|---|---|----|----|----|----|----|----|----|----|----|----|----|----|----|----|----|----|
| Gross req. | 5 | | | 5 | | | 7 | | | 5 | | | 7 | | | 5 | | | 7 | | | 5 | | | 7 |
| Sch. issues | | | | | | | | | | | | | | | | | | | | | | | | | |
| Sch. receipts | | | 15 | | | | | | | | | | | | | | | | | | | | | | |
| Available Inv. | | | | | | | | | | | | | | | | | | | | | | | | | |
| Net req. | | | | | | | | | | | | | | | | | | | | | | | | | |
| Plan. receipts | | | | | | | | | | | | | | | | | | | | | | | | | |
| Plan. release | | | | | | | | | | | | | | | | | | | | | | | | | |

**Fig. 9.8 (Contd)**

**Item C**

| Time period | 1 | 2 | 3 | 4 | 5 | 6 | 7 | 8 | 9 | 10 | 11 | 12 | 13 | 14 | 15 | 16 | 17 | 18 | 19 | 20 | 21 | 22 | 23 | 24 | 25 |
|---|---|---|---|---|---|---|---|---|---|---|---|---|---|---|---|---|---|---|---|---|---|---|---|---|---|
| Gross req. | | | | | | | | | | | | | | | | | | | | | | | | | |
| Sch. issues | | | | | | | | | | | | | | | | | | | | | | | | | |
| Sch. receipts | | | | | | | | | | | | | | | | | | | | | | | | | |
| Available Inv. | 25 | | | | | | | | | | | | | | | | | | | | | | | | |
| Net req. | | | | | | | | | | | | | | | | | | | | | | | | | |
| Plan. receipts | | | | | | | | | | | | | | | | | | | | | | | | | |
| Plan. release | | | | | | | | | | | | | | | | | | | | | | | | | |

**Item D**

| Time period | 1 | 2 | 3 | 4 | 5 | 6 | 7 | 8 | 9 | 10 | 11 | 12 | 13 | 14 | 15 | 16 | 17 | 18 | 19 | 20 | 21 | 22 | 23 | 24 | 25 |
|---|---|---|---|---|---|---|---|---|---|---|---|---|---|---|---|---|---|---|---|---|---|---|---|---|---|
| Gross req. | | | | | | | | | | | | | | | | | | | | | | | | | |
| Sch. issues | 30 | | | | | | | | | | | | | | | | | | | | | | | | |
| Sch. receipts | | | | | | | | | | | | | | | | | | | | | | | | | |
| Available Inv. | 50 | | | | | | | | | | | | | | | | | | | | | | | | |
| Net req. | | | | | | | | | | | | | | | | | | | | | | | | | |
| Plan. receipts | | | | | | | | | | | | | | | | | | | | | | | | | |
| Plan. release | | | | | | | | | | | | | | | | | | | | | | | | | |

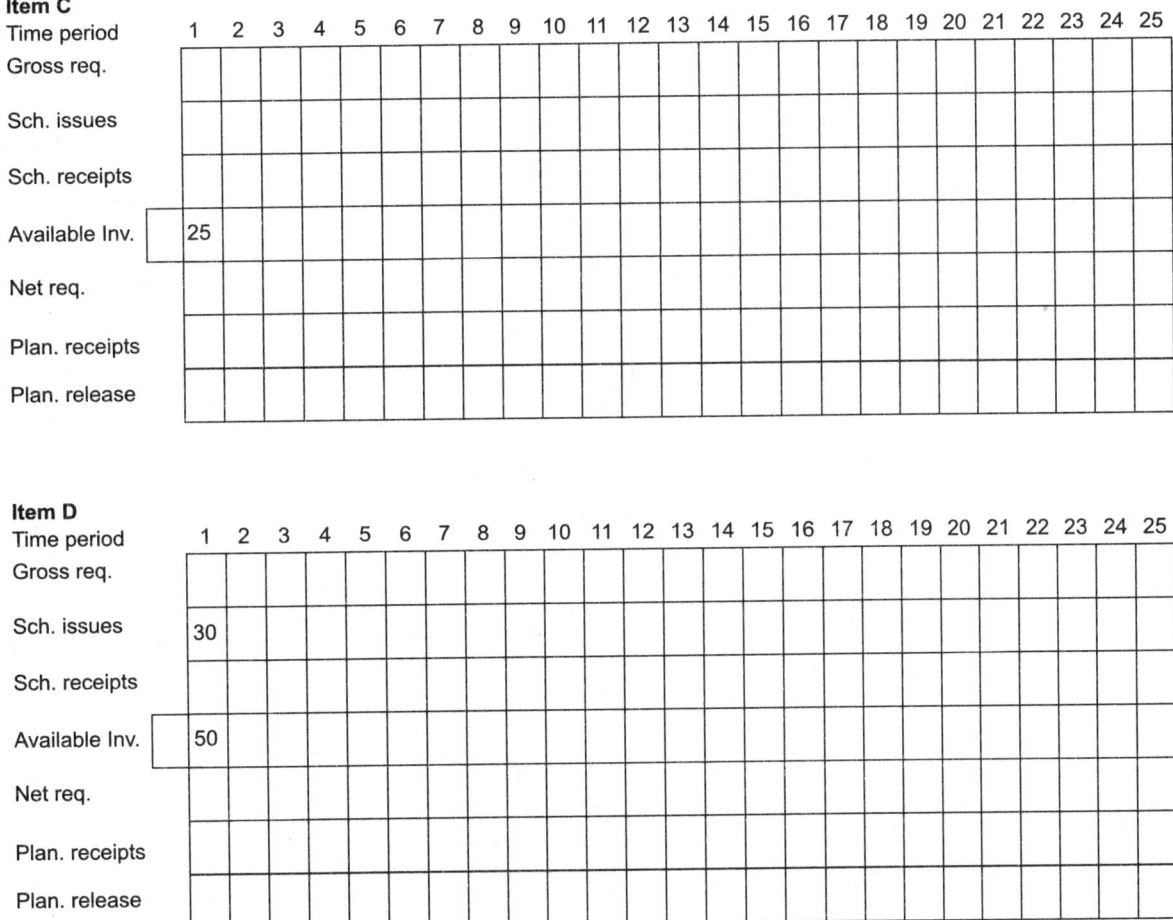

**Fig. 9.8** Tables for MRP calculations in Example 9.1

### Solution

This problem introduces us to the use of an additional row namely 'Scheduled issues' in the MRP tables. Scheduled issues are items, which are ready to be dispatched to the manufacturer of the higher level item or the customer. This may be due to the postponement of some open order in the previous time periods prior to the planning horizon considered here (time periods prior to period 1 in the current plannng horizon of periods 1 to 25). In Fig. 9.8, the table for item D shows scheduled issues of 30 units in period 1.

Note that scheduled receipt in period 3 for item B is an open order that is still not delivered and still not started as component D for this order is still in the inventory of D and is a scheduled issue in period 1 (Fig. 9.8). In all practical situations (such as the one depicted here), despite the given normal lead times, some delays are possible in delivery (scheduled receipts of material for higher level items). Similarly, under exceptional circumstances, the suppliers (internal or external) may agree to the manufacturer's request of sending the supplies earlier than the normal lead time.

The table in Fig. 9.9 for item A shows (20) in period 3 as the scheduled receipt. Similarly, the table for item B shows (15) in period 1 as the scheduled receipt. It should be noted that MRP calculations

### Item A

| | 1 | 2 | 3 | 4 | 5 | 6 | 7 | 8 | 9 | 10 | 11 | 12 | 13 | 14 | 15 | 16 | 17 | 18 | 19 | 20 | 21 | 22 | 23 | 24 | 25 |
|---|---|---|---|---|---|---|---|---|---|---|---|---|---|---|---|---|---|---|---|---|---|---|---|---|---|
| Time period | 1 | 2 | 3 | 4 | 5 | 6 | 7 | 8 | 9 | 10 | 11 | 12 | 13 | 14 | 15 | 16 | 17 | 18 | 19 | 20 | 21 | 22 | 23 | 24 | 25 |
| Gross req. | 10 | | 25 | | 10 | | 15 | | 10 | | 25 | | | 10 | | 15 | | 10 | | 15 | | 10 | | 15 | 10 |
| Sch. issues | | | | | | | | | | | | | | | | | | | | | | | | | |
| Sch. receipts | 20 | | (20) | | | | | | | | | | | | | | | | | | | | | | |
| Available Inv. | 10 | 0 | 0 | 20 | 20 | 10 | 10 | 20 | 20 | 10 | 10 | 10 | 10 | 10 | 0 | 0 | 10 | 10 | 0 | 0 | 10 | 10 | 0 | 0 | 10 |
| Net req. | | | 5 | | | | 5 | | | | 15 | | | | | 15 | | | | 15 | | | | 15 | |
| Plan. receipts | | | 25 | | | | 25 | | | | 25 | | | | | 25 | | | | 25 | | | | 25 | |
| Plan. release | | 25 | | | | 25 | | | | 25 | | | | | 25 | | | | 25 | | | | 25 | | |

### Item B

| | 1 | 2 | 3 | 4 | 5 | 6 | 7 | 8 | 9 | 10 | 11 | 12 | 13 | 14 | 15 | 16 | 17 | 18 | 19 | 20 | 21 | 22 | 23 | 24 | 25 |
|---|---|---|---|---|---|---|---|---|---|---|---|---|---|---|---|---|---|---|---|---|---|---|---|---|---|
| Time period | 1 | 2 | 3 | 4 | 5 | 6 | 7 | 8 | 9 | 10 | 11 | 12 | 13 | 14 | 15 | 16 | 17 | 18 | 19 | 20 | 21 | 22 | 23 | 24 | 25 |
| Gross req. | 5 | | | 5 | | | 7 | | | 5 | | | 7 | | | 5 | | | 7 | | | 5 | | | 7 |
| Sch. issues | | | | | | | | | | | | | | | | | | | | | | | | | |
| Sch. receipts | (15) | | 15 | | | | | | | | | | | | | | | | | | | | | | |
| Available Inv. | 0 | 10 | 10 | 10 | 5 | 5 | 5 | 13 | 13 | 13 | 8 | 8 | 8 | 1 | 1 | 1 | 11 | 11 | 11 | 4 | 4 | 4 | 7 | 7 | 7 |
| Net req. | | | | | | | 2 | | | | | | | | | 4 | | | | | | 1 | | | |
| Plan. receipts | | | | | | | 15 | | | | | | | | | 15 | | | | | | 8 | | | |
| Plan. release | | | | 15 | | | | | | | | | 15 | | | | | | 8 | | | | | | |

### Item C

| | 1 | 2 | 3 | 4 | 5 | 6 | 7 | 8 | 9 | 10 | 11 | 12 | 13 | 14 | 15 | 16 | 17 | 18 | 19 | 20 | 21 | 22 | 23 | 24 | 25 |
|---|---|---|---|---|---|---|---|---|---|---|---|---|---|---|---|---|---|---|---|---|---|---|---|---|---|
| Time period | 1 | 2 | 3 | 4 | 5 | 6 | 7 | 8 | 9 | 10 | 11 | 12 | 13 | 14 | 15 | 16 | 17 | 18 | 19 | 20 | 21 | 22 | 23 | 24 | 25 |
| Gross req. | | 25 | | | | 25 | | | | 25 | | | | 25 | | | | 25 | | | | 25 | | | |
| Sch. issues | | | | | | | | | | | | | | | | | | | | | | | | | |
| Sch. receipts | | | | | | | | | | | | | | | | | | | | | | | | | |
| Available Inv. | 25 | 25 | 0 | 0 | 0 | 0 | 25 | 25 | 25 | 25 | 0 | 0 | 0 | 0 | 0 | 25 | 25 | 25 | 25 | 0 | 0 | 0 | 0 | 0 | 0 |
| Net req. | | | | | | 25 | | | | | | | | 25 | | | | | | | | 25 | | | |
| Plan. receipts | | | | | | 50 | | | | | | | | 50 | | | | | | | | 25 | | | |
| Plan. release | | 50 | | | | | | | | 50 | | | | | | | | 25 | | | | | | | |

### Item D

| | 1 | 2 | 3 | 4 | 5 | 6 | 7 | 8 | 9 | 10 | 11 | 12 | 13 | 14 | 15 | 16 | 17 | 18 | 19 | 20 | 21 | 22 | 23 | 24 | 25 |
|---|---|---|---|---|---|---|---|---|---|---|---|---|---|---|---|---|---|---|---|---|---|---|---|---|---|
| Time period | 1 | 2 | 3 | 4 | 5 | 6 | 7 | 8 | 9 | 10 | 11 | 12 | 13 | 14 | 15 | 16 | 17 | 18 | 19 | 20 | 21 | 22 | 23 | 24 | 25 |
| Gross req. | | 50 | | | 30 | | | | | | 50 | | | 30 | | | | | 25 | 16 | | | | | |
| Sch. issues | 30 | | | | | | | | | | | | | | | | | | | | | | | | |
| Sch. receipts | | | | | | | | | | | | | | | | | | | | | | | | | |
| Available Inv. | 50 | 20 | 45 | 45 | 45 | 15 | 15 | 15 | 15 | 15 | 15 | 40 | 40 | 40 | 10 | 10 | 10 | 10 | 10 | 16 | 0 | 0 | 0 | 0 | 0 |
| Net req. | | 30 | | | | | | | | | 35 | | | | | | | | 15 | | | | | | |
| Plan. receipts | | 75 | | | | | | | | | 75 | | | | | | | | 31 | | | | | | |
| Plan. release | | | | | 75 | | | | | | | | 31 | | | | | | | | | | | | |

(Plan. release also shows **75** in the margin to the left of period 1.)

**Fig. 9.9**  Tables with MRP calculations for Example 9.1

try to utilize the available inventory first. A changed demand from previous MRP calculation is first satisfied with rescheduling of an already open order by either advancing it in an earlier time period or by postponing it to a later time period. Thereafter, planned orders are added. These changes of starting times and finishing (receipt of supplies) times of the open orders are signaled to the users but mostly the original starting and finishing times are left unchanged (because these are already printed on documents in the workshop that identify the order and the material). However, the new starting and finishing times are a base for new planned orders. The figures in parentheses are the new finishing (receipt) times of open orders. In view of the gross requirement of item *A* in period 1 getting satisfied through the 10 units of available inventory, the scheduled receipt of the open order of 20 units can be postponed to time period 3 (and hence, the manufacturer can save on unecessary inventory costs during periods 1 and 2). In time period 3, the gross requirement of 25 units would ensure immediate consumption of the 20 units of this open order and would still be short by 5 units warranting the planning of a new order to be released in period 2 (for planned receipt in period 3). Similarly, for item *B* (see Fig. 9.9), the open order (scheduled receipt) of 15 units in period 3 has to be preponed to period 1 in view of the immediate need to fulfil the gross requirement of 5 units in period 1. This kind of changes in the delivery date for open orders requires the consent of the supplier (internal or external) of such items according to the feasibility on their part. As noted earlier, in this case $D$ is the only component required for making $B$ and in period 1 already 30 units of $D$ are scheduled to be issued. Hence, the supplier (internal or external) of $D$ would be able to easily issue the same in period 1 so that item B can be assembled to fulfil the gross requirement in period 1 itself.

In the table for item $D$ (Fig. 9.9), it is shown that there is a planned release of 75 units in period 0 (one period before period 1). The lead time of item $D$ is given as 3 time periods. Therefore, this order should be (theoretically) released in time period 1 and not period 0 as shown. However, practically time period 0 is the current time and the time prior to it is bygone (past). Hence, the only option here is to release the order right away (in time period 0) with the consent of the supplier (internal or external) to make the delivery with a reduced lead time of 2 time periods instead of the normal lead time of 3 time periods under these exceptional circumstances.

It is mentioned in the problem that fixed order quantities are used in production and these fixed quantities for the four items are given as well. However, in Fig. 9.9, for items $A$, $C$, and $D$ the planned receipts (and releases) during the later part of the time horizon considered have some values other than the fixed quantities mentioned for these items. This is so because we are trying to ensure that there is no inventory to carry forward to periods beyond period 25 (the available inventory for period 26, the starting period for the next planning horizon becomes 0). In most instances, the MRP calculation works as shown. The last demand is treated as if it is the last demand ever, just to ensure that production of a product can be phased out (stopped) and possibly be exchanged by another product (item number) according to the situation prevailing in the market then. This approach is thus different from the one adapted by us in the earlier example of the MRP report.

## Calculation of Order Size in MRP

> There are four methods of calculating the order size in MRP—lot-for-lot method, EOQ method, least total cost method, and least unit cost method.

There are four methods of calculating the order size in MRP. These are as follows
1. Lot-for-lot method
2. EOQ method
3. Least total cost method
4. Least unit cost method

Let us take up a common example to understand all these methods. For an item the following information is given: ordering cost (OC) = ₹50 per order, carrying cost (CC) per week = 0.5%, unit cost price = ₹20, CC per unit per week = $20 \times 0.5\% = ₹0.1$.

| Week | Net requirements |
|------|------------------|
| 1 | 80 |
| 2 | 100 |
| 3 | 90 |
| 4 | 60 |
| 5 | 11 |
| 6 | 50 |
| | 490 |

Now, let us calculate the order size using these four methods as follows.

**Lot-for-lot method**   As the name *lot-for-lot* suggests, the order size or the lot size is the same as the requirements at a point of time.

In the above example, at the beginning of every week the planned order receipts (order size) exactly match the requirements of the item in that week. As shown in the first table of Fig. 9.10, the ending inventory as well as the CC of inventory is zero. There is no accumulation of inventory at any point of time; every week an order is placed, leading to an OC of ₹50. The total cost is ₹300 for this method.

> As the name lot-for-lot suggests, the order size or the lot size is the same as the requirements at a point of time.

**Fig. 9.10** The lot-for-lot and EOQ methods of order-size calculation

**EOQ method** In this method, the annual demand is determined by assuming that the net requirements as given in the six weeks will continue with the same pattern for the whole year. A year contains 52 weeks and in the given six weeks the total demand is 490. Therefore,

$$\text{Anual demand} = \frac{490 \times 52}{6} = 4{,}246.667$$

The CC per unit per week has been calculated earlier as ₹0.1. Therefore,

$$\text{Annual CC (for 52 weeks)} = 0.1 \times 52 = ₹5.2 \text{ per unit}$$

Now, the EOQ can be easily calculated as follows:

$$Q = \sqrt{\frac{2Ao}{c}} = \sqrt{\frac{2 \times 4{,}246.667 \times 50}{5.2}} = 285.773803 \approx 286$$

In Fig. 9.10, the second table, for the EOQ method, shows the above calculations on the right side.

This implies that an order of 286 units only must be placed every time. In Fig. 9.10, the first planned order receipt of 286 units is in week 1. The net requirement in week 1 is only 80 units. Hence, the excess of 206 units forms the closing inventory, for which the CC will be ₹20.6 (206 × 0.1). The OC in week 1 is ₹50. The inventory keeps on decreasing and in week 3 it reduces to just 16 units. Thus, at the beginning of week 4, an order of 286 units is again placed to receive these immediately (assuming zero lead time). The total cost in this method is ₹178.4.

> In the EOQ method, the annual demand is determined by assuming that the net requirements as given in the six weeks will continue with the same pattern for the whole year.

**Least total cost method** In this method, the lot size is determined by extending the time horizon from the smallest unit of time (in our example week 1) to the largest (weeks 1 to 6). In Fig. 9.11, the upper table shows that for the time

In the least total cost method, the lot size is determined by extending the time horizon from the smallest unit of time to the largest.

horizon of week 1, the lot size of 80 units will suffice to meet the requirements with zero CC and an OC of ₹50, resulting in the total cost also of ₹50. When the time horizon is extended from week 1 to week 2, a total of 180 units (80 for week 1 and 100 for week 2) is required. The lot size to satisfy the requirements of this time horizon is, thus, 180 units. Therefore, there is a single order of size 180 units resulting an OC of ₹50. The CC for this time horizon is equal to the CC of 100 units to be stored for one week (as 80 units for week 1 will get consumed in that week only). Thus, the CC is $100 \times 0.1 = ₹10$.

| | A | B | C | D | E | F | G | H |
|---|---|---|---|---|---|---|---|---|
| 1 | Weeks | Lot Size | Carrying Cost | Order Cost | Total Cost | | | |
| 2 | 1 | 80 | 0 | 50 | 50 | | | |
| 3 | 1 to 2 | 180 | 10 | 50 | 60 | | | |
| 4 | 1 to 3 | 270 | 28 | 50 | 78 | | | |
| 5 | 1 to 4 | 330 | 46 | 50 | 96 | Least Total Cost | | |
| 6 | 1 to 5 | 440 | 90 | 50 | 140 | | | |
| 7 | 1 to 6 | 490 | 115 | 50 | 165 | | | |
| 8 | 5 | 110 | 0 | 50 | 50 | | | |
| 9 | 5 to 6 | 160 | 5 | 50 | 55 | Least Total Cost | | |
| 10 | | | | | | | | |
| 11 | Week | Net Requirements | Lot Size | Ending Inventory | Carrying Cost | Order Cost | Total cost | |
| 12 | 1 | 80 | 330 | 250 | 25 | 50 | 75 | |
| 13 | 2 | 100 | 0 | 150 | 15 | 0 | 15 | |
| 14 | 3 | 90 | 0 | 60 | 6 | 0 | 6 | |
| 15 | 4 | 60 | 0 | 0 | 0 | 0 | 0 | |
| 16 | 5 | 110 | 160 | 50 | 5 | 50 | 55 | |
| 17 | 6 | 50 | 0 | 0 | 0 | 0 | 0 | |
| 18 | | | | | | Grand Total | 151 | |

**Least Total Cost Method**

**Fig. 9.11** The least total cost method of order-size calculation

Similarly, for the time horizon of weeks 1–3, the CC = cost of carrying 100 units for one week (requirement of week 2) + cost of carrying 90 units for two weeks (requirement of week 3)
$$= 100 \times 0.1 + 90 \times 0.1 \times 2 = 10 + 18 = ₹28$$

The calculations of the total cost in the time horizon of weeks 1–6 are shown in Fig. 9.11. Note that the CC and OC are most close to each other in value for the time horizon of weeks 1–4 (the values are ₹46 and ₹50, respectively). Thus, this time horizon has the least total cost (where the OC and CC are almost equal). Therefore, the lot size for this interval from week 1 to 4 will be taken as 330 units. For the remaining duration, that is, weeks 5 and 6, we will perform the calculations in a way similar to what was done earlier. First, consider only week 5 for which the CC and OC are 0 and ₹50, respectively. Then consider weeks 5–6, for which the CC and OC are ₹5 and ₹50, respectively. Clearly, for weeks 5–6, the CC and OC values are nearer to each other compared to week 5 alone. Therefore, the least cost lot size is 160 units.

The least unit cost method is an extension of the least total cost method.

In Fig. 9.11, the second table shows the usual total cost calculations, when the first lot of 330 units is ordered and received at the beginning of week 1, while the second order of 160 units is placed at the beginning of week 5. The total cost for this method is ₹151.

**Least unit cost method** This method is just an extension of the least total cost method. As shown in Fig. 9.12, the only difference is that after calculating the total cost for each time horizon, it is divided by the lot size to get the unit cost. Note that the unit cost is lowest for the time horizon of weeks 1–3. Thus, the first lot size will be 270 units. We now do the calculations for time horizons beyond week 3, that is, week 4, weeks 4–5, and weeks 4–6. The least unit cost is for weeks 4–6. Thus the next lot size is 220 units. The total cost for this method has been calculated as ₹149.

The lot-for-lot and EOQ methods are called fixed-period methods, while the least total cost and least unit cost methods are called part-period methods, as various parts of the duration are considered for minimizing the cost. The least total cost and least unit cost methods are based on dynamic lot-sizing techniques. Both these methods result in lower values of total cost compared to the lot-for-lot and EOQ methods (as verified by our example, the least unit cost method results in the lowest total cost of ₹149). At the same time, they are more complicated to implement compared to the lot-for-lot and EOQ methods. See Exhibit 9.2 to learn about Toyota's manufacturing processes.

| | A | B | C | D | E | F | G | H |
|---|---|---|---|---|---|---|---|---|
| 1 | Weeks | Lot Size | Carrying Cost | Order Cost | Total Cost | Unit Cost | | |
| 2 | 1 | 80 | 0 | 50 | 50 | 0.625 | | |
| 3 | 1 to 2 | 180 | 10 | 50 | 60 | 0.3333333 | | |
| 4 | 1 to 3 | 270 | 28 | 50 | 78 | 0.2888889 | Least Unit Cost | |
| 5 | 1 to 4 | 330 | 46 | 50 | 96 | 0.2909091 | | |
| 6 | 1 to 5 | 440 | 90 | 50 | 140 | 0.3181818 | | |
| 7 | 1 to 6 | 490 | 115 | 50 | 165 | 0.3367347 | | |
| 8 | 4 | 60 | 0 | 50 | 50 | 0.8333333 | | |
| 9 | 4 to 5 | 170 | 11 | 50 | 61 | 0.3588235 | | |
| 10 | 4 to 6 | 220 | 21 | 50 | 71 | 0.3227273 | Least Unit Cost | |
| 11 | **Week** | **Net Requirements** | **Lot Size** | **Ending Inventory** | **Carrying Cost** | **Order Cost** | **Total cost** | |
| 12 | 1 | 80 | 270 | 190 | 19 | 50 | 69 | |
| 13 | 2 | 100 | 0 | 90 | 9 | 0 | 9 | |
| 14 | 3 | 90 | 0 | 0 | 0 | 0 | 0 | |
| 15 | 4 | 60 | 220 | 160 | 16 | 50 | 66 | |
| 16 | 5 | 110 | 0 | 50 | 5 | 0 | 5 | |
| 17 | 6 | 50 | 0 | 0 | 0 | 0 | 0 | |
| 18 | | | | | | **Grand Tota** | 149 | |
| 19 | | | | | | | | |
| 20 | | | **Least Unit Cost Method** | | | | | |

**Fig. 9.12** The least unit cost method of order-size calculation

| Exhibit 9.2 | Toyota in India |

For many years after it was founded in 1937, Toyota was derided as a company made up of 'a bunch of farmers'. It hired a lot of farmers to work on its assembly lines and, in fact, the founding family's name Toyoda meant 'abundant rice field' in Japanese. The word Toyota, however, has no meaning in that language. Over a period of six decades, Toyota has acquired the most fearsome reputation in the industry for its exemplary manufacturing system, where costs and inefficiencies are pared not just every day, but every second. During the first three months of 2007, Toyota sold more cars and trucks around the world than any other manufacturer, surpassing General Motors (GM) for the first time ever and ending one of the longest dominance in all of global industry. In 2012, Toyota's worldwide sales of cars and trucks reached 9.75 million as against GM's 9.29 million in the same period.

Let us take a look at its low-fat Bidadi (near Bangalore) operations—the maximum amount of raw material at the factory at any point of time does not exceed two hours production requirement; all finished cars leave the factory within 48 hours, and no dealer is sent more than 15 days stock. So, just how does Toyota do it? The trick lies in its famous 'milk run', which involves picking up small quantities of supplies from vendors throughout the day. This is how it works—every morning small trucks leave a central stocking point (there is one each in Pune, Delhi, and Chennai), picking up supplies from the local vendors.

These trucks then return to the hub, where the supplies are transferred to bigger trucks, which leave for the Bidadi plant every day. For vendors based in and around Bangalore, the milk runs are straight from the plant to the vendor and back.

Transystems Logistics International, a joint venture between Travel Corporation of India and Mitsui & Co., is the sole transport and logistics provider of Toyota to facilitate the JIT supplies for its Bidadi plant. Everyday, 261 trucks of Transystems log more than a lakh kilometres picking up parts from Toyota's 83 vendors in 20 different states of the country, though most of them are near Bangalore. It has three cross-dock facilities in Gurgaon, Chennai, and Pune. On the 25th of every month Toyota sends out a detailed schedule to all its vendors and Transystems, informing them of the raw material requirement and production schedule. Based on this schedule, Transystem does milk-runs at each of the four regions, aggregating the parts at the three cross-docks. Here, the components are loaded on to a bigger truck, which then ferries to Bidadi. All the parts arrive 'just-in-time' to be assembled. Apart from delivering components, Transystems ferries built up vehicles to all of Toyota's dealers in the country. It picks spare parts from the vendors and sends them off to the dealers and ferries imported knocked down kits from Chennai port to the Bidadi plant.

*Source:* Notte (2013).

# Just-in-time

Schonberger (1982) defines the just-in-time (JIT) system as to 'Produce and deliver finished goods just in time to be sold, sub-assemblies just in time to be assembled into finished goods, and purchase materials just in time to be transformed into fabricated parts'. Monden (1981) defines JIT as 'a production system to produce the kind of units needed, at the time needed and in the quantities needed'.

The basic idea of JIT was originally developed by the Toyota Motor Company in Japan. The idea was formalized into a management system when Toyota sought to meet the precise demand of customers for different models and colours of cars with minimum delay. During the early 1970s, this approach to managing manufacturing began to attract wide attention in Japan, and by the mid-1970s many Japanese companies had adopted this approach. At that time, the approach was not known as JIT but was called the 'Toyota Manufacturing System'. The JIT philosophy began to attract significant attention from the West towards the late 1970s. During that time, startling comparisons were made between Toyota's plant in Japan and some American plants as shown in Table 9.3.

**Table 9.3** A comparison between American and Japanese plants during the late 1970s

|  | *Toyota Takaoka plant, Japan* | *American plant* |
|---|---|---|
| Set-up time (h) | 0.2 | 6.0 |
| Set-ups per day | 3 | 1 |
| Lot size | 1 day use | 10 days use |
| Number of employees | 4,300 | 3,800 |
| Number of vehicles produced per day | 2,700 | 1,000 |
| Total labour days per vehicle | 1.6 | 3.8 |

Just-in-time manufacturing has become synonymous with excellence in manufacturing. Sometimes called *lean production*, it is used in a wide variety of industries such as automobiles, consumer electronics, office equipment, electrical equipment, etc. However, there are very few references to the term JIT manufacturing in process industries such as chemicals, plastics, pharmaceuticals, etc. It was originally felt that the use of JIT manufacturing required high volumes and constant demands, it now appears that most aspects of JIT manufacturing are also applicable to low-volume, high-variety products. For example, Boeing implemented JIT manufacturing in spite of the fact that it only produces a few hundred aeroplanes each year and each aeroplane has a unique design.

### JIT Manufacturing

JIT manufacturing in most common terms is the continuous improvement of material flow in either a factory or a combination of factories. There are four techniques in JIT for improving material flow as follows.

**Factory layout revision**   The layout of factories can be revised to introduce assembly lines and manufacturing cells. Sometimes called continuous-flow manufacturing, the purpose of these layout modifications is to minimize material-handling activities and their associated transactions, and to provide faster quality feedback. Assembly lines are typically dedicated to a particular product type, although they may be able to produce multiple models. Manufacturing cells produce a variety of completed parts and the cells are developed using group technology (discussed in Chapter 6). Often, in order to have the capability to handle sudden surges in demand, excess capacity is built into the system.

**Set-up time reduction**   Factories can reduce set-up times in order to reduce lot sizes and smooth production. For example, in manufacturing doors and other sheet metal parts of an automobile, the metal sheet is given various shapes by using heavy presses containing metal dies. This process is called *stamping*. These dies have to be changed every time the body of a new car model is to be manufactured. Before the 1950s, these set-up changes of dies required as long as a day. By the late 1950s, Taiichi Ohno, the then Vice-President of Toyota Motor Company, reduced the time required to change dies from a day to an astonishing three minutes, and eliminated the need for die-change specialists. In the process, he made an unexpected discovery—it actually costs less per part to make small batches of stampings than to run off enormous lots.

> Just-in-time manufacturing has become synonymous with excellence in manufacturing.

> There are four techniques in JIT for improving material flow—factory layout revision, set-up time reduction, pull system implementation, and better coordination with supplies.

Reduced set-up times enable a factory to produce smaller lot sizes economically.

Reduced set-up times enable a factory to produce smaller lot sizes economically. Smaller lot sizes enable a factory to produce a broader variety of products, assemblies, and parts each day. However, preventive maintenance and lowering defect rates are also needed to achieve these lower safety stock sizes.

**Pull system implementation**    Factories can implement a *pull system* of production using *kanban* (a flag or signal in Japanese is a visual aid to convey the message that action is required). In a pull system (in contrast to the MRP-based push system, where inventories of components/parts are pushed into production according to the MPS), final assembly lines only produce actual orders and *kanban* cards are used to signal sub-assembly and part deliveries, and production. MRP may be used, and smooth production facilitates the use of a pull system.

**Better coordination with suppliers**    Factories can work with suppliers to reduce raw material inventories and solve quality problems. The first three techniques are applicable to the suppliers as well, for improving the material flow between a firm and its suppliers. The goal is to make the supplier an extension of the internal material flows, to avoid the problems associated with shifting of inventories from customers to suppliers.

### *Kanban* Visual System

*Kanban* is a Japanese word meaning flag or signal, and is a visual aid to convey the message that action is required. The *kanban* inventory control system was originally pioneered by the Toyota Motor Company in Japan and developed from the ideas of Toyota's Vice-President Taiichi Ohno.

On a visit to the United States, Ohno observed the method adapted by American supermarkets for replenishing empty shelves in racks. Whenever a shelf was found emptied of a product, it triggered the replenishment of the product to the shelf. It was so simple because an empty shelf was easily visible among the other shelves full of products. Ohno thought of implementing the same idea for replenishment at his assembly lines. He adapted this simple but effective method by using a trigger, or *kanban*, to alert the manufacturing area that the assembly area was running low on components. Every component must have its own *kanban* to signal when it nees to be replenished.

The *kanban* system can be explained in the following steps (see Fig. 9.13).

*Step 1*    When a worker requires components, he goes to the racks placed opposite his workstation. These racks contain bins of components required by a workstation, which form the work-in-process inventory. Every bin has the *requisition kanban* card affixed on it, which is removable. This card contains the component name, its identification number, and the rack number and shelf on the rack in the store (opposite the manufacturing cells) where more bins of the component are stored. The workers from the assembly line remove the *kanban* card from the bin, hang it on a hook on the rack, and take away the bin to their workstation for using the components in assembly operations. These hanging *kanban* cards are thus clearly visible from everywhere, signalling replenishment of components from the store.

Kanban is a Japanese word meaning flag or signal, and is a visual aid to convey the message that action is required.

*Step 2*    A supply worker called *mizosomashi* in Japanese keeps on moving in the aisle across the racks with his trolley. When he reaches the racks opposite the assembly line, he removes all the hanging requisition *kanban* cards and the empty bins from the racks. He then takes these along with him through the aisle to the racks in the store opposite the manufacturing cells.

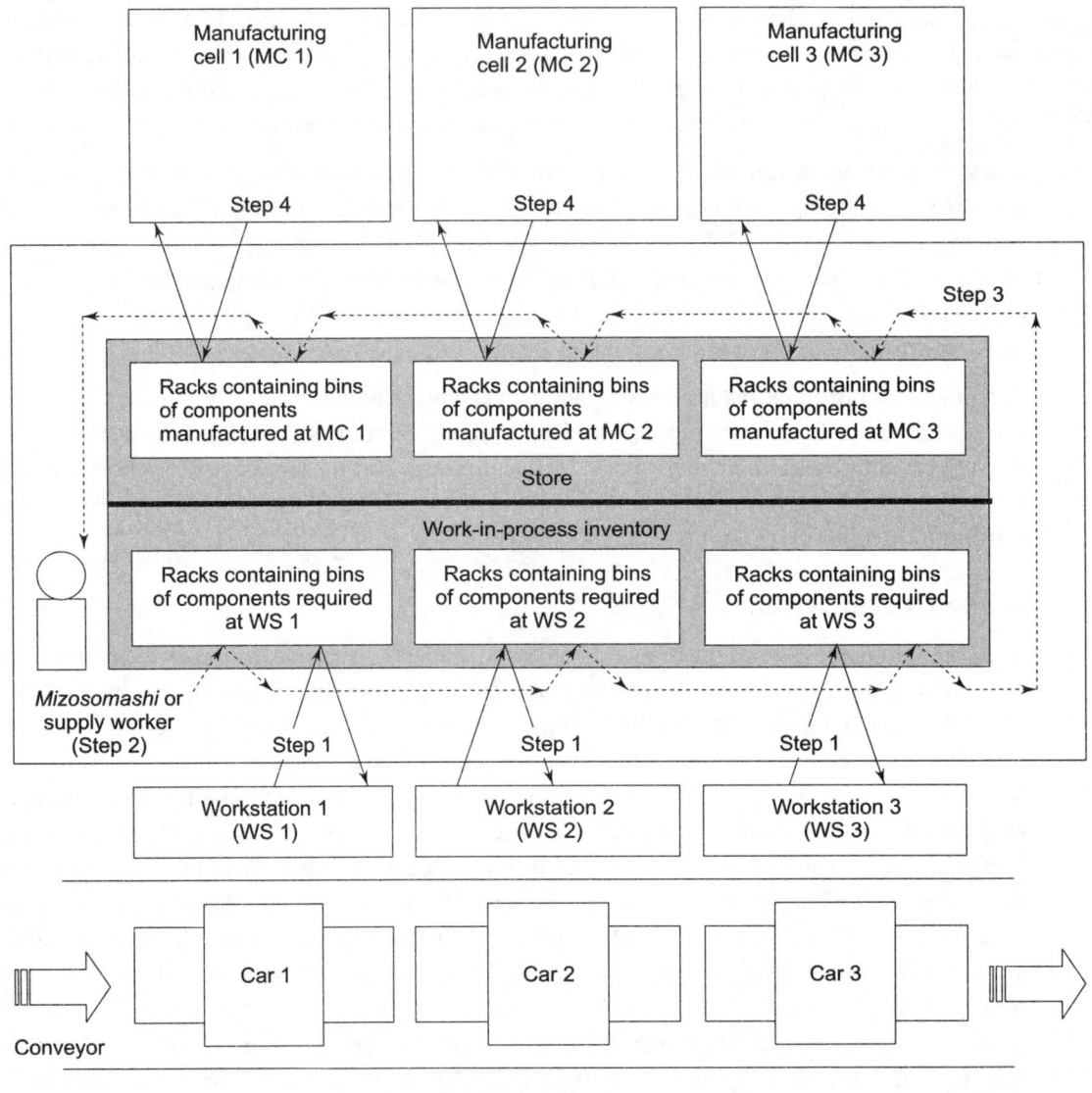

**Fig. 9.13** The *kanban* visual system

**Step 3** *Mizosomashi* looks at the information on each requisition *kanban* card and locates the position of the rack and the shelf on the rack containing the bins full of a particular component. Every bin in the store has the *production kanban* card affixed on it, which is removable. The production *kanban* card contains the name and identification number of the component to be manufactured in the cell. *Mizosomashi* takes off the bins from the racks corresponding to the requisition *kanban* card he had brought with him, and removes the production *kanban* card from these. He hangs these on the hooks on the corresponding racks in the store, attaches the requisition *kanban* cards on the bins, and puts the bins in the trolley. The empty bins that

> The production *kanban* card contains the name and identification number of the component to be manufactured in the cell.

The obvious benefits of using the *kanban* system are reduced inventory and less storage space required.

he had brought with him in his trolley are placed on the racks. After loading all the required bins into the trolley in this way, he takes the trolley to the racks opposite the assembly line and places the bins in the appropriate racks. Thus, the replenishment of the bins at the assembly line has taken place. *Mizosomashi* repeats this process at regular intervals of time.

**Step 4** One worker from each of the manufacturing cells goes to the rack placed opposite his cell with his trolley. He removes the hanging production *kanban* cards and places the empty bins from the rack in his trolley. He takes these to his manufacturing cell, where the different components mentioned on the production *kanban cards* are manufactured in exact quantities so as to fill the empty bins completely. The filled-in bins with the production *kanban* cards attached to them are then taken from the manufacturing cell to the rack opposite the cell and placed on the appropriate shelf mentioned in the production *kanban* card.

JIT is a *pull system*, as opposed to the western norm of making bulk components and storing them 'just in case' they are needed (called a *push system*). The obvious benefits of using the

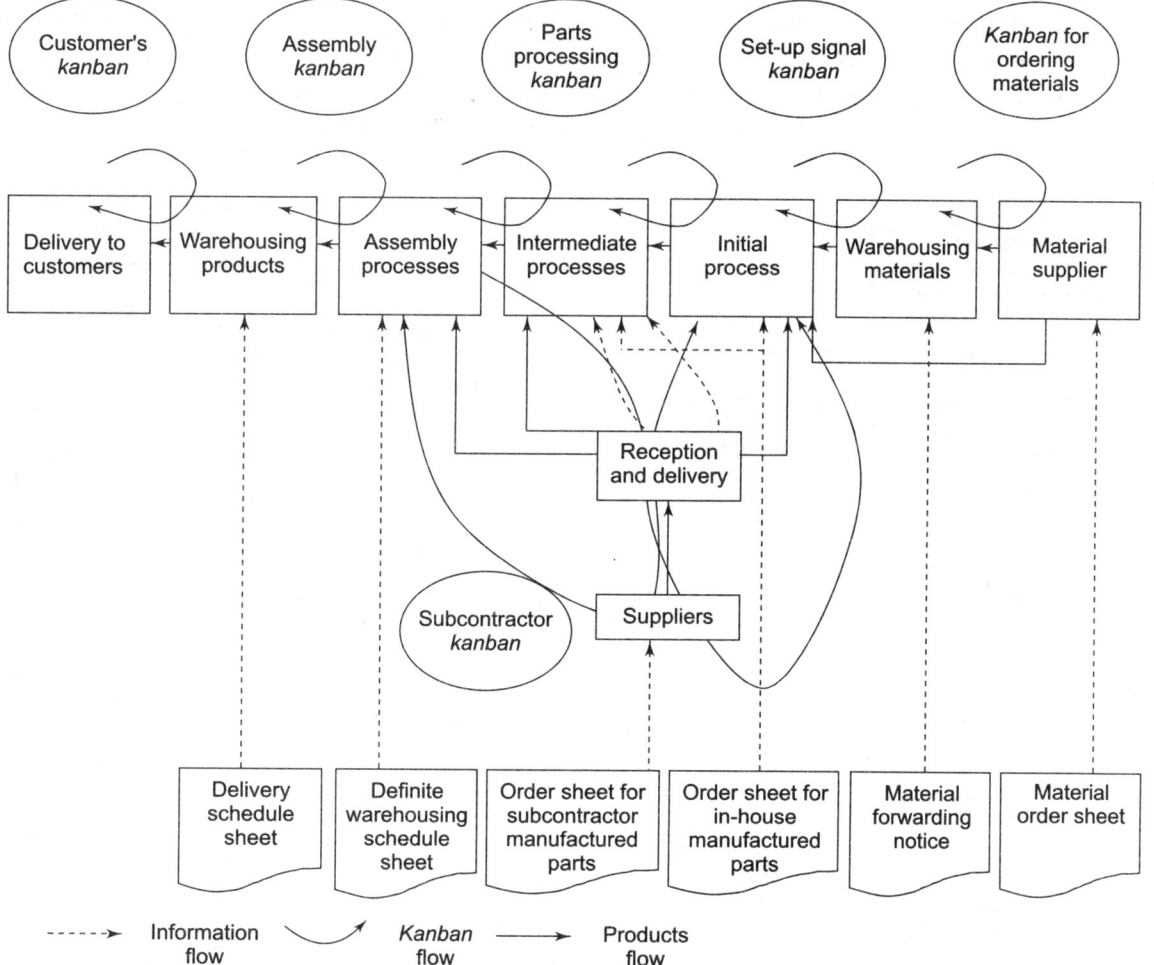

**Fig. 9.14** Use of *kanban* across the supply chain

The overall reduction of inventory across the whole supply chain leads to much lower inventory and material-handling costs.

JIT's first benefit is the heightened awareness of problems and causes in the organization.

*kanban* system are reduced inventory and less storage space required; however, the hidden benefit is the high quality of components. Production of components in small batches makes it easier to immediately detect defects in them. Thus, reduced inventory acts as a buffer against bad quality.

Figure 9.14 shows *kanban* cards being used throughout the supply chain across its various elements, from the material supplier to the end customer, leading to negligible work-in-process inventory everywhere. This overall reduction of inventory across the whole supply chain leads to much lower inventory and material-handling costs, thus reducing the overall cost of production and lowering sales prices compared to those of competitors. The products are able to effectively compete with those of the competitors. We will study this in greater detail in the section Supply Chain Management.

### Benefits of JIT

Figure 9.15 shows the benefits of JIT as explained by Schonberger. JIT's first benefit is the heightened awareness of problems and causes in the organization. This leads to generation of ideas/suggestions on the part of employees. These ideas for continuous improvement are termed kaizens in Japanese. As shown in the figure, these ideas result in smaller lot sizes of materials, JIT production, and better quality control, leading to various advantages.

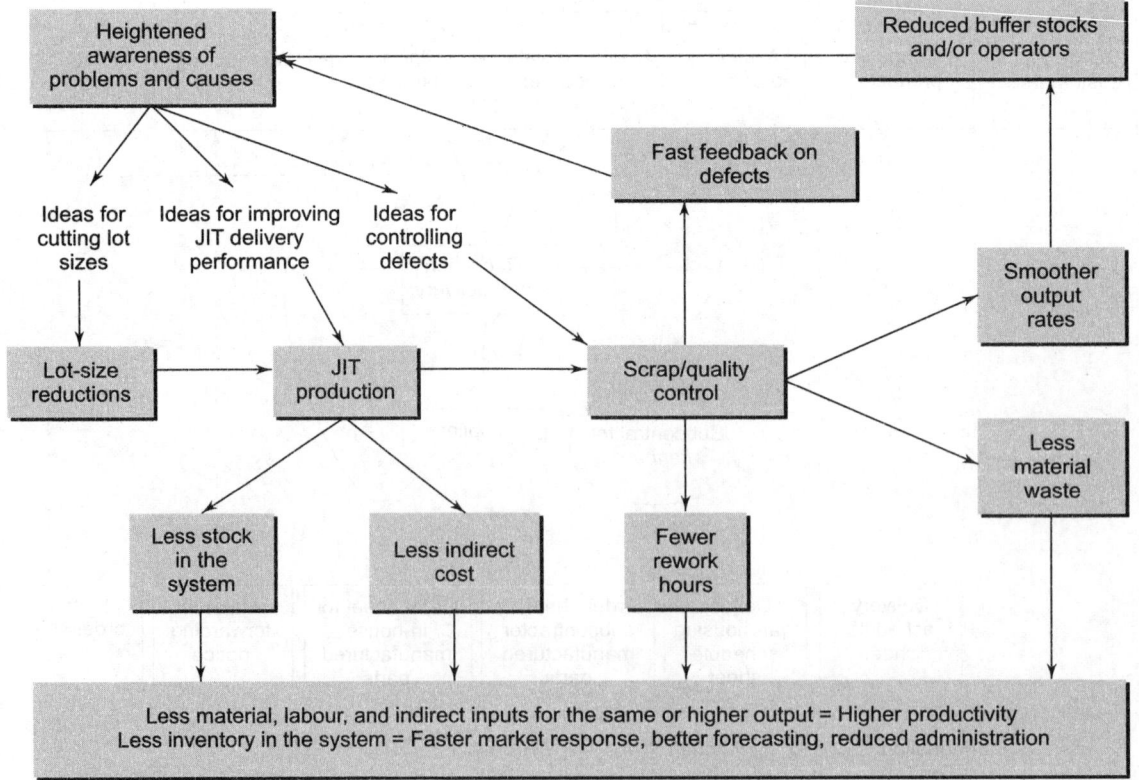

**Fig. 9.15**  Benefits of JIT

---

### Exhibit 9.3   Kirloskar Copeland Ltd

Kirloskar Copeland Ltd (KCL) is a joint venture between Kirloskar Brothers Ltd and Copeland (USA), and manufactures a range of air-conditioning and refrigeration compressors. KCL lists Amtrex, Blue Star, Carrier, and Voltas among its biggest customers, apart from a host of small air-conditioner assemblers. KCL has two plants—one at Atit and the other at Karad, 150 km from Pune.

The kaizen quality technique introduced in September 1997 has gone a long way to help KCL achieve the kind of growth it has witnessed. As a result of kaizen, the set-up change time has been brought down from 30 minutes to 8 minutes, and rejections have been reduced drastically. One particular kaizen implementation in an operation resulted in an increase in per shift output from 175 compressors to 225. Kaizen, introduced for permanent employees and later embracing contract workers too, has everyone contributing now.

The kaizen awards vary from steel tumblers and plates, clocks, and gas stoves for individual achievers, to field trips for teams. A worker with 80 improvements to his credit gets to go on a training course to Copeland's parent plant in the US. S.L. Kalbhor, an operator at the Atit plant, has been the first to achieve 80 plus kaizens. In the US, he intends to study how they ensure zero rejection, and help implement it here when he returns. Kalbhor, a farmer's son who worked his way through an industrial diploma, admits that his colleagues were initially jealous. 'But I explained the advantages to the company, and they understood', he says. Among the improvements he is particularly proud of, are the introduction of an ink bottle within the cycle to automatically put a dot on each compressor when its oil is changed; a safety device to stop the conveyor belt when a shear pin breaks; a modification to prevent couplers from flying off, so that there is no leakage; and a slide fixture so that the operator does not burn his hands lifting down dehydrated compressors.

KCL has achieved an average of three kaizens per employee per year—it wants to increase these to six. Next, the practice is being extended to ancillary suppliers.

---

**Kaizen**   Kaizen in Japanese means *continuous improvement* in every sphere of activity. Kaizen is a sub-system of JIT. The management of the company encourages suggestions or kaizens from employees regarding possible improvements in their respective work areas. The employees are rewarded for giving a large number of useful suggestions (Exhibit 9.3). These rewards are more of recognition, such as 'kaizen man of the month' titles and certificates or small gifts, rather than monetary worth.

## Kaizen Sheet

A kaizen sheet is a useful way of depicting the information relating to the implementation of a kaizen suggested by an individual or a group of workers. Figure 9.16 shows a typical format of a kaizen sheet. The kaizen theme mentioned in this sheet is 'to eliminate cleaning process of centre bolt cut length with saw dust (*muda* of process)'. *Muda* is Japanese for waste. The problem highlighted on the sheet is 'two men engaged on three machines for removing oil from centre bolt cut length with saw dust'. Note that the top right portion of the sheet mentions about the location (machine, department, etc.) of the concerned kaizen to be implemented. A flow chart is helpful in making an analysis of the problem as shown. Cleaning of the centre bolt cut length with saw dust is required because of the oily surface. Notice the 'why?' at each step of the flowchart. It

> Kaizen in Japanese means continuous improvement in every sphere of activity.

becomes clear from the figure marked 'before counter measure' that oil used to be poured from an oil pipe above the straightening rollers on the machine to reduce the heat generated as a result of friction. The root cause of the problem has been identified as excessive flow of oil on the machine so that the job

A kaizen sheet is a useful way of depicting the information relating to the implementation of a kaizen suggested by an individual or a group of workers.

(centre bolt cut length) being processed on the machine used to get wet with oil.

The kaizen idea depicted is to somehow reduce the flow of oil on the machine so that the job does not get wet with oil. The kaizen suggested is to use a sponge/cotton wet with oil touching the straightening rollers. This is pictorially depicted as the 'after counter measure'. The implementation of this kaizen has resulted in the elimination of the need of cleaning with saw dust and thus, a saving of 16 man-hours (i.e., no requirement of two workers employed earlier for this purpose). The following calculations demonstrate a yearly saving of ₹77,857 as a result of this kaizen.

| | Before *Kaizen* | | |
|---|---|---|---|
| 1. | • Oil (diesel) consumption/day | | : 5 Litres |
| | Price/litre (₹) | | : ₹16.66 |
| | • Cost of oil/day (16.66 × 5) | | : ₹83.30 |
| | • Cost of oil/month (83.30 × 26) | | : ₹2,165.80 |
| | • Cost of oil/year (2165.80 × 12) | | : ₹25,989.60 |
| 2. | Salary of 2 persons/year | | : ₹48,000.00 |
| 3. | • Saw dust consumption/day | | : 23.3 KGS |
| | • Saw dust cost/bag | | : ₹21.00 |
| | • Monthly expenses of saw dust | (21.00 × 26) | : ₹546.00 |
| | • Yearly saw dust expenses (546.00 × 12) | | : ₹6,552.00 |
| 4. | Monthly electricity expenses | | : ₹65.00 |
| | Yearly electricity expenses | | : ₹780.00 |
| | Total expenses per year (25,989.60 + 48,000+6,552+780) | | : ₹81,322.00 |
| | After *Kaizen* | | |
| | Yearly expenses of oil (0.7 Ltr/Day × 26 × 12) | | : ₹3,465.00 |
| | Total saving/year (81,322.00 – 3,465.00) | | : ₹77,85,700 |

### Andon

For error prevention and fault-finding in the factory premises, operators must notify supervisors and the management when a problem affects any area within the factory. To enable this, JIT uses

For error prevention and fault-finding in the factory premises, operators must notify supervisors and the management when a problem affects any area within the factory.

a portable *andon* system. The *andon* in the Japanese means an ambulance-style flashing light with a complementary siren. The operator puts the *andon* on whenever he needs to draw the management's attention, highlighting to all the importance of his problem. By reacting instantly to this call for assistance, the management ensures that customers are protected against receiving defective products. In principle, the *andon* system is not effective until most problems are resolved, otherwise the system will be triggered continuously and is not practical.

# KAIZEN SHEET

**BRAR AUTO, JALANDHAR**

| | |
|---|---|
| Machine | : Straightening |
| Unit | : Bar Drawing |
| Date | : 16.07.2005 |

**Kaizen Theme :**
**(WHAT AND WHICH)** To eliminate cleaning process of centre Bolt cut length with saw dust (Muda of process).

**Target and Target date :**
**(HOW MUCH AND WHEN)** To eliminate saw dust cleaning process by 18.07.2005

**(WHERE)**

**Problem :**

Two men engaged on three machines for removing oil from centre bolt cut length with saw dust.

**Counter measure :** Wet waste cotton used instead of flow of oil

**Before Counter Measure:** (HOW)

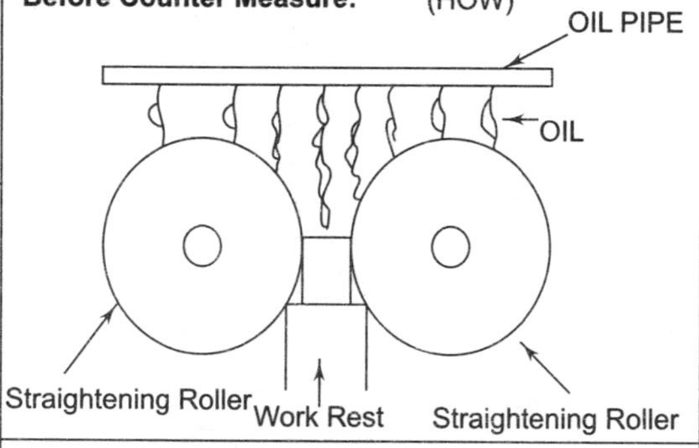

**Analysis :**

Clearing with Saw Dust

→ Why?

Oily Surface

→ Why?

Flow of excessive oil fed on the straightening Rollers to save it from friction/deterioration

**Benefits/Results after Implementation :**
(HOW MANY)

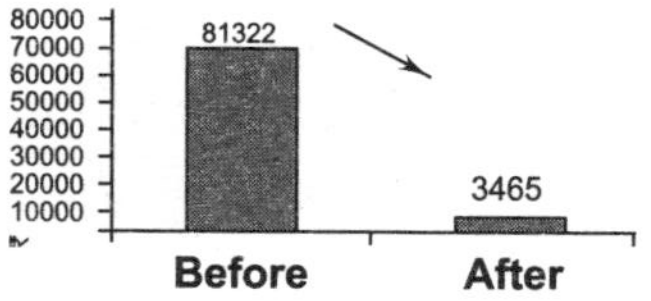

81322

3465

Before          After

Elimination of Clearing with Saw Dust
Saving of 16 Man Hours/Day
Saving ₹77,857.00 / Year

**(SHEET ENCLOSED)**

**Scope and plan for horizontal deployment :**

| Machine | Target Date | Resp | Status |
|---|---|---|---|
| 17 | 20.07.05 | GS | Implemented |
| 18 | 20.07.05 | GS | Implemented |
| | | | |
| | | | |

**Root Cause :** Excessive flow of oil

**Idea :** To reduce oil flow and to eliminate saw dust cleaning process

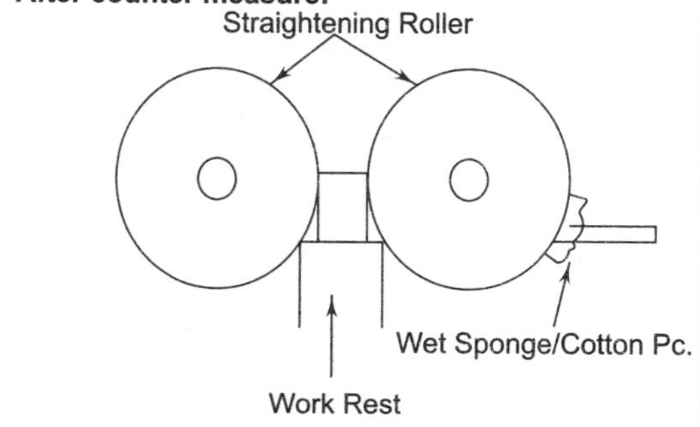

**Implemented by :**
**(WHO)** RS, GS, PS, AS, AS, JS

Kaizen no. : 01 (ZONE-1)

**Fig. 9.16** Kaizen sheet to eliminate cleaning process of centre bolt cut length with saw dust

## Fixed Location Storage

The hidden key to the success of JIT is that there should be a fixed location for all components, parts, tools, and equipment. The handling of parts and tools is minimized if these are properly located in the assembly area and in the stores. Fixed locations assist in knowing the exact location of parts and the number of parts available for assembly. This ease of access increases productivity and also reduces damage to components. Tools and equipment that are common to all workers should be brought back to their locations immediately after a worker finishes his work with them so that other workers may use these whenever required.

## Hybrid MRP-JIT Production System

Figure 9.17 shows how MRP and JIT may be used together in a factory (Lee Choong 1993). The important concept here is that MRP is used only for guiding the purchase department for planning the purchasing needs of the future. The actual supplies are made by the suppliers on the basis of the *kanban* cards received by them (JIT). Note the two outputs generated by the MRP in Fig. 9.17 (the two arrows coming out from the MRP box). One output goes to shop scheduling for guiding the manufacturing cell on the quantity of various parts to be internally produced, and the other output goes to the purchase department for purchase order scheduling. The purchase department sends the purchase orders to the suppliers, but the suppliers know that the actual deliveries have to be made (say, daily) according to the *kanban* cards collected by them from the buyer's factory. The purchase order is only a broad guidance to the suppliers to be prepared for the future demand trends (Exhibit 9.4). Another important advantage of MRP in the hybrid MRP-JIT system is the capacity planning of the internal production facilities as well as those of the suppliers. Note the two arrows emanating from the capacity requirements planning box. One arrow goes to capacity control on the shop floor, while the other goes to the purchasing department for vendor capacity control. Capacity requirements planning means planning the machines, equipment, and manpower required for making the required parts internally, and also at the vendor's end for the vendor-supplied parts. It also means planning the number of shifts for the plant and the overtime required on the part of workers to meet the materials requirement generated by the MRP. Total productive maintenance (TPM) and total preventive control (TPC) are a must for this system in order to avoid equipment breakdowns leading to disruption in production schedules.

## Understanding the Supply Chain

The supply chain has been defined (Cox et al. 1995) as follows:

'The processes from the initial raw materials to the ultimate consumption of the finished product linking across supplier-user companies; and the functions within and outside a company that enable the value chain to make products and provide services to the customer.'

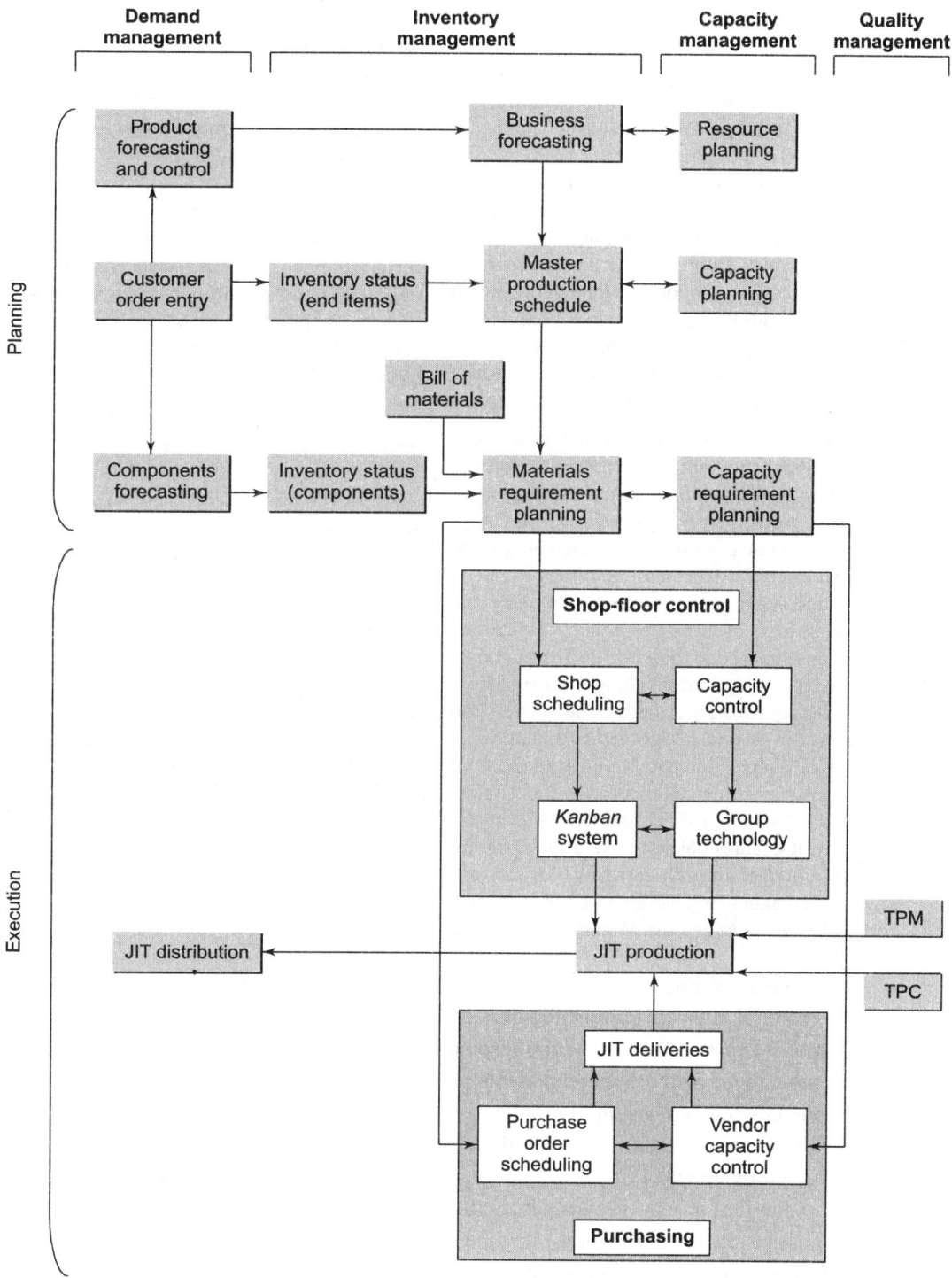

**Fig. 9.17** Hybrid MRP-JIT production system

## Exhibit 9.4 Bajaj Auto Limited

Bajaj Auto Limited is one of India's top ten companies in terms of market capitalization and among the top five in terms of annual turnover. Established in 1945, it was incorporated as a trading company. From 1948 till 1959, it imported scooters and three wheelers from Italy and sold them in India. It then obtained a production licence in 1959 and struck a technical collaboration with Piaggio of Italy in 1960. Scooter production commenced in 1961. Three wheeler production followed in 1962. Its collaboration with Piaggio ended in 1971 and since then the company's scooters and three wheelers are sold under the brand name 'Bajaj'. Earlier, the company sold its products under the brand name Bajaj Vespa.

The company has since then come a long way and has withered under competition from Hero MotoCorp, which currently holds the market leadership position in India. Bajaj Auto is striving hard to dethrone it from the number one position. Bajaj Auto has to keep costs low to enable it to retain its average lead of between 10 and 15 per cent over its competitors in the manufacturing costs of its two-wheelers. The ₹202.01 billion company has divided the 3,000 odd components that go into its scooters into A, B, and C categories. The first category consists of high-value (₹1,000 and above) items; the second category has medium-value components between ₹500 and ₹1,000; and the third category consists of low-value components (below ₹500). This classification translates into lower costs for the company. It enables Bajaj Auto to apply different purchasing strategies to each category. For starters, it allows its managers to build inventories in inverse proportion to the average cost of each genre. Thus,

inventories for category A items are never more than for one shift. Although orders are placed every week, deliveries are made daily, using a just-in-time (JIT) system. To ensure that this inventory level is kept to a minimum, Bajaj Auto has done away with the quality inspection of these products. Instead, it makes it mandatory for vendors to conform to its self-certification programme—under which they guarantee the quality of their output—and feed their supplies directly to the production-line. With 174 of its 1,000 vendors falling in this category, Bajaj Auto saves on both inventory pile-ups and quality-related rejection.

For items in category B, the ordering frequency is once a fortnight and the inventory-ceiling is one week. The ordering cycle of category C items is monthly, but the actual delivery is controlled by the *kanban* process. Under this system, the requirements of the production-line for a particular component are indicated visually through cards, which suppliers use to deliver exactly as much as is required. A variation of this system, using two bins, is followed *inter alia* by the auto-electricals manufacturer, Lucas-TVS. Its production-line and stores have two bins each for a particular component. The moment a bin is emptied on the shop floor, it is traded for a full bin from stores, which passes on the empty bin to the supplier, and picks up a full bin in exchange. The result, for both Lucas-TVS and Bajaj Auto—nobody carries too much inventory, and demand pulls production at every stage. Crucially, this allows Bajaj Auto to pay for only as much as it uses.

*Source:* BSE (2012).

As shown in Fig. 9.18 , a supply chain has the initial raw material supplier at one end. The raw material supplier supplies materials to the Tier-2 supplier, who converts them into some components/parts. The Tier-2 supplier supplies these components/parts to the Tier-1 supplier, who assemble them with other components/parts to form sub-assemblies. These sub-assemblies are supplied by the Tier-1 supplier to the manufacturer, who further assembles them into a finished product. It must be noted here that there may be Tier-3, Tier-4, and so on suppliers between the manufacturer and the initial raw material supplier. The manufacturer supplies the finished goods to the distributor, who in turn passes them on to the retailer. A customer comes to the retailer for purchasing the items only when he or she requires them. Thus, the customer is the most important element of the supply chain and, therefore, the primary objective of the entire supply chain is to meet the customer's requirements.

As shown in Fig. 9.18 , the flow of information and funds takes place from the customer end to the initial raw material supplier, while the product flow takes place in the reverse direction. Any

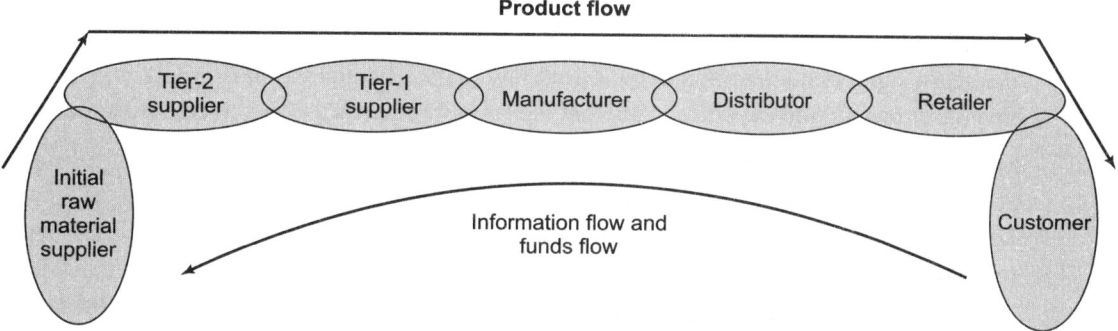

**Fig. 9.18**    The supply chain

hindrance to the flow of information, funds, or product in the supply chain results in inefficiencies. Such hindrances should be eliminated at the earliest to ensure full customer satisfaction.

### The Bullwhip Effect

The *bullwhip effect* is a phenomenon whereby each upstream player in the supply chain tends to carry more and more inventory or capacity due to lack of visibility of actual customer demand at the fag end of the supply chain. As shown in Fig. 9.19, this variability in demand from the customer end to the initial raw material end of the supply chain resembles the 'bullwhip'.

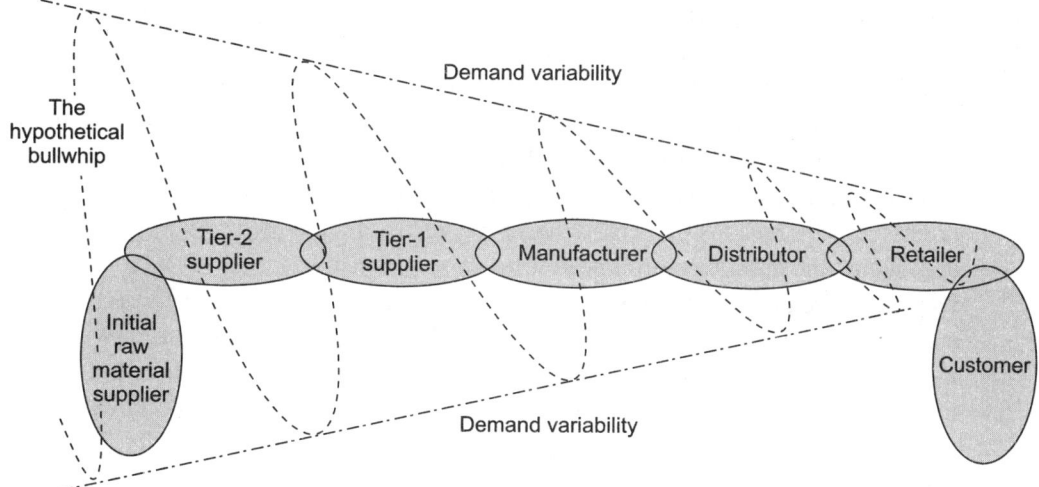

**Fig. 9.19**    The bullwhip effect

The bullwhip effect comes into play when the retailer does not share the exact customer demand with its upstream supply chain partner—the distributor. The distributor, therefore, takes the orders placed by the retailer as the 'demand' and does its forecast planning accordingly, without realizing the fact that the retailer might have slightly exaggerated the size of the order to hedge against the risk of higher customer demand. Similarly, the distributor does not pass on details of the order placed by the retailer to its upstream supply chain partner—the manufacturer. Here also, the manufacturer has to contend with the orders placed by the distributor, without realizing that the distributor would have bloated them up to maintain a high service level for the retailer (meaning, prompt delivery without stock-out). This way, the player at the end of the upstream supply chain, which is the initial raw material supplier, ends up carrying much more inventory/production capacity than what is actually required as per the end-customer demand.

**Methods for coping with the bullwhip effect**   There are several ways for reducing the bullwhip effect:

*Centralizing the demand information*   As discussed in the earlier sub-section, it is imperative to provide visibility to all the players in the supply chain on actual end-customer demand data. This allows them to forecast demand correctly rather than depending on orders from the immediate downstream participant in the supply chain. It must, however, be noted that some amount of bullwhip would remain under any circumstances. Even if all the players in the supply chain employ the same forecasting techniques and similar ordering policy, it results in reduction in bullwhip effect but not its elimination.

*Keeping the end-customer demand even across time*   It has been observed that promotional policies like 'sale' periods make the end-customer demand uneven. Companies following such promotions initially keep the prices on the higher side and reduce them during the end-season sale periods. Naturally, more sales are seen during the sale season compared to the remaining time frame. Such uneven demand increases the bullwhip effect. In order to reduce the bullwhip effect, companies should refrain from such promotional policies and should instead keep the pricing constant throughout the time frame. However, it is easier said than done, as the competitors come up with promotional schemes, which have to be counter-effected by others through similar campaigns.

*Improvising on order placement and execution across the supply chain*   The lead time involved in order placement and execution should be reduced as much as possible to undermine the impact of the bullwhip effect. Information technologies such as the enterprise resource planning (ERP) and electronic data interchange (EDI) are helping in real-time dispatch and retrieval of purchase orders between various players in the supply chain. Techniques like cross-docking are helpful in reducing the order execution lead time.

*Forging strategic partnerships*   Collaborations and partnerships in seamless flow of information are crucial in reducing the impact of the bullwhip effect, as we saw earlier with the centralized information system. Another example of such collaboration is the concept of vendor-managed inventory (VMI) whereby the distributor is directly responsible for placement of stocks on the racks of the retailer's facility, thus automatically having first-hand information about the actual end-customer demand trends.

## Push, Pull, and Push-pull Systems

In this section, we shall study about three types of supply chain strategies, namely push-, pull-, and push-pull-based. As is evident, the third supply chain strategy is a combination of the first two strategies.

**Push-based supply chain**   Let us look at Fig. 9.20 to understand the push-based supply chain concept whereby the material is pushed into the supply chain from the initial raw material end to the customer end on the basis of demand forecasts. At the end of the supply chain, the finished goods await customer orders. Naturally, inventory in various forms (raw material, work-in-

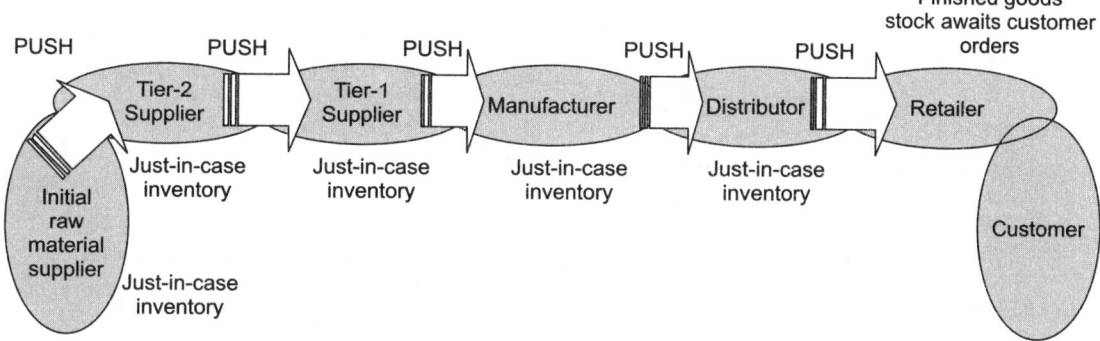

**Fig. 9.20**   The push process view of a supply chain

progress and finished goods) exists at various points in the supply chain, 'just-in-case' it may be required. Inventory costs are, therefore, very high in this system. A lack of transparency of information between various players in a supply chain often results in the 'bullwhip' effect. Another drawback of this supply chain strategy is the lack of flexibility to respond to the rapidly changing customer preferences. Often, inventories accumulated have to face obsolescence, as the changing customer preferences require different set of features in a product compared to what were incorporated while manufacturing them. In other words, the risk of uncertainty is quite pronounced in this supply chain strategy. A typical example of push-based supply chain is grocery stores such as Food Bazaar, Food World, and More. The vegetable and fruits supply chains of these stores use the push-based system.

A major advantage of the push-based supply chain strategy is the responsiveness in terms of ready availability of the product at the retail stores for the customer to come and buy at his or her will. However, a key challenge to the planners is to decide whether to design production capacities keeping in view the peak demand or average demand over a period of time. If the capacity is designed by considering the peak demand, the capacity may remain idle during periods of low demand, thus resulting in wastages and increased cost of production. On the other hand, if the capacity of facilities is based on average demand, it would require overtime during peak demand, which is prone to more defects, higher costs, and frequent machine breakdowns due to excessive usage during a given period. In a nutshell, there is more risk of inefficient resource utilization in the push-based supply chain strategy.

**Pull-based supply chain**   Figure 9.21 illustrates this strategy where a customer order pulls material into the supply chain. However, the catch here is that the customer should be willing to wait during the time the product is being processed in the supply chain. If the waiting time on part of the end-customer is stretched too long, this strategy starts failing. Thus, the pull-based strategy should be deployed when the overall processing time of the product in the supply chain equates to tolerable waiting time on part of the end-customer. A major advantage of this strategy is that in an ideal scenario, there would be zero inventories all across the supply chain. In more realistic situations though, the inventory would be lowest possible, resulting in negligible inventory costs. For example, Toyota utilizes the pull-based supply chain where the material is pulled into the supply chain only when the order for a car is placed by a customer through its retail showrooms. The retail showrooms only display the models of the cars for the customer

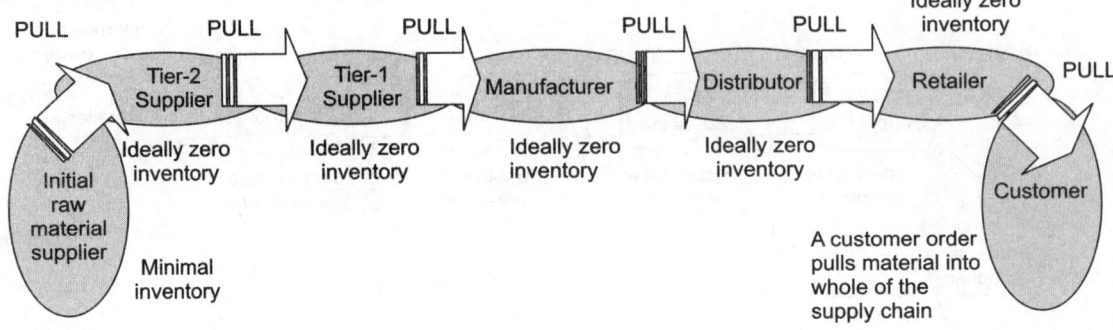

**Fig. 9.21** The pull process view of a supply chain

to choose from. The delivery of the car is promised to the customer sometime within 15 days to three months, depending upon the model chosen by the customer in the order placed along with the booking amount.

The pull-based supply chain strategy is essentially driven by actual demand and requires seamless flow of this information all across the supply chain. This system is more popular by the names just-in-time (JIT) or lean system. Typically, kanban cards are used as flags or signals to pull the materials into the supply chain. Based upon the number of units of the product ordered by the customer, the retailer issues a kanban card to the distributor by detailing out the specifications of the order. By accumulating all such actual orders through the kanban cards received from various retailers, the distributor issues another kanban card to the manufacturer stating the total quantities and other details. The manufacturer, in turn, issues a new kanban card to the Tier-1 supplier to supply the components by considering the number of units of the component required to assemble a unit of the finished product. This chain of kanban cards is thus used to pull material into the supply chain.

Clearly, the inventory costs in a pull-based system are negligible. This system allows the supply chain to respond to the customer requests of customization of the product promptly and in a cost-effective manner. However, the transportation costs are significantly higher due to small quantities of material flow in the supply chain as per the actual customer orders. This system also lacks economies of scale that are inherent in a push-based system due to longer planning horizon based on demand forecasts. Most importantly, the level of coordination and camaraderie required in pull-based system is very difficult to achieve in practical scenarios. Nevertheless, pull-based systems have been used successfully by organizations worldwide, particularly the Japanese organizations that take a lot of pride in their unique organization culture conducive to support this kind of supply chain strategies.

**Push-pull supply chain** A push-pull-based supply chain strategy is a combination of push- and pull-based strategies. The downstream operations from the initial raw material supplier end to another player in the chain are pursued on push-based strategy, while the remaining part of the chain is operated on pull-based strategy. As shown in Fig. 9.22 , the push-pull boundary segregates these two diverse strategies within the same supply chain. Usually this boundary is created at a point in the supply chain where the assembly of goods is about to begin. Thus, it may be at the Tier-1 supplier or the manufacturer.

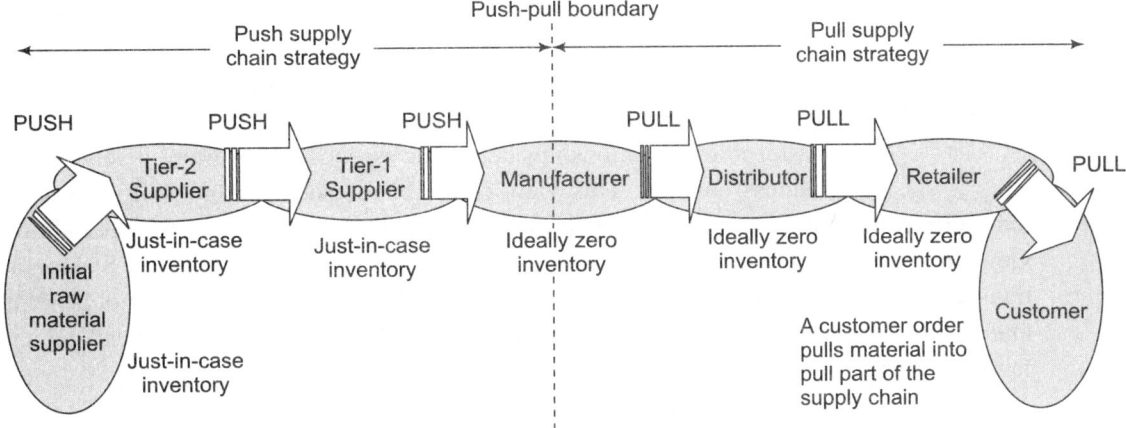

**Fig. 9.22** A push-pull supply chain strategy

Thus, the designing, planning, and procurement of components are done through the push-based strategy by utilizing the *aggregate* demand forecasts for the various models and variants of the product. However, the assembling of the product starts only when the actual customer demand comes in at the retailer's end of the chain. This has two major advantages—first, the actual preferences of the customers on the choice of models and variants becomes known and assembling is performed by using the components and parts accordingly; secondly, the overall lead time is reduced as about half of the supply chain is ready with the components and parts before the assembling starts. Aggregate demand forecast is relatively more accurate and is helpful in reducing uncertainty. A prime example of successful use of push-pull-based supply chain strategy is Dell Computers. It provides estimates of forecast for components to its Tier-1 suppliers and asks them to be ready for delivery at any time (push system). However, it takes actual delivery of these components only after the customer places the order for a computer through its online portal. Thus, a portion of Dell's supply chain follows the push mode, while the remaining portion works on the pull strategy.

Another variant of this strategy is termed as *delayed differentiation*. In this strategy, steps in the production process that lead to product differentiation (for example, colouring of apparels by a garment manufacturer) are performed only when the exact colour preferences of customers come from actual customer orders at the beginning of a fashion season. Thus, a generic product is created (say, white shirts) till the product differentiation stage in the supply chain as per aggregate demand forecasts. However, the steps of differentiation (say, colouring or design pattern printing of white shirts) are performed through pull-based strategy, whereby actual customer orders determine the differential steps to be performed.

## Supply Chain Management

The co-founder of the Honda Motor Company Takeo Fujisawa once said—'Japanese and American management is 95 per cent the same and differs in all important respects.' Fujisawa was, in fact, referring to the softer side of management, that of managing relationships. A fundamental relationship in any business is that between a contractor and a subcontractor—the buyer–seller relationship, managed primarily by the buying firm's purchasing function.

The single-sourcing concept is a point of distinction between the supply chain practices of the US and those of Japan.

Perhaps the most well-known characteristic of Japanese society is its focus on the importance of the group. In the US, it is the individual that counts; in Japan, it is the group. Things get done not by nonconforming lone rangers, but by group consensus. This consensus is possible only through the cultivation of relationships. Relationships define the essence of Japanese society, including business conduct. This view of the buyer–seller relationship stresses upon long-term commitment by both parties. It differs markedly from the transaction, arm's-length view that has been characteristic of the buyer–seller relationship in the United States. In this transaction mode, buyers enter into contracts with suppliers which may or may not be renewed after a short period to time (e.g., one year), depending upon whether the buyer can get a more favourable price in the open market.

### Japanese Supply Chain Management in Practice: The *Keiretsu*

The best examples of relationships among companies in Japan are the *keiretsu*—the powerful business groups. There are six main groups in Japan: *Mitsui, Mitsubishi, Sumitomo, Fuyo, Sanwa, and Dai-Ichi Kangyo*. In addition, large companies become the centre of what are called entrepreneurial *keiretsu*—vertically integrated groups with a dominant manufacturing firm and a network of major suppliers and subcontractors. For example, Toyota, although a member of the Mitsui group, has developed such an extensive network of suppliers and subcontractors that it has become the core company in its own entrepreneurial *keiretsu*.

Figure 9.23 shows that the industry structure in Japan is compartmentalized into families of companies, with no overlap among the Toyota, Nissan, and Honda groups (McMillan 1985). In the United States, no such compartmentalization exists. Major suppliers in the US may do business with any American auto producer, whereas in Japan, reflecting the *keiretsu* arrangement, major suppliers and subcontractors are typically dedicated to doing business with only one of the auto producers.

The single-sourcing concept is another point of distinction between the supply chain practices of the US and Japan, where a major Japanese manufacturer generally uses a single source for various material requirements. This is especially true for firms using the just-in-time operations strategy. Schonberger notes: 'A rule of thumb in the US purchasing trade is to always have at least two suppliers for a given purchased part. Japanese companies, by contrast, hope to evolve to buying a given part from just one supplier—but good one, and one preferably that does little business with other buyer companies; the Japanese buying firm wants to be the dominant reason for the supplier's existence. A supplier selling, say, 60 per cent of its output to a single buyer company will go to great lengths to be responsive.'

Although the vertical *keiretsu* relationships in Japan certainly do develop dependency relationships between the buyer and seller, the fact that these relationships account for only 50 per cent of such trade suggests that a significant portion of the trade takes place on a transaction, arm's-length basis.

### Comparison of Japanese JIT Supply Chain Management and Traditional US Purchasing

The Japanese revolutionized the field of purchasing with the unique concepts of JIT supply chain management (SCM) and made US companies redefine their inventory management concepts in

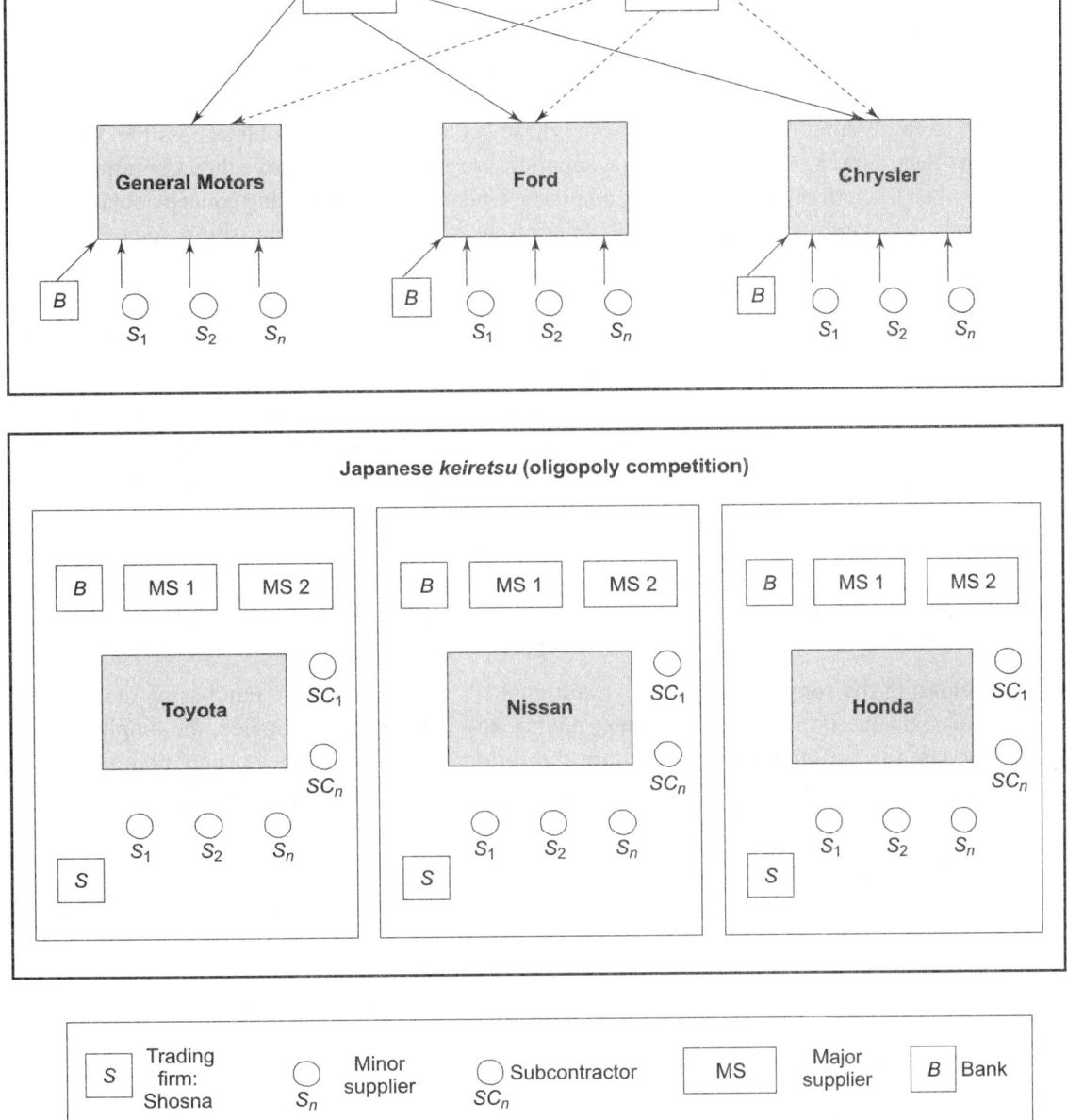

**Fig. 9.23** US and Japanese supply networks

the 1970s and 1980s. Indian companies have traditionally followed US purchasing concepts due to geographical similarities between the two countries (suppliers located at long distances from the plants in contrast to Japan, which has a small geographical area). Let us compare the Japanese JIT supply chain concept with traditional US purchasing with respect to various parameters.

**Purchase lot size**   Under the JIT purchasing practice the emphasis is on the purchase of minimum lot sizes, preferably piece for piece, which allows tighter inventory control, eliminating large stocks of parts between process stages. There are two approaches which can be adopted. The first approach is to develop a freight consolidation programme with various suppliers. In this arrangement, the suppliers share delivery trucks, which carry small quantities of parts from three or four suppliers. Each truck is assigned a time when it can enter the plant and drive directly to the assembly line. The second approach is to select local suppliers as far as possible. When there is no local supplier of a part, potential suppliers are encouraged to move their operations close to the plant through offers of long-term contracts. Under the JIT purchasing concept, obtaining small lot sizes is considered a challenge in spite of obstacles such as higher shipping cost compared to large lot sizes in traditional US purchasing.

Traditional US purchasing is based on purchasing in large quantities, with a delivery schedule specified in the purchase order. This practice allows a company to continue operating even if there are serious delays in supply, although the inventory costs are high.

**Supplier selection**   JIT purchasing involves dealing with a small number of suppliers located nearby—ideally a single source. This is contrary to the typical US purchasing practice, which generally relies on multiple sources of supply for a given part. The advantages of multiple sources of supply are:

1. It provides a broader technical base to the buyer.
2. In times of shortages, it protects the buyer against failure at the supplier's plant.
3. It encourages competition among suppliers for securing the best possible prices and products.
   The advantages of a single source of supply for every part are shown in Fig. 9.24.

**Evaluating the supplier**   Although traditional US and Japanese JIT purchasing practices both emphasize the importance of product quality and delivery performance, the emphasis varies between the two approaches. While in the former, many companies accept about 2 per cent rejects from suppliers, the latter permits no rejects because the supplier has the responsibility to deliver just the right quality of items.

**Receiving inspection**   In JIT purchasing, the inspection of quality is extended back to the supplier's plant, where it is ensured that quality is built in before the part leaves the plant. Therefore, suppliers drive their trucks straight to the assembly line of the buyer's plant (except for new parts and new suppliers).

Under traditional US purchasing, the receiving department of the buyer is responsible for receipt, identification, piece-by-piece counts, and inspection of all inbound freight for quality in accordance with product design specifications.

**Negotiating and bidding**   US buyers provide very exact and rigid product specifications for prospective suppliers, and the traditional bidding process implies that the lowest bid customarily will get the contract. The contracts are short-term and may be terminated whenever more competitive prices are offered by other suppliers.

In JIT purchasing, the buyer and the supplier (due to a single source of supply) agree upon a 'fair' price for both parties. The bidding specifications are not as rigid, and suppliers are encouraged to be innovative in meeting the specified needs, with primary emphasis on product quality.

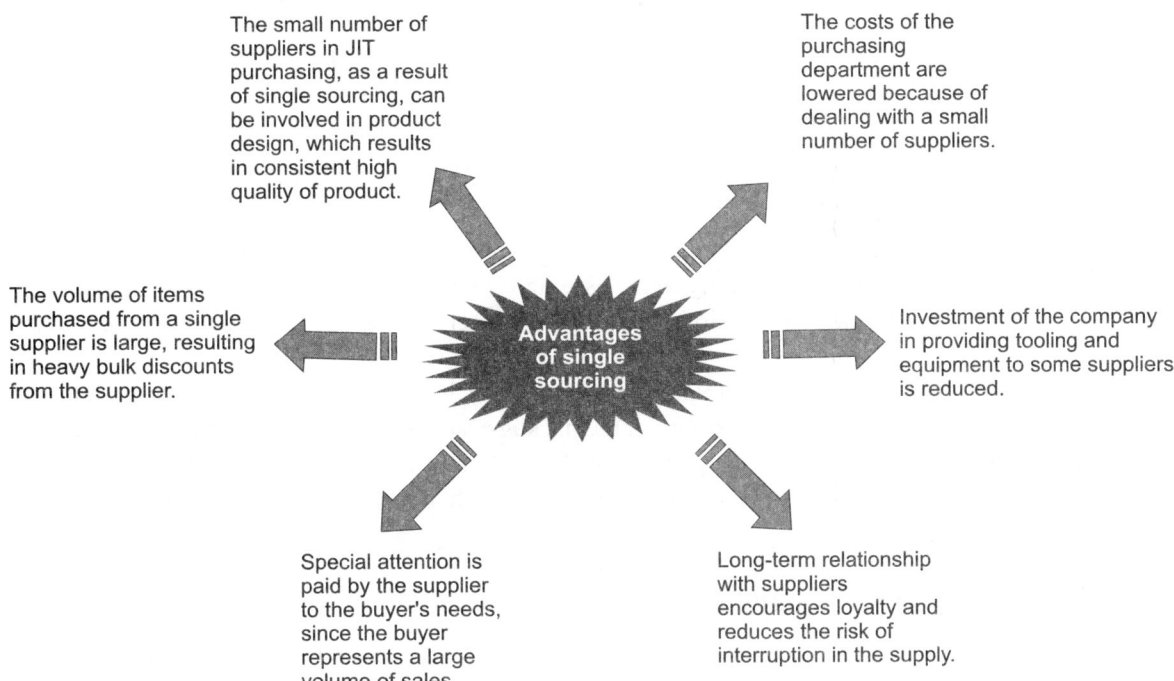

The small number of suppliers in JIT purchasing, as a result of single sourcing, can be involved in product design, which results in consistent high quality of product.

The costs of the purchasing department are lowered because of dealing with a small number of suppliers.

The volume of items purchased from a single supplier is large, resulting in heavy bulk discounts from the supplier.

**Advantages of single sourcing**

Investment of the company in providing tooling and equipment to some suppliers is reduced.

Special attention is paid by the supplier to the buyer's needs, since the buyer represents a large volume of sales.

Long-term relationship with suppliers encourages loyalty and reduces the risk of interruption in the supply.

**Fig. 9.24** Advantages of single sourcing

**Mode of transportation**   In traditional US purchasing, the primary responsibility for scheduling and delivery are generally left to the supplier and the transportation company. The manufacturing traffic managers emphasize upon lowering the outbound freight cost only and not the inbound freight.

Under JIT buying, traffic managers concentrate on both outbound and inbound freight. They are also more concerned with on-time delivery in order to avoid production disruptions in the buyer's plant than with trying to lower outbound costs.

**Product specifications**   In traditional US purchasing, the buyers rely more on design specifications (which describe and identify the composition of materials to be used, their size, shape, and manufacturing method) than on performance specifications. Although the design engineers are responsible for developing the performance specifications also, they rarely interact with the suppliers.

Under JIT, the buyer seeks technical advice and assistance from suppliers in order to design better parts, achieve lower prices, and improve product quality and productivity. The buyer relies more on the supplier's performance specifications and less on narrowly defined design specifications. This allows the supplier to exercise greater discretion in making recommendations and innovations when discussing any problems with the buyer with respect to design and quality.

**Paperwork**   In US purchasing, purchase orders are issued for nearly all requirements, such as purchase requisitions, packing lists, invoices, shipping documents, etc. These activities and their supporting documents require a massive amount of time and formal paperwork. More than 50 per cent of the time of the purchase department gets spent on paperwork and expediting.

In JIT purchasing, the buyer and the supplier agree upon a 'fair' price for both parties.

JIT requires much less formal paperwork, since deliveries are made several times a day using *kanban* cards.

JIT requires much less formal paperwork, since deliveries are made several times a day using *kanban* cards, which trigger the deliveries; long-term contracts are used; and a simple phone call can easily change the delivery timing and quantity level. Therefore, the purchase department has more time on their hands to spend with the suppliers to improve product design specifications, quality, and productivity.

**Packaging**  In JIT purchasing, small standard containers are used for every part type and part number to deliver the parts directly to the assembly line. It allows to keep an easy and accurate count of parts. Precise specifications of parts are written on the containers so as to prevent the buyer from making mistakes.

Traditional US purchasing involves purchasing in large quantities to avail discounts and transportation cost benefits. Therefore, large packages are used in delivery with less attention to the product specifications on the packaging. The different types of products packaged in large boxes have to be sorted out, counted, inspected, and then stored in the warehouse, leading to high handling costs.

## Purchasing, Procurement, and SCM

*Purchasing* refers to the actual buying of materials and the activities associated with it. *Procurement*, on the other hand, has a broader meaning, and includes purchasing, transportation, warehousing, and inbound receiving. Procurement is a closed-loop process that begins with the requisition and ends with payment. *Supply chain management* is a transition from purchasing and procurement towards a more strategic focus, which involves suppliers as strategic partners in warding off the competition.

Figure 9.25 shows the transition from purchasing (tactical focus) to SCM (strategic focus). The outermost circle shows the specific activities which have come into existence due to the long-term strategic focus of SCM. For example, the use of cross-functional teams in supplier qualification and selection means involving people from the engineering, manufacturing, design, and quality control departments in preparing the list of approved vendors. The benefit is that the quality control personnel can specify quality specifications, design personnel can interact with potential suppliers to implement any improvements in the design of supplied parts for better performance, and the manufacturing personnel can determine whether the supplier is capable enough to, say, meet their JIT supply schedules.

The second strategic function of SCM is the early involvement of suppliers in product design through a *concurrent engineering approach*, which means while designing a new product, the design team should include personnel from various related departments, along with personnel from the design department. These departments can be engineering, manufacturing, materials,

Supply chain management is a transition from purchasing and procurement towards a more strategic focus, which involves suppliers as strategic partners.

quality control, finance, and marketing. The team also includes some selected suppliers in the design process, so that they can give their opinion from time to time about any modifications in the design for better performance. The suppliers may also comment on the feasibility of manufacturing certain parts or components to be used in the product being designed. This approach reduces the duration of the design process drastically in contrast to the conventional sequential design approach, in which the design moves from one department

The concurrent engineering approach reduces the duration of the design process drastically in contrast to the conventional sequential design approach.

to another in a sequence. Many times the design gets disapproved in the final stages of this sequence owing to contradictions in opinions, resulting in the wastage of a lot of time and effort.

The other specific activities under the supply chain also have the strategic focus as shown in Fig. 9.25. Note that SCM also includes all the purchasing and procurement activities shown inside the inner circles.

Exhibit 9.5 discusses how Walmart started its supply chain in India.

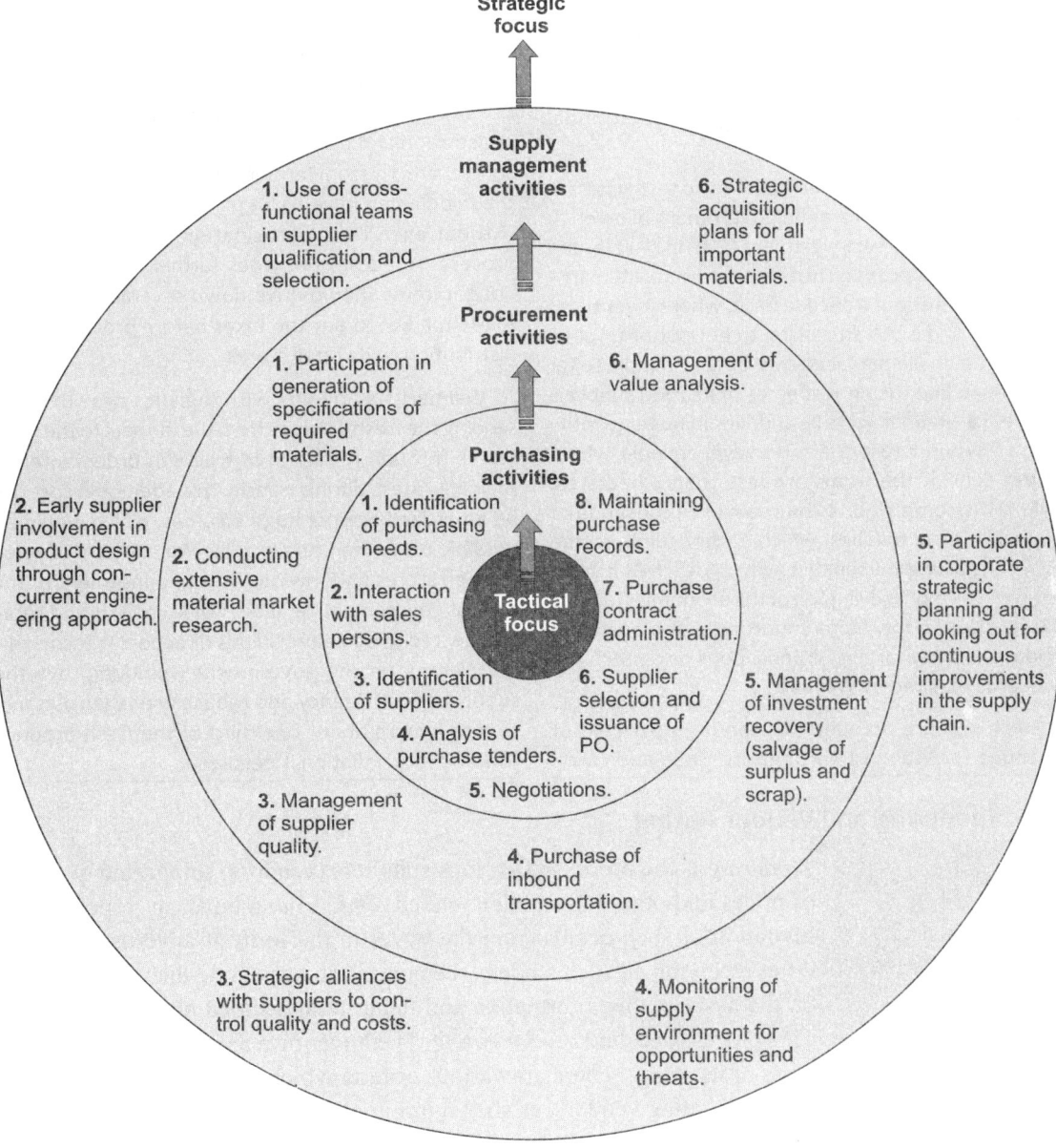

**Fig. 9.25** Activities in supply chain management

---

**Exhibit 9.5    Walmart Creating its Supply Chain in India from Scratch**

Walmart, which is the number one retailing giant in the world, entered India through a joint venture with Bharti Group in 2007. The aim of this venture was to establish wholesale cash-and-carry stores and back-end supply chain management operations in line with the Government of India guidelines. Under the agreement, Bharti and Walmart hold 50:50 stakes in Bharti Walmart Private Limited.The first wholesale cash-and-carry facility named 'Best Price Modern Wholesale' was opened in Amritsar in May 2009 and subsequently in Zirakpur (Near Chandigarh), Jalandhar, Kota, Bhopal, Ludhiana, Raipur, Indore, Vijaywada, Meerut, Agra, Lucknow, Jammu, Guntur, Aurangabad,Bathinda, Amravati, and Hyderabad.

The joint venture allowed Walmart to test waters in the Indian market, before the government allowed 51 per cent foreign direct investment (FDI) in multi-brand retail in September 2012. This is in contrast to Walmart's entry to China about a decade back, where it ventured on its own and is still struggling to get out of trouble. The biggest challenge faced by Walmart in India so far has been to find the right sources of its food supplies. In America, Walmart gets its supplies in huge quantity from a few hundred farmers. However, in India, where 80 per cent of the farms are less than 2 hectares, Walmart is compelled to source from thousands of farmers in small batches, which is very cumbersome from contracting perspective, which deprives it from deriving maximum advantage of the economies of scale that it is known for. More importantly, the quality of produce of most farmers in India does not match the standards required by Walmart.

Fresh produce accounts for about 30 per cent of revenues for Walmart through its 'cash-and-carry'

wholesale outlets in India. As part of its growth strategy, Walmart is planning to signup about 35,000 farmers over the next few years, up from its current tie-ups with about 7,000 farmers. In doing so, Walmart has budgeted for providing the farmers with modern irrigation equipment, quality nutrients, and best possible seeds, while training them right from when the seed is sown to when it is harvested.

Another challenge faced by Walmart in India is the role of the middlemen between farmers and retail chains. The local markets run by the state Agricultural Produce Marketing Committees (APMC) impose registration and transaction taxes even if retail chains source directly from farmers in their region.Moreover, the middlemen have to be paid their full commission without even their participation in the transaction process. To add to the woes further, trucks carrying bought items should drive down several miles to the APMC market to pay the taxes before proceeding for distribution to its retail stores.

Walmart has tie-ups with logistics providers for sending the fresh produce from the farmers to the retail stores through refrigerated trucks in order to retain their freshness during transit. This additional cost can be amortized against huge volumes, which would be possible only when retailers like Walmart are allowed to open stores nationwide. The announcement of the central government to allow FDI in multi-brand retail is expected to be helpful in this direction. It seems this intervention of the government would improve the supply chain efficiency and reduce wastage/costs in a country where about one-third of the fresh produce rots and food inflation is persistent.

---

## Tendering and Vendor Rating

Tendering is the process of various suppliers submitting quotations of prices and other information to a buyer in response to the invitation of such details from the buyer.

*Tendering* is the process of various suppliers (vendors) submitting quotations of prices and other information (called *tenders*) to a buyer in response to the invitation of such details from the buyer in the form of advertisements, etc. After receiving all such tenders, the buyer firm has to rate the various vendors on the basis of this information and the criteria decided upon by the buyers. This process is called *vendor rating*. The buyer firm approves a vendor on the basis of its rating. There are various criteria which may be considered by the buyer for rating vendors, as shown in Fig. 9.26.

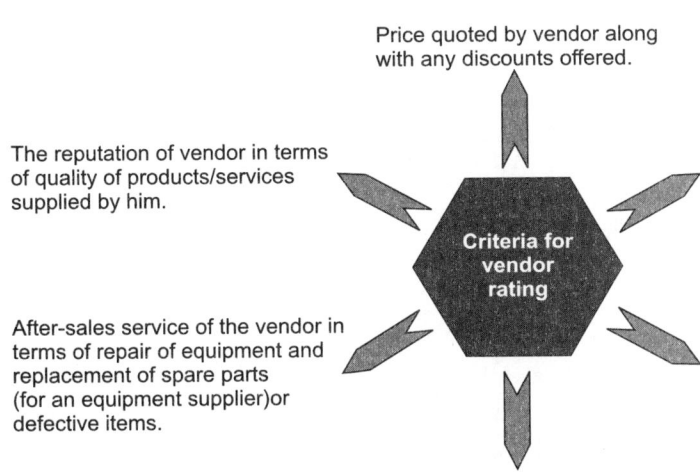

Price quoted by vendor along with any discounts offered.

The reputation of vendor in terms of quality of products/services supplied by him.

Location of vendor in the vicinity of the firm helps in the emergencies of processing rush orders. It becomes very important in JIT settings.

**Criteria for vendor rating**

After-sales service of the vendor in terms of repair of equipment and replacement of spare parts (for an equipment supplier)or defective items.

Inventory policy of the vendor-in JIT settings, the buyers prefer their vendors to have JIT practices, with negligible inventory. For equipment suppliers, buyers prefer vendors with sufficient spare-parts inventory (useful in case of equipment breakdown).

Sole dependence upon the buyer (vendor supplies to only one buyer)—the buyer has better control over the supplier in terms of quality, pricing, supply schedules, etc.

**Fig. 9.26** Criteria for vendor rating

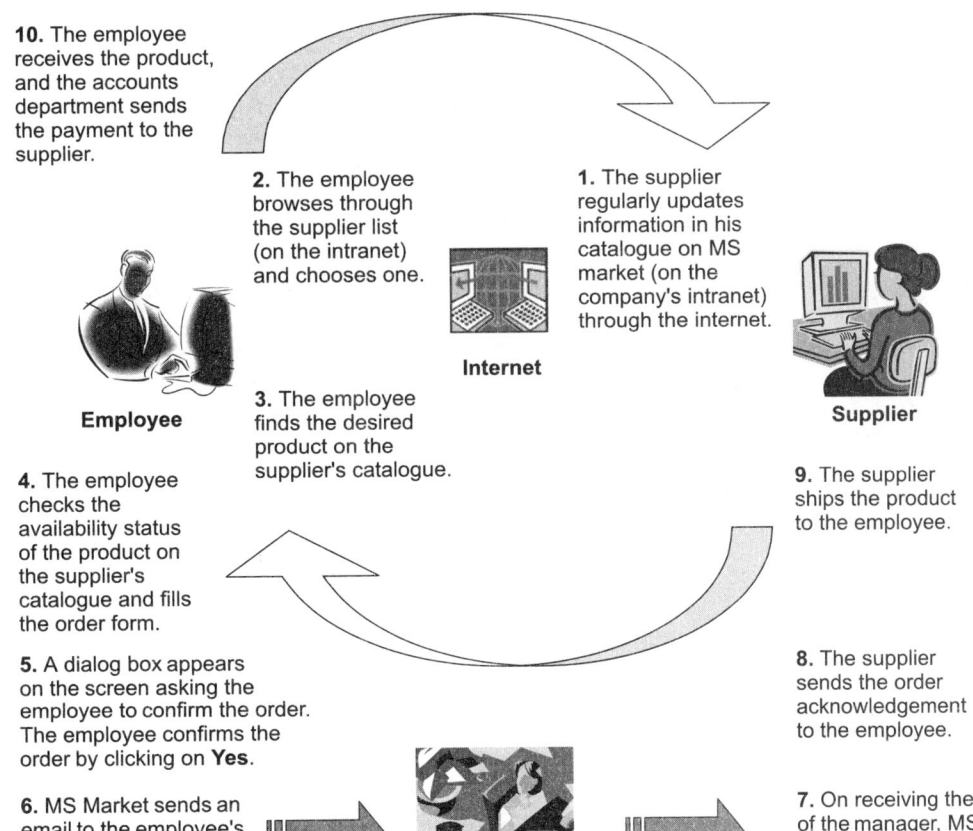

**10.** The employee receives the product, and the accounts department sends the payment to the supplier.

**2.** The employee browses through the supplier list (on the intranet) and chooses one.

**1.** The supplier regularly updates information in his catalogue on MS market (on the company's intranet) through the internet.

**Internet**

**Employee**

**Supplier**

**3.** The employee finds the desired product on the supplier's catalogue.

**4.** The employee checks the availability status of the product on the supplier's catalogue and fills the order form.

**9.** The supplier ships the product to the employee.

**5.** A dialog box appears on the screen asking the employee to confirm the order. The employee confirms the order by clicking on **Yes**.

**8.** The supplier sends the order acknowledgement to the employee.

**6.** MS Market sends an email to the employee's manager for approval of the order.

**7.** On receiving the approval of the manager, MS Market sends the purchase order email to the supplier and a copy to the accounts department.

**Fig. 9.27** E-procurement through MS Market

> Operating resources management (ORM) is the procurement of non-production goods.

### E-procurement and Operating Resource Management

Non-production goods are items that are required to run day-to-day business operations, such as computers, telephones, fax machines, photocopiers, furniture, stationery, maintenance items and services, travel, lodging, catering, entertainment, etc. *Operating resources management* (ORM) is the procurement of non-production goods. Large corporations such as Ford, Microsoft, etc. realized that in the purchase of non-production goods, many employees were wasting time turning requisitions into purchase orders, taking approvals, and trying to follow business rules and procedures—one of the biggest drawbacks of using traditional procurement procedures. It was also experienced that *low-capital transactions* represented 70 per cent of the total volume, but 3 per cent of accounts payable. To save on the procurement costs of such items, Ford implemented the e-procurement software from *Intelisys*, while Microsoft Corp. developed a software called *MS Market* for the same purpose. Figure 9.27 shows the steps in e-procurement through MS Market at Microsoft Corp.

## Summary

*Materials requirement planning* (MRP) is a system for determining order quantities and the time intervals for placing orders of dependent demand items. It requires three inputs, namely, *master production schedule* (MPS), *bill of materials* (BOM), and *inventory status*. It generates three output reports—planned orders report, order release report, and order change report. Just-in-time (JIT) is a manufacturing system in which work-in-process inventories are reduced to minimum levels. Small quantities of materials are supplied by the suppliers to the assembly line directly with the aid of *visual kanban cards*.

MRP and JIT can be used together simultaneously as a hybrid MRP-JIT system, where MRP is used for planning materials requirement only, and the purchase orders sent to the suppliers act only as an indication of the probable requirements of the buyer company. The supplier supplies the goods only according to the JIT system of *kanban* cards.

A supply chain has product flow in one direction and the information/funds flow in the opposite direction. The bullwhip effect should be minimized across the supply chain. Three strategies are used by organizations—push, pull, and push-pull.

*Supply chain management* (SCM) means forging long-term relations with suppliers and treating them as partners in warding off the competition. For example, the Maruti supply chain competing with Hyundai's supply chain and vice versa in order to gain each other's market share. Japanese JIT supply chain management concepts have brought about a revolution, and have replaced the traditional US purchasing practices in many companies worldwide.

Technology is playing a major role in changing the buying practices of firms for non-production items such as furniture, computers, stationery, books, catering, travel, lodging, etc. E-procurement software like MS Market and many others are becoming more and more popular amongst organizations for bringing down the overall cost of procurement of items.

## References

BSE 2012, http://www.bseindia.com/stock-share-price/bajaj-auto-ltd/bajaj-auto/532977/, accessed on 3 February 2013.

Cox, J.F., J.H. Blackstone, and M.S. Spencer (eds) 1995, *APICS Dictionary*, 8th edition, American Production and Inventory Control Society, Falls Church, VA.

Karlsson, C. and C. Norr 1994, 'Total effectiveness in a Just-in-Time system', *International Journal of Operations and Production Management*, vol. 14, no. 3.

Lee Choong, Y. 1993, 'A recent development of the integrated manufacturing system: A hybrid of MRP and JIT', *International Journal of Operations and Production Management*, vol. 13, no. 4, pp. 3–17.

McMillan, Charles J. 1985, *The Japanese Industrial System*, Walter de Gruyler, New York, p. 61.

Monden, Y. 1981, 'Adaptable kanban system helps Toyota maintain Just-in-Time production', *Industrial Engineering*, vol. 13, no. 5, pp. 29–46.

Notte, J. 2013, 'Toyota isn't sweating recall of 1 million cars', http://money.msn.com/now/post.aspx?post=7b577c24-1713-45ab-8625-5f90d-c77653c, accessed on 1 February 2013.

Schonberger, R.J. 1982, *Japanese Manufacturing Techniques: Nine Hidden Lessons in Simplicity*, Free Press, New York.

Westbrook, Roy 1988, 'Time to forget "Just-in-Time"? Observations on a visit to Japan', *International Journal of Operations and Production Management*, vol. 8, no. 4, p. 5.

# Keywords

**Andon** in Japanese means an ambulance-style flashing light with a complementary siren. The operator puts the *andon* on whenever he needs to draw the management's attention, highlighting to all the importance of his problem.

**Bill of materials (BOM)** is a document which tells us about an item's product structure, showing the sequence in which components/sub-assemblies are assembled and their required numbers. It also contains details about the workstations at which the item is assembled.

**Bullwhip effect** is a phenomenon where each upstream player in the supply chain tends to carry more and more inventory or capacity due to lack of visibility of actual customer demand at the end of the supply chain.

**Just-in-time (JIT) system** is defined as 'Produce and deliver finished goods just in time to be sold, sub-assemblies just in time to be assembled into finished goods, and purchased materials just in time to be transformed into fabricated parts'.

**Kaizen** in Japanese means *continuous improvement* in every sphere of activity. Kaizen is a sub-system of JIT.

**Kanban** is a Japanese word meaning flag or signal, and is a visual aid to convey the message that action is required.

**Low-level coding** is a procedure in which the product structure is redrawn and the item which appears at different levels is brought down to its lowest level.

**Master production schedule (MPS)** is an extension of the *aggregate production plan*. It tells us the number of units of different models of a product to be manufactured on a weekly or monthly basis in the coming 6–18 months.

**Materials requirement planning (MRP)** is a system for planning the future requirements of dependent demand items.

**Operating resources management (ORM)** is the procurement of non-production goods.

**Order change report** provides the purchase manager with information about any changes to be made in the *open orders* with the suppliers.

**Order release report** gives information about planned orders to be released on the present date.

**Planned orders report** gives information about planned orders to be released on some future date or during a given interval of time.

**Procurement** includes purchasing, transportation, warehousing, and inbound receiving. Procurement is a closed-loop process that begins with the requisition and ends with payment.

**Product structure** shows a product's build-up. It shows diagrammatically the components required to assemble it, their numbers, and the sequence of assembly.

**Purchasing** refers to the actual buying of materials and the activities associated with it.

**Supply chain management** is a transition from purchasing and procurement towards a more strategic focus, which involves suppliers as strategic partners in warding off the competition.

**Tendering** is the process of various suppliers (vendors) submitting quotations of prices and other information (called *tenders*) to a buyer in response to the invitation of such details from the buyer in the form of advertising, etc.

**Vendor rating** is the process of the buyer firm rating the various vendors on the basis of the tendors supplied by them and the criteria decided upon by the buyers.

CASE STUDY I

# The 'Indian' McDonald's

Come to think of it, McDonald's globally is the symbol of everything wrong—junk, fast, and fattening food, and American to boot. In India though, McDonald's has been a runaway success by being very mindful of local sensibilities and tastes. Localization of ingredients, communication, visible company faces, and consciously not cultivating an international image have been the strategies adopted by McDonald's in India. Where else in the world would you get a McAloo Tikki or a Maharaja Mac? McDonald's is a renowned fast food American chain started by Ray Kroc in 1955. He established a franchising company with brothers Dick and Mac McDonald, who owned the famous McDonald's hamburger stand in California since 1937. Later in 1961, Ray became the sole owner of McDonald's by buying out the stakes of the McDonald brothers. In India, McDonald's was started in 1996 in a unique way. The company got into a 50:50 joint venture with Delhi-based entrepreneur Vikram Bakshi's Connaught Plaza Restaurants to own and operate McDonald's restaurants in the northern parts of the country. On similar lines, Mumbai-based Amit Jatia and his Hardcastle Restaurants were chosen for to own and operate McDonald's restuarants in the western parts of India.

Interestingly, Bakshi was considering a franchisee model for McDonald's North India operations by 2008 for a deeper penetration into the country's growing food and beverages market. By February 2007, McDonald's had 61 outlets in North India and planed to open another 25 joints in the course of the year and invest ₹4 billion over the next three years. It also planned to introduce the McCafé concept in India by the end of 2007. McDonald's India aimed to increase the number of its restaurants from 105 to 155 all over the country by the end of 2007.

It is unfortunate that every year ₹500 billion worth of food produce is wasted in India, despite millions of Indian population deprived of even a single meal in a day. This is mainly because of the lack of proper infrastructure for storage and transportation under controlled conditions. In India, typically one-third of the 150 million tonne production of fruits and vegetables is lost at the post-harvest stage. Most of it is attributed to wastage in storage and transportation, mishandling, and the cost of intermediaries in the supply chain. McDonald's spent a few years setting up a unique cold chain. The cold chain is necessary to maintain the quality of food products and retain their freshness and nutritional value. A cold chain refers to the procurement, warehousing, transportation, and retailing of food products under controlled temperatures. Setting up the cold chain has involved the transfer of state-of-the-art food processing technology by McDonald's and its international suppliers to pioneering Indian entrepreneurs, who have now become an integral part of the cold chain. McDonald's has invested a staggering ₹8 billion in setting up its extensive supply chain in India. Efforts to initiate work on its supply chain started way back in 1992, about four years ahead of opening its first outlet in 1996. Not only was it difficult to identify the right vendors capable of adhering to McDonald's international standards, but also to train them to products as per its stringent specifications. For example, the peas have to be of a particular dimension, otherwise they protrude from the patty (if bigger than the standard size) and get burnt. Similarly, the iceberg lettuces (*band gobhi* in Hindi) have to be of a specific weight.

All suppliers adhere to Indian government's regulations on food, health, and hygiene, while continuously maintaining McDonald's recognized standards. As the ingredients move from farms to processing plants to the restaurant, McDonald's quality inspection programme (QIP) carries out quality checks at over 20 different points in the cold chain system. Setting up of the cold chain has also enabled it to cut down on operational wastage.

The company's hazard analysis critical control point (HACCP) is a systematic approach to food safety that emphasizes prevention within McDonald's suppliers' facility and restaurants rather than detection through inspection of illness or presence of below quality food. Based on HACCP guidelines, control points and critical control points for the company's major food processing plants and restaurants in India have been identified. The limits have been established for those followed by monitoring, recording, and correcting any deviations. The HACCP verification is done at least twice in a year and certified.

The relationship between McDonald's and its Indian suppliers is mutually beneficial. As McDonald's expands in India, suppliers get the opportunity to expand their business; have access to the latest in food technology and advanced agricultural practices;

and the ability to grow or to export. There are many cases of local suppliers operating out of small towns who have benefited from their association with McDonald's India.

## Trikaya Agriculture

Implementation of advanced agricultural practices has enabled Trikaya to successfully grow specialty crops such as iceberg lettuce, special herbs, and many oriental vegetables. The farm's infrastructure features:

- a specialized nursery with a team of agricultural experts;
- drip and sprinkler irrigation in raised farm beds with fertilizer mixing plant;
- pre-cooling room and a large cold room for post harvest handling; and
- refrigerated truck for transportation.

McDonald's buys a third of its 450 tonne annual requirement from Trikaya. The remaining amount is sourced from farms in Ooty (20 per cent), Meena Agritech of Delhi (25 per cent), and Ferracon Farms in Dehradun.

The association with McDonald's has its share of risks because any damage to the crop is borne by the supplier. It accepts only good quality material, so suppliers have to minimize rejections. The lettuce crop is highly vulnerable to weather conditions. It can fail if there is excess rainfall, heat, or hailstorm. McDonald's vast experience comes into play here. To avoid calamities, McDonald's suggested that lettuce seeds be purchased from McDonald's (which imports them) and planted on raised beds or moved to two other non-flood prone locations eight km and forty km away during the monsoon.

Trikaya has also invested in a cooling plant and a refrigerated vehicle to transport the produce. To avoid excessive man-handling, the head of lettuces, which is cut at the base, is placed directly onto a tray which goes into the refrigerated room. It is stored there till the next morning when it is sent to the processing plant.

The lettuce is harvested everyday at 6 a.m., packaged and maintained at a temperature of two degrees celsius in the cooler. It is transported by a truck in a compartment maintained at four degrees celsius. When it arrives at the processing centre, it is processed at eight to twelve degrees room temperature. The product and water temperature is one to four degrees and kept for up to a week before being dispatched to the distribution centre in Thane, a north-eastern Mumbai suburb.

Lettuce is one of the few products sourced by McDonald's from more than one supplier despite the usual norm of having as few suppliers as possible. According to the company, for a burger in Delhi to taste the same as in Chennai, the number of suppliers should be less. In the case of lettuce, given the fragility of the crop, it is always possible for one of the suppliers to have a washed-out crop. Trikaya, with its excess capacity, fills in to maintain the steady flow of supply. Trikaya sells the surplus produce in the local market for which it gets a better price of ₹40 to ₹100 a kg. McDonald's, on the other hand, leverages the economies of scale to buy the vegetable at cheaper prices.

Few years back, pests used to devastate the lettuce crops at Trikaya. Today, with McDonald's help Trikaya uses the right pesticides during different times of the pest's lifecycle and inhibits their growth. Every Monday, the pest scouting data is passed on to McDonald's office and together they work out a solution. Due to this collaboration, pest-related rejections are down to 10 per cent.

## Vista Processed Foods Pvt Ltd

Vista Processed Foods produces a range of frozen chicken and vegetable foods. A world class infrastructure at their plant at Taloja, Maharashtra, has

- separate processing lines for chicken and vegetable foods;
- capability to produce frozen foods at temperature as low as −35 degree celsius to retain total freshness; and
- international standards, procedures, and support services.

Vista, with its state-of-the-art plant, provides 20–30 per cent of McDonald's total purchase of processed food. It deals with 45 suppliers for the 12 products it supplies to McDonald's, ranging from frozen peas and assorted vegetables for vegetable patties to procuring the right quality of birds for the chicken patty.

The process of freezing a patty after preparation is quite interesting. A food expert mixes the vegetables as per McDonald's recipe. It is then mixed with rice as the binding agent. Once this is fed into the automated machine, it goes through the motions of being dipped in batter and then rolled in bread crumbs and fried and frozen; all this in exactly half an hour. The final outcome is a frozen and packaged patty which then has a shelf-life of one year. It is maintained at −18 degree centigrade.

The chicken used in the Chicken McGrill is supplied by Coimbatore-based Suguna Poultry. It provides the frozen deboned meat to Vista. In fact, by the time the meat comes to Vista, it has traveled quite a bit. The eggs are laid in Bangalore. The hatching and contract farming is done out of Pune. The bird is processed in Pune before it is deboned and sent to Vista. The egg hatching and bird killing cycle takes forty five days and another five days are used for processing. Vista picks up 70,000 birds a month from Suguna, which is 20 per cent of its output.

In order to contain costs, Vista strives to minimize rejections. After every batch of patties, a quality assurance expert fries a patty to test it for colour, appearance, internal texture, and flavour. If it passes this test on all the parameters, it is ready to be sent to the distribution centre. If it falls short on even a single parameter, the entire batch is rejected. By constant trial and error, rejections are down from the earlier eight to ten per cent to the current two per cent. The major concerns of Vista in this process are related to temperature controls.

## Dynamix Diary

Dynamix has brought immense benefits to farmers in Baramati, Maharashtra by setting up a network of milk collection centres equipped with bulk coolers. Easy accessibility has enabled farmers to augment their income by finding a new market for surplus milk. The factory has

- fully automatic international standard processing facility;
- capability to convert milk into cheese, butter/ ghee, skimmed milk powder, lactose, casein and whey protein, and baby food; and
- stringent quality control measures and continuous R&D.

Cheese comes in both shredded form and as singles. While the singles go directly to McDonald's two distribution centres, the shredded cheese comes to Vista to be used in a range of concoctions. While Modern Dairy and Amul provide the paneer, the cheese is made by Dynamix, which has set up a separate line for McDonald's. For McDonald's, Dynamix produces sheets of cheese that are then cut into eight slices each. It also churns out cheese singles for biscuit-maker Britannia that are marketed under the brand name Milkman.

## McCain Foods

McDonald's had a troublesome learning experience in sourcing the right kind of potatoes for its French fries in India. One of its suppliers, Lamb Weston, invested heavily in setting up production lines to process Indian potatoes in the early nineties. However, with the quality of the potato crop not up to McDonald's specifications, the project had to be abandoned.

Having burnt its fingers, McDonald's did not want to take any chances. It has continued to import around 1,200 tonnes of potatoes every year for French Fries from New Zealand. Now, it has partnered with its main global supplier, McCain Foods, the world's largest French fries company. Together, they are helping Indian farmers grow the right kind of potatoes. The Indian potato crop was not as good because farmers used seeds from the preceding crop. As a result, not only did they have only one variety of the crop, but the quality was poor. McDonald's specifications are clear and unbending—a certain length, high solid content, and low moisture. Indian potatoes typically have 15–19 per cent solid matter compared to the global standard of 18–26 per cent. Hence, McCain, a leader in agronomy, zeroed in on Deesa and Kheda, two Gujarat towns. It has been helping farmers in these places with better agronomy techniques, including irrigation, sowing seed treatment, planting methods, fertilizer application, and storage. The crop is improving with 21 per cent solid content and McDonald's is now sourcing 350 tonnes of potato from Gujarat for its wedges. It will take a good three or four years before the right quality of potatoes (with 24 per cent solid content) are grown for French fries.

## Radhakrishna Foodland

An integral part of the Radhakrishna Group, Foodland specializes in handling large volumes, providing the entire range of services including procurement, quality inspection, storage, inventory management, deliveries, data collection, recording, and reporting. The salient strengths of this company are

- a one-stop shop for all distribution management services;
- dry and cold storage facility to store and transport perishable products at temperatures up to –22 degree celsius; and
- effective process control for minimum distribution cost.

Once processed, all the products have a minimum of 60 days shelf-life, except for buns, which remain fresh for five days and lettuce, which remains fresh for three days. To transport around 800 tonnes per month of varying quantities of some 250 ingredients from 50 suppliers at varying temperatures, a wider assortment of trucks than Radhakrishna Foodland Ltd (RKFL) currently has, is needed. However, their design contributes to lower McDonald's supply chain costs. Each truck has three levels of variable refrigeration, and the size of each refrigerated compartment can be varied according to the need.

The use of multi-temperature trucks has reduced the number of daily deliveries to McDonald's outlets, which maintain an inventory of 2.5 to 3 days requirement. If on a particular day, lettuce is needed more than ice cream, the compartment with the relevant temperature can be expanded to take in more lettuce. This flexibility is the key to cost control in a situation where some perishables such as tomatoes have to be dispatched daily, while products such as cheese and buns require replenishment every two or three days, depending on demand and shelf-life. RKFL has invested in 24 multi-temperature trucks which offer three different temperatures—ambient, chilled, and frozen.

This has no doubt saved on transportation time and helped RKFL reschedule deliveries based on orders from various outlets. Earlier, transportation productivity was 6 to 7 cases per man-hour. This has gone up to 16 to 17 cases. Moreover, every case was earlier moved manually from the truck to the restaurant. Today, trolleys transport four cases at a time. Even the boxes, which used to be placed haphazardly as in any godown, are well-aligned now.

The supply chain is common for both North and West India managed by Vikram Bakshi and Amit Jatia respectively. The processed food is taken to RKFL's two distribution centres at Thane near Mumbai and Noida near Delhi. The Noida centre also doubles up as a processing unit.

McDonald's always treats its suppliers as partners and strives to help them in every possible way. During its early association with RKFL, it introduced the supplier to Australia's F J Walker to develop the distribution system. In 1996, RKFL's distribution centre had inventories of 35 to 36 days. Now with more sales and efficiencies, it is down to around 10 days—about 175 stock keeping units. Dry goods account for 60 per cent of inventory compared to 20 per cent each of frozen and chilled stuff. This includes both inbound (those picked up and brought to the distribution centre) and outbound (which are taken from distribution centres to the outlets).

There are also systems in place for tracking demand and supply. Every fortnight, RKFL sends rolling projections to the suppliers for the next three fortnights as every purchase order is placed three weeks in advance. The objective is to minimize the conversion of raw materials into finished products. This helps suppliers to control their inventory as well. A big hurdle was the accurate forecast of product movement. Earlier product movement was tracked manually from each of the restaurants. Today, with volumes increasing, it is tracked through the product-mix. Outlets are able to gauge their best-sellers. The distribution business works on stock turnarounds as fixed costs such as storage are distributed over larger volumes. Therefore, RKFL has three turnarounds a month compared to just one when it began operations.

The planning behind McDonald's supply chain is so intense that if a new product hits the market today, its journey is sure to have begun a good two years before that. The competition is way behind for McDonald's in India. Its fellow American food giant Kentucky Fried Chicken (KFC) entered the Indian market around the same time, but is yet to catch up with it. The truly Indian fast food chain, Nirulas of Delhi is trying hard to make its presence felt in Delhi's adjoining states but with a snail's pace. The gusto to take on the international giants such as McDonald's is missing among Indian fast food pioneers. Only time will tell, if they would ever be able to give competition to the likes of McDonald's.

## Discussion Questions

1. McDonald's has been quite successful in extending the life of its raw materials by various innovative methods, which were hitherto deemed in India as 'perishable commodities'. The earliest consumption of these perishable commodities akin to the JIT concept has been defied by McDonald's in a market which prefers fresh food. Discuss.

2. It would have been much more cost effective and convenient if McDonald's would have pursued a local sourcing strategy rather than the current strategy of centralized distribution centres, involving high transportation cost (especially in view of the vast geography of the country). Comment.

3. What was the logic in McDonald's setting up two separate JVs with two different partners in the same country? Was there some point in completely neglecting the southern and eastern parts of the country during its initial years?

4. What are your recommendations to Indian fast food chains such as Nirulas?

CASE STUDY II

# Volvo–Sunwind

Volvo is a Swedish multinational which manufactures cars and trucks. Sunwind is one of its suppliers, which supplies floor panels for the station wagon models of Volvo's 240 and 740 series of cars to Volvo's Torslanda plant in Sweden. Sunwind is a company of some 200 employees, and its product range consists of different interior fittings for the automobile and aeroplane industries. Volvo has been one of Sunwind's main customers since the start.

In the early 1950s, Volvo had severe problems with the quality of the floor panels in their station wagon model *Volvo Deuett*. One of Volvo's employees knew two guitar craftsmen who had their workshop located in the vicinity of Volvo's Torslanda plant. These craftsmen were able to solve Volvo's problems with the help of a different milling technique and a couple of other process improvements. Volvo invited them to continue the relationship, and provided capital to the two entrepreneurs, who left the music business to join the automobile industry. Thus Sunwind was born.

At Sunwind's Save plant, some 100 km from Torslanda, the production rate is 2,000 floor panels per week for the 740 series and 1,000 for the 240 series. The assembly of panels is done in two assembly lines, one for each model. The panels are produced in eight different variants per line (two different covering materials in four colours). The role of Sunwind was like a subcontractor, as Volvo developed the prototypes and supplied the tools and raw materials to Sunwind. The completed floors were delivered to Volvo in different containers, each part in its own container. The product being bulky and colour-dependent, a large storage space, both adjacent to the assembly line at Volvo as well as in Sunwind's own operations, was required. Volvo bought and collected the goods from the Save factory twice a week.

In order to gain cost benefit for both the parties, Volvo and Sunwind initiated a JIT-like delivery schedule. The role of Sunwind has changed into being more of a partner than a subcontractor with an increased responsibility for the development and manufacture of their products to meet Volvo's specifications. The floors are now being delivered from Sunwind in sequence with the demand of the final assembly line of Volvo and transported in custom-built containers in Sunwind's own trucks, which are unloaded less than 100 yards from the assembly point. Each container holds the complete set of floors for eight vehicles, stacked on one another in the same sequence as the vehicles that arrive at the assembly point in Torslanda, where the floors are assembled into the cars.

Every four weeks, a delivery schedule is made by Volvo, containing an estimate of the floor requirements of different colours, grades, etc. According to these forecasts, Sunwind orders their raw materials such as carpet materials and plywood, which are delivered to its plant in Hogsater some 200 km north of Save. Sunwind has reduced the number of suppliers and now relies up to a great extent on single sourcing. Due to economic reasons, the quantity bought at each shipment is the same—one truck load—but the mix of colours is pegged more accurately to the Volvo demand forecast. Volvo sends a specified order to Sunwind approximately ten days ahead of the production schedule. At Hogsater, work begins by milling out the plywood parts and cutting the covering materials to shape. Deliveries are made out of forecasts once a day to Sunwind's Save plant. By reducing set-up times, Sunwind had been able to transfer inventory backwards and, thus, save on the inventory costs.

At Sunwind, the final assembly of floors does not take place until the complete delivery sequence is known, for example, when a certain vehicle has passed through the paints works at Volvo, passed the subsequent quality controls, and reached the next assembly station. Each time a vehicle enters this point on the assembly line, a message is sent to the Save plant with a full assembly specification for the complete floor. The printer is actually standing in the assembly hall in Save and approximately once a minute an order is received. When assembly starts at Sunwind, the car in the Volvo plant in Torslanda is only seven hours away from the assembly point where the floor will be installed into the car. The deliveries of floor panels are made at the Torslanda plant four times a day. When the shipment arrives at the assembly building, it is only one hour until the first floor will be assembled into the car. From the unloading dock, one container at a time is fetched by a forklift operator and delivered to the assembly point (Karlsson & Norr 1994).

## Discussion Questions

1. Volvo has another assembly plant in Kalmar at a distance of some 450 km from Sunwind's Save plant. Can Sunwind be used by Volvo to

deliver floors to its Kalmar plant according to JIT schedules as it does for its Torslanda plant?

2. Are these positive results due to Sunwind transferring the problems on hand to their own suppliers?

3. Summarize the pros and cons of the JIT system from the point of view of Volvo and that of Sunwind.

## Objective Questions

### Choose the correct option

1. The following supply chain strategy is associated with just-in-time (JIT) or lean system:
   (a) push-based
   (b) pull-based
   (c) push-pull
   (d) push-push

2. The following supply chain strategy is suitable for the grocery industry:
   (a) push
   (b) pull
   (c) push-pull
   (d) pool

3. The following is not part of a supply chain:
   (a) manufacturer
   (b) distributor
   (c) bank
   (d) retailer

### State True or False

4. Procurement refers to the actual buying of materials and those activities associated with the buying process.

5. The flow of information and funds takes place from the initial raw material supplier end to the customer end, while the product flow takes place in the reverse direction.

6. In a push-based process, the material is pushed into the supply chain by the initial raw material supplier in anticipation of the customer demand at the other end of the supply chain.

7. JIT systems are based on push-production concept.

8. Business to consumer (B2C) systems are known as e-procurement.

9. A major advantage of the pull supply chain strategy is responsiveness in terms of ready availability of the product at the retail stores for the customer to come and buy at his or her will.

### Fill in the blanks

10. The _____ supply chain strategy should be deployed when the overall processing time of the product in the supply chain equates to tolerable waiting time on part of the end-customer.

11. The indirect materials are commonly referred to as _____ materials.

## Concept Review Questions

1. What is materials requirement planning (MRP)? What are the inputs and outputs required by the MRP processing logic?

2. What is product structure? What is a bill of materials?

3. Give the general format of an MRP report using a hypothetical example.

4. Explain the various methods of determining the order size in MRP.

5. Define the just-in-time (JIT) system and explain the basic concept of JIT manufacturing.

6. What is the *kanban* visual system? Explain the various steps followed in operating the *kanban* system in a plant.

7. Explain the benefits of JIT with a schematic diagram.

8. What is a hybrid MRP-JIT system? How can it be implemented in a factory?

9. Define a supply chain. What is a bullwhip effect, and how can it be minimized?

10. Explain the three types of supply chain strategies.

11. What is supply chain management (SCM)? Explain the concept of keiretsu in Japanese SCM.

12. Compare Japanese JIT SCM with traditional US purchasing. According to you, which one of these is suitable for Indian factories?

13. What is tendering? Explain the various criteria used for vendor rating.

14. What is operating resource procurement? How does e-procurement work at Microsoft Corp. through MS Market?

## Numerical Problems

1. Figure 9.28 shows the product structure of a product *L*. If 500 units of product *L* are required to be manufactured, how many units of the various sub-assemblies/components shown in Fig. 9.28 do we require?

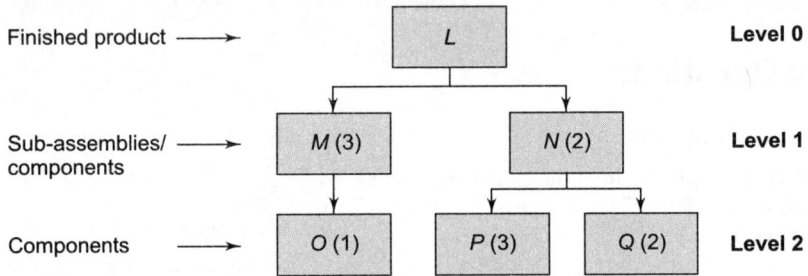

**Fig. 9.28** Product structure of product L

2. Perform the low-lever coding of Product S, whose structure is given in Fig. 9.29.

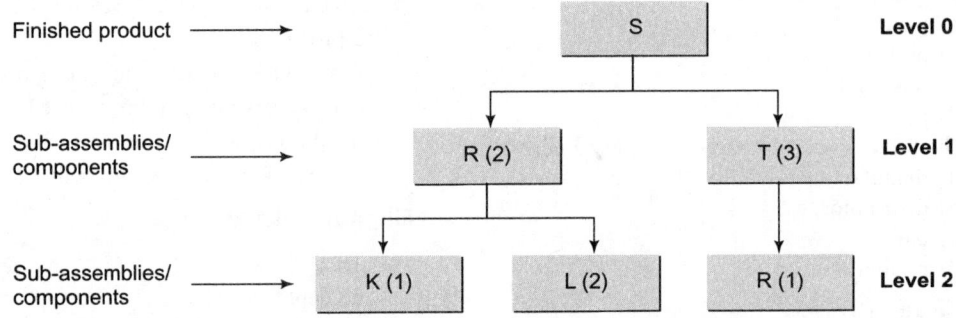

**Fig. 9.29** Product structure of Product S

3. The product structure of item 612, with LT in weeks, is shown in Fig. 9.30. The MPS of item 612 shows the gross requirements as 200 and 400 units in weeks 5 and 8, respectively. Component 485 has a projected on-hand inventory of 200 units in report week 0. Prepare the MRP reports using MS Excel for items 612, 485, and 217 with lot sizing according to the lot-for-lot method.

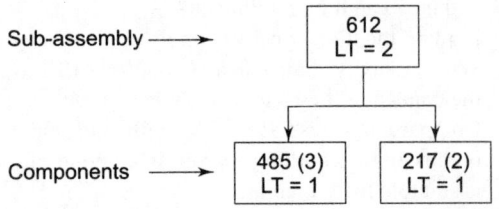

**Fig. 9.30** Product structure of sub-assembly 612

4. Repeat Problem 2 if it is given that the lot size can be a multiple of 250 units for item 612, 400 units

for item 485, and 600 units for item 217. Take the time horizon of 10 weeks from the report week 0.

5. Items *A*, *B*, *C*, and *D* have the following bill of materials (product structures):

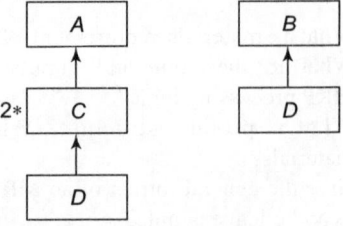

*A* and *B* are end-items. Component *D* is used in items *B* and *C* both (and hence, in item *A* too). The manufacturing of 1 unit of *A* requires 2 units of *C*, and to manufacture 1 unit of *C*, 1 unit of *D* is required. The manufacturing of 1 unit *B* requires 1 unit of *D*. Fixed order quantities are used in production.

Other notable important specifics are as follows:

| Item | Lead-time in time periods | Order quantity |
|------|--------------------------|----------------|
| A | 2 | 25 |
| B | 1 | 25 |
| C | 2 | 50 |
| D | 3 | 50 |

Use the data given in the Master Production Schedules for end-items *A* and *B* (Fig. 9.31) to complete the MRP calculations (in the tables given in Fig. 9.31) for the next 25 time periods for items A, B, C, and D.

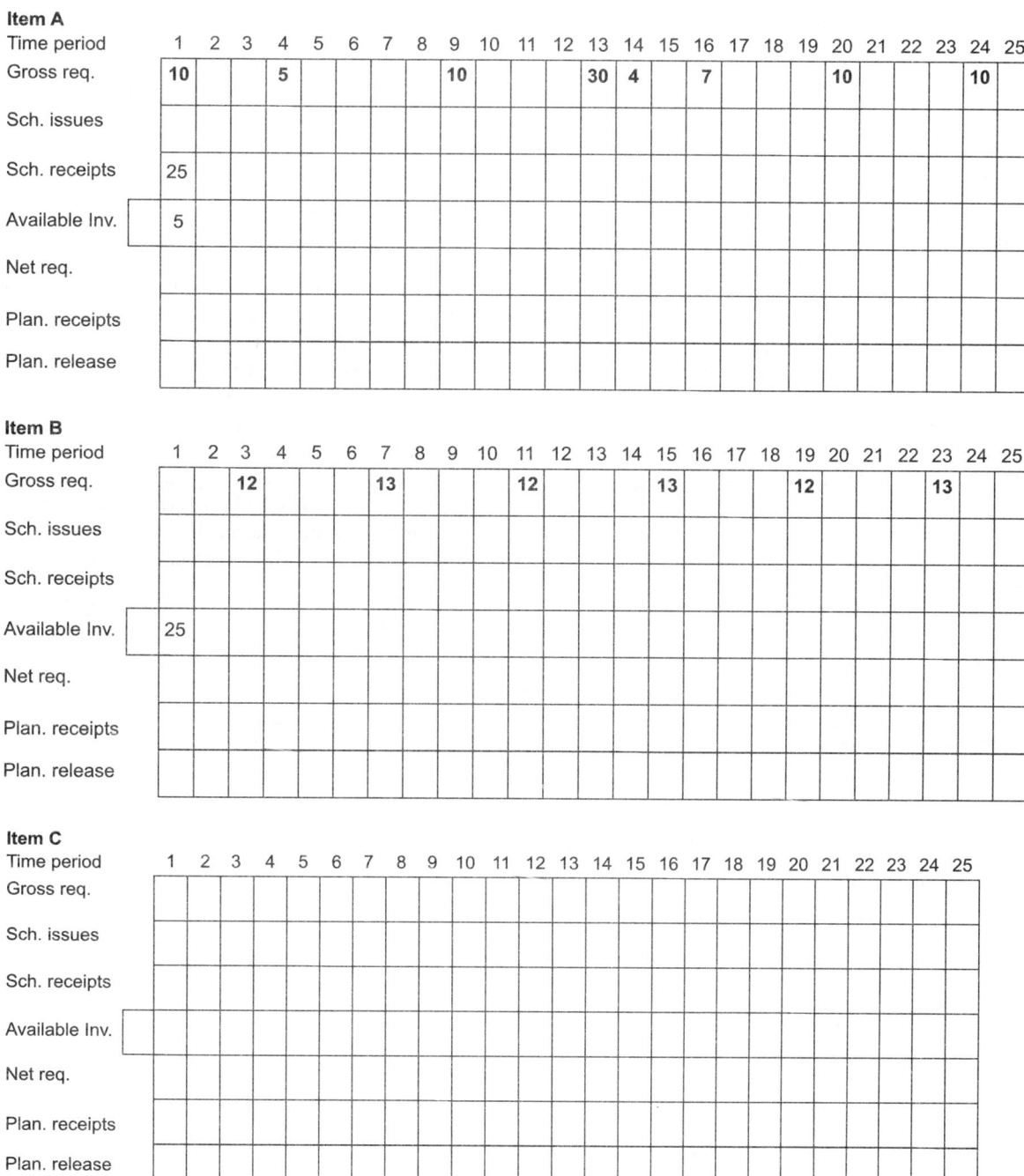

**Fig. 9.31 Contd**

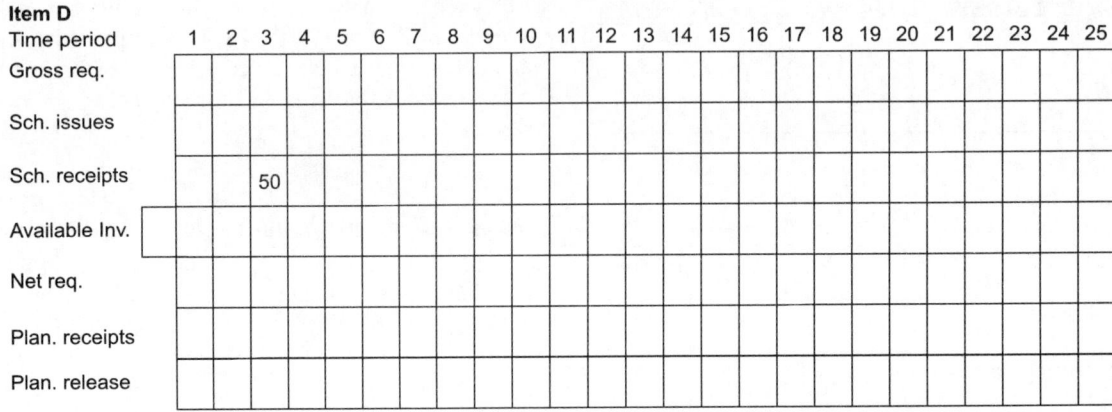

**Item D**

| Time period | 1 | 2 | 3 | 4 | 5 | 6 | 7 | 8 | 9 | 10 | 11 | 12 | 13 | 14 | 15 | 16 | 17 | 18 | 19 | 20 | 21 | 22 | 23 | 24 | 25 |
|---|---|---|---|---|---|---|---|---|---|---|---|---|---|---|---|---|---|---|---|---|---|---|---|---|---|
| Gross req. | | | | | | | | | | | | | | | | | | | | | | | | | |
| Sch. issues | | | | | | | | | | | | | | | | | | | | | | | | | |
| Sch. receipts | | 50 | | | | | | | | | | | | | | | | | | | | | | | |
| Available Inv. | | | | | | | | | | | | | | | | | | | | | | | | | |
| Net req. | | | | | | | | | | | | | | | | | | | | | | | | | |
| Plan. receipts | | | | | | | | | | | | | | | | | | | | | | | | | |
| Plan. release | | | | | | | | | | | | | | | | | | | | | | | | | |

**Fig. 9.31** Tables for MRP calculations in problem 4

6. The following information is given about an item: OC = ₹25 per order, CC per week = 0.2%, unit cost price = ₹10, CC per unit per week = 10 × 0.2% = ₹0.02. Table 9.4 shows the weekly requirements of this item.

**Table 9.4**

| Week | Net requirements |
|---|---|
| 1 | 200 |
| 2 | 300 |
| 3 | 100 |
| 4 | 450 |
| 5 | 250 |
| 6 | 100 |
| 7 | 300 |
| 8 | 400 |

Calculate the total cost for MRP lot sizing using the (a) lot-for-lot method and (b) EOQ method.

7. Using the data of Problem 6, calculate the total cost for MRP lot sizing using the least total cost method.

8. Use the data of Problem 6 to calculate the total cost for MRP lot sizing using the least unit cost method.

9. Fly Aircraft Systems is a Bangalore-based company that manufactures light aircrafts for amateur training. In its aircrafts, an electrical sub-assembly #821 is used with MPS given in Table 9.5.

**Table 9.5**

| Master production schedule (MPS) | June | | | | July | | | |
|---|---|---|---|---|---|---|---|---|
| | Week 1 | Week 2 | Week 3 | Week 4 | Week 5 | Week 6 | Week 7 | Week 8 |
| | | 700 | | | 700 | 700 | | 700 |

The assembly period (lead time) is one week for this sub-assembly, which requires two units of component #633 to be combined to three units of component #597 (Fig. 9.32). These components are sourced from outside suppliers in quantities of 2,000 units and 4,000 units (or multiples thereof) at a time with lead time of 2 weeks and 3 weeks, respectively. Create an MRP report for the sub-assembly and its components.

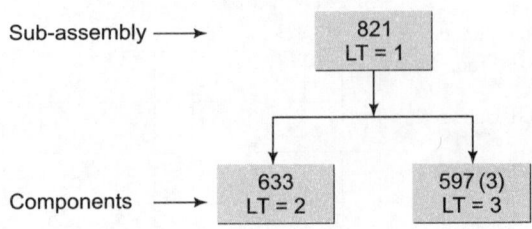

**Fig. 9.32** Product structure of sub-assembly #821

# Project Assignments

1. Visit a factory near you and find out their practices for materials requirement planning of dependent demand items and their relationships with suppliers. Study also the role of the purchase manager of the company, as to up to what extent he acts on the functions you have studied with respect to purchasing, procurement, and SCM. Brainstorm in class the best MRP practices adopted by the factory and critically evaluate the function of the purchase manager.

2. Visit a nearby restaurant and find out their procurement systems of perishable items such as vegetables, milk, meat, chicken, etc. Do they decide on the order placements of these items on the basis of the three inputs of MRP studied by you? Find out also whether they have fixed suppliers for these items or they change their suppliers frequently on the basis of the cost, quality, etc. of these items.

## Answers to Objective Questions

|   |   |   |   |   |
|---|---|---|---|---|
| 1. (b) | 2. (a) | 3. (c) | 4. False | 5. False |
| 6. True | 7. False | 8. False | 9. False | 10. pull-based |
| 11. maintenance, repair, and operation (MRO) | | | | |

# 10

# Total Productive Maintenance

## Learning Objectives

After reading this chapter, you will be able to answer the following questions:
- What is total productive maintenance (TPM)?
- What is the need for maintenance management?
- What are the different types of maintenance?
- How do the various sub-systems of TPM help the organizations in leveraging the advantages of TPM?
- How does 'why-why' analysis help in finding the root causes of problems?

## Total Productive Maintenance (TPM)

All manufacturing organizations possess industrial equipment for various processes in the production of goods. Similarly, services organizations are also using various gadgets such as computers, printers, facsimiles, photocopiers, telephones, etc. as an aid to their daily operations. Maintenance of facilities and equipment is done to ensure that these are in good working condition at any point of time and if breakdowns occur, necessary repairs should be done in order to bring these back to running condition as early as possible. Maintenance management is planning, organizing, and controlling maintenance activities such that the overall maintenance cost is the minimum.

Maintenance is required not only by equipment but also by other facilities such as building, land, etc. Maintaining lawns and gardens of the premises of the factory may be an important aspect of environment protection especially in process industries. However, maintenance of equipment used directly in the production process is much more important for a business enterprise.

Total productive maintenance (TPM) seeks to maximize equipment effectiveness throughout the lifetime of that equipment. It strives to maintain optimum equipment conditions in order to prevent unexpected breakdowns, speed losses, and quality defects arising from process activities. The ultimate aim is zero equipment downtime and zero defects through the eradication of equipment error. Nakajima (1982) suggests that in the ideal factory, equipment should be operating at 100 per cent capacity 100 per cent of the time.

> Total productive maintenance (TPM) seeks to maximize equipment effectiveness throughout the lifetime of that equipment.

Total productive maintenance draws heavily upon the philosophy of total quality management. It involves everyone in all departments and from all levels of the organizational hierarchy. It seeks to highlight plant maintenance and to motivate the workforce through teamwork and training in basic housekeeping, problem-solving, and activities intended to achieve zero defects. Therefore, TPM brings together production and maintenance personnel; unlike in the post-modern manufacturing organization, where, traditionally, production staff operate and maintenance staff fix. According to Suzuki (1992, 1994), TPM can generate substantial measurable improvements in cost, delivery, safety, and morale, thus cementing intra-organizational linkages between functional areas and also developing those linkages between the organization and its suppliers and customers (Exhibit 10.1).

---

### Exhibit 10.1   India—The Epicentre of Aviation MRO Growth

India has experienced extraordinary growth in airline traffic in recent years. In 2001, the number of aircraft departures in India was 2,16,700. This increased to 3,66,700 in 2005, and to 4,38,700 departures in 2006. The country is witnessing rapid growth in fleet; such growth is projected to continue—the fleet of all airlines operating in India grew from 160 in 2004 to 249 in 2005 and is projected to be around 620 in 2014 (see Fig. 10.1). A significant corresponding increase in revenue passenger kilometres has also been recorded. The emergence of multiple carriers in recent years has fuelled the growth. India has witnessed the entry of airlines across the service spectrum, ranging from full service carriers to a large number of low cost carriers such as Spice Jet, Go Air, and IndiGo.

With the rapid growth of the aviation sector in India, airport infrastructure, air traffic control (ATC) requirements, and pilot and engineer shortages have emerged as major areas of concern. The critical aspect of aircraft maintenance has unfortunately not received adequate focus and coverage. A study by Frost & Sullivan estimates that the global market for maintenance, repair, and overhaul (MRO) is valued at US$37 billion; Asia's share of the global MRO market is US$8.1 billion, or eight per cent share of this market; and that India's share of the Asian market is US$615.3, or is 7.6 per cent.

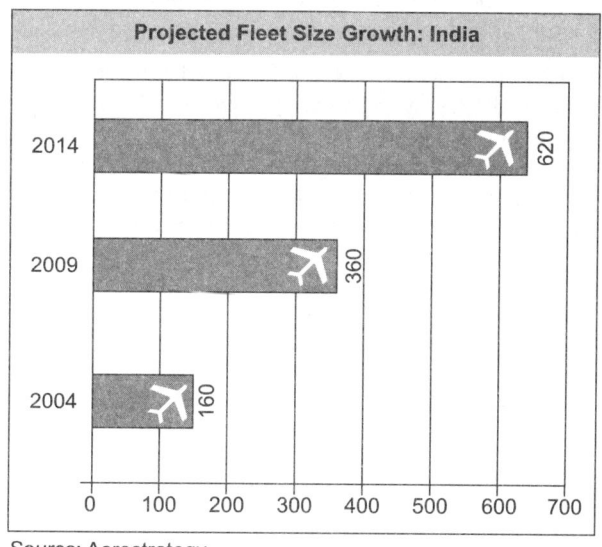

*Source*: Aerostrategy.

**Fig. 10.1**   Projected fleet size growth in India

*(Contd)*

*Exhibit 10.1 Contd*

The Indian maintenance and repair segment is fractured. While the two public sector airlines, Air-India and Indian, have full-fledged maintenance and repair arms, these facilities have just enough capacity to meet their own needs. Jet Airways and, to a lesser extent, Blue Dart Aviation, are the only private carriers that have developed their own maintenance and engineering facilities.

Air India has developed full-fledged facilities for line maintenance (day-to-day servicing) as well as the mandatory periodic checks (C and D checks). However, their capacity for such maintenance work is limited to their fleet requirements alone. Even these facilities will prove insufficient when the airlines acquire new aircraft.

Jet Airways, on the other hand, has one hangar (leased from Hindustan Aeronautics Ltd) in Bangalore, and, following the allocation of a plot of land at Mumbai, the airline has now set up a two-bay hangar in Mumbai, where it will shift much of its maintenance and repair work.

The private maintenance and repair organizations, such as Air Works India and Max AeroSpace & Aviation Ltd, point out that they operate at a disadvantage, with the existing tax structure, land allotment, and policies relating to customs duties and foreign direct investment all loaded against them. Max AeroSpace & Aviation, which was allocated land at the Juhu aerodrome (in suburban Mumbai), says its location precludes it from taking on maintenance work for larger aircraft.

Larger passenger aircraft cannot land at the small airstrip at Juhu, which means the company can carry out only small maintenance and repair work that the big MRO firms are not interested in. Apart from their locational disadvantage, the private MRO firms point out that they are not allowed to develop larger hangar facilities, which also prevent them from working on larger aircraft. The services of Indian MRO firms attract a service tax of 10.2 per cent and a value added tax of 8 per cent. Considering that the cost of spares and labour are on par at home and abroad, MRO firms based abroad have an 11 per cent benefit. While the Indian MRO firms are subject to these taxes, the services of those based abroad are exempt from customs duty.

With a significant and sudden rise in the total fleet size in India, the demand for MRO services has also increased rapidly. Long-standing players such as Air India and Jet Airways have established their own MRO teams and have adequate maintenance capability. However, several new entrants in the market do not have adequate manpower and skills for MRO and therefore source their maintenance requirements from abroad (see Table 10.1). In the table, line maintenance includes entry level transit checks, night halts, and weekly checks; base maintenance includes modification, repairs and alterations of various accessories such as propellers, power systems, seats, window shields, furnishings, etc.; component maintenance includes maintenance and substitution of major accessories such as flight control equipment, engine fuel, wheels and brakes, and air conditioning equipment. With a significantly high growth estimate of 10.2 per cent the aviation MRO market in India is expected to outpace growth in the global market as well as in the Asian market. Low-cost carriers (LCC) like SpiceJet are increasingly outsourcing their fleet MRO requirements.

While leasing is a popular mode of aircraft acquisition worldwide, in India many new airlines have opted for acquisition through purchase. As this puts the onus of maintenance on the airlines, the airlines need comprehensive maintenance contracts. Table 10.1 shows the maintenance relationships established by various airlines. Presently, a lot of such work is being sourced from service providers based in Singapore and Europe.

**Table 10.1** Mode of MRO adapted by airlines in India

| Airline | Line maintenance | Base maintenance | Component repair |
|---|---|---|---|
| Air India | Air India | Air India | Air India |
| Jet Airways | JAECO | JAECO | JAECO |
| Air Deccan | EADS | EADS | EADS |
| Spice Jet | Hamilton | Hamilton | Hamilton |
| Indigo Air | Indigo Air | – | Rockwell Collins |
| Go Air | Go Air | – | (Sahara, Jet, or Indian) |
| Paramount | Paramount | – | GE |

*(Contd)*

*Exhibit 10.1 Contd*

A number of companies have firmed up plans to enter the airline market in India. This signifies enormous growth potential for the MRO market. Air-One, Visa, Royal, Skylark, and Yamuna Air are the proposed airlines which plan to operate in a variety of formats such as chartered carriers, regional discounters, etc.

As in the global MRO market, the engine overhaul segment of the Indian MRO market is the largest, at US$174 million, and is expected to grow to US$490 million by 2014 (see Fig. 10.2). The state-owned airlines have developed capabilities for engine maintenance; the private airlines routinely source their needs from independent MRO firms. In India, 80 per cent of airframe maintenance is done in-house by airlines. The airframe maintenance market in 2004 was US$47 million. Original equipment manufacturers (OEM) have developed a significant share of the component overhaul market in India. The market size of the component overhaul market was US$81 million in 2004 and is expected to grow to US$204 million by 2014. The market for modifications is smaller; it was US$32 million in 2004 and is expected to be US$77.5 million by 2014.

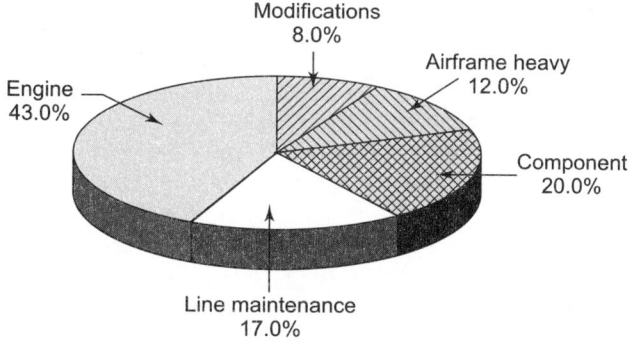

**Estimated 2004 Commercial MRO Market in India: US $405 million**

Modifications 8.0%
Airframe heavy 12.0%
Engine 43.0%
Component 20.0%
Line maintenance 17.0%

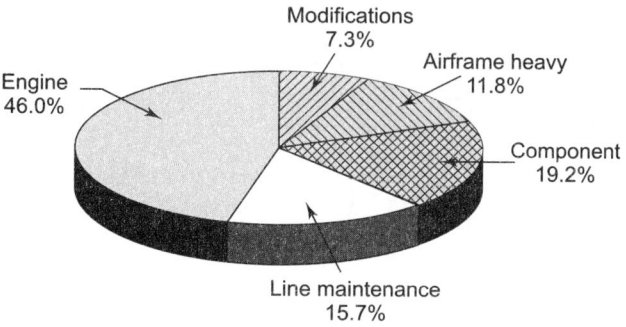

**Projected 2014 Commercial MRO Market in India: US $1065 million**

Modifications 7.3%
Airframe heavy 11.8%
Engine 46.0%
Component 19.2%
Line maintenance 15.7%

**Fig. 10.2**  Commercial MRO market in India: projection for 2014

Already, global players such as Airbus and Boeing have announced their MRO plans. The two competitors are collaborating to set up an MRO facility and an aeronautical fight training centre in Nagpur at an estimated investment of US$185 million. These initiatives from Airbus and Boeing are part of offset agreements with the Government of India in exchange of huge orders from Air India. Engine manufacturer Pratt & Whitney (P&W), a sister concern of the US$42.7 billion UTC Corporation, is exploring alliances with Indian entities such as Hyderabad Aircraft Maintenance Company (HAMCO) and Hindustan Aeronautics Limited (HAL), besides other international players, for its first MRO facility in India.

Two decades ago, about 85 per cent of global engine maintenance was done in-house. Now, this has reduced to 30 per cent. Much of this is because of

*(Contd)*

*Exhibit 10.1 Contd*

the proliferation of low-cost carriers (LCCs), who are turning to third-party MRO firms to cut costs and focus on core activities, to achieve better affordability and more efficient customer service. Many high-cost carriers have also begun following suit.

According to a report by AeroStrategy, a management consulting firm, labour in line and base maintenance (two segments of the MRO market) accounts for nearly 70 per cent of the total cost. Employing highly skilled technicians, who are paid by the hour, only for in-house activities, may, therefore, be too expensive. However, in the component and engine maintenance segment, about 62 per cent of total costs are material-based. This is why a third-party model could succeed well, as players could reduce the risk of their investments on tools and people, thereby offering services for multiple carriers.

Moreover, for domestic players, there also exists a labour arbitrage opportunity. For instance, in Europe and North America, the labour rate per hour is US$50–60. In contrast, the hourly rate in the Asia-Pacific and Indian markets can be as low as US$10 and US$25, respectively. Locating MRO units in India also saves time and resources. (Among Indian carriers, though, there is already talk of converting India into a regional MRO hub.) Having a local facility is better than ferrying aircraft to Singapore, the Middle East, and Europe (thereby incurring fuel costs and delays due to high occupancy rates). Globally, 25 per cent of flight delays happen due to maintenance issues. Research by HAMCO reveals that in India these are as high as 60 per cent. The Boeing report says maintenance costs are as high as 12.2 per cent of the total cost incurred by an aircraft annually.

Setting up an MRO unit, whether third party or in-house, costs a minimum of US$50 million. Regardless of size, an aircraft is made up of about 700 independent components. Hence, maintenance becomes crucial as the number of flying hours increases. It has to undergo a series of routine checks. While some checks such as night halts, transit checks, etc., could be undertaken either on the tarmac or in the hangar, for specific high-level (C and D) checks (including engine, component, airframe maintenance and modification), aircraft are flown to large MRO units. Despite having in-house units, some Indian carriers ferry flights abroad, citing unavailability of space and resources as reasons.

There are about 300 third-party MRO units worldwide, of which more than 65 are located in the Asia-Pacific region; there are none in India. Even the existing in-house units have a long way to go before they meet global standards. For now, the domestic market and sheer growth prediction is in itself a sizeable market to cater to. Assuming that there will be 1,000 aircraft in 2012 (both commercial and business), there would be a need for about 50,000 weekly checks, 3,500 A level checks, and millions of night halts. An aircraft undergoes a check after 600 flying hours. Assuming that an aircraft flies the minimum of 12–14 hours a day, it flies an average of 2,500 hours annually, and therefore goes for a check 3–4 times a year.

There is a long way to go for the aviation MRO business in India, but the early signs are great indicators of its having already become the epicentre of the aviation MRO industry.

## Benefits of Maintenance Management

As shown in Fig. 10.3, there are several benefits of maintenance management. If maintenance activities are planned and executed properly, it will lead to less frequent breakdowns of equipment. Thus, the valuable production time can be devoted to production activities to bring the actual production capacity of the plant to the effective capacity as closely as possible. There are three types of capacity, namely, design, effective, and actual capacity. Design capacity, as the name suggests, is the capacity which was designed in the facility. It depends upon the number

> Design capacity depends upon the number and capacity of machines and equipment coupled with labour.

and capacity of machines and equipment coupled with labour. It represents the maximum rate of output that can be achieved under ideal conditions. In reality, if a facility is used to make different products, the set-up time will be required between batches of different products to be produced. These set-ups are required to replace the raw material and components for the new batch of another product to be processed on the machines. Also, the machines may

> Proper maintenance management helps us to bring the actual capacity as close as possible to the effective capacity of the plant.

require adjustments, oiling, cleaning, etc. Some units of initial output may be lost in quality testing. Thus, it is not practically feasible to achieve design capacity. What can be achieved is the effective capacity. Actual capacity is the maximum output rate which is actually achieved under the constraints of machine breakdowns, labour inefficiencies and absenteeism, defective products, late deliveries of materials by the supplier, and so on. Actual capacity can be equal to or less than the effective capacity. Thus, proper maintenance management helps us to bring the actual capacity as close as possible to the effective capacity of the plant.

Lesser breakdowns will result in less disruption of production schedules, resulting in timely delivery of goods to customers. Also, the idle time of workers during such breakdowns can be avoided. Poorly maintained machines and equipment show high variation in output. The quality control managers have to be on their toes all the time because the control limits set by them are exceeded frequently, prompting them to look for assignable causes and do the rectification to bring the process back in control. Sudden breakdowns can become safety hazards for the workers. For example, some rotating parts may fly off to hit the workers in the absence of proper maintenance. Maintenance management increases the life of equipment and facilities. This is because in the lack of maintenance, certain worn-out and less costly parts and components of the equipment may result in the wearing out of other expensive parts. At some stage, the cost of repairs may exceed the cost of a new equipment suggesting the need for replacement of this poorly maintained equipment.

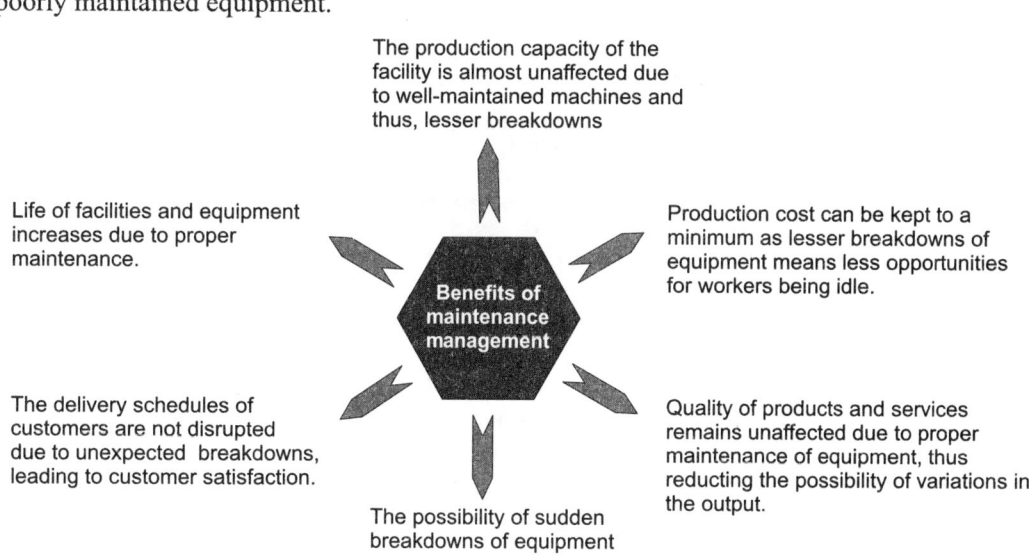

**Fig. 10.3**　Benefits of maintenance management

## Types of Maintenance

There are basically two types of maintenance:
- breakdown maintenance
- preventive maintenance

There are basically two types of maintenance: breakdown maintenance and preventive maintenance.

*Breakdown maintenance* is a reactive approach in which repairs and replacement of parts are performed only when the breakdowns occur. In preventive maintenance, which is a proactive approach, breakdowns are avoided by following regular schedules of oiling, cleaning, adjustment, inspection, and replacement of worn-out parts in the equipment.

Most of the organizations follow a mix of the above two approaches. This is because excessive attention to prevention of breakdowns may become very costly in the long run. The idea here is to find an optimal combination of two approaches, which results in the minimum total cost of maintenance. As shown in Fig. 10.4, as the amount of preventive effort increases, the cost of preventive maintenance increases while the cost of repairing sudden breakdown (which includes the loss in production due to disruption) decreases due to lesser possibility of breakdowns. The optimal effort corresponds to the minimum total cost of maintenance which is the sum to the cost of preventive maintenance and the cost associated with repairs of sudden breakdowns.

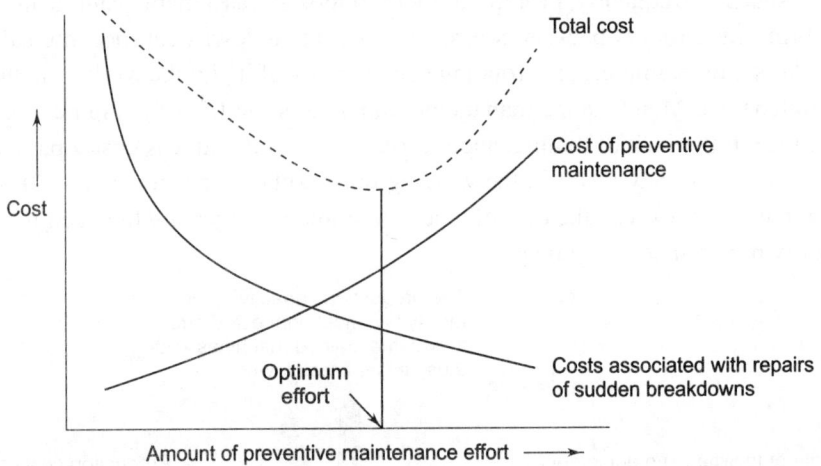

**Fig. 10.4**   Types of maintenance costs

*Preventive maintenance* is a periodic activity in which the time of maintenance can be scheduled either according a calendar dependent upon the predetermined number of operating hours of different equipment or on the basis of inspections of the equipment to find its state and need for maintenance. Total preventive maintenance is the performance of maintenance activities on the equipment by the operators of the equipment themselves. This approach has been popularized by the Japanese companies following the JIT systems. For example, the Maruti Udyog Limited (Maruti-Suzuki) plant at Gurgaon is operated for two shifts for the production of cars, while the third shift (late night shift) is used for maintenance purposes. This approach has certain benefits—the cost of keeping a separate workforce of maintenance personnel can be avoided and also, the workers have an increased sense of responsibility while maintaining their equipment. In this process, the workers become more committed to proper use of the equipment and avoid malfunctioning which may result in breakdowns.

A good preventive maintenance programme is based upon the prediction of possible breakdown time of equipment.

A good preventive maintenance programme is based upon the prediction of possible breakdown time of equipment so that maintenance may be performed just before the breakdown. These predictions can be made by analysing

It is necessary to keep inventories of spare parts required for replacement in case of breakdowns and during preventive maintenance schedules.

historical records of maintenance and breakdowns of similar equipment. Thus, it is necessary to keep such records as the date of installation of each equipment, operating hours, and types of maintenance and repairs required by it with tentative dates.

The ease of maintenance should be kept in mind even during the designing of the equipment. For example, in Maruti Omni and Eeco models, for servicing the engine, the front seats of these cars have to be removed as the engine is below the seats. Thus, it is comparatively difficult to perform the maintenance (service) in these models compared to other models of Maruti. At times, the other aspects of designing such as cost, attractive looks, or a special use of the equipment may be more important compared to ease of maintenance, as in case of Maruti Omni and Eeco models.

As was mentioned earlier, breakdowns cannot be completely avoided. The degree of preventive maintenance will vary from equipment to equipment depending upon the criticality or importance of the equipment in the production process. It is thus, necessary to keep inventories of spare parts required for replacement in case of breakdowns and during preventive maintenance schedules. For equipment which are critical in the production process, if the cost permits, a stand-by equipment can be kept so that it may be used during breakdowns of the equipment.

Aging equipment with frequent, costly breakdowns should be considered for replacement by a new one. This decision is affected by technological advancements when the new equipment is more productive. The replacement of old machines by new ones may result in disruptions during installation of new equipment and more training may be required by workers due to its advanced features. Exhibit 10.2 discusses Bajaj Auto's TPM initiative.

---

## Exhibit 10.2    TPM is Bajaj Auto's 'The Prime Mover'

Bajaj Auto Ltd (BAL) started its total productive maintenance (TPM) initiative in 1999 in its manufacturing plants. In March 2007, the Japan Institute of Plant Maintenance (JIPM) adjudged all its manufacturing facilities as 'TPM Excellence Category –1' winners. In 2008, TPM and quality initiatives at its vendor plants gathered further momentum. Since inception of BAL's vendor quality and vendor TPM awards, the tally of quality and TPM award winners is as follows:

1. Quality award 'Bronze': 2009–10: 24 winners (cumulatively, 108)
2. Quality award 'Silver': 2009–10: 30 winners (cumulatively, 89)
3. Quality award 'Gold': 2009–10: 16 winners (cumulatively, 44)
4. Quality award 'Platinum': 2009–10: 3 winners (cumulatively, 3)
5. 'BAL TPM' award: 2009–10: 11 winners (cumulatively, 29)

In other words:

- Over 50 per cent of BAL's vendors have achieved a status of supplying zero defect components to the company's plants for six straight months at least once during last four years (Bronze).
- Almost 40 per cent achieved zero defect supplies for 12 straight months (Silver).
- 25 per cent of the vendors had zero defect supplies for 24 straight months (Gold).
- Three vendors supplied zero defect components for more than 36 straight months (Platinum).

On 7 April 2010, BAL adopted a wider and more encompassing concept of TPM giving it the acronym of 'The Prime Mover' towards excellence—to build and continuously improve its core competencies. With this in mind, BAL created a 'company-wide TPM kick-off'. This initiative, the first of its kind in India, sought to align all key businesses and activities of the company.

BAL's core competencies rest on its values of innovation, perfection, and speed. TPM is expected to build and continuously improve its core competencies, as also its entire supply chain including its suppliers and dealers.

*Source*: Bajaj Auto (2010).

## The Eight Pillars of Total Productive Maintenance

Figure 10.5 shows the eight pillars of total productive maintenance (TPM).

**TOTAL PRODUCTIVE MAINTENANCE (TPM)**

- JISHU HOZEN (Autonomous maintenance)
- KOBETSU KAIZEN (Individual improvements)
- PLANNED MAINTENANCE
- HINSHITSU HOZEN (Quality maintenance)
- DEVELOPMENT MANAGEMENT
- EDUCATION AND TRAINING
- SAFETY, HEALTH, AND ENVIRONMENT
- TPM IN OFFICES

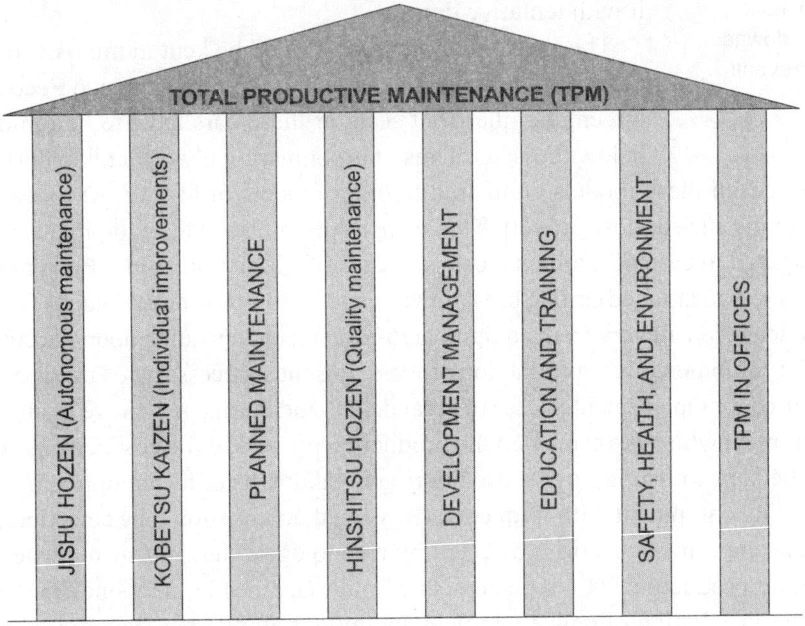

**Fig. 10.5**    The eight pillars of total productive maintenance (TPM)

**Jishu Hozen or autonomous maintenance**    The first pillar is Jishu Hozen (JH), which, in Japanese, means autonomous maintenance. In JH, the workers are taught that cleaning the machine helps in discovering areas of equipment malfunction. The workers are taken to the model machines and explained the procedure of carrying out various activities in cleaning and autonomous maintenance. The first step in JH is the initial cleaning of machines and electrical and electronic parts. During this process of cleaning, if some abnormality is observed (e.g., open wiring in an electrical panel) a red tag is put immediately. The electrician responsible spots the problem and mends the wires at the earliest. The second step involves finding those areas in the machine that are difficult to clean, lubricate, or inspect (such as the insides of machinery parts). Appropriate measures are taken to make changes so as to aid these cleaning, lubricating, and inspecting activities on the machine. For instance, the opaque covering on certain parts can be replaced with transparent ones or can be removed altogether, if possible. Once such parts become clearly visible, efforts are made to eliminate the causes of faults which generate oil leaks, chips, etc. The main objective here is to optimize the machine's working. Machines are rated on criteria ranging from bad to very good on the basis of accessibility for cleaning, lubricating, and inspection in difficult-to-reach areas. The deterioration in the machines can be of two types—natural and forced. The machine operators are trained to look for and eliminate the forced deterioration. In this step, a reducing trend should be shown by the machine cleaning time or the sources of contamination and dirt should be eliminated so that the machines do not require cleaning at all. In the last step of JH, it is examined as to how stickers and other devices can be useful in visual control of the cleaning, lubrication, and inspection process. Visual inspection is necessary to identify areas where malfunction of equipment could take place.

> Kobetsu Kaizen or
> individual improvement
> is to move towards
> zero losses of all kinds.

**Kobetsu Kaizen or individual improvement** Kobetsu Kaizen (KK) or individual improvement is to move towards zero losses of all kinds. Sixteen major kind of losses (such as breakdowns, changeover times, etc.) are identified, their current level calculated, and goals are set for improvement in overall equipment efficiency (OEE).

Each company has to make up their list and collect data. The highest losses will be the priority for the KK pillar. In some companies this list may be different. The following list is an example of such losses.

- Loss no. 2: set-up
- Loss no. 3: tool change
- Loss no. 4: start-up loss
- Loss no. 5: minor stoppages
- Loss no. 6: reduced speed
- Loss no. 9: management loss
- Loss no. 10: operating motion loss
- Loss no. 11: line organization loss
- Loss no. 13: measurement and adjustment loss
- Loss no. 15: tools, jigs, and consumables loss
- Loss no. 16: yield loss

Three major losses can be prioritized in each area to start the work. The objective here is to demonstrate ultimate production efficiency improvement. Kobetsu Kaizen sub-committee comprising seven to eight members and chaired by the plant head is formed, which instructs the project teams to work on specific losses in different machines and areas on a priority basis. In this regard, a master plan is developed in line with the business or factory objectives such as achievement of productivity, quality, costs, delivery, safety, and morale (PQCDSM) targets. Data should be collected for the previous one year before kick-off. The KK committee looks at PQCDSM at the company level and selects areas under each category. An example of this process has been given below.

**P – Productivity/production increase by**
- improvement in OEE of machines,
- improvement in attaining effective man-hours, and
- improvement in labour productivity.

**Q – To bring defects to zero by analysing**
- customer complaints and warranty returns,
- in-house rejections,
- in-house rework, and
- incoming material rejections.

**C – Cost reduction through**
- OEE increase,
- cycle time reduction in bottleneck machines,
- reduction of inventory on cutting tools,
- reduction in consumption of cutting oils, and
- enhancement of tool life.

**D – To maintain delivery performance through**
- OEE increase, and
- improvement of bottleneck machine/process.

**S – To achieve zero accident level by**
- providing training on machine operations,
- identifying unsafe actions and locations and taking corrective actions to avoid accidents,

- motivation of operating personnel through involvement and participation, and
- analysis of accidents happened in the past and near miss accidents through why-why analysis and improved working conditions.

**M – To improve morale of operators through**

- involvement and participation in circle activities, and
- by encouraging generation of kaizens and rewarding for suggestions/improvements carried out.

Usually at least a 5 per cent cost (variable) reduction target should be set as a company objective. Companies should set target for OEE and then set target for P, Q, C, and D. In some cases, P targets are set using takt time calculation or 1.5 times the current production to be achieved in 3 years time. Q targets are set in PPM range and warranty, based on the trend of the last three-years. D target is set for own delivery to customers and also for supplier's performance. Target for safety is zero accidents. Companies should eliminate unsafe actions and locations, and make hand injury zero in the first year. Target for M is in line with the suggestion scheme and any other schemes the organization has, such as QCC, etc. The company-level targets are deployed product-wise and from there on to specific lines and machines. Accordingly, areas of activity with highest losses are given the highest priority. For instance, if the KK sub-committee assigns a task to a project team to reduce set-up time, the machine operators (along with project team members) may study video films recorded during the set-up activity. This study may result in discussions leading to kaizens such as modifying, eliminating, or reducing the elements in the set-up activity. Another example can be reduction of tool change time. Operators detect and inform the early wearing out of tools, and contribute to extending their tool-life.

Cost-benefit analysis can be performed through KK by analysing the data available on each loss. The losses are categorized in the following categories:

- loss of production
- loss of man hours
- loss of material
- loss of energy

Cost-benefit is calculated by evaluating payback periods (e.g., loss on changeover time).

### *Example 10.1*

The calculation of loss on change-over time for a particular type of machine through an evaluation of the payback period has been discussed below.

M/c: MW19, Cell-1(Aluminum), Unit: Actuation, Cell hour rate: ₹5,000

Current changeover time = 3 hrs/changeover

Reduced changeover time = 1 hr/changeover

Saving in the changeover time = (3 – 1) = 2 hr/changeover

No. of changeovers in a month = 10

Total hours saved = 2 hr/changeover × 10 changeovers/month = 20 hours/month

Gross saving is at the rate of ₹5,000, adding up to = ₹5,000 per hour × 20 hours/month = ₹1 lakh per month

Amount spent per variety for achieving reduced changeover = ₹2,000 per changeover

Total amount spent = ₹2000 per changeover × 10 changeovers = ₹20,000

Payback period = (₹20,000)/(₹1 lakh per month) = 0.2 months

Table 10.2 shows the loss-cost matrix for a particular type of machine.

*Rewards for kaizens*   Workers suggesting kaizens can be rewarded either monetarily or non-monetarily. However, the non-monetary awards approach is always considered better.

*Monetary awards*   A spot award of ₹100 can be given to the worker who suggested the kaizen for every kaizen submitted, provided it can be practically implemented and after implementation, an award of 10 per cent of annual saving (max. of ₹20,000) can be given.

*Non-monetary awards*   Grading against P, Q, C, D, S, and M is done for proportionately rewarding kaizens. Monthly kaizen meetings are held to boost the morale of workers suggesting good kaizens. Awards are announced in common forums addressed by the Executive Director or department/unit heads. Presented kaizens are displayed in common places and photographs of the kaizen team who have done the best kaizen for the month are displayed in all units. A rolling trophy for the best kaizens can be instituted. The top 3 kaizens of each quarter should be published in the house journal. Certificates from the CEO and individual recognition through photographs on notice boards are a better approach as compared to monetary rewards.

**Planned maintenance**   The planned maintenance (PM) pillar of TPM has an objective of improving the efficiency of the maintenance department. It comprises the following types of maintenance.

- preventive maintenance
- daily maintenance
- periodic maintenance
- time-based maintenance
- overhauls
- predictive maintenance
- condition-based maintenance (CBM)
- breakdown maintenance
- corrective maintenance

PM helps in extending the life of equipment, stabilizing failures, periodically restoring deterioration, and even predicting equipment life. PM supports the jishu hozen pillar of TPM by encouraging the operators to identify abnormalities and prepare tentative standards for cleaning, lubrication, and inspection by way of on-the-job training of operators.

**Hinshitsu Hozen or quality maintenance**   Hinshitsu Hozen or quality maintenance focuses on setting targets for ensuring the quality of products. These targets can be reduction in process failures, consumer complaints, and retention time of trucks for raw and processed materials and, at the same time, increasing the number of product-related kaizens.

**Early management or development management**   Early management or development management helps in drastically reducing the time taken to receive, install, and set-up newly purchased equipment (known as vertical start-up). Early management can also be used for reducing the time to manufacture a new product in the factory.

> PM helps in extending the life of equipment, stabilizing failures, periodically restoring deterioration, and even predicting equipment life.

**Education and training**   Education and training emphasizes upon 'hard' engineering training, with production operatives becoming familiar with the equipment they operate and gaining the practical skills to operate and maintain it, and with maintenance staff acquiring advanced maintenance skills and predictive maintenance techniques, such as shock pulse monitoring, vibration analysis, oil debris analysis, etc. 'Soft' issue training is needed in the areas of raising awareness of the responsibility of all operatives towards quality, training

**Table 10.2** Loss-cost matrix for particular type of machine

| S. No. | Cost / Losses | Material cost | | Energy/ fuels | Spares | Tool | Consumables | Manhours | | | | Transportation |
|---|---|---|---|---|---|---|---|---|---|---|---|---|
| | | Incoming matl. | In proc ess rej. | Fuel Power | | | | Prodn | Maint. | Quality | Supr. | |
| 1. | Breakdown | | | | | | | | | | | |
| 2. | Set-up | | | | | | | | | | | |
| 3. | Tool change | | | | | | | | | | | |
| 4. | Start-up | | | | | | | | | | | |
| 5. | Shut-down | | | | | | | | | | | |
| 6. | Management | | | | | | | | | | | |
| 7. | Motion | | | | | | | | | | | |
| 8. | Line org. | | | | | | | | | | | |
| 9. | Distribution | | | | | | | | | | | |
| 10. | Meas. and adj. | | | | | | | | | | | |
| 11. | Minor stopp. | | | | | | | | | | | |
| 12. | Speed | | | | | | | | | | | |
| 13. | Defect/rew. | | | | | | | | | | | |
| 14. | Energy | | | | | | | | | | | |
| 15. | Yield | | | | | | | | | | | |

Office TPM focuses on improving the productivity and infusing efficiency in the administrative support functions of the organization by identifying and eliminating losses.

operators to work in teams, and educating all employees about the importance of internal and external customer requirements. The employees are categorized into five levels namely 0 to 4 on the criteria of experience and skill level. A new employee who joined the job recently is categorized in level 0. The level-1 employees are the ones who know what is to be done, but still require extensive exposure and practical training. The level-2 employees are considered reasonably trained, while level-3 are considered proficient. The level-4 employees are capable of training and imparting knowledge to other workers.

**Safety, health, and environment**  The safety, health, and environment (SHE) pillar of TPM strives to achieve the objective of zero accidents and defects and reducing the level of human effort required to attain a given level of production.

**Office TPM**  Office TPM, as the name suggests, focuses on improving the productivity and infusing efficiency in the administrative support functions of the organization by identifying and eliminating losses. The efficiency losses are further broken down into decision-making losses, communication losses, data and document processing losses, etc. Current baselines for office efficiency can be created by using criteria such as time taken in any manual work, inventory turnover ratio, number of places having duplication of work, money spent on communication, and the amount of storage space used in documentation and inventories. On the basis of these criteria, processes and procedures are analysed in order to improve the work efficiency in offices.

**Why-Why analysis**  Why-why analysis was propounded by Taiichi Ohno, the father of Toyota production system. In this concept, Ohno encouraged people to ask five questions starting with 'Why' to get to the root cause of a problem. Why-why analysis is often used in TPM. To illustrate the power of Why-why analysis, Ohno often cited the following example (Ohno 1978):

1. 'Why did the robot stop?'
   The circuit has overloaded, causing a fuse to blow.
2. 'Why is the circuit overloaded?'
   There was insufficient lubrication on the bearings, so they locked up.
3. 'Why was there insufficient lubrication on the bearings?'
   The oil pump on the robot is not circulating sufficient oil.
4. 'Why is the pump not circulating sufficient oil?'
   The pump intake is clogged with metal shavings.
5. 'Why is the intake clogged with metal shavings?'
   Because there is no filter on the pump.
   Action Recommended: Install filter on the pump.

## Summary

Total productive maintenance (TPM) seeks to maximize the effectiveness of equipment throughout its lifetime. It strives to maintain optimal equipment conditions in order to prevent unexpected breakdowns, speed losses, and quality defects arising from process activities. The reactive approach of organizations toward breakdown maintenance is being shifted increasingly to the proactive approach of preventive maintenance. They strive to achieve optimal effort that corresponds to the minimum total cost of maintenance, which is the sum of the cost of preventive maintenance and the cost associated with repairs of sudden breakdowns. The eight pillars of TPM help these organizations in implementing TPM and leveraging its advantages to the fullest. In India, organizations like HUL, Brakes India Ltd, Sundaram Fasteners, TVS Srichakra Ltd. Tata Metaliks Ltd, and Bajaj Auto Ltd have successfully implemented TPM organization-wide.

## References

Bajaj Auto 2010, www.bajajauto.com/report/bal-ar-2009-10.pdf, accessed on 15 March 2013.

Nakajima, S. 1982, *TPM Development Programme*, Productivity Press, Cambridge, MA.

Ohno, T. 1978, *Toyota Production System: Beyond Large Scale Production*, Diamond Inc., Tokyo, Japan.

Suzuki, T. 1994, *TPM in Process Industries*, Productivity Press, Cambridge, MA.

## Keywords

**Hinshitsu Hozen (HH)** or quality maintenance, focuses on setting targets for ensuring the quality of products. These targets may be reduction in process failures, consumer complaints, and retention time of trucks for raw and processed materials and, simultaneously, increasing the number of product related kaizens (suggestions for continuous improvement).

**Jishu Hozen (JH)** is the first pillar of TPM; in Japanese, it means autonomous maintenance. In JH, the workers are taught that cleaning the machine helps into discovering areas of equipment malfunction.

**Kobetsu Kaizen (KK)** or individual improvement is to aim at zero losses of all kinds. Sixteen major kind of losses (such as breakdowns, changeover times, etc.) are identified, their current level is calculated, and goals are set for improvement in overall equipment efficiency (OEE).

**Total productive maintenance (TPM)** seeks to maximize the effectiveness of equipment throughout its lifetime. It strives to maintain optimal equipment conditions in order to prevent unexpected breakdowns, speed losses, and quality defects arising from procss activities.

## CASE STUDY I

## Maintenance Management at Jet Airways

During late 2006, Boeing supplied its innovative, web-based maintenance tool, Maintenance Performance Toolbox (MPT), to three Asian carriers— Jet Airways, Air China, and Nippon Cargo Airlines. Maintenance Performance Toolbox is an award-winning suite of software solutions that is the aviation industry's first set of productivity tools designed to unify an airline's maintenance and engineering operations from start to finish. All three airlines acquired the popular capabilities of MPT, which give airlines quick access to critical maintenance information and the ability to streamline the potentially cumbersome process of customizing online maintenance manuals. In addition, Jet Airways also signed up for tools that will help it generate and automatically track task cards, which are labour-intensive documents required for a wide range of airplane maintenance activities.

Jet Airways' engineering and maintenance facility was set up in 1994 and progressively upgraded to carry out various checks in house including major maintenance up to C check. This is being further upgraded to carry out D check, which is the highest level of check in aircraft maintenance. Its strong engineering team ensures that its aircraft are safe and airworthy at all times at optimal cost to meet on time departures.

Jet Airways' main engineering base is located at Mumbai and its second base is Delhi. It also carries out maintenance activities at its night halting stations at Chennai, Kolkata, and Bangalore. The major maintenance activities, which were earlier performed at Bangalore, are now carried out in its state-of-the-art hangar recently built in Mumbai.

Its engineering team consists of highly qualified and professional engineers, technicians, and other technical services and support staff. The team has proved their competency by achieving the highest dispatch reliability rate (99.2 per cent and above). In recognition, it has received the Boeing Company award for maintaining the 'Best Technical Dispatch Reliability' for the past 2 consecutive years. Jet Airways continues to improve and maintain these standards.

Its maintenance procedures are regulated by the Directorate General of Civil Aviation (DGCA). Regulations framed by the DGCA are based on International Civil Aviation Organization (ICAO) requirements. Its maintenance programmes are based on manufacturers' maintenance planning documents (MPD), which are approved and certified by the DGCA.

The maintenance performed on its aircraft can be divided into three general categories—line maintenance; C or phase 10 checks (C checks); and heavy maintenance checks (D checks). Line maintenance consists of routine, scheduled maintenance checks on its aircraft, including preflight, daily, and overnight checks, and any diagnostic and routine repairs. For instance, C checks for its Boeing aircraft are carried out after a maximum of 4,800 flight hours. These checks take an average of eight days for its Boeing 737 aircraft, and may result in the loss of service of such aircraft for a period of up to 10 days. Heavy maintenance or D checks consist of more complex inspections and servicing of aircraft that require a longer maintenance period. Heavy maintenance checks are performed following a prescheduled agenda of major overhauls defined in an aircraft's manual, which is based on the number of flights flown by the aircraft or the age of the aircraft. A typical D check would result in the loss of service of a Boeing 737 aircraft for approximately 45 days.

Typically, all its line maintenance and C checks are performed by its own experienced technicians. Jet Airways has its own maintenance hangar facility in Mumbai and New Delhi. In addition, it has leased a maintenance facility at Bangalore from Hindustan Aeronautics Limited (HAL) for C checks on its Boeing aircraft. D checks of Boeing aircraft are presently carried out at facilities approved by the US Federal Aviation Administration (FAA) and the DGCA. In fiscal 2006 and 2007, nine and eight Boeing aircraft, respectively, were scheduled to undergo D checks, resulting in the unavailability of approximately one aircraft for the entire duration of such fiscal years. It has established a maintenance hangar complex with workshop and allied facilities at Mumbai that was completed in September 2006. The hangar has been constructed on land leased from the Airports Authority of India (AAI) and provides maintenance and overhaul facilities at Mumbai airport, which is the main base of its operations. The cost of construction

of the maintenance hangar and related workshops and engineering training facilities is US$15 million (₹690 million). The hangar is used for C checks, line checks, storage, and minor rectification of engines and workshops for composite structural repair; it shall include D checks in due course. The construction of the hangar is expected to reduce its maintenance costs and improve its operational efficiency. It has also entered into various contracts in connection with maintenance support for its Boeing 737 fleet, including the following.

- Power by the hour (PBTH) contract with Lufthansa Technik for the repair and maintenance of spares for its Boeing fleet.
- PBTH contract with Israel Aircraft Industries Limited, Bedek Aviation Group, Israel, for the maintenance of auxiliary power units (APU) in its Boeing 737-400 Classic aircraft.
- Contract with Honeywell International Inc., USA, for the repair and overhaul of the APUs in Boeing 737 NG aircraft.
- PBTH contract and technical services contract with MTU Maintenance Hanover GmbH, Germany, for engineering services and engine condition monitoring services in connection with its CFM 56-7 engines in its Boeing 737 NG aircraft.

Jet Airways has a global maintenance agreement and an equipment lease agreement with ATR, the manufacturer of the ATR aircraft, to provide technical support for its ATR 72-500 aircraft. Jet Airways' technical personnel have the capability and required approvals and licences from the DGCA to carry out C checks. All technical personnel are trained by its in-house training programmes (type courses and refresher courses) and also by programmes offered by aircraft and engine manufacturers. These programmes have been approved by the DGCA. It has a quality control division that oversees the compliance of all airworthiness requirements and coordinates with the DGCA for various engineering activities. Its engineering technical services division implements modifications, determines the work scope of repairs and maintenance and plans shop visits for engines and auxiliary power units (APU). This division is also responsible for the engine trend monitoring programme. It has a reliability section that monitors components and analyses defects of systems and components. It also has an engineering planning division that forecasts long-term and short-term maintenance activities. The division is also engaged in optimization of resources and the minimization of the time required for maintaining aircraft. Its technical dispatch reliability, which is the percentage of flights not being delayed for more than 15 minutes for technical reasons, was over 99 per cent for the period 1 January 2004 and 30 November 2004.

*Aircraft Maintenance Costs*
Costs of aircraft maintenance, APU, and engine maintenance and repair are accounted for as incurred, except where such overhaul cost in respect of engines/APU are covered by third-party maintenance agreements and accounted for in accordance with such agreements. From fiscal 2005, Jet Airways has been required to follow Accounting Standard 29 (AS-29) for the treatment of contingent liabilities and estimates, which specifies standards for provisions, contingent liabilities, and contingent assets. Under AS-29,

- *a liability* is a present obligation of the enterprise arising from past events, the settlement of which is expected to result in an outflow of resources, embodying economic benefits, from the enterprise; and
- *a provision* is a liability that can be measured only by using a substantial degree of estimation.

As a result, all the costs associated with heavy maintenance checks of aircraft (for example, D checks) and engines not covered by any third party maintenance contracts are being accounted for as incurred. These costs were provided for in its financial statements at a predetermined rate before 1 April 2004. As an operator of aircraft, Jet Airways is liable for maintaining its aircraft. Its maintenance and repair expenses consist of scheduled and unscheduled maintenance for its aircraft, engines, and other parts. In order to optimize and control maintenance costs, it has entered into long-term and medium-term maintenance contracts, including PBTH contracts for components, APUs, and engines for its Boeing aircraft, and a global maintenance contract with ATR for components for its ATR 72–500 aircraft. Its aircraft currently require a lower level of maintenance relative to airlines with older fleets of aircraft because the average age of the aircraft in its fleet is currently 4.5 years, and many of the parts on its aircraft are under multi-year warranties. As the age of its fleet increases and its warranties expire, its maintenance expenses will increase.

Maintenance and repair costs decreased by 16.6 per cent from ₹1,668 million during the six-month period ended on 30 September 2003 to ₹1,391 million during the six-month period ended on 30 September 2004. This decrease in maintenance and repair costs was primarily due to the introduction of the new accounting standard, AS-29, and the discontinuation of the accrual of certain provisions with effect from 1 April 2004. Under AS-29, certain maintenance costs that were previously accrued on the basis of hours flown are now accounted for on an as incurred basis.

In just over 10 years, Jet Airways has risen to be the number one in India's domestic market with 50 Boeing 737s and has started international services with wide-body aircraft. The carrier has ordered one A330, twelve A350s, and ten 777s in the expectation of owning a fleet of 67 narrow-body aircraft and 22 wide-body aircraft by 2009. Jet Airways is allowed to fly revenue flights abroad, so it gets heavy checks done more economically. Jet Airways sends its 737s for D checks to Singapore and Malaysia.

Jet Airways' chairman Naresh Goyal says the airline now has the critical mass in terms of its fleet size to launch an MRO company. Jet Airways has announced plans to set up its own MRO arm in collaboration with Lufthansa Technik. It has been strengthening its capabilities over the past year to include C checks on 737 NGs and has hired several expatriates, including some from Lufthansa Technik, to spearhead the project. Its first hangar at Mumbai has just been commissioned to move ahead in this direction. The acquisition of Air Sahara by Jet Airways in April 2007 has provided another good reason for the company to set up its own MRO company to service its even larger fleet size (including that of 'Jetlite' as Air Sahara has been rechristened).

## Discussion Questions

1. 'A maintenance strategy involving creation of its own MRO facilities has resulted in higher maintenance costs for Jet Airways compared to its new low-cost rivals such as Air Deccan, SpiceJet, and IndiGo, which outsource their MRO'. Discuss.
2. Why would Lufthansa Technik be interested in helping Jet Airways establish its own MRO arm in India?
3. What steps should Jet Airways take to attract its rivals in India like SpiceJet, Indigo, etc. to utilize its MRO services in place of outsourcing their MRO to foreign orgaizations?

## CASE STUDY II

# Hindustan Unilever Limited

Japan Institute of Plant Maintenance (JIPM) has bestowed its coveted JIPM excellence awards on Hindustan Unilever Limited's (HUL) Sumerpur, Chhindwara, Yavatmal (personal products), and Silvassa (personal products) plants. Dadra and Amli villages near Silvassa are home to the two personal products factories of HUL. The Dadra unit has a production capacity of 5,000 tonnes per annum (tpa) and the Amli unit a capacity of 18,000 tpa. These factories were set up in 1996 and 1997, respectively, and the products manufactured in these factories include fairness creams (Fair & Lovely), lotions, shampoos (Clinic, Clinic All Clear, and Sunsilk—both bottles and sachets), deodorants, talcs (Denim), and toothpaste (Pepsodent). At the Silvassa factories of HUL, the worn-out machine parts are not tossed out to the trash can as in any other factory. The workers collect these failed parts carefully as if these were 'collector's items' from a recently discovered treasure. Formal records of such parts are maintained by the workers and these parts are stored in a specially created 'museum'.

The purpose served by these parts is an opportunity to understand what went wrong leading to the failure of the parts. This understanding helps in modifications of the designing or usage of the parts so that the life of the parts can be extended further. A few years ago, if the factory manager at any of the HUL factories was informed to change the size of Rin bars from 250 gms to 125 gms, he would have shuddered. This meant stopping the production line for a whole shift, resulting in loss of productivity and idle time on part of workers. Today the scene has changed completely with the changeover steps meticulously planned and rehearsed so that a major part of the changeover work is performed even before stopping the production line.

The changeover time has been drastically reduced to 25–30 minutes. A typical example can be of the Amli factory of HUL, where 40 changeovers took place in a 26 week period recently. The concept of seniority at the personal products factory at Daman has seen a transformation. A display board is maintained highlighting the skill level of workers regardless of seniority.

If a senior worker does not know how to align or adjust a particular machine, there is a cross put across his name with respect to this skill on the display board. In order to learn this skill, this worker would have to find his own mentor/trainer who many times may be junior to him. This worker may also have to find co-students in order to make it a feasible group for the training exercise. The result is enhancement of the skill set of workers, irrespective of hierarchy leading to higher productivity and efficiency. At any other factory, purchasing a new machine has a few stereotyped steps such as placing the order for the best machinery, waiting for its delivery at the factory, installation of the machine upon its arrival, and subsequent production. Not any more at HUL factories, where, whenever the need arises for a new machine, a team of employees is sent to the manufacturer of the machinery to suggest design changes in the machine according to the unique requirements of HUL. Also, it is ensured that the new machine starts performing upto the highest efficiency as soon as it is set up, resulting in a huge cost advantage to HUL.

A typical example is demonstrated by HUL's Mangalore facility, where a new form-fill seal machine arrived from the manufacturer during the noon shift and it became fully operational by the night shift. This results in faster payoffs of projects and investments. Outsourcing production to third parties is commonplace in the industry today due to the fact that companies want to concentrate more upon activities such as marketing and distribution that are higher in the value chain. In contrast to this scenario, the HUL factories are gearing up to cut costs so much so that they may bag the most in-house orders.

HUL's Sumerpur factory in Uttar Pradesh has demonstrated outstanding performance in cost cutting so as to win back an in-house order of a particular product, earlier being outsourced to a third party manufacturer. This has resulted in competition within the group factories and cost efficiency. Once upon a time, HUL factories were plagued with trade union troubles. This transformation is a result of three letters: TPM. If you happen to visit any of the HUL factories pursuing TPM, you will find gleaming floors, clearly marked areas for placing raw materials and finished goods inventory, dust covers and sealed areas for polluting substances. The notice boards display details about various improvements brought about by the workers in their areas of activity. At times, you may come across a group of workers discussing further improvements or probable solution for a recently encountered problem. At other times, you may find a mentor conducting a training class for a couple of disciple workers.

**Table 10.3**  TPM costs and benefits over the past three years at HUL

| Manufacturing site | Investment (₹ million) | Benefits (₹ million) |
|---|---|---|
| Silvassa (Personal products) | 15.00 | 210.00 |
| Chhindwara | 8.00 | 24.00 |
| Yavatmal | 6.00 | 60.00 |
| Orai | 4.50 | 60.00 |
| Raipura | 4.20 | 62.00 |
| Mangalore | 6.20 | 111.00 |
| Daman | 10.0 | 139.00 |
| Sumerpur | 2.00 | 23.00 |

Table 10.3 shows the costs and benefits relating to TPM at various factories of HUL. According to HUL officials, TPM is the only business initiative resulting in returns that are 8 to 12 times the investment in the past three years. As seen in this table, the only exception to this norm is the Chhindwara factory, where the returns are 'only' three times the investment. In a typical Indian factory situation, there is almost always a feeling of mistrust between the management and the trade unions. In fact, at HUL, during the initial introduction stage of TPM, the unions considered it as another bargaining lever with the management.

What would the workers get in return if the productivity is increased by a particular amount? It is important to understand the TPM factory organizational structure at HUL. At the top is the corporate TPM-steering committee headed by the HR director. At the next lower level, there is a group comprising the technical heads of HUL, the corporate quality assurance and the TPM head, and the factory managers. Below this level are the 'pillar heads'—to the managers—taking care of each one of the eight pillars of TPM. At the lowest level, there are TPM circles composed by workers and headed by an officer of HUL. Each TPM circle has a unique identity and a name. At the Silvassa unit, there are 20 TPM circles and each worker of the factory belongs to at least one of these circles. The factory-level circles meet once or twice every week, pillar heads meet monthly, and the corporate level meetings take stock of the situation once a quarter. The manager heading a TPM pillar acts as the mentor and the coach. Whenever he notices an abnormality in his area, he has to tag it and come up with one-point lessons (kaizens). These lessons are initially written by TPM circle leaders, in consultation with the workers in his circle. These lessons explain the reasons for the abnormality observed and the know-why associated with it.

At later stages of TPM, the circle leaders encourage the workers to write such one-point lessons, who in turn become the teachers of the future. Over the past few years, HUL has created a pool of 70 odd TPM instructors as if giving itself a status of a 'TPM University', as commented by a team of Japanese auditors sent by JIPM. This intellectual pool has helped HUL to make intelligent deviations from some of the norms set up by JIPM. For example, in the first pillar, jishu hozen (autonomous maintenance), JIPM suggests that there should be a gap of around four to five months in the movement from Step 1 to Step 2. In Step 1, the machines are cleaned and tagged if their condition is not alright so that these may be repaired. In Step 2, these machines are rated from bad to very good on the basis of several parameters.

HUL executives thought that unless Step 2 is performed at the earliest, the machines do not become visibly different in terms of productivity enhancement or wastage reduction so as to enthuse the workers for further improvement. Similarly, JIPM does not recommend the use of office TPM at the preparatory stage of TPM in any organization. HUL had in its view the discounts offered by suppliers if payments are made earlier. HUL knew that 70 per cent of the costs relate to raw materials and processed materials. Therefore, it made no sense not to do TPM in the office—which is where the supplier's bills are processed. An early payment to suppliers requires quicker documentation and here, TPM is of great use to the office employees. In order to replicate the good practices evolved out of kaizens in some of its factories, HUL has created seven-eight knowledge management (KM) teams (equipment-wise). For example, for the form-fill-seal machines used in Chhindwara, Rajpura, and Mangalore, one person was picked from each factory to form a KM team to replicate the good practices elsewhere. Enthused with the results of TPM implementation, HUL management has decided to implement this initiative at every strategic site and all new factories, including Unilever factories in the region.

**Discussion Questions**

1. Why has the TPM programme at HUL overshadowed all other programmes such as TQM?
2. How do you think HUL would have overcome barriers created by trade unions during the introduction of TPM in the organization?
3. Deviating from the norms of JIPM may result in HUL getting disqualified for the JIPM awards in the future. Gve your views.

# Objective Questions

## Choose the correct option

1. TPM stands for
   (a) total precautionary maintenance
   (b) total productive maintenance
   (c) thorough preventive management
   (d) throughput productivity management
2. Jishu Hozen in Japanese means
   (a) breakdown maintenance
   (b) productive maintenance
   (c) quality maintenance
   (d) autonomous maintenance
3. Kobetsu Kaizen in Japanese means
   (a) continuous improvement
   (b) continual improvement
   (c) individual improvement
   (d) team improvement
4. Hinshitsu Hozen in Japanese means
   (a) breakdown maintenance
   (b) productive maintenance
   (c) quality maintenance
   (d) autonomous maintenance

## State True or False

5. A good preventive maintenance programme is based on the prediction of possible breakdown time of equipment so that maintenance may be performed just before the breakdown.
6. At some stage, the cost of repairs may exceed the cost of new equipment suggesting the need for replacement of this poorly maintained equipment.
7. In Kobetsu Kaizen, six major kind of losses are identified, their current level calculated, and goals are set for improvement in overall equipment efficiency (OEE).

## Fill in the blanks

8. _____ focuses on improving the productivity and infusing the efficiency in the administrative support functions of the organization by identifying and eliminating losses.
9. The ease of maintenance should be kept in mind while _____ an equipment.
10. In why-why analysis, _____ questions starting with 'Why' are asked to get to the root cause of a problem.

# Concept Review Questions

1. What is total productive maintenance (TPM)? Enumerate the benefits of maintenance management.
2. What are the two types of maintenance? Explain in relation to the types of maintenance costs.
3. Briefly explain the eight pillars of TPM.
4. Explain the various steps in implementing Jishu Hozen.
5. Give examples of losses to be reduced/eliminated in Kobetsu Kaizen. What are PQCDSM targets? Illustrate with examples.
6. What is office TPM? Is it different from the TPM pursued by manufacturing organizations?
7. Explain why-why analysis by using a suitable example.

# Project Assignment

Visit a hospital in your city to find out what kind of maintenance management systems they have to maintain their medical equipment. Try to figure out which of the eight pillars of TPM they follow knowingly or unknowingly. Also, identify the challenges to be overcome by them for full implementation of TPM there.

## Answers to Objective Questions

| 1. (b) | 2. (d) | 3. (c) | 4. (c) | 5. True |
|--------|--------|--------|--------|---------|
| 6. True | 7. False | 8. Office TPM | 9. designing | 10. five |

# 11

# Aggregate Planning

## Learning Objectives

After reading this chapter, you will be able to answer the following questions:
- What is aggregate production and operations planning?
- What are production planning strategies?
- How is aggregate planning done?
- Is there a relation between the aggregate plan and capacity of a plant?
- Can we make changes in the aggregate production plan when the actual production time is very near?
- How important is vendor relationship management in aggregate planning?
- What are the distribution strategies that can be used in aggregate planning?

## Aggregate Production Planning

Aggregate production planning is planning the number of units of the product to be produced on a weekly or monthly basis for the coming 6–18 months. This plan should be in line with the overall business plan of the company. 'Aggregate' means complete or total. Hence, this plan includes all the various models of the product and gives the complete picture of the future production requirements. The aggregate production plan is based upon the demand forecasts provided by the marketing department.

Aggregate planning is needed to minimize the various types of costs related to unplanned production. Unplanned production leads not only to high costs such as hiring and laying-off costs of workers, overtime costs, inventory costs, etc., but also to shortages of the product (Exhibit 11.1). A shortage or stock out is most harmful to the company, as it results in loss of goodwill on the part of customers. Let us consider an example to understand the relationship between the aggregate production plan and the costs involved as the time horizon of the demand forecasts provided by the marketing department is broadened.

> Aggregate planning is needed to minimize the various types of costs related to unplanned production.

### Example 11.1

Rajasthan Saris is a 100 per cent export-oriented 5,000 million turnover company based at Jaipur. It exports its typical Rajasthani saris to the European countries through a sales agency based at Zurich.

In the last week of October, the sales agency provides a forecast of 2,000 saris for the month of November. In the last week of November, the agency provides the forecast for December as 3,000 saris. A worker produces 100 saris per month. In October, there are 25 workers in the factory. A salary of ₹4,000 per month is paid to a worker. The company has estimated that the cost of hiring a worker

---

## Exhibit 11.1   Boeing

Boeing, the Seattle-based commercial aircraft manufacturer counted on a lean philosophy to restore its tarnished reputation in manufacturing. It revamped its factories in order to gain an edge over its arch-rival Airbus Industrie, the European conglomerate. Boeing had a good order backlog and stable sales and profits, though its manufacturing operations look frayed compared to those of Airbus. In 1997, amid an unprecedented demand for new planes, Boeing tried to double its production overnight. But parts-supply problems and a shortage of workers forced the company to shut down its 747 and 737 assembly lines. Some customers fled to Airbus, and Boeing's commercial-airplane division was smacked with a US$1.6 billion loss, even though it sold a record US$24.5 billion worth of jetliners.

Boeing has learnt a lesson from this bad patch. Cutting waste, shrinking factory space, and eliminating unnecessary inventory are the basic precepts of the lean manufacturing embraced by it. Boeing aimed to use lean manufacturing to compete against Airbus. The goal: a company-wide implementation of gigantic, moving assembly lines—the first of their kind in commercial aircraft history. Such an advance could speed up production by 50 per cent or more and restore profit margins on commercial-plane sales to double-digit levels.

Boeing recognized the potential benefits of moving lines as early as World War II, when it first tested the method on smaller military planes. But scaling up production proved difficult. It succeeded in late 1999 at its Long Beach (California) plant by building its 100-seat 717 aircraft on a 'pulsed' system—a stop-and-go approach that falls just shy of a moving line. Every six days, a 20-tonne cradle pulls the plane in progress a step forward through eight manufacturing stations. At top speed, the plant can put together a 717 in 72 days, one-third quicker than the old way. By next year, when the line speed is increased to a continuous half inch per minute, Boeing can do it in 20 days.

A moving line also depends on engineers creating more standard airplane designs that can be realized with fewer parts. Better design and pre-assembly, meanwhile, require tighter integration with suppliers and just-in-time delivery of parts. Under a lean regime, suppliers also provision the company differently. They spend time on the assembly line with mechanics to figure out more efficient ways to install their parts. Boeing helps out with symposiums, to coordinate schedules with vendors. Suppliers can check the plane maker's master schedule on a web-based procurement system. When a vendor sees that Boeing's inventories have hit a preset minimum, refills can be dispatched automatically. Some suppliers make their own just-in-time daily deliveries to Boeing's storage areas.

The latest showcase for these techniques is Boeing's Renton plant, which assembles the company's highest-volume model, the 150-seat 737 jetliner. A sweeping view of Line No. 2 at the Renton plant shows the results of the revamp. Just next to a row of old-style slanted manufacturing bays, a 737 is tugged by a yellow winch at a rate of two inches per minute. As the unfinished plane creeps along, mechanics stay tethered to the jet. They never leave what they now call the 'circle', which includes the airplane and its assembly cradle. No longer do the workers have to walk long distances to fetch their parts, or travel in the opposite direction to gather their blueprints and tools—rituals that used to wipe out nearly two hours of a mechanic's day. Support people, called 'water spiders', flit in and out of the circle, delivering parts and tools to mechanics who call for them via two-way radio, or through various visual signals.

Paralleling the main assembly line are more than 30 feeder lines, where components are pre-assembled. These staging areas have proved to be big savers of time and cost. For example, mechanics used to take 42 hours to install the 204 parts that make up a 'mixer bay assembly', which circulates and filters the cabin air through a 737. Thanks to the feeder lines, assemblers need to install only 14 parts, and the job is completed in just 16 hours, cutting flow time by 62 per cent. The final target is to cut down by half the current average time from order to delivery, to six months.

(which includes training) is ₹500. The company has to give 20 per cent of the salary as laying-off cost to a worker (when a worker is discontinued from work in the next month). The inventory carrying cost (CC) is ₹10 per sari per month. Prepare the aggregate production plan for the company.

### *Solution*

The first table in Fig. 11.1 shows the production plan prepared by the production manager. In November, 2,000 saris are to be produced according to the forecast provided in the last week of October. Each worker produces 100 saris per month. Therefore, 20 workers are required in November as shown in cell B5 of Fig. 11.1. The total salary to be paid to these 20 workers in November (at the rate of ₹4,000 per worker per month) is ₹80,000 (cell B6). In October, there were 25 workers, while 20 are required in November. Thus, five workers are to be laid off in November (shown in cell B11), for which these workers will be paid a total of ₹4,000 ( = 5 × 800, which is 20% of ₹4,000) as shown in cell B12. The entries in cells B8 and B9 are zero, since no worker is hired in November. There is no inventory in this month, as production is exactly the same as the demand forecast (cells B14 and B15).

| | A | B | C | D | E | F |
|---|---|---|---|---|---|---|
| 1 | **Production plan when forecast is available only one month in advance** | | | | | |
| 2 | Month | November | December | Total Cost | | |
| 3 | Salary | | | | | |
| 4 | No. of units to be produced | 2000 | 3000 | | | |
| 5 | No. of workers required | 20 | 30 | | | |
| 6 | Salary @ ₹4000 per worker | 80000 | 120000 | 200000 | | |
| 7 | Hiring Cost | | | | | |
| 8 | No. of workers hired | 0 | 10 | | | |
| 9 | Hiring cost @ ₹ 500 per worker | 0 | 5000 | 5000 | | |
| 10 | Laying-off Cost | | | | | |
| 11 | No. of workers laid-off | 5 | 0 | | | |
| 12 | Laying-off cost @ ₹ 800 per worker | 4000 | 0 | 4000 | | |
| 13 | Inventory Cost | | | | | |
| 14 | No. of units in inventory | 0 | 0 | | | |
| 15 | Cost @ ₹10 per unit | 0 | 0 | 0 | | |
| 16 | Grand Total of Costs excluding Salary | | | 9000 | | |
| 17 | | | | | | |
| 18 | **Production plan when forecast is available two months in advance** | | | | | |
| 19 | Month | November | December | Total Cost | | |
| 20 | Salary | | | | | |
| 21 | No. of units to be produced | 2500 | 2500 | | | |
| 22 | No. of workers required | 25 | 25 | | | |
| 23 | Salary @ ₹4000 per worker | 100000 | 100000 | 200000 | | |
| 24 | Hiring Cost | | | | | |
| 25 | No. of workers hired | 0 | 0 | | | |
| 26 | Hiring cost @ ₹500 per worker | 0 | 0 | 0 | | |
| 27 | Laying-off Cost | | | | | |
| 28 | No. of workers laid-off | 0 | 0 | | | |
| 29 | Laying-off cost @ ₹800 per worker | 0 | 0 | 0 | | |
| 30 | Inventory Cost | | | | | |
| 31 | No. of units in inventory | 500 | 0 | | | |
| 32 | Cost @ ₹ 10 per unit | 5000 | 0 | 5000 | | |
| 33 | Grand Total of Costs excluding Salary | | | 5000 | | |

**Fig. 11.1**  Aggregate production plan

In the last week of November, the demand forecast for December is 3,000 units (cell C4). Thirty workers will be required for producing these units and a total salary of ₹1,20,000 will be paid to these workers (cells C5 and C6). In November there were 20 workers, and in December 30 workers are required. Therefore, 10 more workers (cell C8) have to be hired, for which a hiring cost of ₹5,000 (at the rate of ₹500 per worker hired) (cell C9) is to be incurred by the firm. The laying-off cost is zero as no worker is laid off in the month of December (cells C11 and C12). There is no inventory, as the number of units produced is exactly the same as the demand forecast (cells C14 and C15). The different total costs are shown in column D, with the grand total of costs excluding salary shown in cell D16 as ₹9,000.

When forecasts for both November and December are available in the end of October, the production manager knows that 2,000 and 3,000 units respectively are to be produced in these two months. He also knows that hiring and laying off workers result in high costs. Thus, he plans for 2,500 units to be produced in November and another 2,500 units in December (see cells B21 and C21 in the second table of Fig. 11.1). The workforce size in October is given as 25 workers. The same workforce can be continued in the months of November and December so that there is no hiring and laying off of workers, and these costs are avoided (cells D26 and D29).

In November, the demand is for 2,000 items, but 2,500 items are produced. The excess 500 units produced form the inventory for November and an inventory cost of ₹5,000 (at the rate of ₹10 per unit per month) is shown in cell B32. In December, these 500 units in inventory will be consumed, as the units produced in this month are 2,500, while the demand is 3,000 units. Thus, in December the inventory and the inventory cost are zero (cells C31 and C32). The grand total of costs excluding the salary is ₹5,000 (cell D33).

Hence, we note that in the two production plans the second plan saves on costs by ₹4,000 (₹9,000 – ₹5,000). The inference is that as the planning horizon is broadened from one month to two months, the total costs tend to fall. Thus, we can expect reduction in costs upon extending the planning horizon to three months, four months, and so on. There is a limit to increasing the planning horizon, beyond which the demand forecasts tend to be more and more inaccurate and the advantages of extending the time horizon fade away. It has been established that the time horizon for production planning should range between 6–18 months for almost all types of industries.

## Steps in Effective Aggregate Planning

Figure 11.2 shows the various steps necessary for aggregate planning to be effective. The aggregate planning process starts with the demand forecast information provided by the marketing department, and the overall business plan provided by the top management. The overall business plan is important for planning future production. For example, the business plan can inform the production manager that the top management wants a huge inventory of finished goods to be accumulated before the coming festive season, despite the demand forecasts for this product not being very good presently. The top management might have some strategies such as aggressive advertising promotion of the product before the festive season, because of which the demand could pick up. Therefore, the production plan prepared by the manager should be in line with this business plan of the company.

As we shall discuss in detail in this chapter, the next step is considering pure planning strategies such as the level output rate plan, chase plan, and varying utilization rate plan. A combination of these pure plans is made, which is called an *intermediate plan*. The intermediate plan is then disaggregated, that is, broken down into smaller time periods, and made to include information on different models of the product. This process of disaggregation gives the *master schedule*.

The next step is the master scheduling process, which requires three inputs—the master schedule, the beginning inventory status, and the customer orders committed so far. Three outputs are generated by this process, namely, the tentative master production schedule (MPS), the projected on-hand inventory

> The aggregate planning process starts with the demand forecast information provided by the marketing department and the overall business plan provided by the top management.

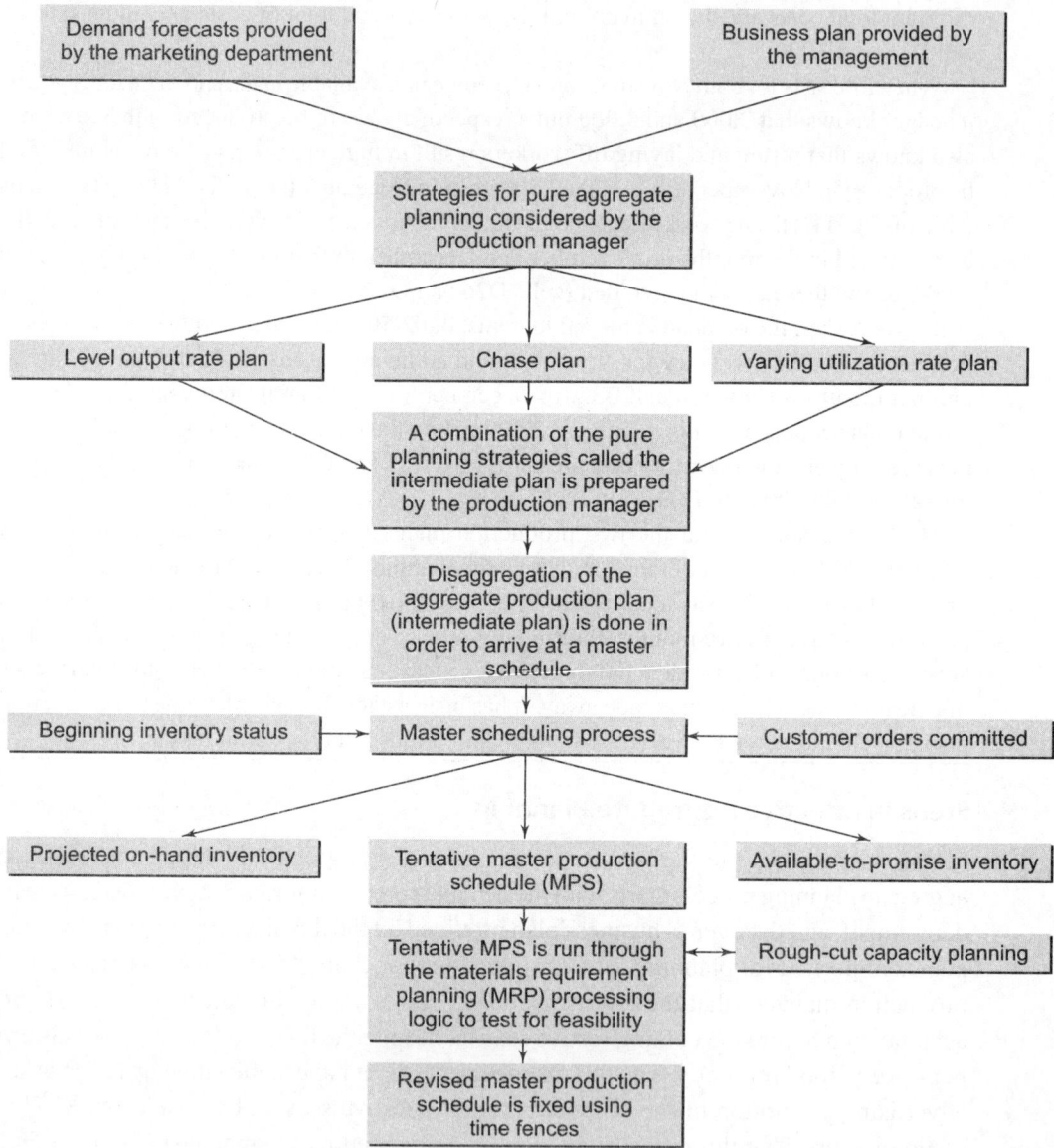

**Fig. 11.2** Steps in the effective aggregate planning process

(inventory available for the next planning period), and the available-to-promise inventory (the number of units the sales personnel can still commit to the customers).

The tentative MPS is run through the materials requirement planning (MRP) software to check the feasibility of the MPS with respect to the available capacities of production in the company as well as those of the suppliers. This process of checking the feasibility of the master schedule with respect to the available capacity is called *rough-cut capacity planning*. The MPS may require some modifications according to the available capacities and the revised MPS is fixed using time fences. The MPS cannot be changed near the actual

> This process of checking the feasibility of the master schedule with respect to the available capacity is called rough-cut capacity planning.

production time. If changes are made at this stage, the whole exercise of production planning will become useless. Therefore, the production managers set various time intervals called time fences to regulate changes in the MPS.

Go through Exhibit 11.2 to know about the production problems related to Airbus' ambitious A380 aircraft.

---

### Exhibit 11.2 Airbus A380

The A380 aircraft is the most ambitious project of Airbus SAS till date. The mammoth-sized double-deck airplane is so large that few airports over the world have runways that can accommodate the aircraft's landing and take-off. Touted by Airbus as the world's biggest and most advanced commercial passenger aircraft, the A380 can seat as many as 840 passengers. This is, however, one project which presented Airbus with a myriad of unforeseen production problems and embarrassing delays. These delays incurred severe monetary penalties to Airbus to be paid to those airline companies that had placed orders for the A380 superjumbo. On a wider scale, the production difficulties revealed deep organizational and structural problems that dealt a blow to Airbus' reputation.

Originally conceived as a European contender to usurp the traditional US dominance of the aviation market, the European Aeronautic Defence and Space Company (EADS) formed Airbus Industrie to challenge the supremacy of Boeing. The company, however, suffers from chronic stalemate, as its German and French partners grapple for power and influence in the aviation and space group, which also produces helicopters, military aircraft, and weapons systems.

The image of EADS was tarnished by a series of mishaps since the maiden test flight of the A380 superjumbo in 2005. Top executives were ousted and a massive restructuring plan was put into action that resulted in 10,000 job cuts over four years. The setbacks cost the company billions in profits and saddled Airbus with its first-ever operating loss in 2006. Until the company resolves its problems with the A380, Airbus will be crippled and unable to launch any major new projects—and this at a time when management should be turning its attention to the new 350 jet, a product meant to compete with Boeing's new, long-range, fuel-efficient 787 Dreamliner.

Amid revelations of management errors, technical woes, and huge severance payments for departing executives, it was revealed that the CATIA computer tool used in the airplane's digital design was not sufficiently accurate when it came to designing electrical systems. The problem was made worse by Airbus' switch to aluminium wiring when the model was designed for copper wiring, which has different physical properties. According to Airbus officials, the complexities were exacerbated due to extensive customization made by different airlines to airplane interiors. Other problems detected on Airbus' A380 superjumbo included problems with sections of the fuselage.

The manufacturing process adopted by Airbus for creating its planes is scattered across four countries in Europe, namely, France, Germany, Spain, and the UK. Production of the airline parts in different countries creates a logistical nightmare, especially since the various components have to be transported to landlocked Toulouse in France, for final assembly. Due to all these obstacles Airbus has been forced to delay delivery of its A380 by more than a year.

In November 2010, one of the A380 in service with Quantas caught fire in one of its engines immediately after take-off from Singapore, thus putting a big doubt over the performance of the plane. Its engine manufacturer Rolls-Royce was on the firing line due to the possibility of design flaws.

In yet another blow to Airbus, hairline cracks were discovered on the wings of in-service A330 planes of Emirates Airlines in January 2012. The root cause of the cracks, which are unusual in a new fleet of aircraft, was found to be unforeseen stresses on the wings during the manufacturing process and not due to any design flaws. Airbus had to undertake inspection of all the A380s in operation in order to regain trust of its airline customers. However, these incidents benefited Boeing—the arch rival of Airbus. As Fig. 11.3 shows, Airbus has a lot of catching up to do in order to fulfil its outstanding orders of A380 to various airlines.

*(Contd)*

*Exhibit 11.2 Contd*

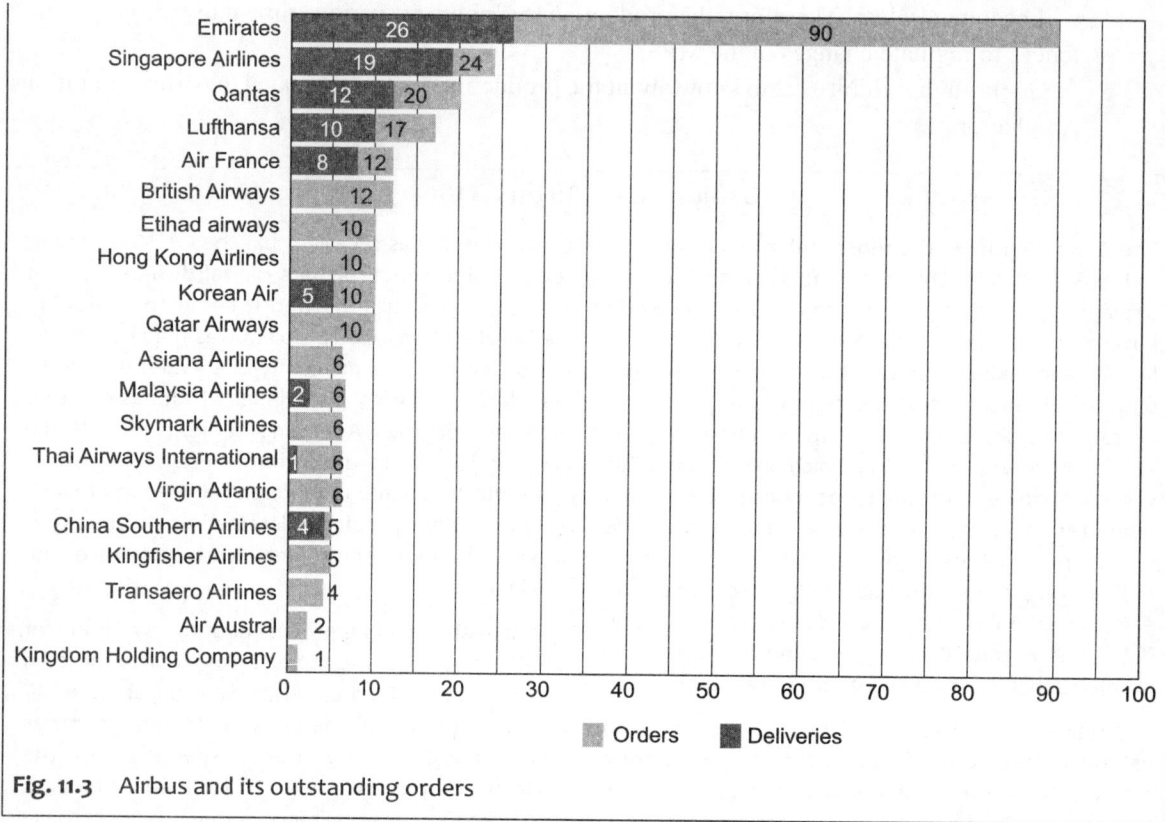

**Fig. 11.3** Airbus and its outstanding orders

## Production Planning Strategies

The basic production planning strategies are based upon three variables: workforce size, utilization of workers, and inventory size. In each one of these strategies, one variable is varied and the other two are kept constant. The following are three basic production planning strategies.

### Level Output Rate Plan

The inventory size is varied keeping the workforce size and utilization of workers constant. The number of workers (workforce size) is kept constant throughout the time period under consideration. During months of low demand, the excess units produced over demand are accumulated as inventory. During the months of high demand, the units required over the units produced are taken from the inventory. The advantage of this plan is that the cost of hiring and training new workers is zero. Also, the cost of laying off workers is zero, as the workforce size is constant. The employee morale is high due to a sense of job security. During periods of low demand, there is a high inventory cost due to its large size.

> In the inventory, size is varied keeping the workforce size and utilization of workers constant.

### Chase Plan

The workforce size is varied according to demand, keeping the utilization of workers and inventory size constant. During months of low demand, the

<table>
<tr><td>In the varying utilization plan, utilization of workers is varied keeping the workforce size and inventory size constant.</td></tr>
</table>

workforce size is decreased and the extra workers are laid off. Similarly, during months of high demand, more workers are hired. The hiring and laying-off costs are substantial in this plan. The worker's morale is also low due to a sense of insecurity. The production of items is in tune with the demand requirements, thus the inventory is almost negligible. Therefore, the inventory cost is also negligible. During the months of heavy demand, overtime may be required on the part of workers, for which the company incurs overtime cost.

## Varying Utilization Plan

The utilization of workers is varied keeping the workforce size and inventory size constant. The number of workers is kept constant in this plan. During the months of low demand, the workers produce less so as to match the demand, and they have a lot of idle time. On the other hand, during the months of high demand, the excess units required over regular production are produced by overtime on the part of workers. The idle time on the part of workers during months of low demand is a loss to the company, which pays full wages to its employees. On the other hand, the company incurs overtime costs during periods of high demand. Overtime is usually expensive compared to the regular wages given to workers. In addition, excess overtime leads to less efficiency on the part of workers and more accidents due to lack of concentration. Still, the company saves on inventory costs, which are almost negligible, in this plan.

These basic planning strategies should preferably not be used in isolation from each other, as each one of these has typical drawbacks. A combination of these strategies is used in preparing the aggregate production plan. Let us understand how to use a combination of these strategies in Example 11.2.

### Example 11.2

PC Mark (P) Ltd is a personal computer assembling company based at Hyderabad. Its marketing department has given the demand forecast shown in row 4 of Fig. 11.4 for its PCs throughout the country in the coming six months from January to June. Every worker assembles two computers a day. The overtime cost is ₹3 per day per unit in excess of the maximum capacity of the factory, that is, 200 units. The company wants to find the total cost involved in the following plans: (a) level output rate plan, (b) chase plan, and (c) an intermediate plan (a combination of level output rate and chase plans).

*Level output rate plan* We have to first determine the optimum size of the workforce. Row 5 in Fig. 11.4 shows the cumulative demand in the various months. The demand in a month is added to the total demand till the previous month. In row 6, we find the number of working days in the various months. Row 7 shows the cumulative number of days in various months. Note that in row 8 we have calculated the number of units to be produced to meet the demand obtained by dividing the demand forecast for a month by the number of working days in that month. For example, in cell B8 of the spreadsheet, we have put the formula **=B4/B6**, which yields 41.66667 and is approximated as 42 units in cell B9 of the next row 9. Similarly, other values of the rows 8 and 9 are calculated.

Now plot a curve between cumulative demand (in units) (plotted along the *y*-axis) and the cumulative number of working days (plotted along the *x*-axis). The first point to be plotted is (24,1000), the second point is (49,4000), and so on (Fig. 11.5). These points are joined to form the *cumulative demand curve*. Next, draw a straight line starting from the origin and touching the cumulative demand curve such that the whole of this curve remains under the line. This line is a tangent to the cumulative

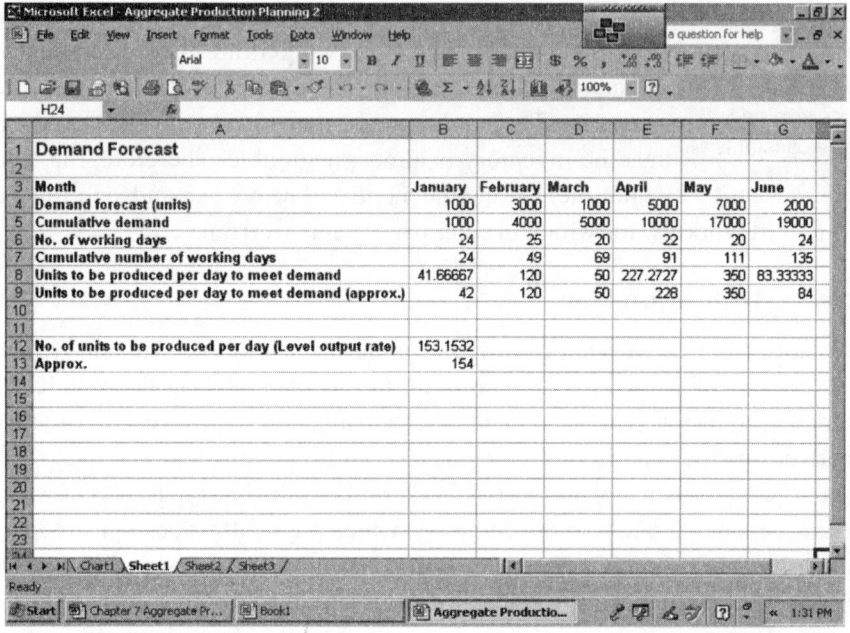

**Fig. 11.4** Demand forecast

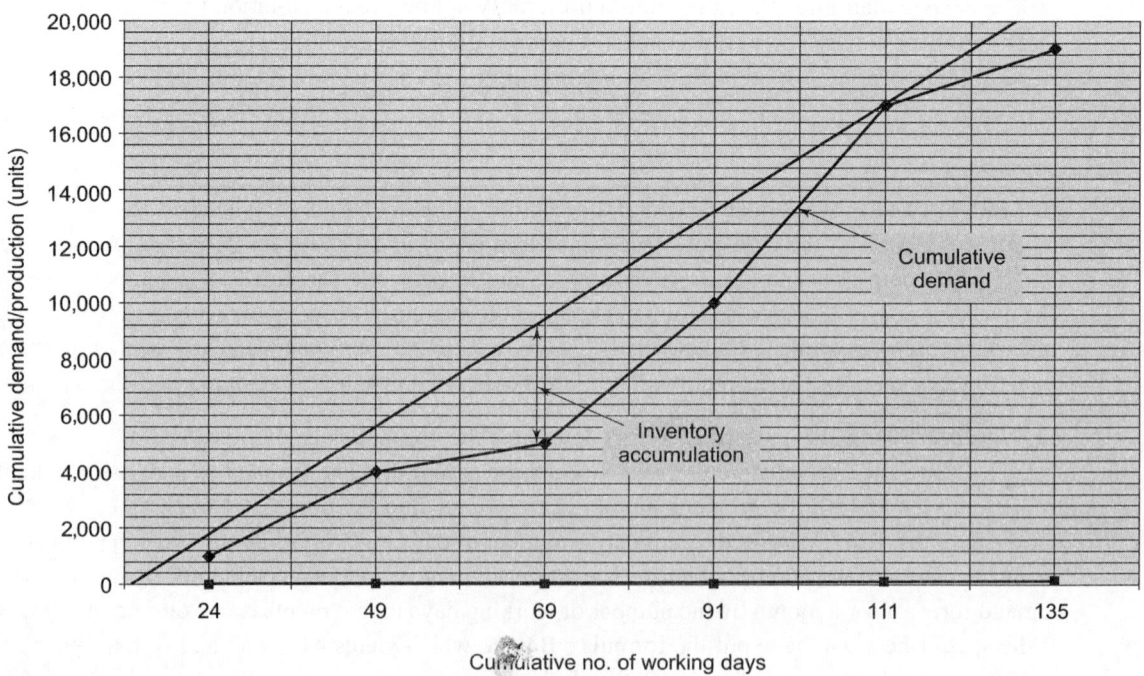

**Fig. 11.5** Cumulative demand vs cumulative number of working days

demand curve. We call this curve the *cumulative production curve*. The cumulative production curve is always above the cumulative demand curve, because at any point of time the production will always be more than demand, ensuring no shortages at all. As shown in Fig. 11.5, the vertical distance between the two curves represents the inventory accumulation at that point of time. Notice that at 111 cumulative days, the inventory accumulation is zero, that is, whatever inventory was accumulated earlier has become zero. After 111 cumulative days, the inventory again starts to build up.

Let us find the slope of the cumulative production curve. This slope represents the rate of production (in units per day). The point (111,17,000) lies on the cumulative production curve. Slope of a straight line is determined as follows:

$$\text{Slope} = \frac{\text{Change in } y\text{-direction}}{\text{Change in } x\text{-direction}}$$

We will use the $x$ and $y$ coordinates of the point (111,17,000) as the changes in $x$ and $y$ directions, respectively. Thus, in cell B12 of Fig. 11.4 we have used the formula = **F5/F7** to get the level output rate as 153.1532, which is approximated as 154 units in cell B13. Every worker assembles two units of PCs every day. Therefore, if 154 units are to be produced per day every day from January to June, 77 workers (154/2) are required per day (constant workforce sze).

Let us now calculate the cost involved in the level output rate plan. Figure 11.6 shows the demand forecast in row 4 and the number of working days in each month in row 5. Note that in row 6, the output rate is shown as 154 units per day for every month. The output in every month can be calculated by multiplying the output rate with the number of working days in the month. In row 7, for example, cell B7 contains the formula =**B5\*B6**. Thus, the output in January is 3,696 units. Similarly, the output in other months is calculated as shown in Fig. 11.6.

Row 8 contains the beginning inventory of every month, row 9 contains the net additions (or subtractions) to (or from) the inventory, and row 10 contains the ending value of the inventory for

| | A | B | C | D | E | F | G | H |
|---|---|---|---|---|---|---|---|---|
| 1 | **Level Output Rate Plan** | | | | | | | |
| 2 | | | | | | | | |
| 3 | **Month** | January | February | March | April | May | June | |
| 4 | **Demand forecast (units)** | 1000 | 3000 | 1000 | 5000 | 7000 | 2000 | |
| 5 | **No. of working days** | 24 | 25 | 20 | 22 | 20 | 24 | |
| 6 | **Output Rate (units/day)** | . 154 | 154 | 154 | 154 | 154 | 154 | |
| 7 | **Output (units)** | 3696 | 3850 | 3080 | 3388 | 3080 | 3696 | |
| 8 | **Beginning Inventory** | 0 | 2696 | 3546 | 5626 | 4014 | 94 | |
| 9 | **Net Addition (or Subtraction)** | 2696 | 850 | 2080 | -1612 | -3920 | 1696 | |
| 10 | **Ending Inventory** | 2696 | 3546 | 5626 | 4014 | 94 | 1790 | |
| 11 | **Average Inventory** | 1348 | 3121 | 4586 | 4820 | 2054 | 942 | 16871 |
| 12 | | | | | | | | Total |

**Fig. 11.6**   Level output rate plan

a given month. For January, assume the beginning inventory to be zero. In this month, the units demanded are 1,000, while the units produced are 3,696. Thus, net additions to the inventory in January are 2,696 units (3,696 − 1,000). Thus cell B9 contains the formula **=B7−B4**. The ending inventory in a month is the sum of the beginning inventory and net additions (or subtractions) to the inventory. In January, the ending inventory is 2,696 units (0 + 2,696); cell B10 contains the formula **=B8+B9**. Row 10 contains the average inventory for the various months. The average inventory in a given month is given by

$$\text{Average inventory} = \frac{\text{Beginning inventory} + \text{Ending inventory}}{2}$$

In January, the average inventory is given in cell B11 using the formula **=(B8+B10)/2**, and the result is 1,348. Note that in any given month the beginning inventory is the same as the ending inventory of the previous month. Therefore, in February the beginning inventory is the same as the ending inventory of January (cell C8 contains the formula **=B10**). The calculations for all the months are done as explained for the month of January. In cell H11, we have found the sum of the average inventories from January to June; cell H11 contains the formula **=SUM(B11:G11)**. The result is 16,871 units. The inventory CC is given as ₹2 per unit per year. Therefore, for six months the CC will be ₹1 per unit. In the level output rate plan, the total average inventory is 16,871 units. The total CC will be ₹16,871 for this plan. There is no other type of cost associated with this plan. Hence, the total cost of the level output rate plan is ₹16,871.

***Chase plan*** In this plan, the production output is planned so as to follow the demand forecasts in every period. In every period (say, month), the number of units planned for production are in accordance with the number of units demanded according to forecasts. This is why this plan is called the *chase plan*. In Fig. 11.4, we had calculated the approximate number of units to be produced per day to meet the demand in various months in row 9. For example, in January 42 units are to be produced per day. Every worker assembles two PCs a day. Therefore 21 workers are required per day in the month of January. Similarly, in February 60 workers are required per day to assemble 120 units of PCs, and so on. Note that this change in the output rate every month will result in hiring and laying off workers, leading to extra costs. The cost of changing the output rate is given in the second table in Fig. 11.7. When the output rate in a month changes by 1–100 units per day compared to the previous month, the hiring, training, and laying off costs are estimated at ₹2,000. Similarly, these costs are ₹5,000 for output rate changes in the range 101–200, and so on.

Now let us do the cost calculations for the chase plan. Figure 11.7 shows the output rate required in the various months to meet the demand requirements in row 6. In January, the output rate is 42 units per day. Therefore the output in January is 1,008 units (42 units per day × 24 days in January), as shown in cell B7. Note that the output is 8 units more than the demand of 1,000 units in January. This is because of our approximation, while computing the output rate, of 41.66667 units to 42 units. These extra 8 units produced will be the net additions to the inventory as shown in cell B9. In January, assume the beginning inventory to be zero (cell B8). Thus, the ending inventory in January is 8 units (0 + 8). The average inventory is 4 units. Similarly, find the average inventories for various months. The total average inventory is shown in cell H11 as 92 units. Thus, the inventory CC (at the rate of ₹1 for six months) is ₹92 according to the chase plan.

Row 12 in Fig. 11.7 shows the change in output rate in a given month compared to the previous month. For example, assume that in January, the change in output rate is 0. In February, the output rate required is 120 units per day as shown in cell

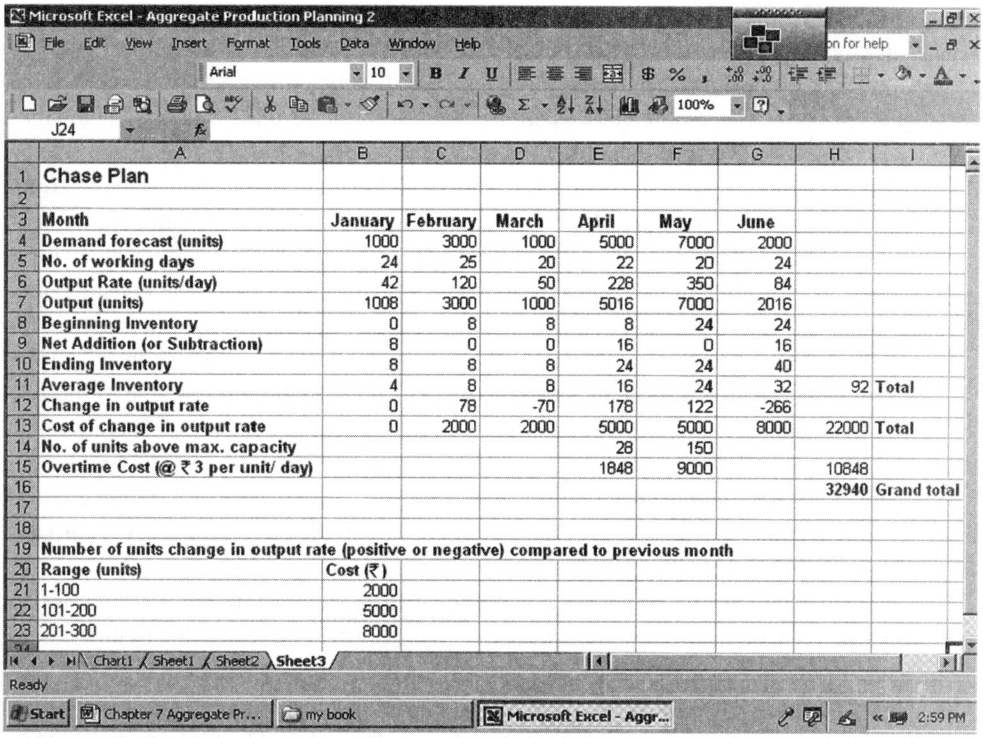

**Fig. 11.7** Chase plan

C6, while in January it is 42 units per day. Thus, the change in output in February is 78 units (120 – 42). In cell C12, put the formula =**C6–B6**. The change of 78 units in the output rate falls in the range 1–100 units. Therefore, from the second table in Fig. 11.7 the cost of change in the output rate is ₹2,000 for the month of February, as shown in cell C13. Similarly, find the costs of change in output rate for other months and then sum up these in cell H13 by putting the formula =**SUM(B13:G13)** to get ₹22,000. Note that there are two months, namely, April and May, in which the output rate is more than the maximum capacity of the plant, that is, 200 units.

The limited number of machines, equipment, and manpower does not allow production beyond the maximum capacity of the plant. Therefore, the workers are required to work overtime, for which they charge overtime cost from the company. The overtime cost is ₹3 per unit short per day in a given month. In April, the output rate is 28 units more than the 200 units of maximum capacity. The overtime cost in April is ₹1,848 (₹3 per unit per day × 22 days × 28 units) as shown in cell E15. In this cell, enter the formula =**3\*E5\*E14** to get the result 1,848. Similarly, find the overtime cost in May as ₹9,000 in cell F15. In cell H14, find the sum of all the overtime costs using the formula =**SUM(B15:G15)** and get the result 10,848. In the end, we find the grand total of costs for the chase plan in cell H16 by selecting cells H11 to H16 and then clicking on the Σ button on the Excel toolbar. The result is ₹32,940, which is much higher than ₹16,871, the total cost of the level output rate plan.

*Intermediate plan*　　We have seen that in the chase plan, despite negligible inventory cost, the cost of change in the output rate and the overtime cost led to a high overall cost. On the other hand, in the level output rate plan, the inventory cost is very high despite there being no overtime cost and cost of change in the output rate. Now try an *intermediate plan*, which is a combination of the earlier two plans. We know that frequent changes in the output rate result in high costs, therefore we will change

The intermediate plan is a combination of the chase plan and the level output rate plan.

the output rate in the new plan only once. We also know that producing more than the maximum capacity of 200 units is costly in the form of overtime cost. Hence, in the new plan we will ensure that the output rate is always within this limit.

In the chase plan, notice that in the first three months, January, February, and March, the output rate required to meet the demand is much less compared to the next three months. Thus, in April, May, and June, keep the output rate at the maximum capacity of 200 units in the intermediate plan shown in Fig. 11.8. During the months of January, February, and March, let us keep the output rate at 100 units and see the result. The total inventory cost shown in cell H11 is only ₹4,350. The output rate changes only once during the considered time horizon in the month of April, resulting in a cost of ₹2,000. The total cost of the intermediate plan is ₹6350.

Note that the ending inventory in May is negative at ₹–1,700 as shown in cell F10. This represents a shortage or backlog of orders by customers, which are highly undesirable as these lead to not only loss of potential profit but also loss of goodwill on the part of customers. Therefore, we need to make slight changes in the output rate. We cannot increase the output rate in April, May, and June, as these are already at the maximum capacity of the plant and any increase here will lead to overtime costs, which we want to avoid. Therefore, increase the output rate in the months January, February, and March to 125 units per day; the new intermediate plan is shown in Fig. 11.9.

Note that now there is no ending inventory with a negative value. The cost of this plan is ₹14,212.5, which is less than that of the level output rate plan (₹16,871) and also that of the chase plan (₹32,940). Thus, this intermediate plan is the best among the three plans considered here. The output rates in the various months of the intermediate plan are to be decided subjectively by trial and error. Therefore, there is a lot of variation possible in the total cost of the plan. The planner should try to find the plan with the least total cost, but one that does not lead to any further significant reduction in cost is also appropriate.

| | A | B | C | D | E | F | G | H | I |
|---|---|---|---|---|---|---|---|---|---|
| 1 | **Intermediate Plan** | | | | | | | | |
| 2 | | | | | | | | | |
| 3 | Month | January | February | March | April | May | June | | |
| 4 | Demand forecast (units) | 1000 | 3000 | 1000 | 5000 | 7000 | 2000 | | |
| 5 | No. of working days | 24 | 25 | 20 | 22 | 20 | 24 | | |
| 6 | Output Rate (units/day) | 100 | 100 | 100 | 200 | 200 | 200 | | |
| 7 | Output (units) | 2400 | 2500 | 2000 | 4400 | 4000 | 4800 | | |
| 8 | Beginning Inventory | 0 | 1400 | 900 | 1900 | 1300 | -1700 | | |
| 9 | Net Addition (or Subtraction) | 1400 | -500 | 1000 | -600 | -3000 | 2800 | | |
| 10 | Ending Inventory | 1400 | 900 | 1900 | 1300 | -1700 | 1100 | | |
| 11 | Average Inventory | 700 | 1150 | 1400 | 1600 | -200 | -300 | 4350 | Total |
| 12 | Change in output rate | 0 | 0 | 0 | 100 | 0 | 0 | | |
| 13 | Cost of change in output rate | 0 | 0 | 0 | 2000 | 0 | 0 | 2000 | Total |
| 14 | No. of units above max. capacity | | | | | | | | |
| 15 | Overtime Cost (@ ₹ 3 per unit/ day) | | | | | | | 0 | |
| 16 | | | | | | | | 6350 | Grand total |
| 17 | | | | | | | | | |
| 18 | | | | | | | | | |
| 19 | Number of units change in output rate (positive or negative) compared to previous month | | | | | | | | |
| 20 | Range (units) | Cost (₹) | | | | | | | |
| 21 | 1-100 | 2000 | | | | | | | |
| 22 | 101-200 | 5000 | | | | | | | |
| 23 | 201-300 | 8000 | | | | | | | |
| 24 | | | | | | | | | |
| 25 | | | | | | | | | |
| 26 | | | | | | | | | |
| 27 | | | | | | | | | |
| 28 | | | | | | | | | |
| 29 | | | | | | | | | |
| 30 | | | | | | | | | |
| 31 | | | | | | | | | |

**Fig. 11.8** Intermediate plan

**Fig. 11.9**   New intermediate plan

| | A | B | C | D | E | F | G | H | I |
|---|---|---|---|---|---|---|---|---|---|
| 1 | Intermediate Plan | | | | | | | | |
| 2 | | | | | | | | | |
| 3 | Month | January | February | March | April | May | June | | |
| 4 | Demand forecast (units) | 1000 | 3000 | 1000 | 5000 | 7000 | 2000 | | |
| 5 | No. of working days | 24 | 25 | 20 | 22 | 20 | 24 | | |
| 6 | Output Rate (units/day) | 125 | 125 | 125 | 200 | 200 | 200 | | |
| 7 | Output (units) | 3000 | 3125 | 2500 | 4400 | 4000 | 4800 | | |
| 8 | Beginning Inventory | 0 | 2000 | 2125 | 3625 | 3025 | 25 | | |
| 9 | Net Addition (or Subtraction) | 2000 | 125 | 1500 | -600 | -3000 | 2800 | | |
| 10 | Ending Inventory | 2000 | 2125 | 3625 | 3025 | 25 | 2825 | | |
| 11 | Average Inventory | 1000 | 2062.5 | 2875 | 3325 | 1525 | 1425 | 12212.5 | Total |
| 12 | Change in output rate | 0 | 0 | 0 | 75 | 0 | 0 | | |
| 13 | Cost of change in output rate | 0 | 0 | 0 | 2000 | 0 | 0 | 2000 | Total |
| 14 | No. of units above max. capacity | | | | | | | | |
| 15 | Overtime Cost (@ ₹3 per unit/ day) | | | | | | | 0 | |
| 16 | | | | | | | | 14212.5 | Grand total |
| 17 | | | | | | | | | |
| 18 | | | | | | | | | |
| 19 | Number of units change in output rate (positive or negative) compared to previous month | | | | | | | | |
| 20 | Range (units) | Cost (₹) | | | | | | | |
| 21 | 1-100 | 2000 | | | | | | | |
| 22 | 101-200 | 5000 | | | | | | | |
| 23 | 201-300 | 8000 | | | | | | | |

# Disaggregating the Aggregate Plan

The aggregate plan gives information about production requirements in general terms, as it includes different models of the product in the number of units to be produced. No specific information is given by the aggregate plan as to how many units of different models of the product are to be produced. Different models of the product may, in general, require common parts and components, but some parts may be specific to the models. Some models may also require specific labour skills for their processing. Thus, for materials and labour planning of different models, information about what quantity of different models is to be produced is required. The aggregate plan is an intermediate planning stage, and in the next stage the aggregate plan is to be disaggregated (broken down into parts) to include information about the different models of the product to be produced.

### Master Schedule

*The master schedule shows the quantity and timing of specific end items for a time horizon, often spanning six to eight weeks.*

A master schedule is the result of the disaggregation of an aggregate plan. The master schedule shows the quantity and timing of specific end items for a time horizon often spanning six to eight weeks. In a master schedule, the time horizon is divided into many time periods usually expressed in weeks. The time periods in a master schedule called *time buckets* may not be equal throughout the time horizon considered. The time periods in the near future may be smaller (say,

*Courtesy:* BMW. Used with permission.

The completely robotized welding of the motor compartment of a car at the Spartanburg plant (USA) of BMW. The motor compartment is the first step of the X5 production line, where the options and build sequence of each X5 are confirmed.

in weeks) than the time periods in the distant future (say, in quarters or months). The master schedule is more and more tentative for the distant future than that for the near future.

There is no upper limit on the duration of the time horizon for a master schedule, but there is a lower limit. The duration of the time horizon has to cover at least the cumulative lead time of production of end items. For example, if the production of an end item requires three days for procurement of raw materials, four days for manufacturing components, two days for putting together sub-assemblies, and one day for the final assembly, the cumulative lead time will be 10 days. Thus the master schedule must cover a time horizon of 10 days.

The aggregate plan covers a duration between 6–18 months, while the master schedule covers a few weeks to two or three months. Thus, the aggregate plan is disaggregated in phases or parts into the master schedule. The master schedule may be revised on a monthly basis in order to accommodate any changes in the actual demand being experienced in comparison to the demand forecast. For example, if the actual demand in January for an end item turns out to be far less than the demand forecast for January, leading to accumulation of excessive inventory, the master schedule for February and March may be updated or revised to incorporate changes in the planned output.

**Rough-cut capacity planning**　The initial master schedule is tentative in nature, as in reality the capacity of the production system may not be able to support its practical implementation. Thus, the initial master schedule must be run through the MRP system as a trial to check whether sufficient production capacities, such as machines, equipment, labour, warehouses, capacities at the supplier's end, etc., exist or not. If the available capacities are not sufficient to support the master schedule, either the

> There is no upper limit on the duration of the time horizon for a master schedule.

schedule can be revised to match the production capacities, or the production capacities expanded. For example, the workers may be required to do overtime, or the number of production shifts may be increased. Subcontracting some of the work to outside vendors is another means of temporarily satisfying the master schedule requirements. This process of checking the feasibility of the master schedule with respect to the available capacity is called *rough-cut capacity planning*.

## Master Production Schedule

The master schedule provides details about the quantities and delivery timings of a product, but not the production plan. For example, if according to the master schedule, 1,200 cars of a particular model are to be delivered to the customer in week 1 and 1,000 cars of the model are already in the inventory, then only 200 units have to be produced in this week. On the other hand, if there are 1,500 units of this model of the car in the inventory, there may be no requirement of any production in this week.

The MPS gives details about the quantities and timing of the planned production of a product. It is derived from the master schedule by taking into account the inventory status of the product in a given time period.

Refer to Example 11.1. Let us assume that the master schedule for saris for the eight weeks during the two-month period is as shown in row 5 (represented by demand forecast here onwards) of Fig. 11.10. Note that the sum of master schedule values in the first four weeks (in January) is

### Master Production Schedule (MPS)

|  | week 1 | week 2 | week 3 | week 4 | week 5 | week 6 | week 7 | week 8 |
|---|---|---|---|---|---|---|---|---|
|  | | January | | | | February | | |
| Demand Forecast (units) | 300 | 200 | 100 | 500 | 800 | 900 | 600 | 700 |
| Customer Orders (committed) | 350 | 100 | 50 | 300 | 400 | | | |
| Initial inventory in period week 0 = 500 units | 500 | | | | | | | |
| Net inventory before MPS | 150 | -50 | 850 | 350 | -450 | -350 | 50 | -650 |
| Master Production Schedule (MPS) | | 1000 | | | 1000 | 1000 | | 1000 |
| Projected on-hand inventory | 150 | 950 | 850 | 350 | 550 | 650 | 50 | 350 |

### Master Production Schedule (MPS) with Available-to-promise Inventory

|  | week 1 | week 2 | week 3 | week 4 | week 5 | week 6 | week 7 | week 8 |
|---|---|---|---|---|---|---|---|---|
|  | | January | | | | February | | |
| Demand Forecast (units) | 300 | 200 | 100 | 500 | 800 | 900 | 600 | 700 |
| Customer Orders (committed) | 350 | 100 | 50 | 300 | 400 | | | |
| Initial inventory in period week 0 = 500 units | 500 | | | | | | | |
| Net inventory before MPS | 150 | -50 | 850 | 350 | -450 | -350 | 50 | -650 |
| Master Production Schedule (MPS) | | 1000 | | | 1000 | 1000 | | 1000 |
| Projected on-hand inventory | 150 | 950 | 850 | 350 | 550 | 550 | 50 | 350 |
| Available-to-promise inventory (ATP) (uncommitted) | 150 | 550 | | | 600 | 1000 | | 1000 |

**Fig. 11.10** Master production schedule

1,100 units and in the next four weeks (in February) is 3,000 units, according to a new aggregate plan made by the operations manager. Row 6 shows the orders already committed to the customers in the coming few weeks, row 7 shows the inventory in week 0 as 500 units. This inventory will be available at the beginning of week 1. Let us assume that the lot size of manufacture is 1,000 units, that is, in each production run 1,000 units of saris are produced.

In row 8, we calculate the net inventory before the MPS. For example, in week 1 the inventory on hand is 500 units (cell B7), while the maximum demand is 350 units (the higher one out of the demand forecast and customer orders committed to). Thus, the net inventory before the MPS is the difference between the two, that is, 150 units (500 – 350). Projected on-hand inventory is the inventory available for the next period (week). In week 1, the projected on-hand inventory is the same as the net inventory before MPS, that is, 10 units.

In week 2, the available inventory is 150 units. The demand forecast of 200 units is greater than the 100 units of customer orders committed. Thus, the net inventory before MPS is—50 units (150 – 200). To avoid this shortfall, a new lot of 1,000 units will be produced in week 2 (cell C9) so that the projected on-hand inventory (available for the next week) is 950 units (1,000 – 50). The rule of thumb is that whenever the net inventory before the MPS becomes negative, a new lot of items is scheduled for production in the MPS of that time period.

In week 3, the available inventory is 950 units. The demand forecast of 100 units is greater than the 50 units of customer orders committed. Thus, the net inventory before the MPS is 850 units (950 – 100). The same 850 units are available for the next period and form the projected on-hand inventory for week 3. In week 4, the available inventory is 850 units. The demand forecast of 500 units is greater than the 300 units of customer orders committed. Thus, the net inventory before the MPS is 350 units (850 – 500). The same 350 units are available for the next period and form the projected on-hand inventory for week 4.

In week 5, the available inventory is 350 units. The demand forecast of 800 units is greater than the 400 units of customer orders committed. Thus, the net inventory before the MPS is—450 units (350 – 800). To avoid this shortfall, a new lot of 1,000 units will be produced in week 5 (cell F9) so that the projected on-hand inventory (available for next week) is 550 units (1,000 – 450).

In week 6, the available inventory is 550 units. The demand forecast is 900 units and there are no customer orders committed to so far. Thus, the net inventory before the MPS is—350 units (550 – 900). To avoid this shortfall, a new lot of 1,000 units will be produced in week 6 (cell G9) so that the projected on-hand inventory (available for next week) is 650 units (1,000 – 350).

In week 7, the available inventory is 650 units and the demand forecast is 600 units. Thus, the net inventory before the MPS is 50 units (650 – 600). The same 50 units are available for the next period and form the projected on-hand inventory for week 8.

In week 8, the available inventory is 50 units. The demand forecast is 700 units and there are no customer orders committed to so far. Thus, the net inventory before the MPS is—650 units (50 – 700). To avoid this shortfall, a new lot of 1,000 units will be produced in week 8 (cell 19) so that the projected on-hand inventory (available for next week) is 350 units (1,000 – 650).

**Available-to-promise inventory** It is necessary for sales personnel to know how many units of the product at maximum they can commit to customers in a given time period. Available-to-promise inventory gives them this information (Exhibit 11.3). In Fig. 11.10, the second table shows the calculations of available-to-promise inventory. In week 1, the inventory available from

The master produc-
tion schedule cannot
be changed near the
actual production time.

the previous period is 500 units. The customer orders booked in this week are 350 units. Thus, the difference between the two, that is, 150 units (500 – 350), is the available-to-promise inventory.

Apart from the first period in which the initial inventory is available from previous week, available-to-promise inventory is found for only those periods in which an MPS value is scheduled. In week 2, the MPS is of 1,000 units. There is no MPS for the next two periods (weeks 3 and 4). The customer orders in weeks 2, 3, and 4 are 100, 50, and 300 units, respectively (shown in the shaded cells C22, D22, and E22). These orders upon summing up are 450 units. The available-to-promise inventory in week 2 can be determined by subtracting these 450 units from the scheduled MPS of 1,000 units. Thus, the available-to-promise inventory in week 2 is 550 units (1,000 – 450).

In week 5, the committed customer orders are 400 units and the MPS is 1,000 units. Note also that in week 6 the MPS is of 1,000 units. Therefore, in week 5, for finding the available-to-promise inventory, we need to use only the customer orders in week 5. The available-to-promise inventory in week 5 is 600 units (1,000 – 400). Similarly, in week 6 the MPS is of 1,000 units, but there is no customer order committed in this week as well as in week 7. Hence, the available-to-promise inventory in week 6 is 1,000 units (1,000 – 0). Finally, the available-to-promise inventory in week 8 is also 1,000 units (1,000 – 0) as the MPS in this week is of 1,000 and no customer orders are committed.

**Time fences**  The MPS cannot be changed near the actual production time. If changes are made at this stage, the whole exercise of production planning will become useless. Therefore, production managers set various time intervals called *time fences* to regulate changes in the MPS. For example, three time fences may be fixed at time intervals of one, two, and three months. Before three months of the actual production time, any changes in the MPS may be made. Between two and three months (time fences), product models may be substituted, provided the required components are available. Between the time fences of one month and two months, changes are avoided, but minor ones may still be permitted. The last fence of one month before actual production takes place is strictly frozen, that is, no changes are allowed during this time.

## Exhibit 11.3  Volvo Wheel Loaders

Volvo Wheel Loaders (VWL) is mainly a make-to-order company, which assembles equipment called *wheel loaders* used in construction work for moving material from one place to another. VWL has a plant at Eskilstuna in Sweden, where it assembles the models Volvo L50 and Volvo L70. It has another plant at Arvika, where it assembles five more models of wheel loaders. VWL is a part of the Volvo Construction Equipment (VCE) group of the Volvo Corporation. The components required by VWL for assembling are supplied by another company within VCE called Volvo Construction Equipment Components AB (VCEC) based at Eskilstuna. VCEC manufactures axles, transmissions, and frames for wheel loaders, and many other components for Volvo

factories in Brazil and the US.

After every quarter of a year, the marketing department of VCE provides new market forecasts for the coming 15 months based upon estimates provided by the selling companies and the distributors. A delivery plan, or the sales programme, is prepared from these forecasts every month by a team comprising officials from the marketing department of VCE, aggregate planning managers from the two plants of VWL, and one official from Volvo Construction Equipment Cabs AB in Hallsberg, where cabins and hydraulic cylinders are produced. A manufacturing plan is made from the delivery plan by the aggregate planning manager,

*(Contd)*

*Exhibit 11.3 Contd*

| | A | B | C | D | E | F | G | H | I | J | K |
|---|---|---|---|---|---|---|---|---|---|---|---|
| 1 | **MPS for option 95821 for weeks 5 to 12 at week 5** | | | | | | | | | | |
| 2 | | | | | | | | | | | |
| 3 | Week | week 5 | week 6 | week 7 | week 8 | week 9 | week 10 | week 11 | week 12 | week 13 | week 14 |
| 4 | Forecasted Balance (MPS) | 1 | | | | | | | | | |
| 5 | Forecast MPS | 2 | 3 | 1 | 1 | 4 | 3 | 5 | 2 | 1 | 3 |
| 6 | Real customer orders | 0 | 2 | | | | | | | | |
| 7 | | | | | | | | | | | |
| 8 | | | | | | | | | | | |
| 9 | **MPS for option 95821 for weeks 7 to 14 at week 7** | | | | | | | | | | |
| 10 | | | | | | | | | | | |
| 11 | Week | week 7 | week 8 | week 9 | week 10 | week 11 | week 12 | week 13 | week 14 | week 15 | week 16 |
| 12 | Forecasted Balance (MPS) | 4 | | | | | | | | | |
| 13 | Forecast MPS | 1 | 1 | 4 | 3 | 5 | 2 | 1 | 3 | 4 | 1 |
| 14 | Real customer orders | 0 | 1 | | | | | | | | |
| 15 | | | | | | | | | | | |
| 16 | | | | | | | | | | | |
| 17 | **MPS for option 95821 for weeks 9 to 16 at week 9** | | | | | | | | | | |
| 18 | | | | | | | | | | | |
| 19 | Week | week 9 | week 10 | week 11 | week 12 | week 13 | week 14 | week 15 | week 16 | week 17 | week 18 |
| 20 | Forecasted Balance (MPS) | 2 | | | | | | | | | |
| 21 | Forecast MPS | 4 | 3 | 5 | 2 | 1 | 3 | 4 | 1 | 2 | 0 |
| 22 | Real customer orders | 3 | 1 | | | | | | | | |
| 23 | | | | | | | | | | | |

**Fig. 11.11**   MPS Volvo Wheel Loaders

taking into consideration the number of working days, utilization of workers, and the required safety stock inventory. This manufacturing plan is reworked into batches of units to be produced on a weekly basis, and this becomes the concrete MPS.

Hundreds of variants of wheel loaders are possible, with variations in air conditioning, seats, hydraulic equipment, transmissions, load buckets, etc. The MPS consists of the two standard models of wheel loaders and several hundreds of pieces of special equipment (which are called 'nine numbers' as their ID numbers begin with the number 9 and these are product structures for some special equipment or option). There is a problem with these changeable product structures: they sometimes lead to double reservation of materials. For example, there is an option which makes it possible to move the load bucket horizontally and another option making it move vertically. Each of these options requires a fastening plate assembled on the grip arm. If a customer wants both these options together, only one fastening plate is required and not two. This problem is overcome by VWL by a manual cancellation or the addition of a wrong inventory record.

The MPS is updated by VWL regularly as given in the Excel worksheet in Fig. 11.11. Let us assume that the MPS for the 10-week period of an option, say, 95821 (note the 'nine number'), is as shown in the first table. The total lead time for this option is, say, 8 weeks. Thus, at week 5 the MPS up to week 12 is fixed, that is, the forecasted MPS values during this period cannot be increased or decreased in any week. Any increase in the MPS value during this period will lead to a suggestion of raw material purchases in the past weeks (before week 5), and if according to this MPS customer orders are booked, this will lead to delays in delivery to customers if the suppliers of raw materials take the normal lead time. Any decrease in the forecasts in this period may result in delays in the delivery of real orders booked by the customers, due to less units assembled.

At the beginning of week 5, the forecasted balance (excess units remaining due to less real customer orders than the forecasted MPS in the previous weeks) is 1. In week 5, the forecasted MPS is 2 units, but the actual orders from the customers turn out to be 0. Thus, the forecasted balance for week 6 becomes 3 units. During

*(Contd)*

*Exhibit 11.3 Contd*

week 6, the forecasted MPS was 3 units, but the real orders received are 2 units. Thus, again the forecasted balance increases by 1 unit and is now 4 units. The planner has to decide now whether or not to reduce this forecasted balance (which acts as a buffer stock now) in the coming weeks. A large buffer unnecessarily ties up the capital while a small or zero buffer may lead to stock outs (worse customer service). Let us assume that the planner decides that the buffer is alright. The second table in the worksheet shows that at week 7, the forecasted balance is kept at 4 units.

At the beginning of week 7, again the real orders received are 0 while the forecasted MPS is 1 unit. The forecasted balance thus increases again by 1 unit and

becomes 5 units. At the beginning of week 8, the real orders exactly match the forecasted MPS at 1 unit. Thus, at the end of week 8 (beginning of week 9) the forecasted balance remains at 5 units. Let us assume that the planner now feels that the buffer of 5 units is on the higher side and reduces it to 2 units at the beginning of week 9 (as shown in the third table). According to this revised MPS, the requirement of raw materials/components in the near future has decreased. Therefore, the open orders of components, etc. according to the MRP (based upon the earlier MPS) should be postponed. The planned orders to start within the next four days (the remaining part of the lead time of eight days from week 5) should be released as open orders.

## Vendor Relationship Management

Developing and maintaining healthy working relationship with vendors (players in the upstream supply chain—towards the end raw material supplier) is an aspect critical to the success of the aggregate plans of an organization. Vendors and buyers need to have trust in each other so as to fulfil their expectations. Many organizations today are trying to develop relationships with vendors so as to transform them into 'business partners' closely linked to the success of their enterprise. Chakraborty and Philip (1996) identified three variables in defining the relationship construct between vendors and buyers. Let us understand these three variables:

**Task structure**    As the relationship between the buyer and the vendor grows, the tasks assigned to the vendor for execution become less structured in nature due to increasing confidence of the buyer on the vendor's capabilities. In highly structured task environments, the buyer provides detailed specifications of the tasks to be carried out by the vendor, including vendor's role, responsibilities, and benefits of compliance to the prescribed specification. However, in an unstructured task environment, the buyer provides generic requirements to be fulfilled by the vendor, while leaving the detailing part to be taken care of by the vendor himself. Clearly, in such an environment, a lot of trust is reposed in the vendor to find his own ways in accomplishing the desired results from the part, component or sub-assembly to be supplied by him.

For example, while designing the famous Scorpio model of their car, Mahindra & Mahindra utilized extremely close relationships with their major vendors. For the vendor, who was entrusted with the task of designing a suitable air-conditioning system for the car, they just provided generic requirements—say, the air conditioner should be capable of bringing down the temperature inside the cabin of the car from 40° Celsius to 20° Celsius in 5 minutes. Normally, automakers provide detailed specifications like the air conditioner should have four vents and should throw air at the speed of 10 metres per second. Thus, in case of Scorpio, vendors demonstrated highest level of craftsmanship, which is now evident in the humungous success of the car in the Indian and international markets.

**Length of the contract**    The length of the contract which buyers enter with their vendors is another important variable in determining the relationship between them. A long-term contract (duration would vary from industry to industry) would naturally imply a strong relationship between the buyer and the vendor. It would indicate the mutual trust they repose in each other. The average model life cycle of the product (how long a model of a product would survive in the market place on an average) is often used to determine the duration of a long-term contract. In the automotive industry, the average model life cycle is about four years. Thus, contracts to vendors given for four or more years are treated as long-term.

For example, Bharti Airtel has entered into long-term contracts with Nokia, Siemens, and Ericsson for creating and maintaining the telecom network infrastructure for Airtel. Similarly, it has engaged the services of IBM through long-term contracts for providing IT-related infrastructure and support.

Long-term contracts are a typical feature of Japanese organizations, while traditionally, American organizations preferred short-term contracts with their suppliers. Long-term contracts help the Japanese organizations in exercising better control over their vendors in ensuring on time (just-in-time) deliveries with highest quality standards.

**Selection of vendors**  The level of trust, confidence, and comfort between the buyer and the vendor is determined by the selection procedure followed before awarding the contract to a vendor. Vendor relationship with the buyer would be deemed as strong when the buyer deploys less formal/less structured procedures in vendor selection. There are three types of selection methods used, which are as follows.

*Open tendering*  In this method, any possible vendor is allowed to bid for the tender opened by the buyer. Generally, the lowest bidder is selected in open tendering as cost is the primary criterion of vendor selection here.

*Closed tendering*  Only the approved vendors of the buyer organization are allowed to bid for the tender in the closed tendering method. The vendors are approved on the basis of past experiences of the buyer with them. The selection criteria are usually cost and the past experience with the vendor.

*Direct selection*  This method of direct selection is used when the buyer is absolutely confident that there is only one supplier that is best suited for supplying a particular component or part. Here, the buyer organization approaches the vendor directly with a proposal. It is up to the vendor to accept or deny such an invitation.

From the aforementioned methods of supplier selection, it is evident that the direct selection method denotes the closest relationship between the vendor and the buyer.

## Types of Distribution Strategies

Aggregate planning should also consider the downstream players (towards end customer) in the supply chain and the distribution strategies to supply the finished goods to them. Three types of outbound distribution strategies are used, as follows.

**Direct shipment**  As the name of this distribution strategy suggests, here the transportation of goods takes place directly from the manufacturer to the retailer, thus bypassing the distributor or wholesaler. Clearly, in this scenario there would be a major saving in terms of not creating/ maintaining a distribution centre and the lead time would be reduced drastically as there is no major stopping point en route from the manufacturer to the retailer. However, the transportation cost may tend to rise as the manufacturer may have to send separate trucks filled with goods (some of which may not be fully loaded) to several retailers in different directions. This issue can be overcome if the retailers involved are big enough to order full-truck loads every time, which is true for prominent retail chains such as Big Bazaar and Reliance Mart. In fact, it may be these very retailers that may force the manufacturer to use the direct shipment distribution strategy in order to satisfy their demand for shortest possible lead time. It may be a genuine need on part of retailers dealing in perishable commodities like groceries.

**Cross-docking**   In this distribution strategy, trucks from different manufacturers with different goods arrive at the cross-dock at the same time to redistribute goods amongst each other according to the requirements of the respective retailers they are supposed to supply to. This redistribution of goods takes place within a short duration of time, say within a few hours at the cross-dock. Clearly, this distribution strategy requires seamless coordination between the manufacturers, the transporter (logistics provider), the retailers, and the cross-dock manager. Real-time flow of information between all these players is a must for making this distribution strategy successful. The retailers should provide point-of-sale data to the manufacturers and the logistics provider with exact requirements for every product. The scheduling of trucks has to be done in such a way that they reach the cross-dock more or less at the same time for exchanging the goods carried by them as per the requirements of the retailers. It must be kept in mind that this approach of cross-docking is useful when a large number of big retailers are being processed simultaneously to justify full-truck loads reaching them. For example, Trans Systems Ltd is the logistics provider for Toyota's plant at Bidadi near Bangalore. It has two cross-docking facilities—one at Gurgaon and the other at Pune.

**Transshipment**   Transshipment involves transfer of goods between facilities at the same level in the supply chain. For example, two or more retailers may transfer goods between each other depending upon the requirement. If one retail store is facing a stock-out for a particular product, it may source it from another nearby store belonging to the same retail chain. It requires real-time visibility of inventory levels at any store, which is not difficult to achieve in today's times when information technology aids in a big way. Transshipment requires availability of one or more small transport vehicles to allow movement of goods in small quantities between these facilities or for direct delivery to the customer's home, who went back without getting the desired product from the store. In this distribution, a virtual risk-pool is created by considering the combined inventory of nearby retail stores as a single warehouse/distribution centre. Naturally, this distribution strategy is not possible between retail stores belonging to competitors. For example, Trust chain of medical stores in Bangalore provides the facility of home delivery of medicines, which are not readily available in a particular store. This store checks the availability of the medicine with the other nearby Trust store and arranges to get it from there for delivery to the customer's door.

# Summary

*Aggregate production planning* is planning the number of units of the product to be produced on a weekly or monthly basis for the coming 6–18 months. It is required to minimize costs such as worker hiring and laying-off costs, inventory costs, overtime costs, etc. Various pure planning strategies such as level output rate plan, chase plan, and varying utilization plan are available for preparing the aggregate plan. In practical situations, though, a combination of these pure planning strategies is used.

A *master schedule* is the disaggregation of an aggregate plan, as it includes information about the number of various models and sub-models of a product required in a given duration. The master schedule shows the quantity and timing of specific end items for a time horizon often spanning six to eight weeks. The duration of a master schedule is much less than that of the aggregate plan. The process of checking the feasibility of a master schedule with respect to the available capacity is called *rough-cut capacity planning*.

The master schedule provides details about the quantities and delivery timings of a product, but not the production plan. A *master production schedule* (MPS) gives details about the quantities and timing of the planned production of a product. It is derived from the master schedule by taking into account the inventory status of the product in a given time period. *Available-to-promise inventory* provides the sales personnel with information about how many units of a product they can commit to customers in a given time period according to the MPS. *Time fences* are used to establish periods of varying flexibilities for making changes in the MPS.

It is important to manage relationships with the upstream as well as downstream partners in the supply chain for successful aggregate planning. Similarly, suitable distribution strategies for downstream partners in the supply chain should be considered as part of aggregate planning.

# References

Chakraborty S. and T. Philip 1996, 'Vendor development strategies', *International Journal of Operations and Production Management*, vol. 16, no. 10, pp. 54–66.

Paul, J. and A. Mukherjee 2004, 'ATMs and cash demand forecasting: a study of two commercial banks', *International Conference on Applied Business Research*, Thailand, Bangkok, 1–4 December.

Segerstedt, Anders 2002, 'Production and inventory control at ABB Motors and Volvo Wheel Loaders, two examples of MRP in practical use', *Production Planning and Control*, vol. 13, pp. 317–325.

Sinha, G.P., B.S. Chandrasekaran, N. Mitter, G. Dutta, S.B. Singh, A.R. Choudhury, and P.N. Roy 1995, 'Strategic and operational management with optimization at Tata Steel', *Interfaces*, vol. 25, no. 1, pp. 6–19.

Tata Steel 2005, Presentation to Fund Managers and Analysts on 12 September 2005, http://www.tatasteel.com images Presentation_to_Fund_Managers_ and_Analysts_on_12th_ Sep'05.ppt, accessed on 2 March 2007.

# Keywords

**Aggregate production planning** is planning the number of units of the product to be produced on a weekly or monthly basis for the coming 6–18 months. This plan should be in line with the overall business plan of the company.

**Available-to-promise inventory** provides the sales personnel with information about how many units of a product they can commit to customers in a given time period according to the MPS.

**Chase plan** is a pure planning strategy in which the workforce size is varied according to demand, keeping the utilization of workers and inventory size constant.

**Level output rate plan** is a pure planning strategy in which the inventory size is varied, keeping the workforce size and utilization of workers constant.

**Master production schedule (MPS)** gives details about the quantities and timing of the planned production of a product.

**Master schedule** is the result of the disaggregation of an aggregate plan. The master schedule shows the quantity and timing of specific end items for a time horizon often spanning six to eight weeks.

**Rough-cut capacity planning** is the process of checking the feasibility of the master schedule with respect to the available capacity.

**Time fences** are various time intervals set by production managers to regulate changes in the MPS.

**Transshipment** involves transfer of goods between facilities at the same level in the supply chain.

**Varying utilization plan** is a pure planning strategy in which the utilization of workers is varied, keeping the workforce and inventory size constant.

## Jamsetji Tata and Tata Steel—the Saga of Great Indian Pride

Jamsetji Nusserwanji Tata is one of the most revered names in the history of Indian business. An illustrious industrialist, nationalist, humanist, and the founder of the Tata group, Jamsetji Tata was a first generation entrepreneur who established Tata Steel, the country's first integrated steel plant.

Nothing of Jamsetji's childhood suggested he would create his own destiny. Born on 3 March 1839, in the sleepy town of Navsari in Gujarat, he was the first child and only son of Nusserwanji Tata, the scion of a family of Parsi priests. Many generations of the Tatas had joined priesthood, but the enterprising Nusserwanji broke the mould by becoming the first member of the family to try his hand at business.

Raised in Navsari, Jamsetji joined his father in Mumbai, what was known as Bombay then, at the age of 14. Nusserwanji got him enrolled at Elphinstone College, from where he passed out in 1858 as a 'green scholar', the equivalent of today's graduate. The liberal education he received would fuel in Jamsetji a lifelong admiration for academics and a love of reading. Those passions would soon take a backseat to, what Jamsetji quickly understood was the true calling of his life, business.

In 1868, at the age of 29 and wiser from the experience garnered by nine years of working with his father, Jamsetji started a trading company with a capital of ₹21,000. The budding entrepreneur was by now accustomed to the fickleness of business life, being witness to the failure of his father's banking enterprise. This episode blighted his first visit to England, where he was besieged by creditors. However, Jamsetji also learned a lot on this trip, most significantly, about the textile business.

Jamsetji's maiden expedition to England, and others that he made in subsequent years, convinced him that there was tremendous scope for Indian companies to make a dent in the then prevailing British dominance of the textile industry. Jamsetji started his textiles business in 1869. He acquired a dilapidated and bankrupt oil mill in Chinchpokli in the industrial heart of Mumbai, renamed the property as Alexandra Mill, and converted it into a cotton mill. Two years later, Jamsetji sold the mill for a significant profit to a local cotton merchant.

Jamsetji believed he could take on and beat the colonial masters at a game they had rigged to their advantage. The prevailing wisdom of the time dictated that Mumbai was the place to set up the new project, but Jamsetji's genius told him otherwise. He figured he could maximize his chances of success if he factored three crucial points into his plans—close proximity to cotton-growing areas, easy access to a railway junction, and plentiful supplies of water and fuel. Nagpur, near the heart of Maharashtra's cotton country, met all these conditions. In 1874, Jamsetji had floated a fresh enterprise, the Central India Spinning, Weaving and Manufacturing Company, with a seed capital of ₹15 million. Three years later, his venture was ready to realize its destiny. On 1 January 1877, the day Queen Victoria was proclaimed the Empress of India, the Empress Mills came into existence in Nagpur. At the age of 37, Jamsetji had embarked on the first of his fantastic odysseys.

The period following the establishment of Empress Mills was the most significant of Jamsetji's busy life. In hindsight, it was also the most poignant. From about 1880 to his death in 1904, Jamsetji was consumed by the three great ideas of his life—setting up an iron and steel company, generating hydroelectric power, and creating a world-class educational institution (Indian Institute of Science Bangalore) that would tutor Indians in the sciences. None of these would materialize while Jamsetji's lived, but the seeds he laid, the work he did, and the force of will he displayed in fulfilling his dreams ensured they would find glorious expression.

The iron and steel idea got sparked when Jamsetji, on a trip to Manchester to check out new machinery for his textile mill, attended a lecture by Thomas Carlyle. By the early 1880s he had set his heart on building a steel plant that would compare with the best of its kind in the world. This was a gigantic task. The industrial revolution that had transformed Britain and other countries had, by and large, bypassed India. Officious government policies, the complexities of prospecting in barely accessible areas, and sheer bad luck made matters worse. Jamsetji found his path blocked at every other turn by what his biographer, Frank Harris, called 'those curious impediments which dog the steps of pioneers who attempt to modernize the East'.

The torturous twists and turns the steel project took would have defeated a lesser man, but Jamsetji remained steadfast in his determination to see the venture come to fruition. Along the way he had to suffer the scorn of people such as Sir Frederick Upcott, the Chief Commissioner of the Great Indian Peninsular Railway, who promised to 'eat every pound of steel rail (the Tatas) succeed in making'. There is no record of where Sir Frederick was when the first ingot of steel rolled out off the plant's production line in 1912. Jamsetji had been dead eight years by then, but his spirit, as much as the efforts of his son Dorab and cousin R.D. Tata, made real the seemingly impossible.

The brick-and-mortar endeavours that Jamsetji planned and executed were but one part of a grander idea. How much of a man of the future he was can be gauged from his views about his workers and their welfare. Jamsetji offered his people shorter working hours, well-ventilated workplaces, and provident fund and gratuity long before they became statutory in the West. He spelled out his concept of a township for the workers at the steel plant in a letter he wrote to Dorab Tata in 1902, five years before even a site for the enterprise had been decided. 'Be sure to lay wide streets planted with shady trees, every other of a quick-growing variety,' the letter stated. 'Be sure that there is plenty of space for lawns and gardens. Reserve large areas for football, hockey and parks. Earmark areas for Hindu temples, Mohammedan mosques and Christian churches.' It was only fair that the city born of this sterling vision came to be called Jamshedpur.

President Abdul Kalam visited the Tata Steel plant at Jamshedpur on 13 February 2004. He commended the company for 75 years of continuous cordial industrial relations. The last reported strike at the steel plant dated back to 1929. Kalam had wholesome praise for the many welfare schemes introduced by the company, many of which were of a pioneering nature even on the global scale, such as the eight-hour shift or the provision of housing to employees. The elegantly designed and well-laid out museum at Jamshedpur is replete with many such 'firsts'.

In the earlier model of steel-making, the raw material was shipped to where the primary steel-making capacities existed, which were inevitably near the markets the steel was sold in. In the pre-globalization era, when leading steel makers set up shop, the concept of owning assets in other countries was unthinkable because of closed national boundaries. In addition to this, high tariff barriers made it prohibitively expensive to move goods between countries. Therefore, steel was made in the country it was sold in, regardless of whether the raw material was available in that country. In fact,

this is one of the reasons some of the largest steel companies in the world have a limited international footprint. Tata Steel was no exception to this rule and could embark upon its international presence only in mid 2000.

Globalization and the World Trade Organization's pressure to lower tariff barriers have been gradually changing these factors. This has been forcing the century-old industry to change the way it churns out steel. Another reason to look at things in a different light has been soaring freight costs. A shortfall in global shipping capacity, fuelled by China's insatiable demand, has raised freight costs by 344 per cent since 2002. Shaken, the largest steel companies have started questioning the wisdom of transporting bulky raw materials such as ore and coal across continents. It is much more sensible to make primary steel closer to the raw materials and then ship the semi-finished steel, which is far less bulky, near the final markets for finishing.

The other reason for this global shift in manu-facturing philosophy is that long-term links with raw material suppliers are becoming critical. There is a shortage of iron ore and coking coal in the world. The mining industry did not foresee China's appetite for more than 250 mt of steel a year. Therefore, it will take some time for the new mining capacities to kick in.

Tata Steel's rare advantage is that it has captive iron ore mines with capacities far in excess of its current needs. Therefore, it makes imminent sense to expand its primary steel-making facilities in India and look for finishing capabilities elsewhere. The capacity at Jamshedpur is being expanded to 7.4 mt from the current 5 mt and a new plant of 6 mt will be ready in Orissa by 2008.

As a part of this strategy, on 16 August 2004, Tata Steel acquired the steel business of Singapore-headquartered NatSteel in a ₹13.03 billion (US$289.5 million), all-cash transaction. At ₹13.03 billion NatSteel is a relatively inexpensive acquisition. Compare this with the ₹100 billion the company is spending in Jamshedpur and the ₹80 billion in Orissa. It takes about ₹32 billion to set up a one mt green-field steel plant. Therefore, it was a smart acquisition on part of Tata Steel. The challenge for Tata Steel is to bring down the high cost of production at NatSteel. One way is to supply NatSteel with billets (semi-finished steel) from India. Orissa and Jharkhand are dotted with small rolling mills that have been lying idle due to shortage of coal and iron ore. Tata Steel will supply these mills with both these resources and buy billets from them. If NatSteel's electric arc furnaces are shut and scrap is substituted by billets, then its cost of production will come down by about US$100 a tonne.

Tata Steel has always been innovative in its production planning. During 1986, work began on a mixed integer linear programming (MILP) model that would optimally allocate scarce resources so as to maximize profits. This emphasis on optimal profits represented a significant change in thinking. Up to that time the spotlight had always been on maximizing tonnage without paying too much attention to that policy's overall impact on profit. It was wrongly assumed that tonnage and profit were almost equivalent.

Tata Steel is a fully integrated iron and steel-making plant that consumes vast amounts of energy. An early focus of the modelling effort was the impact of scarce power resources on production planning. In metropolitan areas, power availability for Tata Steel fluctuated by time of day and season and, in some instances, the reduction of power was abrupt. One critical set of decisions involved determining which production activities to shut down as power resources

declined. Before the model had been implemented, the policy was to shut down finishing mills first and later primary mills as power became scarcer. The model demonstrated that the optimal strategy was really to shut only a few of the finishing mills before starting to turn off the primary mills. The decisions as to which mills to turn off were represented in the model as 0-1 variables. The first major success of the model occurred in November 1986. The model enabled Tata Steel to generate more profits than the month before even though there was less available power and total production was down. It is estimated that in the first year of implementation, the MILP model increased Tata Steel's profits by US $73 million as it shifted the company's focus to maximizing profit rather than tonnage. The model has since been applied to other parts of the company and its affiliates that produce tubes, tinplate, and steel wire rope (Sinha et al. 1995). Figure 11.11 shows the projected production plan of Tata Steel for the financial year (FY) 2005 in relation to the actual production of hot metal, crude steel, and saleable steel during FY 2003 ad FY 2004.

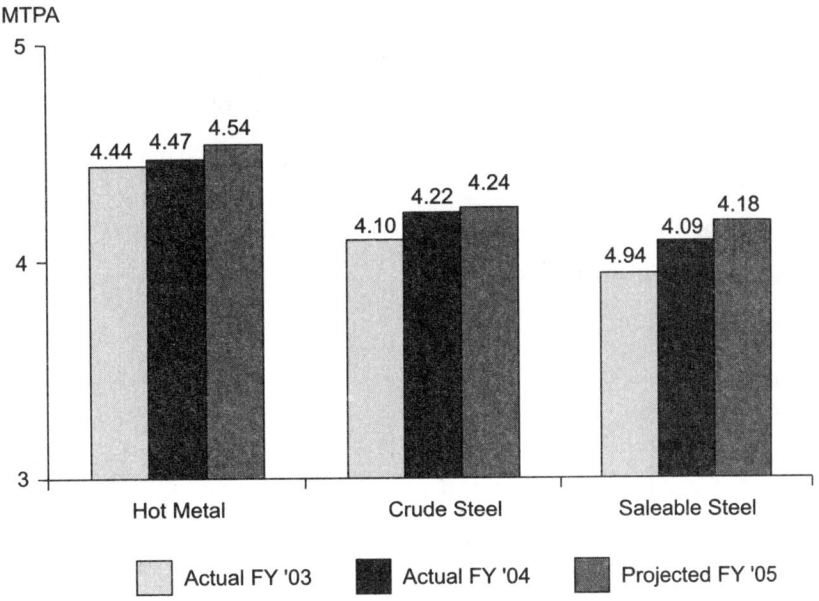

**Fig. 11.12** Projected production plan for financial year 2005

Fig. 11.13 shows the projected sales plan for FY 2005 in relation to FY 2003 and FY 2004. Various varieties of steel such as hot rolled (HR), cold rolled (CR), galvanized steel (Galv), longs, and semis are considered. Theoretically, the only difference between hot rolled and cold rolled steel is that hot rolled steel is rolled to its final dimensions while hot enough to

scale (over 1700 degrees F) while cold rolled steel is rolled to its final dimensions well below scaling temperatures. The finished tolerances on hot rolled steels are looser than on cold rolled. Not only the plus or minus tolerance from nominal size, but the 'squareness' of the product. One other difference is that if you buy cold rolled steel, you can be pretty sure that it has close to 0.18 per cent carbon content and few other impurities. However, the specifications for hot rolled steel can let the carbon content go as high as 0.29 per cent and it can contain many more impurities. More carbon makes it harder to forge. Generally a customer has to pay about twice for cold rolled steel as for hot rolled steel, for reasons which are probably obvious from above.

Galvanized steel goes through a chemical process to keep it from corroding. The steel gets coated in layers of zinc since it is resistant to rust. For countless outdoor, marine, or industrial applications, galvanized steel is an essential fabrication component.

Flat steel products are largely used as inputs to make the category of steel products called cold rolled products, which are used for making consumer durables and automobiles. The long steel category consists of products for the construction and infrastructure industry.

Semis refer to semi-finished steel, which may be in the form of blooms, billets, or slabs. It requires finishing to be given before finally being used in various applications.

Figure 11.14 shows the actual daily production of Tata Steel during April and August 2005 and Fig. 11.15 displays the results of maximizing hot metal ratio at Tata Steel during the last few years. Figure 11.16 shows the crude steel production and manpower productivity at Tata Steel with projections for the year 2006.

January 2007 saw Tata Steel acquiring the London-based Corus, one of the world's largest producers of steel and aluminium. Corus was formed in 1999 following the merger of Dutch group Koninklijke Hoogovens N.V. with the UK's British Steel Plc on 6 October 1999. It employs 47,300 people worldwide and 24,000 people in the UK. This acquisition has

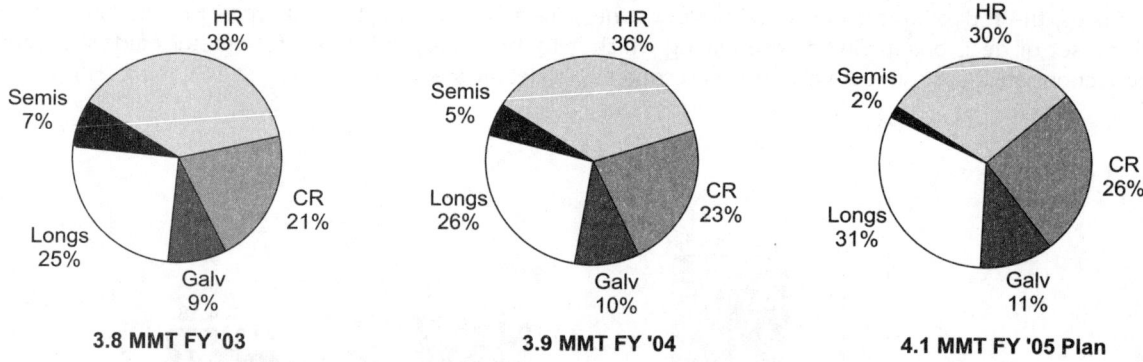

**Fig. 11.13**    Projected sales plan or FY 2005

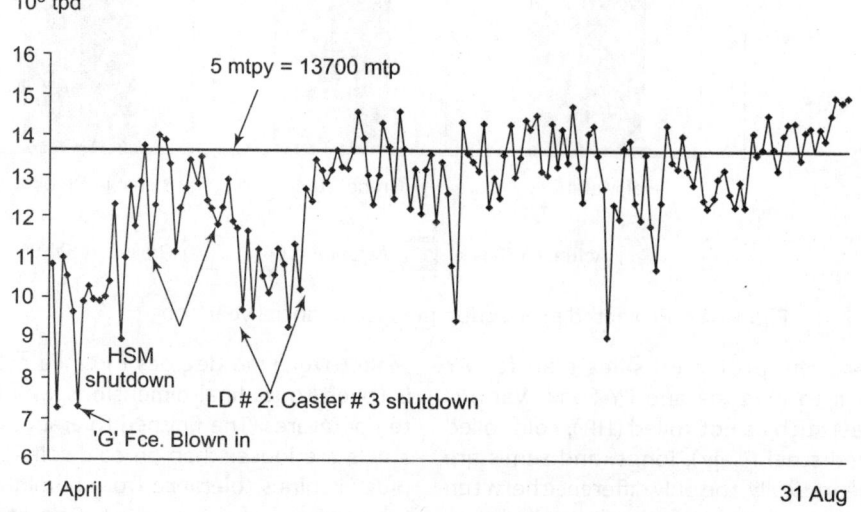

**Fig. 11.14**    Daily crude steel production at Tata Steel during April–August 2005

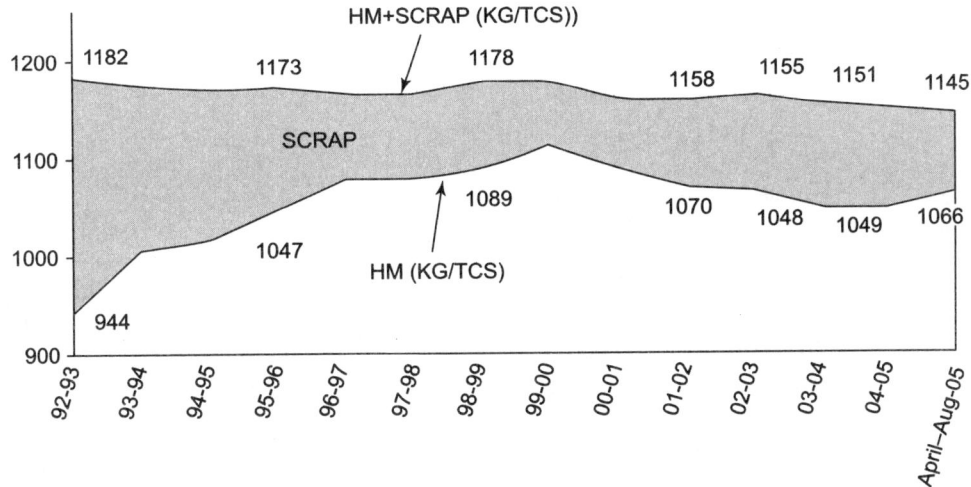

**Fig. 11.15** Maximizing hot metal ratio at Tata Steel

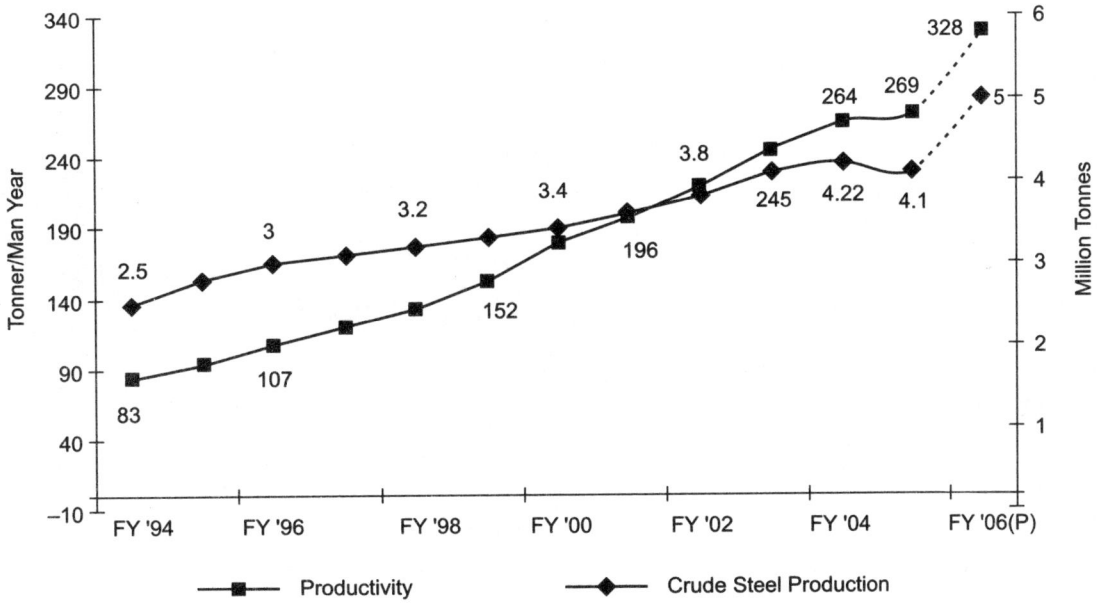

**Fig. 11.16** Production and manpower productivity at Tata Steel

made Tata Steel fifth biggest producer in the world (the world's biggest producer being Mittal–Arcelor).

## Discussion Questions

1. How does the projected production plan for the financial year 2005 in Fig. 11.12 relate to the actual daily production at Tata Steel during April to August 2005 (Fig. 11.14)? Do you think the actual production is in line with the projection?

2. What kind of aggregate production planning method is suitable for Tata Steel in view of the fact that the demand for steel in the coming few years in India as well as rest of the world would be much more than the supply?

3. In Fig. 11.13 what is the reason for increase in sales projections for all other types of steel at the expense of hot-rolled and semis?

4. Labour productivity at Tata Steel (Fig. 11.16) is constantly rising. What reasons can be attributed to this rise?

## CASE STUDY II

# ABB

ABB Motors is based at Vasteras (Sweden) and produces different types of electrical motors, which it supplies to customers throughout Europe. In a year, it produces 2,000 different varieties of motors with seven main sizes. ABB is mainly a make-to-stock company with about 300 different motors of standard configurations stored in the finished goods inventory, so that a customer order from within Europe may be fulfilled within 24 hours. The customized orders take around three to four weeks time, and such motors are manufactured only after the order is placed by the customer.

ABB sources components such as bearings, aluminium bars, iron plates, etc. from outside vendors, while it manufactures the main components such as shields, rotors, stators, etc. in its own production facility. Various meetings are conducted by the marketing manager, the executive officers of various divisions, and the aggregate production planning manager to

finalize the aggregate production plan, consisting of how many units of main motor sizes will be manufactured per prodction day.

The aggregate production plan consists of the level 1 shown in Fig. 11.17. The number of units of main motor sizes to be manufactured per production day is converted into batches per week and fed into the Master Production Schedule Planning (MPSP) software. This software explodes the forecasts to levels 2 and 3 shown in the figure.

The planning bill for the MPS in the figure shows that the motors of sizes S1 and S2 are manufactured at assembly line L1, sizes S3 and S4 at L2, and sizes S5, S6, and S7 at L3. A motor of size S1 at level 1 can be made by processing at machines M1, M2, M3, or M4. Out of the total number of units of size S1 to be assembled, 70 per cent are produced on machine M1 and 10 per cent on each one of M2, M3, and M4. Similarly, for other

*Courtesy*: ABB. Used with permission.

The Galactica production line of ABB's LV AC Drives factory in Helsinki, Finland, for manufacturing frequency converters. Alongside the robots, advanced software, and latest production techniques, the human workforce is a key factor for streamlining the implementation of producion plans.

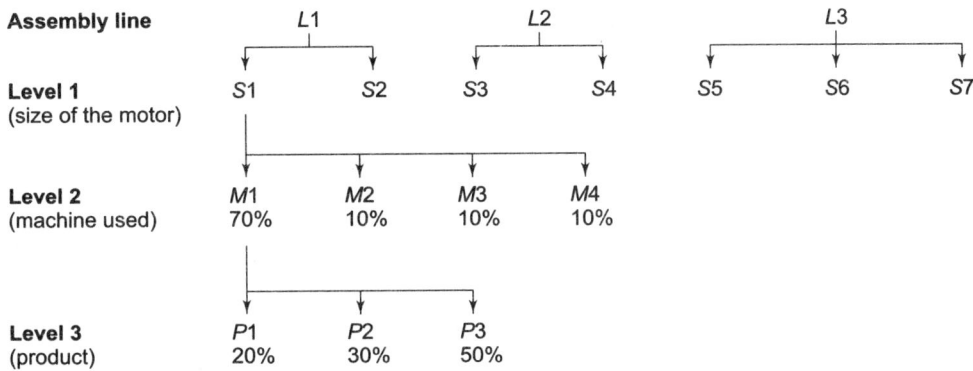

**Fig. 11.17** Planning bill of MPS

| | A | B | C | D | E | F | G | H |
|---|---|---|---|---|---|---|---|---|
| 1 | **MPS at ABB** | | | | | | | |
| 2 | | | | | | | | |
| 3 | Week | 31 | 32 | 33 | 34 | 35 | 36 | 37 |
| 4 | Forecasted Demand | 65 | 46 | 38 | 29 | 42 | 55 | 41 |
| 5 | Other requirements | 10 | | 10 | | | | |
| 6 | Customer orders booked | 70 | 50 | 43 | 20 | 17 | 29 | 14 |
| 7 | Inventory at the end of week 30 | 45 | | | | | | |
| 8 | Scheduled receipts (MPS) | 100 | | | | | | |
| 9 | Master Production Schedule (MPS) | | | | | | | |
| 10 | Projected-on-hand inventory | | | | | | | |
| 11 | Available-to-promise inventory | | | | | | | |
| 12 | | | | | | | | |
| 13 | | | | | | | | |
| 14 | | | | | | | | |
| 15 | | | | | | | | |
| 16 | | | | | | | | |
| 17 | | | | | | | | |
| 18 | | | | | | | | |
| 19 | | | | | | | | |
| 20 | | | | | | | | |
| 21 | | | | | | | | |

**Fig. 11.18** MPS at ABB

motor sizes, this classification of machines is done (not shown for the sake of simplicity). At level 3, the real end products manufactured on any machine are shown. For example, out of all the motors produced on machine M1, 20 per cent are P1, 30 per cent are P2, and the remaining 50 per cent are P3.

The division producing the two main components of the motors (rotors and shafts) also supplies to some other plants of the ABB group. This external demand is incorporated into the MPSP software so that this division may get information about the complete demand.

On assembly line L1, the size S1 is produced for 10 days, after which size S2 is produced for the next 10 days. This cycle is repeated after every 10 days. The sequence of the various models of motors of a particular size to be assembled on the line is decided by the operators themselves, such that the total set-up time is minimized. Figure 10.18 shows how the MPS is generated for a motor by ABB's MPSP software using the forecasts, other requirements (interplant orders for service parts, and orders for filling up inventories within the ABB group), and the orders already committed to the customers (Segerstedt 2002).

### Discussion Questions

1. Calculate the MPS and available-to-promise inventory for weeks 31–37.

2. Is it right to leave the sequencing decisions for different models of motors to workers according to you? Discuss.

3. What is the need for the planning bill of the MPS used by ABB?

## Objective Questions

### Choose the correct option

1. The time periods considered in a master schedule are termed as
   (a) time horizons
   (b) time buckets
   (c) time zones
   (d) time mugs

2. The 'available-to-promise inventory' data is helpful for
   (a) finance department
   (b) HR department
   (c) IT department
   (d) marketing department

3. A product structure is part of
   (a) inventory
   (b) demand forecast
   (c) bill of materials
   (d) master production schedule

4. The term 'aggregate' in aggregate production planning signifies
   (a) average
   (b) mean
   (c) medium
   (d) complete

5. The term 'level' in level output rate plan represents
   (a) varying
   (b) constant
   (c) high
   (d) low

### State True or False

6. The approach of cross-docking is useful when a large number of big retailers are being processed simultaneously to justify full-truck loads reaching them.

7. In the level output rate plan, the employee morale is high due to a sense of job security.

8. Kanban cards are used as prompts to 'push' material into the production system.

9. Master schedule and master production schedule are one and the same.

10. In low-level coding, the items found at various levels in the product structure are brought together at the highest level.

11. The material requirements planning is one of the inputs to the master production schedule.

### Fill in the blanks

12. _____ involves transfer of goods between facilities at the same level in the supply chain.

13. Aggregate production planning is done in order to ascertain the number of units of a product to be produced on a _____ basis for the coming _____ months.

14. If the time period considered is too long, the chances of the forecasts being less accurate _____ and the validity of aggregate production plans _____.

15. Higher the quantity of the product to be produced, _____ would be the material required.

16. In contemporary times, MRP has become an integral part of _____ software.

## Concept Review Questions

1. What is meant by aggregate production planning? Why is it required?

2. Why do costs decrease when the time horizon of planning is broadened? Is there a limit to the duration of planning?

3. What are the pure planning strategies in aggregate production planning? Why are these practically used in combination with each other?

4. What are the advantages and disadvantages of the level output rate plan?
5. What are the advantages and disadvantages of the chase plan?
6. What are the advantages and disadvantages of the varying utilization rate plan?
7. What is the need for disaggregating the aggregate production plan? What is a master schedule?
8. How is a master schedule different from the master production schedule?
9. What is rough-cut capacity planning? Why is it required?
10. What is available-to-promise inventory? How does it help the sales personnel?
11. Why are time fences used in master production schedules?
12. Explain the variables used in defining the relationship construct between vendors and buyers.
13. Explain the various types of distribution strategies.

## Numerical Problems

1. Sun Computers is a desktop PC assembler located in Bangalore. It sources all the components and parts from various suppliers and compiles them as per customer specifications. It serves a niche clientele in Bangalore and adjoining regions. Its marketing team provides forecasts for the coming month only by the end of a given month. It has a variable workforce, which keeps on fluctuating as per the demand projections for a given month. Each worker (assembler) is given a salary of ₹5,000 per month. Hiring cost has been estimated at ₹1,000 per worker, while the laying-off cost has been found as ₹1,500 per worker. Each worker assembles 100 PCs per month. During the month of July, there were 50 workers on the rolls of Star Computers. The inventory carrying cost is ₹20 per unit per month. At the end of July, the marketing department provides forecasts for August as 4,000 units. When the month of August was about to elapse, the marketing department came up with the demand projections for September as 6,000 units. Advise the production manager on the production plan, while calculating the overall costs involved. If the time horizon for demand forecasting becomes two months (i.e., forecasts for a month become available two months in advance), suggest changes in the production plan.

2. Western Air Conditioners is an AC assembling company based at Bhopal. Table 11.1 shows the demand forecast provided by its marketing department for ACs throughout the country in the coming six months, from January to June. The cost involved in changing the output rate compared to the previous month is ₹3,000 for 1–20 units, ₹4,000 for 21–50 units, and ₹6,000 for 51–70 units. Each

worker assembles one AC per day. The overtime cost is ₹4 per day per unit in excess of the maximum capacity of the factory, that is, 60 units. Find the level output rate for the given data and prepare the level output rate plan. Find also the total cost in this plan. Assume carrying cost as ₹1 per unit for 6 months and back-ordering cost as ₹1 per unit per month.

**Table 11.1**

| Month | Demand forecast (units) | No. of working days |
|---|---|---|
| January | 800 | 21 |
| February | 1,400 | 23 |
| March | 900 | 25 |
| April | 1,700 | 22 |
| May | 2,200 | 24 |
| June | 700 | 20 |

3. For the data given in Problem 2, prepare a chase plan and find the total cost involved in this plan.
4. Prepare an intermediate plan (a combination of the level output rate and chase plans) for the data given in Problem 2 and find the total cost involved in this plan.
5. National Furniture House is a prominent furniture manufacturer in Thiruvananthapuram. Its marketing offices in Mumbai, Delhi, and Chennai have provided a consolidated demand forecast from July to December as given in Table 11.2. Advise the production manager to create the level output rate plan such that neither there is excessive inventory nor a stock-out at any stage.

**Table 11.2**

| Month | July | August | September | October | November | December |
|---|---|---|---|---|---|---|
| Demand forecast (units) | 2000 | 5000 | 3000 | 6000 | 9000 | 4000 |

6. Table 11.3 shows the data provided by the marketing department of Jumbo Electronics on the demand forecast for the coming eight weeks and the number of televisions committed to its distributors so far. For a manufacture lot size of 5,000 units, prepare the MPS schedule and the available-to-promise inventory for the given duration of eight weeks.

**Table 11.3**

|  | Weeks in January | | | | Weeks in February | | | |
|---|---|---|---|---|---|---|---|---|
|  | 1 | 2 | 3 | 4 | 5 | 6 | 7 | 8 |
| Demand forecast (units) | 1,000 | 3,000 | 2,200 | 4,100 | 1,800 | 2,700 | 3,600 | 1,700 |
| Customer orders committed | 1,100 | 3,400 | 2,000 | 2,900 | 500 | | | |
| Initial inventory in week 0 = 1,000 units | 1,000 | | | | | | | |

7. Powertone Gensets is a Bangalore-based company, which manufactures electrical generators for industrial use. The marketing department of Powertone Gensets has provided the data given in Table 11.4 on the demand forecasts for the coming eight weeks and the number of generators committed to its institutional customers so far. For a manufacture lot size of 300 units, prepare the MPS schedule and the available-to-promise inventory for the given duration of eight weeks.

**Table 11.4**

|  | Weeks in June | | | | Weeks in July | | | |
|---|---|---|---|---|---|---|---|---|
|  | 1 | 2 | 3 | 4 | 5 | 6 | 7 | 8 |
| Demand forecast (units) | 76 | 89 | 163 | 204 | 88 | 40 | 112 | 134 |
| Customer orders committed (units) | 85 | 121 | 170 | 154 | 72 | 20 | 11 | |
| Initial inventory in week 0 = 50 units | 50 | | | | | | | |

8 Wave Electronics is a manufacturer of colour televisions in Faridabad. Its primary market is the Delhi/NCR region, though it has its marketing presence in nearby states such as Uttar Pradesh, Haryana, and Rajasthan. The weekly demand forecast generated by its marketing department for its popular 'Sigma Slim' flat TV for the months of June and July is shown below. Some of the distributors of their TVs have already placed orders for this period, as shown in Table 11.5 (Customer Orders – committed). The initial inventory in week 0 (week prior to the period considered) is 300 units. Prepare the master production schedule when the production batch size is kept constant at 700 units. Also, find the available-to-promise inventory.

**Table 11.5**

|  | June | | | | July | | | |
|---|---|---|---|---|---|---|---|---|
|  | Week 1 | Week 2 | Week 3 | Week 4 | Week 5 | Week 6 | Week 7 | Week 8 |
| Demand forecast (units) | 180 | 130 | 80 | 420 | 710 | 540 | 60 | 555 |
| Customer orders (committed) | 260 | 140 | 150 | 230 | 670 | 110 | 170 | |

## Project Assignments

1. Visit a manufacturing organization nearby and find out how aggregate production planning is done there. Is there a link between the demand forecasts provided by the marketing department and the production plans prepared? What type of time fences are used in the MPS? Is rough-cut capacity planning

done to check the feasibility of the MPS? Form groups and prepare a detailed checklist, and verify the findings of the visit.

2. Visit a restaurant near your place and find out how they plan to meet future demand, especially before festive seasons. Is there a link between the capacity of the restaurant and the master schedule prepared? How is the MRP done with respect to the MPS?

## Answers to Objective Questions

| | | | | |
|---|---|---|---|---|
| 1. (b) | 2. (d) | 3. (c) | 4. (d) | 5. (b) |
| 6. True | 7. True | 8. False | 9. False | 10. False |
| 11. False | 12. Transshipment | 13. weekly or monthly; six to eighteen | | |
| 14. increase; diminishes | | 15. more | 16. ERP | |

# 12

# Work Design

## Learning Objectives

After reading this chapter, you will be able to answer the following questions:
- What is work design and what are its constituents?
- What is job design and what are the various techniques used in it?
- What is work measurement?
- How are time standards set for jobs performed by workers?
- How can sampling theory be useful in the measurement of work?
- What is productivity? How can productivity be measured?
- What measures can be taken in order to improve productivity?

## Work Design

Work measurement is the measurement of the performance time of a job in order to set a time standard for it.

*Work design* is an umbrella term used to collectively address the issues of *job design* and *work measurement*. Job design is allocating tasks to be performed by a worker in his daily routine. Work measurement is the measurement of the performance time of a job in order to set a time standard for it. These time standards serve as a benchmark to assess the performance levels of various employees performing the same job (Exhibit 12.1).

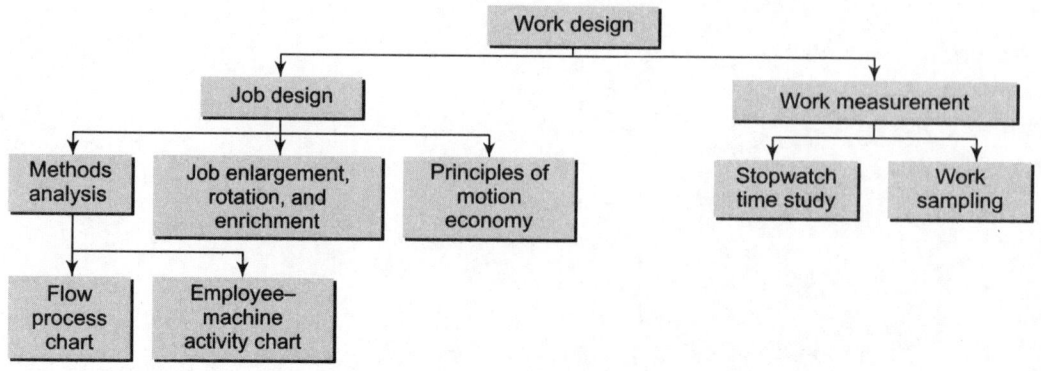

**Fig. 12.1**  Components of work design

> Work measurement can be done using techniques such as stopwatch time study and work sampling.

Figure 12.1 shows the various components of work design. As shown in this figure, a good job design requires the use of techniques such as job enlargement, rotation, and enrichment; methods analysis; and principles of motion economy. Methods analysis can be performed using tools such as the flow process chart, the employee–machine activity chart, and the principles of motion economy. Work measurement can be done using techniques such as stopwatch time study and work sampling. We will discuss all these concepts in detail in the subsequent sections.

---

### Exhibit 12.1   BMW

The German car maker BMW has pioneered many innovations in its labour practices, despite Germany being renowned for its stringent labour laws. In doing so, it has created the world's most flexible and productive factories. Whenever the demand for its cars soars higher, BMW ramps up its assembly lines to 110 hours per week, with negligible overtime costs. On the other hand, when the demand slides, production is brought down to 78 hours per week without firing any workers. The new facility of BMW at Leipzig will be much more flexible, with production swinging from 60 hours to 140 hours a week when the demand soars.

This initiative was started by BMW way back in 1985, when it introduced Saturday shifts. Capital intensive operations in the press and paint shops are run round the clock. In addition, the highly skilled assembly workers work longer hours without charging high overtime rates. The ultimate goal is to match output with demand by boosting up production.

*Courtesy:* BMW. Used with permission.
At BMW's Dingolfing plant, for reasons of ergonomics and better access, cars are turned longitudinally in the swivelling assembly process.

The trade unions have agreed with the system of putting the extra hours spent by a worker (above, the union agreed to 35 hours) during periods of high demand into an account, which he can withdraw later in the form of days off. The system is 9 hours a day for four days in a week, with three days off. The workers get long weekends in exchange for working on some Saturdays. BMW's plants thus operate near full capacity with reduced set-up times, avoiding loss-making periods when capacity use plunges.

BMW also has flexibility in switching models from plant to plant, as all its plants are capable of making at least two different models of cars. The Dingolfing plant was made chiefly to produce the 7 series and 5 series, but when the demand on the 3 series surged last year, the same plant was geared up to boost the production of this model. If one of the factories in Bavaria is getting strained due to work and the other one is slackening, workers are transferred daily by buses to the factory under stress.

*Source:* Edmondson (2003).

# Job Design

Job design means assigning various tasks to a job to be performed by a worker in his daily routine. The behavioural approach to job design calls for not only assigning tasks to a job while designing it, but also ensuring that the job does not become monotonous for the worker. This is because if a worker is genuinely interested in his job, the performance is definitely better. It reflects in the quality and quantity of the products produced or the service delivered. In highly specialized work as in assembly lines, a worker's job may be fitting the tail lights of vehicles. After doing the same work day after day, month after month, the worker may feel frustrated with the job. His value addition to the whole manufacturing process of the vehicle is fitting tail lights only. There is no skill enhancement for the worker beyond fitting tail lights. This results in absenteeism and high turnover of workers.

The job design process should always result in a job description document describing the details of the job. This is important, as this document can be referred to by various workers performing the same job. In addition, new workers find it useful for understanding the job easily. This document is also a requirement in implementing quality systems in the organization based upon quality standards like ISO 9000. It is always beneficial to take the opinion of the concerned worker in the job design process to avoid any resistance later on by the worker in the performance of the job.

## Job Enlargement, Rotation, and Enrichment

There are certain concepts in job design which need the job designer's attention. These are job enlargement, rotation, and enrichment. *Job enlargement* is the *horizontal loading* of a worker's job. This means certain tasks of the same skill and mental level as being handled by the worker presently are added to his job. For example, a worker on the assembly line fitting the tail lights may be given the additional task of affixing the car and company logo at the back of the car. This will give him a sense of pride, though this may not be very long lasting.

A better solution in this case may be *job rotation*. In job rotation, highly repetitive tasks like in assembly lines are swapped (interchanged) amongst workers after a suitable interval of time. For example, a worker fitting the tail lights may be shifted after a suitable interval of time to the workstation where the steering wheel of the car is fitted, and so on. This helps in removing the monotony of a worker up to a great extent.

*Job enrichment* means giving some additional responsibilities to a worker, which are slightly more dignified than the routine tasks being handled by him. This is also called *vertical loading* of the worker's job. For example, in addition to doing his own work, a worker fitting the tail lights at a workstation on the assembly line may be given the responsibility of supervising work at the two workstations adjacent to his. This will have two advantages—first, the worker's monotony will be broken and, second, the number of supervisors may be reduced, thus saving on the cost of supervision. Job enrichment of workers can also be done by the formation of *self-directed teams*. These teams of workers are given the liberty to initiate changes in the work processes in their domain for initiating improvements. These workers are given proper training in process improvement, kaizen, and teamwork.

Job enlargement, job rotation, and job enrichment should be implemented with great care, as these may have some negative impacts also. Job enlargement may be taken by a worker as additional workload without any incentives, if it is implemented without any involvement of the worker while planning the enlargement of the job. It is important to make the worker understand the reason why some additional activities are being assigned to him. Similarly, the time interval between job rotations should be decided upon very carefully because extremely frequent job rotations may result in poor performance on the part of the worker. By the time the worker becomes adept at doing one job properly, job rotation may take place. Finally, job enrichment of workers may be viewed by the supervising staff as a threat to their job security. Supervisors have to be informed beforehand about the benefits of job enrichment for workers and convinced about their future role in the organization.

## Job Task Discretion

Breaugh (1985) identified three types of job task discretion that can be exercised by workers on a factory floor.

***Work method*** This type of discretion allows workers to modify the way a work is performed. They may be given the liberty to suitably modify the standard operating procedures (SOPs) for performing a given task.

***Work criteria*** In this type of job discretion, the workers may be involved in deciding about the criteria that would be used for assessing the quality of their work. This may include their involvement in evolving product specifications.

***Work schedule*** Workers are allowed to decide on scheduling, sequencing, and timing of the activities to be performed.

Conti and Warner (2001) cite examples in which discretion given to workers to take decisions for improvement of their tasks resulted in disaster. In one such instance, the assemblers of car doors at an automotive plant participated in telephonic surveys of their car customers, who were complaining about the difficulty in closing the doors on the hill. The workers redesigned the door to reduce the closing force required and such complaints dried up subsequently. However, new complaints about water leaking through car doors during heavy rains surfaced.

In another similar incident at a factory giving discretion to its workers, a machinist replaced the stainless steel nozzle being manufactured in the gas valves with an aluminium alloy one. This reduced the cost of production, as aluminium is relatively cheaper, easy to be machined, and fits more easily to the connecting parts. However, the machinist did not know that the design engineer had chosen stainless steel to resist corrosive effects of the high-speed gas flow. Several thousands of gas valves with aluminium nozzle failed after use by customers for a few months and had to be recalled, resulting in heavy replacement costs for the company.

Conti and Warner (2001) proposed a matrix for deciding the level of discretion to the workers to allow for creativity and aesthetics as desired by the customers (Fig. 12.2).

The matrix has complexity of the product along the *x*-axis and utility of product variability along the *y*-axis. Utility of product variability signifies the desire of the customers to have novelty in each unit of the product—meaning that no two units of a product should be alike. For example, customers of famous fashion designers such as J.J. Valaya, Ritu Kumar, and Manish Malhotra expect that a dress created by them would be unique and have no replicas.

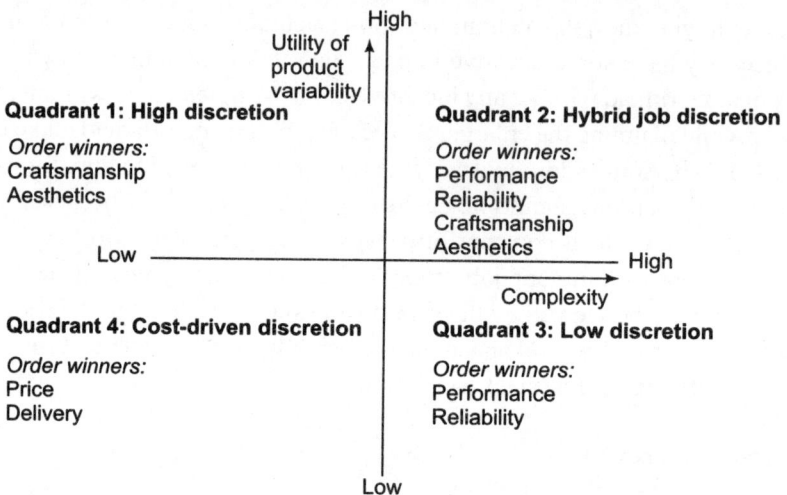

**Fig. 12.2**  Job task discretion matrix (Conti and Warner 2001)

Quadrant 1 in the matrix has low complexity of product and high utility of product variability. Manufacturers of handmade pottery, bone China crockery, handmade embroidery in apparels, etc. fall in this category, as they depend heavily upon the skill of their craftsman and allow them high discretion in designing the products as well as creating them. The craftsmanship and aesthetics of products, thus created, become the order winners.

Quadrant 3 has high complexity of product and low utility of product variability. Thus, the product has to be uniform in all respects and customers have expectation of best performance and reliability. Most car manufacturers fall in this category—they deploy standard operating procedures (SOPs), quality standards such as ISO 9000 and poka-yoke devices to make sure that workers do not deviate from established procedures. Therefore, there is low job task discretion on the part of workers.

Quadrant 4 has low complexity of product as well as low utility of product variability. Low price and quick delivery are the order winners here. Local furniture manufactures fall in this category, as they allow discretion to their workers on designing, creating, and delivering the furniture to the customers as long as the price-point and delivery times are met.

Quadrant 2 represents high complexity of the product as well as high utility of product variability. Here, the customers 'want it all'—performance, reliability, craftsmanship, and aesthetics. Some products fit into this category—for example, Jaguar Land Rover (JLR) cars are manufactured like any other car on an assembly line to achieve the attributes of performance and reliability. The workers on the assembly line are expected to demonstrate highest level of discipline in following the SOPs. However, the department within JLR factories that creates interiors for its cars bestows upon its workers full discretion to its craftsmen to choose the right kind of wood veneers for creating the dashboard, suitable leather for sewing the leather upholstery, etc. Thus, 'hybrid' job discretion is exercised here.

## Methods Analysis

Methods analysis is a tool which can be used to prepare a good job design. Methods analysis can be applied to a new job design as well as to the improvisation of an existing one. In the case of

Methods analysis is a
tool which can be used
to prepare a good job
design.

analysing an existing job design, the job is usually broken down into various steps or procedures. The workplace arrangement, tools and equipment used, materials used, and the worker's skill set required for performing the job are all studied in detail. The workers and supervisors are also involved in the methods analysis to give their opinions about ways of improving the current methods in a job. These people are directly involved in the performance of the job and know the intricate details. Involving them at all stages of the methods analysis also helps during the implementation of the improvisations in the job.

In the case of a new job design, the imaginative skills of the analyser in imagining the various steps of the job, the materials to be used, tools and equipment required, workplace arrangement, and the worker's skill set requirements come into play. The self-directed teams discussed earlier provide a means of methods analysis performed by the workers themselves in order to improvise their work methods. In Japanese manufacturing, the term kaizen (meaning continuous improvement) is synonymous with methods analysis, as the workers are encouraged to give kaizens (suggestions) for improvements in their job methods.

Methods analysis is required whenever a new product is being designed, keeping in view the existing facilities and resources to be used to manufacture it. It is also required whenever changes in tools and equipment, materials used, or workplace arrangement are made. Methods analysis is also needed in case of repeated accidents reported during the performance of a job. It is performed by using flow process charts, employee–machine activity charts, and principles of motion economy, which are discussed next.

**Flow process chart**  As the name suggests, a flow process chart shows the flow of materials, labour, and products (semi-finished and finished) from one place to another in the facility. It helps in identifying the various sources of delay in the process, which may be eliminated in order to achieve better efficiency.

| Operation | Movement | Inspection | Delay | Storage |
|-----------|----------|------------|-------|---------|
| O | ⇒ | □ | D | ▽ |

Methods analysis is
required whenever
a new product is
being designed,
keeping in view the
existing facilities and
resources to be used
to manufacture it.

**Fig. 12.3**  Symbols used in a flow process chart

Figure 12.3 shows the various symbols used in a flow process chart for various types of activities. Figure 12.4 shows the various steps involved in the process of payment to a customer in a bank through the clearance of a cheque. Note that the various steps shown are typically followed in banks excluding those which have done methods analysis for identifying the unnecessary activities in this process. As a result of this methods analysis, we find that many banks have introduced teller facilities, in which many steps in the process shown in Fig. 12.4 are avoided to serve the customer more efficiently.

A flow process chart
shows the flow of
materials, labour, and
products (semi-finished
and finished) from one
place to another in the
facility.

**Employee–Machine activity chart**  An employee–machine activity chart shows the various time instants and the activities of an employee and a machine simultaneously. Figure 12.5 shows the employee–machine activity chart for the process of an employee making milkshakes at a fast food centre. Note that the

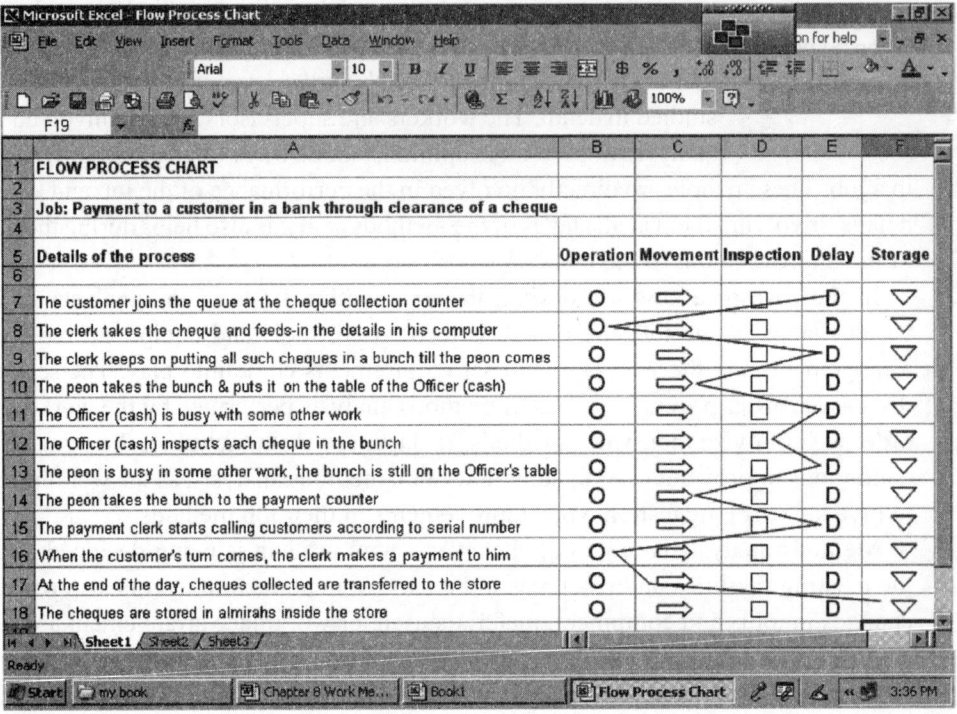

**Fig. 12.4**  Flow process chart

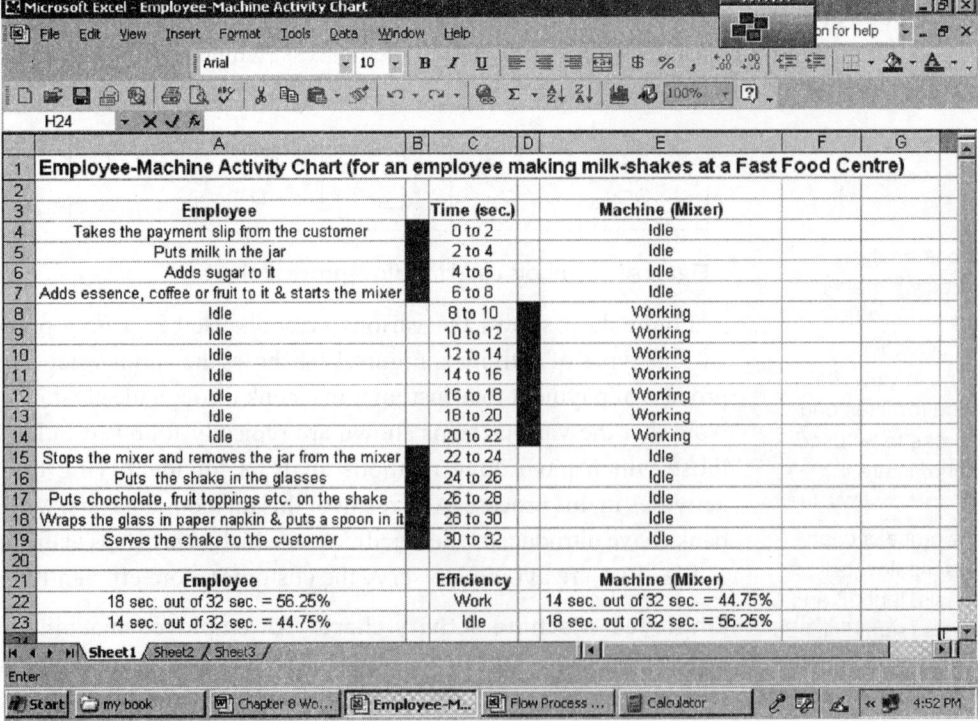

**Fig. 12.5**  Employee–Machine activity chart

mixer remains idle from time instants 0 to 8 s and then from 22 to 32 s. Similarly, the employee remains idle from time instants 8 to 22 s. As calculated in Fig. 12.5, the machine has an efficiency of only 44.75 per cent and the employee has an efficiency of 56.25 per cent. Thus, there is scope for increasing the work efficiency of both the employee and the machine, depending upon the demand of milkshakes in the centre. One way is to make the employee handle two mixers such that his idle time is minimized. The other way is to have two employees with a common mixer in order to utilize the idle time of the mixer.

In some other situations, there is a possibility that both the employee and the machine may be working simultaneously for some time. Thus, employee–machine activity charts help in methods analysis of jobs for improving the efficiency of employees and machines.

### Principles of Motion Economy

The principles of motion economy aim at minimizing the fatigue of workers due to repetitive motion of the different parts of the body, such as hands, feet, and eyes, thus, maximizing the efficiency of the worker during the performance of a job. The human body works best under certain predetermined ways. For example, while pedalling a bicycle the typical movement of the legs is comfortable for the human body. Similarly, pulling up a bucketful of water from a well using a rope is strenuous without the use of a pulley. Some of the principles of motion economy are summarized here:

1. Both the human hands can work simultaneously. Thus, jobs can be designed to use both the hands of a worker effectively.
2. All the tools and equipment, materials, and switches for control should be in the vicinity of the worker (to avoid unnecessary movement). In addition, tools, equipment, and materials should have definite places to avoid wasting time and effort in locating these.
3. Pedalling tasks can be performed comfortably only when the worker is in a sitting position.
4. The worker should be provided with a comfortable chair according to the requirements of the job so that work may be performed continuously for longer hours without frequent breaks.
5. Proper working conditions should be provided for the workers such as suitable temperature, humidity, light, ventilation, noise, and vibration levels.

## Work Measurement

### Sampling Theory

Sampling theory is useful in stopwatch time study, work sampling, statistical quality control (SQC), etc. It is important to understand some basic concepts relating to sampling theory in order to apply this theory to all these topics. Sampling means choosing some samples of items out of a large number of items at random (chosen in any order without any particular sequence). In SQC, samples are chosen from, say, a consignment of items sent by the suppliers. These samples chosen at random consist of a small number of items compared to the size of the consignment, which are inspected to check whether these have the desired quality or not. Depending on the outcome of

An employee–machine activity chart shows the various time instants and the activities of an employee and a machine simultaneously.

The principles of motion economy aim at minimizing the fatigue of workers due to repetitive motion of the different parts of the body.

Sampling theory is useful in stopwatch time study, work sampling, and statistical quality control (SQC).

the inspection, it is decided whether to accept the consignment or to reject it and send it back to the supplier. Let us understand some basic concepts of sampling theory.

**Universe mean** The *universe* in sampling theory refers to the total number of items, people, or things considered. Let us take up an example. Suppose six people are there in a departmental store and have made purchases worth the amounts (in ₹) shown in Table I of Fig. 12.6. These six people constitute the universe or the population in this example. Note that the average or mean money spent by any person is calculated in cell B10 as ₹100. Select cells B4 to B9 by clicking the left mouse button at cell B4 and dragging it up to cell B10. Click on the small arrow next to the Σ button in the MS Excel toolbar. Choose the **Average** option from this pull-down menu. The average value ₹100 appears in cell B10. This is called the *universe mean* or average, as this is the average money spent by any one of the six people constituting the universe.

**Distribution of Sample Means**

Table I

| Person | Amount spent (Rs) |
|---|---|
| A | 100 |
| B | 150 |
| C | 90 |
| D | 100 |
| E | 60 |
| F | 100 |
| Average | 100 |

Table II

| Amount spent (Rs) | Frequency |
|---|---|
| 60 | 1 |
| 90 | 1 |
| 100 | 3 |
| 150 | 1 |

Table III

| Sample | Sample Mean (Rs) |
|---|---|
| AB | 125 |
| AC | 95 |
| AD | 100 |
| AE | 80 |
| AF | 100 |
| BC | 120 |
| BD | 125 |
| BE | 105 |
| BF | 125 |
| CD | 95 |
| CE | 75 |
| CF | 95 |
| DE | 80 |
| DF | 100 |
| EF | 80 |
| Average | 100 |

Table IV

| Sample Mean (Rs) | Frequency | Sample (s) |
|---|---|---|
| 75 | 1 | CE |
| 80 | 3 | AE, DE, EF |
| 95 | 3 | AC, CD, CF |
| 100 | 3 | AD, AF, DF |
| 105 | 1 | BE |
| 120 | 1 | BC |
| 125 | 3 | AB, BD, BF |
| Total frequency | 15 | |

**Fig. 12.6** Distribution of sample means

Now, we choose samples of two persons each at a time and find the mean of the money spent by them. Table III in Fig. 12.6 shows the various combinations of two persons possible and the respective sample means. The first sample is *AB* with person *A* having spent ₹100 and person *B* having spent ₹150. The average is (100 + 150)/2, that is, ₹125, as shown in cell B14. The average of all such sample means is calculated in cell B29 as ₹100. As calculated earlier, the universe mean is also ₹100. Thus we conclude that the mean or average of all the sample means is always the same as the universe mean. Observe also that out of the 15 possible combinations of the samples, only three have the same mean values as the universe mean, ₹100. The rest

The universe in sampling theory refers to the total number of items, people, or things considered.

of the samples have a mean different from the universe mean. Thus, samples represent only an estimate of the universe, they may not possess all the characteristics of the universe.

In Table IV (Fig. 12.6), we find the frequency of the different values of sample means found in Table III. For example, the sample mean value ₹75 occurs only once in Table III for the sample *CE*. Similarly, the sample mean value ₹80 occurs three times in Table III for samples *AE*, *DE*, and *EF*. Thus, the frequency of the ₹75 sample mean is 1, while that of ₹80 is 3. In the same way, we find the frequency of other values of the sample mean. We plot Table IV on a graph as shown by the bold line in Fig. 12.7. Note that the universe mean, ₹100, is also the mean of the sample means, is shown distinctly by a vertical dotted line. In Table II of Fig. 12.6, we find the frequencies of the different amounts of money spent by the six people in the departmental store. For example, the values ₹60, ₹90, and ₹150 have the frequency 1, as only one person has spent each of these amounts. On the other hand, the value ₹100 has the frequency 3, as three people have spent ₹100 each in the store. We plot Table III (frequency distribution of the universe . values) on the graph, shown by the other dotted line in Fig. 12.7.

**Confidence interval, confidence level, and desired accuracy**   Table III in Fig. 12.6 shows the frequency distribution of sample means. From this frequency distribution, certain predictions

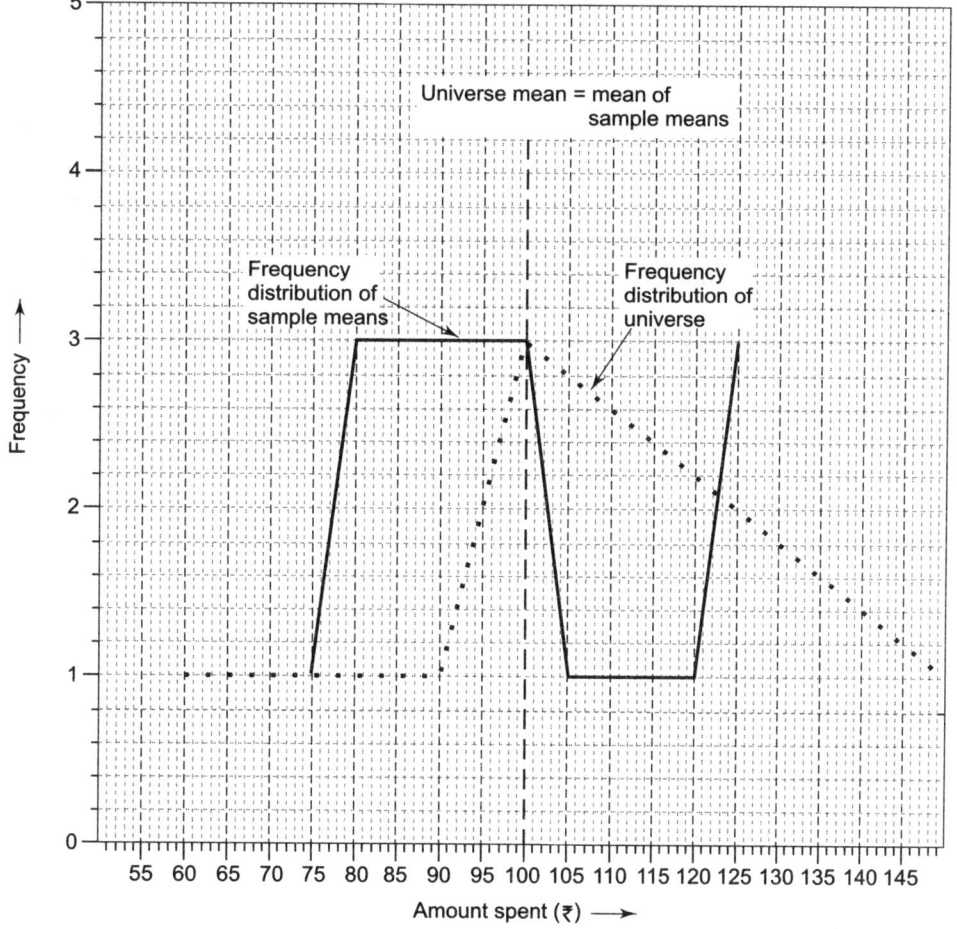

**Fig. 12.7**   Frequency distribution of universe and sample means

> The central limit theorem states that for large samples, the frequency distribution of sample means is approximately a normal distribution curve for all practical purposes.

can be made. For example, 46.67 per cent (7 out of 15) of the sample means lie between ₹95 and 105 (i.e., within ₹5 of the universe mean of ₹100 in either direction). Similarly, 73.33 per cent (11 out of 15) of the sample means lie between ₹80 and 120 (i.e., within ₹20 of the universe mean of ₹100). In other words, if a sample of two people is taken at random out of a universe of six people, there is a 73.33 per cent chance that its mean will lie between ₹80 and 120. It can also be said that if 100 samples of two people at a time are taken at random, then the means of almost 73 samples will lie between ₹80 and 120.

In the situation described above, the interval ₹80 to 120 is called the *confidence interval*. A researcher can be 73.33 per cent confident in making the statement that if a sample of two people is taken at random out of a universe of six people, the sample mean will lie between ₹80 and 120. Thus, 73.33 per cent is the *confidence level* of the researcher. The maximum variation considered here is ± ₹20 from the universe mean of ₹100. Thus, the *desired accuracy* of the estimates of sample means is ± ₹20.

**Distribution of sample means for large sample sizes**  When the sample size is large and the universe size is also very large, it is practically unfeasible to form the frequency distribution tables and graphs shown in Figs 12.6 and 12.7, respectively. It is not possible to determine all the possible combinations of samples and then their means under this condition. Then, how can one predict the confidence intervals of sample means in such a situation.

The *central limit theorem* comes to our aid in this situation. It states that for large samples, the frequency distribution of sample means is approximately a normal distribution curve for all practical purposes. The normal distribution curve is a bell-shaped curve and has typical characteristics, which are useful for predicting confidence intervals. Figure 12.8 shows the frequency distribution curve of the universe, which represents the amount of money spent by people who visited a particular departmental store in the past one year. The *y*-axis represents the frequency, that is, the number of persons corresponding to a particular amount of purchases made (plotted along the *x*-axis). Notice that this curve rises initially to a maximum level and then starts falling down. It means that the number of people having very high purchase amounts is very less (the corresponding frequency is less). The other curve shown is a normal distribution curve (bell-shaped) representing the distribution of sample means.

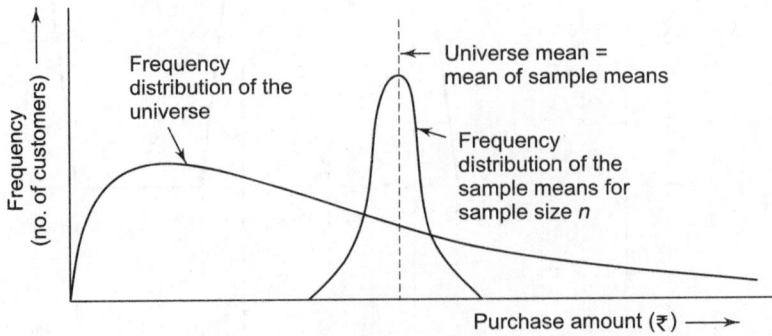

**Fig. 12.8**  Normal frequency distribution curve of sample means

**Standard deviation**  *Standard deviation* σ is a measure of dispersion of a curve. In any frequency distribution (curve), the different values (points on the curve) in the data are scattered around

| | |
|---|---|
| Standard deviation σ is a measure of dispersion of a curve. | the average or the mean value $\mu$ as shown in Fig. 12.9. Standard deviation measures the extent to which these values are scattered around the central (mean) value. It has the same unit as that of the variable being considered and can be determined as follows: |

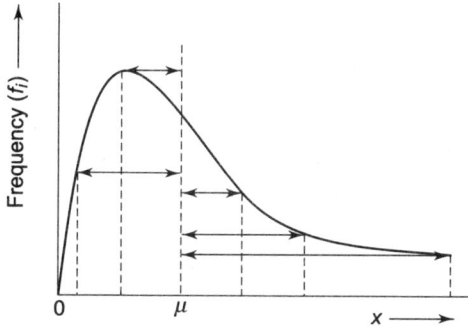

$$\sigma = \frac{\sqrt{\Sigma f_i (x_i - \mu)^2}}{\Sigma f_i} \qquad (12.1)$$

where $x_i$ are different values of the variable $x$, $f_i$ are frequencies of the values $x_i$ of the variable $x$, $\mu$ is the mean or the average of all the $x_i$ values, and $\Sigma f_i$ is the total frequency.

From Fig. 12.8, we can say that $\sigma$ for the frequency distribution curve of the universe is much greater compared to that for the frequency distribution curve of the sample means, though both have the same mean. This is because the points on the universe curve are scattered far away from

**Fig. 12.9**   Mean value $\mu$

the mean value compared to the points on the curve of sample means.

**Standard deviation of the universe and standard error of the mean**   The standard deviation of the distribution of the universe is represented by $\sigma$. The standard deviation of the distribution of sample means is denoted by $\sigma_\mu$ and is called *the standard error of the mean*. The subscript $\mu$ in $\sigma_\mu$ denotes the sample means. There is a useful relationship between $\sigma$ and $\sigma_\mu$:

$$\sigma_\mu = \frac{\sigma}{\sqrt{n}} \quad (12.2)$$

| | |
|---|---|
| The standard deviation of the distribution of sample means is denoted by $\sigma_\mu$ and is called the standard error of the mean. | where $n$ is the size of the sample (i.e., number of persons, things, etc. considered in one sample).<br><br>Note that in Eqn (12.2), the sample size $n$ is in the denominator of the right-hand side of the equation. This means, for a constant $\sigma$, upon increasing $n$, the standard error of the mean $\sigma_\mu$ decreases. As shown in Fig. 12.10, the curve for distribution of sample means will contract towards the mean value. |

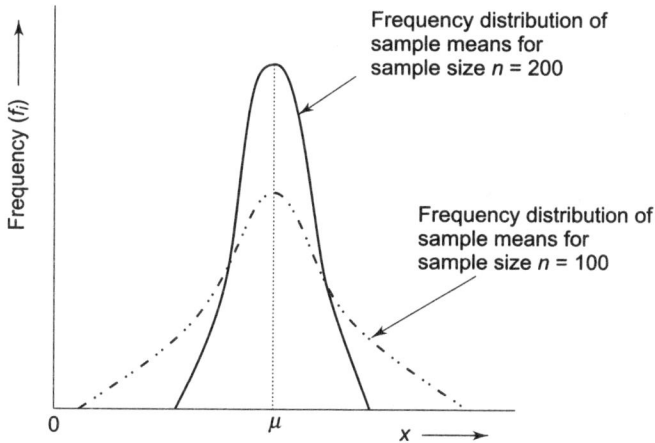

**Fig. 12.10**   The standard error of the mean ($\sigma_\mu$) decreases as sample size ($n$) increases

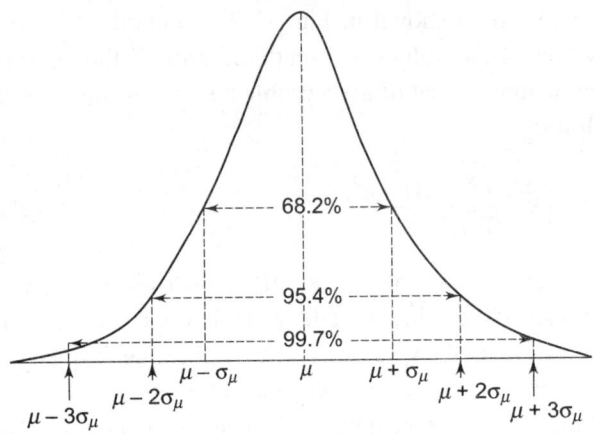

**Fig. 12.11** Typical characteristics of a normal distribution curve

**Typical characteristics of a normal distribution curve** The frequency distribution curve of sample means is represented by a normal distribution curve for large sample sizes. A normal distribution curve has some typical characteristics. As shown in Fig. 12.11, if the values of the mean ($\mu$) and standard error of the mean ($\sigma_\mu$) are available for the distribution of sample means, ($\mu + \sigma_\mu$) and ($\mu - \sigma_\mu$) form the first sigma limits of the normal distribution; 68.2 per cent of the total frequency lies between the first sigma limits. In addition, the area falling below the normal distribution curve between the first sigma limits is always 68.2 per cent of the total area falling under the curve.

Similarly, ($\mu + 2\sigma_\mu$) and ($\mu - 2\sigma_\mu$) form the second sigma limits of the normal distribution; 95.4 per cent of the total frequency lies between the second sigma limits. The area falling below the normal distribution curve between the second sigma limits is always 95.4 per cent of the total area falling under the curve. In the same way, ($\mu + 3\sigma_\mu$) and ($\mu - 3\sigma_\mu$) form the third sigma limits of the normal distribution; 99.7 per cent of the total frequency lies between the third sigma limits, and the area falling below the normal distribution curve between the third sigma limits is always 99.7 per cent of the total area falling under the curve.

When the normal distribution curve represents the distribution of sample means for large samples, the sigma limits are commonly used to represent the confidence intervals, and the percentage of frequency between the sigma limits represents the confidence limits. Note that all the terms used in sigma limits, that is, ($\mu + \sigma_\mu$), ($\mu - \sigma_\mu$), ($\mu + 2\sigma_\mu$), ($\mu - 2\sigma_\mu$), ($\mu + 3\sigma_\mu$), and ($\mu - 3\sigma_\mu$), are similar except for the coefficient of $\sigma_\mu$, which keeps on changing as +1, −1, +2, −2, +3, and −3, respectively. Even the universe mean $\mu$ can be expressed as ($\mu + 0 \times \sigma_\mu$). This typical value is called the $z$-value. Thus, any value of a variable $x$ whose distribution of sample means is represented by a normal distribution curve can be represented as ($\mu + z\sigma_\mu$). Therefore,

$$x = (\mu + z\sigma_\mu) \quad \text{or} \quad z\sigma_\mu x - \mu \quad \text{or} \quad z = \frac{x - \mu}{\sigma_\mu}$$

The $z$-value can assume not only the values +1, −1, +2, −2, +3, and −3, but also decimal values. Note that the vertical line (called the central line) through the universe mean $\mu$ divides the total area under the normal distribution curve into two halves. Thus, 50 per cent of the total area is on one side of this line and 50 per cent is on the other side. We know that 99.7 per cent of the total area lies between the third sigma limits ($\mu + 3\sigma_\mu$) and ($\mu - 3\sigma_\mu$). Half of this area, that is, 49.85 per cent, lies between the central line and ($\mu + 3\sigma_\mu$), the other half, that is, 49.85 per cent, of this area lies between the limit ($\mu - 3\sigma_\mu$) and the central line. The same is true for the first and second sigma limits. The $z$-table given in Table A of the Appendix gives all such areas for different values of $z$.

The frequency distribution curve of sample means is represented by a normal distribution curve for large sample sizes.

**Calculating the sample size necessary for specified accuracy** Let us assume that a departmental store wants to estimate the average money spent by its customers for making purchases in one visit. The store manager wants to have an accuracy of $\pm \text{₹}10$ (represented in our calculations as $a$) of the actual average (which is unknown) in the estimated average. Also, the manager wants to be virtually certain (99.7 per cent confidence level) about the estimated average.

As the confidence level is 99.7 per cent, we will use the third sigma limits, that is, $(\mu \pm 3\sigma_\mu)$. In the general form, we can use $(\mu \pm z\sigma_\mu)$. The desired accuracy is $\mu \pm \text{₹}10$, which in the general form may be written as $(\mu \pm a)$. Here, the confidence interval is represented by both the sigma limits and the desired accuracy. Therefore, we equate both of these to get the following equation:

$$\mu \pm z\sigma_\mu = \mu \pm a \quad \text{or} \quad \sigma_\mu = a \quad \text{or} \quad \sigma_\mu = \frac{a}{z}$$

We know that

$$\sigma_\mu = \frac{\sigma}{\sqrt{n}} \quad \text{or} \quad n = \left(\frac{\sigma}{\sigma_\mu}\right)^2$$

Substituting the value of $\sigma_\mu$, we have

$$n = \left(\frac{\sigma z}{a}\right)^2$$

**Sample size determination when universe standard deviation is unknown** The standard deviation of the universe $\sigma$ is unknown in almost all practical situations. Under such situations, we take a random sample of any suitable size out of the universe and find its standard deviation. The standard deviation of this sample (represented by $s$) is used as an estimate of the actual standard deviation of the universe and is calculated using the formula

$$s = \frac{\sqrt{\Sigma f_i (x_i - \mu)^2}}{\Sigma f_i}$$

Thus, the estimated standard error of the mean is given by

$$s_\mu = \frac{s}{\sqrt{n}}$$

where $s_\mu$ is the estimated standard error of the mean, $s$ is the standard deviation of the sample, and $n$ is the sample size. Therefore, in our calculations we will use $s$ and $s_\mu$ in place of $\sigma$ and $\sigma_\mu$, respectively. These estimated values are a compromise upon the accuracy of our calculations, but for large sample sizes they serve a useful purpose in all practical situations. The formula for sample size can now be modified to

$$n = \left(\frac{sz}{a}\right)^2 \tag{12.3}$$

In our example, $z = 3$, $a = \text{₹}10$, and let us assume a random sample of any suitable size (usually between 10 and 25 units) for which the standard deviation comes out to be ₹40. Then, applying Eqn (12.3), we get

$$n = \left(\frac{40 \times 3}{10}\right)^2 = (12)^2 = 144$$

Thus, 144 persons (sample size) should be selected at random in the departmental store, and the amounts of purchases made by them should be recorded. The average of these amounts will be within ± ₹10 (desired accuracy) of the actual average, or within the third sigma limits (confidence interval). The researcher will have a 99.7 per cent confidence level (virtually certain) of this statement being true.

**Determining sample size for percentages**   In certain situations, one is interested in finding out the percentage of items, persons, or things possessing a particular characteristic. For example, we may be interested in finding the percentage of defective items in a batch of items supplied by a vendor. In such cases, our approach to sampling remains the same as in the case of arithmetic mean or average. The standard error of percentages is given by

$$s_p = \sqrt{\frac{pq}{n}} \qquad (12.4)$$

where $p$ is the percentage of items/persons possessing a particular characteristic in the sample drawn, $q = 1 - p$ is the percentage of items/persons not possessing this particular characteristic in the sample drawn, and $n$ is the sample size. Equation (12.4) can be transformed for the sample size $n$ as

$$n = \frac{pq}{s_p^2}$$

Let us consider a consignment or lot of items sent by a supplier. The company wishes to estimate the percentage of defective items in the lot (universe). The company wants an accuracy of ± 10 per cent from the actual percentage of defective items. It also wants to be virtually certain (third sigma limits) about the above statement. A sample of a suitable size (usually between 10 and 25 units) is drawn from the consignment and it is found that 8 per cent of the items are defective. The sample size $n$ is given by

$$n = \frac{pq}{s_p^2}$$

Let us use the general terms and equate the sigma limits with the desired accuracy.

$$\mu \pm z s_p = \mu \pm a \;\;\Rightarrow\;\; z s_p = a \;\;\Rightarrow s_p = \frac{a}{z}$$

Substituting this value of $s_p$, we have

$$n = \frac{pqz^2}{a^2}$$

In our example, $z = 3$, $a = 10\%$, $p$ (i.e., the number of defective items) $= 8\%$, and $q = 92\%$ ($= 100\% - 8\%$). Therefore,

$$n = \frac{8 \times 92 \times (3)^2}{(10)^2} = 66.24 \approx 67 \text{ units}$$

## Stopwatch Time Study

Stopwatch time study is used for measuring the standard duration of repetitive tasks. Standard duration refers to the time taken by an average worker to perform a task at a sustainable rate under the given facility arrangements. The term 'sustainable' implies that the worker should be able to continue working comfortably at a constant rate for a suitable amount of time (say, the normal working hours in a day). Facility arrangements such as placement of tools and equipment,

Standard duration refers to the time taken by an average worker to perform a task at a sustainable rate under the given facility arrangements.

raw materials, and given procedures are important in the measurement of standard time. Any changes in these arrangements may affect the standard time measurement.

In a stopwatch time study, the task to be studied should be broken down into various small elements (e.g., lifting, pulling, moving, grasping, etc.). The worker involved in the study should be informed about the time study to be conducted, so that the worker does not feel uncomfortable while being studied. Many times, it is observed that the worker being studied tends to slow down his work in order to affect the time study, and later on gain advantage because of lower time standards set as a result of the time study. The manager conducting the study should be observant enough to ensure that the worker is working efficiently while the time study is conducted. The number of observations in the time study depends upon the desired accuracy and the confidence level as discussed in the sampling theory. The number of observations is given by

$$n = \left(\frac{sz}{a}\right)^2 \tag{12.5}$$

where $n$ is the sample size (number of observations in the time study), $a$ is the desired accuracy, $s$ is the standard deviation of the sample drawn, and $z$ is the $z$-value (number of standard deviations for the desired confidence level).

For finding the value of $s$, a simple random sample of suitable size (usually between 10 and 25 units) is chosen, which can be revised later on the basis of the correct sample size calculated using Eqn (12.5). The standard deviation of the sample drawn represents the universe standard deviation here, as it is unknown.

In every observation, the different elements of the job are timed separately using a stopwatch. The benefit of recording the duration of these elements separately is that the company can make a database of standard times for all such elements, which can be used in future for setting standard times of new jobs having these elements. The total cost of time studies of new jobs gets reduced in the future, as only the new elements of the job are required to be timed for setting their time standards.

**Observed, normal, and standard time**   After making all the observations for various elements of the job, the average of all these observations is taken, which is called the *observed time* of that element. All such observed times of various elements of the job are summed up to arrive at the observed time $O$ of the job.

The manager conducting the time study or the management of the company may feel that the performance time of a job expected of the average worker should be more or less than the observed time of the job. The reason may be the observation that the worker being studied was slightly slowing down or rushing up the job during the time study. A *performance rating P* is multiplied with the observed time of the job to arrive at the *normal time N* of the job.

$$N = OP$$

For example, if the observed time of a job is 2 minutes and the performance rating is 0.90, the normal time will be $2 \times 0.90 = 1.8$ minutes. In case the individual elements of the job are timed separately, the performance rating for each element is multiplied by the observed time of that element, and the individual normal times of all the elements are summed up to find the normal time of the job.

In practical working conditions, a worker needs some time for relaxation after working for a long time (say, a few hours). Allowances have to be made for time consumed in adjusting or repairing the machines, workers drinking water or taking rest breaks, etc. One way is to determine these allowances for the whole working day. Another way, which is preferred by many organizations, is to add a suitable *allowance* ($A$) to the normal time of the job. The resulting time is called the *standard time* $S$ of the job.

$$S = N + A$$

### Example 12.1

**Table 12.1**

| *Observation no.* | *Recorded time (min)* |
|---|---|
| 1 | 5.86 |
| 2 | 5.67 |
| 3 | 5.94 |
| 4 | 4.51 |
| 5 | 4.65 |
| 6 | 6.01 |
| 7 | 5.17 |
| 8 | 6.09 |
| 9 | 4.22 |
| 10 | 4.19 |

Heritage Inn is a five-star business hotel at Mumbai. The general manager of the hotel is concerned about a lot of complaints from the customers on the late responses of the bellboys. He conducts a stopwatch time study in order to find the standard time taken by an average bellboy in responding to a customer call. The GM wants to be virtually certain about the estimated average time taken by the bellboy to be studied and also desires an accuracy of ± 10% from the actual average. A preliminary sample of 10 observations is conducted and the recordings are given in Table 12.1. Calculate the sample size of observations in order to achieve the desired accuracy and confidence level in the estimation of the observed time.

### *Solution*

Figure 12.12 shows the calculation of the sample size ($n$) of observations necessary to achieve the desired accuracy and confidence level in the estimation of the observed time using MS Excel. Select the cells B5 to B15 (one extra cell for displaying the average value). Click on the small arrow adjacent to the Σ button in the Excel toolbar. Choose the average option from this pull-down menu. The average of the recorded times appears in cell B15, as shown in the figure.

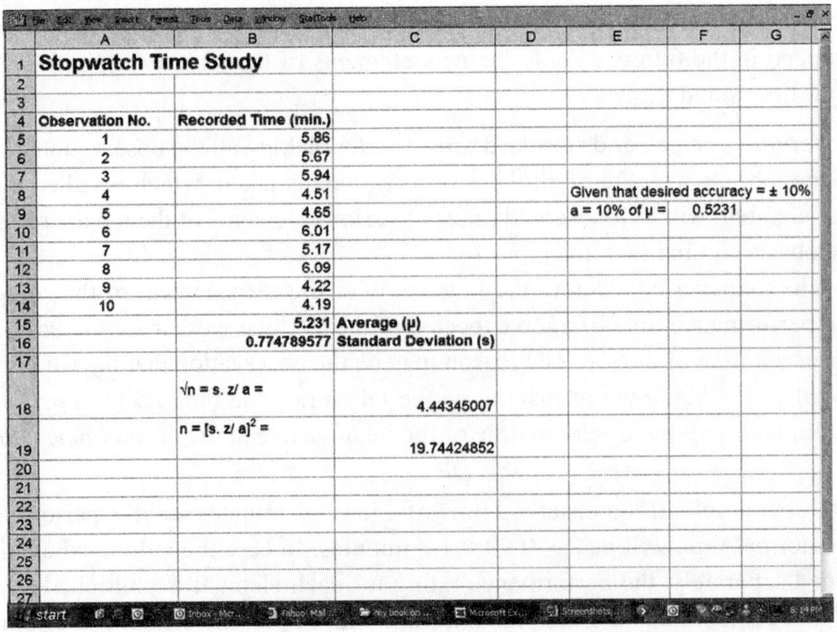

| | A | B | C | D | E | F | G |
|---|---|---|---|---|---|---|---|
| 1 | Stopwatch Time Study | | | | | | |
| 4 | Observation No. | Recorded Time (min.) | | | | | |
| 5 | 1 | 5.86 | | | | | |
| 6 | 2 | 5.67 | | | | | |
| 7 | 3 | 5.94 | | | | | |
| 8 | 4 | 4.51 | | | Given that desired accuracy = ± 10% | | |
| 9 | 5 | 4.65 | | | a = 10% of μ = | 0.5231 | |
| 10 | 6 | 6.01 | | | | | |
| 11 | 7 | 5.17 | | | | | |
| 12 | 8 | 6.09 | | | | | |
| 13 | 9 | 4.22 | | | | | |
| 14 | 10 | 4.19 | | | | | |
| 15 | | 5.231 | Average (μ) | | | | |
| 16 | | 0.774789577 | Standard Deviation (s) | | | | |
| 18 | | √n = s. z/ a = | 4.44345007 | | | | |
| 19 | | n = [s. z/ a]² = | 19.74424852 | | | | |

**Fig. 12.12** Stopwatch time study

In cell B16, we calculate the standard deviation of the sample of observations. Select cell B16 and enter the = sign in it. Select the **Function** option from the **Insert** menu on the toolbar. The **Insert Function** dialog box as shown in Fig. 12.13 appears. In this dialog box, from the **select a category** pull-down menu, select **Statistical**. From the **Select a function** scrolling text box, select **STDEV** (i.e., standard deviation) and then click on **OK**. The **Function Arguments** dialog box as shown in Fig. 12.14 appears. Select cells B5 to B14 and this range automatically appears in the **Number1** text box. Click on **OK** and the value of standard deviation, that is, 0.774789577, appears in cell B16.

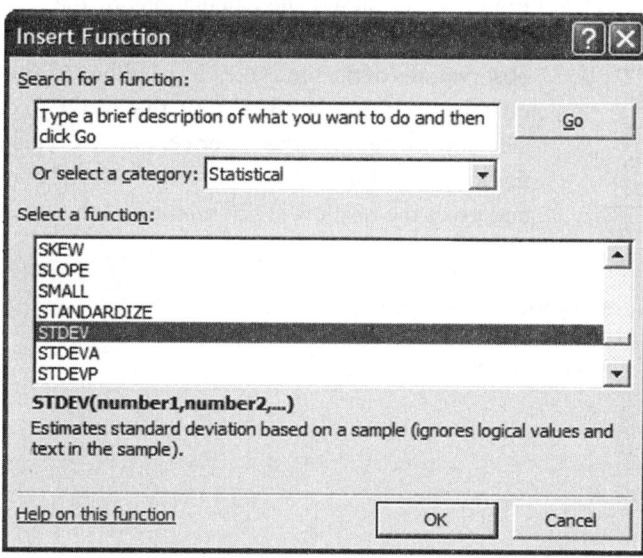

**Fig. 12.13**   The Insert Function dialog box

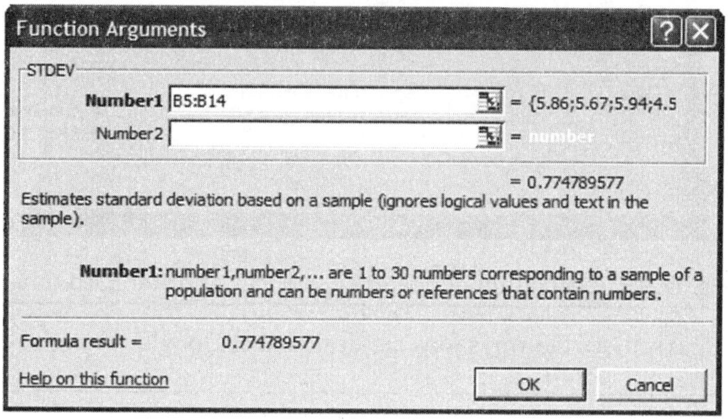

**Fig. 12.14**   The Function Arguments dialog box

The desired accuracy is 10 per cent of the average value ($\mu$) of the sample. In cell F9, we have put the formula =**0.1\*B15** (i.e., 10% of $\mu$). The result 0.5231 is displayed in cell F9. In cell C18, we calulate the value of $\sqrt{n} = sz/a$ by entering the formula =**B16\*3/F9**. In cell C19, we find the value of $n$ by entering the formula =**B18\*B18**, that is, by finding the squre of the value of $\sqrt{n}$. The displayed result in cell C19 is the sample size necessary for the desired accuracy and confidence level. It is 19.7442, which may be approximated as 20. Thus, 20 observations are required.

### Example 12.2

**Table 12.2**

| Observation no. | Recorded time (min) |
|---|---|
| 11 | 5.24 |
| 12 | 4.81 |
| 13 | 5.66 |
| 14 | 6.23 |
| 15 | 5.34 |
| 16 | 4.49 |
| 17 | 5.58 |
| 18 | 6.18 |
| 19 | 4.96 |
| 20 | 5.04 |

In continuation of Example 12.1, the observations shown in Table 12.2 are recorded. It is given that the performance rating $P = 1.10$ and the allowance $A = 5$ per cent of the normal time $N$. Find the observed, normal, and standard times for the job of the bellboy in the hotel.

### Solution

Figure 12.15 shows the calculations of the observed, normal, and standard times. The observed time $O$ as shown in cell B25 is the average of all the 20 observations of the time taken by a bellboy in attending to customers. Cell B26 contains the formula =**B25*1.10**, that is, $OP$ to calculate the normal time ($N$). The allowance, given as 5 per cent of $N$ is calculated in cell G27 by putting the formula =**0.05*B26** in this cell. Cell B27 contains the formula =**B26+G27** and gives the result 6.11226 minutes as the standard time.

| | A | B | C | D | E | F | G |
|---|---|---|---|---|---|---|---|
| 1 | **Stopwatch Time Study** | | | | | | |
| 2 | | | | | | | |
| 3 | | | | | | | |
| 4 | **Observation No.** | **Recorded Time (min.)** | | | | | |
| 5 | 1 | 5.86 | | | | | |
| 6 | 2 | 5.67 | | | | | |
| 7 | 3 | 5.94 | | | | | |
| 8 | 4 | 4.51 | | | | | |
| 9 | 5 | 4.65 | | | | | |
| 10 | 6 | 6.01 | | | | | |
| 11 | 7 | 5.17 | | | | | |
| 12 | 8 | 6.09 | | | | | |
| 13 | 9 | 4.22 | | | | | |
| 14 | 10 | 4.19 | | | | | |
| 15 | 11 | 5.24 | | | | | |
| 16 | 12 | 4.81 | | | | | |
| 17 | 13 | 5.66 | | | | | |
| 18 | 14 | 6.23 | | | | | |
| 19 | 15 | 5.34 | | | | | |
| 20 | 16 | 4.49 | | | | | |
| 21 | 17 | 5.58 | | | | | |
| 22 | 18 | 6.18 | | | | | |
| 23 | 19 | 4.96 | | | | | |
| 24 | 20 | 5.04 | | | | | |
| 25 | Average | 5.292 | Observed Time (O) | | | | |
| 26 | | 5.8212 | Normal Time (N) = O x P | | Given that Performance Rating P = 1.10 | | |
| 27 | | 6.11226 | Standard Time = N + A | | Allowance = 5% of N = | | 0.29106 |
| 28 | | | | | | | |
| 29 | | | | | | | |
| 30 | | | | | | | |
| 31 | | | | | | | |

**Fig. 12.15** Calculation of observed, normal, and standard times

Exhibit 12.2 discusses the ways jobs are designed at Google.

---

## Exhibit 12.2  Google

Google Inc. is a US$38 billion organization that has revolutionized the way jobs are designed for knowledge workers. Apart from staggering salaries and perks to its employees, it provides a work culture that exudes creativity. The founders of the company have intentionally retained the entrepreneurial spirit in the organization culture. The organizational structure is flat and there is no real hierarchy in the organization. The decision-making process is highly 'consultative', not the traditional 'control and command'.

Google operates in small groups, with each group acting as a small start-up organization. Therefore, Google is essentially an amalgamation of several start-up ventures within itself. Any individual is free to

*(Contd)*

*Exhibit 12.2 Contd*

change his or her group as per his or her wishes without any permission or having to go through any human resource channel. This is to instil a sense of freedom and authority in one and all. About 20 per cent of the time can be spent by an employee on a personal project about which he or she is passionate about. Services such as Gmail, Google News, Orkut, and AdSense originated from this endeavour of Google.

'Googleplex' is the name given by employees to its headquarters in California. Employees can show up at Googleplex for work anytime as per their will, come in pyjamas, bring their pets, eat gourmet cuisine free of charge, work out at the fitness centre under the guidance of a trainer free of charge, see an on-site doctor in case of sickness, take a bath or wash their clothes, or enjoy free drinks at the espresso at each corner of their workplace. This relaxed, fun-filled and serene environment is conducive for innovation that drives Google. In a nutshell, Google thrives on 'I think I can' spirit rather than the traditional 'No, you can't' bureaucracy.

## Work Sampling

Work sampling is a method used to determine the fraction of idle time of machines or workers during a day, or to determine the time spent by workers on different types of tasks. This method is suitable for jobs which are non-repetitive in nature. As the name suggests, sampling is done to make observations. In contrast to time study, work sampling does not require one to time the activities of workers. Whether a machine or worker is working or sitting idle is observed, and, if working, the kind of activity being performed is recorded.

For example, an employee who is an architect is expected to utilize most of his time making drawings of buildings rather than talking to clients. It does not imply that the architect should not be talking to clients, as understanding the requirements of the clients before making a drawing of the building is also important. At the same time, more meetings and less drawings compared to other architect employees in the company may result in less increments in this employee's pay.

A work sampling exercise is useful in the performance appraisal of employees involved in non-repetitive activities. In each observation, what the employee is doing at that moment is observed and recorded. It is necessary to determine the number of observations required in order to achieve the desired accuracy and confidence level. The number of observations (sample size *n*) is given by

$$n = \frac{pqz^2}{a^2}$$

> Work sampling is a method used to determine the fraction of idle time of machines or workers during a day, or to determine the time spent by workers on different types of tasks.

where $p$ is the percentage of items/persons possessing a particular characteristic in the sample drawn (say, the percentage of observations in which the worker/machine was idle), $q = (1-p)$ is the percentage of items/persons not possessing this particular characteristic in the sample drawn (say, the percentage of observations in which the worker/machine was working), $a$ is the desired accuracy, and $z$ is the desired confidence level (the $z$-value). The sample drawn should be of a suitable size (say, 10–25 observations) for finding the values of $p$ and $q$.

### Example 12.3

The administrative officer of Centurian Associates (a major law firm based at Kolkata) desires to conduct a work sampling study for estimating the idle time percentage of a photocopy machine in the office. Assuming that there are 9 working hours per day and the study will be conducted during a period of 10 days starting from the 1st of July, make a time schedule for 10 observations to be made in the work sampling. Assume that the working time is from 8 a.m. to 5 p.m. every day and there will be no holiday between the 1st and 10th of July.

### Solution

Take an initial sample of 10 observations to estimate the values of $p$ and $q$. It takes just a moment to see whether a machine is working or not for each observation. It is important to take the observations at random time instants, for which we will use random numbers as shown in Fig. 12.16. In each of the cells A4 to A9, put the formula =**RAND()** and then press **F9** on the keyboard. A random number is generated between 0 and 1 in each of these cells. To make the random number completely visible, double click on the boundary to the right of the column A heading. The benefit of using the F9 key is that the random number generated in a cell will not change every time the worksheet is opened. Otherwise, every time the worksheet is opened, MS Excel regenerates a new random number in the given cell. The random-number table (Table B of the Appendix) can also be used in place of the random numbers generated by MS Excel.

| | A | B | C | D | E | F | G |
|---|---|---|---|---|---|---|---|
| 1 | **Work Sampling** | | | | | | |
| 2 | | | | | | | |
| 3 | **Random Numbers** | **Serial No.** | **Day** | **Hour** | **Minute** | **Time** | **Date** |
| 4 | 0.927582689 | 1 | 9 | 0 | 42 | 8:42 | 10th July |
| 5 | 0.0000911121 | 2 | 2 | 0 | 11 | 8:11 | 3rd July |
| 6 | 0.159442981 | 3 | 7 | 0 | 0 | 8:00 | 8th July |
| 7 | 0.100843405 | 4 | 5 | 1 | 34 | 9:34 | 6th July |
| 8 | 0.594405051 | 5 | 8 | 1 | 5 | 9:05 | 9th July |
| 9 | 0.86333008 | 6 | 2 | 1 | 59 | 9:59 | 3rd July |
| 10 | | 7 | 6 | 2 | 44 | 10:44 | 7th July |
| 11 | | 8 | 8 | 1 | 5 | 9:05 | 9th July |
| 12 | | 9 | 9 | 1 | 5 | 9:05 | 10th July |
| 13 | | 10 | 0 | 5 | 18 | 13:18 | 1st July |
| 14 | | | | | | | |
| 15 | | | | **Observation No.** | **Date** | **Time** | |
| 16 | | | | 1 | 1st July | 13:18 | |
| 17 | | | | 2 | 3rd July | 8:11 | |
| 18 | | | | 3 | 3rd July | 9:59 | |
| 19 | | | | 4 | 6th July | 9:34 | |
| 20 | | | | 5 | 7th July | 10:44 | |
| 21 | | | | 6 | 8th July | 8:00 | |
| 22 | | | | 7 | 9th July | 9:05 | |
| 23 | | | | 8 | 9th July | 9:05 | |
| 24 | | | | 9 | 10th July | 8:42 | |
| 25 | | | | 10 | 10th July | 9:05 | |

**Fig. 12.16** Work sampling

Column B in Fig. 12.16 shows the serial numbers of the 10 observations to be taken. In column C, we find the days on which the observations will be taken using the random numbers. The random number displayed in cell A4 is 0.927582689. We have to conduct the work sampling in 10 days, which we represent from 0 to 9. The first digit after the decimal in the random number of cell A4 is 9. Thus, on day 9 we will select a sample observation as shown in cell C4. The next digit is 2, thus on day 2 a sample observation will be made as shown in cell C5. Similarly, the next seven digits in this random number represent the days on which observations will be made, that is, days 7, 5, 8, 2, 6, 8, and 9, as shown in cells C6 to C9. So far, we have selected days for nine observations.

Therefore, for selecting the day for the 10th observation, move to the next random number shown in cell A5. In this random number, that is, 0.0000911121, the first digit after the decimal is 0. Hence, we will make the 10th observation on day 0, as shown in cell C13.

It is given that there are 9 working hours per day for workers, which we will represent by numbers 0 to 8. In the random number in our consideration, the next digit is 0 (in the second place of decimal). We will therefore conduct the observation on the zeroth hour of day 9 as shown in cell D4. Similarly, the next two digits in the random number are both zero and appear in cells D5 and D6. The next digit is 9, which will be neglected, as the hour to be considered is represented by numbers from 0 to 8 only. The subsequent digits 1, 1, 1, 2, and 1 appear in cells D7 to D11. For the value in cells D12 and D13, choose the first and second digits after the decimal in the next random number 0.159442981 (cell A6), that is, 1 and 5, respectively.

Now let us select the exact time (to the minute) for each observation. We know that the highest minute in an hour is 59, after which the hour changes. Thus, this time we will select two digits together from the random numbers to represent the minutes of an hour. We will start from the random number under consideration, from the third digit after decimal, as its earlier digits have been used to represent the hours. The next two digits in the random number give the value 94, which is higher than the maximum possible value 59. Thus, these will be neglected. The next two digits are 4 and 2, which are selected to give the 42nd minute of hour 0 on day 9 as shown in cell E4. Similarly, other values of minutes are chosen as shown in cells E5 to E13.

The time and date of the various observations can now be found. Day 9 is July 10, as the study will start from July 1 (day 0). The working hours start from 8 a.m., so the zeroth hour is the time between 8 and 9 a.m. Thus, the first observation details, as shown in cells F4 and G4, are 8:42 a.m. and 10th July, respectively, that is, on July 10 at 8:42 a.m., the first observation will be made. Similarly, calculate the time instants and dates of the other nine observations. These are arranged in a chronological order as shown in cells E16 to E25 and F16 to F25, respectively. Note that on July 9, the observation to be made at 9:05 a.m. is repeated twice (observation numbers 7 and 8). This happens very rarely and one of such observations may be neglected, so that we have nine observations to be made.

### Example 12.4

In continuation of Example 12.3, the nine observations are made as scheduled and the recordings are made for a machine being busy or idle during the observations, as shown in Table 12.3. If the officer wants an accuracy of ±15 per cent from the actual percentage and a confidence level of 95.4 per cent (second sigma limits), determine the sample size necessary for achieving the desired accuracy and confidence level.

**Table 12.3**

| Observation no. | Date | Time (h:min) | Working | Idle |
|---|---|---|---|---|
| 1 | 1st July | 13:18 | Yes | No |
| 2 | 3rd July | 8:11 | Yes | No |
| 3 | 3rd July | 9:59 | Yes | No |
| 4 | 6th July | 9:34 | No | Yes |
| 5 | 7th July | 10:44 | Yes | No |
| 6 | 8th July | 8:00 | No | Yes |
| 7 | 9th July | 9:05 | No | Yes |
| 8 | 10th July | 8:42 | Yes | No |
| 9 | 10th July | 9:05 | Yes | No |

### Solution

In three out of nine observations, the machine has been idle. Thus, $p = 3/9 \times 100 = 33.33\%$, $q = 100\% - p = 100\% - 33.33\% = 66.67\%$, $z = 2$ (second sigma limits), $a = 5\%$. Therefore,

$$n = \frac{pqz^2}{a^2} = \frac{33.33 \times 66.67 \times 2^2}{15^2} = 39.50 \text{ observations} \approx 40 \text{ observations}$$

## Productivity

Productivity is defined as the ratio of output produced to the input used in its producion.

$$\text{Productivity} = \frac{\text{Output}}{\text{Input}}$$

Output is usually in terms of units of the product produced, while input can be in terms of units of any one resource, a combination of resources, or all the resources taken together. For exaple,

$$\text{Productivity} = \frac{\text{Number of units produced}}{\text{Man-hours used}}$$

or

$$\text{Productivity} = \frac{\text{Number of units produced}}{\text{Capital employed}}$$

or

$$\text{Productivity} = \frac{\text{Number of units produced}}{\text{Machine-hours used}}$$

or

$$\text{Productivity} = \frac{\text{Number of units produced}}{\text{Man-hours used} + \text{Machine-hours used}}$$

Productivity can be calculated for an individual, a machine, a department, a company, an industry, or even an economy. The input resource considered in productivity calculations depends upon the requirement of the organization. An organization may be considering labour as the only input factor in productivity calculations because it wants to take effective steps to increase labour productivity. In case inputs being considered are different resources, for example, labour, materials, power, etc., in productivity calculations, a common unit of these inputs has to be considered. It can be the cost of labour, cost of materials, cost of power, etc.

$$\text{Productivity} = \frac{\text{Number of units produced}}{\text{Cost of labour} + \text{Cost of materials} + \text{Cost of power}}$$

### Example 12.5

Aqua Plastics manufactured 2,00,000 units of thermos flasks in the last financial year. It utilized 10 workers and 5 machines working for 8 hours per day (h/d) during 200 working days of the year in the production of these flasks. What is the productivity of the company with respect to labour and machine inputs taken together?

### Solution

$$\text{Productivity} = \frac{\text{Number of units produced}}{\text{Man-hours used} + \text{Machine-hours used}}$$

$$= \frac{2,00,000 \text{ units produced}}{(10 \text{ workers} \times 8 \text{ h/d/ worker} \times 200) + (5 \text{ machines} \times 8 \text{ h/d/ machine} \times 200\text{d})}$$

$$= \frac{2,00,000 \text{ units produced}}{16,000 \text{ h} + 8,000 \text{ h}} = \frac{2,00,000 \text{ units produced}}{24,000 \text{ h}} = 8.33 \text{ units/hour}$$

It is the ultimate aim of every organization to increase the overall productivity of the organization, that is, to produce as many units of output as possible by utilizing as little of the input as possible. It is necessary to have productivity measurement systems in place in order to have an idea about the current productivity levels. The organization can set reasonable goals with respect to increase in productivity and take appropriate steps to achieve them. The involvement of workers is very important in this process as their suggestions (kaizens, in Japanese) for improvement of productivity may be most useful for the organization.

Technology also plays a major role in productivity enhancement. In fact, a company may leapfrog in terms of productivity by making significant advances by using the latest technology in its operations. Finally, the productivity increases need to be measured, and the individuals responsible for such increases should be given suitable recognition through rewards, certificates of apprecation, etc.

## Summary

*Work design* has two main constituents—*job design* and *work measurement*. Job design is allocating tasks to be performed by a worker in his daily routine. *Methods analysis* is a technique which can be applied to a new job design as well as to the improvisations of jobs established earlier by using tools such as *flow process chart, employee–machine activity chart*, and *principles of motion economy*.

Work measurement is the measurement of the performance time of a job in order to set a time standard for it. These time standards serve as a benchmark to assess the performance levels of various employees performing the same job. Work measurement can be done using techniques such as *stopwatch time study and work sampling. Sampling theory* is used in both these techniques. The important concept of sampling theory is the fact that the mean or average of all the sample means is always the same as the universe mean. For large sample sizes, the distribution of sample means is a normal distribution curve for all practical purposes.

*Stopwatch time study* is a method of work measurement used for measuring the standard duration of repetitive tasks. *Work sampling* is a method used to determine the fraction of idle time of machines or workers during a day, or to determine the time spent by workers on different types of tasks. This method is suitable for jobs which are non-repetitive in nature. *Productivity* is defined as the ratio of output produced to the input used in its production. It is important to have proper productivity measurement systems in place in order to have an idea about the current productivity levels. The organization can set reasonable goals with respect to increase in productivity and take appropriate steps to achieve them.

## References

Breaugh, J. 1985, 'The measurement of work autonomy', *Human Relations*, vol. 38, no. 6, pp. 551–570.

Conti, R.F. and M. Warner 2001, 'A customer-driven model of job design: towards a general theory', The Judge Institute of Management Studies, Cambridge, UK.

Edmondson G. 2003, 'BMW's labour practices are cutting-edge, too', *Business Week*, http://www. businessweek.com/stories/2003-06-08/bmws-labor-practices-are-cutting-edge-too, accessed on 1 February 2013.

Thompson, P. and T. Wallace 1996, 'Redesigning production through team working: Case studies from Volvo Truck Corporation', *International Journal of Operations and Production Management*, vol. 16, no. 2.

# Keywords

**Central limit theorem** states that for large samples, the frequency distribution of sample means is approximately a normal distribution curve for all practical purposes.

**Employee–machine activity charts** help in methods analysis of jobs for improving the efficiency of employees and machines. It shows the various time instants and the activities of an employee and a machine simultaneously.

**Flow process charts** show the flow of materials, labour, and products (semi-finished and finished) from one place to another in the facility. They help in identifying the various sources of delay in the process, which may be eliminated in order to achieve better efficiency.

**Job design** means assigning various tasks to a job to be performed by a worker in his daily routine.

**Job enlargement** is the horizontal loading of a worker's job. This means certain tasks of the same skill and mental level as being handled by the worker presently are added to his job.

**Job enrichment** means giving some additional responsibilities to a worker, which are slightly more dignified than the routine tasks being handled by him. This is also called *vertical loading* of the worker's job.

**Job rotation** is swapping (interchanging) highly repetitive tasks like in assembly lines amongst workers after a suitable interval of time.

**Methods analysis** is a technique in job design in which the job is usually broken down into various steps or procedures. The workplace arrangement, tools and equipment used, materials used, and the worker's skill set required for performing the job are all studied in detail in order to devise better methods.

**Normal time** ($N$) of a job is the performance rating ($P$) multiplied by the observed time of the job.

**Principles of motion economy** aim at minimizing the fatigue of workers due to repetitive motion of the different parts of the body such as hands, feet, eyes, etc. and, thus, maximizing the efficiency of the worker during the performance of a job.

**Productivity** is defined as the ratio of output produced to the input used in its production.

**Self-directed teams** are teams of workers given the liberty to initiate changes in the work processes in their domain for initiating improvements.

**Standard deviation** ($\sigma$) is a measure of the dispersion of a curve. The standard deviation of the distribution of sample means is denoted by $\sigma_\mu$ and is called standard error of the mean.

**Standard time** is the time taken by an average worker to perform a task at a sustainable rate under the given facility arrangements. It is also the normal time plus allowances. Allowances have to be made for time consumed in adjusting or repairing machines, workers drinking water or taking rest breaks, etc.

**Stopwatch time study** is a method of work measurement used for measuring the standard duration of repetitive tasks.

**Work design** is an umbrella term used to collectively address the issues of job design and work measurement.

**Work sampling** is a method used to determine the fraction of idle time of machines or workers during a day, or to determine the time spent by workers on different types of tasks. This method is suitable for jobs which are non-repetitive in nture.

---

## CASE STUDY I

## Taj Hotels

Indian Hotels Limited (IHL), belonging to India's prestigious Tata Group, operates one of the largest hotel chains in the country under the brand Taj Hotels Resorts and Palaces. Its history begins more than 100 years back when the group's founder, Jamsetji N Tata, opened the first hotel, the Taj Mahal Palace and Tower, in Mumbai in the year 1903.

Legend has it that Jamsetji set his mind on building it after being denied entry into one of the city's hotels for being an Indian during the British rule. His sons, friends, and business associates were sceptical. His sisters asked him, 'Are you really going to build a *bhatarkhana* (eating house)?' The Taj turned out to be a bit fancier than that. By the time of its completion in 1903, it had cost ₹42.1 million. Soaked in luxury, it was the first building in Bombay to use electricity and the first hotel in the country to have US-made fans, German elevators, Turkish baths, English butlers, and whole lot of other innovative delights.

Today, the brand 'Taj Hotels Resorts and Palaces' comprises 58 hotels across India and 17 hotels in international locations. The hotels are grouped into three categories—luxury, leisure, and business. The Taj Luxury Hotels offer lavish accommodation, gourmet specialty restaurants and bars, fitness centres and spas, and well-equipped business and banquet facilities. The Taj group pioneered the concept of authentic palace hotels in the country with the Rambagh Palace of Jaipur and idyllic beach resort at Fort Aguada, Goa. These properties have gone on to become popular tourist destinations. Table 12.4 shows the international properties of the group (excluding the Taj Boston, which was the erstwhile Ritz Carton Hotel acquired and renamed).

**Table 12.4** International properties of the Taj Group

| Location | IHL property |
| --- | --- |
| New York, USA | The Pierre |
| London, UK | 51 Buckingham Gate, Crowne Plaza London St. James |
| Dubai, UAE | Taj Palace Hotel |
| Sana's, Yemen | Taj Sheba Hotel |
| Sohar, Oman | Sohar Beach Hotel |
| Lusaka, Zambia | Taj Pamodzi |
| Wolmar, Mauritius | Taj Exotica Resort & Spa |
| Maldives | Taj Exotica Resort & Spa, Taj Coral reef Resort |
| Seychelles | Taj Denis Island |
| Bentota, Sri Lanka | Taj Exotica |
| Colombo, Sri Lanka | Taj Samudra, Airport Garden Hotel |
| Langkawi, Malaysia | Rebak Marina Resort |
| Sydney, Australia | Hotel Blue Sydney |

As a support to its hospitality business, IHL runs a professionally managed travel agency providing total travel management solutions under the brand name Inditravel. Inditravel offers services such as air and rail ticketing, hotel bookings, car rentals, visa and passport assistance, foreign exchange assistance, global telecards, and medical insurance. IHL also operates Taj Air, a luxury private jet operation with two state-of-the-art Falcon 2,000 aircrafts, and Taj Yachts, two 3-bedroom luxury yachts that can be used by guests in Mumbai and Kochi (Kerala). It also operates an airline catering service under the brand name TajSATS

Air Catering as a joint venture with Singapore Airport Terminal Services, a subsidiary of Singapore Airlines. TajSATS caters to international and domestic flights operating in New Delhi, Mumbai, Kolkata, and Chennai.

Taj Hotels has launched a programme across its hotels known as Taj Brand Standards that identifies standard operating procedures to ensure consistency in guest experience. In order to ensure that these standards are consistently implemented and sustained across the organization, a robust third party audit system has also been initiated.

The hotel Taj President in Mumbai recently witnessed a peculiar problem in its main kitchen. Breakages in the main kitchen were high due to incorrect flow of cutlery and crockery during washing. The Konkan Café and the Thai Kitchen, the two restaurants at Taj President, were also facing problems due to the depth of the sink and mixing up of metal and chinaware. The hotel decided to set up a kaizen team comprising Chef Ananda Solomon, Rajkishore Mahto, and Wilfred Rebello—who immediately sprung into action. The team studied the problem and set about to rectify it.

The system of 'one piece at a time' into the dishwasher was implemented. The layout of the dishwashing area was changed to facilitate single-piece flow. The result—the breakage of crockery came down by 28 per cent. Savings from the stoppage of breakages are at ₹6,00,000 per annum. In the main kitchen, gains are around ₹1,75,000 per annum and in the Konkan Café and Thai Kitchen, the gains are around ₹2,00,000 each.

This is not a one-off incident at the Taj group. Over the past two years, the group has institutionalized both the kaizen approach and the total productivity maintenance (TPM) approach. This is embodied in the Tata business excellence model (TBEM), which all the Tata group companies have adopted. The TBEM model adopted by the Taj group offers the JRD QV Award that is built along the lines of the Malcolm Baldrige National Quality Award in the US.

This whole process has been institutionalized in the Taj group. There is an apex council headed by the Managing Director and comprises around 12 people. There is a business council of each strategic business unit (SBU). Each Taj Hotel in India has a quality council headed by a general manager. An average Taj Hotel has around 14 process implementation teams. They report to the quality council of their respective hotels. The quality council in turn reports to the SBU. However, some of the major Taj hotels such as the flagship

Taj Mahal Hotel in Mumbai, may have up to 20 process implementation teams. These cover every major area, including housekeeping, front office, coffee shop, and other facilities.

This process enables any best practice adopted in any of the hotels to be picked up across the chain. For example, the cross-functional team in Taj Holiday Village, Goa, reorganized room service work floor resulting in savings of ₹7,00,000 per annum and released 150 sq metre of space where a staff activity centre was set up. The transformation has been marked. The savings were ₹75 million within one year of implementation. Indirectly, the savings added up to around ₹150 to 200 million.

So how has the Taj group gone about implementing the TPM and the kaizen approach? For starters, the top officials of the group personally visited the world's leading hotel chains such as the Ritz Carlton and Four Seasons to learn about their best practices. The Taj team not only visited the leading hotel chains but also other leading organizations such as Motorola and FedExpress which have implemented the Malcolm Baldrige model.

The Taj group benchmarked with Ritz Carlton on 'customer satisfaction measurement' in luxury hotels. The Ritz Carlton, which adopted the Malcolm Baldrige model in 1989, won its first award in 1993. Today it is the highest profit-making company of the Marriott group. The Taj group has also adopted its 'three steps to service' philosophy, which is used for defining performance requirements of employees at all levels—warm welcome, anticipatory service, and fond farewell.

After returning from there, the Taj team installed 'customer listening posts' as practised by Ritz Carlton to update guest history data, which is deployed in all guest contact areas, to deliver anticipatory service. The group has also implemented a foolproof guest service tracking system (GSTS) to keep the auditing process clean. This was developed indigenously with the help of IMRB–CSMM market research agency. Each group hotel receives around 2,500 responses every month from its residents, which add up to around 6,000 responses every quarter. These responses are analysed across the 63 questions covered. The responses are then segregated across the areas of operation. The scores are audited by market research firm IMRB, which then suggests ways of improvement. The MD selects the ten best teams across the chain every year. There are performance-linked bonuses and reward mechanisms. The scores on all fronts have been going up, which is itself a proof of the success of the system.

The group also tracks the processes in every hotel. There are about 30 process engines involved. The basic poser is, 'is your hotel vibrant and dynamic in building and strengthening the TBEM framework?' Every hotel has to provide a compliance report on this front. The Taj group currently ranks among the best three hotel chains in Asia. Its aim is to be among the top chains in the world.

The Taj Group of Hotels won the Hermes Award 2002 for the best innovation in human resources in the global hospitality industry for its special thanks and recognition system (STARS). This system was devised in 2001 to encourage employees, to make them go beyond their call of duty, to motivate them to have fun, and to introduce joy at the workplace.

The STARS programme runs from April to March every year and has five distinct recognition levels. Level 1 or the silver grade requires an employee to earn 120 points in three months, level 2 or the Gold grade can be reached with 130 points within three months of reaching the silver level. Level 3 or the Platinum grade requires an employee to accumulate 250 points within six months of reaching the Gold level. The highest grade at the corporate level is the MD's Club (at 760 points and above), below which at 510 points and above an employee can be part of the Chief Operating Officer's (COO) club.

Each hotel in the group has a general manager, an HR manager, and a training manager, who evaluates all suggestions and nominations. The entire process is web-enabled and is regularly monitored. The programme allows employees to win points (at the recommendation of a colleague or a guest). This gives them access to different levels of standing that go hand-in-hand with specific rewards. Accumulation of points enables employees to pin star on their lapel. Still more points gets them into exclusive clubs that can fetch gift vouchers, cash prizes, and holidays in a Taj hotel of their choice. In addition, employees are strongly encouraged to make suggestions and recommend innovations that may be applied to the group as a whole.

For example, a bellboy received an American guest recently after a late-night flight. While escorting him to the room, he realized that the guest had the beginnings of a cold. The guest, though, declined his offer to fetch a doctor. So, of his own accord, the bellboy got the guest a glass of warm water spiked with some ginger and honey (a home remedy). The guest was surprised and delighted. He wrote a note about this gesture and this added to the employee's points.

There was also a suggestion by an employee for guests who were received in the afternoons, 'Why keep morning papers in the pickup van for guests who must have already read them in the flight? We should be keeping Mid Day and some magazines.' The suggestion was implemented and the employee was rewarded 10 points and this best practice was shared with Taj hotels all over the country by email. Another suggestion was made by an employee that cars owned by in-house guests and parked in the hotel overnight should be cleaned and a small note left behind for the guest saying, 'Your car has been cleaned'. This act was thought to dazzle and delight the hotel guests.

During 2001, the winners in the programme were honoured at an Oscars style ceremony in the Taj, Mumbai. Clips about the winners were screened and the MD gave away the awards. This served as a huge morale booster across the group. After this ceremony, every hotel—even those that did not take the programme seriously earlier—pulled up its socks and is vying to get there. The programme has generated plenty of enthusiasm and has improved the guest satisfaction levels. Employees are getting acknowledged and service standards have gone up. Since this links directly to the hotel's business in the form of repeat customers, STARS is not only a feel-good operation, but also a strategic success, a programme that has been patented by the Taj Group.

In January 2007, Boston's famous Ritz-Carlton hotel was taken over by the Taj group and renamed Taj Boston. The purchase of the hotel in Boston by Indian Hotels for US$170 million, at first sight, is just one among many big-ticket acquisitions by Indian companies. This acquisition is unusual because of the complex brand transition that is under way. The deal involves only the Boston property, not the brand. The Boston hotel, located next to the famous Boston Public Garden, is the oldest to carry the Ritz Carlton brand and has been operational since 1927. It was the first hotel in the US to offer private baths in guest rooms. Indian Hotels' operational performance in running the erstwhile Ritz-Carlton of Boston will determine the ranking the Taj brand attains internationally.

## Discussion Questions

1. The STARS programme of Taj group of hotels is in a way, an extension of methods analysis performed by the employees themselves for giving improvement suggestions. Discuss.
2. There seems to be an overlap between the STARS programme and the kaizen or TPM initiatives of the Taj group. What are the key differences and similarities in these approaches? Is it alright if these initiatives co-exist?
3. Unlike manufacturing set-ups, it is difficult to measure the increased levels of productivity in services set-ups such that of Taj hotels. Is it necessary to measure the productivity levels of employes in such services?

---

## CASE STUDY II

# Volvo Truck Corporation

Volvo Truck Corporation (VTC) is a vertically integrated multinational organization, manufacturing the full range of commercial vehicles from cars to trucks and buses. VTC has an engine plant at Skovde (Sweden), which has three distinct production environments: process, manufacturing, and assembly. The process environment is in the foundry area, which is a capital-intensive single-flow process implementing a just-in-time (JIT) system. Maintenance workers have to be highly mobile so that they can quickly be at a system breakdown point when a problem occurs. Teams are linked to distinct process areas—melting, forming, cleaning, core making, heat treatment, etc.—with each having around 50 employees with one supervisor, split into a number of what they call 'semi-autonomous work teams'. The operator is not greatly responsible for the quality, maintenance, productivity, and decision-making, with total responsibility devoted to the supervisors. The units have no team leaders, nor do they meet in any form of quality circle, although they do have some job rotation within, or rather between, phases.

At Skovde, the manufacturing environment is linked to automated production in a multi-machine set-up. The finished shafts and casings are transferred from the foundry to either the D factory where they are machined into crankshafts, transmission covers, and camshafts, or to the A factory where they are machined into cylinder heads and cylinder blocks. In both the plants, teams are organized around specific production lines and shifts with a philosophy of job rotation, payment is linked to the achievement of competences, providing a more cost-effective production environment. In a functionally flexible environment and with the machines running themselves, operators are released to perform indirect tasks associated with material supply, quality, housekeeping, and task allocations within the teams. Operators are responsible for some control and programming functions, product quality, machine set-ups and retooling—which reduces down time, ordering of material as well as machine operations, and also planning their own work. It is the team which is looking to define and make its own 'continuous improvements' and it is the teams, rather than the managers, which are responsible for solving quality problems.

The truck engine assembly at Skovde has a dual production strategy in place, with all common operations being carried out on an automatic flow line. At the end of the automated element production, the engines go into one of the 12 docks in which the customized elements are added manually. The flow line system is automated, with manual loading and unloading at the start and end of the process, and with units carried from machine to machine by a roller system. Each unit is loaded onto the carrier system, which contains a computerized sensor that records information every time an operation is carried out. This is linked to a computer which sends a message to the store, which then sends out material by automatic carriers to the relevant station. There is a loose, task-rotating structure that is fluid enough to allow operators to wander around the system helping each other.

VTC has its Umea plant situated in Northern Sweden, which cuts, presses, assembles, and paints cab parts to be delivered to assembly plants in Sweden, Belgium, and Scotland. Production is based around a series of short flows—a combination of flow line and dock technology, with each flow consisting of four stations organized sequentially in a square formation. There are two operators per station with a *floating ninth person* who also acts as the team leader and an operator replacement as and when required. The position of the team leader is appointed and not rotated. He continues to operate as a blue-collar worker and to spend some of his time in helping reduce the number of supervisors by being responsible for the introduction and use of new short flows, deciding when to get rid of people and who to get rid of, and juggling labour shortages. In other words, he carries out some of the more mundane traditional supervisory functions. The plant manager observes that 'We cannot expect a guy to be a craftsman when he is doing the same job 15 or 20 times a day. If you expand the work it will give [the operator] value. I am not talking about doing the usual work for two hours instead of 30 minutes, I am talking of adding more complicated work outside the usual work by expanding frontiers' (Thompson & Wallace 1996).

### Discussion Questions

1. Why does VTC have different sets of resp-onsibilities for operators in the process, manufacturing, and assembly departments of its Skovde plant?
2. In which department of the Skovde plant do you find the approach to job design the best?
3. In your view, is it right to appoint a team leader like it is done at VTC's Umea plant? Is the concept of a floating ninth person suitable in a facility?

## Objective Questions

### Choose the correct option

1. Which one is not a formal method of work measurement?
   (a) time study method
   (b) elemental standard data approach
   (c) post-determined data approach
   (d) work sampling method
2. Which one is not a formal method of job design?
   (a) time study method
   (b) methods analysis
   (c) job enlargement
   (d) principles of motion economy
3. Which one is not a job task discretion that can be exercised by workers on a factory floor?
   (a) work method
   (b) work criteria
   (c) work enlargement
   (d) work schedule
4. Which one is not considered in stop-watch time study?
   (a) observed time
   (b) elapsed time
   (c) normal time
   (d) standard time

## State True or False

5. A 'work standard' is the work required for trained workers to complete a task by following prescribed methods with normal effort and skill.
6. Work measurement is the process of creating work standards based on the judgement of industrial engineers or skilled observers.
7. Job enrichment is the horizontal loading of a worker's job.

## Fill in the blanks

8. A _____ chart shows the flow of materials, labour, and products from one place to another in the facility.
9. An _____ chart shows the various time instants and the activities of an employee and a machine simultaneously.
10. _____ study is used to is used for measuring the standard duration of repetitive tasks.

# Concept Review Questions

1. What is work design? What are its constituents? Explain using a schematic diagram.
2. What is job design? What are the behavioural aspects in job design?
3. What are the three types of job-task discretion?
4. Explain the job-task discretion matrix using suitable examples.
5. What is methods analysis? How are flow process chart and employee–machine activity chart helpful in methods analysis?
6. What are the principles of motion economy? Why are these required?
7. What is meant by sampling? Using a simple example, explain how the mean of all the sample means is always the same as the universe mean.
8. What is the nature of the distribution of sample means? How can predictions be made by using a distribution of sample means? Explain with an example.
9. What is a confidence interval for a given confidence level?
10. State the central limit theorem of statistics. How is it useful in sampling theory?
11. How can the sample size required for a desired accuracy and confidence level be determined?
12. What is stopwatch time study? What are the observed, normal, and standard times of a job?
13. What is work sampling? How is it different from stopwatch time study?
14. Define productivity. How can it be measured? How can the productivity of an organization be increased?

# Numerical Problems

1. Raipur Bank has its main branch at Raipur. The branch manager of the bank conducts a stopwatch time study in order to find the standard time taken by a teller in making payments to the customers. The manager wants to be virtually certain about the estimated average time taken by the teller to be studied and also desires an accuracy of ±10% from the actual average. A preliminary sampling of 10 observations is conducted and the recordings made are given in Table 12.5. Calculate the sample size of observations in order to achieve the desired accuracy and confidence level in the estimation of the observed time.

2. In continuation of Problem 1, Table 12.6 shows eight more observations. Given that the performance rating $P = 1.15$ and allowance $A = 5\%$ of the normal time $N$, find the observed, normal, and standard times for the job of the teller in the Raipur main branch of the bank.

**Table 12.5**

| Observation no. | Recorded time (min) | Observation no. | Recorded time (min) |
|---|---|---|---|
| 1 | 3.68 | 6 | 3.23 |
| 2 | 3.45 | 7 | 3.82 |
| 3 | 2.81 | 8 | 4.21 |
| 4 | 4.3 | 9 | 2.85 |
| 5 | 3.71 | 10 | 3.52 |

**Table 12.6**

| Observation no. | Recorded time (min) | Observation no. | Recorded time (min) |
|---|---|---|---|
| 11 | 3.15 | 15 | 3.46 |
| 12 | 2.98 | 16 | 3.33 |
| 13 | 4.17 | 17 | 2.81 |
| 14 | 3.72 | 18 | 3.6 |

3. The managing director of Yashowardhan Exports is interested in estimating the percentage of time his

secretary spends in taking shorthand dictations from him and then typing. The rest of the secretary's time is spent in filing and mailing the letters, which the MD feels is a wastage of her talent. He sanctions a work sampling study to be conducted in this regard. Assuming that there are nine working hours per day and the study will be conducted in a period of 10 days starting from November 1, make a time schedule for 10 observations to be made in the work sampling. Assume that the working time is 8 a.m. to 5 p.m. every day and there will be no holiday (including Sundays) between the 1st and 10th of November.

4. In continuation of Problem 3, the 10 observations are made as scheduled, and the type of work handled by the secretary during the observations is recorded as shown in Table 12.7. If the MD wants an accuracy of ± 10% from the actual percentage and a confidence level of 95.4% (second sigma limits), determine the sample size necessary for achieving this.

**Table 12.7**

| Observation no. | Date | Time (h:min) | Shorthand/typing | Filing/mailing |
|:---:|:---:|:---:|:---:|:---:|
| 1 | 1st Nov. | 9:16 | Yes | No |
| 2 | 1st Nov. | 15:27 | Yes | No |
| 3 | 2nd Nov. | 12:34 | No | Yes |
| 4 | 2nd Nov. | 16:42 | No | Yes |
| 5 | 3rd Nov. | 8:26 | Yes | No |
| 6 | 4th Nov. | 10:22 | No | Yes |
| 7 | 5th Nov. | 12:27 | Yes | No |
| 8 | 7th Nov. | 13:50 | Yes | No |
| 9 | 7th Nov. | 16:03 | Yes | No |
| 10 | 10th Nov. | 16:40 | No | Yes |

5. Oriental Fans manufactured 1,00,000 units of fans in the last financial year. It utilized 8 workers and 6 machines working for 8 hours a day during the 210 working days of the year in the production of these fans. What is the productivity of the company with respect to labour and machine inputs taken together?

# Project Assignments

1. Visit a nearby branch of a nationalized bank and perform a time study to measure the time taken by a teller in making payments to a customer. Then repeat the same time study in a nearby branch of a private-sector bank. Make a report highlighting the time difference between these two measurements.

2. In your institute library, study the activities of a library attendant responsible for issuing books using work sampling. Determine the percentage of time during which the attendant is busy issuing or taking back books. Make suitable assumptions and discuss among groups in the class.

**Answers to Objective Questions**

1. (c)        2. (a)        3. (c)        4. (b)        5. False

6. True      7. False     8. flow process    9. employee-machine activity

10. Stopwatch time

# 13

# Operations Scheduling

## Learning Objectives

After reading this chapter, you will be able to answer the following questions:

- What is operations scheduling?
- What are the various functions or steps to be performed by an operations manager in scheduling?
- What is sequencing or prioritization?
- Which are the different ways of scheduling various jobs or activities in an organization?
- Is there a relationship between the capacity of a work centre and scheduling?

## Operations Scheduling

Operations scheduling is one of the planning functions of an operations manager. This function of the operations manager is most important in job shop processing. This is because in job shop processing, the variety of items is large, the number of items to be produced in a batch is usually less, and the machines and workers are versatile and hence perform different types of jobs. In continuous and semi-continuous production processes (such as assembly lines), scheduling is automatically done at the time of designing the facility, as the product has almost no variety and the production volumes are very large (various types of production/operations processes have been discussed in the section 'Process Design' of Chapter 1). Operations scheduling in job shops involves the following activities:

1. Assigning job orders to different machines (or work centres)
2. Deciding the sequence of processing on different machines on the basis of some priority rule (called *sequencing* or *prioritization*)

> In continuous and semi-continuous production processes, scheduling is automatically done at the time of designing the facility.

3. Planning the route of movement of material from one department to another during processing (called *routing*)
4. Issuing dispatch lists to the various work centres containing information about the work centres a customer order should be processed at, the customer order to be processed first, the amount of time the processing should take, and so on (called *dispatching*)

When a proper schedule is prepared for job orders, the overall set-up time of machines is reduced by sequencing jobs such that similar jobs are processed one after the other.

5. Tracking the progress of various scheduled jobs and the implementation of schedules, revising the schedules in case of delays, and expediting the completion of certain jobs (called *expediting*)

The absence of proper scheduling may lead to various problems as shown in Fig. 13.1. The workers may take up any job order at random and start processing it. It is likely that this job order had a much later due date compared to a job order whose due date was close. This will result in delays in meeting the due dates of customer orders, and the random processing of jobs will result in high work-in-process (WIP) inventory. This is because, in the processing sequence of various jobs at different work centres, jobs are chosen at random, so that many jobs have to wait for a long time, resulting in high WIP. In the absence of scheduling, the overall set-up time increases. All these problems (higher waiting/ordering time, higher set-up time, etc.) result in a high average completion time of each job order. In addition, the operations manager will have no information about the current status of a particular job, as the workers themselves will decide about processing a job randomly. At some point of time, at some work centres, workers and machines will be overburdened with work, while at other work centres, they may be idle, waiting for jobs to come to their work centre in sequence. Hence, there will be low utilization of workers and machines leading to a high cost of operations. When a proper schedule is prepared for job orders, the overall set-up time of machines (oiling, cleaning, changing of tools, etc.) is reduced by sequencing jobs such that similar jobs are processed one after the other. Thus, in the absence of scheduling there will be complete turmoil in the shop floor of the facility. In order to avoid such an undesirable situation, operations scheduling is a must for every organization.

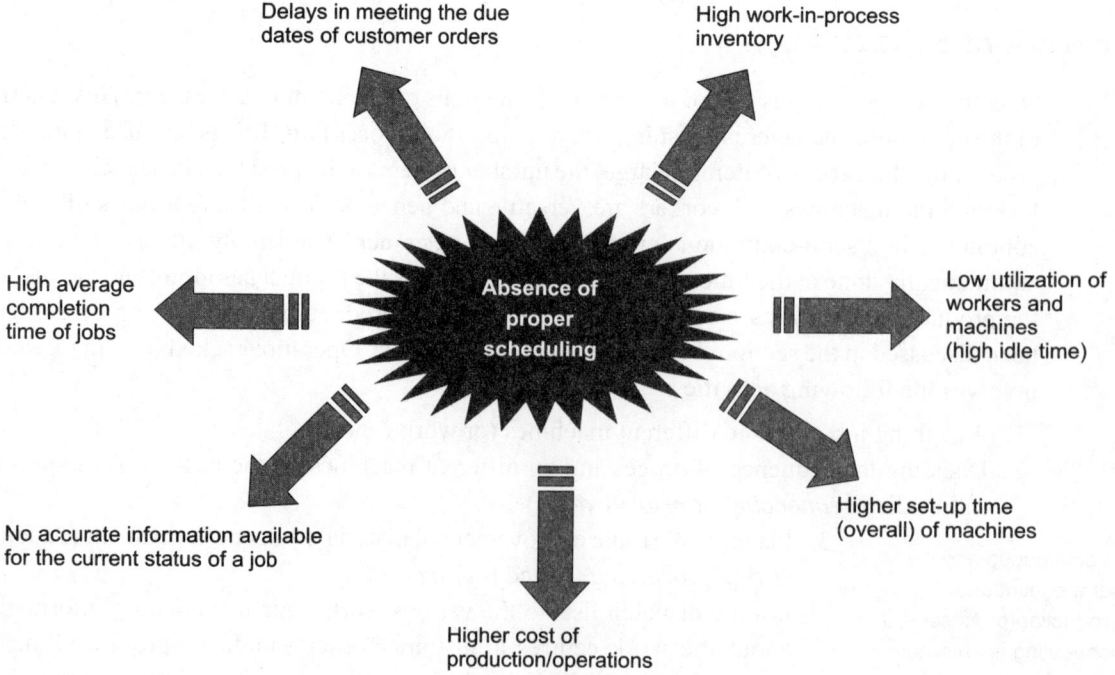

Delays in meeting the due dates of customer orders

High work-in-process inventory

High average completion time of jobs

Absence of proper scheduling

Low utilization of workers and machines (high idle time)

No accurate information available for the current status of a job

Higher set-up time (overall) of machines

Higher cost of production/operations

**Fig. 13.1**   Problems due to the absence of proper scheduling

## Routing, Prioritizing, Dispatching, and Expediting

In job shops, the operations manager designs a product according to customer requirements, and decides the order of work centres or departments through which the product should be processed. This is called the *routing plan*, which specifies the route to be followed by a semi-finished good from one department to another (e.g., drilling, spinning, welding, forging, fitting, etc.). The semi-finished product reaching a department for processing may be accompanied by drawings, specifications, product description documents, etc. as guidance to the worker regarding the processing requirements of the product.

The operations manager must send information about the detailed schedule of various orders (work centres, processing order, processing time, and so on) to the production supervisor in the form of dispatch lists. This is called *dispatching* the dispatch lists. Determining the priority or importance of each customer order for processing is another important task in scheduling. This is called *prioritization* of orders or *sequencing*. After processing the order, the worker informs the supervisor, who in turn informs the operations manager. The operations manager then issues a *move ticket* to the material handlers, specifying the movement of semi-finished goods to the next department according to the routing plan.

The operations manager has to keep track of the progress of various jobs. In practical situations, there are instances when there are deviations from the schedule during the implementation of jobs. This may be due to machine breakdown, delay in the delivery of raw materials, some last minute rush orders (which the company may be forced to accept keeping in view the bright future prospects with a new customer), etc. In such situations, the schedule may have to be revised by the manager and some jobs expedited or handled on a special priority basis. This is called *expediting* in scheduling terminology.

## Forward and Backward Scheduling

Forward scheduling means assigning customer orders or jobs to various work centres based on the 'as early as possible' approach. Thus, a job is scheduled at a work centre as soon as it is free to process a job. The job is then finished as soon as possible. This approach is based on the assumption that a customer is ready to receive the goods as soon as these are produced. This scheduling approach may result in high WIP inventory if the subsequent work centre in the processing sequence of the product is busy with some other job.

Backward scheduling is another way of scheduling, which is based on the 'as late as possible' approach, with the condition that the jobs are finished by their due dates for delivery to the customer. Thus, the planning process starts with assigning the job to the last work centre in the processing sequence. Then, according to the processing time of the job at the various work centres, the schedule is worked out towards the beginning of the processing sequence. The lead times of the earlier processes have to be accurate enough to support this scheduling approach. This approach results in a significant reduction of WIP.

> Forward scheduling means assigning customer orders or jobs to various work centres based on the 'as early as possible' approach.

## Finite and Infinite Loading

*Loading* means assigning tasks to work centres or machines. Gantt charts are very useful tools in this process. These charts were originally developed by Henry Gantt. Every machine or work centre has a maximum production capacity for

Loading means assigning tasks to work centres or machines.

Infinite loading means overlooking the maximum capacity of a machine or work centre while assigning tasks to it.

a normal working day. Keeping in view this maximum capacity when loading is called finite loading. Thus, finite loading involves assigning tasks to work centres such that the maximum capacity of the work centre is not exceeded at any time. Finite loading is shown in Fig. 13.2. Note that the load does not exceed the maximum capacity at any given time.

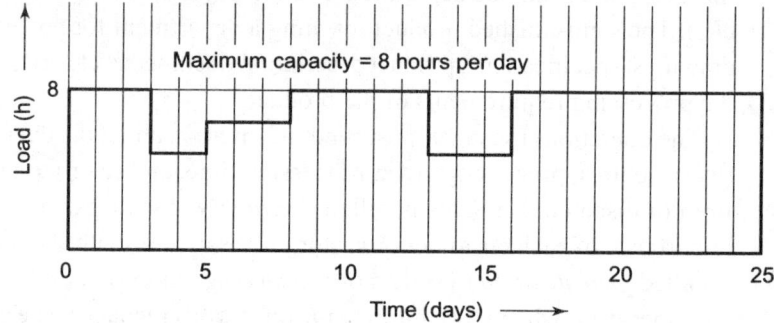

**Fig. 13.2** Gantt chart showing finite loading of a machine

Infinite loading means overlooking the maximum capacity of a machine or work centre while assigning tasks to it. As shown in Fig. 13.3, during some time periods, tasks are assigned to the machine beyond its maximum capacity of eight working hours per day. Infinite loading is done when the operations manager knows that the excess work scheduled during some time periods can be shifted to other work centres or time periods. Another option is to do overtime or subcontracting of work during such times. This is termed as *capacity expansion* of machines or work centres.

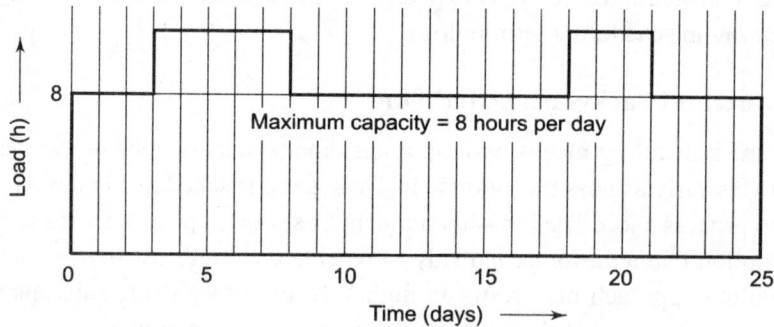

**Fig. 13.3** Gantt chart showing infinite loading of a machine

**Schedule Gantt chart**  Gantt charts are also used to show the job schedules on a timescale. Bars or rectangles are used to show the various jobs, with the extreme left side of a bar corresponding to the scheduled starting time and the extreme right side to the scheduled finishing time of a job. This representation of jobs in Gantt charts helps the operations manager to track the progress of various jobs at any point of time.

We had used such a Gantt chart with MS Project 2000 in Chapter 5, as shown in Fig. 13.4. The right side of the figure shows the Gantt chart for the schedule of a project having

Gantt charts are also used to show the job schedules on a timescale.

various jobs according to given precedence requirements. Note the dates shown above the Gantt chart, which help the project manager to know the start and end dates of a job. On any particular date, the manager can examine the status of progress of a job, that is, whether the job is delayed or ahead of schedule.

Exhibit 13.1 discusses how IndiGo uses hub-and-spoke scheduling to operate efficiently.

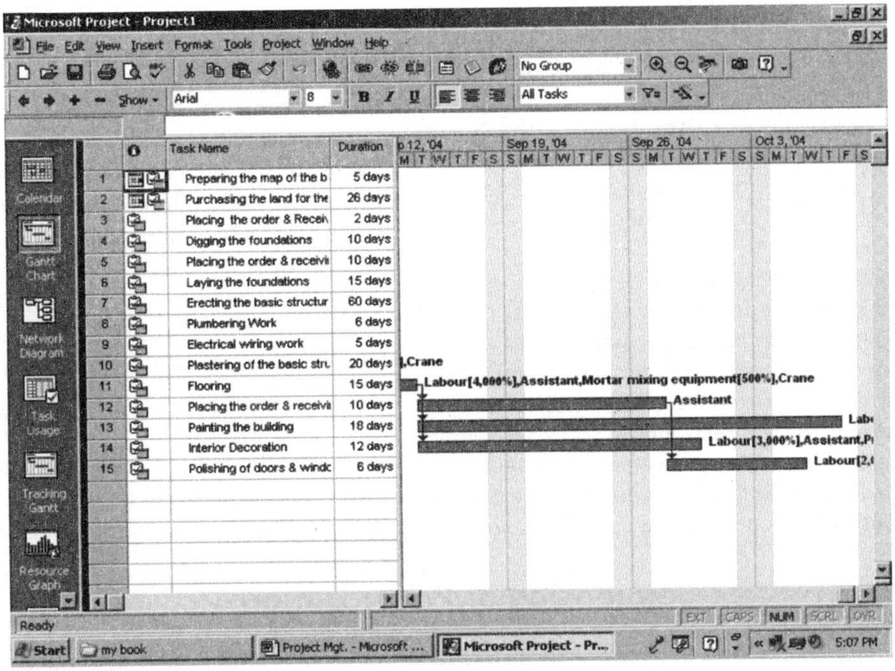

**Fig. 13.4** Gantt chart

## Exhibit 13.1 IndiGo's Hub-and-spoke Flight Scheduling

Founded by Rakesh Gangwal and Rahul Bhatia of InterGlobe Enterprises in 2006, IndiGo became the largest airline in India in terms of market share in August 2012. It was the only airline in India that kept on posting profits even during the lean period of global recession. The low-cost carrier is known for its low fares, on-time performance, and hassle-free boarding of flights.

In June 2005, IndiGo placed a firm order for 100 Airbus A320 aircraft about a year before starting its operations. The firm order for the world's best-selling aircraft gave it a huge pricing advantage. The choice of the aircraft and the quantity ordered were a winning proposition. Having the same aircraft in the fleet is extremely helpful in efficient and cost-effective maintenance. It reduces the training requirements for pilots and staff, who can be easily swapped on different routes as the same aircraft model is used everywhere in the network. In 2011, IndiGo signed another deal with Airbus for A320s, this time ordering 180 aircraft out of which 150 would be of the Neo variety. A320 Neo is a fuel efficient and environment-friendly aircraft, which flies with reduced

fuel consumption by up to 15 per cent and has a much lower engine noise. Since the low-cost carrier does not serve hot meals in its flights, there is no metal cutlery used and hence, reduces the weight of the aircraft further, resulting in even lesser consumption of fuel. All the aircraft are configured to have only economy-class seating with no business- or first-class and no inflight entertainment system. Clearly, the focus of the airline is on the cost-conscious customer, who wants value for money. During the past few years of global recession, even corporations had started using the low-cost carriers for their executive travel. IndiGo has emerged as the biggest gainer of this changing trend in India.

IndiGo is the only airline in India that schedules its flights on the hub-and-spoke model, with Delhi, Mumbai, Kolkata, and Chennai as its regional hubs. This model is akin to a chariot wheel, whereby the spokes are connected to the central hub and the traffic flows in and out of the hub in the direction of the spokes. In this model, if a passenger has to go from Thiruvananthapuram to Srinagar, he or she has to

*(Contd)*

*Exhibit 13.1 Contd*

change IndiGo flights at Bangalore and Delhi (its two regional hubs) to reach Srinagar. This is in contrast to the point-to-point model followed by all other airlines in India, whereby they either choose to schedule a flight directly between two points (for example, Thiruvanathapuram and Srinagar, depending upon sufficient passenger numbers on the route to fill up the aircraft regularly) or choose not to ply over that route at all.

Pioneered by Delta Airlines in the US in 1955, the hub-and-spoke model has its challenges. First, it inconveniences the passenger who has to change flights en-route to his or her final destination. Unless the pricing is lucrative enough to justify it, passengers would prefer to fly direct. IndiGo's low fares more than make up for this inconvenience, especially so when no other airline flies direct on this route. Second, scheduling of flights needs to be done meticulously so

that the waiting time for passengers on regional hubs should be minimal. At that, the actual implementation of schedules should be seamless—any delay in a flight may adversely impact the timing of all the connecting flights, resulting in acute hardships for passengers or losses for the airline for accommodating passengers into other flights. IndiGo seems to have mastered the art of on-time performance, which is key to the success of this model. All its aircraft are fitted with aircraft communications addressing and reporting system (ACARS). The exact departure and landing times are automatically (without any human intervention) recorded by the ground stations using this technology, through which the aircraft remains in constant touch during the flight. Third, the baggage transfer between connecting flights needs to be quick and accurate. Here again, IndiGo has demonstrated operational excellence.

## Sequencing or Prioritization

> Sequencing or prioritization is deciding the order or sequence of various jobs to be performed on the given machines or work centres on the basis of some priority rule.

Sequencing or prioritization is deciding the order or sequence of various jobs to be performed on the given machines or work centres on the basis of some priority rule. Figure 13.5 shows the various sequencing situations and the methods used for sequencing. Note that this figure shows the assignment of jobs to machines as one of the functions of the operations manager in scheduling. The assignment model discussed earlier in Chapter 6 is applicable to the assignment of jobs to machines or work centres.

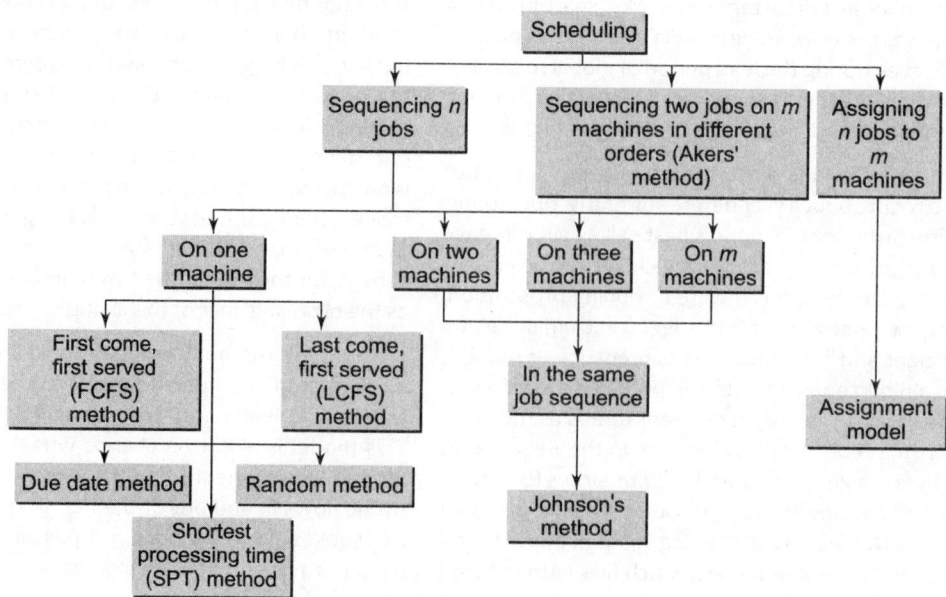

**Fig. 13.5**   Different methods of sequencing/assignment of jobs to machines

The most common comparison criteria for the various methods or priority rules are total flow time, mean flow time, and average lateness.

Sequencing $n$ jobs is shown separately from sequencing two jobs on $n$ machines in different machine sequences, because these have to be solved using different methods. Sequencing $n$ jobs on one machine problems can be solved using different priority rules, out of which the shortest processing time rule is the best, as we will discuss in detail. Johnson's method is used in solving the problems of sequencing $n$ jobs on two or more machines, provided the processing order of the machines is the same for all the jobs. In the next section, we will discuss each one of these methods in detail.

## Sequencing $n$ Jobs

**Sequencing $n$ jobs on one machine**   In sequencing $n$ jobs on one machine, the processing time of each job and their due dates of delivery are required. A priority rule is then decided upon in order to sequence the various jobs accordingly. Various priority rules are possible, some of which are given below.

***First come, first served (FCFS) method***   In this method, the top priority of assignment is given to the job whose order was placed the earliest. Jobs are sequenced according to their dates of arrival. The job order received the latest is scheduled at the end of the sequence.

***Last come, first served (LCFS) method***   In this method, the job order received in the end is scheduled at the beginning of the sequence. Jobs are sequenced according to their dates of arrival. The job order received the earliest is scheduled at the end of the sequence.

***Due date method***   In this method, jobs are sequenced according to their due dates of delivery. The job with the earliest due date is scheduled at the beginning of the sequence.

***Random method***   As the name suggests, jobs are selected for processing at random by the workers. The processing sequence may vary from individual to individual.

***Shortest processing time (SPT) method***   In this method, the priority rule of sequencing is based on the processing time of the various jobs. The job with the shortest processing time is scheduled first. The remaining jobs are sequenced according to their processing time lengths. The job with the maximum processing time length is scheduled at the end of the sequence.

It has been established that the SPT is the best method in terms of all the comparison criteria. The most common comparison criteria for the various methods or priority rules are total flow time, mean flow time, and average lateness. Let us take up an example in order to understand these criteria.

### *Example 13.1*

**Table 13.1**

| Jobs (in the order of arrival) | Processing time (days) | Due date (days from) the start) |
|---|---|---|
| A | 3 | 9 |
| B | 7 | 10 |
| C | 4 | 7 |
| D | 2 | 4 |
| E | 5 | 8 |
| F | 8 | 12 |

Ganapati Typesetting Solutions is a major typesetter of printing material based at Indore. It has recently received six orders for typesetting printing material. Table 13.1 shows the six jobs in the order of their arrival, their processing times, and due dates (days hence) of delivery to the customers. Sequence the given jobs according to the priority rules of FCFS, LCFS, due date, random, and SPT. Compare these methods on the criteria of mean flow time and average lateness.

## *Solution*

Figure 13.6 shows the analysis of sequences of jobs according to FCFS and LCFS methods. In the FCFS method, the schedule of jobs as shown in cells A6 to A11 is according to the time of their arrival. The flow time is calculated in cells D6 to D11. In cell D6, the starting time of job $A$ is day 0 and the processing time, 3 days, of job $A$ is added to it to get the flow time of 3 days. In cell D7, the starting time of job $B$ is day 3 and the processing time, 7 days, of job $B$ is added to it to get the flow time of 10 days. Similarly, the flow times of other jobs in the sequence are calculated in cells D8 to D11, with the total flow time shown in cell A13 as 93 days (the sum of flow times of various jobs).

**Fig. 13.6**  FCFS and LCFS methods of scheduling *n* jobs on one machine

The mean flow time is the total flow time (93 days) divided by 6 (for six jobs). The mean flow time for the FCFS method is shown in cell A14 as 15.5 days. In column $E$, we calculate the lateness of jobs. In cell E6, the lateness of job $A$ is shown as 0. This is because the flow time of job $A$ is day 3, that is, it will be over on day 3, and its due date of delivery is day 9. Thus, there is no delay or lateness at all in the delivery of job $A$. Similarly, the lateness of job $B$ is 0 as shown in cell E7. For job $C$, the lateness is 7 days $(14 - 7)$ as shown in cell E8 (as its flow time is day 14, while its due date is day 7). In the same way, the lateness of other jobs can be calculated. We calculate the average lateness of the FCFS method in cell E12 as 8.17 days. Now, we analyse the LCFS method in the second table of Fig. 13.6. Note that the sequence of jobs in this method is $F, E, D, C, B$, and $A$, with a total flow time of 110 days, mean flow time of 18.33 days, and average lateness of 10.67 days.

We now do these calculations for the due date and random methods as shown in Fig. 13.7. In the due date method, the sequence is made according to the due dates of the jobs. Job $D$ has the nearest due date of day 4. Thus, it is scheduled first, followed by jobs $C, E, A, B$, and $F$. In the random method, the sequence has been randomly decided as $B, F, D, A, C$, and $E$. This sequence may vary from individual to individual.

File Edit View Insert Format Tools Data Window StatTools Help

**Scheduling n jobs on one machine**

**Due Date Method**

| Schedule of jobs | Processing time (days) | Due Date (days from now) | Flow Time (days) | Late by no. of days | |
|---|---|---|---|---|---|
| D | 2 | 4 | 0 + 2 = 2 | 0 | |
| C | 4 | 7 | 2 + 4 = 6 | 0 | |
| E | 5 | 8 | 6 + 5 = 11 | 3 | |
| A | 3 | 9 | 11 + 3 = 14 | 5 | |
| B | 7 | 10 | 14 + 7 = 21 | 11 | |
| F | 8 | 12 | 21 + 8 = 29 | 17 | |
| | | | | 6 | Average |
| Total Flow Time = 2 + 6 + 11 + 14 + 21 + 29 = 83 days | | | | | per job |
| Mean Flow Time = 13.83 days | | | | | |

**Random Method**

| Schedule of jobs | Processing time (days) | Due Date (days from now) | Flow Time (days) | Late by no. of days | |
|---|---|---|---|---|---|
| B | 7 | 10 | 0 + 7 = 7 | 0 | |
| F | 8 | 12 | 7 + 8 = 15 | 3 | |
| D | 2 | 4 | 15 + 2 =17 | 13 | |
| A | 3 | 9 | 17 + 3 = 20 | 11 | |
| C | 4 | 7 | 20 + 4 = 24 | 17 | |
| E | 5 | 8 | 24 + 5 = 29 | 21 | |
| | | | | 10.83333333 | Average |
| Total Flow Time = 7 + 15 + 17 + 20 + 24 + 29 = 112 days | | | | | per job |
| Mean Flow Time = 18.67 days | | | | | |

start ... Inbox - Mic... Yahoo! Mail... WebCT - Mi... Screenshot... My POM 1e... Fig. 12.7D... 12:44 AM

**Fig. 13.7** Due date and random methods of scheduling *n* jobs on one machine

File Edit View Insert Format Tools Data Window StatTools Help

**Scheduling n jobs on one machine**

**Shortest Processing Time (SPT) Method**

| Schedule of jobs | Processing time (days) | Due Date (days from now) | Flow Time (days) | Late by no. of days | |
|---|---|---|---|---|---|
| D | 2 | 4 | 0 + 2 = 2 | 0 | |
| A | 3 | 9 | 2 + 3 = 5 | 0 | |
| C | 4 | 7 | 5 + 4 = 9 | 2 | |
| E | 5 | 8 | 9 + 5 = 14 | 6 | |
| B | 7 | 10 | 14 + 7 = 21 | 11 | |
| F | 8 | 12 | 21 + 8 = 29 | 17 | |
| | | | | 6 | Average |
| Total Flow Time = 2 + 5 + 9 + 14 + 21 + 29 = 80 days | | | | | per job |
| Mean Flow Time = 13.33 days | | | | | |

**A comparison of the various methods**

| Method | Average lateness per job | Mean flow time |
|---|---|---|
| FCFS | 8.17 | 15.5 |
| LCFS | 10.67 | 18.33 |
| Due Date | 6 | 13.83 |
| Random | 10.83 | 18.67 |
| SPT | 6 | 13.33 |

start ... Inbox - Mic... Yahoo! Mail... WebCT - Mi... Screenshot... My POM 1e... Fig. 12.8 S... 12:40 AM

**Fig. 13.8** SPT and a comparison of the various methods for scheduling *n* jobs on one machine

Figure 13.8 shows the calculations for the SPT method. It also shows the comparison of various methods. Note that the SPT method has the lowest mean flow time (and the lowest total flow time) and the lowest average lateness. Thus, it is now verified through this example that SPT is the best amongst all the methods.

**Johnson's method**   Johnson's method is used in problems where *n* jobs have to be sequenced on two, three, or more machines. The procedure is almost the same in all cases, with only slight modification.

Let us understand the application of this method for the following cases:

1.   Sequencing *n* jobs on two machines
2.   Sequencing *n* jobs on three machines
3.   Sequencing *n* jobs on *m* machines

### Sequencing n jobs on two machines

In sequencing *n* jobs on two machines, the processing order of all the jobs on the two machines is always the same. The processing times of all the jobs on the two machines are given. Let us take up a simple example to understand the method of solving problems of sequencing *n* jobs on two machines using Gantt charts.

### Example 13.2

| | M1 | M2 |
|---|---|---|
| J1 | 3 | 9 |
| J2 | 5 | 11 |

Sundaram Machining Works is an ancillary unit at Pune. The production supervisor of Sundaram has to schedule two jobs *J*1 and *J*2, each of which requires machining on two machines *M*1 and *M*2 in the order *M*1, *M*2. The machining time (in hours) required by the two jobs on the two machines is shown below. Determine the sequence in which the jobs should be scheduled to minimize the total machining time?

### Solution

We first make a Gantt chart for processing jobs in the sequence *J*1, *J*2. Figure 13.9(a) shows a Gantt chart in which we plot time (in hours) along the *x*-axis and show machines *M*1 and *M*2 along the *y*-axis. Job *J*1 requires machining for 3 hours on machine *M*1; therefore it is scheduled as shown. While machine *M*1 is busy processing job *J*1, machine *M*2 will be idle.

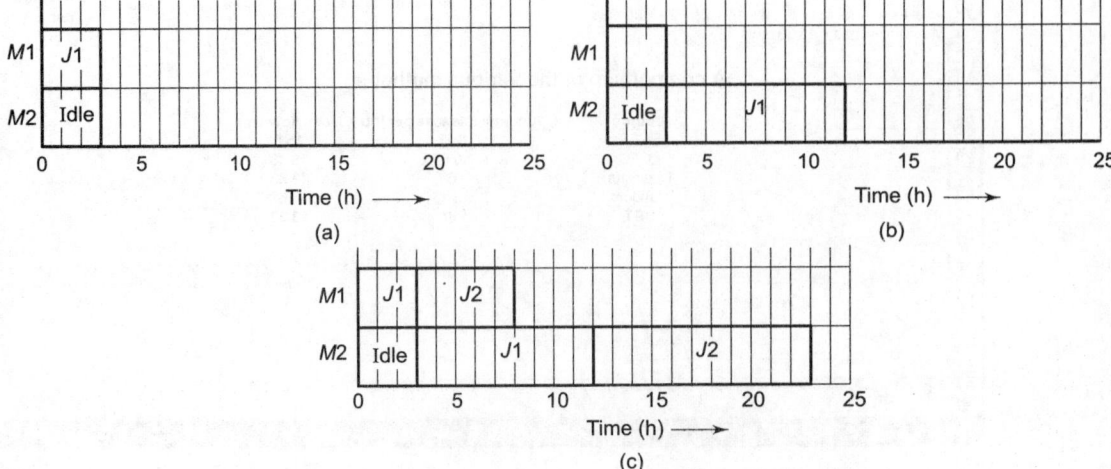

**Fig. 13.9**   Gantt chart for jobs performed in the sequence *J*1, *J*2

After processing on $M1$ is over, $J1$ can be scheduled on $M2$ for 9 hours as shown in Fig. 13.9(b). Job $J2$ can also be scheduled now on $M1$ for 5 hours as shown in Fig. 13.9(c). After the processing of $J1$ on $M2$ is over, $J2$ can be scheduled on it for 11 hours. The total processing time of the two jobs in the sequence $J1$, $J2$ is, therefore, 23 hours.

Figure 13.10 shows the scheduling of the two jobs in the sequence $J2$, $J1$. The total processing time in this sequence for the two jobs is 25 hours. Thus, the sequence $J1$, $J2$ is better than the sequence $J2$, $J1$, as it requires a lower total processing time, of 23 hours.

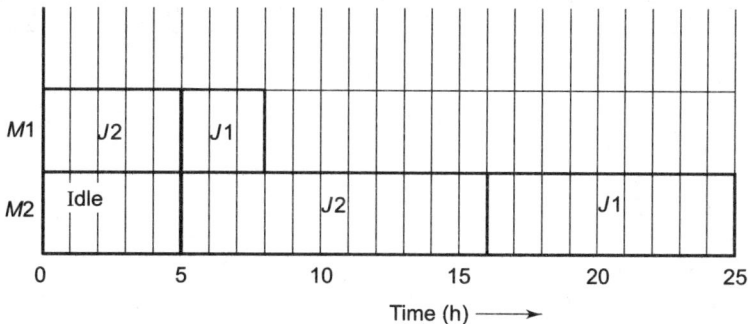

**Fig. 13.10**  Gantt chart for jobs performed in the sequence $J2$, $J1$

Using a Gantt chart in a simple problem like this one has yielded the optimal sequencing solution. However, in problems with more jobs, this method becomes very complicated, as for each possible combination of job sequences, a separate Gantt chart is to be made. Johnson's method on the other hand is very easy to use. Let us now take up an example to understand the application of Johnson's method.

### Example 13.3

**Table 13.2**

| Job | M1 | M2 |
|-----|----|----|
| A | 9 | 2 |
| B | 5 | 4 |
| C | 8 | 10 |
| D | 3 | 5 |
| E | 4 | 6 |
| F | 1 | 11 |
| G | 7 | 6 |

Rajeshwar Engineering Works at Patna has been given a contract to make seven components by Indian Railways. Each of these components requires processing on two machines $M1$ and $M2$ in the order $M1$, $M2$. The time (in hours) required by each of these jobs for processing on the two machines is given in Table 13.2. Find the optimal sequence for processing the seven jobs.

### Solution

We will use Johnson's method for solving this problem. Figure 13.11 shows the various steps in the application of Johnson's method in Tables I–VI. Note that in Table I the smallest processing time is 1 hour for job $F$ on $M1$. Whenever the job with the smallest processing time is on machine $M1$ (the first machine in the order $M1$, $M2$), that job is scheduled at the beginning of the processing sequence. Thus, job $F$ is scheduled first (cell E14) in the optimal processing sequence shown in row 14 of the figure.

In Table II, we shade the row of job $F$, as this job is already scheduled and need not be considered for scheduling any further. The smallest processing time in the remaining jobs is 2 hours for job $A$ on $M2$. According to Johnson's method, whenever a job has the smallest processing time on $M2$ (the second machine in the sequence $M1$, $M2$), it should be scheduled at the end of the sequence. Therefore, we schedule job $A$ at the end of the sequence (cell K14). We shade the row for job $A$ in Table III.

In Table III, the lowest value of processing time in the remaining jobs is 3 hours for job $D$ on $M1$. Thus, job $D$ is scheduled in the beginning of the optimal sequence after job $F$ (cell F14); we shade

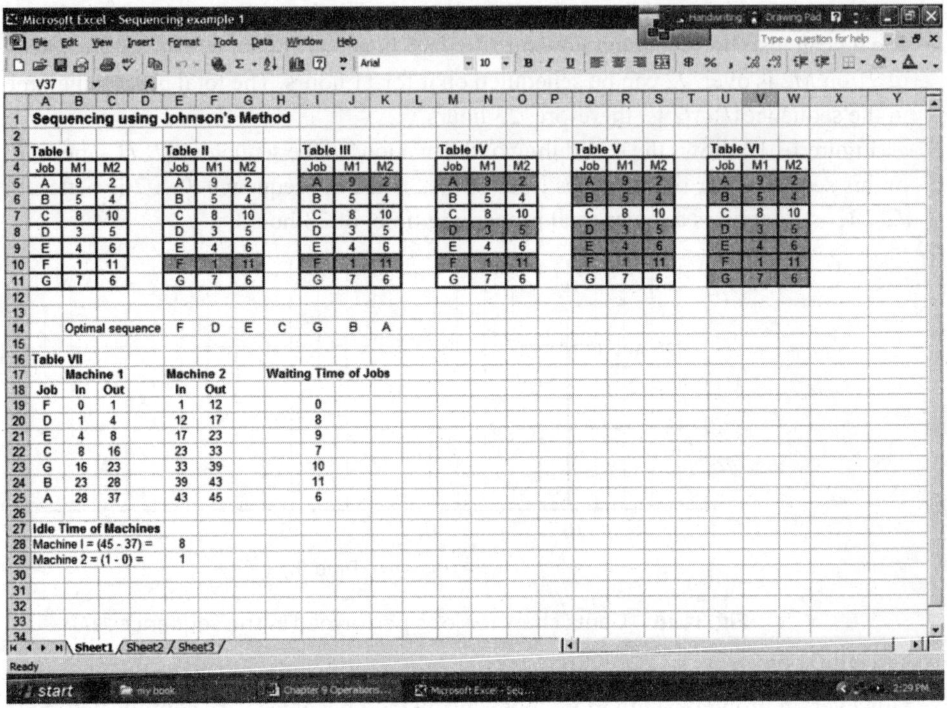

**Fig. 13.11** Sequencing using Johnson's method

job *D* in Table IV. In Table IV, the smallest processing time is 4 hours for jobs *E* and *B* on *M*1 and *M*2, respectively. We schedule job *E* after job *D* and job *B* before job *A* in the optimal schedule, and shade jobs *E* and *B* in Table V. In Table V, the lowest value of processing time is 6 hours for job *G* on *M*2. Thus, job *G* is scheduled before job *B* in the optimal sequence, and we shade the row of job *G* in Table VI. The only remaining job, *C*, is placed in the remaining slot in the optimal sequence (cell H14).

In Table VII, we calculate the total performance time of all the jobs according to the optimal sequence determined above. The first job in the sequence is *F* with a processing requirement of 1 hour on machine *M*1. Thus, at time instant 0 (cell B19) its processing will start on *M*1. It will be over by time instant 1 (cell C19). Job *F* is to be processed now on machine *M*2 for 11 hours. It will be sent to *M*2 at time instant 1 and the processing will be over by instant 13. The waiting time of task *F* is 0 as shown in cell I19.

Machine *M*1 is free from job *F* at instant 1, so the next job in the sequence, job *D*, starts at *M*1 at instant 1 and gets over at instant 4, as it requires 3 hours of processing on this machine. At time instant 4, job *D* is ready to be processed at *M*2, but *M*2 is not free until time instant 12 (as it will be processing job *F* till that time). Therefore, job *D* has to wait for 8 (12 − 4) hours, as shown in the column for the waiting time of jobs (cell I20). Similarly, other jobs in the sequence are shown in Table VII, such that the overall processing time of all the jobs comes out to be 45 hours (cell F25). The idle time of machine *M*1 is 8 hours (= 45 − 37) (cell E28), as its last job, *A*, gets over at time instant 37, after which it becomes free. The final processing on machine M2 gets over only at instant 45. For machine *M*2, the idle time is 1 hour (=1 − 0) (cell E29), as its first job, *F*, starts at instant 1, though the processing at *M*1 starts at instant 0.

In some of the problems of sequencing *n* jobs on two machines, two or more optimal sequences may result. In the following example, four optimal sequences result upon the application of Johnson's method. Each of these sequences will have exactly same total processing times. Therefore, we calculate the total processing time for any one of these optimal sequences.

## Example 13.4

**Table 13.3**

| Job | M1 | M2 |
|-----|-----|-----|
| A | 2 | 7 |
| B | 5 | 3 |
| C | 1 | 4 |
| D | 6 | 7 |
| E | 2 | 8 |
| F | 3 | 9 |
| G | 5 | 10 |
| H | 1 | 2 |
| I | 6 | 1 |
| J | 8 | 5 |

There are ten jobs to be processed through two machines $M1$ and $M2$ in the order $M1$, $M2$. The processing time required by each job (in hours) is given in Table 13.3. Find the optimal sequence for the performance of these jobs in the minimum possible time.

### Solution

Tables I–V in Fig. 13.12 show the steps in the application of Johnson's method to the given problem. Note that there are four optimal sequences generated here, as shown in rows 16–19.

In Table I, there are three jobs having the lowest processing time of 1 hour. These are jobs $C$, $H$, and $I$. Job $I$ has a processing time of 1 hour on machine $M2$, while jobs $C$ and $H$ have a processing time of 1 hour on machine $M1$. Therefore, job $I$ has to be scheduled at the end of the sequence (cell N16). Jobs $C$ and $H$ can be scheduled at the beginning of the sequence in the order $C$, $H$ or $H$, $C$. Thus, two possible sequences can be formed. The optimal sequence I (shown in row 16) has $H$ as the first job followed by $C$, while the optimal sequence II (shown in row 17) has $C$ as the first job followed by $H$. We shade the jobs $C$, $H$, and $I$ in Table II.

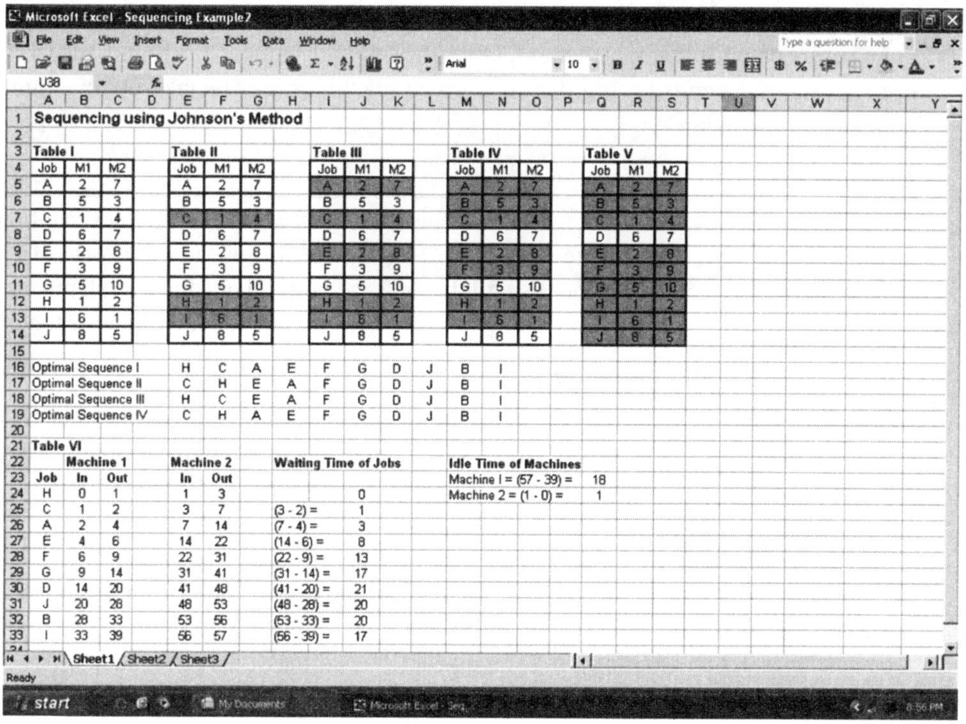

**Fig. 13.12** Sequencing *n* jobs on two machines using Johnson's method

In Table II, the lowest processing time in the remaining jobs is 2 hours for jobs $A$ and $E$ on machine $M1$. Thus, these jobs have to be scheduled at the beginning of the sequence after jobs $C$ or $H$ in the optimal sequence I or II, respectively, in the order *A, E* or *E, A*. Note that now two more optimal sequences, III and IV, have been formed according to the combinations of sequences of the jobs *H, C, A,* and *E*. Note that job *I* is at the end of all the four optimal sequences.

In Table III, we shade jobs *A* and *E*, as these have already been scheduled. In the remaining jobs, the lowest processing time is 3 hours for jobs *F* and *B* on machines *M*1 and *M*2, respectively. Therefore, we schedule job *B* at the end of the sequence before job *I*, and job *F* at the beginning of the sequence after the four jobs *H, C, A,* and *E* already scheduled in various orders in the four optimal sequences. Similarly, we schedule the other jobs and complete the four optimal sequences, each of which will have exactly same overall processing times for the 10 jobs. We calculate the overall processing time of optimal sequence I in Table VI as in the earlier example. The waiting times of the jobs and idle times of machines are also shown in Fig. 13.12.

**Sequencing *n* jobs on three machines** Johnson's method can be applied in problems of sequencing *n* jobs on three machines only when certain conditions are fulfilled. These conditions are as follows:

Minimum processing time on machine *M*1 ≥ maximum processing time on machine *M*2

Minimum processing time on machine *M*3 ≥ maximum processing time on machine *M*2

If any one or both of the above two conditions are satisfied, Johnson's method can be applied. Two hypothetical machines *X* and *Y* are considered. The processing time of various jobs on machine *X* is the sum of the processing times of the corresponding jobs on machines *M*1 and *M*2. Similarly, the processing time of various jobs on machine *Y* is the sum of the processing times of the corresponding jobs on machines *M*2 and *M*3. Then, we proceed to solve the problem as done before using Johnson's method. Once the optimal sequence is found, the overall processing time is calculated considering the three given machines. Let us take up an example in order to understand this method.

### Example 13.5

**Table 13.4**

| Job | M1 | M2 | M3 |
|-----|----|----|----|
| A | 1 | 7 | 8 |
| B | 3 | 3 | 10 |
| C | 7 | 8 | 9 |
| D | 9 | 2 | 11 |
| E | 4 | 8 | 9 |
| F | 5 | 6 | 14 |
| G | 2 | 1 | 12 |

Table 13.4 gives the processing times (in hours) of seven jobs to be processed on three machines *M*1, *M*2, and *M*3 in the order *M*1, *M*2, *M*3. Sequence these jobs using Johnson's method and find the overall processing time. Also find the waiting times of the jobs and the idle times of the three machines.

### Solution

In Table 13.4, the minimum processing times of machine *M*1 is 1, maximum processing time of machine *M*2 is 8, and minimum processing time of machine *M*3 is 8. Since, maximum of *M*2 = minimum of *M*3, Johnson's method can be applied.

In Fig. 13.13, Table II, we have shown the two hypothetical machines *X* and *Y*. Note that in cell G5, the processing time of job *A* is 8 (sum of processing times 1 and 7 on machines *M*1 and *M*2 for job *A*) on machine *X*. In cell H5, the processing time of job *A* is 15 (sum of processing times 7 and 8 on machines *M*2 and *M*3 for job *A*) on machine *Y*. Similarly, the processing times of other jobs on machines *X* and *Y* are calculated in Table II. We proceed further and calculate Tables III–VI. Two optimal sequences are found as shown in rows 18 and 19. Note that having found these optimal sequences, we proceed to find the total processing time for the optimal sequence *I*, considering the processing times of the jobs on the three machines given in the original Table *I*. The overall processing time is 76 hours. The waiting times of the jobs and idle times of the three machines are also shown in Fig. 13.13.

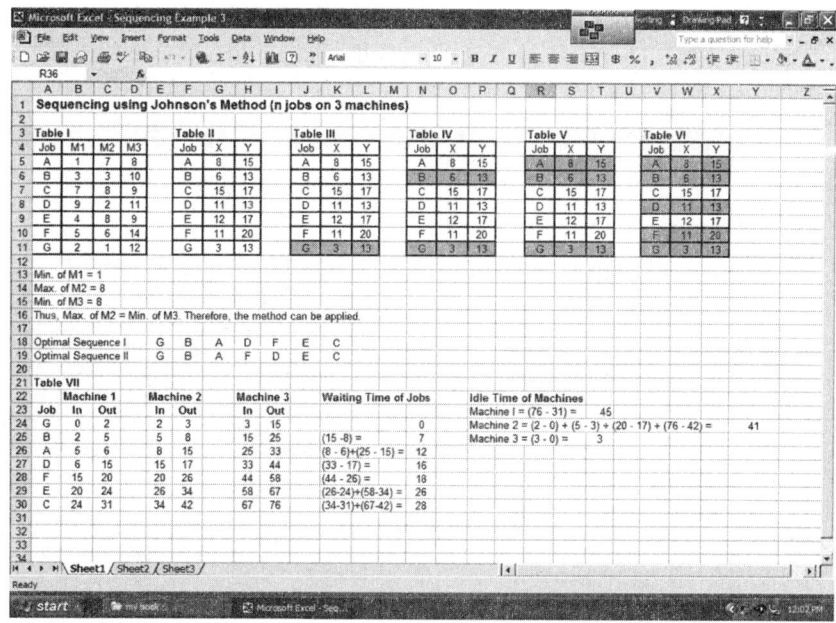

**Fig. 13.13** Sequencing n jobs on three machines using Johnson's method

**Sequencing n jobs on m machines**  Johnson's method can be applied in problems of sequencing n jobs on m machines M1, M2, …, Mm in the order M1, M2, …, Mm only when certain conditions are fulfilled. These conditions are as follows:

Minimum processing time on machine M1 ≥ maximum processing time on machines
$$M2, M3, …, M(m-1)$$

Minimum processing time on machine Mm ≥ maximum processing time on machines
$$M2, M3, …, M(m-1)$$

Here, Mm is the last machine amongst m machines and M(m − 1) is the last but one machine in the processing order of the jobs on m machines. If any one or both of the above two conditions are satisfied, Johnson's method can be applied.

Two hypothetical machines X and Y are considered. The processing time of various jobs on machine X is the sum of the processing times of the corresponding jobs on machines $M_1$, $M_2$, …, M(m − 1). Similarly, the processing time of various jobs on machine Y is the sum of processing times of the corresponding jobs on machines M2, M3, …, Mm. Then, we proceed to solve the problem as usual using Johnson's method. Once the optimal sequence is found, the overall processing time is calculated considering the given m machines. Let us take up an example in order to understand this method.

**Table 13.5**

| Job | M1 | M2 | M3 | M4 |
|-----|----|----|----|----|
| A | 3 | 1 | 4 | 12 |
| B | 8 | 0 | 5 | 15 |
| C | 11 | 3 | 8 | 10 |
| D | 4 | 7 | 3 | 8 |
| E | 5 | 5 | 1 | 10 |
| F | 10 | 2 | 0 | 13 |
| G | 2 | 5 | 6 | 9 |

*Example 13.6*

Table 13.5 gives the processing times (in hours) of seven jobs to be processed on four machines M1, M2, M3, and M4 in the order M1, M2, M3, M4. Sequence the given jobs using Johnson's method and find the overall processing time.

*Solution*

From Table 13.5, minimum of M1 = 2, maximum of M2 = 7, maximum of

*M*3 = 8, and minimum of *M*4 = 8. Thus, minimum of *M*4 = maximum of *M*3, and minimum of *M*4 > maximum of *M*2. Therefore, one of the specified conditions is satisfied and Johnson's method can be applied.

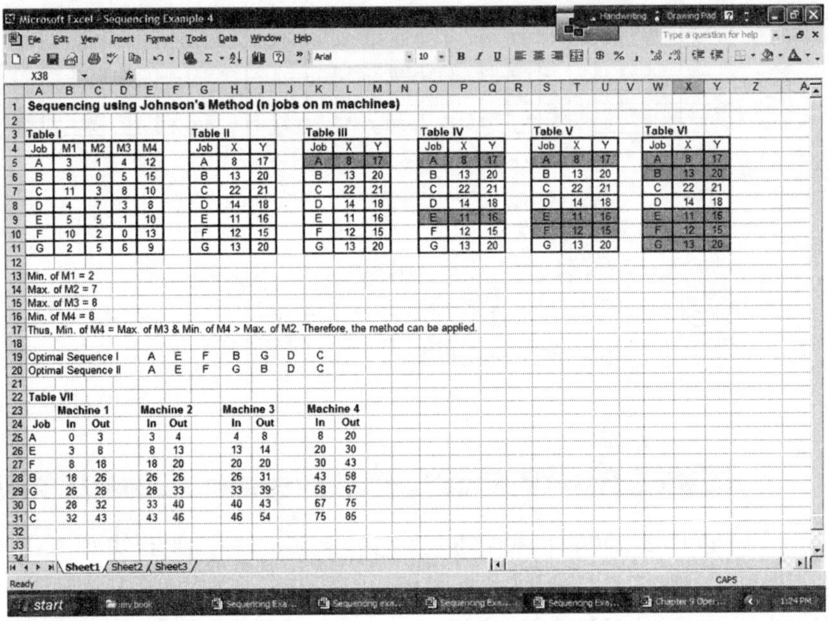

**Sequencing using Johnson's Method (n jobs on m machines)**

**Table I**

| Job | M1 | M2 | M3 | M4 |
|---|---|---|---|---|
| A | 3 | 1 | 4 | 12 |
| B | 8 | 0 | 5 | 15 |
| C | 11 | 3 | 8 | 10 |
| D | 4 | 7 | 3 | 8 |
| E | 5 | 5 | 1 | 10 |
| F | 10 | 2 | 0 | 13 |
| G | 2 | 5 | 6 | 9 |

**Table II**

| Job | X | Y |
|---|---|---|
| A | 8 | 17 |
| B | 13 | 20 |
| C | 22 | 21 |
| D | 14 | 18 |
| E | 11 | 16 |
| F | 12 | 15 |
| G | 13 | 20 |

**Table III**

| Job | X | Y |
|---|---|---|
| A | 8 | 17 |
| B | 13 | 20 |
| C | 22 | 21 |
| D | 14 | 18 |
| E | 11 | 16 |
| F | 12 | 15 |
| G | 13 | 20 |

**Table IV**

| Job | X | Y |
|---|---|---|
| A | 8 | 17 |
| B | 13 | 20 |
| C | 22 | 21 |
| D | 14 | 18 |
| E | 11 | 16 |
| F | 12 | 15 |
| G | 13 | 20 |

**Table V**

| Job | X | Y |
|---|---|---|
| A | 8 | 17 |
| B | 13 | 20 |
| C | 22 | 21 |
| D | 14 | 18 |
| E | 11 | 16 |
| F | 12 | 15 |
| G | 13 | 20 |

**Table VI**

| Job | X | Y |
|---|---|---|
| A | 8 | 17 |
| B | 13 | 20 |
| C | 22 | 21 |
| D | 14 | 18 |
| E | 11 | 16 |
| F | 12 | 15 |
| G | 13 | 20 |

Min. of M1 = 2
Max. of M2 = 7
Max. of M3 = 8
Min. of M4 = 8
Thus, Min. of M4 = Max. of M3 & Min. of M4 > Max. of M2. Therefore, the method can be applied.

| | | | | | | | |
|---|---|---|---|---|---|---|---|
| Optimal Sequence I | A | E | F | B | G | D | C |
| Optimal Sequence II | A | E | F | G | B | D | C |

**Table VII**

| | Machine 1 | | Machine 2 | | Machine 3 | | Machine 4 | |
|---|---|---|---|---|---|---|---|---|
| Job | In | Out | In | Out | In | Out | In | Out |
| A | 0 | 3 | 3 | 4 | 4 | 8 | 8 | 20 |
| E | 3 | 8 | 8 | 13 | 13 | 14 | 20 | 30 |
| F | 8 | 18 | 18 | 20 | 20 | 20 | 30 | 43 |
| B | 18 | 26 | 26 | 26 | 26 | 31 | 43 | 58 |
| G | 26 | 28 | 28 | 33 | 33 | 39 | 58 | 67 |
| D | 28 | 32 | 33 | 40 | 40 | 43 | 67 | 75 |
| C | 32 | 43 | 43 | 46 | 46 | 54 | 75 | 85 |

**Fig. 13.14** Sequencing *n* jobs on *m* machines using Johnson's method

In Table II of Fig. 13.14, note that cell H5 shows a processing time of 8 units for job *A* on hypothetical machine *X* (sum of processing times 3, 1, and 4 units on machines *M*1, *M*2, and *M*3, respectively). Cell I5 we shows a processing time of 17 units for job *A* on hypothetical machine *Y* (sum of processing times 1, 4, and 12 units on machines *M*2, *M*3, and *M*4, respectively). We now solve this problem using Johnson's method, as discussed earlier in the problem of sequencing *n* jobs on three machines.

## Sequencing Two Jobs on *m* Machines in Different Orders (Akers' Method)

In the case of processing two jobs on *m* machines, a graph is used to solve problems where the order of processing on the machines is different. Let us take up an example.

### *Example 13.7*

Thai Cuisine is a famous restaurant in Chandigarh. It prepares two Thai dishes using six different pieces of equipment such as a microwave, grill, stove, boiler, and frying pan. The order in which these are used is different for the two dishes as shown in Table 13.6. Find the optimal cooking time for the two dishes cooked simultaneously by a chef in the restaurant. Assume that one unit each of the six pieces of equipment is available.

### *Solution*

Figure 13.15 shows a graph in which we plot dish 1 along the *x*-axis and dish 2 along the *y*-axis. We show the sequences and time requirements of the equipment used for making the two dishes along the two axes. For dish 1, the first equipment required is *B* for 2 hours. We show this along the *x*-axis.

**Table 13.6**

| | Dish 1 | | Dish 2 | |
|---|---|---|---|---|
| *Equipment sequence* | *Duration (h)* | | *Equipment sequence* | *Duration (h)* |
| B | 2 | | E | 1 |
| F | 3 | | A | 4 |
| A | 1 | | D | 2 |
| C | 4 | | C | 6 |
| E | 2 | | B | 3 |
| D | 5 | | F | 5 |
| | 17 | | | 21 |

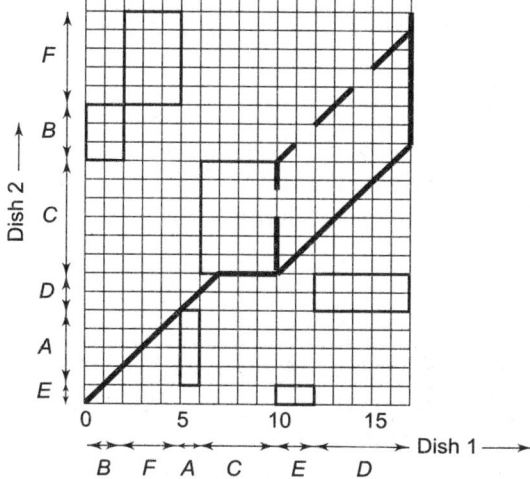

**Fig. 13.15**

Next is *F* for 3 hours, which is shown after equipment *B* along *x*-axis. Similarly, other equipment is shown along the *x*-axis. Along the *y*-axis we show the equipment required for making dish 2. Equipment *E* is required first for one day, which is shown along the *y*-axis. Next is equipment *A* for four days, and so on.

Now, we make rectangles on the graph to represent areas showing the overlapping of the requirement of the same equipment by the two dishes. For example, along the *x*-axis, the first equipment shown is *B* for 2 days, so we make a rectangle corresponding to the 3 days requirement of *B* along the *y*-axis and the 2 days requirement along the *x*-axis. Similarly, we draw other rectangles.

Starting from the origin, we have to now make a line at 45° (the bold line). This line represents the two dishes being made simultaneously using different equipment. Whenever this line comes across a rectangle, a horizontal or vertical movement is made in order to avoid crossing the rectangle. The rectangle cannot be crossed, as this will require the simultaneous use of the same equipment for the preparation of the two dishes, which is not possible. A horizontal movement means dish 1 is being prepared while dish 2 is waiting. A vertical movement means dish 2 is being prepared while dish 1 is waiting. We have to always try to use the 45° line as much as possible, as it results in the simultaneous preparation of the two dishes, saving on overall time.

After moving horizontally to avoid crossing the rectangle of equipment *C*, there are two further paths possible as shown by a dotted line and a bold line. Note that wherever possible, we make the line move along 45°. Now, we have to decide which path is better (i.e., the path for which the overall cooking time of the two dishes is minimum). The simple way to measure the overall duration of a path from the graph is to first take the total horizontal distance covered (17 hours in our example), and then add to it the total vertical distance covered by a path (the bold line covers 7 hours vertically, while the dotted line also covers 6 + 1 = 7 hours vertically). Thus, the total time taken by the bold as well as the dotted line is 17 + 7 = 24 hours.

The other way to measure the duration is to consider the total vertical distance (21 hours total cooking time of dish 2 given in the table), and add to it the total horizontal distance covered by a line

(3 hours for both the bold and dotted lines). Thus, again the total time taken by the bold as well as the dotted line is 21 + 3 = 24 hours. Therefore, both the lines represent the optimal overall preparation time for the two dishes. We make a Gantt chart for the bold line as shown in Fig. 13.16 to verify that the overall cooking time of the two dishes is 24 hours.

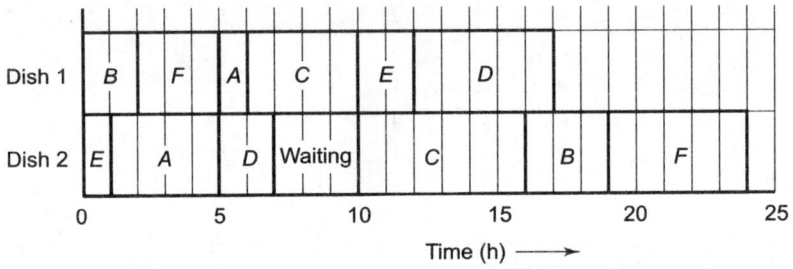

**Fig. 13.16** Gantt chart for dishes 1 and 2 made in the given sequences

> The assignment model is a heuristic, which is used to assign jobs to various machines in such a way that the total processing time is minimum.

## Assignment Model for Scheduling

The assignment model is a heuristic, which is used to assign jobs to various machines in such a way that the total processing time is minimum. The various steps followed in the application of the assignment heuristic can be understood with the help of the example that follows.

### Example 13.8

**Table 13.7**

|    | A  | B  | C  | D  | E  |
|----|----|----|----|----|----|
| J1 | 74 | 34 | 15 | 66 | 38 |
| J2 | 52 | 67 | 92 | 84 | 41 |
| J3 | 59 | 73 | 87 | 70 | 18 |
| J4 | 22 | 50 | 28 | 37 | 24 |
| J5 | 29 | 93 | 82 | 55 | M  |

In the machine shop of XML Motors Ltd, there are five jobs (*J*1–*J*5) to be assigned to five lathe machines *A*, *B*, *C*, *D*, and *E*. The processing times (in minutes) of various jobs on the machines, from past experience, are given in Table 13.7. Job *J*5 cannot be assigned to machine *E*, as this machine does not have proper automation to handle this job. Assign the jobs to the machines such that the total processing time is minimum. Also find the minimum total processing time of the jobs.

### Solution

The assignment heuristic can be applied in the following steps.

**Step 1** Find the smallest value in every row and subtract it from each cell value in the corresponding row (see Fig. 13.17). For example, in the first row the smallest value is 15; subtract 15 from each cell value of the first row. Similarly, the smallest value in the second row is 41, which is subtracted from each cell value of the second row. Thus, the revised table shown in Fig. 13.17 (step) is obtained.

**Step 2** Find the smallest value in every column and subtract it from each cell value in the corresponding column. For example, in the first column the smallest value is 0; subtract 0 from each cell value of the first column. Similarly, the smallest value in the second column is 19, which is subtracted from each cell value of the second column. Thus, the revised table shown in Fig. 13.17 (step 2) is obtained.

**Step 3** Make horizontal and vertical lines to cover all the zeros in the table [shown by grey shaded rectangles in the figure (step 3)]. The lines drawn can be all horizontal, all vertical, or a combination of horizontal and vertical lines in whatever way possible. If the number of lines required to cover all the zeros in the table is equal to the number of machines (or the number of jobs, as both are equal), the

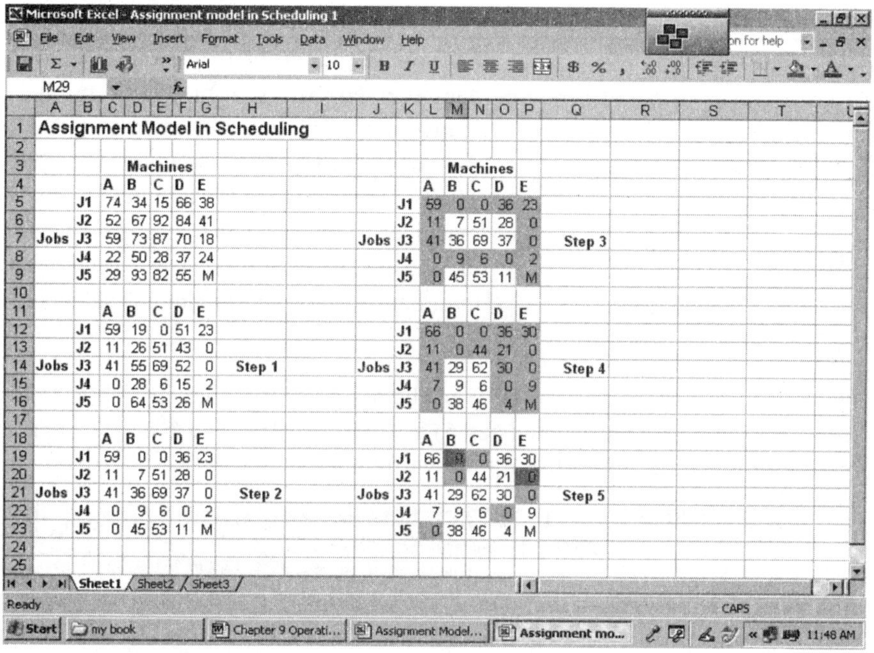

Assignment Model in Scheduling

| Jobs | A | B | C | D | E |
|---|---|---|---|---|---|
| J1 | 74 | 34 | 15 | 66 | 38 |
| J2 | 52 | 67 | 92 | 84 | 41 |
| J3 | 59 | 73 | 87 | 70 | 18 |
| J4 | 22 | 50 | 28 | 37 | 24 |
| J5 | 29 | 93 | 82 | 55 | M |

Step 1

| Jobs | A | B | C | D | E |
|---|---|---|---|---|---|
| J1 | 59 | 19 | 0 | 51 | 23 |
| J2 | 11 | 26 | 51 | 43 | 0 |
| J3 | 41 | 55 | 69 | 52 | 0 |
| J4 | 0 | 28 | 6 | 15 | 2 |
| J5 | 0 | 64 | 53 | 26 | M |

Step 2

| Jobs | A | B | C | D | E |
|---|---|---|---|---|---|
| J1 | 59 | 0 | 0 | 36 | 23 |
| J2 | 11 | 7 | 51 | 28 | 0 |
| J3 | 41 | 36 | 69 | 37 | 0 |
| J4 | 0 | 9 | 6 | 0 | 2 |
| J5 | 0 | 45 | 53 | 11 | M |

Step 3

| Jobs | A | B | C | D | E |
|---|---|---|---|---|---|
| J1 | 59 | 0 | 0 | 36 | 23 |
| J2 | 11 | 7 | 51 | 28 | 0 |
| J3 | 41 | 36 | 69 | 37 | 0 |
| J4 | 0 | 9 | 6 | 0 | 2 |
| J5 | 0 | 45 | 53 | 11 | M |

Step 4

| Jobs | A | B | C | D | E |
|---|---|---|---|---|---|
| J1 | 66 | 0 | 0 | 36 | 30 |
| J2 | 11 | 0 | 44 | 21 | 0 |
| J3 | 41 | 29 | 62 | 30 | 0 |
| J4 | 7 | 9 | 6 | 0 | 9 |
| J5 | 0 | 38 | 46 | 4 | M |

Step 5

| Jobs | A | B | C | D | E |
|---|---|---|---|---|---|
| J1 | 66 | 0 | 0 | 36 | 30 |
| J2 | 11 | 0 | 44 | 21 | 0 |
| J3 | 41 | 29 | 62 | 30 | 0 |
| J4 | 7 | 9 | 6 | 0 | 9 |
| J5 | 0 | 38 | 46 | 4 | M |

**Fig. 13.17** The assignment model in scheduling

optimal solution has been obtained and we can skip step 4 and directly go to step 5. In our example, the number of lines required to cover all zeros is four, that is, less than the number of machines. Therefore, we follow step 4.

**Step 4** Select the smallest value out of those not covered by any of the lines. In our example, it is 7. Subtract this value from all the values not covered by any of the lines (i.e., 7, 51, 28, 36, 69, 37, 45, 53, and 11) and add it to those at the intersection of any two lines (i.e., 59, 23, 0, and 2). Again, make horizontal and vertical lines to cover all the zeros in the table (Fig. 13.17, step 4). If the number of lines required to cover all the zeros in the table is equal to the number of machines (or the number of jobs), the optimal solution has been obtained. In our example, five lines now cover all the zeros (equal to the number of machines). Hence, the optimal solution has been obtained.

**Step 5** A single zero in any row or column is assigned first. For example, the fifth row contains a single zero, which is assigned (shaded grey in Fig. 13.17, step 5). This means that job *J5* has been assigned to machine *A*. Similarly, the third and fourth rows contain single zeros, which are assigned, implying that jobs *J3* and *J4* have been assigned to machines *E* and *D*, respectively. The first and second rows contain zeros in two cells; therefore, we try to find a column which contains any of these single zeros. The third column contains a single zero, which is assigned, implying that job *J1* is assigned to machine *C*. Shade the other zero in the first row dark grey. Now, excluding this dark grey shaded zero, there is a single zero in the second column and it is assigned. Thus, job *J2* is assigned to machine *B*. Shade the other zero in the second row dark grey. Hence, all the jobs have been assigned to the given machines—*J1* to *C*, *J2* to *B*, *J3* to *E*, *J4* to *D* and *J5* to *A*. The total minimum material-handling cost can be found by adding the costs from Table 13.7, with respect to the assigned cells in the table shown in Fig. 13.17 (step 5). Thus, the minimum total processing time is 15 + 67 + 18 + 37 + 29 = 166 minutes.

### Example 13.9

**Table 13.8**

|    | M1 | M2 | M3 | M4 | M5 |
|----|----|----|----|----|----|
| J1 | 12 | 18 | 11 | 22 | 16 |
| J2 | 10 | 10 | 8  | 7  | 20 |
| J3 | 17 | 5  | 16 | 18 | 10 |
| J4 | 9  | 7  | 19 | 21 | 14 |
| J5 | 13 | 12 | 20 | 4  | 17 |

Samuel Engineering Company is based at Trivandrum. It has received orders from a large public-sector company to manufacture five components ($J1$–$J5$) to be used in aircraft. Allthe jobs require processing on the same type of machines. The processing times (in minutes) of the various jobs on the machines, from past experience, are given in Table 13.8. Assign the jobs to the machines such that the total processing time is minimum. Also find the minimum total processing time of the jobs.

### Solution

Figure 13.18 shows the various steps of the assignment model applied to this problem. Note that the optimal assignment schedule (step 5) is $J1$-$M1$, $J2$-$M3$, $J3$-$M5$, $J4$-$M2$, and $J5$-$M4$. The optimal processing time is $12 + 8 + 10 + 7 + 4 = 41$ minutes.

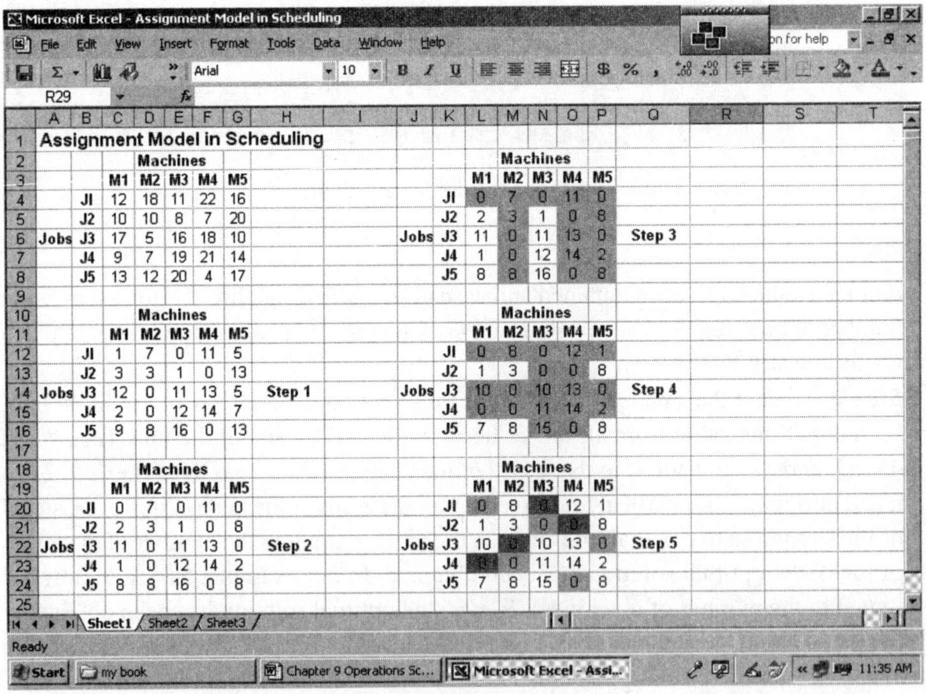

**Fig. 13.18** The assignment model in scheduling

## Summary

*Operations scheduling* is the organizing function of the operations manager. Scheduling involves various activities such as assigning jobs to work centres, sequencing jobs according to priority rules, deciding the routing plan of jobs, sending dispatch lists to supervisors, and expediting in case of delays in the implementation of schedules. Scheduling can have two approaches—*forward scheduling* and *backward*

scheduling. In forward scheduling, the criterion is 'as early as possible', that is, all the jobs are scheduled as early as possible, to finish as early as possible. On the other hand, in backward scheduling the criterion is 'as late as possible', but at the same time meeting the due date of the orders is essential.

The term *loading* implies the assignment of jobs to work centres or machines. Loading can be finite or infinite. *Finite loading* means assigning tasks to work centres or machines such that the maximum capacity of the work centre or machine is not exceeded. *Infinite loading* is done when there is a provision for shifting work to other centres or time periods; the maximum capacity of the work centre is overlooked while assigning the jobs. Overtime and subcontracting of the excess load over the maximum capacity are other options in infinite loading.

*Schedule Gantt charts* are useful in tracking the progress of jobs scheduled earlier. Various sequencing or prioritization rules are possible for sequencing n jobs on one machine, the *shortest processing time rule* being the best one. *Johnson's method* is used for sequencing n jobs on two, three, or m machines. *Akers' method* is used for sequencing two jobs on m machines in different sequences. The *assignment model* is used for assigning jobs to machines.

# Keywords

**Backward scheduling** is a way of scheduling, which is based on the 'as late as possible' approach, with the condition that the jobs are finished by their due dates for delivery to the customer.

**Dispatching** Information sent by the operations manager about the detailed schedule of various orders (work centres, processing order, processing time, and so on) to the production supervisor in the form of dispatch lists.

**Expediting** is tracking the progress of various scheduled jobs and the implementation of schedules in case of delays, revising the schedules, and expediting the completion of certain jobs.

**Finite loading** is assiging jobs to machines or work centres keeping in view their maximum capacity.

**Forward scheduling** means assigning customer orders or jobs to various work centres based on the 'as early as possible' approach.

**Infinite loading** is assigning tasks to a machine or work centre, overlooking its maximum capacity.

**Loading** means assigning tasks to work centres or machines.

**Routing** is planning the movement of material from one department to another during processing.

**Sequencing or prioritization** is deciding the job processing sequence on different machines on the basis of some priority rule.

---

## CASE STUDY

## IndoChem

IndoChem is the Indian subsidiary of a multinational corporation. It is based at Ahmedabad, and manufactures and sells chemical products. By local standards, its sales volume makes it a typical medium-sized company. Most of the productive capacity is used to supply the domestic market, while any temporary excess capacity is used to produce exportable products. Owing to international competition, these products are mostly sold to countries such as Sri Lanka, Thailand, and Bangladesh at discount prices. Since the profit margins of the company are typically low, exports are still less profitable but desirable in periods of lower demand, to utilize the full capacity and increase total profits.

The globalization process and increased market competition have forced a significant drop in the market share position of the company. By the same token, the same process conjugated with reduced import tariffs has made the company lose its profitability. The

productivity has lowered and, unless overtime work is widely used, delivery dates are often not met.

Although the production is by process, as is usual in the chemical industry, the specific requirements of each customer impose a batch or 'made-to-order' kind of production. Each product is made from the same basic compound, but is unique according to customer specifications. These products have variations obtained by the application of additives which change the basic physical and chemical characteristics of the product, such as colour, shock resistance, and transparency.

The greatest challenge faced by the company was overcoming its low productivity, as measured by the larger than expected gap between nominal capacity and effective production. The reason for this inefficiency seems to be related to the unproductive time required for cleaning the mixers when a new batch is introduced. Cleaning times vary from 20 to

200 minutes, a significant 10 times variation depending on the preceding and succeeding product pair. Thus, poor sequence planning would generate enormous production inefficiency. For small orders, the production run was even shorter than the cleaning operation. Figure 13.19 shows the production process at IndoChem. The main activity is the mixer and its output, a powder product, which, if the customer desires, can be further processed into a granulated product.

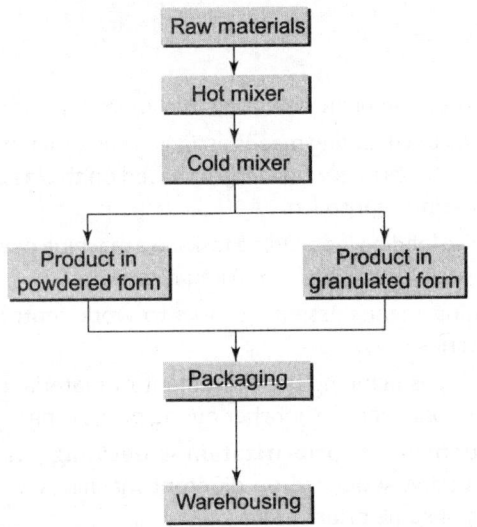

**Fig. 13.19** Production process at IndoChem

The company normally operates in two shifts and the maximum capacity depends on the sequence, variety, and quantity of each batch produced. Every order placed by the customers would specify the quantity and due date. However, many customers prefer to split their orders to receive the product on two or more delivery dates. This created the alternative policies of splitting production or producing in batches, which led to earliness costs. Very often, customers asked for a change in the quantities ordered or advanced the due dates. Thus, a revision of the orders already placed constituted the norm rather than an exception. Such a complex environment is a challenge to a company which does not have a clear and round approach to customer needs. Therefore, the absence of a production sequencing routine contributes to the resulting low efficiency, poor customer service, and lack of competitiveness.

To solve the production sequencing problem, the methodology in practice is a kind of trial and error approach. Production would prioritize lots, according to their due dates, in order to avoid excessive lateness. In periods of lower demand, the existence of idleness would make this policy appear satisfactory. However, in periods of stronger demand, this policy would only be possible at higher production costs, with intensive use of overtime work.

There are many conflicts of the production department with the sales department. This is due to the pressure exerted by the sales department to improve customer service in a difficult environment, where customers tend to react nervously to their own uncertainties. Thus, the deficiency of production sequencing procedures add to the internal and classical conflict between production and sales. In addition, the physical distribution system of the company was largely affected by the inefficiencies of the production system as it stood.

The company has a policy of accepting small orders. Small orders usually represent a new or special product, typically requiring long set-up times and short production times. The company believed that these orders were unprofitable, due to the long idle times and special laboratory arrangements required to satisfy them. Despite this, the management was usually willing to accept such orders as a way to please customers and eventually open new market opportunities. Nevertheless, the effective cost of these orders constituted an open question.

## Discussion Questions

1. Is it strategically right on the part of the company to accept small orders?
2. What should IndoChem do in order to measure set-up costs?
3. Suggest a suitable sequencing method for IndoChem to alleviate its problems.

# Objective Questions

## Choose the correct option

1. Which one is not a type of scheduling on one machine?

   (a) first come, first served
   (b) last come, first served
   (c) due date method
   (d) Johnson's method

2. Loading is of two types:
   (a) loading and unloading
   (b) correct and incorrect
   (c) finite and infinite
   (d) true and false
3. Forward scheduling is based upon:
   (a) as late as possible
   (b) as quick as possible
   (c) as lax as possible
   (d) as early as possible
4. Backward scheduling is based upon:
   (a) as late as possible
   (b) as quick as possible
   (c) as lax as possible
   (d) as early as possible

**State True or False**

5. The shortest processing time (SPT) method results in lowest mean flow time as well as lowest average lateness.
6. In the due date method of sequencing, jobs are selected for processing at random.
7. Johnson's method can be used for sequencing *n* jobs on two machines, on three machines, and on m machines.

**Fill in the blanks**

8. A _____ plan specifies the route to be followed by a semi-finished good from one department to another.
9. Determining the priority or importance of each customer order for processing is called _____.
10. Assigning tasks to work centres or machines is called _____.

## Concept Review Questions

1. What do you understand by operations scheduling? What are the problems faced in the absence of scheduling?
2. What are routing, dispatching, prioritization, and expediting? Explain.
3. What is the difference between forward and backward scheduling? Which one is better?
4. Why is infinite loading of work centres done? How is it different from finite loading?
5. Make a flow diagram to show all the different methods/priority rules of sequencing.

## Numerical Problems

1. Medical Care Pathology is based at Andheri (W), Mumbai and specializes in pathology tests of various types. It has recently received six cases for conducting pathology tests. Table 13.9 shows the six jobs in the order of their arrival, their processing times, and due dates (days hence) of delivery of reports to the patients. Sequence the jobs according to the FCFS and LCFS priority rules. Find the total flow time, mean flow time, and average lateness for both the methods.

**Table 13.9**

| Schedule of jobs | Processing time (days) | Due date (days from the start) |
|---|---|---|
| A | 11 | 20 |
| B | 8 | 10 |
| C | 5 | 11 |
| D | 9 | 15 |
| E | 6 | 9 |
| F | 10 | 16 |

2. In Problem 1, sequence the given jobs according to the priority rules of the due date and random methods. Find the total flow time, mean flow time, and average lateness for both the methods.
3. In Problem 1, sequence the given jobs according to the priority rule of the SPT method. Find the total flow time, mean flow time, and average lateness for this method and compare the methods in Problems 1, 2, and 3 based on these criteria.
4. At an aircraft maintenance facility located in Chatrapati Shivaji International Airport, Mumbai, there are six aircraft A, B, C, D, E, and F that arrived in this sequence for certain maintenance work. The processing time (for maintenance activities) and due date of completion of maintenance (in the number of days from now) are given in the Table 13.10. Let us assume that the maintenance facility can process only one aircraft at a time.

   Find the mean flow time and average lateness per job for various methods of scheduling the above jobs.

**Table 13.10**

| Schedule of jobs | Processing time (days) | Due date (days from now) |
|---|---|---|
| A | 5 | 11 |
| B | 2 | 8 |
| C | 7 | 9 |
| D | 1 | 10 |
| E | 3 | 6 |
| F | 6 | 7 |

5. DuPont Tractors is a tractor manufacturing company based at Trivandrum with a 5,000 million turnover. Its machining division has to manufacture seven components for the latest model of tractors to be introduced by the company. Each of these components requires processing on two machines $M1$ and $M2$ in the order $M1$, $M2$. The time (in hours) required by each of these jobs for processing on the two machines is given in Table 13.11. How can the operations manager find the optimal sequence of processing the seven jobs? How much is the total processing time for the optimal sequence? Find also the waiting times of the various jobs and the idle times of the two machines.

**Table 13.11**

| Job | M1 | M2 |
|---|---|---|
| A | 6 | 8 |
| B | 3 | 2 |
| C | 1 | 10 |
| D | 5 | 4 |
| E | 2 | 8 |
| F | 9 | 6 |
| G | 9 | 7 |

6. There are ten jobs to be processed through two machines $M1$ and $M2$ in the order $M1$, $M2$. The processing time (in hours) required by each job is given in Table 13.12. Find the optimal sequence for the performance of these jobs in the minimum possible time.

**Table 13.12**

| Job | M1 | M2 | Job | M1 | M2 |
|---|---|---|---|---|---|
| A | 1 | 5 | F | 7 | 3 |
| B | 4 | 3 | G | 6 | 2 |
| C | 2 | 1 | H | 1 | 2 |
| D | 4 | 8 | I | 5 | 7 |
| E | 5 | 6 | J | 3 | 4 |

7. Table 13.13 gives the processing time (in hours) of seven jobs to be processed on three machines $M1$, $M2$, and $M3$ in the order $M1$, $M2$, $M3$. Sequence the jobs using Johnson's method and find the overall processing time. Also find the waiting times of the jobs and the idle times of the three machines.

**Table 13.13**

| Job | M1 | M2 | M3 |
|---|---|---|---|
| A | 7 | 6 | 10 |
| B | 10 | 3 | 9 |
| C | 11 | 1 | 15 |
| D | 14 | 2 | 13 |
| E | 21 | 5 | 18 |
| F | 17 | 4 | 11 |
| G | 8 | 1 | 9 |

8. Table 13.14 gives the processing times (in hours) of seven jobs to be processed on four machines $M1$, $M2$, $M3$, and $M4$ in the order $M1$, $M2$, $M3$, $M4$. Sequence the jobs using Johnson's method and find the overall processing time.

**Table 13.14**

| Job | M1 | M2 | M3 | M4 |
|---|---|---|---|---|
| A | 17 | 4 | 5 | 12 |
| B | 15 | 2 | 9 | 16 |
| C | 10 | 5 | 7 | 19 |
| D | 19 | 8 | 2 | 23 |
| E | 20 | 1 | 6 | 21 |
| F | 22 | 4 | 1 | 18 |
| G | 13 | 3 | 8 | 13 |

9. Bose Electronics of Kolkata makes two types of customized electronic sensors for a multinational electronics company. The two sensors require testing on six different pieces of equipment. The order of use of these pieces of equipment is different for the two sensors, as shown in Table 13.15. Find the optimal testing time of the two sensors simultaneously on the various equipment. Assume that one unit each of the six pieces of equipment is available.

**Table 13.15**

| Sensor 1 | | Sensor 2 | |
|---|---|---|---|
| Equipment sequence | Duration (h) | Equipment sequence | Duration (h) |
| A | 3 | D | 2 |
| B | 5 | B | 4 |
| C | 2 | F | 5 |
| D | 1 | A | 2 |
| E | 4 | E | 3 |
| F | 3 | C | 4 |

10. There are four jobs ($J1$–$J4$) to be assigned to five machines ($M1$–$M5$). The processing times (in hours) of the various jobs on the machines from past experience are given in Table 13.16.

    Assign the jobs to the machines such that the total processing time is minimum. Find also the total processing time of the jobs. (**Hint:** Add a fifth row for a dummy job $J4$ with all the cells having 0 processing time.)

**Table 13.16**

|     | M1 | M2 | M3 | M4 | M5 |
| --- | -- | -- | -- | -- | -- |
| J1  | 2  | 3  | 6  | 9  | 10 |
| J2  | 1  | 2  | 5  | 7  | 4  |
| J3  | 5  | 4  | 2  | 1  | 7  |
| J4  | 7  | 6  | 8  | 3  | 5  |

## Project Assignments

1. Visit a nearby factory which operates as a job shop. An ancillary unit of a big plant may be ideal for your study. Ask the production manager about the priority rules/sequencing methods followed by them for sequencing the various orders. Analyse these methods and whether a better alternative is possible and debate its advantages in the classroom.

2. Conduct a study on the sequencing of customer orders in a prominent restaurant in your area during rush hours. If permitted by them, study how the chefs prioritize making dishes belonging to different customer orders. Find out their reasons for this scheduling. Suggest some better options, if possible.

### Answers to Objective Questions

1. (d)    2. (c)    3. (d)    4. (a)    5. True
6. False    7. True    8. routing    9. prioritization or sequencing
10. loading

# 14

# Quality Management

## Learning Objectives

After reading this chapter, you will be able to answer the following questions:
- What is quality? What are its dimensions?
- What is the cost of equality?
- How can we use statistics to measure and control quality?
- How is quality monitored at each stage of the transformation process?
- What is Six Sigma? How can an organization use it for competitive advantage?
- What is ISO 9000? How is it different from ISO 14000?

## Quality

The quality guru J.M. Juran defined quality as 'fitness for purpose'. For assessing the quality of a product or service, the criterion of 'fitness for purpose' is highly subjective, which may vary from individual to individual. The perception of the quality of a product or service from the point of view of a customer may be different from that of the producer. The producer's problem is aggravated by the fact that the number of customers may be too many, and each one may be having a different perception of quality. If a third party, such as a quality certification agency, has to decide the quality of the product or service, its perception may be different from that of both the customer and the producer.

This criterion of 'fitness of purpose' for perfectly suitable only at a particular stage of production. This is the stage of designing the product or service. The marketing department of the company prepares *a product definition document,* in which it specifies the expectations and requirements of the customer from the product (here onwards we use the term product for products as well as services). This document is passed on to the design department, where the designs of the product are prepared keeping in mind the 'fitness for purpose', that is, the expectations or requirements of the customer. The designs so prepared are rated good or bad according to the extent to which these are able to satisfy the requirements mentioned in the product definition document.

In all the subsequent stages, however, such as development, engineering, production, distribution, and after-sales service, quality is defined and measured in terms of 'conformance to specifications'—as stated by another quality guru, Philip Crosby. During the development of

> A quality system is defined as the collection of the resources, organization, equipment, people, and procedures that implement the quality policy.

the product, various specifications are evolved. These specifications have to be adhered to in all the stages of production in order to achieve the desired quality. Conformance to these specifications can be verified by objective evidence in contrast to the subjective approach of the 'fitness for purpose' criterion.

*Quality control is defined as maintaining requisite standards in products or services.* ISO 8402 defines quality control as the operational techniques and activities that are used to fulfil quality requirements. It defines quality assurance as planned and systematic actions necessary to provide adequate confidence that a product or service will satisfy the given quality requirements.

A quality system is defined as the collection of the resources, organization, equipment, people, and procedures which implement the quality policy. Total quality control is an effective system for integrating the quality-development, quality-maintenance, and quality-improvement efforts of the various groups in an organization, to enable marketing, engineering, production, and service at economical levels which allow for full customer satisfaction.

*Six Sigma* (Fig. 14.1) is a quality philosophy for ensuring the reduction of the number of defective products to ideally zero. This Herculean task can be achieved only when each and every employee in the organization has the ability to measure and control quality in his domain

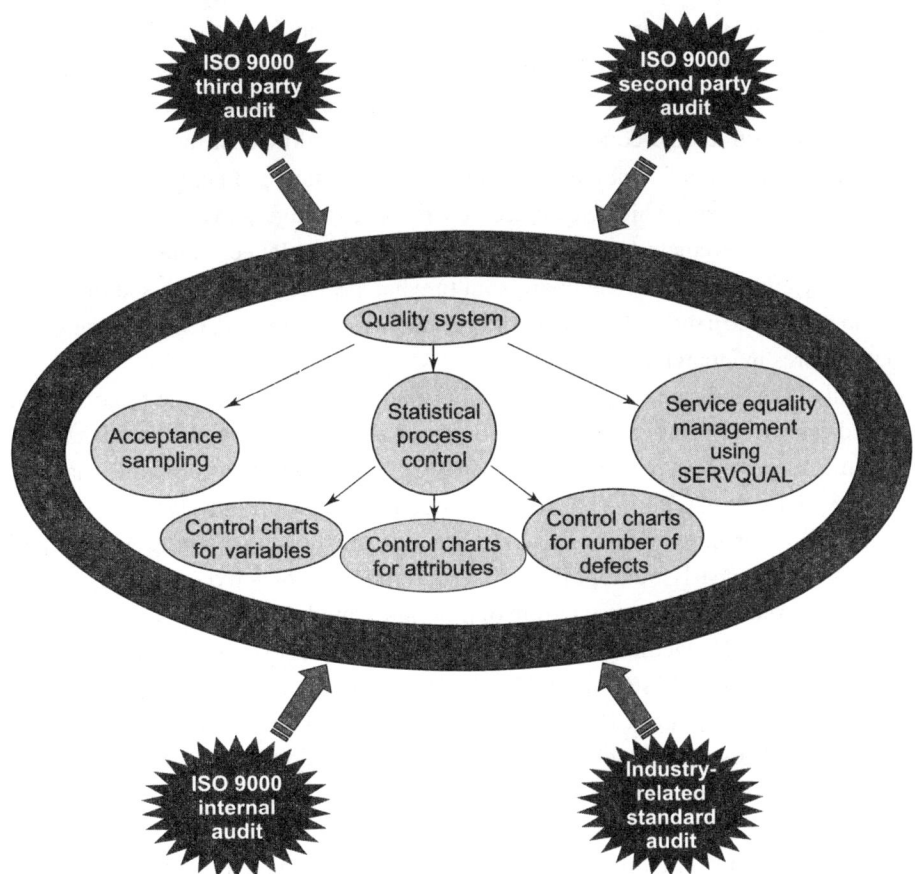

**Fig. 14.1** Quality management

| Six Sigma is a quality philosophy for ensuring the reduction of the number of defective products to ideally zero. |

of activity. Thus, Six Sigma involves the rigorous training of all the employees in various quality control techniques. Quality certification bodies like ISO conduct quality audits (inspection by third party external trained and authorized quality auditors) of the quality system before certifying an organization. It is a requirement in ISO 9000 that an organization seeking ISO certification has to conduct *internal quality audits* on a regular basis. These audits, also called first party audits, can be conducted by the trained employees of the organization to ensure that the quality system is maintained properly.

Second party quality audits may be conducted by an institutional customer of the organization to ensure the quality standards mentioned in their contract. There may be some industry-related standards (especially in defence, aerospace, and nuclear organizations) which may require quality audits from time to time. We will discuss in detail all these aspects of quality management in this chapter.

## India Inc. Riding High on the Quality Bandwagon

Professor Robert S. Kaplan (known for developing concepts such as the balanced scorecard and activity-based costing) of Harvard University recently made an observation that Indian firms need to move from being quality driven and must position themselves as strategy focused, to compete in the global business environment. According to him, 'Indian firms are good at quality. It's time they embrace strategy. While quality in improvement of products can be measured, strategy deals with abstract and conceptual thinking. A purely low-cost model would not be a sustainable business proposition for Indian firms in the wake of rising competition. Management must focus on developing a strategy, which creates a competitive advantage, and ensure its effective implementation. Strategy must percolate from top to each and every employee. India's intangible skills in terms of creativity and data management are akin to what US possessed and used in 1980s to compete with Japan, which had a more efficient workforce. India may be lacking China's tangible product processes, but it scores in intangible assets.'

India is on the same journey of quality that Japan was after the Second World War. In fact, world-renowned TQM expert, Professor Yasutoshi Washio, has predicted that the quality of Indian manufacturing will overtake that of Japan in 2013. Many Indian companies have got Deming prizes (Table 14.1). So far, China has not even entered the Deming radar.

Indian companies seem to be in the favourites list of the Deming Awards of Japan. The 2003 Deming list is nearly monopolized by Indian companies—five out of eight. The other three are also from Asia. The Japanese Union of Scientists and Engineers (JUSE) started the Deming prize in 1951, when Dr Deming donated the earnings from the sale of his papers (the stenographic records of his speeches compiled by JUSE) to JUSE. Initially, this prize was open only to the Japanese industry, but in 1985 it was thrown open to the rest of the world. The prize has three categories. The first category is the Deming Application Prize, which is given to companies or divisions of companies that have enhanced performance through total quality management (TQM) in a given year. The second category is the Deming Prize for Individuals, that is, TQM scholars and practitioners. The third category of the prize is the Quality Control Award for Operations Business Units given out for exceptional implementation of TQM.

**Table 14.1** Deming award winners from India

| Deming Application Prize | |
| --- | --- |
| Sundaram-Clayton Limited, Brakes Division | 1998 |
| Sundaram Brake Linings Ltd | 2001 |
| TVS Motor Company Ltd | 2002 |
| Brakes India Ltd Foundry Division | 2003 |
| Mahindra and Mahindra Ltd, Farm Equipment Sector | 2003 |
| Rane Brake Linings Ltd | 2003 |
| Sona Koyo Steering Systems Ltd | 2003 |
| SRF Limited, Industrial Synthetics Business | 2004 |
| Lucas-TVS Limited | 2004 |
| Indo Gulf Fertilisers Limited | 2004 |
| Krishna Maruti Limited, Seat Division | 2005 |
| Rane Engine Valves Limited | 2005 |
| Rane TRW Steering Systems Limited, Steering Gear Division | 2005 |
| Asahi India Glass Limited, Auto Glass Division (India) | 2007 |
| Rane (Madras) Limited (India) | 2007 |
| Reliance Industries Limited, Hazira Manufacturing Division (India) | 2007 |
| Tata Steel Limited (India) | 2008 |
| National Engineering Industries Limited (India) | 2010 |
| Sanden Vikas (India) Limited | 2011 |
| SRF Limited, Chemicals Business (India) | 2012 |
| Mahindra & Mahindra Limited, Farm Equipment Sector, Swaraj Division (India) | 2012 |
| *Quality Control Award for Operations Business Units* | |
| Hi-Tech Carbon GMPD | 2002 |
| Birla Cellousic, Kharach: A unit of Grasim Industries Ltd | 2003 |
| *Japan Quality Medal* | |
| Sundaram-Clayton Ltd, Brakes Division | 2002 |
| Mahindra & Mahindra Ltd, Farm Equipment Sector | 2007 |

The five winners of this prestigious honor in 2003 (termed as the Nobel prize in the world of manufacturing) include Rane Brake Linings, Mahindra & Mahindra (farm equipment and tractor division), Brakes India (foundry division), Sona Koyo Steering Systems, and Grasim Industries (Birla Cellulosic, Kharach unit). While the first four companies got the Deming Application Prize, Grasim Industries' unit got the Quality Control Award for Operations Business Units. It is not just winning a medal. Indian companies have entered the record books. For instance, Mahindra's tractor unit is the first tractor unit in the world to win the Deming. Similarly, Rane Brake Linings became the world's second brake lining manufacturer to become a Deming company. The first one was also an Indian company—TVS group's Sundaram Brake Linings in 2001.

From 1998 onwards, Indian companies started figuring in the Deming prize list, with Sundaram Clayton's brakes division claiming the honour first. Till 2002, the Indian winners belonged to the 27-unit TVS group—Sundaram Brake Linings (2001) and TVS Motor Company (2002).

Apart from Deming, the group outfits have been winning other quality medals. In 2002, Sundaram Clayton's brakes division got the Japan Quality Medal, also awarded by JUSE. TVS Srichakra Tyres has won the Total Productive Maintenance (TPM), Excellence Award—First Category, from the Japanese Institute of Plant Maintenance (JIPM).

It may not be wrong to call the TVS group as the Deming group. The winds of quality excellence are blowing across all the group units, irrespective of their size.

Says V. Narasimhan, Executive Director, Brakes India: 'Our quality manual was written within two years of our start-up'. And that was 22 years ago. Those were the times when a majority of Indian industries was blissfully unaware of various quality and customer satisfaction concepts.

Similarly, Sundaram Brake Linings' quality excellence strategy started 15 years back. The first non-TVS Indian company to figure in the Deming list is Hi-Tech Carbon (2002), a part of the US $6 billion Aditya Birla group. Like the TVS group, Deming is not new to the Aditya Birla group.

Two of the group's Thailand-based companies (Thai Acrylic Fibre Company and Thai Carbon Black Public Company) have won the prestigious quality award in 2001. Given this position, it is heartening to note that the 2003 Deming list contains non-TVS/Aditya Birla group outfits too.

'We were not pressured by Sundaram Brake Linings or other TVS group companies winning the award. It is just that we wanted to go forward', says S. Sundar Ram, President, Rane Brake Linings.

What is remarkable is that Rane Brake Linings won the award in the shortest time—three years—from the date of starting its TQM practice.

Speaking about the company's pre-Deming days, Ram says: 'We were focusing only on production value. The company had a high level (2.1%) of plant-level rejections and customer returns. There were small individual kaizens (continuous improvement programmes). No systematic initiatives for improvements were in place'.

One may wonder as to how Indian auto ancillaries are increasingly reaching the quality summit. Not long ago, domestic car manufacturers allowed 10 per cent defective parts in supplies. A car normally has around 10,000 parts. In all probability, every car that was rolled out of a factory had some defective parts fitted in, as the production capacity was also low.

Manufacturers have realized that quality actually contributes to the bottom line, in terms of reduction in scrap/waste, inventory turnover, productivity, and lead time to execute an order. The road to success is not smooth. It is really years of hard grind even before the companies think of challenging the award.

Apart from auto ancillaries, other industries are also resorting to TPM, such as manufacturers of cement and condoms. Says J. Srinivasan, Managing Director, TTK LIG, the world's largest condom manufacturing company: 'Our productivity has improved manifold, and waste has come down drastically. There is no company in the world that can meet our production costs now. Today we are catering to the global demand from here.' The company has won the award for TPM Excellence—Second Category from JIPM this year.

While groups such as TVS, Birla, Mahindra, and Rane follow the Japanese quality processes, the Tata group has its own model—the Tata Business Excellence Model (TBEM)—a derivative of the American Malcolm Baldrige quality model. Tata Quality Management Services (TQMS), an arm of Tata Sons, benchmarks the quality standards and systems to be followed by the Tata companies. The company that excels in various parameters is awarded the JRD QV award, instituted by the group.

### The Maruti Factor

Looking back, the quality movement among the domestic auto ancillaries, actually, was initiated by the country's premier car manufacturer, Maruti Udyog, through its cluster approach. Maruti got 11 of its vendors to adhere to quality systems and processes. The idea was to showcase a couple of units so that the others could follow too. Today, the cluster approach is what is being practised to teach small-scale units to adopt quality practices. Many of the auto ancillaries that have won the Deming award are members of the cluster, and some others are in the Deming race. Brakes India's foundry division, a Deming winner in 2003, is also a cluster member.

With many foreign auto ancillaries setting up shop in India (Korean ancillaries tagged along with Hyundai Motors, and Visteon with Ford Motors), the domestic units had to perforce upgrade themselves to ward off competition within India, and also to take advantage of the export possibilities. Not a day passes without an overseas automobile manufacturer announcing sourcing possibilities from India. However, they have laid down stiff qualifying norms. For instance, Ford Motor Company has mandated that its vendors should be Q1-certified.

What do these awards really signify for the domestic companies? In addition to increased exports, it gives the confidence to go global. After getting the production process right in India, replicating the same in other parts of the globe will not be an issue. Such a trend has already started. Auto ancillary groups such as TVS and Kalyani are putting up and buying out units abroad. Sundaram Fasteners is setting up a high-tensile fastener unit in China, and has announced its intention to buy the UK-based forging company Dana Spicer. Two-wheeler manufacturer TVS Motor Company is planning a unit in Indonesia.

Bharat Forge, the flagship company of the Pune-based Kalyani group, acquired Carl Dan Peddinghaus, Germany. In the long run, the positive rub-off of quality awards such as Deming on the Indian industry will be the improvement of the image of the domestic manufacturing sector and the realization of its human resources and capabilities.

From being looked at as the global brain base (many multinational companies are setting up their research and development wings here), India is now seen as a quality manufacturer. A positive image alone will not result in increased foreign investment, thereby making India the production base for global markets, say, like China. Technical capability alone will not attract industrial investments. It is the existence of good infrastructure such as roads, ports, and power which would entice multinational corporations to set up their shop floors here.

According to industry officials, China may be a volume player, but when it comes to quality engineering products, India is way ahead. Not very long ago, Indians looked at the Japanese products with disdain because of its poor quality. Now the elephant is gathering speed.

Infosys, Wipro, I-flex, TCS—all leading Indian software companies—are in the forefront of the quality bandwagon. For most of these software companies, attaining SEI-CMM Level 5 has been considered as the pinnacle in their journey to attain the peak of quality. The motivation for Indian IT software and services companies to attain SEI-CMM Level 5 assessment dates as far back as 1995, when Motorola's unit in India acquired this certification. The seed of quality was thus sown, and the following years have been that of 'quality transformation'. The gold standard in the quality-certification business is the capability maturity model (CMM), which sets out specific steps needed for the completion of an effective development process. The CMM was conceived by the Software Engineering Institute at Carnegie Mellon University in Pittsburgh. It is a group funded by the U.S. government because it wanted a standardized way to assess the work of contractors. CMM certification is awarded by consulting firms that can charge companies to evaluate and train their personnel in CMM methods.

According to the Software Engineering Institute, in 2002, only 18 Chinese companies were CMM-certified, compared with 153 Indian companies. In 2005 that number of Chinese companies climbed to 243, compared with the 387 Indian companies. The NASSCOM strategic review points out that today, India-based centres (both Indian firms as well as MNC-owned captive units) constitute the largest number of quality certifications achieved by any single country. As of December 2006, over 440 Indian companies had acquired quality certifications with 90 companies certified at SEI CMM Level 5—higher than any other country in the world.

## Quality Management—A Conceptual Framework

According to the Oxford dictionary for the business world, *quality* is defined as the degree of excellence.

Quality guru J.M. Juran defined quality as

'Fitness for purpose.'

Quality guru Philip Crosby defined quality as

'Conformance to specifications.'

*Quality control* (QC) is defined as maintaining requisite standards in products or services.

ISO 8402 defines *Quality Control* as

'The operational techniques and activities that are used to fulfill requirements of quality.'

ISO 8402 defines *Quality Assurance* as

'All those planned and systematic actions necessary to provide adequate confidence that a product or service will satisfy the given requirements for quality.'

Quality guru A.V. Feigenbaum defines *Total Quality Control* (*TQC*) as

'Total quality control is an effective system for integrating the quality-development, quality-maintenance, and quality-improvement efforts of the various groups in an organization to enable marketing, engineering, production, and service at the most economical levels which allow for full customer satisfaction.'

## Dimensions of Quality

Quality should, first and foremost, be perceived from the customer's point of view. This is because it is the customer who decides whether or not to buy a product or service according to his or her perception of quality (Fig. 14.2). Performance is the most basic customer requirement from a product. A refrigerator which does not cool is a bad quality product. Similarly, an electric iron, which does not heat up is not a good quality product. The customer also expects the product

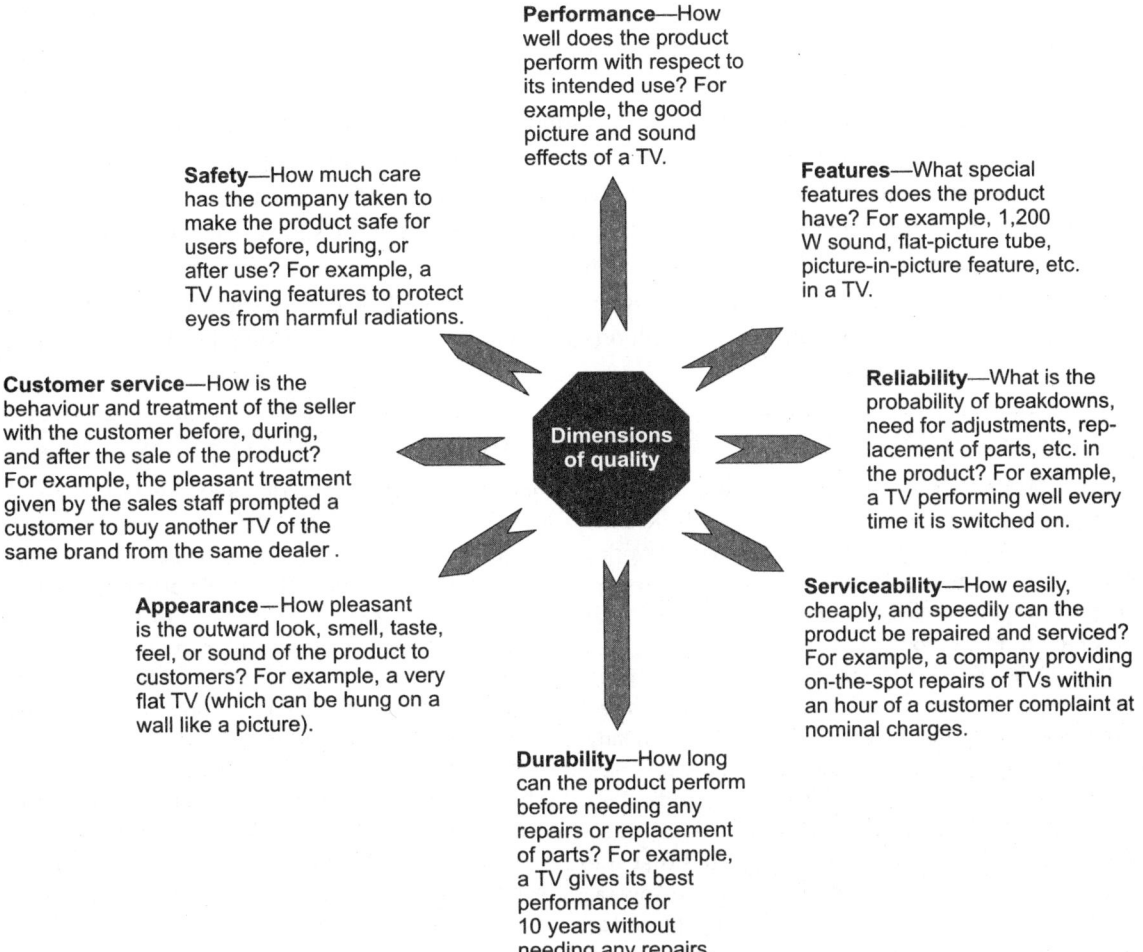

**Performance**—How well does the product perform with respect to its intended use? For example, the good picture and sound effects of a TV.

**Features**—What special features does the product have? For example, 1,200 W sound, flat-picture tube, picture-in-picture feature, etc. in a TV.

**Safety**—How much care has the company taken to make the product safe for users before, during, or after use? For example, a TV having features to protect eyes from harmful radiations.

**Reliability**—What is the probability of breakdowns, need for adjustments, replacement of parts, etc. in the product? For example, a TV performing well every time it is switched on.

**Customer service**—How is the behaviour and treatment of the seller with the customer before, during, and after the sale of the product? For example, the pleasant treatment given by the sales staff prompted a customer to buy another TV of the same brand from the same dealer .

**Dimensions of quality**

**Serviceability**—How easily, cheaply, and speedily can the product be repaired and serviced? For example, a company providing on-the-spot repairs of TVs within an hour of a customer complaint at nominal charges.

**Appearance**—How pleasant is the outward look, smell, taste, feel, or sound of the product to customers? For example, a very flat TV (which can be hung on a wall like a picture).

**Durability**—How long can the product perform before needing any repairs or replacement of parts? For example, a TV gives its best performance for 10 years without needing any repairs.

**Fig. 14.2**   Dimensions of quality

to be reliable, that is, perform well without requiring repairs, adjustments, etc. frequently. For example, an LCD projector purchased by an institute drips every half an hour due to heating. It has to be put off for an hour to allow it to cool down, and then restarted for another half an hour of performance. Is this a reliable product? The obvious answer is a big 'No'. Ease of service is another quality criterion for the customer. For example, Maruti Suzuki Ltd has a big advantage over its competitors in India with respect to this factor. The service network of Maruti is very extensive, probably because it started its operations in India much earlier than any of its competitors. People doing extensive touring in cars prefer a Maruti car due to the fact that it can be easily repaired even on a highway. The durability of a product refers to its lifespan. Customers expect a quality product to last very long. This lifespan extends to a point in time where repairs become costlier than the replacement of the product with a new one. Aesthetic sense in creating the outer appearance is the first impression of quality given to a customer.

Usually, it is the outer appearance of a product which induces a customer to enquire further about it (with a possibility of an eventual purchase). With the intense competition today, the most important dimension of quality, which was overlooked so far by many companies especially in India, is customer service. In India, the domestic industry can overcome the threat of foreign MNCs by focusing on this aspect of quality. Manufacturing organizations must focus on after-sales service as an important opportunity for creating a difference in quality for competitive advantage.

Last but not the least, *safety* is an aspect of a quality product which cannot be neglected by a manufacturer. Exhibit 14.1 provides Toyota's passenger safety initiatives. For example, electrical equipment must have proper earthing to prevent electric shock. The instructions manual accompanying the equipment must clearly explain the precautions for safe use. Automobile companies are heavily spending on R&D for the safety of their customers while driving their cars. Collapsible steering, the air balloon safety concept, steel rods inside doors, etc. are a result of this R&D effort.

---

### Exhibit 14.1   Toyota

Toyota Motor Corporation has come a long way since its inception in 1936 by Kiichiro Toyoda. Kiichiro Toyoda was managing Toyoda Automatic Loom Works, founded by his father, Sakichi Toyoda, after he travelled to Europe and America to acquaint himself with automobile production.

It is believed this is the reason behind the striking resemblance between the first Toyoda model created in 1936 and the Chevrolet car. Initially, the company was christened Toyoda after the name of the founder. Toyoda in Japanese means 'fertile rice paddies'. In order to disassociate the company from old-fashioned farming, some family members suggested that the name of the company should be changed to Toyota. The company was thus registered as Toyota Motor Company Limited in 1937.

During the 1950s, the company faced huge financial crisis and was on the verge of bankruptcy. However, it survived the critical phase and rebuilt itself, strength by strength. In the early 1980s, Toyota started selling its cars in the US and created its first plant there in collaboration with General Motors (GM) in 1984. There was no looking back for Toyota since then.

Toyota has been the ultimate name in quality in the automotive industry for almost three decades until 2009 when its impeccable image witnessed irreparable damage. The company that propounded concepts such as just-in-time (JIT) during the 1970s struggled with its image in the US.

In 2008, Toyota became the largest car manufacturer in the world by ending GM's 77 years of domination. That Toyota would land in such turmoil within a year was beyond imagination. The problem surfaced in August 2009, when the Saylor family in the US succumbed to death while travelling in Toyota's Lexus model. Ironically, they had loaned the vehicle from the dealership where they had given their own Toyota for servicing. The earlier loaner had suspected that there was some problem with the accelerator pedal, which was getting stuck under the floor of the mat. The dealership, however, ignored his complaint.

This incident later mothballed, with the National Highway Traffic Safety Administration (NHTSA) springing into action against Toyota. Toyota had to recall a record 9 million vehicles in the US, Europe, and China. It had to stop production-cum-sale of its eight models affected by the recall, though temporarily. This recall is the biggest ever in the history of automobile manufacturing worldwide. CTS Corporation, the supplier of accelerator pedals to Toyota, refused to take the blame. There was confusion galore, as Toyota struggled to find the root cause of the sudden unintended acceleration (SUA) problem in the affected vehicles.

The media frenzy surrounding Toyota's recall of its vehicles is unprecedented. Experts argue that despite this mammoth controversy, Toyota executives were not forthcoming in sharing their views with the media. It faced criticism for mishandling the whole issue.

Akio Toyoda, the current Chief Executive Officer (CEO) and President of Toyota, had to eventually give a testimony before the Committee on Oversight and Government Reform in the US, to justify that enough steps were being taken by the company to ensure safety of passengers in Toyota cars. He announced the formation of a quality advisory group of outside experts from across the globe and the establishment of an 'Automotive Centre of Quality Excellence'. Besides, he also announced the creation of a new position—product safety executive.

*Source:* Maynard (2010).

The importance of these dimensions call for the adoption of a systematic approach to quality management in production processes and customer service. It starts with the establishment of a quality system in the organization. The documented quality system sets out, in a formal framework, the basis of control for the critical activities of an organization, which demand a systematic approach, that is, quality management. It is very necessary to create an awareness of the need to manage quality in the whole organization, and of the role of the individual in this, as well as in the system, in order to control the activities.

Various techniques such as acceptance sampling, statistical process control (SPC), and service quality management using SERVQUAL have to be used to control quality in every sphere of activity in the organization. In SPC, we prepare control charts for variables, attributes, and the number of defects, as will be discussed later.

## Costs of Quality

*Quality is Free* is the title of the famous book by quality guru Philip Crosby. On the other hand, quality guru J.M. Juran is known for the concepts propounded by him regarding the costs of quality. Figure 14.3 shows the four types of costs of quality. It should be emphasized here that there is an inverse relation between the cost of prevention of defects and the other three types of costs. If the money spent on prevention of defects is increased, usually the costs of detection of defects, scrap and rework, and warranty claims tend to decrease. Companies such as Motorola,

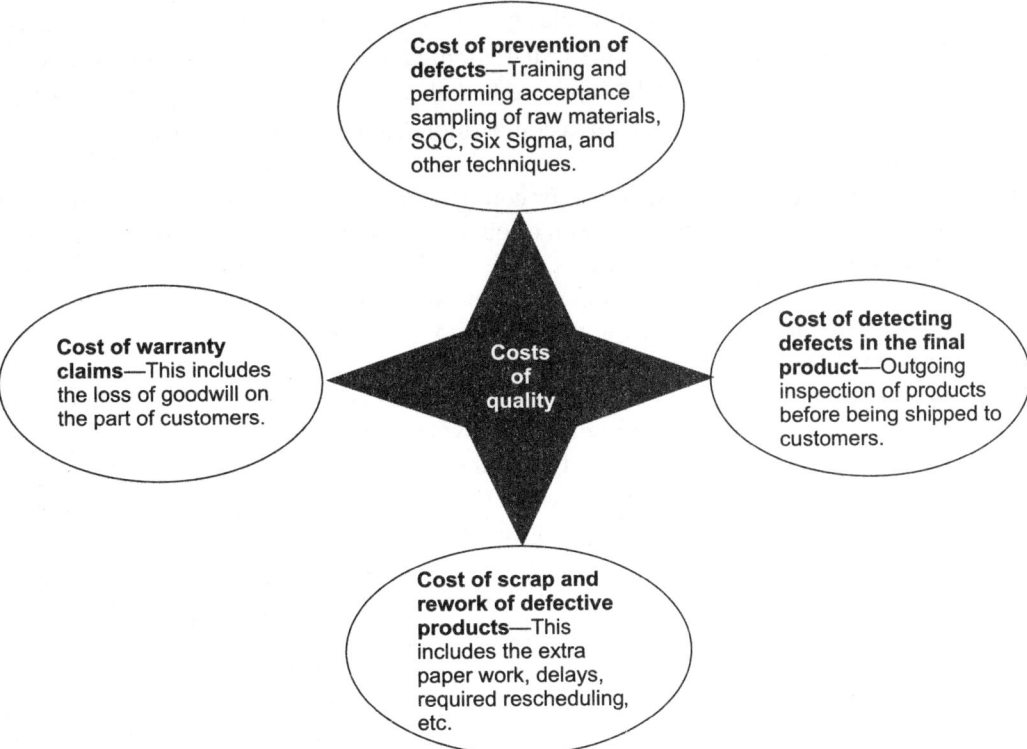

**Fig. 14.3**  Costs of quality

GE, and Texas Instruments etc. have saved billions of dollars by initially incurring a high cost for implementing quality philosophies like Six Sigma for the prevention of defects in their products.

## Deming's Contribution to Total Quality Management

W. Edwards Deming (1900–93) has been the most influential quality guru not only for the Japanese, but also for the rest of the world. The only difference is that the world came to know about him very late compared to the Japanese, who listened to him carefully when nobody else was listening and implemented his concepts to become world leaders in quality.

Deming was awarded his doctorate in mathematical physics in 1928. He then worked in the US Government Service for many years, particularly in statistical sampling techniques. He became particularly interested in the work of statistician Walter Shewhart, and believed that his principles could be equally applied to non-manufacturing processes. Deming started to run statistical courses to explain his and Shewhart's methods to engineers, designers, etc. in the US and Canada. In 1943, he published a technical book—*Statistical Adjustment of Data*.

After World War II, American companies experienced a boom because of the large capacities of their plants now available, which were earlier devoted to the war effort. The countries devastated in the war were willing to buy anything, no matter of what quality, and the Americans were ready to supply. The Americans were, thus, not bothered about quality at all at that time.

On the other hand, Japanese managers and engineers realized that they required new techniques to build their devastated country and economy fast. They invited Deming for his lectures on statistical quality control. In the early 1950s, he lectured engineers and senior managers throughout Japan, including in his lectures principles now regarded as a part of total quality management, or company-wide quality. Only in the year 1970 did the Americans recognize Deming's efforts, but it was too late by then, as the Japanese had already made inroads into the world markets, and the Americans were facing a tough competition from them. Deming's famous 14 points are summarized below.

1. Consistency of purpose is a must for continual improvement of a product. Managers have to ensure that the company's vision of quality is understood by all the employees and that they move continuously towards it.
2. Continuous change and innovation is a must for survival. In today's complex business situations, it is not possible for a small group of managers to identify and sort out quality problems. Thus, all the employees have to be involved in this process.
3. Quality cannot be achieved only by inspection. Inspection wastes valuable production time and adds to the product's cost without any value addition. Inspections may not be perfect, causing some defects to be passed on to the customer. Defects are symptoms removed by inspection, while the disease (root cause) remains intact. Inspections create a gap between the people and processes that introduce defects and the people and processes that detect defects.
4. Wastes should be eliminated in every functional area, not just production. Even processes in accounting, HRM, customer service, and sales affect the quality of the product and, thus, generate waste. Therefore, the whole organization should contribute towards the enhancement of quality.
5. The attitude of supervisors and managers towards workers should be that of a facilitator. Errors by workers should be treated by supervisors as an opportunity to learn the process and systems better. Teamwork should be promoted and rewarded.

6. The barriers between departments and individuals should be removed. Problems should not be handled within strict functional limits and the concerns raised by related functional areas should not be ignored.

7. Posters and slogans should be eliminated. These must not be used to tell the workers to work harder. Instead, they should be provided with tools and training so that they work smarter, leading to better quality.

8. Remove obstacles in the good workmanship of hourly workers to instil a sense of pride in them.

9. Vigorous programmes of retraining and education of employees are a must.

10. Numerical targets and work standards may affect quality. Reasonable numerical targets make the workers complacent, while excessively demanding ones may lead to a compromise on quality in order to achieve the targets. Such targets cannot be eliminated, but can be set such that quality is not compromised.

11. Encourage workers to give quality-improvement ideas without fear. Workers refrain from giving new ideas of change because they may have to work with new and unfamiliar methods in place of known and comfortable, though inefficient, methods. They also feel that if their ideas fail it may affect their performance appraisal, eventually leading to job insecurity.

12. Employees should be trained on the job. Training on quality techniques should be continual, as learning never ends.

13. The lowest price should not be the sole criteria for selecting a supplier. Suppliers asking for lowest prices often offer low-quality products, leading to an increase in the overall cost to the buyer due to the increased expenses of inspection, scrap, rework, inventory to replace defective items, etc. Thus, the supplier offering the lowest total cost should be selected.

14. The top management's commitment for ever-improving quality is a must.

## Quality at Every Stage

The ultimate aim of every organization is to deliver quality products to its customers. For achieving this objective, quality should be monitored at every stage—from input to the output (Fig. 14.4). *Acceptance sampling* is a method of ensuring that the inputs, such as raw materials, parts, components, and labour skills, are of desired quality levels. It is also used for the outgoing inspection of finished goods before distribution to customers.

Acceptance sampling is applied at the input and output stages of the transformation process. If a defect arises during the production of a batch of items, all the items of this batch will have to be rejected as scrap. This will be of immense loss to the company. Thus, in addition to acceptance sampling at the input and output stages, the quality of items has to be monitored during the transformation process. Thus, samples of items produced are inspected for quality at regular intervals of time. If variations are found from the previously fixed standards, the reasons for such variations are determined (e.g., wear and tear of a tool due to prolonged use, change in the concentration of a chemical, etc.) and rectified. This method of ensuring quality during the transformation process is called statistical process control or statistical quality control (SQC).

> Acceptance sampling is a method of ensuring that the inputs are of desired quality levels.

### Statistical Quality Control

During the transformation process of a batch, samples of items are taken at regular intervals and inspected for any variations from the established standards.

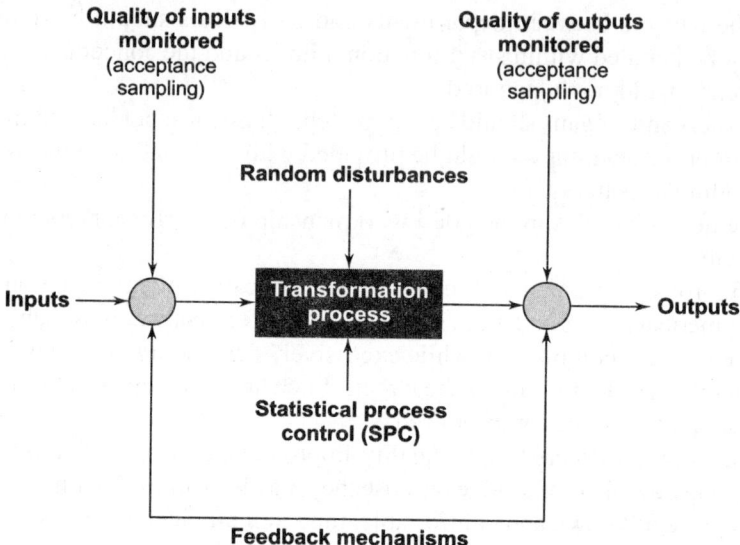

**Fig. 14.4** Monitoring quality levels at every stage of the transformation process

Any variations found prompt the quality control (QC) manager to find the cause. If a cause such as worn-out tool, mistake on the part of a worker in processing the item, and improper adjustment of the machine is found, it is termed as an *assignable cause*. Whenever variations are due to assignable causes, the process is said to be out of control. The assignable causes of the variation are rectified to bring the process under control.

Certain variations are due to the inherent nature of the process and are called *random variations*. In every process some random variations are present, which is expected. The process is said to be in control if variations are only due to random variations. For example, in the process of filling urea in sacks by an automated machine, the machine puts a particular weight of urea into every sack. There is some variation in the weight of urea filled in by the machine in different sacks. In one sack the weight may be 100.005 kg, in another it may be 100.01 kg, and in still another one it may be 99.998 kg. The machine is not designed to be capable of detecting variation in weight up to the third place of decimal in kg. Therefore, it is expected that this much variation in weight will take place because of the inherent nature of the machine. Such small variations bother neither the manufacturer nor the customer. Hence, whenever a variation beyond a certain limit is observed by the QC manager, it is time to look for assignable causes.

> Acceptance sampling is applied at the input and output stages of the transformation process.

There are two ways of monitoring the variation. The first way is to monitor all the physical variables such as tools, machines and equipment, and labour skills acting on the material inputs in the transformation process. Are all the machines working in ideal conditions? Are the workers working according to specified methods? Are the tools properly calibrated? The problem with monitoring variations in physical variables is that these are usually too many in number. Thus, the second way is easier to implement compared to the first way.

> Certain variations are due to the inherent nature of the process and are called random variations.

The second way is to monitor the variations in the output product or service. If the output product satisfies the product definition document specified by the marketing department and the specifications evolved during its development

The limits set by the manufacturer at the design stage of the product or specified by a customer for the value of a variable characteristic of the product are called its specification limits or tolerance limits.

stages, it possesses the desired quality. Samples of the output are inspected at regular intervals of time and any variation from previously established standards can easily be detected.

This second way of monitoring the output is most popularly used in all industries to monitor variation. At the same time, the first method of monitoring the output is also pursued by organizations in combination with the second method, though in a much less specific approach. ISO 9000 and other certification standards require various steps to ensure that the quality system in the organization is maintained properly. The various clauses in these standards relating to calibration of instruments, documentation procedures, methods of processes, maintenance of equipment, working environment, and the skill set required by workers ensure that an overall quality system takes care of variations in the physical variables in the transformation process.

***Specification and control limits***    No item in the world can be a true copy of another item. Some variation is ought to be there in some attributes of items. Therefore, while specifying the desired value of a variable during the design and development stages of a product, it is not expressed in absolute values but in terms of a range. For example, the diameter of a pencil is expressed by its manufacturer not as 7 mm but as 7 mm ± 0.05 mm. Thus, the diameter of a pencil produced by the manufacturer can vary from 6.95 mm to 7.05 mm. If these limits are exceeded by the diameter of a particular pencil produced, the pencil is rejected as scrap.

These limits set by the manufacturer at the design stage of the product or specified by a customer for the value of a variable characteristic of the product are called its *specification limits or tolerance limits*. It is very important for a QC manager to ensure that the specification limits are never exceeded for any unit during the production process, because if this happens, the defective unit produced will be rejected as scrap leading to a loss for the company.

In our example of the diameter of a pencil, we show these specification limits along the vertical axis in Fig.14.5. The value 7.00 mm is shown as the central line (CL) and is called the *targeted or aimed-at value*, because theoretically it is aimed that every pencil produced should have a diameter of exactly 7.00 mm, no more and no less. Due to random variations, though, the diameter of the pencils produced may vary slightly on either side of the CL. The value 6.95 mm becomes the lower specification limit (LSL) and 7.05 mm becomes the upper specification limit (USL).

**Fig. 14.5**   Specification limits for the diameter of a pencil

In order to ensure that the specification limits are never exceeded, certain limits called *control limits* are established inside the specification limits. These limits serve as a danger signal or indication for the QC manager. Whenever these limits are exceeded by the output, he has to look for assignable causes. As shown in Fig. 14.6, the control limits are inside the specification limits in our example of diameter of pencils. The lower control limit (LCL) is set usually at $M - 3\sigma_M$ and the upper control limit (UCL) at $M + 3\sigma_M$, that is, at the third sigma limits (see Fig. 14.6). Here, $M$ is the targeted or aimed-at value of the diameter of all the pencils to be made, that is, 7.00 mm, and $\sigma_M$ is the standard error of the mean (i.e., the standard deviation of the distribution of sample means).

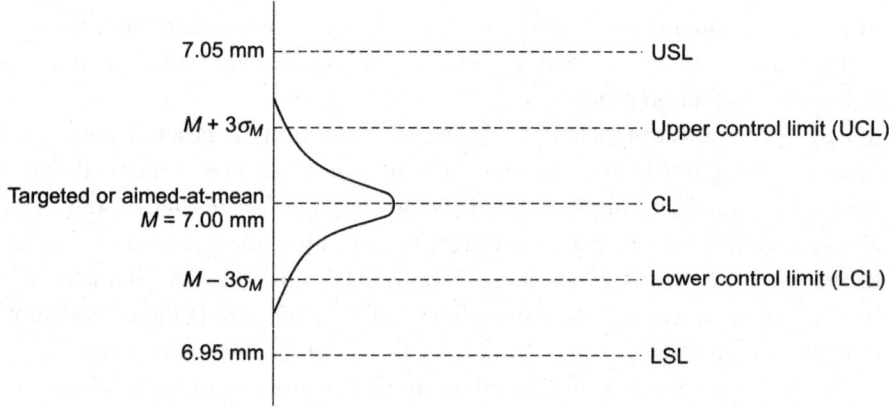

**Fig. 14.6** Specification and control limits for the diameter of a pencil

Here, we are considering the distribution of sample means because samples of pencils (of sample size *n*) are drawn at random and their diameters are measured, and the mean of these measurements is taken. This sample mean should fall within the control limits. If the sample mean for any sample falls either above the UCL or below the LCL, the process is out of control. The QC manager will have to start looking for any assignable causes for this variation. (It is strongly recommended here that the concepts of sampling theory explained in Chapter 12 are revised before proceeding further in this chapter, because the concepts explained here are based on sampling theory.)

**Type I and Type II errors**   The three sigma limits contain between them 97.73 per cent of the sample means. This means that 0.27 per cent of the sample means will cross the control limits, that is, will fall outside the UCL or LCL. In other words, out of every 10,000 samples, 27 samples will have their mean outside the control limits. Thus, when a sample mean overshoots a control limit, there is a possibility that the process may not be out of control. In that case, when the QC manager looks for assignable causes, he is able to find one and correct it to bring the process back under control. At the same time, there is a possibility that the process may be in control and the sample mean exceeding the control limits may be one of those 27 out of every 10,000 samples due to random variations. Two types of errors (summarized in Fig. 14.7) are possible in SQC.

**Type I error**   This error takes place when the process is in control but the QC manager is trying to find some assignable causes. This error leads to wastage of effort, time, and money in finding an assignable cause, which in fact does not exist.

| | Assignable causes are searched for | Assignable causes are not searched for |
|---|---|---|
| Process is in control | **Type I error** | Correct approach |
| Process is out of control | Correct approach | **Type II error** |

**Fig. 14.7** Type I and type II errors

*Type II error* This error takes place when the process is out of control but the QC manager is not looking for any assignable causes. This error is harmful to the quality system as some defective products may be produced during this time as long as the process is out of control.

**Control charts for variables** When the quality of a product depends on some measurable physical quantity or variable (e.g., dimension, weight, concentration, etc.), which is to be controlled, control charts called *control charts for variables* are made. In our example of the diameter of pencils, the diameter is the variable to be controlled, that is, to be kept within the specification limits 7 mm ± 0.05 mm. In order to understand how control charts for variables are made, let us extend our example further. Let us assume that we draw samples of size 3 each after every hour. That is, we choose three pencils as they are produced at random in a sample after every hour and measure their diameters. The data given in Table 14.2 is obtained.

Note that 10 samples of size 3 units each are taken at intervals of one hour starting from 8 a.m. As expected, there are variations in the values of diameters of the various pencils. Let us find the mean of the diameters of each sample and also the range (i.e., the difference between the maximum and the minimum value of the diameter of pencils in each sample). This is shown in cells F6 to F15 and G6 to G15 in the MS Excel spreadsheet of Fig. 14.8.

To find the average of the diameters of pencils in sample 1, select cells C6 to F6 and click on the small arrow adjacent to the Σ tool in the toolbar. A pull-down menu appears, from which we select **Average**. The average of the three values appears in cell F6 as 6.997967. Similarly, find the average of all the other samples. To find the range, say, for sample 1, select cell G6 and put the formula **=D6–C6** in it. Upon pressing **Enter** on the keyboard, 0.0077 appears in cell G6. This is the range of sample 1. The range is a measure of dispersion, that is, it is the difference between the maximum and the minimum values in a sample. In sample 1, the maximum value is in cell D6, while the minimum value is given in cell C6. Therefore, we have taken the difference of these values to get the range for sample 1. Similarly, we find the range for all the other samples.

**Table 14.2** Data table

| | | Diameter of pencils (mm) | | |
|---|---|---|---|---|
| *Time* | *Sample no.* | *Unit 1* | *Unit 2* | *Unit 3* |
| 8 a.m. | 1 | 6.9935 | 7.0012 | 6.9992 |
| 9 a.m. | 2 | 7.0271 | 6.9932 | 6.9815 |
| 10 a.m. | 3 | 6.9838 | 7.0024 | 7.0124 |
| 11 a.m. | 4 | 7.0236 | 6.9789 | 6.9994 |
| 12 noon | 5 | 6.9912 | 7.0072 | 7.0344 |
| 1 p.m. | 6 | 6.9461 | 6.9483 | 6.9494 |
| 2 p.m. | 7 | 7.0186 | 6.9947 | 7.0025 |
| 3 p.m. | 8 | 6.9972 | 7.0176 | 6.9925 |
| 4 p.m. | 9 | 6.9562 | 7.0533 | 6.9949 |
| 5 p.m. | 10 | 6.9993 | 7.0005 | 7.0034 |

If one carefully examines the average or mean values of the various samples in Fig. 14.8, it will be noticed that there is some variation of these values from the targeted or aimed-at value of the diameter of a pencil, that is, exactly 7.0000 mm. Thus, the QC manager should always try to control the process of manufacturing pencils such that the sample averages or means are as close as possible to the targeted value. The mean or average is called the *central tendency* of a distribution. Thus, we conclude that the central tendency of the process has to be controlled.

The range values found in column G of Fig. 14.8 also show variation for various samples. Ideally, the QC manager will try to control the process such that the range of all the samples becomes zero, that is, all the pencils in a sample have exactly the same value of the diameter. In that case, the difference between the maximum and the minimum value in the sample will be zero. Practically, it may not be possible for the range of all the samples to be zero due to random variations. Still the QC manager must try to keep the range as low as possible. Since range is a measure of dispersion, we conclude that in addition to controlling the central tendency (i.e., the mean), we need to control the dispersion (i.e., the range).

**Mean of sample means ($\mu$) chart and mean range ($\bar{R}$) chart** In our earlier discussion, we concluded that we have to control not only the central tendency (i.e., the mean of the sample means), but also the dispersion (i.e., the range) in order to keep the process in control. Two control charts are made to control the process. One chart controls the average or the mean ($\mu$) of the process and is called the *mean of sample means* ($\mu$ or $\bar{x}$) *chart.* The other chart controls the mean range $\bar{R}$ of the process and is caled the *mean range* $\bar{R}$ *chart.*

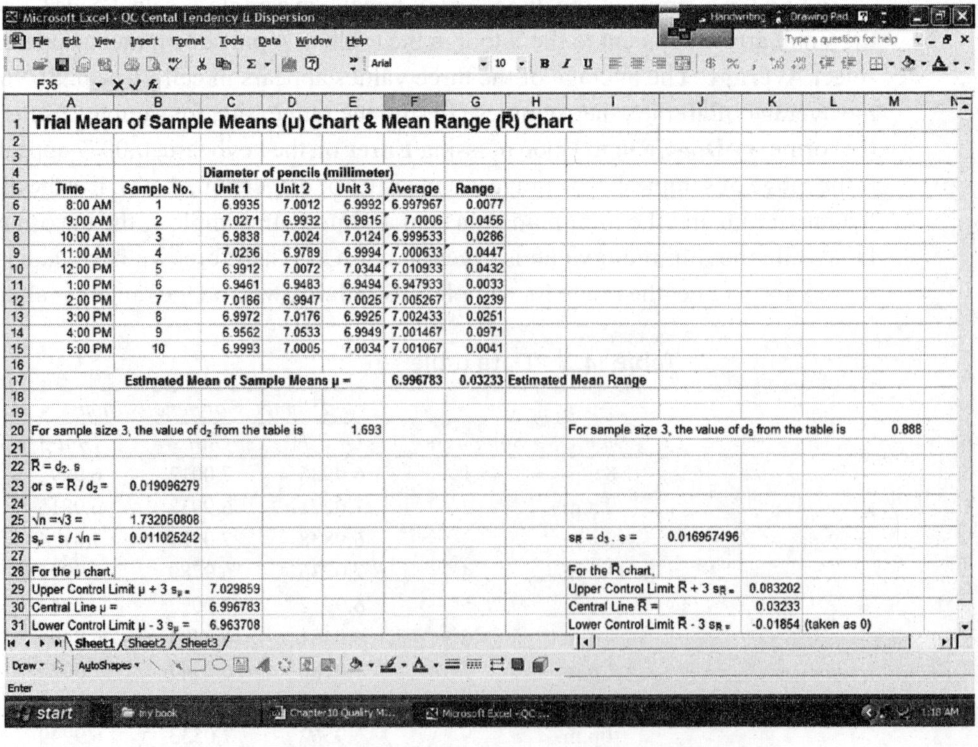

| | A | B | C | D | E | F | G | H | I | J | K | L |
|---|---|---|---|---|---|---|---|---|---|---|---|---|
| 1 | **Trial Mean of Sample Means (μ) Chart & Mean Range (R̄) Chart** | | | | | | | | | | | |
| 2 | | | | | | | | | | | | |
| 3 | | | | | | | | | | | | |
| 4 | | | **Diameter of pencils (millimeter)** | | | | | | | | | |
| 5 | **Time** | **Sample No.** | **Unit 1** | **Unit 2** | **Unit 3** | **Average** | **Range** | | | | | |
| 6 | 8:00 AM | 1 | 6.9935 | 7.0012 | 6.9992 | 6.997967 | 0.0077 | | | | | |
| 7 | 9:00 AM | 2 | 7.0271 | 6.9932 | 6.9815 | 7.0006 | 0.0456 | | | | | |
| 8 | 10:00 AM | 3 | 6.9838 | 7.0024 | 7.0124 | 6.999533 | 0,0286 | | | | | |
| 9 | 11:00 AM | 4 | 7.0236 | 6.9789 | 6.9994 | 7.000633 | 0.0447 | | | | | |
| 10 | 12:00 PM | 5 | 6.9912 | 7.0072 | 7.0344 | 7.010933 | 0.0432 | | | | | |
| 11 | 1:00 PM | 6 | 6.9461 | 6.9483 | 6.9494 | 6.947933 | 0.0033 | | | | | |
| 12 | 2:00 PM | 7 | 7.0186 | 6.9947 | 7.0025 | 7.005267 | 0.0239 | | | | | |
| 13 | 3:00 PM | 8 | 6.9972 | 7.0176 | 6.9925 | 7.002433 | 0.0251 | | | | | |
| 14 | 4:00 PM | 9 | 6.9562 | 7.0533 | 6.9949 | 7.001467 | 0.0971 | | | | | |
| 15 | 5:00 PM | 10 | 6.9993 | 7.0005 | 7.0034 | 7.001067 | 0.0041 | | | | | |
| 16 | | | | | | | | | | | | |
| 17 | | **Estimated Mean of Sample Means μ =** | | | | **6.996783** | **0.03233** | **Estimated Mean Range** | | | | |
| 18 | | | | | | | | | | | | |
| 19 | | | | | | | | | | | | |
| 20 | For sample size 3, the value of d₂ from the table is | | | | 1.693 | | | | For sample size 3, the value of d₃ from the table is | | | 0.888 |
| 21 | | | | | | | | | | | | |
| 22 | R̄ = d₂. s | | | | | | | | | | | |
| 23 | or s = R̄ / d₂ = | 0.019096279 | | | | | | | | | | |
| 24 | | | | | | | | | | | | |
| 25 | √n =√3 = | 1.732050808 | | | | | | | | | | |
| 26 | s_μ = s / √n = | 0.011025242 | | | | | | | s_R̄ = d₃ . s = | 0.016957496 | | |
| 27 | | | | | | | | | | | | |
| 28 | For the μ chart, | | | | | | | | For the R̄ chart, | | | |
| 29 | Upper Control Limit μ + 3 s_μ = | | 7.029859 | | | | | | Upper Control Limit R̄ + 3 s_R̄ = | | 0.083202 | |
| 30 | Central Line μ = | | 6.996783 | | | | | | Central Line R̄ = | | 0.03233 | |
| 31 | Lower Control Limit μ - 3 s_μ = | | 6.963708 | | | | | | Lower Control Limit R̄ - 3 s_R̄ = | | -0.01854 | (taken as 0) |

Fig. 14.8 Trial $\mu$ chart and $\bar{R}$ chart

The distributions of sample means as well as sample ranges may be taken as normal distribution curves for all practical purposes. The mean of the sample means is calculated in our example in cell F17 of Fig. 14.8. Select cells F6 to F17 and choose **Average** on the Excel toolbar as explained earlier to get the value of $\mu = 6.996783$. Similarly, find the average of the sample range values in cell G17 as $\bar{R} = 0.03233$. If $\sigma$ represents the standard deviation of the population (in our example, it represents the dispersion in the values of the diameters of all the pencils manufactured in this production proces), the mean range $\bar{R}$ is expressed as

$$\bar{R} = d_2\,\sigma \tag{14.1}$$

where $d_2$ is a constant whose value depends on the sample size $n$ (values of $d_2$ for various values of $n$ are given in Table C of the Appendix). For our example, the value of $d_2$ for sample size $n = 3$ (since we have three pencils in each sample) is 1.693. As in our example, in any practical situation, the value of standard deviation $\sigma$ of the population is not known. Thus, we find the estimated values of the standard deviation of the population $s$ fom Eqn (14.1) as

$$\bar{R} = d_2 s \quad \text{or} \quad s = \frac{\bar{R}}{d_2}$$

The estimated value of $\bar{R}$ in cell D17 is 0.03233. The value of $s$ has been found in cell B23 of Fig. 14.8 as 0.019096279. We call this value the estimated value $s$ because it is based upon the sample value of $\bar{R}$ and not the actual value of the standard deviation of the population (i.e., all the standard deviations of the diameters of all the pencils manufactured through this process).

For the distribution of sample means, the estimated standard error of the mean is given by

$$s_\mu = s/\sqrt{n} \tag{14.2}$$

In our example, the sample size $n$ is 3 and we have already calculated the value of $s$. Thus, the value of $s_\mu$ is calculated using Eqn (14.2) in cell B26 of Fig. 14.8 as 0.011025242. Now, we calculate the UCL and LCL for the $\mu$ chart as $\mu + 3s_\mu = 7.029859$ in cell C29 and $\mu - 3s_\mu = 6.963708$ in cell C31, respectively. Note that in cell C29, we have put the formula =F17+3*B26. The value of CL for this chart is $\mu = 6.996783$, as shown in cell C30. The $\mu$ chart thus obtained is shown in Fig. 14.9.

The standard deviation of the distribution of sample mean ranges is given by

$$s_{\bar{R}} = d_3 s \tag{14.3}$$

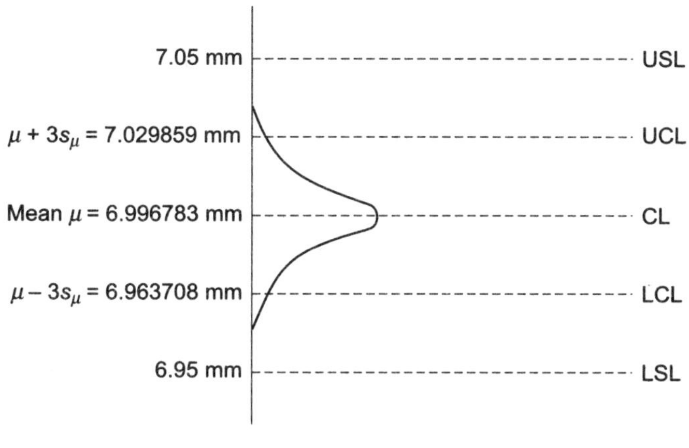

**Fig. 14.9** Trial mean of sample means control chart for the diameter of pencils

where $d_3$ is a constant whose value depends on the sample size $n$ (the values of $d_3$ for various values of $n$ are given in Table C of the Appendix). For our example, the value of $d_3$ for sample size $n = 3$ (since we have three pencils in each sample) is 0.888.

Let us now calculate the values of UL and LCL for the $\bar{R}$ cart. The value of $s_{\bar{R}}$ is calculated using Eqn (14.3) in cell J26 of Fig. 14.8 as 0.016957496 with the formula =M20*B23. Now, we calculate the values of UL and LCL or the $\bar{R}$ chart as $\bar{R} + 3$ $s_{\bar{R}} = 0.08322$ incell K29 and $\bar{R} - 3\ s_{\bar{R}}$

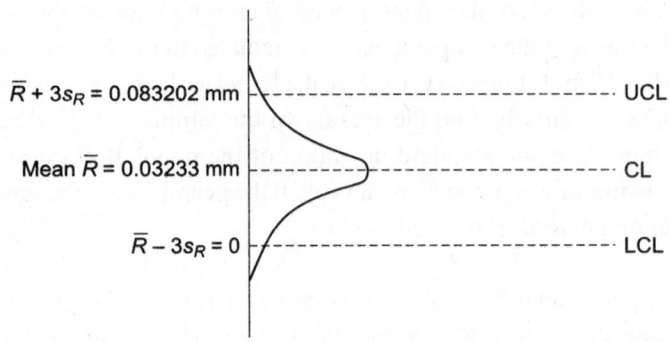

$\bar{R} + 3s_R = 0.083202$ mm ----UCL

Mean $\bar{R} = 0.03233$ mm ----CL

$\bar{R} - 3s_R = 0$ ----LCL

**Fig. 14.10** Trial mean range control chart for the diameter of pencils

$= -0.01854$, which is taken as zero, in cell J31, respectively. Note that in cell C29, we have put the formula $=$**G17+3\*J26**. The value of LCL in this chart is taken as zero as the range (or dispersion) can have a minimum value of zero but can never be negative (remember range is the difference between the maximum and minimum values in the sample). The value of CL for this chart is $= 0.03233$ as show in cell J30. The chart thus obtained is shown in Fig. 14.10.

**Stable $\mu$ and $\bar{R}$ charts** The control charts discussed so far are called *trial control charts*. This is because some of the sample values of $\mu$ may exceed the control limits in the $\mu$ chart and some of the values of the sample range may exceed the control limits in the $\bar{R}$ chart. For example, in Fig. 14.8 note that the value of the sample mean for sample 6 (cell F11) is 6.947933. This value is less than the LCL of the $\mu$ chart, that is, 6.963708. We have plotted all the sample means on a graph generated by the software SPSS as shown in Fig. 14.11. In this figure, note that for sample

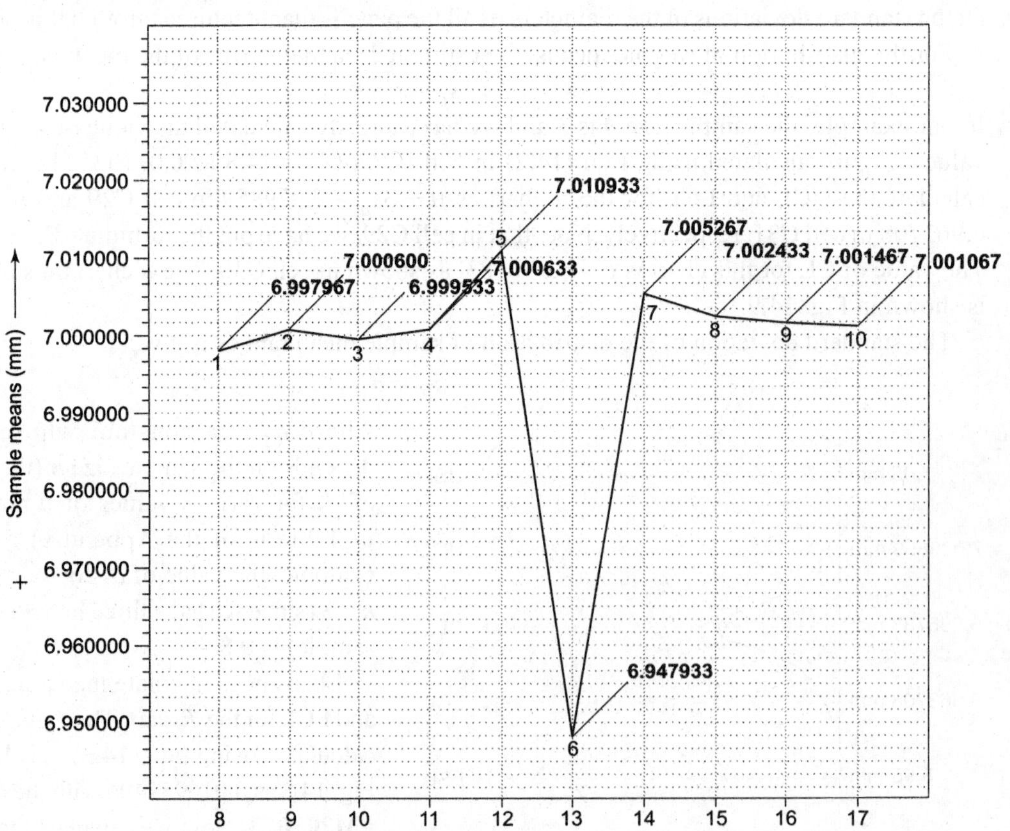

**Fig. 14.11** A plot of sample means (diameter of pencils)

6, the plot is exceeding the LCL value. All the other points plotted are well within the control limits. Therefore, the $\mu$ chart has to be revised by neglecting sample 6, as we cannot use an out of control value in the construction of the chart, which will be used as a benchmark to assess out of control situations in the near future.

Similarly, if one observes the sample range values given in column G of Fig. 14.8, it is found that for sample 9 the value 0.0971 exceeds the UCL of the $\bar{R}$ chart, that is, 0.083202. Thus, we need to revise the $\bar{R}$ chart by neglecting sample 9, as we cannot use an out of control value in the construction of the chart, which will be used as a benchmark to assess out of control situations in the near future.

Figure 14.12 shows the revised mean of sample means $\mu$ (after neglecting the average of sample 6) as 7.002211 mm in cell F18. Similarly, cell G18 shows the revised mean range (after neglecting the range of sample 9) as 0.025133. All further calculations for preparing the trial $\mu$ and $\bar{R}$ charts are revised to arrive at the stable chart values shown in Fig. 14.12. The stable $\mu$ and $\bar{R}$ charts are shown in Figs 14.13 and 14.14, respectively. Note that in these charts, all the values (excluding the neglected values) are well within the control limits. Now, these stable charts serve as benchmarks for assessing out of control situations in the near future. There may be more than one trial chart to be made before arriving at a stable control chart. Therefore, after making each trial control chart, it is required to be checked whether or not all the data values are within the control limits. If some values exceed the control limits, the chart has to be revised by neglecting such values until a stable chart is obtained. Stable control charts also need to be revised at regular intervals of time as new data come in.

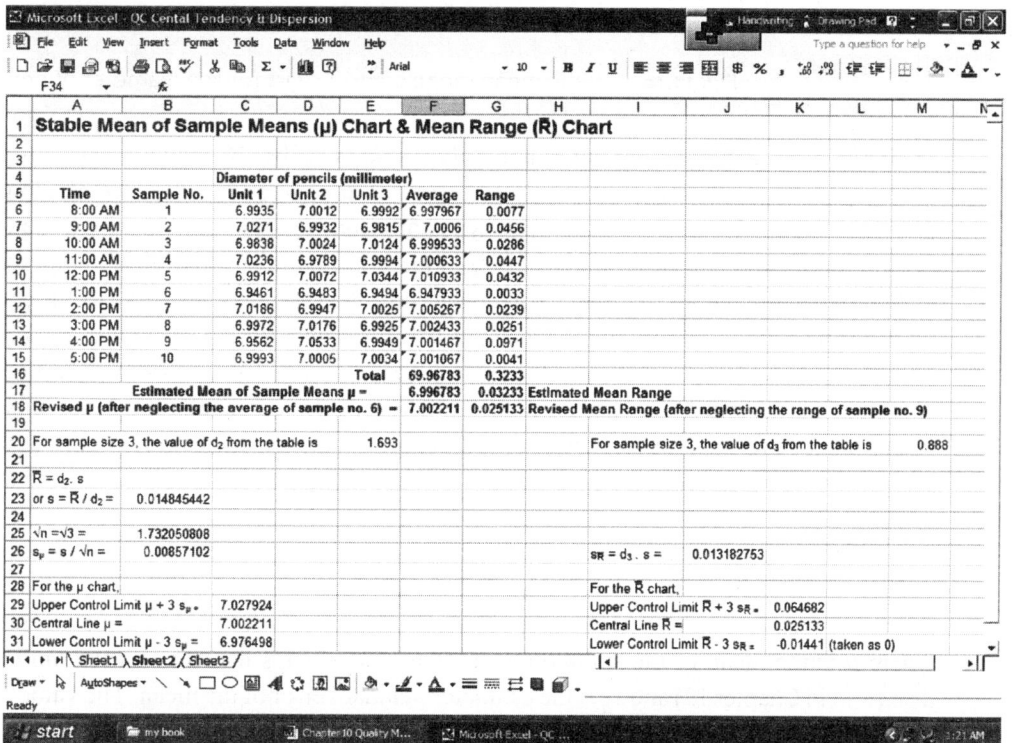

**Fig. 14.12** Stable $\mu$ chart and R chart

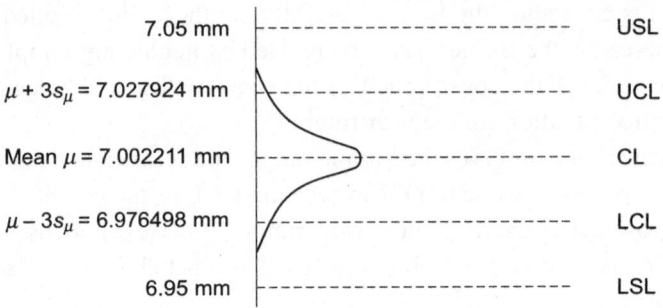

**Fig. 14.13**   Stable mean of sample means control chart for the diameter of pencils

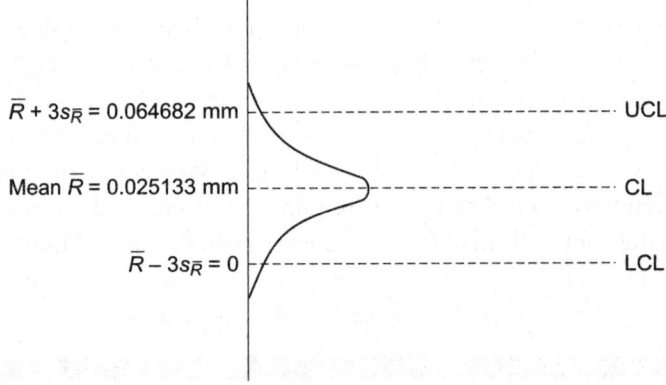

**Fig. 14.14**   Stable mean range control chart for the diameter of pencils

***Trends in $\mu$ charts suggesting out of control situations***   The QC manager has to monitor trends of the points (sample mean values) plotted on the $\mu$ chart with time plotted along the $x$-axis direction. Figure 14.15 shows the three types of trends or situations in which the QC manager gets the indication that there is possibility of an out of control situation of the process.

In some organizations, in order to make the control charts more sensitive to variations, another set of limits called *warning limits* are set at $\mu \pm 2s_\mu$. Thus, $\mu + 2s_\mu$ becomes the *upper warning limit* (UWL) and $\mu - 2s_\mu$ becomes the *lower warning limit* (LWL) as shown in Fig. 14.16. The commonly used criteria is whenever any two out of three successive points cross a warning limit, the QC manager should look for assignable causes. At the same time, it is observed that introducing the warning limits makes the control charts more complex, and the simplicity of implementation is lost.

***Natural tolerance limits***   In the construction of stable control charts, we have considered the sample values of the mean and the range. The control chart is made by assuming that the distribution of sample means follows a normal distribution curve. Thus, the control limits are set at $\mu \pm 3s_\mu$, where $\mu$ is the mean of the sample means (which is always the same as the *universe mean* as discussed in Chapter 12) and $s_\mu$ is the estimated standard error of the mean. The value $s_\mu$ is given by

$$s_\mu = s/\sqrt{n}$$

where $n$ is the sample size and $s$ is the estimated standard deviation of the population.

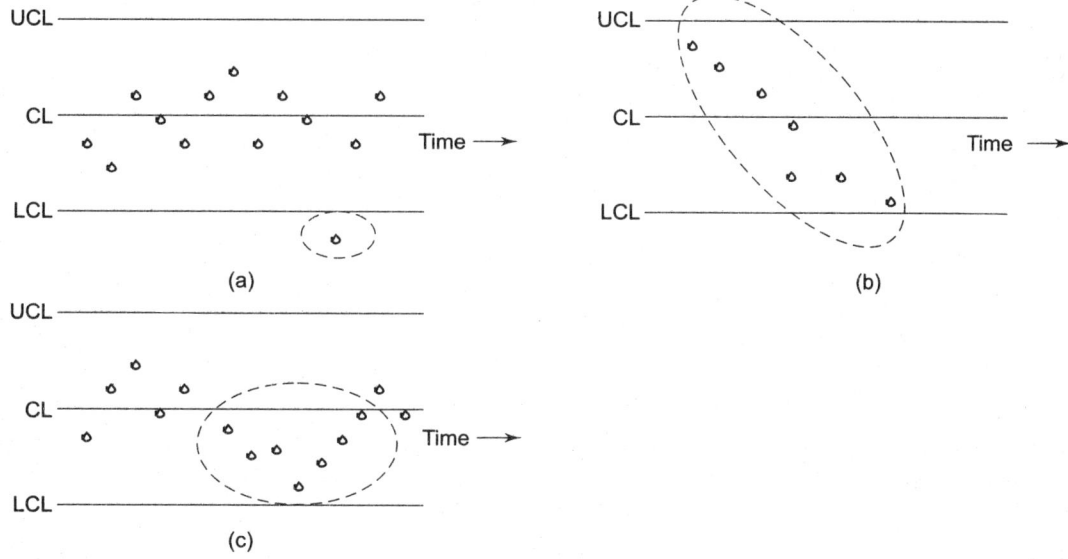

**Fig. 14.15** Trends in $\mu$ chart suggesting an out of control situation (a) A point exceeding the LCL (or UCL) (b) A decreasing (or increasing) trend of seven or eight successive points (c) Five or more successive points on one side of the CL

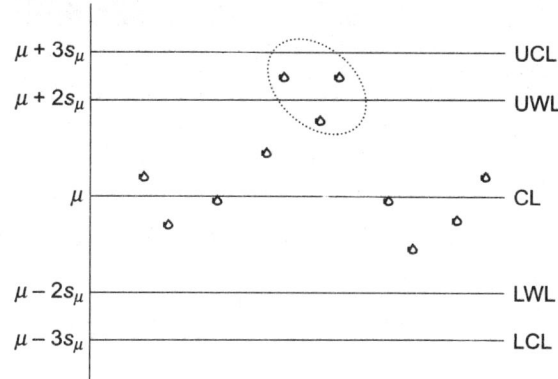

**Fig. 14.16** Warning limits in $\mu$ chart (two out of three successive points beyond a warning limit suggest an out of control situation)

Here, the value $s$ is important for us, as it tells us the extent to which the individual values of the diameters of pencils are dispersed around the estimated mean value $\mu$. If we construct certain limits at $\mu \pm 3s$, the natural tolerance limits (NTLs) of the process are obtained. We do the calculations for these limits in the MS Excel spreadsheet shown in Fig. 14.17. The value of $s$ shown in cell B9 is taken from the stable $\mu$ chart calculations done in Fig. 14.12.

Thus, $\mu + 3s$ becomes the upper NTL (UNTL) and $\mu - 3s$ becomes the lower NTL (LNTL), as shown in Fig. 14.17. The values of UNTL and LNTL have been calculated in cells E20 and E22, respectively. Note that there is no relationship between the specification limits and the NTLs for a variable. The specification limits are set by the customer in the contract document, and the supplier has to ensure that the NTLs of their production process are well within the specification limits in order to fulfil the requiremens of the contract.

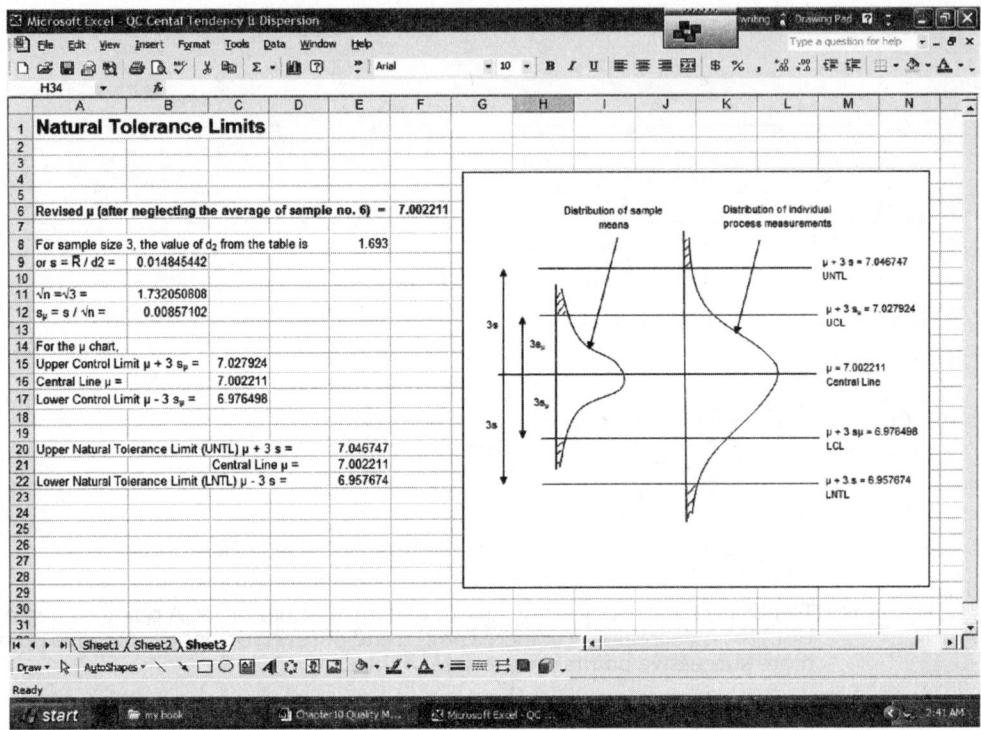

**Fig. 14.17** Natural tolerance limits

**Process capability ratio** As the name *process capability* suggests, this ratio is used to measure the capability of the production process with respect to the specifications of the product provided by the customer.

In Fig. 14.18, we have shown three situations. Let us start with situation *A* first. Assume that a customer has specified the specification limits of a variable in the product (say, a dimension of the product), shown in the figure as USL and LSL. It is but obvious that the customer will not accept a product having values of the variable exceeding these limits. Let us assume that the standard deviation of the process (population) at the producer's end is $s_3$ and the NTLs of the process ($\mu \pm 3s_3$) far exceed the specification limits as shown in the figure.

The producer thus understands that a large number of produced items will have their dimensions outside the specification limits and will be rejected leading to a loss to the producer. He takes remedial measures such as proper training of workers, replacement of worn out tools in the machines, and purchasing new machines so that the process variation reduces to $s_2$. At this stage, the NTLs of the process ($\mu \pm 3s_2$) are exactly equal to the specification limits as shown in situation *B* of the figure. This means that out of every 10,000 items, 27 items will have their dimensions beyond the specification limits and, thus, will be termed as defective or non-conforming.

> The process capability ratio is used to measure the capability of the production process with respect to the specifications of the product provided by the customer.

Thus, the producer takes further steps as mentioned earlier to reduce the variability of the process, and ensures that the standard deviation of the population reduces further to $s_1$. This is shown in situation *C* of Fig. 14.18. Note that the NTLs of the process are well within the specification limits. Thus, a very large amount of the output will certainly fall within the specification limits, leading to very few defective items. In this entire discussion, we notice that the producer has ensured that the capability of the process to produce good items (non-defectives) increase.

*Process capability ratio* (PCR) is defined as the ratio of the difference between the two specification limits to the Six Sigma spread of the process population distribution.

$$PCR = \frac{USL - LSL}{6s}$$

Note that the denominator $6s$ represents the difference between the two NTLs (UNTL and LNTL). This difference is also called the *Six Sigma spread,* because in between these NTLs we have six times the standard deviation distance. Thus, a PCR ratio of 1 will represent situation *B* of Fig. 14.18. Similarly, PCR < 1 will represent situation *A* and PCR > 1 will represent situation *C*. Therefore, it is desirable for any producer that the PCR for a process is greater than 1.

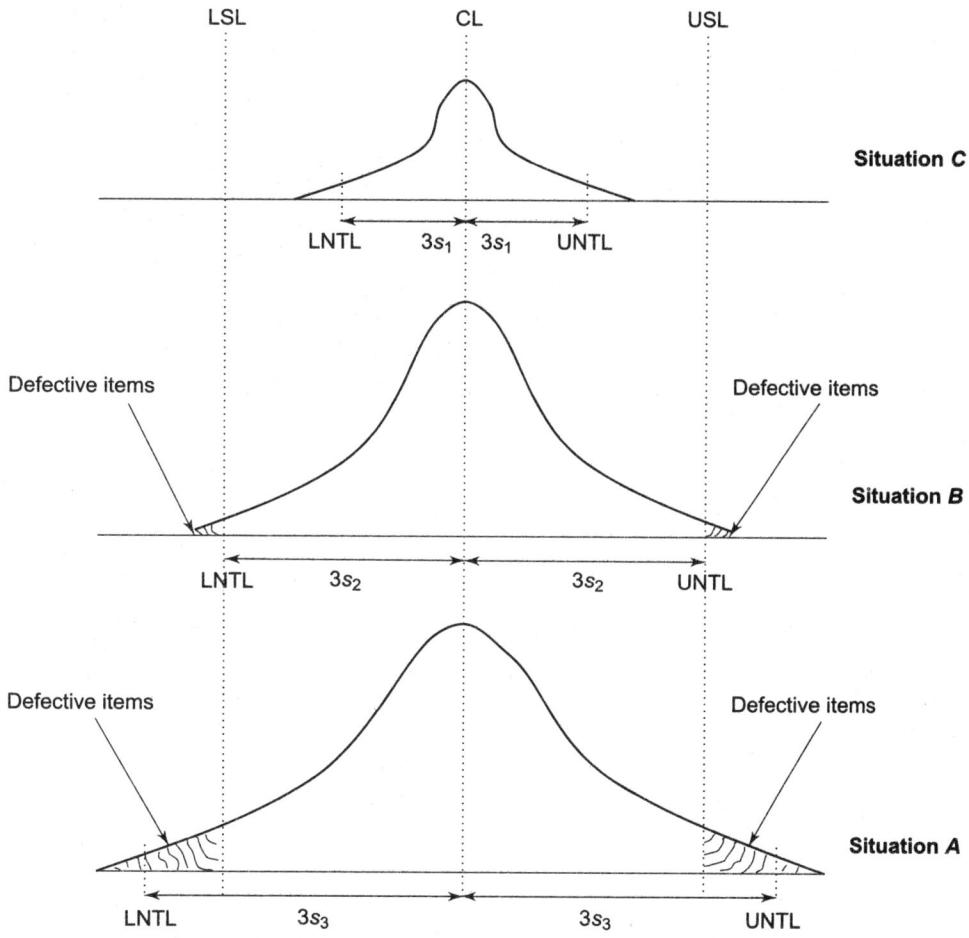

**Fig. 14.18**   Effect of decreasing the process capability ratio

In our example of the diameters of pencils, USL = 7.05 mm and LSL = 6.95. We have calculated the estimated standard deviation $s$ as 0.01484. Therefore,

$$PCR = \frac{7.05 - 6.95}{6 \times 0.014845} = \frac{0.1}{0.089} = 1.1236$$

Here, the PCR is greater than 1, suggesting situation $C$ in Fig. 14.18, which is desirable for any producer.

***Process capability ratio for an off-centre process*** So far, we have discussed the process capability of a process when the central tendency (mean value) is at the centre of the two specification limits (USL and LSL). In all practical situations, there is a possibility that the process mean may shift, over a period of time, in either direction, that is, towards the USL or the LSL. This may result in more defective (non-conforming) items than expected. This shift of the process mean is called the *off-centring* of the process.

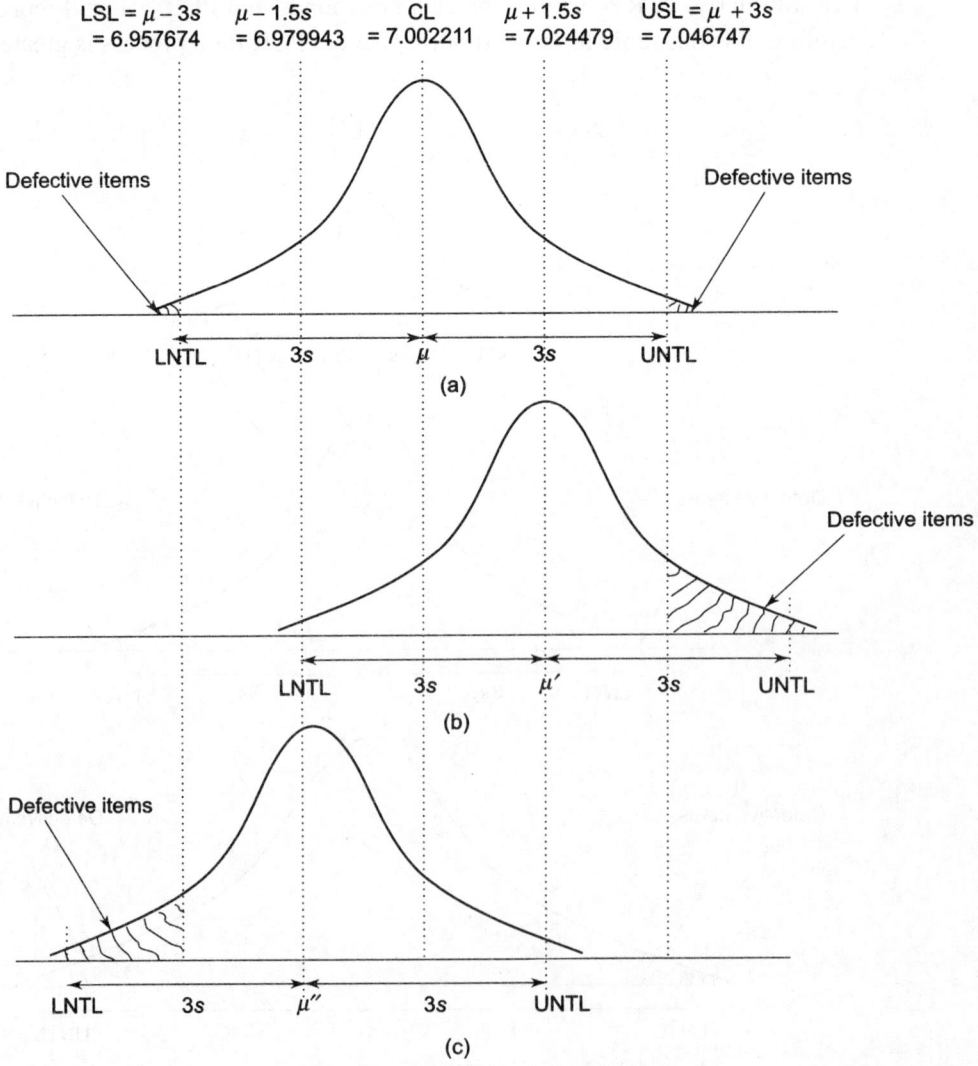

**Fig. 14.19** Effect of shift in the process mean

Let us take up our earlier example of diameters of pencils in order to understand the concept of the off-centring of a process. Assume that in our example, the customer changes the specification limits given earlier, that is, 7 mm ± 0.05 mm, to the NTLs of the process, that is, $\mu \pm 3s$. As a result, things become difficult for the producer because out of every 10,000 pencils produced, 27 will be defective (outside the specification limits, which are equal to the NTLs). Part (a) of Fig. 14.19 shows this situation.

Part (b) of Fig. 14.19 shows the off-centring of the process mean, in which the mean shifts to the $\mu + 1.5s$ position (we have intentionally taken the shift to 1.5 sigma limits in order to explain Motorola's concept of Six Sigma later). Note that the number of defectives produced due to this off-centring of the process is much higher compared to the situation shown in part (a) of Fig. 14.19. Part (c) shows the off-centring of the process towards the LSL by 1.5$s$, which has the same effect as the situation in part (b).

For one-sided specifications, we define the PCR for the USL as

$$PCR_U = \frac{USL - \mu}{3s}$$

and for the LSL as

$$PCR_L = \frac{\mu - LSL}{3s}$$

The PCR that takes process centring into account is given by

$$PCR_k = \min(PCR_U, PCR_L)$$

where 'min' denotes the minimum of the two values $PCR_U$ and $PCR_L$. The value of $PCR_k$ is calculated for comparison with the value of PCR without any off-centring.

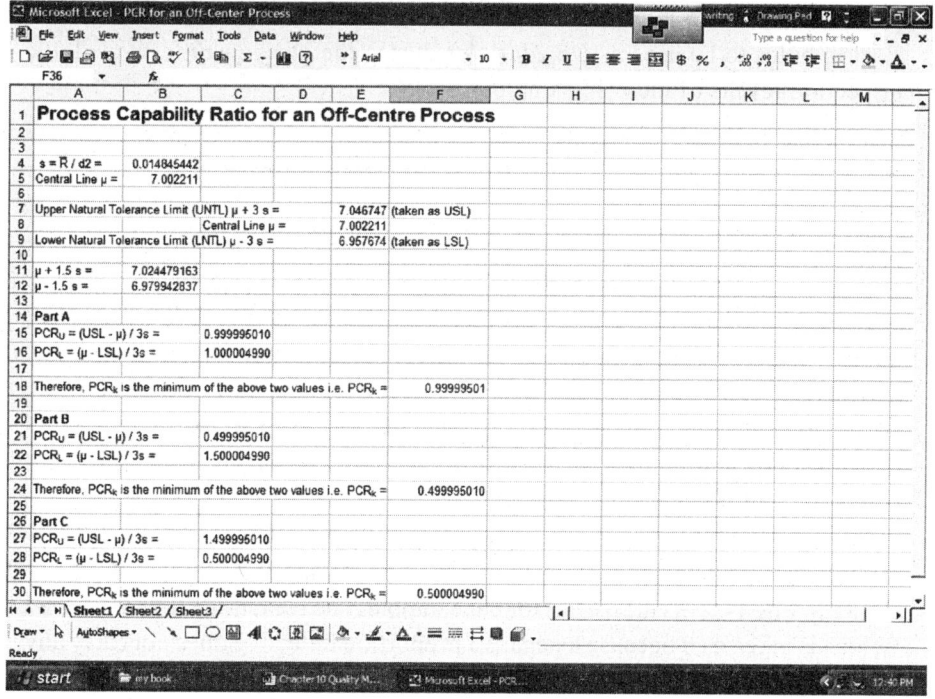

**Fig. 14.20**   Process capability ratio for an off-centre process

Let us calculate the value of $PCR_k$ for parts (a), (b), and (c) of Fig. 14.19. Note that the values of $s$, USL, and LSL will be same for all the parts of the figure. These values are shown in cells B4, E7, and E9, respectively, of Fig. 14.20. For part $A$, the value of $\mu$ is 7.002211 from our calculations of the stable $\mu$ chart earlier. For part $B$, the mean shifts to the $\mu + 1.5s$ position, that is, the new value of the mean, $\mu'$, as calculated in cell B11 is 7.024479163. For part $C$, the mean shifts to $\mu - 1.5s$ position, that is, the new value of the mean $\mu''$ as calculated in cell B12 is 6.979942837.

For part $A$, the value of $PCR_k$ is 0.99999501 as shown in cell F18, which may be taken as 1. Thus, for part $A$, $PCR_k = PCR$; for part $B$, $PCR_k = 0.499995010$. Therefore, here $PCR_k < PCR$. For part $C$, $PCR_k = 0.500004990$. Therefore, here $PCR_k < PCR$ too. This means whenever the value of $PCR_k$ is less than that of PCR, we say that the process is off-centred. For a situation with no off-centring, that is, a perfectly centred process, $PCR_k = PCR$.

**Control chart for attributes ($p$ chart)**   In certain products, a particular characteristic or attribute is of prime importance for quality determination. For example, in case of an electric bulb, the most important attribute is whether the bulb glows or not. In such situations, items are inspected to determine whether or not they possess that particular attribute. Control charts are prepared for the fraction or proportion defective ($p$). In sampling theory (Chapter 9), the standard deviation for a distribution of sample percentges is given by

$$\sigma_p = \sqrt{pq/n}$$

where $p$ is the proportion of items possessing a particular attribute (say, the defective or bad items), $q$ is the proportion of items not possessing this attribute (say, the correct or good items), and $n$ is the sample size. Thus, $q = 1 - p$.

Let us take up an example to understand the construction of control charts for fraction defectives (also called $p$ charts). Fifteen samples of size 100 units each are taken from a consignment of electric bulbs to be used as *Diwali lights* during the *Deepawali* festival. Table 14.3 shows the inspection results of these 15 samples.

**Table 14.3**   Inspection results

| Sample no. | 1 | 2 | 3 | 4 | 5 | 6 | 7 | 8 | 9 | 10 | 11 | 12 | 13 | 14 | 15 |
|---|---|---|---|---|---|---|---|---|---|---|---|---|---|---|---|
| No. of defective bulbs | 6 | 3 | 0 | 5 | 2 | 8 | 18 | 7 | 3 | 9 | 8 | 1 | 4 | 6 | 5 |

We find the proportion defectives in all these samples in cells C4 to C18 of Fig. 14.21. For example, in sample 1 there are 6 defectives out of 100 (sample size). Thus, the proportion defective is 6/100, that is, 0.06. The average of proportion defectives is calculated in cell C19 as 0.056667. This is the mean proportion defective, which we represent by $p$ (and is called the $p$ bar). We calculate $q$ in cell E21 as 0.9433. The standard deviation $\sigma_p = \sqrt{pq/n}$ is calculated in cell D23 by putting the formula =**SQRT(C20\*E21/100)**. Thus, the CL is $p$, that is, 0.056667 (shown in cell D27).

The UCL is calculated as $p + 3\sigma_p$ in cell D26 by putting the formula =**C20+3\*D23**. Similarly, the LCL is calculated as $p - 3\sigma_p$ in cell D28 by putting the formula =**C20 – 3\*D23**. The chart shown in Fig. 14.21 is the $p$ chart for our example. The UCL is 0.126081 and the LCL is $-0.01268$ (which is taken as 0 because a negative proportion defective does not carry any meaning). Note that sample 7, with proportion defective 0.18, exceeds the UCL, that, 0.126081. Therefore, the control chart made by us is a trial control chart, which has to be revised by neglecting sample 7.

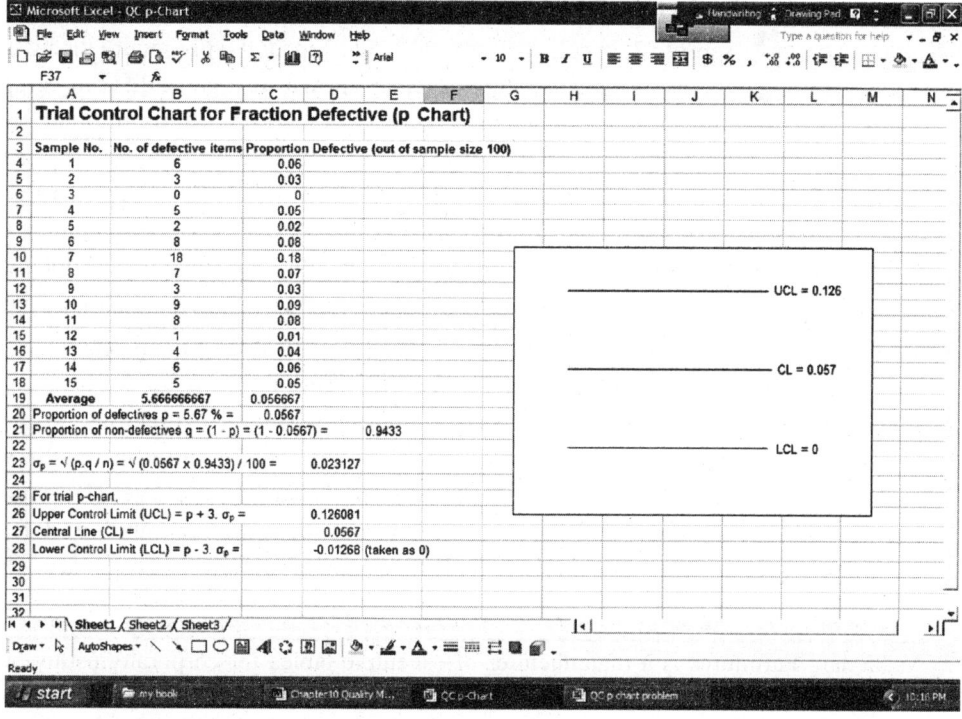

**Fig. 14.21**   Trial control chart for fraction defective

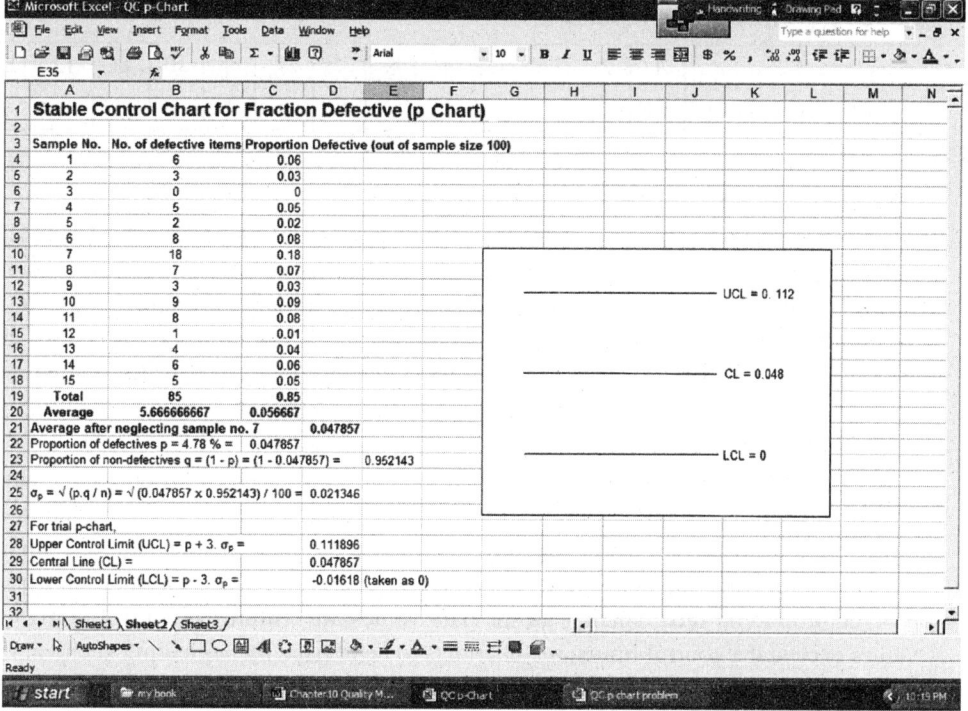

**Fig. 14.22**   Stable control chart for fraction defective

The criterion for deciding the quality of a product in certain situations is the number of defects each unit of the product has.

In Fig. 14.22, we find the average proportion defective, after neglecting sample 7, in cell D21 as 0.047857. Repeat the procedure discussed for the trial $p$ chart to get the stable $p$ chart shown in Fig. 14.22. This graph is used for controlling proportion defectives in the near future. In other problems, more than one trial chart may be required before arriving at a stable control chart. Therefore, after making each trial control chart, it is required to be seen whether all the data values are within the control limits or not. If some values exceed the control limits, the chart has to be revised by neglecting such values until a stable chart is obtained.

**Control chart for number of defects (c chart)**   The criterion for deciding the quality of a product in certain situations is the number of defects each unit of the product has. For example, a furniture company evaluates the quality of the dining tables made by it on the basis of the average number of scratches (defects) per dining table. In such situations, we prepare control charts for the number of defects, or $c$ charts. For all practical purposes, the distribution of the number of defects may be assumed to follow a normal distribution curve. The standard deviation for such a distriution is given by $s_c = \sqrt{c}$ , where $c$ is the average number of defects per unit of the product. Let us take an example to understand the preparation of a $c$ chart.

### Example 14.1

Vadhodara Furnitures is a manufacturer of executive tables for corporate institutions. In order to control the quality of its tables, the QC manager selects 15 tables at random and inspects for the number of scratches on each one of them. The results given in Table 14.4 are obtained. Prepare a stable $c$ chart based on this data.

**Table 14.4   Inspection results**

| Sample no. | 1 | 2 | 3 | 4 | 5 | 6 | 7 | 8 | 9 | 10 | 11 | 12 | 13 | 14 | 15 |
|---|---|---|---|---|---|---|---|---|---|---|---|---|---|---|---|
| No. of defective tables | 13 | 9 | 19 | 7 | 8 | 10 | 12 | 0 | 2 | 5 | 7 | 11 | 9 | 13 | 1 |

### Solution

The average number of defects per table is calculated in cell B19 of Fig. 14.23 as 8.4. The estimated standard deviation of the distribution of defects is calculated in cell C23 by putting the formula **=SQRT(B19)**. The UCL is calculated in cell D26 by putting the formula **=B19+3\*C23**, that is, $c + 3s_c$. Similarly, LCL is calculated in cell D28 by putting the formula **=B19– 3\*C23**, that is, $c - 3s_c$. Note that the value of LCL is a negative number, which is taken as 0, as the number of defects in an item cannot be negative. The CL of the $c$ chart is the value of $c$ that is, 8.4. This is a trial $c$ chart. Let us check if the number of defects in any case, exceedsthe UCL, that is, 17.095.

The number of defects in sample 3, that is, 19, exceed the UCL of our trial $c$ chart. Therefore, the trial $c$ chart has to be revised by neglecting sample 3. The revised calculations for obtaining the stable $c$ chart are shown in Fig. 14.24. In other problems, more than one trial chart may be required before arriving at a stable control chart. Therefore, after making each trial control chart, it is required to be seen whether all the data values are within the control limits or not. If some values exceed the control limits, the chart has to be revised by neglecting such values until a stble chart is obtained.

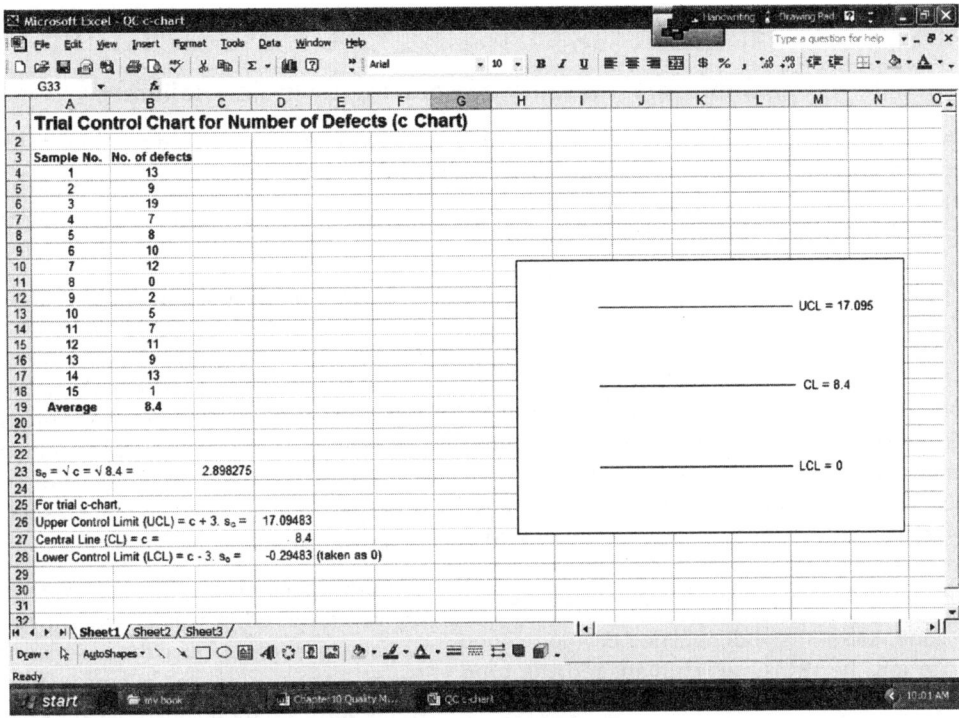

**Fig. 14.23**   Trial control chart for number of defects

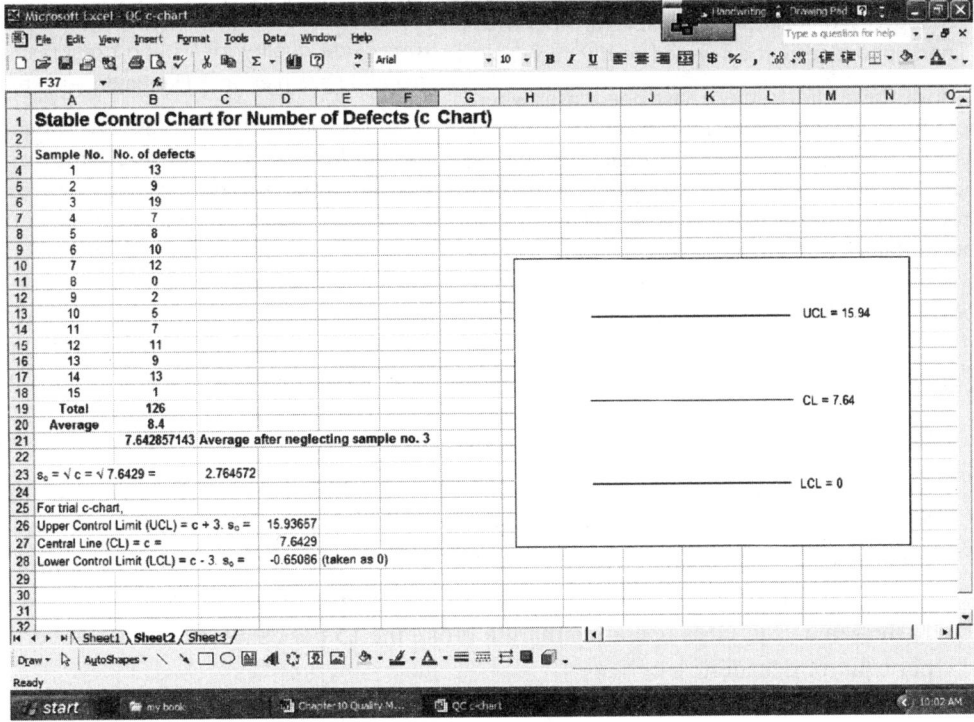

**Fig. 14.24**   Stable control chart for number of defects

Exhibit 14.2 illustrates the quality-related issues of Indian Railways' catering services.

---

### Exhibit 14.2 Quality of Catering by Indian Railways

Indian Railways is the fourth largest rail transportation system in the world. It employs more than 1.4 million employees, while carrying over 30 million passengers and 2.8 million tonnes of freight daily.

The Indian Railway Catering and Tourism Corporation (IRCTC) Limited is a subsidiary of Indian Railways, which provides various types of services to its passengers, such as online ticketing, hotel booking, and catering.

Food on board was introduced to fulfil travellers' needs through innovative marketing strategies. Reports indicated that IRCTC has confirmed plans to set up over 50 multi-cuisine meal plazas at significant railway stations throughout the nation. However, soon its catering services received a lot of criticism from the passengers for the quality of food provided on passenger trains.

In 2008, Kalka Shatabdi obtained ISO 9001: 2000 certification. The IRCTC, which managed the food supply in trains then, revamped the entire food services on-board in the train. The Kalka Shatabdi expanded the menu and introduced sugar-free beverages for passengers as a drive to improve passenger satisfaction. After the success of Kalka Shatabdi, several other trains also lined up to receive the coveted certification.

Despite these efforts, there have been cases where people have voiced their dissatisfaction over the government's inability to better the quality of catering services in trains. The woes of passengers relating to the food served on trains seem to be endless. In one of Indian Railways' premier trains, Shatabdi, running between Amritsar and New Delhi, passengers were served fungus-infected bread past the expiry date. Another Shatabdi running between Ludhiana and Delhi faced similar problems, as the food served by a contractor was often cold and unpalatable.

With these mounting problems, in 2010, the then Railways Minister Mamata Banerjee transferred a majority of IRCTC's catering business to Indian Railways.

Indian Railways was initially planning to create a base kitchen at a station to serve hot, hygienic, and delicious food to the passengers on the train. However, the plan has now been shelved. Passengers, who have seen the on-board pantry of Shatabdi, have often complained about the prevailing unhygienic conditions. They have also expressed their expectations of increasing the variety of food available on trains, especially the low-calorie food required by senior citizens.

During their study visits to ascertain the quality of water served in trains and railway stations, a parliamentary panel found the use of normal tap water stored in tanks, unsealed mineral water bottles, and water bottles without labels of expiry dates.

Such cases have prompted the railways to chalk out a comprehensive plan to keep a tab on the quality of food served to the passengers. Efforts are being made to provide quality meals and breakfast on all trains, including premier ones like Rajdhani Express.

In his railway budget (2012–13) speech, the then Railway Minister, Dinesh Trivedi, emphasized the need to redefine the railways' approach towards catering and the need to address demands of the entire spectrum of passengers. He said that a pilot project was planned to be launched on a few premium trains to introduce international expertise on Indian Railways for catering services. However, it remains to be seen how efficiently these plans would pan out and see action.

---

### Six Sigma

Motorola pioneered the Six Sigma program in 1987. It took five years to yield significant results. Motorola attributes US $15 billion in savings over the past 11 years to Six Sigma. In 1997, General Electric CEO Jack Welch invested US$380 million in it at GE, mostly for training, and in the same year GE received US$700 million in documented benefits from increased productivity. In the same year, GE's operating margin broke the 15 per cent barrier after hovering around 10 per cent for decades.

In a 1997 letter Welch sent to GE stockholders, he stated, 'The Six Sigma quality initiative, very briefly, means going from approximately 35,000 defects per million operations, which is average for most companies, including GE, to fewer than four defects per million in every element in every process that this company engages in every day'. This program has been adopted as a quality philosophy by companies such as Texas Instruments, Allied Signal, Eastman Kodak, and in India by ICICI.

In order to understand the meaning of Six Sigma, let us take up our example of diameters of pencils once again. We have so far used the third sigma limits in our discussion of NTLs in the process of manufacturing pencils. For the sake of better understanding, assume that for this process the specification limits are the same as the NTLs, that is, $\mu \pm 3\sigma$ as shown in Fig. 14.25. Thus, 99.73 per cent of the pencils will have their diameters within the specification limits, while the remaining 0.27 per cent, or 0.27 per 100, or 2,700 per 10,00,000, or 2,700 per million pencils will be defective.

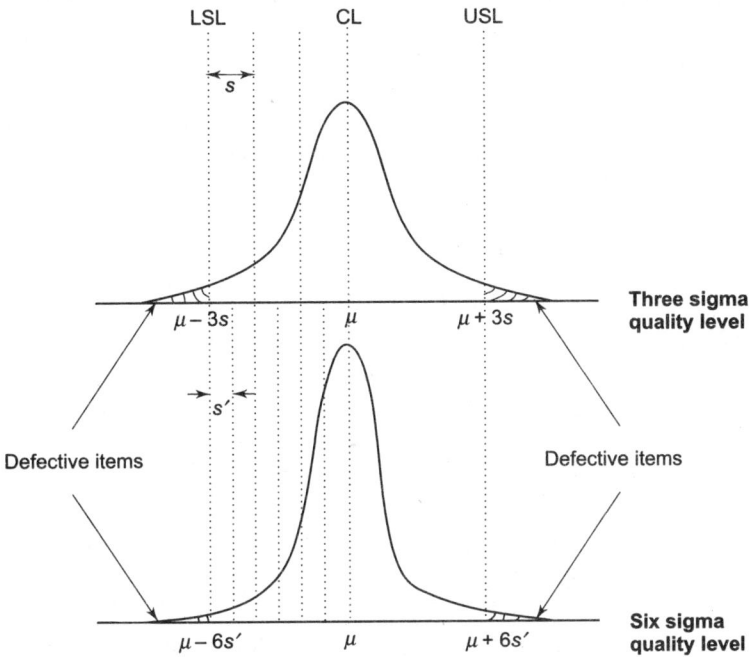

**Fig. 14.25** The Six Sigma and three sigma quality levels

The standard deviation of the population is $s$. The company wants to take every measure to reduce this variation. Therefore, it trains every employee on statistical techniques to measure every critical factor responsible for variation. Then, steps are taken to improve the process and reduce the variation in it. For example, workers are trained to reduce mistakes on their part, processes are redesigned for better performance, maintenance of machines is improved, etc.

Thus, the standard deviation of the process gets reduced to $s'$ such that now there is a 12 sigma spread between the USL and the LSL. Note that in Fig. 14.25, now there are six standard deviations between the CL and the USL or LSL. The values $\mu \pm 6s'$ are now at the specification limits. Now, out of every one million pencils produced, only 0.002, that is, practically no pencil, will be defective. This is Six Sigma quality level meaning zero defectives per million opportunities (DPMO).

Motorola's Six Sigma quality level allows an off-centring of the process up to 1.5 sigma. Table 14.5 shows the number of defectives (parts per million) for specified off-centring of process and quality levels. Note that the first row shows the DPMO when there is no off-centring of the process. At the 3 sigma quality level, the DPMO is 2,700, while at 6 sigma it is 0.002, that is, 2 defects per billion. For an off-centring of 1.5 sigma (row 7) and the quality level of 6 sigma, the DPMO is 3.4.

Thus, Motorola has a quality level such that 3.4 defects per million are allowed. For a process without off-centring, 3.4 defects per million lie somewhere between the 4 and 5 sigma quality levels. In row 1 (for zero off-centring), the 4 sigma quality level has 63 DPMO, while the 5 sigma quality level has 0.57 DPMO. Thus, the value 3.4 lies somewhere between 0.57 and 63 (i.e., between the 4 and 5 sigma quality levels without off-centring). Most businesses currently operate at the 3 sigma quality level with an off-centring of 1.5 sigma, that is, they produce 66,803 defectives out of every million units produced. Thus, Motorola and GE have made a quantum leap in quality enhancement.

**Table 14.5** Number of defectives (parts per million) for specified off-centring of process and quality levels (Tadikamala 1994)

| Off-centring (Sigma) | Sigma/quality level | | | | | | |
|---|---|---|---|---|---|---|---|
| | 3 | 3.5 | 4 | 4.5 | 5 | 5.5 | 6 |
| 0 | 2,700 | 465 | 63 | 6.8 | 0.57 | 0.034 | 0.002 |
| 0.25 | 3,577 | 666 | 99 | 12.8 | 1.02 | 0.1056 | 0.0063 |
| 0.5 | 6,440 | 1,382 | 236 | 32 | 3.4 | 0.71 | 0.019 |
| 0.75 | 12,288 | 3,011 | 665 | 88.5 | 11 | 1.02 | 0.1 |
| 1.0 | 22,832 | 6,433 | 1,350 | 233 | 32 | 3.4 | 0.39 |
| 1.25 | 40,111 | 12,201 | 3,000 | 577 | 88.5 | 10.7 | 1 |
| 1.5 | 66,803 | 22,800 | 6,200 | 1,350 | 233 | 32 | 3.4 |
| 1.75 | 1,05,601 | 40,100 | 12,200 | 3,000 | 577 | 88.4 | 11 |
| 2.0 | 1,58,700 | 66,800 | 22,800 | 6,200 | 1,300 | 233 | 32 |

**Steps for implementation of Six Sigma**    The following steps are followed while implementing Six Sigma in an organization.

**Step 1: Define the priorities of the customers with respect to quality**    In this step, attributes of the product that are considered most important by the customers in evaluating the quality of the product are identified. These attributes are called *critical to quality* (CTQ) *characteristics*. The customer's perception of quality attributes is updated from time to time by conducting customer surveys.

**Step 2: Measure the processes and the defects arising in the product due to the process**    The important processes influencing the CTQ characteristics are identified, and performance measurement techniques are established for these processes. The processes are measured and thus the defects arising in the product due to processes are identified.

**Step 3: Analyse the process to determine the most likely causes of defects**    The key variables most likely to be responsible for variation in the process are identified to find the reason for defect generation.

***Step 4: Improve the process performance and remove the causes of the defects*** Specification limits of the key variables are fixed and a system for measuring the deviations of the variables is established and validated. The process is improvised in order to keep the variables within specification limits.

***Step 5: Ensure that the improvements are maintained over time*** The modified process is subjected to vigil at regular intervals of time to ensure that the key variables do not show any unacceptable variations (beyond specification limits).

**Application of DMAIC** Let us take a hypothetical example to understand how DMAIC (define, measure, analyse, improve, control) can be applied for quality improvement in a process. A call centre in Bangalore is experiencing the problem of long waiting time for customers calling to enquire about their credit card transactions.

**Define** In this phase of DMAIC, the priorities of the customers with respect to the quality of a product or a service are defined. These priorities are known as critical to quality (CTQ) characteristics. In the example, customer surveys indicate that prompt response to their calls is one of the CTQs for the customers. This has been the weak area for the call centre, of late, and the top management wants to urgently do something to alleviate this problem. The customers have been complaining that the automated reply message keeps playing, and even after waiting for a reasonably long time, nobody responds to them. This project is identified by the manager of the call centre as a quality improvement project, and he forms a team of four people to work on it. The team includes two call centre operators (who have earlier worked on credit card operations in the call centre before being transferred to another operation), a supervisor, and a member from the IT team.

**Measure** In the measure phase of DMAIC, key parameters impacting the CTQ are measured by using suitable measuring methods/instruments. In the example, the project team sets out to measure the average waiting time on part of the customers to get first-hand information about the current status. The team member from IT activates the system to measure the waiting time of callers for every operator (there are three operators attending to three different phone lines dedicated to credit card-related queries). This data is collected for four days and the results are plotted on a histogram (Fig. 14.26).

As can be seen in Fig. 14.26, the average waiting time for callers attended by Operator 2 has the highest average waiting time of about 11 minutes.

**Analyse** This phase of DMAIC requires analysis of measurement data collected in the measure phase and application of quality tools to analyse the root cause of the quality problem. Ishikawa's fish bone diagram (Fig. 14.27) is often found quite useful here. The project team decides to apply the fish bone diagram to analyse the different possible causes leading to the high average waiting time for Operator 2.

An analysis of the various possible causes for the 'effect' (high average waiting time for Operator 2) is done. The analysis reveals that the root cause of the problem is the

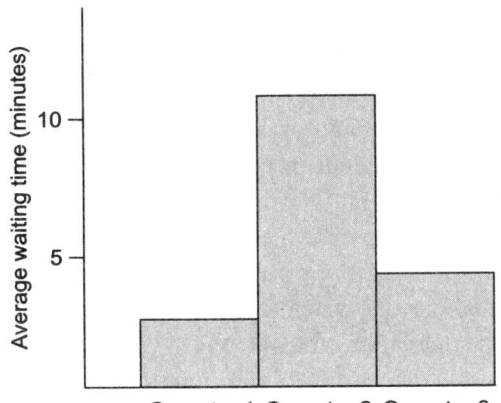

**Fig. 14.26** Histogram for average waiting time

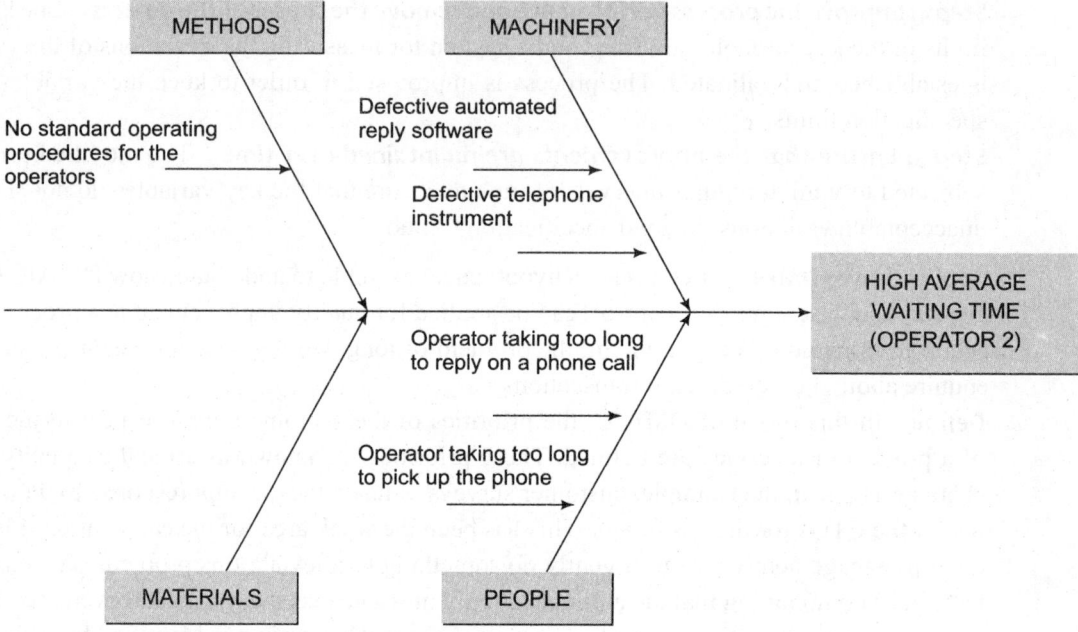

**Fig. 14.27** Ishikawa's fish bone diagram

absence of any standard operating procedures (SOPs) for the operators to attend the phone calls. The project team decides to record some of the calls attended by Operator 2 to understand the procedure adapted by him. The recorded conversations reveal that this operator often takes too long to retrieve the information about the credit card for a customer and he puts this customer on hold till the time the system is retrieving the data. Naturally, other customers in the electronic queue also keep waiting (listening to the pre-recorded message). The project team talked to the operator to know what he does during the time the data for a customer is getting downloaded. The operator could not reply satisfactorily. The project team member who had been an operator himself identified the root cause of the problem. This new operator was not aware that during the time data is being downloaded for a customer, the software allows the operator to start interacting with the next waiting customer. Thus, by the time the data gets retrieved for the earlier customer, the operator could have easily talked to the next customer and entered his details into the system for information retrieval. The team realized that this happened because of the absence of SOPs.

**Improve**   In this step of DMAIC, the root cause of the problem is eliminated through an appropriate solution. Having found the root cause of the problem in the example, the team decides to create the SOPs for the operators, which would not only form part of their training programme but also be installed permanently on the computer machines of the operators for ready reference. The team also decides to install a Poka-Yoke device in the software, which would display a message on the computer screen as soon as the system gets busy to download the data for a customer. This message would remind the operator to attend to the next call by the time the data for the earlier customer is retrieved. The new operator is retrained into the system and the average time taken is again measured by the team. It is found that the average time for Operator 2 is now more or less close to that of other operators.

***Control*** In this last phase of DMAIC, it is ensured that the solutions for the problem initiated in the earlier phase are working fine on a sustained basis. In our example, the project team decides to measure the average time taken by Operator 2 to answer the calls at the end of every week. After doing so for a couple of weeks, the team finds out that the solution is working fine and the problem has not relapsed.

Thus, DMAIC serves as a great tool for quality improvement and is the backbone of the Six Sigma initiative in organizations.

**Defects per million opportunities (DPMO)** The DMAIC process in Six Sigma starts from the customer. It is of prime importance to understand the needs of the customers, before one can define the defects, units, and opportunities in the process. Quality function deployment (QFD), surveys, and focus group interviews should be used to gather customer comments/quotes and translate them into issues and specifications. These comments, issues, and specifications are the origin of the customer CTQs (critical to quality)—product or service characteristics that must be met to satisfy a customer specification or requirement.

A defect is defined as any part of a product or a service that does not meet customer specifications or requirements, or causes customer dissatisfaction, or does not fulfil the functional or physical requirements.It should be noted that the term customer includes both internal and external customers.

The next step is to define the product/service units. A unit is something that can be quantified by a customer. It is a measurable and observable output of the business process. It may manifest itself as a physical unit or, if a service, it may have specific starting and end points.

Let us try to understand the meaning of opportunities. In Six Sigma terminology, opportunities are the total number of chances per unit to have a defect. Each opportunity must be independent of other opportunities and, like a unit, must be measurable and observable. The final requirement of an opportunity is that it directly relates to the customer CTQ. The total count of opportunities indicates the complexity of a product or a service. For example, a watch may have three opportunities of defects: it may not show the correct time; its glass may have scratches; or it may not show the correct date. Any one or more of these three defects may result in a watch being called defective.

Defects per million opportunities (DPMO) are calculated as follows:

$$DPMO = \frac{Total\ number\ of\ defects\ detected \times 10,00,000}{Number\ of\ units\ produced \times Opportunities\ of\ defects\ per\ unit}$$

Let us take some more examples to understand the concepts discussed in this section.

### Example 14.2

**Area**: Excellent Publications

**Customer expectation**: 'I can't tolerate typing errors in the books I purchase.' **CTQ name**: Typographic quality **CTQ measure**: Number of typographical errors

**CTQ specification**: Zero typographical mistake **Defect**: Any typographical mistake **Unit**: A word

**Opportunities of defects per unit**: Number of words per book

**Number of defects**: 7 typographical errors

**Total number of units (words) in the book considered**: 2,50,000 (500 words/page × 500 pages in the book)

$$\text{DPMO} = \frac{\text{Total number of defects detected} \times 10,00,000}{\text{Number of units produced} \times \text{Opportunities of defects per unit}}$$

$$\text{DPMO} = \frac{7 \times 10,00,000}{25,00,000 \times 1} = 2.8$$

From Table 14.5, this DPMO corresponds to a sigma level of above 6σ (with off-centring of 1.5σ).

### *Example 14.3*

**Area**: A company manufacturing printed circuit boards

**Customer expectation**: 'Boards must function when I plug them in.' **CTQ name**: Board functionality
**CTQ measure**: Non-functioning or improperly functioning boards **CTQ specification**: All boards function properly (a board will not function properly if any individual component is bad) **Defect**: Any non-functioning or improperly functioning board **Unit**: A board **Opportunities of defects per unit**: Total number of parts plus solder points = 70 (1 board + 17 resistors + 7 capacitors + 3 diodes + 42 solder points)

**Number of defects**: 26 boards

**Total number of units (boards) considered**: 2000 boards

$$\text{DPMO} = \frac{\text{Total number of defects detected} \times 10,00,000}{\text{Number of units produced} \times \text{Opportunities of defects per unit}}$$

$$\text{DPMO} = \frac{26 \times 10,00,000}{2,000 \times 70} = 186$$

From Table 14.5, this DPMO corresponds to a sigma level of 5.1σ approximately (with off-centering of 1.5 σ).

## Contrasting Six Sigma and TQM

The most intriguing question faced by most executives implementing Six Sigma in their organization is—how is it different from TQM? The TQM movement dominated the quality scenario from the 1970s to the mid 1990s. The late 1990s saw the emergence of Six Sigma as GE brought it to the forefront. Initially, it seemed as if the American companies were trying to produce an answer to the Japanese TQM concept in the form of Six Sigma. The reality is that Six Sigma has become a much broader umbrella compared to TQM, which was mainly confined to the manufacturing sector. Within the manufacturing sector also, TQM remained mainly focused on the production department and its associated departments such as design and engineering. Six Sigma on the other hand is successful not only in the manufacturing sector, but also in the services sector such as banks, financial institutions, insurance companies, healthcare, and education. Barney (2002) has contrasted Six Sigma and TQM as shown in Table 14.6. Six Sigma relies upon executive ownership while TQM depends on self-directed work teams. This is true as, in Six Sigma, the management takes the responsibility of training the employees, making the project teams, selection of projects, and execution of the projects for improvements. TQM, on the other hand, is guided by self-directed teams such as quality circles, and kaizen. Six Sigma is the business

> Six Sigma is a business strategy execution system as it starts with the customer and results in improved profit margins and customer delight, while TQM is only a quality initiative.

strategy execution system as it starts with the customer and results in improved profit margins and customer delight, while TQM is only a quality initiative. As mentioned earlier, Six Sigma is truly cross functional and covers all functional areas including the ones with service focus, while TQM remained mainly focused on production and related functions only. Six Sigma in an organization starts with the focused training of all the employees of the organization in statistical tools by creating training hierarchies with a verifiable return on investment. This focused mass training approach is missing in TQM. Lastly and most importantly, Six Sigma is business results oriented, that is, seeks to improve the bottom-line of the company, while TQM remains only quality oriented. In a way, Six Sigma can be thought of as a much bigger quality movement that embodies TQM in itself in a big way (Exhibit 14.3).

**Table 14.6** Contrasting Six Sigma and total quality management (Barney 2002)

| *Six Sigma* | *Total quality management* |
| --- | --- |
| • Executive ownership | • Self-directed work teams |
| • Business strategy execution system | • Quality initiative |
| • Truly cross functional | • Largely within a single function |
| • Focused training with verifiable return on investment | • No mass training in statistics and quality with return on investment |
| • Business results oriented | • Quality oriented |

## Exhibit 14.3   Mahindra & Mahindra

It is 7:00 a.m. and the siren sounds high at Kandivli (a suburb of North Mumbai) plant of Mahindra & Mahindra's (M&M) Tractor division, signalling the starting time of the morning shift. Hardly any worker has turned up. Reporting late on duty is a norm for the workers here. Seldom does the morning shift start before 7:30 a.m. During the day shift, it was an ominous scene to find workers stretching out under the trees and relaxing during the working hours. The union leaders hang around the factory without doing any work at all. A few days back, the workers in the night shift had beaten up a milkman for creating a lot of noise in the wee hours of the morning and thus, disturbing their sleep during their working hours. Things were worse at the other plant of M&M in Nagpur. But this was all in the 1980s. M&M has come a long way since then—it has won the most coveted Deming prize for quality, and started a farming equipment assembling plant in the USA. After the huge success there, the company opened a second assembly plant and a distribution centre in Georgia. Now, the company is in the process of establishing assembling units in Canada to locally produce and market a range of low horsepower cab tractors with features such as AC heater (keeping in view the cold weather conditions for the farmers there), personal stereo, and even a sun roof. It has also acquired Jiangling Tractors in China, which it would use to develop low cost products suited to plough deeper into the US farm equipment market. Now, the fourth-largest tractor company in the world, M&M, has four tractor plants in India (Mumbai, Nagpur, Rudrapur in Uttrakhand, and Jaipur). It has been maintaining its market leadership for the past two decades. During the late 1980s, the company tried to apply TQM concepts such as quality circles without getting any success. M&M was the market leader in the tractors segment at that time, but in view of the looming multinational threat in the near future, its internal situation was very fragile. During 1990–94, the company started the use of statistical process control and tried to perform business process reengineering. Its journey towards the Deming prize was initiated in 1994, with the appointment of Prof. Yasutoshi Washio, a Japanese expert, in the implementation of the Deming guidelines. The same year, the company was rechristened M&M Farm Equipment Sector (FES).

Initially, Prof. Washio was skeptical about the Indian companies and workers. He felt that the Indian

*(Contd)*

*Exhibit 14.3 Contd*

companies are more like the American companies, which feel that results are important. On the other hand, for the Japanese, the process is more important. Moreover, he had serious doubts about the attitude of the Indian workers with respect to teamwork—a Deming prerequisite—as he felt that Indians were individualistic. He was proved wrong by the M&M workers. In his own words, 'The Indians can be good team workers, much better than the young in Japan today and, in that sense, perhaps, Deming is better suited to Indian companies'. In the initial few years of interaction with the management of FES, Washio found himself isolated due to disagreements on various fronts. Washio had major difficulties in making most of the Indian companies understand the importance of implementation over creating a perfect framework. In his own words, 'Indians are very good with framework and the big picture, but are poor with implementation. The kaizen is weak.' Kaizen means gradual, orderly, and continuous improvement in work processes. It took a while for Washio to make the FES personnel understand that good kaizen hinges on implementation, so there is no need to spend too much time creating a perfect framework. Once you start implementing these, the rest will happen automatically. The FES created a team to implement the Deming guidelines. The team identified eleven key areas to be fulfilled:

1. top management leadership and involvement
2. creating and maintaining TQM frameworks
3. quality assurance
4. management systems
5. human resource development
6. effective utilization of resources
7. understanding TQM concepts and values
8. use of scientific methods
9. organizational power
10. relationship with stakeholders
11. enabling of unique TQM activities

In addition, there is another Deming must-do: eliminate dependence on inspection to achieve quality by building quality into the product in the first place. The system at FES earlier was that at the end of the assembly process or at the customer's place, there used to be a final inspection. If a product showed serious flaws then, it was sent again to the shop floor. This wasted a lot of time and effort, and it did not add to the improvement in the quality of the manufactured product. In order to change this system, computers were installed on the shop floor for showing the standard operating procedure (SOP) of a particular process to make the workers understand the various steps in a process. This reduces the chances of human error and acts as a natural check. At the end of every complete process, a check is performed by a trained worker, who also follows an SOP. Employee involvement is the first step in ensuring the success of any quality initiative. At FES, the workers would dictate terms to the shift supervisors by saying that they would not do different tasks on many machines. The management took time to convince them by giving them examples such as: if your wife can do multiple tasks of cleaning the house, feeding the children, and washing the clothes, why can't you do the same? The workers were explained the multinational threats looming large. They were told that, if they did not mend their ways, the company might shut down the factory, or even worse, a multinational may take it over and would invariably lay off all the problem-creating workers. Examples of companies shut down in Mumbai due to the changed scenario were given. The entire programme was termed 'Ashwamedh' and analogies were drawn from mythology and the current competitive situation. This brought a complete transformation in the workforce that was now willing to perform multiple tasks, double their productivity, and maintain shift discipline by reporting on time. The workers were informed by the management about every difficulty faced by the company in beating the competition in the marketplace. Some of the workers were sent with the marketing staff to meet the farmers using the company's products and facing problems. This was called 'Operation *Hamla*'. The workers came back chastised and sobered when they realized that a small mistake on the shop floor could cost a farmer his season's crop. The company even sent some of the union leaders for short training courses in the USA and UK.

This sustained effort on part of the company has paid rich dividends. Costs are down by 15 per cent and the market share has risen by one per cent to 27.3 per cent (10% higher than its closest competitor), despite an overall decline in the tractor demand. The break-even point for a new model of a tractor has decreased to 30,000–32,000 from the 54,000 tractors three years ago. The worker productivity levels have increased by 100%. Tractor exports from the company have increased 100 per cent over the past 10 years, with 70 per cent

*(Contd)*

*Exhibit 14.3 Contd*

to the USA alone. The quality of tractors has improved drastically with the number of complaints per 1,000 tractors dropping from 228 to 90. The rejection rate for components bought from vendors, rejection and rework in machining, and rejection at final testing have all been brought down to near zero levels. FES has introduced 15 new models in accordance with the

requirements in the international markets. The journey to world-class quality is not over yet. The company now aims at matching the world benchmarks in productivity and quality to establish a cost leadership in the Indian industry. At the end of 2012, the combined market share of MM and Swaraj (its subsidiary) stood at 42 per cent.

*Source:* Madhavan (2012).

## Acceptance Sampling

The process of performing a check of raw materials, components, and parts supplied by vendors is called *incoming inspection*. Similarly, before dispatching a batch of finished goods to the customers, an *outgoing inspection* is done. These inspections may be done in two ways. One way is to check each and every item in the lot. This requires considerable time, effort, and resources. If the inspection is destructive in nature, this approach to testing will not be a good idea. For example, while testing consumer perishables (eatables) for quality, these have to be consumed to check the taste. Thus, it is not possible to check each and every unit. At the same time, the accuracy of such an inspection is the highest.

The other, easier to implement, way is to resort to sampling. One or more samples may be drawn out of the lot and tested for quality. A decision may be made to accept or reject the lot or consignment depending upon the number of defective items found in the samples. This process of using sampling in incoming or outgoing inspection is called *acceptance sampling*.

**Types of sampling plans**  Different types of sampling plans can be used for acceptance sampling depending upon the number of samples drawn from the lot.

*Single-sampling plan*  In this plan, a single sample is drawn from the lot of items. For example, if the consignment sent by a supplier contains 10,000 items, a sample of 100 units may be drawn at random from the lot. Thus, universe size $N = 10,000$; sample size $n = 100$. It may be decided by the QC manager beforehand that a lot will be accepted if the sample of 100 units drawn at random contains, say, 5 defective units or less. Otherwise, the lot will be rejected. This limiting number of defective units used to take a decision about accepting or rejecting a lot is called the *acceptance number 'a'*. In our example, $a = 5$. The number of defective items in a sample may be represented by $d$. Thus, if $d \leq a$ (in our example $d \leq 5$), the lot will be accepted; if $d > a$, the lot will be rejected.

*Double-sampling plan*  As the name of the plan suggests, we take two samples in this plan for inspection. For the first sample of 100 units drawn from a lot of, say, 10,000 units, the QC manager decides beforehand that if the number of defective items in the sample $d \leq 5$, the lot will be accepted; if $d \geq 12$, the lot will be rejected; and if $6 \leq d \geq 11$, a second sample of 100 units will be drawn.

Now, the second sample is inspected and the number of defective items in it is determined. In the combined sample (first and second samples combined to form a combined sample of 200 units), if $d \leq 17$, the lot will be accepted. Otherwise, it will be rejected.

*Multiple sampling plan*  As discussed in the double-sampling plan, when more than two samples are chosen, we have a multiple-sampling plan.

> This process of using sampling in incoming or outgoing inspection is called acceptance sampling.

We note that as we move from the single-sampling plan towards the multiple-sampling plan, the complexity of implementation of the plan increases. The single-sampling plan is the most simple in implementation and is most commonly used in various organizations. We will discuss the single-sampling plan in detail.

**Single-sampling plan and the operating characteristics curve** In the single-sampling plan, the criteria for accepting or rejecting a lot is the acceptance number $a$. We will continue with our earlier example of the single-sampling plan and take $a = 5$. Thus, if $d \leq a$, the lot will be accepted; if $d > a$, it will be rejected. Let us assume that in reality the proportion of defectives in a lot of size $N = 10{,}000$ is $p$. It has been found that the probability of acceptance ($P_a$) of a lot with $d$ defectives in a sample of size $n$ can be represented by a Poisson distribution function as

$$P_a(d) = \frac{e^{-\mu}\mu^d}{d!}$$

where the mean value of the distribution $\mu = np$ and the exponential value $e = 2.718$.

When the proportion defective in the lot ($p$) is zero, the probability of acceptance of the lot ($P_a$) will be maximum, that is, 1. In Fig. 14.28, we show this maximum probability in row 9. In row 10, we calculate the value of $P_a$ for $p = 0.01$. For this value of $p$, the value of $\mu$ is

$$\mu = np = 100 \times 0.01 = 1$$

This value of $\mu$ is shown in cell B10 of the figure. For acceptance number $a = 5$, the lot will be accepted if the number of defectives $d$ in the sample is either of the following: 0, 1, 2, 3, 4, or 5. Note that all these situations are mutually exclusive, that is, no two values can occur at the

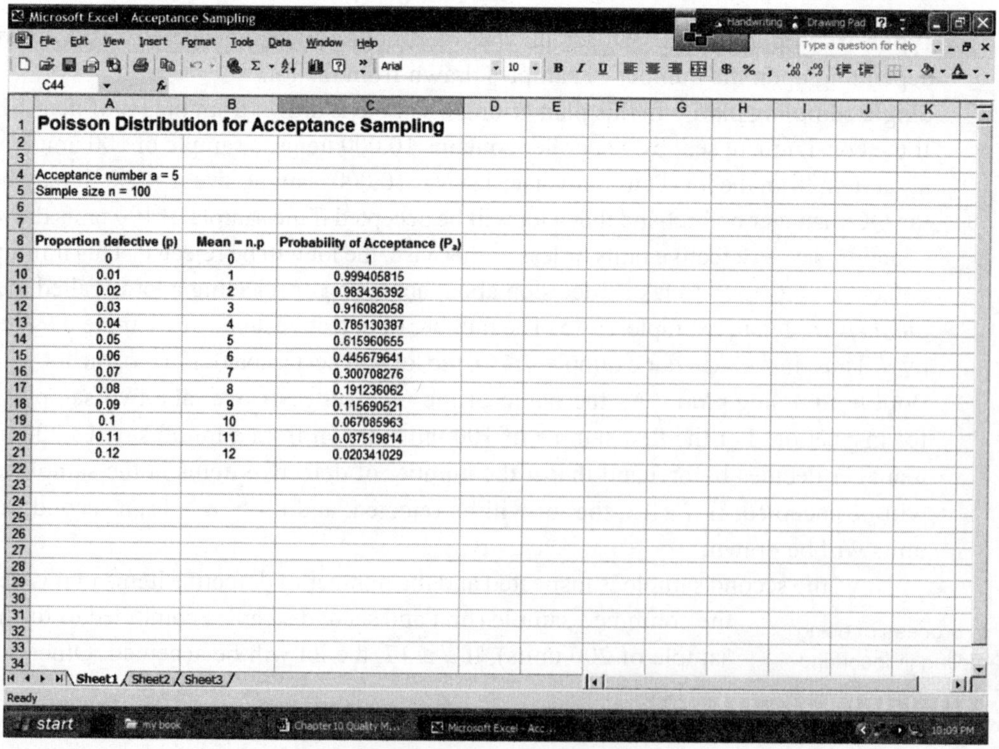


| Proportion defective (p) | Mean = n.p | Probability of Acceptance ($P_a$) |
|---|---|---|
| 0 | 0 | 1 |
| 0.01 | 1 | 0.999405815 |
| 0.02 | 2 | 0.983436392 |
| 0.03 | 3 | 0.916082058 |
| 0.04 | 4 | 0.785130387 |
| 0.05 | 5 | 0.615960655 |
| 0.06 | 6 | 0.445679641 |
| 0.07 | 7 | 0.300708276 |
| 0.08 | 8 | 0.191236062 |
| 0.09 | 9 | 0.115690521 |
| 0.1 | 10 | 0.067085963 |
| 0.11 | 11 | 0.037519814 |
| 0.12 | 12 | 0.020341029 |

**Fig. 14.28** Poisson distribution for acceptance sampling

same time. For example, it is not possible that the sample of size 100 has no defective as well as one defective. Thus, for $p = 0.01$, the probability of acceptance will be

$$P_a(p = 0.01) = P_a(d = 0) + P_a(d = 1) + P_a(d = 2) + P_a(d = 3) + P_a(d = 4) + P_a(d = 5)$$

$$= \frac{(2.718)^{-1} \times (1)^0}{0!} + \frac{(2.718)^{-1} \times (1)^1}{1!} + \frac{(2.718)^{-1} \times (1)^2}{2!}$$

$$= + \frac{(2.718)^{-1} \times (1)^3}{3!} + \frac{(2.718)^{-1} \times (1)^4}{4!} + \frac{(2.718)^{-1} \times (1)^5}{5!} \qquad (14.4)$$

It is very easy to calculate the value of the above expression using MS Excel. In Fig. 14.28 to calculate the value of $P_a$ ($p = 0.01$) in cell C10, select cell C10 and click on the **Insert** tool on the toolbar. From the pull-down menu, select **Function** so that the dialog box shown in Fig. 14.29 appears. In this dialog box, select the **Statistical** category and the **Poisson** function. Upon clicking **OK, the Function Arguments** dialog box shown in Fig. 14.30 appears.

In the **Function Arguments** dialog box, enter the value 5 for $x$ (the value of the acceptance number $a$). We have already calculated the value of the mean $\mu$ as 1, which we enter in the **Mean** text box. Enter **true** in the text box of **Cumulative** and then click on **OK**. The value 0.999405815 appears in cell C10 as shown in the figure. Cumulative here means that we have to add the $P_a$ terms for all the $d$ values—0, 1, 2, 3, 4, and 5—to get the total $P_a$ value for $p = 0.01$.

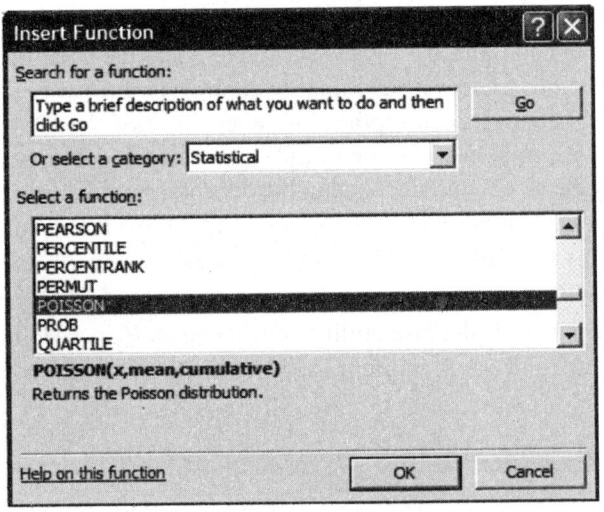

**Fig. 14.29** Insert Function dialog box

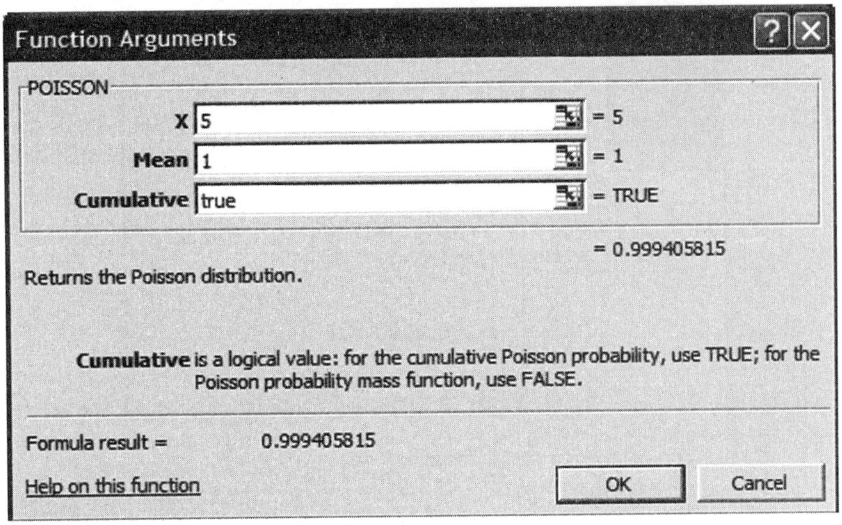

**Fig. 14.30** Function Arguments dialog box

> A good sampling plan ensures that the good lots are always accepted, while the bad ones are always rejected.

In Fig. 14.28, we calculate the value of $P_a$ for different values of $p$, from 0 to 0.12, as shown in column C. We will now make a plot of the proportion of defectives in the lot $p$ and the probability of acceptance $P_a$ using SPSS 10.0. The graph of SPSS is very clear and easy to manipulate.

Paste the columns of $p$ and $P_a$ in the **SPSS Data Editor** as shown in Fig. 14.31. Select the two columns in the **Data Editor**, click on **Graphs** on the toolbar, and from the pull-down menu choose **Interactive**. Then, choose **Line** so that the **Create Lines** dialog box appears as shown in the figure. Drag **var00001** into the text box for the *x*-axis and **var00002** into the text box for the *y*-axis. Upon clicking **OK**, the graph shown in Fig. 14.32 appears.

This curve as shown in Fig. 14.33 is called the *operating characteristics* (OC) *curve*. Acceptance sampling decisions, that is, whether to accept or reject a batch of items are based on this OC curve. A good sampling plan ensures that the good lots are always accepted, while the bad ones are always rejected. The OC curve can be made stricter (stricter quality control) in three ways.

1. By increasing the sample size $n$, while keeping the acceptance number constant.
2. By decreasing the acceptance number $a$, while keeping the sample size $n$ constant.
3. By simultaneously increasing the sample size $n$ and decreasing the acceptance number $a$.

As shown in Fig. 14.34, when we increase the sample size $n$ (100 in our example) while keeping the acceptance number a (5 in our example) constant, the OC curve comes closer towards the origin. Note that for $n = 200$ and $a = 5$, the OC curve is closer to the origin compared to that for $n = 100$ and $a = 5$. For proportion defective $p = 0.05$, the probability of acceptance $P_a$ as seen in the graphs of Fig. 14.34 is 0.6160 for $n = 100$ and $a = 5$, while it is approximately 0.24 for $n = 200$ and $a = 5$.

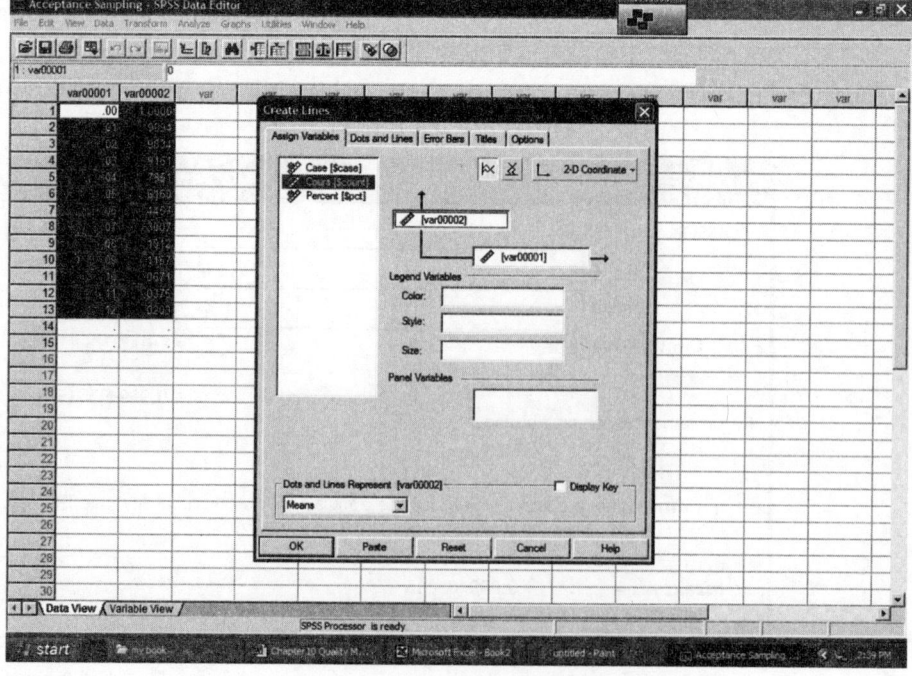

**Fig. 14.31** SPSS Data Editor

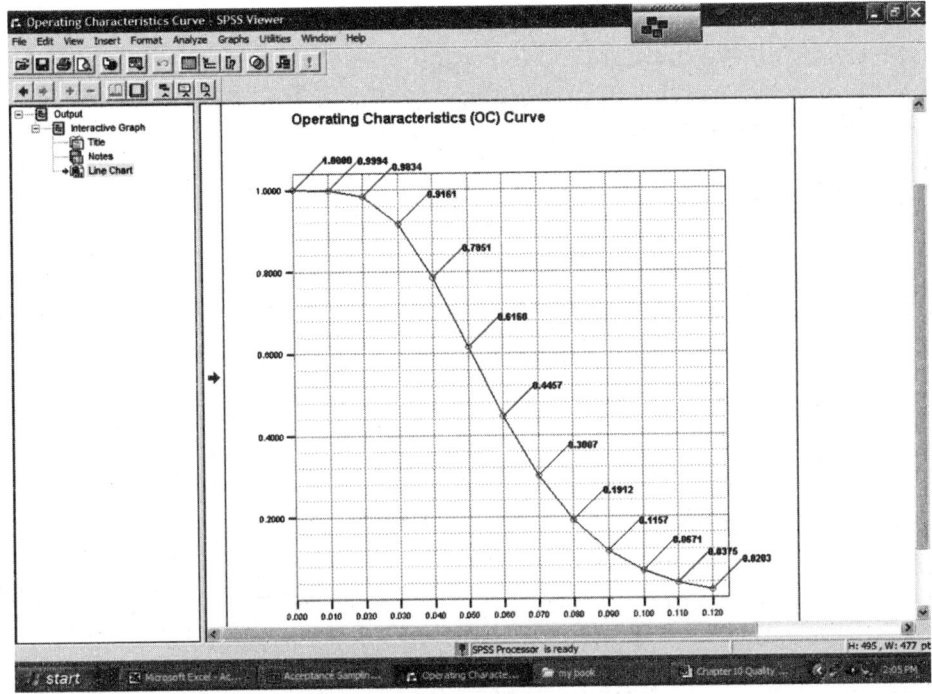

**Fig. 14.32** Operating characteristics curve

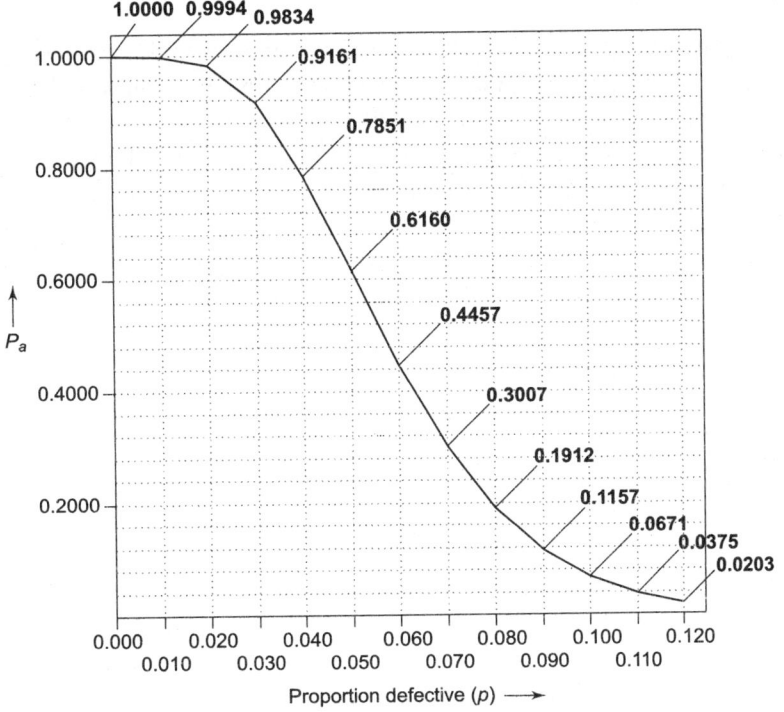

**Fig. 14.33** Operating characteristics curve

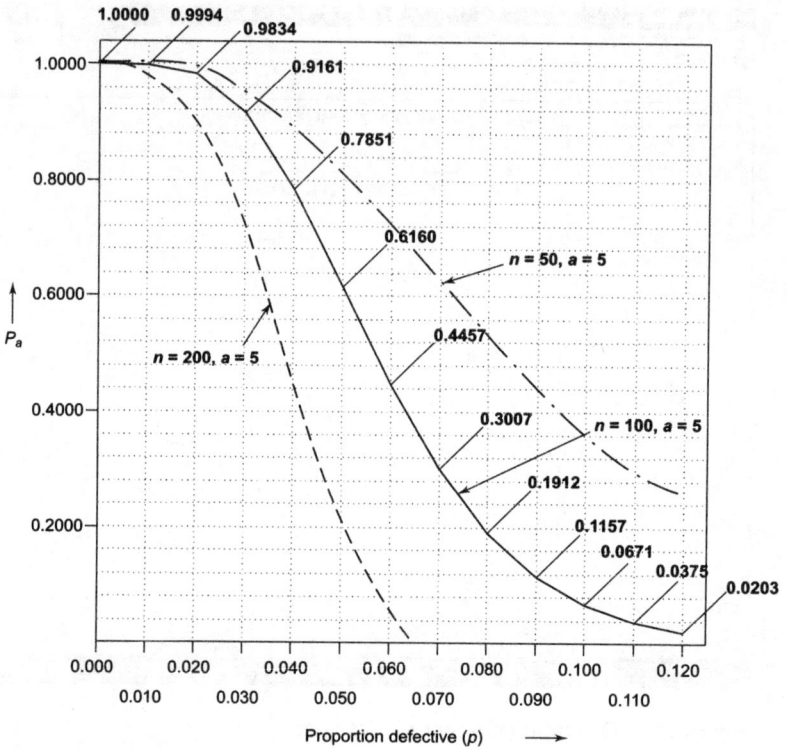

**Fig. 14.34** Effect of increasing the sample size *n* on the OC curve

Thus, the chance of acceptance of a batch of items is far less when sample size *n* is increased from 100 to 200 while keeping the acceptance number *a* constant. It is very logical, as earlier we were accepting a lot when out of 100 units (sample size *n*), 5 or less defectives were found. Now, when the sample size is increased to 200, we accept a lot when out of 200 units (sample size *n*), 5 or less defectives are found.

The second way of making the OC curve more strict for acceptance sampling is by decreasing the value of acceptance number *a*, while keeping the sample size *n* constant (at 100 units in our example). When we decrease the acceptance number *a* from 5 to 3, we accept the lot when out of a sample of size *n* = 100 units, 3 or less defectives are found, compared to 5 or less defectives earlier. Thus, the sampling plan has become stricter.

Note that in Fig. 14.35, the value of $P_a$ for *p* = 0.05 when *n* = 100 and *a* = 5 is 0.6160, while for *n* = 100 and *a* = 3 it is approximately 0.1000. The figure also shows that when the acceptance number *a* is increased to 7, the sampling plan becomes loose, that is, less strict.

When the sample size *n* is increased and acceptance number *a* is decreased simultaneously, both the earlier effects take place together, making the acceptance sampling plan stricter.

**Ideal OC curve**  In our example, we have *n* = 100 and *a* = 5. If we inspect the whole lot, that is, all the 10,000 items (if the sample size is 10,000), we will find the proportion defective exactly. This will be in contrast to sampling, in which sampling errors are always possible. Our decision of accepting or rejecting the lot will be clear, as we would accept the lot if 5 or less defectives are found in every 100 units (sample size *n*). This ratio 5/100 is same as 5 per cent or 0.05. Thus, if

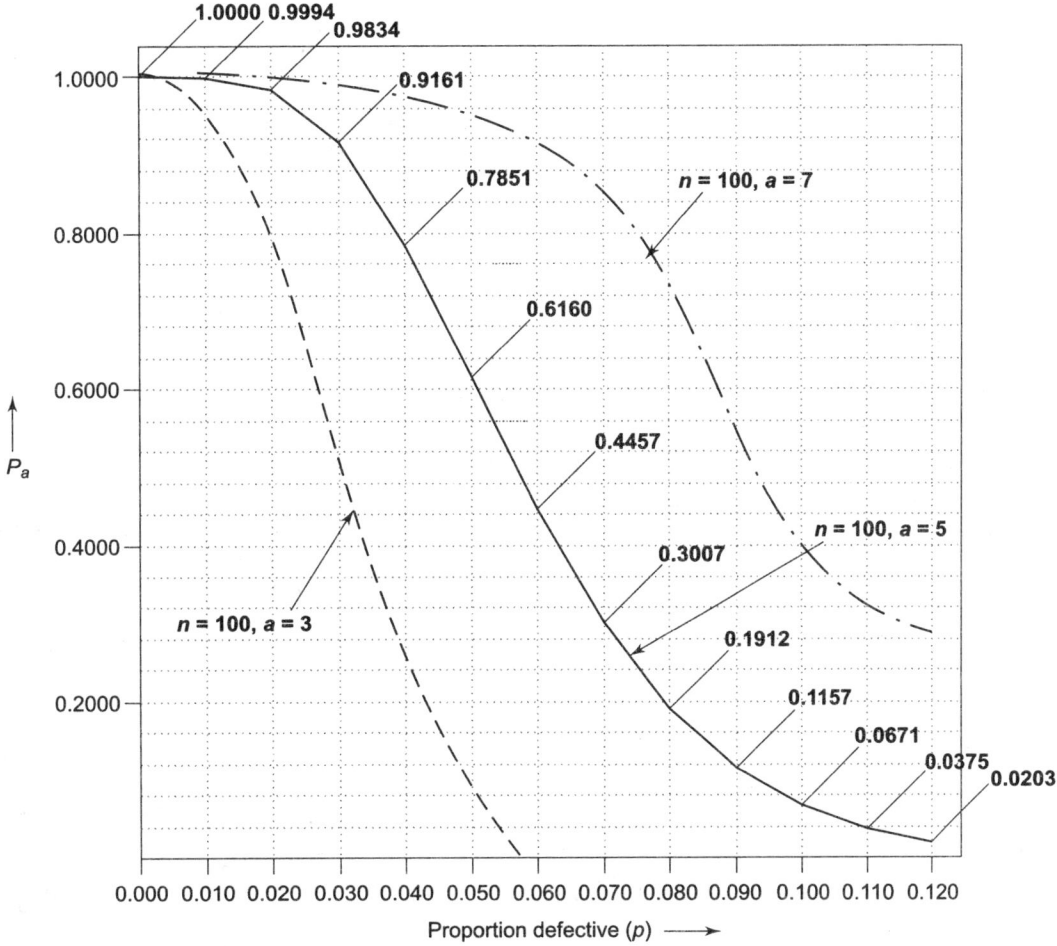

**Fig. 14.35** Effect of decreasing the acceptance number *a* on the OC curve

the actual proportion defective found by inspecting the whole lot is 0.05 or less (i.e., 500 units or less out of 10,000 are defective), we would definitely accept the lot, and otherwise reject it. Figure 14.36 shows this ideal situation by the bold thick curve called the *ideal OC curve*. In this curve, note that for all the points less than or equal to $p = 0.05$, $P_a$ is 1 (the maximum). The value of $P_a$ for all the points greater than $p = 0.05$ is zero. Therefore, if the proportion of defectives found after inspecting the whole lot is more than 0.05, the lot will definitely be rejected ($P_a$ is zero). Practically, the whole lot is seldom inspected, that is, sampling is invariably adopted. Therefore, practical OC curves are like the thin line (the curve based upon our example) shown in Fig. 14.36. Note that this curve passes through the point (0.05,0.160).

When we increase *n* to 1,000 and *a* to 50, while maintaining the same ratio (50/1,000 = 0.05), the dashed curve shown in the figure is obtained. Note that this curve also passes through the point (0.05,0.6160) and is closer to the ideal OC curve compared to the OC curve for $n = 100$ and $a = 5$. All these curves including the ideal OC curve pass through the point (0.05,0.6160) because the ratio of *a* and *n* for all these curves is equal to the proportion defectives in the lot, that is, 0.05.

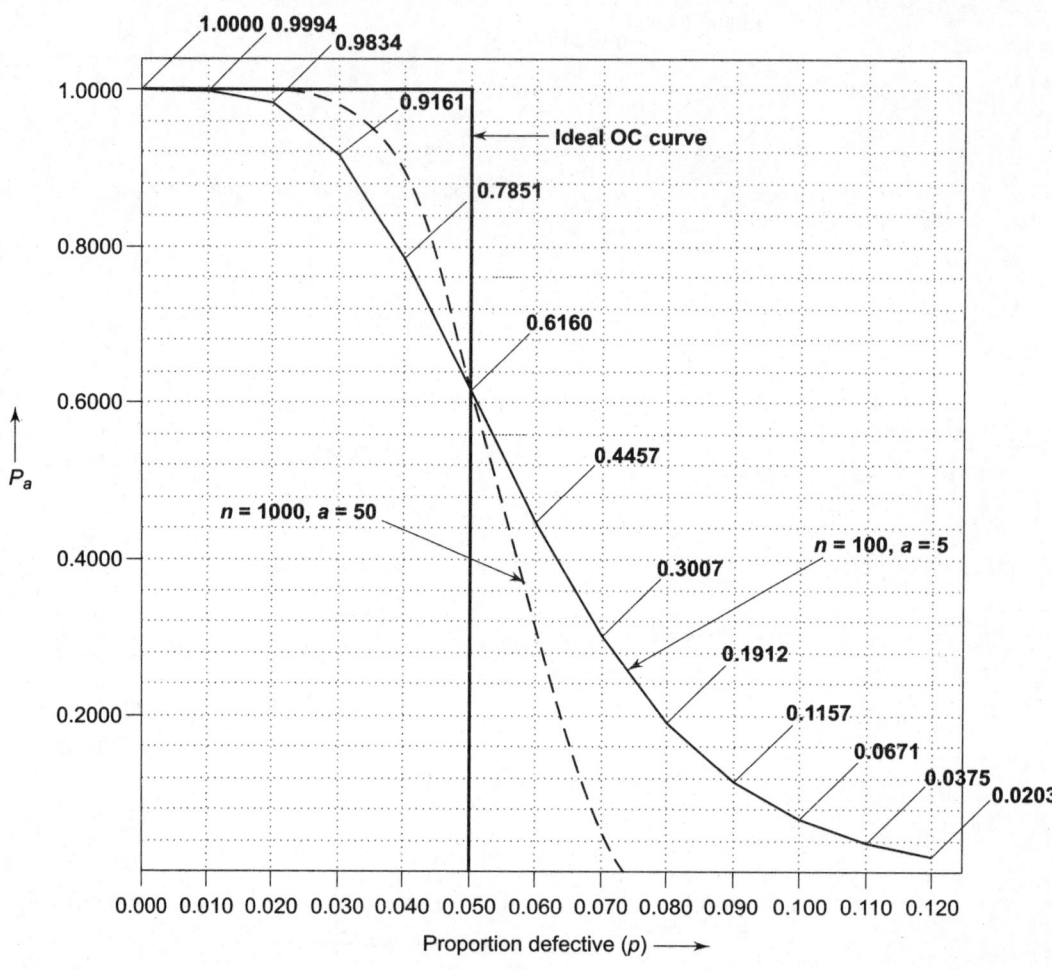

**Fig. 14.36** Ideal OC curve shown by the bold curve

**Producer's and consumer's risk**  Due to sampling variations, it is always possible that a bad lot is accepted and a good lot is rejected. It is a producer's risk that a good lot is rejected by the consumer. In our example, say, by chance in a sample of 100 units, 7 units were defective, though in the whole lot of 10,000 units, only 10 units were defective. Out of these 10 defective items, by chance 7 appeared in the sample drawn at random and *a* being set at 5, the lot is rejected. Thus, the producer faces the risk of rejection of a good lot by the consumer.

Similarly, due to sampling variations the consumer faces the risk of accepting a bad lot (i.e., a lot containing a large number of defects). In our example, suppose there are 700 defective items in a lot of 10,000 units. When a sample of 100 units is drawn at random and inspected, by chance only 2 units are defective and the lot is accepted (as *a* is 5). Thus, the consumer accepts a lot which contained a large number of defectives.

> Due to sampling variations, it is always possible that a bad lot is accepted and a good lot is rejected.

The consumer and the producer negotiate with each other and arrive at two limiting values of proportion defectives in a lot. One value is the *acceptable quality limit* (AQL). Let us assume in our example that an AQL of *p* = 0.03 is agreed upon by both the consumer and the producer (see Fig. 14.37). If the proportion of defectives in a lot is equal to or less than the AQL, the consumer will have to definitely accept the lot. Otherwise, the consumer may accept or reject the lot (he will be indifferent about accepting or rejecting the lot).

The other limiting value is called the *lot tolerance per cent defective* (LTPD). Let us assume in our example that the LTPD of $p = 0.08$ is agreed by both the consumer and the producer (see Fig. 14.37). If the proportion of defectives in a lot is equal to or more than the LTPD, the consumer will definitely reject the lot. Otherwise, the consumer may accept or reject the lot (he will be indifferent about accepting or rejecting the lot). The region between $p = 0$ and $p = 0.03$ (the AQL in our example) is called the *acceptable quality region*. The region above $p = 0.08$ (the LTPD in our example) is called the *unacceptable quality region*. The region between AQL and LTPD is called the *region of indifference*, as in this range of proportion defectives there is no clear-cut criterion for the acceptance or rejection of a lot.

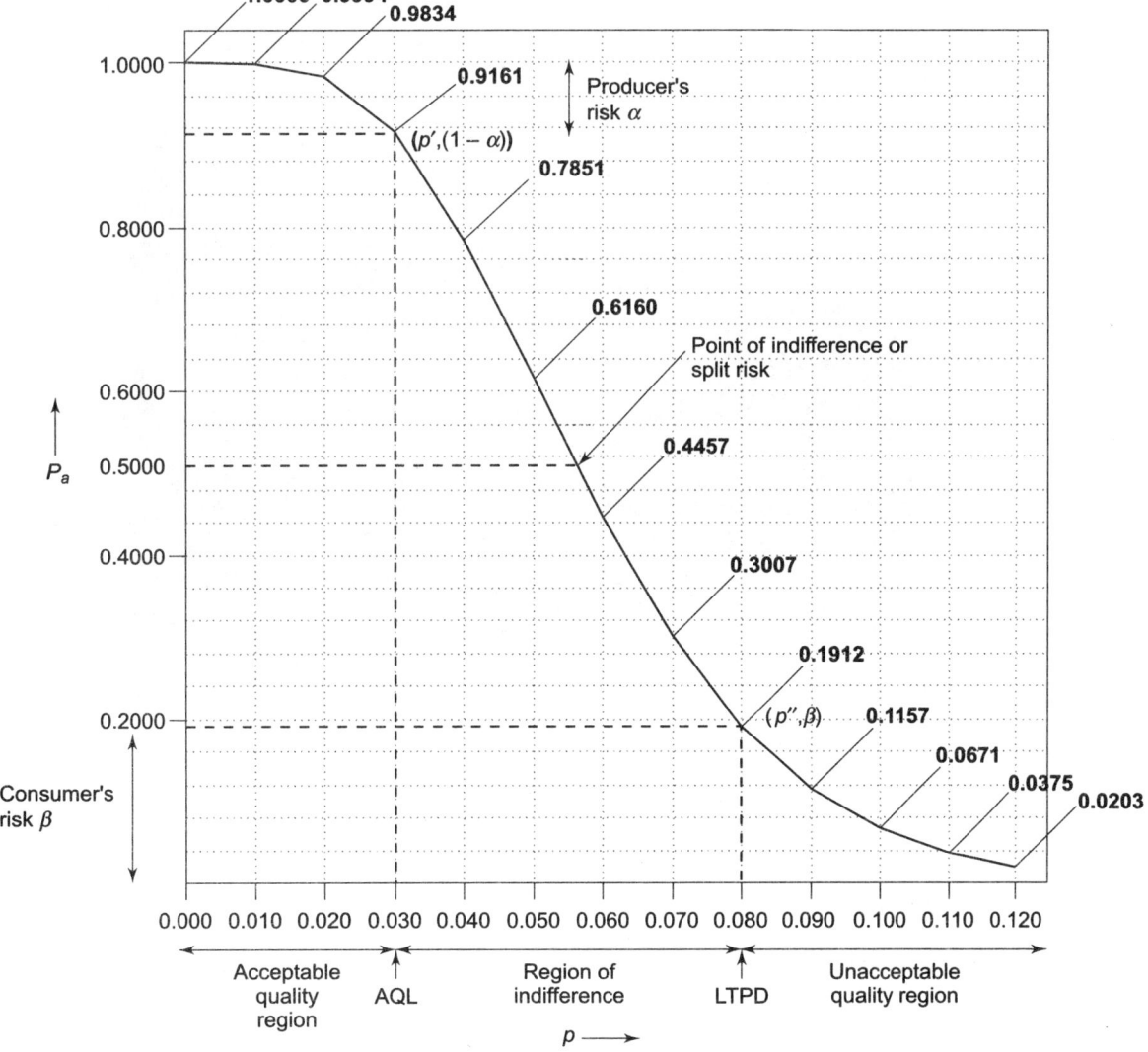

**Fig. 14.37** Producer's and consumer's risk

Practically, despite setting the AQL and LTPD, the whole lot is seldom inspected in normal situations. Thus, there is a risk due to sampling variations of a lot having proportion defectives less than AQL being rejected by the consumer. This is called the *producer's risk α*. In Fig. 14.37, $\alpha$ is shown as the probability of rejection $(1 - P_a)$ corresponding to the AQL. Thus,

$$(1 - P_a) = \alpha \quad \text{or} \quad P_a = 1 - \alpha$$

Similarly, there is a risk due to sampling variations of a lot having proportion defectives more than LTPD being accepted by the consumer. This is called the *consumer's risk (β)*. In Fig. 14.37, $\beta$ is shown as the probability of acceptance $(P_a)$ corresponding to the LTPD. Thus, the consumer and producer negotiate with each other and agree upon four values: AQL $= p'$, LTPD $= p''$, producer's risk $= \alpha$, consumer's risk $= \beta$.

Thus, two points are agreed upon by the consumer and the producer. These are $(p', (1 - \alpha))$ and $(p'', \beta)$. One more point called the *point of indifference* or *split risk*, which corresponds to the value of $P_a = 0.5$, is also agreed upon. An OC curve is then found by the trial-and-error method (by varying the values of $n$ and $a$), which fits these three points. Once such an OC curve is found, it is used for acceptance sampling.

Courtesy: BMW.
At BMW's Spartanburg (USA) facility, during final inspection, cars are driven at 85 miles per hour inside a closed room called the roll booth to check for jumps and vibrations.

## Quality System Standards

Quality system standards are used as minimum requirements of quality systems in organizations. Quality standards are of two types.

**Generic standards** These standards are set by national and international quality certification bodies as a guidance, development, or evaluation of quality system in an organization. 'Generic'

Quality system standards are used as minimum requirements of quality systems in organizations.

means that the same standards can be applied to any organization—large or small, producing any product or service, and in any sector of activity—it could be a business enterprise, public administration department, or a government department (Exhibit 14.4). In India, we have the Bureau of Indian Standards (BIS) as a national organization for setting quality standards and the most popular international standard is ISO 9000. ISO 14000 is a generic standard relating to establishing an environment management system in an organization.

**Industry-related standards** These standards are set by purchasing bodies for a particular industry as the basic requirements for purchasing products/services. For example, defence, aerospace, nuclear industries, etc., usually have a set of guidelines for purchasing due to overriding safety requirements. A new standard came into existence in 1995–96 called COPC–2000 for customer service providers such as BPOs. The Capability maturity model (CMM) is another standard that has been developed by the Software Engineering Institute, Carnegie Mellon University, USA, and is applicable to software organizations. Eighty Indian software companies, including our software majors such as Infosys, Wipro, and TCS, have attained CMM Level-5 out of a total of 117 global companies. India has the largest number of annual bulk drug filings (77) with the US Food and Drug Administration (USFDA). India is home to the largest number of pharma plants approved by USFDA outside USA. Indian pharma companies have also got certification from European and Australian drug authorities. Agmark is another industry-related standard used in the grading and standardization of agricultural and allied commodities.

Quality standards serve the following three purposes:

Quality standards provide guidance to an organization implementing a quality system for the first time.

- Quality standards provide guidance to an organization implementing a quality system for the first time.
- Quality standards are used for assessing the quality system already in place in an organization.
- Quality standards are used for creating quality assurance requirements to be specified in the contract with a supplier.

## Exhibit 14.4 Asia's First ISO Certified Salon

What is the common strand between giant industrial groups such as TVS, the Tatas, Birlas, and the humble Ramesh Gents' Hair Stylist on the upmarket Nungambakkam High Road in Chennai? A coveted ISO quality certification, of course. The salon is the first personal care establishment in Asia to be awarded this prestigious quality certification in this service category. It was certified by the Mumbai-based ISO auditors, International Certification Services (Asia). Says ISO consultant, Ayyan Thiruvalluvar, CEO, IQ International Consultancy Services, 'It took us three months to map and systematise the entire process involved in running the salon'.

Proprietor G. Ramesh, who entered the hair-care profession at the age of twelve, clearly articulates the reason for becoming ISO certified, 'We want to

go global and set up our business overseas and also meet competitive threats at home.' While the personal products company, CavinKare, notched a milestone when it started its unisex salon in this southern metro, the Chennai hairstylist has finalized plans to start operations in Malaysia with a local partner. In addition, Ramesh plans to strengthen his branding in India by establishing a presence in other Indian metros and convert his sole proprietorship into a private limited company. Though planning to corporatize, Ramesh emphatically rules out the franchising route to prevent his standards from being diluted. 'Prior to the certification, we didn't fix prior appointments.

Service was on a first come, first served basis,' says Ramesh and adds, 'with the ISO certification, the salon has systematized all its operations. Every

*(Contd)*

*Exhibit 14.4 Contd*

time a customer comes to the salon, a job card is prepared listing details such as personal preferences and allergies to products.' Records of visits are maintained and reminders about the next appointment are sent to customers. The salon uses disposable equipment, sterilized grooming kits, neck capes, imported disposable shaving kits, and offers shower facilities. A health club with sauna, jacuzzi, ayurvedic massage, and a gym are on the cards. Ramesh has an envious roster of clients which includes well-known cine and television stars, industrialists, bureaucrats, ministers from the state and central governments, and an assortment of MPs and MLAs, who cut across party affiliations to have their tonsorial services.

*Source*: Adapted from Venkatarman (2005) and Ramanathan (2004).

# Bureau of Indian Standards (BIS)

In 1982, India was among the first few countries to develop a national standard known as the IS 10201-quality system in six parts. The Bureau of Indian Standards (BIS) is the national standards body of India, and is governed by the Bureau of Indian Standards Act, 1986. BIS had formulated a standard called IS 13967: 1993 on environment management systems (EMS) before ISO 14001 came into existence. The Indian Constitution contains provision for environmental protection through its Articles 48A and 51A(g). BIS provides the following services to the Indian citizens as outlined in its Citizen Charter.

**Formulation of Indian Standards**   BIS seeks proposals from any ministry of central government, state governments, union territory administrations, consumer organizations, industrial units, industry associations, professional bodies, members of the bureau, and members of its technical committees for establishing a standard, or for revising, amending or cancelling an established standard. BIS has created technical committees by drawing experts from all the concerned areas. These committees are used to formulate standards in the most transparent manner through a consensus process.

**Certification schemes**   The certification schemes operated by BIS are product certification and systems certification schemes. For *product certification*, BIS gives the licence to the manufacturers of products for the use of the standard ISI mark that indicates conformity to the relevant Indian standard. This licence is granted by BIS only if it is satisfied with the availability of the required infrastructure and capability of the producer to produce and test the product, conforming to the relevant Indian standard on a continuous basis. BIS draws samples of the product from the production lines of the manufacturer as well as directly from the market and gets these tested in independent laboratories to ensure that they conform to the relevant Indian standard. This licence is valid for one year, and is renewed only after a reassessment. Four categories of product certification have been discussed below.

The Bureau of Indian Standards (BIS) is the national standards body of India and is governed by the Bureau of Indian Standards Act, 1986.

*Mandatory certification*   The ISI mark scheme is essentially a voluntary scheme, that is, organizations can decide whether to go for this type of a licence from BIS or not. However, for products falling in the categories of mass consumption, consumer safety, health, and energy conservation, etc., the central government has made it mandatory for organizations to obtain this license for using the ISI mark. The Essential Commodities Act, PFA Act, etc. have been used for creating this mandatory requirement.

> The certification schemes operated by BIS are product certification and systems certification schemes.

*Hallmarking of gold jewellery* This is a purity certification scheme of the BIS. Hallmarking means that the jewellery articles have been independently tested and the jewellery conforms to the marked fineness. The BIS logo is marked on the jewellery tested along with the fineness (e.g., 916 for 22 carat gold). The jewellery is assessed only at the BIS recognized assaying and hallmarking centres.

*Certification schemes for imported goods* There are two certification schemes in this category—one for foreign manufacturers and the other for Indian importers. These schemes are essentially similar to the product certification scheme of the BIS for the domestic industry, apart from slight differences necessary for the operation of these schemes. Only foreign manufacturers can seek the BIS licence for products falling under the mandatory certification scheme, while for the rest of the products, both the foreign manufacturer as well as the Indian importer can apply for the licence.

*The Eco mark scheme* This scheme is operated by BIS for the labelling of household and other consumer goods which conform to certain environmental criteria along with quality requirements in the relevant Indian standards.

The following *system certification* schemes are operated by BIS:

*Quality systems certification* This scheme is operated by BIS for organizations with respect to the ISO 9000: 2000 series of standards. This scheme of BIS has been accredited by Raad Voor Accreditatie (RVA), Netherlands. BIS certifies the capability of the suppliers of goods and services against the ISO 9000: 2000 standards.

*Environmental management systems certification* This certification is done by BIS for organizations complying with the ISO 14000 standard.

*Hazard analysis critical control point (HACCP) scheme* For food processing units, BIS operates this certification with respect to ISO 9000 and ISO 15000 standards under a single audit scheme. Hazard analysis and critical control point (HACCP) is a process control system designed to identify and prevent microbial and other hazards in food production. It includes steps designed to prevent problems before they occur and to correct deviations as soon as they are detected. Such preventive control systems with documentation and verification are widely recognized by scientific authorities and international organizations as the most effective approach available for producing safe food. HACCP involves a systematic approach to the identification of hazards, assessment of chances of occurrence of hazards during each phase, raw material procurement, manufacturing, distribution, usage of food products, and in defining the measures for hazard control. In doing so, the many drawbacks prevalent in the inspection approach and in reliance

> Hazard analysis and critical control point (HACCP) is a process control system designed to identify and prevent microbial and other hazards in food production.

only on microbial testing are overcome. HACCP enables the producers, processors, distributors, exporters, etc., of food products to utilize technical resources efficiently and in a cost effective manner in assuring food safety. Food inspection too would be more systematic and therefore hassle-free. It would no doubt involve the deployment of some additional finances initially, but this would be more than compensated in the long run through consistently better quality and hence better prices and returns.

# Agmark Grading and Standardization of Agricultural and Allied Commodities

Quality standards for agricultural commodities in India are framed on the basis of their intrinsic quality. The objective of these standards is the promotion of grading and standardization of agricultural and allied commodities under the Agricultural Produce (Grading and Marking) Act, 1937. Food safety factors are being incorporated in the standards to compete in world trade. Standards are being harmonized with international standards keeping in view the WTO requirements. Certification of agricultural commodities is carried out for the benefit of the producer/manufacturer and the consumer. Certification of adulteration-prone commodities, namely butter, ghee, vegetable oils, ground spices, honey, wheat *atta*, etc., is very popular. Blended edible vegetable oils and fat spread are compulsorily required to be certified under Agmark. Facilities for the testing and grading of cotton for the benefit of cotton growers is provided through six cotton classing centres set up in the cotton growing belt in the country. During the year 1999–2000, agricultural commodities worth ₹4,29,767 were graded and marked under Agmark. A check is kept on the quality of certified products through 23 laboratories and 43 offices spread all over the country. Organizations desirous of grading their commodities under Agmark have to obtain the certificate of authorization. For this purpose, they should have adequate infrastructure to process the commodity and access to an approved laboratory for the determination of quality and safety factors.

Quality has been a tradition in the spice trade of India. To maintain this tradition while keeping up with the modern developments in the field of standardization of agricultural produce, the government of India has prescribed standards for almost all spices. Spices such as pepper, dry ginger, cardamom, dry chillies, turmeric, garlic, coriander, fennel, fenugreek, cumin, celery seeds, and curry powder are graded compulsorily under the law before export. The grades adopted for various spices are those prescribed under the Agricultural Produce (Grading and Marking) Act 1937; and these grades are popularly known as Agmark grades. The scheme of compulsory quality control and pre-shipment inspection on certain spices was introduced by the government in 1963 and from then on the scheme is being introduced to cover all the spices in a phased programme. The pre-shipment inspection scheme is operated by the Directorate of Marketing and Inspection (DMI), Ministry of Agriculture, Government of India.

The grade specifications have been drawn up on the basis of age-old and familiar trade names such as Malabar pepper, Alleppey green cardamom, Snnam chillies, Alleppey finger turmeric, Cochin dry ginger, etc. so as not to disturb the traditional terms. Detailed specifications have been prescribed in the rules taking into account the individual characteristics of the spices concerned and broadly based on physical characteristics, such as colour, size, density, moisture content, presence of extraneous matter, and damaged produce.

Importers of spices from India are well advised to place orders on the basis of Agmark grades or ascertain from the exporters the specific Agmark grades of the spices proposed to be exported. In orders being placed on the basis of samples also, the specific grade under which such goods will be graded could be ascertained so that the importer is assured of the quality characteristics of the spices for which orders are placed. Table 14.7 shows the commodity-wise Agmark grading for domestic trade 2003–04.

**Table 14.7**  Commodity-wise Agmark grading for domestic trade 2003–04

| Commodity | Quantity (million tonnes) | Value (₹ Lakh) |
|---|---|---|
| Besan | 49,934.90 | 11,454.43 |
| Dalia | 54.90 | 8.08 |
| Maida | 5,808.54 | 669.02 |
| Suji | 2,969.16 | 303.09 |
| Wheat Atta | 51,118.10 | 5,580.39 |
| Pulses | 12,618.42 | 3,638.67 |
| Rice | 45,443.50 | 7,588.82 |
| Ground Spices | 71,331.31 | 39,755.27 |
| Turmeric | 4,747.00 | 1,012.30 |
| Cardamom | 2.73 | 24.86 |
| Chillies | 6.00 | 5.04 |
| Black Pepper | 40.73 | 28.85 |
| Cumin Seeds | 423.81 | 236.90 |
| Poppy Seeds | 15.76 | 13.01 |
| Ajwain Seeds | 164.05 | 70.28 |
| Ginger | 0.18 | 0.19 |
| Coriander | 1,470.21 | 301.83 |
| Fennel | 82.20 | 29.36 |
| Fenugreek | 61.93 | 20.90 |
| Compounded Asafoetida | 351.83 | 1,040.39 |
| Seedless Tamarind | 124.98 | 41.23 |
| Tamarind Seeds | 1,590.00 | 86.28 |
| Nutmeg | – | – |
| Clove | 0.23 | 0.73 |
| Mace | – | – |
| Vegetable Oils | 4,91,573.42 | 1,95,182.94 |
| Oil Cake | 18,253.70 | 1,697.41 |
| Honey | 2,370.87 | 2,127.16 |
| Gur | 15.00 | 1.55 |
| Tapioca Sago | 5,242.20 | 760.66 |
| Maize | – | – |
| Ghee | 1,23,509.62 | 1,64,222.36 |
| Creamery Butter | 31,989.63 | 32,687.66 |
| Fat Spread | 144.59 | 145.29 |
| Table Eggs* | 4,664.25* | 67.77 |
| Desicated Coconut | 30.00 | 30.00 |
| Grapes | 2.61 | 0.24 |
| Mango | 5.00 | 0.40 |
| Onion | – | – |
| Oranges | – | – |
| Table Potatoes | 3,862.44 | 136.23 |
| Mustard Seeds | 287.79 | 104.98 |
| Sesame Seeds | – | – |
| Isabgol Husk | 10.73 | 0.31 |
| Grand Total | 9,25,658.07 | 4,69,074.88 |
| | 4664.25* | |

* means "000" numbers

# International Organization for Standardization

The 'International Organization for Standardization' has been abbreviated as ISO, and not IOS, because at the outset, when this organization was being named, it was found that the abbreviations for its name would be different in different languages. For example, in French its name would be *Organisation Internationale de Normalization* so that the abbreviation would become OIN. It was therefore decided that the abbreviations would be derived from the Greek word *isos*, meaning *equal* implying that without any discrimination to any country or language, the organization would be called ISO.

ISO is a non-governmental organization with a central secretariat in Geneva, Switzerland, and represents a network of national standards organizations of 150 countries (one member per country). Our very own Bureau of Indian Standards (BIS) is a member of ISO. ISO is the world's largest developer of standards of various types. From the day of its inception till today, ISO has published over 15,000 international standards. In 2003, ISO published 995 new and revised international standards. Initially, in 1946, delegates from 25 countries met in London to create a new international organization with an objective of 'facilitating the international coordination and unification of industrial standards'. Thus, ISO was born on 23 February, 1947.

ISO itself does not perform certification to its ISO 9000 and ISO 14001 management system standards and does not issue ISO 9000 and ISO 14001 certificates. There are around 750 certification bodies active around the world that issue these certificates to the organizations after conducting proper audit of their quality/environmental management systems.

> ISO 9000 is a series of international quality standards that serves as a guidance to suppliers and purchasers about the minimum requirements of a quality system.

***ISO 9000*** This is a series of international quality standards that serves as a guidance to suppliers and purchasers about the minimum requirements of a quality system. The first edition of ISO 9000 standards was completed in 1986 by ISO Technical Committee 176 and it was published in 1987. Ralli Wolf was the first company in India to get ISO 9001 certified in the year 1988 by BSI, UK.

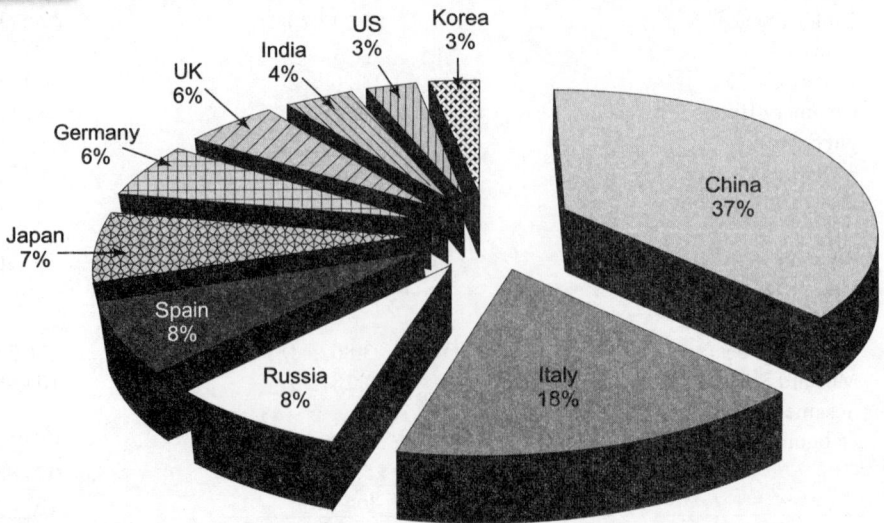

*Source:* ISO.org 2010

**Fig. 14.38** Top ten countries for ISO 9001: 2010 certificates

'The requirements specified are aimed primarily at achieving customer satisfaction by preventing non-conformity at all stages from design through to servicing.'

***ISO 9001***   This is the most comprehensive of the certificates for an organization engaging in development/design, production, installation, and servicing.

Two documents are provided by ISO as guidance to organizations for understanding various aspects of a good quality system:

***ISO 9000***   This document explains principle concepts and applications, and guide to selection and use.

***ISO 9004***   This document explains principle concepts and applications, guide to quality management, and quality system elements.

Figure 14.38 highlights the top ten countries for IS 9001: 2010 certificates.

### Benefits of ISO 9000 Certification

Skrabec, et al. conducted a survey in 1997 with a sample randomly drawn from 2,000 ISO-registered companies and a matched sample (size, industry, and sales) of non-ISO companies. Table 14.8 enumerates the top five actual benefits of ISO 9000 certification according to this survey.

**Table 14.8**   Top 5 actual benefits of ISO 9000 certification

| | *Benefits* | *Per cent agreeing* |
|---|---|---|
| 1. | Improvement in documentation | 84.5% |
| 2. | Improvement in quality awareness | 77.4% |
| 3. | Improvement in operating standards | 74.5% |
| 4. | Improvement in perception of product quality | 64.7% |
| 5. | Everyone's responsibility became more clear | 63.7% |

*Source*:   Skrabec, et al. (1997).

### Clauses and Sub-clauses of ISO 9001: 2010

An organization willing to have ISO certification needs to fulfil the requirements as shown in the brief summary of clauses 4 to 8 of the year 2010 version of ISO 9000 in Fig. 14.38. The organization is required to establish a quality management system (QMS) which is the basis of control for the critical activities of an organization which demand a systematic approach, that is, quality management. For an organization going for ISO 9000 certification for the first time, an external audit is conducted by ISO 9000 certifying bodies. The quality system of the organization is audited against the 5 clauses of the standard. If no non-conformances are found, certification is granted to the company, which is valid for 3 years. After this duration, for renewing the certification, again an external audit by the auditors of the certification bodies is required. As pointed out in Clause 8.2.2 of the standard, internal quality audits have to be conducted by the organization from time to time in order to ensure that the quality system is maintained in the future. The internal quality audits can be performed by the trained employees of the organization, who have received formal training in conducting the quality audit. In case the organization does not have trained employees for conducting the internal quality audit, external

An organization willing to have ISO certification is required to establish a quality management system.

The quality management system provides a framework for ensuring that the entire organization is involved in ensuring quality in every sphere of activity.

auditors may be hired. In the subsequent paragraphs, we give a brief summary of the five clauses of ISO 9001: 2010.

***Quality management system (Clause 4)***  As seen in Fig. 14.39, this clause of ISO 9001: 2010 has two sub-clauses: general requirements (4.1) and documentation requirements (4.2). The general requirements are concerning whether the organization has a well-written quality management system (QMS) implemented or not. This documented QMS would ensure that a long-term strategy with respect to quality management is in place in the organization. Over a period of time, the organization must ensure that the QMS is improved further continually. The QMS provides a framework for ensuring that the entire organization is involved in ensuring quality in every sphere of activity. If the organization is outsourcing some of its processes, formal procedures should be there to control the quality issues in relation to outsourced processes. The QMS should be in accordance with all the clauses of the standard.

The documentation requirements of the standard expect the organization to have a written-down quality policy and quality objectives. The quality policy is the long-term strategic quality plan, while the quality objectives are comparatively short-term (e.g., annual objectives), and have to be in line with the quality policy. It is also expected that the organization maintains six mandatory records, namely, procedures for control of documents, control of quality records, internal audit, control of non-conforming product, corrective action, and preventive action. A document called 'quality manual' is also to be maintained. This manual is usually structured according to the various clauses of the standard, while elaborating about how it is configured according to the unique requirements and business processes of the organization. Control of documents is a sub-clause here. It is to be ensured that any document is to be approved for adequacy before issuing. Also, updating and re-approval of documents should have proper control procedures. The documents should be clearly legible and should be easily found at the appropriate location for use. Obsolete documents, if any, should be removed as soon as possible to avoid any sort of confusion. The sub-clause on the control of records demands that records that provide objective evidence to the auditors should be legible, easily identifiable, and retrievable. Here, the records have been separated from the regular documents because these are the forms, etc. to be filled after conducting certain activities and serve as objective evidence for the auditors.

***Management responsibility (Clause 5)***  This clause of ISO 9001: 2010 is based upon the saying of quality guru Edwards W. Deming that no quality management programme can be successful without the full commitment of the top management of the organization. The sub-clause on management commitment demands that the top management should provide evidence that it is keenly interested not only in the development and implementation of the QMS, but also in its improvement. It is expected that the top management conducts management reviews at regular intervals of time, and the minutes of such reviews should be recorded so as to become objective evidence that aid the auditors in verification.

The sub-clause on customer focus expects the top management to determine continually the requirements and expectations of the customer and take appropriate measures to satisfy these. The quality policy sub-clause is based upon ensuring that the quality policy should be in line with the purpose of the organization and should be flexible enough to be modified, if the management reviews demand so. It should be communicated properly and understood by the employees of the organization, so that they may direct their actions towards the achievement of the quality objectives.

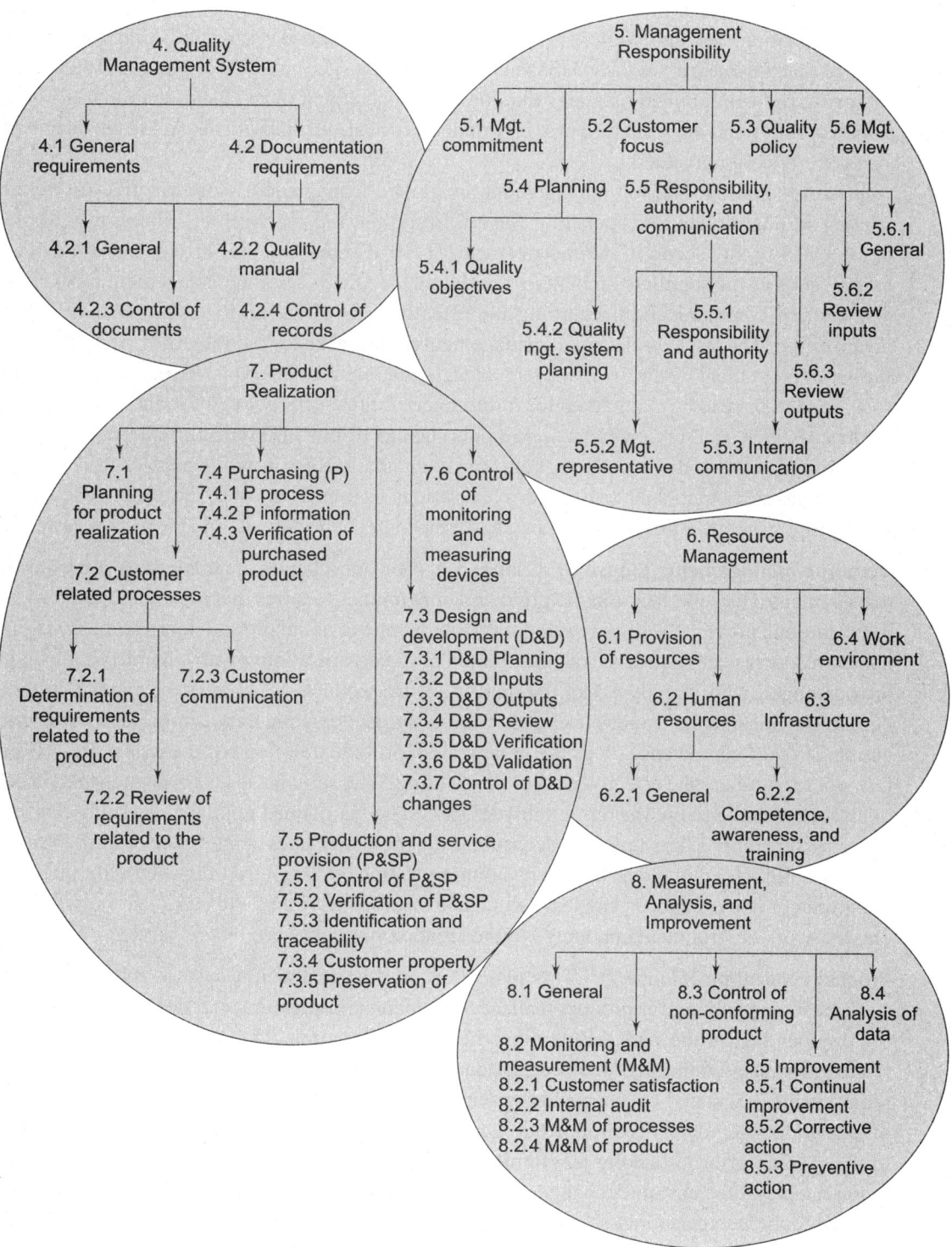

**Fig. 14.39** Various clauses and sub-clauses in ISO 9000: 2010

First, the sub-clause on planning involves establishing measurable quality objectives for the relevant functional areas (such as marketing, HR, operations, finance, etc.) and levels of the organization. Second, while planning any changes in the QMS, establishing whether it is ensured that the integrity of the QMS is maintained or not. The next sub-clause on responsibility, authority, and communication states that the top management must ensure that quality-related responsibilities and authority are properly defined for various individuals and departments and are properly communicated.

It is expected that the top management appoints a management representative for matters relating to quality. He is responsible for informing the top management about any problem in the QMS or any scope in its improvement. He is also responsible for liaison with external parties, such as the suppliers, in matters relating to the QMS. The top management must ensure that internal communication regarding the effectiveness of the QMS takes place within the organization. The last sub-clause on management review asks for the review of the QMS for its further improvement by the top management at regular planned intervals. Also, proper records of such reviews have to be maintained for future reference (especially for the auditors for objective evidence). Each such review must seek inputs such as results of internal or external audits, the status of corrective and preventive actions, recommendations for improvement, etc. Each review should generate outputs such as decisions and actions on improvement of the effectiveness of the QMS, improvement of product according to the customer expectations, and the resources needed.

*Resource management (Clause 6)*    There are four sub-clauses in this clause on resource management. The sub-clause on the provision of resources requires that the organization should determine and provide the resources required to implement, maintain, and improve the QMS. The human resources sub-clause seeks the attention of the organization towards identifying whether the personnel, who directly affect the quality of the product, are competent enough in terms of qualifications, skills, experience, etc. If there is a gap existing between the desired and the current level of competence, does the organization provide training to these employees? If yes, how does it measure the effectiveness of the training? The sub-clause also demands that records of all such training to the various employees should be maintained regularly. The sub-clause on infrastructure emphasizes upon the determination, provision, and maintenance of infrastructure such as building, equipment, transport, communication, etc. required for achieving quality in the product to be produced. The last sub-clause on work environment seeks that organizations create a work environment conducive to the creation of quality product or service.

*Product realization (Clause 7)*    This clause on product realization has six sub-clauses. The sub-clause on planning for product realization demands for planning and developing processes for product realization and maintaining the relevant records. The sub-clause on customer-related processes emphasizes the need for determining requirements specified by the customer, requirements not stated by the customer but necessary for the intended use of the product, or other statutory/regulatory requirements. The organization must review the requirements related to the product prior to making a commitment to the customer to supply the product. If some requirements of the customer change on a later date, the relevant documents must be amended and the concerned personnel should be made aware of such changes. The organization should establish proper communication channels with the customer to know about product information, amendments (if any), customer feedback, complaints, etc.

The next sub-clause is on design and development (D&D) and it seeks that the organization answer questions such as the following.

- How does the organization plan the D&D stages of the product and how does it manage the interface between the groups of individuals involved in this process?
- Are the responsibilities assigned clearly in this process of D&D?
- What are the inputs required in D&D? Are proper records maintained for the same?
- Does the output of D&D provide appropriate information for purchasing, production, service provision, and product characteristics for its safe and proper use?
- Is the D&D process reviewed, verified, and validated?
- Are there established procedures for identifying changes in D&D?

The sub-clause on purchasing ensures that the organization has proper procedures and criteria for evaluation and selection of suppliers. The organization must establish proper controls on the suppliers in accordance with the extent to which the sourced component will have an effect upon the quality of the final product. The purchasing information should describe the characteristics and specifications of the product to be purchased from the suppliers. The organization should establish procedures for the verification (inspection) of the supplies made by the supplier. It can also get into contracts with suppliers, whereby the inspection activities have to be performed by the supplier at his premises according to the procedures stated in the contract.

The production and service provision sub-clause instructs the organization to plan its production and service provision and accordingly execute the plan. Procedures must be established to verify and validate the processes for production and service provision. Does the organization have established procedures to identity and trace back the components used in the final product? This is necessary in situations where the final product may have to be recalled for correction due to customer complaints and the whole batch of the product may have the same manufacturing defect (say, due to faulty component, faulty equipment used, etc.). Here it is also necessary to mention the batch number of production on every unit of the final product for identification and traceability. If a customer's property is under the organization's control, does the organization have procedures to identify, protect, and safeguard it? This is applicable, for example, to post sales service organizations for consumer durables, which have to keep the goods of the customers with them for some duration during correction. Similarly, the intellectual property of the customer should also be treated as customer property. The organization should have suitable procedures for the preservation of the product during internal processing and during delivery to the intended destination. This includes identification, handling, packaging, storage, and protection.

The last sub-clause focuses on the control of monitoring and measuring devices. The organization should establish procedures for the calibration of monitoring and measuring instruments. The instruments should be protected from damage and deterioration during handling, maintenance, and storage. When some equipment is found to be non-conforming, the organization should have established procedures for appropriate action on any product affected due to some measurements done previously. If some software is used in measurement and monitoring devices, is there a procedure to confirm its ability in this regard?

> The organization should have established procedures for monitoring, measurement, analysis, and improvement to demonstrate the conformity of the product.

**Measurement, analysis, and improvement (Clause 8)**   The organization should have established procedures for monitoring, measurement, analysis, and improvement to demonstrate the conformity of the product and to continually

Product release and service delivery should not take place till all the planned arrangements are satisfactorily completed and the authorized person approves the release of the product.

improve the effectiveness of the QMS. These procedures include the use of statistical techniques, but the extent of their use must be determined. Under the sub-clause of monitoring and measurement, the organization must assess and monitor customer satisfaction using the methods established by it. The organization must conduct internal audits at regular intervals by using an audit team comprising members who have been selected to ensure objectivity and impartiality of the audit process. The internal auditors (most of the time employees of the organization) should not be allowed to audit their own work area. The responsibility of correcting the non-conformities found in the internal audits of an area without undue delay should be given to the management responsible for that area. The follow-up activities to the audit must include verification of the actions taken and reporting of the verification results. Various QMS processes should be monitored and measured regularly. Similarly, the characteristics of the product manufactured should also be monitored and measured at appropriate stages of the product realization process. Product release and service delivery should not take place till all the planned arrangements are satisfactorily completed and the authorized person approves the release of the product.

The next sub-clause deals with the control of the non-conforming product. The organization must ensure that the non-conforming products are identified to prevent their unintended use or delivery. If the non-conforming product is corrected, it should be subjected to re-verification to demonstrate conformity with the requirement.

The sub-clause on analysis of data recommends the collection and analysis of data to demonstrate the suitability and effectiveness of the QMS and its continual improvement. The data may be generated as a result of monitoring and measurement and from other relevant sources (e.g., supplier's data).

The last sub-clause focuses on improvement. It emphasizes continual improvement and corrective and preventive action. The organization should strive for continual improvement of the QMS and should take action to eliminate the cause of non-conformities in order to prevent recurrence. The corrective and preventive actions taken should be recorded and reviewed by the organization. See Exhibit 14.5 to learn how ISO 9000 helped in improving the performance of the Bangalore World Bank Health Project.

---

### Exhibit 14.5    Application of ISO 9000 at the Bangalore World Bank Health Project

Taking the example of the Bangalore World Bank Health Project, this section demonstrates how ISO 9000 helps in improving performance.

Bangalore, capital of Karnataka state in India, is one of the fastest growing cities in Asia. Unprecedented migration from backward areas to urban areas during the last decade has resulted in growing slum areas with inherently poor sanitary conditions and meagre health care facilities. In response, the Bangalore City Corporation initiated the 'India Population Project VIII' (IPP VIII) in 1994–95, funded by the World Bank. Its broad objective was to provide free primary health and maternity services to women and children in Bangalore's urban slums, encompassing family planning, health care for mothers, immunization for children, post- and ante-natal care, and ultimately to reduce infant mortality. IPP VIII is a community development programme covering some 8,50,000 urban poor residing in over 500 slums in a city corporation area of 225 sq. km. Highly experienced doctors holding senior positions in the government health sector were appointed as project managers, and community leaders, non-governmental organizations, and link workers from the local areas became involved in health education, and in mobilizing the community

*(Contd)*

*Exhibit 14.5 Contd*

to make use of the services. To date, 55 health centres and numerous maternity homes have been established in city areas close to the slums. Innovative awareness building programmes have helped lay the foundations of the project by educating the target population and encouraging participation in the family welfare and maternal and child health programmes. These activities have included video films, printed material, folk media, and health check-up camps.

## Improving Performance Through ISO 9000

Once IPP VIII had taken shape, the project managers decided that ISO 9002 quality management system (QMS) implementation would improve health centre performance and help achieve project goals. It was also felt that early success with ISO 9002-based systems would act as a stabilizing influence before embarking on more ambitious projects. So, an initial 25 primary health centres were chosen to undergo the process. It was virtually unheard of for government organizations in the country to pursue ISO 9000 certification, particularly in the health care sector. Only a few major private hospitals and diagnostic centres had achieved certification at that time. So, when the project managers announced the certification objective, there were mixed reactions among staff. Some, particularly at top level, welcomed the move, believing it would help encourage a more systematic approach. Many others, including some senior officers, felt that the quality of work in the primary health centres was already fairly high and that ISO 9000 systems would not bring any significant improvement. Middle level employees were initially concerned that their documentation workload would increase substantially. A number of lower level staff were already worried that the flexibility they enjoyed in remote villages would be a thing of the past when posted to urban areas under the scrutiny of senior officers. They felt that ISO 9000 implementation would demand greater accountability. However, most of the medical officers in charge of the health centres were on contract employment, and saw an opportunity for their services to be regularized in government jobs if they showed sufficient commitment to the certification process. At the same time, there was a desire at the top and middle levels to make the IPP VIII health centres stand apart from other government units, be perceived as highly service oriented, and distance them from the stigma of apathy and inefficiency generally attached to government organizations. More than anything else, the respect accorded to project officers and the organizational discipline they established helped generate staff enthusiasm for ISO 9000 certification. This did not mean that problems were brushed aside. They were painstakingly addressed by project managers who used their experience to find effective solutions. The World Bank also closely monitored the programme.

Some service quality elements drawn from ISO 9000 were dropped because of inadequate infrastructure and the hierarchical constraints of a government institution in making even small changes, for example, to modify or improve a prescribed format. Subsequently, the implementation and problem solving phase took about four months.

### Audits and Review

A group of selected medical officers in charge of some of the centres were trained as internal quality auditors. Practice audits were used to help them prepare for the real thing. Technical audits carried out in a few centres by recognized experts in community medicine and witnessed by the trainee auditors identified numerous weaknesses, ranging from inadequate knowledge in some areas to poor implementation and practices.

These included practices not fully in line with procedures, child immunization schedules and post-natal cases not monitored effectively, need for further improvement in immunization practices including vaccine storage, incomplete information recorded on antenatal cards, emergency kits incomplete or containing out-of-date drugs, inadequate follow up of high risk pregnancies, and monthly staff meetings that failed to cover quality issues or progress towards objectives.

Senior officers were shocked to find that such problems existed despite extensive training and periodic technical inspections. Audit findings were discussed with project managers and the centres. All identified problems were investigated and appropriate corrective actions were taken. This was the 'moment of truth' which prompted significant re-training of personnel concerned and reinforcement of the need for continual monitoring and improvement. Subsequently, two rounds of internal quality audits were carried out at all centres by the trained auditors, first on technical aspects only and then on the system itself. Again, all discrepancies and observations were discussed by those concerned. This information sharing and pooling

*(Contd)*

*Exhibit 14.5 Contd*

of knowledge led to common solutions, consistency of practice, and enabled individual centres to anticipate problems before they occurred. We then carried out independent audits of all primary health centres to assess both system and technical aspects. While most of the earlier non-conformities had been eliminated, problems included poor monitoring of performance against immunization targets, crude birth rate, infant mortality and maternal morbidity statistics, inconsistencies in identifying high-risk pregnancies, and inadequate monitoring of the activities of field staff. These issues were discussed by project managers and all centres and necessary corrective measures were implemented.

**Problems Faced**

Achieving certification was not entirely smooth sailing. Considerable difficulties and problems were encountered. For example, project managers repeatedly assured employees that they were already doing good work and all that was required for certification was to maintain appropriate records. Such over simplification proved counterproductive. Workers were lulled into a false sense of security, and it took considerable effort later on to alert them to the reality of the situation. There was the feeling at certain levels that as the health services are provided free of cost, the target population should be content with the treatment they receive. To change such attitudes, everybody was given a docu-ment explaining their duties and responsibilities in clear, unambiguous terms and provided further explanation in open forums. The importance of each individual's contribution, however simple, was strongly emphasized. In addition, the sense of individual self-fulfilment and recognition, and the benefit to customers in achieving organizational goals, was highlighted.

There was little appreciation of the process linkages and interactions. Individual activities were perceived as 'stand alone' which led to inadequate performance monitoring and measurement. The concepts of process approach and systems approach were communicated to improve overall effectiveness. The perception of insufficient time for the additional work in achieving ISO 9002 implementation was widespread. Therefore, it was emphasized that quality was not a 'bolt on' addition, but an integral part of the organization's activity. New personnel brought into the system midstream added a new dimension. This called for repeat training programmes on a number of occasions. But, in retrospect, this helped ensure uniformity and consistency of practices and a greater in-depth understanding of the requirements of ISO 9002.

All 30 primary health centres were successfully certified in accordance with ISO 9002 at the first attempt, and became the first multi-site state agency project in India to do so.

*Source:* Ramachandran (2002).

# ISO 14000

ISO 14000 is a generic standard primarily concerned with 'environmental management'. This refers to the steps an organization takes to minimize harmful effects on the environment caused by its activities, and to continually improve its environmental performance. The Bureau of Indian Standards (BIS) had formulated a standard called IS 13967: 1993 on the environment management system (EMS) before ISO 14001 came into existence. The Indian Constitution contains provisions for environmental protection through its Articles 48A and 51A (g). Figure 14.40 shows the clauses and sub-clauses of ISO 14001.

# COPC-2000

COPC-2000 is a certification mark of Customer Operations Performance Centre Inc., USA, and this standard was created in 1995–1996. World majors such as Microsoft, Compaq (now a part of Hewlett Packard), Intel, Novell, Dell, American Express, L L Bean, and Motorola were among the development team of this standard for improving the level of service provided by the customer service providers (CSPs). This standard is based upon the United States' Malcolm Baldrige

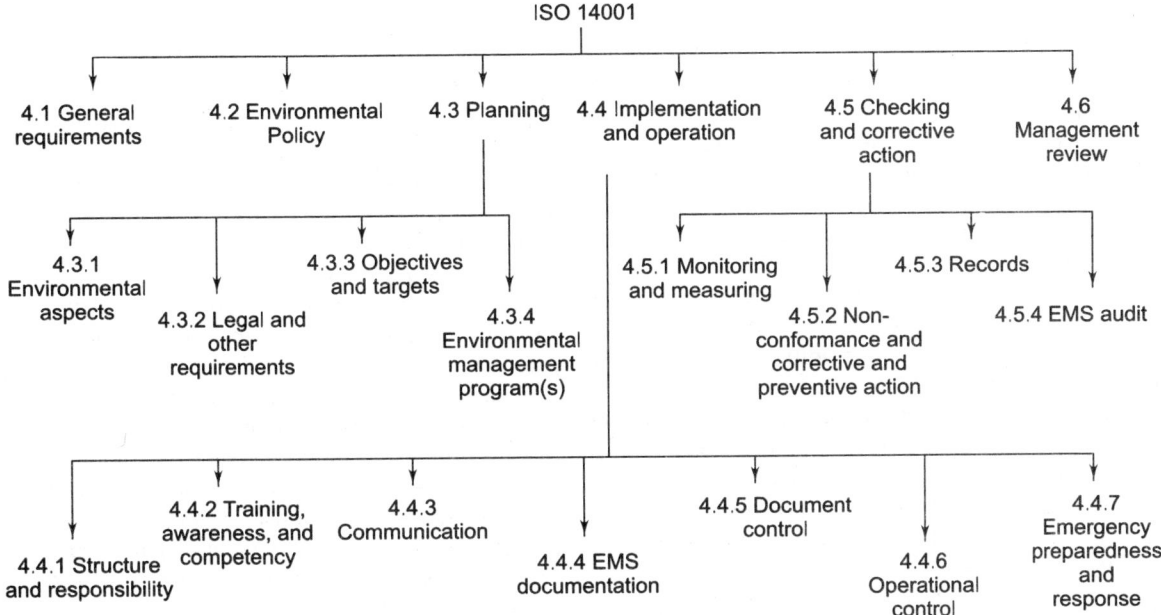

**Fig 14.40** Clauses and sub-clauses of ISO 14001

National Quality Award. However, a few changes were incorporated keeping in view the unique requirements of this industry. The CSP industry is composed by inbound and outbound customer contact centres (popularly known as 'call centres', that interact with customers using telephone, email, web, text messaging, or traditional mail or fax for providing services such as technical support, reservations, and operator services), business process outsourcing (BPO) organizations (providing services such as records management, claims processing, and new account set up and activation), fulfilment centres (providing services such as warehousing, light assembly, picking, packaging, and shipping), remittance processing centres (providing credit card payment services), field service operations (dispatching service personnel to customer locations for repairing or replacing products covered under warranty/service contracts) and collection/recovery services (contacting customers to recover funds). The certification process typically takes 9 to 18 months to complete and involves a rigorous audit by COPC to determine how well a CSP organization meets its client obligations as well as the requirements of the COPC-2000 Standard. The Gold version of this standard is slightly more advanced compared to its Base version as it contains some extra sub-clauses that have raised the performance bar for the CSP organizations keeping in view the rising international competition.

ICICI OneSource (now Firstsource Solutions Ltd), one of India's leading third-party BPO service providers and a member company of ICICI Bank, India's largest private sector bank, became the world's first BPO service provider to achieve COPC-2000 CSP Certification for back-office processing. In addition to back-office processing services, ICICI One Source also received full (COPC) Customer Operations Performance Centre certification for its inbound customer contact centre services.

# Summary

Quality is defined in two ways—*fitness for purpose* and *conformance to specifications*. The fitness for purpose criterion is suitable only in the design stage of the product. The conformance to specifications criterion is suitable in the rest of the stages of a product, namely, engineering, manufacturing, distribution, and after-sales service. The quality of a product has various dimensions such as performance, features, reliability, appearance, etc. Quality has costs such as the costs of preventing defects, detecting defects, scrap/rework, and warranty claims.

Quality gurus Deming, Juran, Feigenbaum, Crosby, and others, emphasize on the need to make quality an organizational issue rather than confining it to a particular department. This approach to quality management is called *total quality control* or *total quality management*. Quality has to be ensured at every stage of the transformation process. Thus, the raw material and finished goods must be inspected using *acceptance sampling*.

During the production process, *statistical process control* (SPC) should be used to ensure that whenever a variation takes place in the process, it is immediately detected and corrected. Various types of control charts, such as the $\mu$ chart, $\bar{R}$ chart, $p$ chart, and $c$ chart, are used in SPC. Most organizations operate at the three sigma quality level, but companies such as Motorola and GE have saved billions of dollars by implementing the Six Sigma quality level. *Six Sigma* is a rigorous application of statistical methods in the whole organization in order to measure and decrease variations in any process critical to the quality of the product.

Quality guru Taguchi suggested that the customer is concerned more with the overall variation between the targeted value and the specification limits, rather than the difference between a variable just inside or just outside a specification limit. Thus, there is a compelling need to reduce the variations in a process as much as possible because the customers are becoming more and more demanding.

Quality standards like *ISO 9000* are being used by organizations as a marketing tool in addition to enhancement in the quality levels of the product. These standards provide a basis to start the process of continuous improvement in an organization.

# References

Barney, M. 2002, 'Motorola's Second Generation', *Six Sigma Forum Magazine*, May.

Deming, W. Edwards 1943, *Statistical Adjustment of Data*, Dover, New York.

http://www.toyota-central.com/safety.html, accessed on 1 February 2013.

ISO survey of ISO 9001: 2000 and ISO 14001 Certificates–2003, ISO Central Secretariat, Geneva, Switzerland.

Madhavan, N. 2012, 'Ploughing ahead', Business Today, 23 December, http://businesstoday.intoday.in/story/case-study-punjab-tractors-success-after-mahindra-took-it-over/1/190220.html, accessed on 4 February 2013.

Maynard, M. 2010, 'An apology from Toyota's leader', *New York Times*, http://www.myties.com/2010/02/25/business/global/25toyota.html?_r=0, 24 February.

Nimwegen, Johan Van and Brian H. Kleiner 2000, 'Harley-Davidson motor company', *Management Research* News, vol. 23, no. 7/8.

Parasuraman, A., V.A. Zeithaml, and L.L. Berry 1988, 'SERVQUAL: A multiple-item scale for measuring customer perceptions of service quality', *Journal of Retailing*, vol. 64, no. 1, pp. 12–40.

Ramanathan, S.K. 2004, 'A cut above the rest', Business Standard, 10 February, http://www.business-standard.com/india/news/a-cut-aboverest/184511/, accessed on 1 February 2013.

Ramachandran, D.V 2002, 'Bangalore World Bank Health Project benefits from ISO 9000', *ISO Management Systems*, May–June.

Skrabec, Q. R., T.S. Ragunathan, S. Rao, S. and T. Bhal Bhatt 1997, 'ISO 9000: Do the benefits outweigh the costs?', *Industrial Management*, Nov–Dec, vol. 39, no.6, p. 26

Tadikamala, P. 1994, 'The confusion over Six Sigma quality', *Quality Progress*, November, pp. 83–85.

Venkatarman,S. 2005, 'Haircut? Head to Asia's only ISO certified saloon', 30 September, rediff.com, http://www.rediff.com/news/2005/sep/30hair.htm, accessed on 1 February 2013.

# Keywords

**Acceptable quality limit (AQL)** If the proportion of defectives in a lot is equal to or less than the AQL, the consumer will have to definitely accept the lot.

**Acceptance sampling** is a method of ensuring that the inputs, such as raw materials, parts, components, labour skills, etc., are of desired quality levels.

**Assignable causes** are causes such as a worn-out tool, mistake on the part of a worker in processing an item, and improper adjustment of the machine.

**Consumer's risk ($\beta$)** is a risk due to sampling variations of a lot having proportion defectives more than LTPD being accepted by the consumer.

**Control limits** are certain limits established inside the specification limits in order to ensure that these limits are never exceeded.

**ISO 9000** is a series of international quality standards, which serves as a guidance to suppliers and purchasers for the minimum requirements of a quality system.

**Lot tolerance per cent defective (LTPD)** If the proportion of defectives in a lot is equal to or more than the LTPD, the consumer will definitely reject the lot.

**Process capability ratio (PCR)** is defined as the ratio of the difference between the two specification limits to the Six Sigma spread of the process population distribution.

**Producer's risk ($\alpha$)** is a risk due to sampling variations of a lot having proportion defectives less than AQL being rejected by the consumer.

**Quality control** is defined as maintaining requisite standards in products or services.

**Quality** is defined as the degree of excellence.

**Random variations** are certain variations caused by the inherent nature of a process.

**Six Sigma** quality initiative, very briefly, means going from approximately 35,000 defects per million operations, which is average for most companies, to fewer than four defects per million in every element in every process that a company engages in every day.

**Specification or tolerance limits** are limits set by the manufacturer at the design stage of a product or specified by a customer for the value of a variable characteristic of a product.

**Statistical process control (SPC)** is a method of ensuring the quality of a product during the transformation process.

**Total quality control** is an effective system for integrating the quality-development, quality-maintenance, and quality-improvement efforts of the various groups in an organization, to enable marketing, engineering, production, and service at economical levels which allow for full customer satisfaction.

**Type 1 errors** take place when the process is in control but the QC manager is trying to find some assignable causes. This error leads to wastage of effort, time, and money in finding an assignable cause which in fact does not exist.

**Type 2 errors** take place when the process is out of control but the QC manager is not looking for any assignable causes. This error is harmful to the quality system, as some defective products may be produced during this time as long as the process is out of control.

---

## CASE STUDY I

## 'Pure for Sure' with Bharat Petroleum

In November 2005, Manjunath, a 27 year old Area Sales Manager of Indian Oil Corporation Limited, (IOCL), was shot dead in Gola Gokrannath in Lakhimpur Khiri district of Uttar Pradesh, reportedly after he blacklisted a petrol pump for stocking adulterated oil. An Indian Institute of Management (IIM), Lucknow graduate of the 2001 batch, Manjunath is said to have discovered 3,000 litres of adulterated petrol and diesel at the Mittal petrol pump in the area. Manjunath had seized the petrol pump in September, forcing it to close down for almost a month. However, a month later, the pump started operating again, prompting him to conduct a surprise raid. He had taken samples of fuel to check for adulteration. On 19 November, he went back to Mittal petrol pump for inspection. He left the petrol pump at 6:00 pm but returned around 9:30 pm, after realizing that he had left some equipment behind. It was then that the petrol pump owner decided to take his revenge. Adulteration and cheating on quantity are common in small towns and rural petrol stations. Officials are often part of such malpractices, however, since Manjunath refused to follow the pattern, he was punished in the most severe manner. Manjunath had earlier warned several other petrol pumps in the area to clean up their act or face action. The gruesome murder of a young man has brought into focus the flaws in the system that can make one's job dangerous.

The Centre for Science and Environment (CSE), a Delhi-based non-governmental agency, did an independent assessment of the fuel adulteration problem in the National Capital Territory of Delhi (NCT) and the National Capital Region (NCR) following a directive from the Environment Pollution (Prevention and Control) Authority (EPCA) under the Supreme Court order dated 22 November 2001. EPCA was directed by the Supreme Court to constitute an agency, which would independently carry out random inspection at petrol pumps, oil depots, and tank lorries in Delhi and give a report with regard to the quality of petrol and diesel. CSE started working on this project on 20 December 2001 and submitted the first draft to the EPCA on 2 February 2002. The findings of CSE confirmed that adulteration is rampant, but it is difficult to detect.

**Tests are inadequate to detect adulteration**

The current fuel quality specifications and testing methods for fuel quality monitoring as prescribed by the Bureau of Indian Standards (BIS) are not adequate to catch adulteration.

## Failure of laboratories

CSE had deliberately sent three adulterated diesel samples for testing to check if these would show up in the tests prescribed for BIS standards. CSE mixed kerosene with diesel in the following proportions—10, 15, and 20 per cent. The Society for Petroleum Laboratory (SFPL) was able to detect only the sample contaminated with 15 per cent kerosene but declared the samples with 10 and 20 per cent kerosene contamination as conforming to all the BIS specifications of diesel. The only parameter in which the sample contaminated with 15 per cent kerosene failed is sulphur content.

BIS specifies a broad permissible range for each fuel parameter which allows sufficient margin to cushion some amount of adulteration without violating the specifications. This essentially means that checking for compliance with fuel quality standards does not necessarily imply testing for adulteration. Since it is possible to adulterate without violating the standards, the tests carried out by the laboratory as specified by BIS do not detect adulteration.

Since fuel adulterants belong to similar hydrocarbon families as that of automotive fuels, though of varying composition, some amount to mixing is possible without changing the overall parameters of the fuel specifications. Unless tests are designed to track this variation as evidence for adulteration, a wide gamut of adulteration will never be caught. Both kerosene and light diesel oil, which are the most popular adulterants for diesel, are so similar in chemical structure of diesel that these mix with almost no aberration in the properties of automotive diesel fuel. However, experts point out that prolonged use of such a mix may impair engine performance and raise emissions. Moreover, just not the environmental consequences but also the misuse of government pricing policy and subsidy are of equal concern too. Illegal use of subsidized kerosene affects the country's economy.

Detecting adulterants in petrol is difficult under the current BIS specifications. An intelligent mix of adulterants can be mixed with petrol such that the outer limits of the specifications are not exceeded. CSE found that it is possible to manipulate BIS specifications. For instance, 91 octane petrol can be adulterated with 15 per cent low aromatic naphtha and still meet the minimum limit of 88 octane. Even if we consider 89 octane petrol, it can still take 6 per cent naphtha mix. However, 10–15 per cent adulteration can be immensely profitable for the retailers. By mixing only 15 per cent naphtha with petrol a retail outlet can reap more than ₹25,000 profit per day.

## Sulphur content

CSE compared the fuel specifications of different batches of fuels as recorded at the Mathura refinery of IOCL, Bijwasan depot (the fuel terminal in Delhi) where fuel comes through a pipeline from the Mathura refinery and the retail outlets. IOCL provided the detailed fuel specifications spanning over a month (3 December 2001 to 7 January 2002). Any abnormal variation from the refinery specifications can be an indicator of something having gone wrong. CSE was stunned to note inexplicable variation in sulphur levels in fuel from the refinery to the retail end.

While the sulphur level in diesel at the refinery level ranges from 400–480 parts per million (ppm), it reduces to a uniform consistent level of 200 ppm at the depot level. In the case of petrol, it is even more dramatic. While the Mathura refinery specifications show a range between 350 ppm and 450 ppm, the depot specification shows a ridiculously low level of 110 ppm.

In comparison, sulphur content in diesel at many retail outlets varies between 200 ppm and 300 ppm, and astonishingly, nearly 3 per cent of the samples record a 100–149 ppm level—a level which refineries do not even produce. The petrol sulphur specifications at the retail end vary between 200 ppm and up to 500 ppm sulphur content. Clearly, there is a problem if fuel sulphur at the depot and the outlet is so dramatically lower than what refineries are producing. The oil industry attributes this to the margin of reproducibility of the test methods that are allowed when tests are conducted in different laboratories under the current test methods. According to them, it could be due to instrumentation and calibration problems. When quizzed by CSE further, they dismissed the problem as very common and of no serious consequence, as long as the standards were met. However, according to CSE, any test method with reproducibility variation of as much as 75 per cent as the case appears to be, is not acceptable.

## Possibility of adulteration during the transportation of fuels

Table 14.9 shows the comparison of prices of fuels and possible adulterants. There is considerable scope for malpractice during transportation of fuel, as oil companies do not take responsibility for the quality of fuels during transit. There are two oil depots or terminals in Delhi that receive petroleum products from refineries—Bijwasan and Shakurbasti. While the Bijwasan depot is connected with a pipeline to the Mathura refinery and receives products almost entirely from that refinery, Shakurbasti receives products from refineries at Panipat, Koyali, and from the Jamnagar refinery of Reliance Petroleum Ltd. Shakurbasti receives the entire stock in tankers. From the two depots, tank lorries carry products to the respective retail outlets. Maintaining strict quality control is necessary during fuel transit. According to the estimates available from the state level coordinator, around 10 per cent of the tankers of the total fleet are owned by the oil companies for fuel transportation. The rest are all contracted out to transporters. Among these, retail outlet owners or petroleum dealers in the region own nearly 50 per cent of the tankers. The industry guidelines on transport discipline, governs the contractual agreement with the transporters. This section describes the various key issues in the transportation of fuel.

**Table 14.9** Comparison of fuel prices of fuels and possible adulterants

| Sr. no. | Fuels and solvents | Price |
|---|---|---|
| **Transportation Fuels** | | |
| 1. | Diesel | ₹17.90 per litre |
| 2. | Petrol | ₹28.00 per litre |
| **Industrial Solvents** | | |
| 1. | SBP spirit/SBP solvents | ₹21.00 per kg |
| 2. | C-9 Solvent/Raffinates | NA |
| 3. | C-6 Raffinates | NA |
| 4. | Pentane | ₹42.06 per kg |
| 5. | Cixon | NA |
| 6. | Solvent 90 | ₹26.40 per kg |
| 7. | Hexane | ₹17.12 per litre |
| 8. | Heptane | NA |
| 9. | Resol | NA |
| 10. | NGL (Non-fertilizer Naphtha) | ₹12.95 per kg |
| 11. | Mineral Turpentine Oil | ₹14.26 per litre |
| 12. | Aromex | ₹18.26 per kg |
| 13. | Iomex | NA |
| 14. | Furnace Oil (Fuel Oil) (Not available in NCT) | ₹8.93 per litre |
| 15. | Light Diesel Oil | ₹12.95 per litre |
| 16. | Kerosene | ₹15.00 per litre |

Note 1: Prices are indicative may not be exact market prices in 2002

*Source*: Compiled from the following:

1. Solvent, Raffinate and Slop order (acquisition, sale, storage and prevention of use in automobiles) 2000
2. Naphtha Control Order (GSR 518)

## Industry quality control manual

The Industry Quality Control Manual (IQCM) absolves the oil companies from taking any direct responsibility of quality of the product being delivered to the retail outlet.

The responsibility of the oil companies for its products ends as soon as the loading in the tanker is completed. According to the IQCM, 'transporters shall be responsible for providing tank lorry fit in all respects to carry petroleum products and transporting/ delivering the same in good condition, as per specifications, to the dealers/consumers/receiving locations and shall be held accountable for any malpractice/adulteration enroute. The transporters are held responsible for any malpractice enroute.'

While the design and fittings of the tank lorry is approved by the Department of Explosives, the calibration certificate is issued by the Department of Weights and Measures. The onus of inducting trained crew to carry fuels also lies with the transporters as per the stipulations of the Motor Vehicles Act, and the driving licence of the driver is endorsed by the road traffic authorities. The discretion of taking any action against a particular tank lorry or fleet owner lies solely with the quality control department of the oil company. The IQCM states that a 'tank lorry caught for having indulged in malpractices shall be immediately suspended by the location-in-charge. However, an investigation shall be conducted as per the procedure of the company, and approval of the appropriate authority obtained before the tank lorry is blacklisted.' The manual further states that the period of the ban shall be two years. The decision for lifting the ban again lies with the oil company imposing the ban. A list of all such blacklisted or banned tank lorries showing their registration numbers along with their engine and chassis numbers shall be prepared and circulated to other regions and other oil companies so that tank lorries banned by one location or oil company are not engaged by other locations or oil companies. The locations are supposed to maintain all records of all such blacklisted or banned tank lorries with all relevant details in a register and exchange this information with their counterparts in other oil companies periodically.

## Responsibility for loading and unloading

The oil industry does not even take responsibility for loading and unloading of tankers. The bulk transport contract agreement of IOCL states that 'the loading of tank trucks at the installation or depot or any other storage points or the unloading thereof will be the sole responsibility of the contractor even though the same is done with the help of the personnel of the Corporation.'

## Sampling

When a tanker is caught having committed adulteration, the companies do not pick up samples to check its quality. The responsibility lies with the district administration. An illustrative case is the recently reported case that CSE investigated in Meerut. The company, Vishal Roadlines, which was caught with adulterated stock, is an authorized transporter of petrol and diesel. This agency had the authority to transport both petrol and diesel to retail outlets and solvents for industrial use. It was supposedly using its workplace to adulterate diesel with kerosene. BPCL officials informed the CSE inspection team that, though the tanker was authorized to transport fuel by the company, it was not the responsibility of the company to check adulteration cases by conducting their own tests.

Serious lapses were noted in the vigilance system. While the visiting team in Meerut observed five tankers at the site that were seized from the accused, the police records showed only two. In fact, local police officials requested the CSE representative not to collect samples from more than two tankers so that it would not create problems later on. The team took samples from three tankers and found the other two empty!

Field investigation shows that fragmentation of responsibility and penalty makes the system more vulnerable to malpractices as there is no clear pressure from within the system to keep the operation clean across the entire supply chain. If all parties across the supply chain are held liable then there would be counter checks on different parties.

## Pilferage to adulteration

The following is a first hand account of fuel pilferage near Bijwasan depot, Delhi. On the morning of 19 January 2002, a team from CSE went near Bijwasan depot of IOCL. The vehicle in which they travelled was parked about 15 metres away from an enclosed area. The gate of this area was marked as Lotus Nursery with white paint. Lotus Nursery is located about 50 metres from the depot of the IOCL. Within a few minutes of parking the vehicle, a truck with the number DL 1GA8370, came near the gate of the nursery and parked itself at the side of the road. Within seconds, about three to four workers came out of the nursery with 50 litre capacity cans and started drawing out fuel from the hoses attached to the tanker. The team could not make out if the locks (of the new locking system) were actually opened or some other mechanism was used to siphon off fuel. However, it was clear that though the tanker was locked, fuel was pilfered. Soon a Tata Indica with the number plate HR 26N4551 came and parked itself near the truck. Some people started filling the Tata Indica from the cans filled with fuel drawn from the tank lorry. The team could not see whether the driver of the Indica paid any amount for the fuel.

Meanwhile, other tank lorries coming out of the depot with numbers DL 162498 (belonging to Dalip Service Station), HR 474848, and HR 387081, also came and stood outside the nursery gate and the same operation of fuel being drawn out from the hoses of the lorries was carried out. About 15 minutes after this, another lorry with number HR 81G 41715 came out from inside the nursery, which had a number of cans, similar to those in which fuel was being filled from the fuel tankers. These cans were covered with a blue plastic sheet. The entire chain of events took place within a span of just 25 to 30 minutes. While returning from the site, the team spotted a policeman under whose nose this illegal activity was taking place. He seemed to be monitoring the whole process. The CSE team only saw pilferage, but if this is possible, then adulteration should be possible as well.

Very little is known about the impact of adulterated fuel on emissions and vehicle engine components. Maruti Udyog Limited (MUL), one of the largest car seller in India, has provided some information on the effect of adulterated fuel on the vehicle.

A large number of fuel pump failures on the Maruti model of Esteem were reported in 1998. MUL, therefore, collected fuel samples from affected vehicles. The samples were sent to Indian Institute of Petroleum (IIP), Dehradun, a petroleum research organization and an accredited certification agency for mass emissions tests for vehicles in India. IIP initially confirmed that all samples met BIS requirements. However, on further investigation, it found that some paint solvent was mixed with the fuel. This shows how initially adulterated fuel met the specifications

and adulterant was not detected in routine tests. In May 2001, similar problems occurred in Nagpur, Maharashtra. Four-stroke engines reported failures due to poor octane rating of the fuel. Similar problems have been reported in the North-East too and it is again suspected to be a case of fuel adulteration.

The automobile industry feels that oil companies do not respond to clarifications or guidance sought on problems like this. It feels that fuel quality assurance from oil companies shall have a definite impact on manufacturers to extend warranties. The automobile industry is worried that if Euro III emissions standards make on board diagnostic II (OBD) requirements mandatory, then adulteration would pose a serious problem. To offer any technology to meet this requirement, consistency of fuel, and the right quality is important. These controls should be in place before OBD is mandated. The automobile industry demands that fuel testing laboratories be totally independent in nature to ensure proper checks.

## BPCL's 'Pure for Sure' campaign

At the time of India's independence, Burmah–Shell had a dominant presence in India, with a market share of 67 per cent. However, nationalization of oil majors was inevitable and Bharat Petroleum Corporation Limited (BPCL) was formed in 1976 consequent to the nationalization of the erstwhile Burmah–Shell Oil Storage and Distribution Company, and Burmah– Shell Refineries. There were many constraints imposed by the government and it was little surprise that the company's share collapsed to a meagre 15 per cent. After a period of three years of further decline and inaction, BPCL embarked on an effort to resurrect itself. This involved extensive representations to the government to increase its share of allocation of new business opportunities. In today's competitive world, it is acknowledged that it is the human factor that gives a company its edge. Acting with far reaching vision and foresight, BPCL has consistently nurtured its employees and picked the best entrepreneurs as its dealers. It has thought of customers in an era of public sector dominance where customers were taken for granted. It has several 'firsts' and 'largest'—it was the first to introduce premium fuel and first bottled gas, largest loyalty programme, and largest convenience store network to name a few.

BPCL's efforts have all along been to build a superior understanding of customer needs and relentlessly work towards fulfilling these needs. The company is consciously working towards providing added value to customers, both in fuel and non-fuel areas. Initiatives, some of them pioneering efforts, have been introduced based on need gaps articulated by consumers during focus group discussions and extensive market research.

BPCL recognized that the basic need of the customer is the quality and quantity of fuel. As one of the major initiatives in this direction, it triggered a virtual movement at select retail outlets (petrol pumps) to guarantee pure quality and correct quantity to its customers. This 'enhanced fuel proposition' movement, which is the sign of a new revolution, has been gaining nation-wide momentum after its initial launch at a few centres. Retail outlets enrolled in the movement display the 'pure for sure' signage very prominently at the outlet. It is this out-of-box thinking of the company that saw its per station monthly throughput grow at least 20,000 litres more than the industry average.

This is done on the basis of certification of quality and quantity for supply point (depot), distribution (lorry tankers), and dispensing point (retail outlets) by an audit check by Germany-based TUV (TÜV Rheinland Sicherheit und Umweltschutz GmbH). It is also possible to de-certify any retail outlet at any point of time. At the retail outlet level, the following criteria are taken into account to certify a dealer or retail outlet as 'Pure for Sure':

1. Seminars and workshops are held with dealers to make them aware of the need for assuring quality to the customer.
2. Special meetings are held with the dealers to discuss the inefficiencies at the retail outlets and how they can be removed. For example, traffic jams in front of pump, problems with dispensing units, and so on.
3. Delivery salesmen at the outlet are trained by BPCL officials and surveys are conducted to evaluate their adherence to prescribed rules and regulations.
4. Inspection of stocks for the outlets not participating in the 'Pure for Sure' campaign is conducted once every quarter. The participating dealers' stocks are checked every 45 days.
5. Samples are collected every month from the outlet and they are tested for every specification in BIS including octane rating.
6. Delivery accuracy meters fixed at the outlet, which are checked every fortnight by officials.
7. Mystery audits are conducted by mystery customers, who are asked to go and visit the outlet, and give their feedback to BPCL about the particular outlet.

## Monitoring the supply chain

At the depot, tankers are not filled using conventional overhead manhole type filling covers. Tankers are filled through the process of bottom loading since it minimizes losses due to evaporation and leakage. Apart from this, BPCL is in the process of installing a complete vapour recovery system at the Bijwasan depot and also at one of the retail outlets as a pilot project to minimize losses caused by evaporation.

All lorry tankers carrying fuel to these retail outlets are specially designed to integrate devices to minimize chances of pilferage and adulteration on the way. For example, these tankers employ a six point sealing system and an Abloy locking system. Apart from this, all the important joints from where pilferage may occur are welded so that, if anyone tampers with them, these will immediately break, (for example, the flag joint and discharge line). Specially designated people from the company, who also carry out surprise checks along the way, physically handle all locks. Every time a lorry tanker decants in a 'Pure for Sure' retail outlet, two samples are drawn for testing. The frequency at which samples are drawn from retail outlets is also increased and a strict check is kept on the samples. All samples are drawn and tested by officials from TUV, which is an independent laboratory.

## BPCL Ghar

BPCL's efforts began with re-modelling and upgrading its retail outlets to world-class standards in 1996. Retail outlets have been equipped with state-of-the-art modern infrastructure, including the multi-product dispensers to pre-set price and quantity of fuel and electronic air gauges to check the precise inflation of tyres. Attractive canopies are suitably designed to provide shelter and adequate lighting of the forecourt at most retail outlets.

On the non-fuel front, BPCL has introduced the 'errand mall' concept successfully at select markets. Branded as *In & Out*, these malls offer the customer a broad range of facilities and brands to choose from. Courier services, cybercafé, laundry, photo studio, music, fast food, greeting cards, bill payments, movies/entertainment tickets, ATM, etc. have made BPCL's retail outlets a rewarding experience for motorists.

BPCL Ghar is a one stop proposition with all the comforts to meet the needs of 'truckers and tourists'. These outlets are located on all major highways across the country. There are dedicated BPCL officers at these outlets. The outlets personalized service all through the day with a host of facilities. Hence, the drivers call it a 'home away from home'.

At BPCL Ghars, customers can experience many convenient facilities such as dhaba services, secure parking space, essential items, emergency assistance, medical facilities, messaging service, smart route assistance, and many more.

*'Pure for Sure'* Fuel All the Ghars offer the customer guaranteed quality and quantity of fuel. Therefore, customers can set aside their worries about compromising on the quality and quantity of fuel.

*Secure Parking* BPCL understands that it is very important to secure customers' loaded trucks. Hence, Ghars provide the customers with a safe parking space free of cost. Customers can rest aside their worries for loaded trucks while their driver eats, sleeps, or shops with BPCL.

*Shop, Eat, or Simply Relax* Truckers and tourists can avail of many more convenient facilities. They can eat hygienic food at the Dhaba at extremely affordable prices. They can even sleep and relax in the resting cots, and bathe and refresh themselves, if they wish to. In fact, they can also shop for essential items such as toiletries at these outlets.

*Health Care Facilities* At select BPCL Ghars, drivers are provided with free medical consultations for minor problems during certain timings. They can also benefit from first-aid medication at the BPCL Ghar outlets whenever the requirement arises. To complement this facility in remote areas, BPCL has launched innovative telemedicine services known as Sanjivani at select Ghars. With this proposition, customers would not be required to search for medical assistance while on the highway, the company will serve them with world-class consultancy and advisory services from one of the best hospitals in India.

*Emergency Assistance* With BPCL Ghar, drivers need not worry about unforeseen situations. In case an emergency does arise, these outlets have arrangements to provide truckers and tourists with assistance such as auto-electrical repairs, automobile mechanic, crane, ambulance, insurance agent, and even RTO assistance.

*SmartFleet Dak Service* Today contacting a driver using SmartFleet has become very easy. An email message is sent to the driver through the SmartFleet Dak service, which is presently available at select BPCL Ghar outlets. The drivers can also contact their transporters through email from these outlets.

*Smart Route Assistance* Using Smart Route Assistance, it has become easy for drivers to navigate their way. With SmartFleet Route Service, all the Ghars are equipped with an e-atlas of India. Customers are helped to reach their destinations. They can avail host of information such as the name of the place from the pin code, location of important spots, etc. from this e-atlas.

To make life more convenient and rewarding for customers, BPCL has introduced the *Petro card* for individual customers and the SmartFleet card for fleet owners. Using the Petro card entitles the customer to PetroMiles under the PetroBonus rewards programme. BPCL has also pioneered the concept of convenience stores at select petrol pumps. These stores operate under the name Bazaar. These stores provide a wide range of convenience items and fast food to customers in a clean, air-conditioned, and friendly environment.

BPCL is leading the show in terms of providing excellence service, innovative concepts, and above all, a surety of quality in all its products. These initiatives will go a long way in ensuring its success in the wake of competition from new private sector competitors such as Reliance, which is opening its exclusive fuel outlets with a high degree of professional service.

### Discussion Questions

1. If you were in place of Manjunath, how would you take action against the defaulters, while ensuring your own safety?
2. BIS specifies a broad permissible range for each fuel parameter which allows sufficient margin to cushion some amount of adulteration without violating the specifications. What is your reaction to this statement?
3. What are your recommendations to avoid adulteration of fuel during transportation?
4. Why have the other petrochemical companies such as, IOCL, HPCL, IBP, and Reliance avoided using an explicit quality-related campign as the one initiated by BPCL?

---

CASE STUDY II

# Harley-Davidson

Harley-Davidson Motorcycle Company was established in 1903. It soon became a leading manufacturer of motorbikes in the US and the neighbouring countries. After World War II, Harley-Davidson had a monopoly in the motorbikes market due to the closure of its main rivals. It was easy, therefore, for the company to increase its market share and production, but the quality of the product became a secondary consideration. The problems for Harley-Davidson started only when Honda entered the US market and started to cut into its market share. Using the total quality management principles of Edward Deming, Honda's products were increasingly better in terms of quality at a time when Harley-Davidson's products were low on the quality front. By 1981, Honda almost pushed HarleyDavidson to the verge of closure.

The management of Harley-Davidson was wondering how Honda was able to manufacture motorbikes much better in quality and at a much lesser cost compared to its products. Initially it attributed this to the cheap Japanese labour, huge advertising budgets, and dumping practices on part of Honda. Over a period of time, Harley officials found the three real reasons for Honda's success— kaizen, just-in-time (JIT), and extensive use of statistical methods to measure quality. Using JIT, Honda was turning its inventory 20–30 times a year compared to Harley-Davidson and other American companies at that time, who were turning their inventory only four times a year. Harley had by now understood how fewer inventory turns affect product cost and quality. Earlier in 1978, it had tried to implement the quality circles concept in its organi-zation, but could not sustain it for a long time, in complete contrast to kaizen's continuous improvement concept evolved and successfully implemented by Japanese companies.

The top management of Harley-Davidson was very conscious of *employee involvement* programmes having had a bad experience with *quality circles*. They did not want to thrust upon their workers various types of programmes for inventory reduction, quality improvement, work methods improvement, cost reduction, etc. simultaneously leading to confusion. Instead, they focused on a single most important agenda—quality. They felt that this umbrella term contained in an implicit way all the other improvement programmes. This simple goal of achieving quality in all the spheres of activity was something which every worker could relate to easily. Improving quality in everything you do gives a sense of pride and commitment. Harley-Davidson's managers were so focused on their goal of quality that they were not opposed to making investments in order to improve the quality of their product. If new equipment could increase productivity and quality in addition to fostering a climate of contin-uous improvement,

the company would go for it even without financial justification.

Another important decision on the part of Harley-Davidson officials was not to send rigid rules and regulations to their multiple facilities with diverse manufacturing environments. It was felt that doing so will kill employee participation in the quality initiative. The management provided the plant managers only with the direction in which the company was willing to go and told them the principles and concepts to be applied, but gave them the freedom to do it in their own way. This was a drastic shift from the white-collar and blue-collar discrimination existing in American companies at that time.

A typical example of this radical change in the thinking of top management can be demonstrated with an example of the company's plant at York. The company wanted to have the paint facility enclosed at the plant to keep it cleaner and have proper lighting. The employees made the designs of the enclosures themselves and asked the management if they could choose the colour of its walls. The usual response would have been that we have to follow the standard colour scheme, but the management responded with consent to the workers' request. This resulted in a clear demonstration of the management's commitment to change and the workers reciprocated in the same way.

Harley-Davidson started the employee involvement group (EIG) in order to solve quality problems. It was the same *quality circles* programme which was a disaster earlier. This time the company gave workers the liberty to choose a suitable name for the concept. The employees at the Milwaukee engine plant opted for 'quality circles', while the York assembly plant workers decided to call this as 'employee involvement groups'. Now, the company has a full-fledged employee involvement programme, in which the company formally trains employees in problem-solving, though participation is voluntary. Harley-Davidson does not quantify the cost benefits as a result of these EIGs, as it does not want to shift the company's focus from quality to cost reduction. Harley's turnaround has been highlighted in a big way in terms of its financial recovery and manufact-uring improvements, though what is not reported is the vision of Harley-Davidson in promoting employee involvement (Nimwegen and Kleiner 2000).

### Discussion Questions

1. Is it right on the part of Harley-Davidson to focus only on quality improvement by even overlooking cost considerations?

2. Up to what extent has Harley-Davidson been successful in the international and domestic US market compared to Honda according to you?

3. Is the EIG a unique innovation of Harley-Davidson?

## CASE STUDY III

# Made in China

The last decade witnessed dramatic changes in the manufacturing scene the world over. Outsourcing, shifting of plants from the West to the East, and sourcing from vendors globally is all part of the game. This period has seen the emergence of China as the 'factory of the world', with Chinese products stacking the racks in the supermarkets of every nook and corner of the world.

In the past, Japan enjoyed the legendary status as the manufacturing powerhouse. But, with the rise in Chinese products across the world, Japan's status is gradually diminishing.

The success of China, however, has been blemished by quality-related furore in different parts of the world. The year 2007 saw a series of product recalls and import bans on Chinese products by the West. The trouble started in March 2007, when a Canadian company, which sourced pet food from Chinese manufacturers, complained of animals dying after consuming the products. Investigations revealed the presence of melamine, a chemical used in the production of plastics, in the pet food.

Reports came about Chinese manufacturers admitting that they added melamine to increase the nitrogen count in the pet food, which makes the protein content of the food higher.

Soon, American toy-manufacturing companies, such as RC2 Corporation and Mattel, recalled all their toys sourced from China, due to excessive presence of lead in the paint used on the toys. However, Li Changjiang, the then chief of China's quality watchdog, defended the products.

He commented that the whole issue was politically motivated and blamed the client companies of not being able to detect exactly which toys had dangerous levels of lead content, thus rejecting the whole lot from China.

Strangely enough, Mattel later admitted that the recalls made by them were due to the flaws in designs of the toys given by them to the Chinese manufacturers and not due to manufacturing faults.

Another blow to China came from Europe, where two of its toothpaste brands were detected to contain diethylene glycol (DEG) as a substitute for glycerol, which is used to thicken the toothpaste. Glycerol is a safe ingredient used by prominent manufacturers worldwide; however, DEG is hazardous to health and may result in mass poisoning.

In July 2007, China executed the former chief of its State Food and Drug Administration (FDA), Zheng Xiaoyu, on charges of taking bribes from Chinese drug manufacturers, who manufactured sub-standard drugs leading to several deaths in the country. The year 2008 proved to be equally difficult for China, when the milk-products scandal broke out. Six infants died; about 900 were admitted to hospitals; and more than 3,00,000 affected people were identified after consuming Chinese milk products.

Several countries instituted a ban against importing Chinese milk products. The presence of melamine in these products was found to increase the protein count, which actually increased the chances of kidney stones in its consumers.

Paul Midler, the author of *Poorly Made in China: An Insider's Account of the Tactics behind China's Production Game*, has tried to identify the root cause of the overall quality problems in China. In his view, the current quality woes in China are a result of 'relationship imbalance and asymmetrical information sharing' between American buyer companies and Chinese suppliers. The Chinese suppliers try to cut corners to save costs, while the American buyers pressurize them to meet high quality standards at reasonable prices.

More often than not, the Chinese suppliers know that they are compromising quality to save costs, but they let their American buyers presume where the problems are. The real issue in his view is the reduction of specifications by the Chinese and devising ways to 'fool' laboratory test equipment and inspection processes.

### Discussion Questions

1. Critically analyse if the root cause of quality problems in China is quality planning or quality control.

2. Suggest ways in which the Chinese government could tackle the issue of relationship imbalance and asymmetrical information sharing.

3. Explore if incomplete designs and lax specifications from American clients have landed the Chinese companies in soup.
4. Recommend ways through which the Chinese government should increase awareness in Chinese companies about the value of quality over cost.
5. Guide the Chinese government in taking suitable measures to rebuild trust and confidence in the world, for its products.

## Objective Questions

### Choose the correct option

1. Quality is defined as fitness for purpose by
   (a) W. Edwards Deming
   (b) Joseph M. Juran
   (c) Philip B. Crosby
   (d) Armand V. Feigenbaum
2. Quality is defined as conformance to specifications by
   (a) W. Edwards Deming
   (b) Joseph M. Juran
   (c) Philip B. Crosby
   (d) Armand V. Feigenbaum
3. Which one is not a dimension of quality?
   (a) safety
   (b) features
   (c) cost
   (d) performance
4. Deming summarized his preaching into
   (a) 10 points
   (b) 16 points
   (c) 12 points
   (d) 14 points

### State True or False

5. Quality control is defined as maintaining requisite standards in products and services.
6. Quality assurance is same as quality control.
7. Quality standards are basically categorized into generic and industry-related standards.

### Fill in the blanks

8. _____ limits are established inside the specification limits.
9. The steps in Six Sigma implementation are abbreviated as _____.
10. The process of performing a check raw materials, components, and parts supplied by vendors is called _____.

## Concept Review Questions

1. Define quality and quality control. How is quality control different from total quality control?
2. What are the various dimensions of quality? What are the costs of quality?
3. Name the prominent quality gurus? What are the sayings of W. Edwards Deming in relation to total quality management?
4. What is statistical process control? How is it different from acceptance sampling? What are type I and type II errors?
5. Explain the difference between specification limits, control limits, warning limits, and natural tolerance limits.
6. What is process capability ratio? What do you understand by the off-centring of a process?
7. Explain Taguchi's concept of cost of variability.
8. What is Six Sigma? How is it implemented?
9. How many types of sampling plans are possible in acceptance sampling? Explain each of them.
10. How can we make an acceptance sampling plan strict? What is an ideal OC curve?
11. What are the producer's and consumer's risks in acceptance sampling? How are these related to acceptable quality level and lot tolerance per cent defective?
12. What are quality standards? Why are these required?
13. What are the various types of certification in ISO 9000? What are the major clauses of ISO 9001?
14. What is ISO 14000? It is relevant to the Indian industry?

## Numerical Problems

1. Precision AutoShafts is a manufacturer of steel shafts and supplies its products to various automotive companies. It has received a contract from a major auto company for shafts of diameter 15 mm

± 0.30 mm. In order to control the quality of shafts, Precision takes ten samples of size 3 at regular intervals of 1 hour. The data of diameter measurements obtained is given in Table 14.10. Prepare a stable mean of a sampl means ($\mu$) chart and a mean range $\overline{R}$ chart for the given data.

**Table 14.10**

| Time | Sample no. | Diameter of shaft (mm) | | |
|---|---|---|---|---|
| | | Unit 1 | Unit 2 | Unit 3 |
| 8 a.m. | 1 | 15.0034 | 15.0167 | 14.9975 |
| 9 a.m. | 2 | 14.9925 | 15.0287 | 15.0002 |
| 10 a.m. | 3 | 14.9822 | 14.9759 | 15.0427 |
| 11 a.m. | 4 | 15.2238 | 15.1756 | 15.1182 |
| 12 noon | 5 | 14.8896 | 14.9992 | 15.2761 |
| 1 p.m. | 6 | 14.982 | 14.9775 | 14.9743 |
| 2 p.m. | 7 | 15.1002 | 15.1165 | 14.9749 |
| 3 p.m. | 8 | 15.0034 | 14.9812 | 14.9672 |
| 4 p.m. | 9 | 14.9853 | 14.9993 | 15.1728 |
| 5 p.m. | 10 | 15.2549 | 14.9536 | 14.9831 |

2. National Power Corp. has commissioned a new power plant at Vellore. During the initial run of the plant, the following observations (see Table 14.11) were made by drawing 10 samples (of sample size 4) drawn at equal intervals of 1 hour.

**Table 14.11**

| Sample No. | Voltage of power generated (Volts) | | | |
|---|---|---|---|---|
| | Observation 1 | Observation 2 | Observation 3 | Observation 4 |
| 1 | 211 | 223 | 217 | 215 |
| 2 | 215 | 218 | 215 | 214 |
| 3 | 228 | 224 | 217 | 222 |
| 4 | 214 | 218 | 221 | 212 |
| 5 | 220 | 225 | 221 | 223 |
| 6 | 216 | 222 | 216 | 213 |
| 7 | 223 | 233 | 235 | 230 |
| 8 | 214 | 218 | 223 | 220 |
| 9 | 205 | 214 | 230 | 211 |
| 10 | 212 | 218 | 224 | 221 |

Create stable sample means and sample range charts by using the data given in Table 14.11. Also create the natural tolerance limits.

3. For the data of Problem 1, find the stable NTLs and the $PCR_k$ for off-centring.

**Table 14.12**

| Sample No. | No. of defective ICs | Sample No. | No. of defective ICs |
|---|---|---|---|
| 1 | 9 | 9 | 4 |
| 2 | 11 | 10 | 17 |
| 3 | 4 | 11 | 15 |
| 4 | 1 | 12 | 8 |
| 5 | 0 | 13 | 5 |
| 6 | 9 | 14 | 3 |
| 7 | 12 | 15 | 2 |
| 8 | 10 | | |

4. Fifteen samples of 100 units each are taken from a consignment of integrated circuits (ICs) manufactured by Apollo Electronics based at Bangalore. Table 14.12 shows the result of inspection of these 15 samples. Prepare a stable fraction defective ($p$) control chart for the data.

5. Calcutta Glass is a manufacturer and supplier of window panes for a major constructions group. In order to control the quality of its window panes, its QC manager selects 15 panes at random and inspects each of them for manufacturing defects. The results shown in Table 14.13 are obtained. Prepare a stable $c$ chart based on the data.

**Table 14.13**

| Sample No. | No. of defective ICs | Sample No. | No. of defective ICs |
|---|---|---|---|
| 1 | 3 | 9 | 9 |
| 2 | 12 | 10 | 11 |
| 3 | 21 | 11 | 10 |
| 4 | 3 | 12 | 11 |
| 5 | 7 | 13 | 8 |
| 6 | 8 | 14 | 7 |
| 7 | 3 | 15 | 2 |
| 8 | 1 | | |

6. A pen manufacturing company has identified three opportunities for a pen to be defective: a blunt nib, leakage in the ink tube, and crack in the plastic shield of the pen. In a batch of 1,00,000 pens, the company has found 105 defects. Calculate the defects per million opportunities.

7. Prepare an operating characteristics curve for sample size 50 and acceptance number 3.

# Project Assignment

Search the Internet and your library for the sayings of the following four quality gurus: W. Edwards Deming, J.M. Juran, Philip Crosby, and A.V. Feigenbaum. Conduct a group discussion on the topic *quality gurus—similarities and differences in their sayings.*

**15**

# Demand Forecasting

## Learning Objectives

After reading this chapter, you will be able to answer the following questions:
- What is demand forecasting? Do organizations require it?
- What are the various methods of demand forecasting?
- Are there specific methods for demand forecasting of new products?
- In which situations is a particular method of demand forecasting more suitable than the other methods?
- How can we measure the errors in demand forecasting?
- How can we control the forecasting errors to remain within specified limits?

## Demand Forecasting

Demand forecasting is predicting the future demand of the products or services of an organization. To forecast is to estimate or calculate in advance. Why do organizations require demand forecasting? There are many reasons, as shown in Fig. 15.1. The external environment may be offering opportunities to an organization to maximize its market share, but in the absence of demand forecasting the organization will not be aware of such opportunities. At the same time, certain threats from the external environment, such as a major MNC entering the market with similar products, may not be visible to the organization in the absence of demand forecasting. Otherwise, the organization could prepare for such threats in advance.

If the organization is doing something to increase demand, such as aggressive advertising campaigns, the absence of demand forecasting will result in the organization not knowing the exact impact of such actions in terms of increase in demand. Thus, the organization may not be prepared to reap the maximum advantage of such a situation. Similarly, demand forecasting may help an organization to take counter measures in order to offset the effect of such actions taken by the competitors. We have studied earlier in Chapters 9 and 11 that demand forecasts serve as inputs in these planning processes. Thus, in the absence of demand forecasting, all such plans will be in disarray.

> Demand forecasting is a guiding factor in deciding the capacity and location of a new facility.

Demand forecasting is also a guiding factor in deciding the capacity and location of a new facility being planned by an organization. The capital expenditure on the new facility depends on the capacity of the facility. The staffing decisions should be in line with the demand forecasts for the coming

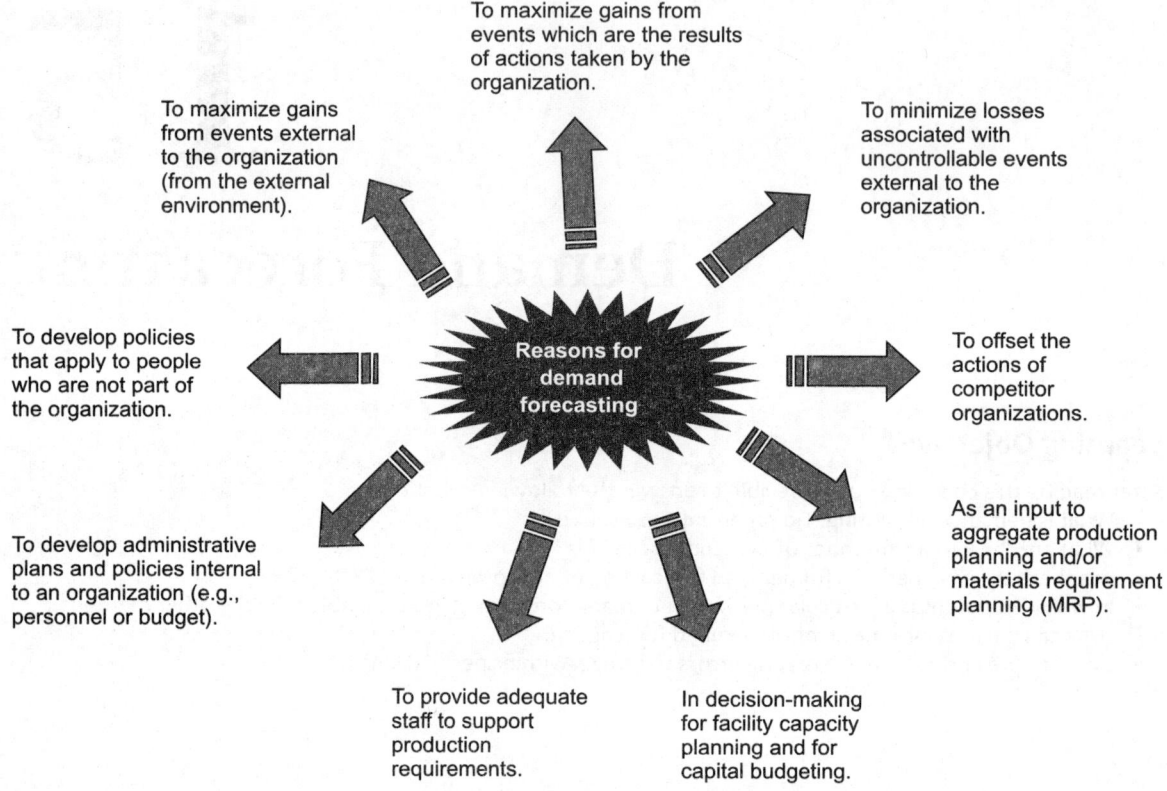

To maximize gains from events which are the results of actions taken by the organization.

To maximize gains from events external to the organization (from the external environment).

To minimize losses associated with uncontrollable events external to the organization.

To develop policies that apply to people who are not part of the organization.

**Reasons for demand forecasting**

To offset the actions of competitor organizations.

To develop administrative plans and policies internal to an organization (e.g., personnel or budget).

As an input to aggregate production planning and/or materials requirement planning (MRP).

To provide adequate staff to support production requirements.

In decision-making for facility capacity planning and for capital budgeting.

**Fig. 15.1**  Reasons for demand forecasting

future. If the forecasts for the future are bleak, retrenchment (lay-offs) of the workforce may be required. Administrative plans and policies are also affected by these forecasts. Low demand forecasts for a particular product indicate less administrative work in some situations, thus requiring the administrative staff to be shifted to other divisions of the company (for product lines experiencing heavy demand). Policies relating to people who are not a part of the organization, for example, suppliers, also depend on demand forecasts. For example, if the demand forecast for a product in the near future is good, the suppliers can expect to have good orders for their supplies from the company.

Demand forecasting may be performed using qualitative methods or quantitative methods, as shown in Fig. 15.2. Qualitative methods are subjective in nature and are at times based upon the judgement of experts. These methods are especially suitable in situations where historical data are not available for quantitative analysis and the forecasts have to be prepared quickly in a short period. We will discuss here various qualitative methods such as customer survey, sales force composite, executive opinion, Delphi method, and past analogy in detail.

In quantitative analysis, there are basically two types of techniques available for demand forecasting. These are *time series analysis* and *causal analysis*. As the term 'time series analysis' suggests, we require a time series of historical demand data with respect to time intervals (periods) in the past to make predictions for future demand. We will discuss in detail the most popular time

> Demand forecasting may be performed using qualitative methods or quantitative methods.

series analysis methods such as simple moving average, simple exponential smoothing, Holt's double-exponential smoothing, Winters' triple-exponential smoothing, and time series forecast by linear regression analysis.

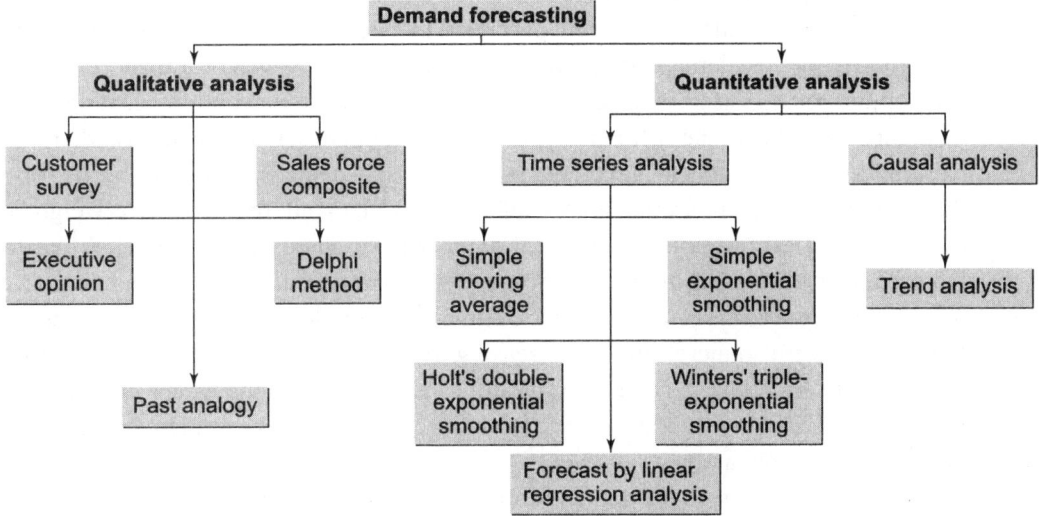

**Fig. 15.2**  Various methods of demand forecasting

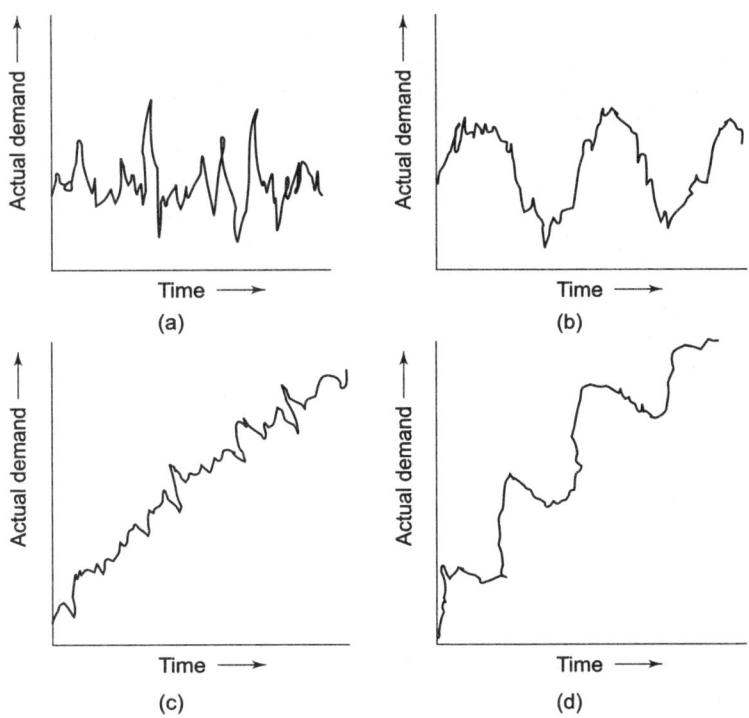

**Fig. 15.3**  (a) No growth/decline trend; no seasonal variation. (b) No growth/decline trend; seasonal variation. (c) Linear growth (or decline) trend; no seasonal variation. (d) Linear growth (or decline) trend; seasonal variation.

Linear regression analysis is a popular method used in the causal analysis approach to demand forecasting.

As the term 'causal analysis' suggests, here we perform demand forecasting using a cause-and-effect relationship. For example, the rent of shops in a locality may be dependent on the level of sales experienced by shops in that locality. Here, the level of sales is the cause of the level of rent of shops in a locality. Similarly, the extent of rainfall in the preceding few weeks can be an indicator of the demand for umbrellas in the coming few weeks. Linear regression analysis is a popular method used in the causal analysis approach to demand forecasting.

Figure 15.3 shows the different types of demand patterns. In situations where the demand patterns in the past do not have any increasing and decreasing trend, that is, only random fluctuations are present around a particular level of demand, the simple (or weighted) moving average method or simple exponential smoothing methods are suitable. When there is no increasing or decreasing trend but there are seasonal variations (note the similar crests and troughs in the curve at regular intervals of time), the simple moving average method is suitable. In situations with an increasing or decreasing trend with no seasonal variations, Holt's double-exponential smoothing is most appropriate. Finally, in situations where there is an increasing or decreasing trend with seasonal variations, we apply Winters' triple-exponential smoothing or linear regression analysis.

Exhibit 15.1 discusses the demand forecasting for cash in ATMs.

---

## Exhibit 15.1    Demand Forecasting for Cash in ATMs of Banks

The amount of cash to be maintained in an automated teller machine (ATM) is meticulously calculated by its associated bank branch. Paul and Mukherjee (2004) highlighted several factors, as follows, that are considered in demand forecasting for cash in ATMs:

- Prevent a stock-out while avoiding unnecessary idle cash in the ATM
- Minimize the lead time to take and fill cash in the ATM
- Minimize the cost of taking and filling cash in the ATM
- Create supply chain architecture (especially when outsourced agencies are involved in the process of taking and filling cash in the ATMs) conducive to the achievement of the previous objectives
- Seasonal factors like weekends and festivals result in higher demand for cash through ATMs
- Banks servicing salary and pension accounts experience more cash withdrawals from their ATMs on the dates immediately after salary/pension is credited in the accounts.

Both time-series and judgemental methods are employed by banks to arrive at this decision. For applying time-series analysis, usually banks use cash-withdrawal data of an ATM for the past three months.

Just before the start of a given month, linear projection of demand for cash through an ATM is done for that month. Such projections are also done for all ATMs combined in a particular region to arrive at trends that are increasing, decreasing, or stagnant. However, such projections are just guiding points, as seasonality and other judgemental factors need to be taken into account for arriving at more accurate forecasts.

Judgemental factors commonly considered by banks in this regard are as follows:

- *Safety margin*, whereby the lead time taken by the banks to send the cash from the branch for loading into the ATM is considered in deciding the amount of cash. For ATMs that are located far off from the branch, the amount of cash loaded should be sufficient for two days of disbursal at the normal disbursal rate through those ATMs. Similarly, for banks that are closed on Saturdays and Sundays, the cash loaded on to the ATMs on Friday should be sufficient to last through the weekend.
- *Cash inflows and outflows* expected from the bank branch, which impact the available cash in the branch at a given point in time.
- The *average volume of transaction* through an ATM per day and its categorization by the

*(Contd)*

*Exhibit 15.1 Contd*

bank branch. Table 15.1 shows a sample categorization.

**Table 15.1** Categorization of ATMs

| Category | Average cash dispensed per day (₹) |
|----------|-----------------------------------|
| A | >7,50,000 |
| B | 5,00,000–7,50,000 |
| C | 1,50,000–5,00,000 |
| D | <1,50,000 |

Limits for cash loading are set by the bank branches according to the categorization done earlier. The methods of setting these limits may vary from bank to bank. Table 15.2 shows an indicative method of setting such limits.

**Table 15.2** Indicative method of setting cash limits for ATMs

| | |
|---|---|
| 'A' Category | 7.5 lakhs × 3 = 22.50 lakhs |
| 'B' Category | (7.5 + 5 lakhs)/2 × 3 = 18.75 lakhs |
| 'C' Category | (5 + 1.5 lakhs)/2 × 3 = 9.75 lakhs |
| 'D' Category | 1.5 lakhs × 3 = 4.5 lakhs |

# Qualitative Methods of Forecasting

There are certain situations in which forecasts have to be prepared quickly without using historical data. The time available is not enough for objectively determining the forecasts using quantitative methods. At other times, historical data may not be available. For example, in the launch of a new innovative product, there is no data available from past experience on the sales of the product. In a country facing economic and political turmoil, the available historical data may become redundant, resulting in qualitative analysis as the only available forecasting method. There are five qualitative methods of forecasting.

### Customer Surveys

It is the customer who determines the demand for a product or service. Therefore, it is but natural to involve the customer directly in the forecasting method. Since it is practically not possible to identify all the potential customers or to contact all the existing customers, sampling of customers is resorted to. While designing customer survey questionnaires, care has to be taken to frame questions such that the true responses of the customers are solicited. Similarly, the implementation and analysis stages of the survey have to be carefully handled to ensure that the conclusions drawn from the survey reflect the exact pulse of the customers. Surveys can be time-consuming and expensive; at the same time, they may provide valuable information about the customers' changing preferences, which may not be easily available elsewhere.

### Sales Force Composite

This approach to forecasting is much less expensive compared to customer surveys. The sales force of a company is in direct contact with the customers. Thus, they may be advised to give their estimates about the likely sales of the product in their region. They may be required to give three estimates of expected demand, namely, the pessimistic estimate (the lowest expected demand), the most likely estimate (having the highest chance of occurrence), and the optimistic estimate (the highest expected demand). The marketing manager may compile these estimates for different regions to arrive at the overall estimate of the demand forecast for the product.

This approach to forecasting has its disadvantages. The sales person's estimates may not be as accurate as customer surveys, which give first-hand information about the customers' current preferences and intentions about the purchase of a product. Sales people, on the other hand, may be influenced by their recent experiences with the sales of a product. For example, if a sales person is experiencing low sales in his region for a prolonged period, he is most likely to give lower forecasts for a product. In addition, if the performance appraisal of sales personnel is linked with achieving sales targets, they are more likely to give lower projections of demand in order to gain incentives later on.

## Executive Opinion

A jury of top executives of the company from different functional areas such as marketing, finance, human resources, production, etc. are brought together to give their opinion about the forecast of a new product to be launched. This approach to forecasting is particularly suitable for new products, which do not have any past history of sales. In such situations, there is no other option except to depend upon the vast experience of these senior executives in providing the forecast for the new product. At the same time, there is a risk that the opinion of any one individual expressed in an impressive manner may overshadow the opinion of other experts. Thus, the responsibility of the forecast arrived at as a result of this approach is spread over the entire group, with less individual accountability to arrive at a correct forecast.

## Delphi Method

This method is named after an ancient Greek astrologer Delphi. In this method, a questionnaire email is sent to experts from various diversified streams, seeking their opinion on the forecast of a (usually highly advanced technology) product. For example, forecasting the year by which only high-bandwidth internet will be used in India and low-bandwidth internet will be almost extinct. This method is different from *executive opinion*, as here the experts may not necessarily be top executives. The experts may be technology forecasters, sales persons with varied experiences in promoting path-breaking high-tech products, etc. The opinions expressed by these experts as responses to the questionnaire are kept anonymous. Thus, even experts on the lower rung of the hierarchy feel free to express their opinion, which may be completely divergent from that of their immediate superiors, who may also be part of the same expert group.

The responses of the experts are compiled and summarized. These responses usually contain many new facts, which were not included in the questionnaire. Thus, a new questionnaire is prepared with a summary of these responses, with a special mention of the extreme views of the forecast compared to the average forecast. This new questionnaire is sent back to the same experts, giving them the discretion to revise their views in the light of the summary. This is done in order to ideally arrive at a consensus forecast. The advantage of the Delphi method is that the opinion of experts based at far-off global locations can be taken without much expense. At the same time, the main disadvantage is that the condition of anonymity of the experts takes away the accountability and responsibility of the forecast so generated.

> In the Delphi method, a questionnaire email is sent to experts from various diversified streams, seeking their opinion on the forecast of a product.

## Past Analogy

For forecasting the sales of a new product, an analogy of the sales growth trends of other existing products may be taken. These products may be substitutes of the new product, complimentary products, or products related to consumers belonging to income groups similar to that being targeted by the new product. For example, a watch manufacturing company launching a designer range of watches may study the buying patterns of customers who patronize fashionable sunglasses or clothes designed by high-profile fashion designers, etc.

# Quantitative Methods of Forecasting

In quantitative methods of forecasting, we will discuss time series analysis first. Later in the chapter, we will discuss the other quantitative method of demand forecasting, namely, the causal analysis.

## Time Series Analysis

As the term 'time series analysis' suggests, we require a time series of historical demand data with respect to time intervals (periods) in the past to make predictions for future demand. Five popular methods are used in time series analysis:

1. Simple moving average
2. Simple exponential smoothing
3. Holt's double-exponential smoothing
4. Winters' triple-exponential smoothing
5. Forecasting by linear regression analysis

Let us discuss each one of these methods one by one.

**Simple moving average**   The simple moving average method of forecasting is suitable under situations where there is neither a growth nor a decline trend, that is, there is a horizontal trend shown by the actual past data used for forecasting. There can also be seasonal variations in this past data. This method involves finding the simple average of the past data used for forecasting. For example, if we have past data of the actual sales of a product for the months of January, February, and March, we take the simple average of these sales figures for the three months. This simple average becomes the forecast for the next month, that is, April. Similarly, when the actual sales data for the month of April is available, we take the average of the sales data for the months February, March, and April to get the forecast for the month of May. Therefore, to arrive at the forecast for a given month, the actual sales data of the three preceding months is considered. Thus, in this example, it becomes a three-month simple moving average. The term 'moving' here means that the data of the most distant period (here month) is discarded as the data for a new period becomes available. In mathematical terms, moving average forecast can be expressed as

$$F_t = \frac{A_{t-1} + A_{t-2} + \dots + A_{t-n}}{n}$$

> The simple moving average method of forecasting is suitable under situations where there is neither a growth nor a decline trend.

where $F_t$ is the simple moving average forecast for the coming period $t$, $A_{t-1}$ is the actual demand in the period $(t-1)$, $A_{t-2}$ is the actual demand in the period $(t-2)$, $A_{t-n}$ is the actual demand in the period $(t-n)$, and $n$ is the number of periods considered in the moving average.

MS Excel has a data analysis tool for finding the moving average. Let us take up an example to understand the procedure of determining the moving average.

### Example 15.1

**Table 15.3**

Kids Toys (P) Ltd is a toy marketing company at Mumbai. The sales figures (in units) of a particular toy during the past 20 weeks are given in Table 15.3. Calculate the four-week and eight-week moving average forecasts for the given 20 weeks.

| Week | Actual demand (units) |
|------|----------------------|
| 1 | 1,634 |
| 2 | 1,821 |
| 3 | 2,069 |
| 4 | 1,952 |
| 5 | 2,178 |
| 6 | 1,597 |
| 7 | 1,834 |
| 8 | 1,852 |
| 9 | 1,771 |
| 10 | 2,014 |
| 11 | 2,395 |
| 12 | 2,683 |
| 13 | 1,936 |
| 14 | 2,076 |
| 15 | 2,103 |
| 16 | 1,699 |
| 17 | 2,387 |
| 18 | 1,854 |
| 19 | 1,521 |
| 20 | 1,726 |

### Solution

In the MS Excel toolbar, click on **Tools**. From the pull-down menu, select **Data Analysis**. If this option is not available, then choose **Add-Ins** from the pull-down menu. A dialog box as shown in Fig. 15.4 appears. Select the **Analysis ToolPak** option and click on **OK**. Now, the data analysis option will become available in the pull-down menu under **Tools**. Upon choosing the **Data Analysis** option, the dialog box shown in Fig. 15.5 appears.

In this dialog box, choose **Moving Average** and click on **OK**. Another dialog box, shown in Fig. 15.6, appears. In this dialog box, there is a small button with an arrow in the text box for **Input Range**. When you click on this button, the dialog box shrinks. Now, on the spreadsheet shown in Fig. 15.7, select cells B4 to B23 (containing the actual demand values). This range is automatically reflected in the shrunk dialog box. Again, click on the small button with the arrow in the **Input Range** text box. The dialog box resumes its original shape again.

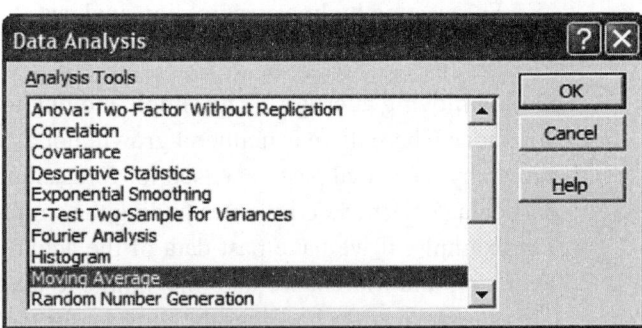

**Fig. 15.5** Data analysis

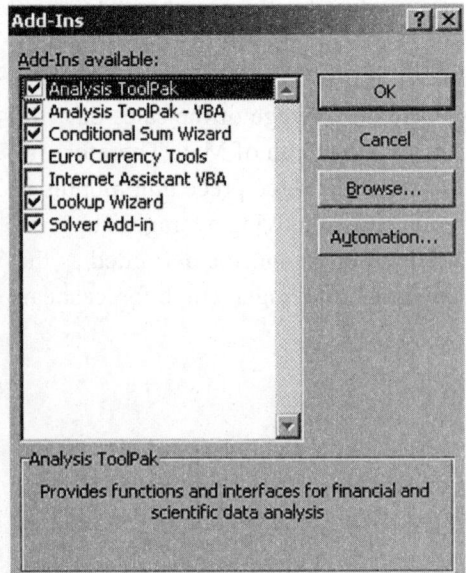

**Fig. 15.4** Add-ins

**Fig. 15.6** The Moving Average dialog box

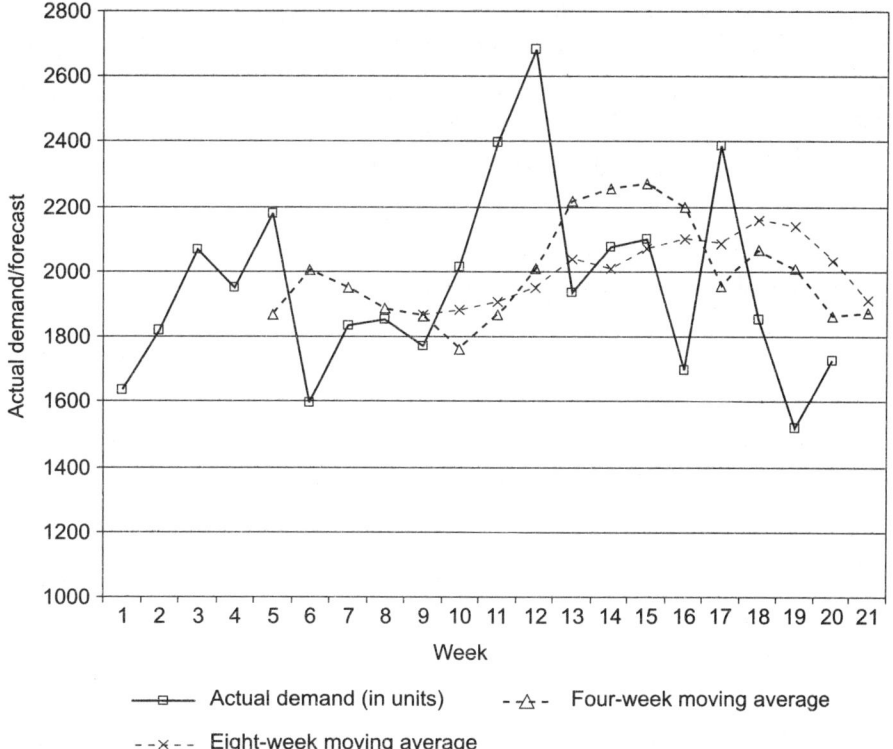

**Fig. 15.7**   Simple moving average

| Week No. | Actual Demand (in units) | Four Week Moving Average | Eight Week Moving Average |
|---|---|---|---|
| 1 | 1634 | | |
| 2 | 1821 | #N/A | #N/A |
| 3 | 2069 | #N/A | #N/A |
| 4 | 1952 | #N/A | #N/A |
| 5 | 2178 | 1869 | #N/A |
| 6 | 1597 | 2005 | #N/A |
| 7 | 1834 | 1949 | #N/A |
| 8 | 1852 | 1890.25 | #N/A |
| 9 | 1771 | 1865.25 | 1867.125 |
| 10 | 2014 | 1763.5 | 1884.25 |
| 11 | 2395 | 1867.75 | 1908.375 |
| 12 | 2683 | 2008 | 1949.125 |
| 13 | 1936 | 2215.75 | 2040.5 |
| 14 | 2076 | 2257 | 2010.25 |
| 15 | 2103 | 2272.5 | 2070.125 |
| 16 | 1699 | 2199.5 | 2103.75 |
| 17 | 2387 | 1953.5 | 2084.625 |
| 18 | 1854 | 2066.25 | 2161.625 |
| 19 | 1521 | 2010.75 | 2141.625 |
| 20 | 1726 | 1865.25 | 2032.375 |
| 21 | | 1872 | 1912.75 |

**Fig. 15.8**   Simple moving average chart

We will find the four-month moving average first. Hence, enter 4 in the **interval** text box. Now, select the **Output Range** as cells C5 to C24. Note that our output will appear up to week 21. This is done intentionally to ensure that the moving average forecast for a week should appear in the same row as the actual demand for that week. To get a chart output, one can click on the **Chart Output** check box.

Now, click on **OK** to get the four-week moving average forecast values in cells C5 to C24. Note that cells C5 to C7 display **#N/A**. This is because MS Excel requires the actual demand forecast for the past four weeks to calculate the forecast for a week. The actual demand for the past four weeks is available only from week 5 onwards, for which MS Excel has generated the forecast. On selecting cell C8, note that **Average(B4:B7)** appears in the formula text box above. This means the cell C8 contains the average of actual demand in weeks 1, 2, 3, and 4. In the same way, we calculate the eight-week moving average forecast for the given weeks in cells D5 to D24.

Now, select the whole table in Fig. 15.7 and click on the chart icon on the Excel toolbar. The chart dialog box guides us through to get the chart shown in Fig. 15.8. Note that the curve for the four-week moving average follows the actual demand trends more closely compared to the eight-week moving average, which smoothes out all the random fluctuations in the actual demand.

**Weighted moving average** In calculating the simple moving average, actual demand data in all the past periods considered are given equal importance. Sometimes it is felt that while finding the moving average, the data in the recent past periods should be given more weight or importance compared to the data in the periods far off from the current time. For example, let us suppose that for a product the actual demand in months 1, 2, and 3 is 20, 30, and 10 units, respectively. For calculating a three-month moving average forecast for month 4, the company may decide to give 50 per cent importance (weight 0.5) to the data in week 3, 30 per cent importance (weight 0.3) to the data in week 2, and 20 per cent importance (weight 0.2) to the data in week 1. Thus, the weighted three-month moving average forecast for week 4 will be given by

$$F_4 = \frac{0.2 \times 20 + 0.3 \times 30 + 0.5 \times 10}{0.2 + 0.3 + 0.5} = 4 + 9 + 5 = 18 \text{ units}$$

Note that the sum of all the weights should always be 1. The general formula for calculating the weighted moving average may be stated as

$$F_t = w_{t-1} A_{t-1} + w_{t-2} A_{t-2} + \ldots + w_{t-n} A_{t-n}$$

where $F_t$ is the $n$-period weighted average forecast for period $t$, $w_{t-1}$ is the weight for the period $(t-1)$, $w_{t-2}$ is the weight for the period $(t-2)$, $w_{t-n}$ is the weight for the period $(t-n)$, $A_{t-1}$ is the actual demand in the period $(t-1)$, $A_{t-2}$ is the actual demand in the period $(t-2)$, $A_{t-n}$ is the actual demand in the period $(t-n)$, and $n$ is the number of periods considered in the moving average.

> In calculating the simple moving average, actual demand data in all the past periods considered are given equal importance.

The weighted moving average gives better forecasts than the simple moving average method, but at the same time is cumbersome in application. Commonly available softwares such as MS Excel, and SPSS do not have the tools for calculating the weighted moving average. In addition, the weights assigned to various periods have to be subjectively decided based on past experience. The simple exponential smoothing method discussed next is more popular in the industry.

**Simple exponential smoothing** Simple exponential smoothing is the most popular forecasting method. It is very simple in application and, in addition, the past data required is limited to just the last period's actual demand and its forecast. In the forecasting methods discussed by us earlier, that is, simple and weighted moving averages, the past data of several periods had to be maintained to forecast for the next period. The forecast using simple exponential smoothing is given by the following equation:

$$F_t = F_{t-1} + \alpha \left( A_{t-1} - F_{t-1} \right) \tag{15.1}$$

Forecast for period $t$ = forecast for period $(t-1) + \alpha$ [forecast error in period $(t-1)$]. Here, $F_t$ is the forecast for period $t$, $F_{t-1}$ is the forecast for period $(t-1)$, $A_{t-1}$ is the actual demand in the period $(t-1)$, $(A_{t-1} - F_{t-1})$ is the forecast error in period $(t-1)$, that is, the actual demand compared with the forecast for period $(t-1)$, and $\alpha$ is the smoothing constant, whose value ranges between 0 and 1.

From Eqn (15.1), it is clear that we require data only for the last period to arrive at the forecast for the next period. Therefore, the data for past periods excluding the most recent one is not required. This method has the term 'exponential' in its name because every period in the past is given a weightage of $\alpha(1-\alpha)^n$, where $n$ represents the number of periods in the past. Hence, $n$ is the exponent used in the weight $\alpha(1-\alpha)^n$ attached if we have to consider data which is $n$ periods away in the past. For example, if we use data which is two periods (say, two months) away from the current time, the weight attached will be $\alpha(1-\alpha)^2$, though we have already seen in the above equation that if the most recent data is available, we do not need any other previous data for calculating the forecast for the next period. Equation (15.1) may also be written as

$$F_t = F_{t-1} + \alpha \left( A_{t-1} - F_{t-1} \right) = \alpha A_{t-1} + (1-\alpha) F_{t-1}$$

We define another constant called the *damping factor $\alpha'$*, which is simply

$$\alpha' = 1 - \alpha$$

Thus, Eqn (15.1) may be written as

$$F_t = (1-\alpha') A_{t-1} + \alpha' F_{t-1} \tag{15.2}$$

MS Excel provides an excellent tool for the calculation of the simple exponential smoothing forecast. Let us take up the data of Example 15.1 to understand the use of MS Excel in this calculation. In the toolbar of MS Excel, click on **Tools** and then select **Data Analysis** from the pull-down menu. The dialog box shown in Fig. 15.9 appears. Choose **Exponential Smoothing** and click on **OK**. The dialog box as shown in Fig. 15.10 appears.

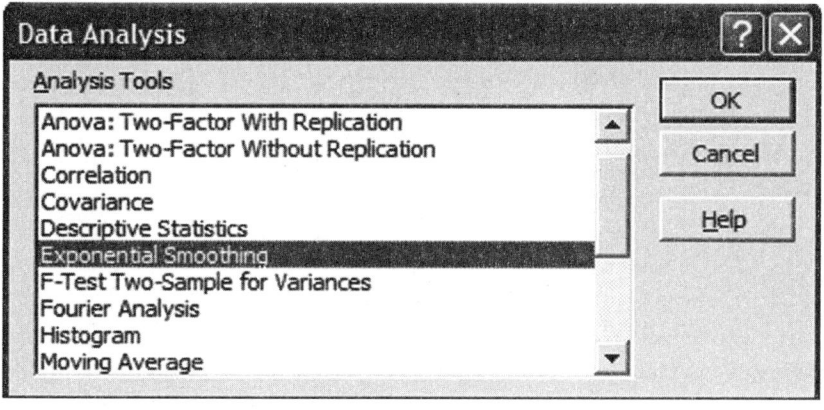

**Fig. 15.9** The Data Analysis dialog box

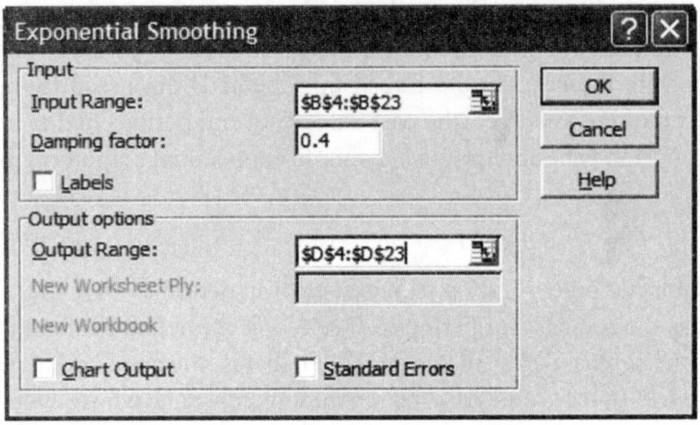

**Fig. 15.10** The Exponential Smoothing dialog box

We have pasted the data for the number of weeks and actual demand (in units) from Table 15.3 as shown in columns *A* and *B* of Fig. 15.11. In the **Exponential Smoothing** dialog box, we choose the **Input Range** as B4:B23 and **Output Range** as C4:C23. Let us assume that the smoothing constant $\alpha = 0.6$. However, in the dialog box, we have to enter the damping factor $\alpha' = 1 - \alpha = 1 - 0.6 = 0.4$. Click on **OK** to get the forecast for $\alpha = 0.6$ as shown in cells C4 to C23 of Fig. 15.11. Similarly, find the simple exponential forecasts for $\alpha = 0.4$ and $\alpha = 0.2$ in columns *D* and *E* as shown in the figure. Select the whole table in Fig. 15.11 and click on the chart icon on the MS Excel toolbar. The chart wizard guides us through to get the chart shown in Fig. 15.12.

On selecting cell C6 in Fig. 15.11, we note that the formula displayed in the formula toolbar is **=0.6\*B5+0.4\*C5**. Here, cell B5 has the actual demand and cell C5 has the simple exponential forecast for week 3. Thus, the calculations done by MS Excel are in line with Eqn (15.2) discussed earlier. In the chart shown in Fig. 15.12, note that the curve for $\alpha = 0.6$ follows the actual demand curve very closely compared to the other curves for lesser values of $\alpha$. In addition, note that the

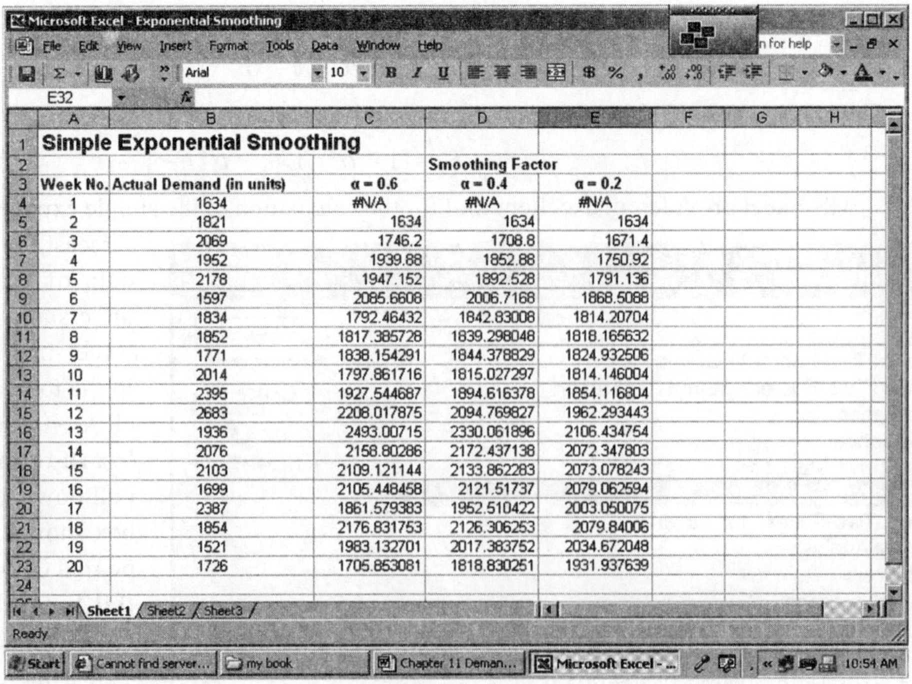

## Simple Exponential Smoothing

| Week No. | Actual Demand (in units) | Smoothing Factor | | |
| --- | --- | --- | --- | --- |
| | | α = 0.6 | α = 0.4 | α = 0.2 |
| 1 | 1634 | #N/A | #N/A | #N/A |
| 2 | 1821 | 1634 | 1634 | 1634 |
| 3 | 2069 | 1746.2 | 1708.8 | 1671.4 |
| 4 | 1952 | 1939.88 | 1852.88 | 1750.92 |
| 5 | 2178 | 1947.152 | 1892.528 | 1791.136 |
| 6 | 1597 | 2085.6608 | 2006.7168 | 1868.5088 |
| 7 | 1834 | 1792.46432 | 1842.83008 | 1814.20704 |
| 8 | 1852 | 1817.385728 | 1839.298048 | 1818.165632 |
| 9 | 1771 | 1838.154291 | 1844.378829 | 1824.932506 |
| 10 | 2014 | 1797.861716 | 1815.027297 | 1814.146004 |
| 11 | 2395 | 1927.544687 | 1894.616378 | 1854.116804 |
| 12 | 2683 | 2208.017875 | 2094.769827 | 1962.293443 |
| 13 | 1936 | 2493.00715 | 2330.061896 | 2106.434754 |
| 14 | 2076 | 2158.80286 | 2172.437138 | 2072.347803 |
| 15 | 2103 | 2109.121144 | 2133.862283 | 2073.078243 |
| 16 | 1699 | 2105.448458 | 2121.51737 | 2079.062594 |
| 17 | 2387 | 1861.579383 | 1952.510422 | 2003.050075 |
| 18 | 1854 | 2176.831753 | 2126.306253 | 2079.84006 |
| 19 | 1521 | 1983.132701 | 2017.383752 | 2034.672048 |
| 20 | 1726 | 1705.853081 | 1818.830251 | 1931.937639 |

**Fig. 15.11** Simple exponential smoothing

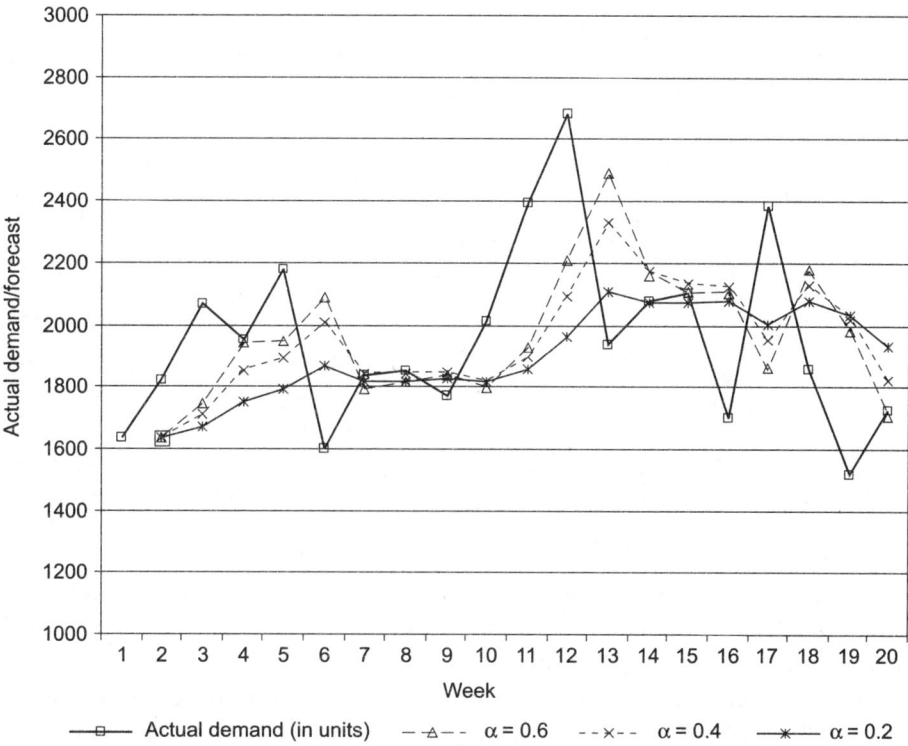

**Fig. 15.12** Simple exponential smoothing chart

forecasts lag behind the increasing or decreasing trend in the actual demand (forecast curves are below the actual demand curve during the increasing trend followed by the actual demand curve. Similarly, the forecast curves are above the actual demand curve during the decreasing trend followed by the actual demand curve). Holt's double-exponential smoothing method discussed next takes care of this lagging effect of the forecast.

**Holt's double-exponential smoothing** As mentioned earlier, Holt's double-exponential smoothing is suitable when the actual demand follows either an increasing or a decreasing trend. In simple exponential smoothing, we had seen that the forecast lags behind the actual demand whenever the actual demand follows an increasing or decreasing trend. In Holt's double-exponential smoothing, we use two smoothing constants. One is the smoothing constant $\alpha$, as used earlier, and the second is $\gamma$, which is used to adjust the trend effect.

In Holt's double-exponential smoothing, the forecast including trend (FIT) for a period $t$ is given by

$$\text{FIT}_t = F_t + T_t$$

where

> Holt's double-exponential smoothing is suitable when the actual demand follows either an increasing or a decreasing trend.

$$F_t = \text{FIT}_{t-1} + \alpha \left( A_{t-1} - \text{FIT}_{t-1} \right) \tag{15.3}$$

$$T_t = T_{t-1} + \gamma \left( F_t - \text{FIT}_{t-1} \right) \tag{15.4}$$

Here, $(t-1)$ is the period prior to period $t$, $F_t$ is the exponentially smoothed forecast for period $t$, and $T_t$ is the exponentially smoothed trend for period $t$.

MS Excel does not have a tool for Holt's double-exponential smoothing, but SPSS 10.0 does. Let us take up an example in order to understand Holt's double-exponential smoothing using SPSS 10.0.

***Example 15.2***

**Table 15.4**

| Week | Actual demand (units) | Week | Actual demand (units) |
|------|------|------|------|
| 1 | 954 | 11 | 1,527 |
| 2 | 1,045 | 12 | 1,573 |
| 3 | 1,162 | 13 | 1,598 |
| 4 | 1,189 | 14 | 1,677 |
| 5 | 1,250 | 15 | 1,754 |
| 6 | 1,291 | 16 | 1,821 |
| 7 | 1,368 | 17 | 1,956 |
| 8 | 1,325 | 18 | 2,054 |
| 9 | 1,372 | 19 | 2,298 |
| 10 | 1,499 | 20 | 2,386 |

Digital Peripheral Devices is a firm dealing with HP printers and peripheral computer devices and is based at Hyderabad. The actual demand (in units) experienced by it for its HP printers during the past 20 weeks is given in Table 15.4. Find the forecast for the given 20 weeks using Holt's double-exponential smoothing. Take $\alpha = 0.5$ and $\gamma = 0.5$. Find also the forecast for the given 20 weeks using simple exponential smoothing ($\alpha = 0.5$). Make a graph showing the two forecasts with the actual demand.

***Solution***

As shown in Fig. 15.13, paste Table 15.4 in the SPSS data editor. Select the table and click on the **Analyze** tool on the SPSS toolbar. From the pull-down menu, choose **Time Series** and then **Exponential Smoothing**. The dialog box shown in Fig. 15.13 appears. Our actual demand data is **Var00002**. Select Var00002 in the **Variables** text box in the dialog box. Select also the check box for **Holt** (double-exponential smoothing). Then, click on the **Parameters** button in the dialog box. An **Exponential Smoothing: Parameters** dialog box as shown in Fig. 15.14 appears. In this dialog box, put the values for **General (Alpha)** = 0.5 and **Trend (Gamma)** = 0.5. The **Initial Values** have

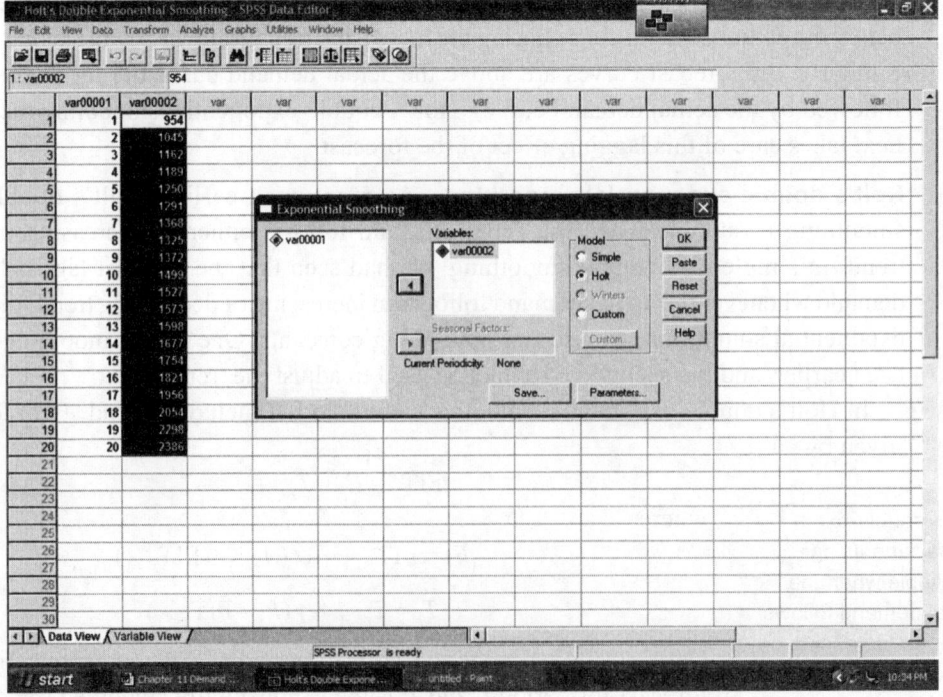

**Fig. 15.13** Holt's double-exponential smoothing

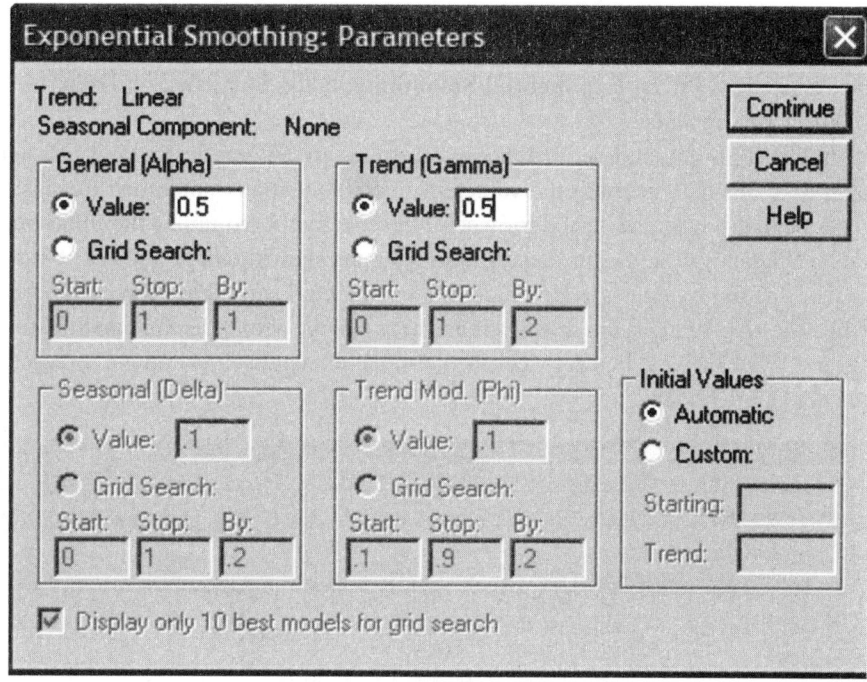

Fig. 15.14

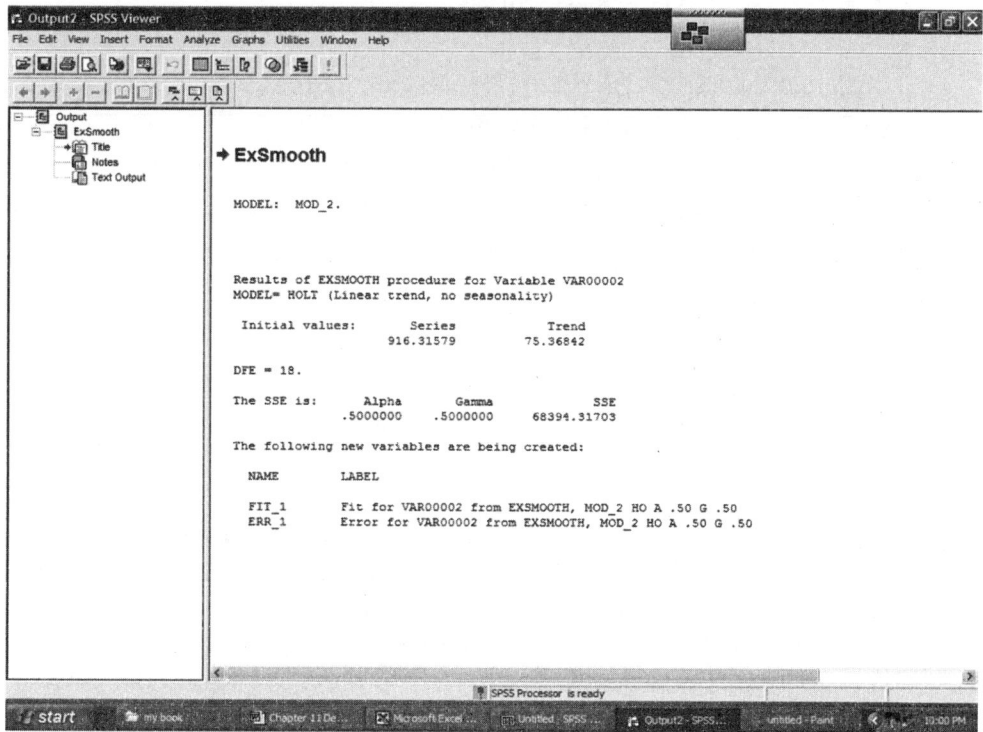

Fig. 15.15

a default setting of **Automatic**. Leave it as it is so that the software automatically selects the initial values of forecast and trend for week 0. Click on the **Continue** button so that the parameters dialog box disappears. In the **Exponential Smoothing** dialog box, click on **OK**. The SPSS output shown in Fig. 15.15 appears.

In the SPSS output, note that the initial values are automatically taken as: **Series** 916.31579 and **Trend** 75.36842. These are the values of $F_1$ (exponentially smoothed forecast for week 1) and $T_1$ (exponentially smoothed trend for week 1), respectively. Minimize the SPSS output and note that in the SPSS data editor, the third and fourth columns show the **fit_1** and **err_1** values as shown in Fig. 15.16. The **fit_1** values are Holt's double-exponential smoothing forecasts for the given 20 weeks, while the **err_1** values are the difference between the actual demand and the forecast values for the given 20 weeks. Note that for week 1, the actual demand is 954 and the forecast is 991.6842, so that the **err_1** is –37.6842.

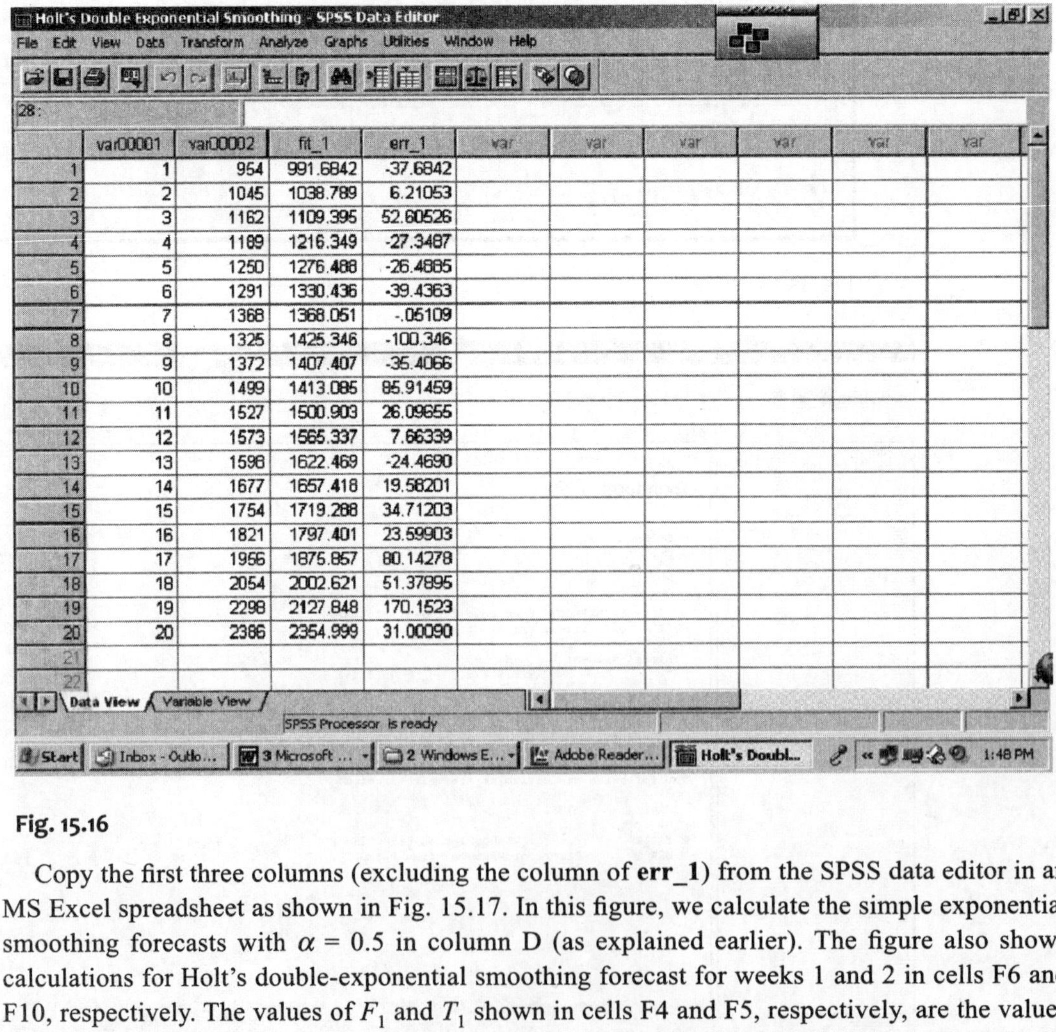

| | var00001 | var00002 | fit_1 | err_1 |
|---|---|---|---|---|
| 1 | 1 | 954 | 991.6842 | -37.6842 |
| 2 | 2 | 1045 | 1038.789 | 6.21053 |
| 3 | 3 | 1162 | 1109.395 | 52.60526 |
| 4 | 4 | 1189 | 1216.349 | -27.3487 |
| 5 | 5 | 1250 | 1276.488 | -26.4885 |
| 6 | 6 | 1291 | 1330.436 | -39.4363 |
| 7 | 7 | 1368 | 1368.051 | -.05109 |
| 8 | 8 | 1325 | 1425.346 | -100.346 |
| 9 | 9 | 1372 | 1407.407 | -35.4066 |
| 10 | 10 | 1499 | 1413.085 | 85.91459 |
| 11 | 11 | 1527 | 1500.903 | 26.09655 |
| 12 | 12 | 1573 | 1565.337 | 7.66339 |
| 13 | 13 | 1598 | 1622.469 | -24.4690 |
| 14 | 14 | 1677 | 1657.418 | 19.58201 |
| 15 | 15 | 1754 | 1719.288 | 34.71203 |
| 16 | 16 | 1821 | 1797.401 | 23.59903 |
| 17 | 17 | 1956 | 1875.857 | 80.14278 |
| 18 | 18 | 2054 | 2002.621 | 51.37895 |
| 19 | 19 | 2298 | 2127.848 | 170.1523 |
| 20 | 20 | 2386 | 2354.999 | 31.00090 |
| 21 | | | | |
| 22 | | | | |

**Fig. 15.16**

Copy the first three columns (excluding the column of **err_1**) from the SPSS data editor in an MS Excel spreadsheet as shown in Fig. 15.17. In this figure, we calculate the simple exponential smoothing forecasts with $\alpha = 0.5$ in column D (as explained earlier). The figure also shows calculations for Holt's double-exponential smoothing forecast for weeks 1 and 2 in cells F6 and F10, respectively. The values of $F_1$ and $T_1$ shown in cells F4 and F5, respectively, are the values which were automatically taken as initial values by the SPSS software. The value of $FIT_1$ is the sum of cells F4 and F5. Remember that for a given period $t$ (here week 1),

$$FIT_t = F_t + T_t$$

| Week Number | Actual Demand (in units) | α = 0.5 & γ = 0.5 | α = 0.5 | | | |
|---|---|---|---|---|---|---|
| 1 | 954 | 991.6842 | #N/A | | | |
| 2 | 1045 | 1038.789 | 991.6842 | $F_1 =$ | 916.3158 | |
| 3 | 1162 | 1109.395 | 1015.2366 | $T_1 =$ | 75.36842 | |
| 4 | 1189 | 1216.349 | 1062.3158 | $FIT_1 =$ | 991.6842 | |
| 5 | 1250 | 1276.488 | 1139.3324 | | | |
| 6 | 1291 | 1330.436 | 1207.9102 | $F_2 =$ | 972.8421 | |
| 7 | 1368 | 1368.051 | 1269.1731 | $T_2 =$ | 65.94737 | |
| 8 | 1325 | 1425.346 | 1318.61205 | $FIT_2 =$ | 1038.789 | |
| 9 | 1372 | 1407.407 | 1371.979025 | | | |
| 10 | 1499 | 1413.085 | 1389.693013 | | | |
| 11 | 1527 | 1500.903 | 1401.389006 | | | |
| 12 | 1573 | 1565.337 | 1451.146003 | | | |
| 13 | 1598 | 1622.469 | 1508.241502 | | | |
| 14 | 1677 | 1657.418 | 1565.355251 | | | |
| 15 | 1754 | 1719.288 | 1611.386625 | | | |
| 16 | 1821 | 1797.401 | 1665.337313 | | | |
| 17 | 1956 | 1875.857 | 1731.369156 | | | |
| 18 | 2054 | 2002.621 | 1803.613078 | | | |
| 19 | 2298 | 2127.848 | 1903.117039 | | | |
| 20 | 2386 | 2354.999 | 2015.48252 | | | |

**Fig. 15.17**

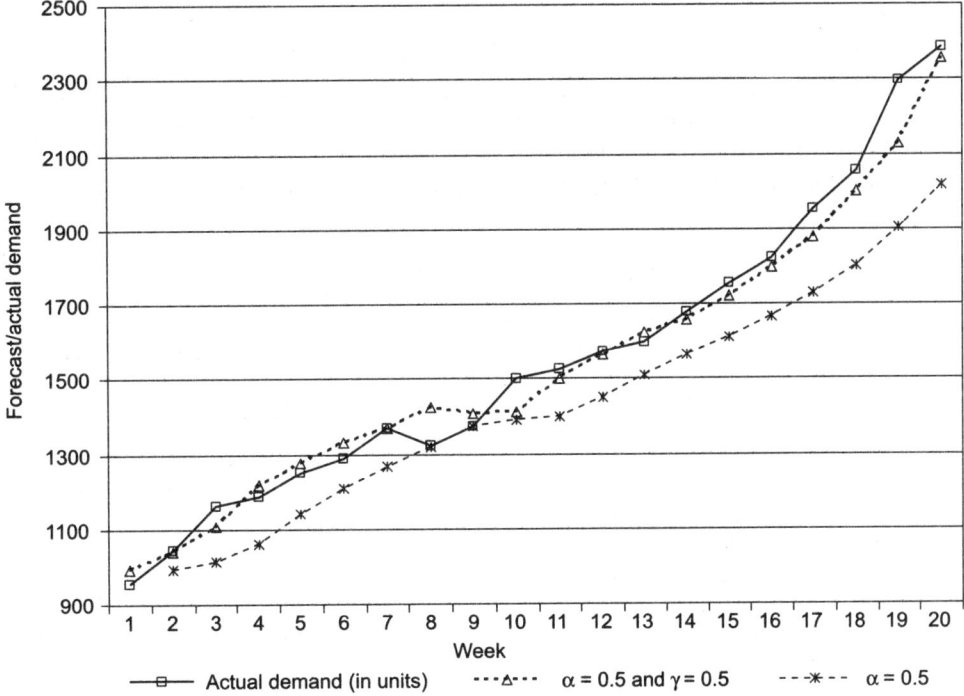

**Fig. 15.18**   Holt's double-exponential smoothing curve

We calculate the values of $F_2$ and $T_2$ for week 2 in cells F8 and F9 by putting the formulae **=C3+0.5\*(B3 – C3)** and **=F5+0.5\*(F8 – C3)**, respectively. These calculations are based on Eqns (11.3) and (11.4). The value of $FIT_2$ shown in cell F10 is the sum of cells F8 and F9. Note that the values of $FIT_1$ and $FIT_2$ calculated in cells F6 and F10 are same as the values calculated by SPSS in cells C3 and C4, respectively.

Now, select columns A, B, C, and D in Fig. 15.17 and click on the icon for the chart wizard in the MS Excel toolbar. The chart wizard guides us through to get the chart shown in Fig. 15.18. Note that the curve for Holt's double-exponential smoothing forecast ($\alpha = 0.5$ and $\gamma = 0.5$) follows the actual demand curve much more closely compared to the curve for simple exponential smoothing ($\alpha = 0.5$). The trend lag in simple exponential smoothing has been overcome by Holt's double-exponential smoothing.

**Winters' triple-exponential smoothing**  In situations where there is an increasing or decreasing trend with seasonal variations, Winters' triple-exponential smoothing is applied. The mathematical treatment of Winters' triple-exponential smoothing is beyond the scope of this book. We will discuss the application of this method of forecasting using SPSS 10.0.

As discussed earlier, Holt's double-exponential smoothing method is able to overcome the trend lag effect of simple exponential smoothing. In situations of an increasing or decreasing trend with seasonal variations, Holt's double-exponential smoothing method is not able to closely follow the seasonal variations in the actual demand as Winters' triple-exponential smoothing method does. Like in Holt's method, Winters' method also uses the general smoothing constant $\alpha$ and the trend smoothing constant $\gamma$. In addition to these smoothing constants, it uses a third smoothing constant $\delta$ for seasonal variations.

Let us take up an example to understand Winters' triple-exponential smoothing method using SPSS 10.0.

### *Example 15.3*

Anandi Beach Resort is a popular resort at Goa. Table 15.5 gives the details of actual demand (in units), which represents the number of registrations of customers the resort received in the past four weeks (28 days). Apply Winters' triple-exponential smoothing to arrive at the forecasts for the 28 weeks taking $\alpha = 0.5$, $\gamma = 0.5$, and $\delta = 0.5$. Find also the forecasts by applying Holt's double-exponential smoothing taking $\alpha = 0.5$ and $\gamma = 0.5$. Make a graph to compare the actual demand pattern with the forecasts.

### *Solution*

Paste the column for actual demand (in units) in the first column of the SPSS data editor as shown in Fig. 15.19. For using Winters' method, we need to define dates for the given data. Select the column of actual demand (in units) in the SPSS data editor and click on the **Data** tool on the toolbar. From the pull-down menu, select **Define Dates**. The dialog box shown in Fig. 15.20 appears. In this dialog box, select **Weeks,**

**Table 15.5**

| Day | Actual demand (units) | Day | Actual demand (units) |
|-----|-----|-----|-----|
| 1 | 721 | 15 | 1,503 |
| 2 | 801 | 16 | 1,386 |
| 3 | 854 | 17 | 1,264 |
| 4 | 826 | 18 | 1,432 |
| 5 | 802 | 19 | 1,589 |
| 6 | 897 | 20 | 1,671 |
| 7 | 969 | 21 | 1,713 |
| 8 | 1,078 | 22 | 1,789 |
| 9 | 1,192 | 23 | 1,631 |
| 10 | 1,064 | 24 | 1,597 |
| 11 | 1,005 | 25 | 1,697 |
| 12 | 1,275 | 26 | 1,743 |
| 13 | 1,392 | 27 | 1,875 |
| 14 | 1,458 | 28 | 1,931 |

**days** in **Cases Are**. In the **First Case Is** section, enter 1 for **Week** and 1 for **Day** and click on **OK**. Dates are defined automatically by SPSS as shown in columns **week_**, **day_**, and **date_** o Fig. 15.19.

| | var00001 | week_ | day_ | date_ |
|---|---|---|---|---|
| 1 | 721 | 1 | 1 | 1 SUN |
| 2 | 801 | 1 | 2 | 1 MON |
| 3 | 854 | 1 | 3 | 1 TUE |
| 4 | 826 | 1 | 4 | 1 WED |
| 5 | 802 | 1 | 5 | 1 THU |
| 6 | 897 | 1 | 6 | 1 FRI |
| 7 | 969 | 1 | 7 | 1 SAT |
| 8 | 1078 | 2 | 1 | 2 SUN |
| 9 | 1192 | 2 | 2 | 2 MON |
| 10 | 1064 | 2 | 3 | 2 TUE |
| 11 | 1005 | 2 | 4 | 2 WED |
| 12 | 1275 | 2 | 5 | 2 THU |
| 13 | 1392 | 2 | 6 | 2 FRI |
| 14 | 1458 | 2 | 7 | 2 SAT |
| 15 | 1503 | 3 | 1 | 3 SUN |
| 16 | 1386 | 3 | 2 | 3 MON |
| 17 | 1264 | 3 | 3 | 3 TUE |
| 18 | 1432 | 3 | 4 | 3 WED |
| 19 | 1589 | 3 | 5 | 3 THU |
| 20 | 1671 | 3 | 6 | 3 FRI |
| 21 | 1713 | 3 | 7 | 3 SAT |
| 22 | 1789 | 4 | 1 | 4 SUN |
| 23 | 1631 | 4 | 2 | 4 MON |
| 24 | 1597 | 4 | 3 | 4 TUE |
| 25 | 1697 | 4 | 4 | 4 WED |
| 26 | 1743 | 4 | 5 | 4 THU |
| 27 | 1875 | 4 | 6 | 4 FRI |
| 28 | 1931 | 4 | 7 | 4 SAT |
| 29 | | | | |
| 30 | | | | |

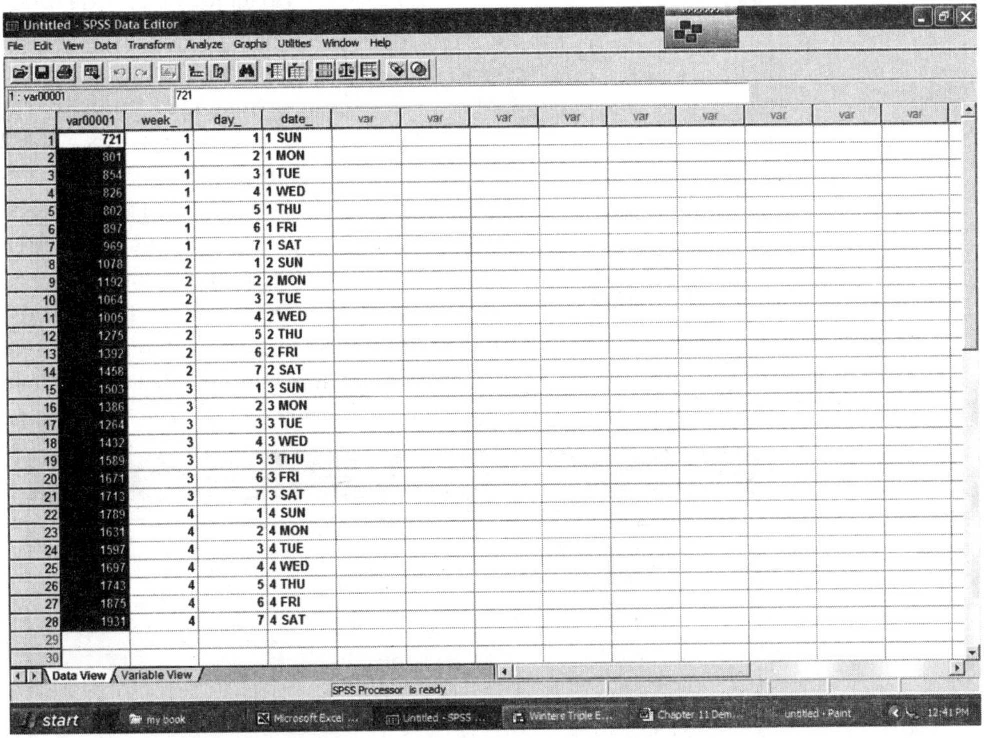

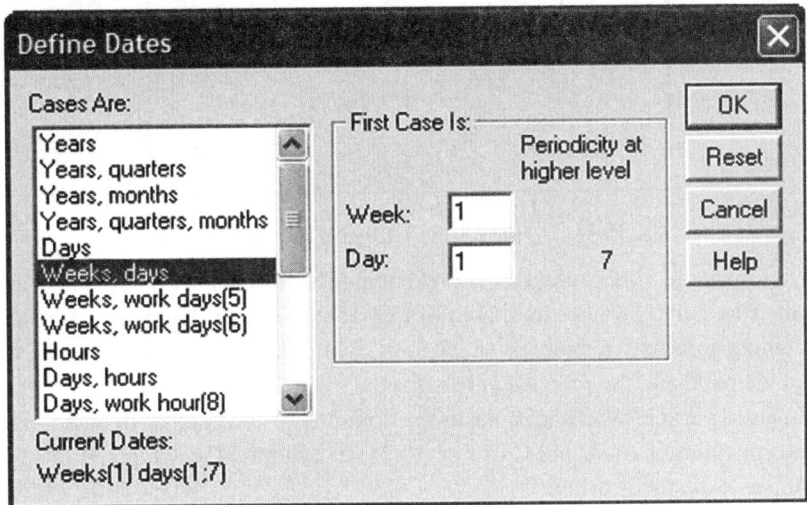

**Fig. 15.19** SPSS Data Editor

**Fig. 15.20** The Define Dates dialog box in SPSS 10.0

Select the four columns in the SPSS data editor and click on the **Analyze** tool on the SPSS toolbar. From the pull-down menu, choose **Time Series** and then, **Exponential Smoothing**. The dialog

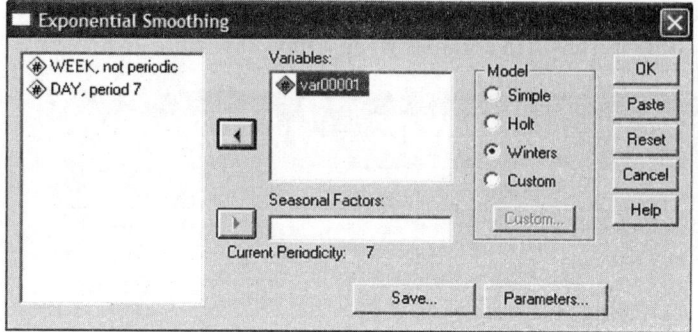

**Fig. 15.21**   The Exponential Smoothing dialog box

box shown in Fig. 15.21 appears. Our actual demand data is **Var00001**. Select **Var00001** in the **Variables** text box in the dialog box. Select also the check box for **Winters** (triple-exponential smoothing).

Next, click on the **Parameters** button in the dialog box. The **Exponential Smoothing: Parameters** dialog box shown in Fig. 15.22 appears. In this dialog box, put the values **General (Alpha)** = 0.5, **Trend (Gamma)** = 0.5, and **Seasonal (Delta)** = 0.5. The **Initial Values** have a default setting of automatic. Leave it as it is so that the software automatically selects the initial values of forecast and trend for day 1. Click on the **Continue** button so that the Parameters dialog box disappears. In the **Exponential Smoothing** dialog box, click on **OK**. The SPSS output is generated.

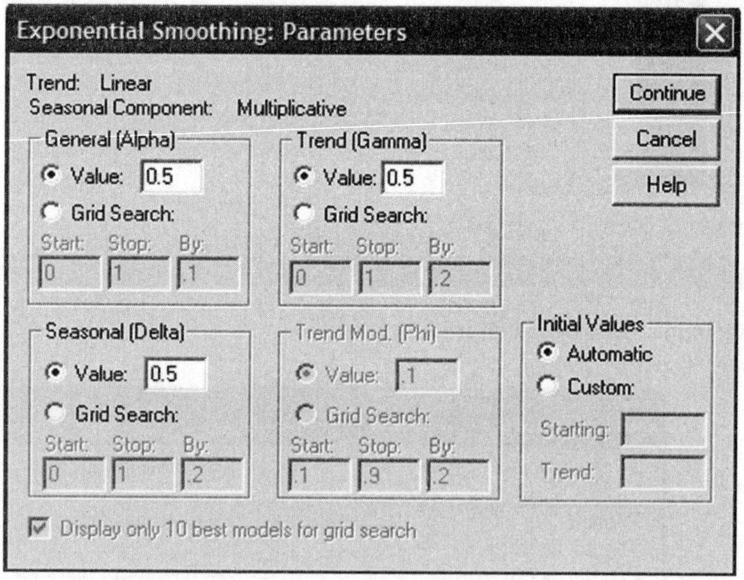

**Fig. 15.22**   Exponential Smoothing: Parameters

Minimize the SPSS output and note that in the SPSS data editor, the fifth and sixth columns show the **fit_1** and **err_1** values as shown in Fig. 15.23. The **fit_1** values are Winters' triple-exponential smoothing forecasts for the given 28 days, while the **err_1** values are the difference between the actual demand and the forecast values for the gven 28 days.

In an MS Excel worksheet, paste the columns of day, actual demand, and Winters' forecast as shown in columns A, B, and C of Fig. 15.24. In column D, calculate Holt's forecast for $\alpha = 0.5$ and $\gamma = 0.5$ as explained earlier.

Now select columns A, B, C, and D in Fig. 15.24 and click on the chart wizard icon on the toolbar. The chart wizard guides us through to get the chart shown in Fig. 15.25. Note that the curve for Winters' triple-exponential smoothing forecast ($\alpha = 0.5$, $\gamma = 0.5$, and $\delta = 0.5$) follows the actual demand curve much more closely, especially the seasonal variations in actual demand, compared to the curve for Holt's double-exponential smoothing ($\alpha = 0.$, $\gamma = 0.5$).

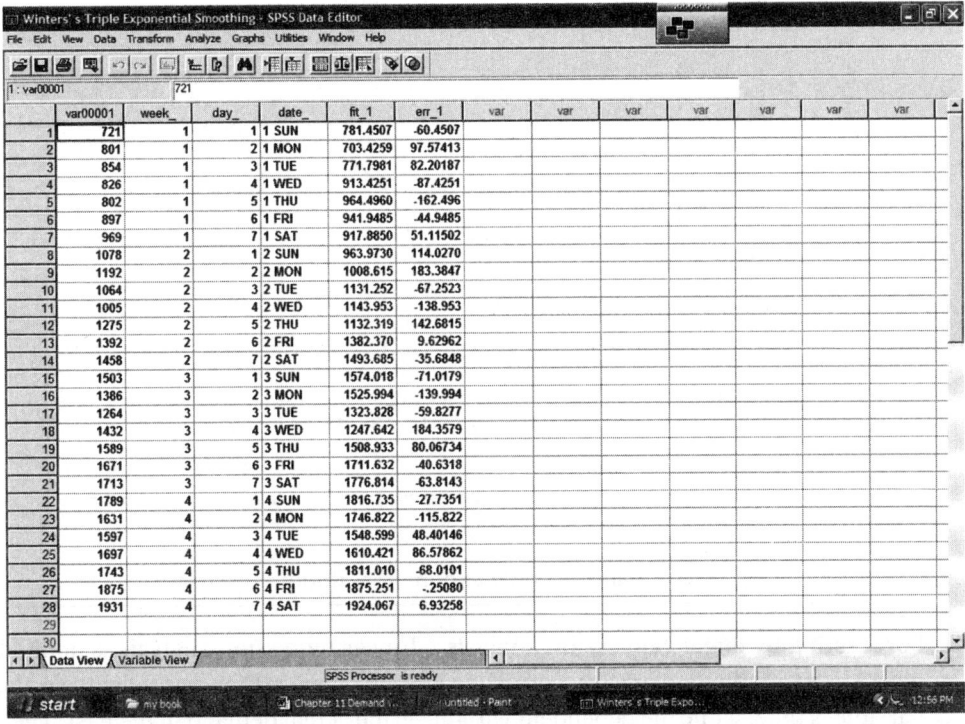

**Fig. 15.23** Winters' triple-exponential smoothing

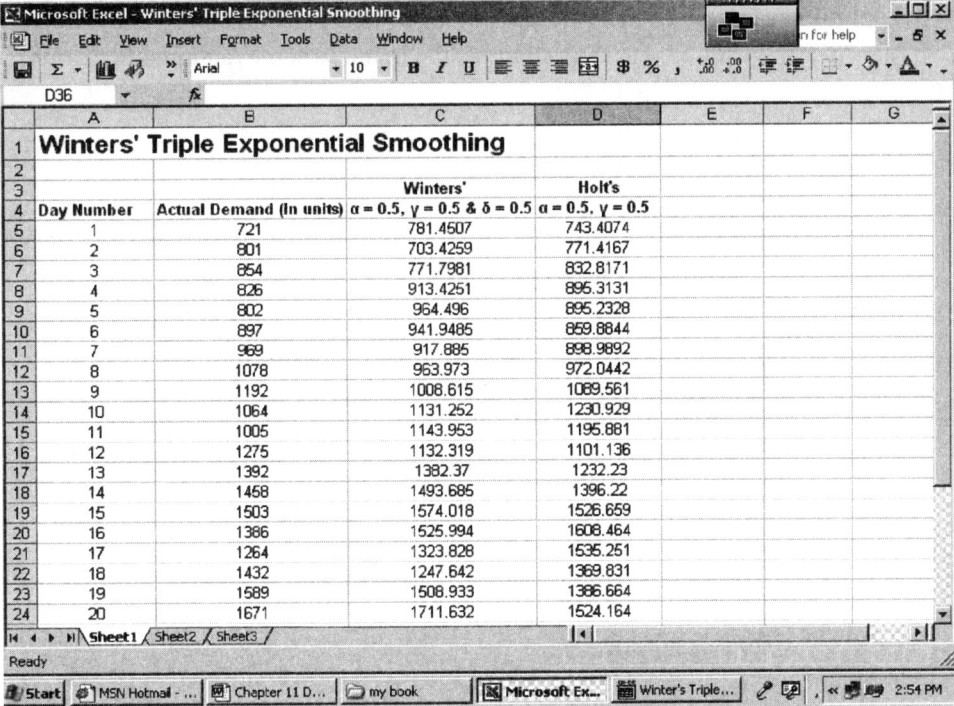

**Fig. 15.24**

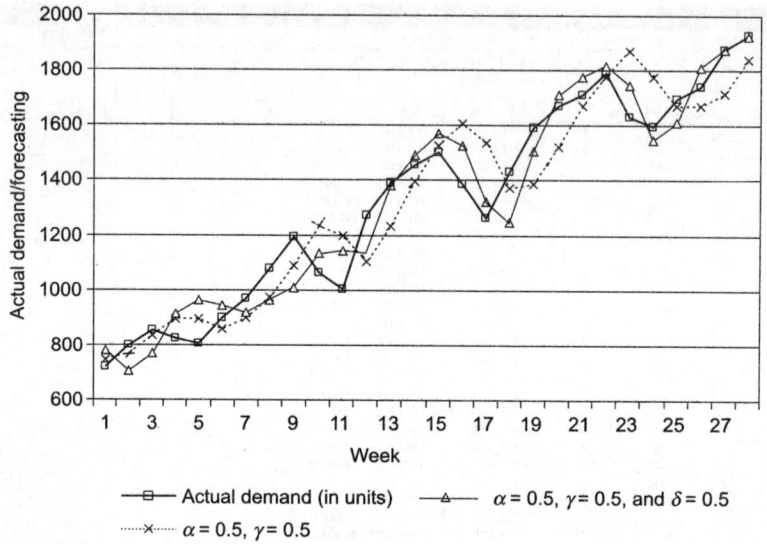

**Fig. 15.25**  Winters' triple-exponential smoothing chart

**Forecasting by linear regression analysis**  Linear regression analysis is applied in situations where two variables are linearly correlated to each other. In time series analysis, the independent variable is time, while the dependent variable is the actual demand in the past. The term 'linearly correlated' means when a graph showing the points for the corresponding values of the two variables is made (called the *scatter diagram* as shown in Fig. 15.26), these points should display an approximately linear trend (increasing or decreasing). It is not practically possible for these points to always follow a perfect straight-line trend, as some random fluctuations will be present

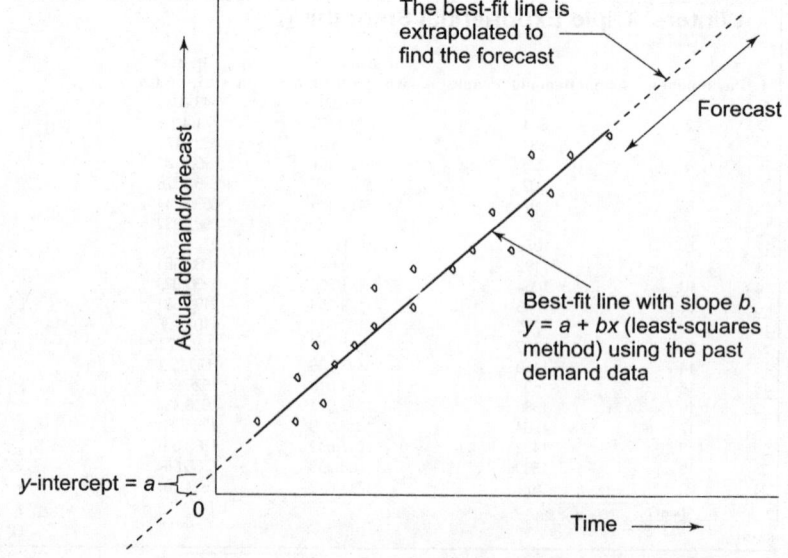

**Fig. 15.26**  Scatter diagram and best-fit line (forecasting by linear regression analysis)

Linear regression analysis is applied in situations where two variables are linearly correlated to each other.

in the demand. Therefore, we find a best-fit straight line, which can be the best representative of the linear trend shown by these points.

The best-fit line is represented by the straight-line equation

$$y = a + bx \qquad (15.5)$$

where $y$ is the actual demand in the past time periods, $x$ represents the time periods, $a$ is the $y$-intercept of the best-fit line, and $b$ is the slope of the best-fit line.

In linear regression analysis, the best fit is determined such that the sum of the squares of the $y$ distances of all the points in the scatter diagram from the best-fit line is the least, that is, $\Sigma(y' - y)^2$ is minimum. Here, $y'$ is the $y$-coordinate of a point in the scatter diagram and $y$ is the coordinate of the corresponding point on the best-fit line at the corresponding time instant. Therefore, this method of finding the best-fit line is called the *least-squares method.*

For finding the best fit, we thus need to find the constants $a$ and $b$ in Eqn (15.5). The best-fit line can be extrapolated (extended further as shown in Fig. 15.26) to find the forecast. We will not be using the mathematical formulae for finding the constants $a$ and $b$ of the best-fit line. MS Excel provides an excellent tool for finding the forecast using linear regression analysis as we will see in the example that follows.

### *Example 15.4*

Take the data for actual demand (in units) up to day 20 from Example 15.3 and find the forecasts for days 21–25 by linear regression analysis.

### *Solution*

Paste the data for day and corresponding actual demand up to day 20 in columns A and B of an MS Excel worksheet as shown in Fig. 15.27. We have to find the forecast by linear regression analysis for

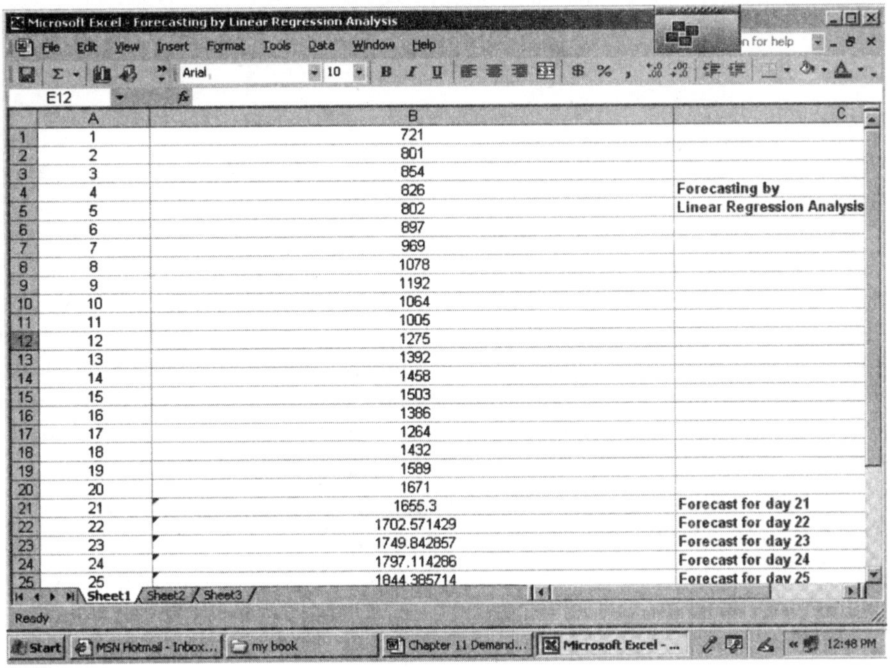

| | A | B | C |
|---|---|---|---|
| 1 | 1 | 721 | |
| 2 | 2 | 801 | |
| 3 | 3 | 854 | |
| 4 | 4 | 826 | Forecasting by |
| 5 | 5 | 802 | Linear Regression Analysis |
| 6 | 6 | 897 | |
| 7 | 7 | 969 | |
| 8 | 8 | 1078 | |
| 9 | 9 | 1192 | |
| 10 | 10 | 1064 | |
| 11 | 11 | 1005 | |
| 12 | 12 | 1275 | |
| 13 | 13 | 1392 | |
| 14 | 14 | 1458 | |
| 15 | 15 | 1503 | |
| 16 | 16 | 1386 | |
| 17 | 17 | 1264 | |
| 18 | 18 | 1432 | |
| 19 | 19 | 1589 | |
| 20 | 20 | 1671 | |
| 21 | 21 | 1655.3 | Forecast for day 21 |
| 22 | 22 | 1702.571429 | Forecast for day 22 |
| 23 | 23 | 1749.842857 | Forecast for day 23 |
| 24 | 24 | 1797.114286 | Forecast for day 24 |
| 25 | 25 | 1844.385714 | Forecast for day 25 |



**Fig. 15.27** Forecasting by linear regresion analysis

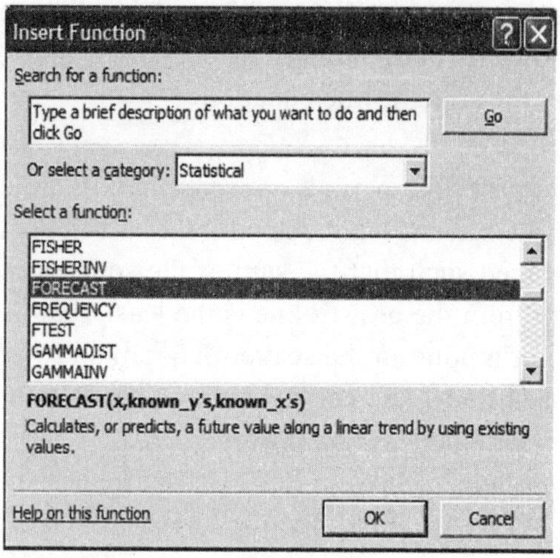

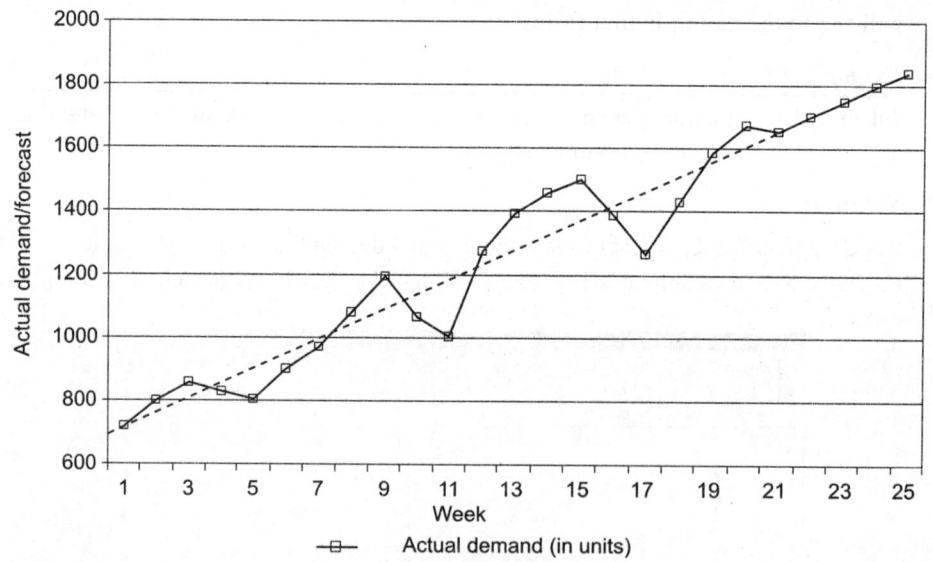

**Fig. 15.28**

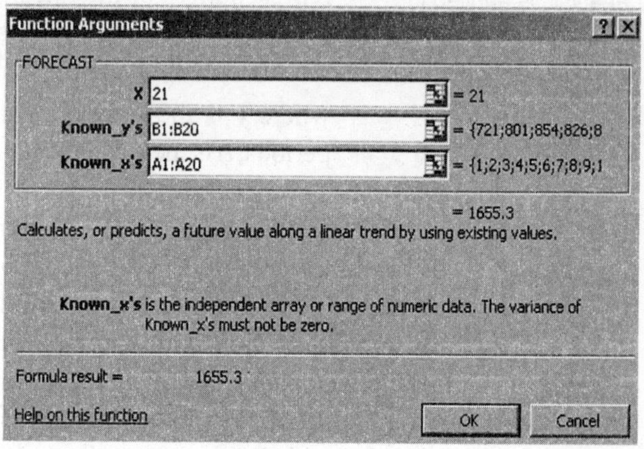

**Fig. 15.29**

**Fig. 15.30** Best-fit line using the least-squares method

days 21–25. These days are shown in cells A21 to A25. Select cell B21 and click on the **Insert** tool on the toolbar. From the pull-down menu, choose **Function**. A dialog box named **Insert Function** shown in Fig. 15.28 appears. In this dialog box, select the category **Statistical** and then select the function **Forecast**. Click on **OK** so that a dialog box named **Function Arguments** shown in Fig. 15.29 appears.

In the **Function Arguments** dialog box, enter 21 in the text box for **X**, as we have to find the forecast for day 21. Click on the small button with an arrow in the text box for **Known_y's** so that the dialog box shrinks. Now, in Fig. 15.27 select cells B1 to B20. Again, click on the shrink button in this text box so that the dialog box expands to its original shape. Repeat the same process to fill in A1:A20 in the **Known_x's** text box as shown in Fig. 15.29. Click on **OK** so that the forecast for day 21 appears in cell B21 as 1655.3 units. Repeat the same process to get the forecasts for days 22–25 in cells B22 to B25, as shown in Fig. 15.27.

Now select columns A and B in Fig. 15.27 and click on the chart wizard icon on the toolbar. The chart wizard guides us through to get the graph shown in Fig. 15.30. Note that in this graph, the forecast points for days 21–25 form a straight line, which is the best-fit line. We can extrapolate this straight line backwards (shown by a dotted line) to get the complete best-fit line.

## Trend Analysis

> Trend analysis is a forecasting method used in the causal quantitative analysis.

Trend analysis is a forecasting method used in the *causal quantitative analysis*. Trend analysis is also based upon linear regression analysis. The only difference is that in trend analysis the independent variable can be any other variable except time. The dependent variable should have a causal relationship with the independent variable, that is, the dependent variable should be the effect of a cause, which is the independent variable. For example, the sale of raincoats and umbrellas in the coming few days depends upon the level of rainfall in the past few days. Here, the level of rainfall is the cause, while the sale of raincoats and umbrellas is the effect. Let us take up an example to understand trend analysis using MS Excel.

### *Example 15.5*

Table 15.6 shows the average sales of shops (in ₹ '000/day) in various localities of Mumbai and the corresponding rent of a shop in the same locality (in ₹ '000/month). Using trend analysis determine the rent of the shop in three localities where the average sales of shops (in ₹ '000/day) is 110, 115, and 120, respectively.

### Table 15.6

| Average sales of shops in a locality (₹ '000/day) | Rent of a shop in the locality (₹ '000/month) | Average sales of shops in a locality (₹ '000/day) | Rent of a shop in the locality (₹ '000/month) |
|---|---|---|---|
| 10 | 5.4 | 60 | 21.2 |
| 15 | 7.1 | 65 | 24.8 |
| 20 | 9.6 | 70 | 35.9 |
| 25 | 10.7 | 75 | 27.2 |
| 30 | 15.3 | 80 | 28.8 |
| 35 | 13.5 | 85 | 30.7 |
| 40 | 15.1 | 90 | 31.6 |
| 45 | 16.7 | 95 | 43.2 |
| 50 | 19.8 | 100 | 35.4 |
| 55 | 21.3 | 105 | 47.9 |

### *Solution*

Paste Table 15.6 in columns A and B of an MS Excel worksheet, as shown in Fig. 15.31.

We have to find the trend values for the rent of a shop in three localities where the average sales of shops (in ₹ '000/day) is 110, 115, and 120, respectively. Therefore, in cells A25, A26, and A27, we put the values 110, 115, and 120, respectively. Select cell B25 and click on the **Insert** tool on the toolbar. From the pull-down menu which appears, choose **Function**. A dialog box named **Insert Function** as shown in Fig. 15.32 appears. In this dialog box, select the category **Statistical** and then select the function **Trend**. Click on **OK** so that the dialog box named **Function Arguments** shown in Fig.15.33 appears.

| | A | B |
|---|---|---|
| 1 | **Trend Analysis** | |
| 4 | Average Sales of Shops in a Locality (In '000 Rs per day) | Rent of a Shop in the Locality ('000 Rs per month) |
| 5 | 10 | 5.4 |
| 6 | 15 | 7.1 |
| 7 | 20 | 9.6 |
| 8 | 25 | 10.7 |
| 9 | 30 | 15.3 |
| 10 | 35 | 13.5 |
| 11 | 40 | 15.1 |
| 12 | 45 | 16.7 |
| 13 | 50 | 19.8 |
| 14 | 55 | 21.3 |
| 15 | 60 | 21.2 |
| 16 | 65 | 24.8 |
| 17 | 70 | 35.9 |
| 18 | 75 | 27.2 |
| 19 | 80 | 28.8 |
| 20 | 85 | 30.7 |
| 21 | 90 | 31.6 |
| 22 | 95 | 43.2 |
| 23 | 100 | 35.4 |
| 24 | 105 | 47.9 |
| 25 | 110 | 43.32578947 |
| 26 | 115 | 45.35070175 |
| 27 | 120 | 47.39253526 |

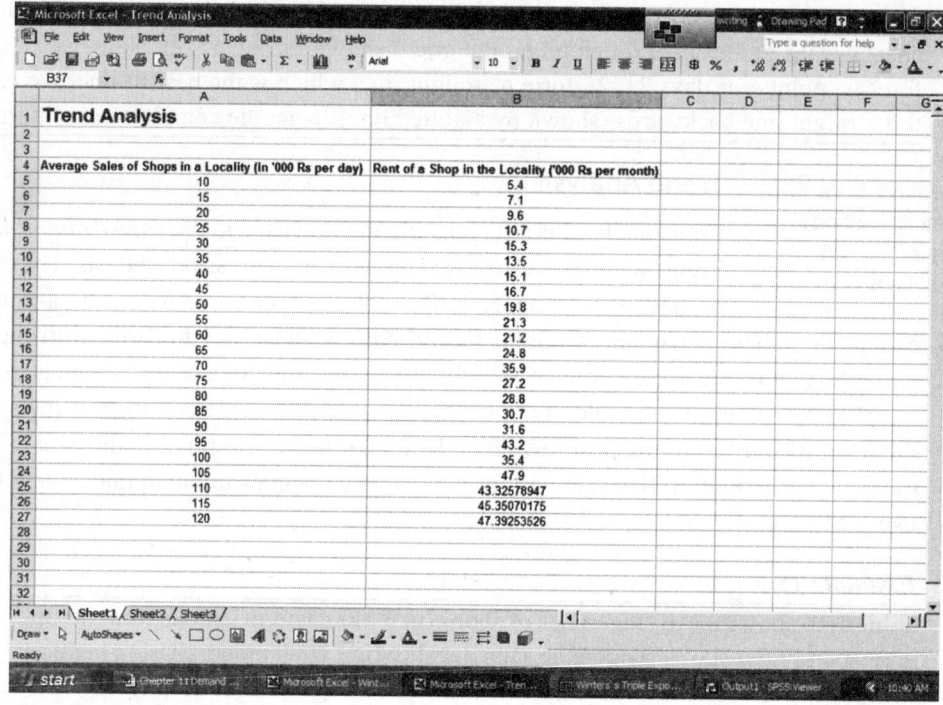

Fig. 15.31 Trend analysis

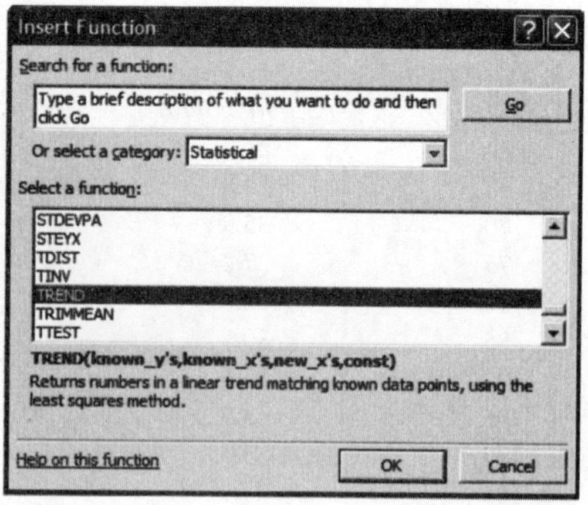

Fig. 15.32

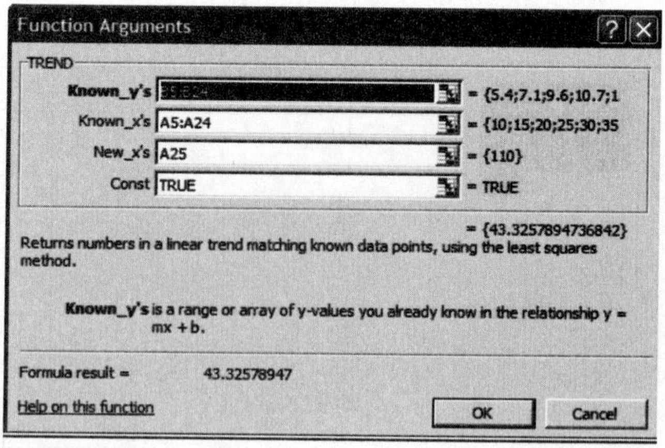

Fig. 15.33

In the **New_x's** text box, put A25, that is, the cell for which we have to find the trend value. In the **Const** text box, type **TRUE** because we want the value of the $y$-intercept (the constant $a$ in the equation of the best-fit line $y = a + bx$) to be calculated normally. If we choose **FALSE**, the value of $a$ will be omitted, which is undesirable. Click on **OK** so that the trend for average sales of shops at ₹1,10,000 per day appears in cell B25 as 43.32578947. Repeat the same process to get the trend values in cells B26 and B27 shown in Fig. 15.31.

Now select columns A and B of Fig. 15.31 and click on the chart wizard icon on the toolbar. The chart wizard guides us through to get the graph shown in Fig. 15.34. Note that in this graph, the trend points for days 21–23 form a straight line, which is the best-fit line. We can extrapolate this straight line backwards (shown by a dotted line) to get the complete best-fit line.

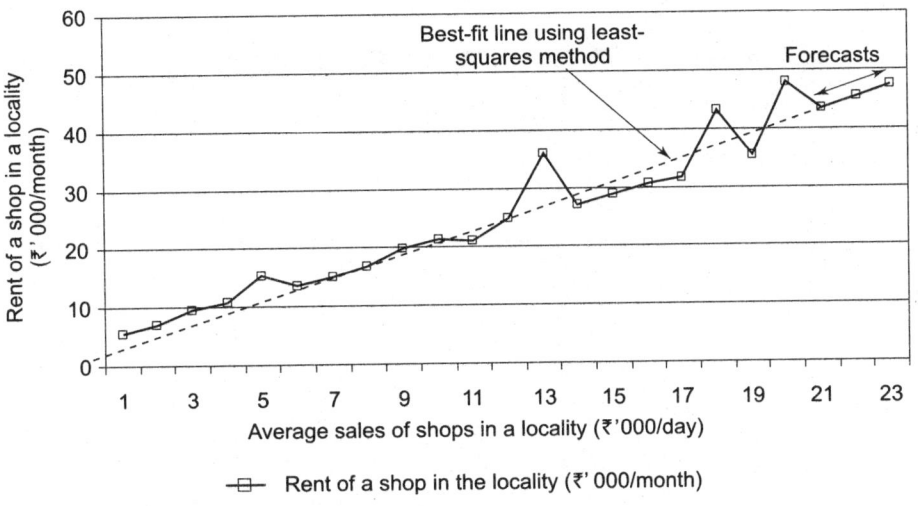

**Fig. 15.34** Trend analysis chart

## Measurement of Forecasting Errors

It is always desirable that demand forecast values should be as close as possible to the actual demand in the coming periods. Practically, some forecasting errors (deviations from the actual demand values) do take place. Therefore, we need to measure these errors and then try to minimize them as much as possible. There are various measures of forecast errors, as follows:

1. Running sum of forecast errors
2. Mean forecast error
3. Mean absolute deviation
4. Mean squared error
5. Mean absolute percentage error
6. Tracking signal

Let us take up Example 15.2 once again in order to understand these measures of forecasting errors. Copy the second, third, and fourth columns from the SPSS spreadsheet of Fig. 15.16 and paste them into columns B, C, and D of an MS Excel spreadsheet as shown in Fig. 15.35. Column A in the figure contains weeks 1–20. Column B contains the actual demand $D$, column C contains Holt's forecast $F$, and column D contains the deviation $D - F$. Select cells D7 to D27 and click on the $\Sigma$ sign on the toolbar. The sum of deviations in the given 20 weeks appears in cell D27 as 287.39891. This is the *running sum of forecast errors* (RSFE). Divide RSFE by 20 (weeks) to get the *mean forecast error* (MFE) in cell D29 as 14.3699455.

In column E, we determine the *absolute deviation* $|D - F|$, that is, we drop the negative signs (if any) for values in column D to get the absolute values (magnitudes) in column E. Select cells E7 to E27 and click on the small arrow adjacent to the Σ sign in the toolbar. From the pull-down menu, choose the **Average** option. The average or mean of absolute deviations called *mean absolute deviation* (MAD) appears in cell E27 as 63.7566375.

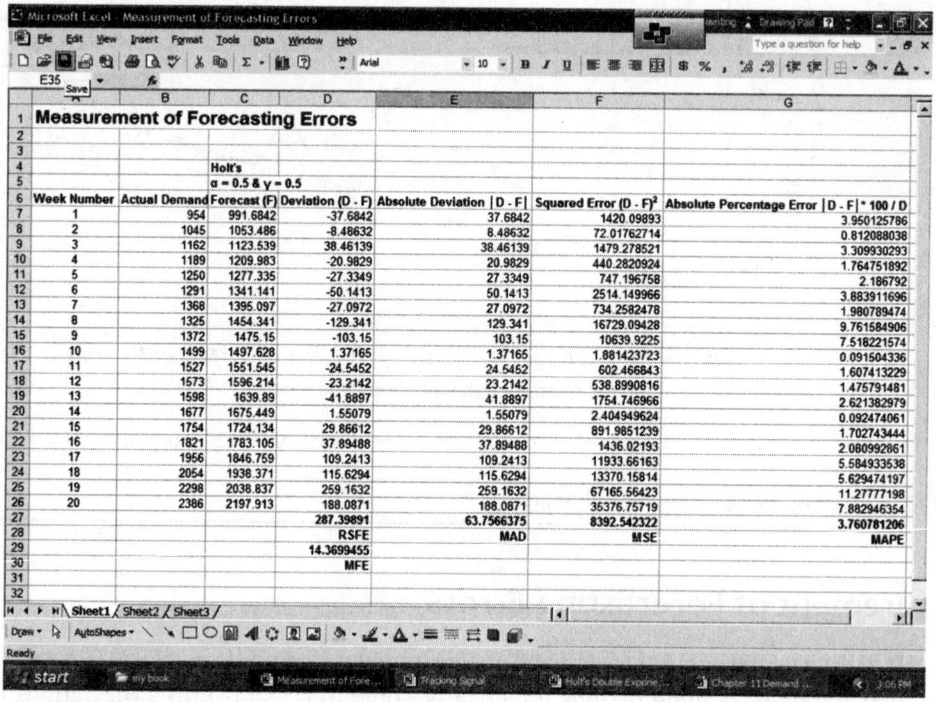

| Week Number | Actual Demand | Forecast (F) | Deviation (D - F) | Absolute Deviation \|D - F\| | Squared Error (D - F)² | Absolute Percentage Error \|D - F\| * 100 / D |
|---|---|---|---|---|---|---|
| 1 | 954 | 991.6842 | -37.6842 | 37.6842 | 1420.09893 | 3.950125786 |
| 2 | 1045 | 1053.486 | -8.48632 | 8.48632 | 72.01762714 | 0.812088038 |
| 3 | 1162 | 1123.539 | 38.46139 | 38.46139 | 1479.278521 | 3.309930293 |
| 4 | 1189 | 1209.983 | -20.9829 | 20.9829 | 440.2820924 | 1.764751892 |
| 5 | 1250 | 1277.335 | -27.3349 | 27.3349 | 747.196758 | 2.186792 |
| 6 | 1291 | 1341.141 | -50.1413 | 50.1413 | 2514.149966 | 3.883911696 |
| 7 | 1368 | 1395.097 | -27.0972 | 27.0972 | 734.2582478 | 1.980789474 |
| 8 | 1325 | 1454.341 | -129.341 | 129.341 | 16729.09428 | 9.761584906 |
| 9 | 1372 | 1475.15 | -103.15 | 103.15 | 10639.9225 | 7.518221574 |
| 10 | 1499 | 1497.628 | 1.37165 | 1.37165 | 1.881423723 | 0.091504336 |
| 11 | 1527 | 1551.545 | -24.5452 | 24.5452 | 602.466843 | 1.607413229 |
| 12 | 1573 | 1596.214 | -23.2142 | 23.2142 | 538.8990816 | 1.475791481 |
| 13 | 1598 | 1639.89 | -41.8897 | 41.8897 | 1754.746966 | 2.621382979 |
| 14 | 1677 | 1675.449 | 1.55079 | 1.55079 | 2.404949624 | 0.092474061 |
| 15 | 1754 | 1724.134 | 29.86612 | 29.86612 | 891.9851239 | 1.702743444 |
| 16 | 1821 | 1783.105 | 37.89488 | 37.89488 | 1436.02193 | 2.080992861 |
| 17 | 1956 | 1846.759 | 109.2413 | 109.2413 | 11933.66163 | 5.584933538 |
| 18 | 2054 | 1938.371 | 115.6294 | 115.6294 | 13370.15814 | 5.629474197 |
| 19 | 2298 | 2038.837 | 259.1632 | 259.1632 | 67165.56423 | 11.27777198 |
| 20 | 2386 | 2197.913 | 188.0871 | 188.0871 | 35376.75719 | 7.882946354 |
| | | | 287.39891 | 63.7566375 | 8392.542322 | 3.760781206 |
| | | | RSFE | MAD | MSE | MAPE |
| | | | 14.3699455 | | | |
| | | | MFE | | | |

Fig. 15.35 Measurement of forecasting errors

In column F, we find the squared error $(D - F)^2$. Put the formula =**D7*D7** in cell F7 and press **Enter** to get the value 1,420.09893. Select cell F7 and right click to choose **Copy**. Now select cells F8 to F26 and right click to choose **Paste**. The values shown in cells F8 to F26 of Fig. 15.35 appear. Select cells F7 to F27 and find the average value 8,392.542322 in cell F27 as explained earlier. This value is the *mean squared error* (MSE).

In column G, we find the absolute percentage error $100\,|D - F|/D$. Put the formula =**E7*100/B7** in cell G7 and press **Enter** to get the value 3.950125786. Copy the formula and paste it in cells G8 to G26. The values shown in cells G8 to G26 of Fig. 15.35 appear. Select cells G7 to G27 and find the average value 3.760781206 in cell G27 as explained earlier. This value is the *mean absolute percentage error* (MAPE). We will discuss the last measure of forecasting errors—tracking signal—in detail in the next section.

## Tracking Signal

Tracking signal is a dynamic measure of forecasting errors, as it can be updated after every time new actual demand data is added to the earlier data.

The RSFE can be calculated as cumulative deviation $D - F$ at the end of every given time period. Similarly, MAD can be calculated at the end of every given time period. At the end of a given time period, *tracking signal* (TS) is defined as

$$\text{TS} = \frac{\text{RSFE}}{\text{MAD}}$$

Tracking signal is a dynamic measure of forecasting errors, as it can be updated after every time new actual demand data is added to the earlier data. Let us try to understand the calculation of TS by taking up Winters' forecasts of Example 15.3. Copy the first, fifth, and sixth columns from the SPSS spreadsheet of Fig. 15.23 into columns B, C, and D of an MS Excel spreadsheet as shown in Fig. 15.36. Column A contains days 1–28, column B contains the actual demand $D$, column C contains Winters' forecast $F$, and column D contains the deviation $D - F$.

In column E, let us calculate the RSFE for each of the given days. Copy cell D4 into cell E4, which is the RSFE for day 1. Put the formula **=E4+D5** in cell E5 and press **Enter**. The cumulative deviation 37.1234, that is, RSFE for day 2 appears in cell E5. Copy the formula and paste it in cells E6 to E31. The values shown in cells E6 to E31 appear. These are the RSFE values for the given 28 days. In column F, we determine the absolute deviation $|D - F|$ by dropping the negative signs (if any) for the deviation values given in column D.

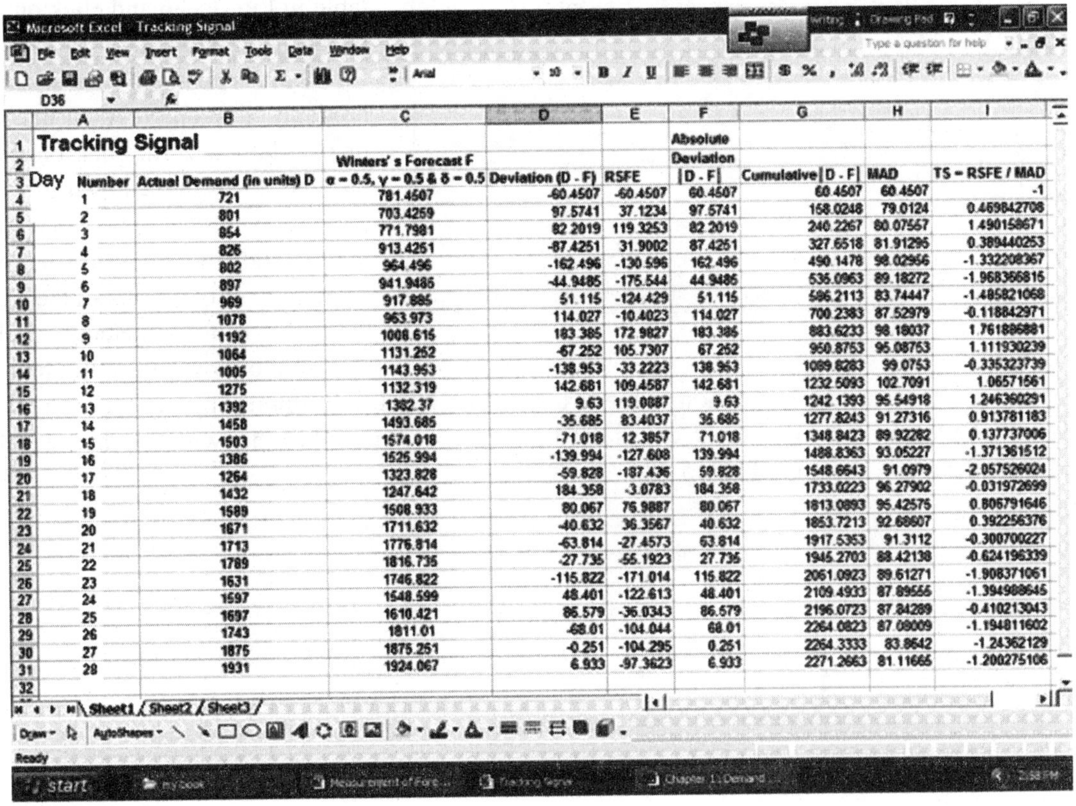

| Day Number | Actual Demand (in units) D | Winters' s Forecast F α = 0.5, γ = 0.5 & δ = 0.5 | Deviation (D - F) | RSFE | Absolute Deviation \|D - F\| | Cumulative \|D - F\| | MAD | TS = RSFE / MAD |
|---|---|---|---|---|---|---|---|---|
| 1 | 721 | 781.4507 | -60.4507 | -60.4507 | 60.4507 | 60.4507 | 60.4507 | -1 |
| 2 | 801 | 703.4259 | 97.5741 | 37.1234 | 97.5741 | 158.0248 | 79.0124 | 0.469842708 |
| 3 | 854 | 771.7981 | 82.2019 | 119.3253 | 82.2019 | 240.2267 | 80.07557 | 1.490158671 |
| 4 | 826 | 913.4251 | -87.4251 | 31.9002 | 87.4251 | 327.6518 | 81.91295 | 0.389440253 |
| 5 | 802 | 964.496 | -162.496 | -130.596 | 162.496 | 490.1478 | 98.02956 | -1.332208367 |
| 6 | 897 | 941.9485 | -44.9485 | -175.544 | 44.9485 | 535.0963 | 89.18272 | -1.968366815 |
| 7 | 969 | 917.885 | 51.115 | -124.429 | 51.115 | 586.2113 | 83.74447 | -1.485821068 |
| 8 | 1078 | 963.973 | 114.027 | -10.4023 | 114.027 | 700.2383 | 87.52979 | -0.118842971 |
| 9 | 1192 | 1008.615 | 183.385 | 172.9827 | 183.385 | 883.6233 | 98.18037 | 1.761886881 |
| 10 | 1064 | 1131.252 | -67.252 | 105.7307 | 67.252 | 950.8753 | 95.08753 | 1.111930239 |
| 11 | 1005 | 1143.953 | -138.953 | -33.2223 | 138.953 | 1089.8283 | 99.0753 | -0.335323739 |
| 12 | 1275 | 1132.319 | 142.681 | 109.4587 | 142.681 | 1232.5093 | 102.7091 | 1.06571561 |
| 13 | 1392 | 1382.37 | 9.63 | 119.0887 | 9.63 | 1242.1393 | 95.54918 | 1.246360291 |
| 14 | 1458 | 1493.685 | -35.685 | 83.4037 | 35.685 | 1277.8243 | 91.27316 | 0.913781183 |
| 15 | 1503 | 1574.018 | -71.018 | 12.3857 | 71.018 | 1348.8423 | 89.92282 | 0.137737006 |
| 16 | 1386 | 1525.994 | -139.994 | -127.608 | 139.994 | 1488.8363 | 93.05227 | -1.371361512 |
| 17 | 1264 | 1323.828 | -59.828 | -187.436 | 59.828 | 1548.6643 | 91.0979 | -2.057526024 |
| 18 | 1432 | 1247.642 | 184.358 | -3.0783 | 184.358 | 1733.0223 | 96.27902 | -0.031972699 |
| 19 | 1589 | 1508.933 | 80.067 | 76.9887 | 80.067 | 1813.0893 | 95.42575 | 0.806791646 |
| 20 | 1671 | 1711.632 | -40.632 | 36.3567 | 40.632 | 1853.7213 | 92.68607 | 0.392256376 |
| 21 | 1713 | 1776.814 | -63.814 | -27.4573 | 63.814 | 1917.5353 | 91.3112 | -0.300700227 |
| 22 | 1789 | 1816.735 | -27.735 | -55.1923 | 27.735 | 1945.2703 | 88.42138 | -0.624196339 |
| 23 | 1631 | 1746.822 | -115.822 | -171.014 | 115.822 | 2061.0923 | 89.61271 | -1.908371061 |
| 24 | 1597 | 1548.599 | 48.401 | -122.613 | 48.401 | 2109.4933 | 87.89555 | -1.394988645 |
| 25 | 1697 | 1610.421 | 86.579 | -36.0343 | 86.579 | 2196.0723 | 87.84289 | -0.410213043 |
| 26 | 1743 | 1811.01 | -68.01 | -104.044 | 68.01 | 2264.0823 | 87.08009 | -1.194811602 |
| 27 | 1875 | 1875.251 | -0.251 | -104.295 | 0.251 | 2264.3333 | 83.8642 | -1.24362129 |
| 28 | 1931 | 1924.067 | 6.933 | -97.3623 | 6.933 | 2271.2663 | 81.11665 | -1.200275106 |

**Fig. 15.36** Tracking signal

In column G, let us calculate the cumulative $|D - F|$ for each of the given days. Copy cell F4 into cell G4, which is the cumulative $|D - F|$ for day 1. Put the formula **=G4+F5** in cell G5 and press **Enter**. The cumulative $|D - F|$ 158.0248 for day 2 appears in cell G5. Copy the formula and paste it in cells G6 to G31. The values shown in cells G6 to G31 appear. These are the cumulative $|D - F|$ values for the given 28 days.

In column H, we find the MAD, which is the cumulative $|D - F|$ up to the corresponding day divided by the number of days. Put the formula **=G4/A4** in cell H4 and press **Enter**. The value

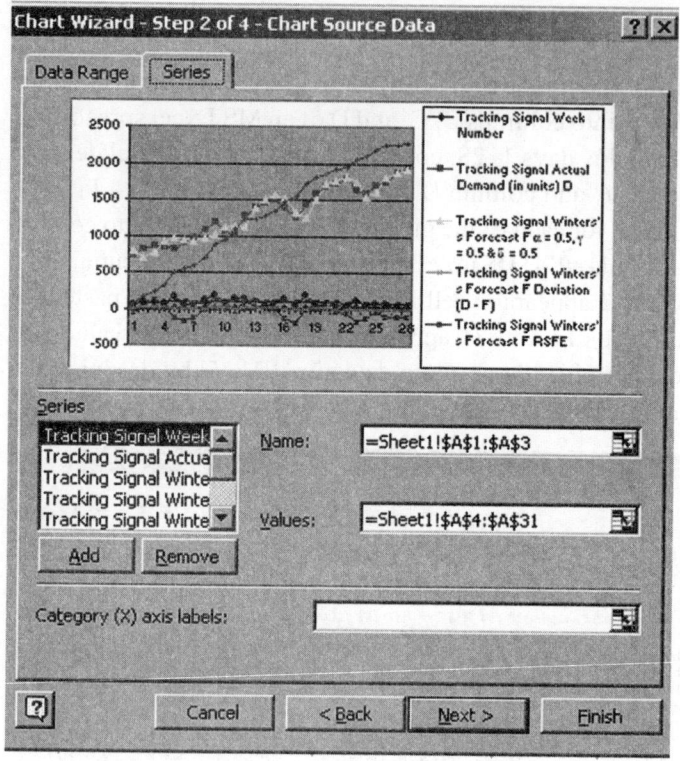

**Fig. 15.37**

60.4507 appears in cell H4. Copy the formula and paste it in cells H5 to H31. The values of MAD shown in cells H5 to H31 appear. In column I, we calculate the TS for the given days. Put the formula =E4/H4 in cell I4 and press **Enter**. The value − 1 appears in cell I4. Copy the formula and paste it in cells I5 to I31. The values of TS shown in cells H5 to H31 appear.

We now make a chart to plot the TS against the number of days. Select the table in Fig. 15.36 and click on the chart wizard icon on the toolbar. Choose **Line** for **Chart type** in the chart wizard dialog box and click on **Next**. In the next step of the chart wizard, click on the **Series** tab; the dialog box shown in Fig. 15.37 appears. Note that the chart view visible in this dialog box shows various plots, but we require only the plot of the TS against the number of days. Hence, click on the **Remove** button below the text box for **Series** until the last option in the text box (for **Tracking Signal**) appears. For the text box of **Category (X) axis labels**, choose cells A4 to A31. Proceed further with the chart wizard to get the graph shown in Fig. 15.38.

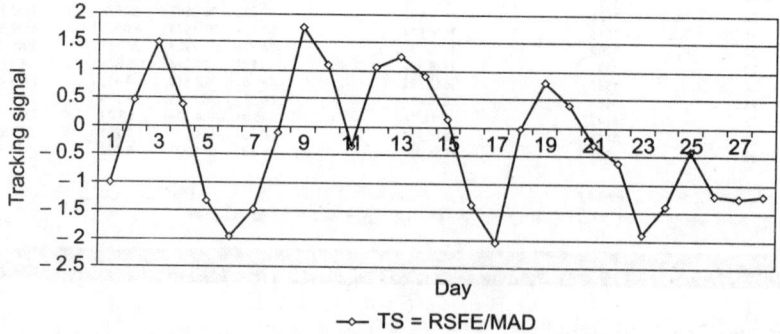

**Fig. 15.38**   Tracking signal plotted against number of days

As shown in Fig. 15.38, the TS values keep on fluctuating around the centre value zero. In an ideal forecast system, the TS value should hover closely around zero. This will mean that the overestimated forecast errors are offset completely by the underestimated ones. The region above the centre zero line shows the situation when the actual demand exceeds the forecast, while the region below the centre zero line shows the situation when the forecast exceeds the actual demand. Some control limits can be established for the TS to ensure that the forecast errors are within acceptable limits. The forecast control limits used in controlling the forecasting errors are usually established using standard deviation based on the MSE rather than the TS. We will discuss forecast control limits in detail in the next section.

> Forecast control charts are made by using individual values of forecast errors rather than cumulative values, as in case of TS control limits.

## Forecast Control Limits

Forecast control charts are made by using individual values of forecast errors rather than cumulative values, as in case of TS control limits. It is assumed here that forecast errors follow a normal distribution curve and are randomly distributed around the mean, which is zero. As discussed in Chapter 14, control charts in statistical quality control are made with control limits usually at three sigma limits. Here also, control limits are usually set at three sigma limits, with the standard deviation $s$ given by

$$s = \sqrt{MSE}$$

Thus, the three sigma limits are given by $0 \pm 3s$, as the mean forecast error is assumed to be zero (see Fig. 15.39). The forecasting system is said to be performing well if all the forecast error points fall within these control limits. Any point exceeding either the upper control limit (UCL) or the lower control limit (LCL) is a signal to the forecaster to start looking for some assignable causes of variation. These assignable causes may be due to temporary shortage or breakdown, natural phenomena such as severe weather conditions, mistakes in calculations of forecasting errors, etc. Random variations within the control limits are always acceptable. Let us take up an example to understand the calculation of forecast control limits.

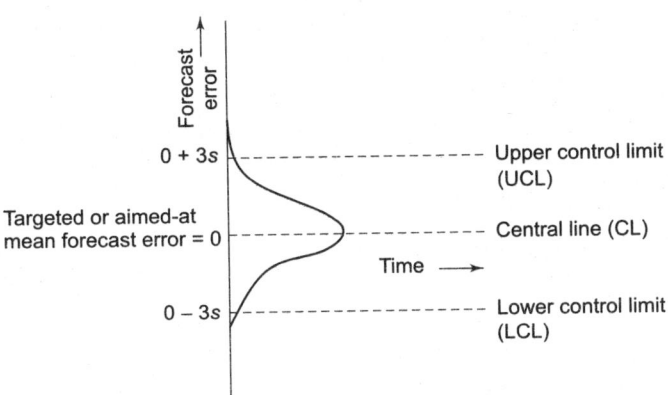

**Fig. 15.39** Forecast control limits

### Example 15.6

Table 15.7 gives the data for actual demand $D$ and forecast $F$ for a product for the past 25 months. Establish a three sigma control chart for the forecast errors using the data of the first 10 months, and then evaluate the remaining data with the control chart.

**Table 15.7**

| Month | Actual demand D (units) | Forecast F (units) | Month | Actual demand D (units) | Forecast F (units) | Month | Actual demand D (units) | Forecast F (units) |
|---|---|---|---|---|---|---|---|---|
| 1 | 1,578 | 1,584 | 10 | 1,685 | 1,673 | 19 | 1,598 | 1,603 |
| 2 | 1,689 | 1,699 | 11 | 1,715 | 1,720 | 20 | 1,564 | 1,529 |
| 3 | 1,795 | 1,724 | 12 | 1,811 | 1,801 | 21 | 1,762 | 1,784 |
| 4 | 1,522 | 1,512 | 13 | 2,136 | 2,124 | 22 | 1,458 | 1,464 |
| 5 | 1,643 | 1,687 | 14 | 2,297 | 2,314 | 23 | 1,579 | 1,571 |
| 6 | 1,894 | 1,901 | 15 | 2,378 | 2,395 | 24 | 1,771 | 1,798 |
| 7 | 2,001 | 1,982 | 16 | 1,678 | 1,673 | 25 | 1,976 | 1,957 |
| 8 | 2,053 | 2,073 | 17 | 1,734 | 1,721 | | | |
| 9 | 1,856 | 1,866 | 18 | 1,873 | 1,888 | | | |

### Solution

Paste the given data in columns A, B, and C of an MS Excel worksheet (Fig. 15.40). To calculate the deviation $D - F$ in column D, put the formula **=B5 − C5** in cell D5 and press **Enter** to get the value − 6. Copy the formula and paste it in cells D6 to D29 to get the values shown in these cells. In column E, we calculate the squared error $(D - F)^2$ for months 1 to 10. Put the formula **=D5*D5** in cell E5 and press **Enter** to get the value 36. Copy the formula and paste it in cells E6 to E14.

| | A | B | C | D | E | F | G | H | I |
|---|---|---|---|---|---|---|---|---|---|
| 1 | **Forecast Control Limits** | | | | | | | | |
| 2 | | | | | | | | | |
| 3 | | | | | | | | | |
| 4 | Month # | Actual Demand D | Forecast F | Deviation (D - F) | Squared Error (D - F)² | | | | |
| 5 | 1 | 1578 | 1584 | -6 | 36 | | | | |
| 6 | 2 | 1689 | 1699 | -10 | 100 | | | | |
| 7 | 3 | 1795 | 1724 | 71 | 5041 | | | | |
| 8 | 4 | 1522 | 1512 | 10 | 100 | | | | |
| 9 | 5 | 1643 | 1687 | -44 | 1936 | | | | |
| 10 | 6 | 1894 | 1901 | -7 | 49 | | | | |
| 11 | 7 | 2001 | 1982 | 19 | 361 | | | | |
| 12 | 8 | 2053 | 2073 | -20 | 400 | | | | |
| 13 | 9 | 1856 | 1866 | -10 | 100 | | | | |
| 14 | 10 | 1685 | 1673 | 12 | 144 | | | | |
| 15 | 11 | 1715 | 1720 | -5 | 826.7 | 28.75239 | | | |
| 16 | 12 | 1811 | 1801 | 10 | MSE | Standard Deviation s = √ MSE | | | |
| 17 | 13 | 2136 | 2124 | 12 | | | | | |
| 18 | 14 | 2297 | 2314 | -17 | | Upper Control Limit = 0 + 3s = | | | 86.257174 |
| 19 | 15 | 2378 | 2395 | -17 | | Central Line = | | | |
| 20 | 16 | 1678 | 1673 | 5 | | Lower Control Limit = 0 - 3s = | | | -86.25717 |
| 21 | 17 | 1734 | 1721 | 13 | | | | | |
| 22 | 18 | 1873 | 1888 | -15 | | | | | |
| 23 | 19 | 1598 | 1603 | -5 | | | | | |
| 24 | 20 | 1564 | 1529 | 35 | | | | | |
| 25 | 21 | 1762 | 1784 | -22 | | | | | |
| 26 | 22 | 1458 | 1464 | -6 | | | | | |
| 27 | 23 | 1579 | 1571 | 8 | | | | | |
| 28 | 24 | 1771 | 1798 | -27 | | | | | |
| 29 | 25 | 1976 | 1957 | 19 | | | | | |
| 30 | | | | 0.12 | | | | | |

**Fig. 15.40** Forecast control limits

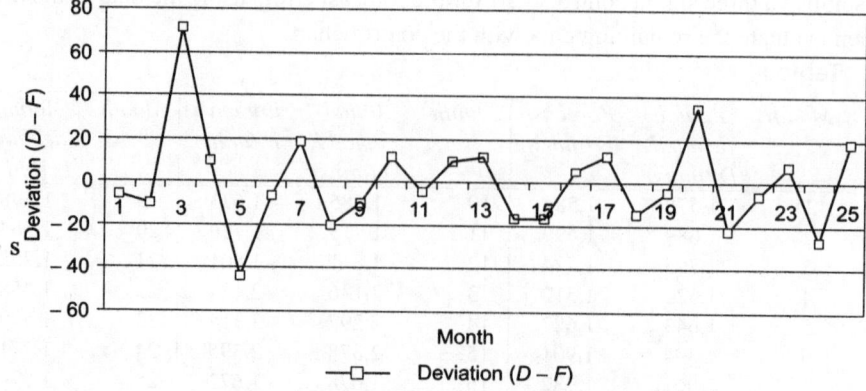

**Fig. 15.41** Forecast control limit chart

Now, select the cells E5 to E15 and click on the small arrow adjacent to the $\Sigma$ tool on the toolbar. Choose **Average** from the pull-down menu so that the value 826.7 appears in cell E15. This is the MSE. Calculate the stanard deviation $s = \sqrt{\text{MSE}}$ in cell F15 by putting the formula =**SQRT(E15)**; the value 28.75239 is obtained. Calculate UCL = 0 + 3$s$ in cell I18 by putting the formula =**3\*F15** to get the value 86.257174. Similarly, calculate LCL = 06 – 3$s$ in cell I20 by putting the formula = **– 3\*F15** to get the alue – 86.257174.

Using the MS Excel chart wizard, plot the graph for deviation $(D - F)$ with respect to the months as shown in Fig. 15.41. Note that all the points are well within the control limits $\pm$ 86.257174. Thus, the forecasting system is under control.

# New Product Demand Forecasting

Forecasting demand for new products is relatively difficult due to lack of past sales data, consumer acceptance, and reactions of competitive forces. Assmus (1984) compiled various models specifically developed for demand forecasting of new products (Fig. 15.42)

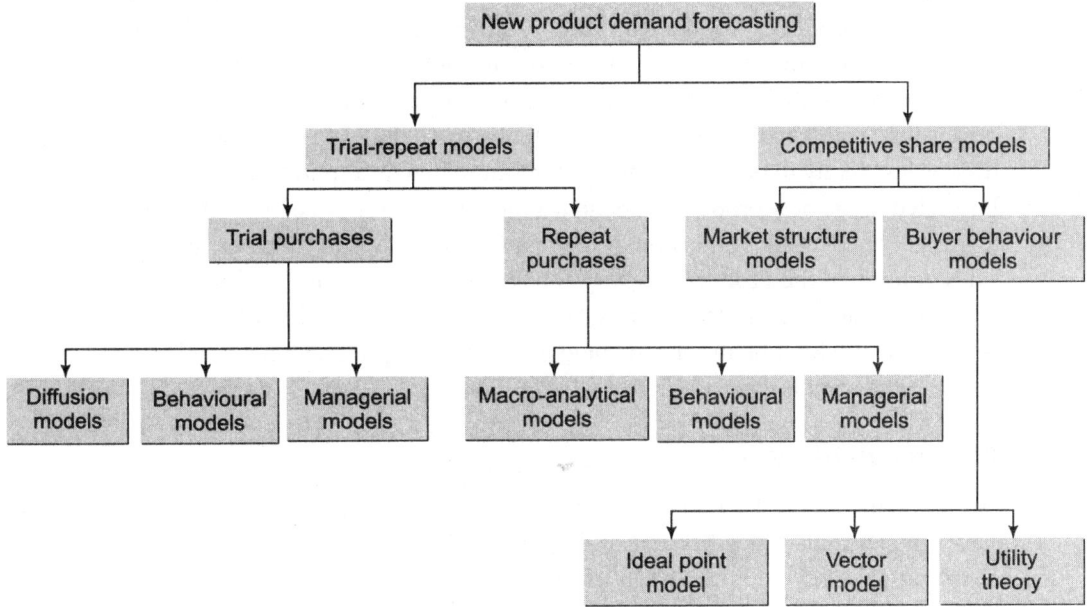

**Fig. 15.42**  Various models for new product demand forecasting

The various models for demand forecasting of a new product can be broadly divided into two categories—trial-repeat models and competitive share models. Trial-repeat models basically focus on potential demand from product trial purchases and, subsequently, from repeat purchases of the new product.

### Trial Purchases

*Trial purchases*, as the name suggests, are the purchases made by customers to try out a new product and experience its unique features. Three types of models, as follows, are used for demand forecasting of trial purchases:

**Diffusion models** These models forecast the trial purchases due to the adoption and imitation tendencies within the population of potential buyers. Trial is assumed to be a function of the social process where a few courageous persons would adopt the product first and lead the way for the followers, who constitute the majority of the total market. The total number of potential trial buyers is affected by the firm's marketing efforts along with external variables, like economic conditions.

**Behavioural models** These models explicitly deal with various stages of potential buyer readiness preceding a trial purchase. The awareness and attitude of a potential consumer population is influenced by advertisements about the new product by the manufacturer/retailer and word-of-mouth promotion by people who have just tried the product. There are four levels of awareness of a new product (Urban 1969): awareness of (a) the brand, (b) its promotional campaigns, (c) specific product appeals, and (d) word-of-mouth recommendations.

**Managerial models** These models identify the variables that can be controlled by the firm to influence product trial rates by the target population. Some of these variables are product sampling programmes, distribution level (availability of the product in retail outlets) across regions, and price of the product. Product sampling programmes involve distributing free samples of the new product amongst the target population. In such programmes, the trial rate is defined as the product of the probability that a person receives a free product sample and the probability that a person who received the sample would actually use it. However, it should be noted that a 'sample trier' is less likely to purchase a product in future than is a 'purchase trier', who was sufficiently interested in the new product to spend his money to familiarize himself with it. The distribution level is defined as the proportion of the retail outlets that carry the new product weighted by the sales volume in the product category. The idea here is that the customer is more likely to buy the new product if it is conveniently available to him. Similarly, if the price of the new product is intentionally kept below the average price of other products in a similar category, it is more likely to induce a higher trial rate of the new product.

## Repeat Purchases

As the name suggests, *repeat purchases* are the purchases by the customers subsequent to new product trials. They become an important component of the demand forecast, particularly if the purchase cycle is relatively short. Three models of repeat purchases are suggested, as follows:

**Macro-analytical models** These models predict repeat purchases on the basis of external factors, such as repeat ratios or brand-switching probabilities. The first repeat ratio is the fraction of the initial buyers who make a second purchase and represents the probability that a first-time buyer would purchase the product for the second time. The second repeat ratio is similarly the fraction of the second-time buyers who make a purchase of the new product for the third time. These ratios tend to grow larger as the group of hard-core loyal customers evolves.

**Behavioural models** After having tried the new product, whether the customer would go for a repeat purchase or not depends upon certain internal factors like experience with the first use of the product. Customers who are ready for a repeat purchase are then identified and their awareness about the new product is translated into intent or predisposition to purchase. However, if the customer would actually go for repeat purchase depends upon intervening variables such as in-store price, displays and facings in the store, and so on. Displays and facings become unimportant after the first repeat purchase; however, relative price changes could cause the buyer to switch to other brands.

**Managerial models**   These models consider the variables that can be controlled by managers in inducing a repeat purchase. Pricing and advertising are such variables. An advertising copy test is conducted to identify the product attributes that were communicated through the advertisement. A consumer use test is then conducted to determine how these attributes were rated by consumers who used the product. These consumer ratings point towards the probability of a repeat purchase on the part of a consumer. Thus, managers may like to bring in changes in the advertisement to highlight different product attributes in order to enhance the repeat rate.

### Competitive Share Models

In competitive share models, an equilibrium market share for the new product is determined either by considering the choice of buyers from a set of competing products in the given market (buyer behaviour models) or by studying the unique characteristics of the market itself (market structure models).

**Buyer behaviour models**   Any of the three approaches can be used to understand the buyer behaviour with respect to the new product viz-a-viz existing similar products in the perceptual space. The first approach is the 'ideal point model', in which an ideal point (ideal combination of product attributes as deemed by the customers) is determined on the product space (represented by quadrants created by axes of different product attributes). The closer the point coordinates of the new product to the ideal point, the better are its chances of capturing the market share upon introduction. The second approach called the 'vector model' is a special case of the ideal point model, in which the ideal limit of any product attribute is considered as infinity. Therefore, the relative position of the point coordinates of the new product with the most successful existing similar product is taken into account to predict its potential market share. The third approach is based upon the 'utility theory', in which coefficients of the utility function reflect the relative importance of relevant product attributes, their interdependencies as well as the risk attitude of the buyer (decision maker).

**Market structure models**   The equilibrium market share for the new product is determined in these models by considering the number of products in the market, their respective shares, and the consumer preference structure. If the customers in a given market demonstrate high switching propensity between brands, the new product is likely to capture a larger market share than if a high loyalty factor prevailed.

## Summary

*Demand forecasting* is predicting the future demand of the products or services of an organization. It is very important for organizations to determine the capacity of facilities at the outset, which is eventually used as an input for production/operation planning, materials requirement planning, etc. Basically, forecasting methods can be divided into two categories: *quantitative and qualitative*. Qualitative methods are subjective in nature and are based on different types of surveys and the judgement of experts. The various qualitative methods are customer surveys, sales force composite, executive opinion, Delphi method, and past analogy.

Quantitative forecasting methods may be divided into *time series analysis* and *causal analysis*. Time series analysis requires a time series of historical demand data with respect to time intervals (periods) in the past to make predictions for future demand. There are five popular methods used in time series analysis: simple moving average, simple exponential smoothing, Holt's double-exponential smoothing, Winters' triple-exponential smoothing, and forecasting by linear regression analysis. Causal analysis is performing demand forecasting using a cause-and-effect relationship. *Linear trend* analysis is a popular method of causal analysis.

It is always desirable that demand forecast values should be as close as possible to the actual future demand. Practically, some *forecasting errors* (deviations from the actual demand values) do get introduced.

Therefore, we need to measure these errors and then try to minimise these as much as possible. There are various measures of forecast errors: running sum of forecast errors (RSFE), mean forecast error (MFE), mean absolute deviation (MAD), mean squared error (MSE), mean absolute percentage error (MAPE), and tracking signal (TS).

*Forecast control charts* are made using individual values of forecast errors rather than cumulative values, as in the case of tracking signal control limits. It is assumed here that forecast errors follow a normal distribution curve and are randomly distributed around the mean, which is zero. The forecasting system is said to be performing well if all the forecast error points fall within these control limits. Any point exceeding either the upper control limit (UCL) or the lower control limit (LCL) is a signal to the forecaster to start looking for some assignable causes of variation.

Forecasting demand for new products requires different approaches such as trial-repeat models and competitive share models.

## References

Assmus, G. 1984, 'New product forecasting', *Journal of Forecasting*, vol. 3, no. 2, p. 121.

Beck, Jeff 1999, 'Statistical process control and selectable forecast calenders reduce GE Aircraft Engine's parts inventory', *Production and Inventory Management Journal,* Third Quarter. (Published with permission of APICS—The Educational Society for Resource Management, Alexandria, Virginia, USA.)

Paul, J. and A. Mukherjee 2004, 'ATMs and cash demand forecasting: a study of two commercial banks', *International Conference on Applied Business Research*, Bangkok, Thailand, 1–4 December.

Urban, G.L. 1969, 'Market response models for the analysis of new products', in King, R.L. (ed.) 1968 *Fall Conference Proceedings*, Chicago, Illinois; American Marketing Association, pp. 105–111.

## Keywords

**Causal analysis** is performing demand forecasting using a cause-and-effect relationship.

**Delphi method** is a questionnaire email sent to experts from various diversified streams, seeking their opinion on the forecast of a (usually highly advanced technology) product.

**Demand forecasting** is predicting the future demand of the products or services of an organization.

**Simple exponential smoothing method** has the term 'exponential' in its name because every period in the past is given a weightage of $\alpha(1 - \alpha)^n$, where $n$ represents the number of periods in the past. Hence,

$n$ is the exponent used in the weight $\alpha(1 - \alpha)^n$ attached if we have to consider data which is $n$ periods away in the past.

**Simple moving average** involves finding the simple average of past data used for forecasting.

**Time series analysis** requires a time series of historical demand data with respect to time intervals (periods) in the past to make predictions for future demand.

**Tracking signal (TS)** is defined as TS = RSFE/ MAD. It is a dynamic measure of forecasting errors, as it can be updated every time new actual demand data is added to the earlier data.

## CASE STUDY I

# Air Traffic Forecasting by Airbus

From its inception in 1970 as a European consortium, in the then American dominated aviation industry, Airbus has grown into a global company employing more than 55,000 people and offering a range of 14 aircraft types that offers unrivalled levels of reliability, innovation, comfort, efficiency, and flexibility.

With its head office in Toulouse, France, Airbus operates out of over 160 international locations, including 16 main development and manufacturing sites in France, Germany, UK, Spain, and three wholly owned subsidiaries in China, Japan, and North America. Specialist facilities around the world include engineering centres in Beijing, Wichita, and Mobile; a joint venture engineering centre in Moscow; fast response spares centres in Hamburg, Frankfurt, Washington, Beijing, and Singapore; state-of-the-art training centres in Toulouse, Hamburg, Miami, and Beijing; and 130 field service offices at key customer locations.

Airbus is 80 per cent owned by the European Aeronautic Defence and Space Company (EADS) and 20 per cent by BAE Systems. Airbus has sold more than 5,500 aircraft to over 200 customers since its inception. The secret of this success is very clear. The company is responsive to customer needs, anticipates future demands, and creates innovative products, which are built to the highest standards of safety and which incorporate the most appropriate mix of leading edge technologies.

Airbus is sensitive to the way an airline's profitability can stand or fall by how closely it matches demand capacity and how quickly it can adapt its fleet. For this reason, Airbus aircrafts offer the highest possible degree of commonality in airframes, onboard systems, cockpits, and handling systems. This benefits pilots, crews, and maintenance staff, while giving airlines lower training and maintenance costs as well as flexibility. For example, pilots who hold a type rating on one Airbus aircraft type require minimal training to become qualified on another.

For almost 35 years the Airbus global market forecast has accurately anticipated market trends and customer demands some 20 years in advance, providing an invaluable resource in guiding the company from newcomer to market leader and in helping airlines plan for the future. With such a strong track record, Airbus is confident when it forecasts that the next twenty years will see demand for 16,600 new passenger aircraft with more than 100 seats (including over 1,200 with more than 450 seats), in addition to 700 new and 2,400 converted freighters. Airbus expects to deliver at least half of all these aircrafts.

The starting point for any aircraft demand forecast is a clear understanding of the issues driving air transport and the way in which they relate to future air traffic and aircraft capacity. Airbus' traffic forecast process is based on four major building blocks—preparatory market research, appropriate market segmentation, econometrics, and importantly, network development (Fig. 15.43).

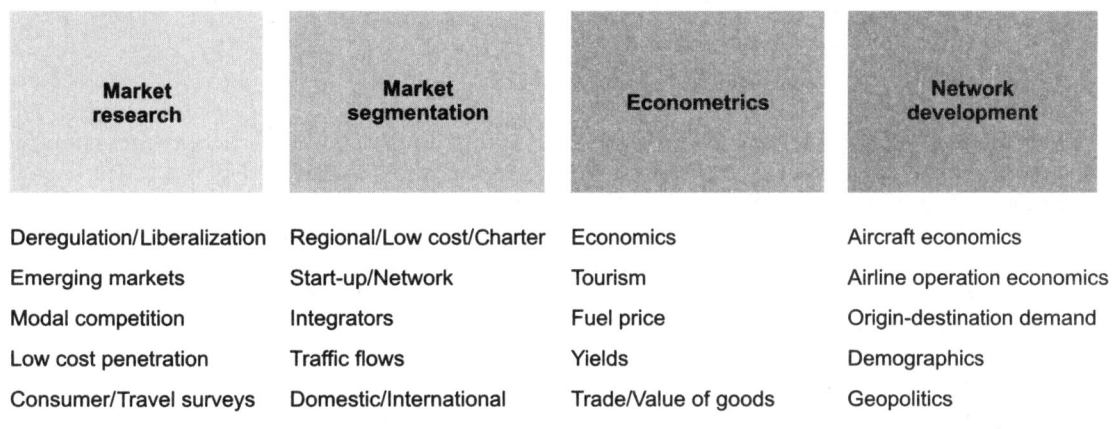

**Fig. 15.43**   Airbus' traffic forecast process

The Airbus global market forecast analyses a total of 152 distinct domestic, regional, and intercontinental passenger sub-markets, segmented according to their degree of maturity and specific characteristics over a period of time. Airbus' market research examines the fundamental drivers of transportation including future consumer behaviour and expectations, the pace of liberalization, the growing importance of emerging markets, and constraints, such as the influence of airport congestion.

The market is segmented by airline business model, region, and traffic flow. This enables the precise circumstances and drivers prevailing on every segment to be fully considered. Econometric data is then used to quantify future air travel demand based on economic, operational, and structural variables. Finally, the derived growth is distributed accordingly across the route network, either through organic growth, such as the addition of traffic on existing routes such as New York to London, or through the addition of brand new routes. This process produces a view of the future aviation network on which to base the micro demand forecast, which essentially takes the form of a large number of airline by airline fleet build ups.

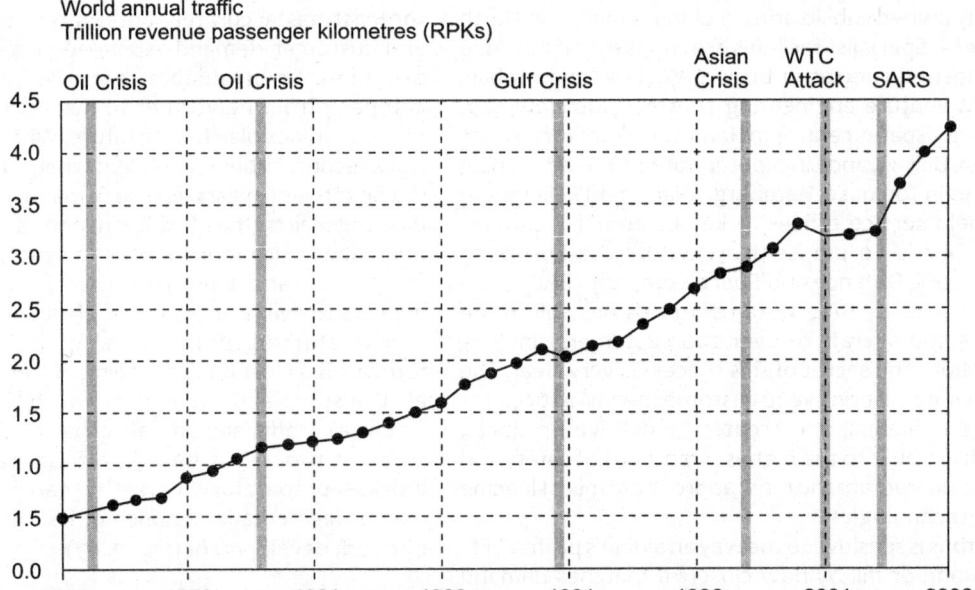

World annual traffic
Trillion revenue passenger kilometres (RPKs)

*Source:* ICAO, Airbus estimate for 2006.

**Fig. 15.44**  Air travel resilient to external shocks

In some market segments, classic econometric modelling is not sufficient to forecast traffic growth. For example, in Asia, the development of low cost carriers (LCCs) is driven by the pace and timing of deregulation within each country and the liberalization between others. In Mexico, a portion of air traffic growth depends on the number of people switching from the popular bus network to air transport, which is a consequence of lower airfares and improved journey time. In the maturing LCC markets of North America and Western Europe, the LCCs' growth will ultimately depend on the number and size of new routes still to be opened on an economic and sustainable basis.

Air travel demand has proven to be resilient to exogenous disruption such as recession, war, terrorism, and disease (see Fig. 15.44). The impact of each crisis has lasted only a short time, after which strong growth has been resumed. After two years of stagnation in 2001, air travel demand increased 14 per cent in 2004, 7 per cent in 2005, and close to 6 per cent in 2006.

Looking forward, the main drivers of traffic growth will be the increasing importance of the Middle Eastern global hubs, the development of new routes, the evolution of domestic traffic in China and India, the Asian economic paradigm shift created by a wave of consumerism, and the continuing traffic stimulation by low cost or low fare airlines.

In terms of the number of available seats, the market share of Asian LCCs grew from 5 per cent in 2004 to 9 per cent in 2006, largely within their own deregulated domestic markets. While there is still a potential for domestic new route development, the growth potential is thought to be much larger for the intra-Asian international markets. The pace of growth in these international markets will largely depend on the pace of liberalization between countries in the region. For example, the Association of South East Asian Nations (ASEAN) is planning for open skies in 2008.

Air travel demand between Asian cities in a fully liberalized market could generate up to 1,600 LCC routes by 2015. The Airbus market forecast conservatively assumes that by 2015, the progressive liberalization within Asia will result in the opening of 920 of these routes. This will increase the number of Asian airports with LCC operations from 37 in 2000 to 292 in 2010. Asian LCCs are anticipated to grow at 11 per cent per year for the next ten years (Fig. 15.45).

Overall, Airbus predicts that for the next 20 years, revenue passenger kilometres (RPKs) will grow at an average annual growth rate of 4.8 per cent. Among the largest submarkets, annual RPK growth on Indian and Chinese flows is expected to average 12.3 per cent

and 8.2 per cent respectively. This reflects increasingly optimistic projections for economic growth in these countries, as well as an increasing tendency for their population to travel by air. Growth will also be driven by increased wealth and improved access to air transportation.

For other, more mature markets, such as the US and the intra-European market, Airbus foresees average annual RPK growth of 2.7 per cent and 4.1 per cent respectively, itself not at all insignificant, due to the already high base of air traffic in these regions.

Although Indian and Chinese domestic flows are set to increase at a quicker pace, by 2025 the total volume of traffic and the actual volume of new RPKs (growth) in the US will still be larger (Fig. 15.46). However, by that time, the flows to and within North America—which has traditionally generated the largest volume of traffic—will have been overtaken collectively by flows based in the fastest growing regions of Asia-Pacific and Europe.

In addition, the combined Middle East traffic flows are also expected to expand rapidly with 6.2 per cent annual growth by 2025. Africa and Latin America are also expected to increase by 5.4 per cent and 5.3 per cent respectively over the next twenty years.

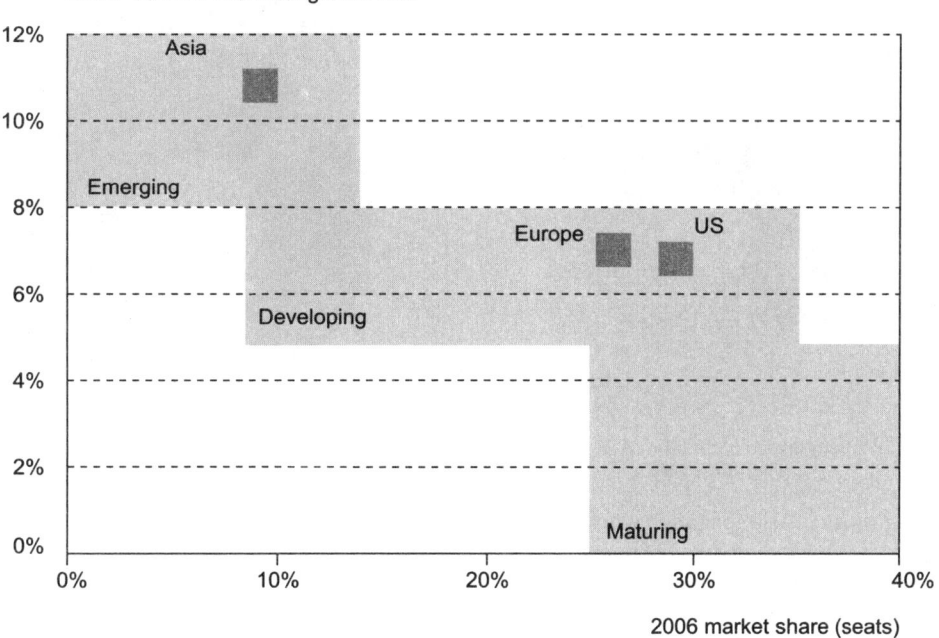

**Fig. 15.45**  Low cost carriers in Asia to continue their strong growth

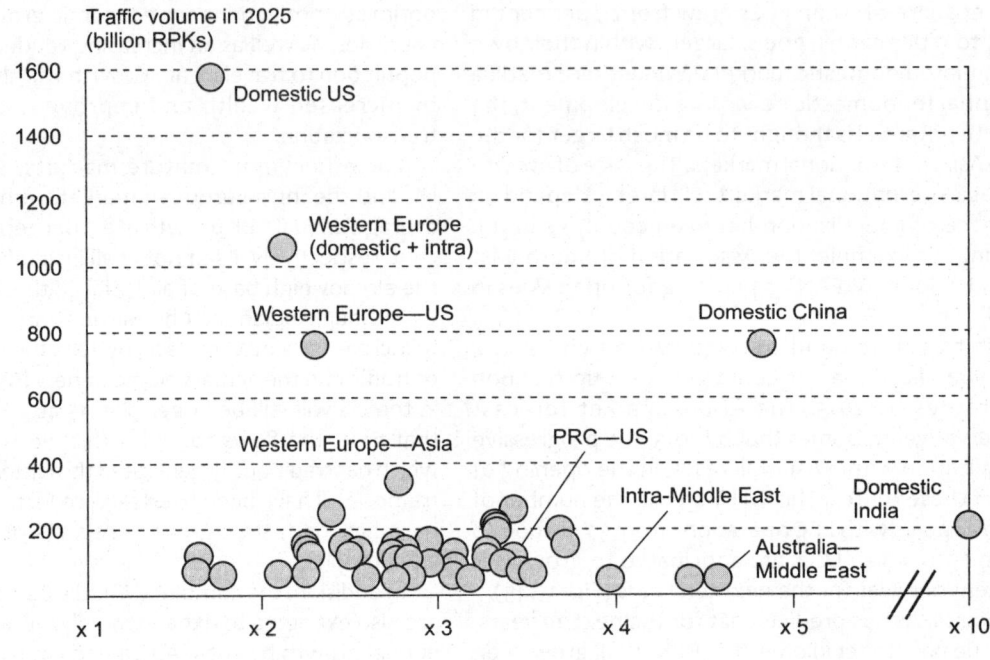

**Fig. 15.46** US and Western Europe remain the largest markets

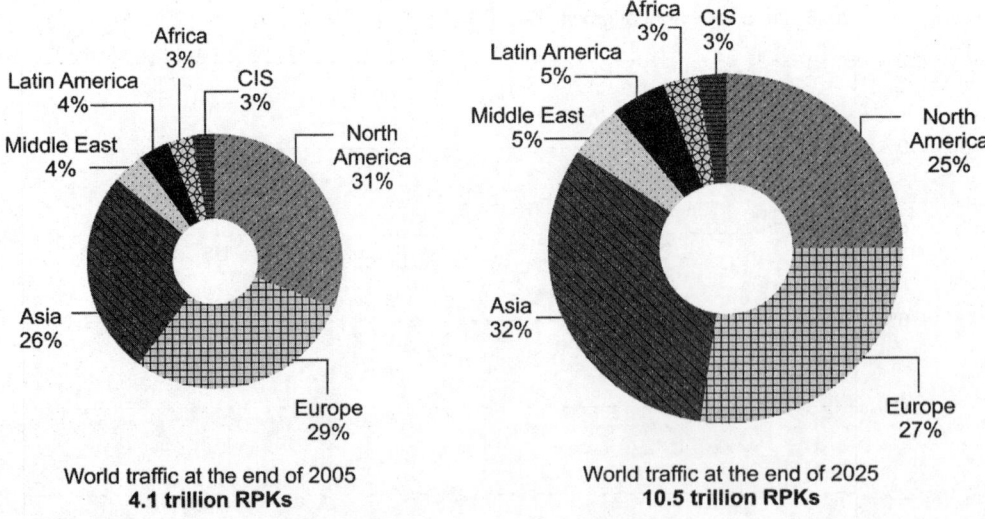

**Fig. 15.47** Asia to lead in world traffic by 2025

Airlines based in the Middle East and Asia are expected to develop more quickly than airlines based in other regions, growing by an average of 6.4 per cent and 6.2 per cent respectively. This is fuelled by the aspirations of airlines and, in some cases the countries themselves, as well as access to burgeoning markets driven by liberalization and a growing propensity to travel.

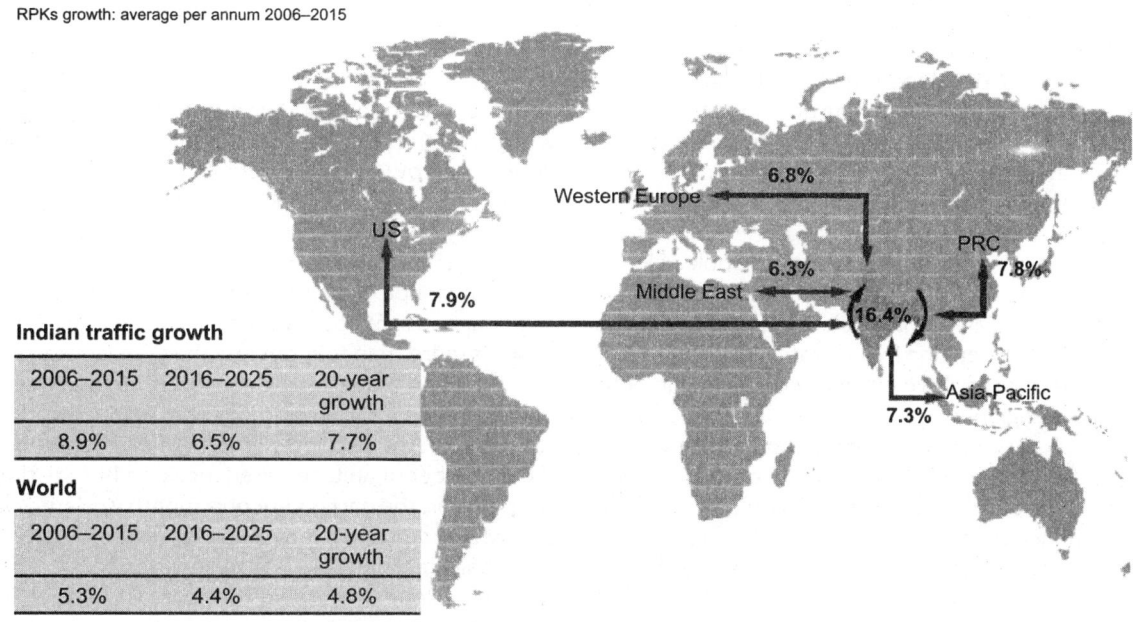

RPKs growth: average per annum 2006–2015

**Indian traffic growth**

| 2006–2015 | 2016–2025 | 20-year growth |
|-----------|-----------|----------------|
| 8.9% | 6.5% | 7.7% |

**World**

| 2006–2015 | 2016–2025 | 20-year growth |
|-----------|-----------|----------------|
| 5.3% | 4.4% | 4.8% |

**Fig. 15.48**   India: International growth high, domestic even higher

The airlines of Latin America, the Commonwealth of Independent States (CIS), and Africa are also expected to register higher growth than the global average during this period, as air transportation and its benefits continue to be more evenly distributed worldwide.

Meanwhile the airlines of North America and Europe—some of the most significant in the world in terms of their aircrafts fleets and traffic—will continue to grow strongly from an already powerful base, averaging 3.9 per cent and 4.6 per annum respectively over the next twenty years.

As a result of these developments, the way that traffic is distributed between regions is expected to evolve. The biggest change will be traffic becoming much more evenly shared across the world, with Asian airlines forecast to represent 32 per cent of traffic, an impressive growth of 6 per cent when compared to the end of 2005 (Fig. 15.47). This having been said, flows which involve North America and Europe are also expected to remain significant. Seven of the top ten flows in terms of actual traffic added are forecast to involve the US, Western Europe, or both. The US domestic market is still expected to add the most RPKs in the next twenty years, with the Chinese domestic, flow next in importance (by this measure). In India, the international growth rate will be high, but domestic growth rate would be even higher (Fig. 15.48)

### Discussion Questions

1. The world annual traffic graph shown in Fig. 15.44 is fairly linear and can easily provide future world annual traffic projections by linear regression analysis. Nevertheless, Airbus follows its four major building blocks (as shown in Fig. 15.42) for making air traffic forecasts. Why?

2. The twenty year time period considered by Airbus for air traffic projections is seemingly too long. Give your views about this statement with proper reasoning.

3. The pie-charts in Fig. 15.47 estimate that the world air traffic proportions for Africa and CIS will stagnate at 3 per cent for the next 20 years. Is this estimate realistic?

## CASE STUDY II

# GE Aircraft Engines

GE Aircraft Engines (GEAE) is the world's leading producer of large and small jet engines for commercial and military aircraft. It also supplies aircraft-derived engines for marine applications and provides aviation services. GEAE's technological excellence, supported by continuing substantial investments in research and development, has been the foundation of growth and helps to ensure quality products for customers. In the early 1990s, GE developed the GE90 turbofan engine to power the large, twin-engine Boeing 777. The GE90 family, with the baseline engine certified on the 777 in 1995, has produced a world record steady-thrust level of 122,965 pounds. To honour this achievement, the GE90-115B was recently named 'the world's most powerful jet engine' by the Guinness Book of World Records. The latest GE90, the GE90-115B, has the world's largest fan (128 inches), composite fan blades, and the highest engine bypass ratio (9:1) to produce the greatest propulsive efficiency of any commercial transport engine.

GEAE has its service parts operation, which supplies parts for its commercial jet engines from an inventory of around 8,000 parts. In 1992, the company's system was confined to forecasting average monthly demand. There were 12 inventory planners with no idea how to identify trends, how to track forecast errors, and how to make provisions for seasonal variations. During this time, the airline industry started facing problems of various sorts and GEAE was forced to reduce costs. The inventory planners were reduced from 12 to 8, with clear instructions to reduce the service parts inventory.

GEAE performed the ABC analysis of its parts and identified that 5 per cent of its parts generated 80 per cent of its business. These 5 per cent parts (called A+ items) were assigned to five inventory planners for micromanaging using a pull-production process. The rest 95 per cent of the parts were assigned to the remaining three planners. Most of these parts did not have smooth demand patterns. Thus, GEAE required a forecasting tool that could handle lumpy and intermittent demand trends. Five hundred items were randomly selected in a pilot test in order to determine how to use selectable forecast calendars to solve forecasting problems.

Initially, for every part, the forecasting calendar is monthly. If the number of units required for a part is less than four per year, the part is put on a semi-annual calendar and refit. If the number of units required for a part is more than four but less than 60 per year, the part is put on a quarterly calendar. If the number of units required for a part is more than 60 but less than 120 per year, the part is put on a bi-monthly calendar. If the number of units required for a part is more than 120 per year, the part is kept on a monthly calendar. A part whose demand has declined for so long that it has essentially reached zero is fitted on a longer duration forecast calendar to make the forecast usable. For example, a part initially on a monthly calendar is moved onto a bimonthly, quarterly, semi-annual, or an annual calendar until its forecast becomes positive. Otherwise, the part is put on an exception list for a manual review.

Once the right calendar is selected for a part, the forecast model accurately represents the underlying demand for the part, resulting in a very low forecasting error. The forecast is revised from time to time to keep the model current with reality by making incremental changes. It also identifies the parts for which the chosen forecast calendar is suspected to

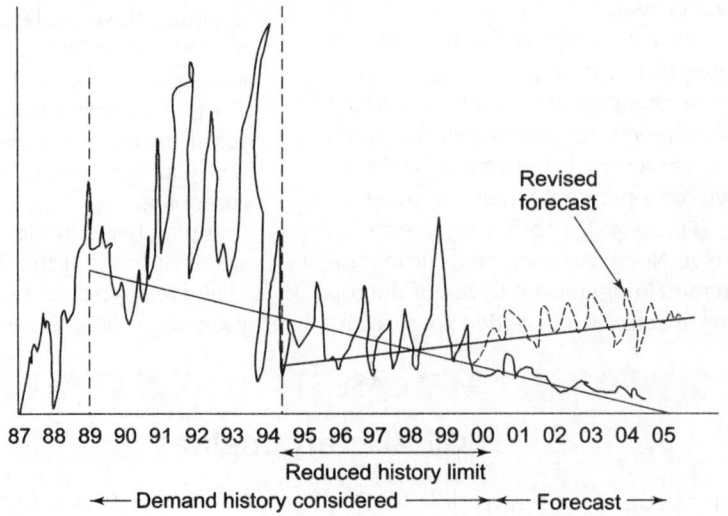

**Fig. 15.49**

**Table 15.8** Calendar comparison for part 3872

| Calendar | Exceptions | Number of history periods | Forecast for coming 12 months (in units) | Error | Relative error (%) |
|---|---|---|---|---|---|
| Semi-annual | None | 6 | 23 | 4.1 | 42.71 |
| Annual | None | 3 | 23 | 5.4 | 56.25 |
| Quarterly | None | 12 | 24 | 6.2 | 64.58 |
| Bimonthly | Error > level | 24 | 25 | 7.8 | 81.25 |
| Monthly | Error > level | 48 | 25 | 9.6 | 100.00 |

be no longer working (i.e., requires fundamental rather than incremental changes). It alerts the planners to investigate the cause of change (e.g., new competition or product changes).

While reviewing the exception list, the planners try all calendars for every part in the list and rank them by forecast error. For example, Table 15.8 shows the calculations of error for various calendars for part 3872. Note that for the various calendars, the forecasts are similar, ranging from 23 to 25 pieces per year, but the errors from the actual demand range from 4.1 to 9.6. The error given here is the standard deviation of the forecast error adjusted for the lead time (for any desired level of service, safety stocks are a constant multiple of the error). Thus, the semi-annual calendar, whose error is only 42.7 per cent of the error using the monthly calendar, needs only 42.7 per cent of the safety stock, compared to the monthly calendar, resulting in an inventory savings of 57.3 per cent.

As discussed earlier, the forecast calendar may

have to be revised in response to an exception. The reason for exceptions is often found by using outside marketing intelligence and then fixed. The demand history limits may be used by planners to fine-tune the exact date the change became apparent. The history that is inappropriate may be discarded. In Fig. 15.49, note that the history limit considered was inappropriate, leading to a linear regression forecast with a high forecast error. Upon reducing the history limit as shown in the figure, the forecast fits the relevant data much better (Beck 1999).

### Discussion Questions

1. How does the selectable forecast calendar approach help GEAE in inventory reduction? Explain in the context of part 3872.
2. Was it necessary for GEAE to perform the ABC analysis of parts? Does it help in inventory reduction?
3. Can the use of control limits help GEAE in its overall effort of inventory control?

# Objective Questions

## Choose the correct option

1. Which one is a market research method of forecasting?
   (a) customer survey
   (b) linear regression analysis
   (c) Delphi method
   (d) trend analysis
2. Which one is a judgemental method of forecasting?
   (a) customer survey
   (b) linear regression analysis
   (c) Delphi method
   (d) trend analysis
3. Which one is not a time-series method of forecasting?
   (a) trend analysis
   (b) simple moving average

   (c) simple exponential smoothing
   (d) linear regression analysis
4. Which one is not a measure of forecast errors?
   (a) mean forecast error
   (b) mean absolute deviation
   (c) running sum of forecast errors
   (d) simple moving average

## State True or False

5. In a time series, the independent variable is time, while actual demand data of the past are the dependent variable.
6. Judgemental methods of forecasting are based on analysing cause-effect relationships between two variables, one of which is an independent variable (the cause) and the other is the dependent variable (the effect).

7. Time is necessarily not a variable to be considered in trend analysis, as otherwise it would become time-series analysis.

## Fill in the blanks

8. _____ methods are preferred when numerical data is available in some form to apply mathematical/statistical models for demand prediction in future.

9. _____ is a dynamic measure of forecasting errors, as it can be updated after every time new actual data is added to the earlier data.

10. _____ charts are made by using individual values of forecast errors rather than cumulative values.

## Concept Review Questions

1. What is demand forecasting? Why is it required by organizations?
2. Explain using a schematic diagram the different methods of forecasting and the situations in which these are appropriate.
3. Explain the various qualitative methods of demand forecasting. In which situations can qualitative methods be useful?
4. In which ways is the simple exponential smoothing method better than the simple moving average method? Explain.

5. What is forecasting by linear regression analysis? How is it different from trend analysis?
6. Explain the various measures of forecasting errors.
7. Define tracking signal. How is it different from forecast control limits?
8. Explain the trial-repeat models of demand forecasting for new products.
9. Explain the competitive share models of demand forecasting for new products.

## Numerical Problems

1. Avaran Exports is a major garment export house based at New Delhi. The sales figures (in 1,000 units) of a particular garment during the past 20 weeks are given in Table 15.9. Calculate the three-week moving average forecast for the given 20 weeks. Make a graph for the actual demand and the three-week moving average forecast for the given 20 weeks and week 21.

**Table 15.9**

| Week no. | Actual demand ('000 units) | Week no. | Actual demand ('000 units) |
|---|---|---|---|
| 1 | 21 | 11 | 19 |
| 2 | 24 | 12 | 22 |
| 3 | 18 | 13 | 26 |
| 4 | 22 | 14 | 24 |
| 5 | 27 | 15 | 17 |
| 6 | 23 | 16 | 21 |
| 7 | 21 | 17 | 29 |
| 8 | 25 | 18 | 27 |
| 9 | 27 | 19 | 23 |
| 10 | 18 | 20 | 25 |

2. Bharat Nirmana Bank has a centralized facility in Chennai for printing and procurement of cheque books for all its account holders across all branches in India. In order to minimise its inventory costs as much as possible, it wants to have a demand forecasting for cheque books such that it gets them printed in numbers that can be dispatched as per the requirements in a given week while having negligible inventory to carry for the next week. You have joined the bank recently and have been asked by your boss to apply 4- and 8-week simple moving average method to the 20-week data shown in Table 15.10 and extend this forecast to Week 21.

**Table 15.10**

| Week no. | Actual demand (units) | Week no. | Actual demand (units) |
|---|---|---|---|
| 1 | 2563 | 11 | 4732 |
| 2 | 5291 | 12 | 6184 |
| 3 | 6698 | 13 | 4216 |
| 4 | 5329 | 14 | 3126 |
| 5 | 3167 | 15 | 1982 |
| 6 | 7103 | 16 | 2766 |
| 7 | 6257 | 17 | 5793 |
| 8 | 3768 | 18 | 7239 |
| 9 | 2591 | 19 | 6108 |
| 10 | 3365 | 20 | 4275 |

3. Find the simple exponential smoothing forecast for the data given in Problem 1. Take the smoothing constant $\alpha = 0.5$. Make a chart using MS Excel to show the actual demand and the simple exponential smoothing forecast.

4. Cupid Bakers are specialists in cakes, pastries, and other bakery products in the city of Jaipur. The actual demand (in units) experienced by them for their popular birthday cakes during the past 20 weeks is given in Table 15.11. Find the forecast for the given 20 weeks using Holt's double-exponential smoothing. Take $\alpha = 0.6$ and $\gamma = 0.7$. Make a graph showing the forecast with the actual demand.

**Table 15.11**

| Week no. | Actual demand (units) | Week no. | Actual demand (units) |
|---|---|---|---|
| 1 | 56 | 11 | 100 |
| 2 | 61 | 12 | 102 |
| 3 | 66 | 13 | 99 |
| 4 | 74 | 14 | 110 |
| 5 | 81 | 15 | 113 |
| 6 | 85 | 16 | 119 |
| 7 | 78 | 17 | 125 |
| 8 | 89 | 18 | 128 |
| 9 | 92 | 19 | 134 |
| 10 | 96 | 20 | 137 |

5. Bhavishya Life Insurance Company has its headquarters based at Chennai. Table 15.12 gives the details of the actual number of insurance policies subscribed by it throughout the country (in units) in the past four weeks (28 days). Apply Winters' triple-exponential smoothing to arrive at the forecasts for the given 28 days by taking $\alpha = 0.7$, $\gamma = 0.4$, and $\delta = 0.8$. Make a graph to compare the actual demand pattern with the forecast.

**Table 15.12**

| Day | Actual demand (units) | Day | Actual demand (units) |
|---|---|---|---|
| 1 | 125 | 15 | 199 |
| 2 | 138 | 16 | 186 |
| 3 | 149 | 17 | 205 |
| 4 | 130 | 18 | 238 |
| 5 | 145 | 19 | 247 |
| 6 | 158 | 20 | 269 |
| 7 | 166 | 21 | 275 |
| 8 | 172 | 22 | 258 |
| 9 | 160 | 23 | 250 |
| 10 | 179 | 24 | 255 |
| 11 | 184 | 25 | 299 |
| 12 | 197 | 26 | 310 |
| 13 | 203 | 27 | 324 |
| 14 | 213 | 28 | 351 |

6. In Problem 5, take the data of actual demand (in units) up to day 20 and find the forecasts for days 21 to 25 by linear regression analysis.

7. Super Mart is a chain of supermarkets across India. Its demand forecasting department has collected all-India data of past sales of plasma TVs across all its stores in the previous 20 weeks (see Table 15.13). It wants to forecast demand for plasma TVs for the coming five weeks (Weeks 21, 22, 23, 24, and 25). You are the manager of the department and decide to apply linear regression analysis. The rest of the team is awaiting your demand projections on this basis.

**Table 15.13**

| Week no. | Actual demand (units) | Week no. | Actual demand (units) |
|---|---|---|---|
| 1 | 1576 | 11 | 8676 |
| 2 | 2438 | 12 | 9691 |
| 3 | 3621 | 13 | 8874 |
| 4 | 4783 | 14 | 10163 |
| 5 | 2109 | 15 | 11631 |
| 6 | 3032 | 16 | 12732 |
| 7 | 4761 | 17 | 11052 |
| 8 | 5526 | 18 | 13721 |
| 9 | 7129 | 19 | 14829 |
| 10 | 6682 | 20 | 15715 |

8. Table 15.14 shows the average rainfall (in cm per day) in Kolkata and the corresponding sale of umbrellas at a particular shop (in ₹ '000/day). Using

**Table 15.14**

| Average rainfall (cm/day) | Sale of umbrellas in Kolkata at a particular shop (₹ '000/day) |
|---|---|
| 5 | 0.8 |
| 10 | 1.1 |
| 15 | 2.9 |
| 20 | 2.7 |
| 25 | 3 |
| 30 | 4.4 |
| 35 | 4.6 |

trend analysis determine the trend forecast for the sale of umbrellas at a particular shop (in ₹ '000/day) corresponding to the average rainfall (in cm per day) in Kolkata at 40, 45, and 50, respectively.

9. The average sales of shops in a given locality have a causal relationship with the rent charged for shops in that locality. A survey was conducted in the city of Chandigarh to collect data on both these parameters and study their inter-relationship. Table 15.15 shows this data collected through the survey. Just after the survey was over, a new shopping mall was inaugurated in a newly developed area in Chandigarh and the shops in the three wings of the mall are experiencing average sales per day of ₹22,000, ₹24,000, and ₹26,000, respectively. A few shops are available for rent in the three wings and the owner of the mall wants your help in ascertaining the rent he should demand from interested parties.

**Table 15.15**

| Average sales of shops in a locality (in ₹ '000 per day) | Rent of a shop in the locality ( ₹ '000 per month) |
|---|---|
| 2 | 4.5 |
| 4 | 8.2 |
| 6 | 12.1 |
| 8 | 15.6 |
| 12 | 20.8 |
| 14 | 24 |
| 16 | 28.5 |
| 18 | 31.3 |
| 20 | 34.5 |

10. For Holt's forecast in Problem 4, calculate the following measures of forecasting error (a) running sum of forecast errors, (b) mean forecast error, (c) mean absolute deviation, (d) mean squared error, (e) mean absolute percentage error.

11. For Holt's forecast in Problem 4, calculate the TS and make a graph to show the TS with respect to weeks.

12. Table 15.16 gives the data for actual demand $D$ and forecast $F$ of a product for the past 20 months. Establish a three sigma control chart for the forecast errors using the data of the first 10 months, and then evaluate the remaining data with the control chart.

**Table 15.16**

| Month | Actual demand $D$ (units) | Forecast $F$ (units) | Month | Actual demand $D$ (units) | Forecast $F$ (units) |
|---|---|---|---|---|---|
| 1 | 98 | 100 | 11 | 195 | 205 |
| 2 | 102 | 110 | 12 | 200 | 191 |
| 3 | 167 | 124 | 13 | 213 | 212 |
| 4 | 128 | 156 | 14 | 239 | 225 |
| 5 | 159 | 146 | 15 | 227 | 235 |
| 6 | 167 | 174 | 16 | 248 | 256 |
| 7 | 172 | 166 | 17 | 255 | 267 |
| 8 | 188 | 182 | 18 | 253 | 262 |
| 9 | 193 | 200 | 19 | 269 | 260 |
| 10 | 174 | 180 | 20 | 274 | 270 |

## Project Assignments

1. Conduct a Delphi method forecasting for the year by which India will send its mission to Mars. Seek the opinion of space scientists (as experts) through a questionnaire. The questionnaire should seek their reasons for choosing a particular year as the forecast. These should be compiled as a summary before the questionnaire is sent back to the experts for any change in opinion in the light of new facts/reasons. Form groups in the class and arrive at a suitable forecast at the end of the exercise.

2. Select a nearby branch office of an insurance company. Meet the branch manager there and request her for data on the number of insurance policies subscribed and the amount insured in the past 12 months. Make a chart of the data to see the pattern, and then select a suitable quantitative forecasting model to predict the number of insurance policies to be subscribed and the amount to be insured in the coming three months.

**Answers to Objective Questions**

1. (a)     2. (c)     3. (a)     4. (d)     5. True
6. False     7. True     8. Quantitative     9. Tracking signal
10. Forecast control

# 16

# Service Operations Management

## Learning Objectives

After reading this chapter, you will be able to answer the following questions:
- What are the typical characteristics of services?
- How to classify the services?
- How to take capacity-related decisions in services?
- What are the key considerations in designing services?
- What is service quality?
- How to measure and improve service quality?

## Services Scenario in India

Services constitute around 60 per cent of the Indian economy. The service industry is growing at a rapid rate. In most developed countries, services contribute more to the GDP as compared to the manufacturing sector. Due to the scarcity of natural resources the economies of countries such as Singapore are driven primarily by services. Such small countries have become an example before the world for their high quality services in every possible domain. India has started exhibiting its prowess in the services domain through its information technology (IT) sector. IT companies such as Infosys, Wipro, TCS; airlines such as Jet Airways; banks such as ICICI; and hotels such as Taj (Indian Hotels) have set new standards in the services sector. Still, Indian companies have a long way to go to match the international quality standards in services. Figure 16.1 shows the contribution of the services sector in the GDP of India.

In its export–import policy 2002–07, the Government of India has given special status to the services sector. It included all the 161 tradeable services covered under the head 'services'. The payment for these services is received in free foreign exchange.

It is noteworthy that after liberalization of the Indian economy in the early 1990s, the service industry has grown faster than other sectors. This is evident in Fig. 16.2, which shows the average growth rates of select services in India over the 1990s. The white bars in the graph depict the significantly liberalized services, the grey bars depict the moderately liberalized services, and the black bars depict the non-liberalized services. It is imperative that the service operations of various services are understood in this new competitive context so that India's domestic

> After liberalization of the Indian economy in the early 1990s, the service industry has grown faster than other sectors.

services industry is able to evolve its own distinguishing set of features to compete well against international services giants.

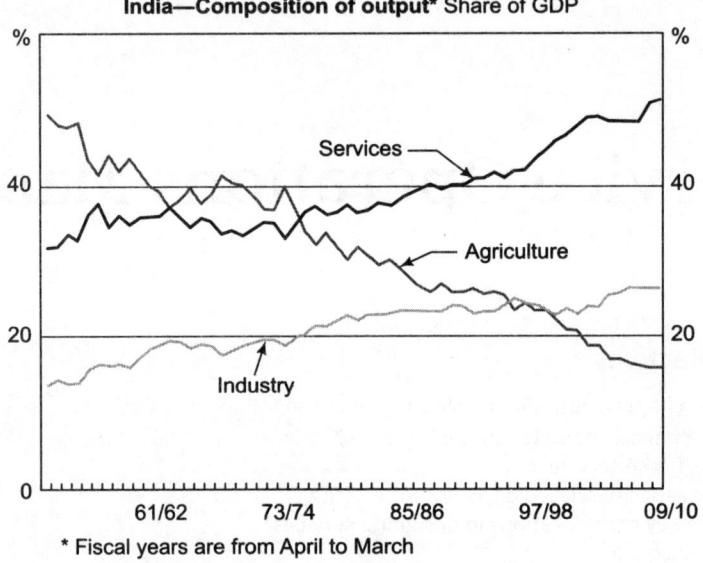

Sources: CEIC; RBA.

**Fig. 16.1**   Composition of India's GDP

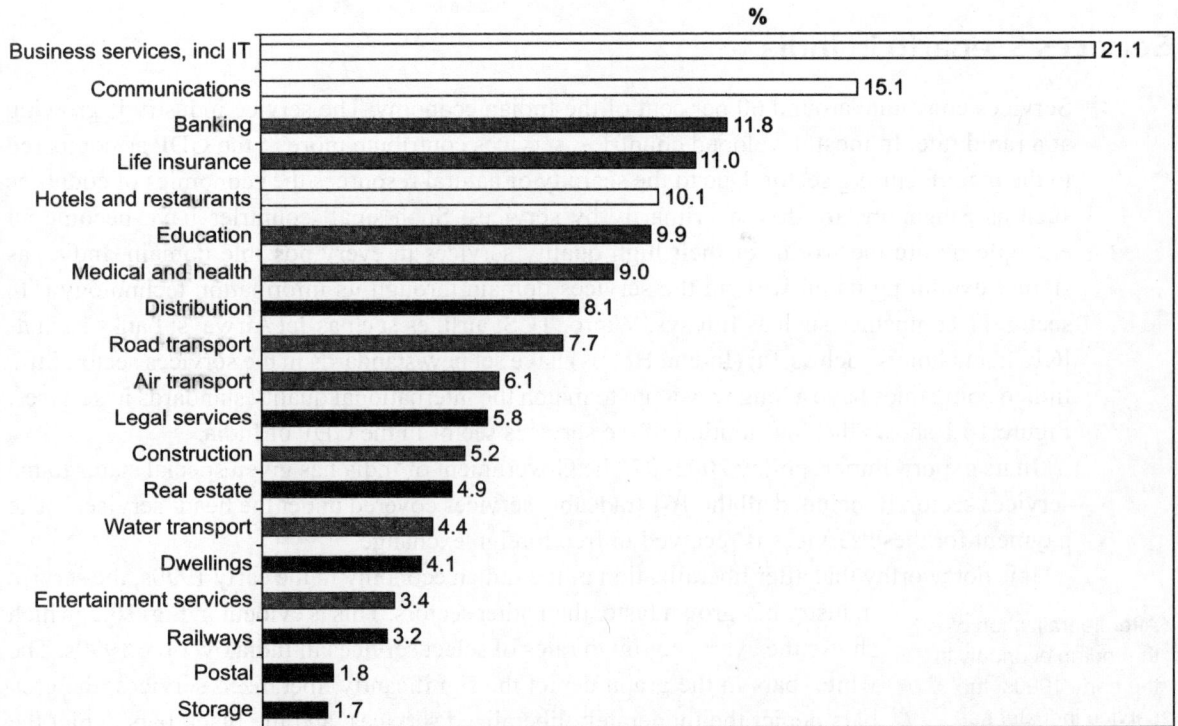

Source: World Bank (2004).

**Fig. 16.2**   Average growth rates of select services in India over the 1990s

# Medical Tourism in India

A liver transplant in the US costs around US $4,50,000. In India a similar surgery costs about US $40,000. A cardiac surgery in India costs as low as US $4,000 to US $9,000, while in the US it costs as high as US $30,000 to US $50,000. An orthopedic surgery costs around US $4,500 in India with the corresponding surgery in the US costing around US $18,000. This is reason enough for anybody to understand why medical tourism in India is flourishing today.

The Indian medical tourism market is projected to swell to US $2 billion by 2015 (Hamid 2012). The key is not just the south or west Asian population that is coming here for treatment; patients from countries such as the UK and the US have also realized the cost effectiveness of getting treatment in India. According to estimates, out of 1,50,000 international patients who visited India recently, three-fourths came from the US and the UK.

There are three factors contributing to this phenomenal growth in health tourism in India. First and most importantly, the international community is confident about the quality of Indian healthcare practitioners. It is said that one of the six doctors in the US is an Indian. Second, Indian private sector healthcare power houses such as Apollo, Wockhardt, and Max have created massive healthcare infrastructure in recent times, equipped with state-of-the-art equipment and manned by the country's most professionally trained staff. Third, of course, the huge cost benefits of getting treated here.

The reasons for indulging in health tours also vary from country to country. Medical tourists from the US can seek treatment here at one-fourth or even one-eighth of the cost at home. Canadian patients who are frustrated by long waiting periods come to India for treatment. The typical UK patient is the one who is not able to wait for treatment by the National Health Services and, in some cases, cannot afford to see a physician in private practice. Then there are patients coming from countries, such as Bangladesh, Kenya, and Vietnam, where it is difficult to get quality treatment.

Indian healthcare offers a holistic approach to the treatment by weaving practices such as yoga, aromatherapy, and Ayurveda into the treatment process. A majority of the clinical population here speaks English and Indian surgeons have world-class skills and surgical exposure. Another aspect that is helping Indian medical tourism is the fact that there are 50 million uninsured US citizens. High insurance premiums have kept a lot of people away from taking health insurance policies in the US.

The health insurance sector in India, however, does not even cover 10 per cent of the population. It is expected to grow soon with health insurance enrolments to peak at about 195 million in 2015 (National Health Expenditure Projections 2010–2020). The growth in health cover would be crucial for the development of the domestic medical care market.

India is now beginning to face overseas competition in medical tourism. Countries such as Thailand, Singapore, and Malaysia are aggressively promoting medical tourism. However, the quality of service and cost effectiveness have helped India to retain the edge.

# Characteristics of Services

In Chapter 1, we briefly discussed the similarities and differences between products and services and how, in many cases, services and products are interwined with each other. In the

> The decision to buy a service is primarily guided by the 'reputation' of the service provider.

product–process continuum, we had noticed that 'pure manufacturing' and 'pure services' form the two extremes of the continuum and are very rare. Let us now discuss certain typical (and generic) characteristics of services, which broadly distinguish them from tangible products.

**Services are intangible** Products are tangible, that is, have physical dimensions, allowing customers to touch, see, and examine their features, while making the buying decision. Services, on the other hand, can only be 'felt' by customers after purchasing. Only after having undergone the 'service process', customers can tell if it was 'good' or 'bad' and accordingly, whether they would like to experience it again or not. Otherwise, the decision to buy a service is primarily guided by the 'reputation' of the service provider. For example, lectures of certain professors are so entertaining and enlightening that students willingly attend their classes, while they prefer to spend time in the canteen or library during the classes of other professors.

According to Fitzsimmons (2004), services are ideas and concepts; products are things. Service innovations are not patentable and in order to derive maximum benefits of a pioneering service concept, the service provider has to expand its operations rapidly in order to preempt the risk of competitors copying the same concept. Franchising is one route to achieve this daunting task in the minimum possible time. In India, the retailing concept of Big Bazaar is rapidly being imitated by new entrants such as FabMall and FoodWorld. Big Bazaar itself was inspired by the retail chain stores in the West. Similarly, the low-cost airline model is being replicated by GoAir, SpiceJet, Indigo, etc. It may be recalled that the Air Deccan model of low cost airlines was adapted from Ryanair of Europe and Southwest Airlines of the US.

**Services inspired the 'just-in-time' concept** In a just-in-time (JIT) system, the production and provision of service starts as soon as the customer arrives to avail the service. The customer's involvement in the service process is imperative. This is known as the 'pull' production system in manufacturing and was inspired by the retailing services in the US supermarkets. The production process is initiated only when the customer places the order for the product and the raw material is 'pulled' into the various constituents of the production process according to the quantity of the order placed by the customer. Taiichi Ohno, the then President of Toyota, observed that in the US supermarkets the replenishment of any empty shelf on the racks is immediate due to the easy visibility of the same from anywhere in the store. He thought of implementing the same concept on the racks alongside the assembly lines of Toyota and the JIT concept (earlier known as the Toyota production system) was born.

Thus, the 'push' production system prevalent in many manufacturing organizations cannot be applied to service organizations. The 'push' production system results in 'pushing' the

> The inability to inventorize services throws up major challenges for the operations manager in terms of capacity planning, capacity utilization, and quality control.

raw material in the production system and creation of inventories (work-in-process or finished goods). This is not possible in services, as they cannot be inventoried. This typical characteristic of services throws up major challenges for the operations manager in terms of capacity planning, capacity utilization, and quality control. Excess service capacity (in terms of manpower, equipment, building space, etc.) results in low capacity utilization during periods of low customer turn-outs. In other words, this excess service capacity is 'perishable'. In a hair salon, if the capacity is created by hiring ten hair dressers and on a

Services are more 'people-centric' due to their labour intensive nature and high customer involvement.

particular day the number of customers turned up amount to the work load of only five hair dressers, the idle time of the excess five hair dressers cannot be carried forward to the next day. This idle time would be wasted completely. This is quite in contrast to manufacturing organizations, where the products can be manufactured in a factory at full-capacity even during days of low demand as the excess goods produced can be stocked for future (when the demand would be higher than the production capacity). See Exhibit 16.1 for more on this.

On the other hand, higher demand than the service capacity would result in waiting time on part of the customers. In today's competitive world, this can be a disadvantage as customers may be attracted to a competitor whose service facility provides prompt services or lesser waiting time. If the service providers are overstressed to process the high number of customers beyond their capacity, the quality of service may suffer, which may again be disastrous for the organization's reputation.

Quality management is easier in manufactured products, which can be inspected during the production process and before customer delivery. A manufacturing organization has ample scope of detecting the defects and repairing these before the product reaches the customer. This is not so in services, where the customer is himself/herself involved in the service delivery process. Any defect in the service delivery has to be detected and corrected then and there.

**Services are more people-centric** Services are more 'people-centric' due to their labour intensive nature and high customer involvement. In most instances, the service providers provide (or are rather forced to do so by the competition) a personalized service to the customer. This complicates the service process manifold. Different customers have varied expectations from a service and employees providing the service have different levels of skill-sets. The interactions between customers and employees may lead to different levels of customer satisfaction or dissatisfaction. The challenge before the operations manager is to try and match customer expectations and develop employees' skill-sets through constant training and development. This will lead to a delightful service experience for the customer and brand loyalty for the service provider. The role of employees involved in the provision of service (especially in direct contact with the customers) is paramount in creating happy customers. Therefore, it is imperative to keep the employees happy and satisfied, so that they provide the best service experience to customers.

---

### Exhibit 16.1   MakeMyTrip.com

MakeMyTrip.com (MMT) started its operations in India in September 2005 and since then, it has transformed the way airline ticketing is done. It is a one stop travel website, which provides customers with a comparative pricing data for various airlines on a route, allowing them to make choice of lowest fares and book their tickets online. The hassles of contacting the travel agents to enquire about the various airline travel options and their pricing have been completely wiped off by MMT. The company's website offers complete travel solutions including online booking of air tickets, hotels, car rentals, weekend packages, and road trips within and from India. During the first year of its operation in India, MMT did a business of US$41 million and currently books about 2,000 air tickets and 150 hotel rooms daily.

The company is a success story of an Indian entrepreneur, Deep Kalra, its founder and CEO. Headquartered in New Delhi, India, MMT has a 450 strong team and offices in New York and Sydney. A recent report by Pho-

*(Contd)*

*Exhibit 16.1 Contd*

CusWright, 'The Emerging Online Travel Marketplace in India', revealed that online leisure/unmanaged business travel gross bookings in India totaled US$295 million in 2005 and estimated that this number will increase nearly sevenfold to US$2.0 billion by 2008. The report also found that in 2005, 2.2 per cent of total travel was booked online in India, and forecasts that the strong growth in Internet connections will cause the percentage of online bookings to approach double digits by 2008. The success of MMT has prompted new entrants into the field such as ClearTrip.com and Yatra.com.

The company was originally funded in 2000 by eVentures. After the fund exited, the management of MMT bought the stake. Currently, Softbank Asia Infrastructure fund has over 50 per cent stake in it. In January 2007, Sierra Ventures, a US$1.5 billion Silicon Valley-based venture capital firm, made a direct investment in MMT. It initially focused on non-resident Indians (NRIs) travelling from destinations such as the US, UK, and Australia to India. Due to its focus on this niche market, it avoided direct competition from mega travel portals such as Travelocity, PriceLine, and Expedia, which dominate the US market. Later, it realized that there is a great need for such a service in the burgeoning domestic air travel sector in India and hence, the operations were started here in 2005. Its entry into India was prompted by the then developments in online bookings. The website of SpiceJet recorded 37,000 bookings on the day of its launch.

In order to attract the price sensitive Indian customer, MMT launched the 'lowest air fare guarantee' that promises to refund the difference if a customer is able to get a domestic airfare cheaper than what is being offered by it. The 'lowest airfare guarantee' is applicable on all domestic airlines, including the low cost ones.

There is cut-throat competition among conventional travel agents in India. Their revenue generation model has seen a paradigm shift over the past one decade or so; from charging commissions from consolidators and airlines for the sale of tickets to just charging service fee from the customers for searching the best itinerary and fares for them. This has resulted in the reduction of ticket distribution costs in the airline industry. Costs have gone down from almost 10 per cent to almost nil over the past decade. Online booking portals such as MMT have further added to the woes of these agents. The large volumes of bookings done by MMT for any airlines

results in heavy discounts for them due to which the fares quoted on their website are the most competitive.

MMT has toll free numbers in India and the US, which are attended $24 \times 7$ by their customer service representatives (CSRs), who have been trained to answer queries from customers relating to flight schedules, itineraries, hotels, fares, foreign currency exchange rates, etc. These CSRs operate in three shifts to cover operations during 24 hours in a day. Many times the same customer calls up MMT repeatedly during different shifts and it becomes necessary for a CSR manning a particular shift to know the itinerary and fare quoted by the CSR in the earlier shift. In addition, MMT wanted to segregate its repeat customers from the new customers to attend to their needs in a much better way. To streamline its operations, it needed automation to

- identify each repeat customer with the transaction history
- manage the lifecycle of each ticket from initiation to delivery and maintain up-to-date status across all the departments of MMT
- update the status on each transaction across the organization
- scheduling of follow-ups for each CSR for each transaction (sending itineraries, cancellations, refunds, etc.)
- tracking of all grievances and queries of the customer with a possibility to assign tasks across shifts
- unification of the customer information and transaction in a single view to have a holistic view of the customer
- making the process of cancellation, rescheduling, and refunds more customer-friendly.

To take care of the above issues, MMT has installed sales and workflow intelligence for travel (SWIFT), a mini-ERP solution based upon the SalesLogix platform. This has facilitated in obtaining the exact costing of every ticket and in searching the data for a customer. Overall, the processing time from order to delivery of a ticket has been reduced by about 24 hours. It has witnessed a steady increase in its gross bookings and gross profit margins since the implementation of this system in July 2004.

*Sources:* Jham and Chotani (2005); makemytrip.com (2013).

Services can be classified into four categories—service factory, service shop, mass service, and professional service.

## Classification of Services

Schmenner (1986) categorized services into four categories in the service process matrix as shown in Fig. 16.3. The four categories are named service factory, service shop, mass service, and professional service. In this matrix, one variable considered is the degree of interaction and customization. The services categorized in service shop and professional service fall in a high degree of interaction and customization. For example, in hospitals every patient has a unique problem and the doctor has to provide a customized prescription for the problem. Similarly, in auto repair shops every vehicle coming for service has unique repair requirements. In professional services provided by lawyers, every lawsuit involves different sections of the law and has its own unique points to be considered.

| Degree of Labour Intensity | Degree of Interaction and Customization: Low | Degree of Interaction and Customization: High |
|---|---|---|
| Low | **Service factory:**<br>• Freight services<br>• Hotels, inns, and motels<br>• Airline services<br>• Amusement parks | **Service shop:**<br>• Auto/electronic service centres<br>• Hospitals and nursing homes |
| High | **Mass service:**<br>• Schools and colleges<br>• Retail shops<br>• Wholesalers and distributors<br>• Selling of insurance policies | **Professional service:**<br>• Specialist doctors<br>• Lawyers and tax consultants<br>• Financial consultants<br>• Hospitals and nursing homes |

*Source*: Adapted from Schmenner (1986).

**Fig. 16.3** Service process matrix

On the other hand, the services categorized under service factory and mass service have a low degree of interaction and customization. For example, airlines provide very few options to the passengers—say, the economy class and business class services. The customers are rarely provided with customized services. The menu service onboard has mainly two options—vegetarian and non-vegetarian. Similarly, in schools, every student in a class is given the same standard treatment and education.

The second parameter considered in the service process matrix is the degree of labour intensity, measured by the ratio of labour cost to capital cost. Mass service and professional service have a high degree of labour intensity. For example, in case of architects, accountants, etc. the capital cost is low (as there is no costly equipment required) compared to the labour cost (there may be a team of professionals of this sort). Thus, the degree of labour intensity is high.

Mass service and professional service have a high degree of labour intensity.

The service factory and service shop categories have a low degree of labour intensity. For example, in airlines the cost of capital required is quite high (as the cost of equipment, that is, the aircrafts, is very high) compared to the

> For professional services (high degree of labour intensity as well as high degree of interaction and customization), there are no standard ways of measuring and improving the service quality.

labour cost. Similar is the case with hospitals, where the cost of equipment such as X-ray machines, CAT scan machines, and pathology labs is very high compared to the cost of labour.

From the service quality point of view, it is easiest to manage the quality of the service factory category of services (low degree of labour intensity as well as low degree of interaction and customization), while it is most difficult to manage the service quality of the professional service category. We shall discuss in a latter part of this chapter, the elaborate criteria for service quality measurement in the airline industry as well as the hotel industry (both examples of service factories). See Exhibit 16.2 to know about Southwest Airlines' service quality. On the other hand, for professional services (high degree of labour intensity as well as high degree of interaction and customization) there are no standard ways of measuring and improving the service quality.

---

### Exhibit 16.2   Southwest Airlines

The pioneer of the 'low-cost airline' concept, Southwest Airlines is one of the largest airline in America and a renowned brand in the airline industry for its exemplary service quality backed by unique organization culture. The magazine *Fortune* recognized Southwest Airlines with the title—'the most successful airline in history.' Many other airlines across the globe have tried to ape its low-cost model, but few could come close to nurturing an organization culture as demonstrated by Southwest.

The salient features of the Southwest way (as they call their organization culture) are as follows (Smith 2004):

- It promotes an 'easy going' relaxed corporate style that provides employees with extensive operational independence.
- It treats its employees as its 'first customers' and passengers as the 'second' (Goldberg 2000).
- With its catchline—'Time flies when you're having fun!', the airline promotes a unique and fun experience for its customers. The flight attendants enjoy the liberty of speaking freely during the passenger announcements and often run humourous contests with awards like free airline return tickets to any destination where Southwest flies. In one such contest, the flight attendant awarded free tickets to the first passenger providing socks with holes (Donlon 1999).
- Suitable provisions for rest and relaxation are made to augment creativity, especially for people experiencing high-stress jobs—at the airline's

corporate office, there are rocking chairs galore and employees are allowed to work in pyjamas for a day (Donlon 1999).

- Its managers acknowledge birthdays, birth, and even death of the loved ones of the employees (Goldberg 2000).
- The values of 'caring for others' are promoted. It was pointed out to the CEO once that the graveyard-shift employees are unable to participate in the company picnics. A special barbeque was organized at 2 a.m. for them in which the CEO and several pilots served as chefs for the picnic (Donlon 1999).
- Most organizations use functional metrics for performance appraisal, which unfortunately leads to finger-pointing between functional departments. Southwest devised team metrics to promote shared goals, shared knowledge, and mutual respect. For example, all Southwest employees (from all functional departments) at a particular airport are expected as a team to keep the percentage of on-time departures as high as possible (Gittell 2003).
- The front-line supervisors at Southwest are 'working supervisors' with the responsibility of training 10–12 front-line workers. This is the lowest supervisor-to-worker ratio in the industry, with the objective of sparing more time for the supervisors for mentoring, guiding, and coaching the workers compared to the competitors (Gittell 2003).

*Sources:* Donlon (1999); Goldberg (2000); Gittell (2003); and Smith (2004).

For service shop and mass service (low–high combination for the two variables in the matrix), service quality management has moderate level of difficulty. The SERVQUAL types of instruments (discussed later) are commonly used in all such service industries.

## Service Capacity

> Service capacity is the maximum level of value-added activity which can be consistently achieved over a period of time under normal operating conditions.

Slack et al. (1998) defined service capacity as the maximum level of value-added activity which can be consistently achieved over a period of time under normal operating conditions. Thus, service capacity may be expressed as the maximum number of patients attended by a doctor per hour, the maximum number of lectures taken by a professor per day, or the maximum number of passengers serviced by a metro train per day. The important consideration here is that the service provider should be able to sustain provision of service at such a rate comfortably under normal operating conditions. It is highly likely that at a given point in time during heavy rush hours, a young enthusiastic employee gives performance beyond expectations and produces service output in terms of number of customers processed beyond the maximum capacity of the service system. However, she may not be able to perform at the same level the whole of the day due to fatigue and exertion. The operations manager has to constantly monitor the quality of service under such extraordinary conditions, and in case it suffers, the employee needs to be told to slow down a little.

### Strategies for Service Capacity Planning

Johnston and Clark (2001) have suggested three pure planning strategies for service capacity planning. These are strategies with

- constant capacity;
- capacity closely following the demand patterns (Chase strategy); and
- demand smoothening.

**Strategy with constant capacity**    As the name of this pure planning strategy suggests, the capacity constituted by key, critical, rare, or costly resources is kept constant throughout. The issues relating to customer expectations and satisfaction have to be managed by the operations manager. This strategy is suitable in conditions, where the service differentiation is too high, with very few competing options available to the customers. For example, patients would be willing to wait for some time for the medical advice of a famous specialist doctor (a rare service resource). Here, it may be known from past experience that, on an average, the doctor spends around 10 minutes per patient and, therefore, three patients can be processed through the service system in half an hour. While giving appointments to patients, over-booking is intentionally done. For example, five patients would be given the appointment of 7 p.m. keeping in view that each patient would require on an average of 10 minutes and two out of these five patients may not actually turn up despite having the appointment. Therefore, effectively three patients who turn up would be easily processed in the half an hour duration with the next batch (of five patients) of appointments scheduled (for five patients) at 7:30 p.m. If all five patients turn up in a given half an hour time slot, it would result in a maximum 20 minutes waiting time for two of these patients in the slot. Also, it would delay all the subsequent batches by 20 minutes resulting in increased waiting time of patients. The patients do not have many alternative options to go elsewhere for a similar service (from another specialist doctor) and, hence, tolerate this kind of an unannounced waiting time.

The bottom-line in this strategy is that the valuable consultation time of the specialist doctor should not go waste at a given point in time. However, the service quality is neglected here at the cost of maximum resource utilization. The American Embassy at New Delhi follows this kind of service strategy, and an appointment system for granting visa to Indian nationals. The Indian applicants eligible to apply at the New Delhi embassy are given a particular time for personal interview and many are surprised to reach at the scheduled time to find that the same time was allotted to numerous other persons; leading to long queues and seemingly endless waiting time at different stages of their service process. This is despite the fact that American Embassy charges a hefty amount as the application fee and gives visa interview appointment after many months. However, the embassy has announced transformation of its processes to enable Indian nationals to get a visa within a month. This is a typical example of how government agencies and departments of even the most developed nations neglect service quality to ensure maximum resource utilization.

In some instances, the demand of an expensive and rare resource may be quite less compared to the fixed built-in capacity. In such situations, possibilities of sharing excess capacity with some allies must be explored. For example, many airlines have this kind of capacity sharing arrangement with their partner airlines. During low demand seasons, a single common flight of both the airlines is made by using a single aircraft of one of the partner airlines. Singapore Airlines and Air India have this kind of a strategic partnership with each other.

**Chase strategy**   This strategy is applicable in situations where there is hardly any service differentiation between the services provided by a number of competitors. The customers are unwilling to wait and would not hesitate to move to a competitor's facility nearby, if faced with long queues at a service facility. Therefore, the constant capacity strategy would be disastrous in this situation. The operations manager would have to take measures to introduce a lot of flexibility in the capacity of the system to take care of peak demand times at the facility. Fast food restaurants are typically faced with this kind of a situation, when customers flock their facilities during certain specific hours of the day. The remaining duration of the day witnesses low demand.

In order to have flexible capacity in the service system, there has to be extra infrastructure to support the fluctuations in the demand. For example, at a fast food restaurant there has to be extra space and cash collection/receipt generation equipment at the front counter facing the customers.

> Chase strategy is applicable in situations where there is hardly any service differentiation between the services provided by a number of competitors.

It will allow extra staff to take charge during heavy rush hours, in addition to the regular staff manning the counter. Depending upon the minimum demand level throughout the day, the operations manager may keep a constant workforce size for the two shifts to cover the whole day. For example, the first shift can be from 6 a.m. to 2:30 p.m. and the second shift can be from 2:30 p.m. to 11 p.m (Fig. 16.4). To take care of the heavy rush hour during breakfast (7 a.m. to 8:30 a.m.), part-time staff may be hired to share the burden of the regular staff. A third split shift of workers can be created over and above the regular two shifts to take care of extra work load during the lunch time slot (12 noon to 3:30 p.m.) and dinner time slot (6:00 p.m. to 1:30 p.m.).

The key challenge before the operations manager in this strategy is to find and train part-time employees (during the morning hours in the example of fast food restaurant).

Another way of pursuing this strategy is by cross-training employees to make them capable of performing a variety of tasks. For example, many banks have introduced a 'single window banking' concept in which a customer can go to any service counter in the bank to avail any service. Earlier, the customers had to go to different counters for cash withdrawals, cash deposits, drafts, and so on. Modern banks have cross-trained their employees, who are now capable of performing a variety of tasks. This has eliminated different work loads at various service counters depending upon the number of customers willing to avail a particular service at a given point in time.

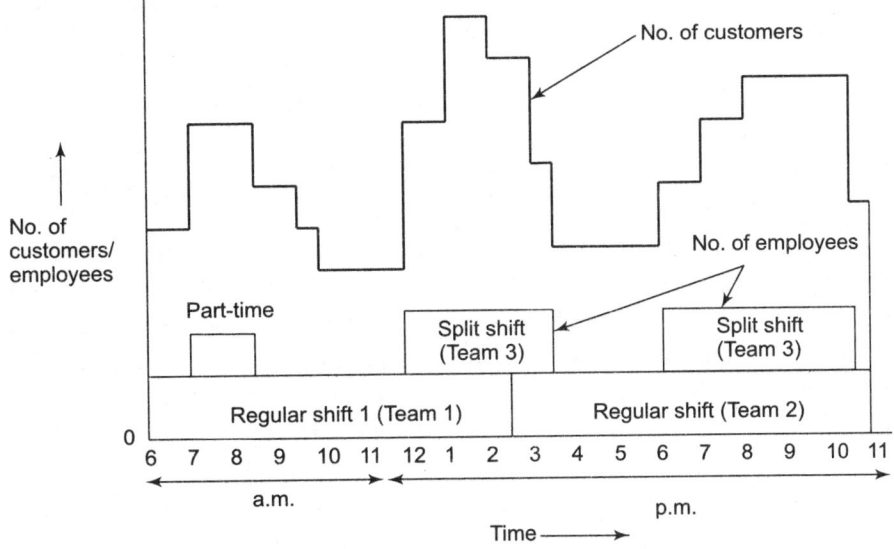

*Source:* Adapted from Johnston and Clark (2001).

**Fig. 16.4**  Chase capacity strategy in a fast food restaurant

**Strategy with demand smoothening**  In this strategy, the operations manager should attempt to smooth customer demand throughout the time period by inducing more customers to avail the service during periods of low demand. This can be done by offering price discounts during these time durations; for example, many airlines offer lower fares on their late night flights as compared to their regular fares. Similarly, many cinema theatres price their morning shows, during weekdays, at one-third of the regular prices. The strategy is to attract elderly people and housewives to this time slot, which is unattractive to working people. The other way to pursue this strategy is to provide less variety of service during the peak hours; for example, many popular restaurants offer a limited menu to the guests arriving during the peak hours. In a way, these are the means of discouraging customers to avail the service during rush hours and induce them to come at other times. Another example of demand smoothening strategy is the use of special television sets and LCD projectors by restaurants during major cricket tournaments in India to induce those customers to visit the restaurants for meals, who would otherwise prefer to have meals at home. The three pure planning service capacity strategies are used in combination by many service providers.

## Yield Management

The concept of yield management has been popularized and used extensively by the airline industry. The hotel industry is also embracing this concept of revenue maximization. The airline industry has different fares for different segments such as first class, business class, and economy class. There are various sub-segments of fares within these segments too. It means that airlines have different fares for the economy class. These fares may be dependent on factors such as advance booking and bulk booking. Hence, two passengers flying in the economy class of the same flight might have bought the tickets at different rates. This system is quite different from that of Indian Railways, whereby every passenger in a particular class (or compartment) pays the same amount for a ticket.

Yield management focuses on the optimal utilization of existing fixed capacity to maximize the overall revenue from a particular flight. In order to achieve this objective, the airline would like to sell as many tickets as possible on full fare for a particular class (which is obviously higher than the discounted fare), though this may not be always possible due to intense competition from other airlines on the same route. It has been observed that there are two main categories of passengers—business travellers and leisure travellers. Business travellers are not price sensitive, but demand comfort and flexibility of change in their travel schedules. Many of these customers book their tickets very close to the flight departure. The leisure traveller usually travels with family and friends. Such customers are price sensitive (i.e., demand lowest fares), are willing to have more or less fixed travel schedules, and usually book tickets much in advance.

The challenge before the operations manager here is to decide whether to sell off the remaining tickets (apart from the ones already sold on full fare) near the departure date at discounted fares or wait for last minute passengers who may be ready to pay full fare due to the emergency of their travel. This decision should be made in such a way so that the total yield (revenue) from the flight is maximized. An important factor is that any empty seat in a flight would mean an unrecoverable loss. The same is true in the hotel industry, where an empty room for a given duration of time would mean a loss. The competition on the same flight route from other airlines adds many more dimensions to this problem on part of the operations manager.

If a rival airline is offering discount fares through their communication channels to the potential customers close to the departure time, while a particular airline is sticking to its full fare, it is obvious that the competitor would be the winner in attracting more customers. The other dimension is that

> Yield management focuses on the optimal utilization of existing fixed capacity to maximize the overall revenue from a particular flight.

if most of the customers get used to getting discounted tickets, they would start preferring to wait for the discounted tickets to be offered by an airline. This may drastically reduce the number of passengers buying full fare tickets and, thus, may create the problem of forecasting customer demand.

If the operations manager decides to wait for full fare passengers up to one day before the departure of the flight and then offer empty seats on discount, the airline should be able to communicate this special offer to the potential

---

**Exhibit 16.3    Air India**

Air India was founded in 1932 by J.R.D. Tata, and at that time, it was called Tata Airlines. A trained pilot, Tata is aptly known as the 'father of civil aviation' in India. The first flight of the airlines carrying airmail was flown by Tata himself from Karachi to Mumbai, the then Bombay. Tata Airlines was made a public limited company in 1946 and rechristened as Air India.

After India's independence, the government acquired 49 per cent stake in the airlines with an option to purchase 2 per cent more at a later date. Air India was designated as the national carrier and was allowed to fly internationally. In 1953, the government exercised its option to buy 2 per cent more stake and, thus, became the majority shareholder of Air India. The Air Corporations Act nationalized the whole of air transportation in India at this time and all the domestic airlines were merged with Indian Airlines to ply on domestic routes.

Air India started getting symbolised with its unique caricature called the 'Maharajah' (meaning the King of Kings) since 1946. It represents the warmth, comfort, and cosiness that one expects in an emperor's abode. Indeed, Air India represented luxury in the air till the time new-generation airlines were born in India.

The monopoly of Air India and Indian Airlines was broken in 1994, when Jet Airways was granted the scheduled airline status after having operated as an air taxi operator since 1992. The next few years witnessed the mushrooming entry and growth of several new airlines in India, including Kingfisher Airlines, Air Deccan (later acquired by Kingfisher Airlines), Sahara Airlines (eventually taken over by Jet Airways), SpiceJet, Indigo, GoAir, Paramount, and so on. Things have gone down for both the national carriers since then. In February 2011, Air India and Indian Airlines were finally merged to form the National Aviation Company of India Limited (NACIL) under the brand name Air India.

Frequent strikes by employees has literally crippled operations and tarnished the reputation of Air India severely. On one occasion in 2008, both the pilots fell asleep during an Air India flight, resulting in the plane going beyond the final destination of Mumbai by about 200 miles, before the air traffic controllers sounded special alarms in the aircraft to wake them up.

In 2010, it is alleged that laxity on the part of a pilot resulted in a tragic accident in Mangalore with 158 persons dead, when the aircraft could not be landed properly on the table-top airstrip. Several incidents of impoliteness and unprofessional conduct have been reported in the recent times, which have further worsened the sagging fortunes of the airline.

---

customers at a short notice. The Internet provides these kinds of real-time communication tools, but most airlines and hotels are yet to fully exploit these possibilities for yield maximization.

Computerized reservation systems such as Semi-automated Business Research Environment (SABRE) are of great use for airlines in making these decisions. According to Kimes (1989), yield management is most effective in services that have relatively fixed capacity with high marginal capacity increase cost. For example, for increasing the capacity of an airline, the purchase of an additional aircraft by the airline would increase its fixed cost. The service should have—advance reservation system; fluctuating demand patterns; various segments/categories of customers; perishable services (for example, an empty seat in a flight is a complete loss, which is irrecoverable); and low marginal sales cost (for example, an additional seat in a flight sold by the airline would have marginal sales cost as the cost of the meal offered to the passenger during the flight, which is a negligible amount).

See Exhibit 16.3 to learn about Air India's sagging fortune and operational inefficiencies.

# Designing Service Processes

Three generic approaches can be used for designing service processes. These approaches depend on the extent of customer involvement in the service process and are as follows:

The three generic approaches used for designing service processes depend on the extent of customer involvement in the service process.

1. Designing high customer contact and low customer contact operation separately.
2. Designing through an assembly line approach.
3. Designing service with technological interfaces.

## Designing High and Low Customer Contact Operations Separately

In any service, it is possible to identify parts of operations having high and low levels of customer contact. For example, at a fast food restaurant, the service counter has the highest level of customer contact. The customers place their orders, make payments, and serve themselves at the counter. All the remaining operations relating to the production of dishes, procurement of raw materials, etc. hardly involve any direct customer contact. Therefore, such operations can be designed in a matter similar to manufacturing organizations, while high customer contact operations need to be designed differently (Chase 1978).

This 'decoupling' of different portions of the service operations is useful for running 'low cost' operations as a factory within the service system. For example, in a laundry, the collection and delivery of clothes from/to the customers are high customer contact operations, while the actual laundry work is a low customer contact operation. Similarly, in an airline, the issue of boarding passes, baggage collection, directing passengers to board the plane, steward services during the flight, etc. are high customer contact operations, while back-end operations such as aircraft maintenance, catering services, cleaning services inside the cabin, and baggage reclaim are low customer contact operations.

The service design of high customer contact operations requires good ambience, smiling and well-behaved employees, personalized attention, and less or no waiting time. Due to the varied service requirements of the customers, the time and effort expended by the front-office staff on each of these may be different. The design of low customer contact operations, on the other hand, can be treated like assembly line operations to achieve the best capacity utilization. These operations are seldom seen by customers, for example, baggage handlers are almost never seen by the airline customers. Therefore, their dressing need not be as flawless as that of air hostesses and other ground staff, who have direct customer interaction. Nevertheless, passengers always prefer to claim their baggage in time. Even though they remain invisible to customers, baggage handlers can improve customer satisfaction levels by their factory-like precision.

There is a need to have efficient communication between the 'decoupled' low and high customer contact operations, for example, the front-office of a laundry should be in continual communication with the back-end operations about the status of work according to the delivery schedules.

## Assembly-line Approach to Service Design

The service design of high customer contact operations requires good ambience, smiling and well-behaved employees, personalized attention, and less or no waiting time.

An assembly line is a system in production set-ups for assembling various components and parts for building a final product. It is constituted by work stations one after the other in the sequence of assembling jobs to be performed. The workers manning these stations use specialized tools and equipment. This approach to service design can be used if the services provided to customers are of little variety and the customer is looking forward to a quick, efficient,

An assembly line is a system in production set-ups for assembling various components and parts for building a final product.

standard quality, and low-priced service. Theodore (1972) suggested this approach to service design, which is followed by most fast-food restaurants such as Nirulas, Pizza Corner, Pizza Hut, McDonald's, Burger King, and KFC.

At such fast-food joints, the service system starts with the customer entering the facility and choosing one of the five or six standard menus displayed on big posters, luminous displays, or menu cards available at the service counter. A typical feature of these fast foods is the acceptance of payment only by cash—no credit or debit card. Therefore, no commissions are paid to any credit or debit card company, resulting in the most economical prices quoted on the menu. After placing the order of, say, a burger meal, the customer pays in cash to the smartly dressed attendant at the service counter, who immediately informs the kitchen attendant behind her about the order placed.

The kitchen is also partially visible to the customer, who is a witness to the cleanliness and promptness of the service process. By the time the burger is prepared, the front-desk attendant starts preparing the tray for the meal—putting the menu sheet on the tray (this serves to let the customer know about new menu items while having her meal and keeps the tray clean), filling the soft drink, putting the French fries into a standard box and putting a few pouches of tomato ketchup and napkins. During the same time, at the back station the attendant picks the bun, cuts it into two pieces laterally, puts the already prepared chicken, fish, or any other stuffing along with vegetable (tomato, onion, etc.) toppings between the two pieces of the bun and grills it for a while in the oven.

The ready burger is put by the back station (kitchen) attendant on the rack behind the front station, from where the front station attendant picks it up and places on the customer's tray. The customer takes away the tray to a table on her own. After savouring the meal, the customer is expected to dispose of the waste on her own by throwing these away into a prominently visible waste bin, while putting the empty tray over it. Thus, customers also take part in the service provision process up to some extent. In this example of the fast-food restaurant, the customer works at the third work station after the service counter by picking up her tray of meal, consuming it, and disposing of the waste.

The attendants are provided with specialized equipment for expending all the tasks in minimum time. These are the automatic soft-drink dispensers, microwave ovens, etc. Most of these fast-food restaurants have extensive supply chains for supplying all the items required for assembling the standard menus offered by them. These items are stored in very limited spaces, which have the capacity of storing only as much can be consumed on a particular day. This is in view of the perishable nature of the raw materials used.

Thus, we note that in this kind of a service design, there is little scope for personalized service as the employees are given a standard set of tasks to be performed in a well-defined sequence. This ensures uniform service experience to customers. The concept of division of labour is fully exploited in this service design for achieving operational efficiency. Exhibit 16.4 discusses how *dabbawallahs* in Mumbai have provided consistent service for 100 years.

## Service Design with Technological Interfaces

The recent technological advances have made it possible to shift all customer contact functions to technical interfaces, with the customer controlling the various dimensions of the service through

## Exhibit 16.4    Mumbai *Dabbawallahs*

The British public was not too happy with Prince Charles' marriage, but Raghunath D. Megde, leader of the 5,000-strong Mumbai *dabbawallahs*, was kicked: '*Yeh hamare yaar ki shaadi hai*'. Camilla Parker Bowles had a wedding present from India no member of the British royalty has ever had. So what if she has to be content with only being called Her Royal Highness the Duchess of Cornwall, and at best Princess Consort, if her husband ascends the throne. In her gifts, she found a traditional *chhavvari* (six yards long) Maharashtrian silk sari and a matching blouse—probably green in colour. Her husband was not overlooked either—he got a traditional *pheta* (turban). These were gifts to the couple from the *dabbawallahs* of Mumbai. Raghunath D. Megde and Sopan Laxman Mare, leaders of the 5,000-strong Mumbai *dabbawallahs* (Nutan Mumbai Tiffin Box Suppliers Charity Trust, the organization that runs this service), were two special invitees of Prince Charles. The Prince remembered the gifts they sent on hearing of his wedding and was touched by their sentiment. The Queen told Megde she knew about the tiffin-carriers of Mumbai from TV and newspapers, while Prince Charles said it was nice of them to come and then added to convey his greetings and good wishes to other members.

No wonder Megde said at the end of the wedding, 'We will never forget the attention we got from Prince Charles. Now we are being given attention by our own VIPs back home too.' He added, 'We felt like being in a fairyland at Windsor. It was like a dream, spending time at a 900-year old castle and treated equal to Dukes, Duchess, and other dignitaries. We are grateful to him as we said in our wedding greetings card "thank you for enlightening the life *dabbawallahs*".' The *dabbawallahs*' tryst with Prince Charles started in 2003, when he was on a visit to India. Megde was elated by Prince Charles' visit. 'We are glad that this "raja of England" (King of England) is interested in our work. Tragically, no leader of India has ever inquired about our work and our troubles,' he said. Megde and the organization's secretary, Gangaram Talekar, garlanded the Prince, placed a shawl on him, and offered him a white Gandhi cap which he politely declined to wear. This brief ceremony took place in the premises of the Western Railway Headquarters, opposite Churchgate station in south Mumbai. Megde and Talekar then explained the intricacies of their business to the Prince,

showing him a long rectangular tray that carries up to 40 boxes. They explained how the boxes that are collected from various houses in the suburbs are sorted and sent to specific stations, where they are sorted to be sent to various offices. Explaining the rationale for the Prince's visit to the *dabbawallahs*, a British High Commission official said the idea was to show him something that was unique to Mumbai. 'I don't think any other city anywhere in the world or even India has such a system,' she said, adding, 'also, the Prince of Wales is always keen to meet people, so we felt this would be ideal.' Back home, after the wedding of Prince Charles, these leaders of the *dabbawallahs* are getting similar attention. Megde, who was invited at Chennai to receive the 'Lucas TVS NIQR' Award, received a standing ovation in Le Royal Meridien. After receiving this award from the National Institution for Quality and Reliability, he said, 'It is surprising to note that after doing business for more than 100 years now, our model of enterprise had become a global case study for MBAs and PhD students.' Their business model had caught the attention of even the hallowed 'Forbes.' The American business magazine conferred the 'Six Sigma' plus rating on *dabbawallahs*, meaning only one error in six million deliveries, alongside the likes of GE and Motorola in terms of efficiency and quality of service. Their modus operandi too has been well documented by the likes of BBC and Dutch and German film makers. There are close to 5,000 *dabbawallahs* operating in Mumbai city supplying 1,70,000 *dabbas* (tiffin boxes) every day. Their operations are so complex that if even one thing goes out of place, it would lead to chaos, so much so that even when Prince Charles came to visit them, they did not delay their operations. A lot of people believe that the food *dabbawallahs* deliver is also cooked by them. In

*Source*: Steve Evans. Reproduced with permission.
*Dabbawallahs* at work in Mumbai.

*(Contd)*

*Exhibit 16.4 Contd*

reality, they only deliver food to the people of Mumbai which is cooked in the homes of the people by their wives, sisters, or mothers. The tiffin box that the food is delivered in also belongs to the customer. *Dabbawallahs* have a unique colour coding system that they put on the boxes. Their ancestors started by first using coloured threads. Then they switched to using pieces of cloth and now *dabbawallahs* use oil paint and symbols. The first colour symbolizes a 'group'. A group comprises 10 to 20 people who service one station. Just like a cricket team, there are a few substitutes in case someone falls ill. Each group picks up about 40 tiffins from their area and delivers them to the local railway station. There they are sorted according to their destination. The alphabet written on the tiffin box stands for the person who collects the tiffins from the house, and the number is for its destination. From the Six Sigma point of view, the *dabbawallahs* have to take care of two critical to quality (CTQ) characteristics—the tiffins must be delivered to the customer in office at the scheduled time without any delay and second, the empty tiffin box must be returned back at the customer's home without any mix up. Rarely do *dabbawallahs* get complaints of someone's tiffin getting mixed up or lost. It happens only once in a month or two when they get a complaint. On following up on the complaint, they generally find that it was stolen by a hungry beggar. They then keep a lookout for it in the market and on spotting it buy it back and return it to the rightful owner. *Dabbawallahs* claim that they never misplace anything due to any confusion on their part. It obviously is a puzzle for many who wonder how they have managed to reach such levels of efficiency with such an untrained work force. Megde says, 'It just depends on hard work and sincerity, only when you fly high can you reach the stars. The uneducated have an ability to memorize and retain more as opposed to the educated who are used to writing down everything.' *Dabbawallahs* charge ₹250–300 per month from a customer. That includes picking up the tiffin from

home, delivering it to the office, and then returning the empty tiffin back home. Every station on Mumbai's western, central, and harbour railway lines has two groups ranging between 15 to 40 people. 'All of us are entrepreneurs who come together to deliver as a whole. We work exactly like the post office with hub and spoke operations,' says the 63-year old Jairaj Surve, a *dabbawallah*. The meals picked up from clients by 9–9.30 a.m. are brought to the closest railway station. Numbers and symbols painted on the aluminium cases help to sort out the *dabbas* according to the destination. Over the next hour, they are loaded in trains and taken to their destinations, where they are once again sorted out on the basis of office, street, and floor. Even as the *dabba* is picked up from a client's home and delivered by one person, it is delivered and picked up from the workplace by another person. It goes through 3 to 4 hands before reaching its destination. Till 1980, it was a worker-employer relationship, whereby there used to be a contractor who would employ 20–25 workers under him. However, the railway strike of 1975 under Datta Samant which lasted for 20–22 days, caused huge losses for the *dabbawallahs*. Their losses were further compounded by the mill strike. This made them wonder what would happen if their workers were to go on strike. This was the reason that every worker was made a shareholder. This way they put in more effort and since everyone is a shareholder, there is no question of a union. There are elections for the post of the president of the trust and the person getting majority votes becomes the president. There is a show of hands and the person getting the most hands wins. There are disputes between *dabbawallahs* at times, but they are settled on the 15th of every month by the Panch Committee. *Dabbawallahs* have their own mini-government which levies a fine on the workers for making mistakes like not turning up for duty or drinking alcohol while on duty. No dispute has ever reached the police or the courts.

these interfaces on his/her own. The automatic teller machine (ATM) is one such example. The ATM machines have easy to learn controls, which the customer learns to use easily by initially taking help of fellow customers or the bank staff. Soon, customers become adept at using all these controls themselves. Thus, the function of a bank teller is shifted over to the customer by the use of such technological interfaces.

Major banks provide money transfer, bill payment, credit card payments, account statement enquiry, etc. through their online banking services using the Internet. Similarly, travel portals such as MakeMyTrip.com allow customers to choose from a variety of air travel options on the desired route with a comparative listing of fares. The simple to use templates guide the customers to make their own itinerary. Portals such as Amazon.com provide a variety of goods for the customers to choose and allow them to place the orders online.

Jet Airways has introduced the system of allowing customers without check-in baggage to issue and print boarding passes through the Jet Airways website. It has also installed automatic machines at the airports, where such passengers can issue their own boarding passes.

It takes sometime to educate customers about a new technology as a replacement for human service providers. Over the period of time, the customers become self-reliant in the usage of such interfaces and start taking a very active role in the provision of a service.

## Service Blueprinting

Service blueprinting is a special type of flowcharting for service operations propounded by Shostack (1984). The term 'blueprint' has been derived from architectural drawings, which use blue lines on charts to show the shape, size, and other dimensions/specifications of various parts of a building. The service blueprints are different from other forms of flowcharts as these demarcate the operations in the visibility of the customers and the back office operations (invisible to the customer). A line of visibility is created between these sets of operations.

This helps in identifying those points of encounter with the customer which result in creating the impression about the service quality. In the blueprints, small circles/ovals with 'F' written inside are used to identify potential points of failures so that effective measures (poka-yoke) may be planned to avoid such failures. Similarly, small triangles with 'W' written inside are used to identify those points (in the visibility of the customer), where the customer has to wait. For certain operations, which are critical to the good service quality, a standard time duration or a time range is mentioned in the service blueprints.

Figure 16.5 shows the service blueprint of issuance of a life insurance policy for a customer. In this blueprint the first failure point is represented by F1, which indicates that there is a chance of failure if a wrong mortality rate is given to the customer by the sales person even after consultation with her manager. If later the headquarter insists upon a different value, it may result in a face-off situation for the organization as a whole. There is even a possibility of the customer refusing to take the insurance policy from this company at a later date due to this misinformation. A *poka-yoke* device is something which helps in avoiding such failures. Quality Guru Shigeo Shingo propounded the concept of 'zero-defect' or 'error-proofing' by using poka-yoke devices of various sorts. To avoid F1, for example, the company can provide the sales person a laptop with appropriate software/company intranet access to easily calculate/check the mortality rate to be charged from the customer according to his age. The failure point F2 is when the cusomer is informed about the date and time of the medical check-up at a hospital, there is a possibility that the customer may not be informed of the precautions to be taken before the required medical tests. For example, there are tests for which the patient is supposed to come empty stomach. The company may devise a checklist (poka-yoke) of all such precautions to be informed to the customer while conveying the date and time of the medical tests. The failure point F3

> Service blueprinting is a special type of flowcharting for service operations propounded by Shostack (1984).

Line of visibility

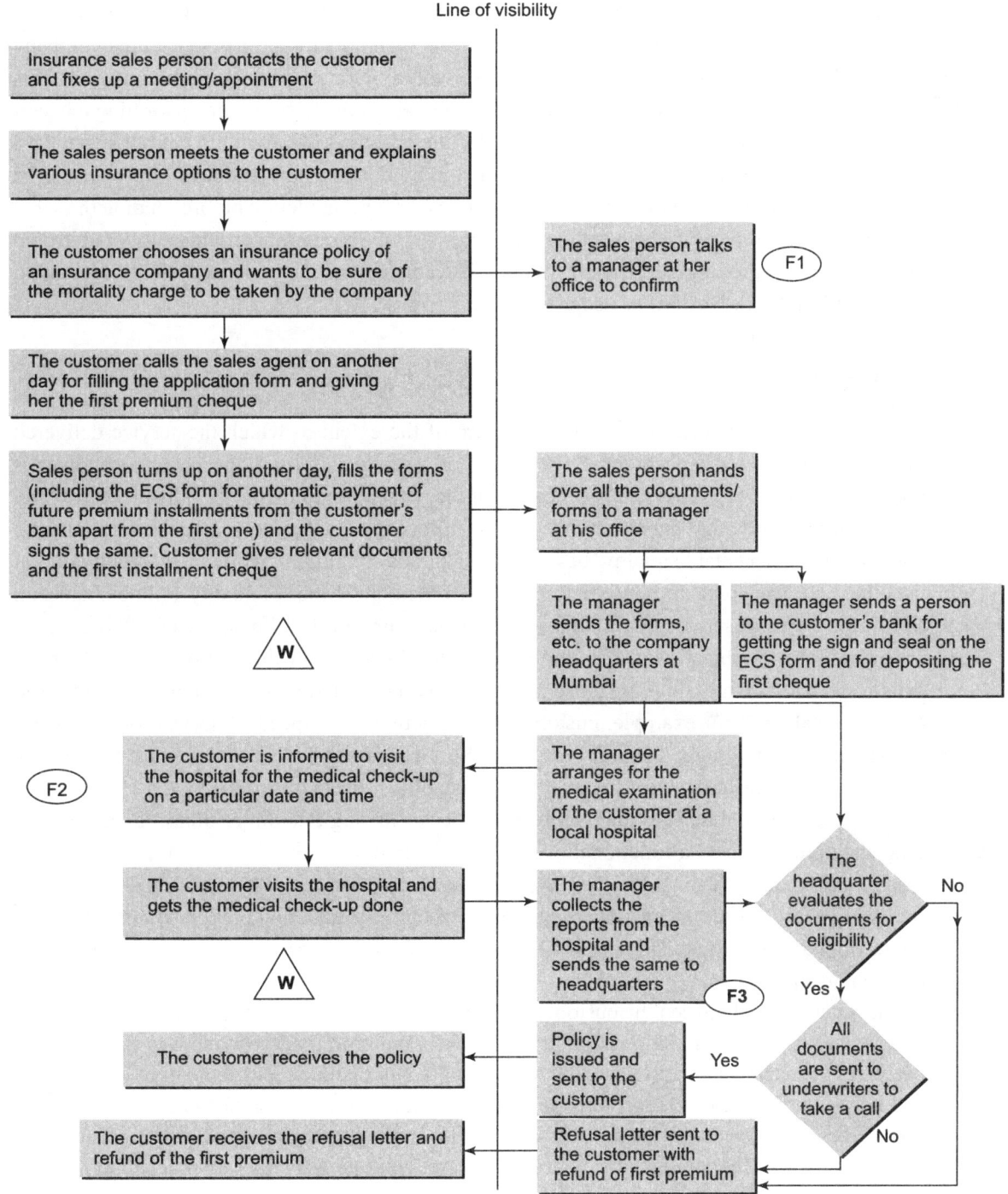

**Fig. 16.5**  Service blueprint of issuance of a life insurance policy for a customer

Service blueprints provide a lot of clarity in designing and improving the service systems.

in the blueprint indicates that there is a possibility that the reports sent by the hospital may be incomplete. If the incomplete report is sent to the company headquarters at Mumbai, these would be returned back for completion. This may involve calling the customer again to the hospital for performing the tests would be very cumbersome for the customer. To avoid this pitfall, a standard form can be devised by the company to be filled in by the hospital conducting the tests on the customer, which can be easily reviewed by the manager for completion before sending the same with the medical reports to the headquarters. Thus, service blueprints provide a lot of clarity in designing and improving the service systems. The concept of 'methods analysis' (discussed in Chapter 12 on Work Design) is also useful in this context.

## Service Quality

'Quality' in a service organization is a measure of the extent to which the service delivered meets the customer's expectations. The nature of most services is such that the customer is present in the delivery process. This means that the perception of quality is influenced not only by the 'service outcome' but also by the 'service process'. The 'perceived quality' lies along a continuum. 'Unacceptable quality' lies at one end of this continuum, while 'ideal quality' lies at the other end. The points in-between represent different gradations of quality. (Ghobadian et al. 1994). Measures of service quality may either be hard or soft. Hard measures are those which are quantifiable or objective; for example, computer downtime or the proportion of telephone calls answered. Soft measures are those which are qualitative, judgemental, subjective and based on perceptual data, for example, customer's satisfaction with speed of service or manager's assessment of staff attitude towards customers. Soft measures of service quality are particularly relevant to the measurement of the quality of intangible aspects of service (Voss, 1985).

Grönroos (1990) describes the quality of service as having two dimensions—a technical or outcome dimension and a functional or process-related dimension. What customers receive is clearly important to them and to their overall evaluation of quality. This could be looked on as 'product quality': what the customer is left with when the production process and the personal interactions are over. Frequently this dimension can be measured objectively because it represents the technical provision.

The interactions between the customer and the service provider—constitute the 'how' of the service provision. This functional quality will have a major influence on the way the customer perceives the technical quality. The functional quality will include such elements as the attitudes and behaviour of staff, relationships among staff and customers, relationships between staff themselves, the appearance and personality of the staff, the service-mindedness of staff, the accessibility of staff to the customer and their overall approachability. These elements are very difficult to measure in any objective way, but may have a disproportionate effect on the customer's overall evaluation of the quality of their service experience.

Soft measures of service quality are particularly relevant to the measurement of the quality of intangible aspects of service.

In addition, Grönroos identifies the corporate image dimension of quality. This image will be built up from the functional and technical quality of the services the organization offers, plus the effects of traditional marketing activities such as advertising, pricing and public relations.

## Dimensions of Quality in Services

Services are different from tangible products as the customer undergoes and experiences the service process himself or herself, while he or she is least interested in knowing about the production process of tangible products and only makes a decision to buy by looking at the final product. Thus, the involvement of the customer in a buying decision is much more in services compared to products. There are several dimensions of quality in services.

**Time**   It is expected by the customers that time would be kept as promised by the service providers. For example, one major attribute of the Indigo airline is the on-time performance of a large majority of its flights.

**Completeness**   In this attribute, the customers expect the service to be completed to a logical conclusion. For example, in a restaurant, meals should be ideally followed by desert, tea/coffee, and so on. If a restaurant does not proffer such items in its menu, its service would be considered as incomplete, and this may impact its business.

**Courtesy**   The employees in a service facility are expected to demonstrate highest standards of courtesy and amicable demeanour. For example, a guest in a hotel expects its staff to greet him or her warmly on arrival and provide him or her any desired information in a courteous manner.

**Consistency**   Consistency means that every time a customer visits a service facility, he or she should have the same experience without any deviation. For example, a customer doing online transactions through the website of a bank would expect easy navigation and seamless execution of transactions each and every time. Any uninformed downtime of the website would lead to customer dissatisfaction.

**Accessibility and convenience**   It is important that the staff of a service facility is well-trained to respond to any queries by the customer (are easily accessible) about the service or help them as per the convenience of the customer. For example, it becomes unbearable for the customer who is made to wait for long on phone after she calls a customer service call centre because of the lack of knowledge of the operator about the service to be able to respond promptly.

**Accuracy**   This refers to the accuracy of information provided about the service by its service providers. For example, in an advertisement of an amusement park, the customers look forward to having accurate information about the opening and closing timings, the various amusement facilities, eating joints, and so on. Any lapse in the provision of such information may later result in customer dissatisfaction.

**Responsiveness**   This attribute demands from the staff of the service facility to come up with solutions even before the customer demands them. For example, in a hospital, a patient would feel delighted if an attendant or a nurse promptly appears as soon as the callbell is pressed.

## Internal and External Measures of Service Quality

Information on service quality can be gathered from internal and/or external data sources. Internal data are those generated by the staff or management inside an organization, enabling the

High staff turnover is a negative internal indicator of service quality.

organization to ensure that it is meeting its own internal specification of service quality. However, internal measurement of service alone may be of little value if an organization has no means of assessing whether or not the service levels set internally are generating customer satisfaction. Customers also inevitably assess the quality of the service during and after its provision. Their assessments (external measures of service quality) result in a level of customer satisfaction. Thus, service organizations may measure service quality not only on the basis of their own internal data but also by using external data, by monitoring customer satisfaction (Silvestro et al. 1990). Table 16.1 shows the various internal and external measures of service quality used by an equipment rental organization and a transport terminal operation. For the equipment rental organization, the number of service calls per product and the average time taken to respond to a client's request (indicating the responsiveness) are internal measures of product reliability. The service engineer's competence in fixing the equipment is measured by the internal measure named first-time fix. High staff turnover (employees leaving the organization for greener pastures) is a negative internal indicator of service quality. When trained and skilled staff quit the job and new employees are hired to replace them, it takes time to train them. During this time, the chances of these employees faltering on the service quality front are obviously more.

Amongst other external measures, mystery shoppers (dummy customers instituted by the company itself) have been used by this equipment rental organization to have first-hand experience of customers with respect to service quality. Similarly, the transport terminal operation uses both internal as well as external measures of service quality as shown in Table 16.1.

**Table 16.1** Internal and external measures of service quality (Silvestro et al. 1990)

| *Internal* | *External* |
|---|---|
| *Equipment Rental Organization* | |
| First-time fix | Number of rental terminations |
| Speed of response to service request | Net gained/lost customers |
| Number of service calls per product | Mystery shopper used to evaluate intangible as well as tangible aspects of service |
| Staff turnover | After-sales telephone call used to moniter customer satisfaction, and adherence to service specification |
| Structure and formal monthly management inspection of intangible as well as tangible aspects of service | |
| *Transport Terminal Operation* | |
| Equipment availability | Number of complaints per 1,00,000 passengers |
| Safety procedure inspection | Customer feedback from comment cards and correspondence |
| Speed of passenger throughout | Customer surveys of satisfaction with a wide range of aspects of service |
| Punctuality | |
| Percentage of outstanding equipment faults | |
| Daily product sampling by managers and formal reporting of quality of intangible and tangible aspects of service to senior managers | |

Parasuraman et al. propounded a model of service quality popularly known as the 'gap model'.

# Measuring Service Quality Using SERVQUAL

All the statistical techniques discussed earlier have been successfully applied to the services set-up as well. Still it is very important to assess the quality of a service from the customer's point of view as the customer experiencing the service has some expectations and perceptions about a quality service. In the manufacturing sector also, there are many support services which require the measurement of quality from the customer's point of view. For example, post-sales service is one such support service, about which the customer has some expectations and perceptions.

Parasuraman et al. (1985) propounded a model of service quality popularly known as the 'gap model'. Fig. 16.6 shows this model with five gaps between various elements in the design and delivery of a service. These gaps are the discrepancies or hurdles in the ultimate customer satisfaction. The customer develops his/her set of expectations from a service through word-of-mouth communication (from friends, relatives, etc. who have experienced such a service), his/her own personal needs from the service, and his/her own past experiences with the service.

**Gap 1** exists between the expectations of the customer (consumer of service) and the perception of the service provider about these customer expectations. For example, the manager of a restaurant might have instructed the waiters to stand somewhere near the customers' table after having served the meals so that if the need be, the customer can easily call the waiter. On

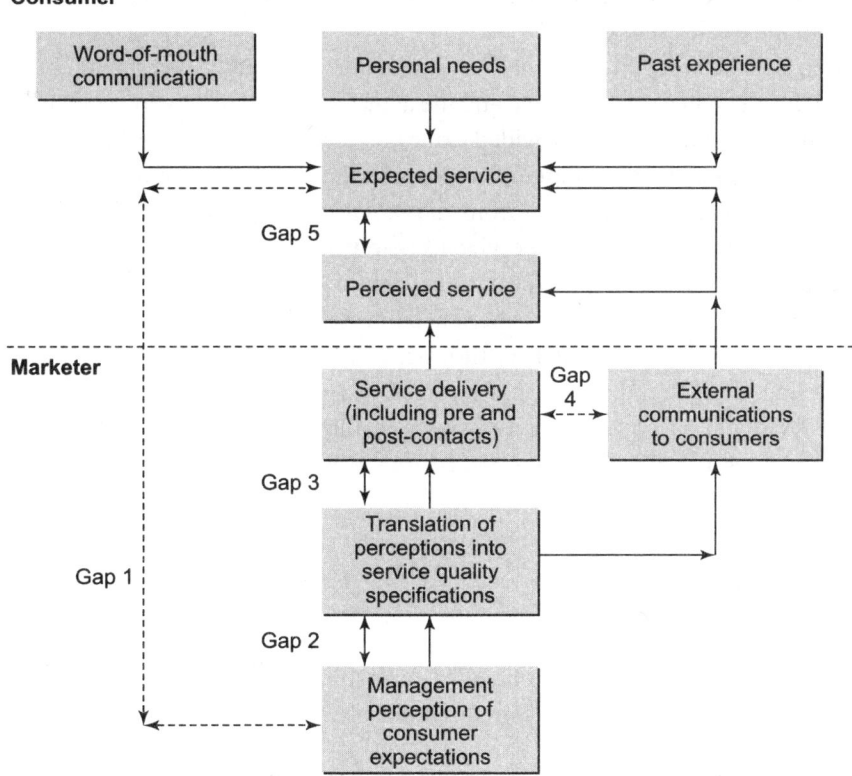

**Fig. 16.6** The Gap model

SERVQUAL is a questionnaire designed to measure the gap between the expectations and perceptions of a customer from a particular service.

the other hand, the customer may feel irritated by the waiter staring at him/her while having the meal. In this situation, the customer expects the waiter to be readily available whenever she needs and at the same time, remain at a sufficient distance to ensure adequate privacy at the customer table. Thus, the manager of the restaurant has to use proper tools and techniques to understand the customer expectations as objectively and precisely as possible.

**Gap 2** exists between the perception of the service provider and the translation of these perceptions into the creation of the specifications of the service. In our example of Gap 1, having understood the expectation of the customer, the manager has to evolve the specifications about the exact distance from the customer table at which the waiters should stand after having served the meals. Also, it should be specified how waiters should not stare at the customer and still be prompt enough to respond to a call/gesture of the customer. If any such required specification is not specified objectively, it would exemplify Gap 2.

**Gap 3** is between the service specifications and service delivery (including pre- and post-contacts with the customer). In our example, let us assume that it has been specified that the waiter should be 5 metres away from the customer's table and look in any vague direction (but not towards any table) with the customer in peripheral vision for detecting any signal/call by the customer. When it came to the implementation of these specifications, it was found that some waiters (who had joined recently) were not following these specifications. During rush hours, waiters had to attend to more than one customer table and the distance specification became difficult to adhere to practically. As the end result, some customers perceived the same problem as with the earlier service.

**Gap 4** is between the external communication (through advertising, etc.) to the consumers about the attributes of the service and the actual service delivery. It is always beneficial to give a realistic view of the service provided to the customers through advertising. Otherwise, consumers get overwhelmed by the exaggerated commercials shown to them on TV, radio, or print media, and have bloated expectations from the service. Subsequently, after having experienced the service they may perceive the service as below standard.

**Gap 5** exists between the expectations of the consumers from the service and their perceptions about the service after having experienced it. Perceived quality of service depends on the size and direction of Gap 5, which in turn depends on the nature of the gaps associated with the marketing, design, and delivery of services.

SERVQUAL is a questionnaire (shown in Table 16.2) designed to measure the gap between the expectations and perceptions of a customer from a particular service. This questionnaire has the following five categories:

- tangibles
- reliability
- responsiveness
- assurance
- empathy

These five dimensions are the result of a factor analysis applied to ten dimensions, initially identified in earlier exploratory research (Parasuraman et al. 1985), namely,

1. tangibles,
2. reliability,
3. responsiveness,
4. communication,

5. credibility,

6. security,

7. competence,

8. courtesy,

9. understanding/knowing the consumer, and

10. access.

> **SERVPERF measures only the performance (PERF stands for performance) of the organization and not the gap.**

There are 22 questions in total in this questionnaire, as shown in Table 16.2. Note that in the questionnaire we have considered a hospital, although this questionnaire can be applied to any service set-up. The responses of customers are recorded on a scale ranging between 1 and 7, with 1 representing 'strongly disagree' and 7 representing 'strongly agree'. For each question, two separate responses of the customer are taken—one for expectation and the other for perception. The difference between the responses for perception and expectation (P–E) is the gap score, which is usually negative. In Fig. 16.7, we have shown the scores given by a hypothetical customer for the 22 questions. Note that in column E most of the gap scores are negative. In column F, we have calculated the average gap score of each category. In Fig. 16.8, column B, we have given weights to various categories according to their importance. The total of the weights should always be 100. These weights are multiplied to the average score obtained by each category (shown in column C) to arrive at the weighted average scores as shown in column D. The average of these weighted average scores is called the SERVQUAL score (shown in cell D11 as –22.2).

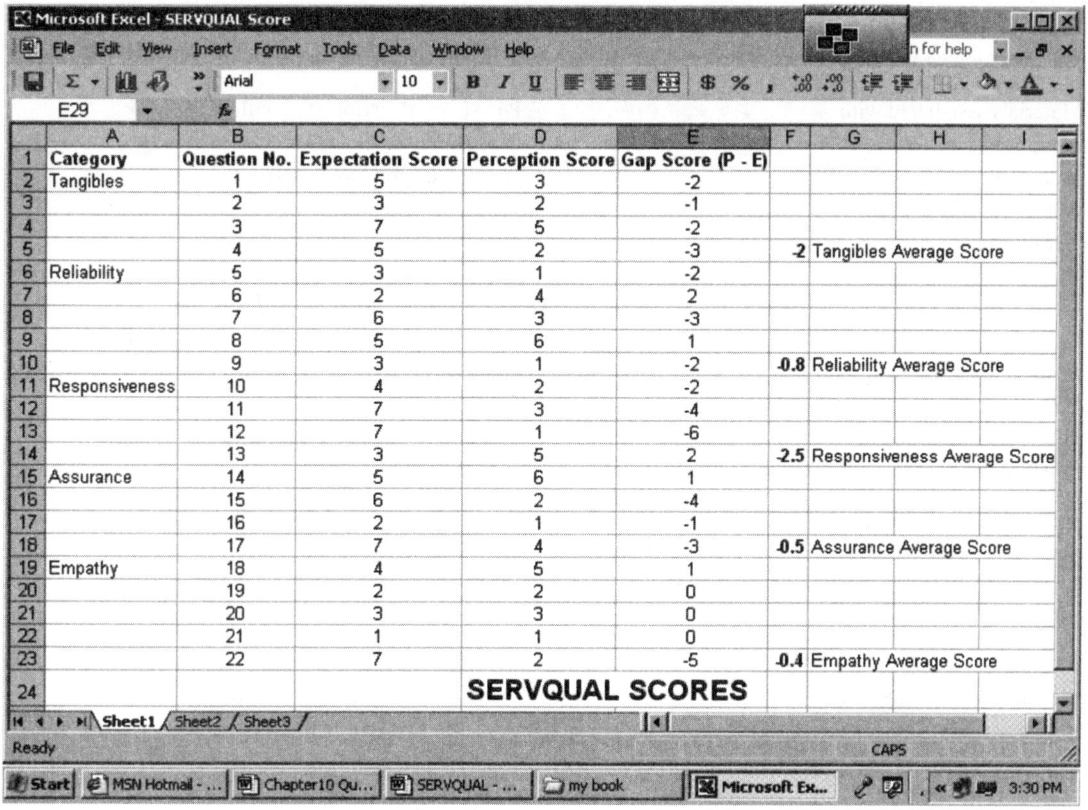

| | A | B | C | D | E | F | G | H | I |
|---|---|---|---|---|---|---|---|---|---|
| 1 | Category | Question No. | Expectation Score | Perception Score | Gap Score (P - E) | | | | |
| 2 | Tangibles | 1 | 5 | 3 | -2 | | | | |
| 3 | | 2 | 3 | 2 | -1 | | | | |
| 4 | | 3 | 7 | 5 | -2 | | | | |
| 5 | | 4 | 5 | 2 | -3 | | -2 | Tangibles Average Score | |
| 6 | Reliability | 5 | 3 | 1 | -2 | | | | |
| 7 | | 6 | 2 | 4 | 2 | | | | |
| 8 | | 7 | 6 | 3 | -3 | | | | |
| 9 | | 8 | 5 | 6 | 1 | | | | |
| 10 | | 9 | 3 | 1 | -2 | | -0.8 | Reliability Average Score | |
| 11 | Responsiveness | 10 | 4 | 2 | -2 | | | | |
| 12 | | 11 | 7 | 3 | -4 | | | | |
| 13 | | 12 | 7 | 1 | -6 | | | | |
| 14 | | 13 | 3 | 5 | 2 | | -2.5 | Responsiveness Average Score | |
| 15 | Assurance | 14 | 5 | 6 | 1 | | | | |
| 16 | | 15 | 6 | 2 | -4 | | | | |
| 17 | | 16 | 2 | 1 | -1 | | | | |
| 18 | | 17 | 7 | 4 | -3 | | -0.5 | Assurance Average Score | |
| 19 | Empathy | 18 | 4 | 5 | 1 | | | | |
| 20 | | 19 | 2 | 2 | 0 | | | | |
| 21 | | 20 | 3 | 3 | 0 | | | | |
| 22 | | 21 | 1 | 1 | 0 | | | | |
| 23 | | 22 | 7 | 2 | -5 | | -0.4 | Empathy Average Score | |
| 24 | | | | **SERVQUAL SCORES** | | | | | |

**Fig. 16.7** The SERVQUAL scores

In certain type of industries, the expectations of the customers are too high and are almost the same for all the parameters. In such situations, only the perception scores are obtained from the customers and the questionnaire is called SERVPERF as it measures only the performance (PERF stands for performance) of the organization and not the gap.

**Table 16.2** The SERVQUAL questionnaire

| *Expectations* | *Perceptions* |
|---|---|
| This survey deals with your opinions of hospitals. Please show the extent to which you think hospitals should posses the following features. What we are interested in here is a number that best shows your expectations about hospitals. | The following statements relate to your feelings about the particular hospital ABC you chose. Please show the extent to which you believe ABC hospital has the feature described in the statement. Here, we are interested in a number that shows your perceptions about ABC hospital. |

| Strongly Disagree      Strongly Agree<br>1   2   3   4   5   6   7    **(E)** | Strongly Disagree      Strongly Agree<br>1   2   3   4   5   6   7<br>**(P) Gap Score (P − E)** |
|---|---|
| **Tangibles**<br>E1. Excellent hospitals will have modern looking equipment.   — | **Tangibles**<br>P1. ABC hospital has modern looking equipment.   — |
| E2. The physical facilities at excellent hospitals will be visually appealing.   — | P2. ABC hospital's physical facilities are visually appealing.   — |
| E3. Employees at excellent hospitals will appear neat. | P3. ABC hospital's reception desk employees appear neat.   — |
| E4. Materials associated with the service (such as forms, pamphlets, and bandages) will be visually appealing at an excellent hospital.   — | P4. Materials associated with the service (such as forms, pamphlets, and bandages) are visually appealing at ABC hospital.   —<br>**Average Tangibles SERVQUAL score** |
| **(E)** | **(P) (P − E)** |
| **Reliability**<br>E5. When excellent hospitals promise to do something by a certain time, they do.   — | **Reliability**<br>P5. When ABC hospital promises to do something by a certain time, it does so.   — |
| E6. When a patient has a problem, excellent hospitals will show a sincere interest in solving it.   — | P6. When you have a problem, ABC hospital shows a sincere interest in solving it. |
| E7. Excellent hospitals will perform the medical treatment right the first time.   — | P7. ABC hospital performs the medical treatment right the first time.   — |
| E8. Excellent hospitals will provide the medical treatment | P8. ABC hospital provides its medical treatment at the time it |

*(Contd)*

Table 16.2 Contd

| Expectations | | Perceptions | | |
|---|---|---|---|---|
| **Reliability** | | **Reliability** | | |
| at the time they promise to do so. | — | promises to do so. | — | |
| E9. Excellent hospitals will insist on error-free records. | — | P9. ABC hospital insists on error-free records. | — | |
| | | **Average Responsiveness SERVQUAL score** | | |
| **Responsiveness** | | **Responsiveness** | | |
| E10. Employees of excellent hospitals will tell patients exactly when services will be performed. | — | P10. Employees in ABC hospital tell you exactly when medical treatment will be performed. | — | |
| E11. Employees of excellent hospitals will give prompt service to customers. | — | P11. Employees in ABC hospital give you prompt service. | — | |
| E12. Employees of excellent hospitals will always be willing to help customers. | — | P12. Employees in ABC hospital are always willing to help you. | — | |
| E13. Employees of excellent hospitals will never be too busy to respond to customers' requests. | — | P13. Employees in ABC hospital are never too busy to respond to your request. | | |
| | | **Average Responsiveness SERVQUAL score** | | |
| | **(E)** | | **(P)** | **(P – E)** |
| **Assurance** | | **Assurance** | | |
| E14. The behaviour of employees in excellent hospitals will instill confidence in patients. | — | P14. The behaviour of employees in ABC hospital instills confidence in you. | — | |
| E15. Patients of excellent hospitals will feel safe with the medical treatment. | — | P15. You feel safe with your medical treatment at ABC hospital. | — | |
| E16. Employees of excellent hospitals will be consistently courteous to customers. | — | P16. Employees in ABC hospital are consistently courteous to you. | | |
| E17. Employees of excellent hospitals will have the knowledge to answer customers' questions. | — | P17. Employees in ABC hospital have the knowledge to answer your questions. | — | |
| | | **Average Assurance SERVQUAL score** | | |

*(Contd)*

Table 16.2 Contd

| Expectations | Perceptions |
|---|---|
| **Empathy** | **Empathy** |
| E18. Excellent hospitals will give customers individual attention. — | P18. ABC hospital gives you individual attention. — |
| E19. Excellent hospitals will have working hours convenient for all their patients. — | P19. ABC hospital has working hours convenient for all its patients. — |
| E20. Excellent hospitals will have employees who give patients personal attention. — | P20. ABC hospital has employees who give you personal attention. — |
| E21. Excellent hospitals will have their patient's best interests at heart. — | P21. ABC hospital has your best interests at heart. — |
| E22. The employees of excellent hospitals will understand the specific needs of their patients. — | P22. The employees of ABC hospital understand your specific needs. — |
| | **Average Empathy SERVQUAL scores** |

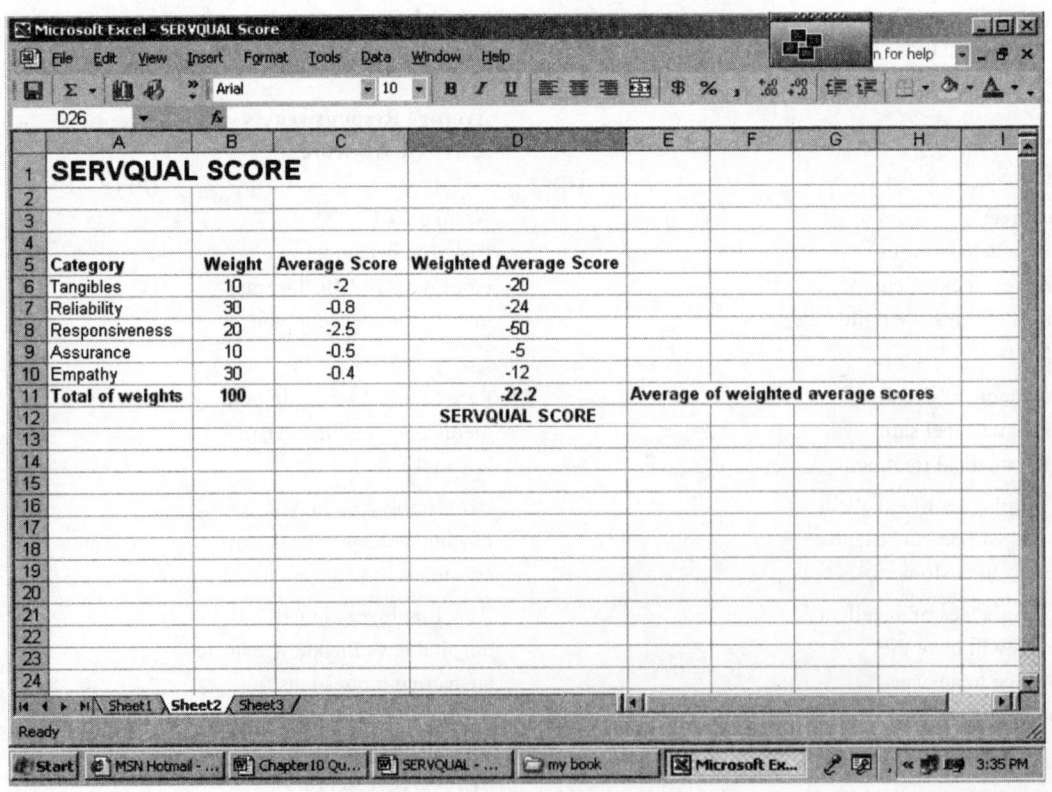

Fig. 16.8   The final SERVQUAL score

### Limitations of SERVQUAL

Cronin and Taylor (1992) concluded that the current performance best reflects a customer's perception of service quality and that expectations are not part of this concept. They performed an empirical test with four alternative service quality models:

- SERVQUAL: Service Quality = Performance – Expectations
- Weighted SERVQUAL: Service Quality = Importance × (Performance – Expectations)
- SERVPERF: Service Quality = Performance
- Weighted SERVPERF: Service Quality = Importance × Performance

From the results of their empirical investigation, Cronin and Taylor (1992) concluded that the unweighted SERVPERF measure (performance only) performed better than any other measure of service quality.

Despite Parasuraman et al.'s (1988) initial claim that the five service quality dimensions are generic, it is generally agreed that this is not the case and that the number and definition of the dimensions varies depending on the context. Indeed, one of the authors (Zeithaml) reaches this conclusion when stating that a two-dimensional service quality model is 'the preferred model for overall perceived quality for our particular application' (Boulding et al. 1993). When measuring the quality of accounting firms, Freeman and Dart (1993) conclude that service quality is a seven-dimensional construct. Robinson and Pidd (1998) propose 19 dimensions of service quality in the context of management science projects.

Developing separate instruments depending upon the purpose and context of the service quality measurement may be the most fruitful way forward. Since the understanding of service quality is so limited, it seems unrealistic to be aiming for a global measurement approach until a much better understanding is obtained. Indeed, it may be that the service quality construct is quite distinct in different domains, and as such it is impossible to obtain a global measurement approach. As much of scientific research has evolved to develop, in some cases, general theorems and laws, so the same could be true of research into service quality.

According to Stauss and Weinlich (1997), a closer look, however, reveals some deficits of attribute-based quality measurement (such as SERVQUAL). First, the data collected by these methods cannot completely reflect the customer's quality perception. A comprehensive listing of all quality aspects would involve a questionnaire by far exceeding the normal customer's willingness to answer. It is thus highly likely that a multitude of problems and positive service contact experiences will not be listed at all, particularly those which do not address the core service and which the management deem to be of secondary importance. Second, the respondents are forced to aggregate their quality experiences in a problematic way. A customer of a bank asked to evaluate the friendliness of customer contact employees of a bank is forced to tick a single point on a scale even if he/she had contacts with three employees whose behaviour and

> Developing separate instruments of the service quality measurement is more suitable than a global measurement approach.

friendliness differed considerably. Third, as the quality items are formulated in a necessarily abstract manner, survey results are not particularly concrete (Bitner et al. 1985). For example, a considerable discrepancy between the expectation and the perception of the attribute 'friendliness of staff' would seem to point to a deficiency in quality, but fails to indicate which concrete behaviour customers perceive as unfriendly and which concrete quality improvement measures should be taken to overcome this deficiency.

## Conformance to Specifications

Quality Guru Philip B. Crosby defined quality as 'conformance to specifications' and recommended the following steps in achieving it:

**Defining the quality characteristics**   In this activity, the priorities of the customers with respect to the quality of a product or service are defined. These priorities are known as 'critical to quality (CTQ)' characteristics. For example, a popular café in Mumbai (Laziz Café) conducted a survey to know about the CTQs of the hot tea served by them, which happens to be the most popular item on their menu. The survey revealed the following CTQs:

- The tea should be really hot.
- The tea should have the typical Laziz Café aroma.
- The tea should have the typical Laziz Café taste.

**Measuring each quality characteristic**   As is evident from the CTQs expressed by the customers in the earlier example of tea, it may be difficult to capture the true expectations of the customer. For instance, in the first CTQ—how hot is 'really hot'? The role of the product designer (in this case, the chef) comes into the picture. Thus, the measurable characteristics implicit in the CTQs have to be decided upon. In our example of tea, the chef of Laziz Café decides the following:

- The temperature of the tea served needs to be measured (to make sure it is 'really hot').
- The time taken by the waiter to take the tea from the kitchen to the table of the customer needs to be measured (to make sure that the tea is served 'really hot').
- The quantity of the tea put into water in the cup (standard size) needs to be measured (to give the typical Laziz Café aroma as well as taste).
- The brand and type of the tea used has to be always the same (to give the typical Laziz Café aroma as well as taste).

**Setting quality standards for each quality characteristic**   Having decided upon the measurable quality characteristics, the engineer/designer needs to set standard values (specifications) for each of them. In our example, the chef comes up with the following specifications:

- The temperature of the tea when ready in the kitchen should be between 100°C and 98°C.
- The waiter should take two minutes ± one minute to take the tea from the kitchen to the customer table.
- The quantity of tea to be put into water in the cup is two table spoons per cup ± one-fourth tablespoon.
- Only Brooke Bond Red Label tea should be used.

**Controlling quality against those standards**   Having created the standards, it is necessary to ensure that the same are followed rigorously and any deviation from the standards can be easily detected. In our example, to control quality against the standards, the following control mechanisms are installed:

- A temperature meter is installed on the microwave oven used for heating the tea with water in the cup. This microwave should be used exclusively for tea making. A standard operating procedure (SOP) is created, which states that the tea with water in the cup must be heated (by one of the cooks) till the temperature displays 100°C and the cup should remain inside the oven as long as the waiter does not come to take it directly to the customer table.
- Another SOP mentions that when the waiter comes to take the tea from the oven, he or she should check the temperature displayed there and if it is less than 98°C, he or she should put

the oven on for a couple of minutes till the temperature display shows 100°C. As a control measure, a buzzer (a form of Poka-yoke or fool-proofing device) is installed in the oven, which starts ringing in case the door of the oven is opened when the temperature displayed is below 100°C. This draws the attention of all in the kitchen, thus alerting the waiter to comply to the SOP.

- Small pouches of Brooke Bond Red Label tea are prepared with exact measurement of two tablespoons, which the cook has to put in the water in the cup while preparing the tea. As a control measure, the chief cook occasionally (once a week) inspects the quantity in a pouch drawn at random from the lot.

**Finding and correcting causes of poor quality**   In order to detect any lapses, a customer feedback form is created and provided to customers chosen at random. In case of any problem reported by customers in the feedback form, corrective action is taken. For example, a new waiter who is found to deviate from the SOPs is re-trained so as to not repeat the same mistakes leading to poor quality.

**Continuous improvements**   No process should be deemed to have achieved the state of perfection, as there is always some scope for further improvisation. Employees know their area of activity in the best possible way and should be encouraged to suggest ideas for continuous improvement.

## Waiting Time Management

Formation of queues and waiting time on part of customers is considered to be a necessary evil by many operations managers. It is an evil indeed, though not necessary. Some managers used to have similar impressions about inventory management in manufacturing facilities before the advent of the JIT concept, but later realized how wrong their impressions were. Service managers and customers have become accustomed to long queues. Invariably each one of us comes across queues every now and then. Do we ever imagine what would our world look like without these queues? Before we discuss the possible ways to eliminate this evil completely, let us briefly discuss how operations managers have tried in the past to provide various formats of queues in a desperate attempt at improving customer satisfaction levels.

**Formats of queues**   There are four basic formats of queues:

1. Classic queue format (multiple servers, multiple queues)
2. Zigzag queue format (multiple servers, single queue)
3. Numbered queue format (multiple servers, single queue with numbered customers)
4. Split queue format (multiple servers, single split queue)

The *classic queue* format shown in Fig. 16.9(a) is the most common format of queuing. The customers have the flexibility of choosing the queue, which they feel is the shortest or is moving at the fastest pace. Even after having joined a particular queue, they may join another queue if it appears to them that the queue they had joined earlier is moving slowly compared to others. It is common to see customers leaving the queue and asking the person behind them to reserve their place. Usually, when the person joins back the queue, he/she is greeted by protests from other customers. In this format, the first come first served (FCFS)

In the classic queue format, the customers have the flexibility of choosing the queue which they feel is the shortest or is moving at the fastest pace.

rule may not apply, as a customer entering the service system late may actually get processed sooner compared to other customers who had come earlier because of joining the faster or shorter queue. This classic queue format is also useful when certain servers are used to provide specialized services. For example, at some Indian Railway reservation centres, there are separate servers for physically challenged persons, foreign tourists, enquiries, etc.

The *zigzag queue* format displayed in Fig. 16.9(b) is often found, at the airports, in front of security checks or immigration counters. The zigzag barricades created by using tapes or steel

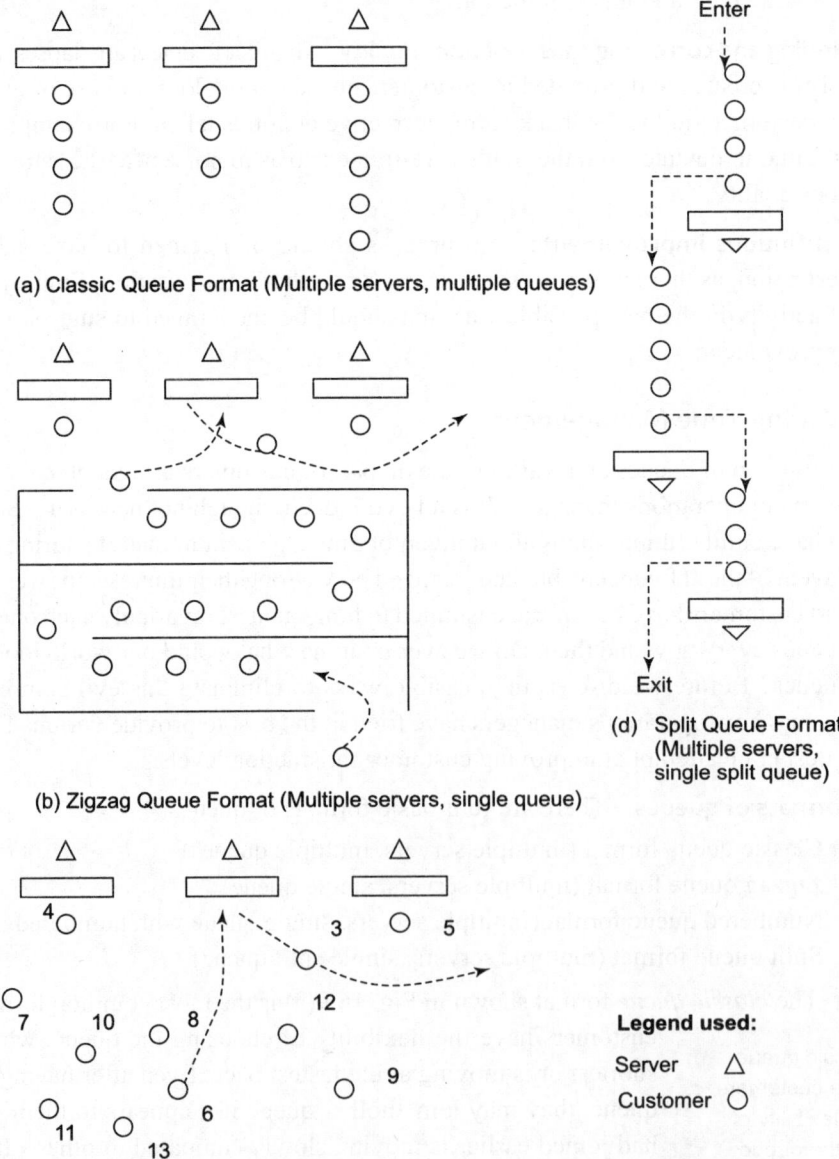

(a) Classic Queue Format (Multiple servers, multiple queues)

(b) Zigzag Queue Format (Multiple servers, single queue)

(c) Numbered Queue Format (Multiple servers, single queue with numbered customers)

(d) Split Queue Format (Multiple servers, single split queue)

Legend used:

Server △

Customer ○

*Source:* Adapted from Fitzsimmons (2004).

**Fig. 16.9** Various queue formats

The numbered queues are a need when the actual waiting area in the facility is not big enough to accommodate a large number of customers.

ensure a single queue with a single entrance and a single exit. The exit leads to many servers, where the customers may move according to availability. A major advantage is a single queue with less chance of customers cutting-in because of the barricades. The FCFS rule is automatically followed here with a surety of least average waiting time for customers when compared to the classic format. This reduces the anxiety on part of the customers as they do not have to worry about other queues moving faster, as in the classic format.

The third format is the *numbered queue* (Fig. 16.9c), whereby customers are given a numbered token, eliminating the need for them to stand in physical queues. The numbered tokens serve as a virtual queue. The server counters (and other strategic locations in the service facility) have easily visible displays of the number being currently processed by them. Therefore, the customers get an idea about the time after which their turn would come. In the meantime, they are free to move around the premises or seat themselves comfortably. This queuing format is quite useful in departmental stores, where in place of getting captured in a physical queue, the customers are free to move around with a chance of buying more items by the time their turn comes up for paying the bill. However, customers can face some anxiety by keeping an eye on the numbers being displayed on the server counters to ensure that their turn is not missed. The *numbered queues* are a need when the actual waiting area in the facility is not big enough to accommodate a large number of customers. Many restaurants face this space problem and customers are encouraged to take their numbered counters and roam around with the promise of SMS alerts being sent by the servers before their turn comes up.

The *split queue* format is shown in Fig. 16.9(d). This format is useful when there are sequential steps in the service provision process. A typical example can be seen in hospitals, where the first split queue can be formed outside the OPD, where the general physician does the initial examination of the patients. After this examination, some patients are sent for different types of tests such as X-ray, pathology tests, and ECG. The patients have to stand again in a queue while waiting for their turn at these test centres. The next stage of the split queue can be outside the room of the specialist doctor, where the patients get their final prescription. It may, however, be noticed that split queues can provide a very torturous experience for customers, especially if all the split queues are not clearly visible to the customer at the outset giving him/her an approximate idea of the total time to be consumed there.

Some organizations use a combination of the four formats of queues discussed above. A typical example is the American Embassy at New Delhi, which follows all the four formats in combination. As mentioned earlier, the visa appointments for personal interviews are given by the embassy months in advance and the appointment specifies an exact time slot (akin to the *numbered queue*) giving the impression that the embassy would be waiting exclusively for the invitee during this time. To the dismay of the applicant, upon reaching the embassy, there is a huge crowd of other applicants across the road opposite to the embassy complex. It is natural on part of the applicants having appointments to reach a bit earlier than the scheduled time (especially since most of them come from outside Delhi). The applicants are allowed to be a part of the *classic queue* format outside the embassy premises (near the road). Television sets are installed at regular intervals of this queue, which display music videos praising the US and intermittently displaying the correct procedure for filling the visa application form.

The applicants are under the impression till this stage that the couple of windows where this queue is culminating are the places for personal interview and they would be free after this process. They would discover later that it is actually only a *split queue*. When their turn comes up at one of the windows, the applicants realize that only the relevant documents (along with the application form) are collected at these windows and they have to now proceed within the embassy for further formalities. There is another split queue for the security check at the entrance, which is hardly visible from the earlier split queue. There is a third queue upon entering the main hall. This queue is for finger printing through a machine installed at the server window. The next step is without any queue. Applicants flock around a cage, where the embassy's authorized outsourcing agency, TTK's personnel ask the applicants to write their address on a slip for dispatch of the passport (with visa stamping), in case the applicant gets the visa. The last queue of the process is a *zigzag queue* facing the server counters. Personal interviews are conducted by the visa officers here. A television set faces the queue with latest speeches of the US heads of the government. After another two hours of wait in this final queue, the applicant gets a chance to interact with the visa officer. It seems more like a test of patience—a personal interview after a total of four hours of standing in different queues. It is clearly stated on their website that it is the sole responsibility of the applicant to convince the visa officer by relevant documents. The visa officer is completely behind the glass window and interacts with the visa applicants through a microphone-speaker system. The saying of the great American quality guru, Joseph M. Juran resounds, 'There is still a lot of work to be done by the quality management professionals, especially in government, healthcare and education.'

**Elimination of queues and waiting time**   Where there is will, there is a way. This statement is relevant to managers who believe that queuing and waiting is a part of life. There are several examples and innovative ways of eliminating the queues and waiting time completely. A red light signal on any square is a typical example of waiting of vehicles for their turn to move ahead towards their destination. Many times a prominent display of the number of seconds of wait remaining is made to make the drivers aware. It is no doubt better than an uninformed wait, but still the wait is very much there. The advent of multiple flyovers for movement in many directions across a square has eliminated this kind of waiting and queuing. It is an expensive option, but is a boon for areas experiencing heavy traffic and frequent traffic jams.

The Internet has helped in eliminating the queues in many walks of our lives. Many banks are providing online banking services through their web portals. It is now easy to check the account statement, transfer money to other accounts, and pay utility bills, such as, phones, electricity, Internet, and insurance premium. ICICI Bank has extended its utility bill payment services free of charge to its credit card customers. For customers who agree to avail this service, an SMS is sent to the credit card holder seeking permission to pay a particular month's (for example, electricity) bill. If the customer responds in affirmative, the bill payment is done by the bank directly to the Electricity Board and the same is reflected in the monthly credit card statement of the customer.

> There are several examples and innovative ways of eliminating the queues and waiting time completely.

The monthly payment for the expenses through the credit card can also be easily done online by Visa Money Transfer (VMT) facility provided by many banks through their Internet banking services. Almost all airlines accept payments using credit cards for bookings made through their websites.

The use of technology will reduce queues and waiting time in the near future.

Indian Railways has its extensive online ticketing services through its Indian Railways Catering and Tourism Corporation Limited (IRCTC) website. All these examples are indicators that the use of technology will reduce queues and waiting time in the near future.

Let us now explore possibilities of eliminating queues or at least reducing waiting time by organizations, which are reluctant to invest in either infrastructure or technology or both for placating their customers. Fitzsimmons (2004) suggests that an excessively long waiting time of customers or idle servers is an obvious indication that the service is not being deployed effectively. Depending on the circumstances, back office personnel may be asked to come forward and open additional service stations parallel to the existing ones in order to reduce the waiting time of customers. For example, in a bank, the back office executives may be asked to open additional teller counters during rush hours. We have already discussed about cross-training employees to enable them to handle multiple activities. The employees should be trained in customer service and they should be motivated to take on additional responsibilities. To fulfil this objective, even the branch manager of the bank should not feel embarrassed to sit on an additional teller counter during busy hours. At Pepsi India, it has been a long practice that every employee (to the highest rank) has to spend a day every month in one of their distribution trucks. This gives the employees a chance to analyse market conditions and product performance.

## Quality Ratings in the Hotel Industry

The hotel industry is one of the rare exceptions amongst all services organizations and has had elaborate criteria for categorizing hotels into the star or diamond ratings on the basis of service quality for a long time now. Exhibits 16.5 and 16.6 discuss the impotance of service in the hotel industry. Let us try to understand the star ratings first.

**Stars**    For hotels, star ratings from one to five are used to assess the standard of quality one can expect.

*

At this level, staff are polite and courteous and provide informal yet competent service. The majority of rooms are en suite and there is a designated eating area with a reasonable choice of food and wines available.

**

Staff are smartly presented and provide competent, often informal, service. All rooms are en suite and have a TV. There is at least one restaurant or dining room with a substantial choice of food and wines available.

***

Staff will be skilled in responding to guests' needs, and there will be a dedicated receptionist on duty. All rooms are en suite and have remote-controlled TV and direct-dial telephone. There is a restaurant open to residents and their guests and a bar or lounge serving drinks.

****

A formal professional service is provided and the staff anticipate and respond to guests' needs. The reception is staffed 24 hours a day, with porters available on request. Bedrooms offer superior quality and comfort than at the three-star level; en suite bathrooms have high-quality toiletries.

Services such as porterage, 24-hour room service, and laundry and dry-cleaning are be available, and the restaurant demonstrates a serious approach to cuisine.

*****

Flawless guest services and professional attentive staff are a must at this level. Accommodation throughout the hotel is spacious and luxurious, with impressive interior design and immaculate furnishings. En suite rooms offer exceptional quality and provide extras such as bath sheets and robes and an evening turn-down service. The restaurant provides dishes created with a high level of technical skill, complemented by superior wines.

**Diamonds**　In the western world, AAA's diamond rating criteria are broad guidelines to designate what is typically found at each rating level. The size, age, and overall appeal of an establishment are considered, in addition to the regional architectural style and design. Diamonds are assigned on the basis of the overall guest impression rather than on individual criteria. Therefore, meeting all of the criteria in certain categories or failing to meet a few criteria will not necessarily affect the diamond rating.

The final factor in determining the diamond rating for a property is professional judgement. This is a very important part of the rating assessment. Tourism Editor expertise is based upon ongoing training and experience in conducting more than 850 evaluations a year.

*One diamond*　These establishments typically appeal to the budget-minded traveller. They provide essential, no-frills accommodations. They meet the basic requirements pertaining to comfort, cleanliness, and hospitality.

*Two diamond*　These establishments appeal to the traveller seeking more than the basic accommodations. There are modest enhancements to the overall physical attributes, design elements, and amenities of the facility typically at a moderate price.

*Three diamond*　These establishments appeal to the traveller with comprehensive needs. Properties are multifaceted with a distinguished style, including marked upgrades in the quality of physical attributes, amenities, and the level of comfort provided.

*Four diamond*　These establishments are upscale in all areas. Accommodations are progressively more refined and stylish. The physical attributes reflect an obvious enhanced level of quality throughout. The fundamental hallmarks at this level include an extensive array of amenities combined with a high degree of hospitality, service, and attention to detail.

*Five diamond*　These establishments reflect the characteristics of the ultimate in luxury and sophistication. Accommodations are first class and the physical attributes are extraordinary in every manner. The fundamental hallmarks at this level are to meticulously serve and exceed all guest expectations while maintaining an impeccable standard of excellence. Many personalized services and amenities enhance an unmatched level of comfort.

---

### Exhibit 16.5　How Marriott Never Forgets a Guest

Marriott International, Inc. is a leading worldwide hospitality company. Its heritage can be traced to a root beer stand opened in Washington DC in 1927 by J. Willard and Alice S. Marriott. Today, Marriott International has more than 2,600 lodging properties located in the United States and 65 other countries and territories. When retiree Ben B. Ussery Jr goes on vacation, he typically spends hours beforehand nailing down golf dates, scouting shops for his wife, and making restaurant reservations. However, last year,

*(Contd)*

*Exhibit 16.5 Contd*

when the Usserys and another Richmond (Virginia) couple chose to spend a week at Marriott's Desert Springs resort in Palm Desert, California, he let the hotel do the legwork. Weeks in advance, Marriott planning coordinator Jennifer Rodas called Ussery to ask what he wanted to do. When all was set, she faxed him an itinerary. She had even ordered flowers for his wife. 'Marriott made it a real smooth experience', says Ussery. 'I'm ready to go back.'

What makes such velvet-glove treatment possible is Marriott International Inc.'s use of customer management software from Siebel Systems Inc. The hotel chain, based in Bethesda, Maryland, is counting on such technology to gain an edge with guests, event planners, and hotel owners. The software lets Marriott pull together information about its customers from different departments, so that its representatives can anticipate and respond more quickly to their needs. It starts with reservations. Says Chairman J.W. Marriott Jr, 'It's a big competitive advantage to be able to greet a customer with: 'Mr. Jones, welcome back to Marriott. We know you like a king-size bed. We know you need a rental car.' Marriott, America's No. 1 hotel chain, is the industry leader in using technology to pamper customers. The company began installing the Siebel software in late 1998 and is spending just under $10 million for the initial pieces. A few other hotel chains are dabbling in customer-information systems, but Marriott is ahead of the pack, says analyst Bryan A. Maher of Credit Lyonnais Securities. 'It's a huge advantage,' he says. The biggest boost from the Siebel software is in the hotel chain's sales operations. Marriott is transforming its sales teams from order-takers for specific hotels to aggressive marketers of all Marriott properties. A salesperson in Dallas—who understands the needs of his local customers as well as the chain's world inventory of hotel rooms and other facilities—can now pitch and book orders for hotels in Hawaii or China.

The process is hassle-free. Early results are promising. In 1998, the sales-force software helped Marriott generate an additional $55 million in cross-chain sales. Anecdotal evidence also suggests there has been a jump in bookings from event planners, who find it easier to give business to Marriott, which has their needs on file, than put it out for bid. Eliminating hassles for guests is the appeal of Marriott's free personal-planning service, too. The software tracks guest preferences, so personal planners can anticipate amenities that repeat guests may want. 'Our spa is very popular', says Doug Mings, Personal Planning Supervisor at Marriott's deluxe Camelback Inn in Scottsdale, Arizona, 'If you don't plan ahead, sometimes you don't get in'. The service also gives Marriott representatives an opening to pitch hot-air balloon rides and other fee-generating activities. Happy customers and fatter sales—with that kind of advantage, no wonder other hotel chains, such as Hilton Hotels Corp., are starting to follow Marriott's technology lead.

## Exhibit 16.6    Kaizen at Taj Hotels

The famous Taj Hotels (₹6.87 billion Indian Hotels Corporation Ltd) belong to the Tata Group. The Taj Hotels chain is ranked amongst the best three hotel chains in Asia, but the aim is to be among the top chains in the world. Over the past three years, the group has institutionalized both the kaizen approach and total productive maintenance. Senior Vice-President (Corporate Quality) Mr. H.N. Shrinivas personally visited the world's leading hotel chains such as the Ritz Carlton (Marriott group) and Four Seasons to pick up best practices. The Taj team not only visited the leading hotel chains, but also other leading facilities such as Motorola and FedEx that have implemented the Malcolm-Baldrige Model. The Taj group benchmarked with Ritz Carlton on customer satisfaction measurement in luxury hotels. It has also adopted its 'three Steps to service' philosophy which is used for defining performance requirements of employees at all levels—warm welcome, anticipatory service, and farewell. According to Mr. Shrinivas, 'We have also installed "customer listening posts" as practiced by Ritz Carlton to update guest history data, which is deployed in all guest contact areas to deliver anticipatory service'. According to Taj Hotels, three functions should happen simultaneously within any organization—maintenance, innovation, and kaizen. Maintenance refers to maintaining the current status, where procedures are set and the standards implemented. Innovation refers to breakthrough activities initiated by top management, buying new machines, new equipment, developing new markets, directing R&D, change of strategy, etc. In the middle there is kaizen, small steps but continuing

*(Contd)*

*Exhibit 16.6 Contd*

improvements 'without large capital investments'. Kaizen should be implemented by the staff at all levels with encouragement and direction from the management. Taj Hotels follow the following ten basic tips for kaizen activities:

1. Discard conventional fixed ideas.
2. Think of how to do it, not why it cannot be done.
3. Do not make excuses. Start by questioning current practices.
4. Do not seek perfection. Do it right away, even if for only 50 per cent of the target.
5. Even if you make a mistake, correct it right away.
6. Do not spend money for kaizen, use your wisdom.
7. Wisdom is brought out when faced with hardship.
8. Ask 'why?' five times and seek root causes.
9. Seek the wisdom of ten people rather than the knowledge of one.
10. Kaizen ideas are infinite.

### Energy Conservation at Taj Bengal, Kolkata

**Before kaizen** Electrical energy was being wasted due to misuse/under use of electrically operated kitchen equipment such as hot ranges, ovens, and salamanders in various kitchens.

**After kaizen** After a proper work study and discussion with the executive chef, all the under-used electrically operated kitchen equipment have been disconnected and removed.

**Before kaizen** Fresh air and exhaust fans were running beyond the operating hours in various kitchens.

**After kaizen** Timers have been provided for fresh air and exhaust fans of various kitchens.

**Before kaizen** Air-conditioners of various offices were running beyond working hours.

**After kaizen** Timers have been provided for the air-conditioners of various offices.

**Before kaizen** Unwanted lights in lobby corridors were on during the night.

**After kaizen** The 300W halogen lights have been replaced with 70W metal halide lamps. Timers have been provided and cabling modified for the alternative hundi lights of lobby corridors.

**Gains from the above kaizens** Annual savings of ₹1.962 million and in terms of savings in electricity, there is a total saving of 4,01,317 kWh annually.

### Maintenance Complaints Handling at Taj Holiday Village, Goa

**Before kaizen** Being such a spreadout property, the staff had to cover long distances on foot for attending to complaints. Staff had to often come back to the maintenance department to collect tools or required spares. These were carried in hand by the staff.

**After kaizen** Bicycles have been introduced to reduce time to attend to complaints. A tool pouch, fastened around the waist, has been designed to hold tools in specially designed slots. Staff attending to complaints now carry wireless sets for easier and faster communication.

**Before kaizen** The repair room was cluttered with broken telephones, since repairs took time due to lack of space and stacking of spares. The maintenance sub-store was also disorganized.

**After kaizen** The store is now using seiri (sort) and seiton (orderliness) so that items can be easily identified and accessed. Telephone repair room has been reorganized, creating more workspace.

**Before kaizen** Communication between the staff executing the complaint and the control room was a problem.

**After kaizen** A job card has been designed for staff attending to complaints. This has also helped in tracking the number of jobs done each day. The time taken for a complaint to be attended to is now being tracked accurately by introducing a maintenance complaint sheet. Complaints received have been recorded and repeated complaints identified to solve the root cause of the problem.

### Gains from the above kaizens

- Workflow has smoothened.
- Reduction of complaints by 70 per cent, eliminating the cause of repeat complaints.
- Items are now easily identified and accessible in the stores, hence time taken to respond to complaints and searching of tools and spares in the stores has reduced.

### Kitchen Utensils Management at Taj President, Mumbai

**Before kaizen** Breakages in the main kitchen were high due to incorrect flow of cutlery and crockery during washing.

**After kaizen** The system of 'one piece at a time' has been implemented.

**Before kaizen** Work flow was not in order at the

*(Contd)*

*Exhibit 16.6 Contd*

Trattoria Washer. Konkan Café and Thai Kitchen also faced problems due to the tedious work area due to the depth of the sink and mixing up of metal and chinaware.
**After kaizen** The layout of dishwashing area has been changed to facilitate single-piece flow.

### Gains from the above kaizens

- Stock level has reduced due to quick turnover of cutlery and crockery.
- The breakages of crockery have come down by 28 per cent. The saving from the stoppage of breakages are ₹0.6 million per annum.
- In the main kitchen, gains are ₹0.17 million per annum.
- In Konkan Café and Thai Kitchen gains are around ₹0.2 million per annum.

### Zero Defect Room at Taj Connemara, Chennai

**Before kaizen** Room requirement for daytime was unknown to housekeeping, hence duty rotas were not planned efficiently.

**After kaizen** Front office hands over details by 7 a.m. to housekeeping regarding the type of room/number of rooms and the time of requirement of rooms according to the guest arrivals. The housekeeping supervisor briefs staff by 7:30 a.m. on the room requirement for the day and amends duty rotas accordingly. Priority is given to attend to vacant and dirty rooms. Front office has been asked to block rooms on the computer system for the entire day. To make the room boys understand the system of '0' defect room, a model zero defect room has been created.

**Before kaizen** The room boys had to strain themselves to replenish supplies because of limitations in trolley layouts.

**After kaizen** The room boy trolley has been modified to accommodate maintenance and minibar supplies adequately and at the same time reduce the weight of the trolley to reduce 'muda (irregularity) and muri (strain and difficulty)' for staff. The supplies in the trolley now include a screwdriver, tester, light bulbs, etc. to enable the room boys do small jobs of maintenance. Hence 'muri' is reduced on maintenance. The room

boys have to check all the fittings everyday—plumbing, electrical, carpentry, etc.—before cleaning and accordingly inform housekeeping, thereby giving the maintenance department some lead-time to rectify any complaints.

### Gains from the above kaizens

- Since the systems are in place the waiting time for guests for rooms has reduced.
- Obtaining the guest flight details has helped reduce the no-show factor.
- Training of staff is easier with model room as reference point.
- Allowances for minibar complaints have reduced by ₹ 0.4 million per annum.

### Goods receiving and handling process at Taj Mahal Hotel, New Delhi

**Before kaizen** High levels of inventory of various provision items.

**After kaizen** Kanban system has been introduced at the main stores. This involves standardizing the reorder level for each provision item as per consumption. A buffer stock of one day is maintained for provision items. Entry of only cleaned and processed vegetables takes place in the main store, where constant checks are performed by the chef and purchase manager.

**Before kaizen** Long procurement time of requisitioned items from the main store for user departments.

**After kaizen** The 'super bazaar' concept has been introduced at the main store. User departments use trolleys to pick up the requisitioned items themselves. Single point check at exit and direct debiting into the system has been introduced.

### Gains from the above kaizens

- Minimum inventory leading to reduction in shelf-stock from 15 days to 4 days.·
- The floor storage area has reduced by 80%.·
- Procurement time for user departments has been reduced from 25 minutes to 10 minutes and there is an increase in trust levels.·
- Reduction in manpower from eight to three members in the main store.

---

> The dominating principle of five S is to create ownership for every object in the organization.

## Five S

Five S is one of the basic tenets of lean manufacturing. It originated in Japan as a work-environment enhancing measure, but the Japanese believe this visually-oriented exercise is useful not just for improving the physical environment,

> The five S practice not only helps to impress the customers but also to establish effective quality processes for good services and products.

but also for improving total quality management (TQM) processes. The five Ss are *seiri* (sorting out), *seiton* (systematic arrangement), *seiso* (spic-n-span), *seiketsu* (standardize), and *shitsuke* (self-discipline).

The dominating principle of five S is to create ownership for every object in the organization, so that nothing is neglected. In the first step (sorting out), individual owners sort their belongings into needs (used regularly/irregularly) and wants (may be used later or scrap).

This is followed by making a systematic layout of the workplace, specifying the storage areas and deciding where to put each item, right from files and documents down to the stapler and pins.

The third phase (spic-n-span) monitors whether the two earlier steps are being regularly and effectively carried out and the workspace is kept clean.

What follows next is to standardize the policies and rules that are to be followed by the entire workplace. These include making timetables and indexes that indicate where you can find what, using charts and visuals. Finally, it is self-discipline that is required to sustain five S.

Many successful organizations have found that by developing a high quality work environment and instilling discipline in the form of procedures and work instructions, employees devoted more energy and time to achieve results. The five S practice not only helps to impress the customers but also to establish effective quality processes for good services and products. Five S is a part of the kaizen family that talks about continuous innovation. The Japanese invented it but it has been adopted by non-Japanese companies ranging from computer giant Hewlett Packard to legendary motorcycles maker Harley Davidson.

In India companies such as Hindustan Unilever practice the principles of five S under the umbrella of their efficiency and quality unimitative, total productive maintenance (TPM). Other Indian companies that have taken up five S include (Bharat Heavy Electricals Limited) and the Aditya Birla group. See Exhibit 16.7 to understand how ICICI Bank implemented five S.

---

### Exhibit 16.7    ICICI Bank

If you are ever in the men's room on the ninth floor of ICICI Towers (the headquarters of the financial services major) in suburban Mumbai, do not be surprised if you find a pillow resting on the two-feet-wide windowsill. It has probably been left behind by a housekeeping employee. Not that the housekeepers at ICICI Bank are sleeping on the job, though they can certainly afford it. That is because the bank has cleaned up its act—literally. It has been just 12 or 14 months since the bank began implementing five S (a management initiative to keep the workplace in order), but compared to other quality control drivers, such as Six Sigma and ISO which have been running for more than four years, five S made a clean sweep almost immediately. In certain cases, such as ICICI's back office for integrated operations at Mahalaxmi (central Mumbai), the company claims to have saved ₹75 million as a result of quality programmes in the current year. However, it was five S that

contributed generously, making up 50 per cent of the savings. At another location, employees confide that earlier, document retrievals would take upto two or three days. Now even the lower rung employees boast of tracing documents in record time—just 30 seconds (naturally, it takes significantly more time to drum up a hard copy from the store). 'Five S is a workplace transformation exercise. When we implemented it across the organization, it appeared functional with many tangible benefits,' says Chanda Kochhar, Executive Director, ICICI Bank. But implementation was nowhere as easy. When ICICI Bank announced the initiative in December 2003, nearly 15,000 employees grudgingly gave up their weekends to come in to office—and clean their workplace! Granted, they did not scrub floors or wash used coffee mugs. But they did everything else, such as emptying out filing cabinets and drawers and retaining only what was absolutely

*(Contd)*

*Exhibit 16.7 Contd*

essential. 'Everybody grumbled in the beginning', recalls an employee, as we admire her impeccable workstation, adding 'but we had no choice because the bosses themselves followed it.' In the process, the bank freed up huge amounts of shelf space. Consider this: in the HR department alone, throwing out old, unwanted résumés cleared up six cupboards. At the central Mumbai back office, too, employees discarded their pack-rat tendencies, freeing about 10 per cent storage space. There was a direct pay-off consequently: ICICI Bank saved more than ₹6,00,000 a year on payments to third-party warehousing companies, since records can now be stored in the office. ICICI Bank may be shedding excess baggage now—and saving money in the process—but it was not so full of good cheer even a year ago. In fact, ICICI's foray into five S highlights issues that could escape the radar when companies grow at top speed as ICICI Bank did. The bank set up retail banking operations in 1994; by 2000, it had half a million retail bank account holders. That number skyrocketed in the next few years; at present, it has 10 million retail bank account holders. The track record in credit cards has been equally awe-inspiring. ICICI Bank claims to be the number one credit card company in the country with 2.5 million cards issued in less than five years. In comparison, Citibank, which was the first to enter the Indian market for credit cards in 1990, has about 2.4 million subscribers. As a consultant puts it, 'The bank was growing furiously in the period 1997–2001, compromising on quality. It's only later that the focus shifted from market share to evaluating the share of the wallet.' ICICI Bank executives accept the charge. Says a middle-level manager, 'By chasing numbers and growing too fast we were losing sight of the customer'. And customer grievances were increasing: from poor service at the branches to interminable waits for re-issue of cards, the laundry list of complaints grew. Calls to the customer care helpline were of no use—it was not unusual to be put on hold for up to half an hour at a stretch. By end-2003, ICICI Bank officials realized they needed to take action fast. A close look at global best practices that could help improve the customer experience turned up 5S, a Japanese concept used mainly on manufacturing shop floors around the world. But they soon realized that the main principles of five S (sorting out, systematic arrangement, spic-n-span, standardize, and self-discipline) could be easily imported into the services sector as well. Another advantage is that 5S could be easily followed by

everybody—from the 'peon to the president', as Sanjiv Kerkar, Senior General Manager, ICICI Bank puts it. Compare that to a statistics-dependent technique such as Six Sigma, where all problems are broken down to mathematic terms—implementing a concept that requires a certain degree of capability. Says Kerkar, 'The best thing about 5S is that it is extremely simple and yet powerful. More importantly, the benefits are visible immediately'. In December 2003, ICICI Bank managers from across the country participated in a one-day leadership programme that included not just 5S but also sessions on workplace improvement and change management. The aim was to help them encourage employees down the line to adapt to 5S. 'It is not enough to just engage zonal heads and branch managers. If 5S has to be successful, it must be owned by the line employees', says Debashis Sarkar, Assistant General Manager, ICICI Bank. The bank followed up the initial sessions with pilot projects across 30 locations, involving 25 people at each location. The 750 employees so covered accounted for just 5 per cent of the total workforce. It took the bank close to six months to implement 5S at all its offices across the country. How is 5S implemented practically? Take the central Mumbai back office that has successfully cleared the two levels of 5S (ICICI Bank splits 5S into just two levels: implementation and sustenance, and continuous improvement) and is considered a model case by ICICI Bank. Here, employees navigate their way through the workplace using colours for reference (orange is for cabinets, blue for workstations, mauve for vaults, and pink for storage). The fetish for life beyond black-and-white does not stop here. Even in the dark-brown key hive (the keys belonging to all departments in the office are hung in a central key hive), each key chain is colour coded according to the department to which it belongs. Anyone taking a key out of the hive has to sign a register, to ensure that it can be easily tracked if necessary. Says Sanjay Tikotekar, Deputy General Manager and Head, Integrated Operations Group (IOG), ICICI Bank, 'This is as user-friendly as it can get'. Life at the back office has become simpler after 5S. The biggest change has been in cataloguing. Earlier, records were filed haphazardly, strewn across cupboards and rooms. Now, they are neatly lined up. A coloured line runs diagonally across all files. This ensures that the file retrieved is returned to its original place, without disturbing the sequence. Instead of letting files flop over, the vacant space when a file is removed is filled

*(Contd)*

*Exhibit 16.7 Contd*

with a dummy, so that the other files remain upright. There is more science to file keeping. Files are now cross-referenced in alphabetical order, by date and by month—making retrieval far simpler. Some regional offices also offer vernacular explanations for 5S, making it easy for even the housekeeping boys to retrieve documents. Finally, 10 minutes at the end of each working day is reserved for a staff meeting, where employees discuss various initiatives and identify problems, and achievers are publicly applauded. Incidentally, for these 10 minutes, lights and computers are switched off to save power. Five S is an entirely people-driven initiative and ICICI Bank has not been slow in recognizing that. In order to sustain employee involvement, the bank awards individual and group efforts with certificates signed by the chairman. There have been two such ceremonies in the past six months alone. The bank has also tied-up 5S project involvement with the performance management systems, so that no employee is caught napping at the workplace. So was it an employee who sneaked in a pillow to the men's room?

## Summary

The Indian economy is currently experiencing immense growth in the service sector. Services have some typical characteristics, such as, intangibility, inability to be inventoried, and greater involvement of customers and employees. Services can be classified into four categories on the basis of the degree of labour intensity, and the degree of interaction and customization. These categories are service factory, service shop, mass service, and professional service. Service capacity is the maximum level of value-added activity which can be consistently achieved over a period of time under normal operating conditions. There are three pure planning strategies for service capacity planning—strategy with constant capacity; strategy with capacity closely following the demand patterns (Chase strategy); and strategy with demand smoothening.

The basic approach in yield management is to utilize existing fixed capacity most optimally to maximize the overall revenue. Services can be designed by using three generic approaches—designing high customer contact and low customer contact operations of a service process separately, assembly-line approach to service design, and service design with technological interfaces. Service blueprinting is a special type of flow-charting for service operations. The term 'blueprint' has been derived from architectural drawings, which use blue lines on charts to show the shape, size, and other dimensions/specifications of various parts of a building.

Quality in a service organization is a measure of the extent to which the service delivered meets the customer's expectations. The nature of most services is such that the customer is present in the delivery process. This means that the perception of quality is influenced not only by the 'service outcome' but also by the 'service process'. The perceived quality lies along a continuum. Unacceptable quality lies at one end of this continuum, while ideal quality lies at the other end. The points in-between represent different gradations of quality. The Gap model (SERVQUAL instrument) is the most popular method of service quality measurement in the service industry.

Queue formation and waiting on part of customers for having a service is deemed by many operations managers as a 'necessary evil' for best utilization of resources. There are four basic formats of queues—classic queue format (multiple servers, multiple queues); zigzag queue format (multiple servers, single queue); numbered queue format (multiple servers, single queue with numbered customers); and split queue format (multiple servers, single split queue). Innovative ways to eliminate queues and the waiting time have been discussed.

The hotel industry has elaborate criteria for categorizing hotels into star and diamond ratings. Hotels have successfully used concepts such as Kaizen to improve the quality of their service operations. Five S is one of the basic tenets of lean manufacturing. The five Ss are—seiri (sorting out), seiton (systematic arrangement), seiso (spic-n-span), seiketsu (standardize), and shitsuke (self-discipline).

## References

Bitner, M.J., J.D. Nyquist, and B.H. Booms 1985, 'The critical incident as a technique for analyzing the service encounter', *Services Marketing in a Changing Environment*, p. 48.

Boulding, W., A. Kalra, R. Staelin, and V.A. Zeithaml 1993, 'A dynamic process model of service quality: from expectations to behavioural intentions', *Journal of Marketing Research*, vol. 30, pp. 7–27.

Chase, R.B., 1978, 'Where does the customer fit in a service operation?' *Harvard Business Review*, Nov–Dec., pp. 137–142.

Cronin, J.J. and S.A. Taylor 1992, 'Measuring service quality: a reexamination and extension', *Journal of Marketing*, vol. 56, pp. 55–68.

Cross, K.P. 1981, *Adults as Learners*, Jossey-Bass, San Francisco.

Donlon, J. 1999,'Air herb's secret weapon', *Chief Executive*, vol. 146, pp. 32–40.

Fitzsimmons, J.A. and M.J. Fitzsimmons 2004, *Service Management: Operations, Strategy and Information Technology*, 4th edn, McGraw-Hill/Irwin, New York, p. 24.

Freeman, K.D., and J. Dart 1993, 'Measuring the perceived quality of professional business services', *Journal of Professional Services Marketing*, vol. 9, no. 1, pp. 27–47.

Ghobadian, A., S. Simon, and J. Matthew 1994, 'Service Quality: Concepts and Models', *International Journal of Quality & Reliability Management*, vol. 11, no. 9, pp. 43–66.

Gittell, J. 2003, *The Southwest Airlines Way*, McGraw-Hill, New York, NY.

Goldberg, L. 2000, 'Southwest's approach still flies', *The Houston Chronicle*, p. 1.

Grönroos, C. 1990, *Service Management and Marketing*, Lexington Books, Lexington, Massachusetts.

Hamid, Z. 2012,'The medical capital's place in history', *The Hindu*,20 August, Chennai,http://www.thehindu.com/news/cities/chennai/article3796305.ece, accessed on 15 March 2013.

Jet Airways, 2005, Draft Red Herring Prospectus, available at http://myiris.com/shares/ipo/draft/JETAIRPR/JETAIRPR.pdf (downloaded on 21 January 2007).

Jham, V. and P. Chotani 2005, 'Building Travelocity through CRM in Travel Industry', *Cases in Management*, edited by B.S. Sahay, R. Stough, and G.D. Sardana, Allied Publishers, New Delhi.

Johnston, R. and G. Clark 2001, *Service Operations Management*, Pearson Education, United Kingdom.

Kimes, S.E. 1989, 'Yield management: A tool for capacity constrained service firms', *Journal of Operations Management*, vol. 8, no. 4, October, pp. 348–363.

Knowles, M. 1984, *Andragogy in Action*. Jossey-Bass, San Francisco.

National Health Expenditure Projections 2010–2020, https://www.cms.gov/Research-Statistics-Data-and-Systems/Statistics-Trends-and-Reports/NationalHealthExpendData/downloads/proj2010.pdf, accessed on 2 March 2013.

Parasuraman, A., V.A. Zeithaml, and L.L. Berry 1985, 'A conceptual model of service quality and its implication for future research', *Journal of Marketing*, vol. 49, pp. 41–50.

Parasuraman, A., V.A. Zeithaml, and L.L. Berry 1988, 'SERVQUAL: a multiple-item scale for measuring consumer perceptions of service quality', *Journal of Retailing*, vol. 64, no. 1, pp. 12–40.

Robinson, S., M. Pidd 1998, 'Provider and customer expectations of successful simulation projects', *Journal of the Operational Research Society*, vol. 49, no. 3, pp. 200–209.

Rogers, C.R. and H.J. Freiberg 1994, *Freedom to Learn*, 3rd edn, Columbus, OH: Merrill/Macmillan.

Schmenner, R.W. 1986, 'How can service business survive and prosper?', *Sloan Management Review*, vol. 27, no. 3, Spring, p. 25.

Shostack, G.L., 1984, 'Designing services that deliver', *Harvard Business Review*, vol. 62, no. 1, pp. 133–139.

Silvestro, R., R. Johnston, L. Fitzgerald, and C. Voss 1990, 'Quality measurement in service industries', *International Journal of Service Industry Management*, vol. 1, no. 2, pp. 54–66.

Slack N., S. Chambers, C. Harland, A. Harrison, and R. Johnston 1998, *Operations Management*, 2nd edn, Pitman, London.

Smith, G. 2004,'An evaluation of the corporate culture of Southwest Airlines', *Measuring Business Excellence*, vol. 8,no. 4, pp. 26–33.

Stauss, B. and B. Weinlich 1997, 'Process-oriented measurement of service quality: Applying the sequential incident technique', *European Journal of Marketing*, vol. 31, no. 1, pp. 33–55.

Theodore, Levin 1972, 'Production-line approach to service', *Harvard Business Review*, Sept.–Oct., pp. 41–52 .

Voss, C. 1985, 'Field service management', in C. Voss, C. Armistead, B. Johnston, and B. Morris, *Operations Management in Service Industries and the Public Sector: Text and Cases*, John Wiley and Sons.

www.makemytrip.com, accessed on 26 February 2013.

# Keywords

**Five S** is one of the basic tenets of lean manufacturing. The five Ss are—seiri (sorting out), seiton (systematic arrangement), seiso (spic-n-span), seiketsu (standardize), and shitsuke (self-discipline).

**Hard measures** of service quality refer to quantifiable or objective measures; for example, computer downtime or the proportion of telephone calls answered.

**Pull production system** is initiated only when the customer places the order for the product and the raw material is pulled into the various constituents of the production process according to the quantity of the order placed by the customer.

**Push production system** results in pushing the raw material in the production system and creation of inventories (work-in-process or finished goods).

**Service blueprinting** is a special type of flowcharting for service operations. The term 'blueprint' has been derived from architectural drawings, which use blue lines on charts to show the shape, size, and other dimensions/specifications of various parts of a building.

**Service capacity** is the maximum level of value-added activity, which can be consistently achieved over a period of time under normal operating conditions.

**Soft measures** of service quality are those which are qualitative, judgemental, subjective, and based on perceptual data; for example, customer's satisfaction with speed of service or manager's assessment of staff attitude towards customers.

**Yield management** tries to utilize existing fixed capacity most optimally to maximize the overal revenue.

---

## CASE STUDY I

## Naresh Goyal and Jet Airways

Naresh Goyal was born in 1949 in Patiala, Punjab. His father, a jewellery dealer, died when he was 10 years old. Naresh used to walk miles to go to his school as he could not afford a bicycle. His mother struggled to pay his fees. However, with the help from her family, Naresh was able to get his basic education. Naresh earned a Bachelor of Commerce degree in 1967.

Many of his friends went to London for higher education and he had a desire to do the same. Since he did not have the money to pursue education abroad, he decided to work with his mother's uncle. His mother's uncle used to run some cinema theatres in India and had an agency with Lebanese International Airline. Naresh heeded his mother's advice and joined as a cashier in her uncle's Delhi-based agency, Continental Travels. For three years he slept in the office and earned about ₹2,000 a month. Later, Naresh joined as a Sales Agent for Lebanese International Airlines. Subsequently, he was appointed as the Public Relations Manager of Iraqi Airways in 1969. From 1971 to 1974 he was the Regional Manager for Royal Jordanian Airlines. During this period, he also worked with the Indian offices of Middle Eastern Airline, where he gained experience in various areas, such as, ticketing, reservations, and sales.

Naresh began to build contacts and, in 1974, with ₹40,000 from his mother, he floated his own Jetair Private Ltd (then known as Jetair Transportation Private Ltd) to provide sales and marketing representation to airlines, such as, Air France, Austrian Airlines, and Cathay Pacific in India. Shortly thereafter in 1975, he was appointed as the Regional Manager of Phillipine Airline where he handled the airline's commercial operations in India.

Naresh's wife, Anita, used to work for the Oberoi hotels in India. In 1979, she joined the marketing department of Jetair. This is when Naresh met her for the first time. Over the years, she grew from a Market Analyst to a General Manager to a Vice President in Jet Airways. She has been looking after pricing, scheduling, network, revenue management, and sales and marketing.

The Indian government nationalized the airline industry in 1953, hence, Indian Airlines (now Indian) and Air India were the only two airlines in the market. The market opened after the liberalization in 1991. The government allowed, what it described as, air taxis to operate—private carriers could fly but they could not print time tables. Naresh spotted an opportunity. In 1993, with the backing of Gulf Air and Kuwait Airways, he leased four Boeing 737 aircrafts and started Jet Airways. Jet Airways started commercial operations on 5 May 1993. Naresh hired talent from airlines he admired. He overcame the constraints of not being able to publish a schedule with inventive zeal. Back in 1993, when other start-ups were inducting Boeing 737-200 aircrafts, Naresh bought new generation Boeing 737-400s. He understood the value of quality and made sure that he hired the best professional talent in the international market. Jet Airways was granted scheduled airline status on 14 January 1995. It became a deemed public company on 1 July 1996. On 19 January 2001, it was reconverted into a private company. Jet Airways became a public company on 28 December 2004.

The government of India came with a civil aviation policy on 29 December 2004. According to the policy, private airlines could fly overseas anywhere in the world except Gulf for three years. Jet Airways started its operations to Singapore on 18 April 2005 and to London on 23 May 2005 (between Mumbai–London Heathrow), shortly followed by its Delhi–London–Delhi service. It also started flights to Kuala Lumpur on 18 May 2005.

In its first year of operation, Jet carried 7,30,000 passengers. In 2005, the company, which now had a fleet of 55 aircraft, carried 10 million people and generated revenues of US $1.4 billion. Today, Jet Airways has evolved into India's largest private domestic airline. Naresh Goyal has an elegant house in a posh locality across Regent's Park in London. The Sunday Times (London) ranked him in 2006 as the sixth richest Asian living in Britain, estimating his wealth at £780 million. He has lived in London since 1991.

Being an NRI based in London only adds to his enigma. He is also said to be a nervous flier who prays before take-off. In his spare time, Naresh is known to be glued to Bollywood films. No wonder that film personalities, such as, Shatrughan Sinha and Javed Akhtar, have served as independent Directors on the Board of Jet Airways. Naresh considers Reliance Industries founder Dhirubhai Ambani as his role model. In the airline industry, he is a great admirer of Lord Marshall, the former Chairman of British Airways, and J.Y. Pillay, the former Chairman of Singapore Airlines.

Since its inception, Jet Airways had a clear strategy of focusing on the business traveller in India. It offers several services directed towards the convenience of the business traveller, including telephone check-in facilities, priority baggage service, high frequency services on major routes, same-day return flights on major routes at convenient timings, point to point connections, providing flight information on cellular phones of customers, its customer loyalty programme, e-ticketing, business class section on almost all flights, and airport lounges for business class passengers at most airports. These facilities and the focus on providing high-quality reliable service have contributed to it becoming the preferred airline for business travellers in India.

Jet currently provides regular scheduled services to 42 destinations in India and operates 1,924 weekly flights. It uses five hubs—Mumbai, Delhi, Chennai, Kolkata, and Bangalore. It maintains engineering and maintenance facilities at each of these hubs. The major hub of its operations is Mumbai followed by Delhi, Chennai, Kolkata, and Bangalore. The use of five hubs helps it to originate flights from these cities.

One of the key elements of the company's business strategy is to maintain high daily aircraft utilization, which represents the average number of block hours operated per day per aircraft for the total aircraft fleet. High daily aircraft utilization allows it to enhance the efficiency of its operations and generate more revenue from its aircraft and is achieved in part by reducing turnaround time at airports so that it can fly more hours on an average in a day. Aircraft utilization is reduced by delays resulting from the following factors, most of which are beyond the control of any airline:

- security requirements;
- air traffic and airport congestion;
- adverse weather conditions, especially in North India during winter months;
- defects or mechanical problems with the aircraft of the airline;
- unavailability of cockpit and in-flight crew;
- strikes or work stoppages; and
- acts of third parties upon which the airlines rely for requirements, such as, fueling and maintenance.

A major cause of concern for Jet is the expansion of its business to include new destinations and more frequent flights on existing routes. This could increase the risk of delays as expansion increases its exposure to congested airports, longer flight durations, and air traffic congestion. Delays could reduce its daily aircraft utilization and, in turn, limit its ability to achieve and maintain profitability as well as damage its reputation. Further, high aircraft utilization increases the risk that once an aircraft falls behind schedule during the day, it could remain behind schedule during the remainder of that day, which could result in disruption in operating performance leading to passenger dissatisfaction. Passengers may get dissatisfied due to delayed or cancelled flights, or missed connecting flights.

## Utilizing aircraft efficiently

**Table 16.3** Various parameters and data relating to the utilization of aircraft efficiency at Jet Airways

| | As of and for the year ended 31 March | | | As of and for the six months ended 30 September | |
|---|---|---|---|---|---|
| | 2002 | 2003 | 2004 | 2003 | 2004 |
| Passengers carried (millions) | 5.82 | 6.41 | 6.91 | 3.27 | 3.78 |
| $ASKM_S$[1] (millions) | 7,780 | 8,496 | 9,162 | 4,542 | 4,796 |
| $RPKM_S$[2] (millions) | 4,777 | 5,291 | 5,852 | 2,771 | 3,245 |
| Passenger Load Factor[3] (%) | 61.4% | 62.3% | 63.9% | 61.0% | 67.7% |
| Number of aircraft at period end | 38.0 | 41.0 | 41.0 | 39.0 | 41.0 |
| Average number of aircraft during period | 34.9 | 38.9 | 40.8 | 40.6 | 41.0 |
| Number of domestic stations served (+ international stations served) | 44 | 40 | 41(+1) | 40 | 42 (+2) |
| Aircraft utilization[4] (hours/day per aircraft) | 9.66 | 9.41 | 9.46 | 9.48 | 9.84 |
| Average stage length (kilometres)[5] | 792 | 805 | 816 | 821 | 818 |

(1) Available seat kilometres represents the average number of block hours operated per day per aircraft for the total aircraft fleet.
(2) Revenue passenger kilometres represents the number of kilometres flown by revenue passengers.
(3) Revenue passenger kilometres expressed as a percentage of available seat kilometres.
(4) The average number of block hours operated per day per aircraft for the total aircraft fleet.
(5) The average number of kilometres flown per flight.

*Source*: Jet Airways (2005).

In fiscal 2004 and the six months ended 30 September 2004, Jet Airways aircrafts operated an average of 9.46 and 9.84 hours per day, respectively (see Table 16.3). By achieving high utilization, it is able to optimize crew movement, and spread its fixed costs over a greater number of flights and available seat kilometres. It achieves high aircraft utilization because:

- newer aircraft can be scheduled to fly more hours per day as they are more reliable and require less maintenance than older aircraft; and
- its staff is able to achieve quick, efficient, airport turnarounds, which enable it to increase the number of daily flights per aircraft.

### Pricing and Revenue Management

Jet Airways offers several fare options as given below:

- Economy and club premier fares;
- Discounted fares for senior citizens and defence personnel;
- Advance passenger excursion, or APEX fares. Using its yield management system, Jet Airways reserves a fraction of seats to be offered on discounts for advance booking (30 days, 21 days, and 15 days before the departure date of the flight);
- 'One fare' scheme that allows passengers to buy four or six coupons for a fixed fare and use them on any sector;
- 'Night saver' fares are offered for night flights, operated by Jet on certain routes. Up to 80 per cent discount is offered in five slabs for these flights due to their odd timings;
- US dollar fares and 'visit India' fares for overseas travellers.
- 'Check fares' are offered to the customers on certain flights with no requirement for advance booking. These are different from APEX fares as there is no need for advance booking with these check fares, which are 30–40 per cent lower than the normal economy class fares. These fares are offered close to the departure date of the flight to ensure minimum number of unsold (empty) seats in a flight. Most of these flights happen to be afternoon flights with less passenger traffic. This is another benefit of the yield management system implemented by Jet due to which the revenues started showing an upward trend.

Its APEX fares are subject to certain advance purchase and cancellation conditions. Yield management and pricing form the backbone of its revenue generation strategy and are strongly linked to its route and schedule planning, and sales and distribution activities. Yield management involves the use of historical data and statistical forecasting models in order to gain knowledge about its markets and maximize the airline's operating revenues.

Its yield management practices enable it to respond to and anticipate market changes. The number of seats it offers at each fare level in each market results from a continual process of analysis and forecasting. Past booking history, seasonality, the effects of competition, and current booking trends are used to forecast demand.

Current fares and knowledge of upcoming events at destinations that will affect traffic volumes are included in its forecasting model to arrive at optimal seat allocations for its fares on specific routes. Jet uses a combination of approaches, taking into account yields and flight load factors, depending on the characteristics of the markets served, to arrive at a strategy for achieving the best possible revenue per available seat kilometre, balancing the average fare charged against the corresponding effect on their load factors. For this purpose, Jet uses SABRE, a state-of-the-art yield management system.

Jet Airways derives its revenues primarily from transportation of passengers on its aircrafts. In addition, it also earns revenues from carriage of cargo, which consists of courier, postal mail, and commercial cargo. Passenger revenues are dependent on 'passenger load factors' and fare levels. These are measured by the following (Table 16.4):

- Capacity measured in terms of available seat kilometres or ASKMs. It is defined as the aircraft seating capacity multiplied by the number of kilometres the seats are flown;
- Utilization measured in terms of revenue passenger kilometres (RPKMs). It is defined as the number of kilometres flown by revenue passengers;
- Passenger load factor, or the percentage of its capacity that is actually used by revenue customers. It is defined as revenue passenger kilometres expressed as a percentage of available seat kilometres.
- Net passenger revenues, representing passenger revenues less commissions paid to GSAs and travel agents;
- Yield, derived by dividing net passenger revenues by revenue passenger kilometres; and
- Break even load factor. It is defined as the passenger load factor that will result in net passenger revenues being equal to total expenses less cargo and non-operating revenues.

**Table 16.4** Parameters and data relating to the passenger revenues of Jet Airways

| | Year ended 31 March | | | Six months ended 30 September | |
| --- | --- | --- | --- | --- | --- |
| | *2002* | *2003* | *2004* | *2003* | *2004* |
| Capacity ASKMs (millions) | 7,780 | 8,496 | 9,162 | 4,542 | 4,796 |
| Utilization RPKMs (millions) | 4,777 | 5,291 | 5,852 | 2,771 | 3,245 |
| Passenger load factor (%) | 61.4% | 62.3% | 63.9% | 61.0% | 67.7% |
| No. of passengers (millions) | 5.82 | 6.41 | 6.91 | 3.27 | 3.78 |
| Gross average revenue per passenger (₹) | 4,057 | 4,173 | 4,655 | 4,650 | 4,785 |
| Growth in average revenue per passenger (%) | – | 2.8% | 11.5% | – | 2.9% |
| Yield (₹) | 4.36 | 4.52 | 5.01 | 50.2 | 5.05 |
| Growth in yield (%) | – | 3.7% | 10.8% | – | 0.6% |

*Source*: Jet Airways (2005).

### Service Quality

The branding tagline of Jet Airways is 'The joy of flying' and it reflects in the quality of services it provides to its passengers. Jet Airways is one of the few airlines in the world to receive the ISO 9001 certification for its in-flight services.

Jet Airways provided on demand audio and video entertainment for the first time ever in the domestic sector. The passengers can select, play, pause, forward, or rewind their favourite programme. It provides over 100 hours of award-winning shows from Hollywood and Bollywood; 8 audio channels and over 70 audio CDs; the largest video screen in the domestic sector with touch screen technology; and an innovative moving airline route map. Jet Airways is renowned for its sumptuous and delicious meals served on every flight even during the flights not covering the meal timings.

Jet Airways has developed systems to track various aspects of its services. On-time performance and the reasons for delays are analysed every day. It receives and analyses over 57,000 service tracker question-naires (see Exhibit 16.8) every month, where passengers are asked to evaluate all its services on a four-point scale. It undertakes quality audits of in-flight and ground services by a dedicated services and product quality team. It endeavours to promptly respond to any customer complaint. The airline believes in meeting and exceeding its customer service expectations. It is evident from the feedback received by the airline during the six months ended 30 September 2004:

- It was rated either 'good' or 'excellent' for overall services by approximately 95 per cent of its passengers who completed its questionnaires.
- Ratings for in-flight services and efficiency were 97 per cent and 95 per cent, respectively.

---

### Exhibit 16.8 Jet Airways Service Tracker

**We look up to you, to help us serve you better**
**JET AIRWAYS**
**THE JOY OF FLYING**

Dear Passenger,

Thank you for choosing to fly with us. On behalf of the entire Jet Airways family, I am delighted to welcome you on board our flight.

For us taking care of you is not just good business but indeed an enduring commitment. We always seek the views of customers such as yourself to help us serve you even better.

I will therefore be very grateful to you if you spare some of your precious time to fill-in this Service Tracker. As the Tracker is a service quality survey, it is not designed to enable you to provide specific feedback. You may, however, for any specific feedback, request our Cabin Crew for a Comment Form.

Once again, we are delighted to have you on board and wish you a very pleasant flight.

Warm Regards,
Wolfgang Prock Schauer
Chief Executive Officer

Flight No. 9W_____ From_____ To_____
Date_____ Seat No_____
Class of Travel o Club Premiere o Economy
1. **Frequent Flyer Programme**
   (a) **Are you a Jet Privilege Member**
       o Yes (Your JP Membership No...................................) o No
   (b) **Your current JP membership status**
       o Platinum   o Gold   o Silver   o Blue Plus   o Blue
2. **Reservation**
   (a) **Where did you make your reservation**
       o Jet Airways Reservation/Ticket Office  o E-ticketing  o Travel Agent
   (b) **In which city did you make your reservation**_____
       o Excellent o Good   o Average   o Poor

*(Contd)*

*Exhibit 16.8 Contd*

**(c)** **In case you used the Jet Airways website (www.jetairways.com), how do you rate it for**

| | | | | |
|---|---|---|---|---|
| (i) Ease of navigation | o | o | o | o |
| (ii) Ease of online booking | o | o | o | o |
| (iii) Information provided | o | o | o | o |

**3. Accessibility**

**(a)** **Accessibility of our telephone nos**

| | | | | |
|---|---|---|---|---|
| (i) Reservations | o | o | o | o |
| (ii) Airport | o | o | o | o |
| (iii) Tele check-in | o | o | o | o |

**(b)** **Handling of tele check-in/enquiry**

| | | | | |
|---|---|---|---|---|
| (i) Staff efficiency | o | o | o | o |
| (ii) Staff courtesy | o | o | o | o |

**(c)** **Overall rating for accessibility**      **o**    **o**    **o**    **o**

**4. Airport Services**

**(a)** **Baggage security screening**

| | | | | |
|---|---|---|---|---|
| (i) Time taken | o | o | o | o |
| (ii) Assistance provided | o | o | o | o |

**(b)** **Check-in-procedures**

(i) Where did you check-in for this flight

     o Airport check-in    o City check-in    o Tele check-in

(ii) How long did you have to wait in the queue before check-in

     o <5 mins    o 5–10 mins    o 11–15 mins    o >15 mins

(iii) Time taken to check-in at the counter

     o <2 mins    o 2–5 mins    o 6–10 mins    o >10 mins

| | | | | |
|---|---|---|---|---|
| (iv) Staff greeting, helpfulness, and warmth | o | o | o | o |
| (v) Staff grooming | o | o | o | o |
| (vi) Staff efficiency | o | o | o | o |
| (vii) How do you rate the check-in process | o | o | o | o |

**(c)** **Boarding procedures**

| | | | | |
|---|---|---|---|---|
| (i) Clarity of boarding announcements | o | o | o | o |
| (ii) Boarding process | | | | |
| At boarding hall | o | o | o | o |
| At the aircraft | o | o | o | o |
| (iii) Friendliness and warmth of staff | o | o | o | o |
| (iv) If your flight was delayed, how well was it handled by our airport staff? | o | o | o | o |

**(d)** **Overall Rating for Airport Services**    **o**    **o**    **o**    **o**

**5. In-flight Services**

(a) Service by Cabin Crew

| | | | | |
|---|---|---|---|---|
| (i) Friendly welcome at the time of boarding | o | o | o | o |
| (ii) Assistance on board | o | o | o | o |
| (iii) Courteous and professional service | o | o | o | o |
| (iv) Responsiveness to your needs | o | o | o | o |
| (iv) Grooming | o | o | o | o |
| (v) Interaction | o | o | o | o |
| (vi) Overall rating for cabin crew | o | o | o | o |

*(Contd)*

*Exhibit 16.8 Contd*

    **(b) In-flight reading material**
       (i)  JetWings       o      o      o      o
       (ii)  Selection of newpaper(s)   o      o      o      o

    **(c) JetKids giveaway**
       (i)  Quality       o      o      o      o
       (ii)  Content       o      o      o      o

    **(d) Announcements**
           **Cockpit Crew**
       (i)  Clarity       o      o      o      o
       (ii)  Diction and fluency   o      o      o      o
           **Cabin Crew**
       (i)  Clarity       o      o      o      o
       (ii)  Diction and fluency   o      o      o      o

    **(e) Others**
       (i)  Cleanliness of the cabin   o      o      o      o
       (ii)  Cleanliness of the washroom   o      o      o      o
       (iii)  Temperature in the cabin   o      o      o      o
             Before take-off
             o Just right   o Too cold   o Too hot
             After take-off
             o Just right   o Too cold   o Too hot

**6. Food**

    (a)  Type of meal enjoyed in this flight
        o Vegetarian   o Non-vegetarian   o Others
    (b)  Meal appropriateness (for time of flight)  o      o      o      o
    (c)  Meal presentation (visual appeal)  o      o      o      o
    (d)  Meal quality (taste)  o      o      o      o
    (e)  Meal quantity  o Just right o Too little      o
                                            Too much
    (f)  Overall rating for food  o      o      o      o

**7. Please rate your total experience with Jet Airways on this trip**
                                    o      o      o      o

**8. Based on your experience on today's flight**
    (i)  Would you travel with Jet Airways for your next trip?
        o Definitely   o Probably   o Definitely not
    (ii)  Would you recommend Jet Airways to your friends?
        o Definitely   o Probably   o Definitely not

**9. Your experience on arrival, of your previous flight on Jet Airways**
    Date_____
    Flight No. 9W_____From_____To_____
    (a)  Waiting time for Tarmac Coach (if applicable)
        o None   o 2–5 mins   o 6–10 mins   o >10 mins
    (b)  Baggage arrival
        o 2–5 mins   o 6–10 mins   o 11–15 mins   o >15 mins
    (c)  Presence of staff at conveyer belt
        o Yes   o No
    (d)  Handling of baggage-related issues (if any)
        - Staff efficiency  o      o      o      o

*(Contd)*

*Exhibit 16.8 Contd*

| | | | | |
|---|---|---|---|---|
| - Courtesy and helpfulness | o | o | o | o |
| - Responsiveness to your query | o | o | o | o |
| (e) Overall rating for baggage handling | o | o | o | o |

**Staff Recognition**

Kindly help us recognize those members of our staff who have impressed you with their outstanding service.

(i) Name _____

Department_____

(ii) Name _____

Department_____

(iii) Name _____

Department_____

(iv) Name _____

Department_____

**We thank you for the time that you have invested in answering our Service Tracker. Your valuable opinion and constant support is our inspiration.**

Jet Airways has received numerous awards that recognize the quality of its service:

- Citibank Diners Club Blue Moon Award for Service Excellence in 1995;
- H&FS Best Domestic Airline of the year Award for Excellence in Hospitality for the years 1996, 1998, 1999, and 2001;
- Air Transport World Market Development Award for the year 2000;
- Financial Express Business Traveller Award (Domestic Airline Category) for Business Class, Economy Class, and Best Service (Airport and In-flight) in 2003 and 2004;
- Best Domestic Airline of Asia by the Asian readers of Travel Trade Gazette for the years 2003 and 2004; and
- The Business-world award for the most respected company in the travel and hospitality sector in 2003.

Jet Airways has also been ranked by Business-world magazine, in 2004, as one of the ten most respected companies in India. As part of its continued emphasis on the quality of its service, in August 2004, the company launched a new programme known as Seamless Customer Care, which involves the participation of employees at the 42 domestic airports it connects. The objective of this programme is to focus on customer care and enhance the overall passenger experience by seeking input from its employees at the airports it connects. A committee of the heads of each operational department chaired by its Chief Operating Officer oversees this programme.

The ride has not been entirely smooth for Jet Airways. Its market share peaked at 46 per cent but has fallen to 35 per cent since the launch of aggressive new low-cost carriers such as Air Deccan, SpiceJet, Indigo, and GoAir. Jet is still growing, but has failed to keep pace with the domestic market, which is growing by up to 25 per cent a year. However, the acquisition of Air Sahara by Jet Airways on 13 April 2007 for 14.5 billion—40 per cent less than the 22 billion original deal in January 2006—after a long-drawn arbitration is indeed a positive development for Jet Airways. The takeover has propelled Jet Airways as the largest private airline in the country having a fleet size in excess of 80 aircraft and around 42 per cent of the market share.

## Discussion Questions

1. The market share of Jet Airways is falling due to intense competition. Should Jet continue its focus on business customers under the current competitive scenario?

2. The service tracker instrument devised by Jet Airways for tracking its service quality is a better instrument than the SERVQUAL instrument. Do you agree with this statement? If yes, why?

3. The current yield management systems used by Jet Airways can be improvised further by prompt communication with potential customers and ensuring full occupancy in all flights. What is your opinion?

████████████████ CASE STUDY II ████████████████

# Narayana Hrudayalaya

A 10 days old Pakistani child, Ahmad was taken by his mother and uncle to Narayana Hrudayalaya (NH), Bangalore, on 28 July 2004. The child had a complex heart defect, known in medical terms as 'transposition of the great arteries'. In Ahmad's case, the right ventricle of the heart was connected to the aorta and the left ventricle was connected to the pulmonary artery, while in normal conditions, it is the reverse — the right ventricle is connected to the pulmonary artery, the left ventricle to the aorta. This is a severe heart condition and required a complex 'arterial switch operation' before Ahmad was two weeks old. His parents had contacted Narayana Hrudyalaya when he was four days old. During the flight to Bangalore, Ahmad developed complications; fortunately a doctor on board examined him and advised immediate intensive medical care. The pilot informed the Hyderabad airport and diverted the flight to Hyderabad. The plane landed there at 10 p.m., where the airport staff and the medical officers rushed him to the nearby Krishna Institute of Medical Sciences (KIMS). Within an hour, the hospital brought the condition of the child to stability. Next day, the airport officials visited the hospital and later that night, the child was brought to Bangalore through another Indian Airlines flight. At Narayana Hrudayalaya, Dr Rajesh Sharma, the paediatric cardiac surgeon successfully operated on the child.

This incident has set a precedent in terms of service operations management in the country, exemplifying a perfect coordination between Indian Airlines, KIMS, and Narayana Hrudayalaya in saving the life of the little child. This is no new feat for Narayana Hrudayalaya, which has the mission of making sophisticated healthcare available to the masses, especially in a developing country such as India. One year earlier, a little Pakistani girl, Noor Fatima came to India to repair her imperfectly formed heart at this hospital. She was born with holes in the heart that in turn caused obstructions in the flow of blood to her lungs. Her parents Nadeem and Tayyaba were ecstatic when the hospital cured their daughter.

Nearly 30 per cent of the patients at Narayana Hrudayalaya are foreigners hailing from 22 countries including Bangladesh, Pakistan, Mauritius, the Middle East, and African countries. The man behind the creation and success of Narayana Hrudayalaya is Dr Devi Prasad Shetty, who has become synonymous with highest quality humanitarian healthcare in India. He operates free for kids below 12 years of age and has performed about 5,000 operations on children out of his 15,000 odd operations in a career spanning almost two decades. He has the distinction of treating Mother Teresa during her illness.

His list of achievements seem endless. For the first time in the world, he used a microchip camera in an open heart surgery to close a hole in the heart. He is credited with performing the first dynamic cardiomyoplasty operation in Asia. He is the first surgeon in India to venture into neonatal open heart surgery. He used an artificial heart for the first time in India. He has the distinction of performing the first surgery in India using blood vessels of the stomach to bypass the blocked arteries of the heart. His biggest achievement for the benefit of the poor has been bringing down the cost of heart related operations drastically. He introduced the concept of 'assembly-line heart surgery', which has helped him in achieving zero mortality and is targeted at reducing the cost of operations.

Dr Shetty's persona is clearly reflected in his statement, 'If given a choice, I would like to treat only poor patients. Unfortunately, the economic reality does not allow me to do that.' It is remarkable to note that the Seva Clinic (a cooperative insurance scheme started in Gujarat in 1992) has funded the operations of about 100 poor patients, who could otherwise have not been able to afford these on their own.

Phase 1 of NH is spread over 25 acres. Presently, it has 1,000 beds with 10 operating rooms with the capacity to perform 25 heart surgeries in a single day. With the onset of Phase 2, NH will sprawl over an impressive 100 acres. The structure will accommodate 780 beds and 30 operating rooms to perform 75 heart surgeries every day. Besides the hospital, it will also accommodate a teaching institute for cardiologists, cardiac surgeons, cardiac anesthetists, nurses, health technicians, and healthcare specialists. Once completed, the entire project will have 5,000 beds and will be known as the Health City with specialty hospitals for every disease. Currently, the hospital performs heart operations on at least 12 children out of 25 odd operations performed every day.

Indian Space Research Organization (ISRO) has

helped the hospital with the funding to realize its dream of 'telemedicine'. It has provided NH with 13 satellite video links with distant hospitals within the country and terrestrial video links including integrated services digital network (ISDN) to connect places outside the country such as Malaysia and Mauritius. The hospital is in the process of establishing such links with Bangladesh, Mauritius, and Tanzania. Bangalore's central prison is one of the unique jails in the country, which has a video link-up with the law courts. This enables the court to listen to the inmates' cases and appeals without the need for their physical presence within the court premises.

The hospital has pioneered in providing its telemedicine facility to the prisoners in this prison through this video link. In January 2006, NH extended its telemedicine facilities to Air India passengers, staff, and crew at the Mumbai Airport and the Air India Clinic at Mumbai. This is done by installing ECG machines at these facilities; the data is then interpreted at the NH facilities at Bangalore. The typical characteristic of a heart attack is that without immediate and adequate treatment, there are 50 per cent chances of the patient succumbing to death. With adequate immediate treatment the mortality rate can be reduced to less than 5 per cent.

Generally, the rural areas have a general practitioner (GP), who neither has the specialist knowledge nor the infrastructure to perform proper diagnosis. In most instances, the GP would diagnose the initial symptoms of a heart problem as indigestion, only to later discover that the patient passed away within the next 24 hours due to a heart attack. The telemedicine facility becomes a boon under such circumstances, whereby the GP can take advice from a heart specialist at NH through telemedicine facility before reaching any conclusions about patient's illness. Out of the 20,000 odd patients treated by NH so far through telemedicine, about a 1,000 had serious heart problems.

It is a common practice for the cardiac experts at NH to see patients through the video links. Simultaneously, they refer to the angiograms, X-rays, and other information of these patients. Dr Shetty is of the view that the doctor needs to touch the patient only when a surgery is to be performed. Therefore, specialist doctors, who are mostly confined to few prominent cities, can make their services available to the public at distant locations using this technology without their physical presence. At the same time, it is necessary for the doctor to 'see' her patients and allow them to see the doctor on the video screen to strike a sense of relationship and compassion with the patient.

The mantra of high quality and cost reduction at NH is the 'economies of scale.' It focuses on high productivity by way of utilizing the infrastructure capacity to the fullest. The number of procedures conducted at NH per day is way ahead of any other hospital of comparable size in the country. The hospital has installed latest digital machines, which help in reducing the running cost, for example, the hospital uses digital X-ray machines without the need of X-ray films.

Narayana Hrudolaya has its sister hospital at Calcutta and the two hospitals, through common bargaining power with suppliers, enjoy heavy discounts due to large volume of supplies sourced by them. Over and above that, Dr Shetty extends his promise of recommending these suppliers to many outside cardiac hospitals as well, which usually honour his advices. Surprisingly, the hospital does not enter into long-term contracts with its suppliers to keep itself free to explore other better suppliers with better pricing and quality over the period of time. The state-of-the-art software installed on the hospital's computers helps them keep the inventory levels to the most economical levels. By sourcing of many cardio-diabetes drugs from the local pharmaceutical company at Bangalore, Biocon Ltd helped NH to contain the costs significantly.

The doctors are paid salaries in place of the common system of sharing the percentage of revenues with them. The 'assembly-line' approach to cardiac surgeries and long hours put in by doctors every day results in bringing down the cost per operation related to doctors. Thus, an open-heart surgery, which costs about ₹2,50,000 to 3,00,000 in any private hospital in the country, costs about ₹1,00,000 at NH.

In order to fulfil its mission of providing cardiac care to people not having the funding, the hospital has developed a unique system of generating data regarding the net revenue generated every day (after deducting the costs of drugs, pro-rated salaries, etc.). This data is used by the doctors scheduling the operations to schedule below-cost surgeries, which are non-urgent in nature, on days having surplus revenue from the paying patients. This stringent accounting system ensures that the hospital is able to pursue its social objective, while keeping itself viable in the long run.

The story does not end here. Dr Shetty's focus on serving the poor and disadvantaged led him to launch Yashasvini, a health insurance scheme, started with the help of the state government in Karnataka in 2003. He was convinced that a majority of poor farmers could not afford expensive surgeries even after selling their small patches of land and cattle. The cooperative societies are quite strong in this state and Dr Shetty used them as a vehicle to launch this unique insurance scheme among the members of these societies, primarily the farmers of the state. A meagre premium of ₹5 per month (₹60 per year) is charged for comprehensive coverage of all surgical procedures and outpatient care to be provided through a network of private hospitals.

The state government allows him to use the post offices for deposit of the premium and issue of Yashasvini Insurance Cards to the farmers and helped its best to create awareness of this scheme as a 'government scheme' among the masses. The scheme enrolled 1.6 million rural farmers in the first year of its operation. The target is to increase it by 2.2 million in its second year. During the first year of operation, around 9,000 surgeries were performed, while about 35,000 patients received outpatient services under this scheme. It is significant to note that a majority of these operations were major surgeries, without which the patients would not have survived. The Yashasvini scheme has become the world's largest health insurance scheme for the rural poor.

It would not be exaggeration to say that Dr Shetty has played the role of Narayana (the Almighty) for the poor and underprivileged. His hospital has truly lived up to its name—Narayana Hrudayalaya, which in Sanskrit, means God's compassionate abode.

## Discussion Questions

1. Specialist surgeons such as Dr Devi Shetty are always short of time. Do you think experts like him would be able to spare enough time for providing diagnosis advice to distant patients through 'telemedicine' in a sustainable manner for a long time?

2. Is it a right operations strategy to get into short-term contract with the suppliers of the hospital?

3. The Yashasvini insurance scheme is based upon the premise that the premium collected from the member farmers would be used for funding the cost of surgeries and OPD for sick patients. The other approach is the one followed by NH in which the net revenues generated by paid-surgeries (mostly by affluent people) is used for partially funding the below cost surgeries. According to you, which model is better in taking care of the poor?

# Objective Questions

## Choose the correct option

1. The period of time during which a customer interacts with a service is called
   (a) service blueprint
   (b) service encounter
   (c) service quality
   (d) service outcome

2. What the customer receives at the end of a service encounter is called
   (a) service blueprint
   (b) service encounter
   (c) service quality
   (d) service outcome

3. Which one of the following is not a key component of a service blueprint?
   (a) competitor actions
   (b) on-stage contact employee actions
   (c) back-stage contact employee actions
   (d) support processes

4. The first-hand testing of a new service, which happens within the organization, is called
   (a) beta testing
   (b) alpha testing
   (c) gamma testing
   (d) delta testing

5. One of the following is not a criteria to distinguish products from services:
   (a) intangibility
   (b) perishability
   (c) homogeneity
   (d) inseparability

6. The following is not a characteristic of services:
   (a) perishability
   (b) heterogeneity
   (c) intangibility
   (d) durability

## State True or False

7. A service, if not consumed at the appropriate time, ceases to exist.
8. Heterogeneity refers to the low variability possible in delivery of services.
9. Another distinct characteristic of services is perishability, which means that they cannot be inventoried.
10. Services that involve high contact with customers are referred to as 'pure services'.
11. The back-stage contact employee actions are visible

to the customer and these employees directly interact with the customer.

## Fill in the blanks

12. _____ is a map that accurately portrays the service systems so that anyone involved with the process can understand and deal with them regardless of what roles they perform in the process.
13. _____ represents the amount of human workforce involved in performing the service operations.

## Concept Review Questions

1. What are the typical characteristics of services and do these make services difficult to manage compared to manufacturing of products?
2. Classify the various types of services according to the degree of labour intensity and degree of interaction and customization. How difficult is it to manage the service quality for services in these categories?
3. What is service capacity? Which strategies can be followed for service capacity planning?
4. Explain the concept of yield management in the airline industry.
5. What are the generic approaches in designing the service processes? Are these approaches industry specific?
6. What is service blueprinting? How can poka-yoke be helpful in service blueprinting? Illustrate by using appropriate examples.

7. What is service quality? What are the internal and external measures of service quality?
8. What is the gap model of service quality measurement? What are the limitations of the SERVQUAL instrument?
9. What are the criteria for rating hotels in star and diamond categories? How can kaizen be applied to improve the quality of services in hotels? Illustrate with examples.
10. Explain the five S concept used in lean manufacturing. Is it applicable in services? Illustrate with examples.
11. What are the steps in achieving conformance to specifications? Explain using appropriate examples.
12. Enumerate and briefly explain the dimensions of quality in services.

## Project Assignments

1. Visit and meet the personnel of a courier company in your town to understand the delivery model followed by them to deliver mails to various locations in the country. Compare their model with that of Mumbai's *dabbawallahs*. Try to explore if it is possible for the courier company to replicate the delivery model of delivery of lunches in the offices of your city.

2. Visit two hospitals in your town—first, a government hospital and then a private hospital. At the outpatient department (OPD) of both hospitals, measure the service quality using the SERVPERF instrument. Critically compare the results with respect to all the five parameters of the instrument. Explore the reasons for lower performance (if found) of one of the hospitals among the two studied by you with respect to these parameters.

| Answers to Objective Questions | | | | |
|---|---|---|---|---|
| 1. (b) | 2. (d) | 3. (a) | 4. (b) | 5. (c) |
| 6. (d) | 7. True | 8. False | 9. True | 10. True |
| 11. False | 12. Service blueprint | | 13. Degree of labour intensity | |

# Appendix: Statistical Tables

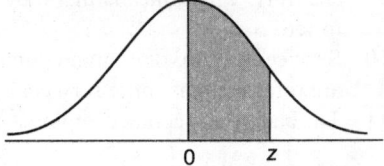

0   z

**Table A**   Areas under the standard normal curve

| z | 0 | 1 | 2 | 3 | 4 | 5 | 6 | 7 | 8 | 9 |
|---|---|---|---|---|---|---|---|---|---|---|
| 0.0 | .0000 | .0040 | .0080 | .0120 | .0160 | .0199 | .0239 | .0279 | .0319 | .0359 |
| 0.1 | .0398 | .0438 | .0478 | .0517 | .0557 | .0596 | .0636 | .0675 | .0714 | .0753 |
| 0.2 | .0793 | .0832 | .0871 | .0910 | .0948 | .0987 | .1026 | .1064 | .1103 | .1141 |
| 0.3 | .1179 | .1217 | .1255 | .1293 | .1331 | .1368 | .1406 | .1443 | .1480 | .1517 |
| 0.4 | .1554 | .1591 | .1628 | .1664 | .1700 | .1736 | .1772 | .1808 | .1844 | .1879 |
| 0.5 | .1915 | .1950 | .1985 | .2019 | .2054 | .2088 | .2123 | .2157 | .2190 | .2224 |
| 0.6 | .2258 | .2291 | .2324 | .2357 | .2389 | .2422 | .2454 | .2486 | .2518 | .2549 |
| 0.7 | .2580 | .2612 | .2642 | .2673 | .2704 | .2734 | .2764 | .2794 | .2823 | .2852 |
| 0.8 | .2881 | .2910 | .2939 | .2967 | .2996 | .3023 | .3051 | .3078 | .3106 | .3133 |
| 0.9 | .3159 | .3186 | .3212 | .3238 | .3264 | .3289 | .3315 | .3340 | .3365 | .3389 |
| 1.0 | .3413 | .3438 | .3461 | .3485 | .3508 | .3531 | .3554 | .3577 | .3599 | .3621 |
| 1.1 | .3643 | .3665 | .3686 | .3708 | .3729 | .3749 | .3770 | .3790 | .3810 | .3830 |
| 1.2 | .3849 | .3869 | .3888 | .3907 | .3925 | .3944 | .3962 | .3980 | .3997 | .4015 |
| 1.3 | .4032 | .4049 | .4066 | .4082 | .4099 | .4115 | .4131 | .4147 | .4162 | .4177 |
| 1.4 | .4192 | .4207 | .4222 | .4236 | .4251 | .4265 | .4279 | .4292 | .4306 | .4319 |
| 1.5 | .4332 | .4345 | .4357 | .4370 | .4382 | .4394 | .4406 | .4418 | .4429 | .4441 |
| 1.6 | .4452 | .4463 | .4474 | .4484 | .4495 | .4505 | .4515 | .4525 | .4535 | .4545 |
| 1.7 | .4554 | .4564 | .4573 | .4582 | .4591 | .4599 | .4608 | .4616 | .4625 | .4633 |
| 1.8 | .4641 | .4649 | .4656 | .4664 | .4671 | .4678 | .4686 | .4693 | .4699 | .4706 |
| 1.9 | .4713 | .4719 | .4726 | .4732 | .4738 | .4744 | .4750 | .4756 | .4761 | .4767 |
| 2.0 | .4772 | .4778 | .4783 | .4788 | .4793 | .4798 | .4803 | .4808 | .4812 | .4817 |
| 2.1 | .4821 | .4826 | .4830 | .4834 | .4838 | .4842 | .4846 | .4850 | .4854 | .4857 |
| 2.2 | .4861 | .4864 | .4868 | .4871 | .4875 | .4878 | .4881 | .4884 | .4887 | .4890 |
| 2.3 | .4893 | .4896 | .4898 | .4901 | .4904 | .4906 | .4909 | .4911 | .4913 | .4916 |
| 2.4 | .4918 | .4920 | .4922 | .4925 | .4927 | .4929 | .4931 | .4932 | .4934 | .4936 |
| 2.5 | .4938 | .4940 | .4941 | .4943 | .4945 | .4946 | .4948 | .4949 | .4951 | .4952 |
| 2.6 | .4953 | .4955 | .4956 | .4957 | .4959 | .4960 | .4961 | .4962 | .4963 | .4964 |
| 2.7 | .4965 | .4966 | .4967 | .4968 | .4969 | .4970 | .4971 | .4972 | .4973 | .4974 |
| 2.8 | .4974 | .4975 | .4976 | .4977 | .4977 | .4978 | .4979 | .4979 | .4980 | .4981 |
| 2.9 | .4981 | .4982 | .4982 | .4983 | .4984 | .4984 | .4985 | .4985 | .4986 | .4986 |
| 3.0 | .4987 | .4987 | .4987 | .4988 | .4988 | .4989 | .4989 | .4989 | .4990 | .4990 |
| 3.1 | .4990 | .4991 | .4991 | .4991 | .4992 | .4992 | .4992 | .4992 | .4993 | .4993 |
| 3.2 | .4993 | .4993 | .4994 | .4994 | .4994 | .4994 | .4994 | .4995 | .4995 | .4995 |
| 3.3 | .4995 | .4995 | .4995 | .4996 | .4996 | .4996 | .4996 | .4996 | .4996 | .4997 |
| 3.4 | .4997 | .4997 | .4997 | .4997 | .4997 | .4997 | .4997 | .4997 | .4997 | .4998 |

(Contd)

## Table A Contd

| z | 0 | 1 | 2 | 3 | 4 | 5 | 6 | 7 | 8 | 9 |
|---|---|---|---|---|---|---|---|---|---|---|
| 3.5 | .4998 | .4998 | .4998 | .4998 | .4998 | .4998 | .4998 | .4998 | .4998 | .4998 |
| 3.6 | .4998 | .4998 | .4999 | .4999 | .4999 | .4999 | .4999 | .4999 | .4999 | .4999 |
| 3.7 | .4999 | .4999 | .4999 | .4999 | .4999 | .4999 | .4999 | .4999 | .4999 | .4999 |
| 3.8 | .4999 | .4999 | .4999 | .4999 | .4999 | .4999 | .4999 | .4999 | .4999 | .4999 |
| 3.9 | .5000 | .5000 | .5000 | .5000 | .5000 | .5000 | .5000 | .5000 | .5000 | .5000 |

## Table B   Random numbers

| | | | | |
|---|---|---|---|---|
| 22 17 68 65 84 | 68 95 23 92 35 | 61 09 43 95 06 | 87 02 22 57 51 | 58 24 82 03 47 |
| 19 36 27 59 46 | 13 79 93 37 55 | 85 52 05 30 62 | 39 77 32 77 09 | 47 83 51 62 74 |
| 16 77 23 02 77 | 09 61 87 25 21 | 16 71 13 59 78 | 28 06 24 25 93 | 23 05 47 47 25 |
| 78 43 76 71 61 | 20 44 90 32 64 | 46 38 03 93 22 | 97 67 63 99 61 | 69 81 21 99 21 |
| 03 28 28 26 08 | 73 37 32 04 05 | 88 69 58 28 99 | 69 30 16 09 05 | 35 07 44 75 47 |
| | | | | |
| 93 22 53 64 39 | 07 10 63 76 35 | 08 13 13 85 51 | 87 03 04 79 88 | 55 34 57 72 69 |
| 78 76 58 54 74 | 92 38 70 96 92 | 82 63 18 27 44 | 52 06 79 79 45 | 69 66 92 19 09 |
| 23 68 35 26 00 | 99 53 93 61 28 | 56 65 05 61 86 | 52 70 05 48 34 | 90 92 10 70 80 |
| 15 39 25 70 99 | 93 86 52 77 65 | 22 87 26 07 47 | 15 33 59 06 28 | 86 96 98 29 06 |
| 58 71 96 30 24 | 18 46 23 34 27 | 49 18 09 79 49 | 85 13 99 24 44 | 74 16 32 23 02 |
| | | | | |
| 57 35 27 33 72 | 24 53 63 94 09 | 44 04 95 49 66 | 41 10 76 47 91 | 39 60 04 59 81 |
| 48 50 86 54 48 | 22 06 34 72 52 | 33 29 94 71 11 | 82 21 15 65 20 | 15 91 29 12 02 |
| 61 96 48 95 03 | 07 16 39 33 66 | 77 21 30 27 12 | 98 56 10 56 79 | 90 49 22 23 62 |
| 36 93 89 41 26 | 29 70 83 63 51 | 87 09 41 15 09 | 99 74 20 52 36 | 98 60 16 03 03 |
| 18 87 00 42 31 | 57 90 12 02 07 | 54 08 01 88 63 | 23 47 37 17 31 | 39 41 88 92 10 |
| | | | | |
| 88 56 53 27 59 | 33 35 72 67 47 | 08 18 27 38 90 | 77 34 55 45 70 | 16 95 86 70 75 |
| 09 72 95 84 29 | 49 41 31 06 70 | 64 84 73 31 65 | 42 38 06 45 18 | 52 53 37 97 15 |
| 12 96 88 17 31 | 65 19 69 02 83 | 24 64 19 35 51 | 60 75 86 90 68 | 56 61 87 39 12 |
| 85 94 57 24 16 | 92 09 84 38 76 | 29 81 94 78 70 | 22 00 27 69 85 | 21 94 47 90 12 |
| 38 64 43 59 98 | 98 77 87 68 07 | 40 98 06 93 78 | 91 51 67 62 44 | 23 32 65 41 18 |
| | | | | |
| 53 44 09 42 72 | 00 41 86 79 79 | 35 55 31 51 51 | 68 47 22 00 20 | 00 83 63 22 55 |
| 40 76 66 26 84 | 57 99 99 90 37 | 37 40 13 68 97 | 36 63 32 08 58 | 87 64 81 07 83 |
| 02 17 79 18 05 | 12 59 52 57 02 | 28 14 11 30 79 | 22 07 90 47 03 | 20 69 22 40 98 |
| 95 17 82 06 53 | 31 51 10 96 46 | 56 11 50 81 69 | 92 06 88 07 77 | 40 23 72 51 39 |
| 35 76 22 42 92 | 96 11 83 44 80 | 33 42 40 90 60 | 34 68 35 48 77 | 73 96 53 97 86 |
| | | | | |
| 26 29 13 56 41 | 85 47 04 66 08 | 82 43 80 46 15 | 34 72 57 59 13 | 38 26 61 70 04 |
| 77 80 20 75 82 | 72 82 32 99 90 | 89 73 44 99 05 | 63 95 73 76 63 | 48 67 26 43 18 |
| 46 40 66 44 52 | 91 36 74 43 53 | 78 45 63 98 35 | 30 82 13 54 00 | 55 03 36 67 68 |
| 37 56 08 18 09 | 77 53 84 46 47 | 24 16 74 11 53 | 31 91 18 95 58 | 44 10 13 85 57 |
| 61 65 61 68 66 | 37 27 47 39 19 | 53 21 40 06 71 | 84 83 70 07 48 | 95 06 79 88 54 |
| | | | | |
| 93 43 69 64 07 | 34 18 04 52 35 | 61 85 53 83 45 | 56 27 09 24 86 | 19 90 70 99 00 |
| 21 96 60 12 99 | 11 20 99 45 18 | 18 37 79 49 90 | 48 13 93 55 34 | 65 97 38 20 46 |
| 95 20 47 97 97 | 27 37 83 28 71 | 45 89 09 39 84 | 00 06 41 41 74 | 51 67 11 52 49 |
| 97 86 21 78 73 | 10 65 81 92 59 | 04 76 62 16 17 | 58 76 17 14 97 | 17 95 70 45 80 |
| 69 92 06 34 13 | 59 71 74 17 32 | 23 71 82 13 74 | 27 55 10 24 19 | 63 52 52 01 41 |

*(Contd)*

## Table B    Contd

| | | | | |
|---|---|---|---|---|
| 04 31 17 21 56 | 33 73 99 19 87 | 53 77 57 68 93 | 26 72 39 27 67 | 60 61 97 22 61 |
| 61 06 98 03 91 | 87 14 77 43 96 | 45 60 33 01 07 | 43 00 65 98 50 | 98 99 46 50 47 |
| 85 93 85 86 88 | 72 87 08 62 40 | 23 21 34 74 97 | 16 06 10 89 20 | 76 38 03 29 63 |
| 21 74 32 47 45 | 73 96 07 94 52 | 25 76 16 19 33 | 09 65 90 77 47 | 53 05 70 53 30 |
| 15 69 53 82 80 | 79 96 23 53 10 | 45 33 02 43 70 | 65 39 07 16 29 | 02 87 40 41 45 |
| | | | | |
| 02 89 08 04 49 | 20 21 14 68 86 | 11 29 01 95 80 | 87 63 93 95 17 | 35 14 97 35 33 |
| 87 18 15 89 79 | 85 43 01 72 73 | 89 74 39 82 15 | 08 61 74 51 69 | 94 51 33 41 67 |
| 98 83 71 94 22 | 59 97 50 99 52 | 87 80 61 65 31 | 08 52 85 08 40 | 91 51 80 32 44 |
| 10 08 58 21 66 | 72 68 49 29 31 | 59 73 19 85 23 | 89 85 84 46 06 | 65 09 29 75 25 |
| 47 90 56 10 08 | 88 02 84 27 83 | 66 56 45 65 79 | 42 29 72 23 19 | 20 71 53 20 25 |
| | | | | |
| 22 85 61 68 90 | 49 64 92 85 44 | 50 14 49 81 06 | 16 40 12 89 88 | 01 82 77 45 12 |
| 67 80 43 79 33 | 12 83 11 41 16 | 77 02 54 00 52 | 25 58 19 68 70 | 53 43 37 15 26 |
| 27 62 50 96 72 | 79 44 61 40 15 | 27 31 58 50 28 | 14 53 40 65 39 | 11 39 03 34 25 |
| 33 78 80 87 15 | 38 30 06 38 21 | 54 96 87 53 32 | 14 47 47 07 26 | 40 36 40 96 76 |
| 13 13 92 66 99 | 47 24 49 57 74 | 10 97 11 69 84 | 32 25 43 62 17 | 99 63 22 32 98 |
| | | | | |
| 10 27 53 96 23 | 71 50 54 36 23 | 04 14 12 15 09 | 54 31 04 82 98 | 26 78 25 47 47 |
| 28 41 50 61 88 | 64 85 27 20 18 | 39 71 65 09 62 | 83 36 36 05 56 | 94 76 62 11 89 |
| 34 21 42 57 02 | 59 19 18 97 48 | 05 24 67 70 07 | 80 30 03 30 98 | 84 97 50 87 46 |
| 61 81 77 23 23 | 82 82 11 54 08 | 44 07 39 55 43 | 53 28 70 58 96 | 42 34 43 39 28 |
| 61 15 18 13 54 | 16 86 20 26 88 | 14 53 90 51 17 | 90 74 80 55 09 | 52 01 63 01 59 |

## Table C    Values of $d_2$ and $d_3$ for sample size n

| Number of observations in sample n | $d_2$ | $d_3$ | Number of observations in sample n | $d_2$ | $d_3$ |
|---|---|---|---|---|---|
| 2 | 1.128 | 0.853 | 15 | 3.472 | 0.755 |
| 3 | 1.693 | 0.888 | 16 | 3.532 | 0.749 |
| 4 | 2.059 | 0.880 | 17 | 3.588 | 0.743 |
| 5 | 2.326 | 0.864 | 18 | 3.640 | 0.738 |
| | | | 19 | 3.689 | 0.733 |
| 6 | 2.534 | 0.848 | 20 | 3.735 | 0.729 |
| 7 | 2.704 | 0.833 | | | |
| 8 | 2.847 | 0.820 | 21 | 3.778 | 0.724 |
| 9 | 2.970 | 0.808 | 22 | 3.819 | 0.720 |
| 10 | 3.078 | 0.797 | 23 | 3.858 | 0.716 |
| 11 | 3.173 | 0.787 | 24 | 3.895 | 0.712 |
| 12 | 3.258 | 0.778 | 25 | 3.931 | 0.709 |
| 13 | 3.336 | 0.770 | | | |
| 14 | 3.407 | 0.762 | Over 25 | – | – |

# Index

# About the Author

**Kanishka Bedi**, Professor, School of Business & Quality Management, Hamdan Bin Mohammed Smart University, Dubai, UAE, has more than two decades of teaching experience at the postgraduate level. He is also the President of the Indian Ocean Comparative Education Society (IOCES), an affiliate of the prestigious World Council of Comparative Education Societies (WCCES).

While working previously for U21Global Graduate School, Singapore, Dr Bedi assumed the role of the Co-Director of the Management Programme for Entrepreneurs and Family Businesses, jointly with N.S. Raghavan Centre for Entrepreneurial Learning at the Indian Institute of Management Bangalore. He has also taught post-graduate students at the Indian Institute of Management Lucknow; Lucknow University; Jaipuria Institute of Management, Lucknow; Asian International College, Singapore; and Hamdan Bin Mohamed e-University, Dubai, UAE.

He has presented research papers at international conferences in India and abroad and published in journals, conference proceedings, and books. He has regularly been engaged as an executive peer reviewer with the *International Journal of Production Research* (*IJPR*), *Computers and Industrial Engineering, Australasian Journal of Educational Technology,* and *International Journal of Education and Development using Information and Communication Technology* (*IJEDICT*).

He has provided consultancy and training to several organizations globally. He has brought about several innovations like the use of digital-storytelling, deployment of the Wiki, authentic assessments, blending synchronous with asynchronous technologies, etc. in designing and customizing executive education programmes to fulfil the unique training and development requirements of corporations. He was conferred in 2010 with an award for excellence in online education by U21Global Graduate School, Singapore and the Chancellor's Award for Innovation in Online Teaching and Learning by Hamdan Bin Mohammed e-University, Dubai, UAE.

Dr Bedi is the author of two more books—*Quality Management* and *Management and Entrepreneurship*—both published by OUP.

# Related Titles

## MARKETING, ASIAN EDITION
[9780198079446]

**Paul Baines**, Professor, Cranfield School of Management, Cranfield University; **Chris Fill**, Director, Fillassociates; **Kelly Page**, Lecturer, Cardiff Business School; **Piyush Kumar Sinha**, Professor, Indian Institute of Management Ahmedabad (IIMA).

Designed for postgraduate students pursuing courses in business management, this textbook will be equally useful to marketing practitioners, particularly because of the real-life case insights presented by marketing professionals. Recognizing the need to go further than the traditional 4Ps approach, the text reflects on newer perspectives, covering topics such as relational, not-for-profit, digital, and postmodern marketing. It provides powerful learning insights into marketing theory and practice, through a series of 'Insight' features: Case Insights, Market Insights, and Research Insights.

**Key Features**
- Separate chapters on digital marketing, relationship marketing, not-for-profit marketing, postmodern marketing, and marketing, sustainability, and ethics
- Deals with contemporary marketing practices with relevant examples drawn from international as well as Asian markets including India
- Well-integrated Online Resource Centre for lecturers and students

## FINANCIAL MANAGEMENT, 2E
[9780198072072]

**Rajiv Srivastava**, Professor, Indian Institute of Foreign Trade, New Delhi; **Anil Misra**, Associate Professor, Management Development Institute (MDI), Gurgaon

The second edition of *Financial Management* is a comprehensive textbook specially designed to meet the requirements of management students specializing in finance. It deals with the core concepts of finance with an emphasis on specialized sub-areas, such as working capital, capital markets, investment decisions, international finance, derivatives, mergers and acquisitions, and risk management.

**Key Features**
- Focuses on managerial applications through case studies of well-known Indian companies
- Carries a number of side-boxes that highlight the crux of the key concepts discussed in each section
- Includes examples, exhibits, and illustrations interspersed in the text
- Contains review questions, practical assignments, numerical problems, and practice problems with each chapter

## STRATEGIC MANAGEMENT
[9780198070795]

**N. Chandrasekaran**, Loyola Institute of Business Administration (LIBA), Chennai; **P.S. Ananthanarayanan**, Consultant and Visiting Faculty, Chennai

The book begins with an introduction to the basic concepts and objectives of strategic management. This is followed by the decision of environmental analysis and forecasting techniques and models. It then goes on to cover corporate strategies including that of mergers and acquisitions and many more, and their formation and implementation. The book also addresses corporate social responsibility and corporate governance, and emphasizes the importance of evaluating and controlling the effectiveness of a strategy.

**Key Features**
- Contains extensive discussion on the importance of governance and corporate social responsibility
- Provides a brief to readers on how to overcome risk-based challenges when applying new strategies
- Discusses the process of strategic cost management to help readers understand how the expenses of a project can be monitored
- Includes 40 case studies on major Indian and global companies including Indian Oil Corporation Ltd, Reliance Industries Ltd, and Oracle Corporation

## CORPORATE GOVERNANCE
[9780198062233]

**T.N. Satheesh Kumar**, D.C. School of Management and Technology, Kochi

*Corporate Governance* is a comprehensive textbook designed to meet the requirements of postgraduate management students. It provides an in-depth analysis of the core concepts of the subject and supplements them with relevant examples, exhibits, and case studies.

**Key Features**
- Expounds on issues and challenges faced by corporates in applications of governance in India as well as abroad
- Includes detailed reports of some of the various committees constituted by SEBI, including the Kumar Mangalam Birla Committee Report, Narayana Murthy Committee Report, and Clause 49 guidelines
- Contains extensive discussion on the European Union approach to corporate governance
- Provides numerous real-world cases such as Jubilant Organosys Ltd and Reliance Industries Ltd

### Other Related Titles

9780198066903  Khatua: *Project Management and Appraisal*
9780198075479  Pai: *Operations Research: Principles and Practice*

### Books by the Same Author

9780195677959  Bedi: *Quality Management*
9780198061908  Bedi: *Management and Entrepreneurship*